SMITH & WOOD'S EMPLOYMENT LAW

Smith & Wood's Employment Law

Seventeenth Edition

IAN SMITH MA, LLB (CANTAB)

of Gray's Inn, Barrister
Emeritus Professor of Employment Law at the University of East Anglia
General editor of Harvey on Industrial Relations and Employment Law

OWEN WARNOCK MA (CANTAB)

Former Partner, Eversheds Sutherland, Solicitors
Emeritus Professor of Employment Law, University of East Anglia
An editor of Harvey on Industrial Relations and Employment Law

GEMMA MITCHELL PHD, LLM, LLB

Associate Professor in Law, University of East Anglia

OXFORD
UNIVERSITY PRESS

OXFORD
UNIVERSITY PRESS

Great Clarendon Street, Oxford, OX2 6DP,
United Kingdom

Oxford University Press is a department of the University of Oxford.
It furthers the University's objective of excellence in research, scholarship,
and education by publishing worldwide. Oxford is a registered trade mark of
Oxford University Press in the UK and in certain other countries.

Fourteenth Edition 2019
Fifteenth Edition 2021
Sixteenth Edition 2023

Published in the United States of America by Oxford University Press
198 Madison Avenue, New York, NY 10016, United States of America

British Library Cataloguing in Publication Data
Data available

Library of Congress Control Number: 2026934403

ISBN 9780198980339

Printed in the UK by
Bell & Bain Ltd., Glasgow

The manufacturer's authorized representative in the EU for product safety is
Oxford University Press España S.A. of Parque Empresarial San Fernando de Henares,
Avenida de Castilla, 2 – 28830 Madrid (www.oup.es/en or product.safety@oup.com).
OUP España S.A. also acts as importer into Spain of products made by the manufacturer.

MIX
Paper | Supporting responsible forestry
FSC® C007785
FSC www.fsc.org

Preface

The previous edition was produced towards the end of the Conservative administration when matters in employment law were relatively calm. However, since then that has been far from the case. First, and perhaps surprisingly, at the very end of that administration there was a flurry of legislative changes (often from private members' bills) introducing new rights relating to neonatal care and leave and carers' leave and making amendments to several other family-friendly provisions and flexible working. Secondly, however, far more major change has come with the change of government in 2024. The incoming Labour administration had campaigned on a proposal to overhaul worker rights across a wide spectrum. Action on this was promised in short order and the result was the Employment Rights Act 2025, a huge piece of legislation. In the collective sphere the Act aims to make it easier for trade unions to recruit members within the workplace and to win recognition for collective bargaining, and it will simplify the procedure for industrial action ballots. On the enforcement of individual rights, it creates a new Fair Work Agency to amalgamate some functions of existing bodies into one place but adding new ones, including a radical new power to bring cases on behalf of individuals. In the individual rights area, it will lead to restrictions on zero-hours contracts and the use of the fire-and-rehire tactic to change contracts, make statutory sick pay and parental rights into day-one rights, and will amend the law on tips, flexible working, and whistleblowing. The original proposal was also to make unfair dismissal a day-one right, but this proved to be particularly controversial, leading to a serious stand-off between the Commons and the Lords (and a protracted legislative ping-pong process); the result was a compromise at the last minute to reduce the existing qualifying period from two years to six months (thus reverting to what it was when unfair dismissal was first introduced in 1972—there is nothing new under the sun in the strange world of employment law).

The Act finally became law at the very end of 2025. However, that was not the end of the matter because these changes are so extensive that the government made it clear at the outset that they would not come into force together or immediately. The only aspect which took effect when royal assent was given was the repeal of the previous government's system enabling employers to secure at least a minimum level of service during strikes within certain important public services—a system that had never in fact been used. In relation to the remainder of the Act the government published a 'roadmap' of phased introductions stretching over a period of up to two years, that is, most of the currency of this edition. A significant proportion of the Act operates not by making straightforward amendments to the existing legislation, but by giving the government powers to do so by regulations. Moreover, the intention in several areas is to do so only after consultation exercises—at the time of writing 26 consultations have been started. This is going to be a long process. The approach in this edition is to set out the amended/new laws as contained in the Act and to give best estimates as to their eventual introduction. It will be necessary for the reader to keep fully abreast of these developments. On top of all of this legislative change, this edition also of course covers the case law since the previous one, which has continued at its usual pace and still throws up important issues of principle and interpretation, even under existing legislation that has been in force for many years.

Ian Smith
Owen Warnock
Gemma Mitchell
January 2026

New to this edition

- Coverage of the major changes made by the Employment Rights Act 2025, in relation to collective labour issues, individual rights, and the administration of those rights.
- Best estimates as to when its provisions are likely to be brought into force throughout the currency of the edition.
- Full updating of other legislative developments and case law since the last edition.

Contents

Table of Statutes

Table of Statutory Instruments

Table of European Legislation

Regulations

Table of Cases

European Court of Justice

1

Introduction

1.1 General

Employment law has been the subject of as rapid a transformation as has been seen in any legal subject in recent times, and it is certainly one of the most difficult areas of law in which to keep up to date. In some ways it is a curious mixture of ancient and modern because much old law lies behind or at the basis of new statutory law and in some cases the old law continues to exist alongside the new (eg the continued existence of the separate actions for wrongful dismissal and unfair dismissal, the former being a common law action and the latter entirely a creation of statute). To take one small example, as late (in legal terms) as 1969 it could still be seriously debated before the Court of Appeal[1] whether a general hiring of an employee (ie one not subject to any express time limitation) was a hiring only for a year, under the old 'presumption of a yearly hiring' which used to apply in the nineteenth century and earlier, principally in order to guarantee year-round employment for agricultural labourers, but which is now totally irrelevant to

[1] *Richardson v Koefod* [1969] 3 All ER 1264, [1969] 1 WLR 1812, CA.

modern employment law. We have come a remarkable distance since then, but it remains the case that ghosts can still clank their chains—particularly in the law relating to contracts of employment, where a strictly contractual approach may not always lead to a realistic result.

However, the subject is unrecognizable from what it was only 50 years ago, with the enormous increase in statute law and the ever-increasing volume of case law on the modern statutes. Thus, the student must be able to exercise the lawyer's skill in dealing both with extensive case law and with major statutes, sometimes of astounding complexity. Moreover, the student must be able to deal with this mass of law with a certain amount of intelligence and discernment, for example being able to tell when a line of old cases, authoritative in themselves, may be so out of line with the modern approach to employment or industrial relations that they are unlikely to be applied in practice, or to tell when a case on a modern statutory provision is merely *illustrative* (however interesting) rather than setting a definite precedent on a point of interpretation—for if this distinction is not borne in mind students will soon find themselves buried alive under the case law, particularly in an area such as unfair dismissal, where so much is vested in the discretion of the tribunal and, furthermore, where any actual point of law which does arise should normally be approached primarily by reference to the wording of the statute. The student will soon realize when reading this book that while a desire to escape from over-legalism in decision-making on employment matters has been one of the dominant themes of modern employment law, it is regularly frustrated by the avalanche of modern legislation, often of great complexity. Case law of course remains important, but equally clearly some cases are more equal than others.

While the approach of this book is avowedly legal, treating the subject as it now has to be treated—as an important area of substantive law which leads in practice to a very considerable amount of litigation—at the same time it must be realized that in certain ways this is law with a difference; this must be reflected in the approach of the student, and it is hoped that it is reflected in this book, which in turn reflects the love–hate relationship to the law adopted by so many employment relations practitioners.

As well as a whole new body of law, employment law is subject to a separate jurisdiction exercised by employment tribunals (with appeal to the Employment Appeal Tribunal (EAT), and only then into the ordinary court structure, with appeal to the Court of Appeal and then to the Supreme Court[2]). Even though tribunals gained some common law jurisdiction (on termination of employment) in 1994, not all matters may go to a tribunal because many common law actions must still go to the ordinary courts (eg an action for breach of the contract of employment during employment, or an action by an employer for an injunction to restrain illegal industrial action). However, the large majority of cases which are brought do in fact go before the tribunals.

All of these developments have led to a mushrooming in specialized sources and materials in employment law, many ephemeral, but some of major practical use to the employment lawyer. Most importantly, this subject is so specialized that there are two dedicated series of law reports, namely the Industrial Cases Reports (ICR)[3] and the Industrial Relations Law Reports (IRLR);[4] preference will be given to citation of these reports throughout this book, as is the case across the subject. The IRLR are of particular

[2] In 2016 there was added the possibility of a 'leapfrog' appeal directly from the EAT to the Supreme Court in the case of points of law of general public importance: Civil Justice and Courts Act 2016, s 65.

[3] These are the official reports, published by the Incorporated Council of Law Reporting for England and Wales; until 1974 they were called the 'Industrial Court Reports'.

[4] Published by LexisNexis UK.

importance, being very up to date and heavily relied upon by practitioners. The leading academic journal is the *Industrial Law Journal*[5] and the leading practitioner work is *Harvey on Industrial Relations and Employment Law*,[6] a six-volume looseleaf and online work (updated seven times per year, with a monthly bulletin) which is used extensively by practitioners, advisers, and tribunals and is frequently cited in court judgments (especially in the EAT). There are of course also various websites covering the subject, which are particularly useful for keeping abreast of it. Some are private, subscription services, but of particular use as open, public services are the websites of the Advisory, Conciliation and Arbitration Service (ACAS); the Department for Business and Trade (DBT, previously BEIS, BIS, and originally the DTI); Parliament (for the progress of legislation); the Information Commissioner (for data protection matters); and the EAT (for very recent case law). As an 'alerter' service, the (free) website of the barrister Daniel Barnett would take some beating; it and the *Harvey* Bulletin form the sources of first recourse for the busy employment law practitioner wanting to keep up to date in this fast-moving subject. Recent case law in the Court of Appeal and Supreme Court is most easily accessed through the website of the legal charity BAILII (the British and Irish Legal Information Institute).

Codes of practice have been of major importance in employment law, allowing the statute to lay down merely the general principle on a topic and then amplifying that principle in a way that is likely to be of more use to the people concerned; they have been used in fields such as unfair dismissal, employment protection, flexible working, settlement agreements, union rights, picketing, the closed shop, health and safety at work, and disability discrimination, and they should be consulted whenever appropriate. In the collective sphere, the Donovan Report,[7] from as far back as 1968, should still be consulted in any historic context, for it formed the analytical background to many of the reforms (successful or unsuccessful) in this area. Finally, many of the bodies connected with industrial relations in the widest sense publish from time to time reports or studies with important impacts upon the legal framework.[8]

1.2 A brief history of legal intervention and the legislation

1.2.1 Origins

The subject of employment law may be split, for convenience if not for accuracy, into three principal areas—industrial safety law, individual employment law, and the law relating to employment relations. Each has a different legal and social background, and until recently the level (and type) of legal involvement was markedly different in each. Industrial safety law has a history of statutory intervention dating back to the beginning of the nineteenth century, with a formidable volume of case law on the statutes and on the actions which could be brought by an injured employee. Individual employment law, however, was based almost entirely upon the common law concept of the contract of employment; it attracted little statutory intervention, and even much of the common law,

[5] Published for the Industrial Law Society by Oxford University Press.

[6] Published in hard copy and online by LexisNexis and referred to in footnotes as '*Harvey*'. The *Harvey* Monthly Bulletin is available free of charge at <http://lexisweb.co.uk/sources/harvey-on-industrial-relations-employment-law-bulletin>.

[7] Report of the Royal Commission on Trade Unions and Employers' Associations (Cmnd 3623, 1968).

[8] The annual reports of ACAS, the CAC, the Certification Officer, the European Court of Human Rights, and the Health and Safety Commission are particularly useful sources of information.

though extensive in theory, was a dead letter in practice, principally due to the inadequacies of the remedies for breach of the employment contract by the employer. Employment relations law was characterized by the voluntary principle and the abstention of the law (once legislation had been used in the latter part of the nineteenth century and the first part of the twentieth to legalize the operations and purposes of trade unions and to protect them and their members from tortious liability for industrial action);[9] it is true that wage negotiation in certain industries used to be encouraged by wages councils which were the creation of statute, but even here the law merely provided a minimum framework and did not attempt to impose legal rights and duties on the substance of the negotiation itself.

Major developments have occurred in the past five decades which have changed the previous picture, in some areas beyond all recognition. In the industrial safety sphere, the first of two revolutionary changes came with the Health and Safety at Work etc. Act 1974, which creates administrative machinery, provides for more effective enforcement procedures, and widens the general duties owed by employers (and others). Second, the substance of our safety laws was subject to major reform in the 1990s from a different source, namely the EU, with increased emphasis on attempting to harmonize laws on major safety matters throughout the Community. Due to constraints on the size of a book such as this, industrial safety law is no longer covered here in detail.

Individual employment law has been the subject of major revision by the provision of new statutory rights for those in employment (and, in the area of sex, race, disability, sexual orientation, religion/belief, and age discrimination, for those seeking employment); moreover, these rights (which usually have little or no dependence upon the theoretical contractual basis of employment) are now the subject of *realistic* enforcement procedures through the tribunal system and so are doubly preferable to most common law rights. These rights are many and various, from what is now a relatively minor matter such as minimum periods of notice according to length of service to the more important employment protection rights; clearly the most important is the right not to be unfairly dismissed, and these cases have always constituted a major part of the tribunals' caseload.

Employment relations law suffered great upheaval under a Conservative government with the Industrial Relations Act 1971, which unsuccessfully attempted to impose an overall legislative framework on industrial relations, giving rights and imposing duties by law as is done in some other jurisdictions. The Act was repealed in toto by the incoming Labour government in 1974 (except for the unfair dismissal provisions, which were re-enacted), but ironically we then saw under that same Labour government the enactment of significant new legal rights for trade unions which were capable of having an effect on some of the most fundamental aspects of collective labour relations, such as recognition, bargaining information, standardization of terms and conditions throughout an industry, prior consultation on impending redundancies, and direct union involvement in safety procedures. Certainly, where employment relations remain on a collective level (and there has been a significant decline in collective bargaining over the past five decades), such relations are still on a voluntary basis and voluntary procedures remain paramount; however, this field is no longer devoid of legal intervention, and the modern legislation has also played an important part in setting up machinery for the settlement of certain industrial disputes (in particular, ACAS and the Central Arbitration Committee (CAC)) and subsequently in placing stringent limitations on what previous Conservative

[9] This culminated in the Trade Disputes Act 1906, which gave a trade union complete legal immunity and its officers and members an immunity applying to all acts 'in contemplation or furtherance of a trade dispute'. This underpinning of the voluntary system and the withdrawal of the law from industrial disputes lasted until the Employment Act 1982.

governments saw as unacceptable forms of industrial action or unacceptable purposes behind such industrial action, while at the same time they sought ever greater deregulation of the labour market itself.

1.2.2 **The early legislation**

The whole subject is thus heavily overlaid with modern statutes.[10] In the employment law area, this process started with the Contracts of Employment Act 1963 (consolidated in 1972), which introduced new rules on notice periods, required an employer to give its employee a written statement of terms of employment, and laid down for the first time the statutory rules on 'continuity of employment', which were to take on much greater significance when more extensive employee rights were later enacted which depended on the concept of continuity (either for qualification for rights or for computation of benefits, or both). The first of these rights was the right to a redundancy payment under the Redundancy Payments Act 1965. As well as attempting to introduce a new, but politically unacceptable, framework for industrial relations, the Industrial Relations Act 1971 was notable for introducing the new law on unfair dismissal, and this was re-enacted by the Trade Union and Labour Relations Act 1974, which repealed the 1971 Act, (a) restored the essentially voluntary nature of industrial relations (abolishing, in the process, the National Industrial Relations Court which had adjudicated cases arising under the 1971 Act), and (b) consolidated the law relating to trade union immunities and internal affairs. The 1974 Act was itself amended by the Trade Union and Labour Relations (Amendment) Act 1976, which made the immunities more watertight, abolished the statutory action against a union for unfair expulsion or exclusion, and tightened up the law on the closed shop.

The Employment Protection Act 1975 made significant steps forward in many directions. On the collective side, it gave statutory backing to ACAS, set up the CAC, and introduced the important new trade union rights mentioned previously; it also set up the Employment Appeal Tribunal (to take the place of the NIRC) and modernized the provisions relating to wages councils. On the individual employment side, it introduced new employment protection rights (eg guarantee payments, time off work for union purposes, a right not to be discriminated against on trade union grounds, and the rights relating to maternity pay and leave) and it made significant alterations to the law on unfair dismissal (particularly as regards the available remedies). By this time, the statute law was something of a jungle and indeed was on one occasion castigated in the House of Lords as a bad example of legislation by reference, in that it was frequently the case that a point of law could only be discovered by referring to separate but complementary provisions in two or more Acts. The *individual* aspects were therefore consolidated into the Employment Protection (Consolidation) Act 1978, which covered particulars of terms of employment, employment protection rights, termination of employment, unfair dismissal, redundancy payments, industrial (now employment) tribunals, and the EAT, and was for years the principal statute.

1.2.3 **The Conservative governments 1979–97**

The Employment Act 1980 marked a major change of direction after the election in 1979 of a Conservative government under Mrs Thatcher with a radically new political agenda based on free market economics. Although it adopted, at the very beginning of that

[10] The statutes currently in force are set out, with annotations, in *Harvey*, Division Q.

government, a 'softly, softly' approach, avoiding a rerun of the Industrial Relations Act 1971, it started the remarkable transformation of employment law that marked the 1980s. On the collective side, it affected statutory trade union rights by repealing the provisions of the Employment Protection Act 1975 relating to the statutory recognition procedure and the extension of terms and conditions of employment by the CAC ('Schedule 11 claims'). It also affected the internal government of trade unions by allowing financial support for union elections and by reinstating a statutory right of complaint to a tribunal for people unreasonably expelled or excluded from a union where there was a closed shop in operation. The law relating to picketing was altered, and new curbs introduced on secondary industrial action. On the individual side, the Act altered certain aspects of unfair dismissal law (principally those relating to the burden of proof, the closed shop, and compensation) and made changes in the rules governing maternity rights and guarantee pay.

The Employment Act 1982, an altogether 'drier' statute by a more established government, contained some new provisions (eg altering the law of unfair dismissal in cases where the persons dismissed were on strike) and a host of minor amendments. However, it was principally designed to tighten up the 1980 Act in two areas—the closed shop and the law on industrial disputes. With regard to the former, it imposed more stringent procedural requirements of balloting, radically increased the compensation payable to an employee unfairly dismissed because of a closed shop, and made it more likely that in such a case compensation will in fact be paid by the union rather than the employer. Also, new provisions were introduced to discourage the inclusion of union labour-only requirements in contracts and tenders. In the area of industrial disputes, the Act basically left alone the restrictions introduced by the 1980 Act (though with a tightening-up of the definition of 'trade dispute' on which the statutory immunities are based); however, the radical change in the 1982 Act was the removal of the union's complete immunity from suit in tort (which the unions had had, with the exception of the years of the Industrial Relations Act 1971, since the Trade Disputes Act 1906), so that now the union itself may be sued (subject to statutory maxima on the damages recoverable) if it contravenes the strengthened laws on industrial disputes.

The Trade Union Act 1984 (following the 1983 election in which 'giving unions back to their members' was a prominent Conservative theme) was the third major statute passed by that government, but in large part marked a significant departure. While Part II can be seen as following on from the Employment Acts 1980 and 1982 by allowing an employer to sue a union (for damages or an injunction) if the union takes strike or other industrial action without the now obligatory strike ballot, Parts I and III were different in that the causes of action contained within them are vested in the union *members*. Part I obliged a union to hold secret ballots for high union offices and Part III introduced compulsory periodic reballoting on whether a union should continue to operate a political fund. This Act was therefore aimed at the *internal* affairs of a trade union, particularly as the events surrounding the miners' strike and certain other major industrial disputes tended to show a greater degree of readiness on the part of union members (or of whole sections of a union) to resort to legal action in order to secure compliance with the union's rules. This process was taken a stage further by the Employment Act 1988 (following the 1987 election and the experiences of the miners' strike of 1984–85, a major event in the evolution of employment law at the time), which tightened up some of the provisions of the 1984 Act (in relation to balloting) and introduced certain new statutory rights for union members (eg rights to ballots before industrial action, to inspect union accounts, to restrain unlawful expenditure by the union, and not to be unjustifiably disciplined); to assist in the enforcement of rights against a union, the Act also established the office of Commissioner for the Rights of Trade Union Members. In one respect, the Act harked back to the early legislation of that government, for it took the changes to the law on the closed shop to their logical conclusion by removing *all* legal protection from it as an institution, so that it is now no longer possible for a union to establish or maintain a legally effective, post-entry closed shop.

While the Employment Act 1989 was largely a tinkering measure, the Employment Act 1990 in several ways set the seal on a decade of change,[11] taking several themes first developed in 1980 to their logical conclusions. In particular, it rendered illegal the *pre*-entry closed shop, made illegal *all* secondary action, and attacked *un*official industrial action. Thus, by 1990 laws were in place which many Conservatives would have liked to have seen in 1980, had they been able to wave a magic wand. Crucially, of course, by that time there had also been a significant decrease in union membership, a radical decrease in union influence, and a very noticeable move away, in many areas, from collectively negotiated terms and conditions of employment and towards more individual contracting, flexibility in employment, and more use of what used to be called atypical employments. Indeed, by the early 1990s the encouragement of such moves had been adopted as government policy,[12] along with continuing deregulation.

After the fourth Conservative election victory in 1992, another Bill was expected, though possibly of a tinkering nature again, meant politically to show that the government had not run out of steam in the hitherto politically profitable area of industrial relations. However, the Trade Union Reform and Employment Rights Act 1993 turned out to be far more than that. It again addressed union elections and ballots, and the financial affairs of unions; it recast members' rights on disciplining and expulsion; further restrictions were introduced on industrial action (including strike notice and a Citizen's Charter right for individuals to challenge industrial action in the public sector). In the individual field, it altered the laws on maternity, employment particulars, redundancy consultation, and transfers of undertakings in response to changes in (then) EC law, and introduced two new heads of unfair dismissal. As a logical, but much criticized, further measure to deregulate the labour market, it finally abolished wages councils.

Outside the mainstream legislation just described, the 1980s also saw very significant changes in social security laws relevant to employment law (especially payment through the employer, through statutory sick pay, and statutory maternity pay), and the Wages Act 1986 introduced new laws on deductions from wages that saw quite remarkable development in the early 1990s. In the field of discrimination law there were, again, consistent developments, but this time largely through the intervention of EC law rather than changes in domestic legislation. If all of this does not provide the reader with enough excitement in life, the Transfer of Undertakings Regulations could be addressed.

Given this quite remarkable series of statutes (and, often, their supporting regulations and orders), we have at least been fortunate in having five major consolidations in the period 1992–96, bringing some order to the chaos. The Trade Union and Labour Relations (Consolidation) Act 1992 consolidated the morass of laws (ancient and modern) on collective labour law, replacing in particular the Trade Union and Labour Relations Act 1974 and most of the Conservative Employment Acts 1980–93. Social security law was consolidated into the Social Security Contributions and Benefits Act 1992 and the Social Security Administration Act 1992; it took a particularly strong river to clean out those Augean stables. The law relating to individual employment matters was finally

[11] Highly recommended reading to set this series of statutes into their political context is Auerbach *Legislating for Conflict* (1990), commented on in Foch et al. 'Politics, Pragmatism and Ideology: The Wellsprings of Conservative Union Legislation' (1993) 22 ILJ 14; and Davies and Freedland *Labour Legislation and Public Policy* (1993). The political progress of the three governments of Mrs Thatcher is set out in excellent and highly readable form in Young *One of Us* (1990).

[12] Employment for the 1990s (Cm 540, 1988); People, Jobs and Opportunity (Cm 1810, 1992).

consolidated in the Employment Rights Act 1996, which replaced the Employment Protection (Consolidation) Act 1978 (as, by then, heavily amended) and the Wages Act 1986, with the law relating to tribunals and the EAT being consolidated at the same time in the Employment Tribunals Act 1996. Outside that framework still lay the Equal Pay Act 1970, the Sex Discrimination Act 1975, the Race Relations Act 1976, and the Disability Discrimination Act 1995.

1.2.4 **Labour 1997–2010: change and continuity**

The 1997 general election saw the end of a period of 18 years of Conservative administrations and a landslide victory for (New) Labour. Dramatic though this political reversal of fortunes was, it was far removed from the previous return of a Labour government in 1974, when the Trade Union and Labour Relations Act 1974 (sweeping away the previous Conservative government's employment laws) was the first statute passed by that incoming government. Instead, Labour seemed to put a relatively low priority on employment law changes (reflecting the equally low priority of the subject at the election), and it had been made clear for some time by the 'modernizers' within the party that there were to be no wholesale repeals of the reforms of the Thatcher administration.[13] Indeed, the first statute passed was the Employment Rights (Dispute Resolution) Act 1998 (reforming tribunal procedures and establishing the ACAS arbitration alternative to tribunals for unfair dismissal cases) that was inherited at Green Paper stage from the previous government. The National Minimum Wage Act 1998 enacted one of Labour's relatively few election commitments on employment law, and the Working Time Regulations 1998 were an obligation under EC law (the previous government's challenge to the legality of the backing Directive having failed in the European Court of Justice); the Public Interest Disclosure (or 'Whistleblowers') Act 1998 was also in many ways relatively uncontroversial and commanded widespread support. It was only with the publication of the White Paper 'Fairness at Work'[14] that a clear idea could be obtained of the likely direction of the new government in this area. Again, however, in spite of some reforms important in themselves, this was hardly a major sea change, and even then the government were accused of some backsliding by the unions on the eventual form of the resulting statute, the Employment Relations Act 1999—especially in relation to the union recognition procedure and the mere lifting of the limit on the unfair dismissal compensatory award (from £12,000 to £50,000) rather than its abolition, as had been mooted in the White Paper. The introduction to the White Paper said that this Act was not to be seen as merely a first step in reforms, because it 'seeks to draw a line under the issue of industrial relations law'—and this was largely the case in the first Labour government, at least in relation to purely domestic legislation.

There was, however, one other legislative innovation during this period which had an effect on employment law, namely the passage of the Human Rights Act 1998, putting the European Convention on Human Rights directly into domestic law. As elsewhere, this led to an element of reassessment of existing employment-related rules to see if they were

[13] 'The abolition of the closed shop was one of the many employment law reforms of the 1980s that were justified and will remain . . . Other measures which will remain include those on picketing, secondary action, ballots and notice before strikes, unofficial action, elections for certain trade union offices and rights to join the trade union of one's choice and not to be unjustifiably disciplined': Fairness at Work (Cm 3968, May 1998), p 22. For the background political changes, especially in relations with the trade unions see McIlroy 'The Enduring Alliance? Trade Unions and the Making of New Labour 1994–1997' (1998) 36 BJIR 537.

[14] See n 13. See generally Taylor 'Annual Review Article 1997' (1998) 36 BJIR 293.

compliant with the Convention's standards. In the area of collective labour law, it will be seen in Chapters 9 and 10 that there have been consistent challenges to laws restricting trade union activities (especially on taking industrial action) under provisions such as Article 10 (freedom of expression) and Article 12 (freedom of assembly and association). In the individual employment sphere, Article 8 (respect for private and family life) has been prayed in aid in cases concerning an employee's privacy at work, and Article 9 (freedom of thought, conscience, and religion) in discrimination cases. However, results here have been mixed and reliance on a Convention right is certainly not a panacea. In particular, in the important context of unfair dismissal, the general approach has been that the substance of Convention rights has already been incorporated into domestic law indirectly in the test as to whether a dismissal was fair in the light of 'equity and the substantial merits of the case', so that a secondary argument that the dismissal was contrary to the Convention usually adds little.[15]

The second Labour government (after the party's emphatic re-election in 2001) saw a renewed increase in the pace of domestic legislation with the enactment of the Employment Act 2002, a bad example of 'Henry VIII' drafting, that is, requiring supplementation by a huge raft of statutory instruments over a prolonged period. The two main themes of this Act were the extension of family-friendly policies (a major plank of Labour policy, covering longer maternity leave, paternity and adoption leave, and the right to request flexible working) and a fairly desperate attempt to halt the inexorable rise in tribunal applications by further reforms of tribunal procedure and (more radically) new 'standard procedures' for grievances and discipline/dismissal which had to be exhausted by both parties before going to a tribunal (backed by a regime of automatic unfairness, striking out of tribunal claims, and significant increases or decreases in compensation).

At the same time as these domestic developments, EC law was becoming more active. Prior to Mr Blair's second election victory in 2001 there had been transposed one Directive in the Part-time Workers (Prevention of Less Favourable Treatment) Regulations 2000, and not long afterwards came the transposition of a second 'atypical worker' Directive in the Fixed-term Employees (Prevention of Less Favourable Treatment) Regulations, though a third and complementary Directive on agency workers did not then find favour with member states and was rejected. Going beyond this area of mainstream employment law, EC law was also by this time powering discrimination law, leading to an upgrading of existing sex, race, and disability discrimination law (in particular introducing a statutory reversal of the burden of proof and a wider definition of indirect discrimination) and the introduction of new laws to combat employment-related discrimination in the areas of sexual orientation, religion or belief, and age. The Information and Consultation Directive 2002 led to enactment of the Information and Consultation of Employees Regulations 2004, giving a legal right to require mechanisms for informing and consulting the workforce (where no such mechanism already exists) in firms of 50 or more. The other major EC law development was the updating of the Acquired Rights Directive, leading to the renewed Transfer of Undertakings (Protection of Employment) Regulations 2006. These introduced some useful reforms but were also a disappointment in other ways, this being an area where the government could only make changes which were allowed by the Directive itself.

The domestic law agenda of this second Labour government was unadventurous after the Employment Act 2002 (the Employment Relations Act 2004 being largely a miscellany of technical amendments to industrial relations law), but at the 2005 election there

[15] *X v Y* [2004] IRLR 625 CA; see 7.5.2.4; for a subsequent reaffirmation of this view see *Garamukwana v Solent NHS Trust* [2016] IRLR 416, EAT, affirmed by the ECtHR ([2019] IRLR 853).

was once again considerable emphasis by Labour on further developments in family-friendly policies and work–life balance. A year after Mr Blair's third election victory, this fed through into the Work and Families Act 2006, which gave extended maternity rights (including the raising of the statutory maternity pay period to nine months, as a stage towards an eventual one year) and paternity rights, and (significantly, given changes to the UK's demographic pattern) extended the right to request flexible working to those with caring responsibilities for the elderly and infirm.

The Employment Act 2008, as well as making several technical amendments (particularly to the national minimum wage legislation), addressed one major problem in employment law that had arisen by that time. The 'standard procedures' for grievances and dismissal (introduced by the 2004 Act to attempt to drive down the tribunal application figures) had proved to be an inflexible, bureaucratic, and (at times) counterproductive failure, to such an extent that they were even producing exasperated criticism from the judges having to try to make sense of them, in language sometimes bordering on the unjudicial. They stand as a warning of two dangers in employment law—trying to impose a one-size-fits-all solution to the myriad forms of employment and assuming that legal provisions alone can resolve an employment law problem. To avoid at least a level of facial egg, the government commissioned an independent review of them (the Gibbons Report) which grasped the nettle and recommended total repeal, a relief to all involved. This was done in the 2008 Act,[16] though (in a good example of 'legislate in haste, repeal at leisure') it took years to purge the system of the last cases to be governed by them. Finally, two other legislative developments occurred towards the end of this government. First, the EU finally agreed a Directive on temporary working and this was transposed into domestic law in the Agency Workers Regulations 2010. Second, a further major consolidation exercise resulted in all six heads of discrimination being put in one place, the Equality Act 2010. In addition to the mammoth task of consolidation, the then government introduced a limited number of substantive changes to the law in this Act, though these were not all uncontroversial politically and the succeeding Coalition government, though generally accepting the consolidatory aspects of the statute, either repealed or refused to bring into force certain of these planned innovations.

1.2.5 **The Coalition government 2010–15**

The 2010 election proved inconclusive in the sense that Labour lost it but the Conservatives did not win it. The result was a Conservative/Liberal Democrat coalition, a factor that has had an effect in employment law because of the compromises that had to be made to possible reforms in this area. It is certainly true that the Conservative side of the Coalition government were not able to make certain changes that their backbenchers would have liked to see; on the other hand, the Liberal Democrats had to agree to other changes that in a wider sense could be seen as not exactly 'liberal' as the price of progress of some of their ideas, in particular extending even further the laws on flexible and family-friendly working. Part of the Coalition agreement was a review of employment law. Possibly as a result of the novelty in this country of Coalition politics, this did not have the sort of ideological consistency of the reforms of Mrs Thatcher's governments, *but* when the eventual proposed changes are taken as a whole they do amount to a relatively large scale of reform, if only of an incremental nature.[17] Some of the initial changes were possible by amending regulations, but then the principal legislation was contained in the Enterprise

[16] See Sanders 'Part I of the Employment Act 2008: "Better" Dispute Resolution?' (2009) 38 ILJ 30.

[17] Hepple 'Back to the Future: Employment Law under the Coalition Government' (2013) 42 ILJ 203.

and Regulatory Reform Act 2013, the Growth and Infrastructure Act 2013, the Children and Families Act 2014, the Small Business, Enterprise and Employment Act 2015, and the Deregulation Act 2015. The principal changes of substance were the increase of the qualifying period for unfair dismissal from one year to two, the capping of unfair dismissal compensation at a year's pay in most cases, the removal of the compulsory retirement age, a new system of fines on employers for breaching employment protection laws, an uplift of compensation for failure to follow a code of practice, a controversial new category of 'employee shareholders' (trading in certain employment rights for a shareholding), tougher penalties for failure to pay the national minimum wage, and an attack on at least one potential abuse of zero-hours contracts. On a procedural level, there were new, simplified Employment Tribunal Rules (with far more emphasis on judge-alone hearings at tribunal and EAT level), a new system of *early* ACAS conciliation (to be undertaken before proceedings are issued in a tribunal), and the imposition of fees for applicants to tribunals and appellants to the EAT. In addition to this, legally important changes of a more technical nature were made to whistleblowing protection, collective redundancy consultation, and transfers of undertakings. Most of the above were driven largely by the Conservative element of the Coalition, but the views of the Liberal Democrat element were seen primarily in one other important area, namely in family-friendly laws. Flexible working was extended to *all* employees with six months' service (thus going well beyond a right for carers) and much emphasis was placed on evolving greater rights for working parents—first, existing parental leave was extended, and then there was a major overhaul of the whole system, introducing *shared* parental leave.

1.2.6 **The Conservative government 2015–19**

While at the outset the 2015 election looked likely to result in another coalition, the eventual result was a narrow absolute majority for David Cameron and the Conservatives. Employment law had not figured greatly in their manifesto for the election, except for a proposal for a further tightening of the laws on industrial action (prompted in particular by strikes on the London Underground). This came about in the Trade Union Act 2016, which, among several separate changes (including to the timing of industrial action, picketing, political objects, and the powers of the Certification Officer), set new requirements for minimum ballot thresholds, essentially requiring at least 50 per cent of those eligible to vote to do so (plus at least 40 per cent of those eligible to vote voting 'yes' in a case affecting 'important public services') if the action is to be lawful. On the individual front, the government introduced the idea of the national *living* wage, in effect increasing the National Minimum Wage for those aged 25 and over from £6.70 per hour to £7.20 per hour, with a commitment to continue raising it. However, any prospect of further gradual progress was dramatically affected by two shocks to the political system. The first was the result of the June 2016 Referendum on continued membership of the EU;[18] the second was the result of the 2017 general election called by Theresa May to strengthen her position, but which in fact lost her the Parliamentary majority she had inherited. With regard to the Referendum, this was initially expected to go one way but went the other, leading to a significant period of uncertainty over what became known inelegantly as 'Brexit'. Clearly, exit from the EU was expected to have fundamental effects on employment law *eventually*, but the key point was that this process was likely to take a protracted period to happen. In the short to medium term, the effect of the European Union (Withdrawal) Act 2018 was to preserve EU-based employment rights in their current form.

[18] Leading to the resignation of David Cameron, of whom it could now be said that nothing so marked his prime ministership as his way of leaving it.

1.2.7 **The Conservative government 2019–24**

In late 2019 the Conservatives, under their new leader Boris Johnson, won a major electoral victory with a large majority. Once again, employment policy played relatively little part in the election, except perhaps indirectly through the idea of policies of 'levelling up' deprived areas of the country, a factor strengthened by the government's success in the so-called red wall of previously solidly Labour seats, which made any idea of a major rolling back of employment protection laws on leaving the EU less likely than before. Britain duly left, subject to a transitional period. However, any further moves in domestic politics and legislation were then badly blown off course by the coronavirus crisis. This had certain direct effects in employment law, particularly in relation to sick pay and the temporary laying-off of staff. In addition, however, there may be other indirect but longer-term implications, a principal example being the widespread adoption of home/remote working which may result in serious changes to work patterns, with which employment law may have to catch up over the next few years. The defenestration of first Boris Johnson and then Liz Truss in 2022 initially led to something of a hiatus in government policy, including in employment law. However, in a strange twist, in the remaining time that that administration had under Rishi Sunak there was a quite remarkable flurry of employment legislation (often originating in private members bills) extending legal protection. Chief among these were the Employment (Allocation of tips) Act 2023, the Neonatal Care (Leave and Pay) Act 2023, the Protection from Redundancy (Pregnancy and Family Leave) Act 2023, the Carer's Leave Act 2024, the Employment Relations (Flexible Working) Act 2023, and regulatory changes in 2024 to paternity leave, maternity leave, adoption leave and shared parental leave.

1.2.8 **The Labour government 2025**

When the Labour Party won the 2024 election by a landslide, one of its major commitments was to a widespread overhaul of employment law, resulting in the Employment Rights Act 2025, the most comprehensive piece of legislation since the 1980s. It covers a wide area. Partly it aimed at dismantling several of the restrictions on trade unions enacted by the previous governments, but also at enhancing certain employment protections. Chief among these were reducing the qualifying period for unfair dismissal to six months, making statutory sick pay and parental and paternity leave day-one rights, giving more rights to zero-hours and agency workers, placing restrictions on fire-and-rehire, extending protection from harassment, amending the procedure for handling redundancies, reforming the law on union recognition, increasing the time limit for bringing tribunal proceedings from three months to six, and (potentially most radically of all) introducing a new Fair Work Agency to give support for individual employees in enforcing their rights, existing and new. This was a very large agenda, too large to all come into force in one Big Bang. Some of the repeals of previous laws (particularly the Trade Union Act 2016) most wanted by the trade unions came into force immediately, but in relation to all the rest, the government opted for a phased process. The Department of Business and Trade has issued (at the time of writing) a 'roadmap' to introduction, stressing all the areas that will require consultations and then setting out an intended timetable, envisaging three major commencements in April 2026, October 2026 and in 2027 (no month specified). Two further points should be noticed: (1) as a matter of style, much of the Act operates by way of amendments to existing legislation, especially the Trade Union and Labour Relations (Consolidation) Act 1992 and the Employment Rights Act 1996; and (2) much of the substance of these new provisions and rights is to be either fleshed out or even contained in statutory instruments, which can be expected to be voluminous. Thus, final enactment of the whole Act is likely to take upwards of two years and be of some complexity.

1.3 Machinery (1): practical dispute resolution

As seen, the voluntary and non-legal nature of British industrial relations has been its dominant characteristic, and there is not an overall statutory framework for compulsory conciliation and arbitration leading to enforceable awards and agreements as may be found in certain other countries. Moreover, we do not formally distinguish between what are conceptually two different types of industrial dispute—those about the negotiation of new and improved terms of employment (disputes of interest) and those about the interpretation, application, and enforcement of existing terms (disputes of right).[19] Arguably there should be separate procedures for dealing with these, particularly as the second type is inherently more amenable to legal adjudication, but in this country any such differentiation will be the exception rather than the rule, and so both kinds of dispute tend (in areas where collective bargaining is still the norm) to be subject to voluntarily negotiated procedures of varying quality (or ad hoc arrangements), leading to non-enforceable collective agreements. However, although the law has been non-interventionist (except for the period covered by the Industrial Relations Act 1971) it has not abstained totally, and has attempted in various ways at various times to provide certain residual machinery to facilitate industrial relations and minimize industrial conflict. Wages councils were historically used (prior to their abolition in 1993) to aid collective bargaining in under-unionized trades, and since the Conciliation Act 1896 there has existed machinery for industrial conciliation. Since the Industrial Courts Act 1919 there has also existed machinery for industrial arbitration; this has always[20] been basically voluntary, that is, by the consent of the parties. Since 1975, these conciliation and arbitration services have been largely provided by ACAS, and they are considered presently.

In the resolution of employment disputes by the intervention of an outside agency there is an important conceptual distinction. On the one hand there is conciliation, which is where the conciliator attempts to bring the parties together in the hope that a common discussion will reveal a means of settlement acceptable to both parties; one variation of this is 'mediation', where the mediator takes a more active role in putting forward detailed solutions, though still with a view to settlement by agreement.[21] These functions are now within the jurisdiction of ACAS, which was originally established by the Employment Protection Act 1975. On the other hand there is arbitration, which is where the arbitrator fulfils a quasi-judicial role in that the parties have agreed to submit their dispute to that person for their *decision* on what should be the result; they therefore have to look into the relevant facts and law, and it is clearly understood that the parties will abide by the decision. This function is now within the jurisdiction of both ACAS and the CAC, which was also established by the Employment Protection Act 1975; as we shall see, it may conduct voluntary arbitrations, but it also has certain powers of unilateral arbitration under

[19] Report of the Royal Commission on Trade Unions and Employers' Associations (Cmnd 3623, 1968) para 60.

[20] Except for the period 1940–59 when, initially as a result of wartime measures aimed at avoiding industrial disruptions, some arbitration was compulsory. In 1951 Order 1376 replaced Order 1305 of 1940; some 1,270 cases were heard before its revocation in 1959: see Cooper's *Outlines of Industrial Law* (6th edn, 1972) 446–51; Kahn-Freund *Labour and the Law* (1983) 151–53.

[21] Mediation may be used particularly (a) where issues cannot be presented in a sufficiently clear-cut manner for arbitration (eg major changes of work linked to a pay settlement) or (b) where one or both of the parties is or are unwilling to submit the matter formally to arbitration (on the principle that a party who agrees to arbitration must ultimately be able to afford to lose). Either way, mediation must be properly understood by the parties—it does not result in an 'award' by the mediator, though there may be considerable moral pressure to comply with the mediator's suggestions.

statute and has specific jurisdictions in relation to the statutory recognition procedure, European Works Councils, and the informing and consulting of employees.

To this division must now be added a third, namely a new system for state *enforcement* of employment right. This is contained in the Employment Rights Act 2025 which provides for the establishment of the Fair Work Agency, a potentially major move away from the basic idea that employment rights are personal to the employee who must choose whether to seek to enforce them in an individual law suit.

1.3.1 **The Advisory, Conciliation, and Arbitration Service**

The composition of ACAS is governed primarily by Part VI of the Trade Union and Labour Relations (Consolidation) Act 1992. It is directed by a Council consisting of a chairman and nine to 15 members (three or four representing employers, three or four representing unions, and the rest 'independents'). ACAS itself is set up as a body independent of the government, in particular independent of the Department for Business, Energy and Industrial Strategy, and appoints its own staff. It maintains a central office in London and regional offices in Scotland and in five regions in England and Wales, and must produce an annual report for the Secretary of State for Business to lay before Parliament.

Among its staff, it maintains 'conciliation officers',[22] who have particular responsibility for conciliating in statutory actions brought by individual employees.

The functions of ACAS are set out in Part IV of the 1992 Act; in addition to the detailed functions considered below, there is a statement of its general duty in s 209, as follows:

> It is the general duty of ACAS to promote the improvement of industrial relations.

This apparently simple formulation has in fact gone through three phases, with considerable symbolic significance (if little practical effect). From 1975 to 1993 the section continued: 'and in particular to encourage the extension of collective bargaining and the development and, where necessary, reform of collective bargaining machinery'. That may well have been the ethos of the 1970s, but after a decade of overt government hostility to any such aims in the 1980s it was hardly surprising that the then government took the opportunity in the Trade Union Reform and Employment Rights Act 1993 to repeal that wording. They substituted 'in particular by exercising its functions in relation to the settlement of trade disputes under sections 210 and 212 [ie by conciliation and arbitration]'. ACAS had certainly proved useful to the Conservative government in certain disputes (a measure of that use being that it was never seriously threatened with abolition, unlike most tripartite bodies of the 1970s), and this formulation reflected that. However, it arguably placed too much emphasis on reactive, problem-solving work ('firefighting', in industrial relations (IR) jargon), and too little on long-term advice work ('fire prevention') which ACAS wanted to enhance. With the change of government in 1997, an increased emphasis on fire prevention could be seen to be consistent with that government's 'partnership' ideas in the White Paper 'Fairness at Work'. As a result, the Employment Relations Act 1999 removed the 1993 wording and left ACAS with the widest possible general duty, as just set out. Of course, the cynic could argue that the extent to which ACAS can increase its proactive work will depend not on a change to its statutory remit but on the resources it is given.

[22] Trade Union and Labour Relations (Consolidation) Act 1992, s 211; they are known as Conciliation Officers Tribunals (COTs) to distinguish them from those specializing in collective conciliation.

The specific statutory functions[23] of ACAS are as follows.

1.3.1.1 **Collective conciliation**

Where a trade dispute[24] exists or seems imminent, ACAS may, at the request of one or more of the parties or on its own initiative, offer its assistance for the purposes of conciliation or mediation. In doing so, it may also refer the parties to a third person for conciliation, and it must where possible encourage the parties to use any existing negotiation or disputes procedures.[25] The traditional form of conciliation is carried out by an individual ACAS officer working directly with the parties, but in recent years there has been an increase in the use of a hybrid form, referred to as 'advisory mediation', aimed at encouraging a cooperative and problem-solving approach by the parties themselves, possibly on a longer-term basis; this tends to be done by the setting up of a joint workshop or joint working party, chaired by the ACAS officer, and may be particularly appropriate for resolving disputes over matters such as handling organizational change.[26] In addition to these forms of voluntary conciliation, ACAS has statutory conciliation functions at certain stages in union claims for disclosure of bargaining information or under the statutory recognition procedure, both of which are considered in Chapter 9.

One area of potential difficulty for ACAS in the context of collective conciliation may arise if it transpires in a particular dispute that the employer is seeking to bring a legal action against the union, initially for an injunction to restrain the industrial action or threat of it and then possibly in a suit for damages. In such a case, any ACAS intervention would have to be more circumspect. However, there is another side to it, since such ACAS intervention might in practice be more likely to resolve an impasse than legal proceedings, and at an early stage the suggestion was tentatively made that the law should be amended to include provision for a judge to stay proceedings in any action arising from an industrial dispute in order for ACAS to attempt conciliation,[27] which, if successful, might well make considerable savings in cost, time, acrimony, and accusations against the courts of partiality in industrial disputes; however, this interesting suggestion has never been taken up. It can be further noted that where the parties engage lawyers the lines of communication may be lengthened and the process of conciliation made more difficult.

1.3.1.2 **Individual conciliation**

Quantitatively, the principal statutory duty of ACAS has always been, through its conciliation officers, to attempt to conciliate in cases brought before tribunals by individuals claiming unfair dismissal or denial of other employment protection rights; this also

[23] These services always were in the past free to the parties, but s 251A of the 1992 Act (inserted by the Trade Union Reform and Employment Rights Act 1993) gave a power to charge fees *and* a power for the Secretary of State to require the charging of fees for some or all services. This change was not wanted by ACAS itself. The principal conciliation functions remain free.

[24] The wide definition as originally contained in the Trade Union and Labour Relations Act 1974, s 29 (and now in the Trade Union and Labour Relations (Consolidation) Act 1992, s 218) continues to apply for this purpose; the narrowed definition for the purpose of immunity from tort action in industrial disputes enacted by the Employment Act 1982 and now in the 1992 Act, s 244 does not apply here. Perhaps an example of governmental propensity to have cake and consume same.

[25] Trade Union and Labour Relations (Consolidation) Act 1992, s 210. In 2024/25 522 collective conciliation cases were received and 417 successfully completed. Of these cases, 65 per cent concerned pay or other terms of employment, 21 per cent recognition, 15 per cent working practices and 2 per cent discipline and dismissal: *ACAS Annual Report 2024/5.*

[26] See Kessler and Purcell 'Joint Problem Solving' (ACAS Occasional Paper No 55).

[27] ACAS Annual Report 1983 para 1.16.

applies to cases of all the heads of modern discrimination law and to the various rights enacted by the legislation for the protection of trade union members, including the statutory redundancy handling procedures.[28] To facilitate this procedurally, the ACAS regional offices have always received copies of originating applications to the tribunals. The general principles applying to this form of conciliation are that:

(1) in all cases, the conciliation officer must consider encouraging the use of established grievance procedures within the firm;

(2) in unfair dismissal cases, the officer must in theory seek to promote a settlement primarily by way of reinstatement or re-engagement, and only attempt a monetary settlement if that is impracticable, or not wanted by the ex-employee;[29]

(3) the conciliation process is confidential, in that anything said to the officer during it is not admissible evidence in subsequent tribunal proceedings without the consent of the person who said it;[30]

(4) finally, it must be emphasized that if the conciliation is successful in leading to an agreed settlement as a consequence of action taken by a conciliation officer under these statutory duties (known because of the form recording it as a 'COT3 settlement'), that is *binding* and so will bar any future tribunal proceedings in the matter,[31] so that the claimant should be certain that they are happy with the terms of the proposed settlement before irrevocably agreeing with it. For this reason alone, it is vital that ACAS should behave, and be seen to behave, entirely impartially as between the claimant and the employer when conducting negotiations; there is, however, an interesting divergence between law and practice here because, while this impartiality is and always has been absolutely fundamental to ACAS practice, in strict law the only duty on the conciliation officer is to facilitate the settlement, not to ensure that it is a 'fair' one.[32]

[28] Employment Tribunals Act 1996, s 18. In 2024/5 ACAS received 124,548 cases under the early conciliation system; 28 per cent were primarily for unfair dismissal, 9 per cent for working time issues, and 33 per cent for discrimination in its various forms; in addition (often added on to the above) 32 per cent included claims for unpaid wages or other terms of employment. In all, 50 per cent were subject to an ACAS settlement; 30 per cent were withdrawn, struck out, or otherwise settled; and only 16 per cent proceeded to a tribunal hearing (arguably the key figure): *ACAS Annual Report 2024.5.*

[29] Employment Tribunals Act 1996, s 18(4). This is wholly ineffective in practice, as can be seen from the consistently low rate of re-employment (whether by order or by agreement): see 7.6.1; Williams and Lewis *The Aftermath of Tribunal Reinstatement and Re-Engagement* (DE Research Paper No 23) pp 31 and 39.

[30] Further, anything communicated to the ACAS officer in this process is covered by the defence of absolute privilege in the law of defamation: *Freer v Glover* [2006] IRLR 521, QBD.

[31] ERA 1996, s 203(2); there are equivalent provisions in the discrimination legislation and the other provisions where ACAS conciliation appears.

[32] In *Moore v Duport Furniture Products Ltd* [1982] ICR 84, [1982] IRLR 31, HL, it was held (a) that the action of the conciliation officer in recording an agreement to accept compensation of £300 on the standard form COT3 was sufficient to bar further proceedings, and (b) that where an officer is presented with such an agreement already worked out by the parties, his or her duty is only to verify the fact of agreement and record it—he or she is not under a further duty to enquire into the 'fairness' of the agreement or to give the applicant any further advice. Likewise, an ACAS official is under no legal duty to explain the law to the applicant and is not bound to adopt any particular formula or approach: *Slack v Greenham (Plant Hire) Ltd* [1983] ICR 617, [1983] IRLR 271, EAT. This approach was strongly reaffirmed in *Clarke v Redcar & Cleveland BC* [2006] IRLR 324, EAT where equal pay claimants were trying to evade a COT3 settlement after receiving further legal advice that they had settled for too little, arguing unsuccessfully that the ACAS officer should have told them that it was too little.

These principles continue to apply, but in 2014 the *method* of this form of conciliation underwent its biggest change since its inception in 1975. Until that time, it had operated primarily once employment tribunal proceedings had been commenced, with a view to their being discontinued. However, as part of the Gibbons Report of 2009 recommending the abolition of the failed statutory procedures, it was proposed that in future, tribunal hearings should be minimized by a new system of conciliation taking place before proceedings are commenced *at all*. After an initial trial on a voluntary basis which proved successful, the whole system was altered to make it compulsory, under the title of 'early conciliation' or 'EC'.[33] The basis of this is that before a person can lodge an employment tribunal claim they must (with a few defined exceptions) contact ACAS by letter, online, or by telephone, giving basic information in prescribed form on themselves and the proposed respondent. This triggers a period of one month in which it is the duty of ACAS to seek to promote a settlement. That period can be extended by up to two weeks if both parties agree and the ACAS officer considers that there is a reasonable prospect of settlement. The hope is that this early concentration of minds will be conducive to agreement before the need arises to start legal proceedings. However, there is no compulsion on the parties to do so. If there is such an agreement, the result will be an abandonment of any claim or a COT3 settlement in the usual way. If, however, there is no such agreement (either after an attempt is made at it, or even where it is clear from the start that there is no prospect of it) or if the period simply expires, ACAS will issue an 'EC Certificate' which proves that the claimant has complied with the legal requirements and which is then the gateway to commencement of tribunal proceedings.[34]

The certificate also sets out the relevant dates, which is important for a separate but important aspect. The statutory employment rights in question tend to have short time limits (traditionally of only three months but put up to six months by the Employment Rights Act 2025) and so there was potentially a problem of fitting the new conciliation period into this long-standing law. The answer is in complex provisions which have the overall effect that while the conciliation period is in operation, the time limit for the right in question is suspended, with the clock only starting to tick again on the terminal date shown in the certificate. This whole system is meant to be a practical help for those willing to use it, not a straitjacket, and fortunately the case law on it has in general shown an appreciation of this point and a wide interpretation, with judges emphasizing the essentially voluntary nature of the system (once its procedure has been complied with) and refusing to rule out claimants because of technicalities, being concerned *not* to hamstring the system with the sort of legalistic hair-splitting that was such a feature of the repealed statutory procedures.[35]

Two further points are worth mentioning:

(1) What is now the position with conciliation *after* proceedings have been commenced? There is a provision stating that there is a duty on ACAS still to attempt conciliation here either if both parties request it or if the conciliation officer thinks there is a reasonable prospect of success.[36] Beyond that, however, there is now merely a *power* for ACAS to act, which means that there can be no expectation of help at this later stage, let alone any right to it, and all would depend on whether there were resources to provide it. This emphasizes the dominance and significance now of early conciliation.

[33] Enterprise and Regulatory Reform Act 2013, s 7, adding new ss 18–18C to the Employment Tribunals Act 1996. The details of the scheme are contained in the Employment Tribunals (Early Conciliation: Exemptions and Rules of Procedure) Regulations 2014, SI 2014/254.

[34] Employment Tribunals Act 1996, s 18A. Without such a certificate, no claim may be commenced. It remains possible for either potential party to approach ACAS to seek this assistance in the first place: s 18B.

[35] For the case law here see *Harvey* PI [286] ff.

[36] Employment Tribunals Act 1996, s 18C.

(2) Can the parties reach a binding settlement by themselves, without using this system at all? The answer is that they can, but it must be in a legally acceptable form. By 1990, the demand for ACAS conciliation had ballooned, with evidence that many employers were reaching private accommodations and just handing the result over to ACAS to ratify (in order to make it final). In that year, ACAS policy was changed so that it would no longer merely rubber stamp an existing agreement, a principle which still applies. However, this left a gap in provision for settlement in the case of a bona fide two-party agreement to compromise a claim, because of the general statutory principle that any attempt to contract out of the protection of the law is void. The answer was the introduction by statute of the concept of a binding 'compromise agreement', acting specifically as an exception to that general principle. Such agreements are now widely used (as an alternative to COT3 settlements) and produce the desired finality. However, there are definite legal requirements, both as to their form and also (arguably most importantly) as to the requirement that before the claimant signs it they must have had advice from an independent (professionally insured) adviser as to the terms of the agreement and its binding nature.[37] In an attempt to raise the profile of such agreements even further, the Coalition government in 2013 renamed them 'settlement agreements' and instituted a system whereby an employer can engage in 'pre-termination negotiations' with an employee (with a view to reaching an agreement for the termination of their employment) on a confidential basis;[38] ACAS then issued a new Code of Practice (No 4) on Settlement Agreements to explain and give guidance on these changes.[39]

1.3.1.3 **Arranging arbitration**

Under s 212 of the Trade Union and Labour Relations (Consolidation) Act 1992, ACAS may arrange arbitration for an actual or anticipated trade dispute if one or more of the parties request it *and* all parties consent to it.[40] This is clearly voluntary arbitration, and the resulting decision will not be legally enforceable per se,[41] though in practice the arbitrator's decision is invariably complied with. ACAS does not automatically have to arrange arbitration; as well as being satisfied that all parties consent, it must also consider whether conciliation might be successful instead, and should not arrange arbitration unless satisfied that existing negotiation and disputes procedures have been exhausted (unless there are special reasons why arbitration should be used *instead* of such procedures). The conciliation stage is important—if successful it removes the need for an arbitration;

[37] Employment Rights Act 1996, s 203(3)–(5). This has been used as a template for the compromise agreement provisions in other employment legislation, in particular the Equality Act 2010, s 147 in relation to discrimination claims. The independent adviser may be a lawyer (including a legal executive), a trade union official (authorized by the union for this purpose), or a worker at an advice centre (similarly authorized).

[38] Employment Rights Act 1996, s 111A. This means that if unsuccessful the details of the negotiations cannot be disclosed in any subsequent proceedings for unfair dismissal. This point was emphasized in the first appellate decision on this section: *Faithorn Farrell Timms plc v Bailey* UKEAT/0025/16. There are, however, exceptions where anything said or done was, in a tribunal's view, improper or connected with improper behaviour. Also, it does not apply where the dismissal falls into one of the categories of automatic unfairness.

[39] Important features are guidance on what is 'improper' under s 111A and suggestions that, as a matter of good practice, an employee should be allowed to be accompanied at the discussions and should have at least ten calendar days to consider any offer.

[40] Mumford 'Arbitration and ACAS in Britain: A Historical Perspective' (1996) 34 BJIR 287.

[41] Pt I of the Arbitration Act 1996 does not apply to this form of arbitration: s 212(5).

if unsuccessful the ACAS conciliation officer then has the task of determining with the parties the precise terms of reference for the arbitrator because it is important in an arbitration that the terms are not themselves a subject for dispute; in fact, the terms of reference are usually kept as simple as possible and, further, nothing of what has happened or been said at the conciliation stage is made known to the arbitrator, who approaches the issue afresh. The usual practice is for ACAS to appoint one person to conduct the arbitration (from the panel of appropriate people whom they use), though occasionally a board of arbitration may be convened; officials and employees of ACAS are *not* used, though ACAS do of course provide the necessary secretarial and administrative services.[42] It is also possible for a voluntary arbitration to be referred to the CAC, though this option has effectively now fallen into disuse. Legal representation at an arbitration is unusual (and indeed usually discouraged if suggested) and although the proceedings may be conducted in a relatively structured manner (aimed at giving both sides a full opportunity to expand upon their written submissions and to query the other side's case), matters of procedure are largely for the arbitrator to determine and will not normally include legalistic forms, such as prolonged cross-examination.

Four particular points about arbitration might be noted here briefly. First, references may come from *standing* arbitration agreements, usually taking the form of a clause in the disputes procedure section of a collective bargain stating that in the absence of agreement on a disputed point through internal procedures, the matter shall be referred to ACAS for conciliation and/or arbitration. This may be a general reference, or the clause itself may cover the procedure that is to be adopted. Second, it is possible for parties to a dispute to approach ACAS to ask them simply to *nominate* an arbitrator to conduct an arbitration which has already been agreed upon, without going through the normal conciliation procedures; such arbitrations do not figure in the annual ACAS statistics.[43] Third, at times there has been considerable interest in and publicity about the form of arbitration variously known as 'pendulum', 'flip-flop', 'straight choice', or 'final offer', where the arbitrator is constrained to choose between acceptance in full of one side's case or that of the other.[44] The aim of this is said to be to narrow the field of dispute and ensure that each side puts forward a realistic (rather than a bargaining) case, capable of being accepted in full. While this may be a natural form of adjudication in disputes of right, ACAS is by no means convinced that it is a panacea in disputes of interest such as pay determinations where flexibility in the arbitration may be just as important. Although ACAS will arrange such an arbitration if the parties desire it, it does *not* adopt it as its policy, preferring to encourage responsible bargaining in other ways and pointing out consistently that the fact that an arbitrator is normally given full discretion in coming to their award does *not* mean in practice that all they do is to split the disputed area down the middle, with half a baby to each. Fourth, there was—what should have been—a promising development in

[42] In 2024/5 there were only seven references to arbitration: *ACAS Annual Report 2024/25*. On the use of third party intervention see Millward et al. *Workplace Industrial Relations in Transition* (1992) 194–96 and 208–11.

[43] This, however, can lead to a problem: the resulting arbitration is *not* an ACAS arbitration within the Act and so the exclusion of the Arbitration Act 1996 by s 212(5) (n 41) does not apply. Thus the 1996 Act could be applicable (if the agreement to arbitrate is in writing) and so the resulting decision could be legally binding (and any recourse to the courts excluded) under that Act, possibly without the parties realizing it at the time.

[44] See the *CAC Annual Report 1984* ch 3 for a discussion of this development. The aim is to avoid the damage arbitration is said to do to conciliation. Parties in negotiation anticipating arbitration tend to 'stand off', leaving a wide band of discretion for the arbitrator. Final offer arbitration encourages them to adopt a more realistic position, even perhaps to reach agreement.

2001 when, pursuant to new statutory powers, ACAS produced a scheme for arbitration in unfair dismissal cases (later extended to flexible working cases), the aim being to siphon off certain cases from the tribunals and subject them to a quicker and cheaper form of resolution. In some ways, this was a return to a much older idea of how the tribunals themselves were originally meant to operate. Perhaps sadly, however, this arbitral alternative proved to be a complete failure in practice, partly due to opposition from lawyers advising potential parties who were particularly concerned not just about formally giving up the right to a tribunal claim and the informality of the process but also about the lack of any appeal from the arbitrator's decision if it went against their client. These provisions technically still remain in force but are now a dead letter.

1.3.1.4 **Advice**

The statutory power to give advice, contained in the Trade Union and Labour Relations (Consolidation) Act 1992, s 213, was altered by the Trade Union Reform and Employment Rights Act 1993. It used to contain 11 particular categories of relevant areas, including matters affecting collective bargaining, worker organization, and recognition of unions. It now reads more simply:

> ACAS may, on request or otherwise, give employers, employers' associations, workers and trade unions such advice as it thinks appropriate on matters concerned with or affecting or likely to affect industrial relations.

As with the change at that time (considered previously) to the general duty of ACAS, this alteration was likely to have little practical effect, but could be seen (in its removal of express references to collective means of resolving employment problems) to be symbolic. Again, references to such matters have not been subsequently reinstated.

The power to advise remains wide and continues to be heavily used, along with ACAS training in employment matters.[45] It covers general advice, specific replies to queries (eg on the meaning of modern employment laws), in-depth surveys and projects, giving conferences or seminars, and the publishing of advisory booklets and increasingly webinars and e-learning sessions.[46] Diagnostic work within a company on a longer-term basis may in fact be the result of one particular problem which arose and was settled through ACAS conciliation—the approach may have been made for the ACAS officer to attempt to find a settlement for the immediate problem on the understanding that the whole area in dispute would be looked at, either by the officer him or herself or, increasingly, by the setting up of a joint working party or workshop under the aegis of ACAS. This latter approach (more recently known as 'advisory mediation': see 1.3.1.1) has expanded and largely replaced the older ideas of externally conducted 'IR audits' for two reasons—(1) it fits the current employment relations realities better, reflecting their more diverse nature with less chance of one desirable model being appropriate, but (2) at the same time it enables ACAS still to make a distinctive contribution towards ideas of *joint* resolution of problems and employee involvement, even in areas where formal bargaining with unions is no longer the norm.[47]

[45] This advice function has always been of great importance in practice: Armstrong 'Evaluating the Work of ACAS' [1985] Employment Gazette 143 and Dix, Hawes, and Pinkstone 'Asking ACAS' (ACAS Occasional Paper No 56).

[46] For the current list of publications see <http://www.acas.org.uk> under 'advice and guidance'. The website also gives details of the e-learning packages for use in advice and training.

[47] Kessler and Purcell 'Joint Problem Solving—Does It Work? An Evaluation of ACAS In-Depth Advisory Mediation' (ACAS Occasional Paper No 55).

The ACAS Helpline came to renewed prominence with the repeal of the standard procedures for grievance and dismissal in 2009. As part of the government's replacement system (aimed at returning to a more voluntaristic and less prescriptive way of resolving individual disputes), the Helpline was expanded by about 50 per cent in order to undertake a subtly different function—previously its function had been largely to give factual information (eg as to a dismissed employee's legal rights) but the idea now is that it should operate more proactively to steer enquiries into the available choices for resolving the possible dispute behind the enquiry *instead* of issuing tribunal proceedings.[48]

1.3.1.5 **Powers of inquiry**

ACAS may on its own initiative hold an inquiry into aspects of industrial relations generally or in any particular industry or firm.[49] It may add its advice to its eventual findings, and it is empowered to publish both if it thinks publication desirable (after hearing any representations on the question by those involved). In cases of greater public interest, however, the Secretary of State may decide to appoint a Court of Inquiry under the Trade Union and Labour Relations (Consolidation) Act 1992, s 215 (a power going back to the Industrial Courts Act 1919). This is a more formal procedure than that adopted by ACAS and results in the laying before Parliament and publication of a formal report.[50] In appointing such a court, the Secretary of State lays down rules regulating its procedure, which may include powers to compel witnesses to provide information or give evidence on oath.

1.3.1.6 **Codes of practice**

Pursuant to its powers of inquiry and advice, ACAS is empowered by the Trade Union and Labour Relations (Consolidation) Act 1992, s 199 to issue codes of practice. The procedure is that a draft code will be drawn up with a view to comment by interested parties. The final draft is then submitted to the Secretary of State, who, if they approve, may lay it before Parliament. If no objection is taken to it, the Secretary of State may then bring it into force by order. Codes of practice have been of increasing importance in modern employment law, to attempt to fill out the bare bones of the legislation and give practical advice on how to put that legislation (often of considerable legal complexity) into effect. A code of practice is not law in itself, so a person will not be liable for its breach; like the Highway Code in motoring cases, however, breach of its terms may be used as evidence against an employer in any proceedings before a tribunal or the CAC.[51] The first three codes of practice issued by ACAS covered disciplinary practices and procedures in employment, disclosure of bargaining information, and time off work for trade union duties and activities; to these were subsequently added codes on settlement agreements and dealing with requests to work flexibly. Arguably, the Code of Practice No 1 on discipline and dismissal has been one of the most important documents in modern employment law, laying down many of the most fundamental principles for unfair dismissal law

[48] In 2024/5 the Helpline received 594,110 telephone enquiries; in addition to this, there were 46,519 web advice sessions, 102,000 people attended webinars, and 41,500 attended ACAS training: *ACAS Annual Report 2024/5*.

[49] Trade Union and Labour Relations (Consolidation) Act 1992, s 214.

[50] Use of this device is rare; a notable example historically was the Report of the Court of Inquiry under Scarman LJ into the dispute between Grunwick Processing Laboratories Ltd and APEX (Cmnd 6922, 1977).

[51] Trade Union and Labour Relations (Consolidation) Act 1992, s 207(2). Under s 203 the Secretary of State for Employment may issue codes of practice (after consultation with ACAS) and any such COP may replace part or all of one already issued by ACAS. This power has been used to issue the COPs in the politically contentious areas of picketing, the closed shop, and union ballots and elections.

and acting as the basis (or even the model) for most of the internal procedures adopted by employers, which—as Chapter 7 will show—are frequently of major importance in unfair dismissal cases.

The present code (reissued in 2015) is actually shorter than its predecessors (to be more user-friendly to non-lawyers), though backed by the much longer 'Discipline and Grievances at Work: The ACAS Guide', which, though not having the formal status of a code of practice, is likely to be of great practical significance in fleshing out the principles set out in the code itself.[52] Taking all this together, the present code contains provisions going back many years, *but* there was one innovation. Wanting to 'beef up' the code (as a replacement for the failed procedures), the government provided in the Employment Act 2008, s 3 (adding a new s 207A to the Trade Union and Labour Relations (Consolidation) Act 1992) that if a tribunal finds that a party before it has unreasonably failed to comply with a code of practice, it may increase or decrease any award or compensation by up to 25 per cent.[53] The novelty of this is that the ACAS Code No 1 (for all its immense practical effect) has *never* previously had any element of legal enforceability, being meant to operate purely in the context of 'best practice'.

1.3.2 **The Central Arbitration Committee**

The CAC, successor to the Industrial Court and the Industrial Arbitration Board, was established by the Employment Protection Act 1975 and its procedure is now governed by Part VI of the Trade Union and Labour Relations (Consolidation) Act 1992. It is a permanent arbitration body, independent of both ACAS and the sponsoring department, and sits centrally in London and elsewhere as the need arises. It consists of a chairman and deputy chairmen and a panel of persons appointed from both sides of industry. It will normally sit with a chairman or deputy chairman and two side members, though if it cannot reach a unanimous decision the power of decision lies with the chairman or deputy chairman, acting as an umpire. It may sit in public or in private, and its decisions made in the exercise of its statutory functions (but not any consensual arbitrations) must be published; these decisions are given in the form of arbitral awards, with the emphasis upon a statement of 'general consideration' and then the terms of the award, rather than being given in the form of a closely reasoned legal judgment. If a question arises as to the interpretation of one of its awards, any party to it may refer the matter back to the CAC for decision. The functions of the CAC were progressively lessened by the Conservative government of the 1980s (which had a general distaste for third party intervention in industrial disputes) and were restricted to the following:

(1) to arbitrate on matters voluntarily submitted to it by the parties through ACAS;[54] the CAC may thus be an alternative to the (more usual) single arbitrator and such a reference may be ad hoc or may be because reference to the CAC is formally built into the relevant procedure agreement between employer and union;

(2) to enforce the disclosure of certain bargaining information.

[52] This view of the supplementary guidance was accepted by the Court of Appeal in *McMillan v Airedale NHS Foundation Trust* [2014] IRLR 803, CA.

[53] This most obviously applies to misconduct cases in unfair dismissal, but it has been held that it can also apply to other categories such as incapability or 'some other substantial reason' if there was an element of *culpability* by the claimant for which he or she was being disciplined: *Hussain v Jurys Inn Group* UKEAT/0283/15; *Holmes v QinetiQ Ltd* UKEAT/0206/15. There is guidance to tribunals as to how to operate these provisions in *Rentplus UK Ltd v Coulson* [2022] EAT 81 and how to fix the appropriate penalty in *Slade v Briggs* [2022] IRLR 216, EAT.

[54] Trade Union and Labour Relations (Consolidation) Act 1992, s 212(1)(b).

The workload of the CAC was therefore drastically reduced from its high point as a major player in employment relations under the Labour governments of the 1970s.

The CAC, however, saw a revival in its use under the New Labour government, being involved in three major developments. The first, and most high profile, was the statutory recognition procedure introduced by the Employment Relations Act 1999 (see Chapter 9); jurisdiction to adjudicate on disputes arising from this procedure is given to the CAC.[55] The second development was the transposition of the European Works Councils Directive 94/45/EC. More significantly, however, the CAC was given important functions under the Information and Consultation of Employees Regulations 2004, in relation to questions both of interpretation and enforcement.[56] The present Labour Government in the Employment Rights Act 2025 have enacted a new union right to access to workplaces for the purposes of recruitment, with complaints for failure lying to the CAC. In addition, it has sought to make the statutory recognition procedure easier to operate and so these two together may increase the CAC's workload.

1.3.3 **The Certification Officer**

In addition to ACAS and the CAC, another principal institution which the reader is likely to encounter in the areas of industrial relations and trade union law is the Certification Officer (CO). The office was established by the Employment Protection Act 1975 and is now governed by Part VI of the Trade Union and Labour Relations (Consolidation) Act 1992, though with major changes made by the Employment Relations Act 1999 and the Employment Rights Act 2025. It takes its name from the major function at that time of certifying trade unions as 'independent', such certification being the key to enjoyment of the new statutory rights given to unions and their members by that Act; the procedure of certification is considered in Chapter 9. However, it becomes immediately obvious that in fact this official is, if not misnamed, at least inadequately named, since their functions now extend far beyond certification (which is now of course quantitatively far less important). In fact, they resemble more the old institution of the Registrar of Trade Unions, with a wide supervisory jurisdiction which has historically been split into three functions—administrative, investigative, and judicial. The *administrative* functions include the listing of trade unions, dealing with the mechanics of union amalgamations, and receiving the audited annual returns and actuarial reports on members' superannuation schemes that are required of trade unions under the Trade Union and Labour Relations (Consolidation) Act 1992. The CO's powers to *investigate* possible breaches of trade union law off their own bat (and if necessary issue enforcement notices) have been the subject of political change; they were strengthened by previous Conservative government in the Trade Union Act 2016,[57] but these were an immediate target of the incoming Labour government and were largely repealed by the Employment Rights Act 2025 (with immediate effect) along with most of the rest of the 2016 Act. In addition, the CO has *judicial* functions, in that they have the power to adjudicate on complaints brought by individuals of infringements of the laws relating to (1) political expenditure by a union, the running of a political fund, and the necessary balloting thereon; (2) the balloting required for a union amalgamation; and (3) the balloting required for the appointment of

[55] In exercising these functions, the CAC 'must have regard to the object of encouraging and promoting fair and efficient practices and arrangements in the workplace': Trade Union and Labour Relations (Consolidation) Act 1992, Sch A1, para 171.

[56] In 2021/22 the CAC received 57 applications; 46 concerned trade union recognition, eight disclosure of information, and three European consultation: *CAC Annual Report 2021/22*.

[57] See Cavalier and Arthur 'A Discussion of the Certification Officer Reforms' (2016) 45 ILJ 363.

union officers; however, the power to impose financial penalties was removed by the 2025 Act. Although the CO is funded and provided with staff through ACAS, they operate independently of it (and of the Department for Business and Trade). They are expressly empowered to regulate their own procedure on any application or complaint, and are to produce an annual report on the year's activities, which is an important source of up-to-date information and statistics on trade unions and their operations.

1.3.4 **The Fair Work Agency**

The whole edifice of modern individual employment rights has largely been based on the idea of individual enforcement by potential claimants, using the statutory rights provided by Parliament. Certain exceptions to this have been established, whereby governmental bodies can enforce certain rights by administrative means, in particular in the laws on employment agencies, the national minimum wage, working time rules, gangmasters, and modern slavery. However, these have been increasingly viewed as being not just too piecemeal but also too reactive and, putting it bluntly, ineffective.[58] One of the principal innovations in the Employment Rights Act 2025 is to enable the setting up by the Secretary of State of a new Fair Work Agency which aims to be not only more comprehensive (replacing the existing bodies and adding new coverage) but also more *proactive* in securing compliance by employers with their legal obligations. These provisions are contained in Part 5 of the Act which is of great complexity, stretching to 161 sections and four schedules. They empower the Secretary of State to exercise these functions, but in practice they will be delegated to the new Agency and its enforcement officers, acting as an executive agency of the Department of Business and Trade.

The functions of the Agency fall into two broad categories, direct administrative enforcement and indirect enforcement by aiding individual enforcement in the tribunals:

(1) Administrative enforcement

This applies to 'relevant labour market legislation' which is defined in Sch 7 as being laws relating to employment agencies, statutory sick pay, financial penalties for non-payment under awards or settlements, the national minimum wage, working time rights, gangmasters, and modern slavery. With regard to these, the Agency has three principal remits to enforce employer compliance:

(i) It has wide powers to investigate employers (including rights of entry) and require them to produce documentation to show compliance with the law.

(ii) It has civil penalties powers. Where the Agency's inspector finds that an employer has underpaid individuals they may issue a Notice of Underpayment, requiring the employer not only to make good the amounts outstanding but also pay a penalty to the government.

(iii) In addition, the Act creates a new concept of labour market offences. Where an officer finds breaches by the employer it may enter into a labour market agreement with it to mend its ways. If this does not work, they may seek from a court a labour market enforcement order, breach of which is a criminal offence punishable by a fine or imprisonment, on top of which the Agency may claim its enforcement costs.

(2) Backing individual enforcement

[58] A government guide to the new Agency cites research showing that 900,000 workers per year have their holiday pay withheld, 14 per cent of the lowest paid workers report that they received no holiday pay and in 2024 19.4 per cent of workers at or around the wage floor were underpaid the national minimum wage.

This second category operates by facilitating individual actions in tribunals, in two ways. First, the Agency may offer legal advice and assistance to individuals who are actual or potential claimants in employment cases. Second, and arguably more radically, it may *bring* proceedings on behalf of an individual worker who, for whatever reason, has not done so themselves.

Three general points may be made at this early stage. First, although the sections themselves are voluminous and complex, there are still elements that have to be fleshed out by regulations. Also, for the future, there is a specific power by regulations to add other areas of employment law to the list of those amenable to administrative enforcement. Second, there is the question of timing. At the time of writing, the government have proposed bringing Part 5 into force in April 2025, but official guidance has referred to the Act as the 'first phase' of its overall programme here, which is to be completed 'over time'. Third, in what may therefore be an extended period for the Agency's full establishment, much may depend not just on its final form but also (as commentators have suggested) on how well *resourced* it is going to be and the extent to which that may affect how many of these functions it is able to exercise at first. In particular, how much time/resources will be left for backing individual cases if the primary forms of administrative enforcement are given priority? On that point, note that there is a statutory obligation on the Agency to produce and publicize a labour market enforcement strategy every three years. The first one of these will be important in answering these questions.

1.4 **Machinery (2): judicial dispute resolution**

The large majority of all employment and employment relations litigation is handled by employment tribunals, which from inauspicious beginnings under the Industrial Training Act 1964 have expanded to assume wide new jurisdictions under the modern employment legislation and now have common law jurisdiction over breach of contract claims, at least on termination of employment.[59] They started life as 'industrial tribunals' but were renamed 'employment tribunals' in 1998,[60] for no apparent compelling reason. As 'industrial juries' they were originally designed to provide a means of speedy resolution of employment cases which will often turn very heavily upon their particular facts, and the Donovan Report in 1968[61] referred to their potential advantages as being ease of access, informality, speed, and inexpensiveness. Rules of procedure (including pre-trial procedures, such as the simplified pleadings) are drafted with this aim in mind, and the tribunals have wide powers to decide most cases in a common-sense way, having regard to 'good industrial practice'. The paradox here, however, is that while the tribunals' procedure may be simplified, the law which they have to apply is often of great complexity and there has in the past been major controversy over how 'legalistic' the proceedings and decisions of tribunals should be. Simple, common-sense access to quick justice may be a

[59] Employment Tribunals (Extension of Jurisdiction) Order 1994, SI 1994/1623 (in Scotland SI 1994/1624); see *Harvey* Division R [778], [788]. One serious limitation in high value claims is that the maximum awardable is £25,000, a figure that has not been increased since 1994. Moreover, a claimant in such a claim cannot claim the first £25,000 in a tribunal (in which eg he or she is claiming unfair dismissal) and then claim the rest in a court because the tribunal decision establishes an estoppel: *Fraser v HLMAD Ltd* [2006] ICR 1395, [2006] IRLR 687, CA.

[60] Employment Rights (Dispute Resolution) Act 1998, s 1. The Industrial Tribunals Act 1996 was renamed the Employment Tribunals Act 1996. All references to these bodies pre-1998 (in cases and legislation) will of course be to 'industrial tribunals'.

[61] Royal Commission on Trade Unions and Employers Associations (Cmnd 3623, 1968).

worthy aim, but there is still a lot of hard law which must be complied with in most of the statutory actions. One indicator of this is the surprisingly low success rate for claimants in cases proceeding to a full hearing,[62] giving the lie to a persistent employer myth over many years that tribunals were Trotskyite plots in which employers were bound to lose.

The original idea of quick and informal justice in a tribunal was consistent with another theme in this area, namely the undesirability of appeals to complicate the matter. Tribunals have always been given primacy on questions of fact, and so one important feature of this whole system is that an appeal from a tribunal decision lies to the EAT only on a question of *law*.[63] As seen presently, this rule is applied rigorously and indeed may well affect the ultimate disposal of an appeal because even if it is successful, a common order will be for the matter to be remitted to the tribunal for final decision on the facts, that is, the EAT will not normally *decide* the case for itself.

1.4.1 **Employment tribunals**

1.4.1.1 **Constitution**

Tribunals sit in most local centres of population, under the auspices in England and Wales of 27 local offices—all under the control of the Head Office in Leicester—and in Scotland five local offices, under the control of the Head Office in Glasgow. Under the original model, a tribunal consisted of three people: a legally qualified chairman (now known as an employment judge) and two lay members, one from a panel kept by the Secretary of State representing employers' interests and one from a panel kept representing employees' interests. The theory is that although expressly appointed from each side of industry, the lay members are to act as independent members of the bench, not in a partisan manner, and so they are full members of the tribunal, which decides its cases if necessary by a majority (even in the unusual case of the judge being in the minority). One of the principal functions of the side members is to use their employment experience to help the tribunal to come to a sensible and practicable decision; however, this approach must not be taken too far, and the Court of Appeal has warned that knowledge of the employment background and industrial common sense (though of great importance in many cases) may *not* be used to take a decision directly against the plain meaning of a statutory provision, even if the side members consider the end result of applying that plain meaning to be unfair or ridiculous.[64]

This original model has, however, been under attack for some years. This started when the Trade Union Reform and Employment Rights Act 1993 amended these provisions as to the composition of a tribunal by establishing a class of case to be heard by a judge *alone*; this was partly to deal with withdrawn or non-contested cases, but it also covered Wages Act cases, applications for interim relief, and the common law proceedings that may now be heard by a tribunal, *unless* they raise matters of fact or law such that they should be heard by a full tribunal. This process was taken further by the Employment Rights (Dispute Resolution) Act 1998, which extended the categories of judge-alone hearings (covering eg guarantee payments and redundancy payments and cases involving union subscriptions)

[62] The overall success rate for claimants in *fought* cases has rarely been above 50 per cent. For many years it hovered around 35 per cent. Interestingly, by 2015/16 Ministry of Justice figures showed an *exactly* 50 per cent figure, but this contained major variations—higher rates tended to be in the more technical actions (eg for unpaid work), whereas the success rate in fought unfair dismissal claims was only 39 per cent. Discrimination cases generally fared even worse (sex 25 per cent; race 17 per cent; disability 30 per cent; age 13 per cent; sexual orientation 31 per cent; religion/belief 18 per cent). Even in whistleblowing cases, long a bugbear for employers, the success rate was only 22 per cent.

[63] Employment Tribunals Act 1996, s 21.

[64] *British Coal Corpn v Cheesbrough* [1988] ICR 769, [1988] IRLR 351, CA.

against the background of a significant increase in tribunal applications.[65] However, arguably the most significant change came in 2012 when the Coalition government added to the list of judge-alone jurisdictions cases of unfair dismissal—for many lawyers the prime area for the use of side members with their industrial expertise. There is still a power to sit with side members[66] but the legislation now makes judge-alone very much the normal default setting in these cases. This is clearly a major derogation from the original model and it has come along with what appears to be another such change, namely a diminution in what was originally seen as an important *inquisitorial* function for a tribunal (given that originally lawyers were not expected to be present); the current emphasis is on the tribunal adjudicating solely on the arguments presented by the parties (the classic adversarial system) and not seeking out the truth off its own bat, even in the case of a litigant in person.[67]

1.4.1.2 **Representation and costs**

The original idea was for tribunals to be accessible, speedy, and *non*-legalistic. Although the reality is now often very different, this original concept can still be seen in relation to representation and costs. The claimant may conduct the case before the tribunal in person or be represented by any other person (sometimes a lawyer, sometimes a trade union official, and the respondent employer may often be represented by a member of the firm's personnel or legal staff);[68] there is no legal aid for representation, though a dismissed employee may be eligible to obtain free preliminary advice from a solicitor, and may also be able to turn to his or her trade union or to the CAB.

Costs are not usually awarded; this 'costs-free jurisdiction' has generally been thought to be a fundamental and desirable element of the tribunal system. However, there is always some pressure politically to curb what are seen as unworthy or time-wasting applications (at the very least adding a significant 'nuisance value' to applications, leading—so the argument goes—to too many undeserving cases being bought off by employers, regardless of their merits). In recent years, this has coincided with the desire of successive governments to curb the major increase in the number of tribunal applications.[69] There has always been a residual power to award costs. Originally this only covered frivolous or

[65] Applications rose sharply from 34,697 in 1990–91 to 71,821 in 1992–93; they peaked at 130,408 in 2000–01. In 2004–05 they fell to 86,181, which seemed to give some credence to the government's dispute resolution reforms in the Employment Act 2002, *but* any hopes of a permanent decrease were then dashed when they increased again to 115,039 in 2005–06. They stayed at well above 100,000 until the introduction of fees and the consequent radical decrease, considered later.

[66] Employment Tribunals Act 1996, s 4(5). Other than this power, the prime area for full tribunals is now discrimination cases.

[67] For a particularly strong steer on this see the judgment of Lady Smith, President of the Scottish EAT, in *Arnold Clark Autos Ltd v Middleton* UKEATS/0011/12 where she overturned a tribunal decision to call witnesses itself when dissatisfied with the parties' cases and went so far as to say that 'employment tribunals are not investigative bodies. It is not for them to decide what issues are to be looked into'. This was later echoed by Langstaff P south of the border in *East of England Ambulance Service NHS Trust v Saunders* UKEAT/0217/14, where, in strongly disapproving of a tribunal conducting its own research into the claimant's disability, he said openly that tribunals should be adversarial, not inquisitorial, bodies. For the extent to which a tribunal may legitimately help a litigant in person to put their case properly see *Mervyn v BW Controls Ltd* [2020] EWCA Civ 393.

[68] Ministry of Justice annual figures for 2021/22 were not available due to a new computer recording system (!), which lasted into 2024/5. Figures for 2019/20 showed that 55 per cent of claimants were legally represented, only 6 per cent were represented by trade unions, and 32 per cent had no apparent representation. For a survey of the experiences of the litigants in person see Busby and McDermont 'Fighting with the Wind: Claimants' Experiences and Perceptions of the Employment Tribunal' (2020) 49 ILJ 159.

[69] This has gone along with concern, at least in the press, about excessive awards by tribunals. However, the statistics do not bear this out. In 2021/2 Ministry of Justice figures showed that the median award for unfair dismissal was £13,541 and for discrimination cases £24,903.

vexatious conduct by a party; in 1980 this was widened to cover cases brought 'otherwise unreasonably', and in 2001 the current rule was introduced under which costs may be awarded (a) where the party or their representative acted vexatiously, abusively, disruptively, or otherwise unreasonably in the bringing or conducting of the proceedings, or (b) where any claim or response had no reasonable prospect of success.[70] The significance of the 'prospects of success' heading is that now a costs application can be made based on the weak *merits* of the case, not just the way it was handled. Costs have thus become a live issue again, with these wider powers. On the other hand, employment judges remain generally wary of introducing wider costs rules into their jurisdiction and, in spite of these changes, actual orders for costs remain relatively rare.[71]

1.4.1.3 **Procedure and the issue of fees**

Apart from specific rules, such as on costs, the tribunals have wide powers to determine their own procedure by virtue of the Rules of Procedure. These Rules were reissued in 2013 after a thorough review by Underhill LJ (a previous President of the EAT) and then again in 2024, aiming at simplifying them and making them more user-friendly for self-representing parties.[72] In recent years there has been much emphasis on case management in tribunals, with the judge expected to play an active part at this preliminary stage. This has become an important feature of the system, but one particular example shows that the matter is not always simple—successive governments have wanted to increase the use of strike-out powers in the case of weak claims, if only to reduce the running costs of the tribunal system, but this aspect above all others has led to what could be seen as a conflict between executive and judiciary because to a significant extent tribunal judges have been loath to comply and the higher courts have always stressed the unusual and draconian nature of a strike-out, particularly in the light of the right to a fair hearing in Article 6 of the European Convention on Human Rights.[73]

In addition to the recast Rules of Procedure, the Coalition government made two novel changes of substance to the tribunal system, for the purpose of effecting what it saw as a necessary rebalancing of the system.[74] The first was the introduction of what is in effect a fine on an employer who has been found to have breached a worker's rights in a way that has 'aggravating features'; the amount is to be 50 per cent of the award, with a maximum of £25,000.[75] Note that although the amount is related to the award to the employee, the

[70] Rule 76(1).

[71] Ministry of Justice figures for 2021/22 showed that there were 184 costs orders, of which 50 were in favour of claimants and 134 in favour of respondents. The largest award was for £600,673 but the median award was £8,818.

[72] The Employment Tribunal Procedure Rules 2024 SI 2024/1155. Details of the rules lie outside the scope of this work: see *Harvey* Div PI and R [3598].

[73] The leading authority is *Ezsias v North Glamorgan NHS Trust* [2007] ICR 1126, [2007] IRLR 603, CA and in *Tayside Public Transport Co v Reilly* [2012] IRLR 755 the Inner House of the Court of Session reaffirmed that normally there should be no strike-out if any facts remain in contention.

[74] See Mangan 'Employment Tribunal Reforms to Boost the Economy' (2013) 42 ILJ 409. The government also addressed the specific issue of the remarkably high rate of failure by employers actually to pay tribunal awards (according to MoJ statistics in 2009, 39 per cent of successful claimants were not paid their awards, with only 53 per cent receiving payment in full; see Mangan 'Assessing Employment Tribunal Awards' (2014) 43 ILJ 212); the Small Business, Enterprise and Employment Act 2015, s 150 (adding ss 37A–37Q to the Employment Tribunals Act 1996) established a much tougher system of enforcement of awards and ACAS settlement agreements, operated by enforcement officers with the power to issue warning and penalty notices.

[75] Employment Tribunals Act 1996, s 12A, inserted by the Enterprise and Regulatory Reform Act 2013, s 16, as from April 2014. Section 12A(10) has the curious provision that the employer is only liable for 50 per cent of the fine if it is paid within 21 days—perhaps echoing a supermarket BOGOF, though here a SOGOF (sack one, get one free).

fine itself is payable to the Secretary of State, being obviously meant to contribute to the cost of running the tribunal system.

It was, however, the second change that had the most profound effect, albeit temporarily. This was the introduction in 2013 of *fees* for bringing tribunal proceedings. These were set out in complex regulations. Essentially the idea was that if the claimant was successful, the fees would be recoverable from the respondent employer, *but* the desired concentration-of-the-mind effect that lay behind the system was that, quite simply, if the claimant failed, the fees would be forfeited. This had an immediate and radical effect, much more so than any previous measures aimed at curbing the increase hitherto in tribunal applications. In the six-month period immediately following the introduction of fees, tribunal applications (on a year-by-year basis) fell by 59 per cent, and in the second six-month period (on a similar basis) by 70 per cent. Not surprisingly, the fee system was highly unpopular in many quarters and was eventually challenged in judicial review proceedings by the union UNISON. This was initially unsuccessful before the Divisional Court and Court of Appeal, but then, in a quite remarkable decision (for constitutional law as well as employment law), the Supreme Court held that although the government had had a legitimate base for imposing fees, this particular scheme was unlawful *at common law* (with illegality under EU law also established as a secondary ground) because of its disproportionate effect on access to justice.[76] The government had no option but to revoke the whole fees system immediately, and indeed also to set up a scheme for reimbursing fees already charged. Toward the end of the Conservative government in 2024 there was some talk of reintroducing an amended system of fees but it did not eventuate and it is uncertain whether it would be seriously considered by the present government (though it cannot be ruled out).

However, there is one other area that is to be altered by the present government, namely the extension of the time limit for bringing tribunal proceedings from three months to six. The existing very short period has often caused problems (especially for litigants in person), spawning much case law on the circumstances where a tribunal may (untypically) be persuaded to extend it. The Employment Rights Act 2025 raises it to six months across the board and while this is still deliberately short by comparison with common law actions (six years in contract, three for personal injury), it is to be hoped that this change (scheduled by the government for introduction in October 2026) will decrease the number of cases on this difficult area.

One final point on tribunals generally concerns the aggregate effect of all of these changes. If one adds together the demise of side members in so many cases, the consequent emphasis on the position of the judge alone (no longer simply the tribunal 'chairman'), the attempts to extend the costs regime, and the inexorable lengthening of hearings, with arguably a significant decrease over the years of the original inquisitorial nature of tribunals, the question might well be asked—are these really still tribunals as originally understood, or simply courts by another name?

1.4.2 **The Employment Appeal Tribunal**

1.4.2.1 **Constitution**

Appeal from a tribunal decision lies to the EAT, a body set up under the Employment Protection Act 1975.[77] The EAT, a superior court of record, is headed by a High Court or circuit judge. As with employment tribunals, there have been significant changes in recent

[76] *R (UNISON) v Lord Chancellor* [2017] IRLR 911, [2017] ICR 1037, SC.

[77] Now the Employment Tribunals Act 1996, Pt II.

years as to its composition. Originally, it consisted of the judge and two lay members, representing both sides of industry and there to lend practical credence and knowledge to its decisions. However, that tripartite system came under attack in two stages. First, it was provided that where a tribunal had sat judge-alone any appeal was to be likewise; as the categories of judge-alone tribunal cases expanded (see 1.4.1.1), so did the incidence of judge-alone appeals. Then the Enterprise and Regulatory Reform Act 2013 changed the statutory basis formally by providing that 'Proceedings before the Appeal Tribunal are to be heard by a judge alone', subject only to a judicial *discretion* to sit with side members.

The constitution of the EAT is laid down in the Employment Tribunals Act 1996, which expressly gives it the powers of the High Court *and* those of the employment tribunals.[78] Its procedure is contained in the EAT Rules laid down in Regulations.[79] As in the case of tribunal proceedings, the parties may be represented by anyone and costs are not normally awarded, unless the EAT considers that the appeal was 'unnecessary, improper, vexatious or misconceived' or there was 'unreasonable delay or other unreasonable conduct in bringing or conducting the proceedings'.

1.4.2.2 **Appeal on a point of law**

The first and most important rule about the appeal to the EAT is that it is an appeal on a point of law *only*;[80] this is a deliberate policy to minimize appeals. The practical significance of this is that the parties must ensure that they argue the facts properly and fully before the tribunal, as if they do not and they lose on the facts (eg by not calling all the relevant evidence or by not presenting it sufficiently persuasively), they may not take the matter to the EAT for a second chance. To appeal to the EAT, the party must be able to show that the tribunal was wrong in law. It has been authoritatively stated in *British Telecommunications plc v Sheridan*[81] by the Court of Appeal that this means one of two things—either (a) an ex facie error of law or (b) that the tribunal's decision was perverse. There had been said to be a third category, that is, where the tribunal misunderstood or misapplied the facts,[82] but that was specifically disapproved in *Sheridan*, since it would have permitted the EAT to allow an appeal simply by taking a different view of the facts.[83]

The judicial approach to perversity has undergone considerable changes over time, against the background of the obvious point that this is the only way in which an appellant can legitimately convert fact into law. Indeed, the developments here could be seen in some ways as reflecting the history of the evolution of our present employment law generally. In the early years of the tribunals' expanded jurisdiction after the inception of unfair dismissal law in 1971, the appellate courts tended to take a wider, more interventionist approach in which if (particularly) the industrial members of the bench agreed that they would not have decided the case that way, the decision was perverse. At a time when the new law was bedding in and basic ground rules were being established, this approach could be seen as natural, but by the mid-1980s a large element of revisionism (based on

[78] Sections 28, 33.

[79] SI 1993/2854, *Harvey* R [714]. These rules are supplemented by the EAT *Practice Direction* reissued in 2024 and set out at *Harvey* PI [1901].

[80] The EAT will not hear appeals where the dispute has in fact been resolved, even if one or both of the parties wish to have a particular point resolved as a matter of principle: *IMI Yorkshire Imperial Ltd v Olender* [1982] ICR 69. Likewise, if there is no real dispute between the parties, who want a ruling for some extraneous purpose: *Baker v Superite Tools Ltd* [1986] ICR 189.

[81] [1990] IRLR 27, CA.

[82] *Watling v William Bird & Son Contractors Ltd* (1976) 11 ITR 70, per Philips J.

[83] If there can be said to be *no* evidence to support a particular finding of fact, that is an error of law under head (1). Note, however, that delay by a tribunal, even if extreme, is not a separate head of appeal even when allied to human rights arguments: *Bangs v Connex South Eastern Ltd* [2005] IRLR 389, CA.

the idea that the system was becoming too legalistic) led to a review of this crucial element of perversity appeals. This was when the current narrow approach to perversity came in (with the corresponding warnings to the EAT not to reverse a tribunal decision merely because they think it wrong on the facts). In *RSPB v Croucher*,[84] Waite P went as far as to call cases of perversity 'exceptional' and said:

> We have to remind ourselves of our duty and our functions as an appellate tribunal. We have to remember that it is our duty loyally to follow findings of fact by an industrial tribunal which has enjoyed the advantages, which can never be ours, of having seen witnesses, sensed the atmosphere prevailing in a particular work-place, gauged the qualities of the different personalities, weighed the impact of their effect each upon the other; and that cases must be very rare indeed where we take upon ourselves to reach the conclusion that a tribunal has arrived at a result not tenable by any reasonable tribunal properly directed in law.

This narrow approach to perversity was approved by the Court of Appeal in *Neale v Hereford and Worcester County Council*,[85] where May LJ said that an appellate court should only reverse a tribunal's decision if it could be said 'My goodness, that must be wrong'.[86] Indeed, even this well-known explanation was thought possibly too liberal in *Piggott Bros & Co Ltd v Jackson*[87] by Lord Donaldson MR, who thought that it might tempt an interventionist EAT into the forbidden land of fact. However, his preferred solution (that perversity could normally only be shown by an error of law or a *total* lack of evidence) was arguably capable of removing perversity as a separate heading. Subsequently, Wood P in the EAT in *East Berkshire Health Authority v Matadeen*[88] complained that *Piggott* was causing difficulties in appeals, and sought to lean back towards the *Neale* approach, stating that the EAT could interfere if the members were satisfied that the tribunal decision was not a permissible option, or was one which offended reason, or was one which no reasonable tribunal could have reached, or was so clearly wrong that it could not stand. This formulation leaves perversity as a freestanding ground, which seems now to have been accepted at Court of Appeal level, though with the clear warnings that any perversity challenge must be fully particularized and should only be upheld by the appellate body if an 'overwhelming case' has been made out. In *Yeboah v Crofton*,[89] the case now normally cited on this point, the position was summed up by Mummery LJ (a previous EAT President) as follows:

> Such an appeal ought only to succeed where an overwhelming case is made out that the employment tribunal reached a decision which no reasonable tribunal, on a proper appreciation of the evidence and the law, would have reached. Even in cases where the Appeal Tribunal has 'grave doubts' about the decision of the employment tribunal, it must proceed with 'great care': *British Telecommunications plc v Sheridan* . . . no appeal on a question of law should be allowed to be turned into a rehearing of parts of the evidence by the Employment Appeal Tribunal.

[84] [1984] ICR 604, [1984] IRLR 425; the passage cited is at 609 and 428, respectively.

[85] [1986] ICR 471, [1986] IRLR 168, CA; moreover it was held in *Campion v Hamworthy Engineering Ltd* [1987] ICR 966, CA that if a case goes to the Court of Appeal on perversity, that court's function is to apply the *Neale* test to the tribunal's decision, *not* to consider whether the EAT's decision on the point was correct.

[86] This is known in some quarters as the 'Biggles test' (see (1987) 16 ILJ 213) due to a flippant remark in the *Harvey* bulletin that although this statement is entirely consistent with the modern approach, its phraseology may appear over-reliant on the writings of Captain WE Johns ('"Gosh" said Biggles as a shell ripped off his right leg').

[87] [1992] ICR 85, [1991] IRLR 309, CA.

[88] [1992] ICR 723, [1992] IRLR 336.

[89] [2002] IRLR 631, CA.

Appeal on a point of law is thus tightly circumscribed and the point has been made repeatedly that the EAT must exercise considerable self-restraint in cases where it disagrees profoundly with the decision of the tribunal on the facts but where there is no definable error of law; in such a case it must not interfere. Moreover, it is now accepted that the EAT will not subject tribunal judgments to minute scrutiny to detect any legal errors; instead, tribunals are cut a considerable amount of slack, provided they make clear findings of fact and set out adequate reasoning on legal points.[90] This is well summed up in the neat judicial aphorism 'what is required is adequacy, not perfection. The Employment Tribunal is not sitting an exam.'[91] Likewise, there have been repeated warnings by the Court of Appeal to appellants and, more particularly, their legal advisers that points of fact are not to be dressed up in the garb of points of law in order to bring an appeal. Moreover, this is backed by an important procedural device. Starting originally with perversity appeals but now applying to all appeals, a notice of appeal is subject to a 'sift' by a judge or the Registrar which is partly to decide (as a matter of case management) which of several procedural routes should be adopted, but which can also be used to ensure that there is a proper point of law at issue (or at least a reasonable prospect of success); if not, the appeal may be struck out at that stage (subject to a right to have this decision reconsidered at a short oral hearing).[92]

1.4.2.3 **Three specific aspects**

Three further points about the EAT are worth noting. The *first* is that it will be most reluctant to admit fresh evidence unless, exceptionally, the existence of the fresh evidence could not have been reasonably known of or foreseen (akin to the 'reasonable diligence' test applied generally by the Court of Appeal);[93] this rule is not to be circumvented by remitting the case to the tribunal for a rehearing including the otherwise inadmissible evidence.[94] This reinforces the point made previously that it is essential that all relevant evidence is placed before the tribunal at the hearing. The *second* point is that, although the EAT is empowered on appeal to substitute its own decision for that of the tribunal if it allows the appeal,[95] if the decision on appeal entails the finding of further facts or the reconsideration of certain existing facts, the proper course will normally be to remit the case to the tribunal for further consideration in the light of the EAT's decision.[96] The *third* point concerns the question of precedent. In theory, the EAT is not bound by a previous decision of its own, but over time it has evolved guidelines as to when it will depart from a previous decision, namely: (1) when that previous decision is *per incuriam* (eg for having

[90] *DPP Law Ltd v Greenberg* [2021] IRLR 1016, CA.

[91] *Sullivan v Bury Street Capital Ltd* [2021] EWCA Civ 1694 per Singh LJ at [42].

[92] EAT Practice Direction, para 11. The institution of this process is explained in detail by Burton P in 'The Employment Appeal Tribunal: October 2002–July 2005' (2005) 34 ILJ 273. *Star Wars* fans may think of this as the Revenge of the Sift. In 2023/24 the EAT received 1,500 appeals and dealt with 1,000 of them. Thirty-one per cent were dealt with at a preliminary hearing. Of these, 31 per cent were dismissed at this stage.

[93] *Borden (UK) Ltd v Potter* [1986] ICR 647. Similarly, the EAT will not normally allow a party to argue a point of law not taken at the tribunal, unless it is a point that the tribunal should have considered on its own motion: *Langston v Cranfield University* [1998] IRLR 172.

[94] *Kingston v British Railways Board* [1984] ICR 781, [1984] IRLR 146, CA.

[95] Employment Tribunals Act 1996, s 33.

[96] This was strongly reaffirmed by the Court of Appeal in *Jafri v Lincoln College* [2014] ICR 920, [2014] IRLR 709, CA and *Burrell v Micheldever Tyre Services Ltd* [2014] ICR 935, [2014] IRLR 630, CA, though with some misgivings because of the potential for lengthening cases. In *Burrell* it was said however that the EAT might be 'robust' in applying *Jafri* rules, ie more ready *not* to remit where the outcome was clear: see *Robinson v Department for Work and Pensions* [2020] EWCA Civ 859 for a good example. In 2023/4 43 per cent of those reaching a final hearing were dismissed, this being 54 per cent of employer appeals and 38 per cent of employee appeals.

overlooked applicable legislation); (2) where there are conflicting previous EAT decisions; (3) where the previous decision is inconsistent with other case law (eg in the High Court); (4) where the previous decision is manifestly wrong; and (5) where there are other exceptional circumstances.[97] Although this seems to limit the EAT's discretion, heads (4) and (5) do suggest a residual power and in the past there have been many instances, in cases raising bona fide matters of law, of a later EAT decision at least altering the *direction* of an area of law away from previous authorities. There is thus a difficult balance to maintain between certainty and legal development, and the student of employment law must realize that in practice the doctrine of precedent is not as strong here, and so, for example, it cannot always be assumed beyond doubt that an ageing EAT decision will always be applied without question. This is one of the reasons why the EAT has always been at the forefront of developing employment law to fit new social and employment realities.

1.4.3 **Proposals for reform**

In addition to the various changes already made to the employment tribunals system, for example in relation to judge-only sittings and the unsuccessful attempt to introduce hearing fees, there have been two more fundamental reviews of the future in recent years. In 2016 Briggs LJ produced a report about tribunals generally. Although this did not specifically include employment tribunals, it did float the idea of a fundamental change to a new Employment and Equalities Court to replace employment tribunals and the EAT and to be integrated more into the general court structure. To date, nothing has come of this. Perhaps more likely to produce change (at least in the longer term) is the Law Commission Report 'Employment Law Hearing Structures' (Law Comm No 390, April 2020). In the past the Commission has been most wary about being asked to inquire into potentially politically controversial areas such as employment law, so this is something of a departure. The principal recommendations were:

(1) time limits should be standardized at six months, with a 'just and equitable' power to extend, which would rationalize standard employment law rights with the existing provisions in discrimination law;

(2) tribunals should have wider powers to deal with common law claims (eg for unpaid wages) more generally (in particular, not restricted to claims arising on termination of employment), up to a maximum of £100,000; this would be extended to be available to 'workers', not just 'employees' (see Chapter 2);

(3) there should be greater rationalization where under the present law there are overlaps in jurisdiction between tribunals and the county court, with the emphasis on the former being used as a matter of course in employment-related matters;

(4) there should be stronger powers to apportion liability between different respondents in order to do justice;

(5) there is a need for further changes to fast-track the enforcement of tribunal awards to successful claimants, delays in which (or simple non-payment) are still causing concern.

Clearly, these are much more bread-and-butter issues than any wholly new court structures, but that very nature may make them more likely to succeed. As one commentator put it, in contrast to various previous governmental attempts at change here, the Law

[97] *Lock v British Gas Trading Ltd (No 2)* [2016] IRLR 316, EAT; for an application of this see *Fentem v Outform Emea Ltd* EA-2020-000851, EAT.

Commission started from a position of understanding the special nature of the employment tribunal system and wanted to retain and improve it.[98] To date, only point (1) above has been acted upon, with the Employment Rights Act 2025 raising the time limits for tribunal actions from three to six months.

Review and Final Thoughts

- This chapter has considered the history of legal involvement in employment matters and some of the vital procedural aspects that will be met time and time again in subsequent chapters. An important divide has been seen immediately between practical mechanisms for resolving workplace disputes on the one hand and legal intervention on the other. This reflects an important choice for an aggrieved employee—do they want an acceptable pragmatic resolution, hopefully without making further employment impossible, or have things got so bad that recourse to the law has become the only route to resolution, whatever its effect on future employment? Is the claimant most interested in an acceptable settlement to draw a line under the whole sad affair and get on with life or do they want to crucify the employer in a legal forum 'as a matter of principle' (the five most feared words for a conciliator or arbitrator)? It is not always obvious to lawyers that the legal route is not always the best one.
- Institutionally, dispute resolution has had three fixed points—(a) ACAS has arguably been the principal success story throughout the whole period of modern employment law, and the change of its individual function to *early* conciliation in 2014 appears to have continued this success (partly due to the tribunals' determination not to let it become mired in legalistic interpretation but to allow it to operate in the realistic and non-prescriptive way that was intended); (b) employment tribunals have always borne the brunt of the expanding litigation, though it must be remembered that their jurisdiction is purely statutory and so there can be more complex issues if a case concerns wholly or partly matters of common law; (c) the Employment Appeal Tribunal (EAT) is the dominant body in the development of employment law and the employment aspects of discrimination law, having a heavy case load and a specialist judiciary whose judgments are followed closely by employment lawyers, particularly when wanting guidance on new legislation or on how venerable rules of employment law are likely to be construed and applied now (a good example being how to apply standard rules on misconduct dismissal to modern concerns about misuse of email and/or social media).
- We have seen that over the years various reforms have been made to the tribunal system. The Briggs Report of 2016 made further recommendations of a 'macro' nature querying the whole future of that system, and the Law Commission Report of 2020 made more detailed recommendations for improving the efficiency of the current system at a 'micro' level. As always, the question then becomes whether Parliamentary time will be forthcoming for these matters to be legislated upon. The present government's Employment Rights Act 2025 makes many changes to the *laws* that the tribunals have to administer, but makes relatively few changes to the system itself.

[98] Levinson 'They've Got It!' New Law Journal, 15 May 2020, p 7.

2

Contracts of employment (1): status, formation, continuity, and change

OVERVIEW

Coverage of the substantive law of employment must always start with an analysis of the most fundamental jurisdictional point of all—who is an 'employee'? This is then complicated in modern employment law by the intermediate category of 'worker' and by the slightly different approach taken by discrimination law.

In this chapter, then, we consider:

- Part-time, fixed-term, and agency workers (under both domestic and EU-inspired law), along with how all of this applies to casual workers (a category not recognized as such by the law, but of some topicality politically).
- Two more technical areas. The first concerns the 'section 1 statement' of basic terms and conditions which has been an obligation on employers since 1963 but which is still not always given. The second concerns the application of the common law concept of illegality to employment cases, both generally and in relation to the difficult question of the extent to which an employer can seek to impose limitations on an employee even after employment ends; this entails the law on restraint of trade clauses and their more recent variant, the garden leave clause.
- The chapter continues with an examination of the rules on continuity of employment. Although continuity differs in being a statutory concept, it is often of practical importance alongside the common law question of status—for example, in calculating compensation for breach of the employee's rights.
- The chapter concludes with consideration of how contracts of employment can be lawfully changed, a topic which may appear simple but which can throw up surprisingly difficult conceptual problems, largely caused by one commonplace of employment law generally—namely, that contracts are inherently static in nature, whereas jobs are often quite the opposite in the modern economy.

Context

It used to be so simple. You could tell an employee because *he* wore a flat cap and overalls; the supervisor/manager wore a bowler hat and waistcoat; the employer owned the company personally and ruled the workplace paternalistically but with a rod of iron. Such employment law as existed featured little in industrial relations, and in contracts even less. Disputes led either to intervention by the employee's trade union or to a sacking for which the law gave little redress. The rest of this book will show just how much all of this has changed, both as to the renewed importance of individual contracts and as to the radically increased coverage of so many aspects of practical employment by statutory rights. However, before proceeding to all of this it is vital to establish who can benefit from these developments, starting with the definition of 'employee'. This has taxed the courts and tribunals for decades and, if anything, has actually become more difficult in recent years because of the increasingly diverse nature of the UK's workforce, as to types and forms of working and (possibly even more important in the long run) the gender of the workforce. Even the old, hallowed 'employee/self-employed' division is now complicated by increasing use in modern statutes of the intermediate term 'worker'. What used to be thought of as 'atypical' forms of employment have in many contexts actually become quite typical and one of the themes of the first part of this chapter is the way in which the law has had to keep up with changing models of 'employment'. In the case of very recent developments in the 'gig economy', including the controversial issue of zero-hour contracts, the reader may form the view that the law has hitherto struggled to do so, though there are some potentially important developments here in the Employment Rights Act 2025.

Employment law generally rarely stands still, as the student of it will soon find out, and that applies equally to this fundamental area of defining the various forms of engagement. The coronavirus crisis led to several innovations of an administrative nature to try to mitigate its economic effects, such as the Job Retention Scheme. While these owed little to classic employment law and have proved largely temporary, it is likely that there will be major *indirect* effects on forms and patterns of employment that will eventually have to work their way through employment law, including in this fundamental area of definition. The key one has been the shift (increasingly *not* temporary) to increased home/remote working. Traditionally, an 'employee' worked manually in a factory and 'home workers' were an unusual sub-set of workers assembling or sewing various things on low piecework rates. Initially and for some time this caused problems with their legal status. Now, however, there will be new issues arising in applying the employee/worker/self-employed model to a very different world of widespread remote working by individuals at the opposite end of the earnings spectrum: old law in new circumstances.

2.1 The relationship of employer and employee; other forms of engagement

The fact that someone is an employee of someone else is a major jurisdictional factor in several areas of law, for example in tort law on the question of vicarious liability, and in the fields of taxation and social security on the questions of assessment, payment, and contributions. In employment law, both ancient and modern, it is often of fundamental importance; most of the common law on employment only applies to employees, and hitherto the same has usually been the case with the important statutory rights, which usually require the claimant to be an employee and to have served a certain qualifying period as such.[1] As the only definition of 'employee' in the Employment Rights Act 1996 and the Trade Union and Labour Relations (Consolidation) Act 1992[2] is 'an individual who has entered into or works under (or, where the employment has ceased, worked under) a contract of employment', the question of what constitutes a contract of employment is left to the courts and tribunals. The major divide here is between employment and self-employment, between a contract of employment and a contract for services (although other relationships such as agency or partnership could perhaps be used to avoid the relationship of employer and employee, and the concept of 'office holders' has occasionally caused problems for such individuals trying to enforce statutory rights).[3] A person with a contract for services is usually referred to as an 'independent contractor' and there may be several reasons why an individual may wish to be classed as such; the prime one is usually taxation, for there may well be tax advantages in being self-employed, whether

[1] For the classic arguments in favour of freeing statutory employment rights from their present basis on the contract of employment, see Hepple 'Restructuring Employment Rights' (1986) 15 ILJ 69; for a criticism that courts tend still to lean too strongly on contractual principles when interpreting employment statutes, see Anderman 'The Interpretation of Protective Employment Statutes and Contracts of Employment' (2000) 29 ILJ 223.

[2] Sections 230(1) and 295, respectively.

[3] In *Lincolnshire County Council v Hopper* [2002] ICR 1301, EAT, a registrar of birth, deaths, and marriages was unable to claim unfair dismissal. See generally the discussion of different kinds of office holding by Morison P in *Johnson v Ryan* [2000] IRLR 236, EAT, where, on the facts, it was held that a rent officer could so claim.

of a legal (ie tax avoidance through being assessed as trading income with payment at least partly in arrears and more generous allowances) or an illegal nature (ie tax evasion through part- or non-disclosure of income, not being under the pay-as-you-earn (PAYE) system for taxation of employees).[4] From the employer's point of view, it may be desirable to hire independent contractors, for this relieves it of the administrative tasks involved in deducting PAYE deductions and national insurance (NI) contributions from wages, and may relieve it of certain other administrative burdens (eg statutory sick pay and statutory maternity pay); further, it may have certain value-added tax (VAT) advantages and help to avoid the need to negotiate with unions (indeed, in an area of large-scale self-employment such as the building industry it may be a long-standing cause of weak unionism generally).[5]

Advantages to the individual, however, tend to be of a short-term nature, and categorization as 'independent' may have certain serious longer-term disadvantages, as most of the industrial safety legislation, some of the most important social security rights (particularly those relating to unemployment and disability), and much of the modern employment protection legislation only applies to employed persons—to put it shortly, the independent contractor may be in a better monetary position while working, but at a grave disadvantage if they fall off a ladder or are sacked. Moreover, categorization as independent may indirectly affect the rights of third parties too—for example, a passerby injured by the acts of that person—for the action then lies only against that independent contractor and *not* against the employer, who may in the realities of the case be the only person worth suing.[6]

2.1.1 Definition of the relationship

2.1.1.1 The original approach—control and integration

In spite of the obvious importance of the distinction between an employee and an independent contractor, the tests to be applied are vague and may, in a borderline case, be difficult to apply.[7] Historically, the solution lay in applying the 'control' test: that is, could the employer control not just what the person was to do but also the manner of doing it? If so, that person was its employee.[8] In the context in which it mainly arose in the nineteenth century, of domestic, agricultural, and manual workers, this test had much to commend it, but with the increased sophistication of industrial processes and the greater numbers of professional and skilled people being in salaried employment, it soon became obvious that the test was insufficient[9] (eg in the case of a doctor, architect, skilled engineer, pilot, etc). There have been certain attempts to modernize it;[10] for example, a couple engaged to look after and manage an agricultural property on behalf of largely absentee owners were

[4] For tax treatment in general, see *Harvey on Industrial Relations and Employment Law* Div BII.

[5] Bird 'The Self Employed: Small Entrepreneurs or Disguised Wage Labourers?' in Pollert (ed) *Farewell to Flexibility* (1991).

[6] There are certain exemptions to this general rule, where an employer can be liable for the acts of its independent contractor, but these have historically been narrow and, in some cases, uncertain.

[7] The tests to be applied are a matter of law, but the *application* of those tests is a question of fact; where it arises in a statutory action, this means that the decision on categorization lies almost entirely with the employment tribunal, with little chance of a successful appeal from their decision: *O'Kelly v Trusthouse Forte plc* [1983] ICR 728, [1983] IRLR 369, CA; *Lee v Chung* [1990] ICR 409, [1990] IRLR 236, PC.

[8] See eg *Performing Right Society Ltd v Mitchell and Booker (Palais de Danse) Ltd* [1924] 1 KB 762; *Mersey Docks and Harbour Board v Coggins and Griffiths (Liverpool) Ltd* [1947] AC 1, [1946] 2 All ER 345, HL.

[9] *Cassidy v Ministry of Health* [1951] 2 KB 343, [1951] 1 All ER 574, CA (a surgeon).

[10] An early example was *Zuijs v Wirth Bros Ltd* (1955) 93 CLR 561, concerning the control which could be exercised over a circus acrobat.

held to have been employees and so able to claim unfair dismissal, their claim not being ruled out by the large amount of de facto discretion that they had in running the property. The point was accepted by the Court of Appeal that in modern circumstances employees may well have such discretion and that what matters in such a case is whether the putative employer has ultimate control over major matters (as was the case here), not whether it exercises day-to-day supervision.[11] In spite of such important developments, however, it has been long accepted that in itself control is no longer the sole test, though it does remain a factor, and perhaps, in some cases, a decisive one.[12] In the search for a substitute test, ideas have been put forward regarding an 'integration' test, that is, whether the person was fully integrated into the employer's concern, or remained apart from and independent of it.[13] Once again, this is not now viewed as a sufficient test in itself but rather as a potential *factor* which may be useful in allowing a court to take a wider and more realistic view—for example, in a case where the individual's initial relationship with the organization was one of relative independence but changed over time as they became gradually more absorbed into it, to the point where in practice they became indistinguishable from an ordinary employee (a common problem in this area).

2.1.1.2 **The multiple approach**

The modern approach has been to abandon the search for a single test and instead to take a multiple or 'pragmatic' approach, weighing up all the factors for and against a contract of employment and determining on which side the scales eventually settle. Two first instance judgments as long ago as 1968 are still regularly cited as starting points in modern judgments on this point. In *Ready Mixed Concrete (South East) Ltd v Minister of Pensions and National Insurance*,[14] Mackenna J put it as follows (using older terminology of master and servant):

> A contract of service exists if the following three conditions are fulfilled: (i) The servant agrees that in consideration of a wage or some other remuneration he will provide his own work and skill in the performance of some service for his master. (ii) He agrees, expressly or impliedly, that in the performance of that service he will be subject to the other's control in a sufficient degree to make that other master. (iii) The other provisions of the contract are consistent with its being a contract of service.

On a slightly different tack, in *Market Investigations Ltd v Minister of Social Security*,[15] Cook J said that the question ultimately is whether the person in question is performing the services as 'a person in business on his own account'. Factors which are usually of importance are as follows: the power to select and dismiss; the direct payment of some

[11] *White v Troutbeck SA* [2013] IRLR 949, CA.

[12] Particularly where the control demonstrates the reality of the relationship (eg in a case where there is more than one possible employer): *Clifford v Union of Democratic Mineworkers* [1991] IRLR 518, CA. Control may also be particularly important in vicarious liability in tort, in a case where employer A 'borrows' an employee from employer B and injury is caused by the employee while working for the latter: *Hawley v Luminar Leisure Ltd* [2006] EWCA Civ 18; if control is actually shared, there may even be joint vicarious liability now: *Viasystems Ltd v Thermal Transfers Ltd* [2005] IRLR 983, CA; see Brodie (2006) 35 ILJ 87.

[13] *Stevenson Jordan & Harrison Ltd v McDonald and Evans* [1952] 1 TLR 101, CA, per Denning LJ.

[14] [1968] 2 QB 497, [1968] 1 All ER 433. The continuing importance of this old case as at least the starting point in this exercise was reaffirmed in *Revenue & Customs Commissioners v Atholl House Productions Ltd* [2022] IRLR 698, CA.

[15] [1969] 2 QB 173, [1968] 3 All ER 732, approved and applied by the Privy Council in *Lee v Chung* [1990] ICR 409, [1990] IRLR 236.

form of remuneration; deduction of PAYE and national insurance contributions;[16] the organization of the workplace; the supply of tools and materials (though there can still be a labour-only subcontract); and the economic realities (in particular who bears the risk of loss and has the chance of profit). However, even this is not an exhaustive checklist, and a court or tribunal must still look at the overall picture in the particular case.[17]

At this point, a particular example may be useful to show not just the breadth of the factors that may be involved, how finely balanced they can be, and how one set of facts can split tribunals and courts, but also that the test may have to be applied in contexts far removed from traditional factory-based employment. In *Stringfellow Restaurants v Quashie*[18] (a favourite case of the newspapers at the time), the claimant was a lap dancer operating in the respondent's club. She was subject to a 'club agreement' and 'house rules' which reflected the general assumption within the trade at the time that dancers were self-employed. She was subject to a definite weekly rota for appearances and had to book holidays. However, she provided her own costumes and could work elsewhere on days not scheduled. The greatest complication came, however, in relation to payment—she had no 'wage' from the club, which instead passed on to her the fees paid by the customers in relation to her dances (having taken a cut), out of which she had to pay 'tips' to the floor manager, hairdresser, and other club functionaries; on a bad night this could exceed her earnings. When her services were dispensed with after 80 weeks, she claimed unfair dismissal, which the club defended partly on the basis that she was not their employee at all. The employment tribunal weighed all the factors, agreed with the respondent and rejected her claim. The EAT reversed that decision, taking particular notice of the level of control exercised by the club on the occasions when she did work for them. However, on further appeal the Court of Appeal reinstated the decision of the tribunal. It concentrated on the issue of payment, which had complicated the case considerably. Of course, direct payment of wages is not an absolute condition for employment, but what then had to be taken into account was that the dancer took upon herself the risk of earning either nothing or at least an insufficient amount to cover the other expenses she had to pay to the club and others on any particular night. This raised the question of another possible approach to defining employment considered previously, namely the 'economic reality' test. Adding these together, Elias LJ said that 'it would, I think, be an unusual case where a contract of service is found to exist when the worker takes the economic risk and is paid exclusively by third parties'. When there was added the factor that it was not part of her case that the whole thing was a sham (see 2.1.1.5) and the facts that she herself had in the contract accepted that she was self-employed, that she had to deal with all matters of tax, and that there was no question of sickness or holiday pay, the overall result was the status of self-employment.

[16] Though perhaps a potent factor, this is not decisive (being primarily a matter between the person and the tax and insurance authorities) and so the non-deduction of these sums does *not* inevitably point to an independent contract if the other factors are against it: *Davis v New England College of Arundel* [1977] ICR 6, EAT; *Airfix Footwear Ltd v Cope* [1978] ICR 1210, [1978] IRLR 396, EAT; *Thames Television Ltd v Wallis* [1979] IRLR 136, EAT; conversely, deduction of these amounts does not per se mean that the relationship is one of employment: *O'Kelly v Trusthouse Forte plc*, see n 19.

[17] *Hall (Inspector of Taxes) v Lorimer* [1994] ICR 218, [1994] IRLR 171, CA.

[18] [2013] IRLR 99, CA. One factual analogy that was used here was with the golf caddy in *Cheng Yuen v Royal Hong Kong Golf Club* [1998] ICR 131, PC, who was licensed by the club to offer caddying services, had a discretion when to work, and was remunerated by the golfers, not the club, which merely administered the payments. The finding there was one of self-employment.

2.1.1.3 **Mutuality and personal service**

A further development in the modern case law (particularly concerning atypical employments) has been the idea of 'mutuality of obligations' as a possible factor, that is, whether the course of dealings between the parties demonstrates sufficient such mutuality for there to be an overall employment relationship. It is true that such an approach can be disadvantageous to certain particularly irregular workers, making it more difficult to establish that they are employees,[19] but on the other hand it has the positive aspect that it is capable of extending employed status to groups of atypical workers (especially of an external or part-time nature) if the relationship with the employer is sufficiently long-standing and stable; thus in *Nethermere (St Neots) Ltd v Gardiner*,[20] outworkers making garments at home on a piecework basis were held to be employees of the garment manufacturer, largely because of the regular, long-standing arrangement which showed the necessary mutuality of obligations (to do and to be provided with the work) in practice, even though the outworkers were not covered by a formal contractual obligation to undertake a particular quantity of work; this was an important development, capable of extending employee status (and thereby employment rights) to workers employed otherwise than on a nine-to-five basis on the employer's premises.

On the other hand, 'mutuality' was used as an argument *against* employee status for 'casual, as required' power station guides in the rather regressive decision of the House of Lords in *Carmichael v National Power plc*,[21] where it was seen as an irreducible minimum for the existence of a contract of employment; indeed, the current approach is to view it as a requirement for any kind of contract to arise between the parties, leading on to a consideration of other factors to see if the contract was one of employment.[22] On a more general level, however, this whole idea of an 'irreducible minimum' is rather worrying because it could cut across the usual approach of weighing *all* the factors (all factors are equal, but some are more equal than others?) and could be seen as the higher courts searching for a philosopher's stone in this area. It was seen again in *Express & Echo Publications Ltd v Tanton*,[23] where the Court of Appeal viewed personal service as an irreducible minimum. While it is true that *Tanton* was 'explained' and restrictively interpreted by the EAT in later cases,[24] the Court of Appeal showed a similar approach again in *Montgomery v Johnson Underwood Ltd*[25] in relation to a necessary amount of control by the employer. We have therefore seen qualifications on the pure 'balancing of factors' approach in the higher courts, but some reluctance to go down such a route in the (specialist) EAT.

[19] *O'Kelly v Trusthouse Forte plc* [1983] ICR 728, [1983] IRLR 369, CA; *Wickens v Champion Employment* [1984] ICR 365, EAT. See 2.1.4.3.

[20] [1984] ICR 612, [1984] IRLR 240, CA.

[21] [1999] ICR 1226, [2000] IRLR 43, HL, applied in *Stevedoring Haulage Services Ltd v Fuller* [2001] IRLR 627, CA, where the employer had set this argument up in advance by saying in the hiring contract that there were to be *no* mutual obligations between the parties.

[22] *Stephenson v Delphi Diesel Systems Ltd* [2003] ICR 471; *Cotswold Developments Construction Ltd v Williams* [2006] IRLR 181, EAT.

[23] [1999] ICR 693, [1999] IRLR 367, CA.

[24] *MacFarlane v Glasgow City Council* [2001] IRLR 7, EAT; *Byrne Bros Ltd v Baird* [2002] ICR 667, [2002] IRLR 96, EAT.

[25] [2001] IRLR 269, CA.

2.1.1.4 **The bottom line?**

Given the vagueness of the tests, there is considerable scope for an 'instinctive' approach in this area, that is, that the judge knows a contract of employment when they see one. In *Cassidy v Ministry of Health*,[26] Somervell LJ said:

> One perhaps cannot get too much beyond this, 'Was the contract a contract of [employment] within the meaning which an ordinary person would give under the words?'

This may be unsatisfactory from an analytical point of view, but it probably reflects the practical position, and indeed may not be as unsatisfactory as it first seems when considered in the context of the modern statutory rights, where it falls to be applied by employment tribunals which may be expected to apply industrial experience in their resolutions.[27] The real problem with a vague test or tests is, however, that it can make advising in advance very difficult; not only is this a problem for the lawyer but also it concerns an area of fundamental importance for both employer and employee, who need to be certain as to the legal basis of their relationship. The parties' primary contact on this matter is likely to be not with lawyers or tribunals but with government departments and agencies, in particular HM Revenue and Customs[28] and the Department of Work and Pensions (DWP); given the practical importance of such contacts, there has unfortunately been evidence in the past of different departments and agencies giving different advice and using different criteria on a person's employment status.[29] However, in the context of taxation, the Revenue have for some years published guidance (initially in leaflets and now on their website)[30] attempting to clarify the distinction between employment and self-employment, using the criteria set out previously. While stressing that no one factor is a conclusive test, the current advice suggest that someone who works for a business is probably an employee if most of the following are true:

- they are required to work regularly unless they are on leave, for example holiday, sick leave, or maternity leave;
- they are required to do a minimum number of hours and expect to be paid for time worked;
- a manager or supervisor is responsible for their workload, saying when a piece of work should be finished and how it should be done;
- they cannot send someone else to do their work;
- the business deducts tax and national insurance contributions from their wages;
- they get paid holiday;
- they are entitled to contractual or statutory sick pay, and maternity or paternity pay;

[26] [1951] 2 KB 343, [1951] 1 All ER 574, CA at 352 and 579, respectively; see also McKenna J's third condition for a contract of employment in the *Ready Mixed Concrete* case, see n 14. *Withers v Flackwell Heath Football Supporters' Club* [1981] IRLR 307, EAT.

[27] *Challinor v Taylor* [1972] ICR 129, EAT; *Thames Television Ltd v Wallis* [1979] IRLR 136, EAT. One limitation on this is now that unfair dismissal cases are now heard primarily without side members, who were always that repository of such industrial experience.

[28] In many cases, the parties will in practice consider that they have successfully created the relationship of self-employment if the Revenue have accepted it and not required the employer to operate the PAYE system. As stated, however, this is not legally conclusive and the Revenue can later decide to reconsider, the second principle of tax law being that the Revenue cannot be estopped (the first principle being that they always win eventually).

[29] See Leighton 'Observing Employment Contracts' (1984) 13 ILJ 86.

[30] The general address is <www.gov.uk/hmrc>; their guidance is at <www.gov.uk/employment-status>.

- they can join the business's pension scheme;
- the business's disciplinary and grievance procedures apply to them;
- they work at the business's premises or at an address specified by the business;
- their contract sets out redundancy procedures;
- the business provides the materials, tools, and equipment for their work;
- they only work for the business or if they do have another job, it is completely different from their work for the business;
- their contract, statement of terms, and conditions or offer letter (which can be described as an 'employment contract') uses terms such as 'employer' and 'employee'.

It is then suggested that someone is probably self-employed if most of the following are true:

- they are in business for themselves, are responsible for the success or failure of their business, and can make a loss or a profit;
- they put in bids or give quotes to get work;
- they are not under direct supervision when working;
- they submit invoices for the work they have done;
- they are responsible for paying their own National Insurance and tax;
- they do not get holiday or sick pay when they are not working;
- they operate under a contract (sometimes known as a 'contract for services' or 'consultancy agreement') that uses terms like 'self-employed', 'consultant', or 'independent contractor'.

While these are *not* authoritative statements of law, and ultimately the decision on a person's status may have to be taken by a court or tribunal, it is to be welcomed that at least an attempt is being made to standardize the rules of the game (in the most important context in which in practice the issue initially arises, that is, tax and NI contributions), though one might be cynical and say that in marginal cases a game is precisely what it remains.[31]

In addition to the general points just made, two particular problems may be noted here: one a specific and recent cause of controversy and the other a general problem that has vexed the courts and tribunals for many years.

2.1.1.5 **Delegation clauses and sham contractual terms**

The first (specific) issue arises if the contract in question contains a 'delegation' or 'substitution' clause, stating in some way that the work need not actually be performed by that individual. The problem is that there is an immediate clash with the idea that *personal* service is at least one of the hallmarks of a contract of employment. As seen, the initial response was a strong one in *Express & Echo Publications Ltd v Tanton*[32] that *any* power to delegate was fatal to employment status. This was then construed restrictively by the EAT and when the matter was reconsidered by it generally in *Staffordshire Sentinel Newspapers*

[31] With the Revenue permanently having the service, through their ability to raise an assessment on the basis that they have decided upon (usually employment requiring use of the PAYE system), leaving it up to the employer and/or 'employee' to appeal and challenge the correctness of that basis. In the light of this, the National Federation of the Self-Employed has argued for a registration system for self-employment, with registration under it being conclusive of a person's status, and at one point the Institute of Directors put forward the most radical proposal, that people should simply be able to *elect* to be self-employed. Neither of these suggestions has been taken up officially.

[32] See n 23.

Ltd v Potter,[33] an important distinction was drawn: if the clause only applies where the individual *cannot* do the work (and so, for example, must arrange a suitably qualified replacement to take the shift) there can still be a contract of employment, but a *general* power to delegate (or indeed to not do the work at all)[34] at the individual's own discretion is inconsistent with a contract of employment. A similar distinction was accepted and expanded upon by the Court of Appeal in *Pimlico Plumbers Ltd v Smith*.[35]

Welcome though this clarification was, it left one particular loose end—what if an employer cynically inserted such a clause into what would otherwise be a normal contract of employment, thus deliberately *avoiding* employment liabilities? In *Staffordshire Sentinel* it was said that a tribunal could avoid such a clause if it was a sham, but what is meant by a 'sham'? When tested, the EAT felt obliged to hold that it would only be a 'sham' if it could be proved that the employer deliberately inserted it to evade legal liabilities;[36] the mere fact that the clause had never actually been activated in practice (ie the individual had always turned up and done the work themself) was not sufficient. This difficult point caused contradictory decisions at EAT and Court of Appeal level for some time but eventually came before the Supreme Court in what is now the leading case, *Autoclenz Ltd v Belcher*,[37] in which the facts raised the point neatly. The contractual arrangements for car valeters were entirely consistent with employment status *except* that the employer inserted both a delegation and a substitution clause (neither of which had in practice ever been used). The Supreme Court in effect struck these clauses down and held that the valeters were not only 'workers' (their principal contention) but also 'employees'. In doing so, they approved the decision of the Court of Appeal below that the answer to this conundrum lies not in trying to apply the inherently difficult concept of a 'sham' (which fits commercial law more than employment law) but in considering more widely whether the clause in question reflected the true agreement between the parties at the time of contracting. Where the offending clause had simply been inserted by the employer because of its superior bargaining position and it was clear from the outset that it would play no part in practice in the actual employment, it could be overlooked when deciding on employment status. Giving the leading judgment, Lord Clark accepted that this involved a level of purposive interpretation which would not normally be adopted in commercial contracts. He approved a passage from Aikens LJ in the Court of Appeal to the effect that in the employment context, employers will often have the power to dictate contract terms which the employee has to accept in order to take the job, and that in this area 'it may be more common for a court or tribunal to have to investigate allegations that the written contract does not represent the actual terms agreed and the court or tribunal must be realistic and worldly-wise when it does so'. Expanding on this, Lord Clark said that the true nature of the agreement will often have to be gleaned from all the circumstances of the case, of which the written agreement is only a part. Thus, although delegation or substitution clauses are not per se illegal and may be proper in certain contracts, this decision

[33] [2004] IRLR 752, EAT.

[34] This is sometimes known informally as the 'duvet test', ie can the individual decide to stay under their (or indeed somebody else's) duvet that morning.

[35] [2017] IRLR 323, CA; see the summary of the law here by Etherton MR at [84]. This was not affected by the later appeal to the Supreme Court ([2018] IRLR 872, SC).

[36] *Real Time Civil Engineering Ltd v Callaghan* (2006) UKEAT/516/05. The classic definition of a 'sham' in a commercial setting is where *both* parties intend to deceive the outside world: *Snook v London and West Riding Investments Ltd* [1967] 2 QB 786, CA per Diplock LJ. This also caused severe problems in the initial case law.

[37] [2011] ICR 1157, [2011] IRLR 820, SC, approving *Protectacoat Firthglow Ltd v Szilagyi* [2009] IRLR 365, CA and disapproving *Consistent Group v Kalwak* [2008] IRLR 505, CA. See Bogg 'Sham Self-Employment in the Supreme Court' (2012) 41 ILJ 328.

of the Supreme Court shows that the scope for their *abuse* has been severely limited. This approach was strengthened even further in the *Uber* case (considered at 2.1.3.3) where the Supreme Court not only followed *Autoclenz* but explained that it was based on an overriding policy consideration of furthering (not limiting) the protection of *statutory* rights, not just contractual ones, which permits a wide application generally.

2.1.1.6 The parties' own classification

The second (long-standing) problem concerns the emphasis (or lack of it) which can be placed upon the statements and intentions of the parties themselves. They may stipulate (orally or in writing) that their contract shall be viewed in one way (usually as an independent contract)—how is the court or tribunal to treat that?[38] In the past the usual approach has been to ignore the statements of the parties and apply an objective test,[39] and this can be seen in the decision of the Court of Appeal in *Ferguson v John Dawson & Partners (Contractors) Ltd*[40] where a man taken on at a building site with no written contract but on an oral understanding that he was on the 'lump'—that is, a labour-only subcontractor—and who was later injured was held to have been in fact an employee (and so able to rely on certain industrial safety provisions in order to bring his action). The majority, Megaw and Brown LJJ, took a clearly objective approach and said that a declaration by the parties, even if incorporated into the contract, should be *disregarded entirely* if the remainder of the contractual terms pointed to the opposite conclusion (though for the purpose of their decision they were prepared to adopt the less stringent approach that such a declaration or statement can be a relevant, but certainly not conclusive, factor). Lawton LJ dissented strongly, stating:[41]

> I can see no reason why in law a man cannot sell his labour without becoming another man's servant even though he is willing to accept control as to how, when and where he shall work. If he makes his intention not to be a servant sufficiently clear, the implications which would normally arise from implied terms do not override the prime object of the bargain. In my judgment, this is just such a case.

In a subsequent Court of Appeal case, *Massey v Crown Life Insurance Co*,[42] however, a different approach was taken. In that case a branch manager who was an ordinary employee asked to change the basis of his contract to self-employment (for tax purposes); the employer consented to this and negotiated a new agreement. When the agreement was subsequently terminated, the manager tried to claim unfair dismissal on the basis that he was in fact an employee all along, but the Court of Appeal held unanimously that he could not do so, since the new agreement had effectively altered the basis of his engagement so that he was no longer an employee. It must be said at the outset that the desire to avoid a position whereby a person could claim various tax advantages during employment, and then argue exactly to the contrary to obtain unfair dismissal benefits at a later stage,

[38] There may be the added complication that the employee is now trying to *change* the basis of the contract, eg where they initially agreed to be self-employed, but have now been injured or dismissed and so need to show that they were in fact an employee in order to claim the appropriate remedy.

[39] For examples, see *Davis v New England College of Arundel* [1977] ICR 6, EAT; *Tyne and Clyde Warehouses Ltd v Hamerton* [1978] ICR 661, EAT; *Thames Television Ltd v Wallis* [1979] IRLR 136, EAT.

[40] [1976] 3 All ER 817, [1976] IRLR 346, CA.

[41] [1976] 3 All ER 817 at 828, [1976] IRLR 346 and 351.

[42] [1978] ICR 590, [1978] IRLR 31, CA, applied in *BSM (1257) Ltd v Secretary of State for Social Services* [1978] ICR 894, EAT and *Calder v H Kitson Vickers & Sons (Engineers) Ltd* [1988] ICR 232, CA.

obviously played a part in this decision,[43] but, in spite of that, the approach to the problem was different from that of the previous Court of Appeal. Lord Denning MR said:[44]

> It seems to me on the authorities that, when it is a situation which is in doubt or which is ambiguous, so that it can be brought under one relationship or the other, it is open to the parties by agreement to stipulate what the legal situation between them shall be . . . So the way in which the parties draw up their agreement and express it can be a very important factor in defining what the true relation was between them. If they declare that one party is self-employed, that may be decisive.

His Lordship distinguished the *Ferguson* case quite simply 'on its facts' and Lawton LJ did likewise (pointing primarily to the lack of a written agreement or, indeed of any particularly reliable evidence as to the relationship in that case), adding:[45]

> *Ferguson* clearly established that the parties cannot change a status merely by putting a new label on it. But if in all the circumstances of the case, including the terms of the agreement, it is manifest that there was an intention to change status, then, in my judgment, there is no reason why the parties should not be allowed to make the change.

However, this wider approach in *Massey* was called into question in the further Court of Appeal case of *Young & Woods Ltd v West*,[46] where a sheet metal worker who had been engaged on a self-employed basis (and had been treated as such by the Inland Revenue) was held to have in fact been an employee so that after his dismissal he could claim unfair dismissal. The court did not indicate that *Massey*'s case was wrong, and did not take as purely an objective approach as the majority in *Ferguson*'s case would have liked to do. They did, however, seek to narrow the effect of *Massey*'s case; in particular they did not accept that if the parties deliberately set out to create a relationship of self-employment, that intention should normally be put into effect by a court or tribunal. A further contribution to this question was made by Lord Hoffmann in *Carmichael v National Power plc*,[47] where 'casual, as required' power station guides were held not to be employees. Pointing out that in reality many employment relationships will not be contained purely in written form, but will also need to be discerned from correspondence and conduct, he envisaged a significant role for the parties' intentions, at least as a factor:

> The evidence of a party as to what terms he or she understood to have been agreed is some evidence tending to show that those terms, in an objective sense, were agreed. Of course, the tribunal may reject such evidence and conclude the party misunderstood the effect of what was being said and done. But when both parties are agreed about what they understood their mutual obligations (or lack of them) to be, it is a strong thing to exclude their evidence from consideration.[48]

Thus, the position now seems to be that, as a matter of practice, the declared intention of the parties may be more important if (a) there has been a deliberate *change* in the basis of

[43] See also the dissenting judgment of Lawton LJ in *Ferguson v John Dawson & Partners (Contractors) Ltd*, n 40.

[44] *Massey v Crown Life Insurance Co* [1978] ICR 590 at 595, [1978] IRLR 31 at 33.

[45] [1978] ICR 590 at 597, [1978] IRLR 31 at 34.

[46] [1980] IRLR 201, CA.

[47] [1999] ICR 1226, [2000] IRLR 43, HL.

[48] [1999] ICR 1226 at 1235, [2000] IRLR 43 at 47. Lord Hoffmann disapproved the view of the majority of the Court of Appeal that the relationship had to be considered purely objectively, disregarding the parties' understandings.

employment, (b) the work in question was of an unusual nature so that an ambiguity as to its true nature might be found more easily,[49] or (c) the arrangement has been entered into in a relatively informal manner and has to be construed in the light of several factors and circumstances, as in *Carmichael*.

On the question of the policy behind the earlier decisions, this can operate in two opposite ways. The court in *Young & Woods Ltd* thought that the danger of allowing employers to avoid the employment protection legislation simply by labelling people as self-employed was an important consideration. When the major *Uber* litigation went to the Supreme Court (considered at 2.1.3.3) this was a dominant factor, given the importance of ensuring that important employment protection rights such as working time rights and the national minimum wage cannot be negated by employers' own classifications of the individuals. On the other hand, in *Young & Woods* the court also recognized the fears expressed (particularly in *Massey*'s case) of injustice being caused by allowing a person to claim to be self-employed for tax purposes during employment, but then to claim on dismissal to have been an employee all along in order to claim unfair dismissal; however, it suggested that this could be overcome by a court or tribunal finding that the person was employed (thereby permitting the unfair dismissal action) but then informing the Revenue of that fact, thereby inviting a reassessment of his or her tax liability for the past years of the engagement on the basis of employment.[50] Knowledge that this is a possibility could be a considerable disincentive to the person who is thinking of trying to alter their status at this late stage.

2.1.2 **Three particular applications**

In addition to these general principles relating to the existence of a contract of employment, three particular applications are worthy of mention. The *first* is that although some of the cases cited on this problem are tort cases concerning vicarious liability, some care may be needed, for the test for vicarious liability is not necessarily identical to that for the existence of an employment relationship in employment law. It is true that it *looks* the same—was there a contract of employment?—but the factors behind it may be different, for in tort (eg in a 'borrowed servant' case,[51] where employer A lends B a crane plus driver and, while acting under B's orders, the driver injures C, should A or B be liable to C?) the court is essentially looking at the liability question at one moment in time, whereas in an employment case (eg on redundancy rights or unfair dismissal) the tribunal may have to assess the legal consequences of a potentially long-term relationship; it may be, therefore, that 'static' ideas of control may be more important in a tort case than in an employment case, where more factors may need to be taken into account to achieve a realistic result. Thus, in the borrowed servant example, it may be that on the facts, B is liable

[49] Both (a) and (b) were considered by Stephenson LJ in *Young & Woods Ltd v West* to have been important aspects of *Massey*'s case; on the latter factor, Mr Massey's position as a manager with a separate agency agreement was more unusual employment than Mr West's job of sheet metal worker (working alongside other people doing exactly the same work, but as employees). The Court of Appeal found that Mr West's circumstances did not raise the sort of ambiguity necessary if the label of self-employment was to be decisive.

[50] Thus it could be that the ex-employee would end up owing more to the Revenue than they gained in compensation for unfair dismissal. In *Young*'s case, Ackner LJ said that Mr West had probably won a 'hollow, indeed an expensive, victory'. The problem from the employer's point of view is that if this happens it will end up liable to pay the employer's NI contributions that should have been paid over the course of the employment; moreover, if the employee is unable to pay the back tax, the Revenue could seek to recover it from the employer on the basis that it should have been operating the PAYE system all along.

[51] *Mersey Docks and Harbour Board v Coggins and Griffiths (Liverpool) Ltd* [1947] AC 1, [1946] 2 All ER 345, HL.

to C,[52] whereas it is clear that for unfair dismissal or employment protection purposes, A remains the employer. Thus, tort precedents may have to be used with care in other contexts. Indeed, when the Supreme Court recently reconsidered and redefined the scope of vicarious liability in tort.[53] Lady Hale specifically said that the intention was *not* to try to align employment law with these amended rules.

The *second* point is that various practical problems may arise over the use of independent contracting, particularly in a system of labour-only subcontracting as traditionally on the 'lump' in the building industry.[54] The Court of Appeal showed some hostility to this in *Ferguson*'s case, particularly as there was clear suspicion in that case of unlawful tax evasion; as it stood, that case could perhaps have been developed by subsequent courts as a way of curbing the overuse of subcontracting by placing stringent limits upon its legal recognition, but even the majority did not feel that they could go as far as to strike down such an agreement as an illegal contract and, in the light of the subsequent case law discussed previously, a major judicial assault on the lump and other such practices is unlikely.[55] Legislative reforms have periodically been suggested in order to rule out all but bona fide contractors but, except in the area of income tax where provisions have been introduced to extend the PAYE system and counter unlawful tax evasion, little has been done specifically. Indeed, the legal issues that have tended to arise recently in relation to the building industry have come from a general change in some legislation to the use of the term 'worker' (rather than 'employee'), which can cover many contractors, even though their tax status is that of a self-employed independent (see 2.1.3).

The *third* point concerns the position of company directors. An ordinary director will not normally be under a contract of employment, even when in receipt of directors' fees. On the other hand, however, there is nothing to prevent a director from being 'employed' (even by their own one-person company)[56] if the relationship is in fact over and above that of ordinary director, as in the case of an executive or managing director. However, the mere fact that a director performs some duties for the company may not be enough[57] and if they wish to establish a contract of employment (eg to be able to claim unfair dismissal

[52] *Donovan v Laing, Wharton and Down Construction Syndicate Ltd* [1893] 1 QB 629, CA; *Sime v Sutcliffe Catering Scotland Ltd* [1990] IRLR 228, Ct of Sess. For variations on this, see *McDermid v Nash Dredging and Reclamation Co Ltd* [1987] ICR 917, [1987] IRLR 334, HL and *Interlink Express Parcels Ltd v Night Trunkers Ltd* [2001] EWCA Civ 360, [2001] RTR 338, [2001] 20 LS Gaz R 43, CA. Control was vital in *Hawley v Luminar Leisure Ltd* [2006] EWCA Civ 18 in holding a nightclub liable for the violence of a bouncer who had been supplied by a security company to whom that function had been contracted out. If there is actually joint control by A and B, there can now be joint vicarious liability in tort: *Viasystems Ltd v Thermal Transfers Ltd* [2005] IRLR 983, CA. Significantly, however, the EAT later held in *Patel v Specsavers Optical Group Ltd* UKEAT/0286/18 and *Fire Brigades Union v Embery* [2023] EAT 51 (14 April 2023, unreported) that in *employment* law there is no place for multiple employers, a good example of the possible divergence here; see Wynn-Evans 'One man, two guvnors: revisiting the principle against two employers' (2024) 53 ILJ 94.

[53] *Barclays Bank plc v Various Claimants* [2020] IRLR 477, SC; *W M Morrison Supermarkets Ltd v Various Claimants* [2020] IRLR 481, SC; noted Buxton [2020] CLJ 217. In addition, there are signs that tax law may also be diverging from employment law on employee status because of different background policy factors: *Revenue & Customs Commissioners v Atholl House Productions Ltd* [2022] IRLR 698, CA.

[54] This is a very old problem—see Clark 'Industrial Law and the Labour-Only Sub-Contract' (1967) 30 MLR 6; Drake 'Wage Slave or Entrepreneur?' (1968) 31 MLR 408; Mordesley 'Some Problems of the "Lump"' (1975) 38 MLR 504.

[55] In *Costain Building and Civil Engineering Ltd v Smith* [2000] ICR 215, EAT an agency-supplied building engineer was held not to have been lawfully appointed by his union as a safety representative because he was not an 'employee' as required by the relevant regulations.

[56] *Lee v Lee's Air Farming Ltd* [1961] AC 12, [1960] 3 All ER 420, PC.

[57] *Stanbury v Overmass and Chapple Ltd* (1976) 11 ITR 7, IT. However, there may be a presumption of employed status if the director is required to work full time for the company in return for a salary: *Folami v Nigerline (UK) Ltd* [1978] ICR 277, EAT.

when their services are dispensed with), they must show further factors. Thus in the old case of *Parsons v Albert J Parsons & Sons Ltd*,[58] the Court of Appeal held that a director was not 'employed', in spite of working full time for the company, since the company records did not contain a written contract of employment for him or memorandum setting out the terms of an oral contract,[59] his sole remuneration was that categorized in the accounts as 'directors' fees', and he had been treated as self-employed for tax and national insurance purposes.

One specific problem of legislative *policy* here has been the possible argument that a director should not be classed as an 'employee' because to do so would be inconsistent with the employment right that that person is trying to claim; the area in which this has arisen to date is the state guarantee for moneys outstanding to 'employees' on a company's insolvency,[60] where it was initially held by the EAT that it would be improper to allow the de facto owner of a one-man company to claim from the state on his own company's insolvency.[61] However, the Court of Appeal later reaffirmed strongly that there was no such rule of law, and that in each case it remains a question of fact—the person's status as a controlling director may well be a *factor* against employment status, but must be balanced against other factors such as the bona fides of the contract, the degree of control exercised by the company, the nature of their remuneration, the position of any other directors, and the conduct of the parties.[62]

2.1.3 'Worker' and the wider definition of employment

It can be argued that the traditional legal dichotomy between 'employee' and 'independent contractor' is now too simplistic to fit our diverse workforce, and leaves too many people potentially in a hole in the middle. One way to avoid (or at least mitigate) this is to move the goalposts and extend the definition of 'employee'.

2.1.3.1 The original applications

This is not a new idea, and it has in the past been done in one of two ways, namely to use the term 'worker' instead (with a correspondingly wider definition) or to retain the term 'employee' but add to the normal definition (ie simply as a person under a contract of employment). Trade union legislation has always used the term 'worker', defining it as 'an individual who works . . . (a) under a contract of employment or (b) under any other contract whereby he undertakes to do or perform personally any work or services for another party to the contract who is not a professional client of his'.[63] The extension in (b) is highly

[58] [1979] ICR 271, [1979] IRLR 117, CA; *Morley v C T Morley Ltd* [1985] ICR 499, EAT; *Eaton v Robert Eaton Ltd* [1988] ICR 302, [1988] IRLR 83, EAT.

[59] As was required by the Companies Act 1985, s 318.

[60] See 3.6.

[61] *Buchan v Secretary of State for Employment* [1997] IRLR 80, EAT.

[62] *Secretary of State for Trade and Industry v Bottrill* [1999] ICR 592, [1999] IRLR 326, CA (director held to be an employee for insolvency guarantee purposes; reasoning in *Buchan* disapproved), as explained and amplified in *Secretary of State for Business, Enterprise and Regulatory Reform v Neufield* [2009] IRLR 475, CA (directors again held to be employees for insolvency purposes in spite of 90 per cent and 100 per cent shareholdings in their companies), where the Court of Appeal approved guidance given by Elias P in *Clark v Clark Construction Initiatives Ltd* [2008] IRLR 364, EAT. How the individual is remunerated is to be viewed realistically, not just considering how it is described: *Department for Employment and Learning v Morgan* [2016] IRLR 350, NICA (payment was for services rendered to the company by the director, even though described as 'dividends'; held to be employment).

[63] Trade Union and Labour Relations (Consolidation) Act 1992, s 296; the 'Wages Act' provisions on deductions from wages use a similar term and definition, see now the ERA 1996, s 230(3) and the recovery of commission by a self-employed investment consultant in *Robertson v Blackstone Franks Investment Management Ltd* [1998] IRLR 376, CA.

significant; it was carried over into the Employment Rights Act 1996, where individuals covered by it tend to be referred to in the jargon as 'limb (b) workers'. Conversely, discrimination legislation has always used the term 'employment' but applied it to employment under a contract of employment or apprenticeship *or a contract personally to do any work*;[64] in other words, it confusingly uses the term 'employee' where it in effect means 'worker'. The Transfer of Undertakings (Protection of Employment) Regulations 2006 (TUPE) use the term 'employee' but define it as working 'for another person whether under a contract of service or apprenticeship or otherwise but does not include anyone who provides services under a contract for services'.[65] While these definitions contain subtle differences (with the TUPE definition being arguably narrowest, with its exclusion of *anyone* under a contract for services), they do show a deliberate extension of statutory coverage. Two important aspects follow from this:

1. Although the use of the term 'worker' may carry with it some historical, political, and/or sociological baggage (not to say Dickensian overtones), the extended legal definition is not restricted to horny-handed sons (and daughters) of toil and can apply (if satisfied on the facts) across a wide spectrum of types of work; for example, it has recently been applied to a part-time judge[66] and a partner in an LLP partnership.[67]
2. It is now generally accepted that case precedents on the 'worker' definition will also apply to the discrimination law's 'employee' definition and vice versa. There is an argument in principle that the two definitions are not identical because of the greater emphasis in the EU law backing the discrimination legislation on wider ideas of economic 'subordination' of the individual to the employing entity as the touchstone here,[68] but the Supreme Court has denied such a divergence between the definitions and held that there was no advantage in 'adding some mystery ingredient of "subordination" to the concept of employee and worker'.[69]

2.1.3.2 **Definition**

Perhaps surprisingly, the case law here was for a long time relatively scarce, though the leading authority of *Mirror Group Newspapers Ltd v Gunning*[70] emphasized the element of 'personal service', and stated that that must be the dominant purpose of the contract in question. In *Cotswold Developments Construction Ltd v Williams*,[71] this area was

[64] Equality Act 2010, s 83(2). This definition does not contain the express exclusion of a professional client, but that was effectively read into it by the Supreme Court in *Jivraj v Haswani* [2011] ICR 1004, [2011] IRLR 827, SC.

[65] SI 2006/246, reg 2(1).

[66] *O'Brien v Ministry of Justice* [2013] ICR 499, [2013] IRLR 315, SC.

[67] *Bates van Winkelhof v Clyde & Co LLP* [2014] ICR 730, [2014] IRLR 641, SC. See Berry 'When Is a Partner/LLP Member Not a Partner/LLP Member?' (2017) 46 ILJ 309. For general consideration of the definition, see Prassl 'Who Is a Worker?' (2017) 133 LQR 366; Bogg and Ford 'Between Statute and Contract: Who Is a Worker?' (2019) 135 LQR 347.

[68] For a recent example of this, see *B v Yodel Delivery Network Ltd* C-692/19 [2020] IRLR 550, ECJ.

[69] Per Lady Hale in *Bates van Winkelhof*, n 67 above.

[70] [1986] ICR 145, [1986] IRLR 27, CA, applied by the EAT in *Sheehan v Post Office Counters* [1999] ICR 734 in holding that a sub-postmaster was not covered by the disability legislation.

[71] [2006] IRLR 181, EAT. See generally Davidov 'Who Is a Worker?' (2005) 34 ILJ 57. A later challenge that the personal service requirement breached art 11 of the European Convention was rejected: *Independent Workers Union of Great Britain v Central Arbitration Committee* [2024] IRLR 148, [2024] ICR 189, SC. The first question (of a contract between the parties themselves) meant that an individual who contracted through his service company was not a worker: *Plastic Omnium Automotive Ltd v Horton* [2023] EAT 85 (28 June 2023, unreported).

reviewed by the EAT under Langstaff J, who suggested that a useful approach would be to consider, first, whether there was the required minimum level of mutuality of obligations between the parties for there to be a contract at all; second (if there was), whether the level of mutuality and control was enough to produce a contract of employment; third (if not), whether there was a sufficient obligation of personal service on the part of the individual to qualify them as a 'worker'; and fourth (if so), whether the usual proviso (that the work must not have been done in the course of the individual's business or profession) applied on the facts. This was followed by further consideration and guidance from Elias P in *James v Redcats (Brands) Ltd*,[72] where a parcel courier (using her own van, working only for the respondent firm, arranging her own timetable and holidays, paid per parcel delivered, and accepted by HMRC as self-employed) was held to be a 'worker' for the purposes of a claim of breach of the national minimum wage.

The relative stability achieved by this case law could have been upset when the matter finally went to the Supreme Court in *Jivraj v Hashwani*,[73] because it concerned the discrimination law definition and raised the point that this definition (as opposed to the definition of 'worker') is backed by EU Directives which have accumulated their own case law on its meaning. These tend to concentrate on whether (a) the individual performs services for reward for another person and (b) they are in a position of economic subordination;[74] some of the arguments in the case sought to drive a wedge between this and the domestic definition in UK discrimination law (and hence the 'worker' definition). The Supreme Court accepted that that domestic definition must now be construed so as to be consistent with EU law and in that context said that the 'primary purpose' test (set out previously) can now no longer be sufficient in itself. *However*, the judgment as a whole shows that the requirement for performing services for reward is simply a form of 'personal service' and that the idea of economic subordination is analogous to the domestic requirement that the individual must not have been acting independently in a business or professional capacity. Thus, properly understood, the case in fact ended up *aligning* the domestic definitions with the relevant EU law requirements, meaning that the existing case law (especially *Cotswolds Developments* and *Redcats*) continues to be authoritative, on both the discrimination law 'employee' definition and the more general 'worker' definition.

2.1.3.3 **Wider application**

This whole matter took on more significance when the wider 'worker' definition was adopted by the Labour government in the Public Interest Disclosure Act 1998,[75] the National Minimum Wage Act 1998,[76] and the regulations on working time and part-time workers.[77] The aim generally has been to move away from the traditional coverage of employees only, especially as many of the individuals most in need of protection will

[72] [2007] ICR 1006, [2007] IRLR 296, EAT.

[73] [2011] ICR 1004, [2011] IRLR 827, SC. The result of the case was that a commercial arbitrator was held not to be a 'worker' and so could not sue for religious discrimination when his services were rejected because he was not of a particular faith.

[74] See particularly *Allonby v Accrington and Rossendale College* C-256/01 [2004] ICR 1328, [2004] IRLR 224, ECJ at paras 67 and 68.

[75] This is because the Act puts new sections into the ERA 1996 and adopts the latter's definition of 'worker'.

[76] Section 54. In *James v Redcats (Brands) Ltd* (n 71) it was thought important for the effectiveness of the national minimum wage legislation that a broad approach be taken to the definition of 'worker', to include just the types of individuals most in need of its protection.

[77] SI 1998/1833, reg 2(1); SI 2000/1551, reg 1(2). The wider definition was not used in the Fixed-term Employees (Prevention of Less Favourable Treatment) Regulations 2002. It was later adopted, however, by the Coalition government in the new scheme for compulsory enrolment in workplace pensions.

come into the middle ground of 'atypicals' that has caused so many problems of definition in the past. Arguably, the 'worker' definition is a more inclusive one, prima facie covering atypical working unless there is good reason why it does not.[78] The way that this was put in the original DTI (now DBT) guides on the national minimum wage and working time may be significant—they both stated that it is only the '*genuinely* self-employed' who will not be covered by these laws. Clearly, there will be as many problems defining this as there are currently in defining a person under a contract of employment; however, it does give a flavour of the intent of the legislation, which can be seen graphically from two earlier cases (both of which concerned the entitlement to statutory holiday pay of individuals who, prior to the Working Time Regulations, would have had no such claim). In *Byrne Brothers (Farmwork) Ltd v Baird*,[79] self-employed building workers (under a subcontracting contract which stated that no holiday pay was due) were effectively laid off by a Christmas/New Year closure by the one firm for whom they worked. Even though they were clearly not employees (being taxed as labour-only subcontractors in the long-standing tradition of the building industry), they successfully sued the firm for paid annual holiday for the period in question under the Working Time Regulations 1998; they were under *a* contract, performing work personally for that firm, and in practical terms were subordinate workers (dependent for work on that firm) and so not genuinely in business on their own account. This result was then seen again when the matter reached the Court of Appeal in *Wright v Redrow Homes (Yorkshire) Ltd*[80] and direct labour subcontracting bricklayers were held entitled to holiday pay because (looking at the realities of the engagement rather than the technical meaning of the ill-fitting contract that they had been given) the intention of the parties was that the individual bricklayers themselves were to perform the work in question.

That is how matters stood for several years, but then the whole topic was revisited in two major cases, both concerning business plans based wholly on the use of self-employed labour, with the added factor in the second one of doing so in the 'gig economy'. In *Pimlico Plumbers Ltd v Smith*,[81] the company used as its workforce 125 'contractors', including the claimant. They wore its uniforms, drove its marked vans, and were represented to customers as its workforce. They were directed to customers by the company, who invoiced for the work. On the other hand, they were described in the agreement as self-employed, they had to look after all matters of their tax and NI, they provided their own tools and equipment, they were responsible for the quality of their work, and they had to be insured. The agreement stipulated a maximum working week over five days, but there was no obligation on either side to give or perform work; although there was some flexibility in who did what work, there was no formal substitution provision. When the claimant's engagement was terminated he claimed unfair dismissal (and certain other mainstream

[78] A potential problem (especially for sporadic work) arose in *Windle v Secretary of State for Justice* [2016] IRLR 628 where the Court of Appeal considered that mutuality of obligations is just as much a requirement for 'worker' as for 'employee'. In *Pimlico Plumbers Ltd v Smith* [2018] IRLR 872, SC the Supreme Court declined a request to rule on whether *Windle* was right on this point but subsequently the Court of Appeal resolved the matter by holding clearly that the employee element of an irreducible amount of mutuality does not apply to the worker definition: *Nursing & Midwifery Council v Somerville* [2022] IRLR 447, CA.

[79] [2002] ICR 667, [2002] IRLR 96, EAT.

[80] [2004] ICR 1126, [2004] IRLR 720, CA. Subsequently to this decision, the employers (with advice) sought to amend their terms of hiring deliberately to exclude 'worker' status, but when a further challenge arose it was held that they had failed to do so: *Redrow Homes (Yorkshire) Ltd v Buckborough* [2009] IRLR 34, EAT.

[81] [2018] IRLR 872, SC. The decision of the Supreme Court is curiously limited in its discussion of the law, being largely concerned with the facts and whether this conclusion was one which was *open* to the tribunal. For a summary of the law, the judgment of the Court of Appeal ([2017] IRLR 323, CA) should still be consulted; nothing in the Supreme Court's judgment casts doubt on it.

employment law rights), disability discrimination, and outstanding statutory holiday pay. From the tribunal up to the Supreme Court it was held on these facts that although he was not an 'employee' within the Employment Rights Act 1996, and so could not claim unfair dismissal (or the allied employment rights), he *was* a 'worker' and *did* come under the wider 'employee' definition in discrimination law, so that his disability discrimination and holiday pay claims could proceed.

In the newsworthy case of *Uber BV v Aslam*,[82] taxi drivers had their contracts carefully drafted to negate legal liabilities including working time rights and the national minimum wage. They were permitted to work for other organizations, had no expectation of any particular amount of work, had to look after their own vehicle and licensing, and had to take care of their own tax affairs. There was no Uber logo for the cars, they did not wear a uniform, and direct control was only in relation to compliance with public hire regulations. When challenged, Uber argued that this was just a hi-tech form of a traditional taxi/minicab business and that it simply provided an app-based service for the independent drivers. However, the tribunal, EAT, Court of Appeal and eventually the Supreme Court held that the drivers were 'workers' and so entitled to the statutory rights. In the latter, there was reliance on the *Autoclenz* principle (considered above) of looking beyond the strict terms of the contract to establish the real relationship, together with the policy imperative of not allowing employers to circumvent statutory rights. On the facts, worker status was shown by the following practical factors:

1. all questions of remuneration were fixed by Uber; the only way the drivers could increase their pay was by working more hours on those fixed amounts;
2. all other contractual terms were drafted and imposed by Uber;
3. drivers could choose when to turn on the app, *but* once logged on the choice of work was subject to constraints by Uber, including disciplinary penalties for too few fares;
4. although the drivers provided the cars, these were subject to conditions by Uber, who provided all the technology and operated their own rating system for drivers and customers; and
5. Uber not only collected all the fares but also deliberately limited a driver's contact with the customer.

Overall, the picture was one of a system tightly controlled by Uber for its own benefit, with little input from the drivers. It was not analogous to a hotel booking system (where the hotel remains in control of the relevant terms and conditions) or (more to the point, given Uber's arguments) to minicab drivers. Moreover, the court found no help from either the golf caddy case (*Cheng Yuan v Royal Hong Kong Golf Club* [1998] IRLR 131, PC) or the lap dancer case (*Quashie v Stringfellows Restaurants Ltd* [2013] IRLR 99, CA). Given that ultimately the question of status where the enquiry goes beyond simply the meaning of contractual terms is one of fact, the tribunal had reached a defensible decision and its decision stood.

The *Uber* case is clearly important in demonstrating the approach to be taken, but of course the ultimate emphasis on it being a question of fact means that these cases will continue to be closely fought. In the post-*Uber* cases, worker status has been successfully claimed by a private hire driver and a motor bike courier;[83] but on facts not a million miles

[82] [2021] IRLR 407, [2021] ICR 657, SC.

[83] *Addison Lee Ltd v Lange* [2021] EWCA Civ 594 and *Stuart Deliveries Ltd v Augustine* [2022] IRLR 56, CA respectively.

from those in *Uber* itself, such status was denied to a parcel deliverer who was held to be independently operating a genuine franchise arrangement and a black cab owner using the respondent's app to access fares but remaining ultimately in business on his own.[84]

2.1.4 **Atypical workers (1)—domestic law**

2.1.4.1 **Background**

It has long been clear that atypical workers may have their employment protection rights jeopardized by a finding that they are independent contractors.[85] An early form of this problem revolved around the position of 'outworkers' (ie people who perform work for another at home rather than on that other person's premises). Part-time workers in factories may have had problems in the past with the old '16 hours per week' rule for computing continuity of employment until its repeal in 1995,[86] but at least there was usually no question that they were in fact 'employed', whereas in the case of an outworker even that might be in doubt, for if on the facts it appears that the work is brought to them, and accepted, purely on an ad hoc basis, the tribunal might take the view that the outworker was not in fact 'employed'.[87] Where, however, the outworker works on a regular basis, the EAT held in *Airfix Footwear Ltd v Cope*[88] that there is no reason why there should not be a finding of a contract of employment, even though the work is done elsewhere than on the employer's premises, if there is sufficient mutuality of obligations; this approach was approved by the Court of Appeal in *Nethermere (St Neots) Ltd v Gardiner.*[89]

2.1.4.2 **Economic developments**

While an arrangement such as homeworking was long generally considered 'atypical', it has been for many years now recognized that nine-to-five employment throughout the year in a manufacturing factory is now much *less* typical, and so increasingly the law has had to consider the position of those working under more diverse and less full-time conditions. In particular, much of the job creation in the economy in the past decades has been in forms hitherto thought to be atypical, but fast becoming the norm in many sectors of the labour market.[90] At the same time, with the decline of traditional manufacturing industries and the expansion of the service and IT sectors, the nature of the employing concern has also been changing, with larger numbers of people now being employed by what hitherto would have been considered 'small firms'.[91]

Part-time and temporary work is now more prevalent[92] and in some areas remote working (the modern form of more traditional homeworking) is increasingly

[84] *Stojavllevic v DPD Group Ltd* EA-2019/000259, EAT and *Johnson v Transopco Ltd* [2022] EAT 6 respectively.

[85] Collins 'Independent Contractors and the Challenge of Vertical Disintegration to Employment Protection Laws' (1990) 10 OJLS 353.

[86] See further discussion in this chapter in 2.5.1.

[87] *Mailway (Southern) Ltd v Willsher* [1978] ICR 511, [1978] IRLR 322, EAT.

[88] [1978] ICR 1210, [1978] IRLR 396, concerning footwear makers.

[89] [1984] ICR 612, [1984] IRLR 240, CA, concerning garment sewers.

[90] See Fredman 'Labour Law in Flux: The Changing Composition of the Workforce' (1997) 26 ILJ 337; Davies and Freedland *Towards a Flexible Labour Market* (2007).

[91] This was strikingly demonstrated by research undertaken in the late 1990s when considering whether to decrease what was then an exemption from the Disability Discrimination Act 1995 for small firms. This showed that 1 m employers in the private sector (95 per cent of the total number of employers in the UK) employing 4.5 m workers were firms employing fewer than 20 people: *Disability Discrimination Act 1995: Employment Provisions and Small Employers* (DFEE, 1998).

[92] The Taylor Report on Modern Employment Practices (2017) contains up-to-date statistics as well as suggestions for reform: see this chapter, 2.1.7.

common.[93] Generally, the workforce has become more flexible,[94] and indeed encouraging such flexibility has long been government policy,[95] since it is seen as a way of encouraging more use of individual contracting, flexible pay, and payment by results—the antithesis of the collective approach to wage determination. However, this development may cause strains in applying laws evolved basically against the background of full-time, 'normal' (not to say 'male') employment. While it is important to remember that, for better or for worse, the juristic basis here remains the traditional contract of employment, it is also important to ensure that there is not too much scope for employers to use devices such as temporary or part-time work in order to evade statutory obligations.[96]

It has been argued for some time now that in Britain we have been in danger of evolving a two-tier labour force—those in traditional full-time employment with a fair degree of job security and statutory protection, and (increasingly) those in part-time, temporary, or otherwise atypical employment with little security, and hitherto generally excluded from statutory protection.[97] In fact, the principal moves towards protection of atypical employees such as part-timers have come through EU law. Initially, this was under EU sex equality laws which apply because of the disparate effect on women of rules prejudicing part-timers; the most notable success lay in the enforced removal (first by court action and then by amending regulations) of the requirement of working 16 hours per week in order to gain continuity of employment (for the purposes of qualifying for the major statutory rights).[98] This approach was then largely superseded by EU law Directives aimed at giving protection *directly* to specific *forms* of atypical employees, relieving them of the necessity of going through the hoops of a discrimination action; this development is considered separately presently.

Finally, note that the coronavirus crisis has had effects in the short term that may well prove rather longer-lasting. The most obvious example of this has been the large increase in home/remote working. One irony here is that although (as seen above) the law's relatively favourable view of this as 'employment' evolved in the context of homeworking by lower-paid manual workers, during the crisis it was largely higher-paid, higher-skilled, and/or professional individuals with easy access to online/Internet technology who were able to adopt this form of working. If it is the case that employers view this as a permanent and desirable aspect of modern working (eg by radically cutting back on overheads for office space in expensive locations and by discovering that individuals' productivity has increased while working remotely) then it will be important that the law continues to regard this form of working as 'real' employment (albeit one that can cause potential problems, eg in applying working time and health and safety legislation).

[93] Even before the COVID pandemic and consequent changes in working patterns, figures from the Office of National Statistics showed that in 2014, 4.2 m people worked from home, splitting approximately one-third female and two-thirds male.

[94] For the history of this movement see Whiteside 'Before the Gig Economy: UK Employment Policy and the Casual Labour Question' (2021) 50 ILJ 610.

[95] See Employment for the 1990s (Cm 540, 1988) and People, Jobs and Opportunity (Cm 1810, 1992) for the then Conservative government's policy; Fairness at Work (Cm 3968, 1998) for the succeeding Labour government's policy.

[96] *Lewis v Surrey County Council* [1987] ICR 982 at 998, [1987] IRLR 509 and 516, HL, per Lord Ackner.

[97] Dickens 'Falling through the Net: Employment Change and Worker Protection' (1988) 19 IRJ 139; Freedland and Kountouris, *The Legal Construction of Personal Work Relations* (2011). One view is that this movement has been a pragmatic reaction to market conditions and business uncertainties rather than deliberate and widespread managerial policy: Sisson and Marguison 'Management: Systems, Structures and Strategy' in Edwards (ed) *Industrial Relations, Theory and Practice in Britain* (1995) 113.

[98] See further discussion in this chapter, 2.5.1.

2.1.4.3 **Casual working generally**

Casual work has always caused problems legally, especially as there is a persistent folk myth among many employers that *because* a person is termed 'casual', *therefore* they cannot have any employment rights. It is important to realize at the outset, however, that 'casual' is *not* a legal term of art, that the word appears *nowhere* in the Employment Rights Act 1996, that the only legal distinction is between those who do and those who do not qualify for employment rights, and that a casual worker may or may not so qualify, depending on the facts.

On the other hand, it has to be accepted that casual workers can have more problems than most in meeting qualification conditions, obviously in relation to continuity of employment, but more fundamentally in relation to employee status itself. This was established early in the history of the modern legislation in *O'Kelly v Trusthouse Forte plc*,[99] which concerned wine waiters used by a hotel organization as and when required. In perhaps a telling phrase, they were referred to as 'regular casuals'. They were kept on a list of preferred individuals for the work and were called in as necessary for catering events; this was their principal source of work and if they refused a particular call they could be taken off the list. The other indicators of status were neatly split between those pointing to employment (working under the control of the organization, which paid them for work done under deduction of tax, provided clothing and equipment, organized rotas, and provided holiday pay and bonuses) and those pointing away from it (no obligation to provide work, no statements of terms and conditions, no notice required to terminate, and a general acceptance in the industry and by these parties that waiters were self-employed). When their services were dispensed with—they said because of trade union membership—they claimed unfair dismissal. The tribunal held that they could not claim because they were not employees; the EAT allowed their appeal but the Court of Appeal reinstated the tribunal's decision, which had been largely based on the lack of any obligations to offer or accept work, leading to the conclusion that this was essentially a commercial arrangement for the provision of ad hoc services.

Although it seemed that the general trend in the succeeding case law was towards extension of legal rights to casuals, this development then suffered some setbacks. In *Clark v Oxfordshire Health Authority*,[100] a 'bank' nurse (being offered and accepting work as and when it was available at any of the authority's hospitals) who was paid at standard rates and charged to PAYE and NI contributions, but who was not guaranteed any regular work, was held by the Court of Appeal *not* to be an employee (after three years working in the authority's hospitals, with only four breaks totalling 14 weeks) and so was unable to claim unfair dismissal.[101] Even more significantly, in *Carmichael v National Power plc*[102] a question was raised as to the employment status of two power station guides employed on a 'casual, as required' basis to show parties around when the need arose, who were given uniforms and charged to PAYE and NI contributions. The Court of Appeal split, with the majority finding that they were employees, in a thoughtful decision in favour of

[99] [1983] ICR 728, [1983] IRLR 369, CA.

[100] [1998] IRLR 125, CA.

[101] There was, however, a major qualification in the judgment. In the tribunal this issue had arguably been confused by considering not just whether there was an employment contract, but whether there was an umbrella contract covering the whole period (discussed below). What had not been considered was whether there was a series of *individual* contracts (for each stint at one of the hospitals), possibly *linked* by the rules on continuity of employment (see now *Cornwall CC v Prater* [2006] ICR 731, [2006] IRLR 362, CA); the result of the decision was a remission to the tribunal to consider this possibility.

[102] [1999] ICR 1226, [2000] IRLR 43, HL. The principal speech is by Lord Irvine LC; the other speech by Lord Hoffmann is of interest on the fact/law distinction as applied to the existence of a contract of employment, holding that the Court of Appeal had been wrong to interfere with the tribunal's decision for the employer *at all*.

extending employment status, perfecting the potentially informal relationship by finding implied terms that (a) the employer would offer each guide a reasonable amount of the work available and (b) each guide would accept a reasonable amount of the work offered. However, on further appeal the House of Lords disapproved this completely and held that the guides were not employees, largely due to lack of a level of mutuality of obligations which Lord Irvine LC said was an irreducible minimum for any contract of employment. This was taken one step further in *Stevedoring and Haulage Services Ltd v Fuller*,[103] where the employer in effect achieved this result in advance by putting a clause into the hiring contract that no mutual duties (to offer work or to turn up for it) were to arise under it. These have been serious blows to any prospect of further general extension of employment status by judicial action, and it is clear that there are difficulties in attaining a fair balance in this area.

2.1.4.4 **Four possible answers**

Perhaps unsurprisingly, there have been attempts to find ways round these problems caused by irregular working, at least in cases eliciting most judicial sympathy, for example where the facts show *regular* working under conditions usually found in employment relationships, and where the employer defence of lack of employment status only comes at a late stage to counter a tribunal claim. As stated, each case must depend on its particular facts, but four possibilities may be mentioned.

1. One legal device that has shown some signs of evolving as a possible remedy in cases where sporadic work (eg on a series of short-term contracts) appears to be being misused is that of the 'umbrella' or 'global contract', that is, a finding that although the employee was only actually working for certain periods (possibly on an irregular basis), there was sufficient mutuality between the parties to justify a finding that in law there was one overall contract governing the whole period in question. This was considered to be an important possibility for countering employer abuse of such arrangements in *Lewis v Surrey County Council*,[104] and, to take one particular example, it succeeded in *St Ives Plymouth Ltd v Haggerty*,[105] where a bookbinder who was kept on a bank of casual workers by a publisher and used with great regularity over a considerable period of time was held entitled to claim unfair dismissal on the basis that although initially the relationship was merely casual, an overall umbrella contract had *evolved* over the whole period due to the conduct of the parties. Elias J said:

> We recognize that in part it may be said that the Tribunal's reasoning is finding the legal obligation arising out of the practical commercial consequences of not providing work on the one hand or performing it on the other. But we do not see why such commercial imperatives may not over time crystallize into legal obligations. Furthermore, there were other factors which were taken into account, including the lengthy period of employment, the fact that the work was important to the employers, and the work was regular even if the hours varied. One might also readily infer, although it was not spelt out, that the employers felt under an obligation to distribute the casual work fairly, rather as did the allocator in the *Nethermere case*.

[103] [2001] EWCA Civ 651, [2001] IRLR 627, EAT. Dockers who had been made redundant as full-time employees and rehired on a casualized basis could not claim statutory rights, even though in fact working consistently for the same employer, because of the clause in the contract. How much of a sham would such a clause have to be in practice before a tribunal would feel able to ignore it?

[104] [1987] ICR 982, [1987] IRLR 509, HL.

[105] UKEAT/0107/08.

So far so good, from the point of view of the casual, but it is also easy to find examples going the other way. The argument very clearly failed in one of the leading cases, *Hellyer Bros Ltd v McLeod*,[106] where trawlermen who had sailed exclusively for one company for many years were held unable to claim redundancy payments when dispensed with, since the facts only established a series (albeit a long series) of separate contracts for each voyage. It can be argued that the case involved a heavy element of maritime law, with its tradition of signing on for 'voyage contracts',[107] but equally it can be pointed out that the umbrella contract argument also failed in the notorious case of the lap dancer held not to be an employee of her club.[108] It is therefore not a panacea and can cause serious problems in trying to second-guess in advance when a tribunal will or will not be interested in its use.

2. Second, an employer defence based on lack of mutuality may be weakened if it only works one way, in particular if the employer seeks to have its cake and eat it by providing that it is not obliged to offer any work but that the individual is bound to take on any work that is in fact offered. This was the case in *Wilson v Circular Distributors Ltd*,[109] where a relief area manager had a statement of terms of employment stipulating that although the company guaranteed no particular hours (and pay would only be for hours actually worked), he was 'required' to act as relief manager to cover for holidays and sickness when needed. Other terms were consistent with employment. After two years of consistent engagements he received no further work and sued for unfair dismissal. The tribunal held that he was not an employee because of the overall lack of mutuality but the EAT allowed his appeal. It held that for there to be an absence of the irreducible minimum of mutuality, there has to be an absence of obligations on *both* sides (as in *Carmichael*), which was not the case here. His claim could proceed.
3. Alternatively, the casual worker can try the argument that there was an individual contract of employment during *each* engagement and then, particularly if the gaps are relatively short compared with the times working, rely on the statutory rules on continuity of employment to establish any period of continuous employment necessary to qualify for the right being exercised.[110] In *Cornwall CC v Prater*,[111] a home tutor for children had no overall contract with the council but worked for it ad hoc over ten years. There was no expectation of any particular amount of work, but when she was assigned to a particular child she expected to complete that assignment and to be paid accordingly. When a dispute arose with the council over her status, she referred it to a tribunal, which held that she was under a contract of employment during each assignment and that these contractual periods were then deemed continuous under the statutory provisions. The EAT and then the Court of Appeal agreed—in a case of a series of individual engagements a tribunal can consider whether each one was under a contract of employment and then whether

[106] [1987] ICR 526, [1987] IRLR 232, CA.

[107] Though even this might be a bit of a stretch, given that they were only 'signing on' each time for a couple of weeks in the North Sea, not for two years sailing round the Horn to hunt the Great White Whale. Possibly more relevant was the fact that they were claiming unemployment benefit between each voyage.

[108] *Quashie v Stringfellows Restaurants Ltd* [2013] IRLR 99, CA; see this chapter, 2.1.1.2.

[109] [2006] IRLR 38, EAT.

[110] These rules are considered in this chapter, 2.5.2. Particularly important is the Employment Rights Act 1996, s 212(3)(b), which covers 'temporary cessations of work' and can apply to both regular gaps between engagements (*Ford v Warwickshire CC* [1983] ICR 273, [1983] IRLR 126, HL) and, more importantly, wholly irregular such gaps (*Flack v Kodak Ltd* [1986] ICR 775, [1986] IRLR 255, CA).

[111] [2006] ICR 731, [2006] IRLR 362, CA.

they were deemed continuous, in which case it is *not* necessary to show the sort of mutuality necessary for an umbrella contract. This was followed in *Drake v Ipsos Mori UK Ltd*,[112] where an individual used by the company for five years as a 'freelance' interviewer on an 'assignment-by-assignment' basis sought to claim unfair dismissal. The tribunal turned his claim down on the basis that the lack of overall mutuality meant that he was not an employee but the EAT allowed his appeal, considering that the tribunal had erred by looking only at whether there was one umbrella contract and should have gone on to consider whether each assignment had been under a contract of employment. It is arguable that this is the most sensible way to address the problems of sporadic casual work—normally it is clear that during the 'on' periods, the individual is indistinguishable from an ordinary employee (especially if under the direct control of the organization and satisfying the other usual indicia of employment as to pay, hours, etc) and the matter can then be left to the application of the normal continuity rules; if they have worked regularly, with relatively short gaps, those rules will usually grant continuity and so extend legal protection to someone who in policy terms deserves it, but if, on the other hand, the relationship was very informal, with short engagements and long gaps, then legal protection is unlikely to be extended to a case which in economic terms departs too far from the accepted model of employment. There is, however, one major obstacle to this apparently neat solution. That is the existence of cases such as *O'Kelly* and *Carmichael*, which hold authoritatively that some relationships are *so* loose and lacking mutuality that they *cannot* in law constitute employment in the first place. There is therefore still a line that has to be drawn here; the problem is knowing where it is when advising.

4. Finally, there is a fall-back position—if the casual worker cannot qualify as an employee (and so cannot claim unfair dismissal or redundancy rights), they may still qualify as a 'worker' (or come within the wider 'employee' definition in discrimination law). This would at least mean that they would qualify for *some* employment rights and have the protection of discrimination law. Of course, such a finding is not automatic because the wider worker definition still has requirements to be satisfied, but it may be that it is more likely now for many casual workers (especially in the gig economy) in the light of the decision of the Supreme Court in *Uber BV v Aslam*, considered above.

2.1.4.5 **The particular problem of agency working**

One other form of engagement which has caused problems at common law of a surprisingly fundamental nature is agency working. This has traditionally been seen by employers as *the* way to keep staff out of employment status and to achieve a high level of flexibility. Although the relationship legally between the agency and the worker has been far from straightforward,[113] it was thought to be clear that the worker could *not* be the employee of the client. This made particular sense (and continues to do so) when the nature of the work is such that the identity of the worker is unimportant, there is a high level of rotation of staff to the particular client, and the demands are fluctuating (ie classic

[112] [2012] IRLR 973, EAT.

[113] The leading case is *McMeechan v Secretary of State for Employment* [1997] ICR 549, [1997] IRLR 353, CA, where it was held that the relationship is a question of fact (ie no rules of law either way) and that there could be two distinct employments with the agency—a general one (to be on the books) and an individual one covering a particular assignment. In *Bunce v Postworth Ltd* [2005] IRLR 557, CA, however, an agency-provided worker working wholly under clients' control was held not to be an employee of the agency at all, through lack of control *and* mutuality of obligations.

'temping'). The situation, however, began to become more difficult through the evolution of a very different form of agency working, where the work is specialized, the worker's own skills are a key point, labour is in short supply, and when the client discovers a good worker it will want to *keep* them. In such a case, the agency in practice is little more than a recruiter; from that stage on, the client takes over 'running' the worker and the agency soon recedes into the background (remaining technically the conduit for payment). That individual worker then works nine-to-five, 52 weeks a year, for that one client for a significant period of time, by the end of which they are virtually indistinguishable from the client's permanent employees doing similar work.[114] It is well known that in similar circumstances a self-employed 'consultant' who ends up working permanently for the one 'client' can transmute over time into an employee. Could that happen with an agency worker?

In *Montgomery v Johnson Underwood Ltd*,[115] an agency worker was held not to be the employee (for unfair dismissal purposes) of the agency because once supplied to the client, she worked for that one client for two years, subject to little or no control, supervision, or direction by the agency. A case such as this suggested that if the worker is not to be cast into the outer darkness with no rights against anyone, a sympathetic tribunal might be tempted to look for another candidate for 'employer', and there is only one—the client. This was generally thought to be legally impossible (without the deliberate, separate hiring of a good temp onto the permanent staff) until the bombshell case of *Motorola Ltd v Davidson*,[116] where the EAT held that it was a possibility. The worker in question was a skilled telephone repairer who was recruited by an agency to the client's own specifications. He then worked wholly for the client for two years, entirely under its control and with no further contact with the agency. When he gave cause for concern, he was disciplined under the client's own disciplinary procedures (though termination was effected through the agency). On his complaint of unfair dismissal, the tribunal held that on these facts there was a contract of employment with the *client*, against whom the action lay. The client's appeal against this finding was dismissed by the EAT. This decision certainly caused a renewal of interest in this area though it was only a first instance decision. It was, however, followed by three Court of Appeal decisions which strongly suggested that there could have been an evolving contract of employment with the client over time. In *Franks v Reuters Ltd*[117] this was obiter, as it was in *Dacas v Brook Street Bureau*,[118] where the court split on the matter. In *Cable & Wireless plc v Muscat*,[119] however, the court upheld a tribunal decision that an agency worker *had* become the direct employee of the client after two years' service. Thus, by 2007 it appeared to be a distinct possibility that consistent use over time (though *quaere* how long?) of an agency-provided worker could lead to a formal employment relationship with the client.

What happened then was a volte-face that was rapid even by employment law standards. Quite simply, the EAT in a series of cases refused to apply this line of authority and consistently held that *no* such contract had evolved. This reached its height in the judgment of Elias P in *James v Greenwich BC*,[120] where an agency worker was supplied to the council, worked for it consistently for three years, tried to claim unfair dismissal when replaced, but was held by the tribunal and EAT not to have been the council's employee

[114] Particularly as good HR practice tends to be to treat 'outsiders' as much like your own as possible; legally, this is exactly what the client should not do.

[115] [2001] IRLR 269, [2001] ICR 819, CA; see also *Bunce v Postworth*, n 113.

[116] [2001] IRLR 4, EAT.

[117] [2003] EWCA Civ 417, [2003] IRLR 423, CA.

[118] [2004] ICR 1437, [2004] IRLR 358, CA.

[119] [2006] ICR 975, [2006] IRLR 354, CA.

[120] [2007] IRLR 168, EAT; see also Judge Clark's judgment in *Cairns v Visteon* [2007] IRLR 175, EAT.

at all. When this decision was appealed,[121] the Court of Appeal unanimously *upheld* the EAT's decision. It said that *Dacas* had not been a good case in which to consider this fundamental point and (more significantly) that *Cable & Wireless* had been a case on unusual facts (true!) which had laid down no general principle. The Court agreed with Elias P that the test for transmutation into an employee by the finding of an implied contract with the client is not merely that the agency worker ends up *looking* like a direct employee; rather, it is the much tougher test that it must be *necessary* to find such an implied contract in order to make sense of the situation *at all*. In a normal case (where, for example, payment remains through the agency, with whom the client still deals) there will be *no* such necessity, no matter how long the engagement lasts. Thus, in practical terms, *James* has stopped this movement towards direct client employment of agency-provided individuals. This obviously came as a major relief to large-scale users of agency workers and as an equally major disappointment to those wanting greater employment rights for agency workers. In his judgment in *James*, Mummery LJ expressed some sympathy with the latter view but said that litigants must not have unrealistic expectations as to what the courts, as opposed to Parliament, can do to change the law here.

Since this decision Parliament has enacted the Agency Worker Regulations 2010 and more recently the Employment Rights Act 2025, which are considered presently, *but* it is important to note that although these provide important new rights for agency workers, they do *not* govern the employment status (or otherwise) of such workers for other purposes such as general statutory rights, which thus remain subject to the above case law.

2.1.4.6 **The particular problem of zero-hour contracts**

The modern phenomenon of the zero-hour contract, whereby the employer declines to stipulate or guarantee any set amount of work but requires the individual to undertake such work as is offered, has caused considerable controversy. A major study in August 2022 by the Chartered Institute of Personnel and Development (CIPD)[122] showed that 3 per cent of the workforce (1.3 million people) were on such contracts, splitting 4 per cent of women and 2.7 per cent of men. Of all employers, 18 per cent made some use of these contracts, with 77 per cent saying they made no use. The principal areas for their use were hospitality, health, education, and the voluntary sector.

From an economic point of view, the zero-hour contract could be viewed as the ultimate form of flexible working for employers in areas where demand is fluctuating (the report found that one-third of employers who used them combined them with part-time working). On the other hand, there is a large element of their use where informal working *suits* the individual's lifestyle. On this point (which, as the report notes, leads to a more nuanced position than just 'good or bad'), 62 per cent of individuals on such contracts said that they were satisfied with their jobs, especially in relation to work–life balance and health/stress issues; these tended to be students, those with intermittent health issues, carers, and older workers approaching retirement, who tended to view the ability to turn down work essential. However, there was also considerable dissatisfaction in relation to contracts and pay, with concerns being widespread about one-sided flexibility benefiting the employer, in particular in relation to short notice being given to individuals as to their shifts. Equally, this form of contracting can be seen as producing unacceptable

121 [2008] IRLR 302, CA.

122 Zero-hours contracts: evolution and current status (CIPD August 2022), available at cipd.co.uk/zero-hours-contracts-report-aug-2022_tcm18-110465.pdf. It contains a wealth of statistical and other evidence.

uncertainty in income and contributing to low pay (even where the hours actually worked comply with the national minimum wage), and as being open to abuse by employers. For present purposes of status, the key issue is whether such contracts could be used to deny employee status and hence employment protection rights.

Employment status

The first involvement of the law has been on the fundamental question of the employment status of zero-hours workers. As with casual working generally, there has (hitherto) been no 'law on zero-hour contracts' and so each case must be decided on its facts, applying the ordinary principles. It is certainly not the case that anyone on such a contract automatically has no legal rights. We have already seen the case of *St Ives Plymouth Ltd v Haggerty*,[123] where it was held that what originally seemed a loose, zero-hour arrangement had over time (with very regular working) transmuted into an umbrella contract. Likewise, in *Pulse Healthcare v Carewatch Care Services Ltd*,[124] the EAT had little hesitation in finding employment status where a care home had sought to avoid it for care workers working consistently to provide a high level of care by putting them on zero-hour contracts and expressing any engagement to be technically only by the day; the devices used here were to find one umbrella contract and to evade the contractual terms by holding that they were so far from the reality of their work as to constitute a sham.

However, it does not pay to be too complacent here, and the case of *Saha v Viewpoint Field Services Ltd*[125] shows the bear traps that can still await the individual. The claimant was taken on as a telephone interviewer by the respondent market research company. She was told what shifts they were looking for and told them which ones she might be able to do. She had a fairly sporadic work pattern, of seven to 43 hours a week. After some time, the company conducted an employment 'audit' (using HMRC guidelines) and decided that their interviewers were not 'employees' (even though they had tended to refer to them as such) and that they needed to take them all back on as formally self-employed, terminating the current arrangement. When the claimant claimed unfair dismissal, she failed before the tribunal because she had not been an employee. Crucial to this decision was a finding of fact that the whole basis of her engagement had been that the company was under no obligation to provide any particular amount of shifts and that she was not obliged to take on any that were offered. Moreover, there had been occasions in practice where she had declined work. The tribunal said that, while she may have passed the normal *Ready Mixed Concrete* tests for employment, she failed the *prior* test of mutuality of obligations (based on *Carmichael*). Her appeal to the EAT was turned down, in spite of the judge's obvious sympathy. The basis for that decision was that the tribunal's finding of fact on lack of mutuality was one that it was entitled to come to, and that that alone was fatal to her claim. Note that here there was a lack of obligations on both sides, hence the point made above about the importance of fact finding in these cases.

The question of the status of those under zero-hours contracts is thus still at a developing stage and in need of more authoritative case law.[126] However, one finding in the report gives some hope that this may not be as big a problem as at first sight. Of employers surveyed who used these contracts, 76 per cent accepted that the individuals were 'employees' and 10 per cent considered them 'workers', with only 6 per cent maintaining that they were self-employed.

[123] See n 105. [124] UKEAT/0123/12. [125] UKEAT/0116/13 (February 2014).

[126] One example of the piecemeal nature of the approach so far is *Agbeze v Barnet, Enfield & Haringey Mental Health NHS Trust* [2022] IRLR 115 where the EAT had to decide a very specific point as to how to determine any wage loss if a person on a zero-hours contract is suspended.

Legislation (1): a small start

On the legislative front, in 2015 the Coalition government attacked one particularly unfair aspect, namely where the employer not only uses a zero-hour contract but within it states that the individual is not to work for anyone else (even where the employer has no work to offer). This is now banned.[127] However, welcome though that was, it did *not* address the overall problem of the legal status of the individual and the consequent possibility of denial of employment rights. The Employment Rights Act 2025 strengthens these existing provisions on exclusivity, but its principal focus lay elsewhere.

Legislation (2): the Employment Rights Act 2025

A key element politically of the incoming Labour government in 2024 in relation to employment law was to 'ban' zero-hours contracts. This then formed Part 1 of the Employment Rights Act 2025. As with the proposal to ban fire and rehire (discussed at 2.6.4) the eventual legislation was more nuanced, concentrating instead on converting zero-hours contract into defined hours contracts and dealing with abuses of shift working schedules, rather than an outright ban. As with much of the Act, it operates by inserting the new provisions into the existing Employment Rights Act 1996.

A 'zero-hours contract' is defined as a contract of employment or other worker's contract under which (a) the undertaking to do work is an undertaking to do so conditionally on the employer making work available to the worker, and (b) there is no certainty that any such work will be made available to the worker.[128] There are then four new rights for a worker under such a contract. The **first** is a right to have the employer make them a 'guaranteed hours offer' at the end of every 'reference period' beginning and ending with 'specified days'.[129] This offer may be either to amend the existing contract or to enter into a new one and must reflect the hours actually worked by the worker in the relevant reference period. There are limitations on the making of other changes at the same time and regulations are to set out the timing and format of the offer and the information that must accompany it. The worker, on receipt of the offer, may accept or reject the offer by giving notice within a prescribed period The **second** is a right to reasonable notice of shifts to be worked by the worker. What is reasonable sounds like a question of fact, but it is then provided that regulations may specify an amount of time before the shift is due to start. **Third,** this right is then extended to a right to reasonable notice of cancellation of or change to a shift. Again, a minimum period for reasonable notice is to be specified. The **Fourth** right is to payment for a cancelled, moved or curtailed shift. A time for this to be paid is again to be specified.

There is a general exception to these rights where the issues raised by them are specifically covered by a collective agreement governing the worker's contract, made between one or more independent trade unions and the employer. In the case of each of these

[127] Employment Rights Act 1996, s 27A, inserted by the Small Business, Enterprise and Employment Act 2015. Remedies are provided separately by the Exclusivity Terms in Zero Hours Contracts (Redress) Regulations 2015, SI 2015/2021. Dismissal for breaching an illegal exclusivity clause is declared to be automatically unfair.

[128] Employment Rights Act 1996 s 27BZ2.

[129] Employment Rights Act 1996 s 27BA. These vital concepts are left to be covered by regulations. When the Bill went to the House of Lords, there was an amendment to apply this only where the worker requested it but this was rejected by the government, reinstating the present simple obligation on the employer.

rights, complaint for breach by the employer lie to an employment tribunal. If the tribunal finds the case proved, it is to issue a declaration to that effect and may award such compensation as is just and equitable, subject to a maximum amount to be set by regulations.

Four particular points may be noted about this novel legislation:

(i) It in fact goes further than zero-hours contracts as such. The title of this part of the 1996 Act is changed from 'zero hours workers' to 'zero hours workers and similar'. This is because these rights are in fact extended to cover a slightly different category, namely where there *are* some *minimum* hours specified in the contract, but these are low (and below a threshold to be set) and in practice the employer demands more in any reference period. This will, in particular, trigger the obligation on the employer to give such a worker a guaranteed hours offer. There are parallel provisions relating to shifts being required beyond a minimum set out in the contract.

(ii) Nothing in these provisions addresses the original question considered above of the employment *status* of a zero-hours worker, though it is of course significant that they use the term 'worker', not 'employee'.

(iii) In the short term, a question concerns timing. At the time of writing, the expressed intent of the government is to bring this all into force some time in 2027. There is much work to be done before that because it is clear that, although these provisions in the Act are long and complex, there is still a large amount of detail to be set out by the Secretary of State in supporting regulations.

(iv) In the longer term, a major question is as to the effect that they will have. In the light of the ability of a worker to reject an offer, this is not an outright ban, but on the other hand, what it is aimed at is stopping the *unilateral* power of an employer to use/abuse these contracts. It is quite possible that the new provisions will hedge this around with so many restrictions as to make it simply not worth carrying on with them in practice.

2.1.5 **Atypical workers (2)—EU intervention**

The principal developments extending legal protection to certain types of employment have come from the EU. One original idea was for a single, overarching Directive covering all atypical workers, but this was always found politically unacceptable, and so the successful approach was to propose individual Directives on specific categories of work, primarily through the medium of 'Framework Directives' agreed between the social partners (European Trade Union Confederation (ETUC), the Union of Industry and Employers (UNICE), and the European Centre of Enterprises with Public Participation (CEEP)) and then merely promulgated by the relevant EU bodies.[130]

[130] This had two main effects in employment law. The first is that the drafting may be vague and aspirational (being more like a supranational collective agreement than a statute), which causes problems for transposition into UK law, with its literalist tradition. The second is that this vagueness means it is unlikely that many parts of such Directives will be precise enough to support direct effect (see *Gibson v East Riding of Yorkshire Council* [2000] ICR 890, [2000] IRLR 598, CA, where even the relatively precise provisions of the holiday entitlement in the Working Time Directive were held to be insufficient).

2.1.5.1 **Part-time workers**

The Directive and the enacting regulations

The Part-time Workers Directive[131] is transposed into domestic law in the Part-time Workers (Prevention of Less Favourable Treatment) Regulations 2000[132] in relation to its primary requirement of a regime of non-discrimination. Thus, a part-time worker has a right not to be treated less favourably than a comparable full-time worker, as regards the terms of their contract or by being subjected to any other detriment by any act, or deliberate failure to act, of the employer, unless the treatment in question is objectively justified.[133] In assessing whether treatment has been less favourable the pro rata principle may be applied[134] (eg half pay for half time, not one-third pay), which could make less than pro rata 'part-timer rates' unlawful and may cause technical problems with terms of employment other than pay (eg in trying to pro rata holidays or bank holiday entitlements, or a firm's car). There may be some scope here for the objective justification defence, but at a more general level it may be difficult to argue for any widespread use for that defence, given the aim of the Directive to enhance the position of part-time work generally—why should part-timers be treated any less favourably than on a pro rata by time basis?

Definition

A part-timer is defined quite simply as any worker who, 'having regard to the custom and practice of his employer in relation to workers employed by the worker's employer under the same type of contract is not identifiable as a full-time worker'.[135] This covers anyone working fewer hours than full time and so is not confined to those working, for example, half time. There must normally be a comparison with a comparable full-time worker, except where a worker changes from full time to part time or has a period of absence for full-time work and returns part time, in which case the comparison may be with their

131 Directive 97/81/EC, applied to the UK by Directive 98/23/EC. For a strong critique of its minimalist approach see Jeffrey 'Not Really Going to Work?' (1998) 27 ILJ 193.

132 SI 2000/1551, *Harvey* R [1288]. One immediate point to note is that these Regulations apply to 'workers', not just 'employees'; for the significance of the wider 'worker' definition, see this chapter, 2.1.3. For an assessment of the first ten years of the Regulations see Bell 'Achieving the Objective of the Part Time Workers Directive? Revisiting the Part-Time Workers Regulations' (2011) 40 ILJ 254.

133 Regulation 5(1), (2). There must be an actual comparator; there is no provision in the Regulations for a hypothetical comparator and EC law does not require it: *Carl v University of Sheffield* [2009] IRLR 616, EAT. The comparison must be with a full-timer; there cannot be comparison with another part-timer, even one doing significantly more hours: *Advocate General for Scotland v Barton* [2016] IRLR 210, Ct of Sess. The Directive says that a part-timer must not be less favourably treated *solely* because of being part time but this requirement (possibly limiting the protection for a part-timer) does not appear in the Regulations. This caused a difference of opinion between tribunals and courts for several years, until eventually the Court of Appeal decided the point by holding that there is *no* such requirement in domestic law: *Augustine v Data Cars Ltd* [2025] EWCA Civ 658, [2025] IRLR 624.

134 Regulation 5(3). It is specifically provided that a part-timer does not qualify for overtime rates until they have completed normal full-time hours, ie they cannot claim such rates at the expiry of their own part-time hours: reg 5(4). For an example of how complex an argument can be as to what is pro rata see *Elsner-Lakeberg v Land Nordrhein-Westphalen* C-285/02 [2005] IRLR 209, ECJ.

135 Regulation 2(2); *Ministry of Justice v Dodds* [2023] IRLR 428, EAT. Regulation 2(3) sets out categories of persons not to be considered as being under the same type of contract. Fortunately for gig economy cases, the EAT have held that being on a zero-hours contract does *not* mean that the individual is on a different type of contract and so can use the regulations if part time: *Roddis v Sheffield Hallam University* [2018] IRLR 706 (effectively ignoring a rather odd decision of the ECJ to the contrary in *Wippel v Peek & Cloppenburg* C-313/02 [2005] IRLR 211).

own previous full-time terms.[136] The normal requirement of comparability lay behind the leading case on the Regulations, *Matthews v Kent and Medway Towns Fire Authority*,[137] which, though an individual action, was a test case for 12,000 part-time ('retained') firefighters and their union's long-standing campaign for equal treatment, especially access to the full-time firefighters' pension scheme. When the Regulations were passed, their expectation was that this campaign would now be successful, but they then had the mortification of losing at tribunal, EAT, and Court of Appeal levels. Even when the case went to the House of Lords the judges split, but this time 3–2 in the firefighters' favour.[138] The point at issue was whether there was a true comparison, because part-time firefighters largely only fight fires, whereas full-timers have much broader duties (eg in relation to licensing, safety promotion, education, and feline de-arborealization). The panels up to Court of Appeal level and two of their Lordships held that this ruled out a comparison; three of their Lordships held that, on balance, there still was a valid comparison. The case shows that a comparison cannot be too easily assumed from a shared title ('firefighter'). Beyond that, one view is that the case establishes little and really only concerned a dispute over fact. However, it may be significant for one passage in Lady Hale's speech where she says that in a case such as this one should start with the similarities of the *core* duties, not with the dissimilarities. To start with the latter may lead to a finding of no comparison largely because of factors inherent in being part time in the first place.

Enforcement

A worker may present a complaint to an employment tribunal that their employer has infringed the Regulations; in such a case the burden of proof is on the employer and if the tribunal finds the complaint established it may make a declaration to that effect, award compensation, and/or recommend action to be taken by the employer within a specified time to obviate or reduce the adverse effect on the complainant.[139]

Less favourable treatment of part-timers because of their status had already been under attack from existing law for many years, on the basis that it constitutes indirect sex discrimination which would be difficult to justify objectively. This had been known to good employers for a long time, and so it is arguable that these Regulations were largely pushing at an already opened door. They should have got rid of any lingering attachment of the less-than-good employer to ideas of 'part-timer rates' for these 'peripheral' staff, and their major advantage legally is that a worker still faced with such antediluvian treatment now has a *direct* cause of action before a tribunal, rather than having to jump through the hoops of a sex discrimination action.

The second part of the Directive

The Directive does, however, have a secondary aim, much more difficult to transpose into UK law. As is clear from the recitals to the Directive and its second half, it aims generally to increase the *value* placed on part-time work within organizations and to encourage the

[136] Regulations 2(4), 3, 4. A worker who considers that the employer may have treated them less favourably on the ground of their being part time has a right to a written statement by the employer of the reasons for the treatment in question: reg 6.

[137] [2006] ICR 365, [2006] IRLR 367, HL.

[138] The final judge count was 11–3 in favour of the fire authority, but sadly for them the '3' were in the House of Lords.

[139] Regulation 8(1), (6), (7). The complaint must be presented within three months, with the usual discrimination law 'just and equitable' ground for extension of the period: reg 8(2)–(5). Compensation is such as is just and equitable having regard to the infringement and the worker's loss; it is not capped, but may not include injury to feelings and is subject to mitigation and compensatory fault (as in the case of unfair dismissal): reg 8(9)–(13). If an employer fails without reasonable justification to comply with a recommendation, compensation may be increased: reg 8(14).

facilitation of movement between full-time and part-time working, which may include 'timely information' on such job opportunities and 'access by part-time workers to vocational training to enhance career opportunities and occupational mobility'. Moreover, it is made clear that part-time working is to be viewed as a realistic and valued option not just for hewers of wood and drawers of water (or even stackers of shelves), but 'at all levels of the enterprise, including skilled and managerial positions'. This sentiment sits easily alongside successive governments' family-friendly and work–life balance policies, but is difficult to put into the usual format of black letter law. The original idea was to produce a code of practice but this was dropped and the eventual solution was DTI (now DBT) Best Practice Guidance.[140] This covers matters such as widening access to part-time work, making more jobs available on that basis, job-sharing, taking requests to change to and from part time seriously, providing information to staff, training, and other measures to facilitate part-time working. Some of this advice is potentially far-reaching and in places could be seen as placing an informal onus on an employer to *justify* any refusal of part-time working. Of course, the lawyer might be tempted to dismiss this all as non-legalistic wishful thinking, but in practice it may be unwise not to take this form of 'soft law' seriously. It is true that the guidance has no direct form of enforcement, but increasingly in areas such as this employment lawyers are having to think laterally and try to envisage how soft law might be *used* in other contexts. Two are mentioned here: (a) a refusal of part-time working might be attacked as indirect sex discrimination, which would require the employer to justify the refusal, at which point the guidance could be powerful evidence (particularly if it suggested that part-time working should be possible in those circumstances); (b) the guidance might be relevant as evidence of reasonable or unreasonable employer action in a case where the refusal was made in such circumstances as to result in the employee leaving and claiming constructive dismissal. Thus, to write the guidance off as 'only' soft law might be a very short-sighted view.

2.1.5.2 **Fixed-term employees**

The Directive and the enacting regulations

The Fixed-term Worker Directive[141] had two principal objectives: to establish a regime of non-discrimination and to require member states to have laws to prevent the perceived abuse of keeping individuals on successive fixed-term contracts for unreasonable periods. The first objective is thus very similar to that in the Part-time Worker Directive but the second is legally much more precise. Both of these objectives are transposed into domestic law in the Fixed-term Employees (Prevention of Less Favourable Treatment) Regulations 2002.[142]

With regard to the first, a fixed-term employee has a right not to be treated less favourably than the employer treats a comparable permanent employee as regards the terms of their contract or by being subjected to any other detriment by any act, or deliberate

[140] 'Part-Time Work: The Law and Best Practice'. The first half contains guidance on the Regulations; the second half contains best practice guidance on the second part of the Directive.

[141] Directive 99/70/EC; *Del Cervo Alonso* C-307/05 [2007] IRLR 911, ECJ; *Impact v Minister for Agriculture and Food* C-268/06 [2008] IRLR 552, ECJ; *Rosado Santana v Consejeria de Justicia de la Junta de Andalucia* C-177/10 [2012] 1 CMLR 534, CJEU; *Kucuk v Land Nordrhein Westfalen* C-586/10 [2012] ICR 682, [2012] IRLR 697, CJEU.

[142] SI 2002/2034, *Harvey* R [1551]. In *Duncombe v Secretary of State for Children, Schools and Families* [2011] ICR 495, [2011] IRLR 840, SC Lady Hale commented that, although the Regulations are important for their stated aims of countering discrimination and abuse, they are not meant to outlaw the proper use of short-term contracts. Note that unlike the Part-time Worker Regulations (discussed previously), these Regulations are deliberately restricted to applying only to 'employees', not to 'workers'.

failure to act, of their employer, unless the treatment in question is objectively justified.[143] As with the part-time provisions, the pro rata principle may be applied in determining whether there has been less favourable treatment.[144]

Definition

The Regulations define a fixed-term contract by adopting the Directive's definition which extends that hitherto used by domestic law—in the latter a contract was only for a fixed term if it was time-limited (ie until an expressed or ascertainable date), but the Regulations cover contracts terminating (1) on the expiry of a specific term, (2) on the completion of a particular task, or (3) on the occurrence or non-occurrence of any other specific event (other than reaching retirement age);[145] heads (2) and (3) extend the definition to what have usually been referred to as 'purpose' or 'task' contracts (eg employment 'until this building is demolished'). There must be a comparison with a comparable permanent employee.[146] An employee may present a complaint to an employment tribunal that their employer has breached this part of the Regulations.[147]

Justification

A key issue under these Regulations will be justification for continuing disparity of treatment (especially in relation to terms and conditions other than pay), for at least two reasons: (a) there is less likelihood of a straight pro rata solution than there is with part-timers and (b) there are known problems of mismatch between those on *short* fixed-term contracts and major, long-term benefits primarily intended for long-term permanent employees (eg generous sickness benefits and pension entitlements). Thus, justification is likely to be a much more live issue here than under the part-time provisions. It may be affected by three particular points under the Regulations:

1. There is a specific provision (inserted at a late stage) that, in determining whether a fixed-termer has been less favourably treated than a permanent employee without justification, one can look at whether the terms of the fixed-termer's employment *taken as a whole* are at least as favourable as those of the comparator. This allows the employer to rely on a 'package' approach rather than a term-by-term approach.[148] This may be particularly useful where the employer pays the fixed-termer *more*

[143] Regulation 3(1), (3). Provided this comparison is shown, these provisions apply, and it is no defence that the employer treats other forms of non-permanent staff equally badly: *Cure v Coutts & Co plc* [2004] All ER (D) 393 (Oct). It is not a 'detriment' to be put onto a fixed-term basis in the first place: *Webley v Department of Work and Pensions* [2005] ICR 577, [2005] IRLR 288, CA. Regulation 3(2) particularizes the right not to be less favourably treated in relation to any period of service qualification for a condition of service, the opportunity to receive training, and the opportunity to secure any permanent position in the establishment. With regard to the last, the employee has a right to be informed by the employer of available vacancies in the establishment, by advertisement or other reasonable form of notification: reg 3(6), (7).

[144] Regulation 3(5).

[145] Regulation 1(2). The Regulations in fact went much further and applied this wider definition to fixed term contracts generally in the Employment Rights Act 1996: see 7.2.1. As under that Act, a fixed-term contract retains its status as such even if it also contains a notice provision: *Allen v National Australia Group Europe Ltd* [2004] IRLR 847, EAT.

[146] Regulation 2. An employee who considers that the employer may have treated him or her less favourably on the ground of being fixed-term has a right to a written statement by the employer of the reasons for the treatment in question: reg 5.

[147] Regulation 8. Such a complaint as to procedure and remedies is subject to the same rules as those applying to a complaint under the Part-time Worker Regulations 2000, see this chapter, 2.1.5.1.

[148] Regulation 4. This package approach is unusual—there is no mention of it in the Part-time Worker Regulations and it is *not* permitted in equal pay law, where the applicant can demand equality on a term-by-term approach (see 5.3.2).

(eg a higher hourly rate) to reflect the fact that they do not qualify for longer-term benefits.

2. Employees on short-term contracts may lawfully be excluded from particular benefits by attaching qualifying periods to those benefits, *provided* that the period in question does not discriminate between fixed-term and permanent employees.[149]
3. Ultimately, an employer could rely on straightforward objective justification for the disparity in treatment. The original BIS Guide to the Regulations suggested a general three-stage test for justification (which must be considered on a case-by-case basis), namely whether the employer can show that the less favourable treatment is to achieve a legitimate objective, is necessary to achieve that objective, and is an appropriate way to achieve it. Specific guidance is given on when it may be justifiable to exclude those on short-term contracts from pension schemes (where the benefit to the employee may be marginal and the administrative problems for the employer great) and from contractual redundancy/assurance schemes (which may be argued to be constructed to compensate permanent employees for the *unexpected* loss of their jobs, this being inappropriate at the end of a deliberately defined period of a fixed-term contract). To these specific points the Supreme Court has added the potentially important general one that a justification argument will be much more impressive in legal proceedings if thought out and explained in advance, rather than being dreamed up after the challenge has been brought.[150]

One final point to note on this first objective of removing discrimination is that one piece of institutionalized discrimination had to be removed. Prior to October 2002 when the Regulations came into force, it was possible for the employer of an employee on a fixed-term contract of two years or more to get the employee to sign away their rights to a statutory redundancy payment at the end of it. This was repealed,[151] so a fixed-term contract can no longer be used for this purpose (common though it was in the past).

The second part of the Directive

Moving on to the second objective of the Directive, the placing of limits on the unfair use of successive fixed-term contracts, the government adopted a hybrid of two of the three approaches permitted by the Directive. A worker kept on successive fixed-term contracts for four years or more is deemed in law to be a permanent employee, unless the employer can objectively justify keeping that person on a fixed-term basis.[152] Justification is not defined, the original BIS Guide contenting itself with repeating the general three-fold test (just set out) here too. It would clearly need a strong business case, which, after four years, may well be wearing thin. One possible candidate would be where the post is paid for by 'hot money funding', that is, where it is supported by some outside source providing the money on, for example, a one- or two-year basis only, with no guarantee

[149] Regulation 3(2)(a); Directive 99/63/EC, cl 4(4) (which adds 'except where different length-of-service qualifications are justified on objective grounds').

[150] *O'Brien v Ministry of Justice* [2013] ICR 499, [2013] IRLR 315, SC.

[151] Schedule 2, Pt I, repealing the Employment Rights Act 1996, s 197(3)–(5). Also abolished were exclusions of those on fixed-term contracts of three months or less from statutory sick pay, guarantee payments, medical suspension, and minimum notice.

[152] Regulation 8. There have to have been *successive* contracts and so an initial contract of five years would not be converted on the fourth anniversary. Where there have been successive contracts, the conversion occurs on that anniversary. Major uncertainty here is caused by the fact that 'successive' contracts are defined simply by adopting the normal statutory rules on continuity of employment (see this chapter, 2.5), under which quite substantial gaps between contracts can be 'forgiven', especially where the contracts themselves are for relatively long periods.

that it will continue into the future. Unfortunately, the only reported case considering justification arose on very unusual facts and in it the Supreme Court upheld as justified a nine-year maximum *duration* for teaching contracts at EU international schools (that limit being provided for by EU rules), without giving any general guidance as to how justification is to apply to more typical cases.[153] One exception provided by the Regulations is that these provisions generally can be disapplied by a collective or workforce agreement and replaced by other controls on abuse, in the form of one or more of the following: (a) a different maximum period for successive contracts; (b) a maximum number of successive contracts; or (c) the laying down of what are to be objective grounds for renewal of fixed-term contracts.[154] An employee who considers that they have become a permanent employee under these provisions is entitled to a written statement from the employer acknowledging this or giving reasons why the employer contends that the contract remains fixed-term. If a dispute arises, the employee may present an application to an employment tribunal for a declaration of permanent status.

Effects

What is likely to be the long-term effect of the Regulations? It is possible that they will have a greater effect than the Part-time Worker Regulations because while part-time working had for some time been exposed to scrutiny under the law of indirect sex discrimination, this had not happened in relation to fixed-term working and so the possibilities for disparate treatment remained greater, particularly as such working has tended to be viewed in managerial folklore as a prime way of keeping workers at arm's length legally and of providing a reservoir of flexible staff with few or no legal rights. As with the Part-time Worker Regulations, a major advantage now is that an employee in that position no longer has to go through the complexities of a sex discrimination action but can instead complain directly under the Fixed-term Employees Regulations that this was unjustified discrimination against fixed-termers.[155]

The Regulations do *not* ban the use of fixed-term contracts, and bona fide use may continue; this point was affirmed by the Court of Appeal in *Webley v Department of Work and Pensions*,[156] partly by reference to some of the recitals to the backing Directive which accept that time-limited contracts can be to the benefit of both parties. What the Regulations may do, however, is alter the economic balance of advantage in using them—if they can no longer be used to lower labour costs, increase flexibility, make redundancies easier and cheaper, and keep those advantages for year after year by keeping individuals on them, what are their remaining advantages? It may be that in many circumstances employers are to be advised to minimize their use (possibly sharpening up probation and redundancy procedures instead), reserving them for where the real need arises and objective justification could, if necessary, be shown. Doubtless there will still be cases where this sea change still has not percolated down to line manager level, where assumptions about the continued desirability of fixed-term engagements may persist that are now either totally inaccurate or, at least, greatly exaggerated. It may now be that if a manager indicates that they wish a new or replacement post to be on a fixed-term basis, an advising lawyer or HR professional will need to start the advice by asking one key question—'Why?'

153 *Duncombe v Secretary of State for Children, Schools and Families* [2011] ICR 495, [2011] IRLR 840, SC.

154 Regulation 8(5). A 'workforce agreement' is an agreement between an employer and its employees or their representatives, satisfying the conditions (as to form, duration, and the election of representatives) in Sch 1 to the Regulations.

155 As happened in *Dorset CC v Omenaca-Labarta* [2008] UKEAT/92/08.

156 [2005] ICR 577, [2005] IRLR 288, CA; the court upheld a practice by the DWP of putting temporary staff (not recruited through the formal Civil Service procedures) onto 51-week contracts only, thereby avoiding unfair dismissal claims (under the previous requirement of one year's service).

2.1.5.3 **Agency workers**

Background to the Directive

For several years there was considerable controversy over EU proposals for an agency worker Directive, extending to such workers a regime of equality with the permanent staff of the client for the time being, akin to that applying to part-timers and fixed-termers. UK employers' associations were strongly opposed, on grounds of cost and administrative inconvenience, pointing out that the UK is by far the heaviest user of agency labour in the EU. One particular flashpoint (if there was to be a Directive at all) was how long a worker should have to be with the one client before the proposed Directive should apply: UK employers wanted a period of months (to exclude all short-term hirings), whereas the EU authorities have tended to want a short qualifying period (weeks only), if any. The matter seemed to go to sleep but in 2008 it suddenly resurfaced on the EU political radar when it was linked to negotiations on amendments to the Working Time Directive. Putting it rather brutally (but reflecting the nature of the political horse-trading involved), the position evolved that the 'price' for the UK keeping its major derogations in the Working Time Directive was agreement to a Temporary Agency Work Directive.[157] It principally required a regime of equal treatment in EU-based legal rights and terms and conditions ('at least those that would apply if they had been recruited directly by that undertaking to occupy the same job'); there were then further requirements on access to employment, collective facilities, training, representation, and information. One key point was that Article 5(4) permits member states to impose a qualifying period before the equality regime applies; the UK government, the Confederation of British Industry (CBI), and the Trades Union Congress (TUC) agreed that in the UK this was to be 12 weeks, thus excluding genuinely short-term agency workers.

The domestic regulations

The Directive was transposed into domestic law in the Agency Workers Regulations 2010,[158] which came into force in October 2011. They apply wherever an 'agency worker' is supplied by a 'temporary work agency' to work for a 'hirer'. The most important limitation to note at this definitional stage is that a 'temporary work agency' (usually known colloquially as an employment agency) does not include an agency which introduces workers to employers for *direct or permanent* employment.[159]

The principal substantive provision is in reg 5(1), which states that a qualifying agency worker is entitled to the same basic working and employment conditions as they would have been entitled to for doing the same job, had they been recruited by the hirer *other* than through an agency. This provides an initial contrast with the Regulations on part-time and fixed-term working, namely that here there is no need for a comparator

[157] Directive 2008/104/EC.

[158] SI 2010/93. See Paz-Fuchs 'It Ain't Necessarily So: A Legal Realist Perspective on the Law of Agency Work' (2020) 83 MLR 558. On implementation, BIS (now DBT) published substantial guidance on the application of the Regulations: Agency Workers Regulations Guidance (URN/11/905).

[159] In *Moran v Ideal Cleaning Services Ltd* [2014] IRLR 172, EAT, *Brooknight Guarding Ltd v Matei* UKEAT/0309/17 and *Angard Staffing Solutions Ltd v Kocur* [2020] IRLR 732, EAT it was held that 'temporary' means time limited, *not* necessarily of short duration. This was upheld by the Court of Appeal in *Lutz v Ryanair DAC* [2025] EWCA Civ 849. An agency worker is defined as an individual (a) who is supplied by a temporary work agency to work temporarily for and under the supervision and direction of a hirer and (b) has a contract with a temporary work agency which is '(i) a contract of employment with the agency or (ii) any other contract to perform work and services personally for the agency'. Note that the last part of this definition frees the application of the Regulations from a formal contract of employment. Hirings through intermediaries are covered but there is an exemption for client/customer relationships of a professional or business nature.

employee (though it is provided that if there is such a comparator and the agency worker works under the same terms and conditions as that person, that is a defence for the hirer or agency). The reference to equality of basic terms looks initially wide but it is a major limitation of the Regulations that they only apply to certain *specified* terms. These are set out in reg 6(1) as (a) pay, (b) duration of working time, (c) night work, (d) rest periods, (e) rest breaks, and (f) holidays. Heads (b) to (f) obviously mirror the normal working time rights[160] and so it is not surprising that the key right is (a) and that this is further defined. The general rule is that 'pay' means 'any sums payable to a worker of the hirer in connection with the worker's employment, including any fee, bonus, commission, holiday pay or other emolument referable to the employment, whether payable under the contract or otherwise'.[161] Once again, the apparently open nature of this definition is immediately qualified by a list of exceptions, including occupational sick pay and pensions; redundancy payments; certain statutory payments; any bonus, incentive payment, or reward not directly attributable to the work (such as loyalty or long-service payments); and any payment under a financial participation scheme. What these have in common is that they are longer-term benefits meant for long-term employees and quite simply *inappropriate* for short-term, temporary workers.

Bonuses are a particular problem, appearing under both what is included and what is excluded. It is thus the case that it is the nature of the particular bonus that must be considered. According to the original BIS Guidance:

> The key question is whether the bonus or incentive payment or reward is directly attributable to the amount or quality of work done. If it is for another reason . . . such as to encourage the worker's loyalty or to reward long-service then it is outside the scope of the entitlement to the same terms and conditions relating to pay.

Obviously, this could lead to differences of opinion in any given case.

The qualifying period and anti-avoidance provisions

One particular issue which arose as to possible evasion of the new rules was as a result of the negotiated position that the above rules were to apply only once the worker has been with the hirer for 12 weeks. This is incorporated into the Regulations in reg 7(2), which defines a 'qualifying agency worker' as one working 'in the same role with the same hirer for 12 continuous calendar weeks, during one or more assignments'. This raised three forms of possible evasion: (a) altering the role undertaken by the worker during the 12 weeks; (b) using separate contracts of up to 11 weeks with breaks in between in the case of any particular worker;[162] and (c) structuring the assignments themselves in such a way as to negate the rules. These three possibilities are covered separately by anti-avoidance provisions which are of very considerable complexity and take up a large proportion of the Regulations. With regard to (a), reg 7(3) enacts a presumption that the worker has been in the same role unless the worker has started a new role with substantially different work or duties and the employer has informed

[160] See 5.5.3. Note that, unlike the regulations on fixed-term working, there is *no* provision for a 'package' approach; thus, the worker can claim the rights to (a)–(f) on a term-by-term basis and an employer cannot justify failure to comply by paying the agency worker more: *Kocur v Angard Staffing Solutions Ltd* [2018] IRLR 388, EAT (upheld by the Court of Appeal on other grounds: [2019] IRLR 933, [2020] ICR 170).

[161] Regulation 6(2). The exceptions are in reg 6(3).

[162] When (prior to 1995) there was a statutory requirement that an employee had to work 16 hours per week in order to qualify for the major statutory rights such as unfair dismissal, the use of 15-hour contracts for part-timers was common.

them of the new type of work in writing. With regard to (b), arguably the major threat, reg 7(5)–(11) unsurprisingly had to enact more complicated sub-rules. The approach here is to deem there to be continuity of employment through seven stipulated forms of absence. These cover any break of up to six weeks (to stop evasion by a series of short breaks with little disruption to the employer), sickness/injury absence (up to 28 weeks), pregnancy/maternity leave (up to 26 weeks), the taking of other leave to which the worker is statutorily or contractually entitled (eg parental leave), jury service, customary breaks (particularly customary holidays and shutdowns), and periods of strike, lockout, or other industrial action at the hirer's establishment.[163] With regard to (c), reg 9 addresses the possible use of the structure of assignments (possibly by the use of intermediaries such as companies related to the principal hirer) to disrupt the acquisition of rights by an individual agency worker. It addresses the problem that, in spite of the above sub-rules, a hirer may still be able to organize assignments so as to avoid qualification by the individual (lawfully but only just). However, if a *pattern* of doing so over a period of time emerges, reg 9 may bite because, most unusually, it then concentrates on whether the hirer's *intention* was to evade the rules. If the worker has completed two or more assignments with the hirer (or with a connected organization) or has worked in more than two roles during an assignment, then an inquiry is to be made as to whether the 'most likely explanation' for this is that the hirer or the agency intended to prevent the worker from being (or continuing to be) entitled to the equality requirement of the Regulations. In so deciding, the following can be taken into account: the length and number of assignments, the number of new roles given to the worker, the number of times they has returned to work in the same role for the hirer, and the period of any breaks. If the correct inference from this is that the necessary intent to evade the Regulations is shown, the end result is that the worker is to be treated as having completed a qualifying period which would have been completed but for the structuring of the assignment(s). It can also mean that a worker does not have to complete a further qualifying period if returning to the hirer in these circumstances. A good example of the possible working of these complex provisions was given in the original BIS Guidance; having stated that the Regulations do not prevent the use of 11-week contracts or gaps of more than six weeks as such, it went on:

> For example, an agency worker completes 2 or more assignments with the same hirer, where they have already worked for 11 weeks with a 6 week break and then a further 11 weeks with another 6 week break. If the agency worker is then taken on for a third assignment, this could be considered an attempt to avoid the completion of the qualifying period but it would need to be clear that the attempt was deliberate. This would be a matter for the tribunal in the event of a claim.

The second part of the Directive

As with the Regulations on part-time and fixed-term working, there is a second part to the protection to be given under the Directive, but here it is less extensive. It simply consists of (a) a right for agency workers to have access to collective facilities and amenities provided for employees such as canteen or similar facilities, childcare, and transport services[164] and (b) a right for an agency worker to be informed during an assignment of

[163] This is a précis of complex provisions, which need to be consulted directly in any given case.

[164] Regulation 12. This is a 'day-one' right, not requiring 12 weeks' service, and is (unusually here) amenable to a justification defence for the employer.

any relevant vacant post with the hirer, in order to give them the same opportunity as a comparable worker to find permanent employment.[165]

Enforcement

An agency worker who considers that any of these rights has been infringed has a right of action to a tribunal and, in preparation for this, has a right to request a written statement from the agency as to why they have been treated in the way they were.[166] The tribunal can, if a complaint is upheld, make a declaration to that effect, award compensation, and/or recommend future action to be taken by the respondent. Where the breach is of the principal right in reg 5 to equality of basic terms and conditions, both agency and hirer can be liable to the extent that each is 'responsible for that breach'; however, an agency is given a defence if it shows that it took reasonable steps to obtain information from the hirer about these terms and conditions and to ensure that the worker was treated by the hirer in the proper manner.

The effects of the Employment Rights Act 2025

While politically the headline of Part 1 of the 2025 Act was controlling the use/abuse of zero-hours contracts (considered at 2.1.4.6), it in fact goes further and enacts similar provisions relating to agency workers. This is done by inserting a new Schedule A1 into the Employment Rights Act 1996. This provides four new rights. The **first** is a right to receive from the hirer a guaranteed hours offer at the end of every reference period. This is an offer to enter into a worker's contract requiring the hirer to provide the worker with work, and for the worker to do the work, for a number of hours reflecting the hours done in the relevant reference period; this includes the days and times of the work. This right itself is set out in some detail, *but* for many definitions and the details of its operation it is heavily reliant on supporting regulations to be drafted by the Secretary of State after consultation in late 2025. Where such an offer is made, the agency worker can accept or reject it. The **second** is a right to reasonable notice of shifts to be worked, to be given by the agency or the hirer. The use of 'reasonable' suggests a purely factual question, but regulations are to specify a minimum time in order to be reasonable. The **third** is a right to be given by the agency or hirer reasonable notice of any cancellation of a shift or any changes to its start and finish time or a reduction in its hours. Again, a minimum reasonable period is to be set out in regulations. Following on from this, the **fourth** is a right to receive from the agency payment for a cancelled, moved or curtailed shift. This right is particularly dependent on the eventual regulations, for example on calculation of the payment. Complaint of failure to comply lies to an employment tribunal, against the hirer in the first right, against the hirer or agency in the second and third and against the agency in the fourth. If the tribunal finds the complaint established it is to make as declaration to that effect and may award such compensation as is just and equitable, subject to as maximum which is to be set by the Secretary of State.

As with the scheme for zero-hours contracts on which it is based, it will be necessary to see the details in the eventual regulations before it is clear exactly how it is to operate. At the time of writing, the expressed intent of the government is to bring these changes into force some time in 2027.

[165] Regulation 13. Once again, this is a day-one right. Note, however, that this is a limited right and cannot be construed as giving an existing agency worker a right to *preference* in the making of a permanent appointment: *Coles v Ministry of Defence* [2015] IRLR 872, EAT, upheld by the Court of Appeal in *Kocur v Angard Staffing Solutions Ltd* [2022] IRLR 437.

[166] Regulations 18 and 16, respectively. There is the usual six-month time limit for a tribunal claim, extendable on the discrimination law 'just and equitable' basis; the usual ban on contracting out of the Regulations; and protection from detriment or unfair dismissal for asserting these rights.

2.1.6 **Associated employers**

When considering the relationship of employer and employee, 'the employer' will normally be readily identifiable. If an employee decides voluntarily to change employer (eg to further their career), it is accepted that they will in doing so lose the rights they have accrued already and will have to start again with the new employer. However, in the realities of modern business in the private sector, the employer is likely to be a body corporate and here it may be more difficult to identify 'the employer', in that the particular company for which the employee works may itself be merely one part of a larger organization. Such an organization may be split down into smaller units, for reasons (usually financial) which have little to do with employment law. It is, therefore, important that there should be provisions ensuring that employees do not lose their rights as a result of the composition of the employing concern and that an excessively technical view of who or what constitutes the employer should not be taken. Such provisions also serve as an anti-avoidance device, ensuring that employers cannot gain by dividing undertakings artificially into small units.

The provisions in question are those relating to 'associated employers', whereby two or more units (such as companies within one group) can be treated as one employer. The most important application of the concept of associated employers is in the context of continuity of employment (a vital factor in modern employment rights, both as to qualification to claim the right in question, such as unfair dismissal or a redundancy payment, and as to quantification of the employee's entitlement under that right). Thus, if an employee transfers (or is transferred) from the employment of one employer to the employment of an associated employer, their continuity of employment is *preserved*, and time spent with the first employer can count as time with the second employer.[167] The concept goes further, however, and can be found elsewhere in the employment legislation. Thus, for example, offers of 'suitable alternative employment' (important in redundancy law and in relation to maternity leave) may be made by the employer or an associated employer.[168]

From these examples, it is easy to see the importance of the concept of associated employers. The definition is contained in the Employment Rights Act 1996, s 231:

> any two employers are to be treated as associated if one is a company of which the other (directly or indirectly) has control, or if both are companies of which a third person (directly or indirectly) has control.

'Control' is thus crucial, and there must be voting control in some form, not just de facto influence, however strong.[169] An extension to this narrow approach was suggested by the EAT in *Zarb and Samuels v British and Brazilian Produce Co (Sales) Ltd*,[170] where it was

[167] See this chapter, 2.6. To be an 'associated employer', it is not essential that the company in question was already employing labour when the employee in question transferred to it: *Lucas v Henry Johnson (Packers and Shippers) Ltd* [1986] ICR 384, EAT.

[168] See 4.3 and 8.1.

[169] *Secretary of State for Employment v Newbold* [1981] IRLR 305, EAT; *Umar v Pliastar Ltd* [1981] ICR 727, EAT. This even applies when the person in question owns 50 per cent of the shares in one of the companies, for that is *not* a voting majority and so the companies are not associated: *Hair Colour Consultants Ltd v Mena* [1984] ICR 671, [1984] IRLR 386, EAT; *South West Launderettes Ltd v Laidler* [1986] ICR 455, [1986] IRLR 305, CA; cf, however, *Payne v Secretary of State for Employment* [1989] IRLR 352, CA, where one person held 50 per cent as a nominee of the other person.

[170] [1978] IRLR 78, EAT. For this principle to apply, it must be the same group of persons exercising control in the case of each company claimed to be associated: *Poparm Ltd v Weekes* [1984] IRLR 388, EAT, approved by the Court of Appeal in *South West Launderettes Ltd v Laidler*, n 169.

held that control by a third person could include control by third *persons*, so that if two or more persons between them own more than 50 per cent of the voting shares of the two companies *and* in practice act together, that may satisfy the definition. However, this approach has caused considerable difficulties, since the Court of Appeal in *South West Launderettes Ltd v Laidler*[171] questioned the correctness of *Zarb* and declined to apply it where on the facts it may have been possible to do so. The position is not absolutely clear because it was not necessary for the court to decide the matter, and in the subsequent case of *Harford v Swiftrim Ltd*,[172] the EAT applied *Zarb* (on the basis that it has been consistently followed) and expressly refused to apply the criticisms of it in *Laidler*. A different division of the EAT under Wood P then declined to follow *Harford* in *Strudwick v Iszatt Bros Ltd*,[173] stating obiter that if necessary the tribunal would have followed the criticisms in *Laidler* and held against any concept of plural control (largely because of the major problems of discovery, evidence, and proof that are capable of arising under such a concept). On the other hand, *Zarb* was applied again by a later EAT in *Tice v Cartwright*,[174] which perhaps showed that the present position (until we have a definitive ruling of the Court of Appeal) is that *Zarb* remains there to be used where common sense and justice demand that two organizations be deemed to be one, especially where (as in this case) the facts concern a very restricted shareholding in a family concern, where the necessary de facto control and common action can be shown.

One significant problem which arose under this definition was that it only refers to *companies* as being associated employers. What was to be the position where the two employers in question were *not* companies (eg in the public sector, bodies such as health trusts, local authorities, or universities) or if *one* of the employers was not a company (eg where one farmer runs two farms, one constituted as a company and the other as a partnership)? There were conflicting EAT decisions on this point. One view was that the definition was not exhaustive (only governing the position where the two employers in fact are companies), so that other bodies can be 'associated' if that is the practical position.[175] The other view was that the definition *was* exhaustive, so that only companies can be associated.[176] This conflict was resolved in *Merton London Borough Council v Gardiner*,[177] where the Court of Appeal held that the definition is exhaustive, so that an employee who was unfairly dismissed by a local authority could only claim to have his compensation calculated by reference to the two years he had worked with that authority, not by reference to the ten years he had previously served with three other local authorities. Thus, except under the first part of the definition ('vertical' associated employers), where one of the employers can be any sort of person provided that they have control of the company which is the other employer, the bodies claimed to be associated must be companies, which is a significant limitation on the definition in the absence of any special statutory exception; the most important such exception now is that employees in local government service and the National Health Service (NHS) are covered by Regulations which deem their employment to be continuous, for redundancy rights purposes, when they move from one local government body to another.[178]

[171] [1986] ICR 455, [1986] IRLR 305, CA.

[172] [1987] ICR 439, [1987] IRLR 360, EAT.

[173] [1988] ICR 796, [1988] IRLR 457, EAT; *Russell v Elmdon Freight Terminal Ltd* [1989] ICR 629, EAT.

[174] [1999] ICR 769, EAT.

[175] *Hillingdon Area Health Authority v Kauders* [1979] ICR 472, [1979] IRLR 197, EAT.

[176] *Southwood Hostel Management Committee v Taylor* [1979] ICR 813, [1979] IRLR 397, EAT.

[177] [1981] ICR 186, [1980] IRLR 472, CA.

[178] See the Redundancy Payments (Continuity of Employment in Local Government, etc) (Modification) Order 1999, SI 1999/2277; *Harvey* R [1186], the Redundancy Payments (National Health Service) (Modification) Order 1993, SI 1993/3167; *Harvey* R [755] and the ERA 1996, s 218(7) which preserves continuity through the movement by teachers between schools maintained by a local education authority and that authority.

2.1.7 **Possible reforms: the Taylor Review**

In the light of concerns about developments in the labour market, especially (but not exclusively) in the 'gig' or 'app' economy, and the apparent conflict of large elements of underemployment and persistent low pay at a time of record low levels of unemployment, the previous government set up a review of employment law under Matthew Taylor. This reported in 2017.[179] It contains a wealth of statistical evidence on the current position[180] and extensive consideration of what constitutes 'good employment' in practice and how best practice can be spread. Moreover, it starts from the premise that in general, our existing flexible labour market (termed 'the British way') is an advantage which must not be discouraged. It does, however, then go on to consider ways in which the legal coverage could be improved by tackling exploitation, increasing clarity on employment rights, and, in the longer term, aligning the law with modern industrial strategy and other policy goals. Although it considers the present law on employment status to be confusing to both employer and employee, it in fact suggests *retaining* the above threefold classification of employee, worker (to be renamed 'dependent contactor'), and self-employed, but seeking ways to simplify the legislation and to give more detailed guidance as to who is what. The idea is that status should be more a matter of clearer rules and less a matter of judicial interpretation. From this rather vague premise (on which, good luck!) it then puts forward several concrete proposals, including:

1. recasting the definition of the renamed dependent contractor, in particular to remove the requirement of 'working personally' in order to avoid the problem of substitution and to bring within it more casual relationships which at present are at the less realistic end of self-employment;
2. reforming tax law to reflect more closely the threefold employment law classification (and to remove at least some of the present tax and NI incentives to be self-employed);
3. amending the national minimum wage legislation (a) to provide an easier and more realistic calculation of working hours, especially for those working remotely ('platform workers'), and (b) to enact a higher rate of national minimum wage for hours actually worked but not guaranteed by the employer (to give at least some compensation for the uncertainty affecting those on zero-hour contracts);
4. ensuring that flexibility, though still a good in its own right, works both ways, not just in the employer's favour;
5. simplifying the rules on continuity of employment, to help casual workers on sporadic hours or with varying work patterns across the year;
6. calculating holiday pay by reference to earnings across the whole year, not just in the previous 12 weeks;
7. enacting a right for an agency worker who has worked for one client for more than a year to request a direct contract of employment with that client;
8. similarly, enacting a right for a person on a zero-hour contract for more than a year to request guaranteed hours;
9. reforming the system of enforcement of employment rights, possibly by placing more emphasis on action by organs of the state on behalf of individuals instead of leaving it all to those individuals.

[179] *Good Work: The Taylor Review of Modern Working Practices* (Gov.UK, 2017). It was subject to considerable criticism for its basic approach: see Bales, Bogg, and Novitz '"Voice" and "Choice" in Modern Working Practices: Problems with the Taylor Review' (2018) 47 ILJ 46 and McGaughey 'Uber, the Taylor Review Mutuality and the Duty Not to Misrepresent Employment Status' (2019) 48 ILJ 180.

[180] It found that 63 per cent still work in classic full-time employment, 26 per cent work part time and 15 per cent are self-employed; 3.5 per cent have a second job, 2.8 per cent work under zero-hour contracts, and 4.6 per cent work in the app-based gig economy.

In December 2018 (after a consultation exercise), the government announced its intention to adopt nearly all of the report's recommendations. It also published the first three sets of regulations (primarily concerning changes to section 1 statements, lengthening the reference period for calculating holiday pay and removing one controversial limitation on agency worker rights) which eventually came into force in April 2020. However, further progress was then subject to the limitations placed on new legislation by the coronavirus crisis, and matters did not progress further. The Employment Rights Act 2025 made important changes to the substantive provisions on zero-hours and agency working but did not attempt any major reforms to the fundamental question behind all of this, that is, the law categorizing individuals as employees, workers, or neither. There was talk of approaching this later and separately.

2.2 Formation

2.2.1 The contractual basis of employment

We have already seen that the relationship of employer and employee arises out of a contract. This, however, was not always so, as before the latter half of the nineteenth century, the relationship was viewed more as one arising out of the 'status' of being a servant. Blackstone refers to master and servant as one of the three great relationships in private life, along with husband and wife and parent and child,[181] and the extensive legislation governing supply and conditions of employment, dating back to the Statute of Labourers 1351, was not finally abolished until 1875.[182] The movement towards contract proceeded throughout the nineteenth and twentieth centuries, becoming firmly established. In *Laws v London Chronicle*,[183] Lord Evershed MR said: 'A contract of service is but an example of contracts in general, so that the general law of contract will be applicable.'

No sooner was this established beyond real doubt than the trend was, if not actually reversed, at least subject to significant qualification. Since 1963, and particularly since the concept of unfair dismissal was introduced in 1971, the employment relationship has been increasingly overlaid with statutory criteria, rights, and duties, to such an extent that it is certainly open to doubt whether we should still accept that contract law alone provides the underlying structure of employment law, or whether we should talk instead of a modern 'status' relationship of some sort or, at the least, of a *sui generis* law of employment which of necessity looks to contractual theories for guidance in given areas.[184] Against that, it must be stressed that employment remains for the most part a voluntary relationship, and the content of most of the terms of employment remains to be negotiated by the parties, either individually or through the medium of collective industrial relations. The contract theory remains fundamental and, if anything, of renewed importance, given

[181] 1 Bl Com 422. [182] See Wedderburn *The Worker and the Law* (3rd edn, 1986) 141.

[183] [1959] 2 All ER 285 at 287, [1959] 1 WLR 698 at 287, CA. This case demonstrates the purely contractual approach to summary dismissal, which can also be seen in the more colourful case of *Pepper v Webb* [1969] 2 All ER 216, [1969] 1 WLR 514, CA.

[184] For general discussion see Rideout 'The Contract of Employment' [1966] CLP 111; Khan-Freund 'A Note on Status and Contract in British Labour Law' (1967) 30 MLR 635; Napier 'Judicial Attitudes towards the Employment Relationship' (1977) 6 ILJ 1; Kerr 'Contract Doesn't Live Here Any More?' (1984) 47 MLR 30; Honeyball 'Employment Law and the Primacy of Contract' (1989) 18 ILJ 97; Anderman 'The Interpretation of Protective Employment Statutes and Contracts of Employment' (2000) 29 ILJ 223; Barmes 'The Continuing Conceptual Crisis in the Common Law of the Contract of Employment' (2004) 67 MLR 435; Freedland 'From the Contract of Employment to the Personal Work Nexus' (2006) 35 ILJ 1; Honeyball and Pearce 'Contract, Employment and the Contract of Employment' (2006) 35 ILJ 30. In particular, Professor Hepple argues that the statutory rights should be freed from their existing contractual basis, in order to avoid 'a multitude of common law snares': 'Restructuring Employment Rights' (1986) 15 ILJ 69.

the moves over the past three decades in many areas away from a collective model of wage and conditions determination and towards an emphasis on individual contracting; we therefore now have to consider the character of the contract, its formation, and its content.

The employment relationship is by its very nature bilateral—at its simplest, work for wages[185]—so much of the case law on this aspect of contract is of little practical importance. It is extensively dealt with in the contract textbooks, which should be consulted as required. Form was traditionally of supreme importance in common law apprenticeship contracts (which have now been superseded by statutory apprenticeships), and still is in the particular case of merchant seamen. It will be noted later that one of the major features of the modern legislation is a revived interest in form generally. Legality, another major doctrine of classic contract law, in the field of employment law concerns principally the doctrine of restraint of trade, a relatively rare oasis where the courts over many decades have adopted an important stance based on public policy. It merits detailed treatment later, along with the way in which the general doctrine of illegality has been imported into unfair dismissal law, occasionally doing it considerable violence. The question of 'intent to create legal relations' plays a major part in the sphere of collective agreements, where it is discussed, being largely responsible for the long-standing rule that collective agreements are not legally binding.

One further significance of the contractual base is that certain tenets of contractual interpretation or modification (common law or statutory) may be argued by one party or the other to good effect. Thus, for example, in *Levett v Biotrace International plc*[186] a managing director benefiting from valuable share options was wrongfully dismissed and then told by the company that those options had lapsed under a clause in his employment contract providing for such lapse on termination of employment. However, the Court of Appeal interpreted the clause as only applying to *lawful* termination (thus preserving their benefit for him), relying on the general contractual rule of construction that a party should not be able to take advantage of his own breach of contract. Similarly, the general contract law rules on penalty clauses could apply to a provision in a contract of employment stating that a set amount must be paid by the employee to the employer in the case of some particular act or default by that employee, for example a failure to give notice when leaving; under ordinary contract principles, such a clause would be void unless the employer could show that it was a genuine pre-estimate of loss to the employer, which in the employment context could be difficult.[187]

Further, two uncertainties arise in the area of statutory coverage of ordinary contract law. The first is whether the Unfair Contract Terms Act 1977 could be relied on in an employment case. At first this was thought unlikely, but in *Brigden v American Express Bank Ltd*[188] Morland J held that the Act could apply, though he went on to find that a clause stating that an employee could be dismissed within the first two years without implementation of the disciplinary procedure was *not* an exclusion clause within s 3 of the Act (with its requirement of reasonableness). However, a finding that the Act applied required the rather artificial reasoning that the employee dealt with the employer

[185] Even here, however, complications can arise in cases of partial performance by an employee, eg when taking part in industrial action short of a strike (such as a go-slow or refusal to perform certain duties)—are they still entitled to payment, and if so how much? See 10.2.

[186] [1999] ICR 818, [1999] IRLR 375, CA.

[187] *Giraud (UK) Ltd v Smith* [2000] IRLR 763. See also *Murray v Leisureplay plc* [2005] IRLR 946, CA where a relatively indulgent approach was taken to what was argued to be a penalty clause, in a case where a stricter approach might have jeopardized the widespread practice of putting 'golden parachute' clauses into the contracts of executives to facilitate termination and minimize litigation.

[188] [2000] IRLR 94, relying on Watson 'Employees and the Unfair Contract Terms Act' (1985) 14 ILJ 323.

'as a consumer' and when the matter arose for the first time before the Court of Appeal in *Commerzbank AG v Keen*[189] (a case where the Act was being used to attack a clause in a bonus scheme which stated that no bonus would be payable if the employee was not in the employer's employment at the date the bonus was calculated), the Court held that in relation to a normal term in a contract of employment it cannot be said that the employee deals as a consumer or on the employer's standard terms of business (the alternative bases for the Act to apply). The decision in *Brigden* was said to be unsatisfactory, and so it now appears that the Act is very unlikely to play any significant role in mainstream employment law. The second uncertainty is whether the Contracts (Rights of Third Parties) Act 1999 could apply. Employment contracts were of course not primarily the contemplation of its framers, but it does provide that third party rights can be established against employers or ex-employers (but not employees). As such rights can generally be excluded or modified by agreement, the lawyer drafting an employment contract may wish to cover this point in any case where a third party right might arise, especially where one of the benefits in the contract might apply to a spouse or dependant of the employee, for example use of a company car or coverage by medical insurance, life insurance, or pensions.[190]

2.2.2 **Recruitment issues**

The recruitment of staff has traditionally been an area of little legal involvement, being largely left as a matter for employer discretion, with few rights at common law for job applicants.[191] Given that the common law basis for employment is contractual, the refused applicant has by definition no contract on which to sue and so even the implied term of trust and respect (so important in safeguarding the legal rights of persons once employed) could not be relied on at this inchoate stage.[192] This common law abstentionism is now subject to five particular qualifications, five by statute and the sixth arising from separate developments in relation to employment references. Important though these are in their contexts, we still do not have any overarching 'law of recruitment'.

2.2.2.1 **Discrimination**

The first and most important intervention of the law is, of course, through the discrimination statutes. Recruitment is a vital area in which to counter discrimination and it has always been clear that it is covered by the laws on sex, race, disability, sexual orientation, religion or belief, and age discrimination, which are considered in detail in Chapter 4.

[189] [2007] IRLR 132, CA.

[190] Smith and Randall *Contracts Actions in Modern Employment Law* (2nd edn 2011) p 30; Milgate 'Third Party Rights' [2000] Employment Law Journal 5.

[191] See the well-known quote from Lord Davey in the foundation case on common law liabilities, *Allen v Flood* [1898] AC 1, HL (set out at 4.1), asserting the employer's right to refuse employment for any reason or none.

[192] One of the stranger cases on direct enforcement of contracts of employment was *Giles & Co Ltd v Morris* [1972] 1 All ER 960, [1972] 1 WLR 307, where specific performance of the execution of an offered job was ordered, largely so that the individual would then, as an employee (technically, if not actually), have common law rights on his 'dismissal'. On the other hand, in *Wishart v National Association of Citizens Advice Bureaux Ltd* [1990] ICR 794, [1990] IRLR 393, CA the Court of Appeal refused to enforce a job offer which was withdrawn in the light of references: there was no subsisting employment relationship to which any argument of trust and confidence could attach; 'instead there is a stillborn relationship to which one party strongly objects' (per Mustill LJ).

2.2.2.2 **Data protection**

The second, and very different, form of statutory intervention came under the Data Protection Act 1998 (now the Data Protection Act 2018). This legislation ostensibly does not affect the process of recruitment but can apply to documentation produced and/or stored as part of that process. However, the guardian of the Act, now renamed the Information Commissioner, has tended to take a wide view of this remit and has issued guidance which arguably strays significantly into the process itself. This guidance is in the form of the 'Employment Practices Data Protection Code Part I: Recruitment and Selection'.[193] It covers advertising, handling applications, verification of details, shortlisting, interviews, pre-employment vetting, and retention of treatment records. It should be consulted in detail on any of these matters, and is likely to have considerable practical significance for HR practitioners. Among its key recommendations (showing its overall approach) are to (a) make a staff member responsible for compliance, (b) make serious data protection breaches by employees handling their information a disciplinary offence, (c) only request data about an applicant that is relevant to recruitment, (d) ensure that job applicants sign a consent form if documents are needed from a third party, (e) inform applicants if automated shortlisting is the sole basis of decision, (f) retain interview notes,[194] (g) establish a retention period for recruitment records,[195] and (h) dispose of salary information from previous employers. This part of the Code has a slightly ambiguous position in employment law. Unlike Part 3 on employee monitoring (which could well be relevant in an unfair dismissal action, eg by an employee dismissed for internet abuse),[196] Part I is unlikely to link indirectly into mainstream employment law, at least in the case of unsuccessful applicants, because they have no subsisting contract on which to sue (and successful applicants are less likely to have a grievance, though it is not impossible). Its effect will therefore be primarily within its own context of enforcement under the Data Protection Act itself; here, the Code states that while it is not law per se and does not *have* to be followed, an employer who does follow it knows that there has been compliance with the Act.

2.2.2.3 **Previous convictions**

The *third* form of statutory intervention—dating back much further, though with some topicality—is under the Rehabilitation of Offenders Act 1974, whereby a person whose conviction or convictions is or are 'spent' is to be treated as not having been convicted. The key point here is of course that a spent conviction does *not* have to be disclosed on a job application form, even in response to a direct question.[197] This is of importance because if the Act does not apply, any false answer at the recruitment stage is likely to be considered fraudulent, leading if necessary to a later lawful dismissal (even if the individual thought

[193] This is available on <www.ico.org.uk>. The other three parts of the Code are on employee records, monitoring of employees, and information about workers' health. The Code continues in force, unaffected by the radical recasting of the basic legislation in 2018.

[194] This would be advised by a lawyer anyway, in case of a later complaint of discrimination by a disappointed applicant (the time limit normally being three months). As these notes may now be obtainable under the Data Protection Act, those conducting interviews must be advised to be careful what appears in them, including 'pen portraits' of the applicant in the margin.

[195] Together with point (c), this shows an application of the general data protection tenet that a data controller should only gather and retain information that is necessary for the purpose; a variant of that here is that not all information relevant at the recruitment stage will be relevant later—any that is not should not automatically be transferred into the successful applicant's personnel file (see also point (h)).

[196] See 3.3.7 and 7.5.2.

[197] Rehabilitation of Offenders Act 1974, s 4. The rehabilitation periods necessary for a conviction to become spent are set out in s 5.

at the time that they had good reason to be sparing with the actualité).[198] Also of major importance here, however, is the Rehabilitation of Offenders Act 1974 (Exceptions) Order 1975,[199] which sets out certain professions, offices, employments, and occupations which are *not* subject to the Act, so that in these cases a conviction can never become spent and must always be disclosed when asked. This has always covered areas such as the legal profession, the medical profession, and law enforcement agencies. More recently, however, there have been significant extensions of the exempted categories in the light of contemporary concerns about cases of sexual or physical abuse; the Order now also covers wide categories of those employed to care for children and vulnerable adults. This necessary change in the law for this purpose was accompanied by administrative changes to establish systems whereby applicants' suitability for jobs involving contact with children and vulnerable adults could be checked against criminal and other records. This was done first of all by the establishment of the Criminal Records Bureau and the Independent Safeguarding Authority, but the Coalition government took the view that this system was inadequate and replaced it in 2012 with the Disclosure and Barring Service, which operates a stronger system of obligations on an employer to check applicants before appointing them to work in what are defined as 'regulated activities'.[200]

2.2.2.4 **Immigration status**

As well as checking criminal records, there are now major obligations on employers to check the immigration status of appointees and their right to work in the UK, with serious penalties for failure to do so. In effect, in the employment context, employers are being made to operate official immigration policy. Under the Immigration, Asylum and Nationality Act 2006 (as amended by the Immigration Act 2016), an employer who knowingly employs illegal labour is liable to criminal prosecution and, on conviction, an unlimited fine and up to five years in prison. However, of much greater significance for employers is the extensive system in place for penalizing *non-deliberate* employment of illegal labour, hence the importance of the necessary checks. Instead of criminal proceedings, the employer here is subject to a 'civil penalty' of up to £60,000.[201] This is enforced by a 'penalty notice' issued by the Secretary of State. Crucially, liability here is *strict*; there are no general defences possible and it is clearly stated that this strict liability is subject *only* to what are referred to in the legislation as the 'statutory excuses'.[202] These operate by requiring the employer to carry out right to work checks before employment is offered. They refer the employer to the Home Office Code of Practice on Preventing Illegal Working: Employer Right to Work Checks,[203] which sets out exhaustively the nature of the checks and in particular the documentation which must be sought. The Code also sets out how the level of the civil penalty will be worked out in any given case; note again that there is no discretion here, to the extent that even where the scheme refers to the employer taking 'reasonable steps' to effect something, this itself is defined in the Code and not left as a matter of general interpretation.

[198] This general rule is strongly set out in *City of Birmingham District Council v Beyer* [1978] 1 All ER 910, [1977] IRLR 21, EAT1. It was applied to concealment of a non-spent conviction in *Torr v British Railways Board* [1977] ICR 785, [1977] IRLR 184, EAT. On the other hand, dismissal because of discovery of a spent conviction is likely to be unfair: *Property Guards Ltd v Taylor* [1982] IRLR 175, EAT.

[199] SI 1975/1023. [200] Protection of Freedoms Act 2012, Pt 5 chs 1–3.

[201] Immigration, Asylum and Nationality Act 2006, s 15(1). Help is available for employers on the government website at <https://www.gov.uk/penalties-for-employing-illegal-workers>; particularly useful is the link to the Home Office publication 'An Employer's Guide to Right to Work Checks' (December 2014).

[202] Immigration, Asylum and Nationality Act 2006, s 15(3); Immigration (Restrictions on Employment) Order 2007, SI 2007/3290.

[203] See *Harvey* S [2701].

This is clearly a major imposition on an employer at recruitment stage in a general sense, but there is one particular concern that could arise in relation to employment law—could this not all lead to allegations of race discrimination? Just *who* is to be considered by an employer as potentially *needing* an immigration check? If this were to be done on the basis of looks, colour, accent, and so on there could be real problems. Fortunately, this was envisaged from the start and is the subject of a second Home Office Code of Practice entitled Avoiding Unlawful Discrimination while Preventing Unlawful Working.[204] Much of this is concerned with explaining the law on discrimination, but the final part gives practical guidance on avoiding unlawful discrimination. The general principle is that the employer should not make assumptions about a person's immigration status or right to work on the basis of their colour, nationality, or ethnic or national origins. The simplest way to avoid liability is 'to treat all applicants fairly and in the same way at each stage in the recruitment process', that is, to check the work status of *all* applicants. While this may be initially cumbersome, in most cases under the Code this can be done merely by the production of a passport. The important point, however, is that documentation is to be required of *all* applicants.

2.2.2.5 **Probationary periods**

Historically, there has been no need for any special legislative coverage of probationary/trial periods for new employees, for the simple reason that there has always been a requirement of 'qualifying employment' before a new employee could claim unfair dismissal. Originally this was six months, but that was subject to change and most recently has been two years. Within that period, an employer could operate a probationary period as a matter of contract (or even informally) without the prospect of a dispensed employee bringing tribunal proceedings for unfair dismissal. There were always two exceptions—(1) certain forms of automatically unfair dismissal where the qualifying period was specifically disapplied, and (2) cases where the dismissal could be challenged under discrimination law. Otherwise, however, the employer was relatively safe. That is going to change under the Employment Rights Act 2025, though not in as radical a way as originally intended.

At the 2024 election the Labour manifesto proposed making unfair dismissal a day-one right, and this appeared in the original form of the Bill, along with complex provisions enacting new rules for a statutory probationary period during which procedures for dismissing for incapability would be simpler. However, this whole idea became one of the most controversial in the whole Bill, ending in a prolonged period of legislative ping pong between the government/Commons and the Lords. Eventually, in order to get the Bill through its final stages at the very end of 2025 the government compromised, dropped the day one principle and substituted a reduction in the existing qualifying period from two years to six months (to come into force earlier than originally planned). In itself this is still an important change and employers will have to organize their probationary periods accordingly. While it is true that employees with between six months and two years continuity will no longer have to try to bring their cases under one of the heads of automatic unfairness in order to avoid the qualifying period altogether (often by pleading whistleblowing as the reason for dismissal), the downside is that this will still be the case for an employee dismissed within the first six months.

2.2.2.6 **References**

The fifth intervention of the law has been in relation to employment references. Hitherto this involvement of the law has been primarily in relation to possible tortious liability for negligent misstatement. Ever since the foundation case of *Hedley Byrne & Co Ltd v Heller*

[204] See *Harvey* S [2601].

& Partners Ltd[205] it has been arguable that the referee owed a duty of care to the potential employer requesting the reference, but for many years there was no development of this in relation to the employee subject to the reference, probably because the tradition in the UK was that the applicant for the job did not see the reference at any stage. The resurgence of interest here of late has been for two reasons—first, it was held in *Spring v Guardian Assurance plc*[206] that the referee owes a duty of care to the *applicant* for the job, who, if turned down because of a negligently bad reference, may be more likely to contemplate legal action (especially in the financial services sector, which has spawned most of the case law), particularly as, second, under the data protection legislation an employment reference may now be seen by an individual. We have thus seen serious changes here (both in the law and the likelihood of it being used), though wholly in relation to the rights of the *subject* of the reference, not its recipient. These matters are considered in Chapter 3, in relation to the employer's duty to exercise care, along with the difficult question whether the law now imposes any positive duty on an employer or ex-employer to *give* a reference (the common law position in the past having been that there is no such duty at all).[207]

Apart from tortious liability, there has been little law on references in the purely employment contract context, except for one important point of definition. When an employer makes an appointment 'subject to satisfactory references' this simply operates in the law of contract as a condition precedent. However, the question could arise as to what is meant by 'satisfactory'. In *Wishart v National Association of Citizens Advice Bureaux Ltd*,[208] the Court of Appeal held that this only meant satisfactory *to the employer*, that is, a subjective test; it is not open to a refused applicant (already pushing a rock uphill in trying to enforce employment) to argue that the reference *ought* to have been satisfactory to a reasonable employer. In addition, there has been one other form of legal involvement in references, but again in the slightly separate context of data protection law. The Employment Practices Data Protection Code Part 2: Employment Records contains advice (in Section 2, part 9) on the handling of reference-giving. It suggests that an organization should have a policy on who can give references and in what circumstances.[209] Moreover, an employer should not provide confidential information about an individual unless sure that that is their wish, and when employment ends they should establish whether the departing employee wishes references to be provided in the future. Breach of this guidance could mean a breach of the Data Protection Act, but it is possible that the Code could also be used as evidence for collateral purposes more specifically within employment law. Apart from tortious liability for negligent misstatement (above), one interesting cross-over can be seen in *TSB Bank Ltd v Harris*,[210] where an employee who left employment when they discovered that highly unfair references were being sent to potential future employers successfully claimed constructive dismissal (for the purposes of an unfair dismissal action); in such circumstances it is possible that any breach of the Code could now be evidence in such an action.

[205] [1964] AC 465, [1963] 2 All ER 575, HL; the case in fact concerned a reference, but as to commercial creditworthiness, not individual employability.

[206] [1994] ICR 596, [1994] IRLR 460, HL.

[207] See 3.3.3.

[208] [1990] ICR 794, [1990] IRLR 393, CA.

[209] *Spring*'s case (n 205) is a prime example of how corporate references should not be given—inaccurate, unchecked statements were made (highly prejudicial to the subject) in an ad hoc exercise by a manager just collecting others' opinions. While there is no law against a bad reference, this could be a recipe for a *negligently* bad reference. Some organizations (especially in the public sector) have policies as to the only information they will give, and the only form in which they will give it, regardless of what the requesting organization may ask.

[210] [2000] IRLR 157, EAT.

Finally, one variant of this tortious liability is still in its infancy but may see further developments. In *Cheltenham BC v Laird*,[211] it was held that a job *applicant* is under a duty of reasonable care when answering questions (especially those in a health questionnaire) posed by the putative employer. The council had sued its ex-managing director for failing to divulge a history of mental/stress problems which she had not disclosed in a pre-appointment health questionnaire; she had taken sick leave for similar reasons not long after being appointed, ending in early retirement at the council's expense. While the claim failed on the facts because the questionnaire was not sufficiently precise to *require* this disclosure (and the background here is the well-established rule that a (non-director) employee need not volunteer information and so it is for the employer to discover it),[212] the case does establish the duty on the applicant and the judge considered that breach of that duty could lead not just to dismissal (if appointed) but also to an action for damages. As a common law action for damages, this was a rare event and in fact this area went to sleep for several years, but then the question arose in the more likely context of unfair dismissal. In *Easton v Secretary of State for the Home Department*,[213] it was held that a career civil servant who applied for and got a post with department A without disclosing (in the form section on previous employment) that he had been dismissed by department B for gross misconduct was fairly dismissed when this was discovered; unlike in *Cheltenham BC*, the question posed was sufficiently clear to require full disclosure of the previous employment history.

2.3 Form

2.3.1 Form generally

According to a doctrine peculiar to English law, a contract must be under seal or based upon consideration. A promise gratuitously to perform services will not be actionable unless it is by deed. Subject to this, however, a contract of employment may be entered into orally at common law, and statute has not intervened to alter this general position. However, some particular contracts of employment or contracts relating to employment may have to be in writing.[214] Thus, under Part 2 of the Employment Rights Act 1996, an employer and employee may agree for the former to make deductions from the latter's wages, provided that the agreement is either contained in a written contract (or in a contract whose effect has been notified to the employee in writing) or otherwise evidenced in writing signed by the employee prior to the making of the deductions.[215] Certain other provisions of the 1996 Act also require writing; thus under s 71 and the Maternity and Parental Leave etc Regulations 1999 a woman claiming to exercise her right to take maternity leave must inform her employer of her intention in writing if so requested by the employer. Similarly, an employee may consent in writing to work beyond the maximum 48 hours per week under the Working Time Regulations 1998.

[211] [2009] IRLR 621, QBD. The employer had sought damages for almost £1 m for waste of council resources and the cost of the early retirement.

[212] See 3.4.4, and in particular *Nottingham University v Fishel* [2000] ICR 1462, [2000] IRLR 471.

[213] [2025] IRLR 420, EAT.

[214] One long-standing example is the employment of seafarers; see now the Merchant Shipping (Maritime Labour Convention) (Minimum Requirements for Seafarers) Regulations 2014, SI 2014/1613.

[215] Section 13: see 3.5.5. There are exceptions in s 14 and obviously certain statutory deductions (such as income tax under PAYE) do not need written consent.

2.3.2 Notice of terms of employment

Although English law is basically informal about the form of a contract of employment, Part 1 of the Employment Rights Act 1996 (first passed as early as 1963 as the Contracts of Employment Act) provides that an employee to whom the Act applies must be given written particulars of the salient terms of their employment. These provisions were amended and extended by the Trade Union Reform and Employment Rights Act 1993, in order to comply with an EC Directive on information concerning employment conditions,[216] which the government of the day were ready to agree to, for two reasons: (a) the existing law was already largely in compliance; and (b) the extensions necessary (which stressed the need to give these written statements on an individual basis) were in line with their policy of encouraging more individual contracting, at the expense of collective negotiation of terms. There were further amendments by regulation in 2020 to enact recommendations in the Taylor Report, considered above, in particular to make receiving the written particulars a 'day-one' right, to lengthen the list of particulars to be given, and (perhaps most radically) to extend the right from 'employees' to the wider category of 'workers'.

2.3.2.1 The status of the written statement

The incontrovertible starting point is that the written ('section 1') statement is *not* per se the contract of employment; it is, however, *evidence* of the terms of the contract. This may seem a technical distinction (especially in a case where a long-standing statement appears to be the *only* tangible evidence), but it has the important consequence in law that it leaves the door open for an employee to argue in later proceedings that the statement was inaccurate as to the real terms on a given matter. The question then becomes how compelling the statement is to be as evidence. It is certainly not conclusive,[217] but it is possible to point to earlier cases where courts showed themselves ready to incorporate terms from the written statement into the individual contract of employment, particularly where the statement appeared to have been accepted without protest for a reasonable period of time.[218] Later cases have, however, shown a tendency to treat the statement with more circumspection in circumstances where a major dispute has arisen as to the accuracy of a particular term, especially where 'acceptance without protest' is relied upon by the employer as showing the correctness of the statement. In *System Floors (UK) Ltd v Daniel*,[219] Browne-Wilkinson J put the position thus:

> It seems to us, therefore, that in general the status of the statutory statement is this. It provides very strong prima facie evidence of what were the terms of the contract between the parties, but does not constitute a written contract between the parties. Nor are the statements of the terms finally conclusive: at most, they place a heavy burden on the employer to show that the actual terms of contract are different from those which he has set out in the statutory statement.

This case concerned the less typical situation of the *employer* arguing that the statement did not properly reflect the contract; the burden is less heavy in the more typical case

[216] Directive 91/533/EEC; see Clark and Hall 'The Cinderella Directive' (1992) 21 ILJ 106 and Kenner 'Statement or Contract?—Some Reflections on the EC Employee Information (Contract or Employment Relationship) Directive' (1999) 28 ILJ 205.

[217] *Turriff Construction Ltd v Bryant* (1967) 2 ITR 292; *Parkes Classic Confectionery v Ashcroft* (1973) 8 ITR 43; see Dumville and Leighton 'From Statement to Contract' (1977) 6 ILJ 133.

[218] *Camden Exhibition and Display Ltd v Lynott* [1966] 1 QB 555, [1965] 3 All ER 28, CA.

[219] [1982] ICR 54, [1981] IRLR 475, EAT. This approach can also be seen in *Jones v Associated Tunnelling Co Ltd* [1981] IRLR 477, EAT in the context of alterations to contractual terms, considered presently.

where it is the employee contesting the correctness of the statement, because as against them the statement will be (in Browne-Wilkinson J's words) 'no more than persuasive, though not conclusive, evidence'. It is therefore open for the employee to adduce hopefully more persuasive evidence that the real term was other than that contained in the employer's statement (eg evidence of what was said at the job interview or in letters of appointment, or even what was accepted in practice from the beginning of the employment). This can be seen from the subsequent decision of the Court of Appeal in *Robertson and Jackson v British Gas Corpn*,[220] in which the above dicta by Browne-Wilkinson J were approved and the employee successfully challenged the accuracy of the section 1 statement on the basis that it did not reflect what was agreed at the commencement of employment on the bonus that was to be paid. At one stage, Ackner LJ seems to go further and say that the statement was not *even* evidence of the terms, but that must be taken in the light of the facts of the case, particularly the fact that the statement was not given until seven years after the commencement of the employment. In the more usual case, where the statement has been given at the time of or shortly after the commencement of employment and not dissented from, it certainly will be evidence, possibly compelling—as in practice these statements assume considerable importance in many employments.

One case that has caused some difficulty in this area is *Gascol Conversions Ltd v Mercer*,[221] where the employer had sent written terms of employment to the employee who had signed them and a receipt which was attached; the Court of Appeal held that this constituted a written contract, governing, inter alia, the question of hours which was in dispute. The result of such a decision is that the written term in question is binding and not to be supplanted by evidence of extraneous matters or implied terms. However, this decision does not compromise the principles set out previously, since it appears that the employee actually signed the written instrument as the new terms of his contract of employment, not just the attached receipt. It is common for section 1 statements to be signed for, but merely signing for receipt will *not* constitute a binding written contract, unlike in *Mercer*'s case where the crucial extra step of signing *as the contract* was present. This view of *Mercer*'s case (and the distinction between signing a contract and signing a receipt) has been accepted in the later cases.[222] It is thus possible for what would normally be a section 1 statement to be transformed into a formal written contract by the parties signing it as such, but if they are to do so it is doubly important that they should ensure that the terms are correct.

2.3.2.2 **Requirements of the written statement**

The obligation on an employer to give the section 1 statement arises whenever a person is taken on as a 'worker', thus excluding (as usual in statutory employment laws) the self-employed. Certain categories of employee are excluded; thus, this part of the Act does not apply to certain types of mariners,[223] or persons working wholly outside Great Britain.[224]

The employer must give a new worker the statement 'not later than the beginning of the employment', containing the required particulars 'in a single document'.[225] In practice many employers will have the statement ready at the beginning anyway, often as part

[220] [1983] ICR 351, [1983] IRLR 302, CA; note Leighton (1983) 12 ILJ 115. The case is also of particular interest on the incorporation of terms from collective agreements: see 3.2.2.

[221] [1974] ICR 420, [1974] IRLR 155, CA; cf *Hawker Siddeley Power Engineering Ltd v Rump* [1979] IRLR 425, EAT. See Hepple (1974) 3 ILJ 164.

[222] *System Floors (UK) Ltd v Daniel*, n 219; *Robertson and Jackson v British Gas Corpn*, n 220.

[223] Section 199.

[224] This appears to be the case on general principles, in spite of the repeal of the Employment Rights Act 1996, s 196 (by the Employment Relations Act 1999).

[225] Section 1(2), as substituted by the 1993 Act.

of a 'starter pack' for new staff (along with other documents, such as a health and safety statement, disciplinary rules, and company handbook). Where there is, subsequent to the giving of notice of particulars, a change in them, the employer has one month in which to issue a statement of the change.[226]

The initial notice must identify the parties and specify the date of commencement of employment and whether any employment with a previous employer is to count as part of the worker's continuous employment.[227] Section 1(4) then provides that certain particulars of the terms of employment must be stated (and if there are no agreed particulars under certain of the heads that fact must be stated too).[228] These particulars are: the scale or rate of remuneration; the intervals at which remuneration is to be paid; terms and conditions relating to hours of work ('normal working hours' and any variations in hours); any terms and conditions relating to holidays (including public holidays and holiday pay), with sufficient information to enable the entitlement to be calculated precisely; incapacity for work due to sickness or injury; any other paid leave and pensions and pension schemes; the length of notice which the worker is obliged to give and entitled to receive to determine the contract; the title of the job which the worker is employed to do;[229] how long the employment is to last if it is not permanent; any applicable probationary period; the place of work; any collective agreements affecting terms and conditions; where the employee is to work outside the UK for more than a month, the period abroad, currency for remuneration, any additional remuneration or benefits, and any terms and conditions relating to their return to the UK; and any terms as to training requirements. One innovation in 2020 was the addition of the catch-all category of 'any other benefits provided by the employer that do not fall within another paragraph'. In addition, s 3 provides that the employer must include a note specifying any disciplinary rules and procedures, how and to whom the worker may apply if dissatisfied with a disciplinary decision relating to them or if seeking redress of any grievance relating to their employment, and any further steps in the employer's grievance procedure, though these requirements do not apply to any rules, procedures, and so on relating to health and safety at work.

One area where there has been change over the years has been in relation to *how* the statement is to be given. In the beginning, there was a fairly wide power for the statement to be drafted to incorporate 'other documents', which (in times of high union density across the economy) meant collective agreements. In later times, when that density had declined, there were reforms to move towards individual contracting, with more emphasis on all particulars being readily discoverable in the documentation itself. The current system since 2020 (along with the lengthening of the above list of required particulars) is to require prima facie 'single document' but with enumerated exceptions. In relation to

[226] Section 4; see 2.6 later in this chapter on changing the terms of employment.

[227] This should be viewed with caution by an employee, for a simple assurance of continuity of employment by a new employer (where such continuity is not preserved by a provision in the relevant statute) is not enough to safeguard continuity for the purpose of a later claim for a statutory right: *Secretary of State for Employment v Globe Elastic Thread Co Ltd* [1979] ICR 706, [1979] IRLR 327, HL, overruling *Evenden v Guildford City AFC Ltd* [1975] 3 All ER 269, [1975] ICR 367, CA; see 8.1.4.

[228] Thus, the obligation is to notify terms that exist, not to have a particular term in the first place: *Morley v Heritage plc* [1993] IRLR 400, CA (no term on accrued holiday pay).

[229] This is not necessarily a full 'job description', but the employer should approach it with care, because the more specific the title is the less the employer will be able lawfully to demand flexibility on the part of the employee, a factor which could be of importance in a redundancy or unfair dismissal case; conversely, the wider the title, the more difficult it may be to establish that a dismissal is for redundancy. This one example of the job title (in addition to other clear examples such as job location clauses) shows how important it is for both employers and employees to treat contracts and/or written statements not as tedious bureaucracy, but rather as documents which may be decisive in actions before tribunals for modern statutory rights.

sickness, other paid leave, pensions, and training, the statement may refer the worker to 'some other document'; in relation to termination by notice, it may refer the worker to the law or an applicable collective agreement; in either case, the other document or collective agreement must be readily accessible for the worker to read during working hours, or in some other way. Finally, to avoid duplication, where the employer goes further and gives the worker an actual contract of employment, or a worker's contract which contains all the prescribed particulars, the employer is deemed to have satisfied this statutory requirement; this also applies to a less formal letter of appointment, and in any case the document must be given not later than the beginning of the employment.

2.3.2.3 **Enforcement**

Contractual rights may of course be enforced by an ordinary common law action and so, for example, a claim that the employer should be paying more in wages under the contract may be tested by bringing an action for those wages in the county court (or in a tribunal, under the guise of the underpayment being a 'deduction for wages'), which may involve a determination by the court or tribunal of the correct contractual term on wages, which in turn may involve a determination of the accuracy of the written statement on the question of wages. In addition to this, however, the Act provides for the *direct* enforcement of the requirement to give the written statement.

Under s 11 the method of direct enforcement of these provisions is by reference of the issue to a tribunal. Where either no statement has been given under ss 1 or 4, or a statement does not comply with those sections, the worker may refer the matter, and where a statement has been given but a dispute has arisen as to the particulars which ought to have been included or referred to in it so as to comply with the statutory provisions, either the employer or the worker may refer the matter. By s 12 the tribunal is given wide powers to determine what particulars ought to have been included, or whether any particulars which were included are to be confirmed, amended, or substituted. These powers of the tribunal should be a considerable incentive for the employer to comply with the requirements of s 1 in the first place; if it does not do so, and a dispute later arises with the workforce over a particular term of employment (eg overtime arrangements), it would be possible for them to take the employer to a tribunal under s 11 and invite the tribunal to write into their statements the version of the term on overtime that *they* say they originally agreed—if they were successful that would in practice end the dispute in their favour.

However, two problems have arisen as to the construction of these powers. The first arises from the fact that they are declared to be only for the purpose of deciding what 'ought to have been included or referred to in the statement *so as to comply with the requirements of* [*these provisions*]'. This means that in a s 11 claim the tribunal may only declare what ought to have been included in the sense of what was agreed on these various enumerated matters between the parties; it cannot therefore go further and *interpret* any terms expressed in the written statement, for that would be to usurp the functions of the ordinary civil courts to whom traditionally the employee had to turn for interpretation and enforcement of their contractual rights.[230] This distinction was accepted in early case law[231] and has subsequently been reaffirmed by the Court of Appeal in *Southern Cross*

[230] Unless the matter has arisen on termination of the employment, in which case a tribunal may have jurisdiction to determine a contract claim under the Employment Tribunals Extension of Jurisdiction Order 1994, SI 1994/1623 or the case may be brought before a tribunal during employment under Pt II of the Employment Rights Act 1996, concerning deductions from pay. This would now cover the case of *Cuthbertson* (see n 230).

[231] See *Cuthbertson v AML Distributors* [1975] IRLR 228, IT; *CITB v Leighton* [1978] IRLR 60, EAT. Arguably, in some cases a tribunal or court succumbed to the temptation to stray into enforcement; see *Owens v Multilux Ltd* [1974] IRLR 113, EAT.

Healthcare Co Ltd v Perkins,[232] which illustrated the point neatly on its facts. The s 1 statements covered the question of holiday entitlement by granting 20 working days, plus up to five more days for long service by an individual. The claimants were on the maximum of 25 days when, in 2009, the statutory entitlement to holidays under the working time legislation went up to 28 days. Did the term in their statements mean that they were entitled to five days for long service on top of the new 28-day entitlement, or did their entitlement merely have to go up to 28 days in total (which would have swallowed up their long-service extra)? The parties locked horns on the issue and the claimants brought tribunal proceedings to have the term construed and its true meaning decided. The tribunal and EAT found for the claimants' construction, but when the case came before the Court of Appeal, the issue of whether the tribunal had jurisdiction at all came to the fore. Applying the principle set out previously, the court allowed the employers' appeal and held that what the claimants were wanting the tribunal to do was to construe and enforce the term in question, but it had no power to do so. That exercise, going beyond merely ensuring compliance with s 1, remained the province of the ordinary courts. Not surprisingly in the light of this, the court declined even to give any indication as to what its view would have been on the construction issue.

The second problem was potentially more far-reaching, for while it was clear on the wording of s 12 that a tribunal could determine a case where there was a partial or total *failure* by the employer to include the necessary terms in the statement, it was argued that it did not have jurisdiction where the employer had indeed given terms but the employee claimed that they were *inaccurate* (ie that they did not reflect what had actually been agreed). This very narrow view could be seen in the judgment of the EAT in *Brown v Stuart, Scott & Co Ltd*,[233] though the pronouncement was obiter. It is true that the wording of s 12 was not explicit on the point (though the use of words such as 'amend' and 'substitute' surely points in the direction of including claims that particulars are inaccurate); however, it certainly seemed that the narrow view was contrary to Parliament's intention and an unnecessary restriction on the tribunals' jurisdiction. As originally drafted, the Employment Bill 1982 contained a provision which would have stated expressly that tribunals could hear complaints about particulars which had been included or referred to in statements, but this provision was removed as unnecessary when the position was rectified by the decision of the Court of Appeal in the important case of *Mears v Safecar Security Ltd*.[234] It is made clear in this case that a tribunal *does* have jurisdiction to hear complaints of inaccurate particulars. However, on its facts the case concerned the *failure* to give particulars,[235] and in this context too the case is important for its clarification and extension of existing principles. Here, Stephenson LJ said that the complaint could be either (a) a complaint that the statement does not contain a term which had actually been agreed, or (b) a complaint that a term had not been included where in fact there had been no express agreement. In the latter case, a tribunal must consider all the facts to determine what term should be implied,[236] and normally there will be sufficient evidence for them to be able to do so (in particular, evidence of general working practices which are obvious at the latest by the end of the two-month period that the employer has

232 [2011] ICR 285, [2011] IRLR 247, CA. 233 [1981] ICR 166, EAT.

234 [1982] 2 All ER 865, [1982] IRLR 183, CA. The case includes a detailed explanation by Stephenson LJ of the original drafting of ss 11 and 12.

235 The particulars in question related to the payment (or non-payment) of sick pay; this aspect of the case is considered at 3.5.2.

236 The case is also important on this general question of the implication of terms into contracts of employment (see 3.2), for the approach of the Court of Appeal was not constrained by old contract law notions of the intent of the parties or business efficacy.

in which to give the written statement). However, a further problem arose because the court went further and said obiter that the obligation upon the tribunal to declare the relevant particulars (on a complaint of failure to give them) applied even in the untypical case where there is no clear evidence at all, in which case the tribunal might ultimately be left to 'invent' them, on the basis of what would be reasonable and sensible terms in all the circumstances. However, the Court of Appeal subsequently disapproved strongly of that extreme position in *Eagland v British Telecommunications plc*,[237] where it was reaffirmed that the tribunal's function is only to declare what has already been agreed in some way, not to impose upon the parties terms which have not been agreed. It adopted the distinction drawn by Wood P in the EAT in the case between 'mandatory' particulars (eg pay, notice, and job title) and 'non-mandatory' particulars (eg hours, holidays, and sick pay).[238] In the case of the latter, if there is no evidence at all of any agreement, the tribunal should simply state that there is no term on the matter.[239] Mandatory terms cause more difficulty. The Court said that it is most unlikely that this problem will arise (an employment relationship with *nothing* ever said about pay?), but if it did a tribunal would have to look at what the law would normally include as the ordinary requirements of an employment relationship (the obvious example being the implication of a term of reasonable notice if there was no evidence of any agreement). However, Leggatt LJ, in a short, concurring judgment, stated what must eventually be the bottom line if no power of invention is allowed:

> If an essential term, such as a written statement must contain, has not been agreed, there will be no agreement.

The question of the enforcement of the s 1 statement arose in the previous Labour government's deliberations on new methods of dispute resolution in order to lessen recourse to tribunals. It took the view that too many essentially contractual disputes were being taken to tribunals, a view borne out by the statistics at the time,[240] and that one reason for this was that it was still the case that in too many such disputes the employee had not been given either a contract or a written statement of terms (the giving of which might have settled the issue in dispute at the beginning). This view was backed by research showing that, in a survey of 2,700 completed tribunal cases, 82 per cent of employers but only 60 per cent of employees said that terms had been given in writing, and that only 51 per cent of employers and 28 per cent of employees said that there were written procedures at the workplace for dealing with the issue or issues that had led to the tribunal application.[241] One obvious problem was that under existing law a s 1 statement could only be enforced by the individual employee (in s 11 proceedings); these remained rare. The Employment Act 2002 addressed this issue of insufficient enforcement in a novel way. Under s 38, where a tribunal hearing a case finds in favour of the employee and discovers that the employer was in a breach of the duty to give written particulars, it must award extra compensation of between two and four weeks' pay (unless there are exceptional circumstances making that unjust or inequitable). The important point here is that there is *no* causative element, that is, it need not be shown that the employee won the substantive claim *because* there was no s 1 statement; thus, this provision simply gives a new responsibility to tribunals to police the giving of these statements.

[237] [1993] ICR 644, [1992] IRLR 323, CA.

[238] [1990] ICR 248, [1990] IRLR 328, EAT.

[239] *Morley v Heritage plc* [1993] IRLR 400, CA.

[240] And still today—in 2024/25 31 per cent of all cases subject to ACAS early conciliation included disputes over pay or other terms of employment: *ACAS Annual Report 2024/25*.

[241] Findings of the 1998 Survey of Employment Tribunal Applications (Employment Relations Research Services No 13, 2002).

2.4 Legality and restraint of trade

2.4.1 The doctrine of illegality generally

2.4.1.1 The basic position

All contracts having objects contrary to statute or common law, or which entail the passing of an illegal consideration, are void. So, for example, an agreement by which an employee purports to permit the employer to make deductions from their remuneration will be void unless there is compliance with the provisions of Part 2 of the Employment Rights Act 1996.[242] So too will a purported agreement to waive a breach of duty imposed by statute on an employer.[243] Sundry other forms of illegality may theoretically apply to contracts of employment as well as to contracts generally, even if in practice they are less likely to do so. One which could arise directly in the context of employment is the rule that a contract of employment must not contain 'servile incidents', which may best be described as harsh terms showing a lack of mutuality, as where a cinema company obtained sole use of an actor's stage name[244] or where the defendant borrowed money from a moneylender on terms which made it impossible for him to change employment, deal with his possessions, change address, and so on without prior permission.[245]

2.4.1.2 Application to employment law

One particular application of notions of illegality has caused problems in the field of employment law. These problems arise when one of the parties (usually the employer) to a tribunal action concerning modern statutory rights (particularly unfair dismissal) argues that the contract of employment in question was in some sense illegal, usually because it contained some element of unlawful tax evasion (eg under-declaration of income payable under it, or the payment of non-declared extra amounts of income). If this is proved, it can lead to a decision that the contract itself is void and, as such a contract is necessary before a claimant can show that they were an 'employee' for the purpose of claiming that statutory right, that the claim must be struck out.[246]

The doctrine of illegality in the law of contract is a complicated subject at the best of times,[247] but in the sphere of employment law can have particularly drastic effects by depriving tribunals of jurisdiction, even where the element of illegality might be incidental and (in the case of tax evasion) where the amount of money concerned is small. Moreover, it can lead to the problem—which arises generally under the doctrine of illegality in contract law—of one party to the contract (here usually the employer) benefiting from its own illegality, for example in a case where the evasion scheme was in fact initiated by the employer who later used it to try to defeat an employee's claim for unfair dismissal.

[242] *Kearney v Whitehaven Colliery Co* [1893] 1 QB 700, CA (case on the now-repealed Truck Acts): see 3.5.5.

[243] *Baddeley v Earl of Granville* (1887) 19 QBD 423; for a strong case see *Wheeler v New Merton Board Mills Ltd* [1933] 2 KB 669, CA.

[244] *Hepworth Manufacturing Co v Ryott* [1920] 1 Ch 1, CA; however, some cinema contracts have validly imposed highly personal restraints on employees' diets, health, personal life, and so on, probably on the ground that they were in the interests of both parties: *Gaumont-British Picture Corpn v Alexander* [1936] 2 All ER 1686. A tie to pay back the cost of training is not illegal (*Strathclyde Regional Council v Neil* [1984] IRLR 11).

[245] *Horwood v Millar's Timber and Trading Co Ltd* [1917] 1 KB 305, CA.

[246] *Napier v National Business Agency Ltd* [1951] 2 All ER 264, CA; *Jennings v Westwood Engineering Ltd* [1975] IRLR 245, EAT; *Tomlinson v Dick Evans 'U' Drive Ltd* [1978] ICR 639, [1978] IRLR 77, EAT. Note, however, that it has been held (thankfully) that merely getting the tax status *wrong* (eg where employer and employee both treated it as self-employment but it is later held by a court or tribunal to have been employment) does *not* render the whole contract void for illegality: *Enfield Technical Services v Payne* [2008] IRLR 500, CA.

[247] Especially as the purely contract law cases tend to be on abstruse facts.

The starting point here is that the general argument that the doctrine of illegality should not apply to contracts of employment (either at all, or at least to the extent of prejudicing statutory actions) on the grounds of employment law policy has clearly been disapproved by the EAT.[248] Thus, the doctrine is applicable and in a series of cases the tribunals have had to work out its effects. It may of course apply to forms of illegality other than tax evasion, as for example in *Coral Leisure Group Ltd v Barnett*,[249] where it was claimed that an ex-employee could not maintain an action for unfair dismissal because part of his job had entailed hiring prostitutes for the employer's clients, thus falling foul of the law on immoral contracts. In this sort of case it is easier to apply the basic common law distinction that contracts illegal in inception are void, but contracts which are legal in inception but later performed in an illegal manner may not be.[250]

2.4.1.3 **The tax evasion cases**

However, that distinction may be more difficult to apply to the more usual cases of tax evasion. The tendency has fortunately been to treat them as illegal only in performance, with the result that 'innocence' is a defence, and so in practice the determining factor has been whether the employee *knew* of the evasion being practised by the employer—if not, they can still claim their statutory rights;[251] moreover, it is clear that knowledge here means actual, subjective knowledge, so that it is an error of law for a tribunal to consider whether the employee ought to have realized what was happening.[252] The most difficult case here is *Corby v Morrison*, where the primary ground for ruling out a claim for unfair dismissal by an ex-employee who had received £5 per week without deduction of income tax was that the contract of employment was illegal *in inception*, which renders the knowledge or otherwise of the employee irrelevant; the EAT did give as a secondary ground of judgment that even if it was only illegal in performance, she knew what was going on and so was ruled out anyway. This second ground of judgment was emphasized in the explanation of the case subsequently in *Newland v Simons and Willer (Hairdressers)*

248 *Newland v Simons and Willer (Hairdressers) Ltd* [1981] ICR 521, [1981] IRLR 359, EAT. It is of course possible for a statute to state expressly that contravention of its terms shall *not* make any resulting contract void for illegality (see eg the Social Security Contributions and Benefits Act 1992, s 97, which covers industrial accidents in the course of illegal employments); it is unfortunate that the Employment Rights Act does not have such an exclusory provision. A later challenge that applying the doctrine of illegality to employment cases was in breach of the Human Rights Act 1998 also failed: *Soteriou v Ultrachem Ltd* [2004] IRLR 870, EAT.

249 [1981] ICR 503, [1981] IRLR 204, EAT.

250 One possible complication for the future is that in *Patel v Mirza* [2017] AC 467, [2017] 1 All ER 811 the Supreme Court subjected the illegality doctrine in commercial law to a major reconsideration, part of which was to rely on a public policy/proportionality test rather that the 'in inception/in performance' idea. The case is difficult because of the splits among the nine Justices. More to the point, however, most of the discussion is on aspects of illegality that are particularly relevant to commercial cases, not employment ones (most of which are not cited). To date, there has been little sign of this new approach percolating down into employment law; see eg *Okedina v Chikale* [2019] IRLR 905, CA and *Robinson v al-Qasimi* [2021] IRLR 774, CA.

251 *Tomlinson v Dick Evans 'U' Drive Ltd*, n 245; *Davidson v Pillay* [1979] IRLR 275, EAT. In *Wheeler v Quality Deep Ltd (in liq)* [2004] EWCA Civ 1085, (2004) The Times, 30 August, CA a determining factor against applying the doctrine was the employee's inability to speak English and lack of knowledge of the UK tax and NI system. *McConnell v Bolik* [1979] IRLR 422, EAT has an interesting twist in the story in that the case concerned non-declaration of income by the employee, so that the crucial question was the state of the *employer's* knowledge. The knowledge in question is as to the facts; lack of knowledge of the illegality of the transaction (ie a mistake of law) will not help the party: *Salvesen v Simons* [1994] ICR 409, [1994] IRLR 52, EAT.

252 *Corby v Morrison* [1980] ICR 564, [1980] IRLR 218, EAT; *Newland v Simons and Willer (Hairdressers) Ltd* [1981] IRLR 359, EAT.

Ltd,[253] but the first ground was not disapproved. However, in *Hewcastle Catering Ltd v Ahmed*,[254] the Court of Appeal clearly leaned towards treating tax evasion cases as illegality in performance, to which the doctrine should be applied sparingly. Beldam LJ stated that the modern law is that it applies only if in all the circumstances it would be an affront to the public conscience to allow the claim to proceed; further, the defence will not be allowed if the defendant employer's conduct in participating in the illegal contract is so much more reprehensible than the employee's conduct that it would be wrong to allow the employer to rely on it. This is an important case because of the facts—the employees were waiters at the employers' club who were involved in operating the employers' VAT fraud, *but* they did *not* derive any personal benefit from it. After the employers were caught (and the employees gave evidence against them), the employees were dismissed and the employers raised illegality as a defence. Had the court simply applied the existing test (did they *know* of it?) the defence would have succeeded, but on the two wider principles above the court was able to disallow it since (a) public policy did not demand its application, and (b) the employers were clearly the more guilty. While this decision does not go as far as to say that an employee with knowledge (though possibly only an unwilling minion) *cannot* be debarred from an action if they made no personal gain, it did allow a decision to be taken much along those lines on the facts. Moreover, it may permit further developments towards what, it is submitted, would be the best solution (given that the doctrine has to apply at all), namely that any incidental tax evasion should only ever make the contract illegal in performance and that for the illegality then to make the contract void the employee must have known of *and benefited from* the evasion to such an *extent* (in comparison with the gain to the employer) that the court or tribunal has no option but to declare the whole contract void.[255]

2.4.1.4 **Three qualifications**

Finally, three points might be noted. The first is that on general principles it is not every form of illegality that can render a contract void—the illegality must be sufficiently grave or of such a nature as to show (in the case of illegality through contravention of a statute) that the intention of the legislation is to affect contracts if necessary, not just to penalize the conduct in question in other ways.[256] It is this principle in relation to *statutory* illegality that prevents, for example, a lorry driver's contract of employment being totally void as soon as they exceed a speed limit. More importantly in practice, it has also been used to avoid a situation where an illegally trafficked vulnerable worker would be denied redress for flagrant breaches of employment laws because of their illegal status under the immigration statutes, which have been construed as intended to penalize the employer, not the employee.[257] However, it cannot help a claimant before a tribunal in a case involving tax evasion, as this is a form of common law illegality, not statutory, and moreover it has so far been the approach of the courts (subject to any possible new emphasis on the respective

[253] See n 248; the same judge presided over the EAT in both cases. *Newland*'s case was clearly viewed as one of illegality in performance, and was remitted to the tribunal to make more precise findings of fact on the employee's knowledge of the evasion.

[254] [1992] ICR 626, [1991] IRLR 473, CA.

[255] *Quaere* whether the proportionality element in *Patel v Mirza* (n 245) might eventually support this idea.

[256] The authority usually cited for this is the judgment of Devlin J in *St John Shipping Corpn v Joseph Rank Ltd* [1957] 1 QB 267, [1956] 3 All ER 683.

[257] *Okedina v Chikale* [2019] IRLR 905, CA. The judgment is notable for stressing this difference between statutory illegality and the much more usual 'common law' illegality and for containing a useful summary of the modern law here: see Bogg '*Okedina v Chikale* and Contractual Illegality: New Dawn or False Dawn?' (2020) 49 ILJ 258.

moral blameworthiness of employee and employer) that *any* element of tax evasion (even if concerning only small amounts, or only extra remuneration[258] on top of basic wages on which full tax may have been paid) is grave enough to activate the rules on illegality; likewise, the tribunals have not accepted the argument that protection of tax revenue can be adequately left to the tax authorities and legislation and does not need to be reinforced by the striking down of contracts, though it has been accepted that employers may be deterred from making illegal payments and then trying to rely on them to defeat statutory claims by the power of a tribunal at the end of the day to transmit the evidence that they have received to the Revenue.[259]

The second point is that a slightly different approach to illegality was taken in the case of *Hyland v J H Barker (North West) Ltd*.[260] In this case, the employee had taken illegal payments for a period of only four weeks (out of a total period of employment of 16 years); it was accepted that this did not render the whole contract void *but* that did not help the employee much, since it transpired that those four weeks fell during his final year before dismissal and thus (as the contract was void for those four weeks) he could not show the year's continuous employment ending with the date of dismissal that was then required in order to bring proceedings for unfair dismissal. The case shows a possibly unfortunate combination of the restrictive rules on illegality and continuity of employment and also, more generally, the harsh effects of the doctrine of illegality in this field.

The third point is that, as a matter of statutory construction and policy, it has been held that the purely contractual doctrine of illegality as such cannot be used to defeat a *discrimination* claim because (unlike unfair dismissal) such a claim does not depend on the existence of a contract of employment; however, in such a claim it has long been accepted that it is still possible for a tribunal to consider whether the claim is so inextricably linked to illegal conduct by the claimant that it could not give a remedy without appearing to condone that activity and, if that is the case and the illegality is sufficiently serious, to rule out the claim on wider grounds of public policy.[261] When, however, the matter finally made it to the Supreme Court in *Hounga v Allen*,[262] it was in an area that had not featured in earlier cases but which had become a matter of some topical concern (as seen above), namely illegal working in this country without the necessary immigration permits, *but* by highly vulnerable people who had been illegally trafficked into the country and then held in conditions virtually of slavery. Here, the policy factors are extremely pressing—on the one hand it is important to uphold immigration law (and the individuals here will usually have the sort of knowledge of the facts that would normally rule their claim out), but on the other hand to rule out discrimination claims based on the dreadful treatment they had been receiving would allow the traffickers a get-out-of-jail-free card.

It was clearly the latter consideration that weighed with the Supreme Court, which allowed the discriminatory dismissal claim to proceed.[263] Unfortunately, however, the Court split 3–2 on reasoning, which makes it potentially a difficult precedent. The majority

[258] If, however, the tax evasion applies only to extraneous payments (eg gifts) which are *not* part of contractual remuneration, the validity of the contract is not affected: *Annandale Engineering v Samson* [1994] IRLR 59, EAT.

[259] A course advocated in *Corby v Morrison* and put into effect in *Newland v Simons and Willer (Hairdressers) Ltd* (n 247).

[260] [1985] ICR 861, [1985] IRLR 403, EAT. As a variant of this, if the illegality has ceased by the time of termination (in an unfair dismissal case) the claimant can still bring the claim, though the previous period of illegality may affect remedies available to them: *Robinson v al Qasimi* [2020] IRLR 345, EAT.

[261] *Leighton v Michael* [1995] ICR 1091, [1996] IRLR 67, EAT; *Hall v Woolston Hall Leisure Ltd* [2000] IRLR 578, CA; *Vakante v Addey & Stanhope School (No 2)* [2005] ICR 231, CA.

[262] [2014] ICR 847, [2014] IRLR 811, SC.

[263] Her ordinary contract-based employment law claims had been ruled out by the tribunal and there was no appeal on this to the Supreme Court.

concentrated so much on the policy factors that they did not directly decide on how (if at all) the older 'inextricably linked' test is to fit in with the public policy approach, using only the latter to hold in the claimant's favour. The minority did consider this point, but held that there is *no* separate public policy test, that inextricable linkage remains a vital element and that it is to be considered along with the severity of the illegality, legal consistency, and the contribution (if any) of the claimant; they held for her primarily on the basis of lack of the necessary linkage between the illegality and her discrimination claim. Their discussion is much clearer but it is not clear whether it is consistent with the majority decision, which arguably was incomplete in its reasoning.[264] The result appears to be that in future similar cases of domestic servitude by trafficked individuals, the doctrine of illegality is unlikely to bar a discrimination action against their persecutors. However, the case may have muddied the waters in future cases on illegality *generally*, which are not complicated by such strong policy considerations. What now *is* the right test to apply?

In addition to these general applications of the doctrine of illegality, much case law has been produced by one particular area of it, the area of restraint of trade. Indeed, now that this has been held to apply to harsh and one-sided contractual conditions during employment as well as after it,[265] it has probably made much of the ancient law on servile incidents redundant. The classic restraint of trade clause in a contract of employment is where the employee agrees not to work in the same trade or not to solicit their employer's customers in a certain area for a certain period after the termination of their employment with that employer. It is to the doctrine of restraint of trade, and the validity or otherwise of such an agreement, that we now turn.

2.4.2 **The doctrine of restraint of trade**

2.4.2.1 **The use of restraint clauses**

The doctrine of restraint of trade is a legal device to attempt to hold the balance between two competing factors—an employee's freedom to take employment as and when they wish, and an employer's interest in preserving certain aspects of its business from disclosure or exploitation by an employee or, more usually, an ex-employee.[266] Both factors are important, and indeed the law will protect the employer if necessary by the implication of a term of fidelity in the contract of employment thereby restraining the employee, inter alia, from divulging confidential information.[267] However, the employer may wish to go further and extract an express promise from the employee (a) not to disclose certain information and, more important, (b) not to place himself or herself in a position in which they may do so, for example by not working for a competitor for a certain period of time within a certain area after leaving the employment. It has been reaffirmed by the Court of Appeal that if the employer wants this protection of actually being able to restrain future employment by a competitor for a certain period (known in the jargon as 'barring out relief'), it must be done through an express restraint clause; reliance merely on the implied duty of fidelity will not be enough.[268]

[264] It arguably leaves open the crucial question whether the previous leading cases remain good law. Another problem is that the assumption made here that vulnerability and illegal immigration status was to be equated with *race* discrimination was subsequently disapproved in *Onu v Akwiwu* [2016] IRLR 719, SC.

[265] *Schroeder Music Publishing Co v Macaulay* [1974] 3 All ER 616, [1974] 1 WLR 1308, HL; *Clifford Davis Management Ltd v WEA Records Ltd* [1975] 1 All ER 237, [1975] 1 WLR 61, CA.

[266] The leading work on this area is Brearley and Bloch *Employment Covenants and Confidential Information: Law, Practice and Technique* (4th edn, 2018) which gives an excellent exposition of the law and practice.

[267] This topic is discussed at 3.4.4.

[268] *Caterpillar Logistics Services (UK) Ltd v de Crean* [2012] ICR 981, [2012] IRLR 410, CA.

It is thus established that an employer can stipulate for protection against having its confidential information passed on to a rival in trade. But experience has shown that it is not satisfactory simply to have a covenant against disclosing confidential information. The reason is because it is so difficult to draw the line between information which is confidential and information which is not, and it is very difficult to prove a breach when the information is of such a character that an employee can carry it away in their head. The difficulties are such that the only practicable solution is to take a covenant from the employee by which they are not to go to work for a rival in trade. Such a covenant may well be held to be reasonable.[269]

2.4.2.2 **Valid or void?**

The question then arises whether any given restraint clause is valid and enforceable against the ex-employee, or void. The modern law on restraint of trade is to be found in *Nordenfelt v Maxim Nordenfelt Guns and Ammunition Co*,[270] *Esso Petroleum Co Ltd v Harper's Garage (Stourport) Ltd*,[271] and *Peninsula Securities Ltd v Dunnes Stores (Bangor) Ltd*.[272] In the *Nordenfelt* case it was established that a restraint clause is to be considered void unless the party alleging its validity can prove that it is (a) reasonable as between the parties and (b) in the public interest. The two principal forms of agreement which have been subject to the doctrine are agreements by the vendor of a business not to compete with the purchaser of it (as in the *Nordenfelt* case) and by an employee not to act in a certain way after finishing the employment, and it has been clearly stated that it will be more difficult to establish the validity of a restraint clause in the latter case—with which we are primarily concerned here—for it concerns not a commercial transaction at arm's length but rather a transaction, potentially between parties of different bargaining strengths, which could have a major effect on an individual's livelihood (future and present) to the disadvantage of that individual and the public interest.[273]

For present purposes, the decision in the *Esso Petroleum* case clarified the law in two major ways. The first was to confirm that not all agreements which restrain a person's freedom of action are subject to the doctrine, for some are so accepted as normal incidents of particular businesses or transactions that they are not subject to challenge.[274] The test for deciding what is subject to the doctrine and what is not caused problems for many years and was finally addressed by the Supreme Court in the *Peninsula Securities* case, but what is important for present purposes is that the House of Lords in *Esso Petroleum* said clearly that restraint clauses by employees in favour of employers are definitely subject to the doctrine and nothing in *Peninsula Securities* (a case on commercial property) contradicts that. The second major effect of the case was to revive the ailing second limb of the rule in *Nordenfelt*'s case, that is, *public* interest. This had been so neglected as to have been virtually ignored,[275] but this can no longer be so, and indeed Lord Reid and Lord Hodson

[269] *Littlewoods Organisation Ltd v Harris* [1978] 1 All ER 1026 at 1033, CA, per Lord Denning MR.

[270] [1894] AC 535, HL, as explained by a subsequent House of Lords in *Mason v Provident Clothing and Supply Co Ltd* [1913] AC 724, HL.

[271] [1968] AC 269, [1967] 1 All ER 699, HL.

[272] [2020] UKSC 36.

[273] See particularly *Herbert Morris Ltd v Saxelby* [1916] 1 AC 688, HL, per Lord Parker at 710 and Lord Shaw at 714.

[274] Tied houses in the brewery trade are valid, whereas 'solus' agreements in the garage trade, not being so widely accepted, have been the subject of several legal cases.

[275] 'Their Lordships are not aware of any case in which a restraint, though reasonable in the interests of the parties, has been held unenforceable because it involved some injury to the public': *A-G of Commonwealth of Australia v Adelaide Steamship Co Ltd* [1913] AC 781, PC, at 795 per Lord Parker. One exceptional case was *Wyatt v Kreglinger and Fernau* [1933] 1 KB 793, CA, followed by *Bull v Pitney-Bowes* [1966] 3 All ER 384, [1967] 1 WLR 273.

intimated[276] that certain past cases which were decided on the first limb—reasonableness as between the parties—might well have been better decided on the second limb. In the employment context this could be of some importance, as there might be certain forms of agreement—as we shall see—such as labour stabilization agreements between two employers, which might be eminently reasonable as between the parties, but would now be subject to challenge on the wider ground of the public interest.

Thus, an employee might validly bind himself or herself in a contract of employment as to future activities, usually when entering the contract, but also possibly during its currency[277] or at its termination, provided in the latter case that the agreement is genuinely referable to the contract of employment, and not just an afterthought 'in gross'.[278] Moreover, it is now established that a clause restraining certain activities by the employee *during* employment may be subject to challenge, as well as one restricting activities upon termination of the employment; in *Schroeder Music Publishing Co v Macaulay*,[279] an agreement whereby the plaintiff, a young and unknown songwriter, gave his exclusive services to the defendants for five years without any obligation on the latter to publish his works or provide him with any livelihood, and whereby the defendants could terminate or extend the contract at their election but the plaintiff could not, was held to be void as in restraint of trade. That was, however, an unusual case; any more normal restraints *during* employment, for example not to work for competitors or not to disclose information, might well be held to be so common as to require no justification, under the *Esso Petroleum* case, and indeed certain standard ones would possibly be implied by operation of law even if not expressed.[280]

Given that restraint clauses in contracts of employment are amenable to challenge, the next relevant questions are: what interests warrant protection; how extensive can the restraint be if it is to be valid; and what remedies are available to the parties?

2.4.3 Protectable interests

The clearest starting point is that an employer cannot simply restrain an ex-employee from competing with it in an ordinary manner; it must go far beyond that, and in the employment context this has traditionally meant that the restraint must be necessary to protect either (a) trade secrets or (b) customer connections.

There appears to be no case in which a covenant against competition by an employee has *as such* ever been upheld by the court. Wherever such covenants have been upheld it has been on the grounds not that the employee would, by reason of the employment or training, obtain the skill or knowledge necessary to equip them as a possible competitor in the trade, *but* that they might obtain such personal knowledge of, and influence over, the customers of the employers, or such an acquaintance with the employer's trade secrets as would enable them, if competition were allowed, to take advantage of their employer's trade connection or utilize information confidentially obtained.[281] The emphasis is therefore on possible *unfair* competition.

[276] [1968] AC 269 at 300 and 319, [1967] 1 All ER 699 at 709 and 721.

[277] *RS Components Ltd v Irwin* [1974] 1 All ER 41, [1973] ICR 535.

[278] *Stenhouse Australia Ltd v Phillips* [1974] AC 391, [1974] 1 All ER 117, PC.

[279] [1974] 3 All ER 616, [1974] 1 WLR 1308, HL, followed in *Clifford Davis Management Ltd v WEA Records Ltd* [1975] 1 All ER 237, [1975] 1 WLR 61, CA.

[280] See 3.4.4.6.

[281] *Herbert Morris Ltd v Saxelby* [1916] 1 AC 688 at 709, HL, per Lord Parker. For a modern reaffirmation of this principle see *Faccenda Chicken Ltd v Fowler* [1986] ICR 297, [1986] IRLR 69, CA.

2.4.3.1 **Trade secrets**

From this basic principle, certain important points arise. The first is that although 'trade secret' is difficult to define, it is an important concept and must be distinguished from the employee's own skill and general knowledge of the trade (albeit gained in the employer's service),[282] knowledge of general business methods and organizations,[283] and information which lacks confidentiality (eg through having been published),[284] none of which merit lawful protection. The subject matter must be something more in the nature of a secret process or formula or the detailed design of a machine (albeit from parts the individual specifications of which are generally known),[285] and in modern circumstances may also cover highly confidential information of a non-technical or non-scientific nature (disclosure of which to a competitor could cause significant harm)[286] or detailed knowledge of the workings of a specialized business.[287] Particularly difficult questions may now arise in the computer and information technology industries, in deciding what remains confidential at the cutting edge and what is merely the (expert) employee's own knowledge, or indeed general knowledge in such a rapidly developing field.[288]

One possible way forward in the future may come from statute. The Trade Secrets (Enforcement) Regulations 2018[289] were passed to implement the EU Trade Secrets Directive 2016/943, which aims to harmonize the law of confidentiality. As the title suggests, the regulations concentrate on providing updated and express remedies for breach of the common law of confidentiality which in substance remains unaffected, but in doing so they include a statutory definition of 'trade secret' (taken from the Directive).[290] In its terms, this only applies for the purposes of the Regulations, but it is not impossible that over time it may be read over into this context of restraint of trade clauses, if only as a convenient starting point.[291]

2.4.3.2 **Customer connections**

The second point is that the phrase 'customer connections' is even more intangible; naturally, an employee in constant touch with customers may in certain circumstances attract a personal following, be they a solicitor's clerk,[292] estate agent,[293] bookmaker's assistant,[294] or milkman.[295] Every case will depend heavily upon the facts, and in essence what must be shown is that there is a *real* possibility of *misuse* of the employee's knowledge of customers; if this is missing, for example because the employee's contact with the customers

[282] *Herbert Morris Ltd v Saxelby*, n 281; *Mason v Provident Clothing and Supply Co Ltd* [1913] AC 724, HL; *Faccenda Chicken Ltd v Fowler*, n 281.

[283] *Commercial Plastics Ltd v Vincent* [1965] 1 QB 623, [1964] 3 All ER 546, CA.

[284] *Mustad v Dosen* [1963] 3 All ER 416, [1964] 1 WLR 109n, HL (though in fact decided in 1928).

[285] *Haynes v Doman* [1899] 2 Ch 13, CA; *Forster & Sons Ltd v Suggett* (1918) 35 TLR 87; and see the detailed knowledge of current research carried on by the plaintiffs in *Commercial Plastics Ltd v Vincent* [1965] 1 QB 623, [1964] 3 All ER 546, CA.

[286] *Lansing Linde Ltd v Kerr* [1991] ICR 428, [1991] IRLR 80, CA.

[287] *Littlewoods Organisation Ltd v Harris* [1978] 1 All ER 1026, [1977] 1 WLR 1472, CA.

[288] *FSS Travel and Leisure Systems Ltd v Johnson* [1998] IRLR 382, CA.

[289] SI 2018/597.

[290] The definition is set out at 2.4.3.3.

[291] The first case to consider the 2018 Regulations adopted this approach at first instance: *Trailfinders Ltd v Travel Counsellors Ltd* [2020] IRLR 448, IPEC, but on appeal the case was decided on other grounds: [2021] IRLR 450, CA.

[292] *Fitch v Dewes* [1921] 2 AC 158, HL.

[293] *Scorer v Seymour-Johns* [1966] 3 All ER 347, [1966] 1 WLR 1419, CA.

[294] *SW Strange Ltd v Mann* [1965] 1 All ER 1069, [1965] 1 WLR 629.

[295] *Home Counties Dairies Ltd v Skilton* [1970] 1 All ER 1227, [1970] 1 WLR 526, CA; *Dairy Crest Ltd v Pigott* [1989] ICR 92, CA.

was insufficiently direct or influential, the restraint will be void.[296] However, once this elusive element is established, it may well be reasonable to restrain the ex-employee from soliciting not only their particular customers at the date of termination of employment but also any other persons who were the employer's customers at any other time during the period of employment or some specified part thereof,[297] though it will not generally be reasonable to restrain solicitation of persons who might become the employer's customers at some time after termination,[298] as for example by a clause restraining a commercial traveller from soliciting anyone in the relevant trade in the area in which they used to travel for the employer, not limiting it to those who were the employer's customers, or from whom they had attempted to solicit custom for the employer.[299]

2.4.3.3 **Extension to cases of solicitation of staff**

The third point is that if the restraint clause cannot fairly be said to protect a trade secret or customer connection, the long-standing view has been that it should be void on the basis that it concerns no protectable interest known to the law, unless the court is to establish a new one. In *Kores Manufacturing Co v Kolok Manufacturing Co*,[300] two neighbouring employers producing similar goods agreed that neither would employ anyone who had been employed by the other within the previous five years. As this mainly concerned labourers there was no question of trade secrets or customer connections, and the sole purpose of the agreement was to encourage a stable labour supply. The Court of Appeal held it to be void on the ground that it was, on its facts, unreasonable as between the parties,[301] but it is submitted that conceptually the prime reason for invalidity should have been that it concerned no known protectable interest, and there are dicta in the judgment in support of this.

This has, however, subsequently caused controversy and a change in the law, at least partially because of moves by employers to prevent leaving employees' solicitation of *other employees*, especially in highly competitive areas such as the City and/or in the case of highly marketable executives. At first, the traditional view was taken that such anti-solicitation clauses were not permitted. In *Hanover Insurance Bros Ltd v Schapiro*,[302] certain standard clauses preventing solicitation of customers were enforced against the company's departing chairman and managing director, but a clause stating that they would not, within one year of leaving, solicit any *employees* to join them in their new venture was held to be unenforceable, the court giving its opinion that staff preservation was not a protectable interest. However, that was swiftly followed by an unreported Court of Appeal case, *Ingham v ABC Contract Services Ltd*,[303] in which it was held that an employer *does* have a 'legitimate interest in maintaining a stable trained workforce in what is acknowledged to be a highly competitive business'. In the light of this, an injunction was granted in *Alliance Paper Group Ltd v Prestwich*[304] by a Chancery judge to enforce a covenant not to entice away certain employees, on the basis that the remarks on protectable interests in *Hanover* were obiter (the actual decision having been that the

[296] *Bowler v Lovegrove* [1921] 1 Ch 642; *SW Strange Ltd v Mann* [1965] 1 All ER 1069, [1965] 1 WLR 629.

[297] *G W Plowman & Son Ltd v Ash* [1964] 2 All ER 10, [1964] 1 WLR 568, CA, applied in *Home Counties Dairies Ltd v Skilton* [1970] 1 All ER 1227, [1970] 1 WLR 526, CA; *John Michael Design plc v Cooke* [1987] 2 All ER 332, [1987] ICR 445, CA.

[298] *Konski v Peet* [1915] 1 Ch 530.

[299] *Gledhow Autoparts Ltd v Delaney* [1965] 3 All ER 288, [1965] 1 WLR 1366, CA.

[300] [1959] Ch 108, [1958] 2 All ER 65, CA.

[301] This case is expressly mentioned by Lord Reid and Lord Hodson in *Esso Petroleum Ltd v Harper's Garage (Stourport) Ltd* [1968] AC 269, [1967] 1 All ER 699, HL as one which should have been decided on the other limb of the *Nordenfelt* test, public interest. It is interesting to note that the agreement was between employers; the existence of such contracts is difficult to discover.

[302] [1994] IRLR 82, CA. [303] (1994) unreported. [304] [1996] IRLR 25.

clause was too wide in any event), and that it was *Ingham* that was to be followed on this point. Likewise, when it went before the Court of Appeal again in *Dawnay, Day & Co Ltd v De Braconier d'Alphen*,[305] where three Eurobond dealers broke away from their employer to join a similar competing venture, the court upheld the decision of Walker J to enforce (inter alia) covenants prohibiting for one year solicitation of certain other employees, again expressly on the basis of the employer's interest in maintaining a stable, trained workforce, within the bounds of reasonableness. Thus, this form of staff retention may now be seen as joining trade secrets and customer connections as a third protectable interest *but* with limits. It does not necessarily mean that *Kores v Kolok* was wrong on its particular facts, and it has been held by the Court of Appeal that in a non-solicitation case the *length* of the restriction period may be particularly important.[306] Moreover, simple attempts to stabilize non-key and non-specialist staff (ie just for administrative convenience) may still not be valid, though some care may be needed here. The cases so far have concerned the solicitation of *senior* staff, in highly competitive industries subject to high turnover and 'head-hunting' of people with instantly marketable skills and knowledge.[307] It is possible that this legal development is confined to such cases, though with two caveats—there could also be arguments for a valid protectable interest in relation to a more junior employee if (a) that person, though junior, is a key employee in terms of skills, for example in computer technology;[308] or (b) that person is a member of a whole *team* being enticed away by the departing employee (sometimes known as a 'swarming' case[309]).

2.4.4 **The extent of the restraint**

Once there is a legally protectable interest, the question which then arises concerns the extent to which the employer can bind the employee's future conduct in order to protect that interest. Cases on this are as infinitely variable, as are the facts upon which they are based, but certain important factors can be discerned. The terms of the restraint must be no more than is reasonably necessary to give the employer adequate protection,[310] and in approaching this the court might first look at the type of business concerned to see how much protection it warrants;[311] in this context it might be significant if the business is either specialized in its product or service or localized in its area of operation. The position of the employee is also a matter for consideration. The closer their contacts with

[305] [1998] ICR 1068, [1997] IRLR 442, CA. This case was also notable for deciding that a joint venture had sufficient interest to protect. For extensive discussion of these cases see *TSC Europe (UK) Ltd v Massey* [1999] IRLR 22.

[306] *Coppage v Safety Net Security Ltd* [2013] IRLR 970, CA. A non-solicitation clause was enforced primarily because it was only for six months.

[307] In *Alliance Paper Group* the restraint related to company employees 'in a senior capacity' and in *Dawnay, Day* to directors or senior employees; in each case the court held that such phrasing was sufficiently precise to be enforceable, on the elephant principle, ie that you cannot define it but you know one when you see it. By contrast, in *Hanover* a non-solicitation clause applying to 'any employees' was too wide.

[308] Readers of Joseph Heller's *Catch-22* will know that the whole Mediterranean theatre of war was in fact run by ex-PFC Wintergreen, not the general staff.

[309] See eg the facts of *Willis Ltd v Jardine Thompson Group plc* [2015] IRLR 844, CA.

[310] *Herbert Morris Ltd v Saxelby* [1916] 1 AC 688, HL; the longstanding test was reaffirmed by Millett J in *Allied Dunbar (Frank Weisinger) Ltd v Weisinger* [1988] IRLR 60, where he disapproved an attempt to replace it with a more flexible concept of 'proportionality' between the extent of the restraint and the benefit of the employer. For a good factual example see *Scully UK Ltd v Lee* [1998] IRLR 259, CA.

[311] The business in question must be that in which the employer is actually engaged, and not one in which it might be interested at some future date: *Bromley v Smith* [1909] 2 KB 235; however, it may be valid for the employer to protect the business carried out by its subsidiaries, provided the restraint does not go wider than that and apply to activities not covered by the group: *Stenhouse Australia Ltd v Phillips* [1974] AC 391 at 404, [1974] 1 All ER 117 at 125, PC.

customers or prospective customers, the easier it will be to justify a restraint.[312] Similarly, the higher the employee is in the hierarchy of employees, the easier it will be. Thus in *M and S Drapers v Reynolds*,[313] where the restraint was imposed on a collector salesman, the court rejected the analogy with a managing director based on *Gilford Motor Co v Horne*[314] and held that in the light of its particular circumstances the restraint was unreasonable. It is nothing more than a question of fact for again, in *G W Plowman & Son Ltd v Ash*,[315] a restraint on a sales representative was accepted as valid.

Given that the business merits some protection from an employee such as the one in question, the major factual problem is how wide the terms of the restraint may be in terms of geographical area and duration of time. There are no rules of law here; a 25-year worldwide restraint was valid in the context of the international armaments trade in the *Nordenfelt* case,[316] but a one-year restraint was held to be void in the context of the plastics industry in *Commercial Plastics Ltd v Vincent*,[317] partly on the ground that it was unlimited in area. The only general rule is that the two factors of geographical area and duration of time tend to be complementary, in that the wider the geographical area, the shorter the period of time that might be considered reasonable, and vice versa—as in *Fitch v Dewes*,[318] where a restraint that a solicitor's clerk in Tamworth would *never* practise as such within seven miles of Tamworth Town Hall upon ceasing the employment was held to be valid in the light of the restricted area. Further than this, all that can be said is that the drafting of a restraint clause may require a delicate balance in order to protect the lawful interests of the employer while at the same time achieving no more protection than is reasonably necessary for that purpose in all the circumstances. After warning of the dangers of 'home-made' restraint clauses, Pearson LJ said in *Commercial Plastics v Vincent*:[319] 'It would seem that a good deal of legal "know-how" is required for the successful drafting of a restraint clause.'

2.4.5 **Enforcement**

2.4.5.1 **Basic principles**

In looking to see if a restraint agreement is valid and enforceable, two initial principles should be noted—(a) validity must be determined as at the date of contracting, not some later date, which means that if the restraint was excessive when entered into it may not be enforced later even if arguably it has *become* reasonable due to later circumstances (in particular the promotion of the employee to a more sensitive position);[320] (b) the court is

[312] It was felt in *SW Strange Ltd v Mann* [1965] 1 All ER 1069, [1965] 1 WLR 629, that a bookmaker's clerk built up no real contact with clients as business was largely conducted on the telephone.

[313] [1956] 3 All ER 814, [1957] 1 WLR 9, CA.

[314] [1933] Ch 935, CA.

[315] [1964] 2 All ER 10, [1964] 1 WLR 568, CA.

[316] See also the permanent, worldwide restraint on a servant of the royal household, preventing disclosure of any personal information on the royal family, in *A-G v Barker* [1990] 3 All ER 257, CA.

[317] [1965] 1 QB 623, [1964] 3 All ER 546, CA; other grounds of invalidity were that the clause covered work in the whole field of PVC, not just that part which was secret, and it applied to any employment, not just research. On the importance of geographical area see also *Greer v Sketchley Ltd* [1979] IRLR 445, CA; and *Marley Tile Co Ltd v Johnson* [1982] IRLR 75, CA. A longer period is more likely to be reasonable in the case of a non-solicitation of customers clause than in that of a non-competition clause: *Dentmaster (UK) Ltd v Kent* [1997] IRLR 636, CA (citing *Office Angels Ltd v Rainer-Thomas and O'Connor* [1991] IRLR 214, CA). The judgment of Slade LJ in *Office Angels* is now often cited as a good summary of the basic law.

[318] [1921] 2 AC 158, HL.

[319] [1965] 1 QB 623 at 647, [1964] 3 All ER 546 at 555.

[320] *Bartholemews Agri Food Ltd v Thornton* [2016] IRLR 432, CA (restraint on senior agronomist could not be enforced because when entered into 19 years earlier as a trainee it was unreasonable), approving *Patsystems v Neilly* [2012] IRLR 979, QB. The Court in *Bartholemews* observed that the onus is on the employer to make sure that its clauses remain up to date and are reissued when appropriate, eg on promotion.

entitled to look at the realities and effect of any stipulation so that, for example, an employer may not disguise a restraint clause by providing that the employee is at liberty to solicit any customers but must pay a premium or commission for any of the employer's customers solicited.[321] This second point is reinforced by the fact that restraint of trade as a doctrine is not confined to bilateral contracts involving the party concerned,[322] and for present purposes the significance of this is that two or more employers cannot evade the doctrine by agreeing between themselves to do that which, if done between each one of them and their employees, would be void. The facts of *Kores v Kolok*[323] were set out in 2.4.3.3; the indirect restraint there, which would clearly have been invalid if put directly into the contracts of employment of the individual employees affected, was held to be void, thus increasing the legal protection given to the employee. However, the question then arose whether the *employee* could challenge such an agreement, for the agreement in *Kores v Kolok* had in fact lasted for 23 years and was only finally challenged because one of the parties became dissatisfied with it. In *Eastham v Newcastle United Football Club Ltd*,[324] a case concerning the 'retain and transfer' system whereby the restrictive agreement between the club and the Football Association and League could have a major effect on the livelihood of the individual players, Wilberforce J held that the individual does in fact have the right to challenge such an agreement even though they are not a party to it, and this was accepted as correct by Lord Upjohn in *Pharmaceutical Society of Great Britain v Dickson*.[325]

2.4.5.2 **Saving a potentially void clause?**

If the restraint clause is void, it cannot be enforced by the employer, but there are two ways in which a court might be able to save a clause even if it is prima facie void. The first is that, although such a clause must normally be construed strictly, it may be the case that the potential invalidity arises from an ambiguity in the wording which, read one way, could mean that the restraint is too wide; if, however, it is possible to read the clause realistically in the sense in which the parties obviously meant it, and in that sense it is valid, the court may feel able so to validate it, as two of many factual examples show. In *Home Counties Dairies Ltd v Skilton*,[326] the agreement was not to 'serve or sell milk or dairy products' and it was pointed out that, taken literally, this could stop the ex-employee from working in a grocer's shop as well as in the capacity of milkman, and was therefore potentially void for being too wide; however, the Court of Appeal held that the true meaning, in the light of the intention of the parties at the time of entering the agreement, was only to restrain future employment as a milkman, and as such the clause was valid. Likewise in *Marion White Ltd v Francis*,[327] it was held that a clause restraining employment in the hairdressing business 'in any way', which could conceivably have prevented the ex-hairdresser from working as, for example, a receptionist or bookkeeper, in fact was intended by the parties to refer only to actual hairdressing and as such was narrow enough to be valid.

The willingness of a court to use this power has varied over the years. In more recent times, two important limitations have been established. First, the Supreme Court has held that this

[321] *Stenhouse Australia Ltd v Phillips* [1974] AC 391, [1974] 1 All ER 117, PC.

[322] See eg *Nagle v Feilden* [1966] 2 QB 633, [1966] 1 All ER 689, CA and *Edwards v Society of Graphical and Allied Trades* [1971] Ch 354, [1970] 3 All ER 689, CA.

[323] [1959] Ch 108, [1958] 2 All ER 65, CA; see also *Mineral Water Bottle Exchange and Trade Protection Society v Booth* (1887) 36 Ch D 465, CA.

[324] [1964] Ch 413, [1963] 3 All ER 139, HC of A.

[325] [1970] AC 403 at 433, [1968] 2 All ER 686 at 701, HL.

[326] [1970] 1 All ER 1227, [1970] 1 WLR 526, CA.

[327] [1972] 3 All ER 857, [1972] 1 WLR 1423, CA.

interpretative solution can only work if the phrase in question is *genuinely* ambiguous; it is not to be used to validate a phrase that is unambiguously too wide.[328] Secondly, a warning had already been given by the Court of Appeal in *Prophet plc v Huggett*[329] that an employer cannot expect a court to rectify what is actually a *mistake* in the drafting, especially where the clause was professionally drafted. Ultimately, it is for the employer to get it right.

The second possible way to validate a potentially void clause or phrase is if the offending part may be *severed*, leaving the valid remainder capable of enforcement. The concept of severance is a difficult one in contract law generally, giving rise to much case law over the years (not always easy to rationalize). Fortunately, the whole question of severance in employment contracts was reconsidered by the Supreme Court in *Tillman v Egon Zehnder Ltd*,[330] in the light of which it should no longer be necessary to go back to that earlier case law. The case concerned litigation by an ex-employer to enforce a non-compete clause in the departing employee's contract prohibiting her from being 'directly or indirectly engaged or concerned or interested in' any competing business for a period of time. The employee argued that, although the rest of the clause was lawful, the phrase 'or interested in' was too wide, meaning that she was not bound by the clause at all. The employer argued that, if it was indeed too wide, it could be severed and the rest of the clause enforced. The problems of adjudication in this context can be seen from the fact that the trial judge granted an injunction, the Court of Appeal allowed the employee's appeal, and the Supreme Court allowed the employer's further appeal, held that the phrase could be severed and reimposed the injunction. The Court set out three principles:

(1) the 'blue pencil test' continues to apply, ie it must be possible to strike out the offending words without having to redraft what remains;

(2) what remains must still be supported by consideration; and

(3) the removal of the wording in question must not generate any major change in the overall legal effect of all the post-employment restraints in the contract.

The burden of proof is on the employer seeking severance. One drafting point to note here is that, in line with longstanding received wisdom, in the light of (1) above it may still be advisable to draft any series of different post-termination restraints in *separate* clauses each containing a separate restraint, to facilitate the use of that blue pencil if necessary.

2.4.5.3 **Enforcement by the employer**

If the restraint clause is held to be valid (either generally or via one of the above validation methods), it may be enforced against the employee, subject to the caveat that if the employer is in fact in breach of the contract of employment, for example by wrongfully dismissing the employee, it loses the benefit of any restraint clauses contained in it.[331]

[328] [2019] UKSC 32, [2019] IRLR 838; the decision involved overruling *Attwood v Lamont* [1920] 3 KB 571, CA, which had been the leading case for nearly a century.

[329] [2014] IRLR 797, CA.

[330] *Tillman v Egon Zehnder Ltd* [2019] UKSC 32, [2019] IRLR 838, applied in *Boydell v NZP Ltd* [2023] IRLR 572, CA.

[331] *General Billposting Co v Atkinson* [1909] AC 118, HL; *Spafax Ltd v Harrison* [1980] IRLR 442, CA; *Rex Stewart Jeffries Parker Ginsberg Ltd v Parker* [1988] IRLR 483, CA. In *Rock Refrigeration Ltd v Jones* [1997] 1 All ER 1, [1997] ICR 938, the Court of Appeal held that this still applies even if the employer has stated that the clause is to apply on termination 'however caused'; *however*, there were dicta in the case that they only so held because they were *bound* by *General Billposting*, not because they agreed with the principle. This caused uncertainty for some years but eventually it was held directly in *Brown v Neon Management Services Ltd* [2019] IRLR 30 QB that the rule in *General Billposting* is still to be followed. Note, however, that a dismissal lawful at common law but unfair under statute does *not* destroy a restraint clause: *Lonmar Global Risks Ltd v West* [2011] IRLR 138.

Provided this is not so, the employer may sue the employee for damages (and indeed either party may seek a declaration on the validity of the clause in question);[332] in practice, however, the real importance of the action to the employer is that it may seek an injunction to restrain the employee from acting in breach of the clause, and in an urgent case may be granted an interim injunction (provided it can show that it will suffer immediate loss, so that the 'balance of advantage' lies in its favour, within the principles in *American Cyanamid Co v Ethicon Ltd*).[333] Normally, the court will not grant an injunction to enforce a contract of employment on the basis that it is a personal contract not amenable to such enforcement;[334] one long-standing exception to this, however, is the rule in *Lumley v Wagner*[335] that the courts will enforce a valid negative restraint clause, provided that to do so will not have the effect of specifically enforcing the actual contract. This will normally mean that an injunction *will* lie for breach of a restraint clause,[336] but in an untypical case an injunction could be refused, as in *Page One Records Ltd v Britton*,[337] where the dismissed manager of a pop group, The Troggs, sought to enforce a clause in their agreement that they would not engage any other person or firm as manager during a five-year period and would not act as such themselves; Stamp J held that as they had to have a manager in order to operate, to enforce the clause would be to force them to employ him, and so no injunction could be granted.

Finally, it can be seen from this discussion that restraint clauses are not simple, either in their framing or in their enforcement, especially as they tend to operate on an 'all or nothing' basis. It is probably this that has led to the search for other, more reliable ways to safeguard the employer's confidences when an employee leaves the employment. One way that has attracted interest is the 'garden leave' clause, which operates on the basis of a very long notice requirement, during which the employee is paid in full (even though not actually working), but with an express obligation on the employee not to work for anyone else during the notice period. Such clauses may be more certain (though more expensive) than restraint clauses and are considered in Chapter 6.

2.5 Continuity of employment

2.5.1 The concept of continuity and the treatment of part-time employees

The concept of 'continuous employment' is an important one in that many accruing rights, privately negotiated or statutory, depend upon it either for qualification for a particular right, or for computation of benefits to be received under it. Thus, various periods

[332] Even if the period of restraint is already over, provided the applicant can prove that they still have a worthwhile interest in pursuing it (eg where an employer has other employees who are subject to the same clause): *Marion White Ltd v Francis* [1972] 3 All ER 857, [1972] 1 WLR 1423, CA.

[333] [1975] AC 396, [1975] 1 All ER 504, HL. For a modern example see *Planon v Gilligan* [2022] EWCA Civ 642, CA.

[334] *Whitwood Chemical Co v Hardman* [1891] 2 Ch 416, CA; cf *Hill v CA Parsons & Co Ltd* [1972] Ch 305, [1971] 3 All ER 1345, CA. Section 236 of the Trade Union and Labour Relations (Consolidation) Act 1992 provides that no injunction may be granted compelling an employee to work. See Ch 6 on remedies for wrongful dismissal.

[335] (1852) 1 De GM & G 604, 42 ER 687; see also *Warner Bros Pictures Inc v Nelson* [1937] 1 KB 209.

[336] Normally, damages will not be considered a sufficient remedy instead; likewise, an injunction should not normally be refused on the ground that the defendant is willing to undertake not to use the trade secrets, etc until final judgment: *Johnson & Bloy (Holdings) Ltd v Wolstenholme Rink plc* [1987] IRLR 499, CA (a case on the duty of confidentiality generally, but the principles should apply to a restraint of trade clause case). In *D v P* [2016] IRLR 355 the Court of Appeal reaffirmed that the normal expectation will be court enforcement, on the simple principle that the employee should honour what they have agreed to in the contract, irrespective of proof of actual damage to the employer.

[337] [1967] 3 All ER 822, [1968] 1 WLR 157; *Warren v Mendy* [1989] ICR 525, [1989] IRLR 210, CA.

are laid down by statute for the purposes of qualification for minimum rights during notice, qualification for redundancy pay, computation of redundancy pay, qualification for protection from unfair dismissal, quantification of a basic award for dismissal, and qualification for various other employment protection rights. These matters are considered in detail elsewhere, but are mentioned to show the direct effect of the provisions that govern the question of statutory continuity (contained in sections 210–219 of the Employment Rights Act 1996).

Three preliminary points should be noted. The *first* is that continuity of employment means generally with one employer,[338] and this has been construed widely to include continuity where the employee has changed department, job, seniority, or even the terms of their contract of employment during the period, provided that they have remained with the same employer.[339] The *second* is that the Act governs which weeks count in computing a period of employment, and generally if a week does not count it will break continuity, so that the employee then loses the accrued period and must start again from scratch;[340] however, there is the qualification that certain weeks (particularly those spent on strike or, for the purpose of redundancy, abroad)[341] do not count but at the same time are deemed not to break continuity, and thereby the position is effectively rendered neutral (the employee is not unduly penalized by losing all accrued continuity, but at the same time does not benefit because they cannot actually use the relevant period for any purpose of computation). The *third* is that there is a statutory presumption of continuity, unless the contrary is shown; thus, in cases of doubt (eg where there is a possibility that some relevant weeks may not count and so break continuity), the burden of proof is on the employer to show that the employee did *not* have the necessary continuity of employment.[342]

2.5.2 **Weeks which count**

2.5.2.1 **'Any week during the whole or part of which the employee's relations with the employer are governed by a contract of employment' (Employment Rights Act 1996, s 212(1))**

This initially had a complex history, but the emphasis now is on looking only at the continuing existence of the contractual relationship, and whether it covers the week(s) in question. In spite of this apparent simplicity, however, there can still be problems for an employee; in particular, there can be issues with regular *but separate* contracts. This can be seen from two cases. In *Hellyer Bros Ltd v McLeod*,[343] trawlermen were held not

[338] *Lee v Barry High Ltd* [1970] 3 All ER 1040, [1970] 1 WLR 1549, CA; *Harold Fielding Ltd v Mansi* [1974] 1 All ER 1035, [1974] ICR 347. It also means in relation to one contract of employment: *Lewis v Surrey County Council* [1988] AC 323, [1987] ICR 982, HL.

[339] *Wood v York City Council* [1978] ICR 840, [1978] IRLR 228, CA; *Jennings v Salford Community Service Agency* [1981] ICR 399, [1981] IRLR 76, EAT; continuity is a purely statutory concept, exhaustively covered by the statutory provisions which are not to be qualified by courts or tribunals: *Carrington v Harwich Dock Co Ltd* [1998] ICR 1112, [1998] IRLR 567, EAT.

[340] Section 210(4).

[341] Sections 216 and 215, respectively.

[342] Section 210(5). The effect of the presumption was considered in *Nicoll v Nocorrode Ltd* [1981] ICR 348, [1981] IRLR 163, where the EAT held that where it is unclear whether an employee had worked the necessary number of qualifying weeks, the employee need only show that *some* weeks during the qualifying period count and the burden of proof then passes to the employer to prove that there were weeks that do not count and so break continuity. However, there is an exception—in *Secretary of State for Employment v Cohen* [1987] ICR 570, [1987] IRLR 169, the EAT held that the presumption does *not* apply to a 'transfer of business' case under s 218 (see this chapter, 2.5.4), though Scott J emphasized that although the burden of proving continuity through such a transfer lies on the employee, a tribunal should not apply an unrealistically high *standard* of proof.

[343] [1987] 1 WLR 728, [1987] ICR 526, CA.

entitled to redundancy payments on the collapse of their part of the fishing industry, for although they had sailed for one particular owner for many years, the court held that the proper construction was that they had been engaged on a series of separate crew agreements, each covering one voyage. This was further emphasized in *Booth v United States of America*,[344] where maintenance workers were put on a series of fixed-term contracts totalling more than two years, but with very deliberate two-week gaps between each. Their eventual claims for redundancy payments and unfair dismissal were disallowed for lack of continuity—the gaps broke normal continuity, which (for technical reasons) could not be covered by one of the 'deemed continuity' provisions, and the bottom line was expressed by Morison P as follows:

> If, by so arranging their affairs, an employer is lawfully able to employ people in such a manner that the employees cannot complain of unfair dismissal or seek a redundancy payment, that is a matter for him. The courts simply try and apply the law as it stands. It is for the legislators to close any loopholes that may be perceived to exist.[345]

2.5.2.2 **A week during which there is no subsisting contract of employment, but which is covered by special statutory provisions**

In order to avoid unfortunate gaps or 'hiccoughs' in continuity, certain exceptions have always been specifically created by the legislation, and these are now contained in the Employment Rights Act 1996, s 212(3). The three specific cases covered by this subsection are as follows.

(1) *Where the employee is incapable of work through sickness or illness (subsection (3) (a)).* 'Incapable' has been held to refer to the job in question and a temporary, lighter job need not break continuity.[346] Absence from work does not normally, in default of express provision in the contract, terminate the contract.[347] If the contract has not been ended, then the weeks of absence count under subsection (1) anyway. This head is an extension stretching into the period after the contract has been determined.[348] It is limited to 26 weeks after a week counting under subsection (1) and must be followed by a week so counting. Theoretically an employee could have a solitary week of employment followed by 26 weeks of illness and a further week of employment, which would both maintain the continuity and permit a further 26 weeks of absence through illness to count.

(2) *Where the employee is absent from work on account of a 'temporary cessation of work' (subsection (3)(b)).* This has in practice been the most important special case, but it is a phrase not without difficulty. No time limit is laid down. The phrase was

[344] [1999] IRLR 16, EAT. This is a particularly harsh decision because, although the employees were formally 'terminated' and had to complete new application forms for the next contract (after a break which the employers insisted had to be for a minimum of two weeks—strangely), in fact when they returned they were given the same employee number and used the same tools and equipment, and even the same lockers. What a coincidence.

[345] [1999] IRLR 16 at 18. As there has been no legislative amendment, the moral of the story seems to be that the more cynical the manipulation of these rules, the more likely the employer is to win.

[346] *Collins v Nats (Southend) Ltd* (1967) 2 ITR 423; *Donnelly v Kelvin International Services* [1992] IRLR 496, EAT.

[347] For the law as to the payment of sick pay see 3.5.2.

[348] There must be a causal link between the absence from work and the incapacity through sickness or injury: *Pearson v Kent County Council* [1993] IRLR 165, CA.

considered by the House of Lords in *Fitzgerald v Hall, Russell & Co Ltd*,[349] where it was held that it refers to cessation of the *employee's* work for some reason, so there is no requirement that the employer's business in which the employee is engaged should have ceased. It was also held that each case under this head must be looked at in the round and, if necessary, with hindsight, to establish whether it was 'temporary' (the statute giving no guidance on this). Thus, if both parties obviously envisaged that it would be only temporary, that would be cogent evidence, but the lack of it would not mean that the arrangement would necessarily be construed to be permanent:

> The effect of that case is that the tribunal is enjoined to look at the matter as the historian of a completed chapter of events, and not as a journalist describing events as they occur from day to day. The importance of that is this, that things are seen, as they unfold, quite differently from the way in which they are seen when one looks back and considers the whole of the chapter in context. What at the time seems to be permanent may turn out to be temporary, and what at the time seems to be temporary may turn out to be permanent.[350]

The essence of most successful cases is that the employee has been 'stood off', in the sense that they were to be recalled later. The fact that a job is taken in the period of cessation does not destroy the position,[351] but it is plainly not meant to cover the situation where an employee moves to a new employer, fails to settle, and quickly moves back to their old job. It may cover situations such as extra holiday periods taken as periods of absence with the employer's agreement at the employee's expense, and, more particularly, periods when the workplace is closed or no work is available[352] (which may arise through many causes, such as a natural calamity like a fire,[353] or the disruption of supplies of materials). In *Ford v Warwickshire County Council*,[354] it was held to cover the case of a schoolteacher who had been employed on eight consecutive fixed-term contracts for the academic year (September to July); thus, the periods of the summer vacations were held not to break continuity so that she could claim unfair dismissal and a redundancy payment when she did not receive a ninth contract. In interpreting the subsection, the House of Lords took a basically similar approach to that in their earlier decision in *Fitzgerald v Hall Russell Ltd* (previously discussed), holding that 'temporary' means 'transient' and adding that

[349] [1970] AC 984, [1969] 3 All ER 1140, HL, approving *Hunter v Smith's Dock Ltd* [1968] 2 All ER 81, 3 ITR 198. 'Work' here means paid work; if that is missing, the paragraph may apply and it is not the tribunal's function to enquire into *why* the paid work is missing: *University of Aston in Birmingham v Malik* [1984] ICR 492. However, at the end of the day it must be the case that there is a 'cessation of work' available for the employee to do—if the work remains but for some reason they are not eligible to do it, the paragraph does not apply: *Bryne v Birmingham City District Council* [1987] ICR 519, [1987] IRLR 191, CA. It is that cessation that must then be 'temporary', not the employee's absence: *Flack v Kodak Ltd* [1986] ICR 775, [1986] IRLR 255, CA. This can have the unfortunate effect that if the work remains available but the employer *refuses* at certain times to offer it to a particular employee (in order deliberately to break continuity, eg by insisting on gaps between fixed-term contracts), then subsection (3)(b) cannot apply and the employee may be unable to claim statutory rights: *Booth v United States of America* [1999] IRLR 16, EAT, considered earlier.

[350] *Bentley Engineering Co Ltd v Crown* [1976] ICR 225 at 228, [1976] IRLR 146 at 148; in this case, periods of 2 years and 21 months were held still to be temporary. The correctness of this decision has been doubted over the years by commentators, but it was reaffirmed by the EAT in *Holt v E B Security Ltd* UKEAT/0558/11.

[351] *Thompson v Bristol Channel Ship Repairers and Engineers Ltd* (1969) 4 ITR 262; affd (1971) 5 ITR 85, CA; *Bentley Engineering Co Ltd v Crown* [1976] ICR 225, [1976] IRLR 146, EAT.

[352] *Hunter v Smith's Dock Ltd* [1968] 2 All ER 81, 3 ITR 198.

[353] *Newsham v Dunlop Textiles Ltd (No 2)* (1969) 4 ITR 268.

[354] [1983] ICR 273, [1983] IRLR 126, HL, overruling *Rashid v ILEA* [1977] ICR 157, EAT.

the application of subsection (3)(b) was not defeated either by the fact that the absences were easily foreseeable in advance or by the fact that the case concerned a series of fixed-term contracts (rather than a series of contracts terminable by notice). The 'transience' requirement makes it clear that the principle in the case cannot be applied so widely as to give previously unheard of rights to genuinely casual/seasonal workers (who, for example, only work for three or four months of each year—there, the gaps would be anything but transient); however, the case may give food for thought to any employer seeking to avoid the application of employment laws by putting an employee on a series of short-term contracts, if it transpires that in fact the gaps are relatively short by comparison with the periods of work (provided that it remains the case that it is the *work* that is temporarily unavailable, not just the fact that it is not being done by that employee).[355] The application of hindsight and an overall view of events, permissible under this subsection, could easily work to the employer's disadvantage in such a case, though it must be remarked that the categorization of transience as a matter of fact for the tribunal would make it difficult to give definite advice in advance in a marginal case on whether the sub-paragraph will apply,[356] the lawyer being faced with the unanswerable question: 'How long is short?'

In seeking to answer that question, two quite different approaches are possible. As stated, *Fitzgerald v Hall Russell Ltd* sets out a 'broad-brush' approach, looking at all the circumstances throughout the period of employment in order to see if any particular gap can be categorized as temporary. However, in *Ford v Warwickshire County Council*, Lord Diplock suggested a narrower 'mathematical' test of looking at whatever period is relevant to the claim in question[357] and, in the case of any gap during that time, comparing its length mathematically with the periods of work on either side of it to see if it was temporary. This latter approach could produce anomalies[358] and the matter was reconsidered by the Court of Appeal in *Flack v Kodak Ltd*,[359] a case on very different facts from those in *Ford*. This case concerned a series of highly irregular work patterns over periods varying from three to 11 years (the employees having been laid off and taken back on again intermittently, depending on season and demand). The tribunal applied the mathematical approach (even to the extent of expressing the gaps as percentages of their surrounding periods in work) and found that in the case of each employee, continuity was broken in the vital qualifying period for redundancy payments. However, the EAT and the Court of Appeal held that this was the wrong test to apply, that the 'broad-brush' approach should be taken, and that the matter should be remitted to another tribunal for reconsideration. The question is where this leaves the law. Although Lord Diplock's statement in *Ford* as to the mathematical test was said to be obiter, it is clear from later cases that that test has not been disapproved. In *Sillars v Charrington Fuels Ltd*, the EAT[360] suggested that the mathematical test should

[355] See *Booth v United States of America*, n 344.

[356] See eg the facts in *Berwick Salmon Fisheries Co Ltd v Rutherford* [1991] IRLR 203, EAT where salmon netters had been employed for 30 weeks on, 22 weeks off, until their final two seasons when they only worked for 23 weeks on, 29 weeks off. This point now has a particular resonance under the Fixed-term Employees (Prevention of Less Favourable Treatment) Regulations 2002, SI 2002/2034, under which these continuity rules are applied in order to calculate whether an employee has been kept on 'successive' fixed-term contracts for four years, thus becoming a permanent employee unless the employer can objectively justify continued use of fixed-term contracts (see this chapter, 2.1.4).

[357] For example, if the question arose as to entitlement to a redundancy payment, that period would be the last two years before the date of dismissal.

[358] If in the relevant period, for example, the employee had a gap of eight weeks with periods in work of only two weeks on each side, that would not be 'temporary' on a straight mathematical comparison. If, however, that was because of short time in times of difficulties prior to their redundancy, and came as a series of late hiccoughs after years of unbroken service, the end result (no redundancy pay because not continuously employed for two years counting back from the date of dismissal) would be ludicrous.

[359] [1986] ICR 775, [1986] IRLR 255, CA.

[360] [1988] ICR 505, [1988] IRLR 180, EAT.

apply to cases, like *Ford*, of *regular* gaps, and the broad-brush approach to cases, like *Flack*, of *irregular* gaps. Unfortunately, the matter was not fully resolved when the case went to the Court of Appeal,[361] as it was there held that (the case being one of seasonal employment with long, regular gaps) the mathematical test was one which it was *open* to the tribunal to have used. Although the distinction drawn by the EAT appears to have been thought too simplistic by the Court of Appeal, if one is looking for a rough rule of thumb it may not be a bad one, pending further authoritative guidance on the matter.

The continued vitality of the 'temporary cessation' exception in cases of irregular employment can be seen from *Cornwall CC v Prater*,[362] where it was held that a children's home tutor who had undertaken assignments for the council on an ad hoc basis over the years (with no expectation of any particular level of work, but who expected to have to complete an assignment once she had undertaken it) but with no overall contract could claim statutory rights because (a) there was enough mutuality of obligations to produce a separate contract of employment for each assignment and (b) these separate contracts could then be put together under paragraph (3)(b).

(3) *Where the employee is absent from work in circumstances such that, by arrangement or custom, he or she is regarded as continuing in the employment of his or her employer for any purpose (subsection (3)(c)).* Under this head any unique local practices are covered, and some potentially unfortunate breaks in continuity avoided. It appears that the agreement or custom must exist when the absence begins, not as an ex post facto afterthought;[363] once this is satisfied the cause of the absence appears to be immaterial—it could be something ad hoc, such as leave of absence for personal reasons[364] or a long-term agreement that the employer might keep the employee on a 'reserve list' to be called upon when necessary.[365]

One area of current interest where reliance has been sought on subsection (3)(c) is contractual career break schemes. These are not covered by statute; where they have been introduced voluntarily (eg as part of a family-friendly package of terms and conditions), they have caused novel problems legally.[366] One question has been whether the employee taking the break could claim that their continuity of employment was preserved under this subsection, on the basis that the scheme constituted an 'arrangement' to regard the employment as continuing. This finally came before the courts in *Curr v Marks & Spencer plc*,[367] where the employee had taken a four-year break (for family purposes) under the employer's scheme. She had commenced her employment with them in 1973 and took the leave from 1990 to 1994. When she was made redundant in 1999 the employers calculated her entitlement to a redundancy payment only back to 1994; she claimed back to 1973 (capped to the maximum 20 years) on the basis that she had continuity through the break. The scheme itself provided that an employee taking the break had to resign and

[361] [1989] ICR 475, [1989] IRLR 152, CA. The mathematical approach was also applied to the facts of *Berwick Salmon Fisheries Co Ltd v Rutherford* [1991] IRLR 203: see n 355.

[362] [2006] ICR 731, [2006] IRLR 362, CA; see Davies (2006) 35 ILJ 196.

[363] *Murray v Kelvin Electronics Ltd* (1967) 2 ITR 622; *Todd v Sun Ventilating Co Ltd* [1975] IRLR 4, EAT. As a matter of simple English, that is clearly the case with a 'custom', but it has also been held to be the case with an 'arrangement': *Welton v Deluxe Retail Ltd* [2013] ICR 428, [2013] IRLR 166, EAT settling a disagreement in earlier EAT decisions. This means that an employee should be wary of *later* employer assurances about respecting continuity.

[364] *Moore v James Clarkson & Co Ltd* (1970) 5 ITR 298; *Taylor v Triumph Motors* [1975] IRLR 369, IT.

[365] *Puttick v John Wright & Sons (Blackwall) Ltd* [1972] ICR 457, NIRC; *Normanton v Southalls (Birmingham) Ltd* [1975] IRLR 74, IT.

[366] An interesting parallel can be seen with PHI schemes (see 3.3.7), which at one point were being enthusiastically introduced as an aid to headhunting, without working out their complex legal implications.

[367] [2003] ICR 443, [2003] IRLR 74, CA.

forfeit continuing staff benefits (eg staff discount, loans, and share options), but that the employers undertook to take the employee back into an equivalent position and that in each year of the break the employee would do two weeks' paid work (to keep up skills). A tribunal found against this employee; a sympathetic EAT allowed her appeal; but the Court of Appeal (while expressing some sympathy for her position and some criticism of the employers for not making the continuity point clear) restored the tribunal's decision. Reaffirming the point that an 'arrangement' must be mutual,[368] they held that here there was no meeting of minds to the effect that the employment was to be considered as continuing, primarily in the light of the requirement on the employee to resign, and the freezing of all employee benefits. Given that this probably represented a fairly typical career break scheme, this case shows that severe problems of continuity are to be expected with such schemes, *unless* an employer (wishing to use one as a positive recruiting tool) very deliberately drafted it so as to preserve continuity by contract.[369] This apart, such a scheme would only come purely within the wording of the subsection if employment was accepted as continuing 'for any purpose' (for example for pension purposes, as instanced by the Court of Appeal), which was not the case here.

2.5.3 **Industrial disputes**

The Act defines strikes and lockouts in similar language.[370] A lockout involves the closing of a place of employment, the suspension of work, or the refusal by an employer to continue to employ any number of its employees. A strike involves cessation of work by a body of employees acting in combination, a concerted refusal to continue work. In the case of both strikes and lockouts these actions must be in consequence of a dispute and in each case the aim of the action must be to coerce the employees or employers, as the case may be, to accept or not to accept terms or conditions of or affecting employment. Both definitions also expressly include similar action taken to aid other employers or employees in dispute.

If an employee is on strike during a week or any part thereof, that week does not count as a period of employment by virtue of s 216(1); however, a compromise is achieved by s 216(2) which provides that the employee's *continuity* of employment is not broken by a strike. In the case of a lockout, s 216(3) provides that continuity is not broken by the fact that an employee is absent from work because of a lockout, but the paragraph says nothing about whether such a period can *count*, so that that question must rely on whether the contract of employment subsists during the lockout.[371] If it does not, presumably the period will not count, though of course continuity will not be broken.

2.5.4 **Change of employment**

Normally when an employee terminates their job with an employer and goes to work for another employer, their continuity ends and they must start to build up continuous service with the new employer from scratch.[372] However, there may be ways in which the continuity can be carried over, so that they are regarded as being employed by the new employer as from the date when they commenced employment with the old employer. The Employment

[368] See n 361, and also *Booth v United States of America* [1999] IRLR 16.

[369] Even here there is a problem—continuity for statutory purposes cannot be established by contract where the statutory definition is not satisfied (see this chapter, 2.5.2), so the employer would need to draft a scheme operating purely in contract even when giving (wholly or partly) the statutory entitlement.

[370] Employment Rights Act 1996, s 235. Note that these definitions are only for stated purposes; they do not apply to the unfair dismissal provisions relating to industrial action: see 10.2.2.

[371] *E and J Davis Transport Ltd v Chattaway* [1972] ICR 267, 7 ITR 361, NIRC.

[372] *Lee v Barry High Ltd* [1970] 3 All ER 1040, [1970] 1 WLR 1549, CA.

Rights Act 1996, s 218 lays down six classes of case in which employment may be deemed to be continuous even though there is a change in employment. The six cases are as follows:

1. Where the trade of business or undertaking is itself transferred. Subsection (2) provides that continuity is unbroken; this is of general application, but particularly important in cases of redundancy. However, to be relied upon at all, the criteria for its application must be satisfied; one is that the employee in question must have been in the relevant employment 'at the time of the transfer' (which raises the problem of a gap in employment over the period of the transfer),[373] but the primary one is—was it a transfer of business, or merely the disposal of certain assets? If the latter, the provision does not apply, even if the employee goes with the asset, so that, for example, the sale of an operating factory may not come within subsection (2) if it is seen merely as the disposal of a surplus asset, particularly if the original employer carries on its business in other establishments.[374] In *Lloyds v Brassey*,[375] Lord Denning MR said:

   > The meaning of [this provision] was considered by the Divisional Court in *Kenmir Ltd v Frizzell*, where Widgery J said 'In deciding whether a transaction amounted to the transfer of business, regard must be had to its substance rather than its form . . . the vital consideration is whether the effect of the transaction was to put the transferee in possession of a going concern, the activities of which he could carry on without interruption.' I think that it is the right test. If the new owner takes over the business as a going concern—so that the business remains the same business but in different hands—and the employee keeps the same job with the new owner . . . his period of employment is deemed to continue without a break in the same job.

   This basic distinction between a transfer of business and a transfer of assets was approved and applied by the House of Lords in *Melon v Hector Powe Ltd*[376] to a case of the sale by the original employer of one of their two factories to another employer in the same trade; in the circumstances it was held that the tribunal had correctly decided that this was merely a transfer of assets, not a transfer of business.

2. Where an Act of Parliament causes one corporate body to replace another as employer: subsection (3).

3. Where the employer, not being corporate, dies and the personal representatives carry on the business: subsection (4).

[373] This was for a long time complicated by the decision of the Court of Appeal in *Teesside Times Ltd v Drury* [1980] ICR 338, [1980] IRLR 72, which permitted a gap to count, but for three different reasons; in *Clark & Tokeley Ltd v Oakes* [1998] 4 All ER 353, [1998] IRLR 577, the Court of Appeal subsequently held that it is Stephenson LJ's judgment in *Teesside Times* that is to be applied, ie that there is no hard-and-fast rule, that a 'transfer' may well take place over an extended period of time, and that continuity will be preserved, provided that the employee was still in employment at the start of that process (a question of fact for the tribunal).

[374] *Kenmir Ltd v Frizzell* (1968) 3 ITR 159; *Woodhouse v Peter Brotherhood Ltd* [1972] 2 QB 520, [1972] 3 All ER 91, CA; *Crompton v Truly Fair (International) Ltd* [1975] ICR 359, [1975] IRLR 250, EAT. There must be a legal transfer of sorts; it is not enough merely that de facto control has been given to someone else: *S I (Systems and Instrumentation) Ltd v Grist* [1983] ICR 788, [1983] IRLR 391. Continuity is preserved even if there is a gap between the two employments, provided that gap is related to the machinery of the transfer: *Macer v Abafast Ltd* [1990] ICR 234, [1990] IRLR 137, EAT. Note that the presumption of continuity in s 210(5) does *not* apply to a 'transfer of business' case under s 218: *Secretary of State for Employment v Cohen* [1987] ICR 570, [1987] IRLR 169, EAT.

[375] [1969] 2 QB 98 at 103, [1969] 1 All ER 382 at 384.

[376] [1981] ICR 43, [1980] IRLR 477, HL. Notice that in this case it was the *employees* who were arguing that there was no transfer of business, in order to be able to claim their redundancy rights from the original employer; this claim was upheld by the House of Lords. See to like effect *Ward v Haines Watts* [1983] ICR 231, [1983] IRLR 285 (concerning sale of the goodwill of a professional practice).

4. Where the 'employer' is a partnership, personal representatives, or trustees, and the composition of the body involved changes: subsection (5). This provision safeguards continuity when, for example, a partner retires and another is appointed.
5. Where the employee is taken into the employment of an associated employer:[377] subsection (6).
6. Where an employee of the governors of a school maintained by a local education authority or that authority itself is taken into the employment of the governors of another such school or the authority: subsection (7).

2.6 Changing the terms of employment

We have already seen that s 4 of the Employments Right Act 1996 states that changes in the terms and conditions relevant to the s 1 statement must be notified to the employee within one month. However, it is important to realize that s 4 only adds a procedural requirement—it does *not* give the employer any substantive right to alter the terms of employment simply by issuing an amending notice. Any such variation must first be lawful and effective under the ordinary law of employment contracts. The obvious form of change is by an express agreement to vary the terms, entered into voluntarily and fully evidenced in writing. However, in the amorphous world of employment relations, things are not always so straightforward. Short of such a change, there are four main possibilities where the employer may still be able to affect a legally recognized variation.

2.6.1 Unilateral right to vary

A first possibility is that there may be certain, untypical, cases where the employment contract itself is drafted to give the employer a right of unilateral variation.[378] In *Wandsworth LBC v D'Silva*,[379] the Court of Appeal recognized that in purely contractual terms such a clause could be valid and effective, but expressed the view obiter that particularly clear language would be necessary to reserve such an unusual power for one party to the contract and that courts should seek to avoid any unreasonable exercise of such a power. However, in *Bateman v ASDA Stores Ltd*,[380] the well-known supermarket had a major legal win on this point. It was proposing changes to the terms and conditions of a large section of its staff: 9,330 employees agreed but 8,700 did not. The management went ahead and purported to impose the changes on the refuseniks under a clause in their company handbook which said that the company 'reserved the right to review, revise, amend or replace the contents of this handbook and introduce new policies from time to time reflecting the changing needs of the business and to comply with new legislation'. In spite of the broad wording, the reference to changing 'policies' (not specifically contractual terms), and arguments that this power was only meant to apply to technical changes, the EAT held (applying *Wandsworth*) that it unambiguously gave

[377] For the definition of associated employers see this chapter, 2.1.6.

[378] The terms and conditions of employment of senior civil servants may be varied unilaterally by the government under the Civil Service Orders in Council. In an ordinary contract of employment, it would be an interesting question as to whether a term allowing unrestricted unilateral variation ('You are employed to do what I say, on any terms I may decide upon') could be held to be void for uncertainty.

[379] [1998] IRLR 193, CA; see also *Securities and Facilities Division v Hayes* [2001] IRLR 81, CA and Smith and Randall *Contract Actions in Employment Law* (2nd edn, 2011) 43.

[380] [2010] IRLR 370, EAT. See further Reynolds and Hendy 'Reserving the Right to Change Terms and Conditions: How Far Can an Employer Go?' (2012) 41 ILJ 79.

the power of unilateral variation of major terms claimed by the employer.[381] From the employee perspective, it is to be hoped that this decision lies at the end of the spectrum of legally acceptable means of change.

2.6.2 **Within managerial discretion to vary**

Less drastically, a second possibility is that it may be that a particular 'variation' in fact falls within the managerial discretion to order changes,[382] either because it is within an area of flexibility envisaged by the contract or because it falls within the scope of an implied term that the employee will adapt to necessary changes in what remains essentially the same job.[383] However, both of these possibilities show the basic problem here: that contracts are essentially static whereas work and work methods may change (sometimes rapidly), and the possibility may equally arise that the employer may wish to effect changes which are *not* envisaged by the contract. In such a case there has to be a legally effective variation; if this does not happen, an employee may insist upon adhering to the original contract and may bring a common law action to underline that adherence (eg by bringing an action in the county court for wages, which are due by virtue of their being willing and able to continue performing their duties under the original, unamended contract)[384] or (in the case of a pay cut) proceedings before a tribunal on the basis that the change constitutes an unlawful 'deduction' from wages. In such a case, an employer who is insistent upon forcing through changes may have to grasp the nettle, dismiss those who still refuse to accept changes, and take its chances before an employment tribunal by seeking to show that the dismissals were fair because of the business's need to alter working patterns.[385]

2.6.3 **Employee consent**

From the employer's point of view, these uncertainties can be avoided if it can be shown that the employee in question in fact *agreed* to the proposed variation in the contract. How is that to be shown? Obviously the clearest case is where the employee has expressly agreed to the variation, either individually or collectively (through negotiations with the relevant union). However, there remains a middle ground (especially where union representation is not involved), which is where the employer 'proposes' a variation simply by

381 In *Wandsworth* it was pointed out that, even if such a clause was contractually valid, an oppressive application of it might breach the implied term of trust and confidence (see 3.3.4). On the facts in *ASDA* the EAT held that there had been no such conduct, especially as the employer had undertaken an extensive consultation exercise with the staff and guaranteed that no existing employees would suffer a decrease in pay.

382 As in the case of the introduction of a no-smoking policy in *Dryden v Greater Glasgow Health Board* [1992] IRLR 469, which was held not to be a breach of contract, so that the employee who left was not constructively dismissed.

383 This was the case with the computerization of Inland Revenue procedures; this was held to be merely an updated version of the plaintiff tax officers' existing jobs (with which they were expected to cope), *not* a substantive variation of their terms of employment: *Cresswell v Board of Inland Revenue* [1984] ICR 508, [1984] IRLR 190, EAT; see 3.4.2.

384 As in *Burdett-Coutts v Hertfordshire County Council* [1984] IRLR 91, where dinner ladies who had refused to accept a unilateral decrease in their hours of work successfully sued their employer for arrears of wages due under their original contract.

385 This is one of the most difficult areas of unfair dismissal, for it is well established that dismissal because of refusal to accept a necessary business reorganization can constitute dismissal for 'some other substantial reason' within the Employment Rights Act 1996, s 98 (see 8.1.2.2 and, again concerning dinner ladies and cost-cutting councils, *Gilham v Kent County Council (No 2)* [1985] ICR 233, [1985] IRLR 18, CA), but to take the final step and hold that that dismissal was *fair* is to give priority to the employer's business considerations over what the employee would normally expect to be their contractual rights (particularly the right not to have the contract altered except by agreement).

announcing it (possibly by reissuing an amended section 1 statement), thus putting the onus on the employee to *object*. If the employee does not object, that gives rise to the argument that they have impliedly *assented* to the variation. If such an argument were easily accepted, the contractual rights of an employee would mean little, and so it was held in *Jones v Associated Tunnelling Co Ltd*[386] that the question of the correct interpretation to be placed on a lack of objection following a unilateral change in terms by the employer must be approached realistically; if the term in question is of immediate practical importance (eg a reduction in wages or alteration of working hours) and the employee fails to object, that may show implied assent on their part, but in the case of other terms of little immediate importance (for example as to sick pay or possible future changes in the workplace) it may be expecting too much of an employee to make immediate objection (even if they understand the full significance of the changes), and so a tribunal in such a case should be slow to infer assent merely from lack of objection.

A particularly useful summary of the legal position here is contained in the following passage from the judgment of Elias P in *Solectron Scotland Ltd v Roper*:[387]

> The fundamental question is this: is the employee's conduct, by continuing to work, only referable to his having accepted the new terms imposed by the employer? That may sometimes be the case. For example, if an employer varies the contractual terms by, for example, changing the wage or perhaps altering job duties and the employees go along with that without protest, then in those circumstances it may be possible to infer that they have by their conduct after a period of time accepted the change in terms and conditions. If they reject the change they must either refuse to implement it or make it plain that by acceding to it, they are doing so without prejudice to their contractual rights. But sometimes the alleged variation does not require any response from the employee at all. In such a case if the employee does nothing, his conduct is entirely consistent with the original contract continuing; it is not only referable to his having accepted the new terms. Accordingly, he cannot be taken to have accepted the variation by conduct.

This 'only referable to acceptance' test was applied in *F W Farnsworth Ltd v Lacy*,[388] but with a twist in the facts. The employer was seeking to enforce a restraint of trade clause against a departing employee but that clause was not in his original (2003) contract. It had been put into a 'revised' contract given to him in 2009, but which he claimed he had never signed or returned to the employer. He argued that he had at no point accepted the new contract and so, as his silence was not only referable to implied agreement, he was not bound by the restraint clause. However, the twist in the facts was that the 2009 contract had also contained for the first time a valuable right to private medical insurance which the employee had taken up. On that basis it was held that he must be taken to have implicitly accepted the whole contract and so the clause could be enforced against him.

More significantly, the test was then approved and applied by the Court of Appeal (to hold this time that the employees had *not* impliedly consented) in *Abrahall v Nottingham City Council*,[389] the facts of which provide a good example of this problem. The council had (as was common at the time) introduced a 'single status' pay system based on a single scale, with annual progression up it for individuals. Unfortunately,

386 [1981] IRLR 477, EAT, applied in *Harlow v Artemis International Corpn Ltd* [2008] IRLR 629, QBD where an employee managed to show that, over many years, he had *never* agreed to any changes to the (contractual) redundancy rights contained in his original contract.

387 [2004] IRLR 4, EAT.

388 [2012] EWHC 2820 (Ch).

389 [2018] EWCA Civ 796, [2018] IRLR 628, CA, applied in *Re Carluccio's Ltd (in admin)* [2020] IRLR 510, HC concerning a high-profile coronavirus-related insolvency.

shortly afterwards it faced financial problems and in late 2010 it proposed to freeze the employees' pay progression for the years 2011 and 2013. The employees' union objected to this and threatened to hold a ballot for industrial action. However, in the event there was insufficient support for this and it did not happen. After that, there was no further collective objection *and* there were no individual objections either. The pay progression freeze took place, but matters then came to a head in late 2013 when it was proposed to extend the freeze for a further period. This time, there was clear objection and the union organized this legal action, claiming back-pay for the progression that should have taken place in the previous two years. The council's defence was in two parts. First, it argued that the pay progression element of the scheme was not contractually binding at all. Secondly, even if it was, the employees had agreed to its variation for the period of the freeze through their lack of objection. The Court of Appeal had little difficulty in holding that the progression was contractual, and so the result hinged on the question of acceptance by lack of objection. The tribunal had held that this had not been shown by the council on the facts and this was upheld by the Court. Giving the principal judgment, Underhill LJ reviewed the case law and laid down three main points:

1. an inference of acceptance must be unequivocal, relying on the judgment of Elias P in *Selectron Scotland Ltd v Roper* to the effect that the lack of objection must be '*only* referable to' acceptance. In other words, ultimately the employees must be given the benefit of the doubt;
2. protest at a collective level may be sufficient, especially where that is the normal means of negotiating terms, and so individual objection is not always required;
3. the reference in *Selectron* to acceptance possibly arising 'after a period of time' may cause problems of definition, but such difficulty may have to be faced and is not fatal to the arguments here.

In deciding that there had not been acceptance here, the judgment goes on to rely particularly on three further factors:

1. the changes here (unlike in *Farnsworth*) had been wholly disadvantageous to the employees; in such a case it will be inherently more difficult for an employer to establish acceptance than in a 'mixed' case of compensating advantages in an overall deal;
2. the fact of no individual objection had to be seen in the light that it had never been put to the employees that their agreement was actually needed—the change had simply been imposed;
3. the decision not to hold the industrial action ballot was not to be construed as positive evidence of acceptance.

Finally, the Court commented that the basic problem here was that there had been uncertainty and equivocality on both sides, which hardly helps in such a case.

2.6.4 **Dismiss and re-engage on new terms**

Finally, there is one other tactic that has featured largely in employers' received wisdom in the past, but which has always been legally more complex than employers have assumed. This is to dismiss all the employees in question (by giving lawful notice) and then re-engage them on the new terms ('fire and rehire'). Purely as a matter of contract law, this can work to substitute the new terms, but there are now several reasons why it can be legally dangerous for the employee. This has gone through three phases:

First, there have been two long-standing statutory reasons—(a) it is possible that the employees could claim unfair dismissal from the old contract and seek compensation to reflect the net loss of value to them of the new contract;[390] (b) this tactic has been held to constitute a 'redundancy' under the wider EU law definition used in the law on collective redundancies, and so if (as will usually be the case, given that the employer is looking to force the change through) there has not been the obligatory period of consultation with trade union or workforce representatives (where 20 or more employees are involved), the employer may lay itself open to protective awards—which could total a significant amount if large numbers of employees have been subject to this tactic;[391] moreover, in any case where the Information and Consultation of Employees Regulations 2004 apply to an employer, using this tactic (or the previous one of simply announcing changes, leaving it to employees to object) as an alternative to discussions with the employees involved may fall foul of the requirement of informing and consulting worker representatives on 'decisions likely to lead to substantial changes in work organization or in contractual relations'.[392]

Second, the courts have more recently had to struggle with a further problem here—what is the position of employees who are *unsuccessful* in the reselection procedure? Given the commonplace nature of the tactic of dismissing all and getting them to 'reapply' for their jobs (which may have a subtext not just of forcing through changes to terms and conditions but also of trying to effect a major reorganization while at the same time disguising redundancies and not being bound by the usual rules of fair selection for redundancy), it is curious that we had not previously seen more case law on it.[393] When the point finally arose directly before the EAT in *Ralph Martindale & Co Ltd v Harris*,[394] it looked as though the law was to be developed in such a way as to give the unsuccessful employee at least some legal redress. The EAT accepted the basic conceptual problem here that the normal redundancy selection rules cannot apply (because *all* are selected—QED) *but* indicated that the tribunal in such a case should impose a 'duty of care' on the employer to ensure that the 'rehiring' exercise is carried out fairly, for example by the use of open procedures with objective reselection criteria. However, when the matter came

[390] This is because of the rule in *Hogg v Dover College* [1990] ICR 39, EAT that an employee can be 'dismissed' from a particular contract and so can claim unfair dismissal even if still in that employer's employment but under a different contract: see *Alcan Extrusions v Yates* [1996] IRLR 327, EAT. Note, however, that the dismissal must still be proved to have been unfair; if the employer had pressing business reasons for the changes and handled it reasonably, that could still be a fair dismissal for 'some other substantial reason': see 8.1.2.2.

[391] *GMB v Man Truck and Bus UK Ltd* [2000] ICR 1101, [2000] IRLR 636, EAT. In two linked cases from Poland concerning hospitals in financial difficulties trying to force through changes in pay the ECJ extended this to cases of a *threat* of collective redundancies if changes are not accepted: *Socha v Szpital Specjalistyczny* C-149/16, [2018] IRLR 72; *Ciupa v II Szpital Miejski* C-429/16. For the law on collective redundancies (including the wider EC law definition and liability for protective awards) see 8.1.3.

[392] SI 2004/3426, reg 20(1)(c): see 9.9.2. This particular obligation is a strong one because the information and consultation must be 'with a view to reaching agreement' (reg 20(4)(d)). Failure by the employer can lead to a fine of up to £75,000.

[393] The EAT had harsh words for the tactic in *Church v West Lancashire NHS Trust* [1998] ICR 423, [1998] IRLR 4, EAT, but then the case was disapproved on its principal issue (of 'bumping' redundancies) in *Murray v Foyle Meats Ltd* [1999] ICR 827, [1999] IRLR 562, HL.

[394] [2008] UKEAT/166/07.

before the EAT again three years later, this novel approach was not built upon, but in fact disapproved. In *Morgan v Welsh Rugby*[395] it was held that *Ralph Martindale* established *no* general principle and that a dismissal under this fire-and-rehire tactic was fair even though the employer had departed from the reselection procedure it had adopted. More importantly, a year later the EAT under Underhill P reconsidered the law in greater detail in *Samsung Electronics UK Ltd v Monte-d'Cruz*[396] and held (again finding fair dismissal on the facts) as follows:

1. There is no absolute requirement of objectivity in selection; there will often be a heavy element of judgment and 'good faith assessments of an employee's qualities are not normally liable to be second guessed by an employment tribunal'.
2. The employer is to be given considerable discretion in choosing whom to retain, especially if the jobs have been changed and there are also external candidates (who, in the absence of discrimination, have no rights).

This is as far as the courts had reached, and it was not very promising for the employee in this difficult situation, but it is to be superseded by the third development.

Third, the whole question of fire and rehire has now been the subject of legislative developments. In 2021 it was the subject of ACAS guidance stressing that it should only be used as a last resort. This was superseded in 2024 by a Code of Practice issued by the Secretary of State which took a tougher line generally against it. However, this too had a short shelf life because more fundamental reform here was a major plank in the incoming Labour government's employment law proposals and these are now contained in the Employment Rights Act 2025. The political approach was said to be to 'ban' the tactic, but the eventual approach is more nuanced. In particular, it enacts a curious hybrid of making a dismissal in these circumstances automatically unfair, *but* then giving the employer a statutory defence; further, it only applies to the making of certain contractual changes.

The Act inserts a new s 104I into the Employment Rights Act 1996 which provides that a dismissal is unfair if the reason for it was to enable the employer to re-engage the employee under a varied contract to carry out the same (or substantially the same duties) as the employee carried out before being dismissed 395. However, as stated above, the strictness of this is then lessened by two factors:

(1) The employer may then seek to avoid the automatic unfairness if it can show that the reason for the variation sought was to eliminate, prevent, or significantly mitigate any financial difficulties affecting or likely to affect its ability to carry on the business as a going concern and that in all the circumstances it could not reasonably have avoided the need for the variation. Where this can be shown, an ordinary unfair dismissal claim subsists but is subject to further control in the section which states that in determining it a tribunal must consider five matters, namely (a) any consultation with the employee, (b) any with a recognised trade union, (c) if no recognized union, any with any other person representing the employee interest, (d) anything offered to the employee in return for agreeing the variation and (e) any further matters specified by the Secretary of State by regulations.

(2) This regime only applies to the variation of certain specified matters, referred to as 'restricted variations'. These are a reduction in pay, a variation in hours (where these determine pay), a variation of a term relating to pensions, a variation of the number of hours the employee is required to work, a variation in the timing or duration of a shift in circumstances to be set out in regulations, a reduction in the amount of

[395] [2011] IRLR 376, EAT. [396] UKEAT/0039/11.

time off to which the employee is entitled, the inclusion of any clause permitting the employer to make changes without the employee's consent and any other variation specified by the Secretary of State in regulations.

Three points may be noted. The **first** is where this leaves use of the tactic to effect a *non*-restricted variation. This is covered in the new s 104J which does not invoke automatic unfairness and does not require the employer to show that the variation is financially necessary to preserve a going concern; what it does is to stipulate that in an unfair dismissal action the tribunal must consider the same five matters (consultation, etc) set out above. The end result is thus that we have two versions of unfair dismissal here, depending on whether the variation is restricted. The **second** is that, as suggested above, this does not constitute a banning of the tactic of fire and rehire, but rather a control over it, with the employer still allowed to use it under certain stipulated conditions. The **third** is that at the time of writing the government intend to bring this part of the Act into force in October 2026.

Review and Final Thoughts

- Ending this chapter with the problems of changing contracts emphasizes two basic points here—(a) the juristic foundation of employment remains essentially contractual, even if in many ways a contract of employment has to be considered to be significantly different from a commercial contract so that certain contractual doctrines (such as illegality) may have to be applied carefully in order to attain a realistic result; (b) one of the reasons for this tension is the apparently simple point that contracts are static in nature (defining the relationship between the parties at one point in time) whereas the jobs that are subject to those contracts are fluid and capable of substantial change over time. Legally, the worst position to be in is that where an original contract of employment no longer reflects what is actually done on the ground—a recipe for litigation if the parties later fall out. How far this may or may not be remediable by reliance on devices such as implied terms will be considered in the next chapter. For further reading see footnotes 184 and 380.
- Before getting that far, however, it has been seen that it is often necessary to ***categorize*** an individual legally, to determine what their rights might be in the first place. Are they an 'employee', the pole position which attracts the most advantageous rights, such as unfair dismissal? That used to be the only question (with several tests being developed over time to try to answer it), but this chapter has seen that in modern statutory employment law we now have a fall-back position that even if employee status cannot be shown it may be possible for a putative claimant to qualify as a 'worker', which is a key to several other, subsidiary rights such as entitlement to the national minimum wage and statutory holidays and limits on working time. However, there is one complication that the reader must get their head around, namely that discrimination law as it applies to employment is expressed to apply to 'employees' but, as seen, the definition in the discrimination legislation in fact aligns this with the ***worker*** definition in employment law—desirable in that it extends the reach of these important laws beyond classic employment, but confusing as a matter of terminology.
- Whichever definition is in play, one bugbear here is the emphasis often placed by the courts not just on the physical features of these statuses (such as work organization, payment methods, and supply of tools and materials), but on the more nebulous concept of 'mutuality of obligations'. Put simply, this causes problems for casual workers who face an inherently wavy line, beyond which they may be held to have been ***too*** casual to qualify

as anything other than the ultimate category of 'self-employed', which, while sometimes giving tax advantages, also has the effect of the removal of basic employment rights. For further reading see footnote 94.

- On this subject, care must be taken with the phrase 'casual worker', because this is ***not*** a legal category, much though it is used in practice. There is no common approach to this phenomenon. Instead, it is a case of applying known legal rules to the facts of the particular form of casual work in question. Beyond that, and as an example of the piecemeal approach here, three individual examples have now been given statutory protection as a result of EU law Directives, namely part-timers, fixed-termers, and agency-supplied workers. Even here, however, this does not go as far as to determine authoritatively their employment *status* in the first place, which can still cause problems.
- While the position of, for want of a better phrase, non-typical workers is always a topic of debate, the focus of particular concern tends to change over time. The legal position of part-timers has been altered significantly (given that until only a little more than 25 years ago they were deliberately excluded from employment rights simply because they were part time), with fixed-termers and agency workers following in due course. Recently, however, the topic of particular concern has become the use by employers of zero-hour contracts.
- The use of such contracts (particularly in areas such as catering, caring, distribution, and hospitality) has grown fast, a good example of the dynamics of employment law generally. This chapter has considered the CIPD report on these contracts (August 2022; see footnote 122), one key point in which was that the topic legally is not as simple as first appears and a more 'nuanced' approach is necessary. Although they are common in the above sectors, only 3 per cent of the workforce operate under one and 77 per cent of employers said that they do not use them at all. Moreover, of workers consulted, three-quarters of those worried about unreliable work systems were *not* on zero-hour contracts, and of those on them 62 per cent were satisfied with the arrangement. On the other hand, they are also prone to major abuse by employers wanting the ultimate in flexibility and to drive down costs at the expense of their workforce. The trick legally is to take legislative steps to suppress the latter without prejudicing the former. This chapter has considered the legislative moves so far against abuse of these contracts.

Finally, note that, although the Employment Rights Act 2025 contains important provisions addressing several of the issues covered in this chapter, there is one major omission—there is *no* attempt in the Act to produce a modern statutory definition of 'employee' or 'worker', one of the most intractable areas here. There has been talk of this being addressed later and separately, but the cynic might take the view that it has disappeared into the drawer marked 'too difficult'.

3

Contracts of employment (2): content and wages

OVERVIEW

At the heart of the contractual element of employment lies the question of the terms of the contract. As in all contracts, it is usually desirable that these are express and clear, but in employment law this is often not the case. Thus:

- The chapter explores where express terms come from, especially if they are not in fact all neatly set out in writing.
- It then goes on to consider how terms become implied. Here, several significant differences between ordinary commercial contracts and employment contracts will be seen, both in the scale of the use of implied terms in employment law to 'perfect' the bargain and in the sheer strength of some of these frequently implied terms, which (contrary to contract law orthodoxy) can in practice be just as important as express terms.
- Having looked at where these terms come from, the chapter goes on to consider the principal duties that they impose on employers and employees. Some of these are old and/or obvious, such as the employer's duty to pay wages and the employee's duty of obedience to lawful orders. On the other hand, some are more recent and more at the cutting edge of modern employment law. The implied term of trust and respect by the employer is the prime example; it is obviously important in its own right, but its wider significance will be seen in Chapter 7 (Unfair dismissal), where it often forms the basis for a departing employee's claim to have been constructively dismissed by reason of the employer's unacceptable behaviour.
- The chapter concludes by considering specifically the legal provisions on what will often be the most important element of the employment relationship, namely the obligation to pay wages. This is a combination of old (but still relevant) common law on matters such as inability or refusal to work and mistaken overpayments, and modern statutory intervention on matters such as sick pay, recovery of unlawful deductions from wages, and the national minimum wage.

Context

The first edition of this book was written in 1980, when statutory coverage of employment matters was becoming established and expanding consistently. This meant that the book started with chapters on industrial relations law and the modern statutory law on employment protection, only then going on to one chapter (only) on all contractual matters, the implication being that over time these would become merely (in cricketing terms) a long stop to fill in any gaps in the statutory coverage. Over the later editions, that prediction proved inaccurate and, especially as the extent and density of trade union membership decreased (most notably in the private sector), the contractual base of employment became *more* important. Now it is important to start with that contractual base before going on to see how statutory rights fit onto it. To take two principal examples: (1) the existence (since 1965) of a right to a statutory redundancy payment of a modest amount provided the classic 'floor of rights' and *encouraged* the development of contractual redundancy schemes of a more generous (sometimes stunningly more generous) nature; and (2) the existence (since 1971) of remedies for unfair dismissal has *strengthened* contractual rights, in that an employer will be much more wary of riding roughshod over them if the result may be a dismissal (actual or more likely constructive) leading to an expensive tribunal claim.

While some contracts of employment in more traditional industries are still essentially collective in nature, with individual employees having little influence over their content (what in French law would be classed as 'contrats d'adhesion', the French for 'take it or leave it'), in many other economic areas there is much more reality to the idea of 'individual contracting' by individuals with skills making them positively in demand. Such contracts (now often of considerable length and detail) are much more likely to be subject to realistic enforcement by aggrieved employees. One other factor indirectly contributing to this movement has been the demise of the idea of a 'job for life' (40 years heavily dependent on one employer, with a clock and if lucky a pension at the end of it) and its replacement with an expectation of multiple employments over time, hopefully with better contractual terms each time. The bottom line is that contracts and their terms (expressed or implied) have arguably become over time more important, not less, as is shown year on year by employment tribunal statistics.

3.1 **Express terms**

3.1.1 **Generally**

While the employer and employee are generally free to determine the content of the terms of employment, there are now legislative provisions in Part I of the Employment Rights Act 1996 requiring the employer to give written notice of certain basic terms. These provisions were considered in Chapter 2, where it was seen that while this notice does not itself constitute the contract it will be strong evidence as to its terms, and indeed, if it is signed as such by the employee, it may be construed as the written contract, according to *Gascol Conversions Ltd v Mercer*.[1] For present purposes, the importance of these provisions is that they require that major terms be put down in writing and probably encourage the employer to give the employee an individual written contract of employment; as with all contracts, written terms are generally to be preferred for the certainty that they bring,[2] and the legislation attempts to minimize the incidence of what was traditionally referred to as 'factory gate employment' where an employee was taken on without having the relevant terms settled, only finding out the governing terms some time later and leaving potentially important matters to later decision by the courts. The advantage of certainty is obvious to the lawyer (even if sometimes it can seem a counsel of perfection by their clients). Three particular areas can benefit from it:

1. Basic terms—the last thing that the parties want is to fall out (potentially expensively) over basic terms of employment such as pay and overtime, either during employment or (even more of a threat to the employer) on termination where the employee, already suing for example for unfair dismissal, also alleges long-standing failures to honour the contract properly.
2. Known legal bear traps—we shall see during this chapter that some apparently simple employment problems can give rise to remarkably complex and underdeveloped legal issues if there is no contractual term applicable and the matter is left to the common law. One example among many is whether an employee unable to turn up for work because on remand for a criminal offence still has to be paid; it might be thought that the common-sense answer is 'no', but we shall see that at common

[1] [1974] ICR 420, [1974] IRLR 155, CA; see 2.3.2.

[2] For a particularly salutary example see *Stubbes v Trower, Still & Keeling* [1987] IRLR 321, CA, where solicitors, in offering articles, omitted to state expressly that the applicant had to pass the requisite examinations before beginning, and the Court of Appeal refused to find that there was an implied term to that effect on the facts; in the words of one commentator, you cannot always rely on common sense and implied terms to rectify a contractual oversight.

law there may be arguments both ways.[3] The answer legally would be for the contract to contain an express term making clear when the employer may suspend the employee without pay. Another good example is what is to happen if an employee cannot attend work because of adverse weather—again, are they still entitled to be paid? The ACAS advice on this merely states that it 'depends on the contract'; in the absence of some express coverage, that leaves the matter subject to possible implied terms and/or custom and practice, which may be highly arguable.

3. New potential problems—changes in technology and other surrounding circumstances can easily have an impact on employment law, which again can lead to controversy. A good modern example is the use of electronic media by employees. When computerization first became common, an initial employer solution was to try to ban *any* personal use while at work, but that soon became unworkable. Thus, *some* usage became common, raising issues of how much and for what purposes (especially for Internet use and especially in the case of use for illegal purposes that could conceivably incur liability on the employer as well as the individual employee). The rise of social media only exacerbated this because it also raised the issue of usage outside working hours, but in a wider sense concerning the employer; examples would be breaches of confidentiality, harassment of fellow employees, or giving vent to workplace frustrations by overt and public criticism of the employer—legitimate freedom of expression, or unacceptable breaches of good faith by the employee? If the employer does not at least attempt to lay down express ground rules in relation to such matters and then is faced with what it considers a possible dismissible offence by an employee, it lays itself open to an argument for unfair dismissal on bases such as lack of clarity ('you never told me that this was not allowed') or disparity of treatment ('Miss X did that six months ago and only got a telling off'). Sound legal advice therefore is to cover such matters expressly in the contract (or at least in sub-contractual documents such as policy statements), although in practice this can demand considerable forethought on the part of the employer, in trying to anticipate the many ways in which it could all go horribly wrong.

Certainty this can, however, work both ways, and if the parties set something down in writing they should ensure that it is accurate, as once it is expressed there is less room for further extrinsic evidence as to their intentions. As an example of this, in *Nelson v BBC*,[4] the contract stated that the employee could be required to work when and where the corporation demanded, but when the corporation closed down the Caribbean service in which he worked, they claimed that it was to be implied that he was only employed for the purposes of that one service and therefore that he was redundant; the tribunal and the EAT accepted this, but the Court of Appeal rejected it, since the express term was in unrestricted language, and as a basic principle of contract law it was impossible to imply a restriction of the kind that the tribunal had found. On the other hand, even in contract law there are exceptions to the rule against extrinsic evidence, particularly where a written contract does not completely cover all the matters upon which the parties had previously agreed. Thus, in *Tayside Regional Council v McIntosh*,[5] a job advertisement for a vehicle mechanic stated that a clean driving licence was essential and this was restated at

[3] See this chapter, 3.5.1.4.

[4] [1977] ICR 649, [1977] IRLR 148, CA; see the discussion of this case in *Cowen v Haden Ltd* [1983] ICR 1, [1982] IRLR 314, CA, which shows the importance of the proper construction to be placed upon the express term in question.

[5] [1982] IRLR 272. This is consistent with the view expressed by Lord Hoffmann in *Carmichael v National Power plc* [1999] ICR 1226, [2000] IRLR 43, HL that it may be necessary to look to several sources to discern the whole contract of employment.

interview. When later the employee lost his licence and was dismissed, he pointed to the fact that the written terms which he had been given upon appointment made no mention of a driving licence, but the Scottish EAT refused to accept that that meant there was no express term as to a licence. The basic distinction between these two case examples (out of many) is that in the latter extrinsic evidence was being properly used to amplify a written agreement which was incomplete, whereas in the former it was being used improperly to alter the meaning of an existing written term.

3.1.2 **Written or oral**

In line with normal contract law, it should also be remembered that to be an express term, it does not have to be in writing, and so an alternative argument may be that something that was said (or promised) went beyond extrinsic evidence and was actually an *oral* express term. Naturally, there may be major problems of proof in such a case (with the defendant swearing blind that no such thing was ever said) and as a matter of fact there may be a difference between things said on a relatively formal occasion (such as a recruitment or promotion interview) and things said more informally.

Two rather bizarre cases illustrate this. In *Judge v Crown Leisure Ltd*,[6] the Court of Appeal held against an employee who alleged that he was contractually entitled to a pay rise promised to him at the end of the firm's Christmas party (hic!). Secondly, *Blue v Ashley*[7] (the 'Sports Direct' case) figured widely in the press, again because of its somewhat 'unusual' facts and the sheer amounts of alcohol involved at the material times. The claimant sued for £15m that he alleged had been promised by the owner of the company if a certain target was reached. The contentious element of the case was that the alleged promise had been in the course of a 'business meeting' on licensed premises that involved an amount of alcohol that to most ordinary mortals would have proved fatal. The defendant owner said that any mention of such a figure had just been banter or a joke. However, the claimant sought to show that this sort of 'informal' management style ('an unorthodox approach to taking business decisions in informal settings while consuming substantial amounts of alcohol') was normal for the defendant and that it was therefore appropriate in these unusual circumstances to find a contractual intent to the offer. The court decided against this and held for the defendant. As Leggatt J commented at the end of his judgment: 'The fact that Mr Blue has since convinced himself that the offer was a serious one, and that a legally binding agreement was made, shows only that the human capacity for wishful thinking knows few bounds.'

One other minefield can arise where, as a drafting matter, a written contract seeks to establish an express term by reference to some other document. The safest way to do this is to incorporate it specifically by reference and attach it to the contract (or state where it can be found). In *Jowitt v Pioneer Technology (UK) Ltd*,[8] the contract promised the employee coverage by a long-term disability scheme which the employer had had underwritten by an insurance company. However, instead of specifically incorporating that policy into the

[6] [2005] IRLR 823, CA.

[7] [2017] EWHC 1828 (Comm). More soberly, in *Prometric Ltd v Cunliffe* [2016] EWCA Civ 191, [2016] IRLR 776 the Court of Appeal held that where professionals (here, HR directors) discuss a significant matter such as pension rights, a court will normally expect any oral agreement then to be *reflected* in subsequent documentation; in the case itself, lack of any such documentation was fatal to the employee's claim of an oral express term (granting him unusually generous pension rights) based on one conversation 16 years earlier. Lack of subsequent documentation was also a factor in *Blue v Ashley* (though *Prometric* was not cited) and subsequently in *Christie v Canaccord Genuity Ltd* [2022] IRLR 672, QB.

[8] [2003] IRLR 356, CA, applied in *Amdocs Systems Ltd v Langton* UKEAT/0093/20.

contract, the employer tried to précis the policy in its own words in the contract itself. In doing so, it got a key element wrong and ended up promising much more than the policy itself underwrote. When the employee made a claim on this benefit, the employer tried to limit its liability to what the policy actually covered (ie what it had *meant* by its précis), but the Court of Appeal agreed with the employee that all that mattered to him was what *his* contract actually said. The employer was thus left to shoulder the wider (uninsured) liability that it had managed to create by its poor drafting.

3.1.3 **Four problems**

Four current uncertainties relating to express terms of contracts of employment are worth mentioning at this stage. The *first* is whether there is any requirement that an express contractual right for an employer (however clearly expressed) must be *exercised* reasonably. The traditional view is that there can be no such requirement; a contract is a contract, and if the employee agrees a term they must abide by it, even if its application by the employer seems harsh (eg where an employer activates an unrestricted mobility clause to require an employee to move hundreds of miles with little or no warning).[9] However, modern case law has suggested a significant modification of that position and this is considered in 3.2.1; if this trend continues, it will be of major importance and marks another departure of contracts of employment from orthodox contract law.

The *second* uncertainty is whether an employer can, in effect, try to pre-empt any attempts by the employee to add to the written terms by casting the employment contract in terms of an 'entire contract'.[10] In the leading case on this developing area of contract law generally, Lightman J put it thus:

> The purpose of an entire agreement clause is to preclude a party to a written agreement from threshing through the undergrowth and finding, in the course of negotiations, some (chance) remark or statement (often long-forgotten or difficult to recall or explain) upon which to found a claim, such as the present, to the existence of a collateral warranty. The entire agreement clause obviates the occasion for any such search . . . For such a clause constitutes a binding agreement between the parties that the full contractual terms are to be found in the document containing the clause and not elsewhere, and that, accordingly, any promises or assurances made in the course of the negotiations (which, in the absence of such a clause, might have effect as a collateral warranty) shall have no contractual force, save in so far as they are reflected and given effect in the document.[11]

Should this development in commercial contracts law apply equally to employment contracts? There is an argument that it should not; commercial contracts are *expected* to be certain and preferably reduced to clear written terms (hence the general dislike of implied terms in ordinary contract law: see 3.2.1), whereas an employment relationship is likely to be far more amorphous, easily entered, and possibly rapidly evolving. An entire contract clause could lead in practice to an even greater danger of the contract terms and employment realities diverging radically than is already inherent in our present contract-based law on employment. The little authority that has hitherto existed in the employment law

[9] *Rank Xerox Ltd v Churchill* [1988] IRLR 280, EAT.

[10] One form of this would be a clause stating to the effect that '[t]his agreement constitutes the entire agreement between us with regard to its subject matter, and supersedes any previous agreement (whether verbal or written) made between us at any time'.

[11] *Inntrepreneur Pub Co v East Crown Ltd* [2000] 3 EGLR 31 at 33.

context has shown a spectrum of approaches. At the pro-employer end, in *White v Bristol Rugby Club Ltd*,[12] a professional rugby player signed up by a club under a contract which provided for an advance on earnings tried to avoid going through with the engagement by arguing that if he returned the advance he was free to go elsewhere. His primary argument was that there was an oral express term to that effect, arising from discussions that he had had before signing the contract with the club's chief executive. The contract, however, contained an entire agreement clause, stating that the contract contained the whole agreement and that the parties had not relied on any oral or written representations made by other persons.[13] The judge held that this clause was applicable and, as a matter purely of construction, covered the circumstances here, so that no oral term could arise. This forced the employee back on to arguments relating to the terms of the contract *as they stood*, and whether under these he had a right not to go through with the engagement; it was held that he did not. In the middle of the spectrum, in *Fontana (GB) Ltd v Fabio*[14] a general manager's contract made no reference to any right to pension contributions (in fact it contained a clause stating that there were to be none), but the manager said that there had been an oral agreement to such a right. When later dismissed, he claimed arrears of pension contributions alongside an unfair dismissal claim. The contract contained a clause stating that it *substituted* previous agreements and arrangements, whether written, oral, or implied. Did this preclude his claim? The EAT held that it did not; it accepted that an entire contract clause can apply to an employment contract but, applying *White v Bristol Rugby Club Ltd*, held that as a matter of construction this particular clause was not strong enough to preclude this claim because it did not expressly claim that the contract contained all the terms. At the pro-employee end of the spectrum, in *RNLI v Bushaway*[15] the EAT had little difficulty in avoiding an entire agreement clause (in a far more run-of-the-mill context than that of a well-known rugby player) by finding ambiguities in the clause's application, allowing a finding that it had not been what the parties had really intended.

The *third* uncertainty concerns the extent to which an employer may use express terms to reserve to itself a right of unilateral variation. Flexibility in employment has been a nostrum of modern managerialism for some time now, and there will certainly be cases where an employer can lawfully claim to have carefully built in flexibility and an ability to change a particular term or, alternatively, that the matter has been so drafted as to remain non-contractual (so that change remains in the employer's discretion).[16] The question is whether a point could be reached where such phrasing became so unconscionable and vague as to be unenforceable; the contractual doctrine of uncertainty would be inappropriate in an employment context because it would render the whole contract void (to the employee's disadvantage), and so far this point has not had to be fully explored by

[12] [2002] IRLR 204, QBD.

[13] There is some discussion in the judgment (at paras 30–35) as to whether the latter half of the clause (no reliance) could be subject to the Misrepresentation Act 1967, s 3, which subjects a clause of a contract excluding or restricting liability for misrepresentation to the reasonableness test that applies under the Unfair Contract Terms Act 1977. The relationship between s 3 and an entire agreement clause remains subject to conflicting authority, as the judge here did not have to decide the issue because the first half of the clause was effective anyway.

[14] UKEAT/140/01.

[15] [2005] IRLR 674, EAT: the case concerned the transmutation of an agency worker into a permanent employee. The entire agreement clause was not permitted to stand in the way of the EAT's decision, which was in effect to look behind the wording of the original contract, at what had happened in practice.

[16] *Airlie v City of Edinburgh District Council* [1996] IRLR 516, EAT (terms of a bonus scheme expressly subject to variation by employer after consultation with the workforce; no requirement of agreement before revision, provided consultation carried out).

the courts. The nearest that they have come is in *Wandsworth London Borough Council v D'Silva*,[17] where, after upholding the employer's contention that a sickness absence policy in a code of practice remained non-contractual and so within the employer's power to change, Lord Woolf MR said obiter that although a party to the contract could reserve a right of unilateral variation, it would take clear language to do it and a court should, in construing the contract, try to avoid a construction allowing a power of unilateral variation of significant employee rights which could produce an unreasonable result. This can be seen in *Land Securities Trillium Ltd v Thornley*,[18] where the employer claimed that a significant change to the employee's duties (from exercising her profession as an architect to managing an office) was permissible under a clause requiring her to perform to the best of her abilities 'all the duties of this post and any other post you may subsequently hold', but the EAT construed this narrowly as only referring to any other post that she had *agreed* to undertake. While this is a significant decision, whether a court could go further in the case of an absolutely clearly drafted power of unilateral variation that was equally clearly inequitable in its result remains to be seen.

The *fourth* uncertainty is the extent to which one or both of the parties to an agreement can try to *entrench* part of that agreement, in particular to describing a term so produced as 'permanent'. In strict contract law, nothing is permanent and any agreement can be remade at a later date. Thus, any attempt to entrench could be seen as, at best, a benevolent wish or, at worst, well-meaning *excreta tauri*. However, any employers taking this view were given a shot across the bows in *Tesco Stores Ltd v USDAW*.[19] USDAW was the recognized union for employees in the employer's distribution centres. In 2007 these were reorganized, with some closures. As part of an agreement with the union, those in closing centres were given an incentive to relocate to open ones in the form of 'retained pay' on top of normal rates, which was referred to in the agreement as being 'permanent' and only changeable by mutual consent. Informal documentation from the employer referred to it as being 'guaranteed for life'. On that basis the claimant employees accepted the moves. In 2021 the employer wished to end it, proposing to buy it out with a lump sum. The employees refused and, faced with an attempt by the employer to force it through by fire and rehire, brought High Court proceedings for an injunction to enforce their rights. This was granted, then discharged by the Court of Appeal, but on further appeal the Supreme Court reinstated the injunction. The employer had argued that at common law there was always a right to terminate on notice which could not be negated by a stipulation that a term was to be permanent, but the court held to the contrary. The permanency stipulation had been an essential element of the original agreement and there needed to be an implied term to enforce it, otherwise the employer could simply override it at any time; such a term was not too wide as it did not in fact guarantee lifetime employment (and would not prevent a lawful, dismissal, eg for misconduct), but it would enforce the employer's original promise for as long as the individual remained in that employment. Clearly this case was on particularly strong facts and it remains to be seen how far it will be developed, but the point is that the principle is established at the highest level.

[17] [1998] IRLR 193, CA. See 2.6 and in particular the decision for the employer in *Bateman v ASDA Stores Ltd* UKEAT/0221/09.

[18] [2005] IRLR 765. The EAT also held that a reference to 'any other duties that may reasonably be required of you' was to be construed in the circumstances of the individual employee (here, a professional who feared losing her skills), not the employer's commercial reasons for the change.

[19] [2024] IRLR 998, [2025] ICR 107, SC.

3.2 The implication of terms

3.2.1 The process of implication

Even when the statutory provisions for written particulars are complied with, there will be areas left in a contract of employment where no terms are expressed, so that if a dispute arises in one of these areas the court or tribunal may have to have recourse to implied terms. The implication of terms is a concept of application to the whole law of contract, but in the context of employment it has evolved along more specialized lines. Starting from orthodox contract theory, the basis of implication is subjective, in that the court or tribunal should look at the likely intention of the parties at the time of contracting, and should not imply terms simply because they appear (objectively) reasonable when the case is viewed in hindsight.[20] The two classic tests for an implied term are (a) that it is necessary to give 'business efficacy' to the transaction as must have been intended by both parties[21] or (b) that it is so obvious that it goes without saying, so that if an officious bystander had suggested that it be expressed, the parties would have testily suppressed him with a common 'Oh, of course!'[22] Moreover, it has been clearly stated that the presumption is against the adding to contracts of terms which the parties have not expressed, particularly if the term in question is of a novel nature.[23] This traditional view of implied terms has, however, been considerably modified in the case of contracts of employment, where historically so many terms (often the basic ones) were not expressed and where the process of implication has been much used to fill in the details once it was clear that an employment relationship existed.[24] It has been modified in three main ways.

3.2.1.1 Inferred terms

Although cases will of course arise where courts find implied terms on the above traditional grounds,[25] there are also cases where they appear to have been more willing to imply terms because they appear reasonable in all the circumstances, rather than because of the supposed subjective intention of the parties, which, in the reality of a vague hiring, may have been non-existent. There is still a large role for the genuine factual implied term but in this context the court or tribunal may feel more ready to imply—or, more accurately perhaps, infer—a term because it seems reasonable in all the circumstances.

[20] *Reigate v Union Manufacturing Co (Ramsbottom) Ltd* [1918] 1 KB 592 at 605, CA, per Scrutton LJ.

[21] *The Moorcock* (1889) 14 PD 64 at 68, CA per Bowen LJ.

[22] *Shirlaw v Southern Foundries Ltd* [1939] 2 KB 206 at 227, CA, per McKinnon LJ; see *Spring v National Amalgamated Stevedores and Dockers Society* [1956] 2 All ER 221, [1956] 1 WLR 585.

[23] *Luxor (Eastbourne) Ltd v Cooper* [1941] AC 108 at 137, HL per Lord Wright. An attempt to widen the approach to implication in commercial contracts, to make it easier to do so, was rejected and orthodoxy reaffirmed by the Supreme Court in *Marks & Spencer plc v BNP Paribas Securities Services Trust Co (Jersey) Ltd* [2015] UKSC 72, [2015] 1 WLR 1843.

[24] Certainty of terms is classically a prerequisite for a binding contract, but this too has been qualified almost to the point of extinction in contracts of employment: see *Powell v Braun* [1954] 1 All ER 484, [1954] 1 WLR 401, CA; and *National Coal Board v Galley* [1958] 1 All ER 91, [1958] 1 WLR 16, CA. The problem is that the result of applying it could be to make the whole contract of employment void (regardless of how long the employee had actually been working for the employer), which is simply not an option in employment law. On the other hand, the doctrine of certainty might apply to one particular aspect or term of the contract, where the rest of the agreement is not in issue: see *Fontana (GB) Ltd v Fabio*, n 14.

[25] See eg *Ali v Christian Salvesen Food Services Ltd* [1997] ICR 25, [1997] IRLR 17, CA, where the question was whether it was possible to imply a term into an 'annualized hours' contract as to what was to happen to an employee leaving part of the way through the year, the parties having failed to cover the point expressly. The EAT thought it was, but the Court of Appeal held to the contrary and the loss lay where it fell.

This more objective approach can clearly be seen in the reasoning of the Court of Appeal in *Mears v Safecar Security Ltd.*[26] The case primarily concerned a complaint of failure to give the obligatory written statement of terms of employment, and the question of whether wages are to be paid during sickness,[27] but (although certain rather extreme dicta that ultimately a tribunal may have to 'invent' a term were later disapproved)[28] it also contains important guidance on the implication of terms into contracts of employment, showing that in the case of such contracts the normal concepts of implied intention of the parties and business efficacy may have little part to play. Instead, a tribunal may have to take a broader approach and be ready to insert a reasonable term based on all the evidence of the relationship between the parties *and* what had happened in practice *since* the employment began (particularly where it is important that *some* term be included, for example whether or not such pay is payable, or where the employee could be made to work).[29] It is true that this case arose under the Employment Rights Act 1996, s 11, and much of what is said about implying terms is inextricably linked to the court's approach to the tribunal's powers to declare or amend terms of employment under that section, but it is submitted that their approach to the implication of terms should be applicable to a common law action as well as a statutory one—it would be ridiculous if different principles were to apply depending on which forum the employee happened to choose; after all, on the facts of the case, the employee could just as easily have gone to the county court and *claimed* sick pay. The same approach can be seen in the later decision of the Court of Appeal in *Courtaulds Northern Spinning Ltd v Sibson*,[30] where, in the context of the necessary implication into a contract of employment of a location/mobility clause (where the contract was silent on the matter, but the question was vital for deciding a point on constructive dismissal), Slade LJ said:

> [I]n cases such as the present where it is essential to imply some term into the contract of employment as to place of work, the court does not have to be satisfied that the parties, if asked, would in fact have agreed the term before entering into the contract. The court merely has to be satisfied that the implied term is one which the parties would probably have agreed *if they were being reasonable.* (Emphasis added.)

3.2.1.2 **Imposed terms**

The contract of employment has long been surrounded not only by terms implied or inferred from the facts of any given employment but also by a quite distinct form of 'implied term', namely the term which will be imposed by the law onto most or all contracts of employment simply because the relationship of employment exists (except in so far as the parties are free to exclude it expressly and do so), which once again has little to do with any supposed intention of the parties. In *Lister v Romford Ice and Cold Storage Co Ltd*,[31] Viscount Simonds said that the question whether there was an implied term that the employer would ensure that the employee was insured had little to do with the facts of a particular contract or any question of business efficacy, but depended instead on more general considerations relating to the very nature of contracts of employment.

26 [1982] 2 All ER 865, [1982] IRLR 183, CA.
27 See 2.3.2 and this chapter, 3.5.2.
28 *Eagland v British Telecommunications plc* [1993] ICR 644, [1992] IRLR 323, CA.
29 See the facts of *Jones v Associated Tunnelling Co Ltd* [1981] IRLR 477, EAT.
30 [1988] ICR 451, [1988] IRLR 305, CA; the dictum cited is at 460 and 309, respectively.
31 [1957] AC 555, [1957] 1 All ER 125, HL.

This approach is clearly seen in the following two dicta. In *Sterling Engineering Co Ltd v Patchett*,[32] Lord Reid said:

> There are cases in which it has been said that the employer's right to inventions made by an employee in the course of his employment arises from an implied term in the contract of employment. Strictly speaking, I think that an implied term is something which, in the circumstances of a particular case, the law may read into the contract if the parties are silent, and it would be reasonable to do so; it is something over and above the ordinary incidents of the particular type of contract. If it were necessary in this case to find an implied term in that sense I should be in some difficulty. But the phrase 'implied term' can be used to denote a term inherent in the nature of the contract which the Law will imply in every case unless the parties agree to vary or exclude it.

In *Scally v Southern Health and Social Services Board*,[33] Lord Bridge referred to the clear distinction between

> the search for an implied term necessary to give business efficacy to a particular contract and the search, based on wider considerations, for a term which the law will imply as a necessary incident of a definable category of contractual relationship.

In *Malik v BCCI SA (in liquidation)*,[34] Lord Steyn referred to such terms as 'default rules', which are standardized terms that are incidents of all contracts of employment.

It is this form of 'implied term' that will be discussed under the headings of 'Employer's implied duties' and 'Employee's implied duties', and it could well be argued that the phrase 'implied term' should be discarded and these duties viewed simply as incidents of the law of employment.

3.2.1.3 **Overriding terms**

One of the most interesting developments over the years in this area is the possible development of the concept of 'overriding terms' in a contract of employment, that is, that certain terms may be so important that they will be applied by the courts irrespective of the parties' intentions.[35] This would have the radical effect that they could even be used to qualify or attack clear express terms of the contract, something that in orthodox contract law no 'implied' term should be able to do. The prime candidate for beatification as an overriding term is the implied term of trust and respect,[36] which, if applied widely, could be seen as having the effect that even where an employer has the contractual right to insist on something, it must do so *reasonably*. If not, the employee would be able to leave and claim constructive dismissal, through the employer's breach of that implied term. Perhaps the clearest example is an unrestricted mobility clause. Can the employer

[32] [1955] AC 534 at 547, [1955] 1 All ER 369 at 376, HL.

[33] [1991] ICR 771, [1991] IRLR 522, HL; the decision in this case is considered in 3.3.7.

[34] [1997] ICR 606, [1997] IRLR 462, HL; the decision in this case is considered in 3.4.

[35] This would mark them off from the above discussion of imposed terms, since the latter (as in the dictum from Lord Reid) are conceived of applying 'unless the parties agree to vary or exclude them'; see also per Lord Steyn in *Malik v BCCI*, n 34. For an interesting argument that the courts should go even further and hold that the employment relationship gives rise to *fiduciary* duties (which could not be excluded) see Clarke 'Mutual Trust and Confidence, Fiduciary Relationships and the Duty of Disclosure' (1999) 28 ILJ 348. The current judicial approach, however, is entirely to the contrary, finding no fiduciary duties in an ordinary employment relationship: *Nottingham University v Fishel* [2000] ICR 1462, [2000] IRLR 471: see Sims (2001) 30 ILJ 101. *Fishel* was approved by the Court of Appeal in *Ranson v Customer Systems plc* [2012] IRLR 769, CA.

[36] See this chapter, 3.3.4.

simply insist on the literal wording and require the employee to move their place of work from Norwich to Carlisle over a weekend and with no prior warning, or can the employee claim that that insistence (though technically within the employer's contractual power) is in breach of the term of trust and respect on the facts? Orthodox contract law is, of course, on the employer's side,[37] but there have been developments. Where there is no express mobility clause and a court is having to imply one, there may be less problem in attaching implied conditions such as reasonable notice.[38] However, what may eventually prove to have been the crucial step was taken by the EAT in *United Bank Ltd v Akhtar*,[39] where there was an express clause allowing the employer to move the employee to any branch in the UK. In spite of that, the EAT held that the employee could claim constructive dismissal when the employer ordered him to move from Leeds to Birmingham on only six days' notice and refused to grant his request for more time because of his personal circumstances. As well as finding an implied term of reasonable notice, the EAT held even more fundamentally that the employers' conduct in exercising their contractual rights was a fundamental breach of the implied term of trust and respect:

> We take it as inherent that there may well be conduct which is either calculated or likely to destroy or seriously damage the relationship of trust and respect between employer and employee which a literal interpretation of the written words of the contract might appear to justify, and it is in this sense that we consider that in the field of employment law it is proper to imply an *overriding obligation* [of trust and respect] which is independent of, and in addition to, the literal interpretation of the actions which are permitted to the employer under the terms of the contract. (Emphasis added.)[40]

At first sight, the subsequent EAT decision in *White v Reflecting Roadstuds Ltd*[41] may appear to resile from *Akhtar*, as it was held that an employee who resigned after a transfer to a lower paid job which was permitted by the contract could not claim constructive dismissal. However, it is suggested that that was because the employee argued simply that a contractual right such as this must always be exercised reasonably; this was too much to accept and Wood P said that *Akhtar* does not establish any such sweeping principle. At the end of his judgment, though, he recognized that there was a problem with unconscionable action by an employer and offered the following solutions:

> As Knox J emphasised in *Akhtar* a purely 'capricious' decision would not be within the express mobility clause. Likewise, in the present case if there were no reasonable or sufficient grounds for the view that Mr White required to be moved . . . then there would be a breach of the clause. Secondly, it must be emphasized that as a result of the *Woods* decision[42] there is the *overriding implied term* as to the relationship of trust and respect between employer and employee and this is where communication is so important. (Emphasis added.)[43]

[37] This straightforward approach was applied as late as *Rank Xerox Ltd v Churchill* [1988] IRLR 280, EAT.

[38] *Prestwick Circuits Ltd v McAndrew* [1990] IRLR 191, Ct of Sess; however, the Court of Appeal had earlier declined to add any 'reasonable exercise' conditions to an implied mobility clause in *Courtaulds Northern Spinning Ltd v Sibson* [1988] IRLR 305, CA.

[39] [1989] IRLR 507, EAT. See also *French v Barclays Bank plc* [1998] IRLR 646, CA, where the termination of an interest-free bridging loan to a relocated employee when it became too onerous was held to be in breach of the term of trust and respect, even though the granting of such a loan was clearly expressed to be discretionary.

[40] At 512, per Knox J.

[41] [1991] ICR 733, [1991] IRLR 331, EAT.

[42] ie *Woods v WM Car Services (Peterborough) Ltd* [1981] ICR 666, [1981] IRLR 347, the leading decision of Browne-Wilkinson P in the EAT on trust and respect; see this chapter, 3.3.4.

[43] [1991] ICR 733 at 742, [1991] IRLR 331 at 335.

The implication must therefore be that in a case such as this, the employee may have a good argument if it is couched properly (in terms of the term of trust and respect, *not* simply as a general allegation of unreasonableness), and that *White* does not negate *Akhtar*.[44]

In addition to mobility and flexibility clauses, similar ideas of the use of the overriding term of trust and respect to qualify or restrain reliance by an employer on its strict contractual rights have been seen in relation to the imposition of disciplinary measures,[45] the exercise of a power to suspend an employee,[46] and (most strikingly of all) the administration of employee pension funds.[47]

The other principal candidate so far for an overriding term is the employer's obligation to take care of the employee's health and safety. The leading case, *Johnstone v Bloomsbury Health Authority*,[48] shows very different approaches to the matter, which in turn shows well the conceptual difficulties yet to be addressed. This was a highly publicized case of a legal challenge to excessive hours by junior hospital doctors. The doctor claimant's contract stated a standard working week of 40 hours but a further 48 hours on call, which was regularly required, sometimes up to 100 hours per week. He argued that this had a detrimental effect on his health[49] and was a breach of the employer's duty to take reasonable care for his health and safety. The proceedings in fact concerned an interlocutory application by the employers to have the claim struck out, as disclosing no cause of action. By a majority, the Court of Appeal allowed it to proceed. Leggett LJ, dissenting, applied orthodox contract law, stating that reliance on a clear express power could not make the employer in breach of an implied term (ie the traditional primacy of express terms; the doctor had signed the contract and must abide by its clear terms). The problem and fascination of the case is that the two majority judges differed in their reasoning. Browne-Wilkinson V-C took a middle path; he said that the extra 48 hours in question were an 'optional right' for the employers, not an absolute right, and, while there must be no blatant conflict between an express term and an implied term, it was not improper to read in a term that, in exercising their *discretion* to call for further hours, the employers had to have regard to the employee's health and safety. However, possibly the more significant judgment for the future is that of Stuart-Smith LJ, who held more simply that although the contract gave the power to require work of up to 88 hours on average, that power had to be exercised subject to other contractual terms, in particular that relating to health and safety. The difference between the two majority judgments would be shown if a contract required a mandatory 88 hours, as Browne-Wilkinson V-C accepted that in that case, that express term would have to be allowed to stand, whereas Stuart-Smith LJ would still have been prepared to make it subject to the requirement of health and safety.[50]

[44] In the unreported decision in *St Budeaux Royal British Legion Club v Cropper* (EAT 39/94) *Akhtar* was applied to hold that a flexibility clause applied in a 'high-handed and irresponsible manner' by the employer (when cutting hours) was a breach of the term of trust and respect.

[45] The idea being that the exercise by an employer of its discretion under a disciplinary procedure must be subject to requirements of reasonableness and proportionality: *BBC v Beckett* [1983] IRLR 43, EAT; *Cawley v South Wales Electricity Board* [1985] IRLR 89, EAT; *Stanley Cole (Wainfleet) Ltd v Sheridan* [2003] ICR 297, [2003] IRLR 52, EAT.

[46] *McClory v Post Office* [1992] ICR 758, [1993] IRLR 159, EAT.

[47] *Imperial Group Pension Trust Ltd v Imperial Tobacco Ltd* [1991] ICR 524, [1991] IRLR 66, where Browne-Wilkinson V-C (applying his own previous decision in *Woods v WM Car Services (Peterborough) Ltd* [1981] ICR 666, [1981] IRLR 347) held that the black and white nature of pension fund deeds and rules should be impliedly subject to the limitation that they must be exercised in good faith and so as not to undermine the employees' trust and respect: see Nobles (1991) 20 ILJ 137.

[48] [1991] ICR 269, [1991] IRLR 118, CA; see Dolding and Fawlk (1992) 55 MLR 562.

[49] Let alone the prospects for a patient (treated in the hundredth hour) of a long and prosperous life.

[50] The judge makes the significant point that even where the contract stipulates high hours, that still only gives the employer a *power* to call for them: 'There is no obligation to require the men to [work] for 88 hours in the week, and if by so doing he exposes him to foreseeable risk of injury he will be liable': [1991] ICR 269 at 277, [1991] IRLR 118 at 121, CA.

3.2.2 **Particular sources of terms**

3.2.2.1 **Collective bargains**

The effect of incorporation

Although its use as the primary form of setting terms and conditions of employment has declined markedly in recent years,[51] collective bargaining was in the past of central importance, and still is in areas retaining such coverage; and yet the precise legal effect of a collective bargain on the contracts of employment of employees potentially affected by it has always been a topic of some difficulty. The bargain is often classified as performing two functions—regulating the relationship between the bargainers, that is, employers' association or employer and trade union, and settling provisions (eg wage rates and hours) intended for the individual contracts of the employees who are covered. The collective bargain itself is generally not enforceable by the union or employer,[52] and, as the individual is a third party not privy to the agreement, it will not generally be directly enforceable by an employee, particularly as the union is not viewed as acting as the employee's agent during negotiations.[53] In *Burton Group Ltd v Smith*,[54] the EAT considered that any agency relationship must be capable of inference from the particular facts of the case and does not arise merely from the relationship of union and member. Thus, the employee will only be legally entitled to any parts of a collective bargain which in some way became terms of their individual contract of employment.[55]

Methods of incorporation—express

A term may be incorporated into a contract of employment from a collective bargain either expressly or impliedly. Express implication may come through the parties agreeing in writing that all or part of a particular collective bargain shall be binding upon them, as in *National Coal Board v Galley*.[56] In the past, this fitted in with the statutory requirements for written particulars in Part I of the Employment Rights Act 1996 (see 2.3.2), which allowed the employer to refer the employee to some other document which the employee has reasonable opportunities of reading, and this 'other document' could well be the relevant parts of the current collective bargain. There may now be less scope for this approach, because of the amendments to Part I in 1993, 2002, and 2020 restricting the employer's right to refer to other documents (except in relation to sickness, paid leave, pensions, training, and disciplinary rules); on the other hand, there was added to the list of matters to be notified in writing 'any collective agreements which directly affect the terms and conditions of the employment', which could be significant in any argument for the incorporation of terms other than those which now have to be given individually.

[51] After reaching a high point in 1979, union membership declined consistently until 2016, with a possible slight recovery since then. By 2024, figures from the Certification Officer's reports and the government's Labour Force Survey showed membership at 6.4m, representing 22 per cent of the workforce. Within this, there is a major disparity between coverage in the public sector and in the private sector.

[52] *Ford Motor Co Ltd v Amalgamated Union of Engineering and Foundry Workers* [1969] 2 QB 303, [1969] 2 All ER 481 (see Selwyn (1969) 32 MLR 377); Trade Union and Labour Relations (Consolidation) Act 1992, s 179; see Ch 1; *National Coal Board v National Union of Mineworkers* [1986] ICR 736, [1986] IRLR 439.

[53] *Holland v London Society of Compositors* (1924) 40 TLR 440; cf *Edwards v Skyways Ltd* [1964] 1 All ER 494, [1964] 1 WLR 349.

[54] [1977] IRLR 351, EAT.

[55] *Hulland v William Sanders & Sons* [1945] KB 78, [1944] 2 All ER 568, CA.

[56] [1958] 1 All ER 91, [1958] 1 WLR 16, CA.

In *Marley v Forward Trust Group Ltd*,[57] the EAT caused a considerable stir by holding that where a collective bargain was expressed to be binding in honour only, a contractual term purporting to incorporate a provision from the bargain was itself therefore of no legal effect; fortunately, this startling decision was quickly reversed by the Court of Appeal and orthodoxy re-established. However, some care may be needed with this form of incorporation (where it is still viable), because reference to a particular aspect of a collective bargain (eg sickness) does not necessarily incorporate other aspects of it (eg the right to lay off employees) which may need specific incorporation,[58] and indeed the parties must be clear which particular collective agreement they are wishing to incorporate—which may not be as simple as it sounds where either there has been a series of agreements over a period of time or where there is, at any one time, more than one agreement possibly applicable.

The latter possibility could well arise where there is both national and local bargaining within an industry, or where there has been a tendency over time to move the emphasis from national to local bargaining.[59] Moreover, in *Burroughs Machines Ltd v Timmoney*,[60] the Court of Session, reversing the EAT, treated a contractual reference to a particular clause in a collective bargain as an independent term of the contract which merely relied on the clause for its exposition and definition, so that the employees continue to be bound by part of the clause that allowed the employer to lay them off in certain relevant circumstances, even though the employer had in fact left the employers' federation which was a party to the collective bargain. In this case the principle of the independent effect of a collective bargain term once incorporated worked to the employee's disadvantage.

However, it is equally likely (if not more so) to work to the employer's disadvantage, as can be seen from *Robertson and Jackson v British Gas Corpn*,[61] where the Court of Appeal held that employees could still claim a bonus which had been incorporated into their contracts even though the collective agreement whence it had originally come had been unilaterally abrogated by the employer. The lesson is clear for an employer wishing to resile from the terms of a collective agreement—it may not be enough just to abrogate the agreement if in fact some of its provisions have been incorporated into individual contracts of employment; it may have to go further and show that those contracts have themselves also been *varied* (which will principally mean by consent: see 2.6) to exclude or amend the terms in question.

Implied incorporation

In the absence of express reference, a tribunal or court may be asked to incorporate a term of a collective bargain by implication, and this may raise difficulties, for if one thing is certain it is that implication is by no means automatic. On a structural level, it cannot be argued that an agreement is incorporated simply because the employer belongs to an employers' association that bargained for that agreement.[62] Further, it must be

[57] [1986] ICR 115, [1986] IRLR 43, EAT; revsd [1986] ICR 891, [1986] IRLR 369, CA, applying *Robertson and Jackson v British Gas Corpn* [1983] ICR 351, [1983] IRLR 302, CA.

[58] *Jewell v Neptune Concrete Ltd* [1975] IRLR 147, IT; *Cadoux v Central Regional Council* [1986] IRLR 131, Ct of Sess; *Alexander v Standard Telephones and Cables Ltd (No 2)* [1991] IRLR 286.

[59] This problem can be seen on the facts of *Gascol Conversions Ltd v Mercer* [1974] ICR 420, [1974] IRLR 155, CA (see 2.3.2). Site-level bargaining was taken into account by the EAT in holding a site bonus to be contractually binding in *Donelan v Kerrby Constructions Ltd* [1983] ICR 237, [1983] IRLR 191.

[60] [1977] IRLR 404.

[61] [1983] ICR 351, [1983] IRLR 302, CA. See, to like effect, *Gibbons v Associated British Ports* [1985] IRLR 376 and *Crabb v Tui Airways Ltd* [2025] IRLR 32, KB.

[62] *Hamilton v Futura Floors Ltd* [1990] IRLR 478, OH. There is a similar rule in the law relating to recognition: see 9.7.3.

remembered that vague reliance upon implied terms from collective bargains (whether national or local) cannot oust or qualify clear express terms of a contract of employment covering the matters in question.[63] In the old case of *Young v Canadian Northern Rly Co*,[64] an employee sued the company for wrongful dismissal on the basis that his dismissal for redundancy was not in accordance with the agreed seniority provisions in a collective bargain; he was not a member of the union but claimed that the company's practice was to observe the terms of the agreement and apply them to all employees, whether or not members of the union. The Privy Council held for the company, refusing to incorporate the necessary collective terms into his contract of employment. They said that he had not shown that the company's implementation of the collective bargain was due to contractual liability, that it was equally explicable on grounds of company policy, and that any remedy for breach, as in this case, was industrial and not legal.

It may be argued that this is too strict an approach, making it too difficult to incorporate a collective bargain even in cases where there are no other clear, obvious terms in the contract of employment itself. All that can be said is that each case will depend on its own facts, and that one of the factors that may sway a court or tribunal is whether the clause of the bargain in question is really relevant to the individual circumstances of the employee claiming the benefit of it; this is sometimes referred to as the test of 'aptness' for incorporation. If the clause concerns larger questions relating primarily to employment relations, such as recognition of one or more unions,[65] machinery for resolving collective disputes,[66] longer-term policy planning on matters such as retraining or redundancy,[67] or the allocation of staff numbers to particular duties,[68] the court or tribunal might decide that the clause is not to be incorporated into the contracts of the individuals concerned. On the other hand, if the correct inference is that it was envisaged that those conducting the bargaining would be binding on those concerned in some relevant matters, the resulting clause might well be incorporated into the individual contracts and so binding, as with the 'no-strike' clause in *Rookes v Barnard*.[69] How difficult this distinction may be in practice can be seen from *Kaur v MG Rover Group Ltd*,[70] where one part of a major restructuring and flexibility deal with the unions (itself cast largely in aspirational terms) contained the remarkably precise statement by the management that there would (in return for the flexibility) be *no* compulsory redundancies. When, nine years later and in a very different economic situation, such redundancies were threatened, an employee

[63] *Gascol Conversions Ltd v Mercer*, n 59.

[64] [1931] AC 83, PC; *Land v West Yorkshire Metropolitan County Council* [1979] ICR 452, [1979] IRLR 174, EAT; revsd on other grounds [1981] ICR 334, [1981] IRLR 87, CA.

[65] *Gallagher v Post Office* [1970] 3 All ER 712. Though cf *City and Hackney Health Authority v National Union of Public Employees* [1985] IRLR 252, CA, where it was thought arguable (on an interlocutory application) that a clause from a Whitley Council agreement concerning shop stewards *was* incorporated into a steward's individual contract of employment.

[66] *National Coal Board v National Union of Mineworkers* [1986] ICR 736, [1986] IRLR 439; the judgment of Scott J is a useful affirmation of the principle.

[67] *British Leyland (UK) Ltd v McQuilken* [1978] IRLR 245, EAT. In *Alexander v Standard Telephones and Cables Ltd (No 2)* [1991] IRLR 286 the court refused to incorporate a term in a collective bargain covering seniority in the redundancy procedure, though in *Anderson v Pringle of Scotland Ltd* [1998] IRLR 64 the Court of Session thought that it was at least arguable (in interlocutory proceedings) that a redundancy handling clause in a collective government had been incorporated (*Alexander* not cited). *Quaere* whether a term quantifying individuals' severance payments might be appropriate for incorporation.

[68] *Malone v British Airways* [2011] ICR 125, [2011] IRLR 32, CA.

[69] [1964] AC 1129, [1964] 1 All ER 367, HL. No-strike clauses may now only be incorporated into individual contracts in restricted circumstances: Trade Union and Labour Relations (Consolidation) Act 1992, s 180.

[70] [2005] IRLR 40, CA.

brought a test case claiming that they would be in breach of her contract of employment. The judge at first instance caused quite a stir by holding that this statement had indeed been incorporated into her contact; on appeal, however, the Court of Appeal reversed this decision and took the more traditional view that that part of the agreement was primarily concerned with large-scale issues of redundancy handling and, in spite of the unusual wording, was not appropriate for incorporation into individual contracts.

Significance of custom and practice

One of the strongest arguments in favour of incorporation would be custom and practice, evidenced by previous changes in the individual's contract in line with changes in the collective bargain; likewise, the collective bargain may itself be used as evidence of custom and practice within an industry where for some reason it becomes necessary to decide on such matters.[71] Two relatively rare modern cases on this point provide good illustrations. In *Henry v London General Transport Services Ltd*,[72] a management buyout involved negotiations with a recognized trade union leading to a 'framework agreement' worsening certain terms and conditions as a cost of retaining jobs. In the past, the company had negotiated annually with the union and changes in terms (beneficial or not) had always ensued from this, though the contracts were silent on the matter. When, two years later, 94 of the employees brought claims for unlawful deductions for wages on the basis that the new terms had never been incorporated into their contracts, the Court of Appeal held that there was a custom or practice of change coming through dealings with that union; that custom was 'reasonable, certain and notorious' (see 3.2.2.2) and so incorporation was proved and the claims failed.[73] In *George v Ministry of Justice*,[74] a prison officer sought to have incorporated into his contract not just a collective agreement term, not just one part of such a term, but one phrase from such a part. As part of an overall reform of prison officers' working (the 'Fresh Start' agreement) there was a right for the authority to call for certain working hours from officers, this being offset by time off in lieu (TOIL). As subsidiary to this, there were provisions in the agreement as to operating the TOIL system, and at one point these said that '[a]ccumulated TOIL will be granted as soon as operationally possible and within a maximum period of five weeks'. The claimant officer argued that this was part of his contract and so legally binding. The judge held against him, on the basis that while the parties had worked for years on the basis that the 'hours and TOIL' system itself was binding—thus raising good arguments on custom and practice—the phrase about the timing of TOIL did not come into that category. There was no evidence of express incorporation into contracts, and on the more difficult question of implied incorporation it was held that the true nature of the phrase was that it was guidance or a target. It was thus not apt for incorporation. That judgment was upheld by the Court of Appeal, which added the observation that its conclusion was strengthened by the fact that it had never previously been argued in the 20-year existence of the phrase that it was legally binding, and indeed there was no evidence that there had ever been any serious disagreements before over the operation of the TOIL system.

[71] *Howman & Son v Blyth* [1983] ICR 416, [1983] IRLR 139, EAT.

[72] [2002] ICR 910, [2002] IRLR 472, CA.

[73] One complication was that in the past any new terms negotiated by the union had been put to a ballot of members; in the difficult circumstances of the buyout this had not been done. Was it an essential part of the custom and practice? This point was remitted to the tribunal. However, as an alternative the tribunal had held that the two-year delay meant that the employees had acquiesced to the new terms anyway and so lost their right to object; the Court of Appeal indicated that this was probably correct.

[74] [2013] EWCA Civ 324 (unreported). The lead judgment of Rimer LJ contains a useful summary of the current law on aptness for incorporation.

Henry in particular shows that this form of incorporation could well defeat objection by dissidents who are union members but are unwilling to accept what the union has agreed. However, there has also been a long-standing and even more difficult problem in the case of the *non*-unionist within a union shop. Ostensibly a similar principle should apply (especially if the non-member had taken the benefit in the past of union-negotiated increases in pay), but what little scrap of authority that exists on the point suggests a different approach. In *Singh v British Steel Corpn*,[75] the employee resigned from the union which subsequently negotiated a new shift system which the employee did not want to work; he refused to work it and was dismissed. One of the questions in the case was whether the new union agreement could be considered to have been incorporated into his contract which would have thereby been modified and would have obliged him to work the new shift system. The tribunal held that it was not incorporated so he remained subject to his original contractual terms. The fact that he was no longer a member of the union obviously weighed heavily with the tribunal, and it will be recalled that in *Young v Canadian Northern Rly Co* the employee was also a non-member and the fact that the employer in practice treated all employees alike was to little avail. To deny a non-unionist the rights (or, as in *Singh*'s case, the obligations) under a collective bargain by not incorporating terms may perhaps seem just, but on the other hand, to say that *because* they were a non-member the term will not be incorporated would appear to be based principally on an agency theory (that the union always acts as agent of its members), which, as seen previously, has been rejected in other contexts.

Effect on interpretation

One final point to note is that the fact that incorporation of collective agreement terms is accomplished contractually may affect not just the incorporation itself but also the *interpretation* of such terms. Although they may in practice have their origins in a loosely drafted collective agreement, probably the result of compromise and horse-trading, once they are incorporated into a contract they take effect as contractual terms and are to be interpreted as such. In *Hooper v British Railways Board*,[76] a sick pay term was incorporated into an employee's contract from an agreement of the Railway Staff Joint Council; the problem was that it was (according to the employers) badly drafted, did not reflect what the employers considered to be the actual basis of agreement, and (when applied literally) produced arguably a bizarre result. The employers argued that the fact that the term came from a collective agreement should be taken into account when interpreting and applying it, and that the court should also look at the real intent of the employers at the time, and at how it had subsequently been applied in practice. The Court of Appeal, however, disagreed and held that it must be construed in the normal contractual way, that is, objectively as it stood, and *not* by reference to any subsequent behaviour of the parties. The case, with its relatively strict contractual approach, shows that even though collective agreements are not themselves legally binding, the drafting of any clauses within them that may be incorporated into individual contracts (either expressly or by implication) should be approached with care.

[75] [1974] IRLR 131, IT.

[76] [1988] IRLR 517, CA. *Anderson v LFEPA* [2013] EWCA Civ 321 (unreported) is another example; arguably it shows more emphasis on coming to a conclusion that is in line with employment realities, but still within the confines of applying normal rules of contractual interpretation.

3.2.2.2 **Custom**

General

Trade usage or custom may have a role to play in filling a gap in the expressed terms of a contract of employment,[77] or perhaps in the interpretation of a particular term (eg an incorporated clause in a collective bargain, as already discussed),[78] as in the old cases of *Sager v H Ridehalgh & Son Ltd*[79] (custom that the employer might deduct sums from weavers' wages for bad work held to be part of the individual weaver's contract) and *Marshall v English Electric Co Ltd*[80] (established practice of using suspension as a disciplinary measure held to be incorporated). To be thus accepted, a custom must be certain, general (eg in a trade or a particular area), and reasonable, but the legal basis for its incorporation into a contract of employment is not certain—is it automatically incorporated once it is certain, general, and reasonable? Or does it have to be known to and, perhaps, freely accepted by the employee? In *Marshall v English Electric Co Ltd* there was a division of opinion, Lord Goddard accepting automatic incorporation but du Parcq LJ (dissenting) considering that mere operation is not enough, there being some further element of acceptance necessary. *Meek v Port of London Authority*[81] is some authority in favour of a requirement of knowledge, but it is a rather unusual case since it involved a change of employer and a custom (the payment by the employer of the employee's income tax if payable) which did not affect the employee when he commenced employment, and had in fact been discontinued by the time the employee might be affected by it. It appears therefore that, although evidence of knowledge and acceptance might be most useful in establishing a binding custom, in some cases a custom might be applied without proof of them, and in particular in three instances:

1. Where the custom is so notorious that the court or tribunal may take judicial notice of it.[82]
2. Where it is so well established that the employee must be said to have accepted employment subject to it. In *Sagar v H Ridehalgh & Son Ltd* the practice of deductions from pay for bad work was widespread in Lancashire factories, and Lawrence LJ said:[83]

> I think that it is clear that the plaintiff accepted employment in the defendant's mill on the same terms as the other weavers employed at that mill . . . Although I entirely agree with the [first instance judge] in finding it difficult to believe that the plaintiff did not know of the existence of the practice at the mill, I think that it is immaterial whether he knew or not, as I am satisfied that he accepted his employment on the same terms as to deductions for bad work as the other weavers at the mill.

[77] Where this is the case, the Court of Appeal in *Mears v Safecar Security Ltd* [1982] ICR 626, [1982] IRLR 183, CA took a broad approach to the evidence that can be taken into account to imply the necessary term, in particular allowing evidence of actual working practices adopted or continued after the employment had commenced (following *Liverpool City Council v Irwin* [1977] AC 239, [1976] 2 All ER 39, HL and *Wilson v Maynard Shipbuilding Consultants AB* [1978] ICR 376, [1977] IRLR 491, CA); this involves stretching ordinary contract law, where terms are not normally to be construed by later conduct, but this may be essential in employment law: *Stevedoring and Haulage Services Ltd v Fuller* [2001] IRLR 627 at 628, CA, per Tuckey LJ.

[78] *Parry v Holst & Co Ltd* (1968) 3 ITR 317; *Dunlop Tyres Ltd v Blows* [2001] IRLR 629, CA, where it was said that later conduct could be used as a guide to interpreting an ambiguous collective agreement.

[79] [1931] 1 Ch 310, CA.

[80] [1945] 1 All ER 653, CA.

[81] [1918] 1 Ch 415. The decision in *Henry v London Transport Services Ltd* [2002] EWCA 488, [2002] ICR 910, [2002] IRLR 472 reaffirmed the 'certain, general and reasonable' formulation but did not address this point of knowledge because it concerned whether the custom existed at all.

[82] *George v Davies* [1911] 2 KB 445.

[83] [1931] 1 Ch 310 at 336, CA.

Much here may depend upon the certainty and generality of the custom, so that the mere fact that it has happened before in one firm may be insufficient.[84] Also there is the 'reasonableness' limb of the test, which might be important.[85]

3. Where a practice grew up while the employee was in that employment and they impliedly accepted it (eg by accepting benefits under it). This might be a less certain area, for it should not cover unilateral practices, and might be subject to du Parcq LJ's caveat in *Marshall v English Electric Co Ltd* that mere continuance at work may not be enough for acceptance, for it might be caused by other factors such as fear of dismissal.

The particular problem of apparently 'ex gratia' payments

One particular application of custom and practice merits special mention. This concerns the question whether payments ostensibly made by the employer on an ex gratia (ie non-contractual) basis, if made frequently or consistently, can be argued to become contractual through custom and practice, so that in future they can be *demanded* by the employees. In *Quinn v Calder Industrial Materials Ltd*,[86] the employers had paid enhanced redundancy terms on four occasions between 1987 and 1994, pursuant to a management policy document but in each case as a result of an individual decision by senior managers. When redundancies were made in 1994 no such enhanced terms were offered and the employees claimed them as a contractual right by virtue of custom and practice. The EAT rejected this argument, on the basis of insufficient evidence that the employers intended the policy to have contractual effect. A similar result was reached in *Warman International v Wilson*,[87] and in *Hagen v ICI Chemicals and Polymers Ltd*[88] the court refused to incorporate a security of employment policy statement into individual contracts.

However, these are ultimately decisions on the facts, and incorporation is legally possible. In *Albion Automotive Ltd v Walker*,[89] the employers' predecessor (Volvo) had carried out six redundancy exercises between 1990 and 1994. Enhanced terms had been agreed with the union for the first, but in fact they were then given on each occasion. In 1995 the current employers took over the business and in 1999 made the applicant employees redundant, offering only the statutory redundancy payments. The applicants claimed the enhanced terms in a breach of contract action and won. Upholding the tribunal decision in their favour, the Court of Appeal pointed particularly to the facts that the policy was known to the employees; it had originally been adopted by agreement and reduced to writing; it had been applied frequently, and automatically on each occasion; the employees had a reasonable expectation of benefiting from it; and the manner in which it was communicated implied contractual intent.

This older case law essentially showed that there exists a possible factual spectrum between *Quinn* at one end and *Albion Automotive* at the other, with the middle ground

[84] *Spencer Jones v Timmens Freeman* [1974] IRLR 325, IT; *Samways v Swan Hunter Shipbuilders Ltd* [1975] IRLR 190, IT.

[85] *Hardwick v Leeds Area Health Authority* [1975] IRLR 319, IT.

[86] [1996] IRLR 126. The EAT relied on the statement of Browne-Wilkinson P in *Duke v Reliance Systems* [1982] IRLR 347 that a unilaterally adopted management policy cannot become contractual on the grounds of custom and practice unless it is at least shown that the policy had been drawn to the attention of the employees or had been followed without exception for a substantial period.

[87] [2002] All ER (D) 94 (Mar).

[88] [2002] IRLR 31 at 42.

[89] [2002] EWCA Civ 946 (unreported). There is the interesting twist that Albion were liable for their *predecessor's* custom and practice; this may be a salutary lesson for lawyers advising on a TUPE transfer.

being highly arguable and therefore inherently difficult to advise on. Fortunately, this whole area has now been subject to detailed consideration by the Court of Appeal in *Park Cakes Ltd v Shumba*.[90] The judgment of Underhill LJ (previously President of the EAT) starts by stressing the factual nature of this issue and stating that it is not profitable to search for definite *rules* here. What he then does, however, is to set out what may well be *factors* helping a court or tribunal to determine one of these cases. These factors (relating primarily to cases of enhanced redundancy payments, but applicable more generally with modifications if necessary) are as follows:

> (a) *On how many occasions, and over how long a period, the benefits in question have been paid.* Obviously, but subject to the other considerations identified below, the more often enhanced benefits have been paid, and the longer the period over which they have been paid, the more likely it is that employees will reasonably understand them to be being paid as of right.
>
> (b) *Whether the benefits are always the same.* If, while an employer may invariably make enhanced redundancy payments, he nevertheless varies the amounts or the terms of payment, that is inconsistent with an acknowledgement of legal obligation; if there is a legal right it must in principle be certain. Of course a late departure from a practice which has already become contractual cannot affect legal rights . . . but any inconsistency during the period relied on as establishing the custom is likely to be fatal. It is, however, possible that in a particular case the evidence may show that the employer has bound himself to a minimum level of benefit even though he has from time to time paid more.
>
> (c) *The extent to which the enhanced benefits are publicized generally.* Where the availability of enhanced redundancy benefits is published to the workforce generally, that will tend to convey that they are paid as a matter of obligation, though I am not to be taken as saying that it is conclusive, and much will depend on the circumstances and on how the employer expresses himself. It should also be borne in mind that 'publication' may take many forms. In some circumstances publication to a trade union, or perhaps to a large group of employees, may constitute publication to the workforce as a whole. Employment tribunals should be able to judge whether, as a matter of industrial reality, the employer has conducted himself so as to create, in Leveson LJ's words, 'widespread knowledge and understanding' on the part of employees that they are legally entitled to the enhanced benefits.
>
> (d) *How the terms are described.* If an employer clearly and consistently describes his enhanced redundancy terms in language that makes clear that they are offered as a matter of discretion—eg by describing them as *ex gratia*—it is hard to see how the employees or their representatives could reasonably understand them to be contractual, however regularly they may be paid. A statement that the payments are made as a matter of 'policy' may, though again much depends on the context, point in the same direction. Conversely, the language of 'entitlement' points to legal obligation.
>
> (e) *What is said in the express contract.* As a matter of ordinary contractual principles, no term should be implied, whether by custom or otherwise, which is inconsistent with the express terms of the contract, at least.
>
> (f) *Equivocalness.* The burden of establishing that a practice has become contractual is on the employee, and he will not be able to discharge it if the employer's practice is, viewed objectively, equally explicable on the basis that it is pursued as a matter of discretion rather than legal obligation.

[90] [2013] EWCA Civ 974. Again, there was the complication that the employer was held potentially liable for its predecessor's practice of paying enhanced redundancy pay over a period of years prior to the TUPE transfer.

Clearly, this is such a disputable area that difficult cases will still arise, but at least employment lawyers now have a starting point, a set of pegs on which to hang their factual arguments, from such an eminent authority.

3.2.2.3 **Works rules, company handbooks, and policy statements**

An employer may lay down works or company rules, and it is possible that these may become, in whole or in part, terms of the contract of employment, particularly if the employee expressly agrees to abide by them or have some particular aspect of their employment governed by them, or if they are sufficiently brought to their notice when entering the employment. Also, some matters covered in a rule book may now be matters of which written notice must be given by statute, and so they may be strong evidence of the terms of employment by virtue of that (see 2.3.2). However, it is clear from *Secretary of State for Employment v Associated Society of Locomotive Engineers and Firemen (No 2)*[91] that not all such rules will have contractual effect. Lord Denning MR said:

> Each man signs a form saying that he will abide by the rules, but these rules are in no way terms of the contract of employment. They are only instructions to a man as to how he is to do his work.

The distinction between contractual and non-contractual rules is significant because if a rule is contractual, (a) it cannot be altered unilaterally by the employer, for that would require consensual variation in some form, and (b) the employee could, in the absence of such variation, insist upon continuing to work that rule and refuse to operate some other rule; if the rule is non-contractual, (a) it can be changed unilaterally by the employer for, being non-contractual, it remains in the sphere of managerial prerogative,[92] and (b) if an employee refuses to operate the amended rule, they are refusing to obey a proper order and so at common law could be dismissed and under the statutes would quite possibly be fairly dismissed. Thus, the more the rules are considered to be contractual, the more restraints are placed upon the manager's prerogative, and where a rule is not expressly made contractual in some way a court or tribunal may have to make a difficult decision whether it is to be considered contractual by implication. A particularly good example (in an area which had plagued human resource managers for several years prior to the smoking ban) is *Dryden v Greater Glasgow Health Board*,[93] where the employers introduced a no-smoking policy into the hospital and the employee, a heavy smoker, left and claimed constructive dismissal. Her claim failed because the EAT held that the no-smoking policy was in the realm of working rules and employer discretion, and so there was no breach of contract on which to base constructive dismissal:

> There can, in our view, be no doubt that an employer is entitled to make rules for the conduct of employees in their place of work, as he is entitled to give lawful orders, within the scope of the contract.[94]

[91] [1972] 2 QB 455, [1972] 2 All ER 949, CA.

[92] See eg *Wandsworth London Borough Council v D'Silva* [1998] IRLR 193, CA, where it was held that the council's sickness absence procedures were non-contractual and so could be lawfully altered by the council.

[93] [1992] IRLR 469, EAT.

[94] [1992] IRLR 469, EAT at 471, per Lord Coulsfield. The employee's second argument (if, as found, there was no contractual entitlement to smoke) was that the introduction of the policy was in breach of the implied term of trust and respect, but this failed on the facts since the employer had adopted a reasonable procedure for introducing it.

This long-standing law on 'works rules', itself rather an old-fashioned phrase, thus retains substantive significance and may be seen in two more current developments in managerial practice. The first is the modern tendency in medium and large firms to produce company handbooks; while these are in many ways a Good Thing (being readily available, relatively informal, and much more of a guide to new employees) and are encouraged by ACAS, they could cause problems in that they may well mix together some matters that are formal contractual terms and others that are mere guidance or rules made within the managerial discretion, without any clear differentiation. *Keeley v Fosroc International Ltd*[95] is a good example of this problem. The handbook clause in question was under the heading 'Employee benefits and rights' and said that employees with two years' service were 'entitled' to an enhanced redundancy payment *but* its amount was to be left to collective and individual consultation. In spite of this lack of certainty, the Court of Appeal held that this clause *was* contractually enforceable, especially as redundancies were common in the firm and this clause was viewed as part and parcel of an employee's remuneration package.

The second development has been the increased use by employers of 'policies' of various kinds.[96] Again, these may or may not have contractual effect, though the cases so far have not accorded them great legal significance. In *Secretary of State for Scotland v Taylor*,[97] prison officers tried to oppose a unilateral decrease in their retirement age by arguing that it was a breach of contract because it contravened their employer's equal opportunities policy which included a reference to age discrimination; the Scottish EAT held that the policy was part of the contract (largely because the employer was hoist by its own petard by having introduced it in a way consistent with contractual intent), but as a matter of construction further held that the parties could not have intended it to outlaw an otherwise lawful retirement provision in the contract. Perhaps more significantly, when in *Grant v South-West Trains Ltd*[98] an attempt was made to establish sexual orientation discrimination as a breach of contract (again because it appeared in the firm's equal opportunities policy), Curtis J held that the policy was not part of the contract at all; it was merely a statement of aims and aspirations. Given the prevalence of various forms of policies, circulars, codes of practice, or (God forbid) mission statements, this distinction is likely to be troublesome for some time to come.

In dismissal law, however, the practical effect of these matters may be diminished by the fact that the modern law on unfair dismissal is not concerned with technical questions of breach of contract but rather with the overall merits of the dismissal, and in this context it is clear that, while breach of the rules (whether contractual or not) may well be important in any given case, it will only be *evidence*, not a determinative factor, and the existence of

[95] [2006] IRLR 961, CA, applied in *Sparks v Department of Transport* [2016] IRLR 519, CA. The 'handbook' may now in fact be electronic (eg as part of an employer's intranet); where, however, there is a changeover from hard copy to electronic, that does *not* give an employer carte blanche to make changes to any parts which had contractual status, ie the change is only to the *format* of the handbook, not to its substance: *Harlow v Artemis International Corpn Ltd* [2008] IRLR 629, (QBD).

[96] See the Code of Practice on sickness absence in *Wandsworth London Borough Council v D'Silva*, n 92. One variation of this problem is where a policy is initially non-contractual but is applied so frequently and/or consistently that it is later argued to have become incorporated into contracts by custom and practice: see this chapter, 3.2.2.2.

[97] [1997] IRLR 608, EAT, upheld by the House of Lords (where the incorporation point was not argued): [2000] IRLR 502.

[98] [1998] IRLR 206, ECJ. One distinction with *Taylor* was that in the latter the employer's circular introducing the new equal opportunities policy had stated that it was being introduced into the employees' contracts of employment. There was no such evidence of contractual intent in *Grant*.

works rules will in no way preclude a tribunal from looking into the overall fairness of the employer's actions. Thus, for example, in *Laws Stores Ltd v Oliphant*[99] the disciplinary section of the works rules said that cases of gross misconduct (including the disregard of till procedures, which was in question) would normally result in immediate dismissal, but the EAT held that such a provision (or even one more mandatory) could not limit a tribunal's jurisdiction and held the dismissal, on the facts of the particular case, to be unfair. This case is perhaps an example of the decline in the purely contractual approach to employment.

3.3 Implied duties of the employer

3.3.1 To pay wages

This obligation is so fundamental that the law relating to it is considered separately in 3.5.

3.3.2 To provide work

The general common law position has been that there is no obligation to provide work for the employee to do; there is only the obligation to pay the wages which may be due under the particular contract of employment concerned. The classic, if now rather nostalgic, statement of this rule was given by Asquith J in *Collier v Sunday Referee Publishing Co Ltd*:[100] 'Provided I pay my cook her wages regularly, she cannot complain if I choose to take any or all of my meals out.'

This means that in such a case the employer will not be in breach of contract by failing to provide work and so may, for example, normally give salary in lieu of notice.[101] However, the law recognized that in certain contracts the opportunity to work is of the essence, and so certain exceptions to the general rule evolved. In particular, it was held that there may be an obligation to provide work for an actor or singer where the publicity involved may be as important as the remuneration,[102] for an employee paid on a piecework[103] or commission[104] basis where actual work is necessary for them to earn their living, and possibly for an employee engaged to fill a specific office (particularly of a professional nature).[105] Outside such exceptional cases, however, the general rule applied, as can be seen in *Turner v Sawdon & Co*,[106] where a salesman on a fixed-term contract at a

[99] [1978] IRLR 251, EAT. An equally good example is the imposition of a disciplinary penalty by the employer—it may technically have had the contractual power to impose the penalty in question, but it is still open to the employee to argue that on the facts of the case it was excessive (thus eg justifying the employee in walking out and claiming constructive dismissal): *BBC v Beckett* [1983] IRLR 43; *Cawley v South Wales Electricity Board* [1985] IRLR 89.

[100] [1940] 2 KB 647 at 650, [1940] 4 All ER 234 at 236.

[101] *Konski v Peet* [1915] 1 Ch 530. It is possible that in some cases, where the contract does not envisage dismissal with wages in lieu (either expressly or impliedly), such a dismissal will be a breach of contract *but* as damages have been paid in anticipation (by paying the wages due in the notice period) this will be a technical breach only and of little legal significance (except possibly where a restraint of trade clause is in issue): *Rex Stewart Jeffries Parker Ginsberg v Parker* [1988] IRLR 483, CA. See 6.2.

[102] *Fechter v Montgomery* (1863) 33 Beav 22; *Bunning v Lyric Theatre* (1894) 71 LT 396; *Marbé v George Edwardes (Daly's Theatre) Ltd* [1928] 1 KB 269, CA; the obligation may be to provide not just work, but work of a particular kind or standard, eg a leading part in a play, as in *Herbert Clayton and Jack Waller Ltd v Oliver* [1930] AC 209, HL.

[103] *R v Welsh* (1853) 2 E & B 357; *Devonald v Rosser & Sons* [1906] 2 KB 728, CA.

[104] *Turner v Goldsmith* [1891] 1 QB 544, CA; *Bauman v Hulton Press Ltd* [1952] 2 All ER 1121.

[105] *Collier v Sunday Referee Publishing Co Ltd* [1940] 2 KB 647, [1940] 4 All ER 234.

[106] [1901] 2 KB 653, CA. *Quaere* whether the position would be different if it was more urgent that the employee should keep in practice, as for example in the case of a surgeon.

fixed salary was given no work to do but was still paid his salary and it was held, distinguishing *Turner v Goldsmith*,[107] that this was merely a contract to retain the employee so that the employer was not in breach of contract, in spite of the employee's assertions that denial of work would make him deteriorate as a salesman. However, some doubt was cast on this principle in *Langston v Amalgamated Union of Engineering Workers*,[108] where an employee involved in an industrial dispute was suspended on full pay by his employer. To succeed in his claim against the union involved under now repealed legislation,[109] he had to show that the dispute had induced a breach of contract, and this would only have been so if he had a contractual right to be provided with work since the employers were continuing to pay his salary. The Court of Appeal thought that the duty to provide work might exist, and in a strong judgment Lord Denning MR said that the previous authorities such as *Collier v Sunday Referee Publishing Co Ltd* were out of date, that the courts now recognize a 'right to work', and that this was one application of it. However, it must be remembered that this decision was only at an interlocutory stage, so that the Court of Appeal had to decide only if there was an arguable case on this point—they then did not have to *decide* the point, and the judgments of the other two members of the court, Cairns and Stephenson LJJ, are much less emphatic on the point than that of the Master of the Rolls. The case was remitted to the National Industrial Relations Court (NIRC), which held in the employee's favour,[110] but on much more restricted grounds than those explored by Lord Denning: Sir John Donaldson P held that this case came within one of the existing exceptions to the old rule, since under the contract the employee was to be paid premium payments for night shifts and overtime, so that he came within the pieceworker exception in that denial of actual work meant denial of opportunity to earn the premium payments. Thus, in its result, the case is in fact compatible with the old common law rule and its established exceptions.

This question of whether and when there is a right to work (or, more accurately, whether a contract requires the provision of work in addition to the payment of wages) had been dormant for many years, but was revived in an unusual context in *William Hill Organisation Ltd v Tucker*.[111] The case concerned an attempt by an employer to construct an implied 'garden leave clause'[112] from the terms of the employee's contract, quite simply because they had omitted to put an express clause in. The contract contained a long (six months) notice provision; when the employee left with only one month's notice, the employers applied for an injunction restraining him from taking work elsewhere during the six-month period, on the basis that they were prepared to pay his wages *and* had a common law right to require him during that period to do no work for them or anyone else. The Court of Appeal held that that depended on whether his contract only required payment of wages (as the employers argued) *or* required the employers to provide him

[107] [1891] 1 QB 544, CA.

[108] [1974] 1 All ER 980, [1974] ICR 180, CA; see also *Breach v Epsylon Industries Ltd* [1976] ICR 316, [1976] IRLR 180, EAT; *Bosworth v Angus Jowett & Co Ltd* [1977] IRLR 374, EAT.

[109] Industrial Relations Act 1971, s 96.

[110] [1974] ICR 510, [1974] IRLR 182, NIRC. It is made clear in the President's judgment that the employee had to work such shifts and hours as the employer stipulated, which made it easier to construe overtime as a contractual requirement; it is submitted, however, that purely voluntary overtime is not an essential part of a contract, and so failure to provide it should *not* be a breach of contract, and so not subject to the reasoning in *Langston*'s case.

[111] [1999] ICR 291, [1998] IRLR 313, CA.

[112] A 'garden leave clause' is an alternative to a restraint of trade clause, whereby an employer puts an employee onto long notice with a provision that during that notice they can be sent home by the employer (to avoid damage to the employer's business) *but* cannot take any other work while still technically employed by that employer: see 6.2.3.

with work as well (in which case the employers would be in breach of contract and the employee could leave to take up other work); it thus revived the old controversy, and for good measure seemed to take an expansive view as to who can claim to have a sufficient interest in actually performing their work in order to claim that the contract is to be interpreted as requiring work to be provided, not just payment. Far from restricting it to theatrical or piecework/commission workers, the court held that this employee, a senior 'spread betting' dealer with a betting organization, *did* have a right to be provided with work; there was thus no inherent right for the employer to put him on garden leave,[113] and so the employer's application for an injunction was refused. Factors leading to that conclusion were that the appointment was a specific and unique one, that the skills involved were those requiring constant practice and experience, and that the contract contained certain provisions (as to obligations on the employee in carrying out his duties, training, and an express power of suspension) which the court thought consistent with an obligation to provide work, provided that it was available. While the first point (a specific appointment) could point to a narrow future application of this case and some of the points on construction of the contract terms are, with respect, highly arguable, it is likely that most contention in any future cases will be over the second point—who will be considered to be in a job whose skills need constant honing and exercise, so as to come within a widened class of employees with some form of 'right to work'?[114]

Two further points might be mentioned. The first is that this uncertain area of law will only be relevant where there is no express term covering the provision of work, and where such provision is important to either of the parties, they are advised to incorporate a clause in the contract putting the matter beyond doubt. The second is that this topic may be allied to the question of the continuation of wages during stoppages of work and for present purposes it might be noted that at common law, suspension without pay will only be lawful if there is an express or implied term in the particular contract to that effect; that failure to provide work may constitute a lay-off, thus activating certain statutory provisions (principally concerned with redundancy—Employment Rights Act 1996, ss 147–154); and that in the absence of continuing contractual payments the employee may be eligible for a statutory guarantee payment under the 1996 Act, ss 28–35.

3.3.3 **To exercise care**

3.3.3.1 **The duty generally**

On a general level, this matter will normally relate to care for the employee's health and safety, as the employer's common law duty of care is one of the bases of the law relating to the compensation of an injured employee. However, four particular applications of it are important also in mainstream employment law. The first is that one of the commonly accepted aspects of this overall duty is that the employer must provide competent and safe fellow employees,[115] for example to protect the employee from practical jokers; one

[113] As Morritt LJ stated at the end of his judgment, the answer of course is for the employer to use an *express* garden leave clause wherever there might arguably be a right to work (more often now, in the light of this case?). In *SG & R Valuation Services Co v Boudrais* [2008] IRLR 770, QBD there was no express clause *but* it was held that the employee's misconduct (soliciting customers before leaving employment) negated his right to be provided with work and the employer was allowed to keep him on a de facto garden leave for the (long) period of his notice.

[114] A similar case in a different context is *Land Securities Trillium Ltd v Thornley* [2005] IRLR 765, EAT, where one factor in construing a flexibility clause narrowly was that the employer was trying to use it to move the employee away completely from her professional work, in which she had an interest.

[115] *Wilsons & Clyde Coal Co Ltd v English* [1938] AC 57, HL; *Hudson v Ridge Manufacturing Co Ltd* [1957] 2 QB 348, [1957] 2 All ER 229.

effect of this is that there may be a positive common law obligation upon the employer to be rid of a potentially dangerous employee and this should be a good defence to an allegation of unfair dismissal by that employee, provided the necessary procedures are used in effecting the dismissal. The second is that the general duty of care may be construed as including an obligation upon the employer to pay attention to complaints from an employee that a particular appliance, method, and so on is unsafe and to act reasonably in dealing with matters of safety; if the employer does not do so, not only may the employee be justified in walking out and claiming, for the purposes of unfair dismissal, to have been constructively dismissed,[116] but also that dismissal may well be automatically unfair.[117] The third is that the employer may be under an obligation to indemnify the employee against expenses necessarily incurred in the course of their employment, which may include the cost of defending legal proceedings, though not where the fault was purely that of the employee and only collateral to the performance of their duties;[118] there is, however, no implied obligation to insure the employee's activities to any greater extent than is required by law.[119] The fourth is that the specialized duty of care will in general not extend to a duty to take care of the employee's belongings;[120] any possible liability for loss of the employee's goods would have to arise on ordinary principles of tort if there was evidence of particular proximity between the particular employer and employee, not just on the employment relationship per se.

In addition to these long-standing applications of the general implied duty on the employer to exercise care, two areas of considerable modern concern have taken this duty much further on than its origins in physical injury to the employee in a workplace accident. These are the expanding law relating to workplace stress-induced injuries (still largely a health and safety issue, but going well beyond traditional accident-based liability) and the possible liability for a negligently written reference (which expands the duty into the employee's or ex-employee's future financial interests).

3.3.3.2 **Stress at work cases**

The expanding case law on psychiatric injury from mental stress at work has been a major feature of personal injury litigation in recent years. It has developed separately from the long-standing law on 'nervous shock' in the law of tort,[121] and at a journalistic level has been much discussed in the press as an example of our alleged 'compensation culture'. Clearly this is an area where it was always going to be difficult to strike the right balance. The dam appeared to burst with (ironically) a first instance decision in a single case,

[116] *British Aircraft Corpn v Austin* [1978] IRLR 332, EAT; cf *Lindsay v Dunlop Ltd* [1980] IRLR 93, EAT.

[117] Employment Rights Act 1996, s 100; see 7.5.4.

[118] *Burrows v Rhodes* [1899] 1 QB 816; *Re Famatina Development Corpn* [1914] 2 Ch 271, CA; *Gregory v Ford* [1951] 1 All ER 121.

[119] *Lister v Romford Ice and Cold Storage Co Ltd* [1957] AC 555, [1957] 1 All ER 125, HL. In a case where insurance cover is likely to be important, the employee is advised to make the position clear with the employer, especially since the decision in *Merrett v Babb* [2001] EWCA Civ 214, [2001] QB 1174, that when the employer went out of business the individual employee could be liable in damages for bad advice given during employment.

[120] *Deyong v Shenburn* [1946] KB 227, [1946] 1 All ER 226, CA; *Edwards v West Herts Group Hospital Management Committee* [1957] 1 All ER 541, [1957] 1 WLR 415, CA.

[121] Nervous shock cases tend to arise from trauma (eg being involved in an accident caused by the defendant), whereas stress cases tend to arise from a process over time, eg incessant excessive work demands. For the effects on this of modern occupational psychology see Davies, 'Stress at Work: Individuals or Structures' (2022) 51 ILJ 403. Of course, there could still be liability to an employee for trauma-induced mental injury at work, but here there is no special protection for an employee, who must still comply with the normal rules for nervous shock: *White v Chief Constable of South Yorkshire Police* [1999] 2 AC 455, [1999] 1 All ER 1, HL.

Walker v Northumberland County Council.[122] A social worker succeeded in a claim for damages for common law negligence against his employers, based on the second, debilitating nervous breakdown that he suffered due to the ever increasing workload placed on him and the failure of the employer to provide help which had been promised after the first breakdown. This widely reported decision (unfortunately not appealed) caused considerable consternation in human resources circles, especially with its ruling that the employer could not raise as a defence that the increased workload was caused by externally imposed financial cutbacks. It raised the interesting prospect of the old common law contractual and tortious duty of care at work taking on a new role as possibly the only counterweight to what has seemed over time an irresistible movement in so many kinds of work to demand more and more of fewer and fewer employees and call it economic efficiency.

It also showed the continuing vitality of the common law in areas not yet covered by protective legislation. Interest in, and concern about, this novel form of liability grew exponentially, straddling employment law and personal injury litigation, and was eventually subject to detailed review in what is now the leading case, *Sutherland v Hatton*.[123] This was in fact four conjoined appeals which gave the Court of Appeal the opportunity to consider the law here generally. The judgment of the court given by Hale LJ (as she then was) contains a survey of the background to this kind of litigation, anchoring it firmly into the principles of negligence and the duty of care on the employer, as extended into the area of mental rather than physical injury. Of crucial importance, at paragraph 43, the judge reduces all of this to 16 'practical propositions' which have become the *locus classicus* on this whole subject. While these should be read in full by anyone dealing with it, the key points are as follows: (a) the ordinary principles of employer's liability apply to this novel area, which therefore focus on foreseeability of the injury to the employer; (b) mental disorder will be inherently more difficult to foresee than physical injury and an employer will normally be entitled to assume that the employee can withstand the normal pressures of the work; (c) there are no inherently dangerous jobs in relation to stress and so much will depend on whether the demands on that employee have been excessive, perhaps evidenced by a history of sickness (including by other employees) and complaints; (d) the employer is normally entitled to take what the employee says at face value (eg if they are denying difficulty in coping); (e) the employer will only be in breach of duty if it has failed to take steps which it could reasonably have been expected to take, which may involve consideration of the size and resources of the firm and the need to treat other employees fairly as well; (f) an employer who offers a confidential counselling service is unlikely to be found to be in breach of duty;[124] (g) if the only way to avoid the danger was to dismiss or demote the employee, an employer will not be in breach of duty by allowing a willing employee to continue working;[125] (h) causation must be proved, which means

[122] [1995] IRLR 35, [1995] 1 All ER 737.

[123] [2002] ICR 613, [2002] IRLR 263, CA.

[124] This proposition was thought particularly important in personnel management; it was elaborated further in *Hartman v SE Essex Mental Health NHS Trust* [2005] IRLR 293, CA, where it was held that if the employee disclosed problems to a counsellor in confidence, telling the counsellor not to disclose them to managers, the employer is *not* fixed with knowledge of them for the purpose of establishing foreseeability of harm. However, a counselling service will not always be a panacea, and the Court of Appeal subsequently took a more cautious approach, especially where the real cause of problems was the workload itself and not the employee's personal difficulties with it: *Daw v Intel Corpn Ltd* [2007] IRLR 355, CA; *Dickins v O2 plc* [2009] IRLR 58, CA.

[125] This point has caused problems in health and safety law generally—the traditional approach was that the relationship is not teacher/pupil and that an employee is an adult and so able to make their own decision to carry on working in the knowledge of the danger (*Withers v Perry Chain Co Ltd* [1961] 3 All ER 676, CA). However, in *Coxall v Goodyear GB Ltd* [2003] ICR 152, [2002] IRLR 742, CA there was liability (for a physical injury) for allowing a willing employee to continue working, and the court envisaged a possible duty on the employer ultimately to dismiss if no other way round the danger could be found.

showing that the injury was caused by the breach of duty, not simply by the stress itself; (i) on causal grounds, where the stress was caused only partly by the work (eg where the employee also had difficulties outside work) the employer must only pay for its share and if necessary the court must apportion the blame when awarding damages.[126] There was a further appeal to the House of Lords (sub nom *Barber v Somerset CC*)[127] but this turned out to be largely a question of the *application* of these principles to the facts of one of the four cases in the original appeal. Thus, it is still to the principles set out by Hale LJ that the lawyer must look as the essential starting point, as accepted by the Court of Appeal in *Hartman v SE Essex Mental Health NHS Trust*.[128]

What these principles seek to do is to hold liable the bad employer but at the same time give viable defences to the good employer who either could not have foreseen what was about to happen or who genuinely tried to cope with it. Contrary to journalistic arguments about our 'compensation culture', *Sutherland v Hatton* can make these cases far from easy for the claimant, especially where they did not show clear signs of difficulties (perhaps deliberately concealing them), then suddenly imploded (perhaps after only one or two altercations with a manager), went off 'with stress', and never returned; in such a case the end result may well be no liability on the employer.[129] Given the amount of concern expressed about the levels of stress litigation after *Walker v Northumberland CC*, the judgment in *Sutherland v Hatton* seemed to provide a balanced and highly desirable settlement of the law.

There are, however, two possible threats to that settlement. The first is the possible effect of disability discrimination law. If the stress-induced injury is sufficiently serious to constitute a 'disability'[130] then different rules come into play in addition; once a claimant alleges breach of the Equality Act 2010, the question becomes not whether the employer could have foreseen the injury but what steps were taken post-injury by way of 'reasonable adjustments' (in particular to ease the way back into employment for the employee absent with the stress-induced condition). While this may be a considerable complication in a case, it is a long-standing one, relatively well understood by employment lawyers, who often have to operate on the cusp between employment law and discrimination law.

However, the second threat came like a bolt from the blue and is capable of constituting a most unfortunate '*Sutherland v Hatton* by-pass', destabilizing the law in this area. In *Majrowski v Guy's and St Thomas' NHS Trust*,[131] the claimant sued for damages for stress-induced injury in relation to alleged bullying and harassment by a line manager.

[126] This apparently obvious approach (on causation grounds) caused problems subsequently. In *Dickens v O2 plc* [2009] IRLR 58, CA it was suggested obiter that a mental injury may, of its nature, be *indivisible*, with the result of the employer being liable for it in full. The EAT refused to follow this in *Thaine v London School of Economics* [2010] ICR 1422. When the question came directly before the Court of Appeal in *BAE Systems (Operations) Ltd v Konczak* [2017] IRLR 893, [2018] ICR 1 a more nuanced approach was taken than in *Dickens*, holding that whether a mental injury is divisible or indivisible is a question of fact in each case, based on the nature of the injury. It is possible to see in the judgment a leaning towards divisibility in most cases, but the actual result on the facts was indivisibility and full employer liability.

[127] [2004] ICR 457, [2004] IRLR 475, HL.

[128] See n 124. This is again an interesting case factually because it concerned six conjoined appeals with facts going across a whole spectrum of difficult types of stress case, including one of mental injury caused by trauma at work. While most of the litigation here will be in tort, *Sutherland v Hatton* is potentially of general application, as the EAT held in *Marshall Specialist Vehicles Ltd v Osborne* [2003] IRLR 672 when applying it in a constructive dismissal case to determine whether the stress in question justified the employee leaving the employment.

[129] As in *Pratley v Surrey CC* [2003] IRLR 794, CA and *Bonsor v UK Coal Mining Ltd* [2004] IRLR 164, CA. In *Yapp v Foreign and Commonwealth Office* [2015] IRLR 112, CA the claimant lost under *Sutherland v Hatton* on liability and also (in relation to financial loss) on remoteness of damage: see Brodie, 'Risk Allocation and Psychiatric Harm' (2015) 44 ILJ 270.

[130] See 4.7.1. [131] [2006] IRLR 695, HL.

As this was not over a long period and he seemed to have done little by way of complaint, he would probably have failed for lack of foreseeability under *Sutherland v Hatton*; moreover, he had brought his action four years later, and so an ordinary personal injury action would have been statute barred anyway. In the light of this, his lawyers sued instead under the Protection from Harassment Act 1997. This Act was clearly meant to give protection to individuals from *stalking* activities; it makes 'harassment' a criminal offence (without defining it) backed by restraining orders, but almost as a side effect attaches a right of civil action for the victim, subject to a *six*-year limitation period and with the possibility of damages merely for 'anxiety' caused by the harassment. Ostensibly, this Act had nothing to do with employment law, but on the other hand the Act is so vague and broadly drafted that nothing excludes it from that area either. When the claimant here brought his action under the Act rather than at common law, the trial judge rejected the claim, saying that it was inappropriate in the employment context. The Court of Appeal reversed this by 2–1, with a strong dissent denying the applicability of the Act at all, but a further appeal to the House of Lords held unanimously that the Act applies to facts such as these. Although only one judge so held with approval, the others feeling compelled to come to that result as a matter of statutory interpretation (and expressing sympathy as a matter of policy with the dissenting judge in the Court of Appeal), the result is clearly that this avenue is now open to a claimant where the cause of the occupational stress is alleged to be harassing action by another at work. The results of this are as follows: (a) although the Act is cast in terms of liability on the actual perpetrator, in a civil action the claimant can sue the employer for being *vicariously liable* for the perpetrator's actions, and vicarious liability is *strict* (requiring no foreseeability by the employer, or indeed any fault at all);[132] (b) 'harassment' is not defined and remains purely a question of fact (with a potentially difficult borderline between active management of an underperforming employee and unlawful harassment);[133] (c) the time limitation is not three years but six (a long time for memories to fade and relevant staff to turn over); (d) damages can be awarded merely for anxiety, thus breaking the link with the mental *injury* which was so important in *Sutherland v Hatton*; (e) if the cause of the harassment was sex, race, disability, sexual orientation, religion or belief, or age, the normal expectation would be action under the relevant discrimination law where the employer would have the defence that all reasonable steps were taken to prevent that or things like it happening, but under the 1997 Act (which apparently can be used as an alternative to a discrimination action as well as to a common law negligence action) there is *no* such defence available to the employer.

While several of their Lordships in *Majrowski* tried to play down the floodgates arguments against allowing the 1997 Act to apply in the employment context,[134] the exact limits of liability are likely to remain disputed. In *Sunderland CC v Conn*,[135] the Court

[132] Majrowski did not sue the individual manager at all, and there was no requirement to do so. Moreover, vicarious liability will be particularly applicable in one of these cases since the law was changed in *Lister v Hesley Hall Ltd* [2001] ICR 665, [2001] IRLR 472, HL to replace the old 'expressly or impliedly authorized' test for when an employee is acting in the course of employment with a much wider 'reasonable work connection' test. If the bullying manager was doing it in working hours, the employer will now almost certainly be vicariously liable, with little chance of showing that the manager was acting 'on a frolic of his own', ie purely personally.

[133] Lady Hale said that it was important for the courts to draw 'sensible lines between the ordinary banter and badinage of life and genuinely offensive and unacceptable behaviour'. The only limitations in the Act are that it must be such that a reasonable person would think the course of conduct amounted to harassment of another (s 1(2)) and that there must indeed be a *course* of conduct (s 1(1)), so that a one-off event is not covered (see *Banks v Ablex Ltd* [2005] IRLR 357, CA).

[134] The Act has been used by employers to protect their staff against threats from outsiders, eg animal rights extremists; in *First Global Locums v Cosias* [2005] IRLR 873 it was successfully used to restrain an ex-employee who had reacted to being disciplined and dismissed by making death threats against fellow employees.

[135] [2008] IRLR 324, CA.

of Appeal showed a more wary approach, holding that two instances of bad temper by a supervisor (only one of which was aimed at the claimant) fell far short of the threshold required to constitute 'harassment' under the Act. In doing so, it said that where that threshold lies may well vary with the nature of the employment, and that it must be serious enough to be potentially *criminal* under the *primary* provisions of the Act. This quasi-criminal standard was then downplayed by a subsequent Court of Appeal in *Veakins v Kier Islington Ltd*,[136] where a more general emphasis on 'oppressive and unacceptable conduct' was preferred, but then in the first instance decision in *Dowson v Chief Constable of Northumbria Police*[137] the quasi-criminal test was again applied. In spite of these arguments, however (and judicial comments that liability under the 1997 Act is not to be found readily), the genie is now out of the proverbial bottle and available for use.

3.3.3.3 **Application to references**

The second area of considerable current interest concerns the application of a duty of care to the giving of references by an employer or ex-employer. There could, of course, be liability for a negligently written reference to the new employer,[138] but the question arose whether the employee as the *subject* of the reference could sue in negligence, for breach of a duty of care. The House of Lords in *Spring v Guardian Assurance plc*[139] (reversing a more cautious decision by the Court of Appeal) held that there could be such a duty on the employer giving a reference; it lies both in tort (according to Lord Goff on a *Hedley Byrne*-style assumption of responsibility, and according to Lords Lowry, Slynn, and Woolf on the basis that this extension of liability is fair, just, and reasonable, and concerning a sufficiently proximate relationship) and also in contract, based upon a breach of this implied term. This decision does not prevent the giving of a bad reference, only a negligently bad reference, and their Lordships were not persuaded by the argument that to impose liability would deter people from writing references. Subsequent case law has explored this new form of liability to the subject of the reference.

One key question is how comprehensive a reference needs to be in order to discharge the duty of care. This point was addressed in the most important explanatory case to date, *Bartholomew v London Borough of Hackney*,[140] where the Court of Appeal adopted from defamation law the rule that the reference must be true, accurate, and fair, but need not necessarily be full and comprehensive. The latter part of this means that the subject has no right to insist on particular information being in it; content remains a decision for the referee provided that the end result is not misleading (either positively or through the effect of an omission). This has been particularly important when addressing a well-known

[136] [2010] IRLR 132, CA. [137] [2010] EWHC 2612 (QB).

[138] Under the ordinary principles of *Hedley Byrne & Co Ltd v Heller & Partners Ltd* [1964] AC 465, [1963] 2 All ER 575, HL.

[139] [1994] ICR 596, [1994] IRLR 460, HL. The decision was 4–1, with Lord Keith dissenting. The majority held that a duty of care did exist on the facts, but this does not mean that an action will always succeed in such circumstances—the question of causation must also be established (did the employee fail to get new employment because of the negligent reference?); where the plaintiff was one of many applicants, that may be difficult to prove.

[140] [1999] IRLR 246, CA, applied in *Kidd v Axa Equity and Law Life Assurance Society plc* [2000] IRLR 301 and *Jackson v Liverpool City Council* [2011] IRLR 1009, CA. In *Legal and General Assurance Ltd v Kirk* [2002] IRLR 125 it was held that, the action lying in tort, an actual reference must have been given in order for a cause of action to arise: the employee cannot sue on the basis that the ex-employer is *proposing* to give a reference in terms to which they object. However, in a different context, it was held in *TSB Bank Ltd v Harris* [2000] IRLR 157 that an employee (still in employment) discovering that misleading references were being given about her could leave and claim constructive dismissal on the basis of breach of the implied term of trust and respect.

problem here—what is the referee to say when the employee left while still subject to unfinished disciplinary investigations? In *Bartholomew* a reference was requested by a potential employer on an individual who had left the referee's employment in a negotiated termination while under investigation for financial irregularities. The reference stated this as a fact and the individual was refused the post. When he sued under *Spring* the Court of Appeal held for the defendant referee; the reference was factually accurate, it did not give a misleading impression, and the individual had no right to demand that it should have contained further explanatory or exculpatory material. However, in *Cox v Sun Alliance Life Ltd*,[141] an ex-employer giving a reference overstepped an important line by going beyond a factual statement that allegations had been made (at a very late stage) against the individual and gave the impression that there was substance to them (so that he may well have been dismissed if he had not resigned), even though these allegations had *not* been investigated, or even put to the individual for his reactions. The Court of Appeal upheld his claim in negligence; the basis for this was that if value judgements are to be made as to guilt and included in the reference, they must (to satisfy the duty of care) be made on the basis of reasonable investigation. Mummery LJ made an interesting analogy here with the law of unfair dismissal, where a dismissal for suspected misconduct will only be fair after a reasonable investigation has led to a positive belief in guilt;[142] if a dismissal requires this, so does a later reference. Short of such an investigation, the referee ex-employer should stick to factual statements and to value judgements only on any parts of the investigation that had been completed.

The law's application to employment references has thus developed beyond all recognition in the past two decades, though entirely in relation to the reference's subject, not its recipient. This is likely to continue because of another development in a different field. Traditionally references on employees were wholly confidential and so, even if the subject suspected that poor opinions were being expressed by the referee (eg if turned down for several jobs, having named the same referee), it was quite likely that they would never actually know that or be able to prove it. Now, however, there has been a major change, almost by a side-wind. Since the passage of the Data Protection Act 1998 (now the 2018 Act) an employment reference, though unavailable to the subject in the hands of the referee, *can* be demanded by the subject in the hands of the recipient (the only exception being if it refers to third parties who have their own confidentiality interest, though this is unlikely in an employment reference).[143]

Finally, one continuing problem is whether there is any implied obligation on an (ex-) employer to *give* a reference; it has normally been thought that there is no such obligation, but in the speech of Lord Woolf in *Spring* there is a passage suggesting that in certain circumstances (where references are known to be an essential element of recruitment) it may be necessary to imply just such an obligation.[144] As with the whole of the case, this could be seen against the factual background of the plaintiff seeking new employment

[141] [2001] EWCA Civ 649, [2001] IRLR 448. Part of the ex-employee's complaint was that a form of reference had been agreed as part of a termination settlement but the employer had ignored this. There could be a problem with an agreed reference as part of a settlement (a common practice)—if it was misleadingly incomplete, to hide misdeeds by the departing employee, there could be *Hedley Byrne* liability to the *recipient* (the new employer); presumably the fact of agreement between referee and subject would be no defence to such liability, provided that damage and causation could be proved.

[142] *British Home Stores Ltd v Burchell* [1980] ICR 303n, [1978] IRLR 379, EAT; see 7.5.2.3.

[143] For the Information Commissioner's advice as to handling requests for references see 2.2.2.

[144] [1994] ICR 596 at 647, [1994] IRLR 460 at 481. In addition, the European Court of Justice (ECJ) has held that if an employer *refuses* to give a reference in retaliation for a sex discrimination complaint made by the employee, that itself can constitute unlawful sex discrimination: *Coote v Granada Hospitality Ltd* C-185/97 [1999] ICR 100, [1998] IRLR 656, ECJ, applied in *Coote (No 2)* [1999] ICR 942, [1999] IRLR 452, EAT.

under the financial services sector rules (with their mandatory references), but equally both these remarks and the case itself are expressed in general terms potentially applicable either to employment generally or at least to types of employment where references play an important part in recruitment. On the other hand, Lord Slynn pointed out that it is open to the reference-giver to state specifically the parameters within which the reference is given (and any limitations on his knowledge of the employee), or, ultimately, to rely on the *Hedley Byrne* aspect of the case to make his agreement to the employee to give the reference subject to an express disclaimer of liability. Further judicial guidance on these important points in the general context (ie not just in the financial services sector) is needed.

3.3.4 **To treat the employee with respect**

3.3.4.1 **Importance of the implied term of trust and confidence**

In modern employment law there has been a restatement of implied duties of mutual respect between employer and employee. In certain employments, particularly of a domestic nature, this may require positive courtesy,[145] while in others it may mean treating each other with such a degree of consideration and tolerance as would allow the contract to be executed. This is, of course, a vague concept which will vary with the circumstances, and if there is a more concrete area of dispute in any given case, questions of want of 'respect' will be of secondary importance.[146] However, an obligation upon the employer to treat the employee with respect and not to act in a manner likely to destroy or seriously damage the relationship of trust and confidence without good cause may be seen as a corollary of the employee's general duty of faithful service, as confirmed in *British Telecommunications plc v Ticehurst*.[147] Given that the line is still strongly held that employment is *not* a fiduciary relationship and so generalized mutual duties of good faith are not to be incorporated in that way,[148] the development of this implied term has meant that more particular duties can be imposed when necessary in order to govern the employment relationship, in particular to restrain inequitable exercises of contractual power by the employer; at times, such duties come very close to fiduciary or 'good faith' ones, but by using a more acceptable contractual analysis.[149] Moreover, it was argued earlier in this chapter[150] that there are developments suggesting not only that this is a well-established and much used implied term, but that it is assuming an overriding nature, capable of qualifying the ability of an employer to rely on a literal application of its rights under a contract of employment.

[145] *Wilson v Racher* [1974] ICR 428, [1974] IRLR 114, CA.

[146] As in *Donovan v Invicta Airways Ltd* [1970] 1 Lloyd's Rep 486, CA.

[147] [1992] ICR 383, [1992] IRLR 219, CA; see this chapter, 3.4.4.6.

[148] *Nottingham University v Fishel* [2000] ICR 1462, [2000] IRLR 471.

[149] For the evolution of the term generally see Lindsay J 'The Implied Term of Trust and Confidence' (2001) 30 ILJ 1, and see Cabrelli 'The Implied Duty of Mutual Trust and Confidence: An Emerging Overarching Principle' (2005) 34 ILJ 284 for an argument that this remains a separate implied term, not an adjunct of the term of reasonable care. Terminology may be significant; the term tends to be expressed in the negative (*not* to act in such a way as to *destroy* trust and confidence/respect) because a positive formulation (that the employer *must* act in a particular way) could suggest a wider, reasonableness test at which courts have baulked. If necessary, however, the term *can* place positive obligations on the employer: *Transco plc v O'Brien* [2002] ICR 721, [2002] IRLR 444, CA. One balance for the employer is the qualification that the employer must not behave in the way in question 'without reasonable and proper cause': *Hilton v Shiner Ltd* [2001] IRLR 727, EAT.

[150] See this chapter, 3.2.1.3.

3.3.4.2 **Development of the term**

The development of such a term is perhaps not so surprising, as the advent of the law on unfair dismissal has restricted the employer's prerogative to dismiss so that good personnel management has become an essential, not an optional extra.[151] The overall requirement of fair dismissal procedures, for example, has meant that more notice has to be taken of the employee's viewpoint, and the employer is expected not just to assess conduct and issue warnings but also to take more positive action to assist or train the employee to meet any required standards of competence or conduct.

Moreover, in one important area of unfair dismissal law, the concept of an implied duty of respect has taken on definite significance: this is in the area of 'constructive dismissal'. This is discussed in detail in Chapter 7, but the essence of it is that the employee can claim to be dismissed, even though they walk out, if they can show that the employer's conduct was such that they were 'entitled' to do so.[152] In *Western Excavating (ECC) Ltd v Sharp*,[153] a case which served to emphasize the underlying contractual nature of the employment relationship, the Court of Appeal held that this meant *contractually* entitled, that is, where the employer's conduct went as far as to repudiate the whole contract; on the face of it, this narrowed the concept of constructive dismissal, for mere unreasonableness by the employer would not be enough per se, but the effect of this case has been considerably reduced by praying in aid the implied term of respect, because if there is such a term and the employer behaves unreasonably (ie with unacceptable disregard for the employee), the employer can be held to have broken the implied term, to have repudiated the contract, and therefore to have constructively dismissed the employee even within the narrower view taken in *Western Excavating (EEC) Ltd v Sharp*.[154]

Reliance on the implied term in this context is common and can arise on a wide variety of facts, to such an extent that it can constitute something of a 'wild card' in employment law, often requiring the employer to think in terms not just of whether contemplated or proposed conduct (eg changes to working practices or terms and conditions) is strictly lawful under the wording of the individual contracts, but whether objection could

[151] In *Cantor Fitzgerald International v Bird* [2002] IRLR 867, breach of the term came from the manner of the employer's dealings with the employees when changing their contracts; in *Stanley Cole (Wainfleet) Ltd v Sheridan* [2003] ICR 297, [2003] IRLR 52 it came from the imposition of an unjustified disciplinary penalty. *Horkulak v Cantor Fitzgerald International* [2003] IRLR 756 (upheld in relation to remedies in [2004] IRLR 942, CA) was notable for its firm disapproval of the idea that if the employer paid a high enough salary it could treat the employee any way it wanted, ie trust and respect always applies, even in the City; similarly, in *McBride v Falkirk Football and Athletic Club* [2012] IRLR 22 a football club could not excuse bad treatment of its manager simply on the basis that an 'autocratic style of management' is the norm in the sport.

[152] Employment Rights Act 1996, s 95; a similar definition applies to redundancy claims—s 136. For an application of similar ideas of a duty of trust and confidence in a common law claim see *Bliss v South East Thames Regional Health Authority* [1987] ICR 700, [1985] IRLR 308, CA.

[153] [1978] 1 All ER 713, [1978] ICR 221, CA.

[154] There is an excellent explanation of this role for the implied term of respect in the judgment of Browne-Wilkinson J in the EAT in *Woods v WM Car Services (Peterborough) Ltd* [1981] ICR 666, [1981] IRLR 347 (approved by the Court of Appeal [1982] ICR 693, [1982] IRLR 413). If employer conduct is bad enough to breach this term, that will invariably be repudiatory conduct for these purposes: *Morrow v Safeway Stores plc* [2002] IRLR 9, EAT. See also the modern case law set out at 2.1.3, and in particular the extension of this term to the area of employees' pension rights in *Imperial Group Pension Trust Ltd v Imperial Tobacco Ltd* [1991] ICR 524, [1991] IRLR 66 and *IBM Holdings Ltd v Dalgleish* [2018] IRLR 4, CA. The latter case applied the decision of the Supreme Court in *Braganza v BP Shipping Ltd* [2015] ICR [2015] IRLR 487 that where what the employee is complaining about is the (unfair) exercise by the employer of a contractual *discretion*, it is necessary for him or her to go further and show that it was *irrational* (in the administrative law '*Wednesbury* unreasonableness' sense).

legitimately be made by affected employees to the *manner* in which the management propose to pursue their goals. This potentially restraining effect may be a significant factor in good personnel/HR practice. Moreover, the trend in recent years has been for the implied term to be used more widely than just in its original home of constructive dismissal. Action which breaches it also constitutes repudiatory conduct generally, which may give rise to other arguments or causes of action. Thus, for example, the implied term has been the basis for extending compensation for wrongful dismissal,[155] for freeing an employee from a restraint of trade clause after leaving because of the employer's conduct,[156] and even for recovering personal injury damages in cases of occupational stress caused by such conduct.[157]

The implied term of trust and confidence finally received the approval of the House of Lords in *Malik v BCCI SA*,[158] where it formed the basis for an unusual claim at common law for 'stigma damages', the employees' argument being that they had had their future job prospects materially damaged (as ex-managers in the collapsed BCCI bank) by reason of the fraudulent conduct of the bank's operations while they had been employed by it, which had breached the term of trust and respect. Lord Steyn referred to the term as a 'sound development' which had met with widespread approval, and which had to be applied to a wide range of situations in order to strike a balance between the employer's interest in managing the business and the employee's interest in not being unfairly and improperly exploited.[159]

3.3.4.3 **During employment, not on termination**

Shortly afterwards, however, in a fashion not uncommon in cases of major developments in the common law, serious uncertainty was introduced into this area as a side effect of the subsequent House of Lords decision in *Johnson v Unisys Ltd*.[160] The principal aim in this decision was to strangle at birth a new head of recovery of wide, general damages for 'stigma' loss *on dismissal*. This had been enthusiastically taken up by claimants' lawyers after *Malik* and was viewed by their Lordships as a highly undesirable development which was to be stopped. They did so by restricting stigma damages to breaches of contract *during* employment (ie confining *Malik* to its own facts). This was achieved in two ways: (a) by holding that a common law wrongful dismissal action is not to be used to outflank the statutory action for unfair dismissal, which is what Parliament intended should be the principal remedy for unfairness in termination (including stigma), with its deliberate imposition of short time limits and a cap on the amount that can be recovered; and (b) by holding that the term of trust and respect is aimed at ensuring that the contract can

[155] *Clark v BET plc* [1997] IRLR 348; see 6.4.2.5.

[156] *Cantor Fitzgerald International v Bird* [2002] IRLR 867.

[157] *Gogay v Hertfordshire County Council* [2000] IRLR 703, CA; *Eastwood v Magnox plc* [2004] ICR 1064, [2004] IRLR 733, HL.

[158] [1997] ICR 606, [1997] IRLR 462, HL; see Brodie 'The Heart of the Matter: Mutual Trust and Confidence' (1996) 25 ILJ 121 (cited with approval in the case); 'Beyond Exchange: The New Contract of Employment' (1998) 27 ILJ 79; 'Mutual Trust and the Values of the Employment Contract' (2001) 30 ILJ 84; and 'Mutual Trust and Confidence: Catalysts, Constraints and Commonality' (2008) 37 ILJ 329.

[159] The Northern Ireland Court of Appeal in *Brown v Merchant Ferries Ltd* [1998] IRLR 682 and the English Court of Appeal in *Transco plc v O'Brien* [2002] EWCA Civ 379, [2002] ICR 721, [2002] IRLR 444 adopted Lord Steyn's formulation of the implied term which stressed that the test was an objective one, ie whether the employee could properly conclude that the employer was repudiating the contract, not whether the employer had intended so to act (see also *Leeds Dental Team Ltd v Rose* [2014] ICR 94, [2014] IRLR 8). It was also established in *Malik* (n 157) that the repudiatory conduct does not in law have to be aimed directly at the employee.

[160] [2001] ICR 480, [2001] IRLR 279, HL.

continue in a reasonable and proper manner and so is *not* applicable at the dismissal stage, where, by definition, questions of continuance no longer arise.

It was this second ground that caused problems. If confined to the moment and mechanics of dismissal (as used in the case itself to rule out stigma damages from the manner of dismissal) it was unobjectionable. However, if ever applied more widely to the whole process leading up to dismissal, it could be disastrous for the proper treatment of employees under discipline, and indeed for constructive dismissal (where the employee would normally want to rely on immediately pre-termination employer misconduct as justifying leaving). This loose end of what was meant by the implied term not applying 'on termination' caused problems for some time and led to a division of opinion in the Court of Appeal.[161] Fortunately, however, the issue was fairly quickly considered by the House of Lords in *Eastwood v Magnox plc*,[162] which concerned appalling behaviour by the employer during employment (leading to serious mental injury) *but* culminating in dismissal. The case thus posed the question neatly: if a narrow interpretation was adopted (only applying the so-called *Johnson v Unisys* exclusion zone at the moment of dismissal) the damage had already been done and the employee could sue; if a wide interpretation was adopted (with the exclusion applying to any facts leading up to an eventual dismissal) the employee's action would be invalid. The House of Lords unambiguously chose the narrow interpretation and held for the employee. Lord Nicholls put it as follows:

> Identifying the boundary of the '*Johnson* exclusion area', as it has been called, is comparatively straightforward. The statutory code provides remedies for infringement of the statutory right not to be *dismissed* unfairly. An employee's remedy for unfair dismissal, whether actual or constructive, is the remedy provided by statute. If before his dismissal, whether actual or constructive, an employee has acquired a cause of action at law, for breach of contract or otherwise, that cause of action remains unimpaired by his subsequent unfair dismissal and the statutory rights flowing therefrom. By definition, in law such a cause of action exists independently of the dismissal.[163]

Straightforward it may be in principle, but there can still be problems applying it to the facts of a case, and perhaps not surprisingly the matter went for a third time to the Supreme Court in *Edwards v Chesterfield Royal Hospital NHS Trust*.[164] Here, a surgeon had allegedly been subject to harsh treatment leading up to his dismissal, which had been effected (he maintained) by the wrong disciplinary procedure, thus constituting breach of contract.[165] On the basis that the end result was in practice the ending of his

[161] In *Eastwood v Magnox plc* [2002] IRLR 447, the Court of Appeal used a wide interpretation to rule out an employee's action, but on very similar facts a different Court of Appeal in *McCabe v Cornwall CC* [2003] IRLR 87 adopted the narrow view and allowed the employee's action to proceed.

[162] [2004] ICR 1064, [2004] IRLR 733, HL. This common law claim was heard at the same time as the appeal in *Dunnachie v Kingston upon Hull CC* [2004] ICR 1052, [2004] IRLR 727, HL, where it was held that non-financial loss for injury to feelings cannot be awarded in an unfair dismissal action (see 7.6.2). The end result is that such damages (and 'stigma' damages more widely) cannot be claimed either at common law or by statute if they arise on termination.

[163] At para 27. Lord Nicholls saw the statutory cap on compensation for unfair dismissal as one of the problems here (leading to a claimant's lawyers wanting to use a common law action as well if actual damages exceed that cap). Giving the other principal judgment, Lord Steyn was even more critical, tracing many of the problems back to *Johnson v Unisys* itself (in which he dissented) and saying that this whole area needs reforming by Parliament.

[164] [2012] ICR 201, [2012] IRLR 129, SC. See 6.4.2.5 for consideration of the case in its specific context of damages.

[165] Had he been successful, he still faced a difficulty on causation, having to show that if the correct procedure had been used he would not have been dismissed.

future career prospects, he quantified his loss at £4.7m, and hence was not interested in a (capped) unfair dismissal action or the minimal damages usually available for an action for wrongful dismissal. What he claimed was damages for breach of the contractual term on discipline, arguing that *those* damages were completely uncapped (in effect, as if he had been *injured* at work and unable to continue). He therefore ran up against the argument that this form of action came within the *Johnson* exclusion zone and was ruled out. The Court of Appeal upheld his claim, to considerable surprise at the time, but the Supreme Court allowed the employer's appeal and restored orthodoxy. It is, however, a complex case with little by way of clarity in the judgments. The Court found for the employer by 4–3, but in both the majority and the minority there were divisions of opinion on the reasoning (in fact, on one view, the result was 3–1–2–1 in the employer's favour!). The end result, however, was the upholding of the *Johnson* exclusion zone in principle (by 6–1) and its application to disciplinary procedures leading up to dismissal (by 4–3). Thus, any challenge to such procedures must be brought under the heading of unfair or wrongful dismissal, and cannot result in open-ended damages. One point to note here is that (unlike *Johnson*) *Edwards* concerned breach of an express term concerning disciplinary procedure, not breach of the implied term of trust and respect, but there is no reason to think that the same principle would not apply also to the implied term, which therefore cannot be used to found a common law action for general damages because of bad treatment the employee received in the *process* of dismissal (hence the point made in the subheading—that the term is available during employment, but not on termination).

3.3.5 **To deal promptly and properly with grievances**

In *W A Goold (Pearmak) Ltd v McConnell*,[166] two salesmen whose commission-based pay had been hit by a change in sales methods tried to raise this as a grievance; in the absence of a proper procedure[167] they tried to do so on several occasions in an ad hoc manner with their manager and then with the new managing director, but with no results. When eventually they sought an interview with the company chairman and were refused, they walked out. Upholding the tribunal decision that this was a constructive dismissal and unfair, the EAT held that it is an implied term in a contract of employment that employers will reasonably and promptly afford a reasonable opportunity to their employees to obtain redress of any grievances they may have. Moreover, this is a fundamental term, breach of which will be sufficiently serious to justify the employee in terminating the employment.

This declaration of a new (possibly overriding?) implied term was of particular significance for three reasons. First, it was a very good example of the use of implied terms set out previously, as a way of the courts governing certain basic contents of the employment relationship and imposing certain standards of behaviour in employee relations. Second, although this point is not mentioned in the judgment of Morison J, the case could be seen as following on from at least two previous decisions in which failures to take up specific forms of complaints arising in the high-profile areas of health and safety[168] and sexual harassment[169] had been held to constitute fundamental breaches of contract for

[166] [1995] IRLR 516, EAT.

[167] As employees, they should have had a written note of the appropriate grievance procedure in their written ('section 1') statement of terms and conditions; see 2.3. This point was used by the EAT to demonstrate Parliament's intention that there should be proper such procedures, properly administered.

[168] *British Aircraft Corpn v Austin* [1978] IRLR 332, EAT.

[169] *Bracebridge Engineering Ltd v Darby* [1990] IRLR 3, EAT.

the purpose of establishing constructive dismissal when the complainant left. *Goold* in effect consolidates such disparate cases into one general principle and in doing so places new emphasis on the efficient administration of grievance procedures. Third, it fits in well with two subsequent developments elsewhere. The first was the extension of the ACAS Code of Practice No 1 in 2000 to cover grievance procedures as well as disciplinary procedures. This was followed by the unsuccessful experiment (in the Employment Act 2002) of making exhaustion of the statutory grievance procedure compulsory. Although that experiment was abolished in April 2009, part of its replacement was a further reissuing of the ACAS Code of Practice No 1, which again clearly covers grievance procedures (this time primarily as a matter once again of best practice rather than overly prescriptive law, though with provision for an uplift or decrease of compensation for breach of statutory rights such as unfair dismissal of up to 25 per cent if the employer or employee unreasonably fails to comply with the Code).[170] For these reasons, grievance procedures have been given an ever higher profile in recent years and proper exhaustion of them by both parties will now usually be very advisable.

3.3.6 **To provide a reasonably suitable working environment**

In *Waltons & Morse v Dorrington*,[171] a non-smoking secretary in a solicitors' firm was moved into a room close to heavy smokers, which she found a problem. Her complaints had only partial effects and eventually she was told to put up with the solution or leave. She left and claimed constructive dismissal, which was upheld by the EAT, who held that it is now an implied term of all contracts of employment that the employer will provide and monitor for employees, so far as is reasonably practicable, a working *environment* which is reasonably suitable for the performance by them of their contractual duties. This term goes beyond the long-standing term of health and safety (discussed previously) (on the facts, eg it would probably have been too soon to show distinct health risks to her), and in formulating it (much more along 'welfare' lines) the EAT adopted much of the phraseology of the Health and Safety at Work etc Act 1974, s 2(2)(e), which provides that the employer must take reasonable care for 'the provision and maintenance of a working environment for his employees that is, so far as reasonably practicable, safe, without risks to health and adequate as regards facilities and arrangements for their welfare at work'. Moreover, although not mentioned in the judgment, this implied term is also consistent with (a) modern health and safety regulations, especially the Management of Health and Safety at Work Regulations 1999, with their emphasis on proactive measures such as risk assessments in workplaces, and (b) the clear coverage of the 'working environment' (not just traditional health and safety) in Article 153 of the EU Treaty. This novel implied term is potentially very wide but, curiously, has seen little by way of further development in subsequent case law.

3.3.7 **Further developments: advice, confidentiality, and PHI schemes**

As seen previously, it is, of course, always open to the courts to extend the scope of these imposed duties on employers. In that context, three developments merit mention.

[170] Trade Union and Labour Relations (Consolidation) Act 1992, s 207A, inserted by the Employment Act 2008, s 3.

[171] [1997] IRLR 488, EAT.

3.3.7.1 **Informing and/or advising the employee**

The first is that in *Scally v Southern Health and Social Services Board*,[172] the House of Lords upheld the finding of an implied term that the employer would *inform* the employee of valuable (but obscure) rights under his pension scheme; when the employer failed to do so and the employee lost those rights due to a time limitation, the employee could therefore sue the employer for breach of contract. Clearly, the facts of this case were unusual, but Lord Bridge drew a principle that there could be such an implied term where (a) the terms of the contract had not been negotiated individually, but resulted from negotiation with a representative body or were otherwise incorporated by reference; (b) the employee could only avail himself of a valuable right under the contract by taking certain action; and (c) the employee could not, in all the circumstances, reasonably be expected to be aware of the term unless it was brought to his attention. Obligations to inform or warn are common in modern health and safety law,[173] and it was interesting to see this development in mainstream employment law (albeit in the specialized context of pensions), because the traditional approach was much more in the nature of caveat employee.[174]

However, subsequent case law has not shown a desire to extend *Scally*, which may eventually turn out to have been the high-water mark here, or indeed to be restricted to its own facts. In *University of Nottingham v Eyett*,[175] it was held that there was no duty on an employer to advise an employee about to retire that his pension would be higher if he delayed slightly (when all that that employee had enquired about was his entitlement on his preferred date of retirement), and in *Hagen v ICI Chemicals and Polymers Ltd*[176] there was again held to be no obligation to give positive advice on pension entitlements through a TUPE transfer; for good measure, the Court of Appeal held in *Outram v Academy Plastics*[177] (alleged breach of duty by employer as pension trustee in not advising the employee to rejoin the scheme when he renewed employment after a break) that if there is no duty under the contract of employment (given this restrictive treatment of *Scally*), the employee will not be allowed to argue for a wider duty in tort. The matter was eventually considered again by the Supreme Court in *James-Bowen v Commissioner of Police for the Metropolis*,[178] where police officers whose conduct had been challenged in civil proceedings against their chief constable sought damages because they alleged that the way he had settled the claim (accepting liability) caused them financial and reputational harm. The decision of the Court was that this was to be treated as a claim in tort

[172] [1991] ICR 771, [1991] IRLR 522, HL. If this case applies, the obligation on the employer is only to use reasonable care to advise, not to guarantee receipt of the information: *Ibekwe v London General Transport Services Ltd* [2003] IRLR 697, CA.

[173] A good example is the decision of Waite J in *Pape v Cumbria County Council* [1992] 3 All ER 211 that there was a common law duty on the employer to warn cleaning staff of the danger of dermatitis from certain cleaning chemicals (*General Cleaning Contractors Ltd v Christmas* [1953] AC 180, [1952] 2 All ER 1110, HL applied).

[174] In *Lister v Romford Ice and Cold Storage Co Ltd* [1957] AC 555, [1957] 1 All ER 125, HL there was no obligation on the employer to organize all matters of insurance (see this chapter, 3.4.3) and in *Reid v Rush & Tompkins Group plc* [1990] ICR 61, [1989] IRLR 265, CA it was held that the employer was under no duty to warn the employee of the risk of economic loss (through not insuring himself adequately when working abroad). The question of insurance cover for the employee should preferably be covered expressly in the contract whenever it is likely to be an issue, especially since the decision in *Merrett v Babb* [2001] EWCA Civ 214, [2001] QB 1174 that when a firm of surveyors went bankrupt one of their employees could be personally liable to a client to whom he had given bad advice; unfortunately he was not insured as he was no longer covered by the firm's previous policy. For arguments in favour of extending the scope of *Scally* see van Bever 'An Employer's Duty to Provide Information and Advice on Economic Risks?' (2013) 42 ILJ 1.

[175] [1999] ICR 721, [1999] IRLR 87. See also *Marlow v East Thames Housing Group Ltd* [2002] IRLR 798.

[176] [2002] IRLR 31.

[177] [2001] ICR 367, [2000] IRLR 499, CA.

[178] [2018] UKSC 40.

(which failed because it was not 'fair, just and equitable' to extend the law to cover these unusual facts); however, in passing, the judgment refers to arguments based on *Scally* and states that that case establishes no general principle, was decided on narrow grounds, and is dependent on its own facts. Thus, unless a case arises which is much closer to the facts of *Scally* (which is now seen as heavily dependent on the inability of the employees to discover the true facts without information from the employer), it is unlikely that any duty to advise will be held to have arisen, still less any wider duty to protect the employee's financial interests.

One interesting point here is that in *Hagen* the claimant employees in fact succeeded on the separate ground that certain information that they had actually been given was misleading and so, their having relied on that to their provable detriment,[179] the employer was liable in tort for *negligent misstatement*. Thus, if an employer *chooses* to give information which the employee will reasonably and foreseeably rely on, care must be taken as to its accuracy. This distinction is well shown by the contrasting decisions in *Crossley v Faithful & Gould Holdings Ltd*[180] and *Lennon v MPC*.[181] In the former, a senior employee arranged his early retirement in a way that was less advantageous than it might have been; he did not know this but his employer did, and when he finally found out the true position he sued the ex-employer for not telling him. In line with the above case law, his claim was dismissed on the basis that there is no positive obligation in general on an employer to advise an employee as to their best interests. However, *Lennon* fell on the other side of the line because there a police officer changing forces had asked an HR officer which was the best way to do so (to preserve certain accrued benefits) and the officer had *undertaken* to find out for him. When the wrong option was advised and he lost the benefits he successfully sued his old force for damages for their loss, on the basis that there was sufficient 'assumption of responsibility' to activate liability under the modern approach to negligent misstatement. The distinction between these two very instructive cases is clear legally, but in practice there could be major issues of fact as to who said or promised what to whom.

3.3.7.2 **Confidentiality**

The second development is the possible extension of ideas of confidentiality in employment. There is a well-developed implied duty of confidence *on* an employee (considered in 3.4.4.3), but is there an equal and opposite duty *towards* an employee? In *Dalgleish v Lothian and Borders Police Board*[182] an interdict was granted, preventing the employers from divulging employees' names and addresses to the council who were chasing community charge defaulters, partly on the ground that this information was confidential, was not in the public domain, and was held by the employers only for the purpose of the employer–employee relationship. Another early sign of such ideas was the decision of the European Court of Human Rights in *Halford v United Kingdom*[183] that interception of telephone calls at work constituted a violation of the Convention rights to respect for private life and family life, home, and correspondence. Clearly, such arguments are now likely to be buttressed by the Human Rights Act 1998, because such matters are now justiciable before the national courts and tribunals. However, the question then becomes whether it is likely that the *result* of that jurisdiction will be to aid the employee.

[179] This element in *Hagen* was unusual—the employees could show causation on the basis that, if their true position had been known to them, they would have objected to the TUPE transfer *and* then the employers would *not* have gone through with it. Normally, employees will have no such de facto power of veto, the transfer would happen anyway, and so what they may or may not have been told in advance would have no causative effect on their later loss, which would have happened anyway.

[180] [2004] ICR 1615, [2004] IRLR 377, CA.

[181] [2004] ICR 1114, [2004] IRLR 385, CA.

[182] [1991] IRLR 422, Ct of Sess.

[183] [1997] IRLR 471, ECtHR.

The Convention rights *look* as though they should back a right to confidentiality, but case law has been difficult.

In *Barbulescu v Romania*,[184] the claimant employee used his business email account to send and receive personal messages. This was discovered by the employer through monitoring for a week and the employee was dismissed because of it. The Romanian court and Court of Appeal upheld that dismissal under their domestic law, but the claimant argued that they should have excluded this evidence because it was obtained in breach of his Article 8 right to privacy and personal communications. This point was referred to the European Court of Human Rights (ECtHR). The court at first instance found that in such a case Article 8 is engaged but it went on to hold that in circumstances such as these the article is not breached because it was reasonable and proportionate for the employer to protect its interests in this way. This decision was viewed as supporting strongly the employer interest here, but in a most unusual development there was then an appeal to the court's Grand Chamber, which by a majority reversed the lower court's decision and found for the employee. In holding that the employer's breach of the employee's confidentiality was *not* justified on these facts, the judgment sets out the following factors as being relevant:

1. whether the employee has been notified of the possibility that the employer might take measures to monitor correspondence and other communications, and of the implementation of such measures;[185]
2. the extent of the monitoring by the employer and the degree of intrusion into the employee's privacy; in this regard, a distinction should be made between monitoring of the flow of communications and of their content;
3. whether the employer has provided legitimate reasons to justify monitoring the communications and accessing their actual content;
4. whether it would have been possible to establish a monitoring system based on less intrusive methods and measures than directly accessing the content of the employee's communications;
5. the consequences of the monitoring for the employee subjected to it and the use made by the employer of the results of the monitoring operation;
6. whether the employee had been provided with adequate safeguards, especially when the employer's monitoring operations were of an intrusive nature.

The problem here, however, is that it is one thing to set out these guidelines but another to *apply* them, and it would appear that the tendency in later cases (both domestic and European) has been to give the employer more leeway that perhaps *Barbulescu* might have suggested. In *Garamukwana v Solent NHS Trust*,[186] the claimant had been in a relationship with a fellow employee. When this ended, he started sending upsetting

[184] [2017] IRLR 1032, ECtHR (Grand Chamber).

[185] In *Argus Media Ltd v Halim* [2019] IRLR 442 (QB) the employer had and operated a clear email policy, well communicated to employees, thus legitimizing the employer's interceptions of emails (*Barbulescu* distinguished).

[186] [2016] IRLR 476, EAT. Note one extension here, in that the information in question was on the claimant's *own device*, not in the employer's system. The result is very much in line with the relatively pro-employer stance taken by domestic courts in validating quite intrusive covert monitoring (eg by video surveillance) of employees suspected of misusing sick pay and leave: *McGowan v Scottish Water* [2005] IRLR 167, EAT; *City and County of Swansea v Gayle* [2013] IRLR 768, EAT; see 7.5.2.4. It is also in line with pre-*Barbulescu* ECtHR case law on covert monitoring: see *Kopke v Germany* Appl no 420/07 (5 October 2010, unreported); again, however, a later case showed a stricter approach to such monitoring (even where it had established guilt): *Lopez Ribalda v Spain* [2018] IRLR 358.

messages to her and others at work. Moreover, anonymous communications followed, leading to a police investigation. This discovered material on his phone suggesting that he was responsible. The police shared this with the employer. After a proper investigation the employer dismissed the claimant for gross misconduct, in relation both to the general messages and the anonymous ones. On his claim of unfair dismissal, the tribunal found that the employer had acted within the range of reasonable responses and had not breached Article 8. The EAT dismissed the claimant's appeal, going further conceptually in holding that in these circumstances the employee had *no* expectation of privacy and so Article 8(1) was not engaged in the first place; for good measure it was said that even if it had been, the employer would have had the Article 8(2) defence when acting proportionately to protect the rights of others at work who had been affected by the correspondence. When the claimant was refused leave to appeal to the Court of Appeal, he made a reference to the ECtHR but this was rejected on much the same grounds as in the EAT.[187] Moreover, in *Lopez Ribalda v Spain*[188] (which concerned a classic case here of covert surveillance of supermarket tills to discover the cause of till shortages), the ECtHR then held that the Spanish court had been correct in holding that, although Article 8 was engaged, the employer had acted proportionately, given that the surveillance was only of the till area, the recordings had only been seen by a restricted group of managers, and the aim was to discover *criminal* activity.

Given these uncertainties in the protection given by the case law (both European and domestic), arguably in practice greater recognition of ideas of employee privacy or confidentiality at work has come from a further, independent source *not* reliant on contractual or human rights ideas, namely data protection law as introduced in 1998 and now contained in the Data Protection Act 2018. Although in itself lying primarily outside employment law, much effort was put into the production by the Information Commissioner of an Employment Code of Practice giving best practice advice on the impact of the legislation in the employment context. Even with the major changes in 2018 to enact the General Data Protection Regulation, the official view of the Commissioner's office is that the Code is unaffected and is to continue in force. A significant amount of this advice is clearly of relevance to the establishment of a level of confidentiality for employees while at work that had hitherto only been argued for in theory. It is perhaps not fanciful to say that the overall approach is based on a simple yet important principle that the employer employs the employee; it does not own them.

The Code is split into four parts. We have already seen Part I: Recruitment and Selection in the previous chapter.[189] Even at this initial stage there are provisions clearly premised on an element of employee confidentiality, in particular the advice to (a) only ask for information that is directly relevant to recruitment, (b) destroy information afterwards unless it is definitely necessary to keep as part of a personnel file, and (c) only ask for sensitive personal data (especially on health records) once a prima facie decision has been made to appoint that person. Part II: Employment Records continues this approach into the question of what information to keep (and how to keep it) on employees once appointed. Key points here are to (a) only keep such records as are necessary (and inform employees what is kept); (b) ensure security of records, limiting access only to those managers who need to have it; (c) use absence records, not detailed schemes records, where possible; (d) have systems to cope with access requests by employees and third parties;

[187] [2019] IRLR 853, ECtHR.

[188] [2020] IRLR 60, ECtHR. As in *Barbulescu*, the Grand Chamber reversed the lower chamber, but in the opposite direction this time.

[189] See 2.2.2.2.

(e) provide references to third parties only where the employee wishes this; (f) ensure that disciplinary records are accurate and only used when necessary and for proper purposes (eg in later investigations); and (g) have a disposal policy for old or spent information. Medical records are dealt with separately in the fourth part of the Code, being in the more specialized category of 'sensitive personal information'. However, it is the third part, 'Monitoring at Work', which is likely to be most controversial in the context of confidentiality. It covers not just obviously intrusive forms of monitoring such as the use of telephone tapping or CCTV cameras, but also the much wider and more sensitive areas of monitoring for email and/or Internet abuse. Here, the simple approach that the machinery belongs to the employer, which can therefore do as it wants, is not sufficient because we are seeing the evolution of at least formative ideas that an employee at work has certain rights or expectations of privacy, especially where personal use is not wholly banned. Key suggestions in the Code are to (a) have clear business reasons for any monitoring, (b) have a policy on the use and abuse of electronic communications and publicize it to staff, (c) keep access to information obtained restricted, (d) use an 'impact assessment' (similar to a health and safety risk assessment) to determine what monitoring is justified by the benefits, (e) ensure that workers and others know the extent of monitoring, (f) where possible monitor traffic, not content,[190] (g) try to use software solutions to present abuse at source (especially downloading of offensive material), and (h) in dealing with any allegations of Internet abuse, remember that inappropriate websites can be accessed by mistake.

Technically, of course, a code such as this is only relevant to data protection issues, and breach of it for no good reason would only be of direct concern in an enforcement action under the Data Protection Act 2018. However, the cross-over into employment indirectly could be considerable for three reasons: (a) in fact the Codes are likely to have a major impact on personnel/HR practice, just as much as if they had been produced under employment law; (b) the Code on Monitoring could well have a major impact in any case concerning discipline or dismissal for email or Internet abuse (eg where the employee has breached a well-known and consistently applied employer policy, drafted in line with the Code);[191] (c) an interesting point would arise if ever an employee sought to use breach of their rights or expectations under the Code(s) (especially that on monitoring) to privacy at work as a reason for walking out and claiming constructive dismissal—would the courts evolve an implied term either to protect privacy generally or (less controversially) to abide by the Codes? If so, the cross-over would become formal, not just informal.

One final point to note is that this area may take on added topicality in the light of the coronavirus crisis and the significant moves towards home/remote working. To what extent are employers going to want to monitor and *control* the way that an employee works in these circumstances? There have been signs of the use of highly intrusive software (spyware?) to record exact hours worked and individual productivity. Is this just a natural extension of the move to remote working, or an unacceptable infringement of personal privacy?

3.3.7.3 The permanent health insurance cases

The third development concerns a modern trend in the employment of more senior employees of offering permanent health insurance (PHI) as part of the remuneration package; paid for by the employer, this can offer major benefits to an employee who

[190] Although sensible generally, this might not be possible in a case of alleged harassment by electronic means, where the content would be vital.

[191] Particularly in the light of the hard line already taken by the EAT regarding such misconduct in *Thomas v Hillingdon London Borough Council* (2002) The Times, 4 October.

becomes permanently incapable of work through illness, but its relationship with ordinary sickness procedures and notice provisions has proved troublesome (as has the potentially difficult relationship between employer, employee, and the insurance company providing the scheme),[192] especially where the PHI has been in the nature of an 'add-on' without thought as to its possible legal effects. In *Aspden v Webbs Poultry and Meat Group (Holdings) Ltd*,[193] the plaintiff was a senior manager who was subject to the firm's PHI scheme for senior staff—if incapable of work for more than 26 weeks, he would be entitled to three-quarters salary until death, retirement, or ceasing to be an employee. However, on engagement he had been given a standard contract which did *not* take the separate PHI scheme into account, and in the case of long-term illness provided for six months' sick pay and then for dismissal. When he became ill (after altercations with the firm over reorganizations) the employer, which suspected he might have been exaggerating his illness, exercised its contractual power of dismissal before he could qualify for the PHI benefits. The employee brought an action for wrongful dismissal; normally this would have been doomed to failure because of the terms of the contract, but Sedley J upheld the employee's claim that on the facts of the case there was an implied term that, save for summary dismissal for cause,[194] the employer would not terminate the contract while he was incapacitated, so as to deprive him of the PHI benefits. The judge acknowledged that this was on the edge of permissibility for the use of implied terms, but was necessary because otherwise an unrestricted power to terminate would completely negate the working of the PHI scheme, which clearly applied to the claimant but had been completely overlooked when his contract had been given to him. Although an adventurous decision, it has been followed by the Outer House of the Court of Session[195] and approved obiter in the Court of Appeal;[196] it marks yet a further move away from strict contract doctrine in the employment field.

3.3.7.4 A wider principle?

One point of considerable importance for future developments here is whether the *Aspden* principle will be applied outside the PHI context. It operates, in effect, by placing a restriction on the employer's normal power to dismiss by giving notice where to do so would negate valuable PHI rights; might it evolve into a wider principle, applying to deliberate attempts by the employer to use the doctrine of notice to deprive the employee unfairly of *any* valuable rights or expectations?

[192] In *Marlow v East Thames Housing Group Ltd* [2002] IRLR 798 the insurance company stopped paying the PHI benefits when it thought the employee was no longer incapable of work; the employee could not challenge this directly (the PHI scheme contract was between the employer and the insurance company) but established that the employer was contractually bound to take all reasonable steps to pursue her claim, on the basis of the implied term of trust and respect.

[193] [1996] IRLR 521.

[194] This was expressed in *Aspden* to be the important protection that the employer needs in such a case; for an example of its application see *Briscoe v Lubrizol Ltd* [2002] EWCA Civ 508, [2002] IRLR 607. However, it now needs to be expanded to cover summary dismissal for cause *and* dismissal for bona fide redundancy, neither of which mean that the employer is trying to frustrate the PHI scheme, and so neither of which would be contrary to the implied term: *Hill v General Accident Fire and Life Assurance Corpn plc* [1998] IRLR 641, OH.

[195] *Adin v Sedco Forex International Resources Ltd* [1997] IRLR 280, Ct of Sess.

[196] *Brompton v AOC Int Ltd* [1997] IRLR 639, CA. In *Villella v MFI Furniture Centres Ltd* [1999] IRLR 468 a similar argument succeeded again, this time where dismissal was used to try to avoid continuing with PHI payments already being made, as in *Briscoe v Lubrizol Ltd* (n 193 above) where the Court of Appeal accepted the *Aspden* principle as established law.

This would be a major inroad into the traditional law on dismissal by notice,[197] but there are signs of such an extension (certainly where there is a close analogy to PHI rights) in *Jenvey v Australian Broadcasting Corpn*,[198] where an employee, alleging that his employment had been deliberately terminated in a way and at a time so as to ensure that he could not claim valuable redundancy rights, successfully bought a common law breach of contract action for the value of those rights. Elias J held that there had been a breach of a specific implied term that where an employer has resolved to dismiss an employee by reason of redundancy, the employer will not (other than for good cause) dismiss that employee for some other reason. Thus, any advance of the law here is suitably cautious and incremental, not based on any wide generalized principle; on the other hand, the case does extend the PHI cases by analogy into an area not previously covered. As in any area of controversy, however, developments are not all in one direction, and the subsequent decision of the Privy Council in *Reda v Flag Ltd*[199] was far less adventurous. It concerned complex contractual provisions for the termination and payment of two senior executives of a Bermudan company; there were three stipulated forms of termination, each with a different compensation package spelled out. When the company dismissed the executives expressly under one of these (with a substantial payment) but with the effect that they could not benefit from a new share option scheme being introduced, they argued on analogy with *Aspden* that this was unlawful and that they were entitled to the benefit of the scheme. The Privy Council turned down their claims. At first sight this appears to go against the flow of the previous cases but it is suggested that the case is best viewed as reliant on its facts—the termination agreement was highly specific and was not to be assailed by reliance on implied terms (whereas such an assault may be more feasible in more normal cases where the employer is just (ab)using the ordinary doctrine of notice, with no large pay-offs); *Aspden* was distinguished, not disapproved (and none of the other previously mentioned case law was mentioned); and in any event, on the facts, the court clearly thought little of the merits of the employees' cases, and said that the employers had had sound commercial reasons ('reasonable cause'?) for acting as they had done. In fact, in the only subsequent case to consider *Reda* (and then only briefly) the Court of Appeal took a narrow approach to it, as being largely explicable on its facts,[200] and so it is suggested that it should not be seen as stopping further development in this area in suitable cases, though it does show that radical arguments such as these are not to be relied on too readily or too widely. Suitability here may well be heavily reliant on the substantive merits of the case. In *Jenvey* the employer had in fact dismissed the employee in a way that was automatically unfair (partly as revenge for tribunal proceedings brought by him over a dispute), but then pleaded that as the reason why he could not claim to have been redundant and so qualified for the enhanced redundancy rights. Faced with the deeply unattractive argument that the employer could rely on its own automatically unfair dismissal to negate the employee's rights (or at least expectations), Elias J ended his judgment with the following instructive passage:

> It follows that I find for the claimant. I confess that I am pleased to be able to do so. The defendant's position lacked merit. It would in my view have been a gross injustice if ABC were to be better off as a result of dismissing the employee for an unlawful reason than it would have been had it dismissed him lawfully by reason of the redundancy that had

[197] See 6.2 and Smith and Randall *Contract Actions in Modern Employment: Developments and Issues* (2nd edn, 2011) pp 97–100.

[198] [2003] ICR 79, [2002] IRLR 520.

[199] [2002] UKPC 38, [2002] IRLR 747.

[200] *Horkulak v Cantor Fitzgerald International* [2005] ICR 402, [2005] IRLR 942, CA.

arisen. The need to preserve the integrity of the legal process recognized in the old adage 'hard cases make bad law' may sometimes compel a court to accept a particular injustice because it cannot properly be remedied in line with legal principle. Fortunately, I am satisfied that I can here do justice without any improper distortion of the legal rules.

3.4 Implied duties of the employee

3.4.1 Obedience

In the days before employment was explained in terms of a contract, the servant's duty of obedience was taken to be a natural element of employment, and indeed, if one delves far enough back, it was accompanied by the master's right to discipline and perhaps chastise the erring servant. It is now explained as an aspect of the contract of employment that the employer may give and the employee should obey a lawful order, and indeed it has been argued that this should be taken a step further and viewed not as a duty of obedience but rather as an example of cooperation. The term 'lawful' order is often used but in this context it means primarily an order which is reasonably within the ambit of the employment in question so that, once again, in any given dispute much or all will depend on the terms of the individual contract of employment, whether express or implied; the task of deciding what is the scope of the employment may be facilitated by the requirements in s 1 of the Employment Rights Act 1996 of written particulars of terms of employment, particularly of the title of the job which the employee is employed to do (s 1(4)(f)). Thus, the employer cannot give orders outside the proper scope of the employment, for example orders of a 'personal' nature such as regulating the length of the employee's hair or their out-of-work activities (unless it can show some special considerations bringing such matters within the scope of employment, such as danger in having long hair when working machines or some form of special interest, employment-related, in outside activities). Also, this principle means that the employer cannot order the employee to change their contract, so that if it is clear that they are not contractually bound to be mobile or work overtime, it will not be 'lawful' to order them to work elsewhere[201] or to put in hours above the basic.[202]

Questions of obedience are naturally bound up with the law on dismissal, and at common law principally with the employer's right to dismiss summarily. In general, refusal to obey a proper order would usually justify summary dismissal, and although such matters tend to change over time with different social attitudes, this is still the basic position with regard to the common law action for wrongful dismissal. However, the statutory action for unfair dismissal is now far more important and the question of fairness depends upon all the factors in the case, not just whether the employee was technically in breach of contract.[203] In the light of this, although the employer may still dismiss summarily in cases of grave misconduct, a single act of disobedience may not necessarily render the dismissal fair, for although it would qualify as a reason concerning 'conduct' within s 98(2) of the Employment Rights Act 1996, the tribunal must go further and consider, under s 98(4),

[201] *O'Brien v Associated Fire Alarms Ltd* [1969] 1 All ER 93, [1968] 1 WLR 1916, CA; *Courtaulds Northern Spinning Ltd v Sibson* [1988] ICR 451, [1988] IRLR 305, CA; cf *Stevenson v Teesside Bridge and Engineering Ltd* [1971] 1 All ER 296; and *United Kingdom Atomic Energy Authority v Claydon* [1974] ICR 128, [1974] IRLR 6, NIRC.

[202] *Pengilly v North Devon Farmers Ltd* [1973] IRLR 41, IT.

[203] *Farrant v Woodroffe School* [1998] ICR 184, [1998] IRLR 176, EAT.

whether the employer acted reasonably in treating it as a sufficient reason for dismissal in all the circumstances of the particular case.

The duty of obedience at common law is subject to two particular qualifications. The first is that the employer may not order the employee to do something illegal;[204] if it does so the employee is entitled to refuse to obey the order, and any purported summary dismissal will be wrongful and, of more importance, very likely to be held to be unfair, as in *Morrish v Henlys (Folkestone) Ltd*,[205] where the employee was dismissed because he refused to falsify accounts. The second qualification is that the employer may not order the employee into danger; in *Ottoman Bank v Chakarian*,[206] an employee was held to have been justified in disobeying an order to stay in Constantinople, where he had previously been sentenced to death and was in danger of being apprehended a second time. However, it appears that for this exception to apply there must be immediate and personal danger, so that in *Bouzourou v Ottoman Bank*,[207] expectation merely of general hostility from the Turkish authorities was not enough to justify refusal of an order to work in Mersina. The same was found with an unspecific fear of IRA activity if sent to work in Eire in *Walmsley v UDEC Refrigeration Ltd*.[208]

3.4.2 **Adaptation to new methods and techniques**

As was pointed out in the previous chapter when considering changes in the terms of employment, problems may arise from the fact that jobs change but contracts tend to be static. What is to happen if the employer introduces new working methods or techniques which the employee is unwilling to accept? In such a case, the employee may argue that the changes are sufficiently fundamental to fall outside the scope of the existing contract; if this is so, the employer must be able to show a consensual variation of the relevant terms before it can insist on the employee accepting the changes.[209] There is extensive case law on this point in the law on redundancy,[210] where the courts have consistently given considerable latitude to employers to alter work practices without being held to have altered the job itself. A second possibility is that the employer may have envisaged the possibility of future changes and, in the light of that, either framed the contractual terms (particularly the job title/description) flexibly, or given itself express contractual authority to make the changes in question. However, the question remains: what is to happen where neither of these solutions applies, that is, where the changes are not fundamental enough to alter the job itself, but changes in methods or techniques are not expressly covered by the contract? Can the employee refuse to adapt?

It appears that in most cases the employee will not be able to refuse, as they will not be deemed to have a right to continue as they always had indefinitely. There is little case law directly on this point, but it is possible that if necessary, the courts would develop an implied term of adaptation. Signs of this can be seen in the judgment of Walton J in *Cresswell v Board of Inland Revenue*.[211] In that case, Inland Revenue officers and clerks refused to operate a new computerized system of PAYE administration when their

[204] *Gregory v Ford* [1951] 1 All ER 121. Semble there must be a clear order if the employer is to be in breach of this principle: *Buckoke v Greater London Council* [1970] 2 All ER 193, per Plowman J; affd by the Court of Appeal: [1971] 1 Ch 655, [1971] 2 All ER 254, CA.

[205] [1973] 2 All ER 137, [1973] ICR 482, NIRC.

[206] [1930] AC 277, PC.

[207] [1930] AC 271, PC.

[208] [1972] IRLR 80, IT.

[209] On variation see 2.6. If no such variation is forthcoming, the employer may have to dismiss the objector employee and defend an unfair dismissal action on the ground that the dismissal was fair because of the business need to change: see 8.1.2.

[210] See 8.1.1.

[211] [1984] ICR 508, [1984] IRLR 190. Napier 'Computerisation and Employment Rights' (1992) 21 ILJ 1.

employers could not guarantee that there would be no compulsory redundancies. They sought a declaration that their employers were in breach of contract in requiring them to operate the computers. It was held, however, that the change to computers was not sufficient to fall outside their contractual duties of tax gathering and that on the facts they were expected to adapt to the new methods: 'There can really be no doubt as to the fact that an employee is expected to adapt himself or herself to new methods and techniques introduced in the course of his employment.'[212]

However, if such an implied term is to be developed, it should be noted that Walton J added a requirement of reasonableness, continuing the same passage as follows:

> Of course, in a proper case the employer must provide any necessary training or retraining . . . [I]t will, in all cases, be a question of pure fact as to whether the retraining involves the acquisition of such esoteric skills that it would not be reasonable to expect the employee to acquire them.

Cresswell was a common law action, but this reasonableness approach could be particularly important in an unfair dismissal action. In *Smith v London Metropolitan University*,[213] a university lecturer in theatre studies was involved in a personality clash with a colleague in that department, as a result of which she was required by the university to move into the English department and teach English literature. She maintained that that was outside her experience and competence and refused to do so, as a result of which she was disciplined and dismissed. When she claimed unfair dismissal the university argued that she had been in breach of the implied term of reasonable adaptation. The tribunal agreed but the EAT allowed her appeal; it held that that implied term applies to adaptation to new methods of performance of existing contractual duties, whereas on the facts here working in the English department would constitute a new *job*, which is not covered by this term.

3.4.3 **The duty of care**

An employee owes to their employer an implied duty of care in carrying out their job. The basic authority for this is usually said to be *Harmer v Cornelius*,[214] even though that case actually concerned a representation that the employee possessed the necessary *skill* for the job, for in subsequent cases skill and care have been treated as roughly equivalent. This duty of care applies generally[215] and could cover, for example, care in using the employer's equipment. However, its principal legal significance arises where an employee in the course of their employment injures a third party or that party's goods. In these circumstances the employer may be sued for damages by the third party as being vicariously liable for the tort of the employee. Once sued, however, the employer has a legal action against the employee for an *indemnity*, and this has caused some difficulty.

[212] pp 518 and 195, respectively. [213] [2012] IRLR 884, EAT.

[214] (1858) 5 CBNS 236. It was held in *Cheltenham BC v Laird* [2009] IRLR 621, QBD that a job *applicant* owes a duty of care when answering questions posed by the employer (eg as to previous health record); the employer's claim for breach of this duty failed on the facts (see 2.2.2). Following this, in *Easton v Secretary of State for the Home Department* [2025] IRLR 15, EAT it was held that failure to disclose a previous dismissal for gross misconduct was a breach of this duty, leading to a fair dismissal when discovered.

[215] Theoretically, breach of this duty could found an action for damages by the employer against the employee: this is most unlikely to happen, though for an example of it, on rather special facts, see *Janata Bank v Ahmed* [1981] ICR 791, [1981] IRLR 457, CA. In *Cheltenham BC v Laird* above the employer had unsuccessfully claimed almost £1m from the employee.

The employer's cause of action arises in two ways:

1. It may sue the employee for breach of contract, because in incurring it in liability to pay damages, the employee is in breach of the implied duty of care. The leading case on this is *Lister v Romford Ice and Cold Storage Co Ltd*,[216] where it was clearly held that this implied duty exists, and the employer's insurers were awarded an indemnity against the employee who had negligently run down a third party (his own father, as it happened) who had sued the employer for damages. In the House of Lords, the employee attempted to mitigate this harsh application of the duty of care by saying that in modern employment law there is a further implied term that the employer will ensure that the employee is insured against liability such as this, but this was rejected by a majority of 3–2.
2. It may sue the employee in tort, because where the employer has been held vicariously liable it and the negligent employee are in law joint tortfeasors, so that it may sue the employee for contribution or a full indemnity under the Civil Liability (Contribution) Act 1978; under this statute, the court may award such contribution as it thinks 'just and equitable having regard to the extent of [the employee's] responsibility for the damage'.

The decision in *Lister*'s case caused some consternation and was at the time heavily criticized on the grounds that the principal rationalization for vicarious liability is the practical one that it is the employer or its insurer who can afford to pay the damages and that a finding by a court that the employee was negligent may be just a means of fixing liability onto the employer or his insurers; on both of these grounds, a right of indemnity would be inconsistent.[217] Two ways round the decision in *Lister*'s case have been suggested. The first was in *Harvey v R G O'Dell Ltd*,[218] where McNair J held that the right of indemnity did not apply to an employee driving a vehicle in the course of his employment when such action was not work he was employed to do but was merely a special occasion on which the employee had assisted his employer by undertaking an unusual task; this, however, is to take a very refined view of what an employee is engaged to do. The second arises from the fact that at common law (before the new cause of action was added by statute in 1935) the rule was that there could be *no* contribution between joint tortfeasors;[219] there was, however, one long-standing exception to this where the party seeking contribution was wholly innocent[220] and only liable by some operation of law such as vicarious liability—*Lister*'s case was an example of this exception, hence the common law indemnity. Thus, if some fault can be attributed to the employer who is seeking contribution, the case does not fall within the exception but comes instead within the rule and so contribution cannot be claimed; such fault could arise, for example, if the employer had given the employee some task beyond their competence or had failed to give them proper instruction, as in *Jones v Manchester Corpn*,[221] where an inexperienced doctor had caused physical injury to a patient who had sued the employing hospital board for damages but when the board sought an indemnity from the doctor, the Court of Appeal, by a majority, refused to allow it since the hospital had also been at fault in failing to provide adequate supervision for the doctor. The practical problem is that even if one can

216 [1957] AC 555, [1957] 1 All ER 125, HL.

217 Glanville Williams 'Vicarious Liability and the Master's Indemnity' (1957) 20 MLR 220 and 437.

218 [1958] 2 QB 78, [1958] 1 All ER 657.

219 The rule in *Merryweather v Nixan* (1799) 8 Term Rep 186.

220 *Adamson v Jarvis* (1827) 4 Bing 66; *Pearson v Skelton* (1836) 1 M & W 504.

221 [1952] 2 QB 852, [1952] 2 All ER 125, CA.

circumvent the contractual action in this way, the court still has the discretion to apportion under the 1978 Act, and so an indemnity may still in the end be awarded against the employee, unless the court could be persuaded that it would not be 'just and equitable' to do so; 100 per cent indemnities under the Act were awarded against employees in *Ryan v Fildes*,[222] *Semtex Ltd v Gladstone*,[223] *Harvey v R G O'Dell Ltd* (discussed earlier), and *Lister*'s case itself.

In the light of these problems, the effects of *Lister*'s case were investigated by a committee of the then Ministry of Labour[224] which concluded that while legislation could alter the position, there was no urgency since in general employers would not seek indemnities because of the effect on employment relations, and insurers (who were most likely to be interested, since when they pay the damages awarded against the employers they are 'subrogated' into their insured's shoes and can exercise their insured's rights in their own favour—it was an insurance company which brought the action in *Lister*'s case, not the employers) have a 'gentleman's agreement' not to exercise these subrogated rights to indemnity against employees (in personal injury cases, where there is no wilful misconduct or collusion). This remains the position and there has been no amending legislation. However, the rights against employees still exist in law (even if not generally exercised by employers or their insurers in practice), as can be seen from *Morris v Ford Motor Co Ltd*,[225] where a third party who was neither the employer nor an insurance company claimed to have acquired the important right of subrogation through a peculiar indemnity clause in a cleaning contract. The third party then sought to sue the negligent employee who had (indirectly) caused him to pay damages, but the Court of Appeal by a majority refused to allow it. There was no *express* subrogation clause in the cleaning contract, so Lord Denning MR disallowed an implied one on the grounds (1) that subrogation was an equitable concept and it would not be equitable to allow it in this case, and (2) that no clause would be implied in the light of employment realities, and James LJ also disallowed it on ground (2). However, this case does *not* remove the legal right to indemnity in the employment sphere, for two reasons—first, it contains no assault on *Lister*'s case, only upon the concept of subrogation which does not directly affect the actual right to indemnity; second, the majority could only decide the case this way because there was no express subrogation provision—if there had been it could not have been negated by an implied term to the contrary, so James LJ at least would presumably have had to decide the other way and that would have produced a majority in favour of the indemnity. The possibility of an indemnity being claimed from a negligent employee therefore continues to exist even if it is rarely enforced in practice.[226] This raises two further points of interest—first, no concerted action has been taken by trade unions to secure insurance cover for employees (the term claimed in *Lister*'s case), and second, it appears to be no one's business or interest to clear up an area where the formal legal position is in no way in accordance with general assumptions or practice.

[222] [1938] 3 All ER 517. [223] [1954] 2 All ER 206, [1954] 1 WLR 945.

[224] See Gardiner (1959) 22 MLR 652.

[225] [1973] QB 792, [1973] 2 All ER 1084, CA.

[226] For a rare recent example see *Padden v Arbuthnot Pensions and Investments Ltd* [2004] EWCA Civ 382 where the Court of Appeal held that an employee who had committed fraud against a client was liable to indemnify the employer against any claim brought by the client. One limitation here, however, is that if what the employee has done is to incur the employer in a criminal or administrative *fine* it may be contrary to public policy to permit the employer to shift some or all of that fine onto another party (here, the employee): *Safeway Stores Ltd v Twigger* [2010] EWCA Civ 1472.

3.4.4 **Good faith**

3.4.4.1 **The general duty of fidelity**

An act which is inconsistent with the terms of the contract, express or implied, and which is injurious to the employer and their interest will amount to a breach of the duty of faithful service. Thus, a manager whose acts were injurious to the interests of the theatre he was employed to manage was held to have been rightly dismissed at common law,[227] and conversely a court saved from attachment an employee who refused to produce material documents in his possession which he held merely in his role of employee, for the court would not infer that he could produce the documents without violating the duty he owned to his employer.[228]

In particular, an employee must not place himself or herself in a position in which their own interests conflict with their duty to the employer.[229] The clash of interest and duty can be seen most clearly in the leading case, *Boston Deep Sea Fishing and Ice Co v Ansell*.[230] The defendant had been employed as managing director of the plaintiff company and he had contracted with a firm of shipbuilders for the supply of certain vessels and had taken from them a commission in respect of the transaction, of which his employers knew nothing. He also possessed shares in an ice-making and fish-carrying company which paid bonuses to those of its shareholders who, being owners of fishing vessels, used the company's ice or its services as a carrier. He was held to the strictest accountability but, apart from that, there was clearly a breach of his duty faithfully to serve, since the temptation to use the company's ice or its services as a carrier conflicted or might conflict with his duty to consider his employer's interests in preference to his own. It was held that he was properly dismissed, and he had to account to his employer for his profits. It is true that this case concerned a managing director and directors may be under a special fiduciary duty anyway,[231] but the general principle may apply to any employee who misuses their employer's property in a way which shows breach of fidelity (eg by borrowing from the till when not allowed to do so: *Sinclair v Neighbour*),[232] or improperly exploits their position of employment in order to make a secret profit or gain. In *Reading v A-G*,[233] Sergeant Reading, who was stationed in Egypt, agreed on a number of occasions to accompany lorries to certain destinations, his uniform guaranteeing that such lorries would avoid inspection by the police. These lorries contained illicit spirits and as a result of his services Reading secured almost £20,000. When the military authorities arrested him, they impounded the money and when he was released from prison he brought a petition of right claiming return of the money by the Crown. The House of Lords not surprisingly held against him, for he had misused his position in the service of the Crown and had to account for his profit.

[227] *Lacy v Osbaldiston* (1837) 8 C & P 80.

[228] *Eccles & Co v Louisville and Nashville Railroad Co* [1912] 1 KB 135, CA.

[229] *Pearce v Foster* (1886) 17 QBD 536, CA provides a good example; see generally Stephens 'An Agent's Duty to Account' (1975) 28 CLP 39.

[230] (1888) 39 Ch D 339, CA. Note that one of the main propositions established in this case, that at common law the employer may rely on misconduct unknown to it at the date of dismissal and only discovered subsequently in order to justify dismissal, does *not* apply to proceedings for unfair dismissal: *W Devis & Sons Ltd v Atkins* [1977] 3 All ER 40, [1977] ICR 662, HL.

[231] *Cook v Deeks* [1916] 1 AC 554, PC; *Cranleigh Precision Engineering Ltd v Bryant* [1964] 3 All ER 289, [1965] 1 WLR 1293; *Industrial Development Consultants v Cooley* [1972] 2 All ER 162, [1972] 1 WLR 443; *Thomas Marshall (Exports) Ltd v Guinle* [1978] ICR 905, [1978] IRLR 174. Under long-standing rules of company law, a director with an interest in a contract with the company is under a duty to disclose that interest to the board of directors.

[232] [1967] 2 QB 279, [1966] 3 All ER 988, CA.

[233] [1951] AC 507, [1951] 1 All ER 617, HL.

Although secret profits and interests may have to be disclosed, and in certain circumstances an employee may have to inform their employer about matters in their knowledge which affect confidential interests of the employer,[234] the duty of fidelity must not be taken too far. Except for the case of directors who are under a fiduciary duty,[235] a contract of employment is *not* a contract *uberrimae fidei* requiring total and voluntary disclosure. Thus, an employee is not under a general duty to declare facts which may prove inimical to the employer, including the employee's own misconduct or unsavoury aspects of their own background. This rule, dating back to the well-known authority of *Bell v Lever Bros Ltd*,[236] was strongly reaffirmed in *Nottingham University v Fishel*,[237] where the employers were seeking to recover damages from their employee, a leading scientist, who had been undertaking private work abroad without telling them, also using other university employees. Their victory was distinctly Pyrrhic because the primary breach of contract (working abroad in university time) had in fact benefited university research so that there was no damage; there was a secondary breach by using the other employees, which gave rise to damages but not to any great amount. On the crucial allegation (for present purposes) that he was in breach by not telling them the truth, the court held that it was important *not* to erect any contractual duties on employees to fiduciary levels and that special duties of disclosure should only exist if expressly provided for in the contract, which was not the case here. Thus, the university's claim under this head failed, very much along the lines of *Bell v Lever Bros Ltd.*

However, this rule has always been subject to the qualification that the employee must not positively *mislead* the employer as to such matters,[238] and the rule does not extend to the telling of deliberate *lies* by the employee.[239] In the important case of *Sybron Corpn v Rochem Ltd*[240] it was further (a) suggested that there may be a duty to disclose the employee's own misconduct which has been fraudulently concealed, and (b) held that there may be on the facts of the case a positive duty to disclose the misconduct of *other* employees (particularly in the case of an employee high in the company's hierarchy, with responsibility for those other employees), even if that involves of necessity disclosing his own misconduct.[241] In *Tesco Stores v Pook*,[242] a senior manager (*not* a director) defrauded the company to the tune of £0.5m, for which he was sentenced to imprisonment. When the company sought to recover another £0.3m in relation to a bribe that he had

234 *Cranleigh Precision Engineering Ltd v Bryant* [1964] 3 All ER 289, [1965] 1 WLR 1293.

235 *Regal (Hastings) Ltd v Gulliver* (1942) [1967] 2 AC 134n, [1942] 1 All ER 378, HL; *Horcal Ltd v Gatland* [1984] IRLR 288, CA; *Item Software (UK) Ltd v Fassihi* [2005] ICR 450, [2004] IRLR 928, CA.

236 [1932] AC 161, HL. Most of these cases involve attempts by an employer to recover golden handshakes given to employees who, after leaving, are discovered to have been defrauding the employer. Note that a 'spent' conviction does not have to be disclosed anyway, under the Rehabilitation of Offenders Act 1974, s 4 (for the application of this Act to unfair dismissal cases see 7.5.2.2).

237 [2000] ICR 1462, [2000] IRLR 471. See also (for another good factual example) *Helmet Integrated Systems Ltd v Tunnard* [2007] IRLR 126, CA.

238 Hence the importance, on recruitment, of the employer asking the right questions (eg at an interview) so that the employee cannot simply refrain from volunteering information and obtain the employment sub silentio. Deliberate fraud in gaining employment will usually be a fair ground for dismissal: *City of Birmingham District Council v Beyer* [1978] 1 All ER 910, [1977] IRLR 211, EAT. Moreover, in the light of *Fishel* (n 236) an employer may be advised to include in the appointed employee's contract a clause specifically requiring disclosure (eg of any other employment or activities to be undertaken) if it is likely to be a significant issue.

239 *Human Kind Charity v Gittens* [2020] IRLR 412, EAT.

240 [1983] 2 All ER 707, [1983] IRLR 253, CA.

241 Applying *Swain v West (Butchers) Ltd* [1936] 3 All ER 261, CA. A case possibly going further is *RBG Resources plc v Rastogi* [2002] EWHC 2782, Ch D (see Lewis (2004) 33 ILJ 278), where it was thought arguable that a senior manager may have a duty not just to disclose misconduct by others but to *investigate* it initially, with a view to disclosing it.

242 [2004] IRLR 618, Ch D.

taken, he counterclaimed for share options that he said he had been denied by the company. The judge dismissed this counterclaim, partly by finding an implied term that the options would not be exercisable if the employee committed dismissible fraud, but also by holding that, at his level of seniority, he had been in breach of contract himself by not disclosing the bribe. While it is true that a bribe may give rise to a fiduciary duty to account for it, and once a fiduciary duty arises it is easier to find a duty to disclose, the judge also relied on *Sybron Corpn*, even though there was no question of misconduct by other employees.

What seemed to be relevant here was the employee's *seniority* and the overall point of interest is whether a case such as this is showing a movement towards extending duties very similar to fiduciary ones down *below* board level, at least to senior managers. If so, arguably the result is that although *Bell v Lever Bros* has not been subject to frontal assault, there have been moves in recent years to undermine it, particularly where the facts of the case (in *Pook*, the bribe) can be used to convince the court that it is 'special' enough to be treated as an exception. On the other hand, the courts may have to be careful that they do not go too far and erect positive duties on ordinary employees that are too onerous. While it is true that in recent years the law has taken major steps to protect those who *choose* to whistleblow,[243] it would be a different matter for the law to develop so as to impose on ordinary employees an actual *obligation* to whistleblow.

From this general discussion of fidelity, we must now turn to four specific ways in which an employee might be in breach of their duty—by competition, misuse of confidential information, making their own inventions, and failing to serve the employer in good faith. In doing so, it may be helpful to read and remember the following very clear explanation of the policy reasons behind what follows (and which may apply across several of these heads) given by Lord Neuberger in *Vestergaard Fransden A/S v Bestnet Europe Ltd*:[244]

> Looking at this case a little more broadly, I would add this. Particularly in a modern economy, the law has to maintain a realistic and fair balance between (i) effectively protecting trade secrets (and other intellectual property rights) and (ii) not unreasonably inhibiting competition in the market place. The importance to the economic prosperity of the country of research and development in the commercial world is self-evident, and the protection of intellectual property, including trade secrets, is one of the vital contributions of the law to that end. On the other hand, the law should not discourage former employees from benefitting society and advancing themselves by imposing unfair potential difficulties on their honest attempts to compete with their former employers.

3.4.4.2 **Competition**

The courts will be most reluctant to impose restraints on a person's spare time and generally an employee's skills are their own (even if learned in the employer's time), so that normally there is no legal objection to an employee taking other employment in their spare time. The courts will, however, interfere in the untypical case where the use of the employee's skill and knowledge can be clearly shown to be harming the employer. This was the situation in the leading case of *Hivac Ltd v Park Royal Scientific Instruments Ltd*.[245] Certain employees of the plaintiff company worked in their spare time on a similar kind of highly specialized work for the defendant company, the two firms being in direct competition. There was no evidence that any of the employees (who were not parties to the

[243] See this chapter, 3.4.4.4. [244] [2013] ICR 981, [2013] IRLR 654, SC.
[245] [1946] Ch 169, [1946] 1 All ER 350, CA.

action) had divulged any confidential information. It was found that the employees had agreed to do and had done work which they knew must harm their employers, that this was a breach of their duty of fidelity, and that the defendant company would be restrained from employing them. The court made something of the fact that because of the abnormality of the times and the operation of an essential work order, the employees could not easily be dismissed, but it is doubtful how far this is relevant, as the principle remains that where the employee harms his employer the law may interfere:

> It would be most unfortunate if anything we said should place an undue restraint on the right of the workman, particularly a manual workman, to make use of his leisure for his profit. On the other hand, it would be deplorable if it were laid down that a workman could, consistently with his duty to his employer, knowingly, deliberately and secretly set himself to do in his spare time something which would inflict great harm on his master's business.[246]

There may, therefore, be cases where the courts will restrain competition, but even then it will only be during the course of employment, and will not apply to competition by an ex-employee.[247] If the employer wishes to fetter competition after the employee leaves it will have to be by an express restraint clause,[248] and, as we have seen in the previous chapter, even then the clause will only be valid if there is some definite element of trade secrets, customer connections, or staff preservation to protect, for the courts will not allow a clause which is aimed simply at stifling competition.[249]

If an employee engages in improper competition, that may be a valid reason for dismissal, though as always in the realm of unfair dismissal, the fact that it is a breach of contract is not conclusive (as it might have been at common law for wrongful dismissal) and the dismissal must still be fair in all the circumstances, including the procedure adopted.[250] If the employer finds that the employee is soliciting customers with a view to setting up in business after leaving, that too may be a valid ground for pre-emptive dismissal, but once again the evidence of this will have to be clear and may require reasonable investigation by the employer before this step is taken;[251] if the further elements of trade secrets or other confidential information being at risk are not present, however, merely planning to leave employment to work for a competitor or to set up in competition will probably not be a fair ground for dismissal.[252]

[246] [1946] Ch 169 at 178, [1946] 1 All ER 350 at 356, per Lord Greene MR. This dictum was applied by the EAT to an unfair dismissal claim in *Nova Plastics Ltd v Frogatt* [1982] IRLR 146, reinforcing the requirement of definite harm to the employer before an ordinary employee can be said to be in breach of this duty; see also *Helmet Integrated Systems Ltd v Tunnard* [2007] IRLR 126, CA.

[247] *JA Mont (UK) Ltd v Mills* [1993] IRLR 172, CA. The combination of the duty on an *existing* employee not to compete and a long notice provision produces a 'garden leave clause': see 6.2.3.

[248] This was reaffirmed by the Court of Appeal in *Caterpillar Logistics Services (UK) Ltd v de Crean* [2012] IRLR 410, CA, where an attempt to extend this form of 'barring out' relief to cases of breach only of this implied term (ie with no express restraint clause to rely on) was rejected.

[249] *Herbert Morris Ltd v Saxelby* [1916] 1 AC 688, HL; *Faccenda Chicken Ltd v Fowler* [1986] ICR 297, [1986] IRLR 69, CA.

[250] *Gibson v National Union of Dyers, Bleachers and Textile Workers* (1972) 7 ITR 324; *Golden Cross Hire Co Ltd v Lovell* [1979] IRLR 267.

[251] *Hawkins v Prickett* [1976] IRLR 52, IT.

[252] *Harris and Russell Ltd v Slingsby* [1973] 3 All ER 31, [1973] ICR 454; *Laughton and Hawley v Bapp Industrial Supplies Ltd* [1986] ICR 634, [1986] IRLR 245; cf, however, *Marshall v Industrial Systems and Control Ltd* [1992] IRLR 294, where a managing director, proposing to leave, had suborned two other employees and approached customers (Laughton distinguished), and *Adamson v B & L Cleaning Services Ltd* [1995] IRLR 193, where the foreman of a contract cleaning firm tendered for a contract in competition with his employer prior to leaving to set up his own firm, and was fairly dismissed.

3.4.4.3 **Misuse or disclosure of confidential information**

During the course of employment the employee is under an implied duty not to misuse confidential information belonging to their employer[253] and this is a duty which may continue to operate *after* the termination of their employment; however, it was pointed out by the Court of Appeal in what has for some time now been viewed as the leading modern case on the subject, *Faccenda Chicken Ltd v Fowler*,[254] that there is a difference in the content and extent of the duty—in the case of an existing employee the obligation of confidentiality is wider (covering matters such as the employee's own particular skills and knowledge acquired generally during the employment) than in the case of an ex-employee, whose obligations to the ex-employer are restricted to the kind of trade secrets or confidential customer connections that could be the subject of a valid restraint of trade clause.[255] To cover this latter case (of an ex-employee), in any employment where questions of confidentiality are at all likely to be material the employer is well advised to extract from the employee such an express restraint clause (or a garden leave clause), which is not only more certain but may in practice also be more effective because, provided that it is valid, it will stop the ex-employee actually entering employment where they may be tempted to divulge confidential information, whereas the implied duty of fidelity could only be used to seek to prevent them from divulging such information once in the employment in question. An express clause is thus preferable, but if the employer omits to negotiate one or if there is an express clause which stops short of imposing any actual restraints on the employee, the courts will usually find an implied term, as in *Robb v Green*[256] where a manager secretly copied out lists of his employer's customers, left the employment, and set up in competition using the lists: the Court of Appeal upheld the injunction which had been granted restraining the ex-employee, and Lord Esher MR said:

> I think that in a contract of service the Court must imply such a stipulation as I have mentioned (ie, that the servant will act with good faith towards his master), because it is a thing which must necessarily have been in view of both parties when they entered into the contract. It is impossible to suppose that a master would have put a servant into a confidential position of this kind, unless he thought that the servant would be bound to use good faith towards him; or that the servant would not know, when he entered into this position, that the master would rely on his observance of good faith in the confidential relation between them.

Thus, in *Sanders v Parry*[257] an assistant solicitor who set up independently, taking away from his employer one of the practice's main clients whose affairs he had looked after, was held to have broken his implied duty of good faith.

[253] *Bents Brewery Co Ltd v Hogan* [1945] 2 All ER 570; see generally Bryan 'The Employee and Trade Secrets Law' (1977) 30 CLP 191.

[254] [1986] ICR 297, [1986] IRLR 69, CA, noted Hepple [1986] 15 ILJ 183; applied in *Roger Bullivant Ltd v Ellis* [1987] ICR 464, [1987] IRLR 491, CA and *Johnson & Bloy (Holdings) Ltd v Wolstenholme Rink plc* [1987] IRLR 499, CA.

[255] Thus, in *Wallace Bogan & Co v Cove* [1997] IRLR 453, CA solicitors leaving their employer to set up their own firm played it 'by the book', doing nothing to infringe the higher duties before leaving, but *then* writing to clients of the old employer announcing the existence of the new firm. *Held*—no general restriction on this form of competition after employment, in the absence of a restraint of trade clause.

[256] [1895] 2 QB 315, CA; the passage cited is at 317.

[257] [1967] 2 All ER 803, [1967] 1 WLR 753. Contrast on the facts *Wallace Bogan & Co v Cove* [1997] IRLR 453, CA, n 254.

In general, the same rules will apply to this implied duty as apply to express restraint of trade clauses, and these are considered in the previous chapter; in particular, the duty will apply essentially to trade secrets and customer connections (those being recognized by the law as protectable interests, increasingly with the addition of staff preservation), there must be a genuine element of secrecy attached to the information in question, the duty will not apply to ordinary skills or knowledge gained during employment, and it will not be allowed in order simply to stifle bona fide competition.[258] However, even though essentially the same principles apply, the express clause remains preferable, for it will normally restrain the ex-employee from entering certain forms of employment during a particular period and so breach of it will readily be shown, whereas the implied duty allows other employment, only restraining the ex-employee from improper disclosure, and this may be far more difficult to *prove*, particularly where there is no tangible evidence such as the deliberate copying out of plans or lists (as in *Robb v Green*).[259] This problem arises because of the difficult borderline between the ordinary use of information and expertise—albeit gained in the previous employment—which is permissible,[260] and the improper misuse of confidential information which may be restrainable; this may be further complicated if the ex-employee is using some information from each category, and the principle has been stated by Lord Denning in *Seager v Copydex Ltd*[261] thus:

> When the information is mixed, being partly public and partly private then the recipient must take special care to use only the material which is in the public domain. He should go to the public source to get it; or, at any rate, not be in a better position than if he had gone to the public source. He should not get a start over others by using the information which he received in confidence.

The difficulties of applying such a principle to any particular set of facts, for example where a technical director has left the employer and gone to work for a competitor on similar work, are great, and in the light of this it may be the case in practice that although there is no legal requirement that the ex-employee should have carried the information away in some tangible (particularly written) form before the duty can be used to restrain them (and so in some cases evidence of deliberate solicitation of customers prior to leaving has been sufficient),[262] the presence of evidence of such conduct could be extremely persuasive and, indeed, in the lack of it the employer could have grave problems of proof.

[258] The assumption has also been hitherto that, like a restraint clause, the implied duty will lapse if the employee is wrongfully dismissed, under the rule in *General Billposting Co Ltd v Atkinson* [1909] AC 118, HL (see 2.4.5). However, *Campbell v Frisbee* [2002] EWCA Civ 1374, [2003] ICR 141 raised at least the possibility of a coterminous equitable obligation of confidence on an ex-employee (in particular not to divulge *personal* information about the ex-employer) which might survive an employer repudiation. The case itself was not determinative because all that the Court of Appeal were doing was to disapprove an order for summary judgment in favour of the claimant (the model Naomi Campbell); the matter was not dealt with on its merits: see Clarke (2003) 32 ILJ 43.

[259] If, however, it *is* the case that the employee leaves with written material containing confidential information, they may expect short shrift from a court, even if they argue that at least some of the information could have been carried away in their head: *Johnson & Bloy (Holdings) Ltd v Wolstenholme Rink plc* [1987] IRLR 499, CA, applying *Roger Bullivant Ltd v Ellis* [1987] ICR 464, [1987] IRLR 491, CA where Nourse LJ stated that it was still of great importance that the principle in *Robb v Green* should be steadfastly maintained.

[260] *Spafax Ltd v Harrison* [1980] IRLR 442, CA; *Faccenda Chicken Ltd v Fowler*, n 253.

[261] [1967] 2 All ER 415 at 417, [1967] RPC 349 at 368, CA. This dictum refers particularly to the position of a third party, which is considered presently, but the principle is applicable to the ex-employee himself.

[262] *Wessex Dairies Ltd v Smith* [1935] 2 KB 80, CA; *Thomas Marshall (Exports) Ltd v Guinle* [1978] ICR 905, [1978] IRLR 174; cf *Hawkins v Prickett* [1976] IRLR 52, IT.

Considering this problem in *Printers and Finishers Ltd v Holloway*[263] Cross J said, in the context of the ex-employee's knowledge of the general workings of the employer's business:

> Recalling matters of this sort is, to my mind, quite unlike memorising a formula or list of customers or what was said (obviously in confidence) at a particular meeting. The employee might well not realise that the feature or expedient in question was in fact peculiar to his late employer's process and factory; but even if he did such knowledge is not readily separable from his general knowledge of the flock printing process and his acquired skill in manipulating a flock printing plant, and I do not think that there was anything improper in his putting his memory or particular features of his late employer's plant at the disposal of his new employer. The law will defeat its own object if it seeks to enforce in this field standards which would be rejected by the ordinary man.

The employer failed on this particular part of the case, essentially because his case was too vague (as in *Baker v Gibbons*),[264] and this is likely to be the case wherever the employer lacks compelling evidence such as deliberate subterfuge and compilation of information.[265]

If an employee or ex-employee is misusing confidential information, what remedies are available to the employer? Until 2018, this was entirely a matter of judge-made law, often going back a long way. However, the UK has now transposed the EU Trade Secrets Directive 2016/943 in the Trade Secrets (Enforcement, etc) Regulations 2018,[266] which provide an *alternative* set of remedies on a statutory basis. As these two systems are to exist in parallel, each will now be considered.

The traditional remedies

If the employee is still in employment, it might well be a good reason for dismissal which is likely to be held to be fair.[267] More importantly in practice, however, if they have already left employment, the employer may seek an injunction to restrain them from passing on information or damages for breach of the implied duty, as in *Sanders v Parry*.[268] In *Vestergaard Fransden A/S v Bestnet Europe Ltd*,[269] the Supreme Court added one novel requirement before such relief is granted, namely that it must be shown that the defendant employee had *knowledge* of the alleged illegal conduct; normally this will be obvious, but on the facts of this case the particular departing employee could show that she did not know of the nefarious acts of a fellow employee leaving with her and genuinely believed that he was using original work of his own, not information unlawfully taken from the old employment. A complication might arise if the ex-employee passes on confidential information to a third party, for example a competitor with whom the ex-employee has taken employment or a company which they have set up in order to take advantage of their

[263] [1964] 3 All ER 731 at 736, [1965] 1 WLR 1 at 6.

[264] [1972] 2 All ER 759, [1972] 1 WLR 693.

[265] This is as a matter of evidence; there is, however, no legal principle that an employee is free to use *anything* carried away only in their head: *Johnson & Bloy (Holdings) Ltd v Wolstenholme Rink plc* [1987] IRLR 499, CA, disapproving dicta in favour of such a principle by Scott J in *Balston Ltd v Headline Filters Ltd* [1987] FSR 330.

[266] SI 2018/597.

[267] *Smith v Du Pont (UK) Ltd* [1976] IRLR 107, IT.

[268] [1967] 2 All ER 803, [1967] 1 WLR 753. See Goulding 'Springboard Injunctions in Employment Law' (1995) 24 ILJ 152. In *Johnson & Bloy (Holdings) Ltd v Wolstenholme Rink plc* [1987] IRLR 499, CA it was held that a plaintiff employer in such a case should normally be entitled to an injunction—it is not enough for the defendant to offer an undertaking not to use the information to compete with the plaintiff (with the prospect only of damages if there is in fact unlawful competition).

[269] [2013] ICR 981, [2013] IRLR 654, SC.

illicit knowledge. This, however, has not proved a problem, as the original employer may sue that third party, seeking an injunction restraining it from taking advantage of the information either on the narrower ground of inducement to breach of contract[270] (particularly if the employee in question is still in employment with the original employer) or on this wider ground of breach of confidence. With regard to the latter, the basis for liability on the recipient was finally considered by the Court of Appeal in *Travel Counsellors Ltd v Trailfinders Ltd*[271] where the law was potentially widened in the original employer's favour by holding that the recipient can be liable, not just if they had actual knowledge of the confidential nature of the information, but also if they *ought* to have known this by making reasonable inquiries. This makes it clear that breach of confidence is capable of being a useful weapon against a third party in cases such as these, as a further ground for an injunction or damages,[272] or, perhaps of more value, as a ground for ordering an account of profits[273] and delivery up or destruction of the material in question.[274] Thus, to take a useful example from an Australian jurisdiction, in *Ansell Rubber Co v Allied Rubber Industries*[275] the plaintiff company made rubber gloves from machines whose parts and principles were known, but the actual construction of which was secret. One of its employees, A, left their employment and set up the defendant company using identical machines, and a fellow employee, G, remained in employment while helping A to do so. In the subsequent action, the court held (a) that the construction of a machine is capable of being a matter of confidence, albeit made from known components; (b) that A was in breach of his contractual duty of fidelity through misuse of confidential information, G was likewise in breach for that reason and through improper competition while still employed, and the defendant company had received and misused confidential information and so was in breach of confidence; (c) that the plaintiff company should be awarded damages against A and G, an account of profits against the defendant company, and injunctions restraining any further use of the information and the machines.

The Trade Secrets (Enforcement, etc) Regulations 2018

When the UK government was first faced with Directive 2016/943 on rationalizing the protection of trade secrets, its first reaction was that it was not necessary to do anything about it because UK law was already ahead of the game and gave the necessary protection. However, on second thoughts it was decided to use this as an opportunity to 'address any possible gaps and to make the existing law more transparent and coherent', at least in relation to *remedies*. This can be seen in two important aspects—(a) the regulations *assume* the existence of the substantive common law of confidentiality, set out earlier, and do *not* seek to replace it; (b) they also preserve the option of using the common law remedies if they provide wider protection, as long as they conform to the basic safeguards of the Directive.[276] The first point can be seen in reg 3(1), which simply states that 'the acquisition, use or disclosure of a trade secret is unlawful where the acquisition, use or disclosure

[270] *Bents Brewery Ltd v Hogan* [1945] 2 All ER 570; *Hivac v Park Royal Scientific Instruments Ltd* [1946] Ch 169, [1946] 1 All ER 350, CA. The injunction may even order the new employer not to proceed with contracts already entered into: *PSM International plc v Whitehouse* [1992] IRLR 279, CA.

[271] [2021] IRLR 450, CA.

[272] *Seager v Copydex Ltd (No 2)* [1969] 2 All ER 718, [1969] 1 WLR 809, CA. Causation must be proved: *Universal Thermosensors Ltd v Hibben* [1992] 3 All ER 257, [1992] 1 WLR 840.

[273] *Peter Pan Manufacturing Corpn v Corsets Silhouette Ltd* [1963] 3 All ER 402, [1963] RPC 45.

[274] *Industrial Furnaces Ltd v Reaves* [1970] RPC 605.

[275] [1967] VR 37; the judgment of Gowans J contains an extensive review of the relevant British and US authorities on confidential information. For a more recent example see *PSM International plc v Whitehouse* [1992] IRLR 279, CA.

[276] SI 2018/597 reg 3(2).

constitutes a breach of confidence in confidential information'. Where this is the case, the trade secret holder can apply for either or both of interim measures against the infringer pending trial[277] or an injunction and corrective measures.[278] In the case of both types of remedy, the Regulations expressly set out the factors that a court should take into consideration when deciding whether to make an order, as follows:

(a) the value and other specific features of the trade secret;
(b) the measures taken to protect the trade secret;
(c) the conduct of the alleged or actual infringer in acquiring, using, or disclosing the trade secret;
(d) the impact of the unlawful use or disclosure of the trade secret;
(e) the legitimate interests of the parties and the impact which the granting or rejection of the measures could have on the parties;
(f) the legitimate interests of third parties;
(g) the public interest; and
(h) the safeguard of fundamental rights.[279]

Two principal matters remain to be seen about these new Regulations. The first is the extent to which they will in future be used in practice as a *replacement* for the common law (even though expressed only to be an alternative). The second arises from one aspect of the Regulations which *does* address a matter of substance (as opposed to remedy). Regulation 2 contains a statutory definition of the age-old phrase 'trade secret', defining it as

> information which (a) is secret in the sense that it is not, as a body or in the precise configuration and assembly of its components, generally known among or readily accessible to persons within the circles that normally deal with the information in question, (b) has commercial value because it is secret and (c) has been subject to reasonable steps under the circumstances, by the person lawfully in control to keep it secret.

While this definition is expressed to be only 'for the purposes of these regulations', it will be interesting to see if courts in fact will read it over into common law actions for breach of confidentiality, and even possibly into the law on restraint of trade (considered in Chapter 2) where it also appears; it certainly has the advantage of giving at least a set starting point to a notoriously difficult exercise in interpretation.

3.4.4.4 Legal protection for whistleblowers

One exception to the duty not to misuse or divulge confidential information arises where disclosure by the employee or ex-employee is in the *public interest*. This might arise where the employer is committing a criminal offence, but it might also go wider than this.

[277] Regulation 11; these may include cessation of the infringement, prohibition of production, marketing, or use of the infringing goods, or their seizure or delivery up to prevent marketing.

[278] Regulation 14; these echo the measures on interim relief, with the additional possibility of the physical destruction of the infringing goods. Note that a large part of these Regulations (regs 4–9) enact complicated time limit provisions on a statutory action. Regulation 10 provides for the confidentiality of trade secrets during any proceedings.

[279] Regulations 12, 15. Where the infringer knew or ought to have known of the infringement, the injured party may also apply for damages, the criteria for which are also set out expressly: reg 17.

The exception evolved at common law, but more significantly is now also covered by statute under the generally used title of 'whistleblowing', and these statutory provisions are now encountered regularly in tribunal proceedings.

Common law

In *Initial Services Ltd v Putterill*,[280] the ex-employee gave to a newspaper details of an unlawful price-protection ring involving the employers (contrary to the Restrictive Trade Practices Act 1956) and of price rises attributed to Selective Employment Tax in order to disguise higher profits. The Court of Appeal held that this was capable of constituting proper disclosure in the public interest, and Lord Denning MR clearly envisaged that this exception went beyond crime and fraud and applied wherever disclosure was justified in the public interest. This principle was applied in *Fraser v Evans*[281] and *Hubbard v Vosper*,[282] but was subject to restriction in *Beloff v Pressdram Ltd*[283] by Ungoed-Thomas J, who thought that it only applied to the disclosure of 'misdeeds of a serious nature' by the employer. However, this restrictive view was later disapproved by the Court of Appeal in *Lion Laboratories Ltd v Evans*,[284] where it was held that public interest disclosure could apply to a wide range of matters, of which 'iniquity' on the part of the employer was only one example. Moreover, disclosure in the public interest may be particularly justified where that disclosure is to a regulatory body with power of investigation and control of the employer's business.[285] This whole area became topical with increasing concern being expressed over attempts by certain employers to prevent any form of disclosure by employees by the incorporation of 'gagging clauses' into their contracts, for example banning them from talking to the press about anything concerning their employment, and making it a disciplinary offence to do so.[286] Particular concern arose over the use of such clauses by the newly independent trusts and other bodies in the NHS.[287] While at one level the incorporation of an express clause could be likened to the (lawful) use of a restraint of trade clause (rather than relying on the general implied term of confidentiality), the suspicion was quick to arise that these clauses were really intended to go further and prevent *any* disclosure or, as it has come to be known, whistleblowing.

Statute—the modern law on whistleblowing

Although the above common law will continue to apply by way of a defence to a civil action, concerns such as those above, allied with certain moves (eg the Nolan Committee) towards more openness about standards in public life, led to calls for more direct protection for the *individual* employee making disclosures in the public interest. This came

[280] [1968] 1 QB 396, [1967] 3 All ER 145, CA.

[281] [1969] 1 QB 349, [1969] 1 All ER 8, CA.

[282] [1972] 2 QB 84, [1972] 1 All ER 1023, CA.

[283] [1973] 1 All ER 241 at 260. The earlier authorities would have restricted it to criminal acts or danger to the state: *Weld-Blundell v Stephens* [1920] AC 956, HL. Note that an employee may in certain circumstances be under a statutory duty to disclose certain material, eg under the Health and Safety at Work etc Act 1974, ss 27 and 28.

[284] [1985] QB 526, [1984] 2 All ER 417, CA. This is an interesting case on the application of the public interest defence, containing, inter alia, a statement by Stephenson LJ that not all that is interesting to the public may be disclosed in the public interest, and a reminder that the press may have a private interest of their own in making disclosures, which may be a factor to be taken into account.

[285] *Re a Company's Application* [1989] ICR 449, [1989] IRLR 477.

[286] Lewis 'Whistleblowers and Job Security' (1995) 58 MLR 208.

[287] Vickers 'Whistleblowers and the NHS' (1995) NLJ 57. One such clause even prevented employees from contacting their MP without going through (protracted?) internal procedures.

about through a Private Member's Bill, backed by the government as a commitment in the White Paper 'Fairness at Work', which became the Public Interest Disclosure Act 1998.[288] This operated by way of additions to the Employment Rights Act 1996 to establish special protection from dismissal[289] or detriment short of dismissal[290] imposed because the worker[291] has made a 'protected disclosure'. There is, however, one gap in the protection, namely the lack of protection under this scheme for a job *applicant*[292] (a point of difference from discrimination law), even though of course a reputation as a whistleblower in previous employment may not be exactly helpful, especially in a specialized or close-knit industry or profession. To date, the only inroad into this gap has been in relation to employment in the NHS, where whistleblowing has been a particularly sensitive issue, given its nature as in effect a monopoly employer.[293]

A protected disclosure is the disclosure of information which, in the reasonable belief of the worker making the disclosure, tends to show a criminal offence, a failure to comply with a legal obligation, a miscarriage of justice, a health and safety danger, environmental damage, or deliberate concealment of any of these.[294] As with the wider view of the common law, this goes well beyond criminal offences, and to that extent the protection is

[288] Lewis 'The Public Interest Disclosure Act 1998' (1998) 27 ILJ 325, 'Whistleblowing at Work: On What Principles Should Legislation Be Based?' (2001) 30 ILJ 169, and 'Providing Rights for Whistleblowers: Would an Anti-Discrimination Model Be More Effective?' (2005) 34 ILJ 239.

[289] Employment Rights Act 1996, s 103A: such a dismissal is automatically unfair, as is any later selection for redundancy for this reason; there is no qualifying period or upper age limit; the cap on the compensatory award for unfair dismissal has been removed completely in these cases and interim relief is available. According to Public Concern at Work (the charity that was the architect of the Act, now renamed Protect), in the first three years of this new law there was a success rate of 46 per cent before tribunals; the highest award was £805,000, the lowest was £1,000, and (perhaps most significantly) the average was £107,117, a remarkably high figure.

[290] Section 47B. 'Detriment' here is not defined, but is to be construed as it is in discrimination law, ie that there is a detriment 'if a reasonable employee might consider the relevant treatment to constitute a detriment': *Jesudason v Alder Hey Children's NHS Foundation Trust* [2020] IRLR 374, CA, applied in *Edinburgh Mela Ltd v Purnell* UKEAT/00411/19.

[291] The 1998 Act adopts the wider definition of 'worker' in the Employment Rights Act 1996, s 230(3), ie a person under a contract of employment *or* under any other contract to do or perform personally any work or services for another (other than a client or customer of any profession or business undertaking carried out by the person): see 2.1.6. In an appropriate case the protection can apply to victimization before employment actually started (*MacLennan v The British Psychological Society* [2025] IRLR 4, EAT), after termination of employment (*Woodward v Abbey National plc* [2006] ICR 1436, [2006] IRLR 677, CA) or even where the disclosure itself only happens after termination (*Onyango v Berkeley Solicitors* [2013] IRLR 338, EAT). For good measure, s 43K on detriment specifically includes agency workers, homeworkers, work trainees, and certain specified NHS staff who might not otherwise have qualified. Although the terminology of unfair dismissal is of course being used, the Act can go wider than the employment relationship because there is no requirement that the divulged information must show evil-doing by the worker's employer (though of course in many cases that will be so).

[292] Sullivan v Isle of Wight Council [2025] IRLR 520, CA.

[293] The Employment Rights Act 1996 (NHS Recruitment—Protected Disclosure) Regulations 2018 SI 2018/579 give an applicant for NHS employment a right not to be discriminated against (note the terminology of discrimination, not employment protection) because of a protected disclosure, with a right of action before an employment tribunal. Unusually, there is also the alternative of a court action for breach of statutory duty.

[294] Section 43B(1). These matters may occur in the UK or abroad: s 43B(2). The reference to the reasonable belief of the worker means that there can still be a protected disclosure if some or all of the allegations are later not substantiated: *Darnton v University of Surrey* [2003] ICR 615, [2003] IRLR 133, EAT; *Babula v Waltham Forest College* [2007] IRLR 346, CA. Moreover, where the worker is acting on information provided by a third party it is enough if they reasonably believe *that* source, even if direct checking of the information is not possible: *Soh v Imperial College of Science, Technology and Medicine* UKEAT/0350/14. On the other hand, however, a worker may not use improper *means* (eg computer hacking) to try to find evidence leading to that reasonable belief: *Bolton School v Evans* [2006] EWCA Civ 1653.

wide. Indeed, in its first 15 years this increasing width led to arguments that it was being applied more widely than Parliament had intended (particularly at the suit of employees dismissed before serving what was then the qualifying employment for ordinary unfair dismissal) and too far away from its roots in protecting the *public* interest, especially as the controversial case of *Parkins v Sodexho Ltd*[295] (the first major EAT decision) applied 'failure to comply with a legal obligation' to complaints about the employee's own contractual terms and conditions, potentially extending the scope for complaint substantially into what some saw as essentially private disputes with the employer, involving little in the way of public interest. In the light of this, the Coalition government took the opportunity with the Enterprise and Regulatory Reform Act 2013 to take the unusual step of reversing *Parkins v Sodexho* by statute; this was done by reading into the above definition of a protected disclosure that it must be 'in the reasonable belief of the worker making the disclosure *and in the public interest*'.[296] This was obviously meant to rule out personal disputes about workers' own grievances altogether and bring the definition back to the original aim in the 1998 Act, but it is uncertain whether that aim has been achieved in the light of the case law on it. The Court of Appeal has held that the new definition was satisfied where the worker blew the whistle on financial irregularities by the employer which had an adverse effect *on employees' bonuses*. It was held that there was sufficient public interest in this.[297] At least in that case there were 100 affected employees; in one other case there was a protected disclosure relating to an overtime dispute affecting *four* employees.[298] The basis for the Court of Appeal's judgment was that the existence of a personal interest does *not* in itself prevent there also being the necessary public interest (a term not defined by Parliament). This is not simply a matter of numbers and is left to be determined by a tribunal on the facts of an individual case. Giving guidance on this, the judgment sets out four factors likely to be important:

1. the numbers in the group whose interests the disclosure served;
2. the nature of the interests affected and the extent to which they are affected by the wrongdoing disclosed—a disclosure of wrongdoing directly affecting a very important interest is more likely to be in the public interest than a disclosure of trivial wrongdoing affecting the same number of people, and all the more so if the effect is marginal or indirect;
3. the nature of the wrongdoing disclosed—disclosure of deliberate wrongdoing is more likely to be in the public interest than the disclosure of inadvertent wrongdoing affecting the same number of people;
4. the identity of the alleged wrongdoer—the larger or more prominent the wrongdoer (in terms of the size of its relevant community, ie staff, suppliers, and clients), the more obviously should a disclosure about its activities engage the public interest.

Having sorted that question out, it then fell to the Court of Appeal to determine a second difficult point of interpretation of the statutory scheme (again producing an essentially

[295] [2002] IRLR 109, EAT.

[296] As part of this redrafting, there was removed the previous requirement that the disclosure must be made 'in good faith'; it was, however, replaced by a provision stating that if a disclosure is not made in good faith any compensation for the whistleblower may be reduced by up to 25 per cent.

[297] *Chesterton Global Ltd v Nurmohamed* [2018] EWCA Civ 979, [2018] IRLR 947. Perhaps the public interest here was of the John Donne variety: 'Any man's death diminishes me' and hence 'Ask not to know for whom the bell tolls: it tolls for thee'. It is perhaps easier to see public interest in *Morgan v Royal Mencap Society* [2016] IRLR 428, EAT, which concerned alleged health and safety breaches by a charity.

[298] *Underwood v Wincanton Ltd* UKEAT/0163/15.

pro-employee result). This arose from the decision of the EAT in *Cavendish Munro Ltd v Geduld*,[299] which stressed that, on its wording, to be a 'disclosure' at all the actions of the employee must disclose *information* showing the wrongdoing in question; the corollary of this is that the protection is not extended to mere *allegations or adverse opinions* about the employer by the employee. The example was given that if a nurse made a complaint that needles were being left unsafely on wards, that could constitute whistleblowing; if, however, the nurse merely aired the opinion that health and safety was not taken seriously at the hospital, that would not be. In itself, this was unexceptionable, *but* the problem then arose that this was interpreted as imposing a simple 'information *or* allegation?' dichotomy, capable of causing problems of application in any case of a *mixture* of the two. There was some questioning of this interpretation in the case law and eventually the matter came before the Court of Appeal in *Kilraine v London Borough of Wandsworth*.[300] In this case the EAT had cautioned that the matter is not so simple, taking the view that what is involved here is a spectrum between the two possibilities, so that, for example, the fact that the claimant was *also* making allegations does not in itself prevent there being *sufficient* information to satisfy the test. The reasoning and result were then strongly upheld on further appeal, in particular the 'sufficiency' test. For good measure, the court added a third category to the above 'nurse' example, stressing the factual nature of the decision here by saying that if that nurse said that health and safety was not being taken seriously *while pointing to sharps lying around*, that could well be sufficient information.

Assuming there to be an acceptable disclosure, it is then necessary to consider *how* that disclosure is to be made; here the drafting makes it clear that the Act is also meant to strike a balance and not simply to allow the whistleblower to go straight to the press on all occasions, especially where the press in question are waving chequebooks.[301] To that extent, it has advantages to an employer too in emphasizing that disclosure is primarily and initially meant to be internal.[302] This is achieved by establishing the forms of disclosure that have protected status, with four categories of disclosure to named persons, backed up by two categories of wider disclosure which are subject to much more stringent conditions. The four 'normal' categories are disclosure:

1. to the employer or, where the worker reasonably believes that the relevant failure relates solely or mainly to the conduct of another person or to any other matter for which another person has legal responsibility, to that person;[303]
2. to a legal adviser, in the course of obtaining legal advice;[304]
3. to a Minister of the Crown (where the worker's employer is appointed by a Minister);[305]
4. to a person prescribed by order by the Secretary of State, where the worker reasonably believes that the relevant failure falls within the order and that the information disclosed (and any allegation contained in it) are substantially true.[306]

Obviously, cases may well arise where one of these is not appropriate (particularly where the person to whom disclosure is primarily meant to be made is actually the culprit—in

299 [2010] IRLR 38, EAT. 300 [2018] EWCA Civ 1436, [2018] IRLR 846.

301 '[The Act] will encourage resolution of concerns through proper workplace procedures, but it will protect those who, in the last resort, have to go public': Fairness at Work (Cm 3968, 1998) para 3.3.

302 Although there is no obligation in the Act for an employer to have a formal whistleblowing policy, this may well be advisable so that complaints/disclosures can be dealt with effectively in-house, thus avoiding the possibility of a protected disclosure to the press.

303 Section 43C. 304 Section 44D. 305 Section 43E.

306 Section 43F. See the Public Interest Disclosure (Prescribed Persons) Order 2014, SI 2014/2418, see *Harvey* R [2924].

this context, of course, the employer) and so the Act then establishes two longstops, where the worker is in effect allowed to 'go public':

1. 'disclosure in other cases'[307]—this applies where (a) the worker reasonably believes that the information disclosed (and any allegations contained in it) are substantially true, (b) the worker does not make the disclosure for personal gain, (c) any one of a series of conditions is met,[308] and (d) in all the circumstances of the case, it is reasonable for the worker to make the disclosure;[309]
2. 'disclosure of exceptionally serious failure'[310]—this applies where (a) the worker reasonably believes that the information disclosed (and any allegations contained in it) are substantially true, (b) the worker does not make the disclosure for purposes of personal gain, (c) the relevant failure is of an exceptionally serious nature (undefined), and (d) in all the circumstances of the case, it is reasonable for the worker to make the disclosure.[311]

The question of gagging clauses is then dealt with directly and briefly by a provision which states that any provision in any agreement between a worker and their employer[312] (*including* a settlement of legal proceedings) is void insofar as it purports to preclude the worker from making a protected disclosure.[313]

Finally, although this law has been with us now for some time and certainly gives a measure of protection for workers that was rarely there previously, there remain concerns about its overall effectiveness, both generally because of its operation through the medium of an individual complaint to a tribunal (with no coverage of job applicants, except in the NHS)[314] and specifically in relation to what some see as still too high an incidence of gagging clauses in pay-offs to departing employees. The Employment Rights Act does not address these directly, but it does give a wide regulatory power to the Secretary of State to make regulations extending the circumstances in which an employee is considered unfairly dismissed after making a protected disclosure and requiring employers

307 Section 43G.

308 The conditions are that (a) the worker reasonably believes that they will be subjected to a detriment by their employer if they make the disclosure to him or her or to a prescribed person; or (b) where there is no prescribed person, the worker reasonably believes that it is likely that evidence relating to the relevant failure will be concealed or destroyed if they make disclosure to their employer; or (c) that the worker has previously made a disclosure of substantially the same information to their employer or a prescribed person: s 43F(2).

309 In deciding on reasonableness, regard is to be had to (a) the identity of the person (or tabloid?) to whom disclosure is made; (b) the seriousness of the relevant failure; (c) whether the failure is continuing or likely to occur in the future; (d) whether the disclosure is made in breach of a duty of confidentiality owed by the employer to any other person; (e) in a case of previous disclosure (under s 43G(2)(c)), any action which the employer or prescribed person has taken or might reasonably be expected to have taken as a result; and (f) in a case of previous disclosure to the employer, whether the worker complied with any disclosure procedure whose use by him or her was authorized by the employer: s 43G(3). The final head shows the possible importance of a whistleblowing policy in ensuring that disclosure follows the correct internal channels, rather than spilling out too easily into the public arena.

310 Section 43H.

311 In deciding on reasonableness, regard is to be had in particular to the identity of the person to whom the disclosure is made: s 43H(2).

312 Whether or not a 'worker's contract' (under the extended definition in the Employment Rights Act 1996, s 230(3)).

313 Section 43J. A disclosure not protected under the Act would not come under this provision and so a gagging clause covering it would be valid *unless* a court were persuaded to strike it down at common law.

314 See Lewis 'Resolving Whistleblowing Disputes in the Public Interest: Is Tribunal Adjudication the Best that Can Be Offered?' (2013) 42 ILJ 35 and 'Stigma and Whistleblowing: Should Punitive Damages Be Available in Retaliation Cases?' (2022) 51 ILJ 62.

to take reasonable steps to investigate any such disclosure made to them. This applies to employers of 50 or more employees, with an annual turnover of £10m or more, operating in the financial sector or vulnerable to money laundering or terrorist financing. These provisions are, at the time of writing, due to come into forced in April 2026.

3.4.4.5 **The employee's inventions**

In the absence of an express term in the contract of employment, the common law position was that the employer was entitled to the benefit of inventions made by the employee if they were referable to the employment. Thus, in *British Syphon Co Ltd v Homewood*,[315] the defendant discovered a new type of soda syphon and applied to patent it; he was employed by the plaintiffs as a chief technician to advise them generally on their business, but he had not been asked to make any new designs and there was no express agreement between them on the matter of inventions. Roxburgh J held that the plaintiffs were entitled to the benefit of the invention which had arisen out of the employment. This was a strong implied term at common law, usually explained on the basis of fidelity, and it would apply if the parties were silent or if an express term was void through being too wide; moreover, it would continue to apply even if the employee went ahead and patented the invention, for then it was held that he held the patent on trust for the employer.[316] It was even held that the employee might be under a continuing duty to do anything necessary to assist the employer to realize the patent.[317]

Not every invention belonged to the employer, however, and much might depend on the nature of the invention and the position of the employee, but the employee was only really safe if the nature of the invention was clearly outside the employer's business interest;[318] however, if it was safely outside those interests, the fact that it was made during working hours or with the employer's materials would not deprive the employee of it,[319] and indeed even an express term giving the benefit of *any* invention to the employer might be void as in restraint of trade.[320] Section 56(2) of the Patents Act 1949 appeared to mitigate this possibly harsh implied term by allowing the comptroller to apportion the benefits of an invention between employer and employee unless satisfied that one party was absolutely entitled, but this was construed restrictively by the House of Lords in *Sterling Engineering Co Ltd v Patchett*[321] so that it did not apply to the majority of employment cases where, by the operation of the implied term, the employer was already absolutely entitled to the invention. The whole area of patent law was overhauled, however, by the Patents Act 1977, and so the common law will now only apply (a) to inventions made before the commencement of the relevant parts of the Act;[322] (b) where the Act does not apply, in particular where the employee was not 'mainly employed in the United Kingdom' but, under the conflict of laws rules, the matter remains generally governed by English law.[323]

For present purposes, the modern legislation made two innovations—it sets out in s 39 when an invention will belong to the employer, and provides in ss 40 and 41 a scheme for compensating an employee inventor which is quite independent of contractual obligations. Now, therefore, nearly all disputes as to employee inventions will be solved by a process of statutory interpretation, not by recourse to the common law rules. Section 39(1) provides that an invention belongs to the employee except in two specified

[315] [1956] 2 All ER 897, [1956] 1 WLR 1190. See also *British Reinforced Concrete Engineering Co v Lind* (1917) 86 LJ Ch 486.

[316] *Triplex Safety Glass Co Ltd v Scorah* [1938] Ch 211, [1937] 4 All ER 693.

[317] *British Celanese Ltd v Moncrieff* [1948] Ch 564, [1948] 2 All ER 44, CA.

[318] *Re Selz Ltd* (1953) 71 RPC 158.

[319] *Mellor v Beardmore* (1927) 44 RPC 175.

[320] *Electrolux Ltd v Hudson* [1977] FSR 312.

[321] [1955] AC 534, [1955] 1 All ER 369, HL.

[322] Patents Act 1977, s 43(1); the 'appointed day' was 1 June 1978—Patents Act 1977 (Commencement No 2) Order 1978, SI 1978/586.

[323] Section 43(2).

instances when, for the purposes of the Act and all other purposes, it belongs to the employer. These are:

1. if it was made *in the course of the normal duties of the employee* or in the course of duties falling *outside his normal duties, but specifically assigned to him*, and the circumstances in either case were such that an invention might reasonably be expected to result from the carrying out of his duties; or
2. if the invention was made in the course of the duties of the employee and at the time of making the invention, because of the nature of his duties, he had a *special obligation to further the interests of the employer's undertaking.*[324]

Unlike the common law position, this owes nothing to concepts of fidelity, and contentious points now are likely to be whether the invention was reasonably to be expected and in what circumstances an employee is under the special obligation mentioned in paragraph (2) (a director under a fiduciary duty would presumably be covered, but the question is how far coverage will extend outside that special case).[325] By s 42, any agreement purporting to diminish the employee's rights in an invention under s 39 is unenforceable to the extent that it does so diminish those rights.

Sections 40 and 41 provide in addition a statutory scheme for compensation for an inventor employee. Under this scheme, the employee may make a claim to the Patents Court or the Patents Office within a year of the expiry of the patent for compensation in one of two circumstances:

1. where the invention belonged to the employer under s 39 and proved to be of 'outstanding benefit'[326] to that employer; or
2. where the invention belonged to the employee under s 39 and they assigned or exclusively leased it to the employer but received benefits from that contract which were 'inadequate in relation to the benefit derived by the employer from the patent'.

The court or comptroller is then empowered to award such compensation to the employee as will secure for them a 'fair share' of the actual or anticipated benefits derived from the patent. 'Fair share' is not defined, but s 41 lays down criteria to be considered. In the case of (1) these are:

(i) the nature of the employee's duties, their remuneration, and any other advantages from their employment or the invention;

(ii) the employee's effort and skill in making the invention;

[324] Emphasis added. For a rare example of litigation under these provisions see *LIFFE Administration & Management v Pinkava* [2007] ICR 1489, CA, where it was held that the invention (in fact, unusually, a business method) had been made in the course of the employee's 'normal employment' and belonged to the employer. The court affirmed that these statutory provisions are to be construed as they stand, not by reference to the earlier case law. Note that if the patent belongs to the employer and an employee breaches it (or, more particularly, an ex-employee does so by divulging secrets to a competitor employer), that is a matter of strict liability requiring no knowledge on the part of the employee (unlike a parallel claim for misuse of confidential information): *Verstergaard Fransden A/S v Bestnet Europe Ltd* [2013] IRLR 654, [2013] ICR 981, SC.

[325] For detailed discussion of these provisions see the Commentary section in the *Encyclopedia of United Kingdom and European Patent Law* and Phillips 'Employee Inventors and the New Patents Act' (1978) 7 ILJ 30; *Reiss Engineering Co Ltd v Harris* [1985] IRLR 232.

[326] 'Outstanding' is a superlative term, not merely a comparative one, and so the burden of proof is a high one: *British Steel plc's Patent* [1992] RPC 117. When the phrase was eventually considered by the Supreme Court (after a 13-year legal battle) it was held that it meant 'exceptional, or such as to stand out', referring to the monetary benefit to the employer, not the inventiveness of the employee: *Shanks v Unilever plc* [2019] UKSC 45 (fair share held to be 5 per cent of the £24.5m benefit to the employer); see Hannan [2020] CLJ 28.

(iii) the effort and skill of any third party involved;

(iv) the significance of any contributions of the employer towards the invention (eg advice, facilities).

In the case of (2), they are:

(i) any conditions in any licences granted under the Act in respect of the invention or the patent;

(ii) any extent to which the invention was a joint project with a third party;

(iii) any contributions by the employer (as in (iv above)).

An order for compensation may be for a lump sum or for periodic payments or both.[327] Any agreement purporting to exclude the employee's right to statutory compensation is ineffective, but these provisions do not apply where the matter is already governed by a collective agreement.[328]

The position with regard to copyright in material produced by an employee is governed by the Copyright, Designs and Patents Act 1988, s 11, which provides that although the first owner of copyright is the author, 'where a literary, dramatic, musical or artistic work or a film is made by an employee in the course of his employment, his employer is the first owner of any copyright in the work subject to any agreement to the contrary'. This straightforward provision does not attempt any more ambitious schemes of recompensing employed authors, such as that seen in the patents legislation, being content instead to leave the matter as essentially one for agreement between the parties. It substantially re-enacts the pre-existing law which was contained in the repealed Copyright Act 1956, s 4, whose effect can be seen from the case of *Stevenson, Jordan and Harrison Ltd v MacDonald and Evans*,[329] where an accountant employed by the plaintiff company wrote a book on business management; part was based on public lectures given during his employment, part was composed while engaged on a particular assignment for the employer, and the rest was written after leaving the employment. The Court of Appeal held that the lectures were not given pursuant to his contract of employment, but that the second part (composed while on the assignment) was produced in the course of his employment, and so the copyright in that part lay with the employer, who could restrain publication of it.

3.4.4.6 **Failure to serve the employer faithfully**

It has been seen in this chapter that the employee must obey proper orders of the employer and that there is a general duty of fidelity upon the employee. This does not give the employer an unrestricted prerogative and in general it will be bound by the terms of the contract of employment, which it cannot change unilaterally. Thus, the employer cannot make the employee work overtime if it is purely voluntary or change the terms of employment (eg by making a day worker work nights where there is no such provision in the contract); to this extent the employee may stand upon the terms of the contract, and, if necessary, withdraw their goodwill, even if this has a disadvantageous effect on the employer's business. However, there may be cases where a lack of cooperation by the employee may be construed not as a lawful insistence upon observation of the contract, but instead as in fact collective industrial action aimed at prejudicing the employer's business. Although the employee may argue that this form of action (known, eg as 'going

[327] The first reported cases of applications by employees under s 40 are set out and discussed in Wotherspoon 'Employee Inventions Revisited' (1993) 22 ILJ 119.

[328] Patents Act 1977, s 40(3).

[329] (1952) 1 TLR 101, CA; see also *Beloff v Pressdram Ltd* [1973] 1 All ER 241.

slow', 'working to rule', or 'working to contract') is merely the insistence on the contractual minimum, it is clear that in some cases it can in fact be a *breach* of contract, in particular the implied duty to serve faithfully. The line between the two arguments can be a thin one, but it exists.

Strict adherence to contractual terms (on a collective level, as part of industrial action) was held capable of being a breach of contract by the Court of Appeal in *Secretary of State for Employment v ASLEF (No 2)*,[330] though the reasoning of the three judges varied. However, the leading case is now *British Telecommunications plc v Ticehurst*,[331] where a college manager took part in industrial action, first by way of a go-slow and work to contract, then escalating to a rolling campaign of strikes. The question arose[332] whether this action was lawful under the contract and the Court of Appeal held that it was a breach of the implied term 'to serve the employer faithfully within the requirements of the contract'. Adopting that formulation from the judgment of Buckley LJ in the *ASLEF* case, Ralph Gibson LJ said:

> It is, in my judgment, necessary to imply such a term in the case of a manager who is given charge of the work of other employees and who therefore must necessarily be trusted to exercise her judgment and discretion in giving instructions to others and in supervising their work. Such a discretion, if the contract is to work properly, must be exercised faithfully in the interests of the employers.

And later:

> The term is breached, in my judgment, when the employee does an act, or omits to do an act, which it would be within her contract and the discretion allowed to her not to do, or to do, as the case may be, and the employee so acts or omits to do the act, not in the honest exercise of choice or discretion for the faithful performance of her work but in order to disrupt the employer's business or to cause the most inconvenience that can be caused.[333]

Although the case concerns a manager, it is suggested that the key to this is not managerial status but, much more generally, employee *discretion* in how to perform the work. It may be that if a job was exhaustively defined in the contract, there could still be a work to contract that would not be in breach,[334] *but* in modern conditions most jobs are not like that; in such circumstances, the decision in *Ticehurst* shows that such action is very likely to be a breach of the implied duty of faithful service in the contract.

Finally, it may be noted that in at least one area the employee may be under a positive obligation to cooperate with their employer, for under the Health and Safety at Work

[330] [1972] 2 QB 455, [1972] 2 All ER 949, CA. The case concerned long repealed provisions of the Industrial Relations Act 1971.

[331] [1992] ICR 383, [1992] IRLR 219, CA.

[332] Whether or not such action is a breach of contract is not particularly relevant in the context of unfair dismissal, since the special provisions on dismissal during industrial action (10.5.3) apply to strikes 'or other industrial action', with the latter *not* depending on proof of breach of contract. However, this case concerned the equally vital question as to whether the employer can *refuse to pay* employees taking industrial action, where the question of breach is central; that aspect of the case is considered in 3.5.1.3.

[333] [1992] ICR 383 at 398, [1992] IRLR 219 at 225, CA. In *Burgess v Stevedoring Services Ltd* [2002] UKPC 39, [2002] IRLR 810 the Privy Council also adopted the narrower views of Buckley LJ in *ASLEF*, rather than the wider views adopted by Lord Denning. While this case is interesting (given the scarcity of recent authority on this abstruse point), it was under Bermudian legislation which has no UK counterpart and *Ticehurst*, n 329 (the leading UK case) was not discussed.

[334] It could, of course, still constitute 'industrial action' for statutory purposes: see n 330.

etc Act 1974, s 7(a), there is a statutory duty upon every employee 'as regards any duty or requirement imposed on his or her employer or any other person by or under any of the relevant statutory provisions, to cooperate with him so far as is necessary to enable that duty or requirement to be performed or complied with'.

3.5 The law relating to wages

3.5.1 The right to wages at common law

3.5.1.1 The basic principles

The obligation upon the employer to pay the wages which are due is a basic term of the contract of employment; details of the scale, rate, or method of calculation of the remuneration should be given to the employee in writing,[335] and they have a statutory right to receive an itemized pay statement upon payment of wages or salary.[336] However, it must be stressed that the details of the obligation upon the employer depend entirely upon the terms of the contract of employment, and there cannot be said to be any overall legal obligation to pay wages as such, since wages are not necessarily the consideration to be supplied by the employer for the work done or service rendered by the employee. Thus, at common law there can be a valid contract of employment, even though no set wages are payable, where the employee is to be rewarded by a commission,[337] by fees, by the receipt of tips from customers,[338] or by being given the *chance* to earn a salary.[339] Likewise, there will be no set wage or salary where the employee is paid on a piecework or hourly basis (with or without an agreed guaranteed minimum wage), though in such a case there may be an implied term that the employer shall provide a reasonable amount of work for the employee to do.[340] Moreover, in an extreme case it might be that the correct construction of the contract is that, in the circumstances, nothing is payable to the employee, as in *Re Richmond Gate Property Co Ltd*,[341] where the managing director of a company in liquidation had never had the question of his remuneration determined by the directors as required by the company's articles, and so Plowman J held that, in the circumstances, he was not entitled to receive anything for services rendered prior to the liquidation. Also, in certain older cases[342] it was held that an agreement which gives the employer the right to fix remuneration, gives it the right to give *no* remuneration. However, this is unlikely to be the case now, as where there is some reference to remuneration, or some discernible understanding that there would be remuneration, or where the contract is just vague on the subject, the employee may be able to recover a reasonable sum on a *quantum meruit* basis, as in *Way v Latilla*[343] where the plaintiff, who had obtained gold mining concessions for the defendant (yielding a £1 m profit) on the vague understanding that the defendant would 'look after his interests', was held by the House of Lords to

[335] Employment Rights Act 1996, s 1(4); on the significance of different forms of remuneration see Freedland 'The Obligation to Work and to Pay for Work' (1977) 30 CLP 175.

[336] Employment Rights Act 1996, s 8. As from April 2019 this right was extended (a) to 'workers' as opposed to 'employees' and (b) to include a requirement to give details of hours worked where the wage or salary varies with those hours. This is of particular importance to those engaged in the 'gig' economy.

[337] *Phillips v Curling* (1847) 10 LTOS 245; *Clayton Newbury Ltd v Findlay* [1953] 2 All ER 826n, [1953] 1 WLR 1194n; *Bronester Ltd v Priddle* [1961] 3 All ER 471, [1961] 1 WLR 1294, CA.

[338] *Pauley v Kenaldo Ltd* [1953] 1 All ER 226, [1953] 1 WLR 187.

[339] *Gaumont-British Picture Corpn v Alexander* [1936] 2 All ER 1686.

[340] See this chapter, 3.3.2.

[341] [1964] 3 All ER 936, [1965] 1 WLR 335.

[342] *Taylor v Brewer* (1813) 1 M & S 290; *Roberts v Smith* (1859) 4 H & N 315. See, however, the explanation of these cases by Vaughan Williams LJ in *Loftus v Roberts* (1902) 18 TLR 532, CA.

[343] [1937] 3 All ER 759, HL. See also *Craven-Ellis v Canons Ltd* [1936] 2 KB 403, [1936] 2 All ER 1066, CA.

be entitled to £5,000 commission on a *quantum meruit* basis when the defendant refused to pay him anything. Likewise, in *Powell v Braun*,[344] a secretary who had been offered an unspecified annual bonus (having regard to the firm's performance) in place of the usual increase in wages was held by the Court of Appeal to be entitled to a reasonable amount on a *quantum meruit* basis for the two years during which her employer had failed to pay any bonus at all, thus establishing that a *quantum meruit* action may be used to recover additional remuneration as well as ordinary wages or salary. However, one procedural caveat to this has emerged recently, namely that such an action cannot be brought before an employment tribunal and so must be litigated in a court.[345]

Some of these stranger forms of remuneration (or, indeed, possible non-remuneration) may of course now have to be read subject to the national minimum wage legislation (discussed presently), but that only specifies a minimum *amount* that must eventually be payable and does *not* mean that these forms in themselves are illegal.

One theoretical problem concerning the common law right to wages has arisen where the employee does not complete the relevant obligation in the contract of employment. In strict theory it may be that *no* remuneration is payable (even on a *quantum meruit* action), as in the old case of *Cutter v Powell*,[346] where a sailor who contracted for 30 guineas to act as second mate for a certain voyage died in the course of that voyage and his widow failed to recover any of the amount agreed upon, since the court held that partial performance of an entire obligation did not give rise to a right to any of the remuneration. This principle is most unlikely to apply to a case today, for most contracts are divisible, not entire, certainly to the extent of definite periods for payment of remuneration.[347] Even if this were not so, an employee could attempt to circumvent *Cutter v Powell* in several ways—first, by claiming that the employer had received substantial performance of the contract and so was not relieved from payment;[348] second, if complete performance was prevented by the employer, by bringing a *quantum meruit* action;[349] third, where the contract was frustrated,[350] by claiming a just amount under the Law Reform (Frustrated Contracts) Act 1943, s 1(3); fourth, by claiming that his wages or salary are to be deemed to accrue from day to day (even though not so payable under the contract) under the Apportionment Act 1870, s 2, which thus apportions 'all rents, annuities, dividends and other periodic payments in the nature of income'—s 5 states that 'annuities' include 'salaries and pensions', and it is accepted that this applies to an ordinary dispute over wages in employment law.[351]

344 [1954] 1 All ER 484, [1954] 1 WLR 401, CA.

345 *Abellio East Midlands Ltd v Thomas* [2022] IRLR 288, EAT.

346 (1795) 6 Term Rep 320, followed in *Sinclair v Bowles* (1829) 9 B & C 92 and *Vigers v Cook* [1919] 2 KB 475, CA.

347 Details of the periods for payment must be given to the employee in writing: Employment Rights Act 1996, s 1(4).

348 *Hoenig v Isaacs* [1952] 2 All ER 176, CA; *H Dakin & Co Ltd v Lee* [1916] 1 KB 566, CA; *Bolton v Mahadeva* [1972] 2 All ER 1322, [1972] 1 WLR 1009, CA.

349 *Planché v Colburn* (1831) 5 C & P 58.

350 See 6.1.2.

351 *Item Software (UK) Ltd v Fassihi* [2005] ICR 450, [2004] IRLR 928, CA. There has, however, been a major disagreement until recently as to whether 'day to day' means using 365 days per annum or the (lower) number of *working* days per annum in the claimant's case. This can matter where, eg the employer deducts a 'day's pay' for a day on strike—by what number is the annual salary to be divided? Previous case law at first instance had treated this as a matter of principle under the Act but had divided on the correct interpretation. When the matter was finally considered by the Supreme Court it was held that the Act merely legitimizes apportionment; it does not lay down the calculation. In the light of this, the correct number of days to use depends in each case on the particular contract: *Hartley v King Edward VI College* [2017] ICR 774, [2017] IRLR 763, SC. In spite of this factual emphasis, there is a strong steer in the judgment that in the case of a professional annual contract (such as the teachers in the case), the correct result is likely to be use of the 365 calendar days. Obviously, the preferable solution is to specify the calculation expressly in contracts.

In addition to this theoretical problem, four points might be mentioned particularly about the employee's right at common law to be paid his wages.

3.5.1.2 **Use as a test case**

The first is that an action for wages due, brought in the ordinary courts or a tribunal, might be used not just as an individual's remedy but also as a way of testing the legal position in what is in essence a collective dispute between employer and workforce (possibly by the device of bringing an action by one named individual, which is viewed in reality as a test case affecting an entire class of employees). In *Burdett-Coutts v Hertfordshire County Council*,[352] the county council purported to vary the terms of employment of school dinner assistants without their consent (indeed, in the face of their positive dissent); they continued to work under protest, accepting the lower wages under the new terms, but brought an action in the High Court claiming, inter alia, payment of the arrears of wages that were due under the pre-existing terms of employment. The judge held that on the facts they had *not* impliedly accepted the employer's variation by continuing to work, and gave judgment for the arrears. The validity of such an action was accepted by the Court of Appeal in *Miller v Hamworthy Engineering Ltd*[353] (enforced short-time working, not covered by the terms of the contract and not agreed to by the employee or his union) and, more importantly, in the short but emphatic decision of the House of Lords in *Rigby v Ferodo Ltd*[354] (unilateral reduction in wages by the employer, not agreed to by the employee or his union). The point about such an action (or the threat of it) is that it may oblige the employer (who wishes still to force through the new terms) to dismiss the employees formally, and then have to defend an action for unfair dismissal.[355]

3.5.1.3 **Applying the principle 'no work, no pay'**

However, the above will only work if the employee is held to have been contractually in the right. This is because the second point is that in *Cresswell v Board of Inland Revenue*,[356] Walton J held that where an employee refuses to perform duties that they are contractually obliged to perform, the simple principle 'no work, no pay' applies, so that an action for wages will then fail. Of course, such a principle begs the monumental question—what duties *is* the employee contractually obliged to perform? In fact, the case hinged on this question, and whether a requirement that the staff start to operate a newly computerized system had or had not altered the nature of the job.[357] The principle has acquired particular significance in a series of cases concerning deductions from wages due to industrial action—if the employee fails wholly or partly to carry out their duties, what can the employer do? An employee in breach of contract may be sued by the employer, but this is unlikely in practice; instead, the employer will wish to avoid paying some or all of the wages in the first place. If the employee fails to perform any of their duties (either through being on strike, or through only being willing to perform certain of their duties, which the employer refuses to allow, sending them home instead), then as in *Cresswell* the

352 [1984] IRLR 91. See also *Gibbons v Associated British Ports* [1985] IRLR 376.

353 [1986] ICR 846, [1986] IRLR 461, CA.

354 [1988] ICR 29, [1987] IRLR 516, HL.

355 As in *Gilham v Kent County Council (No 2)* [1985] ICR 233, [1985] IRLR 18, CA; see 8.1.2 on the application of unfair dismissal laws to this class of case.

356 [1984] ICR 508, [1984] IRLR 190.

357 This aspect of the case is considered in 3.4.2. One significance of applying such a general principle is that the employer has a freestanding right not to pay wages—it does not constitute a 'suspension' and so the employer does not have to comply with any contractual procedures that may exist before it can impose a suspension (so that *Gorse v Durham County Council* [1971] 2 All ER 666, [1971] 1 WLR 775 was distinguished in *Cresswell*).

employer need not pay any wages. However, the position becomes more complex when the employee is permitted by the employer to perform *part* of their duties.

Here, there are two possibilities. If the part not performed is discrete and quantifiable, it seems clear that the employer may refuse to pay the amount of wages representing that part. Thus, in *Royle v Trafford Borough Council*,[358] where a teacher participating in industrial action refused to accept a further five pupils into his class but continued to teach his existing 31 pupils, the education authority were allowed to deduct 5/36ths of his salary. Similar results were reached in *Sim v Rotherham Metropolitan Borough Council*[359] (amounts deducted from teachers' salaries representing their refusal to cover for absent colleagues as part of industrial action) and *Miles v Wakefield Metropolitan District Council*[360] (registrar normally working 37 hours per week refusing to perform marriage ceremonies in the three hours on a Saturday morning as part of industrial action; employer held correct to deduct 3/37ths of his salary). However, there has been a significant divergence of view on the reasoning behind these deductions.[361] In *Sim*, Scott J held that in such a case the employee could sue for his wages in full, but subject to the employer's right of equitable set-off of the amount representing the duties not performed (for which the employer could have sued the employee in separate proceedings). However, in *Miles* the House of Lords took the more fundamental approach that with regard to the three hours in question the employee had *no* right to the pay in the first place since he had failed to provide the consideration for his part of the contract, namely being ready and willing to work. In the case of a quantifiable failure to perform duties, these two approaches produce the same result, but the position becomes more difficult in the case of a more generalized and nebulous failure (eg as part of a general go-slow or withdrawal of goodwill).

This could be particularly important if (a) the industrial action is 'guerilla' in nature,[362] being aimed at inconveniencing the employer while at the same time allowing the employees still to earn most of their wages; (b) it involves employees who have some discretion in how they perform their work; and (c) they work in open premises from which the employer cannot simply lock them out. Under such cases, the employer could counter the action by deducting a 'reasonable sum' (as in *Sim*) representing duties not carried out. However, two later Court of Appeal decisions (*Wiluszynski v London Borough of Tower Hamlets*[363] and *British Telecommunications plc v Ticehurst*)[364] have established that if the employer makes it *clear* that it will not accept the defective performance by the employees, it may lawfully refuse to pay anything *at all* (even if the employees have attended work and performed most of their duties). In *Wiluszynski* this was explained as following on from the reasoning in *Miles* (just discussed), and the important decision in *Ticehurst* takes this further in two ways: (a) it links it in with an implied term that employees with a discretion how to perform their work will exercise that discretion so as to advance the employer's business, not so as to frustrate it;[365] (b) it shows the efficacy of one particular

[358] [1984] IRLR 184. [359] [1986] ICR 897, [1986] IRLR 391.

[360] [1987] ICR 368, [1987] IRLR 193, HL.

[361] Mead, 'We're Miles Apart: Disproportionate Deductions from Wages' (2023) 52 ILJ 1.

[362] This may now be more difficult to arrange lawfully because of the requirement of strike notice introduced by the Trade Union Reform and Employment Rights Act 1993: see 10.3.

[363] [1989] ICR 493, [1989] IRLR 259, CA; see also *MacPherson v London Borough of Lambeth* [1988] IRLR 470.

[364] [1992] ICR 383, [1992] IRLR 219, CA.

[365] This aspect of the case is considered in 3.4.4; as pointed out there, most jobs today are likely to have some discretion in them, rather than being wholly governed by the contract, and so this case doubts the legality in most cases of any form of 'work-to-contract', 'work-to-rule', or 'withdrawal of goodwill'.

employer tactic when faced with guerrilla action, namely to give an ultimatum that the employees must work normally as from a certain date, otherwise the employer will refuse to pay at all as from that date. One final point on this area should be noted: if the employer permits imperfect performance by its employees in such a way as to suggest acquiescence in it, it may be held to have waived the employees' breach and so lost its right to deduct (whether partially or totally).[366]

3.5.1.4 **Inability to work**

The preceding discussion concerns cases where the employee is refusing to work in some way or other. What, however, is the position if they are *unable* to work? The basic common law principle has always been that the employee's consideration for wages is not actual work, but being *ready and willing* to work.[367] There may therefore be cases where the employee does not actually perform work but is still entitled to payment. A simple example would be where the employee attends in the normal way but a supply glitch means there is nothing to do that day. Another would be where the employee is physically unable to get to work, for example through a traffic accident or bad weather. In cases such as these, unless there is a contractual term allowing the employer to withhold payment, there may be a continuing obligation to pay the wages. The question becomes how widely this principle applies, and (for such a mundane issue) the answer may not be simple.

The most obvious instance of inability to work is sickness or injury, and that is treated separately presently. However, in *Miles v Wakefield Metropolitan Borough Council* Lord Brightman envisaged a wider category when he said that that case concerned a deliberate refusal to work and did not apply to 'a failure to work . . . as a result of illness *or other unavoidable impediment*, to which special considerations apply' (emphasis added). It is this phrase that has featured in the relatively few subsequent cases on the point, but without ever being exhaustively defined. The main area of contention has been where the employee is unable to attend work because they have been accused of a crime and remanded in custody pending trial. It may be easy for the employer to assume that payment of wages can somehow be suspended, but on the other hand the employee has not yet been convicted and is still presumed innocent. Is their inability to work 'unavoidable'? In *Burns v Santander UK plc*,[368] the employee was remanded in custody on charges of sexual assault. The employer ceased paying his wages for the six months that this lasted and when he sued for these the tribunal dismissed his claim on the ground that his absence had been 'avoidable'—the proximate cause of his unavailability was the judicial decision to remand in custody, but the employee had by his conduct brought that about. The EAT, in a short judgment, held that this was a permissible decision by the tribunal, one of the factors taken into account being that at the end of the remand the employee had in fact been found *guilty*. The issue arose again in *Ekwelem v Excel Passenger Services Ltd*,[369] but with a different result. Here, a bus driver was accused of inappropriate conduct towards a passenger. His public carriage licence was suspended pending police investigations

[366] *Bond v CAV Ltd* [1983] IRLR 360 (employer's action in not insisting on the employee working on disputed machinery and allowing him to continue working on other machinery held to constitute waiver of the employee's breach).

[367] For a modern reaffirmation and discussion of this old rule in the difficult context of suspension of a doctor accused of medical malpractice see *North West Anglia NHS Foundation Trust v Gregg* [2019] IRLR 570, CA.

[368] [2011] IRLR 639, EAT. See, to the contrary, *Kent CC v Knowles* UKEAT/0547/11 where the employee accused of offences against the employer was not remanded in custody and a suspension of pay while being investigated (without express contractual authority) was unlawful.

[369] UKEAT/0438/12.

and so he could not work for the employer (note that he was not remanded in custody, but the licence suspension raised the same point). Although the employer paid wages for part of this time (and the employee eventually disqualified himself for further payment by refusing alternative work), there was a period during which no wages were paid. In relation to this, a tribunal refused his claim for payment, but on grounds found by the EAT to be legally wrong. The matter was remitted for reconsideration. Technically, therefore, the EAT judgment did not settle the law here, *but* neither did it disapprove of the claimant's argument that *Burns* was distinguishable because the eventual result here was that the bus driver was eventually *acquitted* of the charges. The law therefore seems to be that (in the absence of a contractual term specifically allowing suspension without pay in these circumstances) the continuance of wages will depend on the eventual result of the criminal proceedings, and that the inability to work will be 'unavoidable' if that result is acquittal. This may seem an odd result to any lawyer schooled to be wary of arguments based on hindsight. Moreover, it can put the employer in a cleft stick if the proceedings drag on—a continuing obligation to pay wages for no work may seem unacceptable but if the decision then is to bring that to a halt by dismissing the employee before the result of the criminal investigation is known, that could well be unfair.[370] In spite of the level of legal uncertainty here, what the cases do suggest is that any straightforward assumption that wages are no longer payable because the employee is not present could well be an over-simplification.

3.5.1.5 **Mistaken overpayments**

The fourth point raises legal complications out of proportion to its commonplace nature. What is to happen if the employee is mistakenly overpaid? Can the employer recover the overpayment?[371] What if the employee has already spent the money? Can the employee simply keep quiet about it? Such problems could arise where payment is in cash, but may be more likely to arise now, with payment by direct means the norm. The starting point is that, in the ordinary law of restitution, payments made under a mistake of law are not generally recoverable, but those made under a mistake of fact are. Thus, the first point is to categorize the mistake. Simple inadvertent overpayment (whether by quill pen or computer) is likely to constitute a mistake of fact, thus giving the employer a prima facie right to recover. This was the case in *Avon County Council v Howlett*,[372] where an employee off sick was inadvertently overpaid. The principal defence to the employer's action for repayment was estoppel by representation, in relation to the whole of the overpayment in spite of the admission by the employee that he had only spent *part* of the overpaid amount.[373] This defence succeeded. However, in the subsequent House of Lords decision in

[370] See eg *Z v A* UKEAT/0380/13 (school caretaker's dismissal after a year's suspension but shortly before police investigation discontinued held unfair, especially as it was becoming clear that the case against him was unravelling).

[371] On a technical level, a deduction to recover an overpayment is not an illegal deduction under the Employment Rights Act 1996, Pt II (see this chapter, 3.5.5) since it is covered by an exception in the Employment Rights Act 1996, s 14(1); however, that subsection does *not* give a positive right to recover and so the overall legality of recovery by the employer remains a common law matter, subject to the following rules.

[372] [1983] 1 All ER 1073, [1983] IRLR 171, CA.

[373] A peculiarity of the case, commented on adversely by Cumming-Bruce LJ, was that the evidence showed that the defendant had in fact spent *all* the overpayment before realizing that he was not entitled to it. However, at the trial, counsel for the defence was instructed to proceed on the basis of only *part* expenditure, since the defendant's backers were using this as a test case, seeking to establish (for the purpose of others who had been overpaid) that even partial expenditure could defeat the employer's right to repayment.

Lipkin Gorman v Karpnale Ltd[374] (not itself an overpayment of wages case), Lord Goff said that in future, cases such as *Howlett* should be dealt with not on grounds of estoppel but on grounds of a general defence of 'change of position' in the law of restitution. He said that such a defence should now be evolved in case law and so is likely to be uncertain for some time. However, one relatively certain point is that such a defence would allow only that part of the overpayment actually spent innocently to become irrecoverable, rather than the defence of estoppel which would operate, potentially unfairly, on an all-or-nothing basis.

All of this operates on the assumption that the employee has spent the money innocently. The one thing that they must not do is simply keep quiet about it if they do realize that they have been overpaid, because that can render them guilty of theft, by virtue of the Theft Act 1968, s 5(4), which provides that:

> Where a person gets property by another's mistake, and is under an obligation to make restoration (in whole or in part) of the property or its proceeds or of the value thereof, then to the extent of that obligation the property or proceeds shall be regarded (as against him) as belonging to the person entitled to restoration, and an intention not to make restoration shall be regarded accordingly as an intention to deprive that person of the property or proceeds.

The Court of Appeal held in *A-G's Reference (No 1 of 1983)*[375] that this section (which does not actually create an offence, but rather supplies what might otherwise be the missing elements for a charge of theft under s 1) can apply to payment by direct debit of sorts as well as to payment in cash, and so provided the prosecution can prove dishonesty,[376] the employee may be found guilty of theft through deliberately keeping the overpayment, though the Court of Appeal expressed some disquiet at the involvement of the criminal law in such cases which have the flavour predominantly of civil debt. However, there should only be criminal liability where the defendant deliberately kept it, or spent it *after* realizing that there had been an overpayment. If they had already spent it before so realizing, then in civil law the employer would have lost its right to restitution according to the above cases and so s 5(4) ('is under an obligation to make restoration') would not apply.

3.5.2 **Wages during sickness and statutory sick pay**

3.5.2.1 **At common law**

In most cases, questions of pay during sickness will be governed expressly by the contract of employment, some form of 'topping up' of state sickness benefits being now very common and usually clearly set out (eg as to how many weeks per year are payable, whether

[374] [1991] 2 AC 548, [1992] 4 All ER 512, HL. Lord Goff was of course no stranger to the law of restitution, having written the leading text. In *National Westminster Bank plc v Somer International Bank (UK) Ltd* [2001] EWCA Civ 970, [2002] QB 1286, [2002] 1 All ER 198 (a commercial case) it was held that even where estoppel is still used a court can (in its equitable jurisdiction) rule that only the part actually spent has become irrecoverable; if this is correct, *Avon CC* and *Lipkin Gorman* would now produce the same result.

[375] [1985] QB 182, [1984] 3 All ER 369, CA. The Theft Act 1968, s 5(4) made a definite change here, for under the pre-1968 law an employee keeping an overpayment was not guilty of theft: *Moynes v Cooper* [1956] 1 QB 439, [1956] 1 All ER 450.

[376] This will now be subject to the reformulation of 'dishonesty' in *Ivey v Genting Casinos* [2017] UKSC 67, [2018] All ER 406 (overturning the previous received wisdom in *R v Ghosh* [1982] QB 1053, CA). Under this, the question is basically an objective one, applying the standards of ordinary decent people. While this may often be obvious in one of these cases, there could be latitude for a defence of no dishonesty if, eg the employee kept the overpayment because they were already owed money by the employer who was refusing to pay it. A jury might be sympathetic.

there is any waiting period before it is payable, whether there is a qualifying period for new employees, and at what rate it is payable, bearing in mind receipts from the state).[377] However, there have been cases where the question of whether sick pay is payable has arisen where there has been no express agreement on the matter. The question then arises whether a term is to be implied covering sick pay and, as a matter of law, this has caused problems. Theoretically, the basis of the law here is the general common law tenet that the employee's consideration for wages is 'service' (ie being ready and willing to serve), not the actual performance of work,[378] and this could lead to the inference that, in the absence of anything to the contrary, wages should continue to be paid during sickness even though the employee is unable actually to perform their work. This view that there is a presumption that sick pay is payable was accepted by Pilcher J in *Orman v Saville Sportswear Ltd*[379] and was consistent with the judgment of the Court of Appeal in *Marrison v Bell*,[380] as explained in later cases.[381] Such a presumption could be rebutted by factors such as payment on a piecework basis,[382] a clear custom that nothing was offered or expected,[383] or some form of notice by the employer that they would accept no, or restricted, liability to make any payments.[384]

However, it was still arguable that it was putting matters too highly to say that there was a presumption, and fortunately the matter was clarified by the Court of Appeal in *Mears v Safecar Security Ltd*,[385] an important case not only on sick pay but also on the jurisdiction of tribunals on complaints of failure to give any or proper particulars of the terms of employment[386] and on the whole question of the implication of terms into contracts of employment.[387] In this case it was clearly held that there is in law no presumption that sick pay is payable; if there is no express provision, a tribunal or court must look at all the facts of the case to determine the correct inference. Applying that approach, the Court of Appeal upheld the EAT's decision that nothing was payable on the facts of the case given that it was the employer's well-known practice not to pay, the applicant had been ill during the course of employment and had never asked for payment, and he had only brought his claim seven months after leaving employment, not really expecting to get anything. Stephenson LJ, giving the judgment of the court, did say that there might be a residual presumption that sick pay was payable in a case where there were no factors either way to guide the court on the correct term to be implied, but that this was inherently extremely unlikely to happen, since usually there will be some evidence at least of past custom and practice.

[377] See the statistics in the White Paper 'Income during Initial Sickness' (Cmnd 7864, 1980), which introduced the idea of statutory sick pay.

[378] *Warburton v Co-operative Wholesale Society Ltd* [1917] 1 KB 663, CA; *Henthorn v CEGB* [1980] IRLR 361, CA; *Miles v Wakefield Metropolitan District Council* [1987] ICR 368, [1987] IRLR 193, HL; Elias 'The Structure of the Employment Contract' [1982] CLP 95; cf, however, the different views expressed by Napier 'Aspects of the Wage Work Bargain' [1984] CLJ 337.

[379] [1960] 3 All ER 105, [1960] 1 WLR 1055.

[380] [1939] 2 KB 187, [1939] 1 All ER 745, CA.

[381] *Petrie v MacFisheries Ltd* [1940] 1 KB 258, [1939] 4 All ER 281, CA; *O'Grady v M Saper Ltd* [1940] 2 KB 469, [1940] 3 All ER 527, CA. The problem was that Scott LJ expressed his views on sick pay so strongly in *Marrison v Bell* that it was reported (in the law reports and the newspapers) as laying down a definite right to wages during sickness as a matter of law, leading to claims for it by people who could show little or no contractual backing for entitlement to it; this was rectified in the above two cases.

[382] *Browning v Crumlin Valley Collieries Ltd* [1926] 1 KB 522; *Hancock v BSA Tools Ltd* [1939] 4 All ER 538.

[383] *O'Grady v M Saper Ltd*, n 381.

[384] *Petrie v MacFisheries Ltd*, n 381.

[385] [1982] 2 All ER 865, [1982] IRLR 183, CA, applied by the EAT in *Howman & Son v Blyth* [1983] IRLR 139, where the implication of a term raised questions as to amount and duration of payment.

[386] Employment Rights Act 1996, Pt I; see 2.3.2. The case was brought before a tribunal under s 11 to determine the correct contractual term; it was not a common law claim for actual payment.

[387] See this chapter, 3.2.1.

A clear contractual term covering sick pay entitlement is a good example of the benefits to be gained from a well-drafted contract of employment,[388] or proper compliance with the obligation to give written notice of terms of employment. As stated, such terms are common and, indeed, were for many years an important area for the improvement of terms and conditions by negotiation (eg by increasing payment rates and the entitlement per year, and decreasing or eliminating any qualifying periods), particularly in times of wage restraint. Thus, except in the odd case unfortunately leaving sick pay as a matter to be implied (or not), it could have been said that there was little *law* on sick pay, merely a question of construction of individual contracts. However, that has not been entirely the case since 1983, when there came into force the present scheme of statutory sick pay (SSP) under the Social Security and Housing Benefits Act 1982 (now Part XI of the Social Security Contributions and Benefits Act 1992).[389]

3.5.2.2 **The statutory sick pay scheme**

This scheme came into being pursuant to a White Paper[390] which showed that contractual sick pay terms are common and quantitatively more important than state social security benefits in the maintenance of income during short-term sickness,[391] that such contractual schemes operated usually by taking into account amounts received from the state,[392] and that most illness was in fact short term.[393] From these findings, the government formed the view that the existing system was administratively inefficient:

> given that the great majority of claimants have available a second source of income from their employer, there is duplication of administrative machinery between employers and DSS in that evidence of incapacity has to be provided for both schemes and two sets of arrangements for the calculation and payment of income have to be maintained.[394]

The statutory scheme was therefore designed to prevent duplication in the large majority of claims—where an employee is sick, the employer must now by law pay an amount equivalent to what that employee would have received from the state. This is a flat rate fixed annually by regulations.

As originally enacted, SSP was payable for a maximum of *eight* weeks (either in one period of illness or cumulatively over several illnesses) in one tax year. However, the scheme was viewed as such a success by the government that the Social Security Act 1985 contained a major extension, so that the maximum entitlement is now 28 weeks (put

[388] One complication in some modern cases has been the provision by the employer of permanent health insurance (PHI) on top of the normal sickness provisions in the contract, without really thinking through how the two are to fit together; see this chapter, 3.3.7.

[389] As amplified by the Statutory Sick Pay (General) Regulations 1982, SI 1982/894, *Harvey* R [198].

[390] 'Income during Initial Sickness' (Cmnd 7864, 1980).

[391] Contractual sick pay terms were relatively uncommon in 1948 at the inception of the National Insurance System, but by 1974 (the year used in the White Paper for statistical purposes) 80 per cent of full-time male workers and 78 per cent of full-time female workers were covered by them; in the large majority of cases, employees qualified to claim sick pay either immediately upon becoming employed or at the most within six months.

[392] In 1974, in the case of male workers, eg full pay without deduction was payable in only 11.5 per cent of cases; full pay *less state benefits* was payable in 55 per cent of cases; some other scheme operated in the remaining 33.5 per cent of cases (eg topping state benefits up to 85 per cent of full pay).

[393] '[O]nly a very small proportion of people who qualify for (state) benefit need to draw it for any length of time. No payment is made for the first three "waiting" days of incapacity; 60% of those who qualify for sickness benefit are back at work by the end of a fortnight, 80% within a month and 90% within six weeks. Yet the effort put in by the state in dealing with these short-term claims was considerable': White Paper, n 377, para 3.

[394] White Paper, n 377, para 3.

on to a rolling basis, ie not tied now to the tax year); the overall effect of this is that now the employer is liable for the payment of all short-term sickness benefit due to one of its employees (with the principal function for the government now being the payment of long-term benefits once the extended SSP entitlement has been exhausted in the case of a major illness or disability). Under the original scheme, the employer recouped the full amount of the money paid out as SSP, by deducting it from its NI contributions. However, this position was gradually altered by the Statutory Sick Pay Acts 1991 and 1994, so that the current position is that there is *no* recoupment, so that the employer actually *pays* the SSP; there used to be an exception if an employer faced a particularly large liability in any one payment period, but even this was finally abolished in 2014. This is a far cry from the original scheme under which the employer merely *administered* the payment of SSP.

Space does not permit the setting out of the (considerable) details of the statutory scheme, but three general points may be noticed. *First*, the scheme does not in any way directly affect contractual sick pay terms, which remain matters between the employer and the employee or their union. Thus, contractual sick pay is still to be paid on top of SSP if there is a contractual term to that effect; likewise, if an employer is not contractually obliged to pay sick pay, there is nothing in the statutory scheme to alter that—it will merely be obliged to discharge what was previously the function of the state to pay SSP. *Second*, the abolition, at the same time as the introduction of SSP, of the separate claim for industrial injury benefit (for those injured at work or contracting a prescribed industrial disease) should be seen in the light of this scheme for the administration of sick pay—employees are now eligible simply for sickness benefit when incapable of work, whether or not they are injured in a work-related accident (or incapacitated by an industrial disease), and the SSP scheme will apply to any claim for such benefit by a person in employment. *Third*, receipt of any form of sick pay normally presupposes that the person claiming it is still in employment and there is of course the possibility of the sick employee being dismissed. The statutory scheme provides that an employer cannot evade paying statutory sick pay by dismissing the claimant employee, but does not go further and declare such a dismissal to be in law unfair. However, there is no reason why such a dismissal should not be unfair on general principles, as considered in Chapter 7.

The Employment Rights Act 2025 makes three changes to statutory sick pay:

(1) The requirement that the employee must wait for three days of sickness before being entitled is removed, so that it becomes a day-one-right.

(2) The further requirement that the employee must not have been earning less than the current lower earnings limit for national insurance purposes is removed, thus opening up entitlement to low paid employees.

(3) When the Fair Work Agency comes into being, it will have administrative powers to enforce payment of SSP on behalf of an employee (see 1.3.4).

These changes are, at the time of writing, due to come into force in April 2026.

3.5.3 **Wages during lay-off or short time**

3.5.3.1 **Generally**

Turning to the question of wages during a lay-off or short time, in any employment where this is relevant this too is likely to be covered in some way by a relevant contract or collective agreement, which might define or limit the employer's right to lay off, or provide a guaranteed minimum wage or minimum number of hours per week.[395] In the absence of

[395] See eg *Powell Duffryn Wagon Co Ltd v House* [1974] ICR 123, NIRC.

some express provisions or definite custom, however, the common law position is unclear. The starting point is that, unless it consisted of a dismissal by the employer followed by re-engagement later,[396] a lay-off would be a suspension without pay, and there is no general common law power to do this.[397] This approach would favour the continuance of wages, and indeed in *Devonald v Rosser & Sons*[398] the Court of Appeal held that the employer had no right to close down his work and fail to provide remunerative work for his pieceworkers simply because of a lack of profitable orders. However, in *Browning v Crumlin Valley Collieries*[399] Greer J held that there was an implied term that the employer could lay off without pay where the reason for the suspension (in that case, closure of the colliery for necessary repairs) was outside its control. Moreover, although the employer's argument in *Devonald v Rosser & Sons* that there was a custom allowing lay-offs in the circumstances in question failed, there may well be cases where such a custom could be shown, particularly in an industry where lay-offs are common and accepted (whatever be the usual common law position), and in such a case the court might well find suspension without pay impliedly allowed,[400] thus at least bringing the law into line with the practical position. In *Puttick v John Wright & Sons (Blackwall) Ltd*,[401] the NIRC held that where the employee had been available to do specific jobs for the same employer over a long period of time, being paid for the work done and then laid off until the next work was ready, the correct legal construction was that there existed an ordinary contract of employment for the whole of that period, including an implied term allowing the employer to lay him off without pay in the periods between available work.

In the light of this old case law, it is therefore difficult to state any particular common law rule, but this is of little significance, since most aspects of lay-offs will normally be covered (in a unionized industry) by a collective agreement (which may, eg give a guaranteed minimum week, subject to safeguards for the employer who may be relieved from this obligation in the case of industrial action or events totally beyond its control, thus approximating to what may be the common law position anyway) or by a statutory provision in the modern legislation. Such provisions affect lay-offs in four main ways:

1. by preserving continuity of employment;[402]
2. by allowing an employee subject to lay-offs or short time (in certain circumstances) to treat himself or herself as dismissed and apply for a redundancy payment;[403]
3. by allowing an employee on short time or lay-off to claim social security benefits, even though technically the contract of employment subsists;
4. by providing certain minimal statutory rights to lay-off pay, either generally or in relation to certain particular forms of lay-off.[404]

[396] In which case continuity of employment is preserved if it is a 'temporary cessation of work': Employment Rights Act 1996, s 212(3).

[397] *Hanley v Pease & Partners Ltd* [1915] 1 KB 698; *Gorse v Durham County Council* [1971] 2 All ER 666, [1971] 1 WLR 775; *Neads v CAV Ltd* [1983] IRLR 360.

[398] [1906] 2 KB 728, CA. [399] [1926] 1 KB 522.

[400] *Bird v British Celanese Ltd* [1945] KB 336, CA; *Marshall v English Electric Co Ltd* [1945] 1 All ER 653, CA.

[401] [1972] ICR 457, NIRC. The question whether on the facts there is a series of individual contracts or one global contract in such a case may cause difficulties; this has arisen in the context of trawlermen and the question whether they have continuity of employment between voyages. In *Hellyer Bros Ltd v McLeod* [1987] ICR 526, [1987] IRLR 232, CA it was held that there was not sufficient mutuality of obligations to establish a global contract (and so there was no continuity for redundancy payment purposes). However, in the present context it will not help the employee if the court finds a global contract but then proceeds to imply into it a lay-off clause.

[402] See n 396. [403] Employment Rights Act 1996, s 148; see 8.1.4.

[404] On the various statutory and contractual possibilities in this difficult area see Szyszczak *Partial Unemployment: The Regulation of Short-Time Working in Britain* (1990).

The lack of coherent and comprehensive laws on lay-offs was exposed clearly during the coronavirus crisis, when the problem of continuing employment for employees self-isolating (and unable to work from home) was addressed by the Job Retention Scheme ('furloughing'), which operated as a novel and self-contained administrative scheme, owing *nothing* to the pre-existing law on lay-offs.

3.5.3.2 Guarantee payments

Where an employer is obliged to lay off employees, or is unable to provide them with work at a particular time, salaried and weekly paid employees may not be affected in the short term but those paid by the hour or by output (and those whose contracts provide for suspension without pay) may lose wages. To meet this situation, an obligation to make guarantee payments was introduced in 1975, and is now to be found in the Employment Rights Act 1996, ss 28–35. These provisions are a good example of the 'floor of rights' argument for providing statutory minima, as the amounts which may be received are meagre but the principle is established, presumably in part to encourage the establishment and extension of more generous private schemes (eg to give a guaranteed minimum number of hours per week to hourly paid workers). This approach can be seen in two particular aspects of the statutory scheme. The first is that any contractual payments referable to the workless day are set off against the statutory right (often to the point of extinguishing it), *not* additional to it.[405] The second is that the minister may make exemption orders, exempting from these provisions employers who are parties to a collective agreement or wages order which covers the question of guaranteed remuneration to his satisfaction.[406]

To qualify for a guarantee payment, the employee must have been continuously employed under a contract of employment for the month ending with the last complete week before the workless day in question.[407] This may disqualify casual workers, as in *Mailway (Southern) Ltd v Willsher*,[408] where the EAT held that a woman who was registered as a part-time packer with the employers who offered her work as and when they needed her, and who on average worked more than 16 hours per week (though she had not in fact done so in the four weeks in question), was not eligible for a guarantee payment as this relationship was only a contract to pay for services rendered, not a contract of employment. If an employee is in fact qualified they are entitled to a guarantee payment under s 28 when not provided with work by the employer on a day on which they would normally be required to work; the failure to provide work must be due to either (a) a diminution in the requirements of the employer's business for work of that kind, or (b) any other occurrence affecting the normal working of the employer's business in relation to that work (eg a power failure or natural disaster affecting the factory; it will not extend to extraneous matters such as factory holidays).[409]

The requirement that the workless day be one on which they would *normally* be required to work means that this right cannot be used as a back-door method to gain remuneration for days not in fact envisaged in the contract; for example, where a contract is

[405] Employment Rights Act 1996, s 32.

[406] Section 35; there have been 26 such orders, the last in 1996 (see *Harvey* Q [659]).

[407] Section 29(1).

[408] [1978] ICR 511, [1978] IRLR 322, EAT; aliter where the employer may *oblige* the employee to attend work when it requires them, rather than just offering them work: *Miller v Harry Thornton (Lollies) Ltd* [1978] IRLR 430, IT. In relation to the decision in *Mailway*, note that the employee now does not have to work a minimum of 16 hours per week in order to have continuity of employment.

[409] *North v Pavleigh Ltd* [1977] IRLR 461, IT.

only to work four days a week an employee cannot claim a guarantee payment for the fifth day,[410] nor can they claim one for days during an agreed annual shutdown of a factory.[411] However, there is another aspect of 'normality' that could have negated much of this right in the case of short-time working. If this is simply imposed by the employer there is no problem applying the statute. If, however, the employer and employee (or union) *agree* to short-time working by working fewer days per week (as opposed to lower hours over the same number of days), for example going down from five to four days a week, does that varied contractual position become the 'new normal'? If so, then that workless day would not now be 'normally' worked and so no guarantee payment would be due. Fortunately, this restrictive interpretation was disapproved by the Court of Appeal in *Abercrombie v AGA Rangemaster Ltd*,[412] where it was held that the question is not whether there has technically been a contractual variation but whether whatever has been agreed constitutes a departure from the normal working pattern (particularly if the facts show an intent to go back to the previous pattern of working if things improve).

The employee will lose the right to payment in three cases. The first is where the failure to provide work is in consequence of a strike, lockout, or other industrial action involving his employer or an associated employer.[413] The second is where the employee refuses the offer of suitable alternative work for that day, which may be work outside the contract, provided it is suited to their skill, aptitude, and so on.[414] The third is where the employee fails to comply with a reasonable attendance requirement, so that the employer can in certain circumstances hold the workforce together, at least for part of the day, for example if it is still hoping that vital supplies will be delivered in time.[415]

As stated, the amount of the statutory guarantee payment is small, for although the principle is that the employee is to receive the number of working hours on that day multiplied by the 'guaranteed hourly rate' (as defined), this is all subject to a maximum of £39 per day at the time of writing, and any individual may only claim for a total of five workless days in any period of three months.[416] Where an employer fails to pay all or part of a guarantee payment, an employee may complain to a tribunal within three months of the last workless day (longer if the tribunal finds that it was not reasonably practicable to complain within that period), and if the tribunal upholds the claim it may order the employer to make the necessary payment.[417]

3.5.3.3 **Suspension from work on medical grounds**

Where an employee is suspended from work because of the operation of one of several specified health and safety provisions (eg where the employer has to close down its factory or that part of it where the employee works), they are entitled to be paid a 'week's pay' (as defined in the Employment Rights Act 1996, Part XIV, Chapter II) for each week of suspension, up to a maximum of 26 weeks.[418] It is thus more generous than the more general provisions on guarantee payments, because of the specialized nature of the

[410] *Clemens v Richards Ltd* [1977] IRLR 332, IT; *Daley v Strathclyde Regional Council* [1977] IRLR 414, IT.

[411] *York v Colledge Hosiery Co Ltd* [1978] IRLR 53, IT.

[412] [2013] IRLR 953, CA.

[413] Employment Rights Act 1996, s 29(3).

[414] Section 29(4); *Purdy v Willowbrook International Ltd* [1977] IRLR 388, IT.

[415] Section 29(5); *Meadows v Faithful Overalls Ltd* [1977] IRLR 330, IT.

[416] Section 30. This includes any such workless days in respect of which contractual remuneration has already been paid—the employee cannot claim five *further* days of guarantee pay if five or more days have already been paid for under the contract within the three-month period: *Cartwright v G Clancey Ltd* [1983] ICR 552, [1983] IRLR 355.

[417] Section 34.

[418] Employment Rights Act 1996, ss 64–5; the specified provisions may be in either statutes, regulations, or codes of practice issued under the Health and Safety at Work etc Act 1974, s 16.

reason for the suspension; the relevant health and safety provisions have been considerably shortened and simplified, so that they now only cover parts of the Control of Lead at Work Regulations 2002, the Ionising Radiations Regulations 1999, and the Control of Substances Hazardous to Health Regulations 2002.

Two general points should be noted. The first is that these sections do not give the employer a positive right to suspend when one of these provisions applies; to suspend lawfully the employer must have contractual authority to do so, and only in such a case do these sections apply to give the employee a limited right to further payments. If there is no contractual right to suspend, the employee may have an ordinary contract action for his wages in full anyway, and indeed it is specially provided that any contractual payments received during the relevant period go towards discharging the employer's obligations under the statute, and vice versa.[419] The second point is that these provisions apply to suspension through the effect of the relevant health and safety legislation on the employer's undertaking, not on the health of the employee himself or herself. Thus, if the employee is in fact incapable of work through disease or injury during the relevant time, they cannot claim payment under s 64 for that period of incapacity.[420]

As well as the illness exclusion, an employee will be disqualified from payment if they refuse suitable alternative work or fail to comply with a reasonable attendance requirement, as in the case of guarantee payments. Complaint lies to a tribunal within three months of the last day of suspension (longer if the tribunal finds that it was not reasonably practicable to complain within that period) and the tribunal may order the employer to make the relevant payment.[421]

3.5.4 **Calculation of normal working hours and a week's pay**

The concepts of 'normal working hours' and 'a week's pay' are important in several contexts throughout modern industrial legislation. The principal significance of 'normal working hours' was originally in deciding whether an employee worked more than the magic 16 hours per week and so could claim statutory rights, but that hours limit was abandoned in 1995.[422] However, it is still necessary to know whether an employment has 'normal working hours' for the purpose of ascertaining what the 'week's pay' is and, in turn, it is necessary to know what the 'week's pay' is for the purpose of computing, inter alia, the amount of a redundancy payment, guarantee payment, or basic award for unfair dismissal. Rather than being defined individually for the purpose of each statutory right where they are relevant, these two concepts are each covered for all statutory purposes in one place, namely ss 220–229 and 234 of the Employment Rights Act 1996. However, it must be added that these have always been difficult provisions and have required a considerable amount of statutory interpretation.

3.5.4.1 **Normal working hours**

In many cases it will be obvious what an employee's normal working hours are, in the sense of the number of hours which the employee is *obliged* to work by their contract; there is no overall statutory definition of this, and it is essentially a matter of interpreting the contract. Thus, where the contract expressly states the number of hours this will usually be conclusive of the matter,[423] and the employee should ensure that the contractual term correctly reflects the practical position, for they will be held to that term (eg for the

[419] Section 69(3). [420] Section 65(3). [421] Section 70. [422] See 2.5.

[423] *Gascol Conversions Ltd v Mercer* [1974] ICR 420, [1974] IRLR 155, CA; *Fewell v B & B Plastics Ltd* [1974] IRLR 154, NIRC; *Lake v Essex County Council* [1979] ICR 577, [1979] IRLR 241, CA.

purpose of calculation of a redundancy payment) even if in practice they work longer hours and regard themselves as bound to work those longer hours, *unless* the facts in the case are such as to support an argument that the term of the contract relating to hours has actually been varied by the parties to include the longer hours.[424] This possibility apart, however, it will normally be to no avail that the employee in fact works longer hours than those stipulated in the contract. In *ITT Components (Europe) Group v Kolah*,[425] a clerk was employed under a contract specifying 20 hours per week (at a time when the necessary minimum for qualification for an unfair dismissal claim was 21 hours per week), but she regularly worked a further three hours each week; the EAT, reversing the tribunal decision in her favour, held that this was not in itself a contract for 21 hours or more per week because of the express term for 20 hours, but remitted the case to the tribunal to discover what the correct interpretation of the contract should be, since the clerk had in fact been promoted to supervisor ten months before she was dismissed, and there was at least the possibility that the relevant contractual term might have been varied on the promotion (that being a question of fact for the tribunal to consider).

If there is no express term covering the normal working hours (in spite of the statutory obligation to give written particulars of this, under the Employment Rights Act 1996, s 1(4)), the tribunal must consider the facts and what happens in practice to decide what is the correct term to infer. This may be a difficult exercise where the employee has in fact been working fluctuating hours. In *Dean v Eastbourne Fishermen's and Boatmen's Protection Society Ltd*,[426] a barman worked certain set sessions and at other times when requested to do so by his employer; this produced fluctuating hours, and as the set sessions amounted to less than the 21 hours per week at that time required for qualification for redundancy rights, the tribunal rejected his claim for a redundancy payment when he was dismissed. However, the EAT allowed his appeal, holding that as the contract was silent on the matter the tribunal had to infer the relevant term and in a case such as this, where that term was essentially to work the hours required of him, that meant looking at what happened in practice during a period before the dismissal. The appropriate period appears to be the period required to qualify for the particular right being claimed (in particular, two years for redundancy and for unfair dismissal);[427] in *Dean*'s case the EAT held that, as in the qualifying period of the preceding two years, the employee had worked for more than 21 hours in 86 weeks, the proper interpretation was that his normal working hours exceeded 21 per week and so he was eligible for a redundancy payment.

Whether 'normal working hours' are expressed in the contract or left to be inferred when the need arises, one overall consideration is that in general they will *not* include overtime. This proposition may help to simplify the question, as even if a contract of employment is not specific on the normal working hours (or, to put it another way, the minimum number of obligatory hours), it might well state that overtime is payable after a certain number of hours per week have been worked and where this is the case the Employment Rights Act 1996, s 234, provides that normal working hours shall be that number of hours to be worked before overtime becomes payable. Thus, in *Fox v C Wright (Farmers) Ltd*,[428] an agricultural worker was employed under a contract which did not specify a minimum number of hours to be worked, and he often worked 50 or 60 hours per week as the job demanded; the contract did,

[424] For a case in which it was held that there had been such a variation see *Armstrong Whitworth Rolls Ltd v Mustard* [1971] 1 All ER 598, 9 KIR 279.

[425] [1977] ICR 740, [1977] IRLR 53, EAT.

[426] [1977] ICR 556, [1977] IRLR 143, EAT. See, to like effect, *Green v Roberts* [1992] IRLR 499, EAT.

[427] *Larkin v Cambos Enterprises (Stretford) Ltd* [1978] ICR 1247, EAT.

[428] [1978] ICR 98, EAT.

however, provide that overtime was payable for hours worked in excess of 40 per week, and when he claimed a redundancy payment the EAT held that he was caught by this provision and his normal working hours were therefore 40 (for the purposes of calculating the redundancy payment). Section 234 does, however, create an exception to this in a case where the contract sets a fixed number of obligatory hours which includes a number of hours in fact payable at overtime rates (eg an obligatory week of 40 hours, but with overtime rates payable from 35 hours). In such a case, the normal working hours will remain the obligatory figure even though that includes some overtime. The predecessor of this provision was considered by the Court of Appeal in *Tarmac Roadstone Holdings Ltd v Peacock*,[429] where Lord Denning MR said that for overtime to be included under this exception it must be fully obligatory under the contract, in the sense that the employee must work it *and* the employer must provide it; it is not sufficient if the overtime is voluntary on both sides or if the employee is obliged to work it when requested but the employer is not obliged to provide it in any particular week. Thus, this exception is restrictively construed (in line, it is submitted, with the clear wording of the provision), and so overtime will only be included in the normal working hours if it is clearly obligatory on both sides under the contract.

3.5.4.2 **A week's pay**

The rules governing the calculation of a week's pay for statutory purposes are laid down in Part XIV, Chapter II of the Employment Rights Act 1996 (ss 220–229).[430] There are four different methods of calculation, depending upon the category into which the employee concerned falls; the first three cover cases where there are normal working hours (as defined in the previous paragraphs) but differing or specialized forms of payment for the work done during those hours, and the fourth covers the case where there are no discernible normal working hours. These are now considered in turn.

1. *Where there are normal working hours and the remuneration does not vary with the amount of actual work done.* This is the simplest case, where, essentially, the employee is paid on a time basis, that is, for the hours during which they are at work, and here the 'week's pay' is the amount payable under the contract of employment when the employee works throughout the normal hours of the week, the relevant contractual provision being that in force on the calculation date.[431] This may be simply the basic rate for a time worker, but not necessarily, since it could include any further payments if they are paid on a regular basis, for example a night shift rate or a regular bonus.[432]
2. *Where there are normal working hours, but the remuneration varies with the amount of actual work done.* This obviously covers pieceworkers, but also extends to persons basically on a time rate but eligible for variable bonuses or commission.[433] Here the 'week's pay' is the remuneration for the normal working hours payable at the *average*

[429] [1973] 2 All ER 485, [1973] ICR 273, CA, followed in *Lotus Cars Ltd v Sutcliffe* [1982] IRLR 381, CA.

[430] These longstanding rules were adopted for the purpose of calculating statutory holiday pay: Working Time Regulations 1998, reg 16(2).

[431] Employment Rights Act 1996, s 221(2); calculation dates vary with the particular statutory rights involved, and are laid down individually in ss 225 and 226. This could cause injustice if, eg the contractual term had been varied downwards by the calculation date (eg because of the firm's economic difficulties).

[432] *A & B Marcusfield Ltd v Melhuish* [1977] IRLR 484, EAT. See the inclusion of a site bonus in *Donelan v Kerrby Constructions Ltd* [1983] ICR 237, [1983] IRLR 191, EAT.

[433] Section 221(4); *Jones v Shellabear Price Ltd* (1967) 2 ITR 36. Where, however, commission is based on the success of work (rather than on a greater amount of work being done) then, if it can still be said that remuneration does not vary with the amount of work done, the employee remains under head (i), which may be financially disadvantageous: *Evans v Malley Organisation Ltd* [2003] ICR 432, [2003] IRLR 156, CA.

hourly rate, which is calculated by working out the total numbers of hours actually worked in a period of 12 calendar weeks preceding the calculation date, then the total amount of remuneration actually paid for those hours over that period (excluding any overtime premia paid), and then working out the average payment per hour.[434]

3. *Where there are normal working hours but they are to be worked at varying times and in varying amounts in different weeks.* This category primarily covers employees working rotating shifts, where the pattern of work is set but alternates from week to week, so that here it is necessary to average *both* the rate of remuneration *and* the number of hours worked in a week, once again over a period of 12 calendar weeks preceding the calculation date. The 'week's pay' here is therefore the average weekly number of normal working hours payable at the average hourly rate.[435]
4. *Where there are no normal working hours.* In this residual category, which would cover, for example, the case of a university lecturer, the tribunal must determine the 'week's pay' simply by calculating the amount of the average weekly remuneration received by the employee over the period of 12 calendar weeks preceding the calculation date.[436] This form of calculation could well be the most favourable for the employee since it looks at overall remuneration and is not tied to concepts such as basic hours, so that, for example, in *Fox v C Wright (Farmers) Ltd*[437] the agricultural worker who regularly worked 50 to 60 hours per week was trying to argue that he had no normal hours in order to put the question of averaging at large, but the EAT held that as his contract provided for overtime rates to be paid after 40 hours' work per week he was caught by s 234 (considered earlier), and so he was deemed to have normal working hours of 40 per week.

Those being the four categories of employee covered by the provisions, four general qualifications should be noticed:

1. The 12-week period referred to must consist of weeks during which the employee actually worked in order to earn some pay, and it is that earned pay which is used for the purpose of calculation even if in any given week they worked (and therefore earned) considerably less than usual for some reason; this leads to a possible gap in the legal coverage in the case where work is consistently run down in the 12 weeks (or more) immediately prior to dismissal—as long as the employee actually earned *something*, those weeks will be used for calculation purposes even if they are in fact untypical and decrease what would otherwise have been their statutory entitlement. This requirement of looking at the pay actually earned in any given calculation week excludes matters such as payment during rest days[438] and the payment of fall-back or guaranteed pay for periods when not actually working.[439] If, however, the period of 12 calendar weeks includes a week when *no* work is done to earn remuneration, the tribunal must ignore that week and take an earlier week instead to bring the number up to 12 again.[440] If the employee has not been employed long enough for calculation over 12 weeks, the tribunal must apply the above provisions as closely as it can, looking at certain other factors, such as the remuneration of other persons in comparable employment—though if the employee has just joined the employer in question from another employer and the employment with both is deemed to be

[434] Section 221(3). [435] Section 222. [436] Section 224. [437] See n 428.
[438] *Mole Mining Ltd v Jenkins* [1972] ICR 282, NIRC.
[439] *Adams v John Wright & Sons (Blackwall) Ltd* [1972] ICR 463, NIRC.
[440] Employment Rights Act 1996, s 223(2). *Secretary of State for Employment v Crane* [1988] IRLR 238, EAT.

continuous, a period of employment with the previous employer can be taken into consideration if necessary.[441]

2. The emphasis remains against the inclusion of overtime rates. As seen above, overtime other than fully obligatory and guaranteed overtime is not counted towards 'normal working hours' in the first place. However, for the purpose of calculating the 'average hourly rate' under categories (2) and (3) the tribunal must look at the hours *actually worked* during the 12-week period, and this may include some hours worked at overtime rates; where this is so, however, s 223(3) provides that the amount of overtime premia earned is to be ignored when calculating the total remuneration for that period for the purpose of calculating the average. The employee therefore cannot take advantage of the overtime premia to increase the average,[442] but this only applies to actual overtime and does not disallow the inclusion of amounts under incentive or bonus schemes which may be built into the wage structure, for these are not to be treated as analogous to overtime.[443]
3. The word used throughout the scheme is 'remuneration', but its definition has been left to the case law. It obviously includes wages and salaries, and has been held to include commission[444] and (contrary to long-standing general assumptions) the employer's pension contributions.[445] Moreover, the tribunal must look at the realities of an employee's pay, which may be significant in the case of certain more complicated payment systems; for example, it is not possible for an employer, as a matter of law, to represent that a worker who is paid £1 as remuneration for doing an hour's work is really paid 50p for an hour's work because the parties choose to specify that the rate shall be 50p an hour but one hour's work shall count as two hours' work in calculating pay.[446]

Contractually binding bonuses will be included, in whatever guise they are presented in,[447] and it is specifically provided that if such a bonus is only payable at a time outside the calculation period (eg once per year) it may be apportioned for calculation purposes in such manner as may be just, and taken into account accordingly.[448] In addition to such matters, an employee may in fact receive further indirect benefits which may cause more difficulty. They may, for example, receive an amount labelled 'expenses' which may be simply genuine reimbursement for money of their own actually expended, or may instead be a none-too-subtle form of giving increased remuneration. If the former, it is not to be included, but if the latter it may be brought into account according to the leading case of *S & U Stores Ltd v Wilkes*;[449] such an arrangement may sometimes raise a suspicion of tax evasion, but the general approach has been to ignore this as being basically a matter for HM Revenue and Customs, not the employment tribunals.[450] The case of *S & U Stores Ltd v Wilkes* also establishes that two other indirect benefits are *not*

[441] Sections 228 and 229; on continuity of employment see 2.5.

[442] This caused problems when applied to holiday pay under the Working Time Regulations 1998 because it was arguably inconsistent with the backing directive; see 5.3.8.

[443] *Ogden v Ardphalt Asphalt Ltd* [1977] ICR 604, EAT; the possible intricacies of bonus and overtime schemes in this context are well illustrated by *British Coal Corpn v Cheesbrough* [1990] ICR 317, [1990] IRLR 148, HL.

[444] *Weevsmay Ltd v Kings* [1977] ICR 244, EAT.

[445] *University of Sunderland v Drossou* [2017] IRLR 1087, EAT.

[446] *Mole Mining Ltd v Jenkins* [1972] ICR 282, NIRC at 284, per Sir John Brightman.

[447] *Amalgamated Asphalte Companies Ltd v Dockrill* (1972) 7 ITR 198, NIRC.

[448] Employment Rights Act 1996, s 229(2); *J & S Bickley Ltd v Washer* [1977] ICR 425, EAT.

[449] [1974] 3 All ER 401, [1974] ICR 645.

[450] *S & U Stores Ltd v Lee* [1969] 2 All ER 417, [1969] 1 WLR 626; cf *Jennings v Westwood Engineering Ltd* [1975] IRLR 245, IT.

to be taken into account when quantifying remuneration; these are payments in kind, such as free accommodation or a firm's car, and payments from a person other than the employer. The latter means that a waiter cannot include cash tips in his remuneration for the purpose of calculating his 'week's pay', since these are discretionary payments by a third party.[451] On the other hand, this has been held not to apply to a fixed service charge shared out between the employees, since that is obligatory payment in fact payable by the employer.[452] Likewise, gratuities on credit cards or cheques paid out to waiters (under Inland Revenue pressure) directly through the employer as 'additional pay' may count as part of the week's pay.[453] In recent years, this topic has been complicated by the overlap with the national minimum wage legislation, under which a similar question has arisen (do tips count towards observing the minimum national minimum wage (NMW) hourly rate?), *but* with the caveat that in the case of 'a week's pay' the employee wants them to count (eg to increase a redundancy payment) but in the case of the NMW it is the *employer* who wants them to count (so that less can be paid by way of basic wages). At first, the distinction just stated (paid directly by the customer or paid through the employer) was applied in the NMW cases. One middle ground was where gratuities on credit cards or cheques are paid through the employer into a 'tronc' (independent fund) controlled and distributed by the employees themselves. In *Annabel's (Berkeley Square) v HMRC*,[454] the Court of Appeal held that such gratuities were *not* paid by the employer and so could not be counted by the employer towards the NMW. At the same time, however, the government altered the NMW legislation (pursuant to a political pledge) to state that *no* tips or gratuities are to count. However, that change does *not* apply to rules such as 'a week's pay', where presumably (a) the above distinction continues to apply, and (b) *Annabel's* will govern tronc systems and continue to exclude tronc-based tips (but this time potentially to an employee's disadvantage).

4. If the week's pay calculated as above turns out to be below the applicable rate of the NMW, then as a matter of policy it is the NMW rate that is to be used when working out any statutory entitlement (particularly a redundancy payment or compensation for unfair dismissal).[455]

Finally, note that owing to the coronavirus crisis there had to be a specific alteration of these rules in the case of employees furloughed on 80 per cent of their normal wages; if their pay then has to be calculated (eg if then made redundant and claiming a redundancy payment) it is to be done on their *pre-furlough* wages, to avoid an obvious injustice.

[451] *Hall v Honeybay Caterers Ltd* (1967) 2 ITR 538, IT; *Palmanor Ltd v Cedron* [1978] ICR 1008, [1978] IRLR 303, EAT.

[452] *Tsoukka v Potomac Restaurants Ltd* (1968) 3 ITR 259; *Keywest Club Ltd v Choudhury* [1988] IRLR 51, EAT.

[453] *Nerva v RL & G Ltd* [1997] ICR 11, [1996] IRLR 461, CA (a case on the repealed Wages Councils legislation, but applying the same principle); the waiters' ultimate action before the ECtHR failed: *Nerva v United Kingdom* [2002] IRLR 815.

[454] [2009] EWCA Civ 361, [2009] ICR 1123.

[455] *Paggetti v Cobb* [2002] IRLR 861, EAT; this obviously applies to the basic award for unfair dismissal, which is mathematically based on the week's pay, but less obviously it also applies to the compensatory award, which is to be based on a calculation of what the employee's net wage would have been if paid at the NMW level.

3.5.5 **Protection of wages**

3.5.5.1 **The repeal of the Truck Acts and the effect on cashless pay**

One of the longest-standing pieces of social legislation in English law was the Truck Acts 1831–1940, designed and put into place early in the nineteenth century to protect the employee in the free enjoyment of their earnings.[456] They served two distinct purposes:

1. The original Act of 1831 gave a legal right to payment in 'current coin of the realm', designed to prevent abuse of the then prevalent 'tommy shop' system whereby an employer might pay at least part of the employee's wages in tokens to be spent at the employer's own shop.[457]
2. The later legislation (particularly the Truck Act 1896) then placed restrictions on the making of deductions from wages, principally in respect of the provisions of goods and services by the employer, fines, or bad workmanship; these were of great complexity, but in essence they usually provided that the deduction had to be authorized in writing and be fair and reasonable in the circumstances.

The principal limitation of the legislation was that it only applied to *manual* workers[458] (with certain limited extensions to shop assistants). Persons not covered were therefore left to their contractual rights on both payment methods and deductions.[459] It was recognized for years that the legislation was in need of, at the least, revision, and indeed the last major case on it showed just how unpredictable and unreliable its coverage was.[460] However, the then Conservative government became interested in the area not because of anything concerning deductions, but rather because of the first of the above two effects, that of the right to payment in cash. Britain had long lagged behind other Western countries in the move towards cashless pay (ie pay by cheque or credit transfer).[461] It is true that the strict requirement in the 1831 Act of current coin of the realm had been qualified by the Payment of Wages Act 1960, which permitted cashless pay with the employee's written agreement, but the problem was that that agreement could always be revoked by written notice and so a manual worker could reinvoke his rights under the Truck Act. Banks had for a long time been interested in extending cashless pay, and sometimes they and employers had offered cash incentives to go over to it; the problem with the 1960 Act was that any such agreement was *not* irrevocable. The Conservative government therefore decided to deregulate this area by the repeal of the Truck Acts and the Payment of Wages Act 1960. However, to do so simpliciter would also remove all protection with regard to

[456] The archaic meaning of 'truck' was to exchange or barter; one of the few current usages is the phrase 'to have no truck' with something, in the sense of not wishing to have any dealings with it. The word 'truck' was not actually used in the wording of the legislation.

[457] Such a system was not necessarily vicious, since the employer might have the benefit of discount buying, but obviously it was open to abuse.

[458] This distinction caused great difficulties and a considerable amount of old case law; for a modern example of the problem see *Brooker v Charrington Fuel Oils Ltd* [1981] IRLR 147, Co Ct.

[459] On deduction, however, there was at least the statutory right to have deductions notified, as part of the statutory itemized pay statement under the Employment Rights Act 1996, s 8.

[460] In *Bristow v City Petroleum Ltd* [1988] ICR 165, [1987] IRLR 340 the House of Lords finally held that a deduction from a shop worker's wages in respect of a stock or till deficiency could be a 'fine' within the Truck Act 1896, s 1, thereby resolving a conflict of opinion between different Divisional Courts on the issue. This final decision came too late to affect the decision to repeal the legislation.

[461] In the early 1980s it was estimated that 50 per cent of all workers in Britain and 78 per cent of manual workers were still paid in cash. This compared with 20 per cent of all workers in Holland and Sweden, 10 per cent in France, 5 per cent in West Germany and Canada, and 1 per cent in the USA. Approximately 400,000 workers in Britain were changing to cashless pay each year, but this was considered slow progress.

deductions and eventually this was thought to be too sweeping, particularly in the light of media coverage of certain cases of highly inequitable deduction clauses in employment contracts, particularly in certain areas of retailing.[462] The compromise was contained in Part I of the Wages Act 1986, which repealed the truck legislation (and other related statutes)[463] but also enacted entirely new provisions giving at least partial protection in relation to deductions. The principal feature in favour of this scheme is that it applies to *all* employees, not just to manual workers; one criticism of it, however, is that (with the exception of certain extra protection for retail workers, considered presently) these provisions largely relate to the *mechanics* of making deductions (the principal requirement normally being the employee's written consent), rather than any concept of the substantive *fairness* or otherwise of the deductions. In this sense, they are not as interventionist as the old Truck Act provisions, and the question of the reason for the deduction in question is left largely as a matter of contract.

As seen earlier, however, the matter of deductions was (if not an afterthought) at least a subsidiary matter in the eyes of the government. The principal point was the removal of blockages to cashless pay, and this has been achieved. The repeal of the Truck Acts means that there is now no freestanding legal right to payment in cash and so an employer taking on an employee (manual or otherwise) may lawfully make it a term of the contract that payment will be by cheque or credit transfer.

The Wages Act 1986 was repealed by the Employment Rights Act 1996, and the provisions relating to deductions are now contained in Part II (ss 13–27) of that Act; in employment lawyers' jargon however, and even in ACAS statistics, there remains a tendency even now to refer to an action before a tribunal to recover an unlawful deduction from wages as 'a Wages Act claim'.

3.5.5.2 **Deductions from wages**

Section 13 provides that an employer shall not make deductions from the wages of a worker employed by it unless the deduction is (a) required or authorized by statute (eg PAYE, NI contributions, or an attachment of earnings order), (b) required or authorized by a provision in the contract of employment which has either been given to them or notified to them previously in writing, or (c) agreed to by the employee in writing prior to the making of the deduction.[464]

Application

From such humble beginnings, these provisions became subject to quite remarkable development, for one procedural reason which had little to do with their origins. Until 1994 we were afflicted with a split jurisdiction, so that in the past employment tribunals could

[462] See Goriely 'Arbitrary Deductions from Pay and the Proposed Repeal of the Truck Acts' (1983) 12 ILJ 236.

[463] The Payment of Wages Act 1960; the Shop Clubs Act 1902; the Payment of Wages in Public-houses Prohibition Act 1883; the Checkweighing in Various Industries Act 1919; and various older statutes concerning coal mines.

[464] Section 15 has equivalent provisions concerning the making of payments by workers to employers, instead of operating by way of deduction. 'Worker' is defined widely in s 230(3), as covering not only a person under a contract of service or apprenticeship, but also one under a contract to do or perform personally work or services for another party (other than in a professional–client relationship). The requirement of *prior* written agreement means prior to the event causing the deduction, not just to the deduction itself: *Discount Tobacco and Confectionery Ltd v Williamson* [1993] ICR 371, [1993] IRLR 327, EAT; *York City and District Travel Ltd v Smith* [1990] ICR 344, [1990] IRLR 213, EAT. To be relied on, a contractual provision must be notified to the employee individually, not just by a factory notice: *Kerr v Sweater Shop (Scotland) Ltd* [1996] IRLR 424, EAT.

not deal with common law matters such as non-payment of wages, which had to go to the ordinary courts (doubly annoying if, for example, the ex-employee was already bringing a tribunal action for unfair dismissal). However, a way round this was discovered—if an employee was complaining about a refusal to pay wages, holiday entitlements, and so on, could that be *called* a 'deduction'? If so, the employee could (on the assumption that there was no prior written consent) complain to a tribunal under the Wages Act for its 'recovery'. This reasoning has been largely successful, as can be seen from the very high number of 'Wages Act cases' brought in recent years;[465] it has operated as a de facto transfer of certain common law contractual claims to tribunals. It had been hoped that when an order was finally made by the government giving common law jurisdiction to tribunals, this would be in general terms, and would end the need to extend what is now Part II of the 1996 Act to perform a function for which it was probably not intended. However, this simple hope did not come about, for two reasons: (a) the order[466] in fact only gives common law jurisdiction to tribunals in cases arising on or out of *termination* of employment, and so challenges to non-payment or underpayment of wages or other benefits *during* employment can still only be brought before a tribunal by squeezing them under Part II; (b) even on termination, it may still be tactically advantageous to the ex-employee to claim amounts not paid under Part II rather than directly under the order, since the latter is subject not only to a monetary limit of £25,000 but also, and far more importantly, to an express power of *counterclaim* by the employer which can be avoided by claiming under Part II (leaving the employer to pursue any claim it may think it has through the ordinary courts, which in practice is highly unlikely to happen). Thus claims under Part II are likely to continue at their present high level, and the reported cases show that such an action can be used as a relatively quick and certainly effective way of challenging an attempt by an employer to force through a unilateral variation of contractual terms.[467]

As a matter of law, this development raised two questions of interpretation of the Act—what is a 'deduction' and what are 'wages'? On the first question, s 13(3) gives a broad definition[468] and certain cases have shown an equally broad approach, so that for example there can still be a deduction even if it is so large that it actually extinguishes the wage payment altogether,[469] and the phasing out of a special bonus from a payment system was held to qualify as a deduction.[470] However, the crucial question was whether simple non-payment would qualify—on a straightforward application of s 13 it would, but it

[465] In 2024/25 ACAS received 124,546 cases for early conciliation; 23 per cent of these included Wages Act claims: *ACAS Annual Report 2024/25*.

[466] The Employment Tribunals Extension of Jurisdiction (England and Wales) Order 1994, SI 1994/1623; the Scottish Order is SI 1994/1624. A further point of difference is that Part II applies to the wider category of 'worker' (including some self-employed) but the Extension Order only applies to 'employees' properly so called: *Robertson v Blackstone Franks Investment Management Ltd* [1998] IRLR 376, CA.

[467] *Bruce v Wiggins Teape (Stationery) Ltd* [1994] IRLR 536, EAT (withdrawal of shift bonus); *Morgan v West Glamorgan County Council* [1995] IRLR 68, EAT (disciplinary salary cut in breach of contract); *Saavedra v Aceground Ltd* [1995] IRLR 198, EAT (employer allocating part of waiters' tronc for tips to himself). In each case the employers' actions were held to be unlawful 'deductions'. See *Miller* (1995) 24 ILJ 162. In addition, it has been held that a Wages Act claim can be used to recover unpaid holiday pay under the Working Time Regulations 1998, even though those Regulations contain their own specific tribunal procedure: *Revenue and Customs Commissioners v Stringer* [2009] ICR 985, [2009] IRLR 677, HL.

[468] 'Where the total amount of any wages that are paid on any occasion by an employer to any worker employed by him is less than the total amount of the wages that are properly payable by him to the worker on that occasion.' In considering what was 'properly payable' a tribunal may if necessary construe the true meaning of the contract itself: *Agarwal v Cardiff University* [2018] EWCA Civ 2084. In the case of a zero-hour contract a tribunal may use an average of previous weekly pay: *Rice Shack Ltd v Obi* UKEAT/0240/17.

[469] *Alsop v Star Vehicle Contracts Ltd* [1990] ICR 378, [1990] IRLR 83, EAT.

[470] *McCree v Tower Hamlets London Borough Council* [1992] ICR 99, [1992] IRLR 56, EAT.

could also be argued as a matter of English that non-payment was different in kind from a deduction from wages paid. On the second question, s 27 gives a lengthy inclusive and exclusive definition,[471] although not specifically covering one of the most contentious areas, wages in lieu of notice on a dismissal; could such amounts, if kept by the employer, be recovered under the Act?

Both of these questions caused major disagreements between different divisions of the EAT, but the matter was largely settled by the decisions of the Court of Appeal and House of Lords in the leading case of *Delaney v Staples*.[472] The facts were refreshingly simple. The employee was dismissed, being owed £55.50 commission and holiday pay and £82 in lieu of notice. She claimed both of these amounts, not in the county court, but before a tribunal under the Wages Act. This neatly raised both of the above questions. The Court of Appeal held that the £55.50 could be recovered, because a simple non-payment such as this *does* qualify as a 'deduction', on a literal interpretation of s 13(3), and there was here no prior agreement. That point was not subject to further appeal and so remains governed by the Court of Appeal's decision.

However, the matter of the £82 in lieu went on further appeal to the House of Lords and raised the second question—are payments in lieu of notice 'wages'? Here the matter was resolved not primarily by the wording of the Act but by a broader consideration of the nature of payments in lieu. Lord Browne-Wilkinson said that the essential characteristic of wages (at common law and under the Act) was as 'payments in respect of the rendering of services during the employment'. He then analysed 'wages in lieu' as covering four different possibilities;[473] in only one (where the employer formally gives the correct notice, pays during that period, but does not actually require the employee to work during it, eg in a 'garden leave' case) does the payment still constitute wages during employment, to which the Act could apply. In the case itself, the in lieu payment came into the much more common category of anticipatory *damages* for the employer's breach of contract in dismissing the employee instantly, without proper notice. It was therefore not 'wages' and so the non-payment could not be challenged before a tribunal. Thus, the end result is that non-payment of wages accrued during the employment can be subject to a statutory action under Part II before a tribunal, but in most cases non-payment of wages in lieu cannot be (though of course, as such a case by definition arises on termination, such amounts outstanding *can* now be claimed before a tribunal quite separately under the Transfer of Jurisdiction Order).

One further class of case deserves mention. If it is the *employee* who is in breach of contract by leaving without giving their contractual notice, the employer may be very tempted to hang on to any final wages, contractual holiday pay, and so on still owing to that employee, as 'damages'. In the light of *Delaney*'s reasoning and two earlier cases[474] this is likely to be unlawful in the absence of prior written consent. The moral is simple:

[471] 'Wages' means 'any sums payable to the worker by his employer in connection with his employment'; there are then six categories specifically included and five specifically excluded. The first included is 'any fee, bonus, commission, holiday pay or other emolument referable to his employment, whether payable under his contract or otherwise'. The last two words meant that the Act's procedure could be used to challenge non-payment of a *discretionary* or ex gratia payment, provided the making of such a payment was clearly anticipated by contract, custom, or ad hoc undertaking: *Kent Management Services Ltd v Butterfield* [1992] ICR 272, [1992] IRLR 394, EAT; *New Century Cleaning Co Ltd v Church* [2000] IRLR 27, CA; *Farrell Matthews & Weir v Hansen* [2005] ICR 509, [2005] IRLR 160, EAT. Ultimately, however, the amount being claimed by the employee must be quantifiable: *Coors Brewers Ltd v Adock* [2007] IRLR 440, CA.

[472] [1991] ICR 331, [1991] IRLR 112, CA; affd [1992] ICR 483, [1992] IRLR 191, HL.

[473] These are set out at 6.2, in the discussion of dismissal by notice.

[474] *Pename Ltd v Paterson* [1989] ICR 12, [1989] IRLR 195, EAT; *Chiltern House Ltd v Chambers* [1990] IRLR 88, EAT. A similar rule applies to statutory holiday pay under the Working Time Regulations 1998; an employer may only claim back overpaid holiday pay (where an employee leaves partway through the year) if there is a pre-existing 'relevant agreement' in writing allowing this to be done: *Hill v Chapell* [2003] IRLR 19, EAT.

if the employer wants a power to retain accrued wages in the event of the employee leaving in breach of their notice obligation (especially where the employer wants to be able to rely on that obligation, for example so as to have time to find a replacement), the employer should ensure that there is a clear written term to that effect in the employee's contract.

Exceptions

Section 14 contains a series of exceptions:[475] thus the provisions of s 13 do not apply to deductions in respect of:

1. overpayment of wages, or expenses;[476]
2. disciplinary proceedings held by virtue of any statutory provision;
3. a statutory requirement to deduct from wages and pay over to a public authority;
4. payments agreed to by the worker which are to be made over by the employer to a third party;
5. a strike or other industrial action in which the worker took part;[477]
6. the satisfaction of a court or tribunal order requiring the worker to pay something to the employer.

The primary point to notice about these exceptions is that they do *not* establish an independent, unilateral right for the employer to make such deductions; they only state that deductions made on these grounds do not infringe the procedural requirements of s 13. In any given case, the question of the overall legality of a deduction may well depend on the contractual or other common law propriety of making it at all. If there is no contractual authority to make the deduction, the employee can sue for it in the county court in the normal way. However, the question again arose whether an action could be brought instead in a tribunal. At first that seemed possible, because in *Home Office v Ayres*[478] it was held that the exclusions in s 14 only apply to deductions *lawfully* made on the above grounds; it was therefore open to the employee to argue that the deduction was unlawful at common law and so did not come within the relevant exclusion in s 14. However, this reasoning was later repudiated by the EAT in *Sunderland Polytechnic v Evans*,[479] where it was held, by exercising the courts' power to consider *Hansard*,[480] that Parliament's intention was that s 14 and its exceptions were to be applied literally, leaving any question of the contractual lawfulness of the deduction in question to be fought over in the ordinary courts.[481] There is, however, middle ground: if the employee is merely denying that the relevant ground existed on the facts (eg that they had not actually been overpaid or that they had not actually been on strike) the tribunal can hear the claim and adjudicate on that point, without trespassing into the forbidden territory of the contractual lawfulness of the deduction.[482]

[475] There is also an exception in s 13(4) relating to errors of computation of wages, but this is to be construed narrowly: *Yemm v British Steel plc* [1994] IRLR 117, EAT; *Morgan v West Glamorgan County Council* [1995] IRLR 68, EAT.

[476] One problem here is that what started out as an amount genuinely supposed to cover actual expenses can, over time, simply become an element of pay; see eg *Mears Ltd v Salt* UKEAT/0552/11.

[477] *Norris v London Fire and Emergency Planning Authority* [2013] IRLR 428, EAT.

[478] [1992] ICR 175, [1992] IRLR 59, EAT.

[479] [1993] ICR 392, [1993] IRLR 196, EAT, applied in *SIP Industrial Products Ltd v Swinn* [1994] ICR 473, [1994] IRLR 323, EAT.

[480] *Pepper v Hart* [1993] AC 593, [1993] 1 All ER 42, HL.

[481] The case itself concerned a deduction for taking part in industrial action (s 14(5)), where this policy consideration is perhaps particularly strong; however, the reasoning should apply to all the heads of s 14.

[482] *Gill v Ford Motor Co Ltd* [2004] IRLR 840, EAT.

Retail employment

Due to the discussions prior to the introduction of the 1986 Act and concerns expressed as to certain inequitable deductions made in certain service industries, ss 17–22 of the 1996 Act impose a further limitation on deductions from the wages of workers in retail employment.[483] Where such a deduction is made in respect of cash shortages or stock deficiencies, the maximum that may be deducted is 10 per cent of the gross amount of wages for that particular pay day. While such an extra provision is to be welcomed, two further points should be noticed:

1. this limitation only applies to the *amount* deductible, not to the grounds for deduction, since there is still no requirement that those grounds be fair and reasonable;[484]
2. there is nothing to stop the full amount of a contractually recoverable deficiency being carried forward over successive pay days until fully recovered, provided that only 10 per cent is taken on each occasion; indeed, s 22 states that the 10 per cent rule does not apply to the final pay day if the employee's employment is terminated, when the whole of any outstanding deficiency could be set against the wages payable.

Remedies

A complaint that deductions have been made (or payments demanded) in contravention of s 13 may be presented to an employment tribunal within three months of the date of the last deduction or payment, or if that is not reasonably practicable, within such further period as the tribunal thinks reasonable.[485] If the tribunal finds the complaint well founded, it is to make a declaration to that effect and order the repayment of amounts improperly deducted.[486] In addition (by virtue of an amendment by the Employment Act 2008), a tribunal may award an amount 'to compensate the worker for any financial loss sustained by him' due to the making of the deduction, thus putting the damages at large and no longer restricted to a refund of the deduction. Three final points should be noted on these provisions. The *first* is that s 205(2) states that '[t]he remedy of a worker in respect of any contravention of [sections 13ff] shall be by way of a complaint under section 23 *and not otherwise*'. At first sight, that may appear to rule out a common law action for wages (the traditional remedy to recover improper deductions). However, that is not so since, as pointed out previously, all that the Act does is to apply to deductions from wages certain (albeit important) procedural requirements, particularly as to prior written agreement to the making of such deductions. There may well still be cases where the employee is objecting not just to the procedure adopted (which may have complied with s 13) but rather to the legality of making a deduction at all in those circumstances. In such a case the employee retains the option of a common law action in the county court.[487] The *second* point is that there is a measure of overlap between these provisions and the right in s 11 of the 1996 Act to bring tribunal proceedings against an employer for failing to

[483] 'Retail employment' is defined in s 17(2), referring principally to the direct supply to the public or other individuals in a personal capacity of goods or services (including financial services).

[484] It is therefore still lawful to incorporate a contractual term requiring the refunding of, eg till deficiencies at a petrol station, even where those deficiencies are not the attendant's fault (as, eg where caused by fraud by a customer).

[485] Section 23. One useful point to note (s 23(3)) is that, where there has been a *series* of deductions (eg each pay day) the time limit only flows from the *last* deduction, so that the worker does not have to contemplate a legal complaint after every deduction (see *HMRC v Stringer* [2009] ICR 985, [2009] IRLR 677, HL).

[486] Moreover, those amounts are *not* then to be treated as properly recoverable by further deductions (by whatever means) or by action in the ordinary courts, ie the employer loses the right to them altogether: s 25; *Potter v Hunt Contracts Ltd* [1992] ICR 337, [1992] IRLR 108, EAT.

[487] *Rickard v PB Glass Supplies Ltd* [1990] ICR 150, CA.

give proper notification of deductions from wages in the statutory-required itemized pay statement;[488] s 26 provides that both actions can be brought, but that if that happens there is not to be double recovery of the deduction. The *third* point is that, in potentially an important extension of the tribunal's powers under the Act, the EAT has held that even if the employer does have prior written consent to make a deduction on a particular ground, the employee can argue that the *amount* deducted was excessive and not justified by the written consent; this permits the tribunal to consider whether that particular deduction was sustainable in fact.[489]

3.5.6 The national minimum wage

The advantages and disadvantages of a national minimum wage were a controversial matter in this jurisdiction for some time. It is a device that is widely used in Europe and some states in the US, and an early International Labour Organization (ILO) Convention[490] encouraged such action by states. Its introduction was an election issue in 1997, and immediately on coming into office the Labour government established a Low Pay Commission, at first on an informal basis and then put on to a statutory footing by the legislation, to investigate and make recommendations. The government proceeded to pass the National Minimum Wage Act 1998 (NMWA), which operates in significant areas by giving regulation-making powers; when the Low Pay Commission made its first report,[491] its recommendations were incorporated into the National Minimum Wage Regulations 1999,[492] which contained much of the detailed law. Those regulations have been amended so many times that they were finally replaced and consolidated by the National Minimum Wage Regulations 2015, which sought only to rationalize and simplify, not change, the previous regulations.[493] While obviously the most politically contentious question is the rate at which the minimum wage is set, the most difficult questions legally tend to be those of definition (what is pay? what can be disregarded? how to average? who is covered?), which are particularly acute in a piece of legislation intended to apply to employment across the board, in all its varieties.

3.5.6.1 The minimum wage entitlement

The Act sets out a basic entitlement for any worker (working, or ordinarily working, in the UK under their contract) to be remunerated by their employer in any pay reference period at a rate not less than the national minimum wage fixed by regulations by the Secretary of State.[494] The ambit of this duty is deliberately broad through the use of the wide term 'workers', which covers employees and any other person under a contract (whether express or implied, written or not) whereby the individual undertakes to do or perform personally any work or services for another party to the contract whose

[488] Section 8. [489] *Fairfield Ltd v Skinner* [1992] ICR 836, [1993] IRLR 4, EAT.

[490] Convention No 26 (1928) 'Minimum Wage-Fixing Machinery'.

[491] Cm 3976, 1998. For the Commission's observations on other countries' legislation see Cash 'Lessons from the International Experience of Statutory Minimum Wages' [1998] Labour Market Trends 463.

[492] SI 1999/584. See Simpson 'Implementing the National Minimum Wage' (1999) 28 ILJ 171 and 'The National Minimum Wage Five Years On: Reflections on Some General Issues' (2004) 33 ILJ 22.

[493] SI 2015/621. See the National Minimum Wage Guidance at <https://www.gov.uk/national-minimum-wage/what-is-the-minimum-wage> and Adams 'Understanding the Minimum Wage: Political Economy and Legal Form' [2019] CLJ 42.

[494] National Minimum Wage Act 1998, s 1. The pay reference period is a month or, in the case of a worker who is paid by reference to a period shorter than a month, that period: reg 10. This could cause problems with 'annualized hours' contracts.

status is not that of a client or customer of any profession or business undertaking carried on by the individual.[495] Any attempt to contract out of the protection of the legislation is void.[496]

3.5.6.2 **On-call and travelling time**

The problem of how to count hours spent 'on call' has generated a fair amount of litigation. It is a particularly difficult and controversial area because of its economic consequences—it arises particularly in the care industry, where workers are often on minimum pay but the industry is highly labour intensive, so that any significant increases in labour costs would only add to the already high costs of care.

The basic position is that time spent while available for work and required to be available (eg on a standby arrangement at or near the employer's premises) is to count (reg 32(1)). However, a specific problem arose where a worker is required to be on the employer's premises but is allowed to sleep for at least part of the time of required presence. Here, the Regulations provide that time when a worker may sleep is excluded (reg 32(2)), but for some time the courts construed this narrowly to apply only where the worker could sleep while waiting to work, and as not applying where the worker's job is to be available on shift in case of need—for example, a nightwatchman or person available to answer requests for help.[497] This distinction turned out to be unsustainable in practice and in *Royal Mencap Society v Tomlinson-Blake*[498] the Supreme Court held that this was a mistake traceable to the *Burrow Down* case, and that reg 32(2) is to be applied literally (as in fact the Low Pay Commission had originally meant it to apply), so that the only time that counts for NMW purposes is time when the worker is required to be actually awake for the purposes of working, not when they are merely present and available if necessary. This was clearly contrary to the employee interest in this difficult area (and at the time a considerable relief to employers in the care industry) but it has at least provided clarity here.

The question of travelling time is treated separately in reg 34, which provides that it can count for the payment of the NMW if it is for the purposes of work and at a time when they would normally be working (eg travelling between appointments) but crucially it is *not* to count if it is for the purpose of travelling from home to work and vice versa. While the distinction here is easily understood, the fact that it can cause hardship to an employee was shown in *Revenue and Customs Commissioners v Taylors Services Ltd* [2025] EWCA Civ 956 498. The claimants were agricultural process workers sent by their employer to work on a variety of farms across a wide region. They were supplied with company transport *but* the arrangement was that it picked them up from their homes and returned them there at the end of their day. The facts showed that the time involved

[495] Section 54 (see 2.1.4): there are subsidiary provisions in ss 34 and 35 to ensure (if necessary) that agency workers and home workers are covered. Voluntary workers (eg for a charity or similar organization) are specifically excluded: s 44. At a late stage, under media pressure, au pairs and family workers were exempted: reg 57.

[496] Section 49. The Secretary of State has power to exclude or modify the right in relation to particular persons but, in response to concerns expressed about the width of this when the Bill was going through Parliament, it is specifically stated that this cannot be on the basis of specifying different areas, sectors of employment, sites of undertakings, or occupations: ss 3, 4. In the event, this power has been used in relation to workers of certain ages.

[497] *Burrow Down Support Services v Rossiter* [2008] All ER (D) 49; *British Nursing Association v Inland Revenue* [2002] IRLR 480; *Scottbridge Construction Ltd v Wright* [2003] IRLR 21, Ct of Sess (IH).

[498] [2021] IRLR 466, [2021] ICR 758, SC. In *Walton v Independent Living Organisation* [2003] IRLR 469, [2003] ICR 688, CA the question had been resolved in a different way, by deeming it to be unmeasured work which permitted the parties to reach an *agreement* as to how these on-call hours were to be remunerated. This case was upheld by the Supreme Court.

was substantial and often at anti-social hours. However, their claim for the NMW during these times was rejected by the Court of Appeal. Following *Royal Mencap* by analogy, reg 34 was to be applied as it stood, on which basis they came within the exception, not the rule. The anomaly is that if they had gone to the employer's premises first and *then* been bussed to the farms they would have had a good claim. The court recognized this but said that any change here is to be done by reference of the issue to the Low Pay Commission and/or amending legislation by the Secretary of State.

3.5.6.3 **The level of pay**

Although the introduction of the national minimum wage in 1999 honoured an important commitment by Labour, the rate at which it was set (the principal rate was £3.60 per hour) was substantially below what the unions had argued for. Rates, which are subject to annual review, have risen steadily since then, but more as a recognition of rises in the cost of living than as a change in policy. However, reflecting rising concern that the top rate was not enough to support a family, the Conservative government introduced in 2016, the National Living Wage, set then at £7.20 (and now £12.21), available to workers 21 years and over. This sits alongside the long-standing national minimum wage (NMW) rates, which will now apply only to workers under 21, at the following rates (at the time of writing):

1. £10,00 per hour generally;
2. £7.55 per hour for a worker aged 18 but under 21;
3. £7.55 per hour for an apprentice.[499]

Prior to the introduction of the NMW the Low Pay Commission estimated that about 2 million employees should benefit, with a total recurring cost to industry of £2.4 bn (0.6 per cent of the national average wage bill). In spite of initial concerns to the contrary in some quarters, a study eight years after its inception indicated that the national minimum wage had had either no effect or a positive effect on employment and productivity, and had narrowed the pay gap between men and women.[500]

3.5.6.4 **Calculation of compliance**

In order to determine whether the legal minimum is being paid, it is of course necessary to work out the current hourly rate for the particular individual, which may be easier said than done where the contracting and/or pay arrangements are complex or flexible. The established formula is to take the total of remuneration for the reference period minus the total of reductions to be made, and divide it by the total hours worked in that period.[501] However, the question of 'total hours' is a potential stumbling block, and to try to cover this, the legislation divides work into four possible categories:

1. 'time work', that is, work that is paid for by reference to the time worked (even if depending on the worker's output per hour);[502]
2. 'salaried hours work', that is, where there are ascertainable basic hours in return for an annual salary, not varying with hours actually worked (except for any performance bonus);[503]

[499] Regulations 4 and 4A.

[500] Metcalf 'Britain's Minimum Wage: What Impact on Pay and Jobs?', Winter 2006–07 *CentrePiece* 10 available at <http://cep.lse.ac.uk/pubs/download/CP217.pdf>.

[501] Regulations 7 and 8.

[502] Regulation 30.

[503] Regulation 21. This heading was added to the original draft Regulations, and gives rise to some of the most complex provisions in the Regulations. There may be a difficult borderline with 'unmeasured work', eg in the case of a worker resident on the employer's premises: *McCartney v Oversley House Management* [2006] ICR 510, [2006] IRLR 514.

3. 'output work', that is, work that is paid for wholly by reference to the number of pieces made or processed by the worker, or to some other measure of output (eg number or value of sales or transactions);[504]
4. 'unmeasured work', that is, work not within the previous categories, in particular where there are no specified hours and the worker is required to work when needed or when work is available.[505]

Calculating the hours worked is simplest in the case of time work, where it is simply the number of hours actually worked in the relevant pay reference period. Likewise, there is a simple averaging process over the salary year in the case of salaried hours work if only the basic hours are worked. *If*, however, the salaried worker actually works more than this, a more complicated calculation is set out to take the extra hours into account.[506] More generalized problems are bound to arise with output work and unmeasured work because of the variability of the hours put in by the worker in discharging the duties. Prima facie, the measure here has to be the total number of hours *actually* worked in the reference period, but this could be administratively difficult where there are significant fluctuations, and so the Regulations permit the worker and employer to agree in writing what the worker's *normal* hours are likely to be, so determining what the 'rated output' or 'daily average agreement' are to be for the pay reference period.[507] In the case of output work, the rated output must be determined by a test carried out according to criteria specified in the regulations. In the case of unmeasured work, daily average agreement must be made before the work is carried out and represent a 'realistic estimate' of the average daily hours likely to be spent on the contractual duties. As will be seen in Chapter 5, this approach is similar to that in the Working Time Regulations, laying down default rules but placing major emphasis on fitting the requirements to individual jobs by agreement (though with the difference that in relation to working time the emphasis is largely on collective forms of agreement, whereas here it is on individual agreement). An employer may have much to gain in entering such agreements, especially where fluctuating or ungovernable work patterns may mean at times being technically in breach of the legislation, in the absence of agreed averages.

The other variable which has to be calculated in order to determine whether the worker is being paid the legal minimum is of course the pay in the relevant reference period. The 'total of remuneration' is defined as all moneys paid by the employer to the worker in (or in respect of) that reference period, plus any permitted charge for living accommodation.[508] From this gross amount, a series of reductions is then to be made,[509] essentially in order to comply with the Low Pay Commission recommendation that (however the pay

[504] Regulation 36. [505] Regulation 44. [506] Regulation 28.

[507] Regulations 41–43, 49–50.

[508] Regulation 16. Benefits in kind are excluded (including exchangeable vouchers such as luncheon vouchers), as are (a) loans or advances of wages, (b) any pension or compensation for loss of office, (c) any tribunal award or settlement amount (other than for an amount contractually due), (d) any redundancy payment, and (e) any amount under a suggestions scheme: reg 10.

[509] These cover: (a) payment for work done in a previous reference period, (b) payment for time absent from work, (c) (crucially) overtime or shift premium, (d) special allowances (eg for dangerous work, anti-social hours, or being on standby; however, performance or incentive payments *do* count), (e) reimbursement of business expenses, (f) certain deductions which have been made by the employer (eg for purchase of tools, equipment, or clothing—this may not include deductions to pay for gas and electric bills, as this is deemed duplicative of the allowance for living accommodation: *Leisure Employment Services Ltd v HMRC* [2007] EWCA Civ 92), (g) certain payments by the worker to the employer (similar to the deductions in (f)), and (h) deductions for living accommodation in excess of a set figure per day: regs 7–15. For the meaning of 'deduction' see *Revenue and Customs Commissioners v Middlesbrough Football and Athletic Company (1986) Ltd* UKEAT/0234/19. An unlawful deduction remains so for these purposes even if made for a benign purpose: *Commissioners for Revenue and Customs v Lees of Scotland Ltd* [2024] EAT 120.

is calculated) it is components that comprise pay for standard working that are to count towards the national minimum wage, not premia or other additions for non-standard work. Since 2009 the regulations have expressly provided that tips and gratuities, whether paid directly by customers or by customers to the employer and then to the worker, are not included as pay (previously the latter had been considered pay but the former had not).[510]

3.5.6.5 **Enforcement**

The worker has a statutory right of access to the records which the employer must keep.[511] In a case of non-compliance with the minimum, the individual worker is given a statutory entitlement under their contract to 'additional remuneration' representing the shortfall.[512] As a result of amendments enacted through the Employment Act 2008, the amount of remuneration is calculated according to the greater of the minimum wage at the time of underpayment or the rate applicable at the 'time of determination'.[513] This time will usually be either the time of initiating legal proceedings or the time of enforcement by minimum wage inspectors. The legislation does not give any special procedure for recovery, and so this amount would have to be claimed in an ordinary breach of contract action (in the county court or, on termination, in a tribunal) or as an unlawful deduction for wages under Part II of the Employment Rights Act 1996; in any such proceedings there is a reversal of the burden of proof.[514] There is, however, in an interesting parallel with the old wages council system, an alternative form of enforcement which may be to an individual worker's advantage. In a major shake-up of enforcement in 2008, the Secretary of State was given power to appoint minimum wage inspectors with wide powers to inspect records, require information, and enter premises for these purposes. This function has hitherto been exercised primarily by HMRC which has its specialized compliance officers. If such an officer finds non-compliance with the minimum, they may serve a 'notice of underpayment' on the employer, requiring future compliance, the payment of arrears to the individual(s) concerned, and the payment of a penalty of up to 200 per cent.[515] If the notice is not complied with within 28 days, the inspector may bring proceedings for the arrears on behalf of the worker in a tribunal (under Part II of the 1996 Act) or by way of other civil proceedings.[516] Finally, the individual worker is given a right not to be subjected to any detriment by their employer because of any action taken by them or on their behalf under this legislation, because the employer has been prosecuted, or because they qualify for the legal minimum;[517] in line with other areas of specialized protection in other contexts, a dismissal

[510] Regulation 10.

[511] National Minimum Wage Act s 10: the worker may complain of failure to provide access to an employment tribunal (subject to the usual three-month time limit) and if the complaint is upheld the tribunal must make a declaration to that effect and award compensation of 80 times the hourly amount of the minimum wage: s 11. Details of the records to be kept are set out in reg 59, and because of employer pressure at draft stage they are much less onerous than as originally proposed.

[512] NMWA s 17.

[513] Employment Act 2008, s 8 amends NMWA, s 17.

[514] Section 28. Refusal or wilful neglect to pay the national minimum wage is a criminal offence, punishable on summary conviction by a fine not exceeding level 5 on the standard scale: s 31. After the Employment Act 2008 the offence is triable 'either way' (ie in Crown Court or magistrates' court): s 31(9).

[515] Section 19–19H. The employer may appeal against the notice to an employment tribunal, but only on certain enumerated grounds.

[516] Section 19D.

[517] Section 23. Complaint lies to an employment tribunal, subject to the same procedure as other classes of detriment (Employment Rights Act 1996, ss 48 and 49): s 24.

on these grounds is declared to be automatically unfair.[518] Finally, note that under the Employment Rights Act 2025 these statutory powers are to be transferred to the new Fair Work Agency once it is set up.

3.5.7 **Tips**

Finally, there has recently been legislative action on one specific form of remuneration, namely tips from customers/clients. Concern has been expressed for some time as to whether the employer was always passing these on in full to their workers, especially now that these are so often given by card or electronically, rather than in cash. As a result, the Employment (Allocation of Tips) Act 2023 inserted a new Part 2B into the Employment Rights Act 1996, instituting a statutory regime for the proper payment of tips, gratuities, and service charges. This is of some complexity (running to 23 sections), having to cope with issues of definition and accommodate the continued existence in some industries of a very traditional of tipping, namely through a 'tronc' run by the staff themselves. However, the basic obligation is relatively simple: the employer must ensure that the total amount of tips, gratuities and service charges paid at, or attributable to, a place of business of the employer is allocated fairly between workers at that place of work and that these allocated amounts are paid to the worker by the employer. This must be done no later than the end of the month following the month in which it was paid by the customer. These obligations are backed up by the Code of Practice on Fair and Transparent Distribution of Tips (2024). There are further obligations on an employer to have a written policy available to workers at the place of business on dealing with these amounts and to keep records which are to be retained for three years. The obligation to have a policy is further strengthened by the Employment Rights Act 2025 which adds requirements to consult recognised trade unions, other worker representatives or the workers themselves when drafting it and to keep it under review, at least once every three years. At the time of writing, this is due to come into force in October 2026. Complaint lies to an employment tribunal (subject to a special time limit of 12 months from the failure to comply) which may order the employer to mend its ways to comply with Part 2B and to make good any underpayment to the complainant and any other workers affected and, if it considers it appropriate, to award further compensation to the claimant not exceeding £5,135.

Review and Final Thoughts

- The contractual basis of individual employment law has figured largely in this chapter, as in Chapter 2, and again one theme has been that in order to remain realistic in the amorphous world of employment the approach to contract law in this area sometimes has to be different from that in commercial contract law—sometimes subtly, or sometimes less so. As in any contract, clear express terms covering all key issues are preferable, but here that may be something of a counsel of perfection—you will be lucky if the written part of your employment contract actually covers everything even when you enter it, let alone ten years down the line when parts of your job have changed beyond all recognition. One obvious difference therefore is the extensive use here of implied terms which often have to be used to fill in

[518] Section 25, adding the Employment Rights Act 1996, s 104A. Adopting the usual 'package' approach, a subsequent redundancy on these grounds is also unfair, no qualifying period is required, and the upper age limit does not apply. There is, however, no entitlement to higher levels of compensation.

such gaps in express coverage; in commercial law, by contrast, implied terms are generally viewed as a regrettable necessity, to be used as little as possible, and demonstrating a failure to deal with matters properly.

- It is suggested in this chapter that in employment law we can best view implied terms as being either 'real ones' (ie inferred from the parties' intent/conduct) or 'imposed' ones (ie applicable potentially to *all* employment contracts). The former may have to be determined on less compelling evidence than would be necessary in a commercial case. The latter have a long history of use by the courts and tribunals as a juristic device to impose rules of law on the employment relationship generally; this is largely done as a matter of judicial policy (thus capable always of change or development as new problems arise) but retaining the fig leaf of the contractual language of 'implied term'. That is why, having considered the legal basis for implication (or incorporation from elsewhere), the chapter then went on to enumerate the most important implied terms as simply 'duties' on employer and employee.
- Going one stage further, it has also been suggested that certain *very* fundamental implied terms may be so strongly imposed as a matter of policy that they are, if push comes to shove, capable of *overriding* an express term (an obvious heresy in commercial law). The key one here is the implied term of trust and confidence (so well established that employment lawyers tend to refer to it simply as 'the T&C term'). This may permit a court or tribunal to impose a requirement on the employer not just to stay within the bounds of its contractual authority, but even when doing so to exercise that power in a way that is not oppressive on the employee or likely to make the employment unendurable. If the employer tries this on in order to get an unwanted employee to leave, it can expect to be staring down the barrel of a constructive dismissal action for unfair dismissal, based on breach of the T&C term. For further reading see footnote 148.
- Three other themes may have emerged from this chapter. The first is the 'Ancient and Modern' nature of much of employment law. In relation to the incorporation of terms into contracts from elsewhere, the old law on this evolved from the system of collective bargaining in heavily unionized industries where the question was how industrial realities emerging from such bargaining, often with a heavy element of custom and practice behind it, found their way legally into individual contracts. Of course, that still applies where there is such bargaining, but that is now largely confined to the public sector. In the private sector, however, a parallel issue has arisen for some time now, namely what is the legal status of the ubiquitous company/organization handbook; as seen in this chapter, this can be surprisingly problematic but its resolution involves much the same law as that previously applying to collective bargains.
- The second is the interplay between old common law and modern statutory coverage, which can be seen particularly well in two other topics considered in this chapter. The first is the question of payment of wages or wage substitutes during sickness where (in the absence of a clear express term) recourse may have to be had to some very old case law, or (as a safety net) the modern statutory sick pay system which has evolved through several social security Acts and has served as a model for the later introduction of social security benefits, The second topic is the implied duty on the employee of respecting the employer's confidentiality, which has long raised the question of a possible defence to breach of it if exposing employer misconduct/criminal action. There is considerable old case law on disclosure 'in the public interest', but this was largely superseded in 1998 by the introduction of statutory protection for whistleblowers. This has been of great importance,

often arising in tribunal cases, but by its nature has raised problems of its exact delineation as to where the protection should stop. For further reading see footnotes 285 and 287.

- Finally, and rather more depressingly, what we can sometimes see in employment is new ideas developed at a practical (often human resources) level with little thought for the legal implications, leaving the lawyers to sort all of these out some time later when litigation ensues, having to have recourse to basic principles such as those considered in this chapter. Again, company/organization handbooks are a good example (tending to be written with little consideration as to which bits *are* meant to be contractually binding), but an even more salutary tale has been that of permanent health insurance schemes—thankfully now less common, they were initially introduced as a major new and attractive part of an employment package but soon posed fairly horrific problems as to their wider legal implications. The employment lawyer may perhaps be forgiven the cynical thought: heaven preserve us from good ideas.

4

Discrimination in employment

OVERVIEW

This chapter begins with an exploration of the structure, concepts, and definitions of the Equality Act 2010 as they relate to employment. The remainder of the chapter considers special issues that arise in connection with particular protected characteristics such as sex, sexual orientation, and religion.

The key questions raised by this chapter include:

- How has the law evolved to reflect the growing understanding of the problems of discrimination in the workplace?
- How does the law deal with situations where the employer has an arguably good reason for adopting a policy or way of doing things, and it applies in the same way to everyone, yet in practice it proves harder on some groups than on others?
- How can a worker prove that adverse treatment was based on an illegal reason (race, sex, and so on) when the employer insists it was based on a different reason?
- Is it discrimination to forbid a worker to do things the worker claims are required by religious beliefs?
- How do we balance the rights of different characteristics protected by the Equality Act, such as between certain religious beliefs and same-sex relationships and between certain philosophical beliefs and those who change their gender?
- Why is it lawful to adjust workplace rules and arrangements in favour of disabled workers?
- If the law considers it wrong to discriminate on the basis of age, when and why is it nevertheless lawful routinely to discriminate on the basis of age (eg compulsory retirement ages and age bands in the national minimum wage)?

Context

Discrimination law is the part of employment law which gains the most public attention. It relates to the core issue of the modern world, that of equality for all members of society not just in relation to employment but also in education, housing, civic participation, and nearly all aspects of life. Indeed, the Equality Act 2010 addresses discrimination and equality in many fields and not just in employment. This Act is not the only legal measure that seeks to tackle inequality in the workplace: the myriad rights to leave for family reasons, the prohibition of less favourable treatment of part-time workers, and the law on flexible working also have important roles to play, and these are considered in Chapters 2 and 5.

Over the past 45 years the law has sometimes led, and sometimes lagged behind, public opinion on matters of equality. While prohibitions on certain kinds of discrimination have on occasion helped to change attitudes, it has also become clear that the law alone will not deliver whatever kind and degree of equality society wants: the issues are too complex and too embedded in society and human nature to be solvable only by legal measures.

One problem is that there is no consensus about what kind of equality we are seeking. Is it just equal treatment—for example, that when a Black person and a white person apply for a job, the appointment is made on the basis of who is best suited for the job rather than the colour of their skin? The law seeks to achieve this by outlawing direct race discrimination. Such equal treatment does not necessarily secure true equality; for example, if the Black applicant is less suited to the job than the white applicant, it would not be direct discrimination to appoint the white candidate, even though the Black candidate may have been less suitable because the opportunities and education afforded to them earlier in their career were hindered by disadvantages related to their colour. To put it shortly, equal treatment may not result in substantive equality. So there is a case for striving to achieve equal *outcomes* for all—but how far should one go? Is it enough to seek to eliminate unjustified barriers which disadvantage certain groups (by outlawing indirect discrimination) or should positive action be taken to assist those groups, and should such action go as far as positive discrimination in their favour?[1] In this chapter we will see that the law certainly goes beyond mere equal treatment, but arguably not far enough.

Much of the development of UK discrimination law has been pushed ahead by decisions of the European Court of Human Rights and by legislation and case law from the EU. Since 31 December 2020 new EU legislation has not led to any further changes in UK discrimination law, but decisions of the Court of Justice of the European Union may well continue to shape UK law since cases decided by the CJEU after Brexit will still be taken into account by the UK courts and tribunals when interpreting UK law which implements pre-Brexit EU law.[2] As you will see in this chapter, there has been legislative change to ensure that existing rights are not lost as a result of Brexit.

Further change is also afoot in the form of the Equality (Race and Disability) Bill, which at the time of writing is only at the consultation stage. This chapter will address what this is likely to look like at the time of writing, but this is an area that is liable to change.

A final point worth making is that even though equality law applies in many fields other than employment, the overwhelming majority of discrimination cases brought before the courts and tribunals are about employment, and so both the principles and the details of our discrimination law have largely been established by case law in the field of employment. A practising employment lawyer will typically find that about half of their work relates to cases raising issues of discrimination law.

[1] For more on these issues see Fredman 'Reversing Discrimination' (1997) 113 LQR 575 and Barnard and Hepple 'Substantive Equality' (2000) 59 CLJ 562.

[2] European Union (Withdrawal) Act 2018, s 6(2).

4.1 Historical background

4.1.1 The common law

The common law placed no restrictions on an employer's freedom to decide whether to hire a particular individual—an approach deeply rooted in laissez-faire philosophy, and encapsulated in the following dictum of Lord Davey in *Allen v Flood*:[3]

> [A]n employer may refuse to employ [an individual] for the most mistaken, capricious, malicious or morally reprehensible motives that can be conceived, but [that individual] has no right of action against him.

Thus, a refusal to employ on grounds of sex, race, marital status, disability, or any other ground was not unlawful;[4] still less did the courts reveal any concern to enforce equality in the terms of employment. Indeed, in *Roberts v Hopwood*,[5] Lord Atkinson in the House of Lords castigated the policy adopted by Poplar Council in London of providing equal pay to men and women performing the same work as being motivated by 'misguided principles of socialistic philanthropy'.

4.1.2 Early legislation—sex and race discrimination

The first legislative intervention, the Sex Disqualification (Removal) Act 1919, had a narrow scope, removing the restrictions on the employment of women in certain occupations and vocations. However, this Act did not outlaw discrimination on grounds of sex in the appointment to jobs in those occupations or in the terms of employment. The Race Relations Act (RRA)1968 took the revolutionary step of prohibiting discrimination in employment on grounds of race. However, that Act relied for its enforcement on a combination of voluntary procedures and the institution of proceedings by the Race Relations Board, and was widely considered to have been a failure.

This all started to change in 1975 when two ground-breaking statutes came into force to tackle sex discrimination. The first of these, the Equal Pay Act 1970,[6] introduced a new right to equal terms and conditions for men and women in comparable work for a particular employer. Other forms of discrimination in the workplace between the sexes were forbidden by the Sex Discrimination Act 1975. This introduced broad protection against direct and indirect discrimination in employment (and also in certain other specified areas such as education and the provision of goods and services) on the grounds of sex or marital status. The Act gave an employee a right of complaint to a tribunal in employment cases and also established the Equal Opportunities Commission (EOC) to oversee the operation of the legislation and to enforce it by bringing court proceedings or through the issue of non-discrimination notices.

The Race Relations Act 1976 closely followed the model of the Sex Discrimination Act 1975 and established the Commission for Racial Equality (CRE), with powers similar to those of the EOC.

[3] [1898] AC 1 at 172.

[4] See eg *Weinberger v Inglis (No 2)* [1919] AC 606, HL; *Bebb v Law Society* [1914] 1 Ch 286, CA; *Short v Poole Corpn* [1926] Ch 66, CA.

[5] [1925] AC 578, HL.

[6] Commencement of the Act was delayed for five years to enable employers to remove discrimination in terms and conditions.

In the two decades that followed, legal developments in this area mostly occurred as a result of the influence of European Union law. European law has had a profound impact on UK sex discrimination law, stretching it into areas which were not originally considered to fall within the scope of the domestic legislation, such as equal pay for work of equal value, benefits on death or retirement, and discrimination on grounds of gender reassignment. Whether the UK's withdrawal from membership in the EU will change this still remains to be seen, given that the EU influences have been incorporated into the key UK statute, the Equality Act 2010. As you will see, the main changes so far have been to codify existing entitlements that would have otherwise potentially been lost as a result of Brexit.

4.1.3 **The third limb—disability discrimination**

The next big leap forward came with the enactment of the Disability Discrimination Act (DDA) 1995, the first significant piece of UK legislation to tackle discrimination against people with disabilities. This Act prohibited discrimination against people with disabilities in relation to employment; the provision of goods, facilities, and services; and the sale and letting of property. It also created the Disability Rights Commission along the lines of the existing EOC and CRE.

4.1.4 **Positive duties to eliminate discrimination**

The tragic death of Stephen Lawrence and the subsequent public inquiry[7] led to the introduction of the Race Relations (Amendment) Act 2000. This Act was highly significant, in that it marked a movement away from the traditional, reactive approach to tackling discrimination, which puts the responsibility onto individuals to seek remedies via the courts and tribunals, towards a more proactive approach which 'mainstreams' equality by requiring public authorities to take equality issues into account in the development of their policies and programmes.[8] This wider approach has now been incorporated in the Equality Act 2010 across all of the protected characteristics other than marriage or civil partnership (it remains, however, limited to the public sector). This topic is considered more fully in 4.2.8.4.

4.1.5 **Europe-wide legislation against many strands of discrimination**

In 1999 the Treaty of Amsterdam inserted a new provision into the EC Treaty: Article 13 (now Article 19 Treaty on the Functioning of the European Union (TFEU)), which provided a new basis for Community-wide action to combat discrimination on grounds of sex, racial or ethnic origin, religion or belief, disability, age, or sexual orientation.[9] As a result, in 1999 the European Commission brought forward two Directives: a Race Directive[10] combating discrimination on grounds of racial or ethnic origin in a wide range of areas including employment, and a framework Employment Directive[11] dealing with discrimination in employment and occupation on grounds of religion or belief, disability, age, or sexual orientation. The Race Directive was implemented by amending

[7] The Stephen Lawrence Inquiry: Report of an Inquiry by Sir William Macpherson (Cm 4262-I, 1999).

[8] See Fredman 'Equality: A New Generation?' [2001] 30 ILJ 145; Hepple, Coussey, and Choudhury *Equality: A New Framework* (2000).

[9] See Waddington (1999) 28 ILJ 133; (2000) 29 ILJ 176.

[10] Directive 2000/43/EC.

[11] Directive 2000/78/EC.

the Race Relations Act 1976.[12] The Employment Directive was implemented by a series of Regulations which amended the DDA 1995[13] and introduced new measures prohibiting discrimination in employment on grounds of religion or belief,[14] sexual orientation,[15] and age.[16] Finally, the EU adopted an updated directive discrimination on grounds of sex, pregnancy, and maternity, the Equal Treatment Directive, in 2006.[17]

The result in the UK legislation was a proverbial dog's breakfast, with significant differences *between* the strands (such as discrimination on grounds of sex and of religion) and even differences *within* the strands. One problem, for example, was that domestic law on disability pre-dated EU intervention (and arguably gave greater protection) and was drafted entirely differently. Similarly, domestic race discrimination law permitted different defences than those authorized by the EC Directives, and thus retained them alongside the new European defences—but only for the aspects of 'race' which *were* specified in the Race Relations Act *but were not* covered by the EC Directives.

The situation was marginally improved by the Equality Act 2006, which created the Commission for Equality of Human Rights (now the Equality and Human Rights Commission) to take over from the Equal Opportunities Commission, the Commission for Racial Equality, and the Disability Rights Commission. This body (the EHRC) fills in the obvious gap that, prior to its inception, there was no supervisory body for sexual orientation, religion/belief, or age discrimination. More fundamentally, however, it has broad, general duties,[18] a more specific duty to promote equality and diversity,[19] and a specific remit to promote understanding of, and encourage good practice in relation to, *human rights generally*,[20] thus going beyond the pre-existing boundaries of discrimination law as such.

4.1.6 **Consolidation and limited extension by the Equality Act 2010**

The chaotic state of British anti-discrimination legislation was rectified by a new all-embracing statute, the 2010 Equality Act. This Act brought nearly all the anti-discrimination legislation into a single statute and applied harmonized definitions and concepts to every strand of discrimination. The Act also introduced a small number of extensions to existing legal protections against discrimination.

4.1.7 **Post-Brexit changes**

Brexit means that the Equality Act 2010 can now be amended however a UK government sees fit.[21] There are no plans to change UK discrimination substantively at this stage and, as will be seen, the limited legislative changes introduced have been to expressly incorporate EU case law (eg see definitions of disability at 4.7.2).[22]

[12] Race Relations Act 1976 (Amendment) Regulations 2003, SI 2003/1626.

[13] Disability Discrimination Act 1995 (Amendment) Regulations 2003, SI 2003/1673.

[14] Employment Equality (Religion or Belief) Regulations 2003, SI 2003/1660.

[15] Employment Equality (Sexual Orientation) Regulations 2003, SI 2003/1661.

[16] Employment Equality (Age) Regulations 2006, SI 2006/1031.

[17] Directive 2006/54/EC.

[18] Equality Act 2006, s 3; these duties relate to the development of a society in which (a) people's ability to achieve their potential is not limited by prejudice or discrimination, (b) there is respect for and protection of each individual's human rights, (c) there is respect for the dignity of each individual, (d) each individual has an equal opportunity to participate in society, and (e) there is mutual respect between groups based on understanding and valuing of diversity and on shared respect for equality and human rights.

[19] Equality Act 2006, s 8; under s 11 there is a duty to monitor the effectiveness of equality and human rights enactments.

[20] Equality Act 2006, s 9.

[21] Retained EU Law (Revocation and Reform) Act 2023, s 3.

[22] Equality Act 2010 (Amendment) Regulations 2023.

In terms of how EU case law will impact UK court decisions, the position remains unclear. What we do know is that CJEU decisions from before 2021 will still apply, but that higher courts can depart from these when it is 'right to do so'.[23] UK courts are not bound by any decisions from 2021 onwards, but they may still have regard to them. This means that employment tribunals will have to apply the Equality Act in accordance with pre-Brexit case law on the relevant EU legislation, even if that means reading words in or out of the UK legislation. Until appellate courts have heard cases dealing with the issues of reading words either in or out, and other ongoing areas of uncertainty (see proportionality at 4.2.5.7), it is impossible to know how, or if, UK discrimination law will change.

4.2 The overall scheme of the Equality Act 2010

4.2.1 Application and coverage

The aim of the Equality Act 2010 is to prevent discrimination in various fields of life on the basis of certain 'protected characteristics'. One of the fields covered is that of work, consisting of 'employment' and also appointment to certain offices. 'Employment' is defined as working under a contract of employment or of apprenticeship, or under a contract personally to do work.[24] Using the term 'employment' brings the potential for confusion because it is defined in a way that gives it a much wider meaning than in other employment law statutes. This extended definition is probably coextensive with the definition of 'worker' in other employment law statutes, as discussed in 2.1.3. A person outside this definition of 'employment' may not claim the benefit of the relevant provision, except in the case of 'contract workers' (ie people working for A who have in fact been engaged by B and hired to A under a contract of supply of labour) and certain office holders.[25] As discussed in 4.2.9, the Act prohibits discrimination at all stages of employment: recruitment, employment, and termination. The Act also gives a trade union member a right not to be discriminated against by the union in matters of admission, expulsion, and provision of union benefits, facilities, and so on.[26]

The Act specifies certain exclusions. Thus, the application of the Act is modified in the case of ministers of religion,[27] and the Act also allows women and people who fall within the Act's definition in s 7(2) of 'transsexual' to be excluded from certain parts of the armed forces if the exclusion 'is a proportionate means of ensuring the combat effectiveness of the armed forces'.[28]

4.2.2 Protected characteristics

The Equality Act 2010 sets out the protected characteristics to which it applies: age, disability, gender reassignment, marriage and civil partnership, pregnancy and maternity, race, religion or belief, sex, and sexual orientation.[29] The definition for each of these characteristics is set out in 4.3 to 4.11 below, together with any special rules that apply in relation to each particular characteristic. The definitions are important: to give two

[23] EU (Withdrawal) Act 2018, s 6(3).

[24] Equality Act 2010, s 83(2)(a).

[25] Equality Act 2010, ss 41, 49–52. In *Jivraj v Hashwani* [2011] ICR 1004, [2011] IRLR 827, SC it was held that an arbitrator held too independent an office, and was insufficiently subordinate, for his selection to be covered by the employment provisions of the Act.

[26] Equality Act 2010, s 57. See Homans (1984) 13 ILJ 262.

[27] Equality Act 2010, Sch 9, para 2. This is discussed at 4.4 in connection with sexual orientation discrimination.

[28] Equality Act 2010, Sch 9, para 4.

[29] Equality Act 2010, s 4.

examples, the meaning of 'race' is quite wide and covers colour, nationality, ethnic origin, and national origin; and the definition of 'disability' is complex and leads to a great deal of dispute on matters of law and fact.

4.2.3 The meaning of 'discrimination'—outline of the legal model and some general points

4.2.3.1 The basic model

The basic model for protection applies to discrimination on the grounds of all protected characteristics, such as race, sex, and age (often referred to as 'strands'). The model, expressed in broad terms, is a ban on four types of behaviour:

(1) **direct discrimination**: treating someone less favourably because of a protected characteristic;
(2) **indirect discrimination**: applying a practice or policy to all employees in a situation where this practice or policy puts employees with one of the protected characteristics at a particular disadvantage—unless this can be justified as a proportionate means of achieving a legitimate aim;
(3) **harassment** of another person which is related to a protected characteristic;
(4) **victimizing** a person for making or supporting a complaint about discrimination.

Why do we need to have concepts of both direct and indirect discrimination?

Lady Hale explained this as follows in the leading case of *Essop v Home Office (UK Border Agency) and Naeem v Secretary of State for Justice*:

> [T]he prohibition of direct discrimination aims to achieve equality of treatment. Indirect discrimination assumes equality of treatment . . . but aims to achieve a level playing field, where people sharing a particular protected characteristic are not subjected to requirements which many of them cannot meet but which cannot be shown to be justified. The prohibition of indirect discrimination thus aims to achieve equality of results in the absence of such justification. It is dealing with hidden barriers which are not easy to anticipate or to spot.[30]

If the law only prohibited direct discrimination, less favourable treatment which stemmed from bias against, for example, those of a particular sex or with a particular disability would be illegal, and would deliver 'formal equality'. However, it would not deliver 'substantive' equality in the field of employment since there would be people excluded from jobs because they could not meet some requirement imposed by the employer even when that requirement was not in fact necessary for the job. For instance, a requirement to work full-time when the role could perfectly well be performed by two part-timers might well exclude women, who are more likely than men to have family caring responsibilities. The prohibition of indirect discrimination tackles this issue by banning such requirements except where the employer can show that they are justified, but it does not deliver full substantial equality in the employment field. First of all, such a requirement is lawful if the employer can show it is justified because it is a proportionate means of achieving a legitimate aim of the employer. This has the result that some requirements which have an exclusionary effect on particular groups of people remain lawful. Further, some people with a disability need an employer to provide special equipment to enable them to do a job and this problem is not solved by the law of indirect discrimination. Again, there may

[30] [2017] UKSC 27, [2017] IRLR 558 at para 25.

be those who, because of race discrimination, may not have had the educational opportunities of other job-seekers and thus will not be able to win appointment to jobs which, with a decent education, they could have been capable of. The question of how far the law should go to seek to ensure substantive equality in relation to employment is controversial. The Equality Act goes some way to tackle the examples just referred to: employers must make reasonable adjustments to overcome barriers for disabled employees (see 4.7.3.2) and some positive discrimination towards less favoured groups is permitted, but it is not compulsory (see 4.2.8.3).

4.2.3.2 **Variations on the basic model**

In relation to certain protected characteristics there are some variations on this basic model of four banned types of discriminatory conduct, and these are covered in the relevant parts of 4.3 to 4.11. In addition there is one major exception, which relates to *sex inequality in the contractual terms of employment*. Complaints about that, which are usually referred to as 'equal pay' complaints, must be brought under the 'equality of terms' provisions in ss 64–80 of the Act.[31] The legal model for this equal pay topic is very different and is considered in 4.3.2. It might seem that the law would have been much more straightforward and transparent if the drafters of the legislation had adopted the same model for sex discrimination in contractual terms as for all other aspects of discrimination in employment. However, the different EU legal instruments and approaches to equal pay on grounds of sex and other aspects of discrimination would have made this difficult.

4.2.3.3 **Some general points about the interpretation of anti-discrimination legislation**

This chapter describes the concepts of discrimination based on the language of the statutes, the theories behind that language, and the best of the decided cases. However, no student of this area of law will fail to notice that some cases appear to fly in the face of the theory of anti-discrimination law or the language of the statutes that implement it. An underlying truth about equality law is that it seeks to change behaviour. It does not enter into a world where equal treatment is the status quo, and in which the law need only hold the line against slipping standards. Instead, it enters into a world in which discrimination—not only discriminatory actions but, more importantly, apparently neutral actions that in fact have a discriminatory impact—happens every day, and more often than not because of attitudes or policies that strike those who hold or adopt them as 'common sense'. It may be that there is less blatant discrimination now than when the Sex Discrimination Act (SDA) came on the scene in 1975, but what remains is often more difficult to handle because it is not blatant.

The issue is not just that it is hard to prove, or that people keep it hidden. It is that some of the most intractable discrimination is perpetrated by accident, by 'good' people who simply cannot or will not accept this truth: just because (a) something has always been a certain way, and (b) nobody has had bad intentions in keeping it that way, does not mean that nobody is getting unfairly and unequally hurt by it. Judges are no worse than other people, but neither are they better.[32] As a result, some judicial decisions simply reflect the inability (or unwillingness) of judges to look beyond practices or assumptions with which they have been comfortable for a lifetime, to see the relative disadvantage produced by those practices and assumptions. In other words, some cases are

[31] Equality Act 2010, s 70 provides that anything that counts as equality-of-terms discrimination does not count as sex discrimination.

[32] *Geller v Yeshurun Hebrew Congregation* UKEAT/0190/15 (23 March 2016, unreported), admonishing tribunals to carefully consider the possibility of unconscious or subconscious discrimination.

just wrong, at least when measured against what equality law seeks to accomplish and actually expresses through statutory language. Specific examples of this are noted where relevant in this chapter.

4.2.4 **Direct discrimination**

4.2.4.1 **'Because of a protected characteristic'**

Direct discrimination is defined in s 13 as where the employer, because of a protected characteristic, treats an employee less favourably than a person without that characteristic. This is what one might call the 'popular' understanding of discrimination: treating people differently for prohibited reasons. A key question is whether it is enough for a protected characteristic to be part of the causal chain for the adverse treatment or whether the protected characteristic must be the *reason* why the employer acted in the way it did. To put it another way: is it enough that but for the characteristic the adverse treatment would not have occurred? It has been clearly established at the highest level in the cases of *Nagarajan v London Regional Transport*[33] and *Chief Constable of West Yorkshire Police v Khan*[34] that the reason does matter. Sometimes the reason is obvious; for example, if a job advertisement were to say 'no women', sex would clearly be the reason for not processing the application of a female candidate. However, sometimes it is necessary to look into the mental processes of the person who did the act in order to determine if the less favourable treatment was because of the protected characteristic. In *R (on the application of E) v Governing Body of JFS*,[35] the Supreme Court said that in deciding what were the grounds for an act alleged to amount to direct discrimination it is necessary to address the question of the factual criteria that determined the decision made by the alleged discriminator. It is only where the factual criteria which influenced the alleged discriminator to act as they did are not plain that it is necessary to explore their mental processes in order to discover what facts led them to act as they did, but in doing so one is not seeking to identify the person's motive, simply what facts influenced the person's decision. Lord Phillips gave the following example:

> A fat black man goes into a shop to make a purchase. The shop-keeper says 'I do not serve people like you'. To appraise his conduct it is necessary to know what was the fact that determined his refusal. Was it the fact that the man was fat or the fact that he was black? In the former case the ground of his refusal was not racial; in the latter it was. The reason why the particular fact triggered his reaction is not relevant to the question of the ground upon which he discriminated.

Even if the reason for less favourable treatment is not overtly a protected characteristic, it may still be a case of direct discrimination if the criterion applied is something that is 'inextricably linked' to one of the protected characteristics.[36] For example, in *Dziedziak v Future Electronics Ltd*,[37] a Polish national alleged that she had been subjected to direct race discrimination when she had been reprimanded for speaking Polish in the office—something that had allegedly distracted one of her colleagues. The tribunal found that the

[33] [1999] ICR 877, [1999] IRLR 572, HL.

[34] [2001] ICR 1065, [2001] IRLR 830, HL.

[35] [2009] UKSC 15, [2010] IRLR 136.

[36] See eg *Jyske Finans A/S v Ligebehandlingsnaevnet acting on behalf of Huskic* C:2017:278, [2017] IRLR 665, ECJ, *MH Müller Handels GmbH v MJ* C-341/19, [2021] IRLR 832, ECJE and *Essop v Home Office (UK Border Agency) and Naeem v Secretary of State for Justice* [2017] UKSC 27, [2017] IRLR 558 (Lady Hale at para 17).

[37] UKEAT/0270/11, [2012] EqLR 543.

manager had specifically instructed Ms Dziedziak not to speak 'in her own language', an instruction that had not been given to any other employee. The employer argued that the instruction related to language, which was not the same thing as nationality and, by itself, could not amount to direct race discrimination. The EAT disagreed and held that the use of the words 'own language' demonstrated an intrinsic link with nationality and was sufficient in itself to pass the burden to the respondent to establish that there was another, non-discriminatory, explanation for the instruction, which it had failed to do.

Mixed causes

Care is needed where the employer acts for mixed reasons, not all of which constitute unlawful discrimination. It is clearly established that the unlawful reason need not be the sole reason for the employer's action. In *Owen and Briggs v James*,[38] the Court of Appeal held that where there is more than one operating cause, it will amount to direct discrimination if the unlawful motive is an 'important factor' in the employer's decision; in other words, the unlawful motive must be of sufficient weight in the decision-making process to be treated as a cause, but not necessarily the sole cause, of the act thus motivated.[39]

What if there is a 'good' motive?

A good motive on the part of the employer (eg a belief that the discriminatory action is in the applicant's own best interests) is no excuse for an act of direct discrimination[40] (nor is the fact that the employer has been pressured to discriminate by a third party, eg a trade union, or the applicant's fellow employees).[41] A particularly good example of this can be seen in *Moyhing v Barts & London NHS Trust*,[42] where, to protect male nurses and to reassure patients, the hospital had a rule that male nurses performing intimate procedures on female patients had to be chaperoned; no such requirement applied to female nurses. In spite of the hospital's view that this was a 'common sense' measure, when it was challenged by an aggrieved male nurse it was held to be unlawful direct discrimination. A further example is *James v Eastleigh Borough Council*,[43] a case which was brought at a time when discrimination on the ground of age was not prohibited. The applicant, a man of 61, complained of sex discrimination because he had been charged 75p to swim in the municipal swimming baths, while his wife of the same age had been admitted free under the council's policy of allowing free entry to those who had reached the state pensionable age (of 65 for men and 60 for women). The Court of Appeal had held that there had not been less favourable treatment on the ground of sex because the reason for the concession was to benefit pensioners and not to discriminate against men. However, on further appeal the House of Lords overturned this decision, rejecting the relevance of good motive and affirming that the correct approach is an objective one: 'Would the

[38] [1982] ICR 618, [1982] IRLR 502, CA.

[39] *Nagarajan v Agnew* [1995] ICR 520, [1994] IRLR 61, EAT. In the later case of *Nagarajan v London Regional Transport* [1999] ICR 877, [1999] IRLR 572, HL Lord Nichols referred to the discriminatory reason as having a 'significant influence'.

[40] *Peake v Automotive Products Ltd* [1977] ICR 480, [1977] IRLR 105 (reversed on other grounds, [1977] ICR 968, [1977] IRLR 365, CA); *Grieg v Community Industry* [1979] ICR 356, [1979] IRLR 158; *Din v Carrington Viyella Ltd* [1982] ICR 256, [1982] IRLR 281. While motive is not relevant when determining whether discrimination has occurred, it may be relevant when deciding the level of compensation to be awarded: *Chief Constable of the Greater Manchester Police v Hope* [1999] ICR 338, EAT.

[41] *R v Commission for Racial Equality, ex p Westminster City Council* [1985] ICR 827, [1985] IRLR 426, CA.

[42] [2006] IRLR 860: the fact that the rule was not aimed at him and had actually caused little inconvenience led to a small award of compensation.

[43] [1990] ICR 554, [1990] IRLR 288, HL; revsg [1989] ICR 423, [1989] IRLR 318, CA.

complainant have received the same treatment but for his sex?' On the facts it was clear that the less favourable treatment would not have occurred but for the complainant's sex, and so there was direct discrimination. The fact that the council did not intend to discriminate against the applicant, and that its reason for adopting the policy of concessions to pensioners was an honourable one, was considered to be irrelevant. The case is a good illustration of the fact that, other than in relation to a limited number of specified exceptions which are considered later, there is no 'justification' defence in a complaint of *direct* discrimination.[44]

Attributing a manager's reason to the employer

One important problem in employment discrimination is the question of which manager's thinking is relevant when deciding whether the employer acted adversely 'because of' a protected characteristic. The law previously appeared to be, according to *Reynolds v CLFIS (UK) Ltd*,[45] that the reason for the treatment complained of must be a reason relied on by the relevant decision-maker, not just by someone who advised the relevant decision-maker. If more than one person was involved in a challenged decision, such as where a high-level manager makes a decision based on assessments provided by lower-level managers, it was necessary to prove that the ultimate decision-maker took the protected characteristic into account, so that it was not enough that the lower-level assessments were tainted. This was another 'common sense' decision that was likely to thwart the aims of anti-discrimination law: it encouraged decision-makers to rely on uninvestigated advice, absolved higher-level managers of responsibility to ensure non-discriminatory assessments by their subordinates, and left it to chance whether the employee could discover the actual locus of the discrimination in time to satisfy relevant time limits.

However, the correct understanding of the law on this issue is almost certainly now different as a result of the approach of the Supreme Court in *Royal Mail v Jhuti*.[46] This was a complaint of unfair dismissal, and the issue related to identifying the employer's reason for dismissing the employee, but the reasoning adopted by the Court seems equally applicable to assessing the reason for an employer's less favourable treatment of an employee in a discrimination case. In *Jhuti*, a manager who was above the employee in the hierarchy decided that they should be dismissed for whistleblowing but put forward a case to the dismissing manager based on the employee's alleged poor performance on which, in all innocence, the dismissing manager relied. The Supreme Court held that the reason for dismissal was nevertheless whistleblowing because the employer's reason for dismissal must be taken to include the reason of any manager in the hierarchy above the employee. A similar principle probably also applies where the misbehaving manager is not part of the hierarchy above the complainant but is given some aspect of the investigation of the complainant's situation to undertake and then manipulates the investigation so as to cause another manager to innocently dismiss the employee.[47]

Stereotypes

Given that one of the aims of the legislation is to discourage the treatment of groups en masse as capable of certain things and incapable of others, general stereotypical assumptions (eg that women cannot do heavy work or that Christians will not work on Sundays)

[44] Cf Bowers and Moran 'Justification in Direct Sex Discrimination Law: Breaking the Taboo' (2002) 31 ILJ 307.

[45] [2015] EWCA Civ 439, [2015] IRLR 562; cf *IPC Media Ltd v Millar* [2013] IRLR 707.

[46] [2019] UKSC 55, [2020] IRLR 129.

[47] *Cadent Gas Ltd v Singh* [2020] IRLR 86, EAT, a case of automatically unfair dismissal for a trade union reason.

are likely to be held to be discriminatory, and an employer who acts on such assumptions may well contravene the statute.[48] This consideration can be very sensitively applied, as illustrated in the following summation, given in a case where accusing a worker of 'playing the race card' was found discriminatory:

> Mr Arnett made a comment to the Claimant to the effect that he was alleging racial discrimination. Crucially, the Claimant had said nothing to provoke that comment. It must follow that Mr Arnett said what he did as a result of an assumption—or, to use another word, the application of a stereotype: 'he is a black employee complaining about his treatment by a white colleague—he must, or at least may, be alleging race discrimination'. In our view, on the tribunal's factual findings, Mr Arnett must have been motivated by some such assumption; and it follows that his comment was made on racial grounds.[49]

4.2.4.2 **Associative discrimination**

Prior to the 2010 Act, the SDA 1975 based direct discrimination on the sex *of the applicant* and the DDA 1995 based discrimination on the disabled status *of the applicant*, while other legislation (eg the RRA 1976 and the 2006 Employment Equality Regulations) addressed direct discrimination 'on grounds of' the protected characteristics of, for example, race or sexual orientation. This meant that some legislation was susceptible to the interpretation that it was discriminatory to treat someone less favourably because of their association with a person of a certain race or sexual orientation, while statutes like the SDA expressly ruled this out. The CJEU made it clear in *Coleman v Attridge Law*[50] that the European Directives on discrimination required that such 'associative' discrimination should be illegal. The 2010 Act clears this up by defining all direct discrimination, whatever the ground, as less favourable treatment 'because of a protected characteristic'. This is intended to make the concept of direct discrimination broad enough to encompass, for example, less favourable treatment for caring for a disabled child, or for being married to an Asian man.

4.2.4.3 **Real and hypothetical comparators**

For there to be a finding of direct discrimination it must be shown that the employer has treated the applicant 'less favourably' than the employer 'treats or would treat' others, 'because of a protected characteristic'. Unlike the 'equal pay' provisions of the Act, which work on the basis of a comparison between the treatment of the applicant and that of a named comparator, the rest of the Equality Act is based on a comparison with a real *or* hypothetical comparator. The comparison must be such that there is 'no material difference between the circumstances relevant to each case'.[51] The identification of the appropriate real or hypothetical comparator and the determination of which circumstances are to be considered as relevant are key elements in any discrimination claim, often requiring difficult judgements as to which of the differences between any two individuals are relevant and which are irrelevant. The choice of characteristics 'may itself be determinative of the outcome'.[52] Accordingly, the comparator requirement is considered one of the most problematic elements of discrimination law.[53]

[48] *Skyrail Oceanic Ltd v Coleman* [1981] ICR 864, [1981] IRLR 398, CA; *Horsey v Dyfed County Council* [1982] ICR 755, [1982] IRLR 395.

[49] *Royal Bank of Scotland plc v Morris* [2011] UKEAT/0436/10/MAA (12 March 2012).

[50] Case C-303/06, [2008] IRLR 722.

[51] Equality Act 2010, s 23.

[52] *Shamoon v Chief Constable of the Royal Ulster Constabulary* [2003] UKHL 11, [2003] ICR 337, [2003] IRLR 285 at 292, per Lord Hope.

[53] See Fredman D*iscrimination Law* (3rd edn, 2024) 254–58.

It may be possible to find an actual comparator whose circumstances are the same or not materially different to those of the applicant, in which case that person can perform the role of the comparator, but in most cases this will not be possible, and in such circumstances the tribunal must[54] make a hypothetical comparison by considering how the employer would have treated an employee lacking the protected characteristic. One way of doing this is to see how the employer acted 'in cases which, while not identical, were also not wholly dissimilar',[55] as that evidence may provide a sound basis for inferring how the employer would have treated another employee in the same circumstances as the applicant.

In relation to the requirement that there must be 'no material difference between the circumstances relevant to' the complainant and the comparator, relevant circumstances must not include facts that did not in reality have any bearing on the challenged decision. Therefore a comparison should not be rejected because the comparators have different degrees of work experience if work experience was not a criterion in the challenged hiring/promotion decision: because it was not actually a criterion applied by the employer in making the decision, the fact that the two employees had different levels of experience cannot disprove that the decision was based on a protected characteristic. To give another example, the fact that the manager who made the decision in the complainant's case is different from the person who had made a decision on a similar issue in relation to another employee is not a relevant circumstance that prevents the second employee being a valid comparator.[56]

In an age discrimination case, *Lockwood v Department for Work and Pensions*, the Court of Appeal held that a tribunal treating people over 35 as improper comparators for a 26-year-old woman, because younger women can more easily find subsequent employment, completely misconceived the point of the comparison:

> In a race discrimination case . . . if a black complainant is alleging discrimination at work on the ground of his race, the comparator will usually be a white person who is otherwise in the same, or in a not materially different, position. It is obvious that once such a comparator has been identified, the Tribunal cannot hold the relevant circumstances of the two cases to be different on the ground that the comparator is white and the complainant is black and so regard the comparison as invalid. The whole purpose of the comparison is as an aid to seeing whether or not the way in which the comparator was or would have been treated in the relevant circumstances support the claimant's allegation that he was subjected to less favourable treatment on the ground of the protected characteristic.[57]

This quotation highlights another concern academics raise in regard to discrimination law; that it creates 'powerful conformist pressures'.[58] This is because, as seen in the example above, the comparator tends to be someone who conforms to the dominant norm, be it white, able-bodied, male, or Christian etc.

In determining with whom to make a comparison, circumstances that are related to a protected characteristic but are not direct and unavoidable consequences of it should be taken into account if those circumstances are relevant differences between the two cases.

[54] A tribunal commits an error of law if it does not construct a hypothetical comparator, where one is required, against which to test the alleged discriminatory treatment: *Balamoody v United Kingdom Central Council for Nursing, Midwifery and Health Visiting* [2001] EWCA Civ 2097, [2002] IRLR 288, CA. See also *Chief Constable of West Yorkshire Police v Vento* [2001] IRLR 124, EAT.

[55] *Balamoody v United Kingdom Central Council for Nursing, Midwifery and Health Visiting* [2001] EWCA Civ 2097, [2002] IRLR 288 at 306, per Lord Rodger.

[56] *Olalekan v Serco Ltd* [2019] IRLR 314, EAT.

[57] [2013] EWCA Civ 1195 (Rimer LJ).

[58] Fredman *Discrimination Law* (3rd edn, 2024) 256.

This is best explained by an example: consider a woman with family caring responsibilities who as a result is not promoted to a job which involves working certain shifts which she cannot accommodate because of those responsibilities, so a man who can work those shifts is promoted instead. If she seeks to complain of direct sex discrimination she cannot choose the man who was appointed as her comparator since the ability to work the shifts is relevant to suitability for the promotion. That is to say, his relevant circumstances are not the same as hers because he can do those shifts and she cannot. This means that she has not been the victim of *direct* discrimination, even though her adverse treatment may well be linked to her sex since women are more likely to have caring responsibilities than men (employment tribunals will normally accept this as true without it being specifically proved). However, she may well have a good claim for *indirect* discrimination, since the requirement to work the unusual shifts puts her, and women generally, at a disadvantage, with the consequence that imposing the condition will be unlawful indirect discrimination unless the employer can justify it as a proportionate means of achieving a legitimate aim (as to which see 4.2.5).

4.2.4.4 **'Less favourably'**

Because direct discrimination is based around the concept of 'less favourable' treatment, differential treatment does not in itself amount to discrimination: 'If discrimination is to be established, it is necessary to show not merely that the [comparators] are treated differently, but that the treatment accorded to one is less favourable than the treatment accorded to the other.'[59] This is problematic because it can give rise to the kind of tendentious 'separate but equal' arguments once used to justify racial segregation in the US. Such arguments are excluded in the case of race, as the Equality Act specifically provides in s 13(5) that racial segregation is deemed to be less favourable treatment. In relation to the other protected characteristics, on the whole the courts have been robust in resisting such arguments and have generally accepted that differential treatment is detrimental, although not without the occasional unfortunate lapse. Indeed, in the first case under the SDA 1975 to come before the Court of Appeal, *Peake v Automotive Products Ltd*,[60] the court was prepared to disregard differential treatment on the grounds that it was too minor. In that case, the employer allowed women to leave the factory five minutes before the men, in the interests of safety and to avoid women being caught in the rush to the gates. One of the men complained to a tribunal that this was unlawful discrimination against men. The Court of Appeal rejected this claim on the grounds, first, that the different treatment was in the interests of safety and good administration (in the words of Lord Denning MR: 'it is not discriminatory for mankind to treat womankind with the courtesy and chivalry which we have been taught to believe is right conduct in our society'), and, secondly, that in any event the employer's action was harmless and could be disregarded under the de minimis principle. This is an example of what was mentioned earlier in this chapter: 'common sense' preventing an otherwise clever judge from applying anti-discrimination law as it reads on the tin.

In the later case of *Ministry of Defence v Jeremiah*,[61] the Court of Appeal reconsidered the approach taken in *Peake*. In that case it was held that requiring a man employed in an ordnance factory to perform dirty and unpleasant work making 'colour-bursting' shells when women working in the factory were excused from such work was less favourable treatment within the meaning of the Act, and therefore unlawful. Lord Denning MR

[59] *Smith v Safeway plc* [1996] IRLR 456 at 458, CA, per Phillips J.

[60] [1977] ICR 968, [1977] IRLR 365, CA, restrictively interpreted by the EAT in *Grieg v Community Industry* [1979] ICR 356, [1979] IRLR 158.

[61] [1979] 3 All ER 833, [1979] IRLR 436, CA.

stated that the approach to direct discrimination taken in *Peake* (ie exempting 'sensible administrative arrangements' in the interests of health or chivalry) was wrong and that the decision was only supportable on the alternative ground given (ie that on the facts the discrimination was too minor to be effective, under the de minimis principle). On the facts in *Jeremiah* it was held that requiring only the men to do the work in question was unlawful. This case is an example of the same distinguished judge eventually accepting the change in thinking required by anti-discrimination law.

While the approach of the Court of Appeal in *Jeremiah* showed a stronger adherence to the actual wording of the Act, it still seemed to allow some scope for the de minimis defence. In subsequent cases the courts have tended to take a more robust approach, particularly where the alleged less favourable treatment involves the denial of an opportunity afforded to others. In *Jeremiah*, Brightman LJ suggested that as differentiation is not necessarily discriminatory, a mere deprivation of choice might not of itself be unlawful.[62] However, in *Birmingham City Council v Equal Opportunities Commission*[63] (a case involving access to grammar schools), the House of Lords held that in order to establish less favourable treatment on the grounds of sex, it is enough that members of one sex are deprived of a choice which is valued by them and which (even though others may take a different view) is a choice obviously valued on reasonable grounds by many others. A similarly broad approach to the concept of less favourable treatment was taken in *Gill v El Vino Co Ltd*,[64] where the Court of Appeal held that it was unlawful for a wine bar to refuse to serve women at the bar. In that case Eveleigh LJ stated:

> I find it very difficult to invoke the maxim de minimis non curat lex in a situation where that which has been denied to the plaintiff is the very thing that Parliament seeks to provide, namely facilities and services on an equal basis.[65]

Reverting to the question of 'separate but equal', this issue arose again in *HM Chief Inspector of Education, Children's Services and Skills v Interim Executive Board of Al-Hijrah School*, which concerned a school which segregated girls from boys.[66] The Court of Appeal held that 'separate but equal treatment may constitute unlawful discrimination, and it will do so (subject to statutory exceptions) if such treatment is based on gender and is more detrimental than it would have been but for that gender'. On the facts of the case the school's policy discriminated against both genders—boys and girls each suffered a disadvantage from the segregation: boys, because they were male, could not socialize with girls; and girls, because they were female, could not socialize with boys.

There is, however, an important caveat: the fact that a complainant subjectively considers that they have been less favourably treated does not of itself establish that there is 'less favourable treatment'.[67] The House of Lords has confirmed that in order for treatment to constitute a detriment, the tribunal must find that 'a reasonable worker would or might take the view that the treatment was in all the circumstances to his [sic] detriment'.[68] However, the test is not wholly objective, in that it must be applied by considering the issue from the point of view of the victim.[69]

[62] [1979] 3 All ER 833 at 840, [1979] IRLR 436 at 440.

[63] [1989] IRLR 173, HL.

[64] [1983] IRLR 206, CA.

[65] [1983] IRLR 206 at 208.

[66] [2017] EWCA Civ 1426, [2018] IRLR 334.

[67] *Burrett v West Birmingham Health Authority* [1994] IRLR 7 at 8, EAT, per Knox J. See 4.3.

[68] *Shamoon v Chief Constable of the Royal Ulster Constabulary* [2003] UKHL 11, [2003] ICR 337, [2003] IRLR 285 at 301, per Lord Scott; *Chief Constable of West Yorkshire Police v Khan* [2003] UKHL 11, [2001] IRLR 830 at 835, per Lord Hoffmann.

[69] 'If the victim's opinion that the treatment was to his or her detriment is a reasonable one to hold, that ought, in my opinion, to suffice': [2003] IRLR 285 at 301, per Lord Scott.

A further difficulty with the need to show 'less favourable' treatment is that it enables an employer to argue that since all employees receive equally bad treatment, its treatment of one sex, race, or other group is no less favourable than its treatment of another—what is sometimes referred to by the authors as the 'evil swine' defence: 'But I'm an evil swine to everyone.' This defence does work, although usually it is deployed in a milder form: 'I agree that my company dealt with this disabled employee's grievance incompetently, but that was not because she is disabled, it is just that we are terrible at dealing effectively with all grievances.'[70]

4.2.5 Indirect discrimination

4.2.5.1 The need for a law against indirect discrimination

Discrimination can, of course, take more subtle forms than the overt ones just discussed. In particular, it can take the form of a rule, policy, criterion, or practice which, while not expressly mentioning a protected characteristic, in practice puts one group at a disadvantage because it has a disproportionate impact on the members of that group. For example, a requirement that applicants for a particular post be between the ages of 17 and 28, while gender-neutral on its face, may be held to discriminate indirectly against women because in practice many women would be unavailable for work between those ages because of family commitments.[71] On the other hand, it could be the case that the factor causing the discriminatory effect, such as an ability to lift heavy weights, is in fact necessary for the efficient performance of the job. This means that a balance has to be struck so that legitimate business needs are not jeopardized, while at the same time recognizing that the consequence is to put a person at a disadvantage for a reason relating to their protected characteristic. The statutory compromise is the concept of indirect discrimination, which enables an applicant to raise an inference of discrimination by showing that a provision, criterion, or practice (PCP) of the employer has an adverse impact on a group defined by a protected characteristic, but then permits the employer to escape liability by showing that there is some objective justification for the application of that rule, etc, despite its adverse impact.

4.2.5.2 Summary of the concept of indirect discrimination

The 2010 Act (s 19) says that there is indirect discrimination when the following four conditions are satisfied:

(1) the employer applies a provision, criterion, or practice which applies or would apply equally to those who do not share the claimant's protected characteristic;

(2) it puts or would put people with the claimant's protected characteristic at a particular disadvantage when compared with those who do not share it;

(3) it puts the claimant at that disadvantage;

(4) it cannot be shown to be a proportionate means of achieving a legitimate aim.

The wording of s 19 is slightly different from the provision in the European Equal Treatment Directive that the section is intended to implement. This is discussed below under the heading 'Justification'.

[70] For more see Fredman *Discrimination Law* (3rd edn, 2024) 251–54.

[71] *Price v Civil Service Commission* [1978] ICR 27, [1977] IRLR 291.

In the leading case of *Essop v Home Office (UK Border Agency) and Naeem v Secretary of State for Justice*,[72] Lady Hale gave the following very helpful and clear outline of the nature and purpose of the concept of indirect discrimination:

> The first salient feature is that [there] is no requirement in the Equality Act 2010 that the claimant show why the PCP puts one group sharing a particular protected characteristic at a particular disadvantage when compared with others. It is enough that it does. Sometimes, perhaps usually, the reason will be obvious: women are on average shorter than men, so a tall minimum height requirement will disadvantage women whereas a short maximum will disadvantage men. But sometimes it will not be obvious: there is no generally accepted explanation for why women have on average achieved lower grades as chess players than men, but a requirement to hold a high chess grade will put them at a disadvantage.
>
> A second salient feature is the contrast between the definitions of direct and indirect discrimination. Direct discrimination expressly requires a causal link between the less favourable treatment and the protected characteristic. Indirect discrimination does not. Instead it requires a causal link between the PCP and the particular disadvantage suffered by the group and the individual. The reason for this is that the prohibition of direct discrimination aims to achieve equality of treatment. Indirect discrimination assumes equality of treatment—the PCP is applied indiscriminately to all—but aims to achieve a level playing field, where people sharing a particular protected characteristic are not subjected to requirements which many of them cannot meet but which cannot be shown to be justified. The prohibition of indirect discrimination thus aims to achieve equality of results in the absence of such justification. It is dealing with hidden barriers which are not easy to anticipate or to spot.
>
> A third salient feature is that the reasons why one group may find it harder to comply with the PCP than others are many and various . . . They could be genetic, such as strength or height. They could be social, such as the expectation that women will bear the greater responsibility for caring for the home and family than will men. They could be traditional employment practices, such as the division between 'women's jobs' and 'men's jobs' or the practice of starting at the bottom of an incremental pay scale. There could be another PCP, working in combination with the one at issue, as in *Homer v Chief Constable of West Yorkshire* [2012] IRLR 601, where the requirement of a law degree operated in combination with normal retirement age to produce the disadvantage suffered by Mr Homer and others in his age group. These various examples show that the reason for the disadvantage need not be unlawful in itself or be under the control of the employer or provider (although sometimes it will be). They also show that both the PCP and the reason for the disadvantage are 'but for' causes of the disadvantage: removing one or the other would solve the problem.
>
> A fourth salient feature is that there is no requirement that the PCP in question put every member of the group sharing the particular protected characteristic at a disadvantage . . . Obviously, some women are taller or stronger than some men and can meet a height or strength requirement that many women could not. Some women can work full time without difficulty whereas others cannot. Yet these are paradigm examples of a PCP which may be indirectly discriminatory. The fact that some BME or older candidates could pass the test is neither here nor there. The group was at a disadvantage because the proportion of those who could pass it was smaller than the proportion of white or younger candidates. If they had all failed, it would be closer to a case of direct discrimination (because the test requirement would be a proxy for race or age).
>
> A fifth salient feature is that it is commonplace for the disparate impact, or particular disadvantage, to be established on the basis of statistical evidence. That was obvious from

[72] [2017] UKSC 27.

the way in which the concept was expressed in the 1975 and 1976 Acts: indeed it might be difficult to establish that the proportion of women who could comply with the requirement was smaller than the proportion of men unless there was statistical evidence to that effect. Recital (15) to the Race Directive recognised that indirect discrimination might be proved on the basis of statistical evidence, while at the same time introducing the new definition. It cannot have been contemplated that the 'particular disadvantage' might not be capable of being proved by statistical evidence. Statistical evidence is designed to show correlations between particular variables and particular outcomes and to assess the significance of those correlations. But a correlation is not the same as a causal link.

A final salient feature is that it is always open to the respondent to show that his PCP is justified—in other words, that there is a good reason for the particular height requirement, or the particular chess grade, or the particular CSA test. Some reluctance to reach this point can be detected in the cases, yet there should not be. There is no finding of unlawful discrimination until all four elements of the definition are met. The requirement to justify a PCP should not be seen as placing an unreasonable burden upon respondents. Nor should it be seen as casting some sort of shadow or stigma upon them. There is no shame in it. There may well be very good reasons for the PCP in question—fitness levels in fire-fighters or policemen spring to mind. But, as Langstaff J pointed out in the EAT in *Essop*, a wise employer will monitor how his policies and practices impact upon various groups and, if he finds that they do have a disparate impact, will try and see what can be modified to remove that impact while achieving the desired result.

4.2.5.3 **Provision, criterion, or practice**

The first step in analysing an indirect discrimination claim is to identify a PCP. For example, a requirement to work full time can amount to a PCP, and so result in a finding of indirect discrimination on the ground of sex (owing to the fact that it is substantially more likely that women, who are more likely to have family caring duties, will struggle with the requirement).[73] It is not necessary that a PCP acts as an absolute bar to compliance for the claimant, simply that it places the claimant at a disadvantage.[74] The fact that the definition features the word 'practice' means that a PCP need not be a formal requirement, or written down, or even conscious. An atmosphere at a workplace that made it clear that employees are expected to work long hours was a 'practice'.[75] A single decision or act can be a 'practice' if it carries with it an indication that it will or would be done again in future if a hypothetical similar case arose.[76]

4.2.5.4 **The pool for comparison**

For indirect discrimination the claimant must identify a pool of similarly situated people to compare to the group of people who share the claimant's protected characteristic, in order to prove that the PCP puts (or would put) the claimant's group at a 'particular disadvantage'. An important preliminary point is that 'particular' means that the disadvantage must be particular to them, that is to say it must apply to them, and not that the disadvantage must be serious or significant.[77]

[73] See eg *Allonby v Accrington and Rossendale College* [2001] EWCA Civ 529, [2001] IRLR 364, [2001] ICR 1189, CA; *R v Secretary of State for Employment ex p Equal Opportunities Commission* [1994] IRLR 176, [1994] ICR 317, HL.

[74] *British Airways v Starmer* [2005] IRLR 862.

[75] *United First Partners Research v Carreras* [2018] EWCA Civ 323 at [31].

[76] *Ishola v Transport for London* [2020] IRLR 368, CA; *Pendleton v Derbyshire County Council* [2016] IRLR 580, EAT.

[77] *McNeil v Commissioners for HM Revenue & Customs* [2019] EWCA Civ 1112, [2019] IRLR 915.

In relation to the comparison exercise in indirect discrimination cases, it has been said that 'the isolation of "pools" within which the proportion of disadvantage could be gauged is a task which defeated three decades' judicial attempts to find a workable formula'.[78] Proving disadvantage is often accomplished through statistics, but statistics are not required: the words 'or would put' were added to make it clear that it is possible for the court or tribunal to infer disadvantage from other circumstantial evidence, without hard statistical evidence in every case.[79] However, whether or not a case involves statistical evidence, the court must decide whether the pool of comparators is right or is likely to 'stack the deck' one way or another.[80] The pool chosen should be one which suitably tests the particular discrimination complained of.[81] In *Essop v Home Office (UK Border Agency) and Naeem v Secretary of State for Justice*, Lady Hale cited with approval[82] an observation made by Sedley LJ when giving permission to appeal in the case of *Allonby v Accrington and Rossendale College* [2001] IRLR 364: 'There is no formula for identifying indirect discrimination pools, but there are some guiding principles. Amongst these is the principle that the pool should not be so drawn as to incorporate the disputed condition.'

The best illustration of the difficulty in identifying the pool—and of how to get it right—is given by the history of the case in *Naeem v Secretary of State for Justice*, where the Court of Appeal rejected the claim of a Muslim prison chaplain that a pay system based on length of service constituted indirect discrimination as applied to him.[83] The prison service had only employed Christian chaplains until 2002; the claimant was appointed in 2004, and alleged that Muslim chaplains were put at a disadvantage by service-related pay, because they could not possibly have served as long as Christian chaplains. The ET found prima facie indirect discrimination by comparing Muslim chaplains to Christian chaplains, but the EAT held that this was wrong: Muslim chaplains should have been compared to Christian chaplains who started after 2002. The logic was that a comparison should compare like with like, and the claimant was, for this purpose, like those hired after 2002, not those hired earlier.[84] The Court of Appeal went further, explaining that there was a clearly identified reason for the pay disparity—the fact that Muslim chaplains were hired later—which meant that the pay disparity could not be indirect discrimination because the tribunal had expressly found that the failure to hire Muslims before 2002 was not unlawful discrimination (a finding that was not challenged).

Fortunately for the integrity of anti-discrimination law, the Supreme Court rejected the reasoning of both the EAT and the Court of Appeal. Lady Hale noted that the statute says nothing at all about limiting the pool to those who experience the same disadvantage as the claimant, nor does it exclude cases where the apparent cause is itself lawful: the pool must consist of all those affected by the PCP, *both positively and negatively*, and any disadvantage shown, no matter how lawful or well-intentioned the reason was for applying the PCP, must be proportionate or it is unlawful.[85] The EAT's logic had ignored the fact that the distinction between the claimant and non-Muslims hired before 2002 flowed necessarily from his religion: he could not have been hired earlier because, and only because, he was Muslim and Muslims were not hired before then. The Court of Appeal made an even greater error, suggesting that the lawfulness of pre-2002 chaplain-hiring practice meant that disproportionate consequences more than a decade later could not be examined on

[78] *Eweida v British Airways* [2010] IRLR 322, CA (Sedley LJ).

[79] *Games v University of Kent* [2015] IRLR 202, EAT; *Homer v Chief Constable of West Yorkshire Police* [2012] IRLR 601, SC.

[80] *Grundy v British Airways plc* [2008] IRLR 74.

[81] *Per Sedley LJ in the equal pay case of Grundy v British Airways plc* [2008] IRLR 74, at para 27.

[82] [2017] UKSC 27, [2017] IRLR 558, at para 40.

[83] [2015] EWCA Civ 1264, [2016] IRLR 118.

[84] [2014] IRLR 520.

[85] [2017] UKSC 27, [2017] IRLR 558.

their own merits. The Supreme Court held that a proper analysis would have compared the whole pool of people doing the same work (all chaplains), and found from that this showed there was a prima facie disadvantage, and then decided, in the justification analysis, whether it was proportionate to maintain the PCP. The pool should not be artificially restricted in order to weed out cases which might deserve to fail because the disparate impact is proportionate, and hence justified: that is what the justification aspect is for.

In this case, excluding pre-2002 chaplains from the pool for comparison—or concluding, as the Court of Appeal did, that no comparison is needed where a non-discriminatory cause has been identified—would have foreclosed consideration of whether the previous non-hiring of Muslims rendered the service-related pay disproportionate (eg because it failed to reflect experience by ignoring non-prison service, and did not secure enough loyalty benefit to justify the perpetual maintenance of a significant pay disparity). In the end these errors were corrected by the Supreme Court, but they are cautionary tales about how difficult the judiciary sometimes finds it to accept the logic of indirect discrimination, and how much they can cling to the idea that discrimination is about bad intentions.

4.2.5.5 **Whether the disadvantage applies to the claimant**

Until recently this step in the analysis presented few difficulties: typically the claimant has brought a claim because of the fact that they have experienced the relevant disadvantage. It is not necessary that the PCP actually prevents the claimant from getting a job or promotion, only that it causes disadvantage; and that disadvantage need not be economic or physical, just what a reasonable worker would perceive as a disadvantage.[86]

It is possible, however, that a claimant could demonstrate a group disadvantage and yet not suffer from that disadvantage: a woman might demonstrate that long shifts disadvantage women, but not have any caring or other gender-associated responsibilities that would interfere with complying with the PCP. As a result of the recent case law considered below (*Naeem* and *CHEZ*) it is now possible that in such a case the claimant might succeed.

A less obvious issue was raised in *Essop v Home Office (UK Border Agency)*:[87] does the claimant have to prove that they are disadvantaged *and that this is for the same reason* that the protected characteristic group are disadvantaged? The claimants alleged that the Civil Service's Core Skills Assessment indirectly discriminated against Black and ethnic minority groups. Statistics showed that such groups tended to get lower scores, but nobody could establish why. The ET had maintained that the claimants must show both *why* they failed and that this was for the same reason that their ethnic group as a whole failed. The EAT rejected this view, however, holding that concern with the reason for the discrimination was nowhere to be found in the statutory definition of indirect discrimination.[88] Unfortunately the Court of Appeal could not bring itself to affirm this clearly orthodox and faithful interpretation of the Equality Act, insisting indirect discrimination required showing why the disadvantage arose.[89]

However, the Supreme Court corrected this error in *Essop v Home Office (UK Border Agency) and Naeem v Secretary of State for Justice*.[90] Very simply, the EAT was correct: there is nothing in the statute that requires proof of the actual mechanism by which disadvantage is brought about.

[86] *Shamoon v Chief Constable of the Royal Ulster Constabulary* [2003] UKHL 11, [2003] ICR 337, [2003] IRLR 285.

[87] [2015] EWCA 609 (CA).

[88] [2014] IRLR 592 (EAT).

[89] For a full discussion of why the Court of Appeal decision is wrong, representing a garden variety inability of judges to accept what anti-discrimination law clearly means by its express terms (our words), see Fredman 'The Reason Why: Unravelling Indirect Discrimination' (2016) 45 ILJ 231.

[90] [2017] UKSC 27, [2017] IRLR 558.

4.2.5.6 **Must the claimant be a member of the group that is put at a particular disadvantage?**

Section 19(2)(b) of the Equality Act requires the disadvantage to apply to 'persons with whom [the claimant] shares the [protected] characteristic', so that if a PCP puts employees with a protected characteristic at a particular disadvantage, the claimant can only succeed if they have that characteristic. However, the CJEU held in *CHEZ*[91] that a woman who was not Roma could nevertheless claim that she suffered indirect discrimination on the basis of Roma ethnicity because the PCP in question put Roma people at a disadvantage and also put her at a disadvantage. The PCP was the policy of mounting electric meters high up the supply poles in Roma neighbourhoods to prevent the vandalism and theft which the authorities assumed to be more likely in those areas. The claimant lived in an affected neighbourhood and suffered the disadvantage of not being able to monitor her consumption of electricity because of the policy, even though she was not Roma. The CJEU made it clear first (as one would expect) that an unjustified disadvantage stemming from a PCP which had a discriminatory impact on a protected group was unlawful and second (more surprisingly) that legal remedies should be available to anyone who suffered from the impact of such a PCP—whether or not they were a member of the group that particularly suffered from it. So, there is no requirement under EU law for the claimant to put forward any reason for the disadvantage other than that it was caused by the PCP.

Any potential confusion as to how this would be dealt with post-Brexit was helpfully addressed by a change to the Equality Act. The legislation now expressly allows someone to claim indirect discrimination even though they do not have the protected characteristic, if the person is put at substantively the same disadvantage as people who have the protected characteristic.[92]

This means that, for the first time, men may be able to bring indirect discrimination claims when they are denied flexible working because of their caring responsibilities. Such a claim has been impossible historically because they could not establish the group disadvantage; this was considered, at a group level, to disadvantage only women. As a result of *CHEZ*, men can rely on women's group disadvantage and their own, individual disadvantage, to bring an indirect discrimination claim. Therefore, *CHEZ* presents an opportunity to challenge a main criticism of indirect discrimination; that is, it 'requires adopting and evidencing a traditional model of female care roles' for claims to be successful.[93]

4.2.5.7 **Justification**

Although the Equality Act does not use the word 'justification', this is the word used by lawyers to talk about the concept set out in s 19(2)(d), which is that prima facie indirect discrimination is not unlawful if the PCP represents 'a proportionate means of achieving a legitimate aim'.

Section 19(2)(d) is intended to implement the European law on indirect discrimination, and must be interpreted in accordance with the guidance given by the CJEU on justification.[94] The relevant EU Directives say that a PCP must be 'objectively justified by

[91] C-83/14 *CHEZ Razpredelenie Bulgaria AD v Komisia za zashtita ot diskriminatsia* [2015] IRLR 746 (CJEU (Grand Chamber)).

[92] Equality Act 2010, s 19A. Added by The Equality Act 2010 (Amendment) Regulations 2023, reg 3.

[93] O'Brien 'Confronting the Care Penalty: The Case for Extending Reasonable Adjustment Rights Along the Disability/Care continuum' (2012) 34 *Journal of Social Welfare and Family Law* 5. For consideration of this change, see McCrudden 'The New Architecture of EU Equality Law after CHEZ: Did the Court of Justice Reconceptualise Direct and Indirect Discrimination?' [2016] European Equality Law Review 1.

[94] *Homer v Chief Constable of West Yorkshire Police* [2012] IRLR 601, UKSC at para 22.

a legitimate aim and the means of achieving that aim [must be] appropriate and necessary'.[95] The concept of proportionality comes to European jurisprudence through German law, which developed a doctrine of proportionality requiring that acts or measures of the state be (a) suitable to achieve a legitimate purpose, (b) necessary to achieve that purpose, and (c) proportional in the sense they do not impose burdens or 'cause harms to other legitimate interests' that outweigh the objectives achieved.[96]

The first two components, and part of the third one, were laid down by the CJEU as requirements of justification in *Bilka-Kaufhaus GmbH v Weber von Hartz*[97] and have been repeated in many cases since. In *Bilka-Kaufhaus* the Court said that a PCP was justified 'where it is found that the means chosen for achieving that objective correspond to a real need on the part of the undertaking, are appropriate with a view to achieving the objective in question and are necessary to that end'. Teasing that out:

- The 'real need' component qualifies what can amount to a legitimate objective by requiring a minimum, although vague, degree of importance.
- The requirement that the PCP is 'suitable to achieve' the legitimate aim simply means that the PCP must actually deliver the result aimed for by the employer.
- The requirement that the PCP must be 'necessary' to achieve the aim is more difficult: it means that there must be no other less discriminatory means available to achieve the end. UK courts have consistently baulked at this requirement and interpreted 'necessary' in CJEU judgments as cause meaning 'reasonably necessary'—a position maintained by the Supreme Court in its most recent pronouncement on this issue, *Homer v Chief Constable of West Yorkshire Police*.[98]

The *Bilka-Kaufhaus* test assesses whether the aim being sought by the employer is sufficiently important to potentially justify discrimination and goes on to require that no other, less discriminatory, means is available to achieve that aim, but there is a further important component of proportionality contained within the German principles set out above. This is that the benefits realized by the employer in achieving the aim must outweigh the disbenefits imposed on those who suffer disadvantage as a result. It is now plain that this too is a requirement of EU law, although it is often not so clearly stated in CJEU judgments. A recent case which asserts clearly that this is an essential consideration is *CHEZ*, where the judgment, after setting out the *Bilka-Kaufhaus* requirements, goes on to say:

> [A]ssuming that no other measure as effective as the practice at issue can be identified, the referring court will also have to determine whether the disadvantages caused by the practice at issue are disproportionate to the aims pursued and whether that practice unduly prejudices the legitimate interests of [the people affected by it].[99]

The recent *Homer*[100] case contains the Supreme Court's confirmation that the Equality Act must be read to incorporate a requirement on a court to carrying this exercise of

[95] Art 2(2)(b) of Directive 2000/43/EC in relation to race discrimination, art 2(1)(b) of Directive 2006/54/EC in relation to sex discrimination and art 2(2)(b) of Directive 2000/78/EC in relation to other strands.

[96] Baker 'Proportionality' in Fenwick (ed) *Supperstone, Goudie & Walker: Judicial Review* (6th edn, 2017).

[97] 170/84 [1987] ICR 110.

[98] [2012] IRLR 601 at para 23.

[99] C-83/14 *CHEZ Razpredelenie Bulgaria AD v Komisia za zashtita ot diskriminatsia* [2015] IRLR 746 (CJEU (Grand Chamber)) at para 123.

[100] See n 98.

balancing the benefits of the aim pursued by the employer against the discriminatory impact on those affected by the PCP:

> Part of the assessment of whether the criterion can be justified entails a comparison of the impact of that criterion upon the affected group as against the importance of the aim to the employer.[101]

The current state of play in UK law therefore is that the test of justification as set out in s 19 of the Equality Act must be interpreted in accordance with the European case law save for one important possible divergence. The divergence is, as discussed above, that under European law a PCP can only be justified where it (1) 'correspond[s] to a real need on the part of the undertaking', (2) is suitable to achieve the aim, (3) has a proportionate impact as between the employer's aim and the impact on the employer, and (4) is 'necessary', that is, no less discriminatory alternative is available.[102] This fourth element is not exactly the same as the UK formulation of 'reasonably necessary', which seems to contemplate that an employer might be allowed to reject a less discriminatory PCP if, for example, it would be very inconvenient. This theoretical difference may not in practice have much impact since the CJEU has shown itself willing to accept PCPs as necessary when it is possible to think of other less discriminatory measures that could have been taken.[103] One can defend the UK formulation of 'reasonably necessary' as being a better description of the standard *actually* applied by the courts, including the European Court itself.[104]

Brexit has cast some uncertainty over the future of proportionality in indirect discrimination cases. This is because the EU principle of proportionality, along with other general principles of EU law, have now been abolished.[105] It seems likely that the UK courts will determine that indirect discrimination cases are outside the realm of the general principle of proportionality (which is about ensuring the EU only adopts measures which are proportionate).[106] Therefore, it is predicted that UK courts will continue to apply the same approach to proportionality as described here. Addressing this uncertainty is, inevitably, going to lead to extra delays and costs before the issue is conclusively decided.

Two final points need to be made. First, in assessing justification it is clear that even if a broad policy, such as a disciplinary code, is itself a proportionate means to achieve a real employer need, the policy's application to the claimant must also be proportionate.[107] Second, it is always for the tribunal hearing the case to make the justification decision: its duty goes beyond merely reviewing the employer's approach. In *Hardy & Hansons plc v Lax*,[108] the Court of Appeal ruled emphatically against a subjective application of

[101] [2012] IRLR 601 at para 24.

[102] *Bilka-Kaufhaus* Case 170/84 [1987] ICR 110, 126.

[103] For example, the acceptance by the ECJ in *Handels-og Kontorfunktionaerernes Forbund i Danmark v Dansk Arbejdsgiverforening (acting for Danfoss)* C-109/88, [1989] IRLR 532, [1991] 1 CMLR 8 that the legitimate aim of rewarding experience which enables an employee to perform his duties better justified service-related pay—clearly there would be other less discriminatory ways of rewarding those who perform their work better than others.

[104] For a different view see Lane and Ingleby 'Indirect Discrimination, Justification and Proportionality: Are UK Claimants at a Disadvantage?' (2018) 47 ILJ 531.

[105] Retained EU Law (Revocation and Reform) Act 2023, s 4.

[106] Treaty on European Union, art 5(4).

[107] *Buchanan v Commissioner of Police of the Metropolis* [2016] UKEAT 0112_16_3009 (unreported).

[108] [2005] EWCA Civ 846, [2005] IRLR 726, CA. For a good example of this principle (in the sensitive context of air safety) see *British Airways plc v Starmer* [2005] IRLR 862.

proportionality that would only ask whether the employer's assessment of the striking of the balance was reasonable:

> The principle of proportionality requires the tribunal to take into account the reasonable needs of the business. But it has to make its own judgment, upon a fair and detailed analysis of the working practices and business considerations involved, as to whether the proposal [by the employer] is reasonably necessary. I reject the [employer's] submission . . . that, when reaching its conclusion, the employment tribunal needs to consider only whether or not it is satisfied that the employer's views are within the range of views reasonable in the particular circumstances.

There is no doubt that this is correct, but it does throw up a problem when the alleged discrimination stems from a dismissal and the employee also complains of unfair dismissal. For example, an employee with a long-term health condition which had got worse might start to fall below the employer's attendance standards and be dismissed. Their claim for unfair dismissal would depend on whether the *employer's* decision to dismiss for poor attendance despite the genuine ill-health was *within the range of reasonable responses of an employer* to that situation (see 7.4.4), but their complaint of indirect disability discrimination caused by the application of a PCP in the form of the employer's attendance policy would depend on the *employment tribunal's* decision as to whether the application of the policy to them was proportionate. In theory the employee could lose the unfair dismissal claim and win the discrimination complaint. This issue has come up in several cases where the employee claimed both unfair dismissal and breach of s 15 of the Equality Act by means of unfavourable treatment because of disability (which also involves a proportionality test). The cases are considered at 4.7.3.1 but in short, the courts have recognized that such a 'split' outcome is possible.

4.2.5.8 **Is cost relevant?**

In the real world an employer's reason for not wanting to do something which would eliminate or reduce discrimination will often involve questions of cost. The permissibility of saying 'it would be too expensive' has come up in two ways in the law. First, can cost-saving be a legitimate aim? Second, when assessing the proportionality of applying a PCP, can the cost to the employer be taken into account?

Can cost-saving be a legitimate aim?

On the first question there are two obvious possibilities: first, that cost-saving can be a legitimate aim; second, that it can never be taken into account as legitimate aim. In fact, the law takes a third stance and holds that saving cost *alone* cannot be a legitimate aim which might justify a PCP, but that if there is some other legitimate aim then cost can also be taken into account as an additional aim. This is referred to as the 'cost plus' principle and it derives from rulings of the ECJ.[109] In the UK it was first set out in *Cross v British Airways plc*.[110]

There are a number of problems raised by 'cost plus'. First: why, if cost cannot be relied on when taken alone, can it be relied on when there is another aim too? Second: most other legitimate aims which an employer might rely on for justifying a PCP could be achieved by spending more money rather than imposing the PCP, so in some senses a

[109] In particular from *Hill v Inland Revenue Commissioners* [1998] IRLR 466, ECJ, and *Kutz-Bauer v Freie und Hansestadt Hamburg* [2003] IRLR 368, ECJ.

[110] [2005] IRLR 423, CA.

PCP is always an attempt to save cost. As Elias P put it in *Redcar and Cleveland Borough Council v Bainbridge*:[111] 'Almost every decision taken by an employer is going to have regard to costs. Given an unlimited purse there need be no losers at all.' Indeed, Underhill P indicated in two cases[112] that he thought cost-saving alone should be a permissible legitimate aim. However, following the decisions of the Supreme Court in *O'Brien v Ministry of Justice*[113] and the Court of Appeal in *Heskett v Secretary of State for Justice*,[114] it must now be regarded as settled that cost alone can never justify discrimination.

However, that is not the end of the issue because the rule raises the problem as to what amounts to 'cost alone'. The courts have, it can be argued, sought to avoid the difficulties which the rule causes by relabelling 'cost-saving' as something else such as ensuring a fair distribution of the employer's limited resources, enabling a business to break even year on year, or living within a budget imposed by the government on a public agency.[115] All of these have been held not to amount to relying on cost-saving alone.[116] Can it really be the case that an employer can rely on saving money to justify discrimination if this is necessary in order to break even, but may not do so in order to return profit to a level that will ensure future viability and investment?

Is cost relevant to proportionality?

It is clear that once a legitimate aim has been established, the question of cost can certainly be taken into account in assessing whether it is proportionate, in seeking to achieve that aim, to impose a PCP. An example is the CJEU case of *Ruiz Conejero v Ferroser Servicios Auxiliares SA*,[117] a case about an attendance policy which put some disabled employees at a disadvantage. The Court held that the legitimate aim was combating absenteeism and in considering proportionality it would be necessary for the court deciding the case to consider the direct and indirect costs that had to be borne by companies as a result of absenteeism, whether the measures went beyond what was necessary to achieve the aim pursued, and the adverse effects it was liable to cause for the persons concerned. As Elias P put it in an equal pay case where the employer was seeking to justify an indirectly discriminatory pay protection scheme:

> *Cross* suggests that an employer cannot defeat the right to equality by pointing to financial burdens alone, but he can pray the financial burdens in aid as some support for a decision which is objectively justified on other grounds. Pay protection arrangements provide a good example. Transitional arrangements of such a kind will sometimes be appropriate (and often unavoidable in practice) to cushion the pay of those moving to lower pay. It would theoretically be possible to confer the benefit of the higher pay on everyone, but the cost may reinforce the justification limiting the benefit.[118]

[111] [2007] IRLR 91, [2008] ICR 249, EAT.

[112] *Woodcock v Cumbria Primary Care Trust* [2011] IRLR 119, [2011] ICR 143 and *R (On the Application of Unison) v Lord Chancellor* [2015] EWCA Civ 330, [2016] ICR 1.

[113] [2013] UKSC 6, [2013] IRLR 315, [2013] ICR 499.

[114] [2020] EWCA Civ 1487, [2021] IRLR 132.

[115] See eg *Braithwaite v HCL Insurance BPO* [2015] ICR 713, EAT; *Harrod v Chief Constable of West Midlands* [2017] EWCA Civ 191, [2017] IRLR 539, [2017] ICR 869; and *Heskett v Secretary of State for Justice* [2021] IRLR 132, CA.

[116] An extreme example is *Woodcock v Cumbria Primary Care Trust* [2012] EWCA Civ 330, [2012] IRLR 491, where the applicant, whose post was redundant, claimed age discrimination when he was given notice sooner than he otherwise would have been in order to ensure he left before reaching the age of 50 so as to save the employer a much larger redundancy cost. The Court of Appeal held that the legitimate aim was to avoid a windfall to the employee rather than to save cost.

[117] [2018] IRLR 372.

[118] *Redcar and Cleveland Borough Council v Bainbridge* [2007] IRLR 91, [2008] ICR 249 at para 92.

4.2.6 **Harassment**

4.2.6.1 History of protection under discrimination legislation

The early case law tended to concentrate on sexual harassment. There was, however, a potential problem in that it was not specifically covered by the legislation and so the judges created protection by using the ordinary definition of direct discrimination, with its emphasis on comparison and *worse* treatment. The EAT evolved the idea[119] that some acts are 'gender-specific' (eg the invasion of personal space in a sexual manner) and so it is to be *assumed* that they are discriminatory per se. While this often worked, it always sat uncomfortably with the conceptual basis of ordinary discrimination law, and ultimately it was disapproved by the House of Lords and the fundamental comparative element reimposed.[120]

4.2.6.2 Introduction of an express prohibition of harassment

However, the Equal Treatment Amendment Directive 2002/73/EC then introduced a definition of harassment which avoids most of the problems just considered. This definition was carried over into the 2010 Act.

4.2.6.3 The definition of harassment

The conceptual base for the new approach is that harassment is *not* a subset of ordinary discrimination, but is instead a freestanding contravention of the legislation. The basic definition, which applies to nearly all protected characteristics,[121] states that a person commits harassment if they engage in unwanted conduct related to a protected characteristic that has the purpose or effect:

(a) of violating an employee's dignity, or
(b) of creating an intimidating, hostile, degrading, humiliating, or offensive environment for the employee.[122]

Crucially, this is then fleshed out with an explanatory provision which states that conduct is only to be regarded as having these effects if, having regard to the circumstances, including in particular the perception of the victim, it is reasonable for the conduct to have that effect. The definition uses the words 'related to' rather than 'on the ground of', which means that the harassment does not need to be because of the claimant's protected characteristic, just related to a protected characteristic. For example, it is race harassment repeatedly to use racist language in the presence of the claimant even if the comments are not about people of the claimant's race.[123]

The Act also has a specific provision designed to cover harassing sexual *behaviour*: s 26(2) brings into the scope of harassment (a) engaging in unwanted verbal, non-verbal, or physical conduct of a sexual nature which has the effect of violating the victim's dignity or creating an intimidating, degrading, etc environment; and (b) treating an employee less favourably because they rejected or submitted to any of this unwanted conduct.

[119] This was most obviously applicable in sex discrimination cases, but might also have applied to the other heads.

[120] *Pearce v Governing Body of Mayfield School* [2003] ICR 937, [2003] IRLR 517, HL.

[121] Marriage and civil partnership and pregnancy and maternity are excluded from harassment protection.

[122] Equality Act 2010, s 26.

[123] *Moxam v Visible Changes Ltd* UKEAT/0267/11/MAA (24 November 2011 unreported). See also *Bakkali v Greater Manchester Buses (South) t/a Stage Coach Manchester* [2018] IRLR 906, [2018] ICR 1481, emphasizing that the change in statutory language makes the test for race harassment much broader than under the RRA.

4.2.6.4 **Subjective and objective assessment of the conduct**

A key element of the definition is the attempt to impose a test which is *both* subjective ('unwanted') and objective ('reasonable') for the conduct to have a degrading effect. The problem with a wholly subjective test is that it would enable an over-sensitive complainant who takes offence unreasonably at an innocent comment to bring a claim for discrimination. On the other hand, the use of an objective test could be considered objectionable because it allows scope for value judgements about the extent to which certain words and conduct are painful or offensive to the members of particular groups and might give no protection to a sensitive person even after they had made it clear that they found the actions or words upsetting.

A number of cases decided when the ordinary definition of direct discrimination was used to tackle harassment give useful guidance on the balance between the subjective and objective approaches, and it is likely that they will remain influential even when applying the express requirement in s 26(4) of the Equality Act 2010 to take into account the perception of the victim, the other circumstances of the case, and whether it is reasonable for the conduct to have the effect which the victim alleges.

In *Reed and Bull Information Systems Ltd v Stedman*,[124] the EAT held that although the judgment as to whether conduct amounts to harassment involves an objective assessment by the tribunal of all the facts, the claimant's subjective perception of the conduct in question must also be considered. So, where an employee appears to be unduly sensitive to what might otherwise be regarded as unexceptional behaviour, the question becomes whether by words or conduct they have made it clear that the conduct is unwelcome: 'Provided that any reasonable person would understand her to be rejecting the conduct of which she was complaining, continuation of the conduct would, generally, be regarded as harassment.'[125] On the other hand, a single act may be so clearly unwelcome as to be 'unwanted',[126] thus avoiding the argument that conduct cannot be said to be unwanted until it has been tried and rejected: 'A woman does not, for example, have to make it clear in advance that she does not want to be touched in a sexual manner.'[127]

In considering whether conduct was unwanted, a tribunal must be wary of accepting the argument that an absence of objection on the part of the victim indicates that she was happy with the perpetrator's behaviour. In *Driskel v Peninsula Business Services*,[128] the employment tribunal had found in the employer's favour, heavily influenced by the fact that the complainant did not make an immediate complaint, but the EAT questioned the significance of this, pointing out that 'any instinct to complain must perforce be inhibited by the fact that she wanted the promotion that would come from the approval of [the alleged harasser]'.[129] The EAT has also stressed that where a number of specific incidents are alleged to constitute harassment, the tribunal should not carve up the case into a series of incidents and try to measure the harm in relation to each of them, but should instead consider the cumulative effect of such behaviour, lest it fall into the trap of 'ignoring the impact of the totality of successive incidents, individually trivial'.[130] These issues continue to be debatable under the 2010 Act.[131]

124 [1999] IRLR 299, EAT. 125 [1999] IRLR 299, para 30.

126 See eg *Insitu Cleaning Co Ltd v Heads* [1995] IRLR 4; *Bracebridge Engineering Ltd v Darby* [1990] IRLR 3, EAT.

127 [1999] IRLR 299, para 30. 128 [2000] IRLR 151, EAT.

129 [2000] IRLR 151, para 14. See also *Wileman v Minilec Engineering Ltd* [1988] ICR 318, [1988] IRLR 144 (a tribunal should be slow to infer that the conduct was not unwelcome from the mere fact that the complainant does not complain or delays in making their complaint).

130 [2000] IRLR 151, para 12 ('That which in isolation may not amount to discriminatory detriment may become such if persisted in notwithstanding objection, vocal or apparent').

131 See eg *Weeks v Newham College of FE* UKEAT/0630/11, [2012] EqLR 788, EAT (relatively mild sexist remarks and a clearly offensive cartoon were not directed at the claimant and did not create a hostile environment, so there was no sexual harassment).

The effect on the complainant of the action complained of will also be highly relevant when assessing compensation, because the amount of compensation will depend on the extent of the detriment that the complainant has suffered as a result of the harassment. Here, the complainant's attitudes and sensitivities will have a direct bearing on the compensation awarded. So, for example, in *Snowball v Gardner Merchant Ltd*[132] the tribunal admitted evidence of the complainant's sexual exploits and that fact that she was in the habit of referring to her bed as a 'playpen', the employer arguing that this diminished the injury done to her by the sexual harassment to which she was subjected; and in *Wileman v Minilec Engineering Ltd*[133] the tribunal took notice of the fact that the complainant sometimes wore what was described as provocative clothing to work. Significantly, however, the EAT held in that case that the complainant's willingness to pose for a national newspaper in a flimsy costume was not inconsistent with a finding that she had been sexually harassed by her employer: 'A person may be happy to accept the remarks of A or B in a sexual context, and wholly upset by similar remarks made by C.'[134]

4.2.6.5 **Employers' liability**

Two recent amendments have strengthened protection for workers against sexual harassment. Employers are now required to take 'reasonable steps' to prevent sexual harassment.[135] This means that proactive duties are now placed on employers, rather than the reactive nature of the law previously. When those preventative duties are not discharged, a tribunal can also now award an uplift of up to 25 per cent to any compensatory award.[136]

These changes reflected a watered-down version of an original proposal, which would have required employers to take 'all' reasonable steps. The Employment Rights Act 2025 has now inserted the word 'all' into the legislation, which increases the expectation of employers.[137] They will avoid liability only when there are no further steps that they could reasonably have been expected to take. Whilst the law does not list specific steps required of an employer, The Employment Rights Act 2025 does include a power to create regulations which can specify these. These would include, amongst others:

(a) carrying out assessments of a specified description;
(b) publishing plans or policies of a specified description;
(c) steps relating to the reporting of sexual harassment; and
(d) steps relating to the handling of complaints.[138]

In addition, the EHRC has written some guidance, which is likely to be relied on by tribunals going forward.[139] These changes are expected to come into force by October 2026.

132 [1987] ICR 719, [1987] IRLR 397.
133 [1988] ICR 318, [1988] IRLR 144.
134 [1988] ICR 318, [1988] IRLR 144, per Popplewell J.
135 Equality Act 2010, s 40A. Inserted by Worker Protection (Amendment of Equality Act 2010) Act 2023, s 1.
136 Equality Act 2010, s 124A. Inserted by Worker Protection (Amendment of Equality Act 2010) Act 2023, s 3.
137 Equality Act 2010, s 40A. Inserted by Employment Rights Act 2025, s 20.
138 Equality Act 2010, s 40B. Inserted by Employment Rights Act 2025, s 22.
139 EHRC *Sexual harassment and harassment at work: technical guidance* (2024, available here: https://www.equalityhumanrights.com/guidance/sexual-harassment-and-harassment-work-technical-guidance#reasonablesteps).

4.2.6.6 **Harassment by third parties**

The issue of employer liability for third party harassment has long been contentious. Previously, employers would only be liable if they had failed to protect the employee for a reason which was in itself discriminatory.[140] For a brief period s 40 of the Equality Act 2010 imposed a liability on employers for failing to take adequate steps to protect employees from harassment, but only if the employee had suffered harassment on at least two previous occasions. This confusing provision was unsurprisingly repealed in 2013. Reintroducing liability for third party harassment was proposed and dropped in the drafting of the Worker Protection (Amendment of Equality Act 2010) Act 2023. Nonetheless, the EHRC determined that the duty to take reasonable steps to prevent harassment also applies to third parties. Although positive, this stopped short of allowing individuals to bring standalone claims for harassment perpetrated by a third party.

The Employment Rights Act 2025 has now successfully reintroduced employers' liability for third party harassment.[141] This makes an employer liable when:

(a) the third party harasses the individual in the course of their employment, and

(b) the employer failed to take all reasonable steps to prevent the third party from doing so.[142]

A third party is anyone who is not an employee of the employer.[143] It is important to note that this does not just apply to sexual harassment but to any of the relevant protected characteristics. Further guidance on this is likely to be forthcoming, especially because of ongoing concerns about how this might impact freedom of speech.[144] This change is expected to be implemented by October 2026.

4.2.6.7 **An alternative—the Protection from Harassment Act**

Employees who have suffered harassment sometimes bring claims in the ordinary courts for the statutory tort of harassment contrary to the Protection from Harassment Act 1997. Although this involves a court fee and the risk of an adverse costs order if the claim is unsuccessful, the 1997 Act has some advantages. The detail of the Act is beyond the scope of this book, but in outline the potential advantages are:

- The definition of 'harassment' is very broad (although two instances of harassment are required before the tort is committed).
- The protection applies to harassment on any grounds, not just the protected characteristics, so for example 'fattist' teasing and general bullying are covered.
- Injunctions to stop the harassment are available.
- Although the meaning of 'in the course of employment' for vicarious liability for tort is narrower than under the Equality Act, the employer has no 'reasonably practicable steps' defence available to get out of vicarious liability.
- The limitation period is three years, rather than the period of three months under the Equality Act.

140 *Pearce v Governing Body of Mayfield School* [2003] ICR 937, [2003] IRLR 517.

141 Equality Act 2010, s 40 (1A), inserted by Employment Rights Act 2025, s 21.

142 Inserted by Employment Rights Act 2025, s 21.

143 Equality Act 2010, s 40 (1C). Inserted by Employment Rights Act 2025, s 21.

144 See Busby 'The Worker Protection (Amendment of Equality Act) Act 2023: Implications for Protection Against Sexual Harassment' (2024) 53 ILJ 505.

4.2.7 **Victimization**

4.2.7.1 **Definition**

Victimization applies where a person is subjected to 'a detriment' because they have, or are believed by the discriminator to have, done one of the following 'protected acts':

- brought proceedings under the Act (or prior Acts);
- given evidence in proceedings under one of these Acts;
- done any other thing for the purposes of or in connection with any of these Acts; or
- made allegations in good faith of breaches of one of these Acts.[145]

The language of the Act does not extend to forbidding 'associative' victimization, that is to say situations where an employer imposes a detriment on the claimant because they associate with someone who does a protected act. However, the EU Directives on equality ban 'associative' direct discrimination and harassment and the EAT has accepted that the same must be applied to victimization.[146]

Victimization is committed by an employer even if the allegation or complaint is that someone else other than the employer committed the discrimination, for example a former employer.

The tribunal must ask whether the detriment occurred 'because of a protected act'. The earlier cases of *Nagarajan v London Regional Transport*[147] and *Chief Constable of West Yorkshire Police v Khan*[148] made it clear that it will usually be necessary to understand the thinking of the alleged perpetrator (see the discussion of 'because' in 4.2.4.1), and *Greater Manchester Police v Bailey*[149] confirms that this is still the case. However, provided that the reason for the detriment was that the victim had, for example, complained of discrimination, there is no need to show that the employer's purpose or motive was to punish the employee for alleging a breach of the Act. On that basis the fact that someone who had made a complaint about something other than discrimination would also have had this detriment imposed on them is irrelevant: the employer has still broken the law by penalizing the client for bringing a complaint of discrimination. Whether treatment amounts to 'detriment' depends on whether it was reasonable for the claim to regard it as such.[150]

The Equality Act appeared to have introduced an unintended change to the law through an apparent drafting error in s 39(4) that seemed to say that there was no prohibition against post-employment victimization. The section says that an employer is prohibited from victimizing their own employee, so tribunals were holding that it failed to cover *former* employees who were victimized, for example, by the refusal to provide a reference. In *Jessemey v Rowstock Ltd*,[151] however, the Court of Appeal let sanity prevail, and held that the Equality Act had not intended to remove a protection that had always been understood to exist under previous statutes.

[145] Equality Act 2010, s 27.

[146] *Thompson v Central London Bus Company* [2016] IRLR 9. The CJEU ruling on associative direct discrimination and harassment is in *Coleman v Attridge Law* Case C-303/06, [2008] IRLR 722.

[147] [1999] ICR 877, [1999] IRLR 572, HL.

[148] [2001] ICR 1065, [2001] IRLR 830, HL.

[149] [2017] EWCA Civ 425.

[150] *Warburton v Chief Constable of Northamptonshire Police* [2022] EAT 42, unreported and *Fullah v Medical Research Council* [2022] EAT 45, unreported, applying to victimization the general case law on detriment set out in *Shamoon v Chief Constable of the Royal Ulster Constabulary* [2003] UKHL 11, [2003] ICR 337, [2003] IRLR 285.

[151] [2014] 3 All ER 409.

4.2.8 **Positive action and discrimination**

4.2.8.1 **Introduction**

The Equality Act is generally based on a neutral or symmetrical model of equality. It gives each individual, male or female, majority or minority, the right not to be treated less favourably on protected grounds. As *James v Eastleigh Borough Council*[152] demonstrated, the fact that the defendant acted from a good or worthy motive is no defence to a complaint of unlawful discrimination. It follows that any preferential treatment aimed at redressing the historic disadvantage experienced by women or minority groups and enabling them to compete equally will normally be illegal if it involves the less favourable treatment of another group. Such measures—generally referred to as 'positive discrimination'[153]—must be distinguished from measures which do not involve preferential treatment of one group but which are designed to promote a greater degree of equality of opportunity within the workplace (so-called positive action). While positive discrimination has normally been unlawful, positive action is not prohibited. Measures aimed at promoting equal opportunities which fall short of positive discrimination might include the development of policies and practices designed to assist disadvantaged groups (eg 'family-friendly' policies), encouraging applications from under-represented groups, and the setting of targets to reduce under-representation.

The Equality Act and its predecessors provide for 'positive duties' on public sector bodies to promote equality,[154] and there has long been a limited ability for employers to assist under-represented groups in relation to sex and race, so long as employers did not actually give them preference in appointing them to jobs. Measures were permitted to encourage such persons to apply for jobs and to provide extra training for employees in such groups.[155]

4.2.8.2 **European law on positive discrimination by employers**

In general terms, EU law has tended to adopt the same symmetrical approach to equality as English law. The equality directives and the TFEU have provisions which permit member states to adopt measures to promote equal opportunity for men and women and to compensate for disadvantages linked to protected characteristics. The CJEU has interpreted such provisions narrowly, and has been reluctant to accept them as legitimizing positive discrimination other than within very narrow limits.

Initially, the limits imposed by the CJEU were very narrow indeed. In *Kalanke v Freie Hansestadt Bremen*,[156] the CJEU considered the legality of a so-called tie-break provision in the relevant domestic provisions, whereby women who had the same qualifications as men for the same post were to be given priority in sectors where they were under-represented. The CJEU held that this overstepped the limits of the exception to the principle of equal treatment in Article 2(4);[157] the exception only permitted national measures

[152] [1990] IRLR 288, HL. See also *Jepson and Dyas-Elliott v Labour Party* [1996] IRLR 116, IT (women-only shortlists unlawful), although note now the Sex Discrimination (Election Candidates) Act 2002.

[153] See Fredman 'Reversing Discrimination' (1997) 113 LQR 575; Pitt 'Can Reverse Discrimination Be Justified?' in Hepple and Szyszczak (eds) *Discrimination: The Limits of Law* (1992); McCrudden 'Rethinking Positive Action' (1986) 15 ILJ 219.

[154] Equality Act 2010, s 149.

[155] See Sacks 'Tackling Discrimination Positively' in Hepple and Szyszczak (eds) *Discrimination: The Limits of Law* (1992). Employers were also permitted to target training on under-represented groups within their organization: Sex Discrimination Act 1975, s 48. There were parallel provisions in the Race Relations Act 1976, s 38.

[156] [1996] ICR 314, [1995] IRLR 660, ECJ.

[157] The ECJ held that the provisions in question fell outside this exception by substituting for equal opportunity 'the result which is only to be arrived at by providing such equality of opportunity'.

relating to access to employment 'which give a specific advantage to women with a view to improving their ability to compete in the labour market and to pursue a career in an equal footing with men'.

The decision in *Kalanke* was greeted with dismay (not least by the European Commission), and when the CJEU next had an opportunity to consider the issue, in *Marschall v Land Nordrhein-Westfalen*,[158] there was a noticeable softening of the tone. That case also involved a tie-break provision giving women priority for promotion in the event of equal suitability, competence, and professional performance, but with the crucial addition of a 'saving clause' whereby women were not to be given priority if reasons specific to an individual male candidate tilted the balance in his favour. The CJEU held that a scheme under which preferential treatment to equally qualified women candidates could be lawful if it contained such saving clause which guaranteed 'that the candidatures will be the subject of an objective assessment which will take account of all criteria specific to the individual candidates and will override the priority accorded to the female candidates where one or more of the criteria tilts the balance in favour of the male candidate'. The reality is that the CJEU had changed its mind since the *Kalanke* decision: if the male applicant is superior to the female candidate in relation to some particular criterion then they are not 'equally qualified', and in such a situation even under the *Kalanke* tie-break scheme the woman would not have been appointed.

The *Marschall* approach was followed by the CJEU in the case of *Badeck*,[159] where the court upheld a programme aimed at eliminating the under-representation of women in the public sector which, inter alia, gave priority to equally qualified women applicants in sectors where they were under-represented and allocated at least half the available training places to women in occupations in which they were under-represented—the decisive point being that, as in *Marschall*, the programme did not automatically and unconditionally give priority to women when women and men were equally qualified. One of the more interesting (and, it must be said, ingenious) aspects of the programme in *Badeck* was the approach taken to the evaluation of the candidates' qualifications, in that the scheme in effect sought to assist women by setting out express rules about what the decision-maker could take into account when assessing the 'merit' of the candidates in order to decide who was best qualified for the post. The scheme provided that certain factors were to be taken into account (eg capabilities and experience acquired by looking after children or persons requiring care, insofar as they were of importance for the suitability of applicants), while other factors (eg family status, income of the partner, part-time work, leave, or delays in completing training as a result of looking after children or dependants) were to be left out of the equation.

Another novel aspect of the scheme accepted as lawful by the CJEU in *Badeck* was that the tie-break preference for women was, in five situations, overridden to assist other disadvantaged groups, including promoting disabled persons, ending a period of long-term unemployment, or giving preferential treatment to those who, for family reasons, worked part time and wished to resume full-time employment. The scheme in *Badeck* probably represents the high-water mark of positive discrimination programmes accepted as valid to date by the CJEU.[160]

4.2.8.3 **Positive action and discrimination by employers under the Equality Act 2010**

In the light of these decisions of the CJEU, the Equality Act 2010 not only retained the ability of an employer to take action to encourage under-represented groups to apply for employment and to provide extra training for such groups but also introduced for the

[158] [1998] IRLR 39, ECJ. [159] *Badeck's Application* [2000] IRLR 432, ECJ.

[160] Although cf *Lommers v Minister van Landbouw, Natuurbeheer en Visserij* [2002] IRLR 430, ECJ, where a scheme giving female employees priority for subsidized nursery places was upheld so long as nursery places were available on the same terms to male single parents. For more on this see Sa Ayada, 'What About Men? The Identity and Role of Men Litigants in EU Gender Equality Jurisprudence' (2021) ELR 607, 623.

first time in the UK the right to treat a member of an under-represented or disadvantaged group *more favourably* in hiring or promotion.

Encouragement and training are covered by s 158, a section which uses complicated wording because it covers positive action both in employment and in other fields such as education and the supply of goods and services. The section provides that an employer may act when persons who share a protected characteristic (a) suffer a disadvantage connected to the characteristic, (b) have needs different from those without it, or (c) are disproportionately represented in an activity. If one or more of these circumstances apply, the employer may take any action that is a proportionate means of (a) helping to overcome the disadvantage, (b) meeting those needs, or (c) enabling participation in the activity. Note that this permission, unlike its predecessors, is not limited to steps to encourage under-represented groups to take up employment and the provision of additional training. How far it goes is not clear, but it clearly does not extend to giving any preference in job appointment decisions, since that is covered expressly by s 159 and the CJEU case law on tie-break provisions.

Section 159(1) permits tie-break discrimination where either (a) persons who share a protected characteristic suffer a disadvantage, or (b) those persons are disproportionately represented in an activity. In such a case an employer may act to overcome the disadvantage or enable participation by treating persons with the protected characteristic *more favourably* in recruitment or promotion, but this is allowed only where

(a) the person thus favoured is 'as qualified' as the other to be recruited or promoted;
(b) this is a proportionate means of tacking the disadvantage or under-representation; and
(c) the employer does not have a policy of treating the group of which the favoured person is a member more favourably.

This last condition is obscure; it may be a clumsy attempt to require an employer to have something like the 'saving clause' in the *Marschall* case. However, the wording of the provision does seem to suggest that a *policy* of operating a tie-break preference for an under-represented group would be unlawful, but an ad hoc decision to do so would be lawful. This is surely unwise since a tie-break scheme should be the result of a careful assessment of the situation by the employing organization and the creation of a clearly defined and proportionate policy. It is to be hoped that the courts will interpret this condition to mean 'the employer does not have a policy of treating the group of which the favoured person is a member more favourably *other than* in relation to such a tie-break'.

Positive discrimination and disabled employees

An employer may treat a disabled person preferentially. This is covered in 'Practical application' in 4.7.2.3.

4.2.8.4 **Positive duties on public authorities**

The February 1999 publication of the Stephen Lawrence Inquiry Report,[161] which found clear evidence of institutional racism[162] within the Metropolitan Police, contributed significantly to the later adoption of positive duties for public authorities to avoid discrimination in all their functions and to promote race equality and good race relations.

[161] *The Stephen Lawrence Inquiry: Report of an Inquiry by Sir William Macpherson* (Cm 4262-I, 1999).

[162] Defined in the Inquiry Report as '[t]he collective failure of an organisation to provide an appropriate and professional service to people because of their colour, culture or ethnic origin. It can be seen or detected in processes, attitudes and behaviour which amount to discrimination through unwitting prejudice, ignorance, thoughtlessness and racist stereotyping which disadvantage minority ethnic people.'

This wider approach was extended into the field of sex discrimination in 2007,[163] and has now been incorporated in the Equality Act 2010[164] across all of the protected characteristics other than marriage or civil partnership. The general duty to promote equality extends to approximately 60 categories of public bodies, covering around 40,000 organizations. In addition to the general duty, the Secretary of State is also empowered to impose additional specific duties on some or all public authorities.[165] The introduction of these positive duties represents a highly significant shift in thinking as regards the use of the law to tackle discrimination. Unlike the existing anti-discrimination laws, which are essentially reactive, they reflect a more proactive and strategic approach to tackling discrimination.

The specific duties have, however, been significantly weakened since their initial adoption in the RRA 1976. More demanding measures such as a requirement to publish a Race Equality Scheme have given way to vague requirements to publish whatever information will suffice 'to demonstrate [the public authority's] compliance with' the general Equality Duty.[166] Moreover, the general scheme of positive duties has been criticized as too weak, and perhaps unlikely or even not intended to lead to any serious change.[167]

4.2.9 **Discrimination before, during, and after employment**

4.2.9.1 **Discrimination before employment**

The first stage at which a person may encounter discrimination in employment is in applying for a job. It is unlawful under the Equality Act 2010, s 39(1) for an employer to discriminate in the arrangements[168] for selection, in the terms offered for employment, or by refusing or deliberately omitting to offer the employment. A certain amount of realism is necessary in construing these provisions, so that, for example, it is not necessarily unlawful for an employer to ask a woman a question at an interview which would not be asked of a man; the issue is whether, by asking the question, the woman was treated less favourably because of her sex than a man would be treated.[169] Also, if a person assumes applicant status purely for the purpose of making a claim for compensation, as opposed to genuinely seeking employment, such a person cannot bring a claim since they have not suffered any detriment and so have not been subjected to less favourable treatment.[170]

[163] Sex Discrimination Act 1975, s 76A (added by the Equality Act 2006); Sex Discrimination Act 1975 (Public Authorities) (Statutory Duties) Order 2006, SI 2006/2930.

[164] Equality Act 2010 ss 149–157.

[165] Equality Act 2010, s 153. This has since been implemented through the Equality Act 2010 (Specific Duties) Regulations 2011 SI 2011/2260. The specific race duties adopted prior to the 2010 Act are contained in the Race Relations Act 1976 (Statutory Duties) Order 2001, SI 2001/3458, issued under s 71(2).

[166] The Equality Act 2010 (Specific Duties) Regulations 2011, reg 2.

[167] See eg Fredman 'The Public Sector Equality Duty' (2011) 40 ILJ 405.

[168] On the meaning of 'arrangements', see *Brennan v J H Dewhurst Ltd* [1984] ICR 52, [1983] IRLR 357 (biased interview).

[169] *Saunders v Richmond-upon-Thames London Borough Council* [1978] ICR 75, [1977] IRLR 362. The applicant for a post as a golf professional had been asked questions such as 'Do you think men respond as well to a woman golf professional as to a man?' and 'Are there any women golf professionals in clubs?' The EAT declared that although the questions asked reflected what is now an out-of-date and proscribed attitude of mind, the industrial tribunal was entitled to find on the evidence that they were not asked with the intention of discriminating against the appellant on grounds of her sex.

[170] *Garcia v The Leadership Factor Ltd* [2022] EAT 19 (1 February 2022, unreported), *Keane v Investigo* UKEAT/0389/09 (11 December 2009, unreported) and *Berry v Recruitment Revolution* UKEAT/0190/10 (6 October 2010, unreported). The CJEU has reached the same conclusion in relation to EU law: *Kratzer v R+V Allgemeine Versicherung AG*, C-423/15.

As a result of EU case law, employers can also be liable for discriminatory statements made outside of an active recruitment phase. *NH v Associazione Avvocatura per i diritti LGBTI: Rete Lenford* involved a senior lawyer stating that he would never hire a homosexual person in a radio interview.[171] Although there were no job openings at the firm at the time and there was no identifiable victim, the CJEU found that this was discrimination. The case also confirmed that employers can be liable for such statements made by third parties. Post-Brexit, this has been incorporated into UK law with the introduction of s 60A into the Equality Act 2010.[172] Statements will be considered discriminatory if:

(a) they are directed to the public, and

(b) if the statement were made when making an employment decision, it would amount to direct discrimination.[173]

The legislation also lists factors to be considered when determining if statements by third parties would fall into this section.[174]

Genuine occupational requirement

Section 1 of Schedule 9 to the Act creates an exemption where a protected characteristic is a genuine occupational requirement (GOR) for the job. A GOR can be applied only where this is a proportionate means to a legitimate aim. The GOR defence is designed to avoid some of the more obvious absurdities of complete equality, but it is important that the boundaries of the exception are not stretched too far, lest the protection against discrimination be undermined. The SDA 1975 and the RRA 1976 had contained a more specific series of defences, called genuine occupational qualifications (GOQs), which for example included casting actors in plays and appointing people to work in situations where members of the public are in a state of undress.

The European Equality Directives of 2000 and 2006 state that the protected characteristic must be a 'genuine and determining occupational requirement' and the application of the requirement must be proportionate. The 2010 Act reflects this but omits the word 'determining'. However, this apparent gap is readily closed by the proportionality analysis: the less 'determining' a requirement is, the less weight should be given to the employer's need for it. In any event, the obligation to interpret the Equality Act so as to implement the Directives means that tribunals are likely to read the word 'determining' into the Act.

To give an example of how this might apply, take a requirement for a waiter at an ethnic restaurant to share the ethnicity of the food on the menu. This was a GOQ under the Race Relations Act, but under the current law it would probably struggle to satisfy a proportionality test since the defining characteristic of the job is clearly taking orders and serving food to customers, not having a certain ethnicity. Further, it seems hard to defend the proportionality of a requirement whose sole 'legitimate' aim is to present customers with an apparently ethnically pure dining experience, when the impact of the requirement would be to exclude a talented waiter from much needed employment purely on the grounds of race.

4.2.9.2 **Discrimination during employment**

Under the Equality Act 2010, s 39(2)(b) it is unlawful for an employer to discriminate against an employee during employment in the way they afford or refuse to afford access to opportunities for promotion, transfer, or training,[175] or to any other benefits,

[171] C-507/18. [172] Amended by Equality Act 2010 (Amendment) Regulations 2023.

[173] S 60A(3). [174] S 60A(4)–(6).

[175] This could occur in a redundancy situation where a new job is created but the employer refuses to transfer a person of a particular sex to it (subject to the genuine occupational qualification defence): *Timex Corpn v Hodgson* [1982] ICR 63, [1981] IRLR 530, EAT.

facilities,[176] or services. It is also unlawful to discriminate by subjecting an employee to any 'detriment'. In *Ministry of Defence v Jeremiah*,[177] the Court of Appeal held that subjecting to any detriment is to be given its ordinary, common-sense meaning of 'putting under a disadvantage',[178] and this was confirmed by the House of Lords in *Shamoon v Chief Constable of the Royal Ulster Constabulary*.[179] Their Lordships also confirmed that the test of detriment contains both subjective and objective elements, approving Brightman LJ's formulation in *Jeremiah* that 'a detriment exists if a reasonable employee would or might take the view that the [treatment] was in all the circumstances to his detriment';[180] according to Lord Scott, the test must be applied 'by considering the issue from the point of view of the victim. If the victim's opinion that the treatment was to his or her detriment is a reasonable one to hold, that ought . . . to suffice.'[181]

The emphasis on the reasonableness of the victim's view of the treatment means that 'an unjustified sense of grievance cannot amount to "detriment"'.[182] The need to establish detriment means that differentiation between those in different groups is not in itself unlawful discrimination, for there must be some element of disadvantage, although the courts have generally been prepared to find that differential treatment is detrimental.[183] It may also be possible for a tribunal or court to consider a claimed disadvantage to be so minor as to be disregarded on the de minimis principle, although as seen earlier (see 4.2.4.4), the scope of the de minimis defence is probably very narrow.

Once there is a detriment it will not be a defence for an employer to show that the detriment is removed by compensating those who experience it, for example where only men are obliged to do certain disagreeable work, but receive an extra payment in respect of it.[184]

4.2.9.3 **Discrimination on, and after, termination of employment**

Under the Equality Act 2010, s 39(2)(c) it is unlawful to discriminate against an employee by dismissal,[185] and this can give rise to a complaint to a tribunal. It is likely that in such a case the employee will also have a claim for unfair dismissal, and usually a former employee will make both claims since they each have different advantages. The preliminary burden of proof in the unfair dismissal case is on the employer, and the compensation awarded will, in addition to covering the employee's losses, include a basic award calculated in the same way as a statutory redundancy payment. On the other hand, the discrimination claim has the distinct advantages that the two-year qualifying period

[176] This refers to facilities which already exist: *Clymo v London Borough of Wandsworth* [1989] ICR 250, [1989] IRLR 241, EAT.

[177] [1979] 3 All ER 833, [1979] IRLR 436, CA, disapproving the reasoning on this point in *Peake v Automotive Products Ltd* [1977] ICR 968, [1977] IRLR 365, CA.

[178] [1979] IRLR 436 at 438, per Lord Brandon.

[179] [2003] UKHL 11, [2003] ICR 337, [2003] IRLR 285.

[180] [1979] IRLR 436 at 440.

[181] [2003] UKHL 11, [2003] ICR 337, [2003] IRLR 285 at 301. Note also that to amount to a 'detriment', the disadvantage must arise 'in the field of employment': per Lord Hope at 291.

[182] [2003] UKHL 11, [2003] ICR 337, [2003] IRLR 285 at 291, per Lord Hope. See also *Barclays Bank plc v Kapur (No 2)* [1995] IRLR 87.

[183] See 4.2.4.4. Separate but equal treatment is however specifically deemed to be discrimination when it is on grounds of race—see 4.5.1.

[184] See *Ministry of Defence v Jeremiah* [1978] ICR 984, [1978] IRLR 402; affd by CA: [1979] 3 All ER 833, [1979] IRLR 436.

[185] Dismissal here includes a constructive dismissal: Equality Act 2010, s 39(7). In a 'last straw' constructive dismissal case, the dismissal may still be discriminatory even if the last straw incident itself was not; this depends upon whether earlier discriminatory conduct, even if it occurred more than three months before the tribunal claim was lodged, 'sufficiently influenced' the overall repudiatory breach: *Williams v Governing Body of Alderman Davies Church in Wales Primary School* [2020] IRLR 589, EAT and *De Lacey v Wechseln Ltd* [2021] IRLR 547, EAT.

for unfair dismissal does not apply, the tribunal is expressly empowered to award a sum for injury to feelings,[186] and there is no upper limit on the compensation which can be awarded for discrimination.[187] Also, if it is not certain that the complainant was an 'employee' in the narrow sense of having a contract of service, they can still bring a claim for discrimination so long as they meet the wide definition of 'employee' in the Equality Act. If an employee succeeds with both claims, there can be no double compensation, as the compensation for discrimination cannot take into account any head of loss already included in the compensation for unfair dismissal, and vice versa.

As for less favourable treatment after employment has ended, s 108 forbids discrimination which arises out of and is closely connected with a former employment relationship. The wording of s 108 is wide enough to cover a broad range of claims by ex-employees, including the conduct of internal appeals against dismissal and the provision of references.

4.2.10 **Combined discrimination**

In the UK, there is no protection against dual discrimination. This is where someone is discriminated against because of two or more characteristics, rather than one. For example, a Black woman might be treated differently from both white women and black men, because of the combination of both racism and sexism.[188]

The Equality Act does contain a provision about this, named 'combined discrimination' but it has never been brought into force.[189] This provides that it is direct discrimination to treat a person less favourably because of a combination of two protected characteristics. The current government has opened a call for evidence to bring this into force and this might be included in the Equality (Race and Disability) Bill.[190]

4.2.11 **Proving discrimination**

Proving discrimination can be extremely difficult, as there will usually be little or no direct evidence of discrimination, and most documentary evidence is in the hands of the respondent.[191] In recognition of the difficulties faced by complainants attempting to prove discrimination the EU adopted the Burden of Proof Directive,[192] which is reflected in s 136 of the 2010 Act. It provides that where the complainant proves facts from which the tribunal could conclude, in the absence of an adequate explanation, that the respondent has committed an unlawful act of discrimination against the complainant, the tribunal must uphold the complaint unless the respondent proves that they did not commit that act. The leading case on how to apply the reversal of the burden of proof is the Court of Appeal decision in *Igen Ltd v Wong*,[193] which preceded the Equality Act. The Supreme Court has confirmed that the guidance in *Igen Ltd v Wong* also applies under the Equality Act, subject to a number of clarifications which had emerged in subsequent case law.[194]

[186] Equality Act 2010, ss 124(6); 119(4). [187] See 4.2.9.

[188] For more on this, see Crenshaw 'Demarginalizing the Intersection of Race and Sex' (1989) University of Chicago Legal Forum 139.

[189] S 14. [190] See Fredman *Discrimination Law* (3rd edn, 2024) 218–32.

[191] The advent of SMS messaging and email has however somewhat restored the balance, given the tendency of managers to unwisely record their discriminatory thoughts and actions on their mobile phones.

[192] Directive 97/80/EC. [193] [2005] ICR 931, [2005] IRLR 258, CA.

[194] *Hewage v Grampian Health Board* [2012] UKSC 37, [2012] IRLR 870 and *Efobi v Royal Mail Group Ltd* [2021] UKSC 33, [2021] IRLR 811, [2021] ICR 1263.

The *Igen* guidance sets out 13 detailed points, but the headlines, with those clarifications, are as follows:

- It is for the applicant who complains of discrimination to prove on the balance of probabilities facts from which the tribunal could conclude, in the absence of an explanation, that the respondents have committed an act of discrimination against the applicant which is unlawful. All the evidence as to the facts which is before the tribunal must be considered, not just evidence adduced by the claimant.
- It is important to bear in mind in deciding whether the applicant has proved such facts that it is unusual to find direct evidence of discrimination. Few employers would be prepared to admit such discrimination, even to themselves.
- It is important to note the word is 'could'. At this stage the tribunal does not have to reach a definitive determination that such facts *would* lead it to the conclusion that there was an act of unlawful discrimination.
- In considering what inferences or conclusions can be drawn from the primary facts, the tribunal must assume that there is no adequate explanation of those facts.
- Where the applicant has proved facts from which conclusions could be drawn that the respondents have treated the applicant less favourably on a protected ground, then the burden of proof moves to the respondent to prove on the balance of probabilities that the treatment was in no sense whatsoever because of the protected characteristic.[195]
- Since the facts necessary to prove an explanation would normally be in the possession of the respondent, a tribunal would normally expect cogent evidence to discharge that burden of proof.

In practice, the main hurdle for the applicant will often be the need to provide factual evidence of treatment that could be discrimination sufficient to shift the burden of proof onto the employer. Unreasonable treatment by the employer will not of itself suffice, as the House of Lords has held that the fact that an employer has acted unreasonably towards an employee and that no satisfactory explanation has been given does not oblige the tribunal to infer that there has been less favourable treatment on grounds of sex or race, as the employer could have treated other employees in the same unreasonable manner;[196] having said that, unreasonable behaviour by the employer is likely to require an explanation, and whether the tribunal is satisfied with the explanation 'will depend not on a theoretical possibility that the employer behaves equally badly to employees of all races but on evidence that he does'.[197]

A live issue under the statutory reversal provisions is the *extent* to which the claimant must prove the initial facts. It is clear that it is not enough to reverse the burden for the claimant merely to make an accusation. Moreover, it is also the case that the claimant must show facts from which a tribunal could, in the absence of an explanation, infer

[195] Although this logically establishes a two-stage process, this is not to be applied too technically and so in deciding whether the claimant has made out a prima facie case the tribunal can look at the evidence given by the claimant and the employers: *Laing v Manchester City Council* [2006] IRLR 748, EAT, strongly affirmed by the Court of Appeal in *Madarassy v Nomura International plc* [2007] IRLR 246, *Brown v Croydon LBC* [2007] IRLR 259, and *Appiah v Bishop Douglass RC High School* [2007] IRLR 264.

[196] *Zafar v Glasgow City Council* [1998] IRLR 36. The important judgment of Elias J in *Bahl v Law Society* [2003] IRLR 640, EAT (affd [2004] IRLR 799, CA) on the pre-statutory-reversal law is commonly cited for the proposition that bad treatment is not per se discriminatory treatment.

[197] *Anya v University of Oxford* [2001] EWCA Civ 405, [2001] ICR 847, [2001] IRLR 377 (a race discrimination case).

less favourable treatment *because of* sex, race, and so on. It may be enough to show less favourable treatment *and* a difference in sex, race, and so on. For example, in *Network Rail Infrastructure Ltd v Griffiths-Henry*[198] the EAT held that an employment tribunal was entitled to decide that the burden of proof had been reversed where a Black woman, who claimed race and sex discrimination in not being appointed to one of five posts, showed that she was as well qualified for the role as the five white men who had been appointed.

One particularly difficult issue has always been the extent to which the tribunal may draw inferences of discrimination from statistical evidence, for example, that the employer's workforce is composed almost entirely of men. It is clear that where women are sharply under-represented, it will be easy to persuade a tribunal that a PCP which puts a female claimant at a disadvantage puts women at a disadvantage, because it appears to discourage them from seeking the job in the first place.[199] Moreover, in the context of race discrimination the Court of Appeal has accepted that statistical evidence drawn from ethnic monitoring which reveals a discernible pattern in the treatment of a particular group to which the complainant belongs (eg a regular failure of members of the group to obtain promotion to particular jobs, or under-representation in such jobs) may justify the inference that 'the real reason for the treatment is a conscious or unconscious racial attitude which involves stereotyped assumptions about members of that group'.[200] In other words, statistical evidence, although not in itself conclusive, may be sufficient to raise an inference of discrimination which, in the absence of a satisfactory explanation by the employer, will be sufficient for the complainant to succeed on the balance of probabilities.

4.2.12 **Vicarious liability of employer and personal liability of employee**

4.2.12.1 **Vicarious liability of employer**

The vicarious liability of an employer for discriminatory action by its employees is of huge importance in seeking to tackle discrimination. While management action by a manager superior to an employee will readily be regarded as an action of the employer, s 109 ensures that the employer is also liable for discriminatory conduct on the part of the complainant's fellow employees[201] so long as the conduct took place in the course of their employment. This is so whether or not the conduct was done with the employer's knowledge or approval. This can be particularly important in a harassment case where the harassment is coming from fellow employees rather than from a superior.[202]

The vicarious liability depends on the person causing the disadvantage to the complainant having been acting 'in the course of employment'. In the earlier cases on this provision it was held that the statutory test of vicarious liability was the same as the common law test in tort at that time (ie whether the employee's act was merely an unauthorized or prohibited mode of doing an authorized act, as distinct from an act which

[198] [2006] IRLR 865, EAT.

[199] *XC Trains Ltd v CD* [2016] IRLR 748 (EAT), where the court concluded that, despite the fact that the claimant was the only woman whose childcare responsibilities prevented her from complying with a scheduling PCP, the fact that the employer employed only 17 train drivers nationally (3.04 per cent of drivers) justified finding a disadvantage based on the absence of women in the job, rather than the presence of other women affected by the PCP.

[200] *West Midlands Passenger Transport Executive v Singh* [1988] ICR 614, [1988] IRLR 186, CA, per Balcombe LJ. In that case the Court of Appeal ordered discovery of statistics showing the ethnic origins of those who had applied for the post of inspector in the preceding two years, and those whose applications had been successful.

[201] Section 109 also creates vicarious liability for the acts of an agent of the employer if the agent was acting with the authority of the employer.

[202] See eg *Porcelli v Strathclyde Regional Council* [1986] ICR 564, [1986] IRLR 134, Ct of Sess.

was outside the sphere of what they were employed to do).[203] The problem with that approach, particularly in cases involving sexual or racial harassment, was that the worse an employee's acts, the less likely it was that they would be held to be acting in the course of their employment; indeed, taken to its logical conclusion it might even mean that no employer could ever be held responsible for such acts, as no employee is employed to harass other employees.

It was therefore to be welcomed that the application of the common law test to vicarious liability for discrimination was comprehensively rejected by the Court of Appeal in *Jones v Tower Boot Co Ltd*.[204] In that case, the complainant had been subjected to a number of extreme incidents of racial harassment by fellow employees, including being branded with a hot screwdriver, whipped across the legs, and verbally abused. The EAT had overturned the tribunal's finding that the perpetrators were acting in the course of their employment, holding that the acts complained of could not 'by any stretch of the imagination' be described as an improper mode of performing authorized tasks. The Court of Appeal reversed the EAT's decision and held the employer liable. Giving the principal judgment, Waite LJ held that a purposive approach should be taken to the statutory test, and that the words 'in the course of his employment' should be interpreted in the sense in which they are employed in everyday speech, unclouded by any parallels drawn from the common law of vicarious liability.

In subsequent cases, vicarious liability for discrimination has been interpreted as extending even to social activities occurring outside working hours, where those activities are work-related.[205] There are, however, limits, as was shown in *Waters v Metropolitan Police Comr*,[206] where the Court of Appeal held that no tribunal applying the statutory test could find that an alleged sexual assault by a male police officer on a female officer was committed 'in the course of his employment' when both parties were off-duty at the time and the man was a visitor to her room.[207]

The wide interpretation of 'in the course of employment' places heightened emphasis on the importance for the employer that a defence is available under s 109(4) if the employer can prove that it took such steps as were reasonably practicable to prevent the fellow employee's conduct. It has been held that this defence is made out where an employer has maintained adequate supervision of the employees and publicized a policy of equal opportunities.[208] An employer who has not taken reasonably practicable steps will not be exculpated simply because the particular conduct of the employee would have occurred even if those reasonable steps had been taken.[209] The correct approach is to identify what steps, if any, have been taken, and to consider whether there were any

[203] See eg *Irving and Irving v Post Office* [1987] ICR 949, [1987] IRLR 289, CA (on the equivalent provision in the Race Relations Act 1976, s 32).

[204] [1997] ICR 254, [1997] IRLR 168, CA.

[205] *Chief Constable of Lincolnshire Police v Stubbs* [1999] ICR 547, [1999] IRLR 81, EAT (police authority held liable for harassment of a female police officer while off-duty at a pub with her work colleagues, and while at a work-related leaving party).

[206] [1997] ICR 1073, [1997] IRLR 589, CA. On appeal ([2000] ICR 1064, [2000] IRLR 720), the House of Lords found for the applicant on the grounds that the Commissioner had acted negligently in failing to protect her from victimization and harassment which might cause her physical or mental harm, in breach of the duty of care both under contract of employment and under the common law principles of negligence.

[207] See also *Sidhu v Aerospace Composite Technology Ltd* [2001] ICR 167, [2000] IRLR 602, CA (violence at a social function organized by the employers outside working hours where most of those present were not employees of the employer held to be outside the course of employment).

[208] *Balgobin v London Borough of Tower Hamlets* [1987] ICR 829, [1987] IRLR 401, EAT.

[209] *Canniffe v East Riding of Yorkshire Council* [2000] IRLR 555, EAT (sexual assaults on a disabled female colleague).

further reasonably practicable steps that could have been taken, irrespective of whether taking those steps would have been successful in preventing the discriminatory acts. Adequate steps are likely to include the need for refresher training and action being taken to deal with transgressions: in *Allay Ltd v Gehlen*,[210] the employer had provided anti-harassment training some 20 to 30 months before the harassment occurred but it needed to be refreshed because managers had failed to do anything about racist remarks made by employees. This meant that the employer had not taken all reasonably practicable steps.

4.2.12.2 **Personal liability of employee**

Where the employer is held vicariously liable under s 109, then s 110 provides that the employee who committed the discriminatory act in the course of their employment is also personally liable. By this convoluted process it is possible to hold an employee responsible in law for discriminatory acts even though the statutory duty not to discriminate applies only to employers. The employee remains personally liable under s 110 even if the employer is able to escape vicarious liability because of the s 109(4) reasonably practicable steps defence.

This liability of the fellow employee is subject to a defence under s 110(3) where the employer told the employee that the act was legal (not a contravention of the Act) and the employee reasonably believes this.

4.2.13 **Remedies**

4.2.13.1 **Time limit**

An employee or ex-employee may bring a complaint to an employment tribunal about discrimination in employment.[211] The time limit for the presentation of complaints is three months[212] beginning when the act complained of was done, or, in the case of a deliberate omission, when the person in question decided upon it.[213] Where the act complained of is dismissal, the date of the dismissal for the purposes of a discrimination claim is not necessarily the same as the 'effective date of termination' for unfair dismissal purposes.[214] Moreover, where the dismissal is a constructive one, it appears that the time runs from the date upon which the employee accepted the employer's repudiatory action as terminating the contract.[215]

Discrimination often takes the form of a continuing act extending over a period of time, in which case the time limit runs from the end of that period.[216] However, a continuing act of discrimination must be distinguished from a single act or event of discrimination which has continuing consequences, where the time limit runs from

[210] [2021] IRLR 348, [2021] ICR 645.

[211] Equality Act 2010, s 120.

[212] Or six months for those serving in the armed forces, because of the need to follow the service redress procedures before making a complaint to a tribunal: Equality Act 2010, s 121.

[213] Equality Act 2010, s 123(3)(b). See *Swithland Motors plc v Clarke* [1994] ICR 231, [1994] IRLR 275, EAT ('decided' means 'decided at a time and in circumstances when he is in a position to implement that decision').

[214] *Lupetti v Wrens Old House Ltd* [1984] ICR 348 (under the Race Relations Act 1976); *Gloucester Working Men's Club and Institute v James* [1986] ICR 603.

[215] *Nottinghamshire County Council v Meikle* [2004] EWCA Civ 859, [2004] IRLR 703 at [49]–[53] and *De Lacey v Wechseln Ltd* [2021] IRLR 547, EAT at [72].

[216] Equality Act 2010, s 123(3)(a).

the act itself.[217] So, for example, in *Calder v James Findlay Corpn Ltd*,[218] the employer's refusal to allow the complainant access to a mortgage subsidy scheme was held to be a continuing act of discrimination, entitling her to bring her complaint more than three months after the refusal. In contrast, in *Sougrin v Haringey Health Authority*,[219] a case under the RRA, a grading decision was held by the Court of Appeal to be a single act with continuing consequences, not a continuing act of discrimination, with the consequence that the three-month limitation period started to run on the date of the grading decision.

The distinction can be extremely difficult to draw, especially where a single act of discrimination is repeated or reaffirmed on subsequent occasions.[220] A succession of specific instances of discrimination (eg a failure to regrade over a number of years, or the reaffirmation of a refusal to allow an employee to job-share) may, however, indicate the existence of a discriminatory policy or regime (formal or informal), which can constitute a continuing act extending over a period.[221] In *Hendricks v Metropolitan Police Comr*,[222] the Court of Appeal reviewed the authorities and took a broad view of the concept of a continuing act, holding that the focus should be on whether there is an 'ongoing situation or a continuing state of affairs' in which the alleged incidents of discrimination were linked to one another, rather than on whether it was possible to identify some 'policy, rule, scheme, regime or practice' in accordance with which decisions affecting the treatment of employees were taken.

The tribunal has a wide discretion to consider a complaint out of time if it considers that it is 'just and equitable' to do so.[223] The tribunals have on the whole been reluctant to extend the time limit in discrimination complaints where the delay was caused by the applicant awaiting the resolution of internal grievance or appeal procedures before embarking on litigation.[224]

If the tribunal finds the complaint well founded, it may make three orders—a declaration that the employee's rights have been infringed, an order for compensation, and a recommendation that the employer take action suggested by the tribunal within a specified period in order to remove the discrimination.[225] The first of those remedies, a declaration that the employee's rights have been infringed, is always made—it consists of the tribunal's judgment announcing that the claimant has succeeded.

[217] See eg *Amies v Inner London Education Authority* [1977] 2 All ER 100, [1977] ICR 308, EAT (failure to appoint to a particular post held not to be a continuing act of discrimination). See also *Tyagi v BBC World Service* [2001] EWCA Civ 549, [2001] IRLR 465 (alleged discriminatory recruitment policy not a continuing act).

[218] [1989] ICR 157n, [1989] IRLR 55, EAT, approved by the House of Lords in *Barclays Bank plc v Kapur* [1991] ICR 208, [1991] IRLR 136 (under the Race Relations Act). See also *Littlewoods Organisation plc v Traynor* [1993] IRLR 154, EAT (failure to take promised remedial action in relation to a complaint of discrimination was a continuing act of discrimination by the employer).

[219] [1992] ICR 650, [1992] IRLR 416, CA.

[220] See eg *Rovenska v General Medical Council* [1998] ICR 85, [1997] IRLR 367, CA.

[221] *Owusu v London Fire and Civil Defence Authority* [1995] IRLR 574, EAT (re-grading); *Cast v Croydon College* [1998] ICR 500, [1998] IRLR 318, CA (job-share).

[222] [2003] IRLR 96, CA.

[223] Equality Act 2010, s 123(1)(b). This is a much wider formulation than the 'reasonably practicable' escape clause that applies to the time limit for bringing a claim for unfair dismissal: see *Hutchinson v Westward Television Ltd* [1977] ICR 279, [1977] IRLR 69, EAT; *Clarke v Hampshire Electro-Plating Co Ltd* [1992] ICR 312, [1991] IRLR 490, EAT; *Hawkins v Ball* [1996] IRLR 258, EAT; *British Coal Corpn v Keeble* [1997] IRLR 336, EAT; *DPP v Marshall* [1998] ICR 518, EAT. Cf *London Borough of Southwark v Afolabi* [2003] IRLR 220, CA (a case in which a complaint was allowed nearly nine years after the expiry of the three-month limit).

[224] *Apelogun-Gabriels v London Borough of Lambeth* [2001] EWCA Civ 1853, [2002] ICR 713, [2002] IRLR 116, CA, approving *Robinson v Post Office* [2000] IRLR 804, EAT, and disapproving *Aniagwu v London Borough of Hackney* [1999] IRLR 303, EAT.

[225] Equality Act 2010, s 124(2).

4.2.13.2 **Recommendations**

The tribunal may make a recommendation that the employer should take certain steps for the purpose of obviating or reducing the adverse effect on the complainant of any matter to which a successful complaint is related. An example might be a recommendation that the employer make a public apology or make a statement to correct a false impression about the claimant on the part of fellow employees or the public which was caused by the discrimination.[226] If the employee remains in employment then a recommendation that the employer give managers, or all employees, appropriate training on equal opportunities or harassment may be appropriate even though this is likely to have benefits for employees other than the complainant. So long as the recommended action is relevant to obviating discrimination against the complainant, the fact that it would also have a wider impact does not make it inappropriate.[227] A recommendation might even go so far as requiring the employer to give an undertaking that it would ensure that the claimant did not have to work with two particular managers and that if at some point in the future this became impractical she would be offered termination with a payment equivalent to the employer's redundancy package.[228] However, it would not be right for a tribunal to recommend that an applicant who has been the victim of discrimination in selection for employment should be appointed to the next suitable job that becomes available, because this would be unfair to the other applicants for that post.[229]

If the employer fails to comply with a recommendation without reasonable excuse, the complainant may go back to the tribunal, which may award increased compensation if it considers it just and equitable to do so.[230] In such proceedings the tribunal must take a realistic approach and one of the main factors in deciding whether the employer had a reasonable excuse not to comply may be whether there has been sufficient time to put matters right, because the provisions relating to the recommendation clearly envisage the possibility of longer-term measures.[231]

4.2.13.3 **Compensation**

The tribunal is empowered to award compensation on the same basis as if the complainant had brought an action for damages in tort before an ordinary court. This means that, as far as money can do it, the applicant must be put into the position they would have been in but for the unlawful conduct of the employer.[232]

[226] As a general rule, a recommendation should not require anyone to make a statement (eg by way of apology) which they genuinely believe to be untrue: *St Andrew's Catholic Primary School v Blundell* UKEAT/0330/09, [2010] All ER (D) 68 (Oct).

[227] *Southwark London Borough v Ayton* UKEAT/0515/03 (18 September 2003, unreported). In *Bayoomi v British Railways Board* [1981] IRLR 431 the EAT held that such training could not be recommended because the complainant no longer worked for the employer and the best that could be done by way of recommendation was to the effect that a note be placed on his personal record to the effect that he had been dismissed in circumstances which amounted to racial discrimination in the hope that this would prevent prospective employers drawing an adverse inference from his dismissal, should they seek a reference.

[228] *Hill v Lloyds Bank plc* [2020] IRLR 652, EAT.

[229] *Noone v North West Thames Regional Health Authority (No 2)* [1988] IRLR 530, CA.

[230] Equality Act 2010, s 124(7).

[231] *Nelson v Tyne and Wear Passenger Transport Executive* [1978] ICR 1183.

[232] Equality Act 2010, ss 124(6); 119(2). See *Alexander v Home Office* [1988] ICR 685, [1988] IRLR 190, CA (under the Race Relations Act 1976) and *Ministry of Defence v Cannock* [1994] ICR 918, [1994] IRLR 509, EAT, which contain detailed guidance on the assessment of damages in discrimination cases.

Financial losses

The main component will usually be compensation for financial loss, for example the value of a bonus not awarded because of a discriminatory decision by a manager. In a case of discriminatory dismissal, the compensation will be for lost earnings and will be assessed in the same way as the compensatory award for unfair dismissal—although, as explained below, not constrained by the statutory cap on compensation for unfair dismissal. The normal rules concerning mitigation and discounting for future uncertainties will apply.[233]

Injury to feelings

In addition, there is an express power to award damages for injury to feelings.[234] In harassment cases in particular this may be the only source of substantial compensation, since the complainant may not have suffered any financial loss. An award for injury to feelings has been said to be 'almost inevitable' in a discrimination case,[235] but this does not mean that it is automatic, as the applicant must still persuade the tribunal that some injury has been sustained.[236] A tribunal must take account of the current '*Vento*' guidelines in awarding compensation for injury to feelings—so named after the case in which those guidelines were first laid down, *Vento v Chief Constable of West Yorkshire Police (No 2)*.[237] In that case the Court of Appeal identified broad bands into which such awards should fall. The bands are now updated every year by a Direction given by the President of the Employment Tribunals. The current bands are:

- the top band, for the most serious cases (such as where there has been a lengthy campaign of sexual or racial harassment), should normally be between £36,400 to £60,700 (the most serious cases), with only the most exceptional cases capable of exceeding £60,700;
- the middle band of between £12,100 to £36,400 should be used for serious cases not meriting an award in the highest band; and
- awards of between £1,200 to £12,100 are appropriate for less serious cases, such as isolated or one-off acts of discrimination.

Awards of less than £1,200 should be avoided altogether 'as they risk being regarded as so low as not to be a proper recognition of injury to feelings'.[238]

[233] See *Ministry of Defence v Cannock* [1994] ICR 918, [1994] IRLR 509, EAT; *Ministry of Defence v Hunt* [1996] ICR 554, [1996] IRLR 139, EAT. See also *Ministry of Defence v Wheeler* [1998] ICR 242, [1998] IRLR 23, CA.

[234] Equality Act 2010, ss 124(b); 119(4). The injury to feelings must arise directly from the sex discrimination, not from other, more remote consequences: *Skyrail Oceanic Ltd v Coleman* [1981] ICR 864, [1981] IRLR 398, CA.

[235] *Murray v Powertech (Scotland) Ltd* [1992] IRLR 257, EAT.

[236] *Ministry of Defence v Cannock* [1994] ICR 918, [1994] IRLR 509, EAT. In *Cannock*, the EAT suggested that it will often be easy to prove injury, as no tribunal will take much persuading that the anger and distress caused by the discriminatory act has injured the applicant's feelings. In sexual harassment cases, the EAT has held that compensation must relate to the degree of detriment suffered; this has led to an uncomfortably close examination of the applicant's character and antecedents in some cases: see eg *Snowball v Gardner Merchant Ltd* [1987] ICR 719, [1987] IRLR 397; *Wileman v Minilec Engineering Ltd* [1988] ICR 318, [1988] IRLR 144, EAT.

[237] [2002] EWCA Civ 1871, [2003] ICR 318, [2003] IRLR 102. The tribunal's award of £50,000 for injury to feelings plus £15,000 aggravated damages was held to be excessive, and the Court of Appeal substituted awards of £18,000 and £5,000, respectively; damages for psychiatric injury were left at £9,000.

[238] [2003] IRLR 102 at 110, per Mummery LJ.

Personal injury

The tribunal can also award damages for personal injury (including an award for psychiatric harm caused by the discrimination),[239] and the Court of Appeal has held that, unlike a common law claim for negligence, a personal injury claim in a discrimination complaint is not limited to harm that is reasonably foreseeable, and that all the applicant need show is a direct causal link between the act of discrimination and their loss.[240]

Other kinds of damages

Aggravated damages are available where, for example, the defendant has behaved in a high-handed, malicious, insulting, or oppressive manner in committing the discriminatory act,[241] or where the defendant has defended the discrimination claim in a manner which was designed to be intimidatory and to cause the maximum unease and distress to the applicant.[242] A tribunal can also award exemplary damages but only if, first, the other compensation is insufficient to punish the wrongdoer, and, second, either (a) the conduct is oppressive, arbitrary, or unconstitutional action by the agents of government, or (b) the defendant's conduct has been calculated by him to make a profit which may well exceed the compensation payable to the claimant.[243]

No financial limits on compensation

Until 1993, compensation for discrimination was subject to the same upper limit as the compensatory award for unfair dismissal.[244] However, as in so many other areas of UK sex discrimination law, EU law has made its mark in this area, and this limitation has been removed, the CJEU holding that the upper limit on compensation infringed Article 6 of the Equal Treatment Directive, which requires the provision of adequate remedies which compensate the complainant in full for the loss and damage sustained as a result of the discrimination.[245]

There is a theoretical limitation to the award of damages for unintentional indirect discrimination in that s 124(5) of the Equality Act requires a tribunal, before awarding compensation, to consider whether to make a declaration or a recommendation. In practice, if the claimant has suffered loss flowing from the indirect discrimination, then a tribunal will normally conclude that it should not just make a declaration or a recommendation and that it should award compensation for the loss.[246]

4.2.13.4 **Action by the EHRC**

In addition to the remedies available to the aggrieved employee, the Equality and Human Rights Commission is empowered to take certain direct steps to secure compliance with the statute. In particular, it may conduct a formal investigation into any alleged

[239] *Sheriff v Klyne Tugs (Lowestoft) Ltd* [1999] ICR 1170, [1999] IRLR 481, CA (under the parallel provisions in the RRA).

[240] *Essa v Laing Ltd* [2004] ICR 746, [2004] IRLR 313, CA (also under the RRA).

[241] *Alexander v Home Office*, [1988] ICR 685, [1988] IRLR 190, CA; *Armitage, Marsden and HM Prison Service v Johnson*, [1997] IRLR 162, EAT; *Ministry of Defence v Meredith* [1995] IRLR 539, EAT.

[242] *Zaiwalla & Co v Walia* [2002] IRLR 697, EAT (£7,500 aggravated damages awarded for the way in which the defendant firm of solicitors conducted their defence).

[243] *Kuddus v Chief Constable of Leicestershire Constabulary* [2001] UKHL 29, [2002] 2 AC 122, applied to discrimination cases in *Virgo Fidelis Senior School v Boyle* [2004] IRLR 268, EAT, and *Ministry of Defence v Fletcher* [2010] IRLR 25, EAT.

[244] See 7.6.2.

[245] *Marshall v Southampton and South-West Hampshire Area Health Authority (No 2)* [1994] QB 126, [1993] ICR 893, ECJ.

[246] *Wisbey v Commissioner of the City of London Police* [2021] EWCA Civ 650, [2021] IRLR 691, [2021] ICR 1485.

contraventions, which may result in the issue of an unlawful act notice if it discovers breaches of the Act; such a notice may require the recipient to prepare an action plan for the purpose of avoiding any repetition, and it may contain requirements to be met by the employer, who has six weeks in which to appeal against it to a tribunal. If there is no appeal, or an appeal is dismissed, the notice becomes final, and any further contraventions of it may be restrained by injunction at the suit of the Commission.[247] The Commission may also enter into legally binding agreements to rectify the situation. There are also further, more specific powers given to the Commission to take action against discriminatory advertisements,[248] and to give practical help to individuals to bring discrimination claims against their employers.[249]

4.3 Sex discrimination

It will not have escaped the notice of alert readers that many of the leading cases about concepts such as indirect discrimination and harassment involve sex discrimination. This is because the SDA was the first of the modern anti-discrimination statutes in the UK. As a result, a great deal has already been discussed in this chapter about issues that arise under sex discrimination.

Although protection against sex discrimination has been long-established, sex is not defined within the legislation. We are told 'man' means a male of any age and that 'woman' means a female of any age, but female and male are not defined further.[250] Therefore, the Equality Act does not say whether sex refers to biological characteristics or the socially constructed ideas of gender, which would include trans people living in their affirmed gender.

The Supreme Court recently had to determine which of these definitions of sex was correct in the high profile case of *For Women Scotland v The Scottish Ministers*.[251] The Supreme Court ultimately decided that sex means biological sex, rather than legal sex. Therefore, references to 'man' and 'woman' in the Equality Act describe the sex of a person at birth. The effect of this is that transgender people cannot claim protection from sex discrimination in their acquired gender, even if they have a Gender Recognition Certificate (GRC). This does not mean that transgender people are left with no protection from the Equality Act, as they are still covered by the protected characteristic of gender reassignment (see 4.9). In reaching this decision, the Supreme Court found that there had to be a consistent definition given to the word 'woman' throughout the legislation. It was determined therefore that references to pregnant and breastfeeding women, for example, could only be interpreted as referring to biological females. It was also reasoned that adopting a different definition of sex would undermine the justifications for single-sex spaces.[252]

[247] Equality Act 2006, ss 20–24. On the nature of an appeal against a non-discrimination notice, see *Commission for Racial Equality v Amari Plastics Ltd* [1982] ICR 304, [1982] IRLR 252, CA; if the formal investigation is not carried out in accordance with the stipulated procedure, any resulting non-discrimination notice is void: *Re Prestige Group plc, Commission for Racial Equality v Prestige Group plc* [1984] ICR 473, [1984] IRLR 166, HL.

[248] Equality Act 2006, s 25. [249] Equality Act 2006, s 28.

[250] S 212. [251] UKSC 16. [252] [220].

To say this case and ruling has been controversial is an understatement![253] One of the main controversies has been the impact this will have on single-sex spaces:

> The ruling does not require services to exclude trans people from all single-sex spaces. It does, however, clarify that if a service operates a single-sex space, for example a gym changing room, then exclusion is based on biological sex and not certified sex. Neither the Court nor the government has said how 'biological sex' would be defined or proven.[254]

The EHRC are still in the process of updating their codes of practice in light of the decision, but an interim update followed the above thinking, suggesting that companies can stop transgender people from accessing single-sex spaces in line with their lived gender. This is not only 'extremely distressing for trans people who will be afraid to use the bathrooms and changing rooms that accord with their lived sex-gender' but also very confusing for service providers.[255] After all, service providers cannot simply ask someone's biological sex—doing so, and requiring a trans person to use the facilities associated with their biological sex, risks outing trans people which would of course be discriminatory in and of itself. Yet failing to provide single-sex spaces divided on biology now also risks being discriminatory on the grounds of sex. Service providers are, therefore, put between the proverbial 'rock' and 'hard-place'.

With finalized EHRC guidance yet to be published and more legal action expected on this topic, from those on both sides of the argument, the definition of sex in the Equality Act is likely to remain topical for some time.

This rest of this section deals not with sex discrimination as a whole, but with two important problems that arise under gender discrimination law:

- Dress and appearance rules, which, while not strictly unique to gender, are not often encountered under other grounds; and
- The law on equality of terms of employment between the sexes, which is dealt with by an entirely different legal model usually referred to as 'equal pay'.

Before turning to those points, we should note that there is an exception to liability for sex discrimination which relates to religion. This also applies to sexual orientation and is discussed in 4.4.

4.3.1 **Dress and appearance rules**

It was mentioned above that sometimes courts and tribunals cannot see past time-honoured conventions to give effect to what discrimination statutes clearly require them to do. One such area is dress and appearance rules. It is not uncommon for employers to impose rules on employees concerning their dress and appearance while at work either for operational reasons (eg in the interests of safety and hygiene) or simply because the

[253] For more reading, see Gascoigne 'Sex, Statutory Interpretation and the Supreme Court: A Comment on *For Women Scotland v Scottish Ministers* for Employment Law and Practice' (2025) 54 ILJ 693. On two different sides of the debate, see Cowan 'Trans Rights, Queer Times: In Search of a New Hope' (2025) *47 Journal of Social Welfare and Family Law* 108; and Foran 'Defining Sex in Law' (2025) LQR 141; Foran, 'For Women Scotland: Is Legal Recognition of Biological Sex a Violation of Human Rights?', UK Constitutional Law Blog (15 May 2025) available at https://ukconstitutionallaw.org/.

[254] Maine '*For Women Scotland*: An Interpretation of Equality Rooted in Biology' (2025) Journal of Social Welfare and Family Law 1.

[255] Cowan 'Trans Rights, Queer Times: In Search of a New Hope' (2025) 47 Journal of Social Welfare and Family Law 108, 122.

employer is seeking to promote a particular corporate image. Such rules often impose different requirements on men and women, reflecting current perceptions of conventional appearance, yet it could be argued that, for example, a requirement on female employees to wear skirts and not trousers is subjecting them to less favourable treatment because of their sex. One rationale of the anti-discrimination legislation was to tackle discrimination which results from gender stereotyping, yet arguably what is regarded as 'conventional' in terms of appearance is itself permeated by gender stereotyping.

The approach of the courts and tribunals to this issue has been to hold that there is no infringement of the Act where the employer imposes an appearance code which has different rules for men and women, as long as the code enforces a common principle of smartness or conventionality *and* taken as a whole neither gender is treated less favourably. So, for example, in *Schmidt v Austicks Bookshops Ltd*,[256] the employer imposed a rule that women could not wear trousers at work and had to wear overalls, while men were not allowed to wear T-shirts. A female employee complained that the rule against trousers was unlawful under the Act, but the EAT held against her on the ground that the employer applied rules on clothing to all employees, although in the nature of things the rules were not the same given the difference between the sexes.[257] According to the EAT, an employer is entitled to a large measure of discretion in controlling the image of his establishment, including the appearance of the staff, especially where they come into contact with the public.

The *Schmidt* approach was approved by the Court of Appeal in *Smith v Safeway plc*.[258] In that case, the employers' appearance code placed restrictions on hair length which applied to men only; women were allowed to have long hair provided it was tied back. The complainant was dismissed because he refused to cut off his ponytail. The tribunal, following *Schmidt*, held that the treatment of the complainant was not less favourable than that which would have been accorded to a woman because the code, although different for men and women, enforced a common standard of smartness and conventionality, and taken as a whole it could not be said that either gender was treated less favourably. The EAT upheld the employee's appeal,[259] holding that since the employer's rules restricted only the hair length of men, the treatment of the complainant was self-evidently less favourable, and that the employer's requirements with respect to hairstyle were capable of being applied to both men and women in such a way as to take account of convention (eg by allowing men to have a ponytail), without placing a restriction on hair length for men only. However, the Court of Appeal overturned the EAT in favour of a more conventional interpretation of *Schmidt*. According to Phillips LJ, the starting point of the reasoning in *Schmidt*, which he considered to be 'plainly correct', was that it was necessary to show not merely that the sexes were treated differently, but that the treatment accorded to one was less favourable than the treatment accorded to the other.[260]

256 [1978] ICR 85, [1977] IRLR 360, EAT.

257 See also *Burrett v West Birmingham Health Authority* [1994] IRLR 7, EAT, where it was held that a female nurse who was required to wear a cap as part of her uniform was not less favourably treated on grounds of sex than male nurses who were not required to wear a cap, since the requirement to wear a uniform applied equally to male and female nurses. Her honestly held belief that the requirement to wear a cap was demeaning was held not to be determinative of whether or not there was less favourable treatment.

258 [1996] ICR 868, [1996] IRLR 456, CA.

259 [1995] ICR 472, [1995] IRLR 132, EAT, Pill J dissenting.

260 According to Phillips LJ, the fact that a restriction applied to permanent characteristics such as hair length or colour, and therefore extended beyond the workplace, was a factor to be taken into account in considering whether a code treats one sex less favourably than the other, but does not affect the test itself.

There are, however, four reasons why the existing case law on dress and appearance codes should be approached with caution. First, the imposition of restrictions on how a person chooses to present himself or herself could be seen as an infringement of that person's right to respect for private and family life under Article 8 of the European Convention on Human Rights. Under the Human Rights Act 1998, passed since these cases were decided, tribunals are obliged to interpret statutes, if they can, in such a way as to comply with the Convention.

Second, where a person adopts a particular form of dress in accordance with the customs or requirements of their religion, the imposition of a dress code that conflicts with the requirements of that religion could constitute unlawful discrimination on grounds of religion or belief.[261]

Third, what is regarded as 'conventional' in relation to dress and appearance may change with time, and employers may be expected to modify their dress and appearance rules to reflect those changes. In *G v Head Teacher and Governors of St Gregory's Catholic Science College*,[262] a school dress code prohibiting cornrows was found to be indirectly discriminatory on grounds of race. In *McConomy v Croft Inns Ltd*,[263] a case on discrimination in the provision of goods and services under Part 3 of the Sex Discrimination Act, it was held to be unlawfully discriminatory for a public house to refuse to serve a man for wearing earrings where there was no similar objection to women wearing earrings. Certain employment tribunal decisions in which dress codes prohibiting women from wearing trousers at work have been held to be discriminatory[264] confirm the inherently transient nature of conventions of dress and appearance and indicate that standards of what is 'conventional' in relation to appearance have shifted somewhat in the years since *Schmidt*; but the decision in *Smith v Safeway plc* suggests that the courts are not yet ready to accept as conventional a man who turns up for work wearing a ponytail.

Fourth, since 2010, the protected characteristic of gender reassignment applies to anyone who is proposing to undergo or has undergone a process of gender reassignment, whether or not any medical treatment is involved, and there is much more public sensitivity to trans issues than even a few years ago. An employer who formerly might have been confident about the legality of a rule not permitting an employee of one sex to dress like the other is likely now, rightly, to be cautious about whether such a rule would be indirectly discriminatory against an employee who was changing, or had changed, gender.

4.3.2 **Equal pay**

4.3.2.1 **History of this separate legal regime**

The Equal Pay Act 1970 was aimed at preventing discrimination between men and women as regards terms and conditions of employment. As such, it only applied to the contractual terms of employment and if a case arose concerning alleged discrimination in relation to other aspects of employment, that would come under the Sex Discrimination Act 1975.[265]

This division reflected the separate EU legislation on equality of terms, on the one hand, and on other kinds of sex discrimination, on the other hand. The principle of equal pay for equal work for men and women has always been set out in the fundamental treaty of the European Union,[266] whereas the remainder of the EU law of discrimination is differently

[261] See 4.6. [262] [2011] EWHC 1452 (Admin), [2011] All ER (D) 113.

[263] [1992] IRLR 561, NIHC.

[264] See eg *Owen v Professional Golfers' Association* (January 2000, unreported), ET. [265] See 4.2.1.

[266] Originally in Art 119 of the 1957 Treaty of Rome and now in Art 157 of the Treaty on the Functioning of the European Union.

worded and has always been contained in Directives. This distinction is manifested in the Equality Act 2010 which has a separate Chapter on 'Equality of Terms'. The equality of pay/terms model is very different from the model applicable to the rest of the law on discrimination, although it does adopt some concepts such as 'justification' of indirectly discriminatory practices.

The Equal Pay Act 1970 initially led to a significant shift in relative pay levels as between men and women,[267] but it became clear that it was subject to certain limitations which meant that it could only go so far. However, since the early 1980s the whole area has been revitalized by decisions of the CJEU about the true meaning of the right to equal pay set out in the Treaty on the Functioning of the European Union and its predecessors. Article 157 of the TFEU provides that each member state shall 'ensure and subsequently maintain the principle that men and women shall receive equal pay for equal work'. This article prevails over conflicting provisions of domestic law, and so long as the UK was a member of the EU if domestic law were found wanting when measured against this yardstick, enforcement proceedings could be brought in the CJEU in order to enforce compliance; however since Brexit this option is no longer available.

In Case 61/81 *EC Commission v United Kingdom*,[268] the CJEU held that the Equal Pay Act 1970 did not comply with the treaty requirements because it only enabled a woman to claim pay equal to that of a man who was either doing similar work or had a job that was different but which had been held in a job evaluation study to be of the same value. The CJEU held that equal pay must be accorded in any case where different jobs were 'work of equal value' even if there was no pre-existing job evaluation study. This led to amendments to the UK legislation in 1983.[269]

In another important decision the CJEU held, in *Barber v Guardian Royal Exchange Assurance Group*,[270] that benefits under a contracted-out, private occupational pension scheme fall within the scope of the word 'pay'. This led to the extension of the UK legislation to create a new right to equal treatment in occupational pension schemes, and also resulted in the equalization of state pensionable ages at 65.

While EU law undeniably revitalized the domestic law on equal pay, the current position is far from satisfactory. The relevant principles and procedures are extremely complex and time-consuming (one well-known case involving a group of NHS speech therapists took 14 years to resolve).[271] The pay gap between men and women has declined steadily over the years, but has not disappeared. According to Office for National Statistics data,[272] in 1997 the median hourly pay of female full-time workers was 17.4 per cent less than that of male full-time workers, whereas in 2024 the gap had reduced to 7 per cent. The same statistics show that for part-time employees the median hourly pay of women has for the past 20 years always been greater than that of men (currently by 3 per cent). This may at first sight appear promising, however since part-time jobs are generally less well paid and more women work part-time than men, the gender pay gap for all

[267] By 1977, women's pay as a proportion of men's had risen to 75.5 per cent, compared with 63 per cent in 1970.

[268] [1982] ICR 578, [1982] IRLR 333, ECJ.

[269] Art 157 now expressly confers a right to equal pay for work of equal value: 'Each Member State shall ensure that the principle of equal pay for male and female workers for equal work *or work of equal value* is applied' (emphasis added).

[270] [1991] 1 QB 344, [1990] ICR 616, ECJ.

[271] *Guardian*, 8 May 2000, reporting a £12m settlement for 351 NHS staff, negotiated between the Department of Health and MSF union; *Enderby v Frenchay Health Authority*.

[272] *Gender Pay Gap in the UK: 2024* available at <https://www.ons.gov.uk/employmentandlabourmarket/peopleinwork/earningsandworkinghours/bulletins/genderpaygapintheuk/2024>.

workers (both full- and part-time) in 2024 was 13.1 per cent—much more than the gap in full-time workers' pay. For age groups under 40 years, the gender pay gap for full-time employees is now close to zero—it is 1.3 per cent for those aged 22–29,—but women's pay starts to lag in the 30- to 39-year age band. This gap continues to grow as women get older. This strongly suggests that the pay gap is linked with motherhood.[273]

The main reasons for the gender pay gap have long been known. In 1999, an Equal Pay Task Force identified three main factors which contribute to it: occupational segregation (ie the concentration of women in low-paid jobs such as shop assistants, secretaries, nurses, and teachers); the unequal impact of women's family responsibilities; and pay discrimination.[274] The task force made a number of recommendations, the principal one being a call for the enactment of a legal duty on employers to carry out regular equal pay reviews. It recognized that as most employers do not think they have a gender pay gap, recognizing the issue is the primary hurdle.[275]

This suggestion was eventually followed in 2017, when a power in the Equality Act 2010 was used to adopt regulations which require that employers with 250 or more employees must report their gender pay statistics annually.[276] The reports must cover both average hourly pay and bonuses. These statistics must be published on the employer's public website and be supplied to the government, which makes them available at <https://gender-pay-gap.service.gov.uk/>. The hope is that the risk of scrutiny by the public generally, and by potential recruits to jobs, will encourage employers to seek to reduce their pay gap—or at least to examine whether the pay gap can be justified.

Some minor changes to these rules on gender pay gap reporting could soon be introduced. The Employment Rights Act 2025 includes a power to introduce regulations which would require employers to name the providers or employers of any contract workers.[277] If introduced, this would slightly enhance the requirements placed on employers, but the gender pay gap data would still not include the pay of contract workers. Further regulations could also be introduced which would require employers with 250 employees or more to develop and publish an 'equality action plan,' showing what steps they are taking in relation to gender equality.[278] The current Labour government has also conducted a consultation into extending this reporting duty to the grounds of ethnicity and disability in the expected Equality (Race and Disability) Bill (see 4.5 and 4.7).

Another innovation in the 2010 Act is the s 77 extension of victimization protection to those who engage in 'discussions with colleagues about the terms' of their employment. This effectively outlaws contractual confidentiality clauses forbidding employees to discuss their pay with other employees, as any attempt to enforce it would impose a detriment for engaging in a protected act, and thus constitute victimization.

Since 2013, a new s 139A of the Equality Act 2010 has enabled the making of regulations which compel an employment tribunal which has found an employer to be in breach of the law of equal pay to order the employer to conduct an equal pay audit to identify if there are other breaches within their workforce. This is considered in 4.3.2.9.

273 See Carr 'The Motherhood Penalty' 19 March 2023 available at <https://www.henley.ac.uk/news/2023/the-motherhood-penalty>.

274 <https://www.eurofound.europa.eu/en/publications/all/eoc-urges-new-action-equal-pay#overview>.

275 Other recommendations included reforms to streamline the tribunal process in equal pay cases, the use of hypothetical comparators, and the extension to equal pay cases of the statutory questionnaire procedure for discrimination claims.

276 The Equality Act 2010 (Gender Pay Gap) Regulations 2017, SI 2017/172 and The Equality Act 2010 (Specific Duties and Public Authorities) Regulations 2017, SI 2017/353.

277 Equality Act 2010, s 78 (3A). Introduced Employment Rights Act 2025, s 34.

278 Equality Act 2010, s 78A, amended by Employment Rights Act 2025, s 33.

Equal pay is, unfortunately, an area where UK employees will soon be worse off than their EU counterparts as a result of Brexit. This is because they will miss out on the changes introduced by the Pay Transparency Directive 2023, including:

- obliging employers to provide starting salary or salary range prior to the interview. Candidates cannot be asked about their current or previous salaries.
- employees can request information about their pay and how it compares to others, helping them to identify any pay gaps.
- employers with over 250 employees will have to report their gender pay gap annually, whilst those with 100 employees will have to report it every three years.
- workers will be entitled to compensation when they experience pay discrimination. Employers can face sanctions for discriminatory employers.
- the burden of proof is shifted from the employee to the employer.[279]

This will come into force in June 2026. The UK government has opened a call for evidence about whether these sorts of measures should also be extended to the UK, so they might form a part of the expected Equality (Race and Disability) Bill. Even if the Directive does not directly impact the UK, it is hoped it might still raise awareness and expectations regarding equal pay.

4.3.2.2 **The law on equality of terms—summary**

Under s 66 of the Act, every employee's[280] contract is deemed to include an 'equality clause'[281] to the effect that (a) if any term in the contract is less favourable than a similar term in the contract of a person of the opposite sex, that term is to be treated as modified so that it is not less favourable than the other term, and (b) if the contract does not include a beneficial term which appears in the other's contract, the contract shall be treated as including that term.[282]

It has been established that less favourable treatment in the exercise of discretion authorized under the contract (such as the allocation of share options permitted, but not specified, under the contract) is sex discrimination, not a matter of equality of terms.[283] This reflects the long-standing separate treatment of equal pay between the sexes on the one hand and sex discrimination on the other.

For the equality clause to operate, there must be an actual, rather than merely hypothetical, comparator fellow employee of the opposite sex in one of the three following categories:

- someone employed on 'like work';
- someone employed on 'work rated as equivalent'; or
- someone employed in 'work of equal value'.[284]

These three categories of comparator are considered in detail below in 4.3.2.2–4.3.2.4. The comparator must be 'in the same employment' and this is dealt with in 4.3.2.5.

The effect of this implied equality clause is that where there is a qualifying comparator who has a higher rate of pay or some other better term of employment, this raises a presumption that the difference is due to sex discrimination, and the contract will be

[279] 2023/970. [280] This refers to 'employee' in the extended Equality Act sense: see 4.2.1.

[281] See *Equal Pay Statutory Code of Practice* (Equality and Human Rights Commission 2011).

[282] The effect of an equality clause was considered by the House of Lords in *Hayward v Cammell Laird Shipbuilders Ltd* [1988] ICR 464, [1988] IRLR 257, considered presently.

[283] *Hosso v European Credit Management* [2011] EWCA Civ 1589, (CA).

[284] Three other heads were added in 2005 to deal specifically with equal pay issues in maternity pay.

modified by the equality clause, subject to a 'material factor' defence. This defence (considered in 4.3.2) applies if the employer can show that the difference in terms is genuinely due to some material factor other than the difference of sex, and that the reason for the difference is not unjustified indirect sex discrimination.

The equality clause operates on a term-by-term basis, so an employer cannot for example argue that lower pay for women is balanced out by a right to more annual leave than men: *Hayward v Cammell Laird Shipbuilders Ltd*.[285] An employee is entitled to keep the benefit of those terms which are better than those of her comparator while still being entitled to the equality of basic pay that she had sought all along.[286] This term-by-term approach also applies *within* the category of pay: in *McNeil v HMRC* Simler J said that 'where the contract makes discrete provision for basic pay, bonus, and other benefits, those discrete provisions cannot be lumped together as one term of the contract merely because they provide for total remuneration'.[287]

4.3.2.3 **Like work**

A person who wants to complain of unequal pay has, as a first option, to make a comparison with someone of the opposite sex who is employed on 'like work'. This is defined in s 65(2) as work that is 'the same or broadly similar', such that any differences between the things the applicant does and the things done by the comparator 'are not of practical importance in relation to terms of their work'.

In deciding whether work is the same or broadly similar, the tribunal should take a wide view. Thus in *Capper Pass Ltd v Lawton*,[288] a female cook who prepared 10–20 lunches for directors was held to be employed on like work with two male assistant chefs who helped to provide many more meals at more times of the day in the works canteen, particularly as a generally similar type of work was involved, with similar skill and knowledge required to do it. In deciding upon similarity or otherwise, the tribunal is not confined to the detailed physical processes performed by the employees in question, but may consider more general matters such as differences in responsibility (as in the case of two buyers, where the higher-paid male buyer is in fact employed to buy more expensive goods, thereby incurring greater responsibility if he buys poor goods),[289] or the status of the complainant as a 'trainee'.[290] If matters such as these are taken into account in a bona fide grading scheme, under which the man and the woman are genuinely on different grades, then the man and the woman will not be held to be on 'like work' and the woman will not be able to claim equality.[291]

In looking to see whether any differences are of practical importance the tribunal should take an equally broad approach, as the very concept of 'broadly similar' work necessarily implies differences in detail. These differences should not defeat a claim for equality unless they are such as the tribunal would expect in practice to be reflected in different terms and conditions of employment.[292] Section 65(3) states that in comparing work, 'regard shall be had to the frequency or otherwise with which any such differences occur in practice as

[285] [1988] ICR 464, [1988] IRLR 257, HL (noted Napier (1988) NLJ 341); revsg [1987] ICR 682, [1987] IRLR 186, CA.

[286] This approach is consistent with EU law: *Barber v Guardian Royal Exchange Assurance Group* [1991] 1 QB 344, [1990] ICR 616, ECJ. See also *Jorgensen v Foreningen af Speciallaeger* [2000] IRLR 726 ECJ; *Brunnhofer v Bank der Osterreichischen Postsparkasse AG* [2001] IRLR 571 ECJ.

[287] [2018] IRLR 398, EAT (upheld on appeal, [2019] EWCA Civ 1112, [2019] IRLR 915). See also *Lloyds Banking Group Pension Trustees Ltd v Lloyds Bank Plc* [2018] EWHC 2839 (Ch).

[288] [1977] ICR 83, [1976] IRLR 366.

[289] *Eaton Ltd v Nuttall* [1977] ICR 272, [1977] IRLR 71.

[290] *De Brito v Standard Chartered Bank Ltd* [1978] ICR 650, EAT.

[291] *Capper Pass Ltd v Allan* [1980] ICR 194, [1980] IRLR 236, EAT.

[292] *Capper Pass Ltd v Lawton* [1977] ICR 83 at 87H, [1976] IRLR 366 at 367.

well as to the nature and extent of the differences'. Thus, the tribunal must look at the duties actually performed, not those theoretically possible. In *Shields v Coomes (Holdings) Ltd*,[293] a male counterhand at a betting shop was paid at a higher hourly rate than a female counter-hand, the claimed difference being that the man was there partly as a deterrent to potential troublemakers; the Court of Appeal held that the woman was entitled to equal pay since there was no evidence of the man in question being particularly skilled or specially trained for this extra function or of there in fact ever having been any particular trouble for him to deal with. The Court held that the tribunal, in finding for the employer, had paid too much attention to bare contractual obligations and too little to the practicalities.

A further point is that the tribunal, in making its comparison, must look at the duties performed by the woman and the man, not at the time at which they are performed. In *Dugdale v Kraft Foods Ltd*,[294] female quality control workers performed prima facie similar work to that done by male quality control workers, but the men were paid at a higher basic rate because they worked night shifts and certain Sundays. The tribunal thought that this was a material difference, but the EAT reversed this decision and remitted the case to another tribunal, which eventually awarded equal basic pay to a majority of the applicants in the case.[295] Of course, if the like work done by the male comparator is performed at antisocial hours, or in unfavourable conditions, this may amount to a material difference justifying the payment of extra remuneration (special premia for overtime, night working, Sunday shifts, and so on) provided that such premia genuinely reflect the extra inconvenience and are not so large that they are seen as simply a way of indirectly reintroducing a sex-based distinction. In such cases, the work is 'like work' but the extra payments are permitted by the material factor defence (see 4.3.2.7). For example, in the *Dugdale* case, the Industrial Tribunal ruled that a night shift premium did not offend against the right to equal pay.

Finally, it is implicit in what has already been said that a claim under this head should not be defeated simply on the grounds that the applicant and her comparator have different qualifications (although that may give rise to a 'genuine material factor' defence: see 4.3.2.7). However, in *Angestelltenbetriebsrat der Wiener Gebietskrankenkasse v Wiener Gebietskrankenkasse*,[296] the CJEU surprisingly held that for the purposes of Article 157 and the Equal Pay Directive, graduate psychologists employed as psychotherapists were not to be regarded as doing the 'same work' as trained doctors employed to do the same job, 'where the same activities are performed over a considerable length of time by persons the basis of whose qualification to exercise their profession is different'. The decision can perhaps be defended on its facts, on the grounds that the difference in the qualifications of the two groups probably meant that their level of performance was qualitatively different, but as a general proposition it is respectfully doubted.

4.3.2.4 **Work rated as equivalent**

An alternative is for a claimant to choose a comparator whose work has been rated as equivalent. This means that the two jobs have been given an equal value in terms of the demands on the worker by a job evaluation scheme.[297] The Act does not lay down detailed

[293] [1978] ICR 1159, [1978] IRLR 263, CA; see also *Redland Roof Tiles v Harper* [1977] ICR 349, EAT.

[294] [1977] ICR 48, [1976] IRLR 368. See also *Electrolux Ltd v Hutchinson* [1977] ICR 252, [1976] IRLR 410.

[295] *Dugdale v Kraft Foods Ltd* [1977] IRLR 160, IT.

[296] Case C-309/97 [2000] ICR 1134, [1999] IRLR 804, ECJ. See also *Glasgow City Council v Marshall* [2000] ICR 196, [2000] IRLR 272, HL.

[297] Equality Act 2010, s 64(4). In *Springboard Sunderland Trust v Robson* [1992] ICR 554, [1992] IRLR 261, the EAT held that where a job evaluation scheme operates by awarding points for different criteria, what matters is whether the woman and her comparator have been placed in the same grade under the scheme, and not the precise number of points awarded. If necessary, a woman can compare herself with a man rated *lower* than her (but paid more highly): *Redcar & Cleveland BC v Bainbridge* [2007] IRLR 91, EAT.

requirements for such a scheme,[298] but it is in mandatory terms, so that where there has been such a study a tribunal should act upon its recommendations, even if the parties who drafted it are no longer happy with it;[299] once the scheme has been worked out, it will be binding for the purposes of the Act and may be relied on by the claimant, even if the employer has not in fact put it into effect.[300] However, to be binding the job evaluation scheme must be a valid scheme, in the sense that it must be non-discriminatory, objective, and capable of impartial application:

> [S]ubsection (5) [the predecessor to s 64(4)] can only apply to what may be called a valid evaluation study. By that, we mean a study satisfying the test of being thorough in analysis and capable of impartial application. It should be possible by applying the study to arrive at the position of a particular employee at a particular point in a particular salary grade without taking other matters into account except those unconnected with the nature of the work . . . One which does not satisfy that test, and requires the management to make a subjective judgment concerning the nature of the work before the employee can be fitted into the appropriate place in the appropriate salary grade, would seem to us not to be a valid study for the purposes of subsection (5).[301]

4.3.2.5 **Work of equal value**

The third possibility is for the claimant to assert that their work is 'is equal to [a comparator's] work in terms of the demands made on [the claimant] by reference to factors such as effort, skill and decision, of equal value to that of a man in the same employment'.[302]

The immediate problem is that this takes the tribunals away from matters of relatively observable fact (Is the work the same or similar? Has the employer got a job evaluation study that applies to this woman?) and into the realm of assessment of value and the almost religious mysteries of job evaluation, for which, arguably, a tribunal as a judicial body is not particularly well suited. The compromise has been to keep the procedure judicial but to make it heavily dependent in practice on the opinion of an independent expert appointed by ACAS from a panel kept by it of persons knowledgeable in the techniques of job evaluation.

The equal value procedure has been highly controversial, not least because of the excessive delays which have bedevilled it since its introduction. In the early years, the average

[298] For some guidance on standard forms of schemes, see *Eaton Ltd v Nuttall* [1977] ICR 272 at 278, [1977] IRLR 71 at 74.

[299] *Greene v Broxtowe District Council* [1977] ICR 241, [1977] IRLR 34, EAT.

[300] *O'Brien v Sim-Chem Ltd* [1980] ICR 573, [1980] IRLR 373, HL. For this principle to apply, however, the scheme must have been worked out and accepted as valid by the parties who had agreed to carry it out: *Arnold v Beecham Group Ltd* [1982] ICR 744, [1982] IRLR 307.

[301] *Eaton Ltd v Nuttall* [1977] ICR 272 at 277H, [1977] IRLR 71 at 74. In *Bromley v H & J Quick Ltd* [1988] ICR 623, [1988] IRLR 249 the Court of Appeal held that, to be valid under s 1(5), an employer-commissioned job evaluation must be 'analytical' in nature, ie based on the demands made on employees under various discrete headings rather than on any job 'ranking' or 'felt fair' basis, which would be too vague. Art 1 of the Equal Pay Directive (Directive 75/117/EEC) also has a requirement that an evaluation study must be fair, in the sense of being based on the same criteria for men and women, and so drawn up as to exclude any discrimination on the grounds of sex: see *Rummler v Dato-Druck GmbH* Case 237/85 [1987] ICR 774, [1987] IRLR 32, ECJ.

[302] Equality Act 2010, s 65(6). In *Murphy v Bord Telecom Eireann* Case 157/86 [1988] ICR 445, [1988] IRLR 267, ECJ the employer raised the astonishing defence in an equal value case that the women who were paid less than the male comparator could not claim equality because they were in fact engaged on work of *higher* value than his; this was held by the ECJ to be contrary to Art 141 and so, under EC law at least, a woman can claim equal pay for work that is at least of equal value to that of the male comparator.

time taken to resolve equal value cases was more than two and a half years, and some claims took far longer. It was widely thought that the decline in the number of equal pay complaints during the 1980s was (at least in part) a result of the length and complexity of the tribunal processes concerned,[303] and some even went so far as to suggest that the system was designed to deter claims. By the early 1990s the case for a radical overhaul of the equal value procedures had become overwhelming.

Since then there has been some change.[304] Historically, an independent expert's report as to whether the work was of 'equal value' was required, but these have not been required since 2004. The 2024 amendments detail that tribunals can now decide whether to deal with the matter itself or to require a report at a 'stage one' hearing. If the tribunal can determine this themselves, the case goes straight to a substantive hearing. If a report is required, a 'stage two' hearing will determine the 'facts relating to the question'.[305] The report will focus only on these questions. The report is not considered conclusive at the final, substantive hearing.

The 2004 reforms also placed emphasis on the setting of timetables and a greater element of case management (though with the quid pro quo that the tribunal lost its power to rule out a claim at a very early stage on the basis that it had no reasonable chance of success). Despite these changes, an equal value claim is of necessity complex, and not to be embarked upon by the faint-hearted.

These equal value claims have recently been in the spotlight as a tribunal found that Next store-based staff, who are predominantly female, were found to be doing work of equal value to Next's warehouse-based employees, who are predominantly male.[306] With over 3,500 claimants currently, this is likely to cost the employer millions of pounds in compensation. This is likely to be the first of many similar cases, where large groups of employees bring claims against similar, large retail employers, including supermarkets. Next has also said they will appeal this decision, so watch this space!

4.3.2.6 **The area of comparison**

Unlike the general prohibition on discrimination, which works on the basis of a comparison between the treatment of the applicant and that of a hypothetical comparator, the equal terms claim is based on a comparison with a named comparator (or comparators). The requirement to identify an actual comparator used to be a major hurdle for an applicant, particularly if they work for an organization where jobs are de facto segregated along gender lines. This has to some extent been eased by the introduction of the ability to choose a comparator doing a different job which is of 'equal value' but, as explained in 4.3.2.5, the process of bringing an equal value claim is long and complex.

The general rule on the area of comparison in the Act is that the comparator must be 'in the same employment' as the applicant, in the sense of being, first, employed by the same employer (or by an 'associated employer', which is essentially a limited company in the same group[307]); this must, second, be at the same establishment, or at another establishment at which common terms and conditions of employment are observed, either generally or for employees of relevant classes.[308]

[303] ACAS Annual Report, 1992, p 23; EOC Annual Report, 1991, p 6.

[304] Employment Tribunal Procedure Rules 2024 2024/1155, Sch 2, replaced Employment Tribunals (Constitution and Rules of Procedure) Regulations 2013, SI 2013/1237, Sch 3.

[305] Sch 2, s 6. [306] Thandi and Others v Next Retail Ltd and Next Distribution Ltd 1302019/2018.

[307] Equality Act 2010, s 79(4) and (9).

[308] Equality Act 2010, s 79. There is no statutory definition of 'establishment'; for its construction in the context of redundancy consultation (where it is similarly not defined), see 8.1.3.

It is easy to misunderstand what is meant by 'common terms of employment'. The Supreme Court confirmed in *ASDA Stores v Brierley*[309] that the phrase 'common terms apply at the establishment (either generally or as between A [the claimant] and B [the comparator])' does *not* require common terms as between the claimant and the comparator; rather it means that if the comparator had been employed in his job at the claimant's establishment his terms would still be the same ones he is currently on at his actual place of employment. This is referred to in the cases as the '*North* hypothetical'—named after the UKSC case of *Dumfries and Galloway Council v North*.[310] The purpose of the common terms test is (a) to prevent the comparison being made if the terms are different at the comparator's establishment because of, for example, geographical reasons such as London weighting; and (b) to ensure that equal pay claims are not prevented by an employer allocating groups of employees to separate sites so that for example the people working in 'male jobs' at one site can have different terms than those working in 'female jobs' at a different site.

In applying the *North* hypothetical it does not matter that the employer's operations are different in the two establishments so that no one in the claimant's category would ever work at the other establishment or vice versa.

'Common terms and conditions' in this context means 'broadly similar' rather than 'the same'. In *British Coal Corpn v Smith*,[311] some 1,286 women employed as canteen workers or cleaners at 47 different establishments claimed equal pay for work of equal value with 150 male comparators employed as clerical workers or surface mineworkers at 14 different establishments. The House of Lords held that the applicants were in the same employment as their comparators because in each case the terms and conditions of the comparators were governed by national agreements which also applied to the male clerks and surface mineworkers employed at the applicant's establishment (or would have applied if there had been any such men employed at the particular comparator's workplace), even though local variations relating to incentive bonuses and entitlement to concessionary coal meant that the terms and conditions at different establishments for the same classes of worker were not exactly the same. Lord Slynn interpreted the phrase 'common terms and conditions' purposively:

> The real question is what the legislation was seeking to achieve. Was it seeking to exclude a woman's claim unless, subject to de minimis exceptions, there was complete identity of terms and conditions for the comparator at his establishment and those which applied or would apply to a similar male worker at her establishment? Or was the legislation seeking to establish that the terms and conditions of the relevant class were sufficiently similar for a fair comparison to be made, subject always to the employer's right to establish a 'material difference' defence . . . If it was the former then the woman would fail at the first hurdle if there was any difference (other than a de minimis one) between the terms and conditions of the men at the various establishments, since she could not then show that the men were in the same employment as she was. The issue as to whether the differences were material so as to justify different treatment would then never arise. I do not consider that this can have been intended.[312]

In *Pickstone v Freemans plc*[313] the question arose whether a woman doing job A could claim equality of pay through work of *equal value* with a man doing job B if the employer

[309] [2021] UKSC 10, [2021] IRLR 456, [2021] ICR 786. See the note on this case, Fredman 'Inching Forward: Preliminary Victory for Equal Value at Tesco and Asda' (2022) 51 ILJ 166.

[310] [2013] UKSC 45, [2013] IRLR 737, [2013] ICR 993.

[311] [1996] IRLR 404, HL (reversing the Court of Appeal on this point).

[312] [1996] IRLR 404 at 408.

[313] [1988] ICR 697, [1988] IRLR 357, HL.

simply pointed out that there were in fact other men doing job A, and so on 'like work' with the claimant. This literal interpretation (which raised the possibility of an employer being able to avoid an *equal value* claim by employing a token male in an otherwise all-female workforce on job A) was disapproved by the House of Lords, who held that an equal value claim can be brought in such circumstances.

The wording of the Equal Pay Act envisaged a comparison between a man and a woman working for the same employer (or an associated employer) at the same time. However, under European equal terms law the permitted comparison is wider. In *Defrenne v SABENA*,[314] the CJEU referred to employment 'in the same establishment or service, whether public or private', and this has led to a significant broadening of the scope of the permitted comparison. For example, in *Macarthys Ltd v Smith*[315] the CJEU held, on a reference from the Court of Appeal, that a woman has the right under Article 157 to compare her pay with that of her male predecessor in the same job and that is now set out in s 64(2) of the Equality Act.

Perhaps more importantly, European law means that cross-employer comparisons are now possible in circumstances where the difference in pay can be traced to a common source which can put the inequality right, for example where the applicant and her comparator work for public authorities operating under joint control, or where their pay is covered by the same collective agreement or legislative provision. In *Lawrence v Regent Office Care Ltd*,[316] the CJEU indicated that such comparisons were possible but would depend entirely on the facts of each case. The UK courts gave effect to this because Article 157 of the TFEU was directly applicable to UK law.[317] Since Brexit, this rule has been incorporated with domestic legislation, to ensure that the same rights are retained.[318]

Lawrence was reaffirmed by the decision of the CJEU in *Allonby v Accrington & Rossendale College*,[319] but the claim in *Allonby* failed. The case concerned a part-time college lecturer whose services were dispensed with but who was immediately re-engaged through a private educational provider. The CJEU held that he could not make a cross-employer comparison because there was no 'single source' governing terms and conditions. Significant though this case was in limiting the effect of equal pay legislation in a case of the contracting out of services, arguably the most important decision in this area was *Robertson v DEFRA*.[320] For many years, under both Conservative and Labour governments, it was official policy to split up the civil service into separate departments and agencies, each being a separate employer (albeit subject to central control ultimately), setting its own terms and conditions (as a way of moving away from centralized collective bargaining, even though ultimately the employer remained 'the Crown'). What would have wrecked this (given that the civil service unions could not prevent it industrially) was an equal pay action enforcing common terms between different departments. This was what was tried in *Robertson*, where six male civil servants in the Department for Environment, Food & Rural Affairs (DEFRA) claimed equal pay with two female civil servants in the Department of the Environment, Transport and the Regions (DETR). The Court of Appeal dismissed their claims, holding that (within *Lawrence*) there was no 'single source', not even the Treasury or the Minister for the Civil Service; moreover, the fact that ministers *could* reverse the fragmentation policy and re-establish central control was held to be insufficient.

[314] [1976] ECR 455, [1976] ICR 547. [315] [1979] 3 All ER 325, [1979] ICR 785, CA.

[316] [2003] ICR 1092, [2002] IRLR 822, ECJ.

[317] See eg *Asda Stores Ltd v Brierley* [2019] EWCA Civ 44, [2019] IRLR 535.

[318] Equality Act 2010 (Amendment) Regulations 2023.

[319] C-256/01 [2004] ICR 1328, [2004] IRLR 224, ECJ.

[320] [2005] IRLR 363, CA. In *Armstrong v Newcastle upon Tyne NHS Hospitals Trust* [2006] IRLR 124, CA a policy of devolving of management (including pay determination) was so far advanced that there could not be cross-employer comparisons even between hospitals run by the same Trust.

The CJEU appears recently to have moved to a much wider conception of what constitutes a single source. In *K v Tesco Stores Ltd*,[321] the European Court held, albeit without examining the facts in any detail at all, that Tesco Stores Ltd appeared to be a single source for the terms and conditions of all its employees so that equal pay comparisons could be made across all its establishments. If this interpretation of EU law is accepted by the UK courts (since the judgment is a post-Brexit one the UK courts may to have a discretion as to this) then this would avoid the difficult hypothesizing about what terms a comparator would be employed on which is involved the 'common terms and conditions' route to comparison.[322]

4.3.2.7 The genuine material factor defence

Even if there is a prima facie case of inequality, the applicant may still fail if the employer can show, on a balance of probabilities,[323] that the difference in terms is genuinely due to a material factor which is not the difference of sex.[324] (As will be explained below, there is a further condition if the factor is not sex itself but the factor is indirectly discriminatory because it puts women at a particular disadvantage: in such a case it must be justified as a proportionate means of achieving a legitimate aim.)[325]

The courts will scrutinize factors put forward by an employer carefully, and may well hold that an apparently neutral factor is in fact just a reflection of the difference in sex between the claimant and the comparator, and therefore cannot be relied on as a defence. For example, in *Ratcliffe v North Yorkshire County Council*,[326] the House of Lords refused to accept that the imposition of a pay cut for a group of predominantly female school catering assistants to enable the employer to tender for work at a commercially competitive rate was due to a material factor which was not the difference of sex. In that case, the council had established a direct service organization (DSO) for the provision of school meals following the introduction of compulsory competitive tendering, but its catering staff were forced to take a pay cut after it became apparent that the DSO was unable to compete for the school dinner contracts with commercial organizations, who employed only women, while continuing to pay the staff on their existing local government rates. The House of Lords upheld the tribunal's decision that the material factor was in fact due to the difference of sex, in that the labour market for catering staff was almost exclusively female, whereas the council employees employed on work of equivalent value (road sweepers, gardeners, refuse collectors, and leisure attendants) were mostly men:

> Though conscious of the difficult problem facing the employers in seeking to compete with a rival tenderer, I am satisfied that to reduce the women's wages below that of their male comparators was the very kind of discrimination in relation to pay which the Act sought to remove.[327]

[321] C-624/19, [2021] IRLR 699, [2021] ICR 1524, CJEU.

[322] See Fredman 'Inching Forward: Preliminary Victory for Equal Value at Tesco and Asda' (2022) 51 ILJ 166 and European Union (Withdrawal) Act 2018 s 6(2), 7A and Withdrawal Agreement Act 86.

[323] *National Vulcan Engineering Insurance Group Ltd v Wade* [1978] ICR 800, [1978] IRLR 225. This is consistent with EC law, which placed the burden of proof on the employer where a pay system is marked by a 'total lack of transparency': *Handels-og Kontorfunktionaerernes Forbund I Danmark v Dansk Arbejdsgiverforening (acting for Danfoss)* Case C-109/88 [1991] ICR 74, [1989] IRLR 532.

[324] Equality Act 2010, s 69(1). The employer must prove (a) that the variation is genuinely due to a material factor, and (b) that this is not due to the difference of sex: *Financial Times Ltd v Byrne (No 2)* [1992] IRLR 163; see also *Barber v NCR (Manufacturing) Ltd* [1993] IRLR 95, EAT.

[325] Equality Act s 69(1)(b) and (2).

[326] [1995] 3 All ER 597, [1995] ICR 883, HL.

[327] [1995] 3 All ER 597 at 604, per Lord Slynn. The fact that two men were employed on the same work at the same rate of pay as the applicants did not detract from this conclusion: 'It means no more than that the two men were underpaid compared with other men doing jobs rated as equivalent' ([1995] 3 All ER 597 at 603).

The most obvious examples of genuine non-sex material factors justifying differential treatment are personal differences between the applicant and her comparator, for example factors such as long service, superior qualifications, higher output, or different geographical location,[328] or where the man is on a higher grade under a bona fide, impartial grading scheme, so that, although in fact performing the same sort of work, he is rated more highly at doing it (eg he works more efficiently, or more reliably, and so subject to less supervision).[329]

On the face of things, this concept of a material factor other than sex which justifies a difference in pay is an obvious, straightforward, and fair idea. However, that first impression is deceptive because the material factor which explains the difference in pay may itself be sexually indirectly discriminatory. To deal with that, the CJEU has from its early days imposed a requirement of objective justification like the one that applies in relation to claims of indirect discrimination in the other parts of equality law. This requirement is now expressly set out in s 69(1)(b) and (2) of the Equality Act, which contains the crucial proviso that if the material factor puts A (the claimant) and persons of the same sex doing work equal to A's at a particular disadvantage when compared with persons of the opposite sex, then the material factor must be a proportionate means of achieving a legitimate aim. In other words, if the material factor, while not directly discriminatory against a particular sex, has an indirectly discriminatory effect then, as with ordinary non-pay indirect discrimination, it must be justified as a proportionate means of achieving a legitimate aim.

It is easy to see how this similarity with ordinary non-pay discrimination has led some to talk and write about 'direct pay discrimination' and 'indirect pay discrimination', but this is a potentially misleading shorthand. It is important always to remember that the starting point is quite different in equal pay cases: a claimant needs only to show that her pay (or other contractual term) is less favourable than that of a legitimate comparator of the other sex and she does not need to establish that the reason for this is either direct or indirect sex discrimination. She will win unless the employer can show that the reason for the difference is a material factor which is neither sex-tainted nor indirectly discriminatory.

A further source of confusion is that at one time it appeared that there were two situations in which objective justification of a difference in pay was required, one being where the difference stemmed from a provision, criterion, or practice imposed by the employer ('barrier' discrimination) and the other where statistics showed that a predominantly female group had lower pay than a predominantly male group ('*Enderby* type discrimination', so named after a case in which the CJEU held that this had to be read into what is now Article 157 of TFEU). As Underhill LJ recently opined in *McNeil v Commissioners for HM Revenue & Customs*,[330] the better view now is that these are all subsumed in the concept of material factor: a PCP is a type of material factor and so too is being in a different category of employee (like the claimant in *Enderby*); if the factor puts women at particular disadvantage then it only justifies unequal pay if it is a proportionate means of achieving a legitimate aim.

[328] *Navy, Army and Air Force Institutes v Varley* [1977] ICR 11, [1976] IRLR 408, EAT. In *Danfoss* C-109/88 (n 96) the ECJ held that length of service payments are *inherently* justified. This was challenged 15 years later as too sweeping, but *Danfoss* was reaffirmed: *Cadman v HSE* C-17/05 [2006] IRLR 969, ECJ.

[329] *National Vulcan Engineering Insurance Group Ltd v Wade* [1978] ICR 800, [1978] IRLR 225, CA.

[330] [2019] EWCA Civ 1112, [2019] IRLR 915 at paras 14 and 17.

In relation to the degree of disparity required before justification needs to be shown, this was usefully summarized by Simler J in *McNeil v Commissioners for HM Revenue & Customs*[331] as follows:

> [W]here statistics are relied on to demonstrate particular disadvantage, a mere difference in the statistical outcome for men and women is not sufficient: the disparate effect must be 'to such a degree as to amount to indirect discrimination': see *R v Secretary of State, ex p Seymour-Smith* C-167/97, [1999] IRLR 253 (ECJ) at [60]–[65]. Different adjectives have been used by the courts to describe the extent of the difference that must be shown. For example in *London Underground Ltd v Edwards (No 2)* [1998] IRLR 364 at [22], the Court of Appeal held that there must be a substantial and not merely marginal discriminatory effect (disparate impact) as between men and women, so that it can be clearly demonstrated that a prima facie case of (indirect) discrimination exists.

Section 69 also clarified that a justification is required for a pay disparity even if the employer could point to a reason for the disparity that did not stem from, and was not tainted by, sex.[332] This brings equal pay claims in line with the justification defence for indirect discrimination claims.

However, if the material factor does not put women at a particular disadvantage, then there is no need for it to be objectively justified. There is House of Lords authority for this proposition,[333] although the later decision of the CJEU in *Brunnhofer v Bank der Osterreichischen Postsparkasse AG*[334] contains dicta which appear to require the employer to show objective justification for *any* pay disparity between men and women. Subsequent EAT decisions have disagreed on this issue, but the weight of authority is that there is no need to justify the material factor unless it is shown that the material factor constitutes indirect sex discrimination.[335] This is also what s 69 of the Act says.

Summary on whether a material factor requires justification

In short, where the employer relies on a material factor as the reason for the difference in pay—whether that be a PCP imposed by an employer or the fact that the claimant and the comparator are in different job categories—then:

- the material factor must not be directly discriminatory (in the words of s 69(1)(a), it must not involve treating A less favourably because of A's sex);

and

- if the material factor is indirectly discriminatory (in the words of s 69(2), it puts A and persons of the same sex at a disadvantage compared with persons of the opposite sex), then use of the factor to justify the difference in pay must be a proportionate means of achieving a legitimate aim.

[331] [2018] IRLR 398 at para 26.

[332] *McNeil v Commissioners for HM Revenue & Customs* [2019] EWCA Civ 1112, [2019] IRLR 915 at para 53 (dealt with more fully by Simler J in the EAT below [2018] IRLR 398).

[333] *Strathclyde Regional Council v Wallace* [1998] ICR 205, [1998] IRLR 146, HL and *Glasgow City Council v Marshall* [2000] ICR 196, [2000] IRLR 272, HL.

[334] C-381/99 [2001] IRLR 571, ECJ.

[335] See eg most recently *McNeil v Commissioners for HM Revenue & Customs* [2018] IRLR 398, which supports the proposition put forward in the text.

Some troublesome material factors

A material factor which relates to the particular person involved—such as that the comparator is a particularly high-performing worker—is usually fairly easy to deal with. However, a problem area is length of service: since women more often have interruptions to their career than men, a length-of-service pay scheme may put women at a particular disadvantage. Is such a scheme capable of objective justification? One might have thought not, since longer service does not necessarily result in better performance of the work. However, the CJEU has taken a different view. In *Cadman v Health & Safety Executive*,[336] the Court said that length of service goes hand in hand with experience, which generally places the worker in a better position to carry out his duties, and that as a consequence an employer need not provide any specific justification for rewarding seniority with higher pay—in other words, the courts should accept that service-related pay increases were justified. However, the Court said, this is subject to the proviso that 'evidence capable of giving rise to serious doubts as to whether recourse to the criterion of length of service is, in the circumstances, appropriate to attain the abovementioned objective'. In the UK, Arden LJ held in *Wilson v HSE Executive*[337] that the test for serious doubts is a low one: the claimant must put forward evidence from which it can properly be found that the general rule that longer service means better work does not apply, and if she does so then the employer must provide specific justification to show that higher pay for longer service does reward higher performance.

The courts have found non-personal factors, such as market forces and different bargaining arrangements, to be much more difficult than personal factors. The kinds of problems encountered are illustrated by *Rainey v Greater Glasgow Health Board*.[338] The issue in *Rainey* was whether a material difference under what was then s 1(3) of the Equal Pay Act 1970 could relate to matters outside the personal equation, such as the operation of 'market forces'. The case concerned the expansion of a national health prosthetics department by the recruitment of prosthetists (all male, as it happened) from the private sector on their existing level of remuneration, which was higher than that paid to the existing National Health Service prosthetists (who were principally female and included the applicant). The applicant sought equal pay with one of the male entrants, who it was accepted was employed on like work with her. The House of Lords held that the genuine material difference defence under s 1(3) was not limited to personal differences, but was capable of extending to other objectively justified[339] grounds for the woman being paid less:

> The difference must be 'material', which I would construe as meaning 'significant and relevant', and it must be between 'her case and his'. Consideration of a person's case must necessarily involve consideration of all the circumstances of that case. These may well go beyond what is not very happily described as 'the personal equation', ie the personal qualities by way of skill, experience or training which the individual brings to the job. Some circumstances may on examination prove to be not significant or not relevant, but others may do so, though not relating to the personal qualities of the employee. In particular, where there is no question of intentional sex discrimination whether direct or indirect (and there is none here) a difference which is connected with economic factors affecting the efficient carrying on of the employer's business or other activity may well be relevant.[340]

[336] C-17/05, [2006] IRLR 969, ECJ.

[337] [2010] IRLR 59, CA.

[338] [1987] ICR 129, [1987] IRLR 26, HL.

[339] Lord Keith, giving judgment, states that the test here is the same as that under the Sex Discrimination Act 1975 for the justification of a provision, criterion, or practice (as it now is) which indirectly discriminates against women.

[340] [1987] ICR 129 at 140, [1987] IRLR 26 at 29, per Lord Keith.

On the facts of the case, the House of Lords held that the applicant's case failed because there was objective justification for putting the male entrant on to a higher scale (given the need to expand the prosthetic service within a reasonable time), and for not raising the wages of the applicant and other existing prosthetists to that higher rate (since there were 'sound objectively justified administrative reasons' for maintaining their existing position within the overall NHS collectively bargained pay scales). In so holding, the House of Lords adopted the standard objective justification test for indirect discrimination under Article 157 set out by the CJEU in *Bilka-Kaufhaus GmbH v Weber von Hartz*,[341] where it was held that in determining whether there were any objectively justified grounds for the variation in pay, the court should consider whether the measures adopted by the employer 'correspond to a real need on the part of the undertaking, are appropriate with a view to achieving the objectives pursued and are necessary to that end'.[342]

Court decisions since then have tended to be quite cautious, but in the recent *Next* case, the tribunal rejected Next's 'market forces' defence for paying the predominantly female store workers less than the predominantly male warehouse employees.[343] Next argued that the lower rate of pay was not only equivalent to the market rate for those roles, but also that the higher pay is needed to recruit and retain sufficient warehouse staff. The ET found that Next could have paid their store workers more but prioritized saving labour costs, which alone cannot justify a difference in pay. Indeed, it recognized that accepting such an argument would defeat the purpose of the equal pay legislation. However, the ET did accept that some payments and bonuses that applied solely to warehouse staff were justified as they related to specific challenges of incentivizing and retaining warehouse staff at the particular times when the bonuses were paid. This is only a first instance decision, so it will be interesting to see if higher courts follow this lead.

One particularly awkward issue arises when an employer has sought to protect the pay of the comparator's group of workers by maintaining it at a higher level than, but for history, the employer would have chosen to pay them—for example, because there has been a restructuring and as a result some jobs are less demanding than they had been. The idea of such pay protection is to avoid an employee being faced with a sudden cut in income. Often this is done by 'red-circling' the employees; that is to say, keeping their pay unchanged until inflation causes the salaries of other employees to catch up with the red-circled pay. In many cases pay protection schemes are implemented for the very reason that the employer is seeking to correct a pay structure which was discriminatory on grounds of sex. Can the employer pay the mainly male group of higher-paid employees more until the mainly female group catches up?

The cases establish that pay protection can indeed provide the basis for a valid employer's defence, but the employer must seek to diminish its effect over time.[344] However, if the reason for introducing the new pay scales is to correct past discrimination, then the starting point is that pay 'protection' should be given for the transitional period not only to the (largely) male group who are being overpaid but also to the largely female group. This means keeping the pay of the men at the higher level for the transitional period and increasing the women's pay to that level for the transitional period.[345] This is the

[341] Case 170/84 [1987] ICR 110, [1986] IRLR 317, ECJ.

[342] In *Rainey*, Lord Keith added ([1987] ICR 129 at 143, [1987] IRLR 26 at 30) that he considered that the ECJ's ruling 'would not exclude objectively justified grounds which are other than economic, such as administrative efficiency in a concern not engaged in commerce or business'. See further 4.2.5.7.

[343] *Thandi and Others v Next Retail Ltd and Next Distribution Ltd* 1302019/2018.

[344] *Fearnon v Smurfit Corrugated Cases Ltd* [2009] IRLR 132, NICA.

[345] *Redcar and Cleveland Borough Council v Bainbridge* [2008] EWCA Civ 885, [2008] IRLR 776, [2009] ICR 133.

starting point because any other approach would be to perpetuate the pay discrimination. However, if the employer can provide 'cogent and specific' evidence to show that the cost of doing this is such that it would be unaffordable, it is possible that a discriminatory pay protection scheme might be justified.[346]

4.3.2.8 Equal pay remedies

The remedies

If an equal terms claim is successful the tribunal makes a declaration to that effect and awards arrears of pay or damages for losses resulting from the contravention of the equality clause.[347] There is, however, no power to award general damages (eg for injury to feelings), as would be the case in a sex discrimination claim.[348] There is also a duty on a tribunal, with certain exceptions, to order that the employer undertake an equal pay audit (see 4.3.2.9).

As so many equal pay claims are started, but so few are heard in a full tribunal hearing, the current Labour government has proposed introducing an Equal Pay Regulatory and Enforcement Unit to improve enforcement.[349] This is only at the consultation phase at the time of writing, but it is envisaged that this unit would provide legal advice and representation, as well as bring proceedings by itself. It could also pursue investigations and seek injunctions against employers, as well as facilitating informal dispute resolution and providing training on equal pay and good practice. This is proposed as part of the Equality (Race and Disability) Bill.

Time limits: bringing a claim and duration of arrears

A claim for equal pay may be brought before an employment tribunal.[350] Alternatively, the claimant can sue in the ordinary courts relying on breach of the implied equality clause as a breach of contract. Normally a court will use the power in s 128(1) of the Equality Act to transfer such a case to the employment tribunal on the basis that it can be more conveniently dealt with in the tribunal because that is the forum with more expertise in discrimination law. However, if a claim would be barred in the tribunal because of the six-month time limit (see below) but the claim is within the more generous six-year limitation period for bringing a contract claim in the civil courts, then the civil court should deal with the case.[351]

Under s 129, proceedings before an employment tribunal must be instituted within the 'qualifying period'.[352] This is normally six months after the last day of the employment[353] in question, but the limit is modified in three circumstances: first, where the employer and employee had a 'stable employment relationship', the qualifying date is six months after the end of that relationship, irrespective of the fact that there may have been more

[346] *Bury Metropolitan Borough Council v Hamilton* [2011] ICR 655, EAT. This case and Redcar (n 345) show that although the saving of cost alone cannot justify discrimination (see 4.2.5.4, Can saving cost be a legitimate aim?), if the justification is, for example to protect employees from a sudden decrease in income, affordability can be put in the balance in assessing proportionality.

[347] S 133(1) Equality Act 2010.

[348] *Allan v Newcastle-upon-Tyne CC* [2005] NLJ 619, EAT.

[349] <https://www.gov.uk/government/news/government-launches-call-for-evidence-to-break-down-barriers-to-opportunity-at-work>.

[350] Equality Act 2010, s 120.

[351] *Abdulla v Birmingham City Council* [2012] UKSC 47, [2013] IRLR 38, [2012] ICR 1419.

[352] Equality Act 2010, s 129(2).

[353] Cf *National Power plc v Young* [2001] IRLR 32, EAT, where this phrase in the pre-2003 provisions was held to refer to her employment with the employer, rather than the actual job for that employer in respect of which her claim was made.

than one contract of employment during that period;[354] second, where the employee was under an incapacity,[355] the qualifying date is six months after she ceased to be under that incapacity;[356] and third, where the employer deliberately concealed relevant facts[357] from the employee, the qualifying day is six months after she discovered (or could with reasonable diligence have discovered) the information in question. The provisions on concealment were introduced to meet the point which arose in *Levez v T H Jennings (Harlow Pools) Ltd*,[358] where the CJEU held that the six-month limit infringed the EU legal principle of effectiveness. It is a fundamental principle of EU law that in the absence of EU rules on the matter, it is for domestic legal systems to lay down procedural rules governing the enforcement of EU rights that do not render the exercise of rights conferred by EU law virtually impossible or excessively difficult. The UK six-month time limit infringed that principle because it did not make allowance for an applicant who delayed bringing proceedings as a result of a deliberate misrepresentation by the employer.

The limit on the duration of arrears is now governed by s 132(4) which provides that if an equality of terms claim is successful, the tribunal may award back pay or damages back to the 'arrears day',[359] which is normally six years before the institution of proceedings.[360] This is still less generous than the position in relation to discrimination other than on equality of terms, where there is no limit on how far back the tribunal can go in assessing the claimant's loss.

4.3.2.9 **Equal pay audit**

In addition to awarding a remedy to the one or more employees who have brought a claim, since 2014 tribunals have been empowered by regulations made under s 139A of the Equality Act to order the employer to conduct an equal pay audit in order to identify action to be taken to avoid equal pay breaches occurring or continuing.[361] A tribunal *must* make such an order unless the employer has already completed an audit containing the same information in the previous three years, or it is clear without an audit whether any action is required to avoid equal pay breaches, or there is no reason to think that the breach identified by the tribunal is anything other than a one-off, or the disadvantages of an audit would outweigh the benefits.[362]

The tribunal must specify the categories of employees to be covered by the audit,[363] but the Act and the Regulations give no guidance as to how far beyond the successful claimant they can go. Clearly there must be some latitude since the position of the particular claimant or claimants has already been identified by the tribunal. There is as yet no case law guidance on this.

Once the audit has been conducted, the Regulations provide for its adequacy to be reviewed by the tribunal.[364] The audit must for example not only identify if there are instances of unjustified unequal pay but also identify the reasons for this and the steps that need to be taken to remedy it. If the audit is not carried out or is inadequate and this is not corrected then the tribunal can order the employer to pay a penalty of up to £5,000

[354] Equality Act 2010, s 129(3).

[355] ie a minor or of unsound mind: Equal Pay Act 1970, s 11(2A), as amended.

[356] Equality Act 2010, s 129(3). The exception applies if she was under a disability at any time during what would otherwise have been the six-month limitation period.

[357] ie facts which are relevant to the proceedings, without knowledge of which the woman could not reasonably have been expected to institute the proceedings: Equality Act 2010, s 129(3).

[358] [1999] ICR 521, [1999] IRLR 36, ECJ.

[359] Equal Pay Act 1970, s 2ZB, as inserted by SI 2003/1656.

[360] S 132(4) makes special provision for cases involving disability and/or deliberate concealment, where the arrears day is the day on which the breach first occurred.

[361] Equality Act 2010 (Equal Pay Audits) Regulations 2014, SI 2014/2559.

[362] SI 2014/2559, reg 3(1).

[363] SI 2014/2559, reg 5.

[364] SI 2014/2559, regs 7 and 8.

to the Secretary of State.[365] The audit must be published on the employer's website and be notified to all the employees covered by it.[366]

This remedy of an equal pay audit is potentially powerful in two ways. First, it should compel employers who have been found to be in breach to do more than just correct the pay of successful claimants. Second, the risk of an equal pay audit being ordered will encourage employers to settle claims before they get to a full tribunal hearing.

4.3.2.10 **Pensions and equal pay**

As originally enacted, the Equal Pay Act contained a blanket exclusion for any provision made by an employer in connection with death or retirement,[367] which was considered to be necessary because of the different state pension ages for men and women because many occupational pension schemes had been based on those different ages. However, during the 1980s it became increasingly clear that the breadth of the exclusion in the domestic legislation was incompatible with EU law, in that while the differential state pensionable age itself was outside the scope of Article 157,[368] retirement benefits (and indeed retirement ages) which are based on the state pensionable age were not.

As a result, the government was forced to introduce legislation outlawing discrimination in provisions made in connection with retirement, initially in relation to promotion, transfer, training, demotion, or dismissal,[369] and later in the area of occupational pensions also.[370] These areas have now been brought together in the 2010 Act. The Act establishes a non-discrimination rule (s 61) and a sex equality rule (s 67) for occupational pensions, which are the counterpart, generally, to the equality clause relating to other terms of the employment contract. Past editions of this book have devoted a great deal of space to this area. However, in light of the arcane nature of the subject generally and the need to devote limited space in the book to core employment matters, the authors have chosen to leave the reader with just this tantalizing hint of the pension secrets to be found in Part 5, Chapters 2 and 3 of the Equality Act 2010.

4.4 Sexual orientation discrimination

As a result of the EU Employment Framework Directive,[371] the UK introduced in 2003 a prohibition on discrimination because of sexual orientation in employment and vocational training. This has since been incorporated into and expanded by the 2010 Act. 'Sexual orientation'[372] is defined as being a sexual orientation towards persons of (a) the same sex (covering gay men and lesbians); (b) the opposite sex (covering straight men and women); or (c) both sexes (covering bisexual men and women).[373]

[365] SI 2014/2559, reg 11. [366] SI 2014/2559, reg 9.

[367] Equal Pay Act 1970, s 6. There was an equivalent exclusion in the Sex Discrimination Act 1975, s 6(4).

[368] Art 7 of EEC Directive 79/7 on Social Security allows member states to exclude 'the determination of pensionable age for the purposes of granting old-age and retirement pensions' from the principle of equal treatment, but does not in terms extend to provisions which are tied to the state pensionable age. See *R v Secretary of State for Social Security, ex p Equal Opportunities Commission* [1992] ICR 782, [1992] IRLR 376, ECJ.

[369] Sex Discrimination Act 1986, s 2. [370] Pensions Act 1995, ss 62–66.

[371] Directive 2000/78/EC.

[372] Oliver 'Sexual Orientation Discrimination: Perceptions, Definitions and Genuine Occupational Requirements' (2004) 33 ILJ 1. Stonewall found that 15 per cent of lesbians and gay men had suffered at least one experience of discrimination in their working lives ('Less Equal than Others: A Survey of Lesbians and Gays at Work' (1993)), while the National Survey of Sexual Attitudes and Lifestyles (1990) found that more than 20 per cent of lesbian and gay workers had been harassed due to their sexuality: DTI 'Regulatory Impact Assessment for the Employment Equality (Sexual Orientation) Regulations 2003'.

[373] Equality Act 2010, s 12.

The Act's use of the expression 'because of a protected characteristic' is wide enough to include discrimination based on A's perception of B's sexual orientation.[374] This wording also covers cases where a person is discriminated against by reason of someone else's sexual orientation, for example where a person is discriminated against for associating with gay friends, or for refusing to carry out an instruction to discriminate against gays or lesbians. This breadth was confirmed in *Lisboa v Realpubs, Pring and Heap*,[375] in which the EAT found that where the management of a former gay pub sought to reposition the pub as 'straight', it was direct sexual orientation discrimination to pressure an employee to cooperate in efforts to treat homosexual clients less favourably.

While the definition of sexual orientation does not, by its terms, include sexual practices or sexual conduct, there will often be a correlation between certain types of conduct and particular sexual orientation, so that it is unlikely to be a defence for an employer who has imposed a detriment on a gay employee to say that his reason for doing so was his objection to certain forms of behaviour indulged in by gay men and not the fact of homosexuality itself. So, in *R (Cornerstone (North East) Adoption and Fostering Services Ltd) v HM Chief Inspector of Education*,[376] it was held that a policy that foster carers 'abstained from all sexual sins including . . . homosexual behaviour' was direct discrimination on grounds of sexual orientation.

A number of exceptions affect the protection afforded to sexual orientation. There is of course the general exception for 'occupational requirements' which is discussed at 4.2.9.1, but there is another, more controversial exception which applies where employment is for the purposes of an organized religion.[377] This exception allows employers to discriminate on the basis of sex, gender reassignment, marital status (including divorce), and sexual orientation, in order to comply with the doctrines of the religion or to avoid 'conflicting with the strongly held religious convictions of a significant number of the religion's followers'.[378] Importantly, this kind of discrimination is not required to be a 'proportionate means' of achieving either doctrinal compliance or avoidance of conflict. This exception has been strongly criticized by the Lesbian and Gay Christian Movement as institutionalizing homophobia by permitting religious employers to sack gay and lesbian staff.

The government has claimed that this organized religion exception is consistent with Article 4 of the Directive because 'a requirement which meets the criteria . . . is necessarily a genuine and determining occupational requirement which is applied proportionately'.[379] However, if this were so the requirement would presumably be covered by the standard GOR exception anyway, making the organized religion exception redundant.

There have been a number of cases in recent years that have confronted the apparent clash between the right to exercise one's religion and the protections against sexual orientation discrimination.[380] Most involve a situation where people whose religious faith dictates, in their view, that they refuse to serve or assist (or potentially employ) people who

[374] See 4.2.4.2 for a discussion of 'associative discrimination'.

[375] UKEAT/0224/10, [2011] All ER (D) 188.

[376] [2021] EWCA Civ 1390, [2021] IRLR 993.

[377] Equality Act 2010, Sch 9, para 2. This exception is not spelled out in the Equal Treatment Directive, but the High Court held in *R (on the application of AMICUS) v Secretary of State for Trade and Industry* [2004] EWHC 860 (Admin), [2004] IRLR 420 that is was a permissible implementation of the general power in Art 4(1) for member states to legislation for genuine occupational requirements.

[378] Equality Act 2010, Sch 9, para 2(6). This exception has been held to allow the established Church of England not only to block people from working for the Church because of the conflict or compliance principles, but also to block priests from taking up a position as a chaplain with the NHS: *Pemberton v Inwood* [2018] EWCA Civ 564, [2018] IRLR 542. The chaplaincy was 'for the purposes of an organised religion'.

[379] Explanatory Memorandum to the Draft Regulations, para 24.

[380] *Ladele v London Borough of Islington* [2009] EWCA Civ 1357, [2009] All ER (D) 155; *McFarlane v Relate Avon Ltd* [2009] All ER (D) 233; *Bull & Anor v Hall & Anor* [2013] UKSC 73.

are not heterosexual. The cases are popularly understood to represent a question of which gets higher priority—protection against religious discrimination or protection against sexual orientation discrimination—but this misunderstands the conflict. These cases all share the following characteristics: (a) there is no real question of whether the religious people are behaving in a discriminatory way towards the non-heterosexual people: they clearly are; (b) there is no question of the non-heterosexual people discriminating against the religious people: they clearly are not; and (c) there is only a question as to whether the state or an employer is discriminating against the religious people by preventing them from discriminating against the non-heterosexual people. This means that the issue is not whether protection of religion or sexual orientation is more important; the issue is whether the prohibition on religious discrimination, or the right of people to exercise their religion, entitles them to commit discrimination in the name of their religion.

The Supreme Court in *Bull v Hall*[381] ruled emphatically that there is no such general 'religion exception' to the prohibition against sexual orientation discrimination. In that case Christian hoteliers refused a room with a double bed to a same-sex couple on the ground that they were not married.[382] However, the couple were civil partners, at a time when marriage was not available to non-heterosexuals. The Court ruled, by a 3–2 majority, that this constituted *direct* sexual orientation discrimination, as the insistence on marriage, in the face of a demonstrated civil partnership, meant that the distinction was at root based on sexual orientation (the Court unanimously found that if it were not direct discrimination it would be unjustified indirect discrimination). Baroness Hale, giving judgment for the majority, also dismissed the idea that the right to free exercise of religion changed the analysis:

> We do not normally allow people to behave in a way which the law prohibits because they disagree with the law. But to allow discrimination against persons of homosexual orientation (or indeed of heterosexual orientation) because of a belief, however sincerely held, and however based on the biblical text, would be to do just that.[383]

4.5 Racial discrimination

4.5.1 Definition of 'race'

'Race' in the 2010 Act means colour, nationality, ethnic origin, or national origin.[384] Section 9 of the Act allows for the Secretary of State to order the inclusion of 'caste' as part of the definition of 'race'. This power has not been used and the previous Conservative government was content to allow the courts to develop caste protection, referring specifically to the recent decision of the EAT that caste *can* be considered part of 'race' under the Act, so long as it is sufficiently linked to 'ethnic origins', in the sense that it exists by 'descent'.[385] The EHRC still recommends that s 9(5)(a) be brought into force.

[381] [2013] UKSC 73. Compare *Lee v Ashers Baking Ltd* [2018] UKSC 49 (a non-employment case, where the refusal of a baker to put on a cake a message supporting gay marriage was found not to be discriminatory, because the baker had not refused to serve the claimants because of their sexual orientation but had refused to write the message because he did not support it). The Supreme Court appears to have accepted that the baker would have made the claimants a wedding cake without the message, and concluded that merely refusing to write a message one does not believe in is not 'because of' the sexual orientation of the claimant.

[382] This case did not arise under the Equality Act 2010 but under the Equality Act (Sexual Orientation) Regulations 2007, but the Court made it clear that the relevant provisions could be read across.

[383] See n 381 at para 37.

[384] Equality Act 2010, s 9.

[385] *Chandhok v Tirkey* UKEAT/0190/14, [2014] EqLR 183. See Penny Mordaunt, *Government Response to Caste Consultation: Written statement—HCWS898* (23 July 2018) available at <https://questions-statements.parliament.uk/written-statements/detail/2018-07-23/HCWS898>.

On the question of what counts as 'ethnic origin', in *Mandla v Dowell Lee*[386] the complainant, a Sikh boy, was refused entrance to a private school unless he gave up wearing his turban and had his hair cut, a requirement which conflicted with his religion. This was before the law prohibited discrimination on religious grounds, so he claimed indirect discrimination on the ground of his ethnic origin. The House of Lords held that Sikhs constitute an ethnic group within the meaning of the Act, Lord Fraser commenting that for a group to constitute an ethnic group it must regard itself, and be regarded by others, as a distinct community with a long shared history and a cultural tradition of its own.

It is clearly established that Jews[387] and gypsies[388] constitute identifiable ethnic groups, but Rastafarians have been held not to, on the grounds that although they have certain identifiable characteristics, they have not established a separate identity by reference to their ethnic origins.[389] The fact that some faith groups were able to obtain protection against religious discrimination indirectly via the Race Relations Act while others were not was a source of considerable grievance, hence the importance of the eventual prohibition on religious discrimination.

'Nationality' in this context points to citizenship, and to the existence of a recognized state at the material time, but 'national origin' is a wider concept, turning on the existence of a nation at some point in time, established by reference to history and geography. Thus, in *Northern Joint Police Board v Power*,[390] the issue was whether the applicant, who claimed that he had been rejected for a post of chief constable in Scotland because he was English, had been discriminated against on racial grounds. The tribunal held that there was no discrimination on grounds of nationality; however, discrimination against an English person was held to constitute discrimination on grounds of national origin, since it could not be in doubt that both England and Scotland were once separate nations.[391]

The courts have expressed in obiter the view that a person can have an 'ethnic or national origin' by birth or by adherence. This was stated in the *Mandla*[392] case by reference to membership of any 'racial group' (although the case was about 'ethnic origin'), where Lord Fraser said: 'Provided a person who joins the group feels himself or herself to be a member of it, and is accepted by other members, then he is, for the purposes of the Act, a member.' In *BBC Scotland v Souster*,[393] the Court of Session applied this to 'national origin' and instanced adherence by marriage, or by the person adopting that identity, or through their being perceived to have become a member of that racial group.

Members of a vulnerable group by virtue of immigration status, which flows from being 'non-British' but not from any particular nationality, cannot claim that disadvantage or less favourable treatment for that group is 'because of' the protected characteristic of nationality. This is because some non-British people do have the right to live and work in the UK and so the claimants' less favourable treatment flowed from their immigration status rather than their nationality.[394]

386 [1983] ICR 385, [1983] IRLR 209, HL.

387 *Seide v Gillette Industries Ltd* [1980] IRLR 427, EAT.

388 *Commission for Racial Equality v Dutton* [1989] QB 783, [1989] 1 All ER 306, CA.

389 *Dawkins v Department of the Environment* [1993] IRLR 284, CA.

390 [1997] IRLR 610, EAT.

391 See also, to the same effect, *BBC Scotland v Souster* [2001] IRLR 150, Ct of Sess. The same reasoning naturally applies to Wales and Ireland, although in *Gwynedd County Council v Jones* [1986] ICR 833, the EAT held that the 1976 Act does not apply to discrimination on the grounds of not being able to *speak* Welsh.

392 See n 386.

393 [2001] IRLR 150, Ct of Sess.

394 *Onu v Akwiwu and Taiwo v Olaigbe* [2016] UKSC 31, [2016] 1 WLR 2653; applied in *Mruke v Khan* [2018] EWCA Civ 280, [2018] IRLR 526 ('The fact is it was the socio-economic circumstances of the appellant, and not her nationality, which were the reason for the less favourable treatment').

The Equality Act specifically provides in s 13(5) that racial segregation is deemed to be less favourable treatment. This is unlike other protected characteristics, where protection against 'separate but equal' treatment has been left to case law development.[395]

The Act's use of the 'because of a protected characteristic' language means that it applies where a person suffers a detriment on the basis of *another* person's race, for example where a person is known to have friends who are of a particular race or where a white person is dismissed for refusing to apply a colour bar.[396] In *Weathersfield Ltd v Sargent*,[397] the complainant resigned from her job with a vehicle hire firm after being told not to hire vehicles to Black or Asian prospective customers. The Court of Appeal held that she had been discriminated against on racial grounds, even though it was the race of the prospective customers that was at issue and not her own race. We have also seen that a person can be found to have suffered race harassment even where the harassing comments were not about her race.[398]

Some future change is possible in this area, as it has been proposed that the equal pay rights (considered in 4.3.2) should be extended to people from ethnic minorities, with mandatory pay reporting for large employers with over 250 employees.[399] A consultation has taken place, but it remains to be seen whether this will remain a priority for this Labour Government.

4.5.2 **Exceptions**

The Race Relations Act 1976 set out certain exempted categories of employment where being a member of a particular racial group was a 'genuine occupational qualification' (GOQ) for a job, for example where the holder of the job provided persons of that racial group with 'personal services promoting their welfare' and those services 'can most effectively be provided by persons of that racial group',[400] or where the job involves participation in a dramatic performance, working as an artist's or photographic model, or working in a bar or restaurant, where a person of a particular racial group is required 'for reasons of authenticity'.[401] These GOQs have of course been replaced by the more generic 'genuine occupational requirement' defence in the Equality Act 2010.[402]

The GOR exception allows employers to recruit employees on the basis of their race or ethnic or national origins if it can be shown that, having regard to the nature of the employment or the context in which it is carried out, being of a particular race or of particular ethnic or national origin is a 'genuine occupational requirement', and it is proportionate for that requirement to be applied in the particular case. The new exception is almost certainly narrower than the GOQ exception, and will probably only apply where the employer can show that the employee's race or ethnic or national origin is an essential, defining feature of the job. This is true not only because the Race Directive uses the phrase 'genuine and determining occupational requirement' but also because it would

[395] See 4.2.4.4. [396] See 4.2.4.2 for a discussion of 'associative discrimination'.

[397] [1999] ICR 425, [1999] IRLR 94, CA. This is sometimes referred to as the rule in *Showboat Entertainment Centre Ltd v Owens* [1984] ICR 65, [1984] IRLR 7, EAT. However, the Court of Appeal would not allow this rule to be used *by* an active member of the BNP to claim that disciplinary action against him constituted race discrimination: *Redfearn v Serco Ltd* [2006] EWCA Civ 659, [2006] IRLR 623, CA.

[398] *Moxam v Visible Changes Ltd* UKEAT/0267/11/MAA (24 November 2011 unreported).

[399] Expected in the Equality (Race and Disability) Bill.

[400] See *Tottenham Green Under Fives' Centre v Marshall* [1989] ICR 214, [1989] IRLR 147, EAT; *(No 2)* [1991] ICR 320, [1991] IRLR 162, EAT; *Lambeth London Borough v Commission for Racial Equality* [1990] ICR 768, [1990] IRLR 231, CA.

[401] See Pitt 'Madam Butterfly and Miss Saigon: Reflections on Genuine Occupational Qualifications' in Dine and Watt (eds) *Discrimination Law: Concepts, Limitations and Justifications* (1996).

[402] Equality Act 2010, Sch 9, para 1.

hardly ever be proportionate to exclude a person from employment on racial grounds for a reason that was not an essential, defining feature of the job. See further 4.2.9.1.

4.6 **Religion or belief discrimination**

4.6.1 **Introduction**

In theory, human rights law offers some protection against religious discrimination, as Article 9 of the European Convention on Human Rights declares that '[e]veryone has the right to freedom of thought, conscience and religion', including the freedom 'either alone or in community with others . . . to manifest his religion or belief, in worship, teaching, practice, and observance'. Article 9 does not itself provide for equal treatment on grounds of religion, but Article 14 of the Convention provides that '[t]he enjoyment of the rights and freedoms set forth in this Convention shall be secured without discrimination on any ground such as . . . religion'.[403] These two Articles, in conjunction, are relevant to UK law about religious discrimination in two ways: first, because they enable action directly against public authorities; second, because these human rights must be taken into account by the tribunals and courts in interpreting the Equality Act. It is important to note that the freedom to manifest one's religion in Article 9 is not an absolute right, but may be subject to restrictions which are 'prescribed by law and . . . necessary in a democratic society . . . for the protection of the rights and freedoms of others'.[404] Case law under the Convention has revealed that the requirements of religious observance are likely to take second place to commercial and business considerations and the primacy of contractual obligations.[405]

In UK law the turning point came with the Treaty of Amsterdam, which provided a legal basis for EU-wide action to combat discrimination on a range of grounds, including 'religion or belief'. In 2000 the Council adopted the Employment Framework Directive,[406] and the Employment Equality (Religion or Belief) Regulations 2003[407] implemented this in the UK. Religion or belief is now a protected characteristic under the 2010 Act. As you will see, a key difference with the manifestation of religion or belief, when compared to the other protected characteristics, is that, arguably, direct discrimination can be justified when it is a proportional response (see 4.6.3.1).

4.6.2 **Meaning of 'belief'**

The approach taken in the Employment Framework Directive is to prohibit discrimination on grounds of 'religion *or* belief', thereby avoiding the need to define religion. That approach is reflected in the Equality Act, which provides that:

- 'religion' means any religion;
- 'belief' means any religious or philosophical belief;
- a reference to religion includes a reference to lack of religion; and
- a reference to belief includes a reference to lack of belief.[408]

[403] This is not a freestanding right, but can only be claimed in conjunction with one of the specified Convention rights. The UK government has not yet signed Protocol 12 to the Convention, which would provide a general prohibition on discrimination.

[404] European Convention on Human Rights, Art 9(2).

[405] See eg *Ahmad v Inner London Education Authority* [1978] 1 All ER 574; *Ahmad v United Kingdom* (1981) 4 EHRR 126; *Stedman v United Kingdom* (1997) 23 EHRR CD 168.

[406] Directive 2000/78/EC.

[407] SI 2003/1660. The regulations came into force on 2 December 2003. See Vickers (2003) 32 ILJ 23.

[408] Equality Act 2010, s 10.

The tribunals have favoured a broad interpretation of the statutory language, holding that there is no material difference between the domestic approach under the Equality Act and that under Article 9 of the ECHR.[409] Accordingly, it was held in the leading case of *Grainger plc v Nicholson*[410] that to be a philosophical belief protected by the Act:

- the belief must be genuinely held;
- it must be a belief and not an opinion or viewpoint based on the present state of information available;
- it must be a belief as to a weighty and substantial aspect of human life and behaviour;
- it must attain a certain level of cogency, seriousness, cohesion, and importance;
- it must be worthy of respect in a democratic society, be not incompatible with human dignity, and not conflict with the fundamental rights of others.

The EAT in *Grainger* agreed with the tribunal below that a belief in human-made climate change, and the ethical obligations that flow from such a belief, can count as the protected characteristic of 'belief'. Similarly, 'spiritualism', involving a belief in life after death and communication with spirits 'on the other side', has the necessary cogency, seriousness, cohesion, and importance to fall within the definition of 'philosophical belief' for the purpose of the Act.[411] On the other hand, a belief in the sanctity of copyright law lacked sufficient cogency to attract protection.[412] Unsurprisingly, the beliefs that 'homosexuality was contrary to god's law and nature' and that 'no Jewish people were killed by the use of poison gas in concentration camps during the Second World War' were held not 'worthy of respect in a democratic society' and conflicted with the fundamental rights of others, and could not therefore attract Equality Act protection.[413]

The scope of the fifth *Grainger* criterion, that the belief must be worthy of respect in a democratic society, be not incompatible with human dignity, and not conflict with the fundamental rights of others, may have been narrowed by a recent decision of the EAT in *Forstater v CGD Europe*.[414] The EAT held that

> it is only those beliefs that would be an affront to Convention principles in a manner akin to that of pursuing totalitarianism, or advocating Nazism, or espousing violence and hatred in the gravest of forms, that should be capable of being not worthy of respect in a democratic society. Beliefs that are offensive, shocking or even disturbing to others, and which fall into the less grave forms of hate speech would not be excluded from the protection.

The facts of *Forstater* were that the claimant alleged that she had suffered discrimination because she held gender-critical beliefs, including that sex is biologically immutable (ie that there are only two genders, male and female) and that there is no possibility of any sex in between the two, or that it is ever possible to change sex. The EAT held that the claimant's belief did not fall foul of the fifth criterion.[415] This was questioned in obiter in *Thomas v Surrey and Borders Partnership NHS Foundation Trust and Brett* as Sheldon J

[409] *Grainger plc v Nicholson* [2010] IRLR 4 and *Harron v Chief Constable of Dorset Police* [2016] IRLR 481.

[410] See n 409.

[411] *Greater Manchester Police Authority v Power* [2010] All ER (D) 173 (EAT).

[412] *Gray v Mulberry Co (Design) Ltd* [2018] IRLR 893, [2019] ICR 175, affirmed on other grounds by the Court of Appeal [2019] EWCA Civ 1720, [2020] IRLR 29.

[413] *Ellis v Parmagon Ltd* [2014] EqLR 343.

[414] [2021] IRLR 706, [2022] ICR 1, EAT.

[415] The *Forstater* decision of the EAT and some ET decisions are examined in detail in Cowan and Morris 'Should "Gender Critical" Views about Trans People Be Protected as Philosophical Beliefs in the Workplace? Lessons for the Future from *Forstater, Mackereth* and *Higgs*' (2022) 51 ILJ 1.

noted that to abide by ECtHR case law, a belief might not be protected under the Equality Act 2010 even if it fell short of the *Forstater* standard (pursuing totalitarianism etc), if the belief itself espoused intolerance or discrimination.[416] Although Sheldon J warned that *Forstater* might not therefore be 'the last word on the matter', it does still represent the law and a number of other cases have followed it.[417]

The EAT has held that *Grainger* criteria are not applicable if the claimant is asserting discrimination on account of their *lack* of belief, because someone who does not believe something does not necessarily have a firm belief in the opposite—it may simply be that they have not thought about the issue or are undecided.[418] So, it would appear that it is not necessary for the claimant to establish that the thing in which they do not believe is a coherent belief as to a weighty matter which is worthy of respect etc. This means that the protection for lack of belief is wider than the protection for belief. For example, a job applicant could not complain of non-recruitment because they believed that a global elite was seeking to establish a New World Order—'a secret satanic ideology to enslave the masses and claim control of the world's resources' (a belief which was judged in *Farrell v South Yorkshire Police Authority*[419] not to meet the *Grainger* criteria)—but an applicant refused a job because they did not believe that there is such a global elite could bring a claim for direct discrimination. This is asymmetrical, but it may nevertheless be a satisfactory position for the law to adopt.

The fact that the Act forbids less favourable treatment 'because of a protected characteristic' means it encompasses discrimination based on A's perception of B's religion or belief, and the Act also prohibits discrimination by reason of the religion or belief of someone else, for example where a person is discriminated against for refusing to carry out an instruction to discriminate against Muslims.[420]

4.6.3 **Manifestation of beliefs**

4.6.3.1 **Direct discrimination**

Treating an employee less favourably because of their manifestation of a belief may be direct discrimination, unless it can be justified. In the CJEU case of *Bougnaoui v Micropole SA*,[421] the employee was dismissed for refusing to stop wearing a veil for religious reasons after a customer of her employer had objected. The Court held that this was a case of direct discrimination: less favourable treatment because of religion: she was dismissed for wearing a veil, which was inextricably linked to her religious belief. In *Bougnaoui* the Court pointed out that direct discrimination could only be justified if it were a 'genuine and determining occupation requirement' (see 4.2.9.1) and held that the employer's reason for requiring the employee not to wear a veil—that a customer had requested this—fell short of being such a determining requirement.

This approach of making direct discrimination justifiable has recently been reaffirmed by the Court of Appeal in *Higgs v Farmor's School*.[422] The case involved someone who was dismissed from their job after reposting other people's Facebook posts which were gender critical in nature on her own, private Facebook page. The Court confirmed, first, that less

[416] [2024] EAT 141.

[417] See *Mackerth v DWP and Advanced Personnel Management Group (UK) Limited* [2022] EAT 99.

[418] *Forstater v CGD Europe* (see n 414) and *Mackereth v Department for Work and Pensions* [2022] EAT 99 (29 June 2022, unreported).

[419] [2011] EqLR 935.

[420] See 4.2.4.2 for a discussion of 'associative discrimination'.

[421] C-188/15, ECLI:EU:C:2017:204, [2017] IRLR 447.

[422] [2025] EWCA Civ 109.

favourable treatment of an employee because they have expressed a religious or other protected belief, will be unlawful direct discrimination. However:

> if the [less favourable treatment] is motivated not simply by the expression of the belief itself (or third parties' reaction to it) but by something objectionable in the way in which it was expressed, determined objectively, then. . .the dismissal will be lawful if, but only if, the employer shows that it was a proportionate response to the objectionable feature—in short, that it was objectively justified.[423]

It was found that dismissing her was not a proportionate sanction for a whole host of reasons including, importantly, that the forum and context was outside of work. As this less favourable treatment could not be justified, the employers were liable for direct discrimination.

This arguably makes religion and belief slightly different to the other protected characteristics, where direct discrimination cannot normally be justified (age is the only exception, see 4.8). Underhill LJ makes it clear that this is only relevant to the objectionable manifestation of those beliefs, rather than just expressing them. Nonetheless, Foran argues that the judgment 'threatens to fundamentally, and unnecessarily, change our understanding of the distinction between direct and indirect discrimination'.[424] He also contends that this is unnecessary, because he sees this just as the application of the 'reason why' test (see 4.2.4.1)—the reason was 'not the protected belief but the inappropriate manner in which it was manifested'.[425] Some might have hoped that any confusion would have been cleared up on appeal to the Supreme Court, but the appeal has since been rejected. Addressing a slightly different issue, dismissing an employee for promoting religious views in the workplace was not direct discrimination in *Chondol v Liverpool CC*, because the dismissal was because of the inappropriate proselytizing conduct, not the beliefs themselves.[426] Similarly, the claimant in *Page v NHS Trust Development Authority*[427] held the faith-based belief that it was preferable for a child to be adopted by a man and a woman rather than a same-sex couple and appeared widely on national media saying so. The Trust where he was a non-executive director took the view that this would cause damage to its provision of healthcare to gay people (deterring those with mental illness from coming forward) and so his directorship was not renewed. The Court of Appeal upheld the judgment of the ET that the non-renewal was not because of the claimant's beliefs, nor his manifestation of those beliefs; rather it was the objectionable circumstances of his manifestation of those beliefs—as a director of an NHS Trust.

4.6.3.2 **Indirect discrimination**

More often, disputes will relate to whether rules on leave from work, or on dress and appearance, which particularly disadvantage certain religious or belief groups in comparison with others are unlawful indirect discrimination or whether they can be

[423] [175].

[424] Foran 'It's Not What You Said, It's the Way That You Said It: Manifesting Protected Beliefs in the Workplace Following *Higgs v Farmor's School*' (2025) 54 ILJ 389, 390.

[425] Foran 'It's Not What You Said, It's the Way That You Said It: Manifesting Protected Beliefs in the Workplace Following *Higgs v Farmor's School*' (2025) 54 ILJ 389, 396.

[426] [2009] UKEAT 0298_08_1102. See also *Wasteney v East London NHS Foundation Trust* [2016] ICR 643, EAT where HHJ Eady QC accepted that the protection accorded to religion and its manifestations could extend to protection for proselytizing. This and a contrary view expressed by Sharpston AG in *Bougnaoui v Micropole SA* C-188/15, ECLI:EU:C:2017:204, [2017] IRLR 447 are discussed in Hambler 'Is There "No Place in the Work Context" for Religious Proselytism?' 51 ILJ 2022.

[427] [2021] EWCA Civ 255, [2021] IRLR 391.

objectively justified as being a proportionate means of achieving a legitimate aim. The potential impact of these provisions on working conditions can be seen from the government's own impact assessment:

> Under the new legislation, and in line with best practice, employers may need to accommodate a wide variety of religious and cultural needs of workers such as different dietary requirements and prayer room facilities. Employers may also need to be flexible in order to accommodate cultural or religious holidays and restrictions on hours of work. People should not be discriminated against in recruitment decisions if they cannot work on particular days of the week; particular times of the day; or in particular areas of a business (for example, the meat and alcohol section of a supermarket) unless this can be objectively justified.[428]

An initial hurdle that claimants must clear is that of demonstrating the existence of a disadvantaged group. Even if the asserted religion or belief is accepted as covered, a claimant cannot show indirect discrimination without demonstrating that an identifiable religious or belief-holding group (as well as the claimant himself or herself) was (or would be) placed at a disadvantage by the relevant provision. The application of that principle can be justified by the desirability of ensuring that one person's uniquely zealous interpretation of the requirements of a religion is not to be allowed to render discriminatory a policy that would otherwise not trouble most members of that religion. Such an approach can work against those with minority interpretations or in favour of those who can more readily point to teachings that favour their claim. The Court of Appeal seemed to have some of these concerns in mind when it decided, in *Mba v London Borough of Merton*,[429] that it is an error for a tribunal to require a claimant to demonstrate that her beliefs are 'core' to some established religion or in any way represent a majority or orthodox view. Despite the fact that a refusal to work on Sunday was clearly not a core Christian belief, a PCP that required Sunday work would cause group disadvantage so long as some Christians held that belief: 'it is not necessary to establish that all or most Christians, or all or most non-conformist Christians, are or would be put at a particular disadvantage. It is permissible to define a claimant's religion or belief more narrowly than that.'[430]

Faced with the requirement for group disadvantage, some claimants have sought to argue that in relation to religion and belief discrimination this group disadvantage element of s 19 of the Equality Act must be ignored. The starting point for this argument is the judgment of the ECtHR in *Eweida, Ladele, McFarlane and Chaplin v The United Kingdom*,[431] which held that religious beliefs should be protected even if they are particular to the individual. In *Mba v London Borough of Merton*[432] the claimant relied on this, but the majority in the Court of Appeal held that although it had to seek so far as possible to interpret the law in accordance with the European Convention on Human Rights, s 19 could not be read in such a way as to disapply the expressly stated requirement of group disadvantage. In *Gray v Mulberry Co. (Design) Ltd*,[433] the claimant tried the same approach but sought to bolster the obligation to interpret the law in accordance with the Convention by relying on EU legal obligations to do so under Articles 52 and 53 of the Charter of Fundamental Rights of the EU. The Court of Appeal maintained its position that the requirement of group disadvantage in s 19 could not be ignored, and pointed out

[428] DTI *Regulatory Impact Assessment on the Religion or Belief Regulations* para 6.
[429] [2013] EWCA Civ 1562, [2014] IRLR 145.
[430] [2013] EWCA Civ 1562, [2014] IRLR 145 at para 17.
[431] [2013] IRLR 231, 57 EHRR 8.
[432] [2013] EWCA Civ 1562, [2014] IRLR 145.
[433] [2019] EWCA Civ 1720, [2020] IRLR 29.

that CJEU decisions on indirect discrimination expressly rely on the concept of group disadvantage.[434]

In practice, this group disadvantage issue will often not cause any difficulty because a disadvantaged group can easily be found. In both the *Mba* and *Gray* cases the courts had no difficulty in identifying groups of people who had the same beliefs as the claimant, and indeed it can be argued that for this reason the views expressed by the court in those cases about whether group disadvantage must be shown were obiter.[435]

4.6.3.3 **Justification of indirect discrimination**

Perhaps the biggest problem religious discrimination claimants face is in overcoming the justification argument that their religious practice simply cannot be reconciled with the employer's business needs, that is to say, that it is proportionate for the employer's real business need to outweigh the adverse impact on the employee. In *Azmi v Kirklees MBC*,[436] a teaching assistant was suspended for refusing an instruction not to wear a full facial veil when in a class assisting a male teacher. The EAT upheld the tribunal's rejection of her claim of religious discrimination. It held that there was no direct discrimination because any assistant who wanted to hide their face for any reason would have been treated in the same way. With regard to indirect discrimination, the EAT agreed that there was a provision, criterion, or practice which put the claimant as a Muslim at a particular disadvantage, but upheld the tribunal, finding that this was justified by the school's concerns about the effect that the veil had on her ability to communicate properly with the children and the impracticability of her suggestions for dealing with her requirements in other ways.[437]

The CJEU has shown a willingness to accept policies which enable an employer to present an image of neutrality in relation to religion and politics to its customers or service users.[438] The desire to present such an image is accepted by the Court as a legitimate one, and the more debatable issue is that of justification. The CJEU has made it clear this depends on the circumstances of each case and has sought to impose a high standard by using formulations such as a 'genuine need' on the part of the employer and the policy going no further than 'strictly necessary'. These phrases sound demanding, but they are inherently vague. Moreover, the Court accepted that such a policy might be justified if the employer could provide evidence of customer demand which was sufficiently strong that the employer would suffer adverse consequences to its undertaking if it did not maintain a neutral image.[439]

There are limits, however, to the ability of the employer's needs to trump the religious expression of workers. In *Eweida v British Airways plc*,[440] the employer was held not to have committed indirect religious discrimination by banning the wearing of visible

[434] See n 433 at para 42.

[435] See further Adentire 'Protecting Solitary Beliefs against Indirect Discrimination' (2021) 40 ILJ 196.

[436] [2007] UKEAT 9/07.

[437] One such suggestion, that she should not be required to work with a male teacher, would have had interesting consequences in sex discrimination law.

[438] *Achbita v G4S Secure Solutions NV* C-157115, ECLI:EU:C:2017:203,!20I7IIRI-R466; *IXv WABE* C-8041t8,l202tl rRLR 832.

[439] In *Müller Handels GmbH v MJ*: C-341/19, [2021] IRLR 832 the CJEU held that an employer's rule forbidding the wearing of conspicuous, large-sized political, philosophical, or religious signs, in addition to being unlawful as indirect discrimination unless justified, might also be direct discrimination if the wearing of such large symbols was inextricably linked to one or more specific religions or beliefs. Direct discrimination cannot usually be justified. In the authors' view the facts of *Müller* fall much more aptly into the concept of indirect discrimination.

[440] [2010] EWCA Civ 80.

jewellery as being inconsistent with the employer's uniform, even though this conflicted with the claimant's belief that she must wear and display a cross pendant around her neck. This case went on to be considered by the ECtHR, along with *Ladele*, *McFarlane*, and *Chaplin*.[441] Although the Strasbourg Court upheld the other three domestic decisions (each of which had rejected the religious discrimination claims on the basis that the employer's rule was justified), it found that in *Eweida* there had been insufficient consideration of the relative importance of the employer's objective as against the right to free exercise of religion.[442] The restriction in *Eweida* could not stand because (although the Court did not use this language, which is the property of the CJEU) it did not represent a real need of the business: the facts showed it could have accommodated the cross necklace without doing violence to its objectives, so the restriction was not proportionate.[443] In contrast, in the *Chaplin* case, where a nurse wished to wear a cross hanging from her neck, the ECtHR held that protection of health and safety justified a rule which banned necklaces because of the risk if a member of staff were grabbed by a patient.[444]

One important aspect of the ECtHR's judgment in the *Eweida and others* cases is that (in an express change of opinion from its previous judgments) the Court made it clear that an employer cannot defend itself against a claim of religious discrimination by pointing out that the employee could resign and thereby avoid the challenged restriction.

Although the *Eweida and others* cases were about infringement of the European Convention on Human Rights and not about indirect discrimination contrary to the Equality Act 2010, the UK courts will apply the principles to such cases. As a result, a policy about wearing uniforms for appearance's sake only is unlikely to justify a rule which prevents an employee from wearing a manifestation of her religion. Furthermore, the argument that 'the claimant could always find another job' is unlikely to be held to justify a policy which interferes with the manifestation of religion. These *Eweida* principles will help not only employees affected by dress and appearance rules but also those seeking to avoid working on particular days for religious reasons. Indeed, some have argued that this case has marked a move towards imposing a duty or reasonable accommodation for religion, which is similar to the duty of reasonable adjustment for those living with disabilities.[445]

There has been considerable public controversy about two cases which involve the intersection of religion and sexual orientation: the cases of *McFarlane*[446] and *Ladele*.[447] According to these decisions it is neither direct nor indirect discrimination to (a) require employees at a counselling centre to commit to counselling same-sex couples and (b) otherwise require employees to perform duties to which they conscientiously object because of their religious views about homosexual behaviour. This is true even if the employee could be individually accommodated, because it is a legitimate objective to pursue a

[441] [2010] ET 1702886/2009.

[442] *Eweida, Ladele, McFarlane and Chaplin v The United Kingdom* [2013] IRLR 231, 57 EHRR 8.

[443] It would be a mistake to view this as a general duty to accommodate religion. It does, however, support the idea that the proportionality analysis should take account of whether the employer could easily accommodate the religious exercise, which is really a gentle form of least-discriminatory-means proportionality.

[444] In another nursing case, *Grimmark v Sweden* [2020] IRLR 554, ECtHR, a nurse re-training to be a midwife was refused employment because her religious beliefs precluded her from carrying out abortions—a requirement in all Swedish midwifery posts. Whilst the ECtHR was satisfied that the refusal to conduct abortions was a manifestation of a religious belief and within the scope of Art 9, the interference was found to be justified in pursuance of the legitimate aim of protecting the health of women seeking an abortion, and was found to be 'necessary in a democratic society and proportionate'.

[445] See Pitt 'Taking Religion Seriously' (2013) 42 ILJ 398 and Griffiths 'The "Reasonable Accommodation" of Religion: Is This a Better Way of Advancing Equality in Cases of Religious Discrimination?' (2016) 16 Int J Discrimination & L 161.

[446] *McFarlane v Relate Avon* [2009] All ER (D) 233.

[447] *Ladele v LB Islington* [2009] All ER (D) 148.

policy of non-discrimination on the basis of sexual orientation, and the requirements applied, again, to manifestations of religion or belief, not to the holding of that belief. The logic of these decisions is straightforward, but they have attracted controversy because they are claimed to prioritize sexual orientation protections over protections for religion or belief. Suffice it to say in this regard that no judgments have ever suggested that the prohibition on sexual orientation discrimination would preclude employers from regulating sexual encounters at work, so long as the regulation was orientation-neutral. In other words, the exercise of religion lost out because it could not be reconciled with the employer's objectives, not because society protects sexual orientation more assiduously than religion.

4.6.4 **GORs**

In addition to the general 'genuine occupational requirements' (GOR) exception discussed with respect to other protected characteristics at 4.2.9.1, there is a specific exception to religion and belief discrimination for employment by an organization with 'an ethos based on religion or belief' in cases where holding that religion or belief is an occupational requirement and applying that requirement is a proportionate means of achieving a legitimate aim.[448] It is unclear what an organization needs to show in order to qualify as having an ethos based on religion or belief (can an organization acquire such an ethos merely by proclamation, or must it be of a certain type, and have a suitable track record, in order to qualify?). It is clear that this exception would cover employment as a minister of religion and employment in a school with a religious ethos. However, even where there is a religious ethos, a requirement that an employee be an adherent, or that they comply with the tenets of that faith may not satisfy the test of being an occupation requirement or may not be proportionate.[449]

There is an allied exception which concerns the interrelation of some religious beliefs with matters of sex, sexual orientation, transgender status, and marriage and civil partnership. This exception is not about permitting discrimination on the ground of religion but about circumstances in which the religious requirement of an employer can trump certain strands of discrimination. This exception is discussed at 4.4.

4.7 **Disability discrimination**

4.7.1 **History**

Statistics indicate that people with disabilities account for nearly a fifth of the working-age population in Great Britain, but for only about one-eighth of all people in employment.[450] People with disabilities are more than twice as likely to be unemployed as non-disabled

[448] Equality Act 2010, Sch 9, para 3. The 'religious ethos' GOR is permitted under Art 4(2) of the Directive, which refers to a situation where a person's religion or belief 'constitute a genuine, legitimate and justified occupational requirement, having regard to the organization's ethos'.

[449] See eg *Glasgow City Council v McNab* [2007] IRLR 476, EAT, where the EAT upheld a tribunal's decision that being a Roman Catholic was not an occupational requirement for a pastoral care post in a Roman Catholic school.

[450] See generally Lawson 'Disability and Employment in the Equality Act 2010: Opportunities Seized, Lost, and Generated' (2011) 40 ILJ 359; Thomas *The New Law on Disability Discrimination* (1996); Doyle *Disability Discrimination: Law and Practice* (4th edn, 2003). See also 'Monitoring the Disability Discrimination Act (DDA) 1995' (DfEE Research Series RR119, 1999).

people,[451] and are more likely to be in poverty than non-disabled people.[452] To some extent this can be explained by the effect which a physical or mental impairment might have on a disabled person's capacity to perform the work in question, but there is also strong evidence to suggest that people with disabilities suffer systematic discrimination in relation to employment, often as a result of ill-informed, stereotypical assumptions on the part of employers about the impact of particular disabilities on the work capacity of such employees and the difficulty of adapting working arrangements and premises to accommodate them.[453]

Until the enactment of the DDA 1995 there was no significant legislation tackling the problem of discrimination against people with disabilities in the workplace. The DDA prohibited discrimination against people with disabilities in relation to employment, the provision of goods and services, and the sale and letting of property; it also required educational establishments to provide fuller information about their arrangements and facilities for disabled pupils and students, and imposed some modest requirements as regards accessible public transport for people with disabilities.

In the area of employment, the DDA tried to strike a balance between the interests of people with disabilities (in terms of access to employment and equal treatment in the workplace, and so on) and the interests of employers by introducing two key provisions. One made it unlawful for an employer to discriminate against a disabled employee or job applicant by treating that person less favourably than he treats or would treat others for a reason relating to their disability. The other placed a duty on an employer to make reasonable adjustments to working arrangements and premises (by providing special equipment, altering working hours, arranging training, adapting premises, and so on) in order to accommodate a disabled person who would otherwise be at a substantial disadvantage in comparison with non-disabled persons. In relation to both duties there was an exception if an employer could show that discrimination against a disabled person was justified.

The DDA was given only a qualified welcome by disabled rights campaigners, on account of the perceived deficiencies in its provisions. In particular, concern was expressed about the extent to which employers were able to claim that discrimination against disabled persons was justified, and (at the outset) the absence of a commission similar to the EOC and the CRE with powers to investigate complaints, assist individuals in enforcing their legal rights, or take enforcement action on its own account. The incoming Labour government addressed some of the main criticisms by establishing a Disability Rights Commission, with powers similar to those of the EOC and CRE,[454] and reducing the small employer threshold from 20 to 15.

The case for reform of the DDA was given a major boost by the reaching of agreement in October 2000 on the EU Employment Framework Directive,[455] which required member states to introduce laws tackling, inter alia, disability discrimination in employment. Implementation of the Directive required some changes to be made to the DDA, such as the ending of the exemption for small firms, changes to the DDA's definition of discrimination and the availability of the justification defence.

[451] Department for Work and Pensions *The Employment of Disabled People 2024* <https://www.gov.uk/government/statistics/the-employment-of-disabled-people-2024/the-employment-of-disabled-people-2024#:~:text=For%20disabled%20people%2C%20there%20is,change%20was%20not%20statistically%20significant>.

[452] Joseph Rowntree Foundation *UK Poverty 2025* <https://www.jrf.org.uk/uk-poverty-2025-the-essential-guide-to-understanding-poverty-in-the-uk#:~:text=Disabled%20people%20face%20a%20higher,or%20other%20type%20of%20disability>.

[453] '9 out of 10 disabled people (87%) experiencing negative attitudes and behaviours said that they had a negative effect on their daily lives' Scope *Attitudes Research* https://www.scope.org.uk/campaigns/research-policy/attitudes-towards-disabled-people.

[454] Disability Rights Commission Act 1999.

[455] Directive 2000/78/EC.

The DDA has now been replaced by the Equality Act 2010. A notable feature of the DDA was the extent to which it left many fundamental issues and concepts to be clarified and expanded upon by Regulations, ministerial guidance, and codes of practice. The Equality Act 2010 maintains this approach. There are regulations relating to the definition of disability,[456] and the Secretary of State has issued guidance on 'matters to be taken into account in determining questions relating to the definition of disability',[457] and in addition the EHRC has issued an Equality Act 2010 Employment Code of Practice which contains a lengthy section on disability.[458] The Guidance and the Code of Practice are both admissible in evidence in proceedings before a tribunal, and must be taken into account where relevant. Incorporation of disability law within the Equality Act has made it work more like other discrimination law with regard to direct and indirect discrimination, harassment, and victimization. However, there are additional kinds of discrimination in relation to people with disabilities, which are explained at 4.7.3.

As with race, there may soon be further change as the current Labour government has proposed that the right to equal pay should be extended to those living with disabilities, with mandatory pay reporting for large employers with over 250 employees. It remains to be seen whether the consultation will lead to legislative change.

4.7.2 **The meaning of 'disability'**

4.7.2.1 **The core definition**

The core definition of disability is in the Equality Act 2010, s 6, which states that a disability is:

- a physical or mental impairment
- which has an effect which is both
  - substantial and
  - long-term
- on the ability to carry out normal day-to-day activities.

The core definition has a number of important extensions which are dealt with in 4.7.2.7. This core definition has been criticized for being too narrow and for adopting a medical as opposed to a social model of disability by defining disability in terms of impairments rather than focusing on the ways in which people with disabilities are disadvantaged by the organization, structure, and attitudes of the society in which they live and work.[459] It was recently confirmed that medical evidence should only be required when clearly necessary, but that a tribunal is not bound to accept the conclusions of a medical expert.[460]

[456] The Equality Act 2010 (Disability) Regulations 2010, SI 2010/2128.

[457] Available at <https://www.gov.uk/government/uploads/system/uploads/attachment_data/file/85010/disability-definition.pdf>.

[458] Available at <https://www.equalityhumanrights.com/en/publication-download/employment-statutory-code-practice>.

[459] See eg Hosking, 'A High Bar for EU Disability Rights' 36 (2007) ILJ 228; Lawson, 'Disability and Employment in the Equality Act 2010: Opportunities Seized, Lost and Generated' 40 (2011) ILJ 359; Doyle (1996) ILJ 1. Ironically, EC law may be even narrower because the ECJ held in *Chacon Navas v Eurest Colectividades SA* C-13/05 [2006] IRLR 706 that the Directive does not cover an employee who is merely sick, whereas it was always clear that the DDA can cover those suffering from long-term and debilitating sickness.

[460] Rejection of medical evidence does require substantive reasoning: *Connor v Chief Constable of South Yorkshire Police* [2024] EAT 175.

In *Goodwin v Patent Office*,[461] the EAT held that the tribunal should adopt a purposive approach to the interpretation of the definition and should construe the language of the statute in a way which gives effect to the stated or presumed intention of Parliament, but with due regard to the ordinary and natural meaning of the words. The Equality Act empowers the Secretary of State to issue guidance on applying this definition and a tribunal must take that guidance into account if relevant.[462] The current very extensive and helpful Guidance was issued in May 2011.[463]

4.7.2.2 The meaning of 'likely'

The word 'likely' plays an important part in many aspects of the definition of disability. Most lawyers would interpret the word as meaning 'more likely than not' but this has been authoritatively rejected in relation to the definition of disability under the DDA, and now the Equality Act. In *SCA Packaging Ltd v Boyle*,[464] the House of Lords held that 'likely' means 'could well happen', which is a significantly lower threshold than 'more likely than not'. As will become apparent below, this meaning has the result that many more people are to be regarded as disabled under the Act than might otherwise be the case.

4.7.2.3 Physical or mental impairment

First, there must be a 'physical or mental impairment'. These terms are not defined, but are intended to cover all forms of impairment, including sensory impairments. Mental illness originally only counted as a mental impairment if it was 'a clinically well-recognized illness' but this qualification was removed in 2005. The Court of Appeal set out the correct approach in *McNicol v Balfour Beatty Rail Maintenance Ltd*,[465] holding that the term 'impairment' bears its ordinary and natural meaning, that it 'may result from an illness or it may consist of an illness',[466] and, crucially, that 'it is not necessary to consider how an impairment was caused'.[467] This last point was recently underscored by the CJEU in holding that (a) obesity could be a disability if it constitutes an impairment and has the relevant adverse effects and (b) it does not matter whether the obesity was in some way self-inflicted.[468] Similarly, in *Zagorski v North West Anglia NHS Foundation Trust*, the EAT found that migraines were an impairment and had substantial adverse effects on day-to-day activities even though they were caused by exhaustion, which could have been avoided with a change of lifestyle.[469] It follows that in applying the statutory definition, the focus should be on whether a physical or mental function or activity is affected, rather than on what the exact cause of the impairment is.

A number of conditions are deemed not to be impairments for the purposes of the Act (eg dependency on alcohol, nicotine, or other non-prescribed substance; pyromania; kleptomania; a tendency to physical or sexual abuse of others; exhibitionism; voyeurism;

[461] [1999] ICR 302, [1999] IRLR 4, EAT. [462] Equality Act 2010, s 6(5) and Sch 1, para 12.

[463] 'Guidance on matters to be taken into account in determining questions relating to the definition of disability' available at <https://www.gov.uk/government/uploads/system/uploads/attachment_data/file/85010/disability-definition.pdf>.

[464] [2009] UKHL 37, [2009] IRLR 746, [2009] ICR 1056.

[465] [2002] EWCA Civ 1074, [2002] ICR 1498, [2002] IRLR 711.

[466] [2002] IRLR 711 at 713, per Mummery LJ. See to like effect Lindsay J in *College of Ripon & York St John v Hobbs* [2002] IRLR 185 at para 32 and *Millar v Inland Revenue Commissioners* [2006] IRLR 112, Ct of Sess (IH).

[467] [2002] EWCA Civ 1074, [2002] ICR 1498, [2002] IRLR 711, citing with approval Part 1 of the Guidance.

[468] *Kaltoft v Kommunernes Landsforening* C-354/13 (2014) [2015] IRLR 146, [2015] ICR 322. Some have suggested obesity should be its own protected characteristic—see Flint and Snook, 'Obesity and Discrimination: The Next "Big Issue"?' (2014) 14 Int J Discrimination L 183.

[469] [2024] EAT 164.

and 'seasonal allergic rhinitis'),[470] although impairments which stem from such excluded conditions are not themselves excluded.[471]

4.7.2.4 **Substantial adverse effect**

The impairment must have a 'substantial' adverse effect'.[472] 'Substantial' could mean 'big' or 'quite big' or it could just mean 'having some substance'. It has been held that in this context it means 'more than minor or trivial'[473] and this was subsequently expressly set out in s 212(1) of the 2010 Act. In *Goodwin v The Patent Office*,[474] the EAT emphasized that the Act is concerned with the effect of an impairment on a person's *ability* to carry out activities: 'The focus of attention required by the Act is on the things that the applicant either *cannot* do or can only do with difficulty, rather than on things that the person *can* do.' This approach avoids the danger of a tribunal concluding that as there are many things that an applicant can do, the adverse effect of the impairment cannot be substantial.[475]

The Guidance suggests that in determining whether the effect of an impairment is substantial, account should be taken of factors such as the time taken to carry out the activity (paragraph B2) and the way in which it is carried out (paragraph B3), in comparison with what might be expected if the person did not have the impairment.[476] The Guidance has a useful appendix containing a long list of adverse effects which it would be reasonable to regard as having a substantial effect on day-to-day activities and a list of those which it would not.

Paragraph B1 of the Guidance says that the word 'substantial' reflects 'the general understanding of "disability" as a limitation going beyond the normal differences in ability which may exist among people', but in *Elliott v Dorset County Council*[477] the EAT pointed out that the Guidance was not law and had to give way to the statute. It was clear, the EAT said, that the Guidance was on this point misleading: the question is the impact of the impairment on how the claimant carries out a task as compared with how that *same* person would carry it out without the impairment, and if the adverse effect on that is more than minor or trivial then they are disabled even if some other members of the general population would face the same difficulty.

4.7.2.5 **Long-term effect**

The impairment must have a 'long-term' effect, so that conditions which are only temporary, such as short-term illness, are not disabilities within the meaning of the Act. An impairment will be treated as having a long-term effect if it has lasted, or is likely to last,

[470] The Equality Act 2010 (Disability) Regulations 2010, SI 2010/2128, regs 3 and 4. These exclusions cannot be circumvented by arguing that they are merely symptoms of some other disability: *Edmund Nuttall v Butterfield* [2005] IRLR 751, EAT and *Wood v Durham County Council* UKEAT/009/18 (3 September 2018, unreported) disapproving *Murray v Newham CAB* [2003] IRLR 340, EAT.

[471] *Power v Panasonic UK Ltd* [2003] IRLR 151, EAT (depression resulting from alcohol addiction still capable of being an impairment within the meaning of the Act).

[472] Equality Act 2010, Sch 1, para 3 provides that a severe disfigurement will be treated as an impairment having a substantial adverse effect; deliberately acquired disfigurements such as tattoos or decorative body piercing are excluded.

[473] *Goodwin v Patent Office* [1999] ICR 302, [1999] IRLR 4; *Vicary v British Telecommunications plc* [1999] IRLR 680, EAT.

[474] *Goodwin v Patent Office* [1999] ICR 302, [1999] IRLR 4, per Morison J (emphasis added).

[475] *Leonard v Southern Derbyshire Chamber of Commerce* [2001] IRLR 19, EAT.

[476] The Guidance also advises that it may be appropriate to consider the cumulative effects of the impairment on a range of normal day-to-day activities (para B4), and the cumulative effects of more than one impairment (para B6).

[477] [2021] IRLR 880, EAT.

for at least 12 months,[478] or if it is likely to last for the rest of a person's life (as in the case of a terminal illness).[479] As explained in 4.7.2.2, it was made clear in the *SCA Packaging* case that 'likely' means 'could well happen', and in consequence many people in the first months of a condition such as back pain or reactive depression must now be considered as people with disabilities: even if the medical evidence is that it is more likely than not that the substantial adverse effect will cease within 12 months, nevertheless it 'could well happen' that the substantial adverse effect will last for that long.

In an important extension of the definition, where the impairment is intermittent or sporadic (eg epilepsy or multiple sclerosis) it will be treated as continuing to have a long-term adverse effect, even through periods of remission, if it is likely to recur.[480] It is the substantial adverse effect which must be likely to recur, not just the impairment.[481] Again, 'likely' means 'could well happen' (see 4.7.2.2).

4.7.2.6 **Adverse effect on ability to carry out normal day-to-day activities**

The impairment must have an adverse effect on a person's ability 'to carry out normal day-to-day activities'. Schedule 1 to the DDA contained an exhaustive list[482] of activities which are to be treated as normal day-to-day activities for these purposes, namely: mobility; manual dexterity; physical coordination; continence; ability to lift, carry, or otherwise move everyday objects; speech, hearing, or eyesight; memory or ability to concentrate, learn, or understand;[483] or the perception of the risk of physical danger. However, the Equality Act does not have such a list, leaving the issue to the Guidance, which says (paragraph D2) that no such exhaustive list is possible but does contain an appendix with a long list of adverse effects which it would be reasonable to regard having a substantial effect on day-to-day activities and a list of those which it would not.

'Normal day-to-day activities' are the activities of an ordinary average person, not a person with specialized skills or abilities. In deciding whether an activity is a normal day-to-day activity, the Guidance states that the phrase is not intended to cover an activity which is normal only for a small number of people and that account should be taken 'of how far it is normal for a large number of people and carried out by people on a daily or frequent basis' (paragraph D4). In *Vicary v British Telecommunications plc*,[484] normal day-to-day activities were held to include making beds, doing housework, sewing and cutting with scissors, minor DIY tasks, filing nails, curling hair, and ironing, since they are all 'activities which most people do on a frequent or fairly regular basis'.[485] In *Ekpe v Metropolitan Police Comr*,[486] the tribunal at first instance had held that the ability of a woman to put rollers in her hair and to use her right hand to apply make-up were not normal day-to-day activities because they were 'activities carried out almost

[478] The material time at which the disability must be assessed is the time of the alleged discriminatory act, not the date of the hearing (*Cruickshank v VAW Motorcast Ltd* [2002] ICR 729, [2002] IRLR 24, EAT), although the Guidance states (at para C3) that in assessing the likelihood of an effect lasting for any period, account should be taken of the total period for which the effect exists, including time before and after the point when the discriminatory act occurred. Cf also *Greenwood v British Airways plc* [1999] ICR 969, [1999] IRLR 600, EAT.

[479] Equality Act 2010, Sch 1, para 2(1).

[480] Equality Act 2010, para 2(2).

[481] *Connor v Chief Constable of South Yorkshire Police* [2024] EAT 175.

[482] DDA, Sch 1, para 4(1).

[483] This can cover Asperger's syndrome, on a wide interpretation of 'understanding': *Hewitt v Motorola Ltd* [2004] IRLR 545, EAT.

[484] [1999] IRLR 680, EAT.

[485] [1999] IRLR 680 at 682, per Morison P. See also *Abadeh v British Telecommunications plc* [2001] IRLR 23, [2001] ICR 156, EAT (travelling by Underground and flying held to be normal day-to-day activities because they were normal means of transport used by most people on a daily or frequent or fairly regular basis).

[486] [2001] IRLR 605, EAT.

exclusively by women', but the EAT, allowing the appeal, stated that what is 'normal' for these purposes may be best understood 'as anything which is not abnormal or unusual', and that the exclusion of any activity done by women rather than men (or vice versa) was 'plainly wrong'.[487]

The Guidance states that in some instances work-related activities are so highly specialized that they would not be regarded as 'normal day-to-day activities'.[488] However, under EU law the impact of an impairment on professional life must be taken into account in assessing whether someone is considered a disabled person.[489] The UK courts therefore read this into the interpretation of 'day-to-day activities' so that a substantial adverse effect on the claimant's work activities is sufficient even if there is no adverse effect on activities outside work.[490] To ensure this interpretation is maintained post-Brexit, the Equality Act has been amended to expressly say that in employment claims, a person's ability to carry out 'normal day-to-day activities' includes 'the person's ability to participate fully and effectively in working life on an equal basis with other workers'.[491] A further point to note is that the effects of an impairment may be exacerbated by conditions at work (eg exposure to fumes), and 'it would risk turning the Act on its head' if the employer were able to avoid any obligations under the Act (eg to make reasonable adjustments) by arguing that the employee was not disabled because the impairment only had a substantial adverse effect on normal day-to-day activities while the employee was at work.[492]

4.7.2.7 **Extensions to the definition and other special issues in applying the definition**

Deemed disability

A person with a severe disfigurement other than a tattoo or a non-medical body piercing is deemed to be a disabled person,[493] as is a person who is certified by a consultant ophthalmologist as blind, sight impaired, or partially sighted.[494]

Progressive conditions

There is an extension of the core definition in relation to impairments where there may eventually be a substantial effect on normal day-to-day activities, but the condition does not yet have that effect. If such an employee were not protected as a disabled person there would be a danger that an employer would 'get in quickly' and dismiss them so as to avoid having a protected disabled employee at a later date. Accordingly, the Equality Act Schedule 1 paragraph 8 provides that if in due course the condition is likely to have a substantial effect then as soon as there is some adverse effect, it is deemed to be substantial straight away. 'Likely' means only that this 'could well happen' (see 4.7.2.2).

[487] [2001] IRLR 605 at 609.

[488] Guidance, para D8. See eg *Quinlan v B & Q plc* (EAT 1386/97) (assistant at garden centre not disabled within the meaning of the Act because, although unable to lift heavy objects following heart surgery, he was capable of lifting everyday objects).

[489] *Chacón Navas v Eurest Colectividades* SA C-13/05, [2006] IRLR 706, [2007] All ER (EC) 59, CJEU.

[490] *Chief Constable of Norfolk v Coffey* [2019] EWCA Civ 1061, [2019] IRLR 805, *Igweike v TSB Bank Plc* [2020] IRLR 267, EAT.

[491] Equality Act 2010, Sch1 para 5A. Inserted by The Equality Act 2010 (Amendment) Regulations 2023, regs 1(2), 6.

[492] *Cruickshank v VAW Motorcast Ltd* [2002] ICR 729, [2002] IRLR 24, EAT (occupational asthma exacerbated by exposure to fumes at work).

[493] Equality Act 2010, Sch 1, para 3 and Equality Act 2010 (Disability) Regulations 2010 SI 2010/2128 reg 5.

[494] Equality Act 2010 (Disability) Regulations 2010 SI 2010/2128 reg 7.

This provision does not completely close the 'sack them early' loophole since some progressive conditions have *no* initial effect on the person's ability to carry out day-to-day activities, such as some cancers. To meet that concern the Act also provides that 'a person who has cancer, HIV infection or multiple sclerosis is to be deemed to have a disability'.[495] Those with other progressive conditions will, however, remain unprotected until the condition has some adverse effect, as will a person diagnosed as having a genetic predisposition to a potentially disabling condition.[496]

Conditions with intermittent effects are dealt with in 4.7.2.5.

Impact of medical treatment

The effect of an impairment on normal day-to-day activities must be considered without taking into account any measures which are being taken to treat or correct the impairment,[497] (eg medical treatment,[498] or the use of a prosthesis or other aid). The rationale is that such a person may experience discrimination even if the potentially disabling condition is controlled; so, for example, in the case of a person with diabetes which is controlled by medication, the question of whether or not the effect of the condition is substantial must be decided by reference to what the effects of the condition would be likely to be if that person were not taking their medication.[499] 'Likely' effects are those that 'could well happen' (see 4.7.2.2).

However, where the medical treatment creates a *permanent* improvement, the effects of that treatment *should* be taken into account in assessing the disability, as measures are no longer needed to treat or correct it once the permanent improvement has been established.[500]

Past disabilities

It is unlawful to discriminate against a person who has had a disability in the past, even if they have made a full recovery and are no longer disabled.[501] This recognizes the fact that a person with a history of disability (eg a person with a history of mental illness) may continue to experience discrimination even when no longer disabled. It is an example of the Act adopting a more 'social' model of disability.

[495] Equality Act 2010, Sch 1, para 6. The protection applies from the moment the disease exists even if it has not yet been diagnosed: *Bennett v Mitac Europe Ltd* [2022] IRLR 25, EAT. In the case of cancer, if the cancer has been successfully treated to the extent that no cancer cells remain in the person's body, then the person is no longer a disabled person, but if it is likely that some cancer cells remain then they are still disabled even if the medical evidence is that the cancer is in remission: *Da Silva Primaz v Carl Room Restaurants Ltd* [2022] IRLR 194, EAT.

[496] On the potential for genetic discrimination in employment, see the report of the Human Genetics Advisory Council, 'The Implications of Genetic Testing for Employment' (1999). The DRC has called for the Act's protection to be extended to those with a genetic predisposition: see *Disability Equality: Making it Happen* (2003).

[497] Equality Act 2010, Sch 1, para 5. This does not apply to those with impaired sight which is correctable by spectacles or contact lenses or some other prescribed method.

[498] This can include attendance at therapy or counselling sessions: *Kapadia v London Borough of Lambeth* [2000] IRLR 699.

[499] ie the tribunal must consider the 'deduced effects' of the impairment: *Goodwin v Patent Office* [1999] ICR 302, [1999] IRLR 4.

[500] *Abadeh v British Telecommunications plc* [2001] ICR 156, [2001] IRLR 23, EAT (although note that a person whose disabling impairment has been successfully treated remains protected by virtue of the provisions on past disability).

[501] Equality Act 2010, s 6(4).

Perception a person is disabled

As with other protected characteristics, coverage extends to those who are perceived to have a disability, and those in association with the disabled. This is discussed generally in 4.2.4.2, but some disability examples are instructive. First, refusing a requested job transfer because the employer speculated that existing low-level hearing problems would get worse and interfere with performance constituted discrimination on the basis of a perceived disability.[502] Second, discrimination was held to have occurred when an employer made a mother redundant because he thought she should be at home caring for her disabled daughter.[503]

Discrimination against non-disabled people?

Note that a non-disabled employee cannot claim direct discrimination because a disabled employee has been treated more favourably: s 13(3) expressly permits more favourable treatment. Moreover, the duty to make reasonable adjustments quite often will in practice *require* the employer to treat a disabled employee more favourably (see 4.7.2.3).

Proving disability

The claimant bears the burden of proof in establishing that they are a disabled person (but the general rules on burden of proof apply to whether the way they were treated was discrimination). The tribunal does not have a duty 'to conduct a free-standing inquiry of its own' into whether the claimant is disabled,[504] nor is it required to obtain evidence or to ensure that adequate medical evidence is obtained by the parties.[505] It may, however, exercise its discretion to grant an adjournment to enable the applicant to obtain further evidence, particularly where the applicant is not only in person but also suffers some mental weakness.[506]

One difficult practical issue for the tribunal is the weight to be placed on medical evidence. It is for the tribunal to decide whether the applicant has an impairment which has a substantial adverse effect on normal day-to-day activities, and the EAT has held that a tribunal makes an error of law if it relies too heavily on medical opinion on those issues.[507] The medical report should be confined to the doctor's diagnosis of the impairment, the doctor's observation of the applicant carrying out normal day-to-day activities, and the ease with which he was able to perform those functions, together with any relevant opinion as to prognoses and the effect of medication.[508]

4.7.3 **Additional kinds of disability discrimination**

In addition to the normal kinds of discrimination, the 2010 Act contains two special kinds of protection afforded only to the protected characteristic of disability: discrimination arising from disability (s 15) and the duty to make adjustments (s 20).

502 *Chief Constable of Norfolk v Coffey* [2019] EWCA Civ 1061, [2019] IRLR 805.

503 *McCorry v McKeith* [2016] NICA 47, [2017] IRLR 253.

504 *Rugamer v Sony Musical Entertainment UK Ltd* [2001] IRLR 644 at 652, clarifying the comment of Morison J in *Goodwin v Patent Office* [1999] IRLR 4 that the role of the tribunal 'contains an inquisitorial element'. See also *Morgan v Staffordshire University* [2002] IRLR 190 at 194, EAT.

505 *McNicol v Balfour Beatty Rail Maintenance Ltd* [2002] IRLR 711 at 714, per Mummery LJ.

506 *Morgan v Staffordshire University* [2002] IRLR 190 at 195, per Lindsay P (the President's guidance was approved by the Court of Appeal in *McNicol* [2002] IRLR 711).

507 *Vicary v British Telecommunications* [1999] IRLR 680, EAT.

508 *Abadeh v British Telecommunications plc* [2001] ICR 156, [2001] IRLR 23, per Nelson J.

4.7.3.1 **Discrimination arising from a disability**

The Equality Act 2010 s 15 provides that an employer A discriminates against a disabled person B, if A treats B unfavourably because of something arising in consequence of B's disability and the treatment is not a proportionate means to a legitimate aim. This reason for this provision is best understood by considering an example. In general, the evidence shows that disabled employees have a better attendance record than non-disabled employees, but some disabled employees have a poorer level of attendance or have a long period of absence before, it is hoped, they recover sufficiently to return to work. The intention of Parliament was that such employees should not be dismissed, even if a non-disabled employee would have been dismissed, if this was not justified by a 'substantial and material reason'.[509] In other words, employers were expected to go further in accommodating disabled employees. However, for reasons relating to the need to construe the employment and housing parts of the DDA consistently, the House of Lords interpreted the Act in *Lewisham LBC v Malcolm*[510] in a way which frustrated this aim. Parliament responded swiftly, introducing in s 15 of the 2010 Act the concept of 'discrimination arising from a disability'.

The way the law currently works can be illustrated by the example of the disabled employee with a record of attendance at work which would have led the employer to dismiss a non-disabled employee. If such a disabled employee is dismissed, their claim for direct discrimination will fail because s 23(2) of the Equality Act says that in such a case they must compare their treatment with that of a person with no material difference in their abilities—and a non-disabled person with the same attendance record would also have been dismissed. Instead, such a claimant must rely on s 15, discrimination arising from disability, which requires an employer not to treat them unfavourably because of something arising in consequence of their disability (the attendance record), unless this treatment is a proportionate means of achieving a legitimate aim. The issue for the tribunal will be whether the claimant's poor attendance was so bad that it was proportionate to dismiss them in order to achieve a legitimate aim such as securing a reasonable level of attendance or maintaining an efficient service.

'Unfavourable' treatment

Whether treatment is unfavourable is not to be established by any form of comparison; rather, '[t]he determination of that which is unfavourable involves an assessment in which a broad view is to be taken and which is to be judged by broad experience of life. Persons may be said to have been treated unfavourably if they are not in as good a position as others generally would be.'[511]

Knowledge of the disability on the part of the employer

The Act includes a specific requirement (s 15(2)) that the employer is only liable if it knows, or could reasonably be expected to know, of the disability. However, the case law has made it clear that the employer need not know that the problem results from the disability—it is enough that the employer knows of the disability, and that the treatment imposed by the employer amounts to a detriment 'because of' the disability.[512]

509 Disability Discrimination Act 1995, s 5(1) and (3).
510 [2008] UKHL 43, [2008] IRLR 700.

511 *Williams v Trustees of Swansea University Pension & Assurance Society* [2015] IRLR 885, [2015] ICR 197, EAT per Langstaff P, affirmed [2019] UKSC 65, [2019] IRLR 603.

512 *City of York Council v Grosset* [2018] EWCA Civ 1105 (the employer knew that the claimant suffered from acute anxiety, but did not know that the act of bad judgement for which he was fired resulted from the disability—it was found disproportionate, and thus discriminatory, to dismiss the claimant in these circumstances). See also *Basildon & Thurrock NHS Foundation Trust v Weerasinghe* [2016] ICR 305 (EAT).

Interrelation with the duty to make adjustments

The Equality Act makes no express reference to how s 15 on unfavourable treatment interrelates with the duty to make reasonable adjustments, whereas the DDA had done so. However, the duty to make reasonable adjustments must be relevant to the proportionality question in s 15. To put it another way, it cannot be proportionate to treat a person in a way that results in a detriment for them when reasonable adjustments are available to remove the detriment. For example, if a post delivery worker with a prosthetic leg cannot do their rounds quickly enough, the employer will not be able to argue that it is proportionate to dismiss them if a reasonable adjustment, such as the provision of a mobility aid, would have solved the problem. The Court of Appeal in *City of York Council v Grosset*[513] approved paragraph 5.21 of the EHRC Employment Code of Practice, which says that a failure to make reasonable adjustments will be an important factor in considering whether less favourable treatment is proportionate under s 15.

On the other hand, if no reasonable adjustments are available, or those that are available do not entirely overcome the issue, then the question is simply whether it is proportionate to treat the person in the relevant way. This will not be a complicated analysis where the matter in question is dismissal for being unable to perform the work required by the job. The analysis gets more difficult, however, if the case is more like the postal worker doing a slow round: how slow does it have to be before it is proportionate to dismiss? This question could *also* be analysed as a question of reasonable adjustments: would it be a reasonable adjustment to make a slight relaxation of the usual standard of speed? Some relaxation is reasonable (as we will see in 4.7.2.3), depending on the balance of the cost to the employer and the efficacy for the employee. A third possibility is that question could also be considered as a matter of indirect discrimination: the employer's standard requirement as to speed of delivery is a PCP and so the question arises as to whether the application of that standard to the post worker puts them and other disabled post delivery workers with the same disability at a particular disadvantage (yes), and, if so, is applying the PCP a proportionate means of achieving a legitimate aim? Unsurprisingly, the evidence so far is that all three ways of putting the claim tend to lead to the same result.[514]

Interrelation with unfair dismissal

The previous paragraph discusses the interrelation of three kinds of disability discrimination that might arise on one set of facts, but there is a further important interrelation, which is between these discrimination claims and a claim for unfair dismissal. In an unfair dismissal claim the question for the tribunal is *not* whether the tribunal would, in the employer's shoes, have dismissed the claimant, but whether the dismissal was within the range of reasonable responses (see 7.4.4). Can a tribunal accept that the employer's actions were within the range of what a reasonable employer might do (possibly at the extreme edge of it) but still decide that the dismissal was, for the purposes of s 15 and for any indirect discrimination claim, disproportionate? In *O'Brien v Bolton St Catherine's Academy*,[515] the claimant alleged that his dismissal was both unfair and amounted to unfavourable treatment for a

[513] [2018] EWCA Civ 1105, [2018] IRLR 746.

[514] See eg *The Government Legal Service v Brookes* [2017] IRLR 780, where the refusal to change the format of a skills assessment was held to be discrimination against a claimant with Asperger's Syndrome. It was analysed under indirect discrimination, the duty to make reasonable adjustments, and discrimination arising from a disability. The finding under indirect discrimination that the PCP was not proportionate led almost directly to a finding of a failure to make a reasonable adjustment. See also *General Dynamics Information Technology Ltd v Carranza* [2015] IRLR 43, [2015] ICR 169, where the EAT indicated that cases arising out of dismissal for poor attendance might be better approached as claims under s 15 rather than as claims for failure to make adjustments.

[515] [2017] IRLR 547.

reason arising out of his disability contrary to s 15. The Court of Appeal attempted to suggest that the tension between the two different tests' approaches is not a substantial one. However, the following year the same court, in *City of York Council v Grosset*,[516] recognized, surely rightly, that the difference is a real one and therefore that an employee might win one claim and lose the other. Subsequent EAT cases have followed the *Grosset* line and have indicated that all that the *O'Brien* case says is that often the outcome of the discrimination claim and the unfair dismissal claim will be the same.[517] The reality is that tribunals strive where they can to avoid 'split' outcomes because such results seem nonsensical to employers and employees. In this endeavour the tribunals are helped by the warning given by the EAT that in assessing proportionality they should give a substantial degree of respect to the judgment of the employer as to what is reasonably necessary to achieve the legitimate aim.[518]

4.7.3.2 **The duty to make adjustments**

Section 20 of the 2010 Act places a duty on the employer to make reasonable adjustments in each of these circumstances:

- where a provision, criterion, or practice of the employer places the disabled person concerned at a substantial disadvantage in comparison with persons who are not disabled;[519]
- in relation to any premises occupied by the employer, where any physical feature of buildings, furniture, or equipment or of any other physical thing places the disabled person concerned at a substantial disadvantage in comparison with persons who are not disabled;[520] and
- where the non-provision of auxiliary aids such as hearing loops and screen readers places the disabled person concerned at a substantial disadvantage in comparison with persons who are not disabled.[521]

Adjustments can include the alteration of buildings, the provision of equipment, and the changing of policies.[522] Failure to comply with the duty to make reasonable adjustments will constitute unlawful discrimination under s 21.[523]

The EHRC Employment Code of Practice (6.28) makes the following suggestions about factors to consider in applying the duty:

(a) the extent to which taking the step would prevent the effect in question;
(b) the extent to which it is practicable for the employer to take the step;
(c) the financial and other costs which would be incurred by the employer in taking the step and the extent to which taking it would disrupt any of his activities;
(d) the extent of the employer's financial and other resources;
(e) the availability to the employer of financial or other assistance; and
(f) the nature of the employer's activities and the size of his undertaking.

516 [2018] IRLR 746.

517 *Scott v Kenton Schools Academy Trust* UKEAT/0031/19 (30 September 2019, unreported), *Iceland Foods Ltd v Stevenson* UKEAT/0309/19 (13 February 2020, unreported), *Department of Work and Pensions v Boyers* UKEAT/0282/19 (24 June 2020, unreported), and *Knightley v Chelsea & Westminster Hospital NHS Foundation Trust* [2022] IRLR 567.

518 *Birtenshaw v Oldfield* [2019] IRLR 946.

519 Equality Act 2010, s 20(3).

520 This is the combined effect of Equality Act 2010, s 20(4) and (10) and Sch 8 para 2.

521 Equality Act 2010, s 20(5).

522 For examples of auxiliary aids see Equality Act 2010, s 20(9); Equality Act 2010 (Disability) Regulations 2010 SI 2010/2128, Parts 3 and 4; and the EHRC Employment Code of Practice Ch 6.

523 Equality Act 2010, s 21. A complaint of a failure to make a reasonable adjustment does not depend upon showing that there has been less favourable treatment: *Clark v Novacold Ltd* [1998] ICR 1044, [1998] IRLR 420, EAT.

It is for the employer to satisfy the tribunal that the duty to make reasonable adjustments has been observed. It will not be good enough for the employer to show that the applicant was unable to think of any satisfactory adjustments if the employer has given no thought to the matter.[524] On the other hand, if there were no particular steps which the employer ought reasonably to have taken in all the circumstances, the employer will have a defence, even if it gave no consideration to the matter. As the EAT stated in *British Gas Services Ltd v McCaull*,[525] the test is an objective one: 'The test of whether it was reasonable for an employer to have to take a particular step . . . does not relate to what the employer considered but to what he did and did not do'; an employer does not fail to comply with the duty merely because it has not consciously considered what steps might reasonably be taken. The duty to make adjustments does not arise if the employer does not know, and could not reasonably be expected to know, that the person has a disability which is likely to place him or her at a substantial disadvantage in comparison with non-disabled persons.[526]

One key issue is *how* a tribunal is to judge whether the employer has or has not fulfilled this duty. When it was argued that tribunals should apply a version of the band of reasonable responses (from unfair dismissal law) to the reasonableness of adjustments in *Smith v Churchill Stairlifts plc*,[527] the Court of Appeal disagreed. Although there may have been some policy arguments in favour of giving the employer a 'margin of appreciation' (given how broad and ill-defined the whole idea of reasonable adjustment is), the court held that, under the wording of the statute, the test to be applied by a tribunal is *objective*. This means that the tribunal will simply decide whether *it* considers that all reasonable adjustments were made on the facts of the case. This clearly makes the test potentially more difficult for the employer and more protective for the employee—it is very like the proportionality test in indirect discrimination.

Practical application

Turning to what 'reasonable adjustments' means in substance, we again see a wide and purposive approach by the courts. Any idea that it only means ramps, wider doors, and voice-activated computers is seriously misinformed. The duty may require a large element of lateral thinking by the employer.

The leading authority is *Archibald v Fife Council*,[528] where a council road sweeper became unable to walk. Considerable effort was put into trying to find alternative employment, but all the available posts were at higher levels, for which she would not normally be eligible. The council made the adjustment of allowing her to *apply*, but insisted on continuing with their normal (statute-backed) policy of open competition for such posts. Although she applied for many of them, there was always a better candidate and so (after a considerable period) the decision was eventually taken to dismiss her. The House of Lords took a particularly liberal approach to her position and held that the council had *not* necessarily made all reasonable adjustments: a reasonable adjustment could include actually *appointing* her to such a vacancy, in preference to a better qualified candidate. The decision demonstrates very clearly that, unlike with other protected characteristics,

[524] *Cosgrove v Caesar and Howie* [2001] IRLR 653, EAT.

[525] [2001] IRLR 60, EAT.

[526] Equality Act 2010, Sch 8, para 20. See also *Eastern and Coastal Kent PCT v Grey* [2009] All ER (D) 171. In the case of a disabled applicant, the duty only applies in relation to a person who is, or has notified the employer that they may be, an applicant for the employment.

[527] [2006] ICR 524, [2006] IRLR 41, CA, distinguishing *Jones v Post Office* [2001] EWCA Civ 558.

[528] [2004] ICR 954, [2004] IRLR 651, HL. In *Southampton City College v Randall* [2006] IRLR 18, EAT it was even held that the employer should have *created* a job for the disabled employee, but that was on particular facts (in particular that the college was at the time going through a 'blank sheet of paper' exercise in restructuring all jobs).

the law not only *permits* an employer to treat people with disabilities more favourably than others,[529] but quite often will in practice *require* the employer to do so. As Lady Hale put it in the *Archibald* case, 'to the extent that the duty to make reasonable adjustments requires it, the employer is not only permitted but obliged to treat a disabled person more favourably than others'.[530]

One area that has been much debated in the past, given that the employer has to look beyond the physical requirements of the job, is whether even *contractual terms* such as sick pay schemes may have to be reasonably adjusted. Such a scheme will tend to allow a fixed period on sick pay, so two questions have arisen—(a) in working out the employee's maximum period of entitlement, must the employer 'strip out' any sickness absence due to the employee's disability? (b) Going even further, if the long-term sickness is because of the disability, should the employer disapply the normal sick pay rules and continue to pay full pay for the whole period? In favour of employees, it was argued that both of these should be viewed as reasonable adjustments (especially after the expansive decision in *Archibald*).

With regard to issue (a), in *Royal Liverpool Children's NHS Trust v Dunsby*,[531] the EAT under Judge Richardson held that there is no rule that disability-related absences must always be disregarded in calculating the period for which the employee is entitled to sick pay, thus leaving it as a question to be assessed on the reasonable test in each case.

In *Nottinghamshire CC v Meikle*,[532] the Court of Appeal considered that adjustment (b) would indeed have been a reasonable adjustment. However, that was on peculiar facts, in that the employee's absence with stress (the disability relied on) had itself been caused by the employer's failure to deal properly with the problem that he had been experiencing with worsening eyesight. In *O'Hanlon v HMRC*,[533] the EAT made it clear that *Meikle* was a special case and that normally it would not be reasonable to require the employer to extend the sick pay period. When *O'Hanlon* went on further appeal, the Court of Appeal strongly backed this decision of the EAT.[534]

However, more recently the position appears to have softened somewhat. In *G4S Cash Solutions (UK) Ltd v Powell*,[535] the EAT distinguished *O'Hanlon*, finding that it could be a reasonable adjustment to extend temporary pay protection—keeping the salary the same while the disabled employee is assigned to otherwise lower-paid work that does not conflict with the disability. Noting that the objective of the legislation was to keep people with disabilities in work, the EAT concluded that on the facts, which included the pay protection as part of a package of measures, this was an adjustment the employer was required to make.

In keeping with this more protective approach, the Court of Appeal recently corrected a tendency of the EAT to preclude reasonable adjustment of sick absence disciplinary policies. The issue here is not pay, but whether it can be a reasonable adjustment to permit a disabled employee to accrue more absences before any disciplinary action occurs. Several EAT cases had taken the position that such disciplinary policies did not place people with disabilities at a disadvantage since non-disabled employees would receive the same discipline for the same number of absences.[536] This is of course another example of judicial refusal to give effect to anti-discrimination law as intended. Fortunately

[529] Equality Act 2010, s 13(3).

[530] At para [68]. For a more recent example, see *Wolfe v North Middlesex University Hospital NHS Trust* [2015] ICR 960 (EAT).

[531] [2006] IRLR 751, EAT.

[532] [2004] IRLR 703, CA.

[533] [2006] IRLR 840, EAT.

[534] [2007] EWCA Civ 283.

[535] UKEAT/0243/15 (26 August 2016, unreported).

[536] See eg *Rider v Leeds City Council* UKEAT/0243/11, [2013] EqLR 98, [2013] All ER (D) 271 (EAT) and *Bailey v Hillingdon London Borough Council* UKEAT/0421/12, [2013] EqLR 729, [2013] All ER (D) 205 (EAT).

the Court of Appeal in *Griffiths v Secretary of State for Work and Pensions*[537] stopped the bleeding, making the obvious observation that a requirement for an employee to maintain a particular standard of attendance at work in order to avoid disciplinary sanctions is a PCP with which some people with disabilities would find it harder to comply, and hence would place them at a disadvantage. The upshot is that disapplying a cap on absences can be a reasonable adjustment, but only if it will actually help the employee stay in work: where no end of the absence from work can be identified, it will not be reasonable to extend it indefinitely.[538]

Cost and reasonableness

Employment lawyers had wondered for some time whether the relatively high cost of an adjustment, which clearly can be taken into account, can stand alone as the sole reason for finding a requested adjustment unreasonable. The Court of Appeal answered this question in the affirmative in *Cordell v Foreign and Commonwealth Office*.[539] Although the judgment makes it clear that all of the relevant factors, such as efficacy, size of undertaking, and even what the employer and similar employers have been prepared to spend in the past, must be considered, in the end the decision of the employer turned on its conclusion that the cost of the adjustment was simply unpalatable, even though strictly speaking it could be afforded. The claimant, who was profoundly deaf, needed lip-speakers in a foreign language in order to be appointed to a post abroad, but the cost of this provision was 'five times the claimant's annual salary'. The claimant pointed out that the respondent had a policy of paying for the children of members of the diplomatic service to attend private, British-style schools and travel three times a year to visit their parents, so where an employee had five or more children the costs under that policy could rival those of the necessary lip-speakers. The Court held that the tribunal had considered the competing factors appropriately, and had taken account of the education expense policy, and had reached a lawful decision that the lip-speaker expense was unreasonable under the circumstances. This case does not mean that 'five times the claimant's salary' will become any kind of test. However, it does supply precedent for the idea that cost can make an adjustment unreasonable even if the employer can afford that cost and has decided to afford it for other objectives.

4.8 **Age discrimination**

4.8.1 **History**

At the 1997 election Labour indicated a desire to legislate on this inherently difficult area, but the only result was a low-key and anodyne code of practice that had little effect. The pace of change was eventually forced by the inclusion of age in the Employment Framework Directive 2000/78/EC, albeit with more exceptions than for other protected characteristics. The Directive gave member states until October 2006 to comply and, in the UK, resulted in the Employment Equality (Age) Regulations 2006.[540] In due course these provisions were replaced, with some changes, by the Equality Act 2010.

[537] [2015] EWCA Civ 1265, [2016] IRLR 216.

[538] Whether a particular measure will be effective poses a particular challenge for those with mental disabilities, such as depression, ADHD, or autism, especially because few employers have any idea what will work. For a further discussion of these issues, see Bell 'Mental Health at Work and the Duty to Make Reasonable Adjustments' (2015) 44 ILJ 194.

[539] [2012] ICR 280, [2012] All ER (D) 97.

[540] SI 2006/1031; See Sargeant 'The Employment Equality (Age) Regulations 2006: A Legitimisation of Age Discrimination in Employment' (2006) 35 ILJ 209.

4.8.2 **The meaning of 'age'**

The characteristic protected in relation to age is a person being in a particular age group.[541] An age group can be defined by a particular age or by a range of ages.[542] What this means is that a claimant can pick the age group that most assists their claim, whether that be 'people under 25' or 'people between 45 and 60' or even 'people aged 52'.

4.8.3 **Justified direct age discrimination**

The 2010 Act protects against age discrimination in the standard ways with regard to direct and indirect discrimination, harassment, and victimization. However, there is then one *major* difference from all other heads of illegal discrimination. This is that s 13(2) permits *direct* age discrimination if it is a proportionate means of achieving a legitimate aim. With all other protected characteristics, treating someone less favourably because of a protected characteristic is permitted only on very narrow grounds, usually on the basis of a Genuine Occupational Requirement, but in relation to age the scope for lawful direct discrimination is much wider. This special treatment of age discrimination stems from article 6 (1) of the Equal Treatment Directive which states:

> Notwithstanding Article 2(2), Member States may provide that differences of treatment on grounds of age shall not constitute discrimination, if, within the context of national law, they are objectively and reasonably justified by a legitimate aim, including legitimate employment policy, labour market and vocational training objectives, and if the means of achieving that aim are appropriate and necessary.

The Directive goes on to say that such differences of treatment may include, among others:

> (a) the setting of special conditions on access to employment and vocational training, employment, and occupation, including dismissal and remuneration conditions, for young people, older workers, and persons with caring responsibilities in order to promote their vocational integration or ensure their protection;
>
> (b) the fixing of minimum conditions of age, professional experience, or seniority in service for access to employment or to certain advantages linked to employment;
>
> (c) the fixing of a maximum age for recruitment which is based on the training requirements of the post in question or the need for a reasonable period of employment before retirement.

As can be seen, this provision appears to permit direct age discrimination for the purposes of any legitimate aim, and then state that such aims include employment policies and labour market and vocational objectives followed by some examples. In contrast the UK's implementing legislation, s 13(2), gives no indication of what kinds of aim might be legitimate. However, decisions of the CJEU make it clear that the range of legitimate aims is narrower than in relation to indirect discrimination. These cases were reviewed and very helpfully summarized by the Supreme Court in *Seldon v Clarkson Wright and Jakes.*[543] The Supreme Court declared that it was clear from the CJEU cases that the approach to justification of direct age discrimination is 'significantly different' from justification of indirect discrimination (where any 'real business need' of the employer can be a legitimate aim). Direct age discrimination may only be justified if the relevant

[541] Equality Act s 5(1). [542] Equality Act s 5(2).
[543] [2012] UKSC 16, [2010] IRLR 590, [2012] ICR 716.

treatment seeks to achieve a legitimate aim of a public interest nature such as those listed in Article 6(1)—employment policy, the labour market, and vocational training. So, these limitations on what can be legitimate aims must be read into the ability to justify direct age discrimination given by s 13(2) of the Equality Act.

This ability to justify direct age discrimination has so far been used to justify arrangements such as the following: enhanced redundancy schemes providing bigger payments for older employees than young ones with the same length of service;[544] points for long service in a redundancy selection process;[545] an age threshold for the vesting of pension rights;[546] and a maximum age for recruitment of firefighters in order to ensure that enough firefighters in employment were young and so likely to be fit enough for frontline duties.[547] Many of the cases have been about compulsory retirement ages, some of which have been held to be justified and others not (see below at 4.8.4).

4.8.4 **Compulsory retirement**

Compulsory retirement of an employee at 65 or the normal retirement age (if different) was not legally an issue before age discrimination was prohibited, because the law expressly provided that an employee at or beyond that age could not claim unfair dismissal.[548] This exclusion was repealed when age discrimination was banned, and so an employee of any age can now claim unfair dismissal.[549]

A 'pure' version of age discrimination could have left it at that, that is, with no compulsory (or even fall-back) retirement age, so that an employee could choose to carry on working to any age (subject to a dismissal for incapability). Initially the government decided not to go for such a radical approach and exempted compulsory retirement *at or above age 65* from age discrimination. This was challenged as not transposing the Directive properly in the so-called Heydey application, *National Council on Ageing (Age Concern) v SoS for BERR*.[550] The ECJ ruled that such an exception was potentially permitted provided that it pursued a legitimate aim proportionately. The case returned to the UK High Court, where Blake J ruled that while a compulsory retirement age was in principle acceptable when the Regulations were made in 2006, by 2009 he doubted that an age of 65 could be justified.[551]

The government undertook a consultation exercise on this, which led to repeal of the default compulsory retirement age—not just at 65 but at any age.[552] This does not mean that employees may not be compelled to retire at a given age, just that employers cannot rely on a general statutory exemption and have to be able to justify any compulsory retirement policy they adopt under the general regime for direct age discrimination as set out in 4.8.3.

The CJEU has subjected such policies to intense scrutiny in connection with the legitimacy of their aims and the proportionality of the laws in achieving them.[553] The effect of

[544] *MacCulloch v ICI* [2008] All ER (D) 81.

[545] *Rolls Royce v Unite the Union* [2008] EWHC 2420, [2008] All ER (D) 174.

[546] *Air Products Plc v Cockram* [2018] EWCA Civ 346.

[547] *Wolf v Stadt Frankfurt am Main* C-229/08, [2010] IRLR 244, CJEU.

[548] Employment Rights Act 1996, s 109, repealed by the Employment Equality Age Regulations 2006, SI 2006/1031 as from 1 October 2006.

[549] Note that this applies whatever the ground of dismissal; it is not confined to retirement cases.

[550] Case C-388/07, [2009] IRLR 373, [2009] ICR 1080.

[551] [2009] EWCH 2336 (Admin) [2009] IRLR 1017.

[552] The Employment Equality (Repeal of Retirement Age Provisions) Regulations 2011, SI 2011/1069, reg 5.

[553] *Fuchs and Kohler v Land Hessen* C-159/10, C-160/10, [2011] All ER (D) 97; *Hörnfeldt v Posten Meddelande* C-141/11, [2012] IRLR 785, *Rosenbladt v Oellerking Gebaudereinigung mBh* C-045/09, [2011] IRLR 51.

these cases was helpfully summarized by the Supreme Court in *Seldon v Clarkson Wright and Jakes*,[554] a case which involved a law firm's partnership agreement, which called for partners to retire at 65. Lady Hale said in relation to compulsory retirement ages:

> Two different kinds of legitimate objective have been identified by the Luxembourg court. The first kind may be summed up as *inter-generational fairness*. This is comparatively uncontroversial. It can mean a variety of things, depending upon the particular circumstances of the employment concerned: for example, it can mean facilitating access to employment by young people; it can mean enabling older people to remain in the workforce; it can mean sharing limited opportunities to work in a particular profession fairly between the generations; it can mean promoting diversity and the interchange of ideas between younger and older workers.
>
> The second kind may be summed up as *dignity*. This has been variously put as avoiding the need to dismiss older workers on the grounds of incapacity or underperformance, thus preserving their dignity and avoiding humiliation, and as avoiding the need for costly and divisive disputes about capacity or underperformance. Either way, it is much more controversial. As Age UK argue, the philosophy underlying all the anti-discrimination laws is the dignity of each individual, the right to be treated equally irrespective of either irrational prejudice or stereotypical assumptions which may be true of some but not of others.[555]

Two of the firm's aims fell under the intergenerational fairness heading and one under the dignity heading. The Supreme Court also held that a general policy, as opposed to each retirement on its own merits, could be justified, but that the use of a general policy must be a proportionate means to the legitimate objectives. Once the use of a general policy has been justified, each individual retirement under it is presumed justified.

The Supreme Court's doubts about the dignity aim are surely well placed: this reason for a compulsory retirement age involves getting rid of some employees whose ability may be fading at a particular age at the expense of dismissing others who are still performing well. It is hard to see how this can be a proportionate course of action when proper performance management or individual discussions with the fading employees about their future would surely be perfectly possible. Nevertheless, the CJEU has clearly backed dignity as a legitimate aim. UK courts may be reluctant to hold that it is proportionate to operate a compulsory retirement age in pursuance of that aim: Lady Hale indicated that it might not be proportionate if the employer already had a sophisticated performance management system in place,[556] and when the *Seldon* case returned to the employment tribunal after its trip to the CJEU and the Supreme Court the firm only relied on the intergenerational fairness aim.[557]

Seldon demonstrates that employers *can* adopt a retirement policy but had better consider very carefully their reasons for doing so, whether they are consistent with the policies in the Directive, and whether a general policy is a proportionate means of achieving them (eg is there a way of achieving those aims that does not require direct age discrimination?). The EAT has made it clear that tribunals must scrutinize the proportionality of company retirement schemes much more carefully than does the CJEU in assessing member state retirement schemes; a particular emphasis was placed on considering whether a less discriminatory measure might have met the stated aim.[558] Tribunals can arrive at different decisions on situations which look very similar. This was dramatically illustrated in the contrasting cases of *Pitcher v University of Oxford* and *University of*

[554] [2012] UKSC 16, [2010] IRLR 590, [2012] ICR 716.

[555] [2012] UKSC 16, [2010] IRLR 590, [2012] ICR 716 at [56]–[57].

[556] [2012] UKSC 16, [2010] IRLR 590, [2012] ICR 716 at [61].

[557] [2014] IRLR 748, EAT.

[558] *Sargeant v London Fire and Emergency Planning Authority* [2018] IRLR 302.

Oxford v Ewart.[559] The university's policy provided for compulsory retirement at the age of 67 but with a possibility of individuals applying for an extension. Professor Pitcher applied for an extension but this was refused. Professor Ewart was given a fixed-term extension but on its expiry was required to leave. The legitimate aims relied on by the university were inter-generational fairness, succession planning, and equality and diversity (because new recruits were more diverse than the existing staff). In Pitcher's case the employment tribunal noted that the policy was relatively new and so there was limited evidence of its impact on the stated aims, but, taking into account some survey evidence and the fact that the extension provision provided some mitigation of the impact of the policy, held that it was justified. In Ewart's case there was some statistical evidence on the effect of the policy, which was that it only increased the rate of vacancies by 2–4 per cent. The Ewart tribunal held that the policy, even with the extension provision, was not justified, balancing its 'severe' discriminatory effect on older academics against the extent to which the legitimate aims were achieved. The appeals were heard together by the EAT and both ET decisions were upheld, based on the different evidence before them and the principle that the assessment as to proportionality was an assessment to be made by the tribunal hearing the case. Given the difficulties, dramatically illustrated by these two cases, of being sure that a compulsory retirement policy is lawful, many employers have abandoned their compulsory retirement age.[560]

4.8.5 **Specific exceptions relating to age**

The Equality Act contains a number of specific exceptions in relation to age discrimination. Three important ones are considered here.

First, age discrimination is permitted in relation to the national minimum wage, and so lower rates for younger employees continue.[561] The government's justification for this is that it promotes access of younger employees to the world of work. Second, there is an exception relating to pay and benefits based on length of service.[562] Enhancements in respect of length of service are common and the government was keen not to render them unlawful at a stroke. On the other hand, they do have an indirectly discriminatory effect on younger employees, who are more likely to have short service. Relying on the ordinary justification defence for indirect discrimination might be difficult with a lengthy pay spine (with annual increments) since the facts might well show that it only takes a few years to reach a level of competence in that job. The eventual compromise was, in effect, to give an employer a minimum of five years' grace. Schedule 9, paragraph 10 states that is it not age discrimination to have a service-related reward for up to five years but beyond five years a service-related pay or benefits difference will only be lawful if it reasonably appears to the employer that the way in which it uses the criterion of length of service fulfils a business need of its undertaking. The previous regulations gave examples of such business needs, namely encouraging the loyalty or motivation, or rewarding the experience, of its workers, but this is no longer spelled out in the legislation. This exception is noteworthy in that it depends on the reasonable belief of the employer rather than an assessment of proportionality by the tribunal, and so it may go beyond what was permitted by EU law. However, post-Brexit this UK exception might well be held by the courts to be effective.

A further important exception relates to contractual redundancy payments. The government took the view that the existing age-weighting in the statutory redundancy

[559] [2021] IRLR 946, EAT.

[560] A useful discussion of the factors considered by courts and tribunals in justifying retirement policies can be found in Dewhurst 'Proportionality Assessments of Mandatory Retirement Measures: Uncovering Guidance for National Courts in Age Discrimination Cases' (2016) 45 ILJ 60.

[561] Equality Act 2010, Sch 9, para 11.

[562] Equality Act 2010, Sch 9, para 10.

payments scheme (which is directly discriminatory) and the service-related weighting (which is indirectly discriminatory)[563] was objectively justified. To mirror this, Schedule 9, paragraph 13 provides that a contractual scheme can lawfully give enhanced benefits *provided* that the basic method of increase by age and service is a multiple of the statutory scheme (and/or consists of raising or removing the statutory cap on a week's pay). Many contractual schemes are not simple multiples of the statutory scales, and such schemes would need to be individually justified by the employer if challenged by an employee.

4.9 Gender reassignment discrimination

Protection against discrimination because of gender reassignment was brought into UK law as a result of the decision of the ECJ in *P v S and Cornwall County Council*[564] that the absence of protection was contrary to European law. This led to amendments to the SDA to cover gender reassignment discrimination. This was carried forward into the 2010 Act with a slightly wider definition of gender reassignment and an additional element of protection. Under the 2010 Act the protection extends to anyone who is proposing to undergo, is undergoing, or has undergone a process or part of a process for reassigning their sex by changing physiological or other attributes of sex.[565] The former requirement that this must be under medical supervision has been removed.

In addition to the usual kinds of discrimination applying to gender reassignment, it is also discrimination for a person who is absent from work as a result of undergoing gender reassignment to be treated less favourably than would be the case if the absence was due to sickness or injury (or to some other cause where it is not reasonable for the treatment to be less favourable).[566]

There is an exception to liability for gender reassignment discrimination which relates to religion. This also applies to elements of sexual orientation and is discussed in 4.4.

Although trans people retain this important protection from discrimination, many have been distressed by the recent *For Women Scotland Ltd v The Scottish Ministers* (see 4.3). For example, Cowan argues that this judgment undermines trans people's rights significantly.[567] An example she draws on is that a trans woman bringing an equal pay claim would now have to find a cisgender woman comparator. She notes that:

> not only is this patently illogical and contradicts the social reality of the trans woman's experience, preventing trans women from bringing equal pay claims against cisgender men flies in the face of evidence that trans women, like other women, are routinely underpaid when compared to men. . . .[568]

4.10 Marital and civil partnership status discrimination

Discrimination on the ground of being married, but not discrimination against those who are unmarried, has been illegal since the adoption of the SDA in 1975. The protection has been extended to civil partnership.[569]

[563] See 8.1.4. [564] C-13/94, [1996] IRLR 347, [1996] ICR 795. [565] Equality Act 2010, s 7.

[566] Equality Act 2010, s 16.

[567] Cowan 'Trans Rights, Queer Times: In Search of a New Hope' (2025) 47 Journal of Social Welfare and Family Law 108.

[568] Cowan 'Trans Rights, Queer Times: In Search of a New Hope' (2025) 47 Journal of Social Welfare and Family Law 108, 121–22.

[569] Equality Act 2010, s 8.

Incredible as it may now seem, it used to be common for employees, especially women, to be dismissed if they got married.[570] A more modern example is *Gould v Trustees of St John's Downshire Hill*,[571] where a minister of religion argued that he had been dismissed because of difficulties in his marriage, and that this was less favourable treatment 'because of' his marital status.

Different panels of the EAT have issued conflicting judgments as to whether discrimination based on the actual person with whom the claimant is married or partnered (as opposed to based on the status of being married or partnered) receives protection as discrimination 'because of' marriage or civil partnership.[572] The balance of opinion in the EAT, and surely the better view, is that protection should only extend to the status of being married: as the EAT pointed out in the *Hawkins* case,[573] it will sometimes be legitimate for employers to accord different treatment to employees who are parties to a close personal relationship, for reasons such as conflicts of interest and perceptions of favouritism, and such treatment may be 'less favourable'. If marriage or civil partnership discrimination covered this kind of situation this could lead to inconsistency of treatment between different categories of family member: for example, Mr X could bring a claim because he was married to Mrs X and so not allowed to join her department, but Mr Y could not bring a claim when he was not allowed to join the department of his live-in partner Miss Z.

There is an exception to liability for marital and civil partnership status discrimination which relates to religion. This also applies to elements of sexual orientation and is discussed in 4.4.

4.11 Pregnancy and maternity discrimination

Much adverse treatment related to pregnancy and maternity will amount to sex discrimination. For that reason, the provisions directly outlawing pregnancy and maternity discrimination are limited in extent. Indirect discrimination and harassment do not apply—they are left to protection via sex.[574]

However, there is an additional form of protection: it is unlawful direct discrimination to treat a woman unfavourably because of her pregnancy or because of illness suffered by her as a result of her pregnancy, or for taking statutory maternity leave, at any time during a defined pregnancy and maternity period.[575] Note that no comparison is required here; the case law in relation to unfavourable treatment for disability will apply (see 4.7.3.1).

There have been some amendments to the Equality Act 2010 to ensure that protection is not changed as a result of Brexit. This includes:

- 'Maternity' has replaced 'childbirth' in s 13(6)(b) of the Equality Act, which relates to affording women special treatment. This ensures the more expansive understanding in EU law is reflected in UK law.[576] Section 13(6)(a) has been amended to ensure that less favourable treatment of a woman includes less favourable treatment at

[570] On both the historical context as well as the future of this protected characteristic, see Hand 'The Curious Case of Marriage/Civil Partnership Discrimination in Britain' (2012) 12 Int J Discrimination L 166.

[571] UKEAT/0115/17 (5 October 2017, unreported). The client ultimately lost the case because the tribunal decided that he was dismissed because he fell out with parish officials and not because he was having marital difficulties.

[572] *Dunn v The Institute of Cemetery and Crematorium Management* UKEAT/0531/10, [2012] All ER (D) 173 (holding that it is); *Hawkins v (1) Atex Group (2) Korsvold (3) Malo de Molina (4) Reardon*, UKEAT/0302/11, [2012] All ER (D) 71 (holding that it is not), which was followed in *Gould v St John's Downshire Hill* UKEAT/0002/20 (5 June 2020, unreported).

[573] See n 572.

[574] Equality Act 2010, s 19(3) and 26(5).

[575] Equality Act 2010, s 18.

[576] Equality Act 2010 (Amendment) Regulations 2023, reg 2(2)(a).

work because she is breastfeeding.[577] Previously, discrimination at work expressly excluded this.

- Section 18 of the Equality Act has been amended to ensure that unfavourable treatment which takes place after the end of the protected period but because of the pregnancy and protected period, can still be considered discrimination.[578]

Although not forming part of 'discrimination law', the law relating to maternity leave does, along with other family leave rights, contribute to seeking to achieve more equality of opportunity and equality of participation for women at work. These rights are considered in Chapter 5.

Review and Final Thoughts

- We have seen that prohibitions on direct discrimination, the most intuitive conception of discrimination, could not address the more pervasive and stubborn inequality that results from (usually) unintentionally arranging things in such a way as to suit majority or dominant groups at the expense of minorities, women, people with disabilities, and so on. To deal with this more difficult problem the law has developed concepts such as indirect discrimination, positive action, discrimination arising from a disability, and the duty to make reasonable adjustments. Furthermore, judges have refused to excuse differential treatment simply because there is no discriminatory motive. This generally reflects a shift in focus from the intentions of the accused discriminator to the effects of a decision or policy on the claimant. See footnotes 44, 89, and 155 for further reading.
- The most important way for a claimant to establish that an unequal experience is because of a protected characteristic—even where the employer denies it—is comparison. For direct discrimination, the comparator is another employee (sometimes hypothetical), without the claimant's protected characteristic, whose circumstances are the same in 'material' ways (eg qualifications, job, experience, and so on); if there is no other relevant difference between the comparators, a tribunal can infer that the protected characteristic explains any less favourable treatment. For indirect discrimination the comparison is between groups of employees with and groups without the claimant's protected characteristic.
- Indirect discrimination deals with situations where a provision, criterion, or practice (PCP) intended to be neutral actually puts people with a protected characteristic at a disadvantage compared to most employees. Sometimes this cannot be avoided, but where it happens the law requires that the employer prove that the PCP is proportionate, in that it imposes no more disadvantage than it needs to in order to meet the employer's need, and no more than is justified by that need.
- Anti-discrimination law, by its terms, requires that employers not place unwanted constraints on one sex that they do not place on another. However, a lot of people—and judges are no different—find it difficult to accept that this really means that people can act and dress in ways that are not expected for people of their gender. As a result, despite everything you have read about the law in this chapter, it remains lawful for a woman to be forbidden to wear clothes that a man is allowed to wear, and vice versa.

[577] Equality Act 2010 (Amendment) Regulations 2023, reg 2(2)(b). This gives effect to *Otero Ramos v Servicio Galego de Saude* (C-531/15).

[578] Equality Act 2010 (Amendment) Regulations 2023, reg 2(3)–(10). This gives effect to *Brown v Rentokil Ltd* C-394/96.

- The law forbids discrimination against people because of what they believe or the religion they follow. It does not, however, prohibit negative treatment because of acts done by religious people that are themselves unlawful discrimination or otherwise in conflict with the equality principle. It is therefore not religious discrimination to prohibit adverse treatment on grounds of sexual orientation even when that treatment is motivated by a religious (or other) belief.
- Disability discrimination law is different, and more demanding, than other aspects of equality law because many elements of our society create indirect discrimination against people with disabilities: physical, policy, and other routine aspects of working life have always been designed with non-disabled people in mind. Although for legal clarity it is said that sometimes the law requires more favourable treatment of disabled employees, employers are really being asked to counteract disadvantageous arrangements that were put into place without attention to the needs of people with disabilities. See footnotes 450, 459, 496, and 538 for further reading.
- Age discrimination, meanwhile, is in a strange limbo where society may think in theory that it is wrong to discriminate on the basis of age, but is unwilling to let go of all the many arrangements which are considered to be very appropriate exceptions. It is therefore still lawful, subject to proportionality, to discriminate on the basis of age by paying people less money, not letting them apply for jobs, and forcing them to leave their jobs for no other reason than that they are considered to be the wrong age. See footnotes 540 and 560 for further reading.

5

The work–life balance legislation

OVERVIEW

This chapter deals with specific aspects of the terms and conditions of work (working time, leave, and other adjustments for family reasons and flexible working) that are regulated by legislation rather than by the contract of employment. These rights have three main intended roles:

- to protect against unfairness or exploitation;
- to reduce conflicts between working life and family life, and by means of reducing those conflicts
- to help promote sex equality at work, since those conflicts tend to affect women more than men.

These laws mean generally that either the employment contract must contain terms consistent with them or the legal requirements will be applied instead.

Some key challenges and questions related to this area of regulation are:

- Why is legislative intervention needed in these areas, rather than letting the parties simply negotiate these issues into the employment contract?
- What are the limits on how many hours people can work (or be made to work), and how much rest are they entitled to?
- How have the courts 'filled in the gaps' on key ambiguities contained in the Working Time Regulations and the Directive from which it stems? For example, how much is a worker entitled to be paid while on annual leave and what happens when the worker is ill and unable to take the leave during the year?
- When an employee has a new child, how much time can they take off to care for the baby, and what rights do they have while taking that leave?
- What protections do parents have against employers who resent the time taken off, and what rights do they have when they return to work afterwards?
- When workers with children or adult dependants need time off to care for them, or even long-term arrangements to make it possible to manage their caring responsibilities and keep their job, are they legally entitled to any cooperation from their employers?

Context

This chapter addresses a collection of statutory rights seen as a loosely coherent programme for ensuring that people could balance work with other aspects of life, especially family life. In its simplest sense, work–life balance refers to the idea that preventing exploitative working hours and requiring appropriate accommodation for caring and other duties outside the workplace will improve the quality of life for most people, and possibly productivity for business as well.[1] However, one should be careful with the phrase 'work–life balance' for a number of reasons. First, it can suggest opposition between 'work' and 'life', whereas the legislation explored in this chapter shows how interconnected these are; personal lives will always impact on paid work commitments. Secondly, the language implies that other employment laws are inherently 'life' unfriendly.[2] Thirdly, the phrase 'work–life balance' suggests that regulation seeks to shoehorn things like one's hang-gliding hobby into a busy professional life. Finally, this label means one can overlook one of the most morally insistent bases for the legislative programme: gender imbalance.

As we saw in Chapter 4, low wages and inflexible working patterns tend to hit women a lot harder than men, owing to social arrangements and expectations not controlled in the workplace. Nearly two decades after the introduction of most of these measures there is a pretty clear understanding that the long-hours culture harms women more than men, and that the rights around caring responsibilities are taken up far more by women than by men.[3] Therefore, while the laws considered in this chapter do not address the subject of equality as such—that is left to the Equality Act 2010—they have come to represent an essential element of ensuring that women can participate equally in the world of work.

One could be forgiven for looking at all of the rights for carers and concluding that the point of the legislation is about levelling the playing field for parents as against non-parents. Yes, they are heavily slanted in favour of those who have children, but it could be argued that parenting represents the greatest societal obstacle to work–life balance, making it facially legitimate to choose that as a focus for regulation. The focus is arguably further justified because as a society, we are dependent upon parents raising the next generation of students, workers, consumers, etc. Non-parents still have the right not to work more than 48 hours a week and the right to ask for flexible work to care for *their* parents (or indeed for any purpose they wish). In response to complaints of unfairness from non-parents, under this conception of the problem, one need only observe that the family-friendly rights only partially redress the significant career advantages enjoyed by non-parents.[4]

However, although a major part of the rationale for these rights is to tackle gender inequality at work, in fact these laws probably also *contribute to and reinforce* inequality because in many cases, these parental rights go beyond merely providing more help to parents than to non-parents: they make it financially attractive for parents to stick to long-established divisions of labour, where the mother bears the predominant child-care role and the father does the primary breadwinning. Of course it is true that the rights to request flexible working, to adoption leave, and to parental leave are not openly gendered, and even maternity rights have become largely shareable between men and women by the new concept of 'trading in' maternity leave to obtain instead shared parental leave. However, matters of money have a similar tendency to entrench the role of women as carers.

Only women can benefit from the six weeks of the premium 90 per cent rate of statutory maternity pay. The other leave rights either are paid at a low level (£194.32 a week at the time of writing) or are unpaid. The logical choice for parents is for the lower-paid

[1] Tony Blair's Labour government, which introduced most of the measures under discussion, indicated in its White Paper, 'Fairness at Work' (Cm 3968, 1998), that fairly treated employees, not worn out and demoralized by an impossible struggle to build a career in the face of competing childcare responsibilities, would be more productive and better able to form constructive relationships with employers.

[2] Busby *A Right to Care? Unpaid Care Work in European Employment Law* (2011) 49.

[3] Lyonette 'Part-Time Work, Work-Life Balance and Gender Equality' J Soc Wel & Fam L (2015) 37(3) 321.

[4] See eg Trades Union Congress *The Motherhood Pay Penalty: Key Findings from TUC/IPPR Research March 2016* (2016).

partner to do the caring. So, where the father is the better-paid partner, he is unlikely to take leave.[5] This is the likely situation in heterosexual families because of the gender pay gap. The pay gap between men and women, whether full or part time, is minimal until the age of 30, and does not become significant until the age of 40. However, women are more likely to work part-time at all ages, and part-time jobs are less well paid, so that, for example, the gender pay gap for all employees in their 30s (full- and part-time taken together) is such that in 2021 women of that age range earned 12 per cent less per hour than men.[6] So, for many families, with the mother earning less because she works fewer hours and because the hourly rate is less than that of a full-time male partner, the logical choice is for her to take most of the leave needed to care for their children both when they are babies and when they are older. Thus the family-friendly rights could be accused of doing nothing to change the stereotype of women as carers, and of granting state approval and economic support to a traditional gendered division of responsibility for parenting new-born children.[7]

At least to some degree, caring responsibilities amount to a problem only because they often conflict with the unnecessarily intractable demands of the traditional workplace. There are two potential ways of resolving this, although many would argue that a combination of the two is ultimately needed. The first, although outside the realm of employment law, would be to increase the availability of good quality childcare. Recent legislative changes means that in England, up to 30 free hours of childcare are now available a week for children of working parents aged between nine months and school age.[8] Whilst this is much more generous than the support previously available, concerns remain about the accessibility, real financial cost to parents as well as the quality of the childcare provided. Therefore, many would argue this still needs to be improved if mothers are to be encouraged to return to the workplace.[9]

The second solution would be to create more flexible paid work. After all, many carers would insist that they could balance work and care if they could arrange their commitments around each other, and get jobs commensurate with their skill level, thereby earning higher pay. This so seldom actually happens, however, because of what is known as the long-hours culture. This refers to an attitude, prevailing in most male-dominated professions such as law practice, corporate management, manufacturing, and construction, that the more continuous hours workers commit to the enterprise, the more valuable they are. The problem is compounded by 'presenteeism'—employees need to do their work in the office rather than from home in order for their commitment to be seen. The preference of some employers for long hours has an arithmetic appeal, based on the idea of getting the most hours for a single salary. However, as salaries tend to rise for the most time-committed workers, and because overtime

[5] Available research suggests that only 1–2 per cent of eligible fathers have used shared parental leave, for example. Birkett and Forbes 'Where's Dad? Exploring the Low Take-Up of Inclusive Parenting Policies in the UK' Policy Stud (2019) 40(2) 205.

[6] See the House of Commons Library Briefing Paper No 7068 *The Gender Pay Gap* (7 April 2022) available at <https://researchbriefings.files.parliament.uk/documents/SN07068/SN07068.pdf>. For more gender pay gap information see 4.3.2.1.

[7] See Mitchell 'Shared Parental Leave and the Sexual Family: The Importance of Encouraging Men to Care' J Soc Wel & Fam Law (2019) 41(4) 406.

[8] Childcare Act 2016, extended to include children nine months and older by The Childcare (Free of Charge for Working Parents) (England) Regulations 2022.

[9] Farquharson 'Free Childcare for the Under-2s Will Mean Big Savings For Some Parents—But Wider Impacts Are Anyone's Guess' available at <https://ifs.org.uk/articles/free-childcare-under-2s-will-mean-big-savings-some-parents-wider-impacts-are-anyones-guess>.

hours tend to be the least productive hours, this simplistic calculation probably yields a feeble dividend.

There is also the conviction that workers cannot deliver seriousness, commitment, and competence without round-the-clock availability and the subordination of all home-life concerns. While not a shred of evidence supports this belief, it persists probably because the predominantly male members of these work communities understandably associate success with the successful (male) mentors and associates they have known, almost all of whom will have assimilated with the long-hours culture. It falls beyond the scope of this discussion to prove that an enterprise could derive just as much value from two people working 20 skilled, efficient, and refreshed hours per week as from one exhausted person working 55 hours a week.[10] It suffices to note that because certain professional cultures have at least until very recently held beliefs to the contrary, a person who can only work part time, or can work full time but needs to go home at 5pm every day, will generally not go far in those professions. Male or female, people who turn down extra work to care for their children have tended, in business cultures like these, either to fail or to languish at the lowest levels.

The increased availability of working from home since the COVID-19 pandemic may, in this regard, may be seen as positive. After all, many reported increased productivity when working from home during the COVID-19 pandemic.[11] As employees return to offices, women are continuing to work from home more than men. However, there are concerns that this will disadvantage women as they miss out on opportunities to make vital connections and risk being an 'afterthought'.[12] It is also worth noting that the pressure to be available and present does not necessarily end when someone is working from home. Therefore, although we can remain hopeful that the pandemic has challenged the idea that employees are valuable only when they are working long hours in the office, working from home is not going to solve these problems alone.

Therefore, it could still be argued that caring responsibilities have not been the greatest societal obstacle to work–life balance: the long-hours culture has. If so, that makes the Working Time Regulations 1998 (WTR), heralded in the 1998 White Paper as a measure 'to tackle excessively long working hours', the lynchpin of the regulatory project. In theory, the WTR limit the average working week to 48 hours, but workers can opt out of this and, as just discussed, salaried employees may choose to work long hours to boost their reputation and prospects of advancement. Meanwhile, hourly paid workers often work long hours because they will earn more. They may not enjoy it, but they choose to do it because it enlarges their pay-packet.

One view of the big picture, then, shows the long-hours culture as the primary obstacle to a level playing field for women, and reveals a legislative programme that only makes a feint at dismantling this obstacle while investing its real energy into making mothers and other carers feel a little less put upon by the unequal situation.[13] However, it would

[10] Lufkin 'Why Do We Buy into the "Cult" of Overwork?'<https://www.bbc.co.uk/worklife/article/20210507-why-we-glorify-the-cult-of-burnout-and-overwork> accessed 9 March 2026.*The Return of the Long Hours Culture* (Trade Unions Congress June 2008); Moyes 'Long-hours Culture Hitting Productivity' *The Independent* (26 October 1995) available at <http://www.independent.co.uk/news/uk/longhours-culture-hitting-productivity-1579453.html>.

[11] 'Remote-Work Options Can Boost Productivity and Curb Burnout (Report)' available at <https://www.catalyst.org/reports/remote-work-burnout-productivity/>.

[12] See eg 'Women Warned Home Working May Harm Their Careers' (BBC, 12 November 2021) available at <https://www.bbc.co.uk/news/business-59244992>.

[13] See eg Doan, Leach, & Strazdins 'The Economic Costs of Men's Long Work Hours for Women: Evidence on the Gender Wage Earnings Gap from Australia and Germany' (2025) 179 Social Indicators Research 1073.

be difficult to go further without removing freedom of choice for workers. The Labour government that introduced much of the regulation in this field, and the Trades Union Council (representing, to an extent, the interests of workers), placed choice at the centre of their agendas for work–life balance.[14]

This illustrates the dilemma: must the longer-hours workers surrender their advantage, or must the shorter-hours workers accept their fate as also-rans? Resolving this conflict hinges on the question of whether longer working represents a real, objective virtue, or merely a preference common to a currently empowered group that alone can exercise that preference. One could hardly celebrate a 'work–life balance' achieved by suppressing the desire of some workers to give greater value to their employers. If, on the other hand, social constructs place only certain people in a position to work long hours, and long-hours commitment in itself does not add value over what can be achieved by a more diverse workforce working fewer hours, then perhaps unfettered choice should give way to a playing field in which the available choices are accessible by all, or most, workers. This is the kind of question that should inform discussion of the legislation considered in this chapter.

Meanwhile, it should be remembered that the statutory provisions outlined in this chapter represent a minimum entitlement which may in practice be replaced by more generous contractual arrangements and, while the law may give preferential treatment to working parents, it is clear that many employers with flexibility policies extend the benefit of those schemes to all employees, not just to working parents. Many employers now recognize that promoting flexible working and enhancing pay during family leave not only may boost employee morale and improve retention of skilled staff but can assist in the competition to recruit the best workers. Accordingly, some companies have started introducing entitlements which are not available at national level, including leave for fertility treatment, menopause, and miscarriage. Working Families, which is a charity promoting work–life balance, has many examples on its website.[15] To take some of those as illustrations:

- Ten2Two Limited is a recruitment consultancy which enables all staff to work remotely and flexibly. Flexible options are made visible on job adverts and managers are trained to manage agile teams. Considerate scheduling of meetings and respect for working hours ensure that staff get to enjoy the benefits of flexibility. The success of this is reflected in the 100 per cent retention rate of employees since 2020.
- BNP Paribas has made a parents and carers network and introduced a flagship Bring Your Child to Work Day. Alongside this, practical support such as 20 days of backup childcare and 12 weeks of 'Secondary Care Givers leave' is available.
- Pan Macmillan makes leave available for fertility treatment as well as six months of fully paid maternity leave. Equal leave entitlements are available for all parents regardless of gender or the pathway to parenthood. A hybrid work model, with core hours of 10am to 4.30pm means women returning to the workplace can do this in a way that suits them and their family. External maternity coaching is offered, as well as mentorship and dedicated breastfeeding facilities on site.

[14] 'Fairness at Work' (Cm 3968, 1998); *The Return of the Long Hours Culture* (Trades Union Congress, June 2008) 9 available at <https://www.tuc.org.uk/sites/default/files/extras/longhoursreturn.pdf>.

[15] <www.workingfamilies.org.uk>.

5.1 The Working Time Regulations 1998

5.1.1 Introduction

The Working Time Regulations 1998,[16] referred to hereafter as WTR, came into force on 1 October 1998. They implement the Working Time Directive (93/104/EC) and certain provisions of the Young Workers Directive (94/33/EC),[17] applying statutory limits or entitlements in four main areas:

- the 48-hour maximum working week;
- rules about night working;
- rest breaks;
- paid annual holiday.

The Working Time Directive had a complicated history, which has had important effects politically and in relation to the drafting of the eventual Regulations.[18] The 1992–97 UK government took part in some of the negotiations on the Directive, but strenuously objected to the Directive in its entirety. Partly as a result, the Directive took on a much watered-down form, with major 'derogations' which a member state can adopt in order to lessen the effect of the main requirements.

5.1.2 Impact of the EU origin on the interpretation of the law on working time

The UK's implementing regulations, the WTR, adopt in full all of the derogations permitted by the Directive. The Regulations largely adopt the 'copy out' technique of implementation, with the result that much of the wording comes from the Directive itself. While this ensures that the WTR do not say anything different from what the Directive requires, it also means that the ambiguities inherent in the European wording have been imported into UK law. An example of this is uncertainty as to the meaning of 'working time', which has had to be resolved by several referrals from the UK and other member states to the Court of Justice of the European Union (see 5.1.5). Furthermore, it means that inadequate attention was given to ensuring that concepts adopted by the Directive, often ones which derived from other member states, were adapted to work in the UK law framework. The prime example of this is the failure to address properly in the WTR what EU law intended should be the level of pay to which employees taking annual leave were entitled, which again has necessitated referrals to the CJEU—followed by the UK courts and tribunals having to do some adventurous 'reading in' of words to UK statutes (see 5.1.10.5).

When dealing with referrals from member states on working time, the CJEU has often interpreted the general and vague terms of the Directive in ways in which the words of the UK legislation cannot be read. The response of the UK courts to this has been, in accordance with the *Marleasing* principles, to read words into the WTR in order to deliver the

[16] SI 1998/1833.

[17] They do so in relation to young persons (ie between 15 and 18, and over school leaving age); these provisions were tightened by the Working Time (Amendment) Regulations 2002, SI 2002/3128, primarily to restrict a young worker's working time to eight hours in any day or 40 hours in any week, and to ban night working except in restricted circumstances. In relation to children under that age, the Directive was transposed by the Children (Protection at Work) Regulations 1998, SI 1998/276. On this basis it was held by the EAT that a child cannot claim under the Working Time Regulations (eg for paid holidays): *Addison v Ashby* [2003] 3 ICR 667, [2003] IRLR 211.

[18] See Bercusson *European Labour Law* (1996) ch 21.

outcome mandated by the European Court. As will be seen below, this can have quite dramatic effects on the meaning of the wording approved in Parliament, in effect converting an 'is' to an 'is not'. The practical consequence for lawyers is of course that they cannot take the words of the WTR to mean what they say, but must be alert to case law showing that additional words must be read in.

The CJEU has recently adopted a second route for making its rulings on working time effective in member states, akin to the route taken in relation to equal pay where EU equal pay law is, because it is stated in the founding treaty of the EU, direct law in each member state and does not need implementing legislation in each EU state. In the case of working time, the mechanism is the Charter of Fundamental Rights of the EU, which was adopted in 2007. Article 31(2) states that '[e]very worker has the right to limitation of maximum working hours, to daily and weekly rest periods and to an annual period of paid leave'. The Court has held that this makes its rulings on the rights created by the Directive immediate directly enforceable law in each member state.[19] It appears that notwithstanding Protocol 30 to the Lisbon Treaty stating that the Charter creates no new law in the UK and Poland, the Charter is binding in the UK.[20]

An obvious question is how the UK leaving the EU has impacted the WTR. The Working Time Directive has always been viewed as foreign, and as imposing bizarre unintended consequences on employers (specifically rolled-over leave during sick leave; see 5.1.10.4). Accordingly, many Brexiters considered the WTR a key target for repeal.[21] Some changes that would have been impossible pre-Brexit[22] have indeed been made by The Employment Rights (Amendment, Revocation and Transitional Provision) Regulations 2023, which will be considered throughout this chapter. However, the impact of these legislative amendments is likely to be more minimal than some Brexiters might have hoped for, as they mainly codify existing rights made available through CJEU rulings. Furthermore, existing interpretations made by the CJEU remain effective, although the UK Supreme Court will be free to depart from them. The Working Time Directive and the Charter are no longer binding in the UK and future rulings by the CJEU will not be binding, but it seems likely that those judgments will still be influential on UK courts and tribunals when interpreting these 'copied-out' provisions on working time.

A final point on the 'copy-out' approach to drafting the WTR: this approach also resulted in a set of Regulations which are quite difficult to use because they follow the Directive's logical but non-user-friendly sequence of setting out first the obligations and only later the derogations that are permitted.

5.1.3 **Application**

The WTR use the wide definition of 'worker' as being an individual under a contract of employment *or* any other contract, whether express or implied, oral or written, whereby they undertake to do or perform personally any work or services for another party to the contract whose status is not that of a client or customer of any profession or business undertaking carried out by the individual.[23] The definition of a 'worker' is examined

[19] *Willmeroth v Broßonn* C-570/16, [2019] IRLR 148 and *Max-Planck-Gesellschaft zur Forderung der Wissenshcaten e.V. v Shimizu C-684/16*, [2019] 1 CMLR 1233.

[20] *RFU v Consolidated Information Services* [2011] UKSC 55, [2013] 1 All ER 928, [2012] 1 WLR 3333.

[21] See eg 'What Is the Working Time Directive that Boris and Gove Are Plotting to Scrap?' (TUC 18 December 2017) <https://www.tuc.org.uk/blogs/what-working-time-directive-boris-and-gove-are-plotting-scrap>.

[22] The Retained EU Law (Revocation and Reform) Act 2023, which sweeps away the supremacy of EU law.

[23] Regulation 2(1); see 2.1.4. Thus, the paid holiday right could be claimed by Sch D paying, self-employed subcontractors working for only one employer on a long-term basis: *Byrne Bros (Farmwork) Ltd v Baird* [2002] ICR 667, [2002] IRLR 96; *Wright v Redrow Homes (Yorkshire) Ltd* [2004] ICR 1126, [2004] IRLR 720, CA. There are subsidiary provisions in regs 36 and 42 to ensure that agency workers and non-employed trainees are covered.

in 2.1.3. The Employment Rights (Amendment, Revocation and Transitional Provision) Regulations 2023 means that irregular hours workers and part-year workers are now subject to specific rules on entitlement to, and carry-over of, annual leave (see 5.1.10).[24] A part-year worker is someone who is required to work part of the year and has at least a week a year where they are not required to work and do not have to paid. An irregular hours worker includes those who, after an appraisal, are determined to be working a number of paid work hours that are wholly or mostly variable in each pay period. There are some obvious vagaries in this definition, namely what are 'wholly or mostly' variable hours and what is the 'pay period,' which will require judicial determination.

As originally enacted, the WTR contained three general exclusions in relation to the transport industry, doctors in training, and the activities of services such as the armed forces, police, and civil protection services 'which inevitably conflict with the provision of these Regulations'. However, subsequent amendments to the Directive narrowed the general exemption of transport and introduced special rules relating to certain transport workers,[25] and the wholesale exclusion of junior doctors in training was phased out over time.[26] The exemption of the armed and emergency services remains in place.[27]

5.1.4 **Agreements which can vary or exclude the WTR**

There are three forms of agreement which can vary or exclude the rules set by the WTR. How these agreements can be used is set out in later sections, but it is convenient to define these forms of agreement here. They are:

- *individual agreement by the worker*: this only applies in relation to opting out of the maximum 48 hours per week;
- *a 'collective agreement or workforce agreement'*: this format, importing an obvious collective element of protection, is adopted for some of the major exclusions. A collective agreement is an agreement made between one or more trade unions and one or more employers as defined in the Trade Union and Labour Relations (Consolidation) Act 1992 s 178.[28] A workforce agreement is an agreement between an employer and its employees (or representatives of those employees) which meets the requirements of Schedule 1 to the WTR.[29] A workforce can only apply to workers who do not have any terms and conditions set by a collective bargain.[30] Such an agreement must be in writing, have a specified length of not more than five years, apply to either all the relevant members of the workforce or to all those in a particular group,[31] and be signed by either the representatives of the workforce or group, or (if the employer employs 20 or fewer workers) either by such representatives or by

[24] Working Time Regulations 1998, regulations 15B–D.

[25] See Council Directive No 2003/88 concerning certain aspects of the organization of working time, OJ 2003, L299/9; the Merchant Shipping (Working Time: Inland Waterways) Regulations 2003, SI 2003/3049; the Fishing Vessels (Working Time: Sea Fishermen) Regulations 2004, SI 2004/1713; the Civil Aviation (Working Time) Regulations 2004, SI 2004/756; and, most significantly, the Road Transport (Working Time) Regulations 2005, SI 2005/639 (as amended by the Road Transport (Working Time) (Amendment) Regulations 2012).

[26] Regulation 25A; a maximum of 58 hours was allowed until July 2007, then 56 hours until August 2009.

[27] Regulation 18. There is a further exclusion in reg 19 of domestic service in a private household, which relates to maximum working hours, night work, and pattern of work; this does not appear in the Directive but is justified as being part of the general exclusion of such activities from domestic health and safety law.

[28] Regulation 2(1). As to collective agreements, see 9.7.2.

[29] Regulation 2(1). [30] Sch 1, para 2.

[31] This is defined as a group undertaking a particular function, working at a particular workplace, or belonging to a particular department or unit: Sch 1, para 2.

the majority of the workers.[32] Where use is made of representatives, they must have been 'duly elected' and the Regulations provide the basic electoral rules that must be complied with.[33] There could be overlaps here with representatives elected for other consultative purposes, and this development could be seen as a further 'carrot' towards de facto works councils of sorts.

- *a 'relevant agreement'*: this is any of (1) a workforce agreement, (2) any provision of a collective agreement which forms part of a contract between the worker and his employer, or (3) any other agreement in writing which is legally enforceable as between the worker and his employer—such as their contract of employment.[34]

5.1.5 **'Working time'**

The meaning of 'working time' is important not only because of the weekly maximum permitted hours of working time but also because the phrase defines what counts as a rest break or a rest period: any time which is not working time counts as rest time.[35]

'Working time' is defined by reg 2(1) as any period during which the worker is (1) working, (2) at his employer's disposal, and (3) carrying out his activity or duties.[36] All three conditions must in theory be met for the time to be working time, but in reality the CJEU has only paid lip-service to this, as the *SIMAP* case considered in 5.1.5.1 shows. An illustration of the need to meet all three conditions is given by *Edwards and Morgan v Encirc Ltd*,[37] where a safety representative and a shop steward attended a safety committee meeting arranged by their employer at the workplace. The EAT held that, taking a broad purposive approach to the definition, these employees were working, were at their employer's disposal, and were carrying out their duties. This was because their duties were to be considered in a practical sense rather than through an examination of their contracts of employment.

In the celebrated *Uber* case, the Supreme Court decided that the employment tribunal were entitled to conclude that when drivers were in their territory with their Uber app turned on (and hence subject to being called for a ride), that constituted working time. Even if drivers were not obliged to accept all or even 80 per cent of trip requests, the high level of acceptances required and the penalty of being logged off if three consecutive requests were not accepted within a 10-second time frame justified the conclusion that drivers waiting for a booking were at its 'disposal'. Interestingly, the Supreme Court recognized in obiter that that if a driver had entered into an obligation of the same nature for another taxi company and had both firms' apps switched on, then, as a matter of evidence, Uber would have been able to argue that that driver was not at Uber's disposal.[38]

[32] Schedule 1, para 1(a)–(d); note that a worker disagreeing but in a minority is bound by the agreement. Before making an agreement available for signature, the employer must have provided all the affected workers with copies of the text and such guidance as they may reasonably require in order to understand it fully: para 1(e).

[33] Sch 1, para 3. [34] Regulation 2(1).

[35] This is stated expressly in reg 2(1) in relation to 'rest periods' and is implicit in relation to the 20-minute 'rest break' required after six hours of work.

[36] Also included is any period during which the worker is on a work experience placement ('receiving relevant training') or which has been agreed to be working time under a relevant agreement: reg 2(1) 'working time' (b) and (c).

[37] [2015] IRLR 528. [38] *Uber BV v Aslam* [2021] UKSC 5, [2021] 4 All ER 209.

5.1.5.1 'On-call' time as working time

As with the National Minimum Wage, whether the time spent 'on call' should be counted as working time courts controversy. On occasion the answer may differ between the NMR and the WTR. For the WTR, time on call only counts when the employee is required by the employer to be at or near the place of work: *Sindicato de Médicos de Asistencia Pública (SIMAP) v Conselleria de Sanidad y Consumo de la Generalidad Valenciana*.[39] Clearly these doctors were at their employer's 'disposal' and one could argue that they were therefore also 'working', but if the three conditions of 'working', 'at his employer's disposal', and 'carrying out his activity or duties' are each intended to mean something different, it is hard to see how, when the doctors were not actually carrying out any active work, they were 'carrying out their activity or duties'.

If this rule in *SIMAP* is satisfied, it does not matter if the employee is allowed to sleep (eg in a rest room or in their own accommodation on the employer's premises).[40] This line was drawn a bit more clearly in *Truslove v Scottish Ambulance Service*,[41] where the EAT held that ambulance workers, who were required to spend the night at accommodation within three miles of their posted workstation, were entitled to compensatory rest for the time spent on call. The same applied to Belgian retained firefighters who were required to live within eight minutes' travel of their fire station and who, when on call, had to be able to be immediately contactable and to get to the fire station within eight minutes.[42] Similarly, care staff who live at the hostel or care home where they work have been held by the EAT to be at work during those periods when they are on call: the key issue is not whether they are at home but the restriction on their liberty imposed by being required to be on call at or near the workplace.[43]

In contrast, the CJEU in *SIMAP* also decided that if a doctor was on call but allowed to be at home this was not working time unless the doctor was actually dealing with a call: they did not meet the 'carrying out his activity or duties' condition. For the same reason, on-call time was not working time (except when actually dealing with a call) for an estates officer of a health trust who, when on call, usually received about 40 phone calls over a seven-day period and who had to be immediately contactable but was not required to be in any particular location.[44]

Not being able to be at home because of the needs of the job is not enough to make time working time. Offshore oil platform workers have been considered by the Supreme Court in *Russell v Transocean International Resources Ltd*,[45] the issue there being whether time off shift but at the place of work—on the offshore platform—counted as working time. Their Lordships held that this was not working time, and the same would no doubt apply to a worker who has to travel for business during periods when they are not working but are having a meal, sleeping in a hotel bedroom, or watching the television.

[39] C-303/98 [2000] IRLR 845, ECJ.

[40] *Landeshauptstadt Kiel v Jaeger* C-151/02 [2003] IRLR 804, ECJ; *McCartney v Oversely House Management* [2006] ICR 510, [2006] IRLR 514.

[41] [2014] ICR 1232, EAT.

[42] *Ville de Nivelles v Matzak* C-518/15, [2018] IRLR 457, CJEU.

[43] *MacCartney v Oversley House Management* [2005] ICR 510, EAT and *Hughes v Jones t/a Graylynns Residential Home* UKEAT/0159/08 (14 August 2018, unreported); cf *South Holland District Council v Stamp* EAT/1097/02, [2003] All ER(d) 10 (Jun) which was decided before the CJEU judgment in *Jaeger*.

[44] *Blakeley v South Eastern Health and Social Services Trust* [2009] NICA 62 (14 December 2009, unreported).

[45] [2011] UKSC 57, [20012] IRLR 149, [2012] ICR 185. See further *DJ v Radiotelevizija Slovenija*: C-344/19, [2021] IRLR 479, [2021] ICR 1109, ECJ.

5.1.5.2 **Travel time as working time**

It is generally accepted that the time a worker spends getting to and from the place of work each day does not get counted as 'working time' for the purposes of the WTR, while time spent by a peripatetic worker such as a sales representative or a service mechanic travelling between the employer's customers in the course of a shift does count. But what is the situation if a worker goes straight from home to the first customer and returns from the last customer of the shift to home: is the time spent on such journeys working time? The answer to this question was provided by the CJEU in the *Tyco* case, which related to Spanish workers who installed and maintained security systems throughout Spain.[46] The Court focused a great deal on the fact that the workers could not control the distance between their homes and their first or last clients, in the way most workers control how much of their time is spent on travel to work simply by choosing where to live. The Court opined that while driving to their first assignment the workers were required to be physically present in a particular place (to wit: their cars), which is a touchstone of what it is to be at work. It rejected the claim that driving should be excluded as it formed no part of the workers' core duties, and made analogy with the 'on-call' cases to note that neither (a) intensity of application nor (b) duty-related output were determining characteristics of work. Driving was, in effect, 'activities or duties' for the purposes of the definition because the workers were obliged to be at their employer's disposal during that time.

5.1.6 **Maximum weekly working time**

5.1.6.1 **Average of 48 hours a week**

A worker's working time, including overtime, is not to exceed an average of 48 hours for each seven days in any particular reference period.[47] The fact that this is an averaging process is fundamental, because it does not necessarily mean a maximum of 48 hours per week, and clearly considerable fluctuations can be accommodated. The number of months over which weeks of long hours can be sustained depends upon the period over which the averaging can be done, hence the importance of the 'reference period'. In the first instance this is stated to be 17 weeks, but where one of the 'other special cases' in reg 21 applies, this is increased to 26 weeks.[48] Further, it can be raised by a collective or workforce agreement to a maximum of 52 weeks 'for objective or technical reasons or reasons concerning the organisation of work' (!), which could be highly advantageous to employers wanting variations in hours over certain prolonged seasons in the year;[49] protection for the worker lies in the collective nature of the necessary agreement.

[46] *Tyco (Federación de Servicios Privados del sindicato Comisiones obreras (CC.OO) v Tyco Integrated Security SL)* Case C-266/14, Judgment of 10 September 2015.

[47] Regulation 4(1). Regulations 4(6) and 4(7) set out the formula for calculating the average, and days of annual, sickness, and maternity leave that are not to count. Note that where a worker works for more than one employer, the average applies to the aggregated hours; the Regulations are silent on what the employer(s) is or are to do in these circumstances, but the original Guidance para 2.1.3 intimated that it is up to the employer to find out if a worker is working elsewhere and if necessary to adjust working arrangements accordingly; it did not say on *which* employer any primary responsibility to do so may rest.

[48] Regulation 4(3): a relevant agreement can lay down *which* 17-week or 26-week periods are to be used; failing that, the average must be met over '*any* period of 17/26 weeks in the course of his employment', which could be less advantageous for an employer with predictable variations in hours required.

[49] Regulation 23(b).

5.1.6.2 The 'opt-out'

The 48-hour average maximum is subject to the most striking exception in the Regulations, namely that it does not apply *at all* to a worker who has agreed in writing with their employer that it should not apply in their case;[50] this individual agreement may be either for a specified period or indefinite, but a worker may terminate it by giving seven days' written notice (or longer, up to a maximum of three months, if this is specified in the agreement). The government and business leaders defend this exception on the ground that it respects individual choice. Remember, however, that the Regulations are first and foremost a health and safety measure: regulations requiring workers to wear safety goggles, or to earn a licence before operating certain kinds of machinery, could hardly allow workers to opt out of the requirements simply to protect personal choice.

The quid pro quo for an exclusion agreement was originally an obligation on the employer to keep specified records of actual hours which were to be open to inspection by a Health and Safety Inspector; however, in another rapid about-turn, the Amendment Regulations in 1999 watered this down very considerably, so that now the only requirement is to keep a record of *who* has signed the opt-out.[51]

One possible point of controversy not covered by the Regulations is what is to happen to the worker's wages if they give notice to end an opt-out and their hours have to be reduced to meet the 48-hour average. This will be primarily a matter of contract, so that if, for example, the worker is paid at a fixed amount per hour, the wage will have to go down pro rata to the new number of hours, whereas a worker paid a salary for work done (over however many hours it takes) would have a good argument for breach of contract if the employer reduced that salary (simply because of a new maximum on hours) without their consent. Although it is unlawful to impose any detriment or to dismiss a worker for relying on any right under the WTR,[52] it is unlikely that reducing pay to reflect the reduced amount of work being done would be imposing a detriment. On the other hand, the CJEU has held that an employer may not transfer a worker to other duties, without agreement, because the worker refused to agree to opt out,[53] which is likely to be understood by employment tribunals to mean that such a transfer would be an illegal detriment.

However, the EAT has upheld a surprising decision by an employment tribunal that 'detriment' does not include excluding a worker from the allocation of 'rest day' (ie overtime) work for refusing to sign an opt-out. In *Arriva London South v Nicolaou*,[54] the EAT held that if an employer's motivation for withholding overtime is a desire to avoid the risk, because of a complicated rota and occasional unforeseen events such as snow, that if employees who had not opted were rostered to work rest days they might exceed the 48-hour limit, then the employer has not subjected those workers to a detriment for the exercise of their rights. The employment tribunal had found as a fact that this genuinely was the reason for the policy, rather than any desire to punish the drivers for refusing to sign an opt-out. Given that somewhat surprising finding, the EAT's conclusion was perhaps inevitable. We can expect that tribunals would decide that, for example, it would be imposing a detriment for an employer to refuse to assign workers to certain higher-paying work or posts without the opt-out on the ground that the work is likely to tempt or induce them (the workers) to work more than 48 hours.

[50] Regulation 5(1). [51] Regulation 4(2), as amended.
[52] Employment Rights Act 1996, ss 44A(1) and 101(A).
[53] *Fuss v Stadt Halle (No 1)*: C-243/09, [2010] IRLR 1080. [54] [2012] ICR 510.

Of course, detriment is not the only way in which pressure can be put on a worker to opt out. It is worth remembering here what was discussed in the Context section of this chapter: many industries and organizations have a culture in which working long hours represents career commitment and general worker value. Where the culture honours long-hours working, the message will be clear that those who do not opt out will not advance easily or rapidly. As long as the opt-out exists, male-dominated industries, where such cultures have evolved, will continue to exercise a 'choice' to opt out: a choice that women are much less likely to be able to make without significant social costs. The more that workers make this choice, the more they are reliant on others, often their partners, to make sacrifices in the workplace to meet their caring responsibilities. The opt-out thus permits a vicious cycle where what is a choice for some (mostly men) limits the choices of others (mostly women), which frees the first group to keep making that choice. Thus it is a mistake to view the problems of the opt-out simply in terms of whether the employer consciously imposes a detriment for refusal.

5.1.6.3 **Record keeping**

As the Working Time Directive requires that member states 'take the necessary steps' to ensure working time limits and restrictions on night working are not breached, the UK's WTR have required that employers keep records to prove compliance for each worker (excluding those with opt-outs).[55] This requirement is one that has been changed as a result of leaving the EU, so now the basic requirement to record each worker's daily hours has been removed.[56] Instead, records must be 'created, maintained and kept in such manner and formant as the employer reasonably thinks fit'.[57] This change was only made possible by Brexit and arguably reflects an emphasis on business expediency rather than the worker's welfare, at least under Rishi Sunak's Conservative government (2022–24).

5.1.7 **Night working and risky working patterns**

A night worker's normal hours of work in any reference period are not to exceed an average of eight hours in each 24 hours.[58] A 'night worker' is defined as a worker who normally works at least three hours of daily working time during night time, or such proportion of annual working time as may be specified in a collective agreement or workforce agreement.[59]

As with maximum weekly hours, the averaging process is vital, and the reference period is 17 weeks; a relevant agreement can set out *which* succeeding 17-week periods are to be used, but in default it means *any* 17 weeks (ie a rolling period).[60] Since the average is calculated on the basis of a six-day week even if the worker has, as is more normal,

[55] Regulation 9.

[56] Regulation 9(4)(3), amended by Employment Rights (Amendment, Revocation and Transitional Provision) Regulations 2023, Regulation 7.

[57] Regulation 9(4)(2), amended by Employment Rights (Amendment, Revocation and Transitional Provision) Regulations 2023, Regulation 7.

[58] Regulation 6(1).

[59] Regulation 2(1). 'Night time' means a period set out in a relevant agreement, lasting at least seven hours and including the period between midnight and 5am; in default of agreement, it means 11pm to 6am: reg 2(1). An employer could use this to push back the definition so that workers working late (eg up to 2am in a bar or night club) do *not* work the three hours in the period necessary to be a night worker.

[60] Regulation 6(3). The formula for the average is set out in reg 6(5).

a five-day week,[61] the reality is that for most night workers this limit adds nothing to the weekly 48-hour average required for all workers—save that no opt-out is possible. There is, however, an exception to the averaging process where the night work involves 'special hazards or heavy physical or mental strain', in which case the limit is eight hours in *any* 24-hour period in which night work is done.[62]

On the question of night work, much is left to be determined by agreement; this goes beyond matters of definition, because ultimately it is possible for the rules themselves to be modified or excluded completely by a collective agreement or workforce agreement,[63] a particularly striking example of collective protection being thought sufficient.

Arguably, the night-working provisions are most closely related to the health and safety provenance of the Regulations, and the Directive itself makes clear in its preamble the assumption on which this is based, one of the recitals being:

> Whereas research has shown that the human body is more sensitive at night to environmental disturbances and also to certain burdensome forms of work organisation and that long periods of night work can be detrimental to the health of workers and can endanger safety at the workplace.

In the light of this, two further obligations are laid on employers of night workers, going beyond the regulation of hours. The first is that no adult worker is to be assigned to night work without at least an opportunity for a free health assessment (unless there is an existing such assessment which is still valid), and each night worker must then have the opportunity of further assessments at regular intervals appropriate to his case.[64] A young worker must have the opportunity of such assessments (as to health *and capacity*) whenever assigned to work during the period from 10pm to 6am.[65] Second, the employer must transfer a night worker onto non-night work if a registered medical practitioner advises that the worker is suffering health problems related to night working and it is possible to transfer the worker to suitable work not at night.[66] Significantly, there are no permissible derogations to these duties.

There is also a provision aimed at protecting those whose pattern of work puts them at particular risk, 'in particular because the work is monotonous or the work-rate is predetermined'. However it is very vague indeed: reg 8 simply says that the employer 'shall ensure that the worker is given adequate rest breaks'.

[61] Regulation 6(5).

[62] Regulation 6(7): the actual circumstances in which this applies are left to be determined by a collective agreement or workforce agreement, or in a risk assessment required by the Management of Health and Safety at Work Regulations 1999, SI 1999/3242. If neither of these avenues is used, there could be a health and safety breach by the employer, though the Regulations do not say so specifically.

[63] Regulation 23(a). This is subject to the requirement of compensatory rest under reg 24, though on its wording (applying where 'a worker is . . . required . . . to work during a period which would otherwise be a rest period or rest break') it is more difficult to apply to night working than to the rules on rest breaks.

[64] Regulation 7(1). This rather stark paragraph was considerably fleshed out by paras 4.1.2 and 4.1.3 of the original Guidance, which suggest that (a) while very few people will be unfit to work at night at all, there could be problems with diabetes, heart/circulatory disorders, stomach/intestinal disorders, sleep conditions, chest disorders, and others requiring regular medication; (b) the health assessment (undefined) could start with a screening questionnaire carried out by the employer, with professional opinion being involved in the interpreting of the questionnaire and any necessary follow-up action; (c) while the Regulations are silent on how regularly to reassess, a rule of thumb might be to administer the questionnaire annually.

[65] Regulation 7(2). This does not apply where the work is 'of an exceptional nature' (undefined): reg 7(4). As stated above, the emphasis (since the amendment in 2002) is on the young worker normally not working nights at all.

[66] Regulation 7(6). If the health problems constituted a 'disability' within the Equality Act 2010, this might be required in any event as a reasonable adjustment.

5.1.8 **Rest periods and rest breaks**

A worker is entitled to the following:

1. a daily rest period of not less than 11 hours in each 24-hour work period;[67]
2. a weekly rest period of not less than 24 hours in each seven-day work period (or, at the employer's option, two 24-hour periods in each fortnight or one 28-hour period in each fortnight);[68]
3. a rest break of at least 20 minutes (subject to any longer time agreed in a collective agreement or workforce agreement) where daily working time is more than six hours.[69]

In the case of young workers, these entitlements are increased to 12 hours' daily rest, 48 hours' weekly rest, and a rest break of at least 30 minutes after four and a half hours' work.[70]

In relation to the 20-minute in-work rest break, the EAT has held that the Regulations entitle workers only to one rest period in each shift, no matter how many hours they work beyond the relevant threshold (eg six hours).[71]

As well as the normal derogations (including the ability to modify or exclude entirely all the adult entitlements by collective agreement or workforce agreement),[72] there are special provisions relating to daily and weekly rest periods for two categories of worker. First, reg 22 provides a small flexibility which exempts the employer from providing daily or weekly rest when a worker changes shift, subject to reg 24 requiring compensatory rest where possible (see 5.1.9.2).[73] Second, and more significantly, neither kind of rest needs to be provided, again subject to reg 24 compensation, to workers engaged in activities which involve periods of work split up over the day 'as may be the case for cleaning staff'. In consequence, a cleaner might have to work from 5am to 9am and from 6pm to 10pm for six days a week. They would never get an 11-hour break during those six days, but they would get enough compensatory rest to avoid breach of the WTR.

5.1.9 **The ability to flex or exclude the WTR rules**

There are some exceptions to the strict rules of the WTR and also several ways in which they can be 'flexed' by the worker and/or the employer. One of these, the opt-out on the maximum of 48 hours' work a week, has already been dealt with (see 5.1.6). We will address the remaining three important ones here.

5.1.9.1 **Workers with unmeasured working time**

By virtue of reg 20 the provisions on the 48-hour maximum week, the length of night working, and daily/weekly rest and rest periods do not apply 'in relation to a worker where, on account of the specific characteristics of the activity in which he is engaged,

[67] Regulation 10(1).

[68] Regulation 11(1) and (2). The relevant seven-day period is to be laid down in a relevant agreement, or, in default of that, is to be a week beginning with Monday: reg 11(6). The weekly rest period is not to include any daily rest period, 'except where this is justified by objective or technical reasons or reasons concerning the organisation of work': reg 11(7).

[69] Regulation 12(1)–(3). Whether such rest breaks are to be with pay is a matter of contract, as the Regulations are silent on the matter. A rest break must have a definite beginning and end; it is not enough for the employer to say that the employee in fact has significant periods of 'down time' (during which the worker is subject to recall by the employer): *Gallagher v Alpha Catering Services Ltd* [2004] IRLR 102.

[70] Regulations 10(2), 11(3), 12(4): the derogations applying to adult workers' rest periods do not apply to young workers, but there is a *force majeure* exception applying to them in reg 27 (unforeseen or exceptional circumstances) in relation to daily rest and rest breaks.

[71] *Corps of Commissionaires Management v Hughes* [2011] EWCA 1061, [2011] IRLR 915.

[72] Regulation 23(a).

[73] Shift work is very broadly defined in reg 22(2).

the duration of his working time is not measured or predetermined or can be determined by the worker himself'. The regulation then goes on to repeat the examples given in the Directive: managing executives or other persons with autonomous decision-making powers, family workers, and religious celebrants.

Initially there was some doubt as to whether this exception could apply where the worker had at least *some* element of unmeasured time and discretion in working hours, and initially the WTR provided that in such a case the WTR only applied to the measured part of the work. However, the examples given in the Directive suggest that only those with *complete* control over their hours would come within the exclusion. The CJEU favoured this narrower interpretation, holding that the exception only applies to those workers all of whose working time is unmeasured, and so the WTR was amended.[74] The CJEU has also held that 'relief parents' at a residential facility for children in care were not on 'unmeasured time' even though they were present 24 hours and could decide when to perform their duties.[75] Although they were mostly unsupervised, and could structure their work as they wanted, they had a list of tasks to perform and a general responsibility to tend to the needs of the children in their care. Thus the amount of time they worked corresponded to the demands of the job, not their own choice.

5.1.9.2 **The 'other special cases'**

Regulation 21 ('Other special cases') gives employers extensive powers to flex the limits on the length of night working and daily and weekly rest and the 20-minute rest breaks. Once again the wording is a straight copy-out from the Directive and it again raises as many questions as to the correct interpretation. The regulation identifies so many situations in which flexing can apply that it is set out below verbatim. However, first we need to address the concept of compensatory rest.

Flexing subject to compensatory rest

Where one of the special cases applies and as a result the worker is required to work in what should otherwise have been a rest period or break, reg 24 provides that the employer should 'wherever possible allow him to take an equivalent period of compensatory rest', or, 'in exceptional cases where this is not possible for objective reasons', afford the worker such protection as may be appropriate to safeguard the worker's health and safety. The CJEU has held that this last option of protection instead of an equivalent period of compensatory rest is only available in cases which are 'entirely'[76] or 'absolutely'[77] exceptional. The same requirement in reg 24 of compensatory rest or other protection also applies to any flexing for shift workers or any flexing agreed in a workforce agreement or a collective agreement.

The CJEU has made it clear in the *Jaeger* and *Isere* cases[78] that so far as the *daily rest* and *weekly rest* periods are concerned, the compensatory rest should (1) follow immediately after the period of work in which the rest was not taken (a daily rest cannot, for example, be compensated for several days later) and (2) needs to be of the length of the missing hours of rest (so for example if a worker has an eight-hour daily rest instead of the WTR minimum of 11 hours, then the compensatory rest would be three hours). The compensatory rest need not be given at a time when the employee would otherwise be working: the WTR is directed at providing *rest* for health and safety purposes, not time off in lieu of overtime worked.

[74] *Commission of the EC v United Kingdom* C-484/04, [2006] IRLR 888, [2002] ICR 592.

[75] *Hannele Halva v SOS Lapsikyla ry* C-175/16, [2017] IRLR 942, [2017] ICR 1408.

[76] *Landeshauptstadt Kiel v Jaeger* C-151/02 [2003] IRLR 804, ECJ.

[77] *Union Syndicale Solidaires Isere v Premier Ministre* C-428/09 [2011] IRLR 24.

[78] In *Landeshauptstadt Kiel v Jaeger* C-151/02 [2003] IRLR 804, and *Union Syndicale solidaires Isere v Premier Ministre* C-428/09 [2011] IRLR 24.

One can see how this can work where there are regular fluctuations of work on a short cycle (so that rest breaks can be disapplied at the busy peaks and compensatory rest given during the slack periods), but this may not be possible where rest breaks are disapplied because of a sustained *season* of heavy work possibly lasting for several months (as may be envisaged, for example, in several of the 'special cases' set out in reg 21, for example a 'foreseeable surge of activity' in agriculture or tourism). In such cases it is not currently clear whether the compensatory rest can be provided long after the missing rest period: the *Jaeger* case suggests this might be possible since it refers to the compensatory rest having to immediately follow the period in which the period was missing or curtailed only 'in principle', but the *Isere* case was more stringently stated.

So far as compensatory rest for the *20-minute in-work break* is concerned, the Court of Appeal has pointed out that if this break is not given when originally intended, but the worker takes the 20 minutes later in the shift, then they are having the break required and it is not a case of compensatory rest at all. As a consequence, compensatory rest for this break can take the form of several shorter breaks, possibly ones which are not complete breaks from work responsibilities—such as the need to remain on call.[79]

The special cases as set out in the WTR

Regulation 21 states that the provisions do not apply in relation to a worker:

> (a) where the worker's activities are such that his place of work and place of residence are distant from one another or his different places of work are distant from one another;
>
> (b) where the worker is engaged in security and surveillance activities requiring a permanent presence in order to protect property and persons, as may be the case for security guards and caretakers or security firms;
>
> (c) where the worker's activities involve the need for continuity of service or production, as may be the case in relation to—
>
> (i) services relating to the reception, treatment or care provided by hospitals or similar establishments (including the activities of doctors in training), residential institutions and prisons;
>
> (ii) work at docks or airports;
>
> (iii) press, radio, television, cinematographic production, postal and telecommunications services and civil protection services;
>
> (iv) gas, water and electricity production, transmission and distribution, household refuse collection and incineration;
>
> (v) industries in which work cannot be interrupted on technical grounds;
>
> (vi) research and development activities;
>
> (vii) agriculture;
>
> (viii) the carriage of passengers on regular worker transport services;
>
> (d) where there is a foreseeable surge of activity, as may be the case in relation to—
>
> (i) agriculture;
>
> (ii) tourism; and
>
> (iii) postal services;

[79] *Corps of Commissionaires Management v Hughes* [2011] EWCA Civ 1061, [2011] IRLR 915 and *Network Rail Infrastructure Ltd v Crawford* [2019] EWCA Civ 269, [2019] IRLR 538.

(e) where the worker's activities are affected by—
   (i) an occurrence due to unusual and unforeseeable circumstances, beyond the control of the worker's employer;
   (ii) exceptional events, the consequences of which could not have been avoided despite the exercise of all due care by the employer; or
   (iii) an accident or the imminent risk of an accident;

(f) where the worker works in railway transport and—
   (i) his activities are intermittent;
   (ii) he spends his working time on board trains; or
   (iii) his activities are linked to transport timetables and to ensuring the continuity and regularity of traffic.

The equal vagueness and potential significance of these categories would suggest they would have been subject to extensive litigation. This has not really materialized, however, suggesting that employers are either avoiding any grey areas or negotiating agreements with their workers. In one of the rare cases to consider reg 21, *Gallagher v Alpha Catering Services Ltd*,[80] the Court of Appeal said that these provisions are to be interpreted strictly, and indeed made a very strict interpretation of special case (c). The case related to airport workers employed to replenish the stocks of in-flight meals on aircraft. The employer argued that flexing was available since these workers fell within the description in special case (c): 'where the worker's activities involve the need for continuity of service or production, as may be the case in relation to . . . work at docks or airports', because there was a need for continuous service of food supply to aircraft landing at the airport. The court held that the need for continuity required in order for this paragraph to apply referred to a need not for the *service* to be continuous but for the *worker's work* to be continuous. While it was true, the court said, that the catering company needed to be able to provide a continuous service, there was no need for the workers to work without a break in order to achieve this, because other staff could be employed so as to give them rest, and therefore the employer was not allowed to use reg 21 to flex the rest periods of the workers. The phrasing and structure of the regulation, and the article of the Directive from which it is copied, strongly suggest that the Court of Appeal was wrong on this and that it was intended that working for an employer providing a continuous service should be covered even if, in theory, breaks could be provided by using additional staff.

5.1.9.3 **Flexing by workforce and collective agreement**

Regulation 23 provides that a collective agreement or a workforce agreement (see 5.1.4) may modify or exclude any of the requirements as to night work, rest period, and rest breaks, subject to the provision of compensatory rest or protection under reg 24. This may be particularly useful where the employer will find it difficult to comply with the WTR but the work does not fall within the 'special cases' covered by reg 21.

5.1.10 **Annual leave**

5.1.10.1 **The basic entitlement to paid leave**

Along with the 48-hour maximum working week, the aspect of the WTR to which most publicity was given on their introduction was the entitlement to a statutory minimum period of paid leave in each leave year. Prior to the WTR there was no legal minimum

[80] *Gallagher v Alpha Catering Services* Ltd [2005] IRLR 102, CA.

entitlement to holiday, paid or not, in the UK, although an entitlement to public holidays was implied in contracts of employment unless expressly negatived in the contract. The WTR minimum was set initially at three weeks, but rose to four weeks as from November 1999. It was felt by many to be unfair that public holidays were counted towards the WTR requirement and so in 2000, the WTR was amended to grant an additional 1.6 weeks, which is eight days for a five-day-a-week worker.[81] As will be seen, as these additional eight days are not mandated by EU law, different rules apply (see 5.1.10.3).

The leave year is primarily left to be determined by a relevant agreement; in default of that, the general rule is that it runs from the date of commencement of employment,[82] but of course that could be inconvenient for an employer who will normally wish to stipulate a standardized holiday year for all employees.

The annual leave entitlement applies simply to 'workers', which may include certain casual or temporary workers who would have had no holiday rights by contract prior to the regulations. The entitlement accrues on a monthly basis in the first year of employment.[83] It was proposed, post-Brexit, that this was changed so that workers accrue their annual leave entitlement at the end of each 'pay period' until the end of the first year of their employment.[84] Ultimately, the then government decided to introduce this only for part-year and irregular hours workers (see 5.1.10.5).[85] This means these workers are not necessarily entitled to 5.6 weeks' annual leave. In contrast to other workers, part-year and irregular hours workers annual leave rights accrue retrospectively at a rate of 12.07 per cent of the hours worked in the pay period, up to a maximum of 28 days.[86] The 12.07 per cent figure is used because 5.6 weeks of annual leave equates to 12.07 per cent of full-time workers working time.[87] Therefore, part-year and irregular hours workers will now be working under an 'accrue-as-you-go' system.

The two different pots of leave, one provided under the EU Working Time Directive and the other from UK legislation, have been criticized as being complicated and administratively burdensome, especially because, as will be seen, different rules applied to the different types of leave.[88] Therefore, it was proposed by the previous Conservative government that the two different types of leave be replaced with one pot of annual leave for workers. Indeed, this was considered a benefit of leaving the EU. These proposals have not been carried forward, so the system of two types of leave remain, for now.

5.1.10.2 **Timing of leave**

Regulation 15 sets out a system by which employer and worker can identify the dates on which leave is to be taken. The worker must propose dates at least twice as long in advance as the length of leave which they wish to take, but the employer can reject the request

[81] Regulation 13, supplemented by reg 13A which contains the additional 1.6 weeks.

[82] Regulation 13. Where an employee joins part of the way through a leave year, they are entitled to a holiday period on a pro rata basis: reg 13(5).

[83] Working Time (Amendment) Regulations 2001, SI 2001/3256, reg 15A.

[84] Department for Business and Trade 'Retained EU Employment Law: Consultation on reforms to the Working Time Regulations, Holiday Pay, and the Transfer of Undertakings (Protection of Employment) Regulations' (2023) available at <https://assets.publishing.service.gov.uk/government/uploads/system/uploads/attachment_data/file/1156206/retained-eu-employment-law-consultation.pdf>.

[85] The Employment Rights (Amendment, Revocation and Transitional Provision) Regulations 2023.

[86] Regulation 15B. Amended by The Employment Rights (Amendment, Revocation and Transitional Provision) Regulations 2023, Regulation 15B.

[87] For more on the maths see <https://www.gov.uk/government/publications/simplifying-holiday-entitlement-and-holiday-pay-calculations/holiday-pay-and-entitlement-reforms-from-1-january-2024>.

[88] Department for Business and Trade 'Retained EU Employment Law: Consultation on reforms to the Working Time Regulations, Holiday Pay, and the Transfer of Undertakings (Protection of Employment) Regulations' (2023) available at <https://assets.publishing.service.gov.uk/government/uploads/system/uploads/attachment_data/file/1156206/retained-eu-employment-law-consultation.pdf>.

and if the employer wishes to do so then they must give notice to that effect before half of the worker's notice period has elapsed. However, the employer can also, if it wishes, specify the dates when leave is to be taken. Many employers do so, for example requiring workers to take holiday during a factory's annual shut-down or an educational establishment's vacations. In Wales, legislation now mandates that employers may require covered agricultural workers to take at least two weeks' holiday during the period 1 October to 31 March, but must permit workers to take at least two consecutive weeks of holiday during the summer period 1 April to 30 September.[89]

It is clear that an employer is perfectly free to specify that leave should be taken on a date when the workers would not be working anyway: the Supreme Court held that oil rig workers, whose pattern of work involved an alternation of two weeks on the rig and two weeks' 'field break' on shore, could legally be required by their employer to take their annual leave during 'field break' periods.[90] The Court reasoned that the leave requirement was quantitative, not qualitative, so it did not actually need to be a break from what would otherwise be working time. The Court noted that this was not controversial for schoolteachers who could be required to take leave out of term time.

While this makes good sense on the facts of the case, the implications might not appeal as much taken to their logical conclusion. Lord Hope, for the unanimous Court, opined obiter, without deciding, that the Regulations would not countenance viewing the working week as consisting of six days, Monday through Saturday, and then requiring that workers take their annual leave on Saturday: he distinguished this on the ground that the Regulations speak of 'weeks' of leave, meaning that workers could demand their leave in at least weekly increments. Because this question did not arise from the facts of the case the Court did not decide that workers could insist on their leave in weekly chunks, but it did hold that they could not demand their leave in a four-week block.

This decision leaves open, for example, the possibility that it would be lawful for an employer to operate for only 11 months out of each year and then require that workers all take their leave during the twelfth month. Indeed, it appears that it would be acceptable for a business to shut down for five weeks distributed throughout the year and oblige employees to take their leave during these weeks. However, if such an arrangement resulted in, say, an eight-month period without any possibility of annual leave, it could be argued that the health and safety objectives of the Regulations were thus successfully circumvented.

5.1.10.3 **Interrelation of annual leave and leave for sickness and other reasons**

It was specifically provided in the WTR that the statutory holiday period must be actually *taken*, in the sense that it may not (in whole or, particularly, in part) be either carried forward into the next holiday year or bought out by a payment in lieu (except on termination of employment).[91] So, if the worker failed to take the leave to which they were entitled during the holiday year, that leave entitlement was lost. The rule had generally been thought to be in line with the health and safety provenance of the Regulations (ie that people should actually have the holiday period to rest, in spite of some evidence that holidays with the family can in some cases rate on the stress scale as highly as moving house, public speaking, or Christmas!).

[89] Agricultural Wages (Wales) Order 2025 SI 2025/293, art 34.

[90] *Russell v Transocean International Resources* [2011] UKSC 57, [2011] All ER (D) 53 (Dec).

[91] Regulation 13(9). Subject to a relevant agreement, the general rules on the timing of holidays are that a worker may give notice of intention to take a certain period, of a length twice as long as the time to be taken off; equally, an employer may require a worker to take a particular period by similar notice, or may notify the worker of time that is not to be taken as holiday by notice of a length equal to that to be taken off: reg 15. This gives the employer considerable ability to time holidays, either to bunch them (eg for annual shutdowns) or to spread them among employees to ensure continuity of production.

However, it has long been established that in circumstances where the worker was unable to take leave because of sickness, they are entitled to carry it forward. This was established by the CJEU in *HMRC v Stringer*,[92] which ruled that if sickness prevents an employee from taking holiday leave before the end of the holiday year it must be carried over to the next year, and the worker must be paid in lieu if their employment is terminated before the holiday can be taken. The rationale for this decision was that the purpose of paid annual leave was to permit a worker to rest, and a sick worker is not in a position to benefit from rest. The Court of Appeal confirmed in *NHS Leeds v Larner*[93] that this meant that additional words had to be read into reg 13(9) so as to disapply the ban on carrying forward leave into the next holiday year. The words in italics have to be read in: 'Leave to which a worker is entitled under this regulation may be taken in instalments, but—(a) it may only be taken in the leave year in respect of which it is due, *save where the worker was unable or unwilling to take it because he was on sick leave and as a consequence did not exercise his right to annual leave*.' In the subsequent decision of *Sood Enterprises Ltd v Healy*,[94] the EAT confirmed that this right to carry forward did not extend to the additional 1.6 weeks granted under reg 13(A) because that additional period was not required by EU law.

There are a number of ancillary points to be made. First, although in *HMRC v Stringer* reference was made to the worker being *prevented* from taking the holiday, it has since been confirmed in *Plumb v Duncan Print Group Ltd*[95] that it is in fact sufficient if the worker chose, because they were ill, not to take the holiday: it is not open to the employer to argue that the worker was sick, but not sick enough to be unable to take annual leave. Second, there is nothing in law to stop the employee taking WTR holiday while off sick if they choose—which quite often happens when an employee runs out of sick pay and needs to boost their income by claiming some paid annual leave.[96] Third, if the worker falls sick when about to go on scheduled holiday,[97] or even falls sick while on holiday,[98] they can convert the booked period of annual leave to sick leave—in other words, they can insist, if they wish, on rescheduling their holiday. Fourth, rolled-over leave must be taken within 18 months of the year in which the leave accrued but could not be taken.[99] This period has been codified in the WTR post-Brexit, with express provision for irregular-hours workers and part-year workers.[100]

The CJEU's rationale in judgments meant it always seemed likely that workers would also have a right to carry WTR leave over from one leave year to the next when they were prevented from using their annual leave because they were taking statutory leave such as maternity, paternity or parental leave. This right has now been 'introduced' in the recent WTR amendment for all workers, including irregular-hours workers and part-year workers.[101] The only difference is that leave needs to be taken within the next year, rather than the 18 months prescribed for sickness.

[92] C-520/06 [2009] IRLR 214, [2009] ICR 932.

[93] [2012] EWCA Civ 1034, [2012] IRLR 825, [2012] ICR 1389.

[94] [2013] IRLR 865, [2013] ICR 1361. This approach was confirmed as permissible in a case involving a French law which permitted more leave than the Directive requires: *Dominguez v Centre Informatique Du Centre Ouest Atlantique* [2012] IRLR 321.

[95] [2016] ICR 125.

[96] *HMRC v Stringer* (n 92).

[97] *Pereda v Madrid Movilidad* SAC-277/08, [2009] IRLR 959, CJEU.

[98] *Asociacion Nacional de Grandes Empresas de Distribucion v Federacion de Asociaciones Sindicales* C-78/11, [2012] IRLR 779, CJEU.

[99] *Plumb v Duncan Print Group Ltd* [2016] ICR 125; the 18-month period was based on ILO Convention 132, as nothing is specified in the Directive or the Regulations.

[100] Regulation 13(15) and 15D(4). Amended by Employment Rights (Amendment, Revocation and Transitional Provision) Regulations 2023, Regulation 3(3)(d) and 3(7).

[101] Regulation 13(14) and 15D(3). Amended by Employment Rights (Amendment, Revocation and Transitional Provision) Regulations 2023, Regulations 3(3)(d) and 3(7).

A further post-Brexit amendment codifies CJEU decisions which confirm that if a worker is deterred from taking leave by the employer refusing to pay for it, for example if the employer claims that the worker is self-employed, then the worker should be entitled to roll the holiday forward indefinitely until either the employer lets them take the leave or the employment ends and they receive a payment in lieu.[102] It is commendable that the legislation now requires employers to give reasonable opportunities to take the leave, or even encourage workers to take their leave (again, codifying existing obligations on employers).[103] However, the right now contained in the WTR is somewhat weaker than what was required under EU law. Any rolled over leave must now be taken by 'the end of the first full leave year' in which the workers leave rights have not been interfered with.[104] Yet the CJEU rulings found that the worker should be entitled to roll the holiday forward indefinitely, with no time limit.[105] Therefore, although it is positive that existing rules protecting workers have been codified, the new deadline, that was not permitted under EU rules, limits workers entitlements.

An important caveat is that the additional 1.6 weeks of leave, which are not guaranteed by the Working Time Directive and only the UK WTR, can be transferred over under agreement,[106] but there is no general right to this. The finding in *Snood* remains correct—that if these days are not taken, they are lost. Whether they are not taken because of sickness is irrelevant. However, the post-Brexit amendments do specify that the additional annual leave entitlement can be rolled over into the next year when maternity, paternity, or parental leave has been taken.[107]

5.1.10.4 **Rolled-up holiday pay**

Turning to the form of payment, one device historically used by employers, particularly in cases of sporadic employment where there may be administrative difficulties in working out exact holiday entitlements, was to 'roll up' holiday pay into an enhanced basic pay rate. Is this lawful under the Regulations and the Directive (in relation to the mandatory 5.6 weeks)? When tested before the English Court of Appeal[108] it was held that it could be lawful, provided it was made clear to the employees and was a genuine addition to basic pay and could be calculated. However, when the matter came before the Scottish Court of Session[109] the decision was that the practice was unlawful under the Directive because it could act as a disincentive actually to take the holiday, especially for low-paid workers who ought to have the pay separately at the time of taking the holiday. Eventually the matter was remitted to the ECJ, which handed down a decision that was strange even by its own standards. The court held[110] that the Directive precludes rolled-up payment as a matter of principle (particularly in the light of the health and safety provenance of the holiday entitlement). To that extent the challenge to rolled-up payment seemed to have

[102] *King v The Sash Window Workshop* C-214/16, [2018] IRLR 142, [2018] ICR 693, CJEU. Regulation 13(16)–(18) and 15D(5). Amended by Employment Rights (Amendment, Revocation and Transitional Provision) Regulations 2023, Regulations 3(3)(d) and 3(7).

[103] *Max-Planck-Gesellschaft zur Forderung der Wissenshcaten e.V. v Shimizu* C-684/16, [2019] 1 CMLR 1233. *Smith v Pimlico Plumbers Ltd (No 2)* [2022] EWCA Civ 70.

[104] Regulation 13(18).

[105] *King v The Sash Window Workshop* C-214/16, [2018] IRLR 142, [2018] ICR 693, CJEU.

[106] Regulation 13A(7).

[107] Employment Rights (Amendment, Revocation and Transitional Provision) Regulations, Regulation 13A(7A).

[108] *Blackburn v Gridquest Ltd* [2002] ICR 1206, [2202] IRLR 604, CA.

[109] *MPB Structures Ltd v Munro* [2004] ICR 430, [2003] IRLR 350, Ct of Sess (IH).

[110] Robinson-Steele v R D Retail Services C-131/04 [2006] IRLR 386, ECJ.

succeeded, *but* a second question had been permitted—what if the employer in fact *had* paid out holiday pay in a rolled-up way? Can the employer then set that off against any later claim by the employee to be paid it again at the time the holiday is taken? Here the ECJ held that the rolled-up pay *can* be set off, provided it has been paid 'transparently and comprehensibly' (note the similarity to the original decision of the Court of Appeal). The end result was thus that an employer should not use rolled-up holiday pay, but that if it did there was no effective sanction because the relevant amount had already actually been paid! Thus, in practice the device could continue to be used for the time being *but* the ECJ added that it was for member states to ensure that the Directive is not breached; the BIS guidance currently says: 'Holiday pay should be paid for the time when annual leave is taken. An employer cannot include an amount for holiday pay in the hourly rate (known as "rolled-up holiday pay"). If a current contract still includes rolled-up pay, it needs to be re-negotiated.'[111]

The situation for irregular hours and part-year workers is now more complex following the post-Brexit WTR amendments. Employers now have the option to use rolled-up holiday pay for these workers.[112] This is another watering down of an original proposal to introduce rolled-up pay holiday as an option for all workers.[113] When employers use the option to pay rolled-up holiday pay to eligible workers, it must be calculated at a rate of 12.07 per cent of the worker's pay, paid concurrently with their normal pay, but itemized separately on their pay slip.[114] Employers must still encourage irregular hours and part-year workers to use annual leave and they cannot lose holiday pay when taking sick leave or family leave.[115] Given the health and safety reasoning which justifies the ban on rolling-up holiday pay for other workers, this might be considered a set-back for part-year and irregular hours workers.

5.1.10.5 **What is a week's pay for leave purposes?**

Of course, paying a worker during leave, or making a payment in lieu of leave, requires deciding what the worker's pay should be. This has been the most troublesome issue in the whole of the WTR because the UK legislation, like the EU Directive, has historically not accounted for irregular working patterns.

Initially, the government decided to define the amount to be paid by using the definition of a 'week's pay' in ss 220–223 of the Employment Rights Act 1996 which required an averaging of pay over the 12 weeks preceding the 'calculation date' (in the case of the WTR this is the first day of the holiday). For about a decade, this was thought to exclude commissions or overtime payments in WTR contexts. This meant some workers' holiday pay would be much lower than their normal income, which would clearly disincentivize taking leave.

Luckily, following CJEU precedent,[116] the Court of Appeal ruled that paid commission must be included as part of the 12 week average pay (later increased to 52 weeks),[117] in

[111] See <https://www.gov.uk/holiday-entitlement-rights/holiday-pay-the-basics>.

[112] WTR reg 16A.

[113] Department for Business and Trade 'Retained EU Employment Law: Consultation on reforms to the Working Time Regulations, Holiday Pay, and the Transfer of Undertakings (Protection of Employment) Regulations' (2023) available at <https://assets.publishing.service.gov.uk/government/uploads/system/uploads/attachment_data/file/1156206/retained-eu-employment-law-consultation.pdf>.

[114] WTR reg 16A(2), (3) and (7).

[115] WTR reg 16A(4).

[116] *Lock v British Gas* [2014] WLR(D) 224, [2014] EU, ECJ C-539/12, [2014] IRLR 648, [2014] ICR 813 (22 May 2014), CJEU.

[117] Employment Rights (Employment Particulars and Paid Annual Leave) (Amendment) Regulations 2018 SI 2018/378, reg 10 effective 6 April 2020.

addition to basic pay.[118] A CJEU ruling[119] also meant that the UK courts established that pay for overtime—whether non-guaranteed but compulsory, or whether totally voluntary on the worker's part—should be included in calculating a week's pay for WTR purposes if the pattern of work is sufficiently regular and settled for payments made in respect of it to amount to normal remuneration.[120]

The post-Brexit amendments have codified these rulings, so the four weeks of WTR leave expressly includes:

(a) commission payments, which are intrinsically linked to the performance of tasks which a worker is obliged to carry out under the terms of their contract commissions;

(b) payments for professional or personal status relating to length of service, seniority or professional qualifications;

(c) other payments, such as overtime payments, which have been regularly paid to a worker in the 52 weeks preceding the calculation date.[121]

It is likely that this legislation will create some changes to the law. First, subsection (b) introduces potentially new things to be factored into weekly pay, including length of service pay, or pay related to seniority or professional qualifications. Secondly, voluntary overtime payments have not been included, despite this already being required under case law. It remains unknown if this omission will change workers' rights in this regard, or if the previous case law will be followed. However, if voluntary overtimes are 'regularly paid' to a worker then they will be likely to count under subsection (c). The legislation remains silent on the question most likely to be heard in court proceedings; how frequently does overtime need to be worked in order for it to be classed as 'normal'? This will be a question of fact for tribunals.

Finally, it is unclear whether tips paid under a tronc system might now be included in calculating normal pay.[122] These have traditionally been excluded from calculating a week's pay.[123] Yet the new language of payments which are 'intrinsically linked' to performing the obliged tasks is likely to include restaurant workers, for example. After all, it would be very challenging to argue that tips are not 'intrinsically linked' to servers' pay.

Calculating weekly pay requires that averaging the additional payments made over the previous 52 weeks (or, if less, the number of weeks they have been in the job) and factoring this into holiday pay for the period of leave taken.[124]

Because the extra 1.6 weeks in reg 13A are not driven by EU law, the rulings on commission and overtime do not apply to those eight days, but the 52-week averaging provision does apply to reg 13A. It is not at all clear how employers should deal with this in law but for simplicity most employers will apply the same principles to all annual leave, whether the basic four weeks, the additional 1.6 weeks, or additional contractual annual leave. This highlights one of the benefits of the proposal to amalgamate the two types of

[118] *Lock v British Gas Trading Ltd* [2016] 2 CMLR 40.

[119] *BA plc v Williams* C-155/10, [2011] IRLR 948, [2012] ICR 847.

[120] *East of England Ambulance Services NHS Trust v Flowers* [2019] EWCA Civ 947, [2019] IRLR 798.

[121] WTR reg 16 (3ZA), inserted by the Employment Rights (Amendment, Revocation and Transitional Provision) Regulations 2023, reg 3(8)(e).

[122] Ontroncsystem,seehttps://www.gov.uk/government/publications/e24-tips-gratuities-service-charges-and-troncs/guidance-on-tips-gratuities-service-charges-and-troncs.

[123] *Annabels (Berkeley Square) Ltd v HM Revenue and Customs Comrs* [2009] EWCA Civ 361, [2009] ICR 1123.

[124] WTR reg 15F (3ZC) and (3ZD).

leave into one, which was unfortunately only implemented for irregular hours and part-year workers.

When the possibility first emerged that by excluding the value of commission and overtime payments, employers had for many years been underpaying for holiday, there was great concern on their part that they might find themselves liable for millions of pounds in back pay. The claims would be made in employment tribunals as deductions from wages claims under s 23 of the Employment Rights Act 1996. In response, in 2015 the government amended s 23 for any such claims brought after 1 July 2015 to limit the arrears to a maximum of two years.[125] Employers breathed a collective sigh of relief when the EAT in *Bear Scotland Ltd v Fulton*[126] found that any three-month gap between periods of underpaid holiday would break the chain in a series of arrears and thus severely restrict long deductions claims. However, this decision has now been overturned by the Supreme Court in *Chief Constable of the Police Service of Northern Ireland v Agnew*, so a three-month gap between underpayments of holiday pay does not automatically break a series of deductions.[127] A lawful payment in between unlawful deductions would also not necessarily break the chain of underpayments. Whether employers have made a series of deductions which can be backdated is now a question of fact and requires just some 'similar features of the deductions,' rather than complete similarity.[128] *Agnew* means that employers who have not included bonus, overtime, commission, and allowances in their holiday pay could be liable for millions of pounds. For example, it has been estimated to cost the Police Service of Northern Ireland over £40 million (note that the two-year cap does not apply in Northern Ireland (NI), so the decision will cost employers there more money than those in England, Scotland, and Wales).[129]

Another issue caused by the rigidity of the WTR was the rates of holiday pay for those who are not working the whole year round. Most employers calculated the holiday entitlement of such part-year workers by multiplying their hours worked by 12.07 per cent (this figure is used because the 5.6 weeks holiday workers are entitled to equates to 12.07 per cent of full-time workers working time).[130] In *The Harpur Trust v Brazel*, the Supreme Court found that applying such a pro-rata formula to part-year workers on full-time, continuous contracts, was unlawful because it ran contrary to the definition of a 'week's pay' in the Employment Rights Act 1996.[131] This came as a surprise to many because it meant that part-year workers would receive proportionately more holiday pay than full-year workers. Many employers were worried that they would not only now be liable for increased holiday pay for full-time part-year workers, but that this might also include back payment.

The Employment Rights (Amendment, Revocation and Transitional Provision) Regulations 2023 effectively overruled *Brazel*, as it provides that irregular hours workers and part-year workers are eligible for pro-rata holiday pay, based on average pay over the previous 52 working weeks.[132] This means the approach generally used by employers previously, of multiplying their hours worked by 12.07 per cent is, once again, the correct one.

[125] Deduction from Wages (Limitation) Regulations 2014.

[126] [2015] ICR 221, [2014] UKEAT 0047_13_0411, [2015] IRLR 15, CJEU; [2012] IRLR 1014, SC.

[127] [2023] UKSC 33, [2024] IRLR 56.

[128] *British Airways Plc v Mello* [2024] EAT 53, [2024] IRLR 543, [2024] ICR 967.

[129] <https://www.unison-ni.org.uk/supreme-court-ruling-agnew-absence-payments>.

[130] For more on the maths, see <https://www.gov.uk/government/publications/simplifying-holiday-entitlement-and-holiday-pay-calculations/holiday-pay-and-entitlement-reforms-from-1-january-2024>.

[131] [2022] UKSC 21.

[132] WTR reg 15C, amended by The Employment Rights (Amendment, Revocation and Transitional Provision) Regulations 2023, reg 3(7).

All these uncertainties are the unfortunate consequence of the vague wording of the original Directive combined with the rather thoughtless 'copy-out' approach to the UK implementing legislation. If the UK government had put more effort into the negotiation of the original Directive, rather than simply trying to oppose it, we might have had clearer and more effective legislation from the outset.

5.1.11 **Enforcement**

The way in which the Regulations effectively straddle employment law and health and safety law is particularly noticeable in the area of enforcement. The so-called limitations relating to the 48-hour maximum working week, night working, and patterns of work are enforceable under the health and safety system, with primary responsibility on the Health and Safety Executive.[133] Thus, the principal obligations in these areas are that the employer must 'take all *reasonable* steps' to ensure that the weekly maximum and the night working limit are observed. There is an obligation on employers to maintain records adequate to show compliance, and to keep them for two years.[134]

On the other hand, the 'entitlements' to rest breaks and paid annual leave are enforceable by complaint by an individual worker to an employment tribunal (holiday pay claims can be heard by an employment judge sitting alone).[135] The tribunal or employment judge can make a declaration, award compensation (not subject to a maximum amount) for a refusal to allow one of these rights to be exercised, or, where the complaint is of failure to pay holiday pay, order the employer to pay the amount due.[136] The compensation can include damages for personal injury caused by the breach,[137] but not for injury to feelings.[138]

The individual worker is not given a statutory right to complain of breach of the maximum working week or night work (or pattern of work) provisions, but it is possible that breach of these obligations could be used *indirectly* by an individual in three ways. First, it could be used as evidence of unreasonable conduct by the employer in another form of claim, such as for constructive dismissal or in a personal injury action (as, for example, in *Hone v Six Continents Retail Ltd*,[139] where a pub manager's refusal to sign an opt-out supplied the element of foreseeability of harm necessary for his negligence action against his employer based on excessive workload). Secondly, it is possible that the Regulations could be held to support civil liability, so that in a case of non-compliance

[133] Regulation 28. It is an offence to fail to comply, carrying a fine on either summary conviction or conviction on indictment: reg 29. The HSE (or local authority where that is the enforcing authority) must make adequate arrangements for enforcement (reg 28(2)), but when the Regulations came into force the HSE made clear that they lacked the resources for proactive enforcement by inspector; it may be that enforcement turns out to be reactive, ie following on accidents or other notified events.

[134] Regulation 9. This record-keeping requirement does not extend to records to show that rest periods and rest breaks have been provided, and the decision of the CJEU in *Federación de Servicios de Comisiones Obreras v Deutsche Bank SAE*: C-55/18, [2019] IRLR 753, [2020] ICR 48 suggests that reg 9 may be deficient in this respect.

[135] Employment Tribunals Act 1996 (Tribunal Composition) Order 2009, SI 2009/789.

[136] Regulation 30. The time limit is the usual three-month period, subject to the 'not reasonably practicable' power to extend (reg 30(2)), or the claimant may sue instead under the 'deductions' provisions of the Employment Rights Act 1996, Pt II (Ch 3, heading 5), with their more generous time limit (*HMRC v Stringer* [2009] UKHL 31).

[137] *Grange v Abellio London Ltd (No 2)* UKEAT/0304/18 (7 March 2019 unreported).

[138] *Santo Gomes v Higher Level Care Ltd* [2018] EWCA Civ 418, [2018] IRLR 440, [2018] ICR 1571.

[139] [2006] IRLR 49, CA.

causing definable harm to the worker they could sue the employer for breach of statutory duty.[140] Third, it was held in *Barber v RJB Mining (UK) Ltd*[141] that it is an implied term of the contract of employment that the employer will comply with the maximum working week requirement, so that if an employee is made to work past the 48-hour average (without agreeing to do so), that employee may have a breach of contract action, or may even (according to the judge) calculate when sufficient hours have been worked in that reference period to average 48 per week and then *stop* until the beginning of the next reference period. The same approach was adopted in *R (oao Fire Brigades Union) v South Yorkshire Fire and Rescue Authority*[142] in relation to the limit on the length of night work. Thus, there are several possibilities here that do not appear on the face of the Regulations.

Any provision in an agreement (whether or not a contract of employment) is void if it purports to exclude or limit the application of the Regulations or to preclude a person from bringing proceedings before an employment tribunal (subject to the usual exceptions for ACAS-conciliated (COT 3) settlements and compromise agreements).[143]

In line with most other recent protective legislation, it is provided that any dismissal because of refusal to comply with a breach of the Regulations, to forgo a right, or to sign a workforce agreement, or because of being or seeking to be a worker representative, is automatically unfair;[144] likewise, a worker has a right not to suffer a detriment (short of dismissal) for similar reasons.[145] These guarantees notwithstanding, roughly two-thirds of workers who worked more than 48 hours a week under pressure from their employers had not signed an opt-out agreement of any kind.[146] It is not hard for employers to get workers either to sign an opt-out or to work long hours without complaint.

5.1.12 **Effects and future**

The general impression to date has been that the Working Time Regulations have had little effect in practice. The only notable litigation has been over the holiday entitlement, and even there it has been primarily about holiday pay. As far as the pursuit of the wider social goals of limiting working hours and patterns are concerned, little change can be discerned.[147] Health and safety enforcement has not happened. Some of this will no doubt be due to the Regulations simply being ignored. However, it is also the case that the exceptionally wide derogations and exceptions make the Regulations easy to avoid

[140] This possibility was expressly envisaged in the government's consultation document URN 98/645 para 184. Such liability would not be automatic under the Health and Safety at Work etc Act 1974, s 47(2) because the Regulations were passed under the European Communities Act 1972, not under the 1974 Act; it would therefore be necessary to prove parliamentary intent that they should support civil liability in the usual way. Given this possibility, an employer might be advised to keep records for at least *three* years (the limitation period in personal injury actions) not just the statutory two years.

[141] [1999] ICR 679, [1999] IRLR 308.

[142] [2018] EWHC 1229 (Admin), [2018] IRLR 717.

[143] Regulation 35.

[144] Regulation 32, adding the Employment Rights Act 1996, s 101A. Asserting a right under the Regulations is protected by s 104 of the Act.

[145] Regulation 31, adding the Employment Rights Act 1996, s 45A.

[146] *Slaying the Working Time Myths* (Trade Unions Congress, April 2009); see also Modern Families Index 2018 (Working Families 2018) available at <https://www.workingfamilies.org.uk/publications/mfi2018_employer_summary/>.

[147] ONS 'Average Hours Worked and Economic Growth, UK: 1998 to 2022' available at <https://www.ons.gov.uk/economy/grossdomesticproductgdp/articles/averagehoursworkedandeconomicgrowth/2024-01-22#:~:text=For%20all%20those%20in%20employment,before%20the%20pandemic%20in%202019>.

lawfully;[148] the opting out of the maximum working week by simple written agreement is the most obvious example. Even this limited impact is now likely to be further reduced as a result of the post-Brexit amendments.

5.2 Rights on the birth or adoption of a child

5.2.1 The development of family leave rights

One of the areas of greatest development in recent years has been that of maternity, paternity, and adoption rights.[149] Starting off from basic protections from dismissal or other detriment, these have seen the growth of positive rights to time off and at least an element of replacement pay during pregnancy and parental leave. The entitlement to a year of maternity leave is well established, with statutory maternity pay having gone up to nine months in 2007. Fathers also received first a basic two-week paternity leave, followed by additional paternity leave (and pay) in 2011 (allowing mothers to transfer the unused remainder of their leave and pay entitlements to the father). Finally, effective 5 April 2015, shared parental leave allows both parents to take the unused remainder of the mother's maternity leave and pay concurrently, and in separate blocks. As part of their general social policy, recent governments have extended these rights to adopters. Other rights have been introduced to support parents and others with caring responsibilities, such as unpaid leave to care for an ill child, or the right to request flexible working; those will be discussed in 5.3.

There has been a long history of incremental improvements to family leave and pay rights. Some of this has been driven by EU law developments, but often the UK has been in advance of the EU floor of rights. Although the UK may look generous in its family leave offerings, an important caveat is that the level of take-up of many rights in Britain has been lower than in other EU states—for example, women have taken less maternity leave—because the rights to pay while on leave have been limited in duration and amount.[150]

The trend of incremental change in this area has been continued by the current labour Government, who have removed the eligibility requirements for both paternity and parental leave.[151] The Employment Rights Act has also slightly modified the flexible working provisions and introduced bereavement leave.[152]

A word of warning in this section: it is easy to get bogged down in the complex legislation, especially regarding notice requirements, when delving into this area. Two key things to bear in mind as you work through the legislation are, first, what is the purpose of the legislation, and secondly, how is this being achieved, if at all? Such legislation can

[148] See Barnard, Deakin, and Hobbs 'Opting Out of the 48 Hour Week: Employer Necessity or Individual Choice' (2003) 32 ILJ 223.

[149] See Mitchell 'Encouraging Fathers to Care: The Children and Families Act 2014 and Shared Parental Leave' (2015) 44 ILJ 123; McRae *Maternity Rights in Britain* (1991); Fredman *Women in Labour: Parenting Rights at Work* (1995); McColgan (2000) 29 ILJ 125; James 'The Work and Families Act 2006: Legislation to Improve Choice and Flexibility?' (2006) 35 ILJ 272.

[150] Only a quarter of eligible employees took all or nearly all of the maximum entitlement even before the increases: DTI *Work and Parents: Competitiveness and Choice, a Framework for Simplification* (May 2001). The more generous the maternity provision, the higher the proportion of women returning to work after childbirth: Callender, Millward, Lissenburgh, and Forth *Maternity Rights and Benefits in Britain* DSS Research Report No 67 (1997); see also Forth, Lissenburgh, Callender, and Millward *Family-Friendly Working Arrangements in Britain* DfEE Research Report No 16 (1997).

[151] Employment Rights Act 2025, ss 15 and 16.

[152] Employment Rights Act 2025, ss 9 and 18.

have a number of aims, ranging from promoting gender equality, increasing birth rates, or helping families at a difficult time through to promoting workplace productivity and easing burdens on businesses. The UK legislation is often criticized for focusing more on the latter, even if superficially it aims to achieve the former.[153]

5.2.2 **Maternity leave**

It should be noted that although there is a separate section in this chapter that discusses adoption leave and pay, for the most part adopters are entitled to the same rights as mothers, so almost all of what is discussed in this section applies to adoption as well.

5.2.2.1 **The basic entitlement**

All pregnant employees are entitled to 52 weeks' maternity leave, irrespective of length of service or hours of work. Prior to 2008 maternity leave consisted of 'ordinary' leave and 'additional' leave. Any distinction between the two has since been removed but, owing to the vagaries of the legislative process, the two terms, 'ordinary' and 'additional', continue to exist in the regulations and statutes for now. However, the two kinds of leave are identical and the combination of ordinary and additional leave will hereinafter be referred to as 'maternity leave'. A woman who also enjoys a contractual right to maternity leave may not exercise the statutory and contractual rights separately, but may take advantage of whichever right is, in any particular respect, the more favourable.[154]

During maternity leave the contract of employment continues (unless either party expressly ends it, or it expires) and the employee is entitled 'to the benefit of the terms and conditions of employment which would have applied if she had not been absent'[155] (apart from remuneration, which is specifically excluded).[156] This means that the employee is entitled to continue to benefit from any terms and conditions concerning, for example, the use of a company car or mobile phone, membership of clubs and societies, reimbursement of professional subscriptions, and participation in employee share-ownership schemes. The period of maternity leave counts towards a woman's period of continuous employment for the purposes of qualifying for statutory employment rights and, because the contract continues throughout, the period also counts when assessing matters such as her seniority, pension rights, and other similar rights which depend on length of service (eg contractual pay increments).

5.2.2.2 **Commencement, duration, and return**

Within certain limits, an employee is free to choose the date on which her maternity leave starts.[157] Unless the employee specifies otherwise, she is assumed to be taking her entire 52-week entitlement. However, she cannot choose a start date earlier than the beginning of the eleventh week before the expected week of childbirth (EWC),[158] and her maternity leave period will be *automatically* triggered by any day on which she is absent from work wholly or partly because of pregnancy after the beginning of the fourth week before the

[153] See James and Busby *A History of Regulating Working Families: Strains, Stereotypes, Strategies and Solutions* (2020); Mitchell 'Shared Parental Leave: Can Transferable Maternity Leave Ever Encourage Fathers to Care?' (2022) 52 ILJ 149.

[154] MPL etc Regulations 1999, reg 21. This is commonly referred to as a 'composite' right.

[155] Employment Rights Act 1996, s 71(4), as amended by the Employment Relations Act 1999, Sch 4.

[156] Employment Rights Act 1996, s 71(5). Remuneration is defined for these purposes as 'sums payable to an employee by way of wages or salary': MPL etc Regulations 1999, reg 9.

[157] Employment Rights Act 1996, s 71(3). MPL etc Regulations 1999, reg 6.

[158] MPL etc Regulations 1999, reg 4(2)(b).

EWC.[159] The thinking behind the latter provision is apparently to prevent a woman from delaying the start of her ordinary maternity leave until the last possible moment (thus ensuring the maximum amount of leave after childbirth) by taking sick leave instead of maternity leave, but it could have the unfortunate consequence of encouraging a woman to continue working during the latter stages of pregnancy, even though medically unfit to do so, in order to prevent her maternity leave period from being automatically triggered. This seems a strange way of giving effect to a Directive which is intended to protect the health and safety of pregnant women.[160] If childbirth occurs prematurely, the maternity leave period begins with the day following the day of childbirth,[161] and the employer must be notified of the date of birth as soon as is reasonably practicable.

Duration

The first two weeks beginning with the day of childbirth is a period of 'compulsory maternity leave', which the woman must take.[162] After that, the Act specifically provides for a right to return to work at the end of the 52-week maternity leave period; but an employee who wishes to return to work *before* the end of her maternity leave period may do so, on giving not less than eight weeks' notice to the employer,[163] although she must still observe the compulsory maternity leave period. Dismissal during the maternity leave period brings that period to an end.[164] Such a dismissal will normally be automatically unfair.[165]

Return to old job

On return from maternity leave a woman is entitled to her old job. However, if she returns after more than 26 weeks of leave then there is a limited amount of flexibility available to her employer: if it is not reasonably practicable for her to return to her old job (for a reason other than redundancy) then the employer must return her to another job which is both suitable for her and appropriate for her to do in the circumstances.[166] There is only one small get-out to this obligation to find suitable alternative work: if the employer can find such suitable and appropriate employment with an associated employer, then he can offer that instead.[167] While there is no decided case on the point, it seems highly unlikely that the fact that someone else had been taken into employment for the purpose of covering the work of the employee on maternity leave would make it 'not reasonably practicable' to permit her to return to her job. Such a maternity cover employee can be safely dismissed without it being unfair because of a special provision to that effect in s 106 of the Employment Rights Act 1996.

If a redundancy situation arises during the employee's maternity leave then she may be made redundant, but only if some particular rights are observed. In such a case, where a redundancy situation arises during the employee's maternity leave which makes it

[159] MPL etc Regulations 1999, reg 6(1)(b). Absence from work due to time off for antenatal care does not count. 'Childbirth' is defined as 'the birth of a living child or the birth of a child whether living or dead after 24 weeks of pregnancy': reg 2; the same definition appears in the Employment Rights Act 1996, s 235(1).

[160] The employer can of course choose to disregard days of pregnancy-related illness if the employee wishes to defer the start of her maternity leave period.

[161] MPL etc Regulations 1999, reg 6(2).

[162] It is an offence under the Public Health Act 1936 to permit a woman to work in a factory within four weeks after the date of childbirth.

[163] MPL etc Regulations 1999, reg 11, as amended as from April 2007 to increase the notice from 28 days.

[164] MPL etc Regulations 1999, reg 7(5).

[165] MPL etc Regulations 1999, reg 20. See 5.4.1.

[166] MPL etc Regulations 1999, reg 18.

[167] If an offer of such employment with an associated employer is unreasonably refused then the woman can be dismissed without this constituting an automatically unfair maternity dismissal: MPL etc Regulations 1999, reg 20(7).

impracticable for the employer to continue to employ her under her original contract of employment, then if there is a suitable available vacancy with her employer (or with a successor, or an associated employer) this job must be offered to her. This relates to a vacancy where the work to be done is of a kind which is suitable in relation to the employee, appropriate for her to do in the circumstances, and on terms and conditions (including the capacity and place in which she is to be employed) not substantially less favourable to her than if she had continued to be employed under her previous contract.[168] If the employer has such a vacancy available but makes the employee redundant during maternity leave without first offering it to her, the redundancy dismissal will be unfair.[169] If, however, there is no suitable alternative work available which could be offered to her, she will not be regarded as unfairly dismissed. These provisions mean that in a redundancy situation, if there is alternative employment available for some of the employees holding redundant positions, an employee who is on maternity leave has priority for such positions over the other employees.

In July 2019 the Conservative government announced that the period during which this priority applies would be extended to start earlier for pregnant women (from the date the employer is informed of the pregnancy) and would continue until six months after the return to work. The reason for extending this special provision is that the government was persuaded that there was evidence that women were vulnerable to being selected for redundancy before or shortly after a period of maternity leave.[170] As this was one of the proposed changes in the now shelved Employment Bill, it is unclear if or when such an amendment would be introduced.

5.2.2.3 **Notice requirements**

To take advantage of her right to maternity leave, the employee must satisfy certain notice requirements. Regrettably, shared parental leave has introduced a new set of notifications superimposed on those discussed in this section, but that complexity comes into play only when the mother opts to share her leave. For maternity leave, the employee is now required to notify her employer, at least 15 weeks[171] before her EWC:[172] (a) that she is pregnant; (b) when the expected week of childbirth will be; and (c) the date on which she intends her maternity leave to start. The start date can be varied, provided she provides notice at least 28 days before either the date varied or the new date, whichever is the earlier.[173] If she gives birth before she has notified a date, or before the date she has notified, her maternity leave will start automatically on the day following the day of childbirth, and she must notify her employer as soon as is reasonably practicable (in writing, if so requested) that she has given birth, and of the date on which childbirth occurred.[174]

[168] MPL etc Regulations 1999, reg 10. The offer of alternative employment must be made before the end of her existing contract, and the new contract must take effect immediately on the ending of the previous contract.

[169] MPL etc Regulations 1999, reg 20(1)(b). If the employer offers her a suitable alternative vacancy and she unreasonably refuses it, she may lose her right to a redundancy payment. It was held under previous provisions that whether a vacancy is 'available' is a question of objective fact, not of reasonableness: *Community Task Force v Rimmer* [1986] ICR 491, [1986] IRLR 203, EAT.

[170] See <https://www.gov.uk/government/consultations/pregnancy-and-maternity-discrimination-extending-redundancy-protection-for-women-and-new-parents>.

[171] To be precise, notification must be 'no later than the *end* of the 15th week before the EWC': reg 4(1)(a), as amended.

[172] Or, where this is not reasonably practicable, as soon as is reasonably practicable. Cf *Nu-Swift International Ltd v Mallinson* [1979] ICR 157, [1978] IRLR 537, decided under the old provisions, where it was suggested that a woman may only be allowed to use this exception if she did not know of the time limit and was not put on inquiry about it.

[173] MPL etc Regulations 1999, reg 4(1A).

[174] MPL etc Regulations 1999, reg 4(4), as amended by the MPL (Amendment) Regulations 2002.

One important requirement is that an employer who has received notification of the intended start date of maternity leave must respond by notifying the employee of the date on which her maternity leave will end.[175] Failure to do so will mean that the employee will be protected against detriment or dismissal if she fails to return to work on the due date.[176]

There is no need for the employee to give notice to the employer of her intention to return to work—it is assumed that she will return on the date notified to her by the employer as the end of her maternity leave period—but if she wishes to return to work *earlier* than that date she may do so, on giving the employer at least eight weeks' notice of the date on which she intends to return.[177]

5.2.2.4 **Keep in touch days**

The Work and Families Act 2006 introduced a provision stating that 'an employee may carry out up to ten days' work for her employer during her statutory maternity leave period without bringing her maternity leave to an end'.[178] There is no *obligation* to attend such days and any question of payment remains a contractual matter. This means that the women could just be paid the low rate of maternity pay for a day's work, rather than their contractual rate of pay. This obviously makes keep in touch days unappealing to many new mothers.[179]

5.2.3 **Statutory Maternity Pay**

A pregnant employee who meets certain qualifying conditions based on her length of service and average earnings is entitled to receive Statutory Maternity Pay (SMP) from her employer for up to 39 weeks, with the first six weeks at nine-tenths of the employee's normal pay, and the remaining weeks at a flat rate (currently £194.32 per week). This means the last 12 weeks of maternity leave are unpaid, which explains why the average length of maternity leave taken is 39 weeks.[180] The employer is entitled to recover most of the amount paid out as SMP from the state, by deducting it from PAYE and NI contributions. In effect, therefore, SMP can be seen as a state maternity benefit which is administered via employers. Most of the rules in relation to SMP apply in the same way to statutory pay for paternity and adoption leave. Employers can enhance the level of pay for all of these entitlements and research suggests that 74.1 per cent of UK employers now offer enhanced maternity pay (although the most common enhancement is relatively minor; full pay for six weeks, rather than 90 per cent, followed by the standard statutory rate).[181] However, for those who can only access SMP, the low level of payment means that maternity leave is only 'likely to be of use to those with little outgoings and/or a partner who is able to financially maintain the family expenses whilst the mother is on low paid or unpaid leave'.[182]

[175] MPL etc Regulations 1999, reg 7(6). The notification must normally be given within 28 days of receiving the employee's notification: reg 7(7).

[176] See 5.4.

[177] MPL etc Regulations 1999, reg 11(1). The employee may vary this notified date by giving further notice of at least eight weeks: reg 11(2A).

[178] MPL etc Regulations 1999, reg 12A. This also states that reasonable contact by the employer from time to time (eg to discuss the employee's return to work) does not terminate the leave either.

[179] James 'Enjoy Your Leave but "Keep in Touch"': Help to Maintain Parent/Workplace Relationships' ILJ (2007) 36(3) 315.

[180] The UK does not collect data for uptake of any leave, so the most recent data remains Chanfreau, Gowland, Lancaster, Poole, Tipping, and Toomse *Maternity and Paternity Rights and Women Returners Survey 2009/2010* (Department of Work and Pensions Research Report No 777, 2011) available at <www.gov.uk/government/publications/maternity-and-paternity-rights-and-women-returners-survey-200910-rr777>.

[181] See 'Enhanced Maternity Pay' <https://pregnantthenscrewed.com/enhanced-maternity-pay/>.

[182] James *The Legal Regulation of Pregnancy and Parenting in the Labour Market* (2009) 42.

5.2.3.1 **Qualification**

To qualify[183] for SMP, the employee must satisfy a number of complex conditions:

(a) her earnings must have been at or above the lower earnings limit for the payment of NI contributions;[184]

(b) she must have been employed by that employer[185] for a continuous period of at least 26 weeks ending with the week immediately preceding the fourteenth week before the expected week of childbirth;

(c) she must give the employer medical evidence of the expected week of childbirth,[186] and at least 28 days' notice of the date on which she expects the employer's liability to pay SMP to begin (ie the date on which she expects to start her ordinary maternity leave);

(d) she must have reached the eleventh week before the expected week of childbirth, or have recently given birth (although she does not need to remain in employment beyond the qualifying week); and

(e) she must have stopped work.

A woman who cannot meet these requirements will probably be entitled to maternity allowance, a social security benefit paid directly to her by the state.

5.2.3.2 **The right to payment**

If she can satisfy these conditions, the employee qualifies for SMP at the higher, earnings-related rate for six weeks, and thereafter at the lower rate for the remainder of the maternity pay period, subject to an overall maximum of 39 weeks. Once entitlement to SMP is established in the qualifying week, the employee is entitled to receive her full entitlement to 39 weeks' SMP, even if she leaves the employer's employment before her SMP was due to start. Alternatively, she may continue working right up to the date of childbirth, and still retain her full entitlement to 39 weeks' SMP. The lower rate of SMP is fixed by regulations (at the time of writing, it stands at £194.32 pw).[187] The higher rate of SMP is set at nine-tenths of her week's pay (averaged, if necessary, over the eight weeks prior to the fourteenth week before the expected week of childbirth).[188] For many women the lower rate is far below their normal earnings, and so many women will feel the need to return to work before the right to SMP ceases simply in order to restore the household income.

Payments of SMP must be offset against any contractual payments for the weeks in question (eg under a contractual maternity scheme) and vice versa. Employers are entitled

[183] Social Security Contributions and Benefits Act 1992, s 164.

[184] The EAT has held that the application of the lower earnings limit as a qualifying condition for SMP is not contrary to Art 141 (ex Art 119) of the EC Treaty or the Pregnant Workers Directive: *Banks v Tesco Stores Ltd* [1999] ICR 1141, EAT.

[185] A woman may not count her previous employment with another employer for these purposes; in this respect the system differs from that applying to statutory sick pay.

[186] This should be given not more than 20 weeks before the expected week of childbirth. The employer cannot start paying SMP until the certificate has been received.

[187] Statutory Maternity Pay (General) Regulations 1986, SI 1986/1960, reg 6. If her earnings-related rate is *less* than the prescribed weekly rate, she will receive the lower of the two rates for the remaining weeks.

[188] Social Security Contributions and Benefits Act 1992, s 166, as substituted by the Employment Act 2002, s 19. If the employer subsequently grants a pay rise that covers any part of the maternity leave, it must be taken into account in calculating SMP for the whole period: Statutory Maternity Pay (General) Regulations 1986, reg 2(7), substituted in 2005 to reflect successful challenges to the previous law in *Gillespie v Northern Health Board* C-342/93 [1996] ICR 398, [1996] IRLR 214, ECJ, and *Alabaster v Woolwich plc* C-147/02 [2004] IRLR 486, ECJ.

to recover the 92 per cent of SMP paid out (100 per cent in the case of small employers) plus an additional amount to cover extra NI contributions. Many employers offer more generous maternity pay than the SMP minima, sometimes with a condition that the excess is repayable if the woman does not after her period of maternity leave return to work for at least a minimum period.

To ensure consistency with the maternity leave provisions, the maternity pay period is automatically triggered where a woman is absent from work wholly or partly because of pregnancy or childbirth after the fourth week before the birth. The SMP period usually lasts for the full 39 weeks but it is not payable for any week in which the employee does any work for her employer, and if she starts work for a new employer after childbirth, the entitlement to SMP stops completely. To avoid this being triggered by 'keep in touch' days for the maternity absentee, the Regulations now contain a provision[189] allowing her to work for the employer for up to ten days without her SMP entitlement being affected.

5.2.4 **Adoption leave and pay**

Adoption leave was introduced by the Employment Act 2002.[190] After amendments, the entitlement now very closely mirrors maternity leave; 52 weeks of adoption leave, and 39 weeks of pay are available, for an adoptive parent when a child is newly placed for adoption.[191] Partners of adopters, or adopters who were not identified as the initial recipient of adoption leave and pay, have the same entitlements to Shared Parental Leave and Statutory Shared Parental Pay as fathers and male partners with regard to maternity pay.[192] The leave can be taken by an individual person who adopts, or by one member of a couple who adopt jointly. In the latter case the couple may elect which partner takes adoption leave;[193] the other partner may be eligible for paternity leave.

To be eligible for adoption leave, an employee must be the child's adopter (ie they must have been matched with a child for adoption by an approved adoption agency, including through 'fostering for adoption' or surrogacy).[194] The adopter can choose to start adoption leave from the date of the child's placement, or from a predetermined date up to 14 days in advance of the expected date of placement.[195]

As in the case of maternity leave, the adopter must notify the employer that they intend to take adoption leave, and the requirement is a tight one—notice must be given within seven days of being notified by the adoption agency that they have been matched with a child, although this limit can be extended if it was not reasonably practicable for the employee to comply. The notice must specify the date when the child is expected to be placed with the adopter, and when the adopter wishes the adoption leave to start.[196] The employer can also ask for evidence of the employee's entitlement to adoption leave, in the form of a 'matching certificate' issued by the adoption agency,[197] but the employee will need to provide this in any event in order to claim statutory adoption pay.

[189] Regulation 9A, added from April 2007.

[190] DTI *Work and Parents: Competitiveness and Choice* (December 2000).

[191] PAL Regulations, regs 18(1), 20(2). If the placement ends prematurely during the adoption leave period, the entitlement to leave normally continues for another eight weeks after the end of the placement: reg 22.

[192] SPL Regulations, Part 3.

[193] PAL Regulations, reg 2(1), (4).

[194] PAL Regulations, reg 15. The employee must also have notified the adoption agency that they agree to the placement of the child, and the timing of the placement.

[195] PAL Regulations, reg 16.

[196] PAL Regulations, reg 17(1), (2). This date can be varied on giving 28 days' notice, unless not reasonably practicable to do so.

[197] PAL Regulations, reg 17(3). The certificate must contain certain specified information about the agency, the date of notification of being matched with a child, and the expected date of placement.

Once the employer has received notification of the intended start date, the employer must respond within 28 days by writing to the employee setting out the date on which the adoption leave will end (assuming that the employee takes advantage of the full entitlement).[198] If the employer fails to do so, the employee will be protected against detriment or dismissal if they fail to return to work on the due date.

The protection afforded to adopters during this leave reflects the maternity leave protections. Employees are entitled to the benefit of all their normal terms and conditions of employment, with the exception of terms relating to wages or salary.[199] Statutory adoption pay also mirrors maternity pay so refer to the discussion at 5.2.3.2. Adopters are also able to take 10 'keep in touch days'.[200] There is no need to notify the employer when they plan to return to work, unless they wish to return early, in which case eight weeks' notice of their intended date of return must be given.[201] Returnees from adoption leave are in a similar position to those returning to work after maternity leave and readers should refer to the fuller discussion at 5.2.2.2 'Return to old job'.[202]

5.2.5 **Paternity leave and pay**

Paternity leave was introduced much later than maternity leave, by the Employment Act 2002. The entitlement is modest—only two weeks' paid leave, to be taken within eight weeks of childbirth, and only at the same flat rate as lower-rate statutory maternity pay (at the time of writing, £194.32 pw). Nevertheless, the legislation was significant, as it was the first legal recognition of the fact that fathers have responsibilities around the time of childbirth that are capable of overriding the needs of employers. Paternity leave was also made available to employees following the adoption of a child, although here the adoptive parents are able to choose which parent takes paternity leave and which takes adoption leave.

5.2.5.1 **Qualification and notice requirements**

In order to qualify for paternity leave in relation to the birth of a child, an employee must (a) be either the child's biological father or the mother's husband, partner, or civil partner; and (b) have, or expect to have, responsibility for the child's upbringing.[203] Historically, parents also had to meet the eligibility requirements of been continuously employed for at least 26 weeks at the fifteenth week before the expected week of childbirth (EWC).[204] This requirement has now been removed by the Employment Rights Act 2025, so paternity leave is now a day-one right.[205] There are parallel provisions for paternity leave in relation to adoption.[206]

The notice requirements are similar to those applying to maternity leave: the employee must inform his employer (in writing, if the employer so requests) of his intention to take paternity leave by the fifteenth week before the expected week of childbirth, unless this is not reasonably practicable, and must tell the employer: (a) the expected week of the

[198] PAL Regulations, reg 17(7). [199] PAL Regulations, reg 19.

[200] PAL Regulations, reg 21A. This also states that reasonable contact by the employer from time to time (eg to discuss the employee's return to work) does not terminate the leave either.

[201] PAL Regulations, reg 25. [202] This is covered by PAL Regulations 26–29.

[203] PAL Regulations, reg 4(2). An employee who is the mother's husband, partner, or civil partner but not the child's father must have 'the main responsibility (apart from any responsibility of the mother) for the upbringing of the child'.

[204] PAL Regulations, reg 4(3).

[205] Employment Rights Act 2025, s 15 This amends s 80A and s 80B Employment Rights Act 1996.

[206] PAL Regulations, reg 2(4) and 8(2).

child's birth; (b) the amount of leave which the employee wishes to take (discussed presently); and (c) the date on which he wants his leave to start.[207] The leave must be completed within 56 days of the date of childbirth.[208] Note that while the employee can specify a calendar date on which they want to start paternity leave, the more popular option is to start the leave on the day the child is actually born or a specified number of days after the child is born.[209] This is because by selecting a fixed date, a father risks having his two weeks of leave either before the baby is born or, more likely, some time after it is born! After the child is born, he must notify the employer, as soon as reasonably practicable, of the date of childbirth.[210]

An employer who wants some evidence of the employee's entitlement to paternity leave is entitled to ask for a signed declaration from the employee (in effect, a self-certificate) that the leave is for the purpose of caring for a child or supporting its mother, and that he meets the eligibility criteria,[211] but the employer is not entitled to ask for any further evidence of entitlement.

5.2.5.2 **Extent of the entitlement**

An employee who satisfies the eligibility criteria and notice requirements can choose to take either one week or two consecutive weeks of paternity leave. There is no option to take odd days, or even two separate weeks, and only one period of paternity leave can be claimed in the event of a multiple pregnancy. Similar rules apply where paternity leave is claimed in connection with adoption, except that the timings run from the date on which the child is placed for adoption.[212] After amendments by the Employment Rights Act 2025, parents can now also take paternity leave after shared parental leave.[213]

During statutory paternity leave, most employees will be entitled to receive Statutory Paternity Pay (SPP) from their employer.[214] This is fixed at the same rate as standard-rate SMP (at the time of writing, £194.32 pw) or 90 per cent of average weekly earnings if this is less. Any paternity pay received under the employee's contract during paternity leave will be offset against the statutory entitlement, and vice versa.[215] Employees whose average weekly earnings are below the lower earnings limit for NI purposes will not qualify for SPP, but may be able to claim Income Support while on paternity leave.

During paternity leave a man is in a similar position as regards contractual entitlements as a woman on maternity leave, in that he will be entitled to the benefit of all his normal terms and conditions of employment, except for terms relating to wages or salary.[216] The similarity with maternity leave continues after the end of paternity leave, in that an employee returning to work after a period of paternity leave is entitled to return to the job in which he was employed before his absence,[217] with his seniority, pension rights, and so on as they would have been if he had not been absent, and on terms and conditions

[207] PAL Regulations, reg 6. The employee can vary the chosen start date by giving the employer notice at least 28 days in advance unless this is not reasonably practicable: reg 6(4). The equivalent for adoption is found at PAL Regulations, reg 10.

[208] PAL Regulations, reg 5. If the child is born prematurely, leave can be taken within 56 days of the beginning of the expected week of childbirth. The equivalent for adoption is found at PAL Regulations, reg 9(2).

[209] PAL Regulations, reg 5(3) and 6.

[210] PAL Regulations, reg 6(7).

[211] PAL Regulations, reg 6(3).

[212] PAL Regulations, reg 9.

[213] Employment Rights Act 2025, s 17.

[214] Social Security Contributions and Benefits Act 1992, s 171ZA, as inserted by the Employment Act 2002. Employers can recover SPP in the same way as they can recover SMP, ie 92 per cent of the amount paid out, or more if eligible for small employers' relief.

[215] Social Security Contributions and Benefits Act 1992, s 171ZG.

[216] PAL Regulations, reg 12.

[217] PAL Regulations, reg 13. As with ordinary maternity leave, the position may be different if the paternity leave is not an isolated period of leave, but follows another period of statutory leave.

no less favourable than those which would have applied if he had not been absent.[218] An employee taking paternity leave is also protected against dismissal or detriment for taking or seeking to take paternity leave.[219]

5.2.6 **Shared parental leave (and pay)**

As explained in 5.2.5, it was recognized in 2006 that it should be made possible for a father to take time off work to care for a new baby rather than only giving women this right. This led in 2010 to the creation of additional paternity leave (APL), which enabled mothers to transfer a maximum of 26 weeks of maternity or adoption leave to an eligible father or partner, so they could care for the child when the mother returned to work. This leave could not start before the twentieth week after birth and was required to be taken before the child's first birthday. Some criticisms of these measures, including the fact that mothers were locked in as the primary carers for the first 20 weeks and that parents could not take time off to care for a child together except during the two-week paternity leave period, were answered by the introduction of shared parental leave (SPL), which replaced APL.

Shared parental leave, introduced by the Children and Families Act 2014, allows the mother (or primary adopter) to elect to curtail maternity leave (and pay) and convert all that remains into SPL (and pay). It is very important to note that SPL *can be used by both parents concurrently, or alternately, or in blocks that overlap.* Blocks must be at least one week long, and employers can insist that leave be taken in a single block. Partners may also allocate to SPL whatever remains of SMP at the same statutory rate of pay. For the purposes of simplicity, the remainder of this account of SPL will refer to the more common case of childbirth rather than adoption.

These measures certainly make it appear that legislators are moving away from parental leave arrangements that entrench the role of women as child-carers. However, it only appears that way.[220] These measures do not in any way increase the leave that fathers have as of right, so they can only have leave if the mother chooses to relinquish it. More to the point, the fact that Statutory Shared Parental Pay will continue to be much less than most parents usually earn, and too little on which to support a family, means that pressure will continue for the lower earner in the relationship—usually the woman in heterosexual relationships—to take the leave.[221] This is one key reason why uptake of SPL has remained very low; only 1–2 per cent of eligible fathers have taken any.[222] Research finds that since 2016 there has been a downward trend in take-up of SPL, despite hopes that over time, more fathers would access such leave.[223] A number of proposals have been made to improve fathers' uptake of leave, most of which focus on replacing SPL with a non-transferable, individual right to leave.[224] The Women and Equalities Select

[218] PAL Regulations, reg 14. [219] PAL Regulations, regs 28, 29.

[220] Caracciolo di Torella 'Men in the Work/Family Reconciliation Discourse: The Swallows that Did Not Make a Summer?' J Soc Wel & Fam L (2015) 37(3) 334.

[221] See further Mitchell 'Shared Parental Leave and the Sexual Family: The Importance of Encouraging Men to Care' J Soc Wel & Fam L (2019) 41(4) 406.

[222] Birkett and Forbes 'Where's Dad? Exploring the Low Take-Up of Inclusive Parenting Policies in the UK' Policy Stud (2019) 40(2) 205.

[223] Chartered Institute of Personnel and Development 'Employer Focus on Working Parents: Parental Leave and Pay and Childcare Policies' (Chartered Institute of Personnel and Development, 2022) available at <https://www.cipd.co.uk/Images/employer-focus-on-working-parents-report_tcm18-111075.pdf>.

[224] 'Action Plan to End Pregnancy and Maternity Discrimination at Work' (April 2021) <https://maternityaction.org.uk/wp-content/uploads/AfMR-action-plan-2021-1.pdf>. See further Mitchell 'Shared Parental Leave: Can Transferable Maternity Leave Ever Encourage Fathers to Care?' (2022) 52 ILJ 149.

Committee proposed replacing SPL with a right to 12 weeks of paternal leave: the first four weeks at 90 per cent of salary, followed by eight weeks at the statutory rate of pay.[225] The current Labour Government is currently undertaking a review of the parental leave and pay system, which includes shared parental leave.

5.2.6.1 **Extent of the entitlement**

Shared parental leave carries the same protections (relating to contract terms, return to work, and so on) as paternity leave. It can only be taken (not surprisingly) with the cooperation of the child's mother. The leave can be divided between the partners or not;[226] taken in one continuous block or broken into blocks no smaller than a week (if the employer agrees);[227] and taken concurrently by the partners or in alternation (subject to employer cooperation). It must be determined in advance by notice, and varied only by eight weeks' notice.

During shared parental leave, employees are entitled to the benefit of all their normal terms and conditions of employment, with the exception of terms relating to wages or salary, just as in the case of maternity leave.[228] Returnees are in a similar position to those returning to work after maternity leave and readers should refer to the fuller discussion at 5.2.2.2, 'Return to old job'. In brief, parents who have taken shared parental leave are entitled to return to the job in which they were employed before their absence, with their seniority, pension rights, and so on as they would have been if they had not been absent, and on terms and conditions no less favourable than those which would have applied if they had not been absent.[229] As with maternity leave, this is subject to some exceptions where this is not reasonably practicable for redundancy or other reasons.[230] Finally, as with other types of family-related leave, employees are protected against dismissal or detriment for taking or seeking to take shared parental leave (see 5.5).[231]

5.2.6.2 **Qualification and notice requirements**

Shared parental leave (SPL) involves highly complex qualification scenarios, which is another factor which is likely to have deterred parents from accessing it. Fathers must have been employed continuously for 26 weeks before the fifteenth week before the EWC and remain employed until the week before the first week of SPL.[232] In the paradigm case the mother will also have met the same continuity requirement, which she must meet in order for her to share in the leave;[233] however, a father who meets the 26 weeks' service requirement can enjoy SPL, even if the mother may not, so long as the mother is entitled to maternity leave, SMP, or maternity allowance.[234] Practically speaking this means that if the mother lacks the continuity for SMP, she can still share her *leave* with her partner so long as he meets the continuity period, but she will not be able to share any of her SMP as shared statutory parental pay.

[225] House of Commons Women and Equalities Committee *Fathers and the Workplace: First Report of Session 2017–19* (HC 358, 2018).

[226] SPL Regulations, reg 7.

[227] SPL Regulations, regs 13 and 14.

[228] SPL Regulations, reg 38.

[229] SPL Regulations, regs 40, 41. As with maternity leave, if a redundancy situation arises during adoption leave, the employee is entitled to be offered any suitable available vacancy: SPL Regulations, reg 39.

[230] SPL Regulations, regs 39, 40(2).

[231] SPL Regulations, regs 42, 43.

[232] Shared Parental Leave Regulations 2014 SI 2014/3050 ('SPL Regulations'), regs 5 and 35.

[233] SPL Regulations, regs 4 and 35.

[234] SPL Regulations, reg 5(3).

This arrangement also means that a mother who is self-employed, and therefore entitled to no leave or SMP but entitled to maternity allowance from the state, can share with her partner (so long as the partner meets the continuity requirement) a number of weeks of leave that corresponds to the number of weeks of maternity allowance she has not yet taken.

So, a mother who does not meet the continuity requirement and wants to share her leave must be prepared to fix a 'curtailment date' for her maternity leave, and she can then convert what remains into SPL[235] (which can, if her partner so wishes, be taken by her partner concurrently with her maternity leave). This of course offers much less flexibility than exists for those partners who both meet the continuity requirement.

Shared parental leave introduces a bewildering array of new notice requirements as follows:

Notice of curtailment of maternity leave: the woman taking maternity leave must have given her employer notice that she will be curtailing her maternity leave.[236]

Notice of entitlement and intention to take: this tells the employer, among other things, the name of the two partners, how much maternity leave has been taken (and is intended to be taken), how much SPL is intended to be taken, and by which partner, as well as giving a non-binding 'indication' of when. This notice must be given to the employer of each partner at least eight weeks before SPL is to be taken.[237]

Period of leave notice: this must set out the start and end dates of each period of leave which the employee wishes to take. The person taking SPL must give this notice to their employer at least eight weeks before SPL is to be taken.[238]

The 'period of leave' notice cannot be given before the 'intention' notice, but it can (blessedly) be given at the same time.

The Regulations also provide for variations of the 'intention' notice (reg 11) and variations of the 'period of leave' notice (reg 15); the first may be given an unlimited number of times, while the second can be given only three times. The practical difference is simply that the 'intention' notice varies who gets how much leave—this must be permitted as often as notice periods can be complied with—whereas an amendment to a 'period of leave notice' will convey requests such as to break a previous continuous block of leave into small blocks at specific times, which should not be allowed to become a serial nuisance.

If you have been following along carefully, then, there are three different notices that must be given to the mother's employer, and two different notices that must be given to the father's employer. James argues that these are 'insensitive to the realities of parenting and reflect a lack of consideration of the unpredictable nature of childbirth/care and needs of parents during what can be an incredibly emotionally and physically draining period'.[239] Surely in practice the advice must be for all of the notices to a single employer to be given at once, at least eight weeks before maternity leave is to end and shared parental leave to begin. Keep in mind that the curtailment date will not always be the same as the SPL start date, and can even be after it, so long as only the father takes SPL before the curtailment date.

Bearing in mind these difficulties, it might come as a surprise that the eligibility requirements for shared parental leave are the only ones that have remained intact after the Employment Right Act 2025. Hopefully, this exclusion is because of the

[235] SPL Regulations, reg 6(4).

[236] SPL Regulations, reg 4(2)(d) and the Maternity and Adoption Leave (Curtailment of Statutory Rights to Leave) Regulations 2014, reg 6.

[237] SPL Regulations, regs 8 and 9.

[238] SPL Regulations, reg 12.

[239] James 'Family-Friendly Employment Law (Re)assessed: The Potential of Care Ethics' ILJ (2016) 45(4) 477, 484.

government's wholescale review of shared parental leave, which will bring about more substantive changes.[240]

5.2.6.3 **Keeping in touch days**

SPL reg 37 allows for 20 keeping in touch (KIT) days during the time that SPL 'may be taken', which covers the entire period from the date of birth to the exhaustion of the mother's total leave entitlement. Effectively this means that even if the mother takes several KIT days during maternity leave, there will remain a healthy allowance during SPL, although the 20 will be offset by the number used during maternity leave. There is no *obligation* to attend such days; any question of payment remains a contractual matter.

5.2.6.4 **Statutory shared parental pay**

Statutory shared parental pay (SSPP) is payable at the statutory rate for the number of full weeks during any SPL to the extent that any of the mother's original 39-week SMP allowance is untaken.[241] After the compulsory maternity leave period is over the mother may, if she wishes, curtail her leave and SMP, so that as much as 46 weeks of leave and 33 weeks of pay will remain for the father. This certainly makes it more feasible for fathers to take a substantial amount of leave, but because of the low rate of pay it is still the case that the lower-paid parent will tend to take the leave. In most heterosexual families, that will be the mother.

A complication comes from the fact that some companies give mothers full or enhanced (ie above the statutory amount) pay throughout their period of maternity leave as an employee benefit. Even though the number of employers offering enhanced SSPP has increased, it still lags considerably behind the number of companies offering enhanced maternity pay.[242] This obviously thwarts any intention (assuming there was one) to encourage fathers to take extensive leave. Such a policy was challenged as sex discrimination in *Ali v Capita Consumer Management Ltd* and *Hextall v Chief Constable of Lincolnshire Police*. The Court of Appeal held that because maternity leave and pay are based on protecting the health of the mother, they are fundamentally different from shared parental leave—which is designed to facilitate care of the child—so treating them differently is not discrimination because of the exception permitting more favourable treatment to women in relation to pregnancy and maternity.[243] Likewise, in *Price v Powys County Council* the EAT found that enhancing adoption pay but not shared parental leave pay was not sex discrimination. This was because the primary purpose of adoption leave was not just about childcare, like SPL, but also the establishing a parental bond and creating a safe space for the adopted child.[244] These cases highlight some of the problems with relying on transferable maternity leave as a way to encourage fathers' uptake of leave.[245]

[240] See <https://www.gov.uk/government/calls-for-evidence/parental-leave-and-pay-review-call-for-evidence/parental-leave-and-pay-review-call-for-evidence>.

[241] SSPP Regulations, reg 10.

[242] 'Employers Twice as Likely to Offer Enhanced Parental Leave Compared to Last Year, Study Finds' <https://www.peoplemanagement.co.uk/article/1795671/employers-twice-likely-offer-enhanced-parental-leave-compared-last-year-study-finds>.

[243] [2019] EWCA Civ 900, [2019] IRLR 695.

[244] [2021] IRLR 741.

[245] See further Mitchell 'Shared Parental Leave: Can Transferable Maternity Leave Ever Encourage Fathers to Care?' (2022) 52 ILJ 149.

5.2.7 **Alternatives to full-time return to work**

5.2.7.1 **Return part-time or with more flexible hours**

One major perceived deficiency of the statutory scheme is that it does not give a woman the right to return to work from maternity leave on *different* terms and conditions (eg on a part-time basis or with flexible working hours), yet for many women this may be the only way of reconciling the competing demands of work and family responsibilities, especially in view of the limited availability of affordable childcare.

However, the Employment Act 2002 gave a woman returning to work after maternity leave the right to request flexible working, a right which has now been extended to all employees.[246] A maternity returner can use this procedure to require her employer to consider letting her return on different hours. Unfortunately, as will be explained in 5.5, there is no direct remedy for an unjustified refusal of a request for flexible working. Instead, an employee faced with such a refusal will need to argue that it constitutes indirect sex discrimination. This is what happened in *Home Office v Holmes*,[247] where the woman used the return-to-work provisions to return full time but also claimed that the requirement to continue working full time constituted unjustifiable indirect sex discrimination (in that compliance with it was particularly difficult for women with children). This argument succeeded in the case, which was widely reported in the press and was said by the EOC to be a significant development. However, it does not stretch the imagination to suppose that there could be many circumstances in which a requirement to work full time might be held to be justifiable[248] in economic terms, and the EAT's decision was based very much upon the facts of the particular case[249]—as can be seen from the subsequent case of *Greater Glasgow Health Board v Carey*,[250] where on similar facts it was held that the employer's refusal to allow a full-time health visitor to return on a part-time basis was indirectly discriminatory but was justified by the need for continuity of care by the same visitor.

However, the more recent case of *Hardy & Hansons plc v Lax*[251] resulted in an important victory for an employee refused a move to part-time working on her return. The Court of Appeal held generally that justification has to be judged directly by the tribunal itself (*not* by applying a variant of the 'range of reasonable responses' test in unfair dismissal), which was particularly important here because the tribunal clearly did not believe a word of the employer's evidence as to why it had refused her request. The case suggests that unlawful discrimination in these cases may now be the 'default setting' and that the onus on the employer to prove justification will be a significant one.[252]

[246] See 5.4. [247] [1984] ICR 678, [1984] IRLR 299. [248] See 4.2.5.7.

[249] It is important not to be too sanguine about cases as precedents; at its most basic, all that the EAT was doing was to say that in this case the tribunal was not manifestly wrong in holding that the requirement to work full time was (a) discriminatory and (b) unjustifiable on the facts before it.

[250] [1987] IRLR 484. In coming to this conclusion, the EAT applied the obiter remarks in *Rainey v Greater Glasgow Health Board Eastern District* [1987] ICR 129, [1987] IRLR 26, HL that administrative efficiency, if sufficiently demonstrated, may be an important factor in the justification defence under the Sex Discrimination Act 1975, s 1(1)(b)(ii).

[251] [2005] EWCA Civ 846, [2005] IRLR 726, CA; the case is of general importance in the area of indirect discrimination and the justification defence.

[252] But see Baker 'Proportionality and Employment Discrimination in the UK' (2008) 37 ILJ 305 for a general discussion of how the tribunals have had a disappointing record with justification in discrimination cases.

5.2.7.2 **Career breaks**

In certain sectors (particularly local government, banks, computer companies, the retail sector, and oil companies) there have been significant moves towards allowing women employees to take far more substantial 'career breaks' in order to have a family—breaks of anything up to seven years are offered, and with the possibility of attending several days' training per year during the break in order to maintain contact with colleagues and keep up with changes. For present purposes the main point to notice is that any such scheme can come about only by agreement and as a matter of contract; such breaks are not provided for in the statutory maternity leave scheme. Employers' schemes which improve upon the statutory entitlement can have a sting in the tail, however, particularly where they involve a lengthy career break, because the effect of the career break may be to break the employee's continuity of employment, with potential disastrous consequences for her employment rights.

This issue arose for consideration in *Curr v Marks & Spencer plc*,[253] where the employee was accepted onto a four-year child-break scheme, a condition of which was that she resigned from the company. At the end of the break she returned to work, but was subsequently made redundant. She claimed a redundancy payment covering all her years of service, both before and after the career break, but the employers argued that she was only entitled to count the period since her return from the child break. The Court of Appeal held that the terms of the career break did not constitute a contract of employment, so that her continuity was not preserved on the basis that her contract continued throughout, but neither could she claim that continuity was preserved under s 212(3)(c) of the Employment Rights Act 1996[254] because the employer did not regard her as continuing in employment during the child break (an odd conclusion, it must be said, given that the employee maintained contact with the employer during the break, including returning to work for two weeks each year, but one reached on the basis that the terms of the career-break agreement were quite unlike a contract of employment). The upshot was that Mrs Curr paid a heavy financial penalty for her career break, and the lesson for an employee is to be very cautious about the effect of a career break on their contract of employment, and on their continuity of employment.

5.2.8 **Risk assessment and suspension from work on maternity grounds**

All employers have a duty under the Management of Health and Safety at Work (MHSW) Regulations 1999 to assess the risks to health and safety to which their employees are exposed while they are at work.[255] In addition, as a result of an amendment to the MHSW Regulations in 1994 (implementing the Pregnant Workers Directive)[256] employers of women of child-bearing age have a specific duty to carry out a further risk assessment where the work is of a kind which could involve a risk to the health and safety of a new or expectant mother,[257] or to that of her baby, from any processes or working conditions, or from physical, biological, or chemical agents.[258] Where that risk assessment identifies

[253] [2003] ICR 443, [2003] IRLR 74, CA.

[254] ie that there was an 'arrangement' by which she was absent from work in circumstances such that she was regarded as continuing in employment: see 2.5.2.2.

[255] SI 1999/3242, reg 3.

[256] Directive 92/85/EC.

[257] Defined as employees who are pregnant, have given birth within the preceding six months, or are breastfeeding.

[258] MHSW Regulations, reg 16(1). These are said to include the list of agents set out in Annexes I and II of the Pregnant Workers Directive.

a risk to the health and safety of a new or expectant mother or her baby, the employer is under a duty in the first instance to take action to prevent her from being exposed to the risk by following the requirements of any relevant health and safety regulations (eg by removing the hazard or by providing protective clothing). If the risk cannot be avoided by such means, and it is not reasonable for the employer to alter the employee's working conditions or hours of work, or such an alteration would not avoid the risk, the employer must remove the employee from the risk by suspending her from work for as long as is necessary to avoid the risk.[259] An employer must also suspend an employee from work on maternity grounds where the employee is a new or expectant mother who works at night, and she has a certificate from a registered medical practitioner or registered midwife which shows that it is necessary for her health and safety that she should not be at work for any period of night work identified in the certificate.[260]

Under the MHSW Regulations, the duty to take action by altering working conditions or hours of work, or by suspending an employee from work, does not arise until the employee has notified the employer in writing that she is pregnant, has given birth within the preceding six months, or is breastfeeding,[261] although even in the absence of written notification of pregnancy, an employer who fails to take reasonable action to protect an employee who is known to be pregnant or breastfeeding might well be in breach of the general duty to protect the health and safety of its employees. The duty to conduct a pregnancy risk assessment in the first place is triggered whenever the employer employs a woman of child-bearing age, and does not depend upon there being an employee who is pregnant.[262]

The employer's duty under the MHSW Regulations is mirrored by a series of rights enjoyed by employees suspended from work on maternity grounds.[263] These rights were introduced by the Trade Union Reform and Employment Rights Act 1993, implementing the Pregnant Workers Directive.[264] First, before being suspended from work on maternity grounds, an employee has the right to be offered suitable alternative employment by her employer where there is an available vacancy,[265] with a right to complain to a tribunal if the employer fails to make such an offer.[266] The work must be suitable in relation to the employee, appropriate for her to do in the circumstances, and on terms and conditions which are not substantially less favourable than those under which she normally works.[267] Second, an employee who is

[259] MHSW Regulations, reg 16(2), (3). As this constitutes a form of legitimate discrimination, there is a delicate balance to be struck and the employer should not proceed to a suspension too readily: *New Southern Railways Ltd v Quinn* [2006] IRLR 266, EAT.

[260] MHSW Regulations, reg 17.

[261] MHSW Regulations, reg 18. If the employee has given the employer a medical certificate which arguably indicates that she is pregnant, but without expressly stating that fact, the burden may pass to the employer to show that there was no notification: *Day v T Pickles Farms Ltd* [1999] IRLR 217, EAT.

[262] *Day v T Pickles Farms Ltd*, n 227. That case also established that an employer's failure to carry out such a risk assessment may amount to sex discrimination if a new or expectant mother can show that she has suffered a detriment. See also *Hardman v Mallon t/a Orchard Lodge Nursing Home* [2002] IRLR 516, EAT.

[263] See the Employment Rights Act 1996, ss 66–68. Suspension must be in consequence of a 'relevant requirement' or a recommendation in a code of practice issued or approved by the Health and Safety Commission under s 16 of the Health and Safety at Work etc Act 1974: s 66(1). The Suspension from Work (on Maternity Grounds) Order, SI 1994/2930, specifies reg 17 of the MHSW Regulations as a relevant requirement for these purposes. See also the Suspension from Work on Maternity Grounds (Merchant Shipping and Fishing Vessels) Order, SI 1998/587.

[264] Directive 92/85/EC.

[265] Employment Rights Act 1996, s 67(1).

[266] Employment Rights Act 1996, s 70(4). The right of complaint is subject to the usual three-month time limit, calculated from the first day of suspension: s 70(5); where the tribunal upholds the complaint it may make an award of compensation: s 70(6).

[267] See *British Airways (European Operations at Gatwick) Ltd v Moore and Botterill* [2000] ICR 678, [2000] IRLR 296, EAT, where an offer of ground work to two pregnant cabin crew workers failed the test because it did not include the flying allowances which they received while working as cabin crew.

suspended from work on maternity grounds has the right to be paid her normal remuneration by her employer during the period of suspension, unless she has unreasonably refused an offer of suitable alternative work for the period in question, in which case no remuneration is payable for the period during which the offer applies;[268] once again, there is a right of complaint to a tribunal that the employer has failed to pay the amount due,[269] and where the tribunal finds the complaint well founded it will order the employer to pay the unpaid remuneration to the employee.

5.2.9 **Time off for antenatal care**

A pregnant employee has a right not to be unreasonably refused time off during working hours to attend antenatal care on the advice of a registered medical practitioner, registered midwife, or registered health visitor,[270] irrespective of her length of service. After the first visit, the employer may require the employee to produce a certificate from the doctor, midwife, or health visitor confirming that she is pregnant, and an appointment card or other document showing that an appointment has been made,[271] but for obvious reasons this is not necessary for the first visit. Antenatal care is not defined in the Act, but it can include relaxation and parentcraft classes, as well as medical examinations, provided of course that the attendance is on the advice of a doctor, midwife, or health visitor. The right to time off is not absolute: the Act states that an employee has the right not to be *unreasonably* refused time off, which implies that there may be circumstances where it would be reasonable for the employer to refuse time off; for example, it might be reasonable for an employer to refuse time off to a part-time worker who could reasonably be expected to arrange her antenatal care outside her working hours.

The employee is entitled to be paid at her normal rate of pay during the period of time off.[272] Complaint of unreasonable refusal to give time off, or of failure to pay wages during time off, may be made to a tribunal within three months of the day of the appointment concerned (or within a further reasonable period if the tribunal accepts that it was not reasonably practicable for the complaint to be presented within the three-month period).[273] The Children and Families Act 2014 inserted into the Employment Rights Act 1996 provision for fathers (or other partners) to have time off for two antenatal visits.

5.3 **Rights relating to parenting responsibilities**

As part of the overall project of developing rights to help reconcile parenting with work, parental leave to look after children (not to be confused with shared parental leave!) was in principle an important development, but it suffers from the basic reality that as long as time off is unpaid the take-up rate will be low. This shortcoming is also evident with the very different right to 'emergency' time off for dependants, another piece of the same project, but is not shared with the most recent right, which is for parental bereavement leave and pay.

[268] Employment Rights Act 1996, s 68.

[269] The time limit here is three months (or a further reasonable period where not reasonably practicable) from the day in respect of which the remuneration was not paid: Employment Rights Act 1996, s 70(2).

[270] Employment Rights Act 1996, s 55.

[271] Employment Rights Act 1996, s 55(2).

[272] Employment Rights Act 1996, s 56. See *Gregory v Tudsbury Ltd* [1982] IRLR 267, IT. The amount of pay will usually be calculated by dividing her week's pay by the number of normal working hours in a week.

[273] Employment Rights Act 1996, s 57. Dismissal or redundancy selection for taking time off for antenatal care is likely to be automatically unfair under s 99: see 5.4.1.

5.3.1 **Parental leave**

The Employment Relations Act 1999 introduced a new right to parental leave for male and female employees, implementing the Parental Leave Directive.[274] The detailed provisions on parental leave are contained in the Maternity and Parental Leave (MPL) Regulations 1999,[275] which set out who has a right to parental leave, and certain key elements which apply to everyone. In relation to detail, employers and employees are free to agree a detailed parental leave scheme, via a collective or workforce agreement, which will be valid provided it does not contradict any of the key elements in the Regulations. If no such scheme is agreed then the 'default' scheme in the Regulations applies.

5.3.1.1 **Entitlement to parental leave**

The right to parental leave is available to an employee who has, or expects to have, 'parental responsibility' for a child within the meaning of the Children Act 1989.[276] There was a one year length of service requirement, but this has now been removed by the Employment Rights Act 2025.[277] However, those taking parental leave before the planned implementation of this in April 2026 will still have to meet the old service requirement. After a legislative extension, the leave can now be taken any time before a child turns 18.[278] Such an employee is entitled to at least 18 weeks' parental leave in respect of each child, for the purpose of caring for that child.[279] If the employee works part time, the entitlement to leave is proportionate to the time for which the employee normally works,[280] and if the leave is taken in shorter periods than the employee's normal working week, the individual periods of leave are aggregated together.[281] Employees have a right not to be dismissed or subjected to any detriment by their employer for taking or seeking to take parental leave.[282] A bone of contention is that parental leave is unpaid, unless the employer agrees otherwise. In practice, this means that many employees who might wish to take some parental leave may simply be unable to do so because of the financial consequences. One very unsatisfactory element of the scheme from the point of view of the employee is that, unlike other family leave rights, the employer can refuse to grant the leave if it is inconvenient: the employer may postpone a period of parental leave (other than leave on birth or adoption) where the employer considers that the operation of the business would be unduly disrupted if the employee took leave during the period identified in the notice.

During the period of parental leave, the employee remains in employment but, in the absence of an agreement to the contrary, the employee is only entitled to the benefit of the employer's implied obligation of trust and confidence, and any terms and conditions of employment relating to notice of termination by the employer, redundancy compensation, or disciplinary or grievance procedures. During that period the employee is bound by the implied obligation to the employer of good faith, and any terms and conditions of employment relating to notice of termination by the employee, disclosure of confidential information, the acceptance of gifts or other benefits, or the employee's participation in any other business.[283] An employee who takes parental leave of four weeks or less is entitled to return

[274] Directive 96/34/EC. The Directive was extended to the UK by Directive 97/75/EC. The relevant Directive is now 2010/18/EU.

[275] MPL etc Regulations 1999.

[276] MPL etc Regulations, reg 13.

[277] Employment Rights Act 2025, s 15. Amends Employment Rights Act 1996, s 76.

[278] MPL etc Regulations, reg 2(1). This goes further than required by the Directive.

[279] MPL etc Regulations, reg 14(1). In the case of multiple births, an employee is entitled to 18 weeks' leave for each child.

[280] MPL etc Regulations, reg 14(2).

[281] MPL etc Regulations, reg 14(4).

[282] MPL etc Regulations, regs 19, 20.

[283] MPL etc Regulations 1999, reg 17.

to the job in which they were employed before taking leave,[284] with seniority, pension rights, and so on as they would have been if the employee had not been absent, and on terms and conditions not less favourable than those which would have been applicable to the employee had they not been absent.[285] If the period of parental leave is more than four weeks, the employee is entitled to return to the old job or, if that is not reasonably practicable, to another job which is both suitable and appropriate for the employee in the circumstances.[286]

5.3.1.2 Detailed parental leave scheme: collective or workforce agreements

In line with the current political emphasis on 'partnership' in the workplace, the MPL etc Regulations allow employers and employees to agree a detailed parental leave scheme via a collective or workforce agreement which is incorporated into the contracts of employment of individual employees.[287] Such a scheme may improve upon the entitlements set out in the regulations, but it may not contradict any of the key elements in the regulations (eg by imposing lower age limits, or a later birth or adoption date). A 'collective agreement' is defined for these purposes as an agreement or arrangement made between one or more independent trade unions and one or more employers or employers' associations.[288] A 'workforce agreement' is defined for these purposes in similar terms to those used in the Working Time Regulations.[289] To be valid, a workforce agreement must: (a) be in writing; (b) have effect for a specified period not exceeding five years; (c) apply to all the members of the workforce, or all the members of a particular group of workers who share a function, workplace, or organizational unit (excluding those whose terms and conditions are provided for, wholly or in part, by a collective agreement); and (d) be signed by all the elected workforce representatives (although if the employer employs 20 or fewer employees on the date when the agreement is first made available for signature, it is sufficient if the agreement is signed by a majority of the workforce). In addition, before the agreement is made available for signature, the employer must have provided all the employees to whom it was intended to apply with copies of the agreement, together with such guidance as they might reasonably require to help them understand it.[290] The MPL etc Regulations set out the requirements for the election of workforce representatives,[291] including matters such as candidature, entitlement to vote, and the conduct of the ballot.[292]

5.3.1.3 Detailed parental leave scheme—the default scheme

The Regulations contain a model scheme[293] on parental leave which automatically comes into operation if the parties do not make their own collective or workforce agreement. The key elements of the model scheme are as follows:

(a) parental leave may not be taken in periods other than a week or multiple of a week[294] (except in the case of a child entitled to Disability Living Allowance);

(b) an employee may not take more than four weeks' leave in respect of any individual child during a particular year;

[284] MPL etc Regulations, reg 18(1). [285] MPL etc Regulations, reg 18A.

[286] MPL etc Regulations, reg 18(2). [287] MPL etc Regulations 1999, reg 16.

[288] MPL etc Regulations, reg 2. [289] See 5.1.4. [290] MPL etc Regulations 1999, Sch 1.

[291] Workforce representatives have a right not to be dismissed or subjected to any detriment by the employer for performing (or proposing to perform) any functions or activities as a workforce representative or a candidate for election as a workforce representative.

[292] These requirements are similar to those which apply to the election of workforce representatives under the Working Time Regulations: see 5.1.4.

[293] MPL etc Regulations 1999, Sch 2.

[294] This condition was applied strictly in *Rodway v New Southern Railways Ltd* [2005] ICR 1162, [2005] IRLR 583, CA to rule out the use of this scheme to cover a single day needed for childcare (even though the employee was willing to trade in a whole week's entitlement for the one day off).

(c) the employee must give the employer at least 21 days' notice of the taking of parental leave, and its duration;

(d) fathers wishing to take parental leave immediately after the baby is born must give the employer notice at least 21 days before the beginning of the expected week of childbirth;

(e) employees wishing to take parental leave immediately after the date of placement of an adopted child must give the employer notice at least 21 days before the beginning of the week in which placement is expected to occur, or as soon as reasonably practicable thereafter;

(f) the employer may ask for reasonable evidence of the employee's entitlement to parental leave (eg evidence of the child's date of birth, or date of placement for adoption);

(g) the employer may postpone a period of parental leave (other than leave on birth or adoption) where the employer considers that the operation of the business would be unduly disrupted if the employee took leave during the period identified in the notice;

(h) leave may not be postponed for more than six months, and the employer must notify the employee of the postponement in writing within seven days of receiving the employee's notice, giving the reason for the postponement and specifying the dates on which the period of leave will begin and end.

5.3.2 **Parental bereavement leave**

This right to up to two weeks' paid leave after the death of a child under 18 was introduced by the Parental Bereavement (Leave and Pay) Act 2018, which was a private member's bill which gained government support. This Act inserted new sections 80EA–80EE into the Employment Rights Act 1996 and is accompanied by the Parental Bereavement Leave Regulations 2020[295] (the PBL Regulations) and two sets of regulations dealing with Statutory Bereavement Pay.[296]

The right to parental bereavement leave (PBL) is conferred on all employees, with no minimum service requirement, in relation to the death of a child. A child is defined as a person under 18, including a baby stillborn after at least 24 weeks of pregnancy.[297] The right applies to parents, including adoptive parents and others responsible for the day-to-day care of a child as defined in reg 4 of the PBL Regulations. The parent may take one or two weeks' leave within 56 weeks of the death. The minimum leave is a period of one week. If two weeks are taken, they need not be consecutive.[298] When more than one child dies, the employee is entitled to leave in respect of each child.[299]

A parent wishing to take PBL must notify their employer of the date of the child's death, when the leave will start, and whether one or two weeks' leave will be taken. Notice need not be in writing. If the leave is taken within 56 days of the death then the notice must be given before the first day of leave, but if the leave is taken later than 56 days after the death then there is a minimum notice period of seven days.[300]

[295] SI 2020/249.

[296] Statutory Parental Bereavement Pay (General) Regulations 2020 SI 2020/233 and Statutory Parental Bereavement Pay (Administration) Regulations 2020 SI 2020/246.

[297] Employment Rights Act 1996, ss 80EA(9) and 80EE.

[298] PBLR, reg 5. [299] PBLR, reg 4(10). [300] PBL Regulations, reg 6.

As with other forms of family leave, the contract of employment continues save that the obligation to pay wages or salary is suspended,[301] and the employee has the right to return to their job, with their seniority, pension rights, and so on as they would have been if they had not been absent, and on terms and conditions no less favourable than those which would have applied if he had not been absent.[302] There is the usual protection against dismissal and detriment for taking, or seeking to take, this leave.[303]

An employee who qualifies for PBL is also entitled to Statutory Parental Bereavement Pay (SPBP) provided that they also have 26 weeks' continuous employment and meet the minimum earnings condition of earnings during the eight weeks before the child's death being not less than the NI lower earnings limit.[304] This could be a problem for a parent who has had to take unpaid leave to care for a dying child. The current rate of SPBP is £194.32 per week. As with the other statutory leave payments, the employer is entitled to a 92 per cent reimbursement of SPBP, or for small employers the whole amount is reimbursed.

It is notable that this protection only kicks in after 24 weeks of pregnancy. This gap has now been filled, albeit less generously, by the Employment Rights Act 2025, as considered at 5.4.3.

5.3.3 **Neo-natal leave**

The Neonatal Care (Leave and Pay) Act 2023 creates a day-one right for parents of babies who require neonatal care to take additional leave to supplement their parental leave.[305] The idea is that this would tag onto the end of their existing rights to leave (however note until the eligibility requirements for paternity leave are removed, parents could be entitled only to ne-natal leave). Neonatal care is defined as:

- medical care received in hospital;
- medical care received elsewhere after being discharged from hospital. This care must be under the direction of a consultant and include ongoing monitoring and visits by healthcare professionals; or
- palliative or end of leave care.[306]

Parents are entitled to this extra leave when their child has been in neonatal care for at least seven consecutive days within the first 28 days after birth.[307] The leave accrues by one week for each week the baby is in care, up to a maximum of 12 weeks.[308] This means that a parent is not entitled to neonatal care leave (NCL) as soon as their child is in hospital, but only after they have been in for a full seven days. However, because the week begins the day after the care started, the earliest NCL can actually be taken is on the ninth day following the start of the care. NCL must be taken within the first 68 weeks of the baby's birth.[309]

NCL is split into two tiers. Tier one is when the baby is in hospital, including one week after the care has ended. Tier two is when the baby is no longer receiving medical care. There are (understandably) different notice requirements for these tiers. If parents are

[301] Employment Rights Act 1996, s 80EB(1)(b) and PBL Regulations, reg 9.

[302] PBL Regulations, reg 10.

[303] Employment Rights Act 1996, s 99 (automatically unfair dismissal), s 47C (detriment).

[304] Social Security Contributions and Benefits Act 1992, s 171 and Statutory Parental Bereavement Pay (General) Regulations 2020 SI 2020/233, reg 4.

[305] Employment Rights Act 1996, s 80EF.

[306] The Neonatal Care Leave and Miscellaneous Amendments Regulations 2025, reg 4(1).

[307] The Neonatal Care Leave and Miscellaneous Amendments Regulations 2025, reg 5.

[308] The Neonatal Care Leave and Miscellaneous Amendments Regulations 2025, reg 7(1).

[309] Reg 7(2).

taking Tier 1 leave, the should inform their employer before they are due to start work on the first day of each week of leave, or as soon as possible afterwards.[310] For parents on Tier 2, parents would need to give 15 days of leave.[311] Tier 1 leave may be taken in non-consecutive weeks, but Tier 2 leave must be taken consecutively.[312] Any leave the employee chooses not to take in the Tier 1 period may be taken during the Tier 2 period. Employees who take NCL are entitled to protection from detriment or discrimination in the same manner as those taking other types of family-related leave.[313]

Although NCL is a day-one right, the right to payment is dependent on meeting the same 26 weeks of service required for maternity and shared parental leave pay.[314]

5.4 Rights for non-parents

Although the package of family-friendly rights does mainly benefit parents, there are some limited entitlements which have been made available to a wider range of caring relationships. For a long time, this only included emergency time off for dependants, but a few more meagre (because they are unpaid) offerings have recently been introduced.

5.4.1 'Emergency' time off for dependants

A right for employees to take a reasonable amount of unpaid time off to deal with incidents involving a 'dependant' was introduced by the Employment Relations Act 1999.[315] Like the provisions on parental leave, the provisions on time off for dependants were designed to implement the Parental Leave Directive, which gives a right to time off in family emergencies. The hope and expectation was that these provisions would lead to a reduction in the number of employees taking odd days off sick in order to care for sick children or to cope when domestic arrangements (eg child-minding arrangements) go awry at short notice.

Although colourfully (and sometimes mischievously) portrayed in certain sections of the media as giving employees carte blanche to take time off whenever they wish to attend to the needs of leaking washing machines or sick poodles, the right to time off for dependants is in fact more limited than this. Under the Employment Rights Act 1996, s 57A an employee has the right to be permitted to take a 'reasonable amount' of time off (not further defined or explained) during working hours to take action which is necessary:

(a) to provide assistance when a dependant falls ill, gives birth, or is injured or assaulted;

(b) to make arrangements for the provision of care for a dependant who is ill or injured;

(c) when a dependant dies;[316]

(d) because of the unexpected disruption or termination of arrangements for the care of a dependant; or

(e) to deal with an incident which involves a child of the employee and which occurs unexpectedly during school hours or other time when the child's school is responsible for the child.[317]

[310] Reg 10(4). [311] Reg 10(5). [312] Reg 8. [313] Reg 17.

[314] Employment Rights Act 1996, s 171ZZ16(2), introduced by the Neonatal Care (Leave and Pay) Act 2023.

[315] Employment Rights Act 1996, ss 57A and 57B, added by the Employment Relations Act 1999.

[316] This only covers the making of the necessary arrangements and attending the funeral; it does *not* enact any wider form of bereavement leave: *Forster v Cartwright Black* [2004] ICR 1728, [2004] IRLR 781, EAT.

[317] Employment Rights Act 1996, s 57A(1). No qualifying period of continuous employment is required.

A 'dependant' of an employee has a wide definition, including a spouse, civil partner, child, parent, or a person who lives in the same household as the employee, otherwise than as an employee, tenant, lodger, or boarder.[318] For the purposes of heads (a) and (b) above, 'dependant' also includes a person who reasonably relies on the employee (a) for assistance on an occasion when the person falls ill or is injured or assaulted, or (b) to make arrangements for the provision of care in the event of illness or injury; and for the purposes of head (d), it includes any person who reasonably relies on the employee to make arrangements for the provision of care.

Where time off is taken under these provisions, the employee must tell the employer the reason for the absence as soon as is reasonably practicable, as well as how long the employee expects to be absent from work.[319]

Although the statutory provisions make no reference to the time off only being available to cope with an emergency, the Directive refers to 'time off on grounds of force majeure for urgent family reasons'. Despite what was said in *Royal Bank of Scotland plc v Harrison* which will be considered below, this has influenced the interpretation of the UK provisions. The extent of the entitlement to time off under this head was considered by the EAT in the leading case of *Qua v John Ford Morrison Solicitors.*[320] In that case, the applicant was dismissed for absenteeism having been absent from work for 17 days over a 10-month period as a result of medical problems suffered by her young son.

The EAT gave useful guidance on the interpretation of the statutory provisions, pointing out that the right is to take a reasonable amount of time off in order to deal with unexpected or sudden events affecting dependants, and to make any necessary longer-term arrangements for their care. The right to time off to provide assistance under head (a) 'does not in our view enable employees to take time off in order themselves to provide care for a sick child, beyond the reasonable amount necessary to enable them to deal with the immediate crisis'. On the particular issue raised by the case, that of a parent with a child suffering from a chronic illness, the EAT gave the provisions a narrow interpretation:

> The legislation contemplates a reasonable period of time off to enable an employee to deal with a child who has fallen ill unexpectedly and thus the section is dealing with something unforeseen. Once it is known that the particular child is suffering from an underlying medical condition, which is likely to cause him to suffer regular relapses, such a situation no longer falls within the scope of . . . section 57A at all.

In *Royal Bank of Scotland v Harrison,*[321] the EAT ruled that the 'unexpected' event need not necessarily be the illness of a child. The unexpected cancellation of ordinary childcare qualifies. Furthermore, even where the employee had 12 days' notice of the impending disruption to normal childcare arrangements, the unavailability of replacement care counted as 'unexpected': the employee had expected to be able to find alternative cover but despite her best efforts could not, so the disruption to childcare was 'unexpected' and there was no requirement in s 57A that it also be 'sudden'. In coming to this conclusion the EAT said that s 57A should be read as enacted and was wider than the Directive and so should not be glossed by the references in the Directive to 'force majeure' and 'urgent'. However, the EAT did not dissent from what was said in *Qua* about the right being to take time off to response to an unusual issue rather than a routine care need.

Returning to the *Qua* case, the EAT rejected the argument that each individual request for time off should be considered in isolation, confirming that where an employee has

[318] Employment Rights Act 1996, s 57A(3). [319] Employment Rights Act 1996, s 57A(2).

[320] [2003] ICR 482, [2003] IRLR 184, EAT, applied in *Truelove v Safeway Stores plc* [2005] ICR 589, EAT.

[321] [2009] IRLR 28, EAT.

exercised the right on more than one previous occasion, the employer can take into account the number and length of previous absences in order to determine whether the time sought to be taken off is reasonable and necessary. However, in determining what is a reasonable amount of time off, the EAT considered that 'the disruption or inconvenience caused to an employer's business by the employee's absence are irrelevant factors, which should not be taken into account', on the grounds that the 'operational needs of the employer cannot be relevant to a consideration of the amount of time an employee reasonably needs' to deal with emergency situations.

On the issue of the duty under s 57A(2) to inform the employer, the EAT held in *Qua* that there is no duty on an employee to report to the employers 'on a daily basis' while taking time off work; she must tell the employer the reason for her absence and how long she expects to be absent, but 'there is no continuing duty on an employee to update the employer as to her situation, though of course many employees would no doubt do this as a matter of course'.

A complaint that an employer has unreasonably refused time off under these provisions lies to an employment tribunal, within three months of the refusal, or within a further reasonable period where the tribunal is satisfied that it was not reasonably practicable for the complaint to be brought within that period.[322] Where the tribunal upholds the complaint, it must make a declaration to that effect and may order the employer to pay compensation to the employee of such amount as the tribunal considers just and equitable in all the circumstances, having regard to the employer's default and any loss suffered by the employee which is attributable to the matters complained of. An employee also has the right not to be dismissed or subjected to any detriment by their employer for taking or seeking to take time off for dependants.[323]

5.4.2 **Carer's leave**

After decades of campaigning in the UK, carer's leave was finally introduced by the Carer's Leave Act 2023 and supplemented by The Carer's Leave Regulations 2024.[324] This makes one week of unpaid leave available a year to enable all employees 'to provide or arrange care for a dependent with a long-term care need'.[325] Like the emergency leave entitlement, a wide range of people are defined as dependents, including a spouse, civil partner, child, parent, or somebody who lives in the same household (excluding boarders, employees, lodgers, and tenants) or anyone else who reasonably relies on the employee to provide or arrange care.[326] A long-term care need is defined as:

- someone with a physical or mental injury that requires (or is likely to require) care for more than three months;
- someone with a disability for the purposes of the Equality Act 2010 (this means someone with a mental or physical impairment that has a 'substantial' and 'long-term' effect on their ability to do normal, daily activities); or
- someone who requires care for a reason connected to their old age.

Employees do not have to meet any eligibility requirements. Importantly, unlike the default provision on emergency leave, leave does not have to be taken for the whole week; the minimum amount an employee can take is a half day.[327] This means that the leave also does not have to be taken consecutively, so carers are afforded some flexibility.

[322] Employment Rights Act 1996, s 57B.
[323] Employment Rights Act 1996, ss 47C(2)(d); 99(3)(d).
[324] Employment Rights Act 1996, s 80J.
[325] Employment Rights Act 1996, s 80J(1) and The Carer's Leave Regulations 2024, reg 5(1).
[326] Employment Rights Act 1996, s 80J(2)(a).
[327] The Carer's Leave Regulations 2024, reg 5(2).

Employees do need to give some notice. Although the Regulations are not prescriptive on the form of the notice, employers must be given the earlier of either twice the number of days of leave they are taking or three days' notice.[328] Leave requests cannot be denied, but employers can postpone the leave if they reasonably believe the timing would unduly disrupt the operation of their business.[329]

Whilst the introduction of carer's leave is symbolically important, as it is the first time unpaid carers have been given their own entitlement, the impact of this legislation is likely to be minimal. This is primarily because it is unpaid, so few will be able to afford to take it. Furthermore, the relatively brief period of a week is unlikely to be enough for many carer's to cover their needs. It was proposed that the Employment Rights Act would make this right payable at their usual wage, but this was ultimately not included. However, the current Labour government have committed to reviewing this, so some level of payment may be introduced at some point.

5.4.3 **Bereavement leave**

Historically, the only leave available to those who grieve the loss of a loved one has been emergency time off for dependents. As seen above at 5.4.1, this provides only limited support and only a 'reasonable' amount of time off, which is not defined. This gap has been somewhat filled by the introduction of bereavement leave, which was introduced by the Employment Rights Act 2025 and is expected to be introduced in 2027.[330] This will supplement the existing parental bereavement leave, by making some leave available to employees who lose someone other than a child.[331] Similarly to PBL, bereavement leave will be a day one right with no eligibility requirements. When more than one person dies, the employee will be entitled to leave in respect of each person.[332] Furthermore, employees are eligible to the same protections from detriment and dismissal.

A 'bereaved person' is not defined in the Act, and will only be defined in future Regulations, which are being consulted on at the time of writing. It is clear that this will extend to people experiencing a miscarriage (loss of pregnancy before 24 weeks gestation) and have experienced a failed IVF transfer.[333]

However, the bereavement leave entitlement will be less generous than parental leave in two key ways. First, the entitlement is only for a week.[334] Secondly, it is unpaid. These limitations arguably creates a hierarchy of grief; some losses deserve two weeks' paid leave, some deserve one week of unpaid leave and some might be deserving of no leave at all, depending on how narrowly the list of 'bereaved persons' is drawn in the Regulations. This disparity, as well as the lack of pay, means that this statutory right to leave is likely to have only a minimum impact.

5.5 **Protection from dismissal and detriment for exercising family leave rights**

All employees have the right not to be dismissed or subjected to any detriment by their employer for reasons connected with pregnancy or childbirth (and for some other specified family reasons), regardless of their length of service. In addition, a woman dismissed

[328] The Carer's Leave Regulations 2024, reg 7(3).
[329] The Carer's Leave Regulations 2024, reg 8(b).
[330] Employment Rights Act 2025, s 18.
[331] S 80EA.
[332] Employment Rights Act 1996, s 80EA(7), amended by the Employment Rights Act 2025, s 18(3)(i).
[333] Employment Rights Act 1996, s 80EA(9), amended by the Employment Rights Act 2025, s 18(3)(j)(ii).
[334] Employment Rights Act 1996, s 80EA(5A) amended by the Employment Rights Act 2025, s 18(3)(g).

on grounds of pregnancy or childbirth may bring a claim of sex discrimination, which has the advantage that compensation for sex discrimination is not subject to any upper limit and that compensation for injury to feelings is available.

5.5.1 **Protection from dismissal**

Section 99 of the Employment Rights Act 1996 (as fleshed out by the MPL etc Regulations,[335] the PAL Regulations,[336] and the SPL Regulations[337]) provides that a dismissal will be automatically unfair if the reason or principal reason for the dismissal[338] is connected with:

(a) pregnancy;[339]
(b) childbirth;[340]
(c) suspension from work on maternity grounds;[341]
(d) the fact that she has taken, or sought to take maternity leave, parental leave, or time off for dependants, paternity leave, or adoption leave;
(e) the fact that she has availed herself of the benefits of maternity leave;[342]
(f) the fact that she has failed to return to work after ordinary or additional maternity leave, or additional adoption leave, where the employer had failed to notify the employee of the date of return;
(g) the fact that she has undertaken or refused to undertake 'keep in touch' days;
(h) the fact that she has refused to sign a workforce agreement in relation to parental leave;[343] or
(i) the fact that she has performed (or proposed to perform) any functions or activities of a workforce representative (including standing as a candidate) for the purposes of the provisions on parental leave.

Special rules apply in the case of redundancy. First, a dismissal will be unfair if the employee is made redundant and it is shown that they were selected for redundancy in preference to other comparable employees for one of the family reasons just set out.[344] Secondly, where a redundancy situation arises during the employee's maternity, adoption,

[335] MPL etc Regulations 1999, reg 19, as amended by the MPL (Amendment) Regulations 2002, reg 13.

[336] PAL Regulations, reg 28.

[337] SPL Regulations, reg 42 (the list here is shorter, to reflect that SPL does not involve the period before and two weeks after childbirth).

[338] As in other unfair dismissal cases, it will be for the employer to show the reason for the dismissal. An employee dismissed while pregnant or during ordinary or additional maternity leave is entitled to a written statement of the reasons for dismissal, without requesting it, and regardless of her length of service: Employment Rights Act 1996, s 92(4), as amended.

[339] For a case to come within this (primary) category, the employer must have known that the employee was pregnant (though with a possible extension to a case where the employer dismissed *in case* she was pregnant): *Ramdoolar v Bycity Ltd* [2005] ICR 368.

[340] The protection under this head only applies during the employee's ordinary or additional maternity leave: MPL etc Regulations 1999, reg 20(4).

[341] Ie under a relevant statutory requirement or relevant recommendation in a Code of Practice, as defined by s 66(2) of the 1996 Act.

[342] Ie that during her ordinary maternity leave period (or additional maternity leave period), she availed herself of the benefit of any of the terms and conditions of her employment preserved under s 71: MPL etc Regulations 1999, reg 20(5), applying reg 19(3) and (3A).

[343] See 5.3.1.2.

[344] MPL etc Regulations 1999, reg 20(2); PAL Regulations, reg 29(2); SPL Regulations, reg 43(2).

or shared parental leave which makes it impracticable for the employer to continue to employ them under their original contract of employment, the employee is entitled to be offered alternative employment with their employer (or with a successor, or an associated employer) where there is a suitable available vacancy. This is discussed in 5.2.2.2, 'Return to old job'. If the employer has a suitable alternative vacancy available, but makes the employee redundant during maternity, adoption, or shared parental leave without first offering it to them, the redundancy dismissal will be unfair.[345] If, however, there is no suitable alternative work available which could be offered to them, they will not be regarded as unfairly dismissed. Where the employee's continued employment would be unlawful or contrary to the recommendations of a code of practice, the employee may be suspended from work on maternity grounds (see later in this chapter), and a dismissal connected with such suspension will be unfair.

The Protection from Redundancy (Pregnancy and Family Leave) Act 2023 created the power to extend these protection, which was then utilized via the Maternity Leave, Adoption Leave and Shared Parental Leave (Amendment) Regulations 2024. This extended these same maternity leave protections to cover all pregnant employees at risk of redundancy, from the point the employer is notified of the pregnancy.[346] For those who suffer a miscarriage (ie before 24 weeks of pregnancy) the protection will extend to two weeks following the loss, if the employer already knew about the pregnancy.[347] Existing protections for those on maternity leave, adoption leave or SPL were also extended to 18 months after the birth or placement of a child. For SPL, this extended protection is only available to those taking six continuous weeks or more (if less, it remains at the end of the leave).[348]

Further change is expected in light of the Employment Rights Act, which makes it unlawful, except in exceptional circumstances, to dismiss pregnant employees, those taking maternity leave, adoption leave or SPL, or those returned to work within 18 months after the birth or placement of a child. These will be fleshed out in upcoming Regulations and expected to take effect in 2027.

5.5.2 **Protection from detriment**

The statutory protection from detriment for family reasons was introduced in the Employment Relations Act 1999. Before that Act there was no explicit right not to suffer detriment for family reasons, although in practice detrimental treatment on grounds of pregnancy or childbirth will almost invariably constitute unlawful sex discrimination.[349] The present provisions bring the protection from detriment in line with the unfair dismissal protection, although there are some differences between the two.

[345] MPL etc Regulations 1999, reg 20(1)(b); PAL Regulations, reg 29(1)(b); SPL Regulations, reg 43(1)(b). If the employer offers her a suitable alternative vacancy and she unreasonably refuses it, she may lose her right to a redundancy payment. It was held under previous provisions that whether a vacancy is 'available' is a question of objective fact, not of reasonableness: *Community Task Force v Rimmer* [1986] ICR 491, [1986] IRLR 203, EAT.

[346] Maternity and Parental Leave etc. Regulations 1999, reg 10. Amended by Maternity Leave, Adoption Leave and Shared Parental Leave (Amendment) Regulations 2024.

[347] Maternity and Parental Leave etc. Regulations 1999, reg 10(1A)(b)–(c). Amended by Maternity Leave, Adoption Leave and Shared Parental Leave (Amendment) Regulations 2024.

[348] Maternity Leave, Adoption Leave and Shared Parental Leave (Amendment) Regulations 2024, reg 3(5)(a).

[349] See 4.11.

Section 47C of the Employment Rights Act 1996 (as fleshed out by the MPL etc Regulations,[350] the PAL Regulations,[351] and the SPL Regulations[352]) gives an employee the right not to be subjected to any detriment[353] (other than dismissal) by the employer for the reason that the employee:

(a) is pregnant;
(b) has given birth to a child;
(c) has been suspended from work on maternity grounds;
(d) has taken, or sought to take, ordinary maternity leave, additional maternity leave, parental leave or time off for dependants, paternity leave, or adoption leave;
(e) has availed herself of the benefits of ordinary maternity leave or additional maternity leave;
(f) has failed to return to work after ordinary or additional maternity leave, or additional adoption leave, where the employer had failed to notify the employee of the date of return;
(g) has undertaken or refused to undertake 'keep in touch' days;
(h) has refused to sign a workforce agreement in relation to parental leave; or
(i) has performed (or proposed to perform) any functions or activities of a workforce representative (including standing as a candidate) for the purposes of the provisions on parental leave.[354]

A fascinating example of what might count as detriment comes from the CJEU in *Napoli v Ministero della Giustizia, Dipartimento dell'Amministrazione penitenziaria*.[355] The claimant was offered a promotion subject to taking a training course and passing an exam. The next training course took place during her period of compulsory leave, and it was not clear when the course would be offered again, so she could not secure the promotion until some time in the indefinite future. This violated the Equal Treatment Directive 2006/54, as it imposed a detriment on pregnancy and leave, and did not allow her to return to work on the same terms as she would have without the leave.

The remedy for an infringement of the right not to be subjected to a detriment for family reasons operates through the usual procedures in Part 5 of the Employment Rights Act for protection from suffering detriment in employment. A complaint must be made to an employment tribunal, within three months of the act or deliberate failure to act complained of (or within a further reasonable period where not reasonably practicable),[356] and if the tribunal upholds the complaint it must make a declaration to that effect, and may award the employee such compensation as it considers just and equitable in all the circumstances.[357]

[350] MPL etc Regulations 1999, reg 19, as amended by the MPL (Amendment) Regulations 2002, reg 13.

[351] PAL Regulations, reg 28.

[352] SPL Regulations, reg 42 (the list here is shorter, to reflect that SPL does not involve the period before and two weeks after childbirth).

[353] This includes detriment by any act or by deliberate failure to act: MPL etc Regulations, reg 19(1); PAL Regulations, reg 28(1); SPL Regulations, reg 42(1).

[354] For the detailed interpretation of these grounds, see the discussion of the parallel provisions concerning dismissal. As with dismissal, the protection for childbirth only applies where the detriment takes place during the employee's ordinary or additional maternity leave: reg 19(5).

[355] C-595/12 [2014] ICR 486.

[356] Employment Rights Act 1996, s 48, as amended.

[357] Employment Rights Act 1996, s 49, as amended.

5.6 Flexible working

5.6.1 History

One of the greatest obstacles faced by working parents trying to reconcile the competing demands of work and family life is that they usually have very little control over the pattern of their working lives. This is a particular problem for women returning to work after maternity leave as the statutory provisions on maternity leave give a woman the right to return to the job in which she was employed before maternity leave but do not confer any right to change the job specification to make it easier for her to return to work. Accordingly, the Employment Act 2002[358] introduced a right for those who had (or expected to have) responsibility for the upbringing of a child under six[359] to request a change in their terms and conditions relating to the hours they work, the times when they are required to work, or where they are required to work (ie as between home or on the employer's premises), to enable them to care for the child.[360]

Although the idea of a right to work flexibly received a high level of support, the measures introduced fell well below expectations because they do not give employees an automatic right to work flexibly: they merely give a right to *apply* to work flexibly, and even that right is very restricted in its scope.[361] The authors often refer to this dismissively as 'a right to ask nicely'.

Entitlement to request flexible working has since been extended twice. First, the Work and Families Act 2006 extended the right to carers of partners or adult family members, so that essentially the right was available to anyone who demonstrably had someone they had to care for, of any age. Finally, the Children and Families Act 2014 extended the right to all employees who meet the eligibility requirements.[362] It is no longer necessary to be wanting to change working arrangements to care for someone else; the employee might, for example, want reduced hours in order to be able to go kite-surfing more often.

Since the COVID-19 pandemic, flexible working has been a key legislative agenda for both major political parties which has led to some, relatively minor changes. Further changes are expected in 2027, when the current Labour government's provisions of flexible working in Employment Rights Act are expected to come into force.

5.6.2 Entitlement

All employees may make up to two applications a year to their employer for a change to their contract in relation to any of the following:

- hours of work;
- times of work; or
- place of work, as between home and the employer's place of business.[363]

[358] Employment Rights Act 1996, Pt 8A, as inserted by the Employment Act 2002, s 47. Part 8A is supplemented by the Flexible Working (Procedural Requirements) Regulations 2002, SI 2002/3207, and the Flexible Working (Eligibility, Complaints and Remedies) Regulations 2002, SI 2002/3236.

[359] Or a disabled child under 18. The application must be made at least 14 days before the child's seventeenth (or, if disabled, eighteenth) birthday.

[360] Employment Rights Act 1996, s 80F, as inserted by the Employment Act 2002, s 47.

[361] Employment Rights Act 1996, Pt 8A, as inserted by the Employment Act 2002, s 47. Part 8A is supplemented by the Flexible Working (Procedural Requirements) Regulations 2002, SI 2002/3207, and the Flexible Working (Eligibility, Complaints and Remedies) Regulations 2002, SI 2002/3236.

[362] Flexible Working Regulations 2014, reg 3.

[363] Flexible Working Regulations 2014, reg 3.

Previously, this was only available to employees with 26 weeks service, but the Employment Relations (Flexible Working) Act 2023 made this a day one right. The Act also made it possible to make two requests a year, rather than one. However, employees can only have one request for flexible working with their employer at any one time. Although these minor changes are positive, they are unlikely to lead to substantial change as employees still have to 'ask nicely' to work flexibly.

5.6.3 **Procedure**

The procedure for making and responding to requests for flexible working is set out in the Act, which has been slightly amended by the Employment Relations (Flexible Working) Act 2023.[364] Until 30 June 2014 there were detailed procedures for the handling of applications set out in the Regulations;[365] however, those Regulations were replaced with a simplified version that contains almost no procedural provisions, meaning that the procedural requirements are only those set out in the Act.[366] The employer must deal with the request 'reasonably' and must respond to the employee's application within two (previously three) months of receipt, unless an extension is agreed.[367] The procedure has been made slightly less burdensome as the Employment Relations (Flexible Working) Act 2023 removed a requirement to explain what effect, if any, the employee thinks making the change would have on the employer and how this might be dealt with.[368] A final legislative change is that employers can no longer reject an application without consultation.[369] The ACAS Code suggests allowing the worker to be accompanied at any meeting is good practice, but the statute does not require this. The employer's duty is merely to consider the request; there is no automatic right to work flexibly. The Act specifies the grounds on which an employer may refuse a request, viz:

- the burden of additional costs;
- detrimental effect on ability to meet customer demand;
- inability to reorganize work among existing staff;
- inability to recruit additional staff;
- detrimental impact on quality;
- detrimental impact on performance;
- insufficiency of work during the periods the employee proposes to work
- planned structural changes;[370] and
- any other grounds specified by the Secretary of State in regulations.[371]

It can be seen that this list provides an employer who is minded to resist an application to work flexibly with plenty of ammunition for doing so, particularly when one

[364] This is underpinned by a new, and sparse, ACAS Code of Practice 5 *Handling in a Reasonable Manner Requests for Flexible Working* (April 2024).

[365] Flexible Working (Eligibility, Complaints and Remedies) Regulations 2002.

[366] This is underpinned by ACAS Code of Practice 5 *Code of Practice on requests for flexible working* (April 2024).

[367] Employment Rights Act 1996, s 80G (1)–(1B), amended by Employment Relations (Flexible Working) Act 2023, s1(6).

[368] Employment Rights Act 1996, s 80F(2), removed by Employment Relations (Flexible Working) Act 2023, s1(2).

[369] Employment Rights Act 1996, s 80G (1)(AZA), inserted by Employment Relations (Flexible Working) Act 2023, s1(5).

[370] Employment Rights Act 1996, s 80G, as inserted by the Employment Act 2002.

[371] As inserted by Employment Rights Act 2025, s 9.

appreciates that the employer's refusal is not subject to any test of reasonableness or proportionality. Many might have hoped these grounds would be reviewed in the new Employment Rights Act, but they have remain unchanged. Instead, the legislation introduces a reasonableness requirement; employers now must explain why their reliance on one of these business grounds is reasonable.[372] Furthermore, employers will have to follow a specified process, to be set out via secondary legislation, to reject a request for flexible working, which is expected to be implemented in 2027.[373] It is hoped that, combined, these changes will result in employers accepting flexible working requests, except when they are unreasonable.

The employee has a right to complain to an employment tribunal on the basis that the employer has either:

- failed to deal with the request in a reasonable manner;
- not notified its decision within two months;
- refused the application for a reason other than one of the eight permitted ones
- based a decision to reject the application 'on incorrect facts';[374] or
- their reliance on one of the eight permitted grounds was unreasonable.[375]

This last ground means that for the first time, tribunals can assess the *substantive* reasonableness of the employer's decision. This means that a judgment in favour of the employee is likely to become more probable from 2027, whereas in the past, this was unusual. Until then, tribunals remain entitled to investigate the evidence, which may involve a consideration of what the effects of granting the request would have been on the employer at the time, in order to decide if the employer based its decision on incorrect facts.[376] This stops short of judging the justification for the decision, but does seem to occupy some middle ground of judging the 'correctness' of the decision (not necessarily just the 'facts').

If the tribunal finds for the employee it may issue a declaration, order the employer to reconsider the request, and award compensation of up to eight weeks' pay.[377] The tribunal cannot order the employer to permit an employee to work flexibly. This means that the penalty for an unmerited refusal is so low that it will not deter employers from refusing if they want to.

The weakness of the 'right' meant that historically, the real remedy for an employee who wishes to challenge a rejection of a request to work to a different pattern will usually be a claim for sex discrimination. If the employee is a woman seeking a change to enable her to care for children or other relatives or dependants, for example if she is a maternity returner, she may well be able to satisfy an employment tribunal that a refusal represents a provision, criterion, or practice which has disparate impact on women. If so, then the tribunal does have the power, indeed the duty, to decide whether the employer's refusal is justified, unlike under the current flexible working rules. This is discussed in more detail in relation to return from maternity leave at 5.2.7. (If a man is refused flexibility which he wants for care reasons, then historically, he would have had to rely on *direct* sex discrimination: his complaint to the employer might be, 'You let women who have young children go part-time so your refusal of my request is treating me less favourably because of my sex.' Now, he might also be able to rely on indirect discrimination—see 4.2.5.6.) It will be interesting to see if the changes to the right to request flexible working will result in more claims being made under the legislation, or not. One major reason

[372] Employment Rights Act 1996, s 80G(1ZB), as inserted by the Employment Rights Act 2025, 9(4).
[373] Employment Rights Act 1996, s 80G(1E), as inserted by the Employment Rights Act 2025, s 9(5).
[374] Employment Rights Act 1996, s 80H.
[375] As added by the Employment Rights Act 2025, s 9.
[376] *Commotion Ltd v Rutty* [2006] IRLR 171, EAT.
[377] Flexible Working Regulations 2014, reg 6.

why sex discrimination claims may remain more popular is that the remedies for sex discrimination can be substantial, including lost pay if the employee decides that they have to resign in order to meet their caring responsibilities, and an award for injury to feelings. For employees seeking to change their hours in order to go kite-surfing more often, the amendments do now give them a chance to challenge any refusals or their request, which would have been near impossible before due to there being no discrimination claim.

Employees have a right not to be dismissed or subjected to any detriment for requesting flexible working, or seeking to exercise or enforce any rights thereto.[378]

Some pitfalls do remain for employees, mainly that any contract variation that results from an application under these procedures will be permanent, unless otherwise agreed at the outset. This means there is no automatic right to revert to the old terms. It has been noted that this means the legislation is of limited use to those accommodating fluctuating or unpredictable caring demands.[379]

Review and Final Thoughts

- Governments for more than 20 years have concluded that certain of the terms and conditions of employment must be regulated by law because, at the most basic level, the market and the illusion of a bargained-for employment contract have left workers exposed to exploitation or unfairness. Specifically, (a) regulation was needed to protect a living wage in the face of market pressures; (b) regulation of the number of working hours and rights to rest and leave responded to the danger of employers putting workers' health at risk, or marginalizing those who cannot commit all of their time to the workplace; and (c) rights to time for childbirth and caring responsibilities were needed to prevent outmoded social patterns from keeping women at home caring for children, and men trapped in a breadwinner role. See footnotes 2–4 and 7 and 10 for further reading.
- The Working Time Regulations provide for a maximum 48-hour workweek, daily rest breaks, limits on night working, and 28 days of paid annual leave. There are many exceptions, and even rest breaks can be denied to workers in some circumstances. The 48-hour limit is an average over (usually) 17 weeks, however, and workers can simply opt out in writing if they want to (or sometimes when their employer wants them to). Annual leave must be taken in the year it is earned, unless the worker is on sick leave in which case it rolls over for up to 18 months. If they do not take it because they are taking another form of leave, it rolls over for a year. These regulations have arguably achieved their objectives regarding breaks and leave, but have had little effect on the long-hours culture. See footnotes 146–148 for further reading. Irregular hours workers and part-year workers are now subject to specific rules on entitlement to, and carry-over of, annual leave.
- Several pieces of legislation now guarantee that (a) a mother can take 52 weeks of leave for childbirth, (b) an employee with at least 26 weeks' service can receive 39 weeks of pay during that leave, (c) a father employed for at least 26 weeks can take two weeks of paid leave (but the government aims to remove this by 2027), (d) a mother may share all but two weeks of her leave and pay with the father (subject to conditions and mind-numbing technicalities), and (e) adoptive parents can have corresponding rights. Employees are protected

[378] Employment Rights Act 1996, ss 104C and 47E.

[379] Horton 'Care-giving and Reasonable Adjustment in the UK' in Busby and G. James (eds) *Families, Care-giving and Paid Work: Challenging Labour Law in the 21st Century* (2011) 141.

against detriment or dismissal for exercising these rights or for other consequence of having (or adopting) a new baby.

- Most leave and pay are controlled by the mother, and the low pay (£194.32) together with other restrictions on the rights of fathers means that the vast majority of leave is still taken by mothers. See footnotes 149, 150, and 153 for further reading.
- Parents continuously employed for a year are entitled by statute to take up to 18 weeks' leave in respect of every child for which they have parental responsibility, to be taken before the child is 18 years old, for the purpose of caring for the child. The employer has substantial say in how and when the leave is taken, and after more than four weeks' leave cannot count on returning to precisely the same job. The eligibility requirements may be removed by 2027.
- Employees are entitled from day one to a reasonable amount of time off to deal with emergencies befalling their dependants, which includes adult dependants. All parents are now permitted paid bereavement leave.
- Anyone can request flexible working arrangements, but, subject to the risk of sex discrimination claims, their employer need only consider the request, not grant it.

6

Termination of the employment contract at common law

OVERVIEW

This chapter will tackle the following key questions:

- How can the contract of employment come to an end (terminate) without a dismissal? What about when both parties agree, or when one of them dies or becomes imprisoned?
- What does it take for one of the parties to the employment contract to terminate it? When can employers lawfully dismiss at common law, and what must they do to ensure it is lawful?
- What is a 'wrongful dismissal' at common law, and what are the consequences for the parties when that is found to have happened?
- What is the relationship between wrongful dismissal and unfair dismissal, and now that the latter is in place, does the former matter at all?

Context

This chapter exists on its own, as opposed to forming part of the next chapter on unfair dismissal, in order to emphasize this fundamental characteristic of employment law generally and dismissal law in particular: statutory rights sit, not entirely comfortably, on top of a common law foundation, in some places intertwined and in others just propped on the surface. Both for practical reasons and in the interests of conceptual tidiness, it behoves the student of this area of law first to become familiar with the baseline of this complex composition, before moving on to the arguably more interesting and notorious melody.[1]

The common law on termination continues to apply and can have various effects, including (1) prejudicing statutory rights by providing for there to be the ending of employment in certain untypical cases *without* there being in law a dismissal, (2) establishing the essential law on dismissal by the giving of notice (the usual form of dismissal in practice), and (3) defining when an employer can lawfully dispense with notice and dismiss summarily for 'gross misconduct' (a common law concept of considerable antiquity).

Turning to remedies, perhaps the most important aspect here, media reports of legal cases in this area can be trusted to get it wrong by treating 'wrongful' and 'unfair' as synonymous. The reader will soon realize that this is entirely false. The old common law action for wrongful dismissal is a purely contractual action looking principally at the *way* in which the dismissal was effected, which, in the employment context, has always provided only limited relief for most ordinary employees. Unfair dismissal, by contrast, looks at the *reason* for a dismissal and whether a fair procedure was used. For most ex-employees, this provides a better chance of exonerating themselves from the slur inherent in being dismissed, and its remedies are much more realistic in nature and amount. However, there may be a major limitation here, namely that compensation is subject to statutory limits; in the case of an employee previously on a high salary the traditional action for wrongful dismissal may be more lucrative. The picture therefore continues to be a mixed one. However, one mercy here is that for years now we have not had the traditional split in forum—it used to be the case that a wrongful dismissal had to go to an ordinary civil *court*, but now an employment tribunal can consider both wrongful and unfair dismissal together, though once again subject to statutory limits on amount. A considerable number of tactics can be involved here.

6.1 Modes of termination other than dismissal

Dismissal acts as a prerequisite to some important common law and statutory rights, but there are certain ways in which employment may be terminated other than simply by dismissal. These ways are founded on old common law principles established at a time when an employee had few rights, and the concept of continuity of employment was of little significance. As a result, these hoary doctrines, which could place employees in an extremely vulnerable position, are now heavily qualified (though not actually abrogated) by specialized statutory provisions aimed at mitigating their potentially harsh application to modern employment rights. One such provision is the Employment Rights Act 1996, s 136, which (along with s 139) provides that where an act of the employer or an event affecting the employer (including his or her death) has the effect of terminating the contract of employment by operation of law, that is deemed to be a termination by the

[1] The authors acknowledge a shift in metaphors but insist that they are not mixed, just cumulative.

employer (ie a dismissal), so that the employee can claim payments due for a redundancy *dismissal*. This kind of 'deeming' goes far towards safeguarding the employee's rights in most cases of death, dissolution, or frustration. However, there remain areas not yet covered by ameliorating statutory provisions where the employment lawyer (particularly when representing the employee) has to be wary of the sudden emergence of arguments based on common law notions of discharge of employment which, if accepted, can do great harm to statutory rights.

6.1.1 Death or dissolution of the enterprise

At common law, death would bring the contract of employment to an end, whether it be the death of the employee[2] or the employer, as in *Farrow v Wilson*,[3] where the personal representatives were held not to be liable to continue the engagement of the employee. The employee is discharged from further performance on the death of the employer, not through any breach of contract but as the result of an implied condition that the continued existence of the parties is an essential of the contract. This position is now qualified by statute in three ways. First, if the business does not carry on after the employer's death, the termination of employment is deemed to be a dismissal for redundancy under the Employment Rights Act 1996, ss 136 and 139, so the employee may claim a redundancy payment from the employer's personal representatives.[4] Secondly, if the deceased employer's business is carried on by their personal representatives and the employee continues to work for them there is deemed to be no termination for redundancy purposes,[5] and their continuity of employment for general purposes is not broken.[6] Thirdly, where it is the employee who dies, any pending proceedings of theirs before an employment tribunal may be instituted or continued by his or her personal representatives (or by other persons appointed by the tribunal if there are no personal representatives), and if they die while under notice of dismissal they will be treated for the purposes of unfair dismissal and redundancy as if they had actually been dismissed.[7]

In practice, of course, most employees will be employed by partnerships or companies which do not die; however, they may be dissolved or wound up in certain ways, and the operation of these processes of law upon the contracts of employment concerned must now be considered.

In the case of a partnership, where a partner dies and there is a consequent dissolution of the partnership, the contract of employment will be discharged wherever it is one related to the personal conduct of the deceased person. In *Harvey v Tivoli (Manchester) Ltd*,[8] the death of a member of a troupe of three music hall artists was held to discharge the contract though he had been replaced and the troupe was ready to appear. In *Phillips v Alhambra Palace Co*,[9] one of the defendant partners had died after a contract had been entered into with the plaintiffs, who were also music hall artists. In this case it was held that the obligation continued despite the death of the partner, because the obligation was not of a personal character and the partners, when they booked the artists to appear, were not individually known. In the first case the contract was with three specific persons;

[2] *Stubbs v Holywell Rly Co* (1867) LR 2 Exch 311; *Graves v Cohen* (1929) 46 TLR 121.

[3] (1869) LR 4 CP 744.

[4] Employment Rights Act 1996, s 206(3).

[5] Section 174. It must be shown on the acts that the personal representatives did renew the contract or reengage the employee, but in practice the longer the employee continues to work for them the easier this will be to infer (in the absence of express agreement): *Ranger v Brown* [1978] ICR 603, EAT.

[6] Section 218(4).

[7] Section 206; Employment Tribunals Awards (Enforcement in Case of Death) Regulations 1976, SI 1976/663.

[8] (1907) 23 TLR 592; *Tunstall v Condon* [1980] ICR 786.

[9] [1901] 1 KB 59.

in the second case it was with a firm and the personal element was not paramount. A dissolution of a partnership on account of the retirement of a partner may operate as a wrongful dismissal at common law but the modern approach is that there is no absolute rule, so that it depends on all the circumstances and the intent and acts of the parties;[10] in particular, a continuance of employment under a firm containing some of the old partners may amount to a waiver of common law rights of action.[11] Under statute, even if the dissolution did not constitute a dismissal per se (which it almost certainly does), it would be deemed to be such for redundancy purposes under the Employment Rights Act 1996, s 136, and where the employee continues in the reconstituted firm's employment his or her continuity of employment is safeguarded by s 218(5) of that Act.

In the case of a company, the legal position is complex.[12] The position seems to be as follows. An order of the court for a compulsory winding up of the company operates as notice of dismissal to its employees.[13] The effect of a voluntary winding up depends upon whether the business is to be carried on in some form (as, for example, where it has been taken over by another company); if it is to carry on, *Midland Counties District Bank Ltd v Attwood*[14] decided that it does not operate as notice of dismissal, but if there is no intention of carrying on then it may so operate, as in the case of a compulsory order.[15] The appointment of a receiver is a less drastic step than an immediate winding up, but once again the rules are complicated. The appointment of a receiver by the court terminates contracts of employment,[16] but the appointment of a receiver out of court by the debenture holders, as agent for the company, does not have that effect,[17] except perhaps in four cases:

1. where the receiver is appointed to act as agent for the creditors only, not for the company;[18]
2. where the receiver sells the business, so that there is no continuation;
3. where the receiver enters a new contract of employment with the employee in question which is inconsistent with the existence of the old one;
4. where the continuation of the contract of employment is inconsistent with the appointment of the receiver because of the nature of the employment; this may be the case with a managing director, but it is not necessarily so and will depend upon all the facts of the case.[19]

The case law on these points is at times confusing, for though most of the cases envisage the effect of one of these events, if any, to be the giving of notice, some are capable of

[10] *Rose v Dodd* [2005] ICR 1776, [205] IRLR 977, CA, considering the long-standing authority of *Brace v Calder* [1895] 2 QB 253, CA; see also *Briggs v Oates* [1990] ICR 473, [1990] IRLR 472.

[11] *Hobson v Cowley* (1858) 27 LJ Ex 205.

[12] See Davies and Freedland 'The Effects of Receivership upon Employees of Companies' (1980) 9 ILJ 95; Pollard *Corporate Insolvency: Employment and Pension Rights* (2nd edn, 2000). Questions of continuity of employment may be covered separately by the Transfer of Undertakings (Protection of Employment) Regulations 2006, SI 2006/246; see Ch 8, heading 2, and *Rose v Dodd* [2005] ICR 1776, [2005] IRLR 977, CA.

[13] *Re General Rolling Stock Co (Chapman's Case)* (1866) LR 1 Eq 346; *Re Oriental Bank Corpn Ltd (MacDowall's Case)* (1886) 32 Ch D 366.

[14] [1905] 1 Ch 357.

[15] *Fowler v Commercial Timber Co Ltd* [1930] 2 KB 1, CA: *Reigate v Union Manufacturing Co Ltd* [1918] 1 KB 592, CA; *Fox Bros (Clothes) Ltd v Bryant* [1979] ICR 64, [1978] IRLR 485, EAT.

[16] *Reid v Explosives Co* (1887) 19 QBD 264, CA; *Re Foster Clark Ltd's Indenture Trusts* [1966] 1 All ER 43, [1966] 1 WLR 125; cf *Pambakian v Brentford Nylons Ltd* [1978] ICR 665, EAT.

[17] *Re Foster Clark Ltd's Indenture Trusts* [1966] 1 All ER 43, [1966] 1 WLR 125; *Re Mack Trucks (Britain) Ltd* [1967] 1 All ER 977, [1967] 1 WLR 780; *Nicoll v Cutts* [1985] BCLC 322, CA.

[18] *Hopley Dodd v Highfield Motors (Derby) Ltd* (1969) 4 ITR 289.

[19] On exceptions (2)–(4) see *Griffiths v Secretary of State for Social Services* [1974] QB 468, [1973] 3 All ER 1184.

pointing to instant dismissal (as by operation of law), which, as has been pointed out,[20] could jeopardize common law rights of the employee.

6.1.2 **Frustration of the contract**

It is a general principle of the law of contract that a contract will be terminated automatically if it is frustrated.[21] A contract is frustrated if a change of law or circumstances makes the contract impossible to perform or makes the result of performance radically different from what was originally undertaken in the contract. This doctrine of frustration applies to contracts of employment. Thus in *Morgan v Manser*,[22] it was held that the calling-up for military service of a music hall artist frustrated the contract which he had with his manager, and Streatfeild J formulated the test as follows:

> If there is an event or change of circumstances which is so fundamental as to be regarded by the law as striking at the root of the contract as a whole, and as going beyond what was contemplated by the parties and such that to hold the parties to the contract would be to bind them to terms which they would not have made had they contemplated that event or those circumstances, then the contract is frustrated by that event immediately and irrespective of the volition or the intention of the parties, or their knowledge as to that particular event, and this even though they have continued for a time to treat the contract as still subsisting.

The effects of this doctrine on the contract of employment are threefold:

1. If the contract is frustrated it is terminated automatically, and immediately upon the happening of a frustrating event; there is no need, for example, for the employer to take any steps to terminate the contract or even to indicate that it regards it as terminated.[23]
2. As a consequence of (1), there is no right to any back pay from the date of frustration until any other date (eg a date, if any, on which the employer indicated that it thought the contract had ended).[24]
3. If the contract of employment is frustrated, its termination is due to the operation of law and not to dismissal (either at common law or under the Employment Rights Act 1996, s 95 or s 136), which could have a serious effect on certain common law and statutory rights, particularly unfair dismissal, which may only be claimed if the employee is dismissed.[25]

[20] *Re Patent Floor Cloth Co* (1872) 41 LJ Ch 476 at 477, per Bacon V-C.

[21] *Davis Contractors Ltd v Fareham UDC* [1956] AC 696, [1956] 2 All ER 145, HL. See Mogridge 'Frustration, Employment Contracts and Statutory Rights' [1982] NLJ 795.

[22] [1948] 1 KB 184, [1947] 2 All ER 666; the passage cited is at 191 and 670, respectively.

[23] *Marshall v Harland & Wolff Ltd* [1972] 2 All ER 715, [1972] ICR 101, disapproving suggestions to the contrary in *Thomas v John Drake & Co Ltd* (1971) 6 ITR 146; it is not necessary to be able to date the frustrating event precisely, which is particularly significant in the case of frustration through illness. See also *Egg Stores (Stamford Hill) Ltd v Leibovici* [1977] ICR 260, [1976] IRLR 376, EAT.

[24] *Unger v Preston Corpn* [1942] 1 All ER 200. However, any wages due up to the date of frustration may be claimed under the Law Reform (Frustrated Contracts) Act 1943, either under s 2(4) if the contract can be regarded as divisible and the employee has fully performed those severable parts before the date of frustration, or under s 1(3) if the wages concerned were not actually due at that date but it would be just in all the circumstances for the court to award a sum representing the work done up to that date.

[25] However, where the frustrating event is one relating to the employer (eg his or her death or the destruction of his or her business), s 136(5) of the 1996 Act safeguards the employee's rights to a redundancy payment by deeming that termination to be a dismissal, and this will apply even if the event applies to both employer and employee (eg the passing of new legislation making the whole employment in question illegal), for it is enough that some of the effect is upon the employer: *Fenerty v British Airports Authority* (1976) 11 ITR 1.

6.1.2.1 **Frustration by illness**

For an event or circumstance to frustrate the contract of employment it must be exceptionally grave. Certain wartime factors have been held to have the effect of frustration, such as being called up or interned.[26] However, in practice the most important event is illness on the part of the employee, as if it is sufficiently grave to frustrate the contract, the employee will lose any potential rights which they may have to claim unfair dismissal or redundancy (the latter because this is not an event befalling the employer, so not covered by the Employment Rights Act 1996, s 136(5)). In *Poussard v Spiers*,[27] an opera singer was ill during rehearsals for the opera for which she was engaged and could not take part in the first four performances; this was held to frustrate the contract so that her employer was entitled to treat the contract as ended. This was also the case in *Condor v Barron Knights Ltd*,[28] where the employee was physically unable to play with the pop group in question for seven nights per week through illness and this was held to be a frustration, particularly as the group could not operate on anything less than full time and could not reasonably operate with a part-time substitute. However, some care may be needed with certain theatrical cases, for a court or tribunal may be ready to find frustration in the case of a short-term contract entered with a particular performance or set of performances in mind. It may be more difficult to establish in the case of a long-standing employment of a permanent nature,[29] particularly in view of the old common law principle that in general the consideration for wages is readiness and willingness to serve on the employee's part, not necessarily the performance of actual work.[30] As the question of frustration through illness is so important in the context of the statutory rights, it was reviewed by the NIRC in *Marshall v Harland and Wolff Ltd*,[31] where Sir John Donaldson P laid down the following factors to be weighed by a tribunal in deciding whether a contract was frustrated:

1. the terms of the contract, including any provisions as to sick pay;
2. how long the employment was likely to last in the absence of sickness, for a temporary or specific hiring is more likely to be frustrated;
3. the nature of the employment, in particular whether the employee was in a 'key post' which had to be filled permanently if his or her absence was prolonged[32] or whether it was such that it could be held open for a considerable period;[33]
4. the nature of the illness, how long it has continued, and the prospects of recovery; this may interact with (3) in that if there is no urgency for a replacement, a more distant prospect of recovery may keep the contract alive;
5. the period of past employment, for 'a relationship which is of long standing is not so easily destroyed as one which has but a short history'.

[26] *Horlock v Beal* [1916] 1 AC 486, HL; *Marshall v Glanvill* [1917] 2 KB 87; *Morgan v Manser* [1948] 1 KB 184, [1947] 2 All ER 666; *Unger v Preston Corpn* [1942] 1 All ER 200. However, even something as potentially drastic as internment must have a substantial effect and not be merely transitory: *Nordman v Rayner and Sturges* (1916) 33 TLR 87.

[27] (1876) 1 QBD 410; cf *Bettini v Gye* (1876) 1 QBD 183, where a singer's illness incapacitated her for the rehearsals but not for any of the performances, and this was held not to be a frustration.

[28] [1966] 1 WLR 87.

[29] See eg *Storey v Fulham Steel Works Co* (1907) 24 TLR 89, CA.

[30] *Warburton v Co-operative Wholesale Society Ltd* [1917] 1 KB 663, CA; *Henthorn v Central Electricity Generating Board* [1980] IRLR 361, CA.

[31] [1972] 2 All ER 715, [1972] ICR 101.

[32] *Hebden v Forsey & Son* [1973] ICR 607, [1973] IRLR 344.

[33] *Maxwell v Walter Howard Designs Ltd* [1975] IRLR 77, IT.

Tribunals have regularly followed these guidelines, but in *Egg Stores (Stamford Hill) Ltd v Leibovici*,[34] the EAT pointed out that they raise a particular difficulty in the case of short-term periodic contracts of employment, which may be determined at short notice, for although the doctrine of frustration is necessary in longer-term contracts if it has become impossible for the employee to perform their part, in the case of the short-term contract the employer has the more ready remedy of dismissal on relatively short notice, which may be more appropriate in the circumstances than reliance upon frustration. The EAT also said that a short-term periodic contract could be subject to an event (eg a crippling accident) so drastic that it was obvious that it was frustrated, but that in the more normal case of a lingering illness there are further matters to be taken into account along with those in *Marshall*'s case. These are:

6. the risk to the employer of incurring obligations (in respect of redundancy payments and unfair dismissal) to an employee meant to be a replacement;
7. whether wages have continued to be paid;
8. the acts and statements of the employer in relation to the employment, in particular whether there has been a dismissal of sorts and if not, why not;[35]
9. whether in all the circumstances a reasonable employer could be expected to wait any longer.

All of these factors must be weighed by the tribunal, which will probably be loath to find frustration. If the contract is not frustrated and the employer is found to have dismissed the employee, a claim for unfair dismissal may proceed which must be decided in the normal way,[36] and it has been stated that the tests laid down in *Marshall*'s case are those for frustration, *not* those for deciding whether a dismissal for ill health is reasonable[37]—though if the further factors in the *Egg Stores* case are applied, in particular factor (9), the two tests do begin to look somewhat similar.[38]

6.1.2.2 *Notcutt*, the right to terminate with notice, and disability

At one point, the whole question of the application of the doctrine of frustration to contracts of employment was thrown into confusion by the decision of the EAT in *Harman v Flexible Lamps Ltd*,[39] where it was held not only that the applicant's illness did not frustrate her contract on the facts, but further that the doctrine as a matter of law should only apply to long-term contracts not terminable by notice. However desirable such an approach may be as a matter of policy, the decision was fatally flawed as a precedent since it did not even cite either *Marshall v Harland and Wolff Ltd* or *Egg Stores (Stamford Hill) Ltd v Leibovici* (previously discussed), with both of which it was inconsistent. Not surprisingly, therefore, when the issue went to the Court of Appeal in *Notcutt v Universal Equipment Co (London) Ltd*[40] orthodoxy was re-established—it was accepted that Bristow J was correct to state in *Harman* that a court should be *cautious* about applying frustration to contracts easily terminable by notice (particularly if it is being used as a means of avoiding statutory rights), but to go further and suggest that the doctrine itself is not

[34] [1977] ICR 260, [1976] IRLR 376, further discussed in *Hart v AR Marshall & Sons (Bulwell) Ltd* [1977] ICR 539, [1977] IRLR 51 and *Williams v Watsons Luxury Coaches Ltd* [1990] ICR 536, [1990] IRLR 164.

[35] Emphasized in *Hart v A R Marshall & Sons (Bulwell) Ltd* [1977] ICR 539, [1977] IRLR 51.

[36] See 7.4.

[37] *Tan v Berry Bros and Rudd Ltd* [1974] ICR 586, [1974] IRLR 244.

[38] *Egg Stores (Stamford Hill) Ltd v Leibovici* [1977] ICR 260 at 264G, [1976] IRLR 376 at 378, per Phillips J.

[39] [1980] IRLR 418.

[40] [1986] ICR 414, [1986] IRLR 218, CA, followed in *F C Shepherd & Co Ltd v Jerrom* [1986] ICR 802, [1986] IRLR 358, CA.

applicable was incorrect. In *Notcutt* itself, illness absence of eight months due to a coronary was held to have frustrated the contract of employment of an employee of 27 years' service, who was entitled by law to 12 weeks' notice. The employee's claim was in fact a common law claim in the county court for sick pay (which in the event was not payable due to the frustration of the contract) but it is clear that the decision is also applicable to a statutory action, particularly an action for unfair dismissal. While the court did state that defences of frustration should be treated carefully,[41] it must be accepted that the decision does leave considerable scope for frustration in sickness cases—12 weeks was not an unduly long notice period, and the dominant factor in the case appears to be that the illness led immediately to total and lasting incapacity for work, which is not going to be a rare occurrence in cases of major illness or accident. In such an event, however, the position may now be complicated by a modern tendency in some employments to offer (as part of enhanced terms and conditions) 'permanent health insurance' covering generously employees who are permanently unable to work—in such a case, could this factor be used to defeat an argument for frustration, on the basis that the illness was fully covered by the contract and so not an *unforeseen* frustrating event?[42] If so, could the argument eventually be taken even further and applied to an employment covered by an *ordinary* sick pay term, at least where it is relatively generous and envisages a long period off work while still receiving pay? Given that the original doctrine of frustration relied on the occurrence of an event or consequences not 'contemplated' by the parties, the law in this area appears to have strayed from its roots by accepting the frustration defence in the presence of evidence that the parties made arrangements applicable to the circumstances in question.

One factor that could perhaps curb this tendency to stray is the statutory duty to make reasonable adjustments for disability.[43] In *Warner v Armfield Retail & Leisure Ltd*,[44] the EAT opined:

> In the case of a disabled person, before the doctrine of frustration can apply there is an additional factor which the Tribunal must consider over and above the factors already identified in the authorities—namely whether the employer is in breach of a duty to make reasonable adjustments. While there is something which (applying the provisions of the Equality Act 2010) it is reasonable to expect the employer to have to do in order to keep the employee in employment, the doctrine of frustration can have no application.[45]

In *Warner* the claimant had a stroke which apparently (the employer assumed this rather than exploring it at the time) rendered him incapable of continuing to perform his job. The EAT found that frustration could apply, following *Notcutt*, and that in this case it did apply because there were no reasonable adjustments that should have been made that could have avoided the frustration. However, it was satisfied that frustration did not interfere with the application of anti-discrimination law, and that claims of disability discrimination in relation to the termination of employment could proceed despite the fact that the contract was deemed discharged through frustration. This serves to illustrate how the common law interacts with statutory rights: frustration in this case ruled out an

[41] Further, it was accepted by Mustill LJ in *F C Shepherd & Co Ltd v Jerrom* (n 40) that the existence of a disciplinary procedure covering the event in question (in that case, imprisonment) might be a factor against finding frustration.

[42] This argument was accepted in *Villella v MFI Furniture Centres Ltd* [1999] IRLR 468. For the effect of such permanent health insurance schemes on the giving of notice to persons subject to them see 3.3.7.

[43] Equality Act 2010, s 39(5).

[44] [2013] UKEAT 0376_12_0810; [2014] EqLR 122.

[45] Ibid at para 46.

action for unfair dismissal because that statute requires a common law dismissal, whereas it did not rule out a discrimination action because that statute does not require a common law dismissal.

Warner can also be understood as calling *Notcutt* into question as a sound authority. *Notcutt* was of course decided prior to the enactment of the Disability Discrimination Act 1995, which introduced protections that have essentially been maintained in the Equality Act 2010. Although *Warner* is an EAT case and *Notcutt* a Court of Appeal case, meaning that *Warner* 'followed' *Notcutt*, if *Warner* is correct then *Notcutt* might be decided differently today. There is little doubt that Mr Notcutt would qualify as 'disabled' under the Act, and it is hard to see how honouring a 12-week notice period would not be seen as a reasonable adjustment that would avoid the frustration of the contract. Moreover, the EAT expressed misgivings about the reasoning in *Notcutt* that are shared by the authors, among others:

> We would, however, make the following observations, drawing on the specialist experience for which the Employment Appeal Tribunal was constituted with members from both sides of industry. Most contracts of employment are terminable at short notice and are far removed from the type of commercial contract in the context of which the doctrine of frustration was mainly developed. As a matter of everyday practical reality employers and employees alike expect to deal with issues of disability, sickness, and absence for other reasons—including imprisonment—within the framework of the employment relationship. The short notice period enables them to do so: even quite unexpected turns of event will have limited financial consequences for an employer. Lawyers are familiar with the concept of frustration because it is taught as part of contract law. But there is no general familiarity with it in industry: the lay members of this Appeal Tribunal had scarcely encountered it in their many years of experience. The behaviour of the respondent in this case—simply sending the P45 without enquiry—is neither good practice nor even common practice where there has been a long period of absence. Readers of this judgment should not therefore suppose that we think the application of the doctrine of frustration to everyday contracts of employment to be beyond question.[46]

6.1.2.3 **Frustration by imprisonment**

Varying views as to the proper approach to be taken to frustration can also be seen in the other major area for its potential application to employment contracts, the effect of imprisonment of the employee. Here the complicating factor is not whether the contract is terminable on short notice but rather whether imprisonment constitutes 'self-induced frustration', as it is usually said that the frustrating event must not be self-induced.[47] In *Hare v Murphy Bros Ltd*,[48] the Court of Appeal held that a contract of employment was automatically terminated when the employee was sentenced to 12 months' imprisonment for an assault unconnected with his employment. Lord Denning clearly said that the contract was frustrated and that it was not a case of self-induction, for the frustrating event was the imposition of the sentence (even though that was of course originally caused by the criminal behaviour). The problem was, however, that the other two judgments

[46] Ibid at para 42.

[47] *Bank Line Ltd v Arthur Capel & Co* [1919] AC 435 at 452, HL, per Lord Sumner; *Denmark Productions Ltd v Boscobel Productions Ltd* [1969] 1 QB 699, [1968] 3 All ER 513, CA, at 736 and 533, respectively, per Harman LJ. It is for the party relying on frustration to prove it, but for the other party to prove that it was self-induced (if that be their allegation): *Joseph Constantine Steamship Line Ltd v Imperial Smelting Corpn Ltd* [1942] AC 154, [1941] 2 All ER 165, HL.

[48] [1974] 3 All ER 940, [1974] ICR 603, CA.

were not unequivocally in agreement with this approach, and a major disagreement arose between different EATs as to whether the doctrine of frustration should apply to imprisonment cases. In one sense the end result might be much the same since even if frustration does not apply and an unfair dismissal action proceeds, it is likely that the dismissal of an employee who has received an immediate and substantial term of imprisonment will be fair, provided it is sensibly handled by the employer.[49] However, it remains of considerable interest legally whether the employer can go further and stop an unfair dismissal action dead in its tracks in such a case by pleading frustration. A finding of frustration through imprisonment was upheld in *Harrington v Kent County Council*[50] (even though the employee's sentence was under appeal, which was ultimately successful), and was assumed to be possible (though not proved on the facts) in *Chakki v United Yeast Co Ltd*;[51] to the contrary, however, it was held in *Norris v Southampton City Council*[52] that a contract of employment is *not* frustrated by imprisonment, as a matter of law.

The point was eventually resolved by the Court of Appeal in *F C Shepherd & Co Ltd v Jerrom*,[53] which concerned an unfair dismissal action by an apprentice who lost his employment when sentenced to borstal training for offences of violence halfway through his apprenticeship. The EAT[54] held that imprisonment can frustrate a contract of employment, that *Hare v Murphy Bros Ltd* (discussed previously) does support that proposition, and that *Norris* is wrong. However, it upheld the tribunal's decision that there was no frustration here on rather novel grounds—it honoured the underlying logic of frustration. Seeking to restrict the operation of the doctrine, Waite P reminded colleagues that where, as here, the contract contained a prescribed termination procedure covering the event in question (in this case, incorporated from a national joint agreement governing apprenticeship), that event cannot be an *unforeseen* eventuality and so cannot be a frustrating event. This principle, that where the contract actually addresses a set of circumstances those circumstances were clearly 'contemplated' by the parties, was not adopted by the Court of Appeal. The court allowed the employer's appeal and held the doctrine to be applicable to cases of imprisonment simpliciter, though a version of the EAT's reasoning resurfaced in *Four Seasons Healthcare Ltd v Maughan*,[55] where one of the factors against frustration was the existence in the employee's contract of a power of summary dismissal for just the misconduct of which he was accused, which the employers had chosen not to use. Thus, the point remains a live one.

Returning to *F C Shepherd & Co Ltd v Jerrom*, the Court of Appeal was faced with one remaining problem—was not this frustration self-induced? Further, was it not the case that frustration must not be the fault of *either* party? This was resolved in two ways: Balcombe LJ accepted Lord Denning MR's view in *Hare v Murphy Bros Ltd* that the frustrating event was actually the imposition of the sentence, not the misconduct by the

[49] *Kingston v British Railways Board* [1984] ICR 781, [1984] IRLR 146, CA.

[50] [1980] IRLR 353, EAT. Note that this case concerns an actual sentence of imprisonment; merely being placed on bail is unlikely to frustrate the contract, and the employer cannot 'back date' frustration in the event of a later sentence: *Four Seasons Healthcare Ltd v Maughan* [2005] IRLR 324, EAT.

[51] [1982] 2 All ER 446, [1982] ICR 140, EAT.

[52] [1982] ICR 177 [1982] IRLR 141. The decision in this case involved a strained reading of *Hare v Murphy Bros Ltd*, n 48 and, arguably, an entirely misplaced reliance on *London Transport Executive v Clarke* [1981] ICR 355, [1981] IRLR 166, CA, see 6.4.2.3, which concerned a case of clear repudiation of contract, not frustration.

[53] [1986] ICR 802, [1986] IRLR 358, CA.

[54] [1985] ICR 552, [1985] IRLR 275. The case was newsworthy when decided by the EAT; the idea of a boy sent to borstal for offences of violence receiving compensation of £7,000 for being refused his job back was not treated sympathetically in the tabloid press.

[55] [2005] IRLR 324.

employee, but Lawton and Mustill LJJ took a more fundamental approach—that, properly understood, the rule against self-induction only meant that neither party could rely on his *own* misconduct to establish a defence of frustration. As the employer was relying on the *employee's* fault here, that requirement was satisfied and frustration could succeed; to hold otherwise would allow a party at fault to benefit from his or her own misdeeds, which would not be tolerated. As with *Notcutt's* case in the context of sickness, this decision of the Court of Appeal resolved an unfortunate division of opinion on frustration, and did so by applying a fairly straightforward and orthodox approach again. It leaves one (possibly unanswerable) question—how long does the sentence of imprisonment have to be in order to justify a finding of frustration? This presumably remains a question of fact for the tribunal or court. The other question that remains is how long the courts and tribunals will allow employers to avoid the consequences of events clearly contemplated in most employment relationships—like sudden illness—on the basis of what was originally an exceptional doctrine to deal with unexpected and fundamental changes of circumstance.

6.1.3 Expiry of fixed-term contracts

There used to be a presumption that a general hiring (ie one with no fixed duration) was a hiring for a year, the significance of this being that it guaranteed agricultural labourers employment through all four seasons. This, however, no longer has any place in employment law, and a general hiring now is regarded as a hiring for an indefinite period, determinable by reasonable notice.[56] However, the employer and employee may agree that a contract shall be for a fixed period only (possibly for a probationary period) and at common law that contract terminates automatically at the expiry of the period (a fixed-term contract).[57] Clearly this point had to be taken into account by the framers of the modern statutory employment law, though for many years this was done in a rather ambiguous way. On the one hand, the expiry of a fixed-term contract has always been deemed to be a 'dismissal' for the purposes of unfair dismissal and redundancy law;[58] to have failed to do so would have left a huge gap in the legal protection by allowing the employer to avoid it simply by making the employee's contract fixed term. On the other hand, for many years the employer was allowed to restrict its liability in defined circumstances, in that an employee could sign away his or her unfair dismissal rights in a fixed-term contract of one year or more and his or her redundancy rights in a fixed-term contract of two years or more.[59] The Labour government repealed both of these provisions, the first by the Employment Relations Act 1999 and the second by the Fixed-term Worker (Prevention of Less Favourable Treatment) Regulations 2002.[60]

6.1.3.1 Fixed-term contracts with notice periods

Given this involvement of statute, questions of interpretation not surprisingly arose, and two in particular go to the root of the meaning of fixed term. The first, and most immediately pressing in the early case law, was the possible conflict between a statement that a

[56] *De Stempel v Dunkels* [1938] 1 All ER 238, CA; *Richardson v Koefod* [1969] 3 All ER 1264, [1969] 1 WLR 1812, CA.

[57] *R v Secretary of State for Social Services, ex p Khan* [1973] 2 All ER 104, [1973] 1 WLR 187, CA. See also *Brown v Knowsley Borough Council* [1986] IRLR 102 (contract expressed to be subject to continued external funding held to terminate automatically when that funding ceased).

[58] Employment Rights Act 1996, ss 95(1)(b), 136(1)(b); see 7.2.1.

[59] Section 197, now wholly repealed.

[60] The main purposes of the 2002 Regulations are to enact a no-less-favourable regime for fixed-term employees and to place limitations on the length of time that an employer can keep an employee on successive fixed-term contracts: see 2.1.4.

contract is for a fixed term and the inclusion in it of a provision for termination by notice. In *BBC v Ioannou*,[61] the contract in question was for a fixed period, but with a provision for termination by three months' notice, and this was held not to be a 'fixed-term contract', so that the purported written surrender of redundancy and unfair dismissal rights was ineffective. Termination by notice was held to be inconsistent with a fixed-term contract, which had to be for that term and not terminable during it.

In this case the Court of Appeal was attempting to safeguard the position of those on fixed-term contracts by ensuring that only those *genuinely* on such contracts could sign away their rights (as the law then allowed). When, however, this reasoning was applied to the statutory definition of dismissal it had potentially dire results for the employee,[62] as it meant that if the employer put him on a contract which was ostensibly for a fixed term but used the ploy of inserting a notice provision of sorts, the employer could then have argued that, under *BBC v Ioannou*, that was *not* a fixed-term contract, and so when it expired that was *not* the expiry of a fixed-term contract under the Employment Rights Act 1996, ss 95(1)(b) and 136(1)(b), and so, as it would not qualify as an ordinary dismissal under ss 95(1)(a) and 136(1)(a), there would have been no 'dismissal' and so no possible claims for unfair dismissal or redundancy. This was argued by an employer in *Dixon v BBC*,[63] but in that case the Court of Appeal recognized the absurdity that would arise from this application of *BBC v Ioannou* and so, not wishing to establish two different definitions for 'fixed term' depending on whether the case concerned the legal waiver of rights or dismissal in a non-waiver situation, they reversed as per incuriam that part of *BBC v Ioannou* which dealt with the definition of 'fixed term', and held that a contract for a set period remains a fixed-term contract for statutory purposes even if it also contains a provision for termination by notice during its currency. Thus *Dixon v BBC* is now the ruling case, and so the employer cannot use this simple device to rule out the employee's action, but must instead accept that when a fixed-term contract expires (whether or not there is a notice provision in it) that is a 'dismissal' under ss 95 and 136, and, in an unfair dismissal case, be prepared to justify its reasons for not renewing the contract.[64]

6.1.3.2 **Can an event define the term?**

The second question has become even more fundamental and led to a significant change—what form of expiry is necessary before a contract comes within this category at all? The case law on the legislation as it stood until 2002 made the clear distinction that a fixed-term contract is one which is to expire on a definable *date*, not on the happening of a particular event or the completion of a particular task at some time in the future.[65] There was therefore the possibility of such a 'task' or 'purpose' contract (eg employment until a particular building is demolished) terminating automatically without there being a dismissal in law, which could, of course, materially prejudice statutory rights.[66] If, however, the event or completion in question (eg the end of a particular course in a short-term teaching contract) could in fact be dated with reasonable precision, then it was held that that should be treated as sufficient for the existence of a fixed-term contract; if it were

[61] [1975] 2 All ER 999, [1975] ICR 267, CA.

[62] See Hepple and Napier 'Temporary Workers and the Law' (1978) 7 ILJ 84.

[63] [1979] ICR 281, [1979] IRLR 114, CA.

[64] *Terry v East Sussex County Council* [1977] 1 All ER 567, [1976] ICR 536, approved by the Court of Appeal in *Fay v North Yorkshire County Council* [1986] ICR 133, [1985] IRLR 247, CA. This is also the position for the purposes of the 2002 Regulations: *Allen v National Australia Group Europe Ltd* [2004] IRLR 847, EAT.

[65] *Wiltshire County Council v NATFHE* [1980] ICR 455, [1980] IRLR 198, CA.

[66] *Brown v Knowsley Borough Council* [1986] IRLR 102, EAT is an extreme example of this.

otherwise, it might be easy for an employer to avoid the statutory definition of dismissal by putting the contract in the *form* of an engagement pending a particular event, even if the date of that event could be discerned.

This was, however, subject to major change under the Fixed-term Employees (Prevention of Less Favourable Treatment) Regulations 2002 in order to comply with the wider definition in the Fixed-term Worker Directive 1999/70/EC, which covers task or purpose contracts. Moreover, this change applies not only under the Regulations themselves, but also to the basic definitions in the above sections in the Employment Rights Act 1996. Both the unfair dismissal and redundancy payments provisions now state that there is deemed to be a dismissal where the employee 'is employed under a limited-term contract[67] and that contract terminates by virtue of the limiting event without being renewed under the same contract'. Inserted definitions define 'limited-term contract' as being where '(a) the employment under the contract is not intended to be permanent and (b) provision is accordingly made in the contract for it to terminate by virtue of a limiting event'; 'limiting event' is defined as the expiry of a fixed term, the performance of a specific task in contemplation of which the contract is made or the occurrence or non-occurrence of an event where the contract provides for termination on such occurrence or non-occurrence.[68] Thus, task or purpose contracts are now included in the statutory definitions and, as there has not in the past been any divergence between statute and common law concepts of fixed-term contracts (given that they have been so closely intertwined), it is to be assumed that this new approach would, if ever necessary, be applied at common law too.

6.1.4 **Mutual consent**

As with other contracts, a contract of employment may in general be terminated by the mutual agreement of the employer and employee so to do (just as they may agree to vary the agreed terms of the contract during its operation, provided that the variation is voluntary and without undue pressure on the employee).[69] Thus in *S W Strange Ltd v Mann*,[70] the defendant was employed as the plaintiff company's manager under a contract which included a restraint clause, restricting his post-employment activities. After certain disagreements the parties agreed that the defendant should cease to be manager and instead take over the running of only one department. When he was eventually dismissed, the plaintiff tried to enforce the restraint clause, but the court held for the defendant on the ground, inter alia, that the original contract had been terminated by mutual consent, and the new contract which was entered did not contain the relevant clause. As with other common law concepts, however, 'mutual consent' gained renewed significance with the advent of the new statutory rights, often dependent upon continuity of the employment, and the fact of dismissal.

While the concept of mutual consent in fact worked in the employee's favour in *Strange Ltd v Mann*, it would be more likely to jeopardize an employee's statutory rights if found too readily, for it could break continuity and provide the employer with an argument that there had in fact been no dismissal, only a voluntary parting of the ways. In *McAlwane v Boughton Estates*,[71] an employee was given notice to terminate his employment on 19 April,

[67] This change of terminology here is curious because the Regulations themselves (which of course use substantially the same definition) retain the term 'fixed-term contract'.

[68] Employment Rights Act 1996, s 235(2A), (2B).

[69] *Marriott v Oxford and District Co-operative Society Ltd (No 2)* [1970] 1 QB 186, [1969] 3 All ER 1126, CA.

[70] [1965] 1 All ER 1069, [1965] 1 WLR 629; cf *Cowey v Liberian Operations Ltd* [1966] 2 Lloyd's Rep 45.

[71] [1973] 2 All ER 299, [1973] ICR 470.

but during the notice period he asked if he could leave on 12 April. The employer agreed, and, when the employee claimed a redundancy payment and unfair dismissal, argued that there was no dismissal because the contract had been terminated by mutual consent on 12 April. The NIRC (the relevant forum for such complaints at the time) rejected this argument, holding that this merely constituted an agreed variation of the notice period, so that the employee was still dismissed by the employer. Sir John Donaldson P said:

> We would further suggest that it would be a very rare case indeed in which it could properly be found that the employer and the employee had got together and, notwithstanding that there was a current notice of termination of the employment, agreed mutually to terminate the contract, particularly when one realises the financial consequences to the employee involved in such an agreement. We do not say that such arrangement cannot arise; we merely say that, viewed in a real life situation, it would seem to be a possibility which might appeal to a lawyer more than to a personnel manager.[72]

This decision, and this dictum in particular, was applied by the Court of Appeal (by a majority) in *Lees v Arthur Greaves Ltd*,[73] where, on similar facts, it was once again held that there was no termination by mutual consent.

Mutual consent will therefore be difficult to establish, particularly in a statutory context; this is especially so in an unfair dismissal action, because the Employment Rights Act 1996, s 95(2) provides that where an employee under notice gives their employer notice that they wish to leave before the expiry of the employer's notice, the employee is deemed still to have been dismissed by the employer for unfair dismissal purposes. The applicants in *McAlwane* and *Lees* could not rely upon the equivalent provisions in the legislation at the time[74] since they then required *written* notice by the employee, and this had not been given. The requirement of writing was deleted for unfair dismissal purposes by the Employment Protection Act 1975, but not for redundancy purposes where it is still required.[75] However, termination by mutual consent does remain a possibility, as can be seen from *Lipton Ltd v Marlborough*[76] where an employee, faced with the loss of his job in a reorganization, began to look for other employment, but was hindered by his contract which required him to give six months' notice and contained a restraint of trade clause. During negotiations he requested that he be released from his contract immediately and the employer agreed. When he later claimed unfair dismissal, the tribunal found that he had been constructively dismissed (on the basis that the employer intended to phase out his job), but the EAT allowed the employer's appeal and held that this was a termination by mutual agreement and not a dismissal, Bristow J stating:

> The whole difference between termination by mutual agreement in this context and constructive dismissal is that in the first case the employee says 'Please may I go?' and the employer says 'Yes'. In the second case the employee says 'You have treated me in such a way that I'm going without a by-your-leave'.

Such a case will, however, remain a rarity (either in the specific context of a cross-notice to end employment or more generally), and the fact that the employee did not object to

[72] [1973] 2 All ER 299 at 302, [1973] ICR 470 at 473.

[73] [1974] 2 All ER 393, [1974] ICR 501, CA. See also *Glacier Metal Co Ltd v Dyer* [1974] 3 All ER 21, [1974] IRLR 189.

[74] Industrial Relations Act 1971, s 23(3) (later the Trade Union and Labour Relations Act 1974, Sch 1, para 5(3)) and the Redundancy Payments Act 1965, s 4(2).

[75] Employment Rights Act 1996, s 136(3).

[76] [1979] IRLR 179.

his own dismissal (eg on an agreed redundancy) will not normally prevent it from still being a dismissal;[77] the usual narrow approach was reaffirmed by the EAT in *Tracey v Zest Equipment Co Ltd*,[78] where termination of employment following a failure to return on time from holiday (when the employee, who had been late back before, had agreed beforehand that his employment would be terminated in the event of lateness) was held not to have been terminated by mutual consent but rather to have been repudiatory conduct leading to dismissal, thus allowing the tribunal to consider the substantive question of fairness.

As against that, termination by mutual consent was subsequently found by the Court of Appeal in *Birch v University of Liverpool*[79] in the case of two academics taking early retirement under a scheme adopted by universities and their relevant unions. The facts were exceptional in that the scheme required a high degree of mutual agreement and clearly envisaged that statutory redundancy payments (which the two applicants were now claiming) would *not* be payable on top; the case does, however, show an important potential application of the idea of mutual consent in modern circumstances, particularly where, as Ackner LJ pointed out, the employer calls for resignations well in advance of decreases in the workforce, there is no compulsion, and the employer offers financial inducements well in excess of what would be payable under the ordinary redundancy payments scheme. The decision in *Birch* was taken one step further by the EAT in *Scott v Coalite Fuels & Chemicals Ltd*,[80] where it was held that there was mutual termination where employees took voluntary early retirement while already under notice of dismissal for redundancy. While such a decision may make good industrial sense in a case where early retirement (with a lump-sum payment, but a reduced weekly pension) is negotiated as an *alternative* to redundancy, it does call into question the dictum of Sir John Donaldson cited at the beginning of this section that mutual termination during a current notice period would only be found in 'a very rare case indeed'. Moreover, mutual consent was again found in *Riley v Direct Line Insurance Group plc*[81] 80a where it arose in the context, not of redundancy, but of serious illness and an arrangement to go on to a generous insurance-backed permanent health; scheme. Linguistically, his termination was described as a dismissal, but in reality it was held that the negotiations over this had led to a mutual agreement for that outcome—it was much to his financial advantage, there was no pressure from the employer and he clearly understood what he was agreeing to.

[77] *Burton, Allton and Johnson Ltd v Peck* [1975] ICR 193, [1975] IRLR 87; *White v HC One Oval Ltd* [2022] IRLR 576, EAT. In *Lassman v De Vere University Arms Hotel* [2003] ICR 44 a hotel manager whose job was being downgraded was given the choice (only) of going part time or taking redundancy; when she reluctantly chose the latter, it was held that she had still been dismissed and so could claim unfair dismissal.

[78] [1982] ICR 481, [1982] IRLR 268. The case is in line with the restrictive approach taken at the same time to the analogous area of 'constructive resignation' or 'self-dismissal', as seen in *London Transport Executive v Clarke* [1981] ICR 355, [1981] IRLR 166, CA (discussed presently) which is cited in the judgment of the EAT.

[79] [1985] ICR 470, [1985] IRLR 165, CA, distinguishing *Burton, Allton & Johnson Ltd v Peck*, n 77; noted Freedland (1985) 14 ILJ 243. Compare this to the more recent case of *Khan v HGS Global Ltd* UKEAT/0176/15 (16 November 2015, unreported), where a relocation of activities confronted workers with a choice between moving, accepting different work in the original location, or taking redundancy with a severance package; voluntarily choosing the last option amounted to termination by mutual consent.

[80] [1988] ICR 355, [1988] IRLR 131 (see also *Logan Salton v Durham County Council* [1989] IRLR 99, where an employee under threat of disciplinary proceedings negotiated severance terms and was held to them). It remains the case, however, that there will still be a dismissal (even if in form there appears to be mutual agreement) if either (a) all that the employee has done is to volunteer to be dismissed for redundancy, or (b) pressure has been put on the employee to agree to go.

[81] [2025] EAT 118; at para [23] of the judgment there is a useful summary of the approach to be taken by a tribunal here.

6.2 Dismissal by notice

Most contracts of employment may be terminated by either party giving the necessary notice of termination. At common law, this notice can be given for any reason not expressly prohibited by the contract, a state of affairs starkly distinct from that under the unfair dismissal statute (which of course does not apply for the first two years of employment).[82] The period of notice may be agreed expressly by the parties[83] and, more unusually, the parties may agree to restrict the reasons behind the giving of notice.[84] Usually, however, the right to give notice will not be so restricted and only the mechanics of the period to be given will be laid down. If there is no such express notice provision, and no term can be ascertained from custom or trade usage,[85] the law will read into a contract of employment that it is terminable upon 'reasonable notice'. It may then be a matter of litigation to quantify what is reasonable; as this involves construction of the contract it has in the past been within the jurisdiction of the civil courts, but it can now be raised in proceedings before tribunals, under their common law jurisdiction on termination of employment.[86] There are many reported cases on this question of quantification and all that can be said is that each case must depend upon its own facts, such as the position of the employee within the firm, his or her professional standing, and, in some cases, the intervals for payment.[87] The date on which notice is deemed to have occurred is the date it is received by the employee (eg in the post).[88] To be effective (since it has such a drastic effect) the notice must be definite and explicit. Thus in *Morris v Bailey*[89] it was held that a notice of termination given to the plaintiff's union but not to him personally was not effective to dismiss him, even though most of his contract of employment (including the notice provisions) consisted of terms incorporated from the union's collective agreement. Moreover, the amount of notice must be made known to the employee, so that a mere warning of impending dismissal (eg for redundancy) will not constitute notice.[90] However, once an effective notice has been given by one of the parties, they may not withdraw it unilaterally, and so withdrawal of the notice may only be by mutual consent.[91]

[82] This is important: if no statute applies, employers may dismiss for any reason at all, meaning that in most circumstances in the current qualifying period of their employment workers can be sacked for any reason that does not violate anti-discrimination law.

[83] Written particulars of the notice period should be given to the employee within two months of commencement: Employment Rights Act, s 1(4)(e).

[84] *McClelland v Northern Ireland General Health Services Board* [1957] 2 All ER 129, [1957] 1 WLR 594, HL. It has been held that there is an implied restriction on giving notice to a long-term sick employee where there is a permanent health insurance scheme in operation under the contract.

[85] *George v Davies* [1911] 2 KB 445.

[86] See 1.4.

[87] Thus in *Grundy v Sun Printing and Publishing Association* (1916) 33 TLR 77, CA, an editor was entitled to 12 months' notice, but in *Fox-Bourne v Vernon & Co Ltd* (1894) 10 TLR 647 another editor was only entitled to six months' notice. For a more modern example of this process of quantification see *Hill v C A Parsons & Co Ltd* [1972] Ch 305, [1971] 3 All ER 1345, CA.

[88] *Newcastle upon Tyne NHS Foundation Trust v Haywood* [2018] UKSC 22, [2018] IRLR 644.

[89] [1969] 2 Lloyd's Rep 215, CA.

[90] *Morton Sundour Fabrics Ltd v Shaw* (1966) 2 ITR 84; *Pritchard-Rhodes Ltd v Boon and Milton* [1979] IRLR 19; *International Computers Ltd v Kennedy* [1981] IRLR 28; *Doble v Firestone Tyre and Rubber Co Ltd* [1981] IRLR 300; *Haseltine Lake & Co v Dowler* [1981] ICR 222, [1981] IRLR 25. This is particularly important in the context of the giving of counter-notice by an employee, for the purposes of redundancy law: see 8.1.4.

[91] *Riordan v War Office* [1959] 3 All ER 552, [1959] 1 WLR 1059 (affd [1960] 3 All ER 774n, [1961] 1 WLR 210, CA); *Harris and Russell Ltd v Slingsby* [1973] 3 All ER 31, [1973] ICR 454; *Butcher v Surrey County Council* [2020] IRLR 601, EAT.

Under the common law of employment, the availability to the employer of dismissal by notice could in practice negate what rights an employee might have; for example, an employee might have been justified in refusing to obey an order which was illegal or outside the scope of their employment and the employer could not summarily dismiss them for that refusal, but there was nothing to stop the employer from giving them notice because of the incident, since a dismissal on proper notice was lawful regardless of the motive behind it. If the notice period was only a matter of days or even hours, that could be a powerful threat to the employee. This position is now heavily overlaid by the statutory provisions as to redundancy and unfair dismissal (particularly as the latter entails scrutiny of the merits of the dismissal, not just its technical correctness), but the question of notice was first affected by statute in the Contracts of Employment Act 1963,[92] which attempted to alter the common law in two ways—first, by gearing the period of notice to the length of continuous service, not simply to the status of the employee; second, by safeguarding certain employee rights during the period of notice. The present provisions relating to these two points will now be considered.

The common law rules proved to be inadequate in that they made no distinction for the long-serving employee. Thus an employee on a weekly contract would only be entitled to a week's notice whether they had worked for their employer for one week or for 40 years. Large-scale redundancies emphasized this defect, and certain minimum notice periods are now laid down by statute. Under the Employment Rights Act 1996, s 86, the minimum notice period for an employee with less than two years' continuous employment is one week; where there is more than two years' continuous employment, the employee is entitled to one week's notice for each year up to a maximum of 12 weeks. As for the employee, the statutory minimum which they must give to terminate their employment is one week if they have been employed for four weeks or more. The section states that it does not affect the right of either party to terminate the contract through the other party's conduct, and does not prevent either party from waiving his or her right to notice on any particular occasion.[93] Subsection (3) also states that the section does not prevent a party from accepting a payment in lieu of notice.[94]

6.2.1 **Wages in lieu of notice**

'Wages in lieu' is a common phenomenon, whereby the employer gives the employee the wages which they would have earned during the notice period and instructs them not to work out the notice period, so that the employer is rid of them immediately. This is perfectly lawful if both parties agree to it, and this is as far as the subsection goes. One contentious point, however, is whether the employer has a *right* to give wages in lieu if the employee wishes to work out the notice period. The old tenet of employment law that the employer's only obligation is to provide wages, not work, suggested that dismissal with wages in lieu would be lawful,[95] except in one of the exceptional cases where work also had to be provided.[96] However, the more modern approach has been to look more

[92] Later the Contracts of Employment Act 1972, and now to be found in the Employment Rights Act 1996, ss 86–91.

[93] Waiver of notice includes waiver of any right to payment for the notice period (especially in a voluntary severance case): *Trotter v Forth Ports Authority* [1991] IRLR 419, Ct of Sess; *Baldwin v British Coal Corpn* [1995] IRLR 139.

[94] *Staffordshire County Council v Secretary of State for Employment* [1987] ICR 956, [1988] IRLR 3 (reversed on other grounds, [1989] ICR 664, [1989] IRLR 117, CA).

[95] *Konski v Peet* [1915] 1 Ch 530.

[96] See 3.3.2. This point was particularly taken up (in the context of garden leave) in *William Hill Organisation Ltd v Tucker* [1999] ICR 291, [1998] IRLR 313, CA, which showed a broader approach to who can claim an interest in having the work itself provided.

closely at *how* the dismissal is effected. The renewed interest in this point is not because of its direct effect on wrongful dismissal (since the prima facie measure of damages for wrongful dismissal, the wages themselves, has already been paid)[97] but rather because of three incidental matters which may be affected—(a) whether the protection against unlawful deductions in Part II of the Employment Rights Act 1996 applies to any non-payment of the wages;[98] (b) what is the effective date of termination of the dismissal;[99] (c) whether any restraint of trade clause in the contract survives the termination.[100] In *Delaney v Staples*,[101] the leading case on deductions from wages, Lord Browne-Wilkinson analysed the law on dismissal with wages in lieu; adopting his classification, the position in relation to the above matters appears to be as follows.

1. The employer gives the employee proper notice, but then tells them that they need not work it out; in such a case (including an ad hoc 'garden leave' arrangement) the dismissal is lawful, with advance payment of 'wages'; the effective date of termination is the end of the notice period; and any restraint clause may continue to apply.
2. The contract itself provides for termination by notice *or* by wages in lieu (including a formal 'garden leave' clause if it operates this way); here, the dismissal is lawful, the payment is not 'wages' for the purposes of Part II of the 1996 Act (because not paid under a subsisting contract of employment), the effective date of termination is the date the wages in lieu are given (*not* the end of the period of notice), and any restraint clause may continue to apply.[102]
3. At the end of the employment, the employer and employee agree ad hoc that it will end forthwith, on the payment of the sum in lieu; the results here are as in (2), it being a lawful variation of the normal notice term.
4. The employer summarily dismisses the employee, without his or her agreement, but tenders a payment in lieu of notice; here, the employer is in breach of contract and so the dismissal is wrongful, which means that the payment is *damages*, not 'wages' (but they extinguish any *claim* for damages); the effective date of termination remains the date of the summary dismissal and payment in lieu, *but* any restraint of trade clause now becomes invalid because of the wrongful dismissal.

From this analysis, it can be seen that the employer now has much to gain from putting into the contract of employment a term expressly permitting dismissal with wages in lieu, since it provides the optimum position of a lawful dismissal, no challenge to the payment in tribunal proceedings, an early effective date of termination, and the preservation of any restraint of trade clause. From the employee's point of view, the existence of an express payment in lieu clause is both advantageous and disadvantageous. On the positive side, as the dismissal is lawful, the employee may claim any unpaid wages in lieu as a

[97] Though it can still affect whether the nature of the employee's right is damages or debt (in which case there is no obligation to mitigate loss, and so earnings in new employment need not be taken into account): *Gregory v Wallace* [1998] IRLR 387, CA.

[98] If it does, the ex-employee may challenge any non-payment (total or partial) of the wages in lieu before an employment tribunal, instead of before the ordinary courts: see 1.4.

[99] See 7.2.2. This is relevant because (a) by that date the employee must have the necessary qualifying service and (b) the three-month time limit for claiming unfair dismissal flows from that date. It is thus in the employer's interest to have the EDT early, ie when the employment actually ends, not the (later) date on which notice would notionally have expired.

[100] If the dismissal is wrongful, the restraint clause falls: see 2.4.2.

[101] [1992] ICR 483, [1992] IRLR 191, HL.

[102] *Rex Stewart Jeffries Parker Ginsberg Ltd v Parker* [1988] IRLR 483, CA.

debt due under the contract, not as damages for breach of it; this means that the employee is not under a duty to mitigate his or her loss, which may be of particular importance for a highly paid employee on long notice, who has obtained new employment during what would have been the notice period but who does *not* have to bring those new (equally high?) earnings into account, and so may receive and retain both sums of money in full.[103] On the negative side, however, the fact that the payment in lieu is contractual means that the amount paid is taxable in the employee's hands, since it cannot be construed as 'damages' and hence not subject to income tax (which may be the case with a non-contractual payment: see 6.1.4).[104]

6.2.2 **Rights during notice**

In addition to laying down minimum periods of notice, the legislation also safeguards certain employee rights during the period of notice,[105] though it should be noted that these provisions do not apply where the notice to be given by the employer under the contract is more than a week longer than the statutory minimum as laid down in s 86.[106] These provisions differ slightly depending upon whether or not the employee who is under notice works 'normal working hours'. The construction of that phrase is therefore important, and essentially the test is whether the contract of employment lays down a certain or minimum number of hours which the employee must work; if so, they work 'normal working hours'. Prima facie this might be expected to be exclusive of overtime, but under s 234(3) of the 1996 Act some overtime may count if it is included in the number of hours which the employee must work (eg if they are contractually bound to work 40 hours per week, and overtime rates begin to be payable after 37 hours, then that is still normal working hours of 40 per week); to qualify under this extension, however, the overtime must be compulsory in the sense of being obligatory for the employee and guaranteed by the employer.[107] Where the employee works normal working hours and actually works during the notice period they will be contractually entitled to the correct payment without assistance from the legislation, but s 88(1) ensures that they continue to be paid at the relevant rate for any periods when (a) they are ready and willing to work but the employer has no work for them, (b) they are incapable of work through sickness or injury, or (c) they are away on proper holiday. It is provided that where the employee draws sickness or injury benefit that is to be taken into account in computing the employer's liability to them, since otherwise they might be doubly entitled, through drawing the benefit and receiving full

[103] *Abrahams v Performing Right Society* [1995] ICR 1028, [1995] IRLR 486, CA. However, according to *Cerberus Software Ltd v Rowley* [2001] ICR 376, [2001] IRLR 160, where there is an in lieu clause but the employer refuses to pay under it, the employee is restricted to an action in damages and so must mitigate (even though this in effect allows the employer to benefit from its own misdeed in dismissing wrongfully, rather than lawfully under the in lieu clause).

[104] *EMI Group Electronics Ltd v Coldicott* [1999] IRLR 630, [1999] STC 803, CA; applied to a negotiated settlement in *Richardson (IT) v Delaney* [2001] IRLR 663. It is, however, now clear that a non-contractual payment in lieu of notice (PILON) will not always be free from tax, because the Revenue have issued new guidance restricting non-taxability to payments which are genuinely damages: Tax Bulletin, February 2003, p 999.

[105] Employment Rights Act 1996, ss 87–91.

[106] Section 87(4); *Scotts Co (UK) Ltd v Budd* [2003] IRLR 145, EAT.

[107] See, in the context of the computation of the number of normal working hours, *Tarmac Roadstone Holdings Ltd v Peacock* [1973] 2 All ER 485, [1973] ICR 273, CA, applied to the present context of the definition of normal working hours in *Fox v C Wright (Farmers) Ltd* [1978] ICR 98. The questions of 'normal working hours' and what constitutes 'a week's pay' are discussed in Chapter 3.

pay from the employer.[108] Where the employee does not work normal working hours, the employer must pay them a week's pay (calculated in accordance with Part XIV of the 1996 Act)[109] for each week of the period of notice, provided that they are ready and willing to do work of a reasonable nature and amount to earn it; once again, the employee is specifically entitled to payment during absence through sickness or injury, or while on proper holiday. The legislation contains three main qualifications upon these rights to payment:

1. the employee is not entitled to be paid during time off which they have requested (including time off governed by statute);[110]
2. if the employee breaks the contract during the period of notice and is justifiably summarily dismissed, they are not entitled to further payment as from that dismissal;
3. if it is the employee who has given notice and they go on strike during the notice period, they are not entitled to payment under these provisions at all; where it is the employer who has given notice this qualification does not apply, so that the employee will be contractually entitled to payment for that part of the notice period when they were not on strike.[111]

If an employer fails to give the statutory notice, the rights laid down in these provisions are to be taken into account in assessing damages, and it is further provided that if the employer breaks the contract of employment during the period of notice (eg by wrongfully terminating it summarily) then the benefits that the employee will receive anyway under these provisions are to go towards mitigating any damages payable to the employee.[112]

6.2.3 **'Garden leave' and other restraints during notice**

One final point to notice on the common law doctrine of notice is that it has increasingly been used by employers to safeguard trade secrets or (in businesses which are highly reliant on skilled employees) to prevent head-hunting by other firms, by the incorporation into sensitive contracts of employment of 'garden leave' clauses. These provide for long periods of notice on either side, during which the employee will be remunerated in full (either in the normal way or by an in-lieu payment) but not necessarily required to work. Thus, an employee wishing to leave may be required to give, say, six months' or a year's notice, during which time (provided the employer pays them their full entitlement to wages and benefits) they continue to be subject to the implied term not to compete or breach confidence,[113] or preferably to an express term to like effect. Compared with the traditional restraint of trade clause,[114] this is expensive *but* it is probably more reliable, since restraint clauses are notoriously difficult to draft and enforce. In an appropriate

[108] Employment Rights Act 1996, s 90. The rationale behind this was queried by Dillon LJ in *Notcutt v Universal Equipment Co (London) Ltd* [1986] ICR 414, [1986] IRLR 218, CA, since it may mean paying sick pay during notice to an employee not normally entitled to it; however, as the court held that the contract was frustrated by the sickness, the matter did not arise.

[109] This calculation is considered at 3.5.4.

[110] Employment Rights Act 1996, Part VI; Trade Union and Labour Relations (Consolidation) Act 1992, ss 168, 170.

[111] For the effect on redundancy entitlements of a strike during the notice period see the 1996 Act, ss 140 and 143.

[112] Employment Rights Act 1996, s 91(5).

[113] See 3.4.4.

[114] See 2.4.2. It is possible to have both a garden leave clause and (then) a restraint of trade clause in a contract, though a court would need to consider the reasonableness of them taken together: *Crédit Suisse Asset Management Ltd v Armstrong* [1996] ICR 882, [1996] IRLR 450, CA.

case, a garden leave clause may be enforced by injunction,[115] but it must be remembered that ultimately an injunction is a discretionary remedy and may be refused by a court if it appears that the clause is unconscionable, as, for example, if there is little or no chance of the employer suffering actual damage if the employee does take up a particular new job (albeit in breach of the clause).[116] Moreover, the efficacy of garden leave clauses generally may now be subject to some limitation because of the decision of the Court of Appeal in *William Hill Organisation Ltd v Tucker*.[117] The *ratio* of that case is that a court will not *imply* a garden leave clause in any case where it is arguable that the employee has an interest in doing the work, not just receiving payment,[118] and to this extent it is unexceptionable (merely stressing the advantage of an express term). However, at the end of the judgment Morritt LJ said obiter that it should not be too readily assumed that a garden leave clause will succeed where a restraint clause might fail:

> if injunctive relief was sought then it had to be justified on similar grounds to those necessary to the validity of the employee's covenant in restraint of trade. The court should be careful not to grant interlocutory relief to enforce a garden leave clause to any greater extent than would be covered by a justifiable covenant in restraint of trade previously entered into by an employee.

Interestingly, where the evidence clearly demonstrated a threat to protectable interests and the notice period was not excessive, the court in *SG & R Valuation Services v Boudrais*[119] was willing to imply a power to impose garden leave in a contract that only provided for notice. This may mean that in future there may be more emphasis on the *extent* of the garden leave and what interests it is protecting, and a tougher line on severing or reducing an unreasonably wide clause.[120]

6.3 Dismissal for cause (summary dismissal)

At common law an employer may dismiss an employee summarily (ie without notice) if it has sufficient cause to do so. In old cases, from the nineteenth century and earlier, this was viewed as a natural and necessary aspect of the relationship between master and servant, and of the servant's duty of obedience. The judgment of Parke B in *Callo v Brouncker*[121] was treated for many years as laying down set rules on summary dismissal, which, he said, could be for moral misconduct (pecuniary or otherwise), wilful disobedience, or

[115] *Evening Standard Co Ltd v Henderson* [1987] ICR 588, [1987] IRLR 64, CA (clause requiring a year's notice enforced to prevent a newspaper production manager from taking up employment during that time with a new newspaper venture, the employers undertaking to pay in full during the year); *Euro Brokers Ltd v Rabey* [1995] IRLR 206 (six-month garden leave clause enforced against a money broker wishing to move to a competitor firm); see Freedland (1989) 18 ILJ 112 and Gouldring 'Injunctions and Contracts of Employment: The Evening Standard Doctrine' (1990) 19 ILJ 98.

[116] *Provident Financial Group plc v Hayward* [1989] ICR 160, [1989] IRLR 84, CA (injunction to restrain financial director from taking up new employment towards the end of a long notice period refused because there was little evidence of any actual detriment to the employers).

[117] [1998] IRLR 313, CA; applied in *Symbian Ltd v Christiensen* [2001] IRLR 77, CA.

[118] For this aspect of the case see 3.3.2.

[119] [2008] All ER (D) 141.

[120] For example, in *GFI Group Inc v Eaglestone* [1994] IRLR 119 an over-long garden leave clause was saved by being reduced in length by the court (and then enforced for that shorter period), but this is just what a court will not normally do with a restraint clause, which usually has to stand or fall as originally drafted.

[121] (1831) 4 C & P 518. Several of the points to be raised here are considered at greater length in Smith and Randall *Contract Actions in Modern Employment Law: Developments and Issues* (2000) ch 8.

habitual neglect. However, with the move in the nineteenth century towards viewing employment in a contractual light, the emphasis changed so that the right to dismiss summarily became explicable on the ground that the conduct of the employee was such that it showed a repudiation by them of the contract of employment, which the employer then accepted and treated as terminating the contract immediately.[122] In *Laws v London Chronicle (Indicator Newspapers) Ltd*,[123] Lord Evershed MR said:

> the proper conclusion . . . is that, since a contract of service is but an example of contracts in general, so that the general law of contract will be applicable, it follows that the question must be—if summary dismissal is claimed to be justifiable—whether the conduct complained of is such as to show the servant to have disregarded the essential conditions of the contract of service.

This will apply as a general principle not just to the particular categories listed by Parke B but to any context in which the employee's conduct is sufficiently grave as to be repudiatory, so that, for example, an employee may be summarily dismissed for going on strike.[124] In rare cases, where it destroys the trust between employer and employee, gross negligence (as opposed to gross misconduct) can support a summary dismissal.[125] The principal effect of this contractual approach is that every case must be viewed on its own facts to determine whether the conduct in question was grave enough, and the question is not to be solved by searching for absolute rules covering each particular context (with the result that decided cases may be of little or no assistance). Thus: 'the true question is whether the acts and conduct of the party evince an intention no longer to be bound by the contract'[126] and 'in every case the question of repudiation must depend on the character of the contract, the number and weight of the wrongful acts or assertions, the intentions indicated by such acts and words, the deliberation or otherwise with which they are committed or uttered and on the general circumstances of the case'.[127]

Much will therefore depend upon the context and the nature of the reason, so that, for example, a relatively minor instance of dishonesty may warrant summary dismissal, particularly if the employee's job involves dealing with money.[128] By contrast, mere negligence may in most cases be amenable only to dismissal by notice and a summary dismissal may be wrongful,[129] unless there are other particular factors, such as endangering life by neglect.[130] Also, while an employer may not be justified in dismissing summarily

[122] *Boston Deep Sea Fishing and Ice Co v Ansell* (1888) 39 Ch D 339, CA, particularly per Bowen LJ at 364–65; *Laws v London Chronicle (Indicator Newspapers) Ltd* [1959] 2 All ER 285, [1959] 1 WLR 698, CA; *Pepper v Webb* [1969] 2 All ER 216, [1969] 1 WLR 514, CA.

[123] [1959] 2 All ER 285 at 287, [1959] 1 WLR 698 at 700.

[124] *Simmons v Hoover Ltd* [1977] 1 All ER 775, [1977] ICR 61, not following the distinction between those strikes with and those without strike notice that was drawn in *Morgan v Fry* [1968] 2 QB 710, [1968] 3 All ER 452, CA; the common law position on strikes is now considerably affected by statute.

[125] *Adesoken v Sainsbury's Supermarkets Ltd* [2017] EWCA Civ 22, [2017] IRLR 346.

[126] *Freeth v Burr* (1874) LR 9 CP 208 at 213, per Lord Coleridge CJ, applied by the House of Lords in *General Billposting Co Ltd v Atkinson* [1909] AC 118, HL.

[127] *Re Rubel Bronze and Metal Co and Vos* [1918] 1 KB 315 at 322, per McCardie J.

[128] *Sinclair v Neighbour* [1967] 2 QB 279, [1966] 3 All ER 988, CA.

[129] See eg *Gould v Webb* (1855) 4 E & B 933.

[130] It has been held, however, that the court should look primarily at the negligent act and not at the consequences which flowed from it, as the latter could be too harsh and involve too much hindsight: *Savage v British India Steam Navigation Co Ltd* (1930) 46 TLR 294.

for a single 'offence', a previous history of similar transgressions, even if not as serious as the one leading to dismissal, may be important evidence in the employer's favour.[131] Any particular case should also be viewed with a certain amount of realism, so that in *Jupiter General Insurance Co Ltd v Shroff*[132] the Privy Council said:

> Their Lordships would be very loath to assent to the view that a single outbreak of bad temper, accompanied, it may be, by regrettable language, is sufficient ground for dismissal. Sir John Beaumont CJ [in the court below] was stating a proposition of mere good sense when he observed that in such cases we must apply the standard of men and not angels and remember that men are apt to show temper when reprimanded.

The court went on to make two observations which might be borne in mind. The first was that summary dismissal is a strong measure justified only in exceptional circumstances; the second was that the test to be applied in determining whether a dismissal was justified must vary with the nature of the business and the position held by the employee and that decisions in other cases are of little value. This variable approach can also be seen in *Neary v Dean of Westminster*,[133] where ideas taken from the modern law on the implied term of trust and respect were also introduced, looking at whether the employee's conduct was such as to undermine completely that element of the employment relationship. In the light of all these factors (and particularly the number of old or very old cases on the subject), another important factor may be changing attitudes, modes of organization, or *mores* in general. Thus in *Wilson v Racher*,[134] Edmund Davies LJ said:

> Reported decisions provide useful, but only general guides, each case turning upon its own facts. Many of the decisions which are customarily cited in these cases date from the last century and may be wholly out of accord with the current social conditions. What would today be regarded as almost an attitude of Czar-serf, which is to be found in some of the older cases where a dismissed employee failed to recover damages would, I venture to think, be decided differently today.

Good examples of responsiveness to new needs are the decision in *Denco Ltd v Joinson*[135] that almost any form of deliberate computer misuse during employment will justify summary dismissal, and the decision in *Thomas v Hillingdon London Borough Council*[136] that this is also likely to be the case in most instances of internet and/or email abuse at work, particularly when it concerns downloading pornography. Perhaps the best example of changing language (albeit that probably the norm is consistent with tradition) can be found in *Metroline West v Ajaj*,[137] where the EAT opined that an employee who 'pulls a sickie'—pretending to be ill to get out of work—has committed a repudiatory breach.

[131] *Mbubaegbu v Homerton University Hospital NHS Foundation Trust* UKEAT/0218/17 (18 May 2018, unreported). See also eg *Clouston & Co Ltd v Corry* [1906] AC 122, PC (intoxication); *Pepper v Webb* [1969] 2 All ER 216, [1969] 1 WLR 514, CA (unsatisfactory work), discussed in *Wilson v Racher* [1974] ICR 428 [1974] IRLR 114, CA.

[132] [1937] 3 All ER 67, PC.

[133] [1999] IRLR 288 (Lord Jauncey, sitting as a Special Commissioner for the Visitor to Westminster Abbey).

[134] [1974] ICR 428, [1974] IRLR 114, CA.

[135] [1991] ICR 172, [1991] IRLR 63; see Napier 'Computerisation and Employment Rights' (1992) 21 ILJ 1.

[136] [2002] All ER(D) 202 (EAT).

[137] [2015] UKEAT/0295/15 (unreported) at para 54.

The advent of the modern statutory rights for employees has of course had an effect on summary dismissal, but usually indirectly, since the presence or absence of notice is a procedural matter and as such only of paramount importance in a common law action for wrongful dismissal; the statutory action for unfair dismissal in theory requires an examination of the substantive fairness of the dismissal, and so any question of the presence or absence of notice will be of secondary importance. Under the legislation, the employer is not deprived of its right to dismiss summarily, and the continuance of this common law concept is clearly envisaged in the Employment Rights Act 1996, s 86(6) (rights to minimum periods of notice not to affect cases where summary termination is justified) and the ACAS Code of Practice, 'Disciplinary and grievance procedures'.[138] However, the existence of the unfair dismissal legislation is likely to make employers more wary of dismissing summarily and may perhaps make them more likely to punish misconduct by action short of dismissal (eg suspension) or by dismissal by notice after exhausting a set procedure of warnings and a hearing; this might particularly be the case where the ground for dismissal is incompetence or negligence. The absence of notice would not per se make the dismissal unfair,[139] but might sway the tribunal against the employer on the question whether it acted reasonably. Moreover, the advent of the unfair dismissal action has placed new emphasis on *procedures* and so an employer might be advised to exercise its rights to dismiss summarily in the light of modern personnel management techniques, in particular the desirability of such matters as laying down in the company's rules what conduct may warrant summary dismissal, ensuring that the decision to dismiss is taken at a reasonably high level (certainly higher than immediate superiors), and providing for an appeal structure.[140]

The common law on dismissal for cause is thus heavily qualified by statute and the modern statutory provisions owe little to the existing common law rules. For example, at common law a summary dismissal would be lawful if the employer acted on reason A which was quite inadequate, but later found out about reason B which could in fact justify summary dismissal;[141] however, under the unfair dismissal legislation the relevant reason is the one upon which the employer acted at the time of dismissal, and not anything that it only discovered later.[142] Moreover, at common law there was no obligation upon the employer to give its reasons, but under the Employment Rights Act 1996, s 92, an employee has a statutory right to be provided with a written statement giving particulars of the reasons for his or her dismissal.[143]

[138] Particularly para 22.

[139] *Treganowan v Robert Knee & Co Ltd* [1975] ICR 405, [1975] IRLR 247; *BSC Sports and Social Club v Morgan* [1987] IRLR 391. See the important discussion of the different bases for wrongful and unfair dismissal in the judgment of Judge Clark in *Farrant v Woodroffe School* [1998] ICR 184, [1998] IRLR 176.

[140] ACAS Code of Practice 2015, paras 24, 22, and 26, respectively. It was not enough for work rules to say that summary dismissal will result from 'any breach of the employer's or a client's security rules'; without something more specific in the rule, the conduct was nevertheless required to be wilful or grossly negligent before summary dismissal was justified: *Robert Bates Wrekin Landscapes Ltd v Knight* UKEAT/0164/13 (30 January 2014, unreported). Even where the contract or work rules identify a kind of conduct as warranting dismissal, it must be clear that it is summary dismissal that is envisaged, given the gravity of the action to be taken: *Skilton v T & K Home Improvements Ltd* [2000] ICR 1162, [2000] IRLR 595, CA (reference to 'instant dismissal' is not enough to mean summary dismissal in a case of missing quarterly sales targets; employee still entitled to wages in lieu of notice).

[141] *Boston Deep Sea Fishing and Ice Co v Ansell* (1888) 39 Ch D 339, CA; *Cyril Leonard & Co v Simo Securities Trust Ltd* [1971] 3 All ER 1313, [1972] 1 WLR 80, CA.

[142] *W Devis & Sons Ltd v Atkins* [1977] AC 931, [1977] 3 All ER 40, HL.

[143] See 7.4.1.

6.4 Wrongful dismissal

6.4.1 Meaning

'Wrongful dismissal', at least in terms of establishing liability, is essentially an action for breach of contract. The action typically alleges that some procedural term of the employment contract, such as a notice provision, has been breached. It can, however, involve a breach of a term relating to permissible reasons for dismissal in the rare instance where a contract specifies such reasons. As can be seen from the earlier discussion, the common law on dismissal appears to be about form, not substance, so that, except in the case of a purported summary dismissal for cause, the concept of wrongful dismissal is essentially procedural. However, this kind of form/substance dichotomy is not really helpful, as it tends to obscure the fact that the nature of any wrongful dismissal action depends upon the actual terms of the contract in question. Thus, if a contract is for a fixed term, or expressly stated to be terminable only in certain ways,[144] and it is terminated before the term expires or in an improper way, that may be a wrongful dismissal. More typical, however, is the case where the employer dismissed the employee with no or inadequate notice, or purported to dismiss them for cause where the facts did not justify such action. Wrongful dismissal also includes 'constructive dismissal', discussed further in Chapter 7, which occurs where the employer commits a repudiatory breach of contract which the employee accepts by leaving the employment.[145]

The common law action for wrongful dismissal must be kept separate from the statutory action for unfair dismissal which entails an examination of the substantive merits of the dismissal. For many years, there was also a formal split of forum, with an unfair dismissal claim going to an employment tribunal but a wrongful dismissal claim having to go to the ordinary civil courts; since 1994, however, tribunals have been given jurisdiction over contractual claims on termination of employment,[146] and so can hear a claim for wrongful dismissal (up to the statutory limit of £25,000).[147]

6.4.2 Remedies

6.4.2.1 The rule against enforcement

While the idea of wrongful dismissal is explicable on a contractual basis (ie that the employer has repudiated the contract by its actions), it is when one comes to the nature of the remedies open to the dismissed employee that the inadequacies of contract theory

[144] This is rare in practice: *McClelland v Northern Ireland General Health Services Board* [1957] 2 All ER 129, [1957] 1 WLR 594, HL is an unusual example. In modern circumstances, it might arise if an employer agreed to a contractually binding 'no compulsory redundancy' deal; any redundancy dismissal during its currency would then be wrongful and arguably the damages should not be restricted (as is usual) to wages for the notice period, but should be for the rest of the period of the agreement, subject to mitigation and a discount for the possibility of lawful dismissal (ie on non-redundancy grounds) during that period.

[145] *Atlantic Air v Hoff* [2008] UKEAT 0602_07_2603. Constructive dismissal is a common law concept, but it is discussed more fully in Chapter 7 because it is raised most often in the context of an unfair dismissal claim. One key aspect of common law constructive dismissal which does not appear in the unfair dismissal context is the principle that one cannot give notice and then claim constructive dismissal: the logic is that one has been forced to leave by the employer's repudiatory conduct, so to give notice would be a temporary reaffirmation of the repudiated contract (see eg in *Elsevier Ltd v Munro* [2014] EWHC 2648 (QB), [2014] IRLR 766). This is not an issue in unfair dismissal law, because the statute specifically says 'with or without notice'.

[146] Employment Tribunals (Extension of Jurisdiction) Orders 1994, SI 1994/1623 and SI 1994/1624 (one order applying to England and Wales, another to Scotland): see 1.4.

[147] This cap has not increased with inflation as other compensation caps have, raising the question of why high earners with long notice periods should be shunted to the county courts.

and, as a consequence, the practical ineffectiveness of the common law become obvious.[148] The starting point is the general principle that the courts will not enforce a contract of employment, either directly by specific performance or indirectly by injunction or any other means,[149] the principal explanation being that the contract is of a personal nature, not amenable to enforcement. Thus, in *De Francesco v Barnum*,[150] Fry LJ said:

> I should be very unwilling to extend decisions the effect of which is to compel persons who are not desirous of maintaining continuous personal relations with one another to continue those personal relations. I think the courts are bound to be jealous lest they should turn contracts of service into contracts of slavery; and . . . I should lean against the extension of the doctrine of specific performance and injunction in such a manner.

Moreover, this is now enshrined in statute as far as such an order against an employee is concerned, for the Trade Union and Labour Relations (Consolidation) Act 1992, s 236 provides that no court shall issue an order compelling an employee to do any work or attend at any place for the doing of any work. This sentiment has been applied by the courts equally to cases where the order is sought against the employer, who may not be made to continue employing a particular individual, and so at common law there has never been any general remedy of reinstatement. If an employee is wrongfully dismissed, the general rule is that his or her remedy lies in damages:[151] the employee cannot sue directly for wages—being prevented from doing the work that earns the wages—and cannot get specific performance to make the work available.

6.4.2.2 **Automatic v elective theories**

The unavailability of a meaningful remedy for contractual rights after the employer's repudiation (by way of wrongful dismissal) led some courts to reverse engineer their way to the conclusion that the employer's repudiation must automatically terminate the contract. Such a rule (of automatic termination) might arguably have made practical sense, but it is difficult to explain in contractual terms. In contract law a repudiation is usually of no effect unless accepted by the innocent party—'an unaccepted repudiation is a thing writ in water and of no value to anybody'[152]—and so in theory an employee faced with wrongful dismissal should be entitled to refuse to accept this repudiation and insist on carrying on in the employment. This, however, used not to be the prevailing view and it was said that contracts of employment form an exceptional category in which the employee has no choice but to accept the repudiation and sue for damages, so that the employer's repudiation automatically terminates the contract.[153] Thus, for example, in *Sanders v Ernest A Neale Ltd*,[154] Sir John Donaldson P said:

> The obvious, and indeed the only, explanation is that the repudiation of a contract of employment is an exception to the general rule. It terminates the contract without the necessity for acceptance by the injured party.

[148] For an analysis of the difficult case law on remedies and possible developments see Ewing 'Remedies for Breach of the Contract of Employment' [1993] CLJ 405.

[149] *Whitwood Chemical Co v Hardman* [1891] 2 Ch 416, CA. For a peculiar application of this on the facts (employee not seeking to continue his contract per se, but rather to continue to exercise his contractual rights as a shop steward in spite of being suspended), see *City and Hackney Health Authority v NUPE* [1985] IRLR 252, CA.

[150] (1890) 45 Ch D 430 at 438.

[151] Or, in an appropriate case, a quantum meruit action: *Planché v Colburn* (1831) 8 Bing 14.

[152] *Howard v Pickford Tool Co Ltd* [1951] 1 KB 417 at 421, CA, per Asquith LJ. See *White and Carter (Councils) Ltd v McGregor* [1962] AC 413, [1961] 3 All ER 1178, HL.

[153] *Denmark Productions Ltd v Boscobel Productions Ltd* [1969] 1 QB 699, [1968] 3 All ER 513, CA.

[154] [1974] 3 All ER 327 at 333, [1974] ICR 565 at 571.

In *Vine v National Dock Labour Board*,[155] a dismissal was held to be invalid on the peculiar facts of the case (considered presently), but Viscount Kilmuir LC was at pains to point out:

> This is an entirely different situation from the ordinary master and servant case; there, if a master wrongfully dismisses the servant, either summarily or by insufficient notice, the employment is effectively terminated, albeit in breach of contract.

He approved the decision of Jenkins LJ in the Court of Appeal[156] that:

> in the ordinary case of master and servant the repudiation or the wrongful dismissal puts an end to the contract, and the contract having been wrongfully put an end to a claim for damages arises. It is necessarily a claim for damages and nothing more. The nature of the bargain is such that it can be nothing more.

However, this doctrine of automatic (or 'unilateral') termination was doubted in cases such as *Decro-Wall International SA v Practitioners in Marketing Ltd*,[157] *Hill v C A Parsons & Co Ltd*,[158] and *C H Giles & Co Ltd v Morris*.[159] These decisions noted that the rule against enforcement is not a rule of law but only a question of fact (albeit frequently recurring fact), in that in nearly all cases the basis of mutual confidence has been destroyed and it would be futile to keep the employment relationship in being. Subsequently, this alternative doctrine of elective (or 'acceptance') termination gained ground, for example in the judgment of Megarry V-C in *Thomas Marshall (Exports) Ltd v Guinle*,[160] in the majority decision of the Court of Appeal in *Gunton v Richmond-upon-Thames London Borough Council*,[161] and in the judgment of Hodgson J in *Dietman v Brent London Borough Council*.[162] In *Gunton*'s case the majority, having clearly decided in favour of the elective theory, went on to stress (a) that in most cases the employee will have no option in reality but to accept the employer's repudiation and seek a remedy in damages,[163] and (b) that the rule of practice against specific enforcement of contracts of employment remains strong and may operate independently of the elective theory

[155] [1957] AC 488 at 500, [1956] 3 All ER 939 at 944, HL.

[156] [1956] 1 QB 658 at 674, [1956] 1 All ER 1 at 8, CA.

[157] [1971] 2 All ER 216, [1971] 1 WLR 361, CA, per Salmon and Sachs LJJ; aliter per Buckley LJ. The majority judgments are cogently criticized by Sir John Donaldson P in *Sanders v Ernest A Neale Ltd* [1974] 3 All ER 327, [1974] ICR 565.

[158] [1972] Ch 305, [1971] 3 All ER 1345, CA, per Lord Denning MR and Sachs LJ. The more traditional view that there is a rule of law against enforcement is well set out in Stamp LJ's dissenting judgment at 322 and 1357, respectively.

[159] [1972] 1 All ER 960 at 970, [1972] 1 WLR 307 at 318, per Megarry J.

[160] [1978] 3 All ER 193, [1978] ICR 905.

[161] [1980] ICR 755, [1980] IRLR 321, CA, per Buckley and Brightman LJJ. Shaw LJ dissented on the reasoning, adopting the automatic approach, but concurred in the result on the facts. The later decision of the Court of Appeal in *London Transport Executive v Clarke* [1981] ICR 355, [1981] IRLR 166, CA, though of fundamental importance on the statutory definition of dismissal, was ambiguous on this point of theory.

[162] [1987] ICR 737, [1987] IRLR 259; upheld on appeal [1988] ICR 842, [1988] IRLR 299, CA.

[163] See eg *Dietman v Brent London Borough Council*, n 161, where the acceptance theory was applied, but the court found acceptance established on the facts fairly readily. In *Delaney v Staples* [1992] ICR 483 at 489, [1992] IRLR 191 at 193, HL, Lord Browne-Wilkinson spoke of an unequivocal instant (wrongful) dismissal being 'effective to put an end to the employment relationship, whether or not it unilaterally discharges the contract of employment'. Moreover, in *Marsh v National Autistic Society* [1993] ICR 453 it was held that, even if the elective theory is applied, the demise of the employment relationship will mean that the employee may not sue in debt for continuing wages, but will be confined to the (restricted) action for damages.

so that while, for some purposes,[164] an employee may wish to argue that they did not accept the employer's repudiation, they will not normally be allowed to do so in order to claim specific performance (directly or indirectly). In *Gunton*'s case the elective theory was invoked to attack the validity of a dismissal which had omitted proper observance of a contractually binding disciplinary procedure, the plaintiff claiming that he never accepted this repudiation by the employer; to that extent it succeeded, but given that the employer could have dismissed lawfully by going through the procedure properly, the court held that the normal rule on damages for wrongful dismissal applied and all that the plaintiff was entitled to was his wages until the date on which a proper dismissal could have been achieved after exhaustion of the procedure. The plaintiff thus succeeded in invalidating the original dismissal, but only obtained a short stay of execution and a few weeks' extra pay (representing the time it would have taken to exhaust the procedure). He certainly did not get his job back.

Meanwhile, the automatic theory continued to appeal to some judges; in *R v East Berkshire Health Authority, ex p Walsh*[165] in the Court of Appeal, May LJ stated unequivocally that he preferred the dissenting judgment of Shaw LJ in *Gunton* and the automatic view; Sir John Donaldson MR was clearly not ecstatic about the overruling by the majority in *Gunton* of his own previous decision in *Sanders v Ernest A Neale Ltd*;[166] and in *Boyo v Lambeth London Borough Council*[167] the Court of Appeal applied the *ratio* of *Gunton* (to allow wages for a short extra period that it would have taken the employer to go through the contractual disciplinary procedure properly) but stated its unease at doing so, making it clear that it had grave doubts about the reasoning of the majority in that case.

6.4.2.3 *Geys* and the elective theory

The question of which theory (elective or automatic) was to be preferred remained undecided until the issue reached the Supreme Court in *Société Générale v Geys*.[168] *Geys* was one of the rare cases where it made a great deal of difference whether the contract was held to have terminated when the employer wrongfully repudiated it, or when the employer lawfully terminated according to the terms of the contract. Mr Geys was a managing director of the respondent Bank; under his contract he was entitled to a 'Compensation Payment' upon termination that was more than €5 million higher if his contract ended on or after 1 January 2008 than if it ended before that date. The Bank summarily dismissed Mr Geys, in breach of his contract, on 29 November 2007, but Mr Geys consulted a solicitor, refusing to accept the unlawful dismissal, and the Bank (very unwisely, as it turns out) proceeded to enter into some semblance of severance negotiation with him. When these negotiations went nowhere the Bank lawfully exercised a clause in the employment contract allowing for 'payment in lieu of notice' (PILON) by making a direct deposit into Mr Geys' account, in the required amount of three months' salary, on 18 December

[164] See eg the continued existence of the contractual term restricting the employee's activities during employment in *Thomas Marshall (Exports) Ltd v Guinle* (n 160) in spite of the employee's wrongful resignation, the desire in *C H Giles & Co Ltd v Morris* (n 159) to put the plaintiff into employment in the first place, if only so that his remedies would be better when then dismissed, and the (unsuccessful) attempt to enforce a shop steward's contractual right to enter the employer's premises in spite of being under suspension in *City and Hackney Health Authority v National Union of Public Employees* [1985] IRLR 252, CA. More recently, there have been attempts to seek specific enforcement of contracts of employment in order to insist on disciplinary procedures being properly applied—see 6.4.2.4.

[165] [1984] ICR 743, [1984] IRLR 278, CA. [166] See n 157.

[167] [1994] ICR 727, [1995] IRLR 50, CA. Appearing in person, the employee (who was on a month's notice) had initially argued that, as he had not accepted the employer's repudiation, he was entitled to his wages up to the year 2000(!).

[168] [2013] IRLR 122, [2013] ICR 177, SC.

2007. However, although Mr Geys noticed the deposit at some point before the end of December 2007, the Bank did not inform him what the deposit was for, or that it was activating the relevant contract clause (and in so doing terminating his contract), until after 1 January 2008. The central question in the case, then, was whether the contract ended when Mr Geys was notified of the lawful termination, or when he was subjected to the unlawful summary dismissal that he refused to accept.

Given that the 4–1 majority (Lord Sumption dissenting) agreed that notice of the lawful exercise of the PILON provision was required for it to be effective, and was not achieved by an unexplained bank deposit,[169] the date of contract termination turned exclusively on whether the November 2007 repudiation automatically terminated the contract without Mr Geys' acceptance or 'election'. The Court concluded that it did not, and in so doing settled the automatic/elective theory debate. Although the majority noted that the reasoning behind the automatic theory was fatally circular ('The circularity is that there is no remedy so there is no right so there is no remedy'),[170] the decision turned primarily on the fact that to adopt such a theory would be to depart from normal contract principles only to allow a wrong-doer to benefit from a wrong:

> In proposing that the court should indorse the automatic theory, the Bank invites it to cause the law of England and Wales in relation to contracts of employment to set sail, unaccompanied, upon a journey for which I can discern no just purpose and can identify no final destination. I consider, on the contrary, that we should keep the contract of employment firmly within the harbour which the common law has solidly constructed for the entire fleet of contracts in order to protect the innocent party, as far as practicable, from the consequences of the other's breach.[171]

Thus with regard to the termination of an employment contract by repudiatory breach (and hence with regard to wrongful dismissal), *Geys* has confirmed *Gunton*: the hesitancy to employ specific enforcement remains, and the usual remedy remains damages, but the non-repudiating party must accept the repudiation, by word or deed, before the contract can be deemed at an end. This can work against an employee, such as when they leave without giving contractual notice to work for a competitor and the employer refuses to accept the repudiation, instead securing an injunction to prevent the move.[172]

When one turns to the possible impact of this decision on statutory dismissal rights the picture becomes much more complicated, and in fact it is in the statutory context (usually of unfair dismissal) that most of the active dispute originally arose. It was always a problem with the automatic theory that if applied to the statutory definition of dismissal[173] it could support the idea of 'self-dismissal', that is, that if an employee misbehaves sufficiently badly they can be said to have repudiated their contract of employment, thus automatically terminating it; if this were so, there would be no 'dismissal' by the employer and so the tribunal would be denied jurisdiction to hear a claim of unfair dismissal. The elective theory in fact fits the statutory definition of dismissal much better, for if acceptance of a repudiation is required, the termination of the misbehaving employee's contract is brought about by the employer's acceptance of the repudiation and *is* thus 'dismissal' by the employer;[174] on the other hand, if the *employer* repudiates the contract, termination

[169] [2012] UKSC 63, paras 54–60 (Lady Hale).

[170] [2012] UKSC 63, para 89 (Lord Wilson).

[171] [2012] UKSC 63, para 97 (Lord Wilson).

[172] *Sunrise Brokers LLP v Rodgers* [2014] EWCA Civ 1373, [2015] IRLR 57.

[173] Contained in the Employment Rights Act 1996, s 95 (in relation to unfair dismissal) and s 136 (in relation to redundancy).

[174] Within ss 95(1)(a) and 136(1)(a).

is brought about by the employee's acceptance, but this is specifically covered by statute which deems it to be a 'constructive dismissal'.[175] The *elective* theory is thus important for the actual definition of dismissal.

However, the difficulty arises if one applies it to the *date* of dismissal. It is important to know precisely the date for the purpose of applying the stringent time limits in the statute (particularly the limitation period for starting an unfair dismissal action of three months from the 'effective date of termination'),[176] but if an employee could claim that they had in fact refused to accept the employer's repudiation, they could argue that the time limit either never started to run or, at least, started to run at some time significantly later than the wording of the statutory definition of 'effective date of termination' would suggest. In the interests of certainty, therefore, it is important that the *automatic* theory be applied to questions of limitation.

One commentator has made a strong case for adopting this differential approach in the statutory context,[177] and this now seems to be the position in practice—in *London Transport Executive v Clarke*[178] the Court of Appeal by a majority disapproved of the idea of 'self-dismissal', applying the elective theory, whereas in *Brown v Southall and Knight*[179] and *Robert Cort & Son Ltd v Charman*[180] the EAT rejected arguments based upon that theory when determining the effective date of termination, preferring instead an automatic termination approach based on (a) the wording of the statutory definition of effective date of termination and (b) the need for certainty on this vital concept. As long as this practical compromise is maintained, the position now seems to be satisfactory, and there is no obvious reason to believe that *Geys*, which did not discuss statutory dismissal, would change that. However, if there were in the future any real danger of the reintroduction of the sort of uncertainty that existed prior to this case law, the time would surely be ripe for legislative clarification.

6.4.2.4 **Exceptions to the rule against enforcement**

Returning to the common law position, and accepting that there is at least a rule of practice (if not an absolute rule of law) against enforcing contracts of employment in most cases, we must now consider certain established exceptions.

A negative restraint clause

Where the employee has agreed in the contract not to do certain things (eg not to perform for any other theatre owner during the currency of the contract, or not to work for a competitor within a certain period after leaving the employment),[181] the court will hold them to their promise and enforce that negative stipulation (even if it would not enforce the positive obligations in the contract).[182] It is immaterial that this may indirectly persuade the employee to remain in the employment (ie that it may have indirectly a positive effect), but on the other hand it is well established that the clause must be bona fide, in particular that it must not be in reality a positive obligation, merely expressed in a negative way.[183] Moreover, an injunction will not be granted if the practical effect would

[175] Within ss 95(1)(c) and 136(1)(c): see 7.2.1. [176] See 7.2.2.

[177] McMullen in his very useful article 'A Synthesis of the Mode of Termination of Contracts of Employment' [1982] CLJ 110.

[178] [1981] ICR 355, [1981] IRLR 166, CA. [179] [1980] ICR 617, [1980] IRLR 130.

[180] [1981] ICR 816, [1981] IRLR 437, approved by the Court of Appeal in *Stapp v Shaftesbury Society* [1982] IRLR 326, CA.

[181] See 2.4.2 .[182] *Lumley v Wagner* (1852) 1 De GM & G 604.

[183] *Davis v Foreman* [1894] 3 Ch 654; *Warner Bros Pictures Inc v Nelson* [1937] 1 KB 209, [1936] 3 All ER 160.

be to compel the employee to perform his or her side of the contract or starve (eg where the stipulation is that they will not take any employment for a period after leaving the employment).[184]

The decision in Hill v C A Parsons & Co Ltd

In this case,[185] the plaintiff refused to join a union which had negotiated a closed shop with his employers, who therefore gave him one month's notice of dismissal. He had been employed by them for 35 years as a chartered engineer and had two years to go to retirement, so that the dismissal would affect his pension rights; moreover, the unfair dismissal legislation was due to come into force within six months of the dismissal. The plaintiff sued the employers for wrongful dismissal and claimed an interim injunction restraining them from treating the notice as terminating his employment. This could be construed as enforcing the contract of employment, but the Court of Appeal by a majority (Lord Denning MR and Sachs and Stamp LJJ dissenting) granted the interim injunction. The imminence of the new legislation was obviously a strong background factor (and hence the finding that proper notice would have been at least six months for a man in his position), but to find in the plaintiff's favour the majority had to go against the normal rule against enforcement (the application of which was the basis of Stamp LJ's dissent). To do so they held that that rule is not a fixed rule of law, but a question of fact which therefore permits exceptions in cases where the usual reasons against enforcement do not apply, in particular where there is continued confidence between the parties (as in this case, where both the parties wanted to continue the employment and the pressure to terminate it came from the trade union).[186] Further, Lord Denning said that in this case damages were not an adequate remedy, so it was right that an injunction should be granted, on the principle 'ubi jus ibi remedium'[187] which would allow the court to 'step over the trip-wires of previous cases and to bring the law into accord with the needs of today'.

It may certainly be argued that justice was done to the plaintiff in this case, but it left many questions open which would have had to have been solved had this area of law not been effectively superseded by the introduction in 1971 of the unfair dismissal action, particularly as the case cast doubt on the general principle previously discussed that when an employer repudiates a contract of employment, that automatically terminates the contract and the employee must accept the repudiation and sue for damages; this raised the problem of what circumstances would put a case into the category in which the employer's repudiation might not have this automatic effect, and opened the way for rather refined arguments based on the concept of repudiation which at times, it is submitted, could stray a long way from the realities of employment.[188] In the event, the case did not lead to a radical reappraisal of enforcement of contracts of employment at common law, and was restrictively construed in subsequent cases as a rare case on its facts, relying upon the continued existence of mutual confidence between the parties, which is unlikely to be so

[184] *Rely-a-Bell Burglar and Fire Alarm Co Ltd v Eisler* [1926] Ch 609; *Warner Bros Pictures Inc v Nelson* [1937] 1 KB 209, [1936] 3 All ER 160; *Page One Records Ltd v Britton* [1967] 3 All ER 822, [1968] 1 WLR 157; *Warren v Mendy* [1989] ICR 525, [1989] IRLR 210, CA.

[185] [1972] Ch 305, [1971] 3 All ER 1345, CA.

[186] This view of the facts was disputed by Stamp LJ.

[187] 'Where there is a right, there is a remedy', but in this context perhaps best translated as 'where there is a will, there is a way'.

[188] See eg *Shields Furniture Ltd v Goff* [1973] 2 All ER 653, [1973] ICR 187, NIRC.

in many cases.[189] However, the case is a decision of the Court of Appeal and at least shows that there may be some scope for enforcement of the contract as a remedy at common law.

Subsequently, at times, interest has been rekindled to some extent in the possibility of such a common law remedy. In *Irani v Southampton and South West Hampshire Health Authority*,[190] Warner J applied *Hill v C A Parsons & Co Ltd* to grant an injunction restraining a dismissal in breach of quasi-statutory disciplinary procedures. A similar result was reached by Mervyn Davies J in *Wadcock v London Borough of Brent*[191] and by Morland J in *Robb v London Borough of Hammersmith and Fulham*[192] in the case of contractually binding disciplinary procedures. In *Powell v London Borough of Brent*,[193] the Court of Appeal granted an interlocutory injunction restraining the employers from depriving the employee of a promotion for which she had successfully applied. In *Hughes v London Borough of Southwark*,[194] Taylor J granted an interlocutory injunction restraining the employers from insisting on the employees taking on work which the latter argued was not within their contractual obligations. In *Anderson v Pringle of Scotland Ltd*,[195] Lord Prosser granted an interim interdict to restrain a redundancy dismissal in breach of a LIFO (last in, first out) redundancy agreement which was assumed to be part of the employee's individual contract. In *Peace v City of Edinburgh Council*,[196] Lord Penrose restrained the disciplining (*short* of dismissal) of the employee under a new procedure to which he argued he had not consented as part of his contract. And in *Gryf-Lowczowski v Hitchingbrooke Healthcare NHS Trust*,[197] Gray J restrained a threatened dismissal in breach of contractual procedures which would have prejudiced a doctor's chance of re-employment by a different trust.

In these cases, the basis of the court's power to intervene is clearly seen as the (argued) continued existence of mutual confidence between the parties,[198] with the exception of

[189] *GKN (Cwmbran) Ltd v Lloyd* [1972] ICR 214; *Sanders v Ernest A Neale Ltd* [1974] 3 All ER 327, [1974] ICR 565; *Chappell v Times Newspapers Ltd* [1975] 2 All ER 233, [1975] ICR 145, CA; *City and Hackney Health Authority v NUPE* [1985] IRLR 252, CA. In *GKN (Cwmbran) Ltd v Lloyd* Sir John Donaldson P suggested (at 221) that a further material factor in *Hill v C A Parsons & Co Ltd* was that the actual dismissal had not taken place, so that the court was restraining a proposed dismissal, not putting an employee back into employment after he had been effectively dismissed. This point was also stressed by Lord Prosser in the Court of Session in *Anderson v Pringle of Scotland Ltd* [1998] IRLR 64.

[190] [1985] ICR 590, [1985] IRLR 203. [191] [1990] IRLR 223. [192] [1991] ICR 514, [1991] IRLR 72.

[193] [1988] ICR 176, [1987] IRLR 466, CA; after the plaintiff's successful application for the senior post, one of the unsuccessful applicants claimed that the council's equal opportunity policy had been infringed and so the council purported to negate the promotion and re-advertise the post.

[194] [1988] IRLR 55. In *Ali v London Borough of Southwark* [1988] ICR 567, [1988] IRLR 100 a challenge to threatened disciplinary proceedings that the plaintiff said would be irregular failed on two grounds: (a) no continued mutual confidence; (b) the court will not normally step in in advance to restrain pending disciplinary proceedings (applying the similar rule in trade union cases, in *Longley v National Union of Journalists* [1987] IRLR 109, CA).

[195] [1998] IRLR 64, OH. Lord Prosser stated that 'such exceptional cases as there have been give no very clear picture of the criteria for intervention', but justified his order on the grounds that (a) there was no evidence of loss of trust in the employee (this being a redundancy case) and (b) court intervention was possible before the dismissal was due to take place.

[196] [1999] IRLR 417, OH. Here it was important that it was a breach of contract during employment that was being restrained, and that both parties were assuming that the contract was to continue.

[197] [2006] IRLR 100.

[198] This means either no loss of confidence on the facts or, possibly, that any such loss by the employer is on irrational grounds, and so rectifiable. In *Hughes*, Taylor J said that mutual confidence should not be considered to have gone merely because the employer and employee are in genuine dispute as to the construction or application of certain contractual terms or duties. Note, however, that in *Robb* Morland J took a slightly different approach, saying that, while continued trust and confidence is important where the employee is trying to get his job back, if (as in that case) the employee was only interested in securing use of the disciplinary procedure in order to air his grievances the test should be whether a court order would actually be workable.

Gryf-Lowczowski, where mutual confidence had vanished but it was held that this was outweighed by the factors that timely intervention was possible and the claimant's professional future was at stake. However, the point remains that these are *not* ordinary, everyday dismissal cases (indeed, *Powell*, *Hughes*, and *Peace* are not dismissal cases at all) and while they may point to interesting and useful developments in the use (or threatened use) of the common law to restrain employer misuses of contractually binding disciplinary procedures,[199] it would be premature to consider them as showing a resurgence of common law actions aimed at preserving employment in wrongful dismissal cases generally, particularly as it is equally possible to point to contemporaneous decisions refusing similar relief for traditional reasons.[200]

Where the dismissal is a nullity

In certain public sector cases, a dismissed employee may be able to invoke certain administrative law remedies to argue that his or her dismissal was invalid; if this is accepted, the legal result is that there was no effective dismissal, and so the contract of employment will be indirectly enforced. The two principal bases for challenge are that the dismissal was contrary to the rules of natural justice or was in some way ultra vires.[201] There has been considerable case law on this question, though in the modern case law the emphasis has switched to consideration of how this confusing area of law fits in with the procedure for claiming judicial review under what was originally RSC Order 53 and is now CPR 54. In turn, this has coincided with increased interest in this area of employment law, since it is well appreciated now that in unfair dismissal cases tribunals hardly ever order reinstatement or re-engagement; thus any remedy that may in fact keep the employee in employment such as this may well be worth pursuing, certainly in cases arising in the public sector.

6.4.2.5 **Damages for wrongful dismissal**

The remedies for wrongful dismissal are limited not only by the rule against enforcement but also by the restricted measure of damages recoverable in many cases. The restriction arises once again from the doctrine of notice, because if an employer wrongfully dismisses an employee who should have had, say, two weeks' notice, what has the employee in fact lost? They cannot be said to have lost their long-term livelihood, because at common law they could have been dismissed at any time merely by being given two weeks' notice. Thus, all that they have lost is their two weeks' notice, and so their measure of

[199] Similar proceedings can be seen in *Deitman v Brent London Borough Council* [1988] IRLR 299, CA.

[200] *Alexander v Standard Telephones and Cables plc* [1990] ICR 291, [1990] IRLR 55; *Jakeman v South West Thames Regional Health Authority and London Ambulance Service* [1990] IRLR 62; *Wishart v NACAB Ltd* [1990] ICR 794, [1990] IRLR 383, CA.

[201] Ganz 'Public Law Principles Applicable to Dismissal from Employment' (1967) 30 MLR 288; Freedland *The Contract of Employment* (1976) pp 278–92; Davidson 'Judicial Review of Decisions to Dismiss' (1984) 35 NILQ 121 (written before the decision in *ex p Walsh*, n 164); Fredman and Lee 'Natural Justice for Employees' (1986) 15 ILJ 15; Ewing and Grubb 'The Emergence of a New Labour Injunction?' (1987) 16 ILJ 145; Fredman and Morris 'Public or Private? State Employees and Judicial Review' (1991) 107 LQR 298; Sedley 'Public Law and Contractual Entitlement' (1994) 23 ILJ 201; Laws 'Public Law and Employment Law: Abuse of Power' [1997] PL 455; Freedland (1990) 19 ILJ 199, (1991) 20 ILJ 72; Carty (1991) 54 MLR 129; Smith and Randall *Contract Actions in Modern Employment Law: Developments and Issues* (2002) ch 10. Presumably other public law grounds of challenge such as perversity would be applicable, though less likely to succeed: see *R v Hertfordshire County Council, ex p NUPE* [1985] IRLR 258, CA.

damage is restricted to their pay during that period.[202] This is backed by the general principle that in a damages action, the employers must be assumed to have discharged their contractual duties towards the employee in the way least onerous to them, which will usually mean assuming that they would have ended the contract in any event, as quickly as they could lawfully have done so (usually by giving notice).[203] Basically, therefore, a wrongfully dismissed employee is entitled to damages equal to their wages or salary during their notice period.[204]

Moreover, the common law was always wary of giving further damages under other heads. Thus, in *Addis v Gramophone Co Ltd*,[205] an employee who was paid at a fixed salary plus commission was wrongfully dismissed and claimed damages under the following heads—(a) salary for the six-month notice period, (b) reasonable commission for a six-month period, (c) damages for the humiliating manner of dismissal, (d) damages for loss of reputation leading to future difficulty in obtaining employment. The House of Lords held by a majority that only heads (a) and (b) were recoverable. Also, the law only looked at the definite contractual liabilities of the employer in assessing damages, not at what the employee might in fact have received (eg a discretionary bonus which he might have received during the notice period). In *Lavarack v Woods of Colchester Ltd*,[206] an employee who was wrongfully dismissed had been on a five-year contract with a fixed salary subject to periodic discretionary bonuses. After he had been dismissed (but during the period for which the contract should have continued), the employers discontinued the bonus scheme and increased the wages of their staff. The Court of Appeal held by a majority that the increase in wages should not be taken into account when assessing the damages, since the only fully contractual obligation upon the employers was to pay the fixed salary and anything on top of that was discretionary (whether a bonus or an increase in wages).

[202] A gloss here is that if a contractually binding disciplinary procedure has been breached, a court may look at when the contract could lawfully have been terminated, awarding damages for a short period representing the time necessary to have operated the procedure properly and then the notice period: *Gunton v Richmond-upon-Thames London Borough Council* [1980] ICR 755, [1980] IRLR 321, CA; *Boyo v Lambeth London Borough Council* [1994] ICR 727, [1995] IRLR 50, CA. However, a court or tribunal cannot go further and speculate on the chances of the employee having been kept on if the proper procedure had gone in his or her favour: *Fosca Services (UK) Ltd v Birkett* [1996] IRLR 325; *Janciuk v Winerite Ltd* [1998] IRLR 63, EAT.

[203] This principle, taken from the majority decision in *Lavarack v Woods of Colchester Ltd* [1967] 1 QB 278, [1966] 3 All ER 683, CA, was applied strongly in *Janciuk v Winerite Ltd*, n 201, *Morran v Glasgow Council of Tenants' Associations* [1998] IRLR 67, Ct of Sess and *Mackenzie v Automobile Association* [2022] EWCA Civ 901.

[204] One slight extension here is that the employee may also claim any benefit that he would have qualified for, had he been given and served out the proper length of notice: *Silvey v Pendragon plc* [2001] EWCA Civ 789, [2001] IRLR 685 (proper notice would have taken the employee past the age of 55, which was significant for pension purposes; damages awarded to reflect this). It is of course possible that the contract may itself quantify the amount to be paid on termination (especially in the case of a high earner); a danger with this is that, on ordinary contract principles, it may be attacked as a penalty clause, but in *Murray v Leisureplay Ltd* [2005] IRLR 946, CA the court took an indulgent approach to this and validated such a 'golden parachute' clause.

[205] [1909] AC 488, HL, reaffirmed in *Bliss v South East Thames Regional Health Authority* [1987] ICR 700, [1985] IRLR 308, CA. See *Alexander v Standard Telephones and Cables Ltd (No 2)* [1991] IRLR 286. The employee's remedy lies in damages; he or she may not sue instead in debt for continuing wages into the future: *Marsh v National Autistic Society* [1993] ICR 453.

[206] [1967] 1 QB 278, [1966] 3 All ER 683, CA; *Bold v Brough, Nicholson and Hall Ltd* [1963] 3 All ER 849, [1964] 1 WLR 201. Damages for loss of rights under a share option scheme were refused because of a literal interpretation of the scheme's rules in *Micklefield v SAC Technology Ltd* [1991] 1 All ER 275, [1990] IRLR 218.

Lord Denning MR, dissenting, took the wider view that the dismissed employee was entitled to recover all that he would *in fact* have earned but for the employers' breach of contract.

To this harsh general rule on damages, there are exceptions:

1. *Fixed-term contracts*: Where the contract of employment is for a fixed term, not terminable by notice, the damages recoverable are the amount which the employee would have earned under the contract during the remainder of the term, after the wrongful dismissal (subject to mitigation, which is considered presently).[207]
2. *Additional benefit work*: Certain untypical contracts of employment may be construed as envisaging a greater reward for the employee than the bare wage or salary, so that damages in respect of this further loss can be recovered in addition. Thus in *Marbé v George Edwardes (Daly's Theatres) Ltd*,[208] an American actress wishing to establish her reputation in London contracted to play a particular part for the defendant, who undertook to give her full publicity. When she was wrongfully denied the chance to play the part, the Court of Appeal held that she could recover the salary due to her for the period of the contract plus an amount representing loss of reputation. The extent of this exception outside the theatre is uncertain (quaere, for example, whether it would apply to any case where the courts found that there was a contractual obligation to provide the employee with actual work, not simply to pay wages),[209] but one case which is at least analogous is *Dunk v George Waller & Son Ltd*,[210] where the plaintiff, an apprentice, was wrongfully dismissed during the four-year term in question and was held entitled to his net loss of wages for the rest of the term plus an amount representing loss of tuition and training and diminution of future prospects.

One possible variant of this may be where the extra 'benefit' that the employee expects under the contract is so important that the court will imply a term that the employer will not use the normal power to dismiss by notice so as to deprive the employee of that benefit. This has arisen in the 'PHI cases', where a long-term sick employee is deprived of major financial benefits under a permanent health insurance (PHI) scheme, provided by the employer, through the employer dismissing him by notice before he can qualify under the scheme.[211] In such cases, courts have impliedly restricted the power to give notice in sickness absences where the result would be deprivation of PHI rights. Thus, a dismissal (otherwise lawful under the contractual notice provision) may become wrongful, with the prospect opening up of *general* damages for loss of those rights. An open question then becomes whether the PHI cases could be extended to other analogous contexts. This was done in *Jenvey v Australian Broadcasting Corpn*,[212] where damages were awarded for the loss of valuable redundancy rights under the contract due to an unlawful early dismissal held to be wrongful because of its effect. Another interesting possibility might be where an employee is taken on specifically in order to bring with them particular trade, contacts, or contracts to the new employer: could it be argued that it is an implied term that they will not be dismissed (other than for gross misconduct) as long as the employer

[207] *Hall v London Lions Basketball Club UK Ltd* UKEAT/0273/19.

[208] [1928] 1 KB 269, CA. See also *Herbert Clayton and Jack Waller Ltd v Oliver* [1930] AC 209, HL; *Withers v General Theatre Corpn Ltd* [1933] 2 KB 536, CA.

[209] See 3.3.2.

[210] [1970] 2 QB 163, [1970] 2 All ER 630. Quaere whether the reasoning in this case applies only to apprenticeship, or might be applicable to any contract of employment envisaging vocational training or retraining.

[211] *Aspden v Webbs Poultry and Meat Group (Holdings) Ltd* [1996] IRLR 521; *Adin v Sedco Forex International Resources Ltd* [1997] IRLR 280, Ct of Sess; see 3.3.7.3.

[212] [2003] ICR 79, [2002] IRLR 520; see 3.3.7.

retains that trade, etc, so that general damages for wrongful dismissal could be awarded for any such dismissal?[213]

3. *Loss of statutory rights*: A third exceptional case seemed to have become established but has subsequently been disapproved. It concerned the case where the employer breaks the contract of employment by dismissing the employee with no or short notice, thereby depriving them of their statutory rights (especially the right to claim unfair dismissal) by advancing the effective date of dismissal to *within* the qualifying period. In such a case, the employee would be debarred from claiming unfair dismissal (if that were the right in question), but it was suggested that the employee might be able to bring an action in the ordinary courts for *wrongful* dismissal claiming extra damages representing the loss to them of their potential statutory rights.[214] This seemed to be a practical answer to the possible problem of an employer being able to rely on the relatively rigid rules on dates of termination and qualifying periods through deliberate breach of contract on its own part, and an award of damages on this basis was finally permitted by the EAT in *Raspin v United News Shops Ltd*,[215] where a summary dismissal three weeks short of the unfair dismissal qualifying period was held to have been wrongful *and* in breach of a contractually binding disciplinary procedure, proper exhaustion of which would have taken long enough to have allowed the employee to reach the qualifying period. Unfortunately for employees in this position, *Raspin* was reconsidered by the Court of Appeal in *Harper v Virgin Net Ltd*[216] and was held to have been wrongly decided in the light of later developments in the common law. Thus, the wrongful dismissal action now cannot be used to challenge an employer's cynical use of short notice to avoid an unfair dismissal claim.
4. *Discretionary benefits*: The fourth exception arises from potentially significant applications of the modern term of trust and respect[217] and even wider ideas borrowed from administrative law to the area of damages. In *Clark v BET plc*,[218] a wrongful dismissal claim by a highly paid chief executive on a three-year fixed-term contract, liability was conceded but a major question arose as to quantification of damages because the executive had been heavily reliant for much of his pay package on salary increases and bonuses which, while regularly paid in the past, remained discretionary. On a strict approach (typified by the *Lavarack* case considered earlier and the principle that the employer should normally be assumed to have discharged the contract in the way least onerous to itself) the executive would not have been awarded anything for these heads, because technically the employer could have decided to give *nothing* for the remainder of the contract. However, Walker J avoided that harsh result by looking at what the employers were likely to have paid out (given the firm's known performance over the relevant period) if they had continued to exercise their discretion *in good faith*.

[213] General damages could cause particular problems of quantification in a context such as this; a court or tribunal would have to fix some sort of 'multiplier' to assess the likely period of loss, but without the highly developed 'tariff' system available to perform a similar task in personal injury cases.

[214] *Robert Cort & Son Ltd v Charman* [1981] ICR 816, [1981] IRLR 437, per Browne-Wilkinson J, approved by the Court of Appeal in *Stapp v Shaftesbury Society* [1982] IRLR 326, CA. This analysis does not work if there is an express payment in lieu of notice clause in the contract, because then the instant dismissal is not wrongful: *Morran v Glasgow Council of Tenants' Associations* [1998] IRLR 67, Ct of Sess.

[215] [1999] IRLR 9.

[216] [2004] IRLR 390, CA; damages such as those in *Raspin* were held now to fall foul of the general principles in *Johnson v Unisys* [2001] ICR 480, [2001] IRLR 279, HL: see 7.6.2. *Harper* was applied in *Wise Group v Mitchell* [2005] ICR 896, EAT.

[217] See 3.3.4.

[218] [1997] IRLR 348.

Although only at first instance, this is clearly an important decision in any case where significant elements of remuneration are discretionary, and it does show a significant departure from the straight *Lavarack* approach. A similar result can be seen in *Clark v Nomura International plc*,[219] where an employee who had been a highly successful trader, receiving large annual bonuses clearly linked to his trading profits for the company, was dismissed and awarded a nil bonus for his final year, even though his trading had continued to be profitable. Burton J felt able to quantify what the employee should normally have received on past experience and awarded that as damages. However, he did not do so under the term of trust and respect (which he thought could cause problems of application here, especially if cast in terms of 'capriciousness'); on the other hand, to apply an ordinary test of reasonableness to cases like this would be too low a threshold for controversial legal intervention. His solution was to import the concept of *perversity*, the basis of adjudication being whether the exercise of the employer's discretion was such that no reasonable employer would have behaved in that way (the employer on the facts failing that test here).

Of course, any importation of public/administrative law principles into private law will be both significant and controversial. It was therefore important that this line was then adopted by the Court of Appeal in *Mallone v BPB Industries plc*[220] and *Horkulak v Cantor Fitzgerald International*.[221] In *Mallone* an executive, dismissed due to genuine concerns on the part of the company about his performance, subsequently had his (vested) rights to valuable share options cancelled by the company. This was technically within its powers under the terms of the share option rules (ie within the employer's 'absolute discretion'), but damages for loss of the options were granted on the basis that the company had acted *irrationally* in coming to this decision (especially as there was no documentation showing *how* it had been reached). In *Horkulak* large damages were awarded under an apparently discretionary bonus scheme (as in the two *Clark* cases), and here the Court of Appeal in effect synthesized the two approaches adopted beforehand by finding an implied term that the employer would exercise the discretion genuinely and rationally. Moreover, the court in this case dealt with the old obstacle of *Lavarack v Woods* more directly than in the previous cases, holding that there is no absolute rule that the employer can always exercise a discretion in any way most favourable to itself (especially in a case where the discretionary element is in practice a major element of the payment system).

Arguably, what we are seeing here is the law on damages being used increasingly to control employer discretion, even where that discretion is clearly and deliberately provided for in the contract. Moreover, the end result is coming close to Lord Denning's dissenting view in *Lavarack v Woods* that the employee should be compensated for what, in some sense, they *should* have received in practice. Several implications of this are immediately obvious. The first is that employers may increasingly have to justify their actions not just on the strict wording of the contract but in the light of how and why they exercised the rights or discretions given by that wording (especially on or after dismissal, if there is any suggestion of motives of revenge). The second is that reliance on ideas of perversity or irrationality can provide a wide form of challenge, possibly going beyond pure breach of contract (note that in both *Clark v Nomura* and *Mallone* the dismissals were lawful, and the damages were awarded for the deprivation of the benefits as such, not as part of a wrongful dismissal action). This could provide a wider range of remedies on termination than under traditional analysis. A third implication could arise from ideas expressed in *Mallone* that the vested share option rights were akin to property rights.

[219] [2000] IRLR 766.

[220] [2002] ICR 1045, [2002] IRLR 452, CA; see the discussion in Smith and Randall *Contract Actions in Modern Employment Law: Developments and Issues* (2002) at 101–03.

[221] [2005] ICR 402, [2004] IRLR 942, CA.

Deprivation of such rights can be seen as validating the importation of administrative law ideas—in which case, need they stop at perversity? If emphasis is to be placed on the rationality of the employer's decision (see the concerns of the Court of Appeal about inadequate records), could the employee argue that they have a right to *participate* in the decision-making process (ie a right to be heard)? Might ideas of unlawful bias surface here (eg if two of the three directors on the committee deciding on annual bonuses or the exercise of share options had been responsible for the employee's dismissal in the first place)? This whole area will need much more judicial exploration, but for the moment it seems that at least the foundations have been laid.

Stigma damages

A fifth exception, again appearing to open up wider damages (this time general damages for injury to feelings and/or manner of dismissal), seemed to arise at the highest level but was immediately heavily restricted, being seen as a movement too far in this volatile area. In *Malik v BCCI SA* (in liquidation),[222] ex-employees of the failed BCCI bank claimed damages in respect of injury to their reputation and future employment prospects caused by the bank conducting a dishonest or corrupt business. The House of Lords upheld this claim on the grounds that the conduct of the employer was a serious breach of the implied term of trust and respect (to the evolution of which they gave their clear support).[223] *Addis v Gramophone Co*[224] was subject to considerable scrutiny by Lords Nicholls and Steyn, giving the principal judgments, and was sidestepped partly on the basis that it principally concerned a claim for injury to feelings caused by the wrongful dismissal whereas the claim in *Malik* was clearly for future financial loss caused by the employer's conduct, and partly on the basis that *Addis* was decided well before the development of the term of trust and respect which now occupies a central position in employment law. This new genus of 'stigma damages' caused much interest and was enthusiastically pursued by claimants' lawyers because it seemed to open up a vista into general damages for wrongful dismissal, even though (a) the case was not in fact one of wrongful dismissal but one of breach of contract during employment, and (b) both Law Lords ended their speeches with warnings that the facts in *Malik* were extreme and that in many more ordinary cases there could be severe problems of causation, remoteness, and mitigation.[225] Thus, the case posed the question: a claimant's Pandora's Box or an interesting decision on unusual facts?

Johnson and the 'Johnson exclusion zone'

The argument that *Malik* was *not* meant to allow damages for injury merely to feelings was accepted by the Court of Appeal in *French v Barclays Bank plc*,[226] a common law damages claim involving breach of trust and respect where a head of claim relating to stress and anxiety caused by the breach was disallowed. This was consistent, however, with the view that stigma damages for financial loss would now be claimable, including in a wrongful *dismissal* case, but that view has now been stopped by the further (and very different) decision of the House of Lords in *Johnson v Unisys Ltd*.[227] This was a difficult case on rather unusual facts, since the employee (who had suffered from work-induced stress prior to being summarily dismissed) had already succeeded in an unfair dismissal

[222] [1997] ICR 606, [1997] IRLR 462, HL; see McMullen (1997) 26 ILJ 245.

[223] They added that the trust-destroying conduct did not have to be aimed at the individual, and that it was not necessary that that individual became aware of the conduct while still an employee.

[224] [1909] AC 488, HL.

[225] The claim did indeed finally fail on its facts: *BCCI SA (in liq) v Ali (No 3)* [2002] IRLR 460, CA.

[226] [1998] IRLR 646, CA.

[227] [2001] ICR 480, [2001] IRLR 279, HL.

action, and then brought a substantial claim for damages for wrongful dismissal to the tune of £400,000, alleging that as a result of it he had suffered a nervous breakdown and was unable to work (thus arguably covering both injured feelings *and* future financial loss, though admittedly not in the usual 'stigma' manner). Ruling this claim out, the House of Lords confined stigma damages to the (highly unusual) case of an employee suing the employer for breach of contract *during* employment. Such damages, they said, are *not* available on termination (ie in a wrongful dismissal action), for (it appeared from the logic of the decision) two reasons. The first was that, on an analytical level, the implied term of trust and respect (the basis for *Malik*) was aimed at keeping the contract alive and so, ex hypothesi, was not applicable on termination.[228] The second was the interesting and novel constitutional point that the common law was not to be developed in such a way as to evade or negative statutory employment law. Parliament has provided the law of unfair dismissal to deal with employer abuses of power on termination, but it has laid down limitations such as the short time limit and (crucially) the statutory cap on the amount of compensation that can be claimed and awarded. A new law on stigma damages in a common law wrongful dismissal action could be used to sidestep unfair dismissal, which, said Lord Hoffmann, was the proper action in which to claim more general compensation for an abusive dismissal.[229]

The *Johnson* ruling has been confirmed and clarified in a number of subsequent cases, but perhaps the most contentious has been *Edwards v Chesterfield NHS and Botham v Ministry of Defence*.[230] The Court of Appeal in the two joined cases had given employees a glimmer of hope by ruling that where the employer failed to apply a disciplinary procedure that was enshrined in an express term of the contract, and but for that failure the dismissal would not have happened, there could be a breach of contract action outside the '*Johnson* exclusion zone' (ie the factual area within which the damages could be said to flow from the dismissal, and thus be excluded from a common law action by the reasoning in *Johnson*). This holding was consistent with the first prong of the reasoning in *Johnson*, which attributed the exclusion to the fact that the implied term of trust and confidence had no logical application to a patent dismissal: the breached terms in these cases were express, not implied from the nature of the ongoing employment relationship. Indeed, the dissent, led by Lady Hale, felt that the '*Johnson* line' should be drawn between implied and express terms of the contract, arguing that *Johnson* only held that Parliament, through unfair dismissal, precluded the development of a damages remedy for breach of the implied term of trust and confidence.[231] However, a 4–3 majority of the Supreme Court (with some of the four expressing rationales somewhat divergent from the

[228] This then raised the important question as to the meaning of 'on termination', which governs the width of this exclusion. After the Court of Appeal had split on the point, the House of Lords in *Eastwood v Magnox plc* [2004] ICR 1064, [2004] IRLR 733, HL held that the phrase is to be given a narrow interpretation, restricting the '*Johnson v Unisys* exclusion zone' to distress, psychiatric injury, and so on arising from the dismissal itself. Thus, if the employee has already suffered this damage prior to the eventual dismissal (eg through harassment or bullying before termination, as in *Gogay v Herts CC* [2000] IRLR 703, CA), he or she can bring a common law claim for damages. If, however, they only suffer it because of the dismissal, no such action lies.

[229] This constitutional approach meant that the old authority of *Addis* was not central to the argument of the majority, who accepted that the common law could evolve away from that case but held that it was undesirable to do so. Lord Steyn (dissenting on the reasoning but agreeing with the result on the facts) would have effected such an evolution. Part of Lord Hoffmann's reasoning was that manner of dismissal damages could be awarded for unfair dismissal, but this went against long-standing authority and was strongly disapproved in *Dunnachie v Kingston-upon-Hull CC* [2004] ICR 1052, [2004] IRLR 727, HL.

[230] [2011] UKSC 58. [231] [2011] UKSC 58, para 121.

leading judgment) found that breaches of express terms in the employment contract that lead to dismissal are also within the '*Johnson* zone', such that any damages flowing from the dismissal must be dealt with through the unfair dismissal procedure and subject to its caps. All of the judgments (including concurrences and dissents) treated *Johnson* as having been based exclusively on the logic that Parliament occupied the field of damages for dismissal when it enacted the unfair dismissal laws, making no mention of *Johnson*'s parallel reliance on the paradox of claiming that a dismissal could somehow breach the implied term of trust and confidence (given that all dismissals seek not to maintain the relationship of trust and confidence but to end it).

This is interesting, because the 'Parliament has occupied the field' argument is seductively flexible, making it possible to sidestep contract law principles and simply argue about what Parliament must have intended to preclude. Lady Hale, at least, observed how fanciful it is to assume that either the parties to employment contracts or Parliament 'intend' there to be no remedy for contractual provisions whose breach happens to result in a dismissal. She rightly asked how this logic would hold up in the face of a contract that specifies dismissal only for cause: is the common law to assume that Parliament intended to preclude action for breach of such a clause, and the awarding of damages that naturally flow from that breach?[232] However, the majority was satisfied that wherever the damages sought flow from a dismissal, the *Johnson* zone cannot be 'finessed' by pointing to even an express contract breach which caused the dismissal.[233] Indeed, Lord Phillips added to the already crude logic of a blanket parliamentary preclusion the even more crude claim that because *Addis* ruled out stigma damages for the ordinary notice-breach wrongful dismissal, such damages could not be recovered no matter what rendered the dismissal 'wrongful'.[234] This is crude because it ignores the fact that in the common wrongful dismissal action, such as that addressed in *Addis*, the dismissal could have been effected lawfully, and the stigma would be the same, so the only damage from the wrongful act was the difference in wages between the unlawful and lawful dismissals. In *Edwards*, on the other hand, the central allegation was that the dismissal would not have happened but for the contract breach; in such a case any provable stigma damages flow from the breach.

Where does this leave stigma damages?

Be that as it may, *Edwards* left the law much where it was before the Court of Appeal decided the cases below: any breach of contract, express or implied, that results in or leads directly to a dismissal cannot afford damages at common law other than the notice period and the *Gunton* extension. This leaves stigma only the *Malik* outlet: if some breach of an express or implied contract clause during employment causes a stigma *without* having to pass through a dismissal to achieve it (ie the stigma flows from the earlier conduct, not from the dismissal or the manner of it) then the employee can recover it if they can prove its existence. *Malik* was rare in that the high-profile nature of the employer's fraudulent conduct made it easy to demonstrate that the industry as a whole looked upon former BCCI employees as tainted (and in the event the claimants were ultimately unable to shepherd their stigma claims through the gauntlet of causation, mitigation, and evidence).

A subsequent discrimination case, forced to confront stigma damages because such damages *can* be recovered under the Equality Act 2010, commented on the difficulties involved in proving stigma damages that do not flow from a dismissal. In *Chaggar v Abbey National*,[235] the Court of Appeal noted that much of the stigma loss resulting from the termination of employment is a consequence of being on the job market at a time not

[232] [2011] UKSC 58, para 113.
[233] [2011] UKSC 58, para 76 (Lord Phillips).
[234] [2011] UKSC 58, paras 80–87.
[235] [2009] EWCA Civ 1202.

of one's own choosing. It observed that a job is often easier to get from a state of employment than from one of unemployment, and that employees tend to put themselves on the job market when market conditions are favourable. The court opined that the stigma loss from an unlawful dismissal could easily be proved by reference to the failure of reasonable efforts to secure new employment. However, where a court must exclude dismissal as a causal factor (which would be the case in any *Malik*-style claim), it might reasonably attribute any difficulty finding work to the intervening (but off-limits from a remedial perspective) dismissal:

> The tribunal would have to determine how far difficulties in obtaining employment result from general market considerations and how far from the stigma. In the unlikely event that the evidence of the stigma difficulties is sufficiently strong, it would be open to the tribunal to make an award of future loss for a specific period. But, in the more likely scenario that the evidence showed that stigma was only one of the claimant's difficulties, it may be that a modest lump sum would be appropriate to compensate him for the stigma element in his employment difficulties.[236]

It is difficult to argue with the conclusion that where it is forbidden from awarding stigma damages in connection with a dismissal, a tribunal must require cogent proof that any alleged stigma damages from some unrelated contract breach do not piggy-back on the consequences of the dismissal. However, this illustrates the strained and artificial results brought about by the '*Johnson* exclusion zone' logic. According to the reasoning in *Chaggar*, if a breach of a simple notice provision places an employee on the job market six months earlier than a lawful dismissal would, it is possible that any difficulty in finding work flows directly from being on the job market (a) from a state of unemployment rather than employment, and (b) earlier than, for market reasons, the employee might have chosen had she received her six months' notice. In such a case losses from failure to find work after the end of the notice period might well result directly from the breach of contract, not from the dismissal as such. It is nothing short of fanciful to assume that by enacting a statute providing a remedy for unreasonable dismissal decisions, Parliament intended to wipe away all remedies for losses that flow not from the occurrence of an unreasonable dismissal, but from effecting that dismissal in breach of the employment contract.

6.4.2.6 **Reduction of damages**

Once the prima facie amount of damages has been ascertained, it is subject to reduction in three ways:

Mitigation

The employee is under a duty to mitigate his or her loss, and in the context of the contract of employment this will mean essentially finding another job. This will be particularly important in the case of the wrongful termination of a fixed-term contract which had several years to run, but will apply generally to all wrongful dismissals.[237] What constitutes reasonable steps to mitigate will be a question of fact in each case, but two general points might be made. The first is that the courts apply a realistic standard, so that the dismissed employee is not expected to take any job immediately, irrespective of his or her former

[236] [2009] EWCA Civ 1202, para 99.

[237] If the dismissal is not wrongful, the employee may sue for unpaid wages for the notice period in an action for debt, to which the obligation to mitigate does not apply: *Abrahams v Performing Right Society Ltd* [1995] ICR 1028, [1995] IRLR 486, CA, dicta in this case suggesting that the obligation does not apply even where dismissal is wrongful must be considered to be wrong.

position; thus, they may be allowed a certain amount of time to look around for a position of equal status before resorting to lesser employment, and it may not be reasonable to expect them to take another post inside the firm that dismissed them if that is offered, particularly if it involves a reduction in status.[238] The second point is that issues other than another job could constitute mitigation, but before allowing them as such (with the resultant decrease in the amount of damages to be paid by the defendant employer) the court should be satisfied that they are not too remote to be taken into consideration. In *Lavarack v Woods of Colchester Ltd*, the facts of which were given earlier in this chapter, the employee was debarred by the contract of employment from engaging in, or holding shares in, any other business during his employment. After his dismissal, he became employed by M Ltd (purchasing half of its stock) and invested in V Ltd. The defendant employers claimed that the profits on these investments should be taken into account to mitigate his damages; the Court of Appeal held that the profits from his shares in M Ltd were to be taken into account, since his dismissal had left him free to *partake* in M Ltd and thereby increase the value of those shares, but the profits from his shares in V Ltd were not to be taken into account, since these were too remote, and the mere fact that he could not have invested while in the defendant's employment was not enough to alter that.

Taxation

The general rule on the taxation of damages, laid down by the House of Lords in *British Transport Commission v Gourley*,[239] is that where a head of damage is based on an estimate of lost wages, the court should make allowance for the tax that would have been paid, and so deduct that figure and award the damages net of tax. This applies to damages for wrongful dismissal. However, the basis for the rule is that the amount awarded as damages is not taxable in the claimant's hands, and at the time of *Gourley* this was generally the case. Now, however, under the Income Tax (Earnings and Pensions) Act 2003, s 403 (previously, and for many years, the Income and Corporation Taxes Act 1988, s 148), such 'post-cessation receipts' are taxed to the extent that they exceed £30,000. The end result is that the rule in *Gourley*'s case applies to the first £30,000 of damages for wrongful dismissal, which must be awarded net of tax, but not to any amount over and above that, which must be awarded gross (and will then be taxed by the Revenue).[240]

Deduction of other benefits received

Where a person is unable to work and claims damages because of that, it is likely that they will receive benefits from various sources during the period out of employment; the question then arises whether the amount of those benefits should be deducted from the damages which the defendant must pay. This is obviously of great importance in personal

[238] *Yetton v Eastwoods Froy Ltd* [1966] 3 All ER 353, [1967] 1 WLR 104; *Shindler v Northern Raincoat Co Ltd* [1960] 2 All ER 239, [1960] 1 WLR 1038. The general principles of mitigation in the employment context were summed up by Potter LJ in *Wilding v BT plc* [2002] ICR 1079, [2002] IRLR 524, CA.

[239] [1956] AC 185, [1955] 3 All ER 796, HL.

[240] *Parsons v BNM Laboratories Ltd* [1964] 1 QB 95, [1963] 2 All ER 658, CA. The tax position must be considered realistically, taking into account any tax rebates due to the employee being unemployed after the dismissal: *Hartley v Sandholme Iron Co Ltd* [1975] QB 600, [1974] 3 All ER 475 (a personal injury case). See also *Bold v Brough, Nicholson and Hall Ltd* [1963] 3 All ER 849, [1964] 1 WLR 201; *Basnett v J & A Jackson Ltd* [1976] ICR 63, [1976] IRLR 154; and *Shove v Downs Surgical plc* [1984] ICR 532, [1984] IRLR 17; *Harvey* A [1076]; Powell 'The Taxation of Payments Received on Termination of Employment' (1981) 10 ILJ 239; Bishop and Kay 'Taxation and Damages: The Rule of Gourley's Case' (1987) 104 LQR 211. This is, of course, all on the assumption that the amount recovered by the claimant is damages; if it is simply a debt under the contract (eg a payment in lieu under an express 'in lieu' clause in the contract), it is taxable in the hands of the claimant anyway: *EMI Group Electronics Ltd v Coldicott* [1999] IRLR 630, [1999] STC 803, CA; *Richardson v Delaney* [2001] IRLR 663.

injury claims, where it is well established that insurance payments provided by the claimant's own foresight and payment of the premia are not deductible,[241] whereas most social security benefits are now (since the Social Security Act 1989) recoverable in full by the state through the system of civil recoupment.[242] Outside those areas, however, the position is less clear, particularly since the decision of the House of Lords in *Parry v Cleaver*,[243] which showed a modern tendency not to deduct benefits[244] and concentrated on public policy and overall fairness rather than the older, more technical tests for deductibility such as remoteness, whether the benefit was received as of right, and whether the plaintiff had contributed to the scheme providing the benefit. The problem is that the case itself only concerned a contributory police disablement fund, and indeed their Lordships declined to consider the deductibility of other benefits (such as those more relevant to the dismissed employee),[245] so that any effect that this case may have on other benefits must be by implication.

While in some respects courts subsequently have taken a more straightforward view of quantifying the claimant's actual loss,[246] the approach in *Parry v Cleaver* was strongly reaffirmed by the House of Lords in *Smoker v London Fire and Civil Defence Authority*,[247] where it was held in a personal injury case that private pension benefits were not to be deducted from the plaintiff's damages for loss of earnings, and this was applied directly to an action for wrongful dismissal in *Hopkins v Norcros plc*.[248] As the law stands at present, with regard to other benefits particularly applicable to wrongful dismissal cases, it appears that contractual payments by the employer such as sick pay are deductible (even if provided under an insurance policy maintained by the employer)[249] and that Jobseeker's Allowance (previously unemployment benefit) received by the dismissed employee during the period by which the damages are calculated is deductible;[250] and, after considerable doubt over a long period, the Court of Appeal held that the same rule of deductibility

[241] *Bradburn v Great Western Rly Co* (1874) LR 10 Exch 1.

[242] Social Security (Recovery of Benefit) Act 1997. This special recoupment system does not apply to damages for wrongful dismissal.

[243] [1970] AC 1, [1969] 1 All ER 555, HL. See generally on this question Lewis 'Deducting Collateral Benefits from Damages: Principle and Policy' (1998) 18 LS 15, and 'The Overlap between Damages for Personal Injury and Work Related Benefits' (1998) 27 ILJ 1.

[244] See also *Daish v Wauton* [1972] 2 QB 262, [1972] 1 All ER 25, CA.

[245] See [1970] AC 1 at 19 and 39, [1969] 1 All ER 555 at 562 and 579, per Lord Reid and Lord Wilberforce.

[246] *Dews v National Coal Board* [1987] ICR 602, [1987] IRLR 330, HL; *Hodgson v Trapp* [1989] AC 807, [1988] 3 All ER 870, HL.

[247] [1991] ICR 449, [1991] IRLR 271, HL; see also *Longden v British Coal Corpn* [1998] 1 All ER 289, [1998] ICR 26, HL.

[248] [1994] ICR 11, [1994] IRLR 18, CA; this meant on the facts of the case that the wrongfully dismissed company chairman received £99,604 twice, once from the pension fund and once as damages for lost income. The judge at first instance had pointed out that provision could be made expressly either in an employment contract or in the rules of a pension scheme to prevent such double recovery.

[249] *Hussain v New Taplow Paper Mills Ltd* [1988] ICR 259, [1988] IRLR 167, HL. In an industrial injury case, one way to prevent the employer (by paying sick pay) effectively subsidizing the tortfeasor is to provide in the sick pay clause that, in the event of the injured employee later recovering damages from a third party, amounts paid to the employee as sick pay are refundable to the employer; this should enable damages to be awarded to the employee in full, without deduction of sick pay. Such clauses have been used, eg in agricultural, railway, and police contracts.

[250] *Parsons v BNM Laboratories Ltd* [1964] 1 QB 95, [1963] 2 All ER 658, CA; *Foxley v Olton* [1965] 2 QB 306, [1964] 3 All ER 248n; *Cheeseman v Bowater UK Paper Mills Ltd* [1971] 3 All ER 513, [1971] 1 WLR 1773, CA. In *Nabi v British Leyland (UK) Ltd* [1980] 1 All ER 667, CA, the Court of Appeal applied the *Parsons* case, but thought that the rule was due for reconsideration. However, the House of Lords applied *Parsons* without demur in *Westwood v Secretary of State for Employment* [1985] ICR 209, [1984] IRLR 209, HL.

applies to supplementary benefit (now Income Support).[251] The other major benefit which might be relevant is a redundancy payment, and while there was some authority in earlier cases[252] against deductibility (on the basis that the payment is due on dismissal anyway, whether or not the dismissal is wrongful), the Court of Appeal have held that such a payment *is* deductible, except possibly in a rare case where it can be shown that the employee would have been made redundant anyway.[253]

6.4.3 **Wrongful dismissal and unfair dismissal**

The obvious contrast between the two is that the statutory action for unfair dismissal involves an enquiry into the overall merits of the dismissal (substance and procedure) whereas the common law action for wrongful dismissal is essentially a breach of contract action, and therefore looks typically to the *form* of the dismissal (except in cases where the employer purported to dismiss summarily for cause and the employee alleges that they gave no such cause, or where the contract actually contains terms governing the substantive grounds for dismissal). Thus, at common law an employer could dismiss for any reason provided it gave the correct length of notice (or wages in lieu thereof),[254] but for the purposes of unfair dismissal this previously all-important question of notice is of evidential value only, if that, and the fact that proper notice was given will certainly not mean that the dismissal is necessarily fair. Thus, although a dismissal could be both wrongful and unfair, it could also easily be one but not the other. Fundamental concepts, such as the meaning of 'dismissal', can vary from one case to another, as can the result of that dismissal, so that a finding that an employee was unfairly dismissed will not necessarily put them at an advantage if they wish later, in some other context, to claim that the dismissal was also wrongful, and vice versa.[255] Also, constructive dismissal[256] amounts to a dismissal for both wrongful and unfair dismissal, but the implications are very different: the dismissal will almost by definition be without notice and can result in wrongful dismissal damages for the notice period, but will constitute a mere 'dismissal' for the purposes of unfair dismissal, proving nothing about whether the dismissal was 'unfair'. Finally, the separate principles of compensation operate independently[257] and indeed

[251] *Lincoln v Hayman* [1982] 2 All ER 819, [1982] 1 WLR 488, CA (a personal injury case).

[252] *Yorkshire Engineering and Welding Co Ltd v Burnham* [1973] 3 All ER 1176, [1974] ICR 77; *Millington v T H Goodwin & Sons Ltd* [1975] ICR 104, [1974] IRLR 379; *Basnett v J and A Jackson Ltd* [1976] ICR 63, [1976] IRLR 154. In each of these cases the decision of Arnold J in *Stocks v Magna Merchants Ltd* [1973] 2 All ER 329, [1973] ICR 530 that a redundancy payment should be deducted was not followed.

[253] *Colledge v Bass Mitchells & Butlers Ltd* [1988] ICR 125, [1988] IRLR 163, CA (another personal injury case, where the judge at first instance had made a finding of fact that it was unlikely that the plaintiff would have been made redundant but for the accident).

[254] In *East Coast Main Line Ltd v Cameron* UKEAT/0212/19 a tribunal held that the employee's dismissal was wrongful at common law because the employer had not taken into account his previous 26 years' blameless conduct, but the EAT held that this was completely wrong in law; such matters were relevant only to *unfair* dismissal.

[255] *Turner v London Transport Executive* [1977] ICR 952, [1977] IRLR 441, CA; *Hope v BMA* EA-2021-000187; *Brown v Castlerock Group Ltd* EA-2020-000174. There is certainly no question of cause of action estoppel as such as between the unfair and wrongful dismissal actions, but on the other hand there are cases where a finding of fact by a tribunal has been treated as raising an issue estoppel in later civil proceedings: *Green v Hampshire County Council* [1979] ICR 861; *Automatic Switching Ltd v Brunet* [1986] ICR 542, EAT; *Soteriou v Ultrachem Ltd* [2004] IRLR 870.

[256] See 7.2.1.

[257] *Norton Tool Co Ltd v Tewson* [1973] 1 All ER 183, [1972] ICR 501; *Everwear Candlewick Ltd v Isaac* [1974] 3 All ER 24, [1974] ICR 525; there is, however, a duty to mitigate loss as at common law, imposed specifically by the provisions relating to the compensatory award: Employment Rights Act 1996, s 123(4).

in theory the primary remedy for unfair dismissal is reinstatement or re-engagement, a remedy which, as seen previously, the common law would only countenance in highly unusual cases.

6.4.4 **The residual importance of wrongful dismissal**

The common law doctrine of notice meant that wrongful dismissal was only a theoretical remedy for a large number of employees, since they were on relatively short notice, so that even if such an employee went to the trouble and expense of bringing a common law action their damages would be small, since they were so rigidly tied to the amount of wages during the notice period. The statutory action for unfair dismissal, while not abolishing wrongful dismissal, is now far more important in practice, with its easier procedure, the possibility (at least in theory) of reinstatement or re-engagement, and the more liberal and realistic approach to compensation. On the other hand, there may still be some atypical cases where wrongful dismissal is still important. One class of case would be where the employee does not qualify for the statutory action, in particular where they are in an excluded category. The most important case, however, would be that of a highly paid employee either on a fixed-term contract or entitled to a substantial period of notice—as the compensation for unfair dismissal is subject to statutory maxima[258] which, though perhaps adequate for many employees (certainly when compared with the small amounts recoverable by them for wrongful dismissal), may be a real restriction in the case of the high earner who, if dismissed unfairly *and* wrongfully, may have more to gain by an action for wrongful dismissal which is not subject to the statutory maxima. Such an action continues to be governed by the law as set out previously, but for most practical purposes a modern dismissal case is likely to proceed on the statutory basis and be subject to the separate body of law on unfair dismissal, to which we turn in the next chapter.

Review and Final Thoughts

- The contractual concept of frustration can end an employment relationship as a matter of law, but disability discrimination law and modern sick pay and incapacity insurance arrangements increasingly make ill health an unconvincing basis for frustration; meanwhile, parties can end the relationship by mutual agreement and avoid dismissal consequences, including voluntary redundancy schemes, even where they result in a formal dismissal. See footnotes 12, 21, and 62 for further reading.
- Employers and employees can terminate the employment agreement for any reason they want to at common law (so long as they do not violate a statute such as the Equality Act 2010), unless the contract specifies permissible reasons (which is rare). To do this lawfully the parties must give the amount of notice required in the contract (or by statute if the

[258] At the time of writing, the maximum basic award is £21,570; the maximum compensatory award was for many years kept at a low level, not keeping up with inflation, so that as late as 1999 it was only £12,000. It was raised to £50,000 by the Employment Relations Act 1999 and at the time of writing stands at £118,223, but that could still be a low ceiling in the case of a very high earner. For lower earners the news is worse, as in 2013 the government introduced an additional limit of one year's pay, such that the limit is the lower of one year's pay or the maximum cap.

contract is silent), or pay in lieu, unless the employee is dismissed for a repudiatory breach of contract, which is then a justified summary dismissal.

- 'Wrongful dismissal' is the name for the breach of contract action available to an employee whose dismissal breaches the employment contract (usually by not giving the employee proper notice); it can also cover a purported summary dismissal where the employer cannot show gross misconduct. Damages are not available for the manner of the dismissal or for non-pecuniary damages such as injury to feelings, so it usually involves compensation for the pay lost during the period of notice that was not given. See footnotes 177, 201, 222, 240, and 243 for further reading.
- These common law rules are often overshadowed by the statutory action for unfair dismissal, but because employees can sometimes fail to qualify for it, the common law action may still be relevant. Moreover, as we will see in the next chapter, compensation for unfair dismissal is limited by statute which may mean that the common law action remains relevant for high earners, with its unlimited damages. Remember too that even those who are protected by the unfair dismissal statute can lose their claim, and yet a common law action for failure to give notice will still survive. Finally, in rare cases the common law can be used to prevent a dismissal from taking place before it lawfully should, which is not the case with unfair dismissal.

7

Unfair dismissal

OVERVIEW

The statutory action for unfair dismissal constitutes a major element of modern employment law, giving greater and more realistic remedies than the common law for most employees. This chapter explains this action, addressing, among others, the following questions:

- How should employers handle problems of misconduct or poor performance, before imposing the ultimate penalty of dismissal (sacking)? To what extent, and how, does the law ensure that employers use fair procedures in dealing with such problems?

- What is a dismissal? Are there formal steps that must be followed to make it legal, and can it be avoided by simply pushing people to resign, or not renewing their fixed-term contracts?
- What are the elements of an unfair dismissal action and who must prove them? How can an employer defend itself?
- How does a tribunal decide whether a dismissal is fair, and is the test fair to both sides? Does it focus on what happens to the employee or on the thought process of the employer?
- Do misconduct cases involve a different approach to cases of poor performance? Does it make a difference if the misconduct is online, and do human rights have anything to do with it?
- What are the remedies for unfair dismissal, and do they make sense?

Context

While much of employment law has been subject to fairly consistent change over the years, unfair dismissal law has been notable for how *little* amendment it has undergone. It was first introduced in 1971 in the ill-fated Industrial Relations Act (see Chapter 1) in an attempt to minimize strike action over dismissals (the then-common non-legal way of opposing them). The incoming Labour government in 1975, in s 1 of its very first statute, stated: 'The Industrial Relations Act 1971 is hereby repealed', but then added in effect 'except for this bit' and retained the whole of the 1971 law on unfair dismissal unchanged. Obviously there have been various bits of tinkering over the years, but overall this law has gained a remarkable level of political acceptability (in spite of initial employer mythology that it was a communist plot under which the employer was on a hiding to nothing—the statistics show a very different picture).

Two specific areas have seen different kinds of change: (1) there have been different qualifying periods at different times, ranging from six months' continuous employment to one year to two years; (2) there has been an expansion in the number of categories of automatically unfair dismissal, where governments have wanted to give special protection to employees (with a now-standard package of automatic unfairness, no qualifying period, and enhanced remedies). In the past, these two could interact, in that if a dismissed employee lacked the qualifying employment, their only hope for an unfair dismissal claim (as opposed to a separate discrimination claim if appropriate) is to seek to establish one of these exceptional categories, the principal one being the special protection given to whistleblowers, which over the past few years has placed strains in the case law on the definition of the limits of this widely pleaded category. Hopefully some of these strains will be lessened when the Employment Rights Act 2025 removes the qualifying period and makes unfair dismissal a day-one right.

Clearly, unfair dismissal is a creature of statute, but as will become quickly apparent it has spawned a large amount of case law, in relation to overall matters such as the vital importance of fair procedures (grafted on early in the law's history on the idea that a fair procedure will often produce a fair decision) and specific matters such as guidance on how its very broad principles apply to commonly occurring situations such as dismissal for misconduct, incapacity, and redundancy. However, this case law will only lay down *factors* which a tribunal should *normally* take into account. Ultimately its decision will be largely one of fact, on which it is sovereign; if it gets the law right, the chances of a successful appeal by the losing party will not be good. In the light of this, one statutory change may be viewed as unfortunate—while the move towards employment judge-only hearings may make sense in the more technical areas such as non-payment of wages, its extension to unfair dismissal cases was in a different category—surely this area is one where side members should have been retained in order to contribute their experience as to what, after all the legal arguments, should be found on the facts to be fair or unfair.

7.1 Procedures for discipline, dismissal, and grievances

The core principles for the management of discipline and dismissal in UK employment law were introduced (originally in 1977) in the highly influential ACAS Code of Practice No 1 *Disciplinary and Grievance Procedures* and many employers now have definite rules and procedures (often in work-rules or handbooks) drafted in the light of the Code's recommendations. The Code itself (reissued in expanded form in 2000, then again in 2004, in 2009, and most recently in a revised 2015 version) places great emphasis on involvement of employees and their representatives in the drafting of procedures covering grievances, discipline, and appeal structures. Having an agreed procedure greatly adds to its authority, and to the authority which may be exercised by the management when it takes action clearly in accordance with the agreed rules; tribunals will naturally tend to pay great attention to an agreed procedure as a question of fact and evidence.[1] Where there are set rules on discipline, grievances, and appeals (whether agreed or not), the employer must give the employee written notice of them at the latest on the commencement of employment.[2] For the guidance of employers when drawing up rules and procedures, the Code makes the following general points:

> 2. Fairness and transparency are promoted by developing and using rules and procedures for handling disciplinary and grievance situations. These should be set down in writing, be specific and clear. Employees and, where appropriate, their representatives should be involved in the development of rules and procedures. It is also important to help employees and managers understand what the rules and procedures are, where they can be found and how they are to be used.

When drawing up and applying procedures, employers should always bear in mind the requirements of natural justice. This means that employees should be given the opportunity of a meeting with someone who has not been involved in the matter. They should be informed of the allegations against them, together with the supporting evidence, in advance of the meeting. Employees should be given the opportunity to challenge the allegations before decisions are reached and should be provided with a right of appeal.

7.1.1 Disciplinary measures

Although certain forms of disciplinary action may still lie entirely within the managerial prerogative (eg transferring a general labourer to a different job or refusing to give a discretionary bonus), many other forms will impinge upon the rights and expectations of the disciplined employee (eg fines, suspension, demotion) and so the crucial point about lawful disciplinary measures is that the employer must have the power to impose them, and normally this will involve having the contractual authority (express or implied) to do so. If the employer goes outside this authority the employee may in theory maintain a common law action (eg to recover the amount of a fine unlawfully deducted);[3] of much

[1] *Securicor Ltd v Smith* [1989] IRLR 356, CA.

[2] Employment Rights Act 1996, s 3: see 2.3.

[3] *Gorse v Durham County Council* [1971] 2 All ER 666, [1971] 1 WLR 775. In the example given, there may also be a statutory action under the Employment Rights Act 1996, s 13.

greater significance in modern employment law is the possibility that the wrongly disciplined employee may walk out and claim to have been constructively dismissed, for the purpose of bringing an unfair dismissal action. Therefore, although some managers remain suspicious of setting down their disciplinary powers in writing on the basis that it restricts managerial prerogative, the modern tendency is to put down in written form the company's policy on discipline (which will of course vary from industry to industry) and the procedures to be adopted, which may then form part of the employment contract either expressly or by implication. A leading survey referred to a 'massive spread of formal disciplinary and dismissal procedures across British industry and commerce' in the 1970s as a 'remarkable development in British industrial relations'. Findings of a major study in 1990 showed that 97 per cent of establishments recognizing a union operated a disciplinary and dismissal procedure and (perhaps even more significantly) so did 83 per cent of those not recognizing a union; 93 per cent of procedures were written, 74 per cent provided for union representation of employees, and 65 per cent were jointly agreed.[4] On the other hand, *compliance* with procedures was sometimes a different matter and a 1998 survey by the DTI (predecessor to the Department for Business, Innovation and Skills (BIS)) found that when one looked at cases actually brought to tribunals (itself arguably a sign of failure of the system), they were characterized by a relatively high incidence of lack of procedures or failure to operate them.[5] These findings were influential in the then government's decision to enact mandatory standard procedures in 2002 to try to enforce a higher level of compliance with basic rules. These mandatory procedures came into effect in 2004 but were a serious failure and were repealed as from April 2009. Concluding that the cure had been worse than the disease, the government reinstated the ACAS Code as the key mechanism for ensuring procedural fairness.

Turning to the detailed provisions of the Code, the primary suggestion is that where a disciplinary procedure is established it should be clear and unambiguous so that individual employees may know what is expected of them; in particular, they should be made aware of the likely consequences of breaking the rules and the type of conduct which may warrant summary dismissal.[6] Although it is therefore desirable to lay down the major forms of unacceptable conduct in the circumstances of the particular industry involved, and the likely consequences of each form, the list should not necessarily be exhaustive, otherwise novel forms of transgression could be construed as permissible (in the sense of not attracting a valid penalty).

A system of warnings (considered further in this chapter) may be an integral part of a disciplinary system (as well as leading up to a dismissal), but if warnings are ignored

[4] Millward et al. 'Workplace Industrial Relations in Transition' (the ED/ESRC/PSI/ACAS Survey) (1992) ch 6. A similar pattern was found in the preliminary results of the 1998 exercise: Cully et al. 'The 1998 Workplace Employee Relations Survey: The First Findings' (ESRC/ACAS/PSI, 1998; URN 98/934).

[5] Earnshaw, Goodman, Harrison, and Marchington 'Industrial Tribunals, Workplace Disciplinary Procedures and Employment Practice' (DTI Employment Relations Research Paper, 1998); see Edwards (1998) 27 ILJ 362.

[6] COP paras 2 and 24; a statement that an employee is 'liable to' dismissal for particular misconduct is probably strong enough: *Procter v British Gypsum Ltd* [1992] IRLR 7. If the rules are ambiguous as to the seriousness of a particular matter but then the employer dismisses for the first breach (ie without warning), a tribunal may well consider that unfair: *Trusthouse Forte (Catering) Ltd v Adonis* [1984] IRLR 382. On the other hand, the fact that particular conduct is absolutely banned by the rules and stated to warrant mandatory dismissal does not mean that such a dismissal will automatically be fair, for the rules cannot oust the jurisdiction of the tribunal to look into the overall merits: *Laws Stores Ltd v Oliphant* [1978] IRLR 251; *Ladbroke Racing Ltd v Arnott* [1983] IRLR 154, Ct of Sess; *Taylor v Parsons, Peebles NEI Bruce Peebles Ltd* [1981] IRLR 119. This may cause problems in striking a reasonable balance between certainty and flexibility.

and the misconduct repeated, the employer, in a case not warranting dismissal, may wish to impose a lesser sanction. Fines or deductions must be permissible under the contract of employment if they are to be valid, and must also comply with the requirements of Part II of the Employment Rights Act 1996.[7] Suspension with pay will usually be lawful,[8] and may be the proper step to take for a brief period while a serious allegation against the employee is under investigation.[9] However, it must be seen as a disciplinary sanction, not as an automatic response to the need for an investigation: suspension is not neutral, and therefore there must be some grounds for using it as a disciplinary punitive measure.[10] For longer periods, however, it is tantamount to a holiday and the more obviously punitive sanction is suspension *without* pay. It is here, however, that the question whether the employer has contractual authority to act becomes particularly vital because, in the absence of express or implied incorporation into the contract, there is *no* common law power to suspend without pay, for this would contravene the employer's basic obligation to pay wages.[11] Thus, as in the case of lay-offs, the employer is clearly allowed to suspend without pay only where it incorporates a clause to that effect in the contract, either directly or via the works rules or a collective agreement. Moreover, the ACAS Code, while not forbidding it, does not give its imprimatur to the use of suspension as a punitive measure.

Other discipline may take forms such as reprimands, temporary withdrawal of privileges, or demotion or transfer; once again these are in theory only lawful if allowed by the contract, though the practical position, particularly in the case of demotion or transfer, may be that even if the legality is dubious the employer may go ahead and then, if the employee walks out and claims constructive dismissal, accept that there was a dismissal, but argue that it was fair because of the urgent need to remove the employee from their previous position. These are, however, all matters which are amenable to inclusion in a contract of employment in the first place (possibly via a set disciplinary code for the firm).

Although the form, then, of any disciplinary procedure will vary, the Code of Practice states that all disciplinary procedures should:

- be put in writing;
- allow for matters to be dealt with without undue delay;
- tell employees what disciplinary action might be taken;
- say what levels of management have the authority to take disciplinary action;
- require employees to be informed of the complaints against them and supporting evidence, before a meeting;
- give employees a chance to have their say before management reaches a decision;
- provide employees with the right to be accompanied;[12]

[7] See 3.5.5.

[8] Except perhaps in cases where the employee claims a right actually to work, not just to be paid wages: *Langston v AUEW* [1974] 1 All ER 980, [1974] ICR 180, CA. This category of case might expand in the light of *William Hill Organisation Ltd v Tucker* [1998] IRLR 313, CA, which emphasized the advantage to an employer of having an express power to suspend with pay.

[9] COP para 8.

[10] *Crawford v Suffolk Mental Health Partnership NHS Trust* [2012] IRLR 402, CA, at [71] per Elias LJ; *London Borough of Lambeth v Agoreyo* [2019] IRLR 560, [2019] ICR 1572, CA.

[11] *Hanley v Pease & Partners Ltd* [1915] 1 KB 698; *Bird v British Celanese Ltd* [1945] KB 336, [1945] 1 All ER 488, CA.

[12] COP s 14. This must now include the absolute right to choose the identity of the person to accompany the employee, provided the person comes within ERA 1999, s 10 (union representative or other employee of the employer). *Toal v GB Oils* [2013] UKEAT 0569_12_2205, [2013] IRLR 696.

- provide that no employee is dismissed for a first breach of discipline, except in cases of gross misconduct;
- require management to investigate fully before any disciplinary action is taken;
- ensure that employees are given an explanation for any sanction;
- allow employees to appeal against a decision.

7.1.2 **Warnings, hearings, and appeals**

7.1.2.1 **Warnings**

A system of warnings has become an integral part of modern employment procedures, particularly where there is a possibility of dismissal. Warnings may seem particularly appropriate to cases of misconduct by the employee, but the general requirement for them has also been applied to cases of lack of capacity (such as inefficiency, bad workmanship, and incompetence)[13] and, in line with the principle that discipline should be constructive as well as punitive, a warning to the employee should not just point out the unsatisfactory conduct but may also be expected to specify any required improvements. Many employers will have a definite warning procedure built into their disciplinary code (which may be in the firm's rules or jointly agreed with a trade union), and may operate on a 'rule of thumb' basis such as 'one oral and two written'; there is no magic in a particular combination, but the Code does lay down this general advice:

19. Where misconduct is confirmed or the employee is found to be performing unsatisfactorily it is usual to give the employee a written warning. A further act of misconduct or failure to improve performance within a set period would normally result in a final written warning.
20. If an employee's first misconduct or unsatisfactory performance is sufficiently serious, it may be appropriate to move directly to a final written warning. This might occur where the employee's actions have had, or are liable to have, a serious or harmful impact on the organisation.
21. A first or final written warning should set out the nature of the misconduct or poor performance and the change in behaviour or improvement in performance required (with time-scale). The employee should be told how long the warning will remain current. The employee should be informed of the consequences of further misconduct, or failure to improve performance, within the set period following a final warning. For instance that it may result in dismissal or some other contractual penalty such as demotion or loss of seniority.
22. A decision to dismiss should only be taken by a manager who has the authority to do so. The employee should be informed as soon as possible of the reasons for the dismissal, the date on which the employment contract will end, the appropriate period of notice and their right of appeal.

Further to this general guidance, three particular points should be noted. First, the existence of a warning system places emphasis upon writing and the keeping of detailed personnel records by the employer,[14] who must be able, if necessary, to provide documentary

[13] *Winterhalter Gastronom Ltd v Webb* [1973] ICR 245, [1973] IRLR 120, NIRC.

[14] The warning should usually be given to the employee personally; giving it to his or her trade union may not be enough: *W Brooks & Son v Skinner* [1984] IRLR 379, EAT.

proof of previous warnings;[15] this leads, for example, to the practices of giving written confirmation even of an 'oral' warning and of requiring the employee's signature of acknowledged receipt of a warning. This may lead to an increased personnel function within a firm, but is inevitable with the modern movement towards increased legalization. Second, the employer's system should include some time limit on warnings, so that after a set period they lapse.[16] The effect of a lapse is that the warning no longer supports progression to the next step; however, it does not mean that it can never be considered to support a dismissal: past, even lapsed, warnings without improvement can inform a decision about whether a later transgression warrants dismissal.[17] Third, a warning should be reasonably specific, identifying the precise ground of complaint by the employer. One consequence of this is that a warning on ground A (eg swearing) should not be used as a step in the procedure to dismiss on ground B (eg bad workmanship), so that one employee may be subject to more than one series of warnings concurrently if they are deficient in different respects; this must be viewed realistically, however, and there may come a point when a multitude of warnings on different matters add up overall to reasonable grounds to dismiss, particularly if some of the grounds are not dissimilar, and the employer may genuinely issue one final warning on generally unsatisfactory conduct.[18]

The presence or absence of warnings may be a most important factor in determining the fairness or otherwise of a dismissal, though as always on matters of procedure it is not necessarily conclusive. Thus, there may be circumstances in which lack of a warning is reasonable; summary dismissal for gross misconduct is still permissible,[19] and a warning might also be dispensed with where the employee has made it clear that they do not intend to 'improve' (eg where they are at odds with the company's policy),[20] where their incapability is so bad as to be irredeemable, or where (as in the case of senior management) the employee already knows exactly what is required of them, so that a warning would be irrelevant.[21] If a warning forms the basis of a later dismissal, and is subsequently found to be itself unfounded, the fairness of the dismissal will depend on how much of a role the warning played—if it in any way tipped the scales towards dismissal then the dismissal will probably be unfair.[22]

[15] In most cases the warnings will be previous but, counterintuitively to say the least, it is possible for an employer to rely on a warning that happens after the conduct being investigated for possible dismissal, so long as the (very rare) circumstances do not offend natural justice: *Sweeney v Strathclyde Fire Board* UKEATS/0029/13 (12 November 2013, unreported) (the employer was considering dismissal based on domestic violence charges which were under investigation; then the employee engaged in further misconduct, and then he was found guilty of the domestic violence offences which, taken together with the intervening misconduct, justified dismissal). See also *John-Charles v NHS Business Services Authority* UKEAT/0105/15 (12 October 2015, unreported).

[16] This requirement was reaffirmed in *Diosynth Ltd v Thomson* [2006] IRLR 284, Ct of Sess (IH), even in the sensitive area of disciplining for health and safety breaches following a fatal accident. A firm's disciplinary procedure may permit an appeal against a warning; a warning which is under appeal may be considered by an employer when dismissing, but the fact that the appeal has not yet been heard should also be taken into account: *Tower Hamlets Health Authority v Anthony* [1989] ICR 656, [1989] IRLR 394, CA.

[17] *Stratford v Auto Trail VR Ltd* UKEAT/0116/16 (31 October 2016, unreported).

[18] *Auguste Noel Ltd v Curtis* [1990] ICR 604, [1990] IRLR 326 is a particularly strong case on this point. One innovation was the concept of a 'first and final' warning, to apply to cases of serious misconduct just falling short of warranting dismissal; this provides more flexibility, with a halfway house between instant dismissal and exhaustion of the full warning system. The idea was finally taken up in the 2000 revision of the Code and is now implicit in the warnings system in the 2015 Code.

[19] COP para 23. Note that summary dismissal means without notice, not without a hearing.

[20] *Retarded Children's Aid Society Ltd v Day* [1978] ICR 437, [1978] IRLR 128, CA.

[21] *James v Waltham Holy Cross UDC* [1973] ICR 398, [1973] IRLR 202. For a particularly good example (involving an NHS Trust financial director) see *Perkin v St George's Healthcare Trust* [2005] IRLR 934, CA, where a dismissal for 'awkward personality' was fair even though no warnings had been given.

[22] *Bandara v BBC* UKEAT/0335/15 (9 June 2016, unreported).

7.1.2.2 **Hearings and appeals**

In addition to warnings, the employee who is in danger of dismissal should normally be allowed a hearing of sorts, which may be built into the firm's disciplinary procedures, or may be arranged ad hoc. This may perform two functions: first, at the investigative stage, to ascertain the true facts of the incident in question; second, at the disciplinary stage, to allow the employee to make representations on the question whether they ought on those facts to be dismissed (when they may wish to refute the charges against them, or accept them but put forward matters such as length of service or previous good conduct in mitigation); where these two functions are separated (eg where the second is considered by a higher level of management), the employee should normally be given a proper opportunity to be heard at each stage.[23] It is important to recall, however, that this relates to conduct and capability dismissals; redundancy has its own rules, but dismissals for 'some other substantial reason' do not necessarily require a meeting in order to be fair, if the reason for the dismissal is external to the employee's work or conduct.[24]

It will usually be of the essence of a fair hearing that the employee must be made aware of the charges against them[25] (unless they are obvious),[26] but the precise form of the required hearing will vary with the circumstances and the emphasis is on the overall failures of the procedure adopted, rather than any rigidly prescribed format.[27] At a minimum, though, a statement of 'charges' must identify a specific act: it is not enough to accuse a worker of dishonesty; they must be accused of a specific act or acts of dishonesty.[28] Although the basic requirement of a hearing is akin to the rules of natural justice (which are sometimes prayed in aid in such cases), it must be remembered that these are *not* court proceedings, and so there is no inalienable right to appear in person,[29] to receive witness statements,[30] or to be allowed to cross-examine 'witnesses'.[31] Article 6 of the European Convention on Human Rights, which guarantees the right to a fair trial, applies only to the tribunal hearing of the unfair or wrongful dismissal case, not to the disciplinary proceedings,[32] even

[23] *Budgen & Co v Thomas* [1976] ICR 344, [1976] IRLR 174; *Tesco (Holdings) Ltd v Hill* [1977] IRLR 63. It is normally for the employer to take the initiative in operating the procedure; it is not enough to say that the employee could have used the grievance procedure: *Clarke v Trimoco Motor Group Ltd* [1993] ICR 237, [1993] IRLR 148, EAT.

[24] *Hawkes v Ausin Group* (UK) Ltd UKEAT/0070/18/BA (14 June 2018 unreported) (the dismissal in this case was because the claimant had been called up on Reserve Army duty and would be unable to work for a substantial period of time).

[25] *Louies v Coventry Hood and Seating Co Ltd* [1990] ICR 54, [1990] IRLR 324; *Spink v Express Foods Group Ltd* [1990] IRLR 320, EAT; *Sattar v Citibank NA* [2020] IRLR 104, CA.

[26] *Fuller v Lloyds Bank plc* [1991] IRLR 336, EAT.

[27] There is, however, a very useful summary of the key points normally expected of a fair hearing in the judgment of Wood P in *Clark v Civil Aviation Authority* [1991] IRLR 412 at 415.

[28] *Celebi v Scolarest Compass Group UK and Ireland* [2010] All ER (D) 136.

[29] *Ayanlowo v IRC* [1975] IRLR 253, CA. Moreover, it has been emphasized that the rules of natural justice do not constitute an independent head of challenge to the fairness of a dismissal in this context: *Slater v Leicestershire Health Authority* [1989] IRLR 16, CA. Normally the dismissing officer will conduct a hearing with the employee personally, but this is not mandatory in all circumstances: *Charalambous v National Bank of Greece* [2023] EAT 75.

[30] *Hussain v Elonex plc* [1999] IRLR 420, CA; on the facts, the tribunal had taken the view that the employee had been made sufficiently aware of the allegations in other ways.

[31] *Khanum v Mid-Glamorgan Area Health Authority* [1979] ICR 40, [1978] IRLR 215; *Santamera v Express Cargo Forwarding* [2003] IRLR 273. There may, in particular, be cases where an informant wishes to remain anonymous for fear of reprisals; Wood P laid down guidance on how to deal with the situation in *Linfood Cash and Carry Ltd v Thomson* [1989] ICR 518, [1989] IRLR 235, EAT, though even this may be impracticable in an extreme case, when the ultimate test of reasonableness in all the circumstances will have to be applied: *Ramsey v Walkers Food Ltd* [2004] IRLR 754.

[32] *Mattu v University Hospitals of Coventry and Warwickshire NHS Trust* [2012] EWCA Civ 641, [2012] All ER (D) 153.

where a disciplinary procedure can feed into a procedure where the employee's civil rights are determined (eg the right to continue working with children). Article 6 only applies to the later procedure, not to the disciplinary procedure that feeds in.[33]

On the other hand, a fair hearing procedure (in whatever form) should normally give the employee a reasonable opportunity to hear the allegations against them and to attempt to refute them.[34] One particular aspect of this is that once the charges have been laid against the employee, the employer should *not* add in more charges (especially of a more serious nature) as the hearing progresses; if evidence of different and/or more serious misconduct arises, the proper procedure is to adjourn and start again with new charges.[35] However, the analogy with the rules of natural justice must not be exaggerated, especially in the difficult area of potential bias, because it may not always be practicable to expect a complete separation of powers between the person dismissing and the person holding the disciplinary hearing (or appeal), since they may both be ordinary line managers; as long as there is substantive fairness in the internal procedure, it is not to be attacked with rules of natural justice on bias which evolved in different contexts.[36]

Where the employee is to attend a formal hearing, they should normally be allowed to be represented if they so wish (by a trade union representative or a fellow employee); this has always been good practice, but in addition the Employment Relations Act 1999, ss 10–13 give a statutory right to be accompanied at a disciplinary hearing[37] by a trade union official or another of the employer's workers; that person is to be permitted to address the hearing (but not answer questions on behalf of the worker)[38] and to confer with them during the hearing, and is to be given paid time off work for the purpose.[39] If the chosen companion is not available at the time proposed for the hearing, the employer must postpone it to an alternative time proposed by the worker (provided it is reasonable and falls within the next five working days). Complaint of breach of this right lies to an employment tribunal (subject to the usual three-month time limitation provisions), which may order compensation of up to two weeks' pay.

[33] *R (G) v Governors of X School* [2011] UKSC 30, [2011] IRLR 756.

[34] *Bentley Engineering Co Ltd v Mistry* [1979] ICR 47, [1978] IRLR 437. For subsequent examples of findings of unfair dismissal based on breach of natural justice (in these cases, the rule on potential bias) see *Moyes v Hylton Castle Working Men's Social Club and Institute Ltd* [1986] IRLR 482 and *Campion v Hamworthy Engineering Ltd* [1987] ICR 966, CA; cf, however, *Slater v Leicestershire Health Authority*, n 29.xyz

[35] *Strouthos v London Underground Ltd* [2004] IRLR 636, CA is a modern reaffirmation of this basic rule of natural justice.

[36] *Rowe v Radio Rentals Ltd* [1982] IRLR 177, where the (unsuccessful) ground of challenge was that the person hearing the appeal had been told of the facts beforehand by the person who dismissed the employee, and the latter person had been present at the appeal hearing: *R v Chief Constable of South Wales, ex p Thornhill* [1987] IRLR 313, CA. However, wherever possible (especially in a large organization), it is highly desirable to have separate levels of management dealing with the different stages: *Sartor v P&O European Ferries (Felixstowe) Ltd* [1992] IRLR 271, CA; *Byrne v BOC Ltd* [1992] IRLR 505, EAT.

[37] This means a hearing that could result in a formal warning, the taking of some other action, or the confirmation of either: Employment Relations Act 1999, s 13(4); what the employer calls it is not particularly relevant, as it is the statutory definition that must be applied: *London Underground Ltd v Ferenc-Batchelor* [2003] IRLR 252. Note that this right also applies to grievance hearings 'which concern the performance of a duty by an employer in relation to the worker': s 13(5). Guidance on this right is found in paras 13–17 of the ACAS Code of Practice.

[38] The wide definition of 'worker' is used in relation to this right, which is itself extended to cover agency workers and home workers: Employment Relations Act 1999, s 13(1)–(3).

[39] Section 10(6), (7). Section 12 extends the usual package of employment protection measures (concerning detriment and dismissal) to both the worker relying on this right and the chosen companion (when in that employer's employment).

In addition to a hearing, most disciplinary procedures in other than small firms will include some form of appeal from an adverse decision; this is prescribed by the Code of Practice, paragraph 26, and may take many forms, from a simple further hearing by a more senior manager up to a formal appeal hearing by a joint management–union committee or even ACAS-organized arbitration. The importance of such an appeal as an integral part of the internal procedure (lack or denial of which may per se make the dismissal unfair) has been recognized by the House of Lords.[40] This has been emphasized even further subsequently by the evolution of the rule that a bad initial dismissal may be 'cured' by a fair appeal; for many years it was thought that this only applied if the appeal hearing took the form of a complete rehearing (not just a review of the initial decision), but when this point was reviewed by the Court of Appeal it was held that there is no such limitation and that the only test is the overall fairness and open-mindedness of the appeal process, whatever its form.[41] If a successful appeal by the employee finds the dismissal unwarranted, this reinstates the employment relationship as if it were never interrupted.[42]

7.1.2.3 The implications of flawed procedure

As in the case of a warning, a hearing and appeal may well be expected in most cases, but lack of them will not necessarily make a dismissal unfair. There may be definite classes of case where it is highly arguable that a hearing would have been inappropriate, such as where the employee clearly refuses to accept the employer's legitimate requirements, where the employee's conduct 'is of such a nature that, whatever the explanation, his continued employment is not in the interests of the business'[43] (particularly where the employment in question is of a delicate or sensitive nature),[44] or where the employee is already being investigated by the police with a view to criminal charges being brought.[45] More generally, however, this is clearly an area where views may differ, and indeed we have seen definite changes of judicial approach to the whole question of fair procedure over the years. In the 1970s (in the infancy of the unfair dismissal law), great emphasis was placed on proper procedures, but this was then perceived to have gone too far and a reaction set in, from two directions—first, through a generally more relaxed approach to procedural requirements beginning with the decision of the Court of Appeal in *Hollister v NFU*,[46] taking the view that a lapse in procedure (such as failure to give a hearing) is merely one factor to take into account; second, and more specifically, through the evolution and widespread application of the rule in *British Labour Pump Co Ltd v Byrne*[47] that an element of procedural unfairness (such as the lack of a hearing) could be 'forgiven' if the employer could show that even if the proper procedure had been carried out it would have made no difference. The potential inroad of the *Byrne* principle into any general requirement of a hearing hardly needed to be spelled out.

That is why its overruling in the leading House of Lords decision in *Polkey v A E Dayton Services Ltd*[48] was of such great importance, and led to a general swing back of the

[40] *West Midlands Co-operative Society Ltd v Tipton* [1986] ICR 192, [1986] IRLR 112, HL.

[41] *Taylor v OCS Group Ltd* [2006] IRLR 613, CA, overruling on this point *Whitbread & Co Ltd v Mills* [1988] IRLR 501.

[42] *Patel v Folkestone Nursing Home Ltd* [2018] IRLR 924, [2019] ICR 273, CA. This is true even if the employee would have preferred to consider himself dismissed and pursue unfair dismissal, as he did in this case.

[43] *James v Waltham Holy Cross* UDC [1973] ICR 398, [1973] IRLR 202.

[44] *Alidair Ltd v Taylor* [1978] ICR 445, [1978] IRLR 82, CA.

[45] *Carr v Alexander Russell Ltd* [1979] ICR 469n, [1976] IRLR 220, applied in *Parker v Clifford Dunn Ltd* [1979] ICR 463, [1979] IRLR 56, EAT.

[46] [1979] ICR 542, [1979] IRLR 238, CA.

[47] [1979] ICR 347, [1979] IRLR 94, EAT.

[48] [1988] ICR 142, [1987] IRLR 503, HL; see 7.4.3 and Collins (1990) 19 ILJ 39.

pendulum, with more emphasis again being placed on procedure in general, and hearings in particular. The court emphasized that the task of a tribunal is to assess the reasonableness of what the employer actually did at the time, not what it might have done, and that the question whether at the end of the day the employee actually suffered injustice goes only to compensation, *not* to liability. The case of *McLaren v National Coal Board*[49] is a good example of the result of once again taking procedures seriously. The employee was accused of assaulting a working miner during the strike; normally the matter would have been investigated by the local manager but in the circumstances this was thought to be impracticable and so it was left to the police and the court—once the employee was convicted, he was automatically dismissed without a hearing. The tribunal held that this was fair given the surrounding circumstances of industrial warfare, but the Court of Appeal held that it was unfair, Sir John Donaldson MR stating:

> [N]o amount of heat in industrial warfare can justify failing to give an employee an opportunity of giving an explanation . . . You have the position that acceptable reasons for dismissing may change in a varying industrial situation, but *the standards of fairness never change. They are immutable but are applied in a different situation.* (Emphasis added)

The pendulum may therefore be seen as having been swung much of the way back; there will still be cases where lack of a hearing is explained sufficiently to the tribunal's satisfaction to produce a finding of fair dismissal, and it remains ultimately a matter of fact for the tribunal.[50] Moreover, even on general principles, in entertaining an employer's case that it was reasonable to dispense with a hearing, a tribunal might do well to bear in mind the words of Megarry V-C in *John v Rees*:[51]

> [T]he path of the law is strewn with examples of open and shut cases which, somehow, were not; of unanswerable charges which, in the event, were completely answered; of inexplicable conduct which was fully explained; of fixed and unalterable determinations that, by discussion, suffered a change. Nor are those with any knowledge of human nature who pause to think for a moment likely to underestimate the feelings of resentment of those who find that a decision against them has been made without their being afforded any opportunity to influence the course of events.

What kind of procedure is required in order to make a dismissal fair depends, of course, on the reason for the dismissal. The ACAS Code for discipline is not designed for cases of incapacity owing to ill health, but is required in any case with a disciplinary element.

Finally, note one possible development here. In *Burn v Alder Hey Children's NHS Foundation Trust*,[52] a case concerning the construction of a particular medical disciplinary procedure, Underhill LJ in the Court of Appeal speculated that the time may have

[49] [1988] ICR 370, [1988] IRLR 215, CA; the passage cited is at 377 and 218, respectively.

[50] This can be seen from the decision of a differently constituted Court of Appeal in *Dillett v National Coal Board* [1988] ICR 218, where on facts similar to those in *McLaren* the court confirmed a decision that a dismissal without a hearing in the middle of the miners' strike was fair, but largely on the ground that that had been the view of the tribunal on the particular facts of the case and it was not open to an appellate court to reverse them.

[51] [1970] Ch 345 at 402, [1969] 2 All ER 274 at 309.

[52] [2022] IRLR 306, [2022] ICR 492, CA; *Holmes v QinetiQ Ltd* UKEAT/0206/15 (26 April 2016, unreported) (COP not applicable to ill-health dismissal as such); but see *Hussain v Jurys Inn Group* UKEAT/0283/15 (3 February 2016, unreported) (COP applicable to 'some other substantial reason' (SOSR) dismissals with some additional disciplinary element); *Rentplus UK Ltd v Coulson* [2022] EAT 81 (COP applicable to a sham redundancy case).

come to 'discover' an implied term in employment contracts that the employer will conduct disciplinary processes *fairly*. Although this was obiter (and said to be for another case to decide) it may well have laid the groundwork for such an implied term, especially coming from such an eminent employment lawyer; it could raise the profile of procedural fairness even further, both in common law actions and in constructive dismissal cases by statute, adding another term capable of being breached fundamentally by the employer.

7.1.3 **Workplace procedures and government policy**

As has already been mentioned, from 2004 to 2009 there existed something called 'mandatory standard procedures'. This was a statutory arrangement which, inter alia, made a dismissal unfair if specific statutory procedures were not followed, intended to ensure that more cases were resolved in the workplace rather than the tribunals. For reasons which it exceeds the ambitions of this chapter to discuss, this system failed miserably to reduce litigation, which prompted a consultation, which resulted in the Gibbons Report.[53] This led—in the blink of an eye, by legislative standards—to the repeal of the standard procedures scheme and a return to the *Polkey* position,[54] under which the ACAS Code is the presumptive but not strictly required standard. The Employment Act 2008 scrapped the statutory discipline and grievance procedures, and replaced them with a revised ACAS Code of Practice for Discipline and Grievance Procedures. However, one innovation was that since April 2009 tribunals have been authorized to adjust compensation in unfair dismissal cases up or down by as much as 25 per cent against any party who unreasonably fails to comply with provisions of the new ACAS Code.[55] The EAT has given guidance in two cases on the operation of this scheme. As to when to make this statutory uplift, the first case[56] suggested that the tribunal consider four questions:

1. Is the case one which raises a matter to which the ACAS code applies?
2. Has there been a failure to comply with the ACAS code in relation to that matter?
3. Was the failure to comply with the ACAS code unreasonable?
4. Is it just and equitable to award an uplift because of the failure to comply with the ACAS code and, if so, by what percentage, up to 25 per cent?

In the second case,[57] guidance was given more specifically as to amount. It was said that the tribunal must consider all the circumstances of the case including the seriousness and motivation for the breach; there is no requirement of 'exceptionally' bad conduct. In addition, the tribunal must be careful not to produce overlap with other forms of damages awarded and at the end of the exercise must look at the result in the round to make sure that it is 'proportionate'. It can be seen from this that, subject to the proportionality point, this is very much in the tribunal's discretion and its decision is unlikely to be upset on appeal.

[53] *Better Dispute Resolution* (DTI, March 2007). [54] See 7.4.3.

[55] TULR(C)A 1992, s 207A. The power to adjust awards applies to jurisdictions other than unfair dismissal, but only to employees, not to workers: *Local Government Yorkshire and Humber v Shah* UKEAT/0587/11, UKEAT/0026/12 (19 June 2012, unreported).

[56] *Rentplus UK Ltd v Coulson* [2022] EAT 81; the EAT upheld a decision to apply the full 25% where the ET found that both the redundancy dismissal of the claimant and the handling of their appeal were shams to get rid of them.

[57] *Slade v Biggs* [2022] IRLR 216, EAT; the claimants had already received substantial damages, but the EAT again upheld a 25% uplift (an equally substantial amount) on evidence that the employer had engineered their dismissals when they became pregnant.

7.2 The definition of dismissal and the date of termination

7.2.1 Dismissal

The existence of a dismissal is a vital jurisdictional factor in the laws relating to unfair dismissal and redundancy. In most cases it is obvious that there has been a dismissal, but in cases of doubt the onus is upon the applicant to prove that they are dismissed; if they fail to do so, they cannot proceed with their claim. In particular, a tribunal will have no jurisdiction to hear the claim if the true construction of the facts is that the termination of employment was brought about by some factor other than dismissal (eg frustration or mutual consent)[58] or that the employee resigned (see later discussion). Dismissal is therefore a central concept in this area of law and has not been without its problems.[59]

7.2.1.1 The definition of dismissal

Dismissal is defined for the purposes of unfair dismissal and redundancy in ss 95 and 136, respectively, of the Employment Rights Act 1996. These definitions are similar and envisage dismissal arising in one of three situations:

1. where the contract is terminated by the employer either with or without notice;
2. where a limited-term contract expires or otherwise terminates without being renewed;
3. where the *employee* terminates the contract, with or without notice, in circumstances such that they are *entitled* to terminate it without notice by reason of the employer's conduct.

Category (1) covers the usual case of dismissal, where the employer clearly dispenses with the employee's services either summarily or by giving them notice (or by giving them wages in lieu thereof). As it means the termination of a particular contract, there can be a category (1) dismissal (and hence a claim for unfair dismissal) even though the employee is still working for the same employer under a new contract (which may be particularly useful for the employee where the employer has unilaterally insisted on radically different terms of employment, sufficient to constitute a 'new' contract, rather than just a modification of the existing one).[60] It has also been held to cover cases where at first sight the employee appears to have resigned, but evidence then clearly establishes that the resignation was procured by the employer either by fraud,[61] pressure,[62] or ultimatum ('resign or be sacked');[63] this has been done by concentrating, as a matter of fact, on the question

[58] For modes of termination other than dismissal see 6.1.

[59] Elias 'Unravelling the Concept of Dismissal' (1978) 7 ILJ 16 was a seminal early consideration of this area.

[60] This is the rule in *Hogg v Dover College* [1990] ICR 39, which, while only likely to apply on strong facts (of a major change in terms imposed by the employer on a reluctant workforce), was affirmed and applied in *Alcan Extrusions v Yates* [1996] IRLR 327. Its importance is that, unlike constructive dismissal (the usual possibility in a case of unilateral change by the employer), the employees can claim unfair dismissal while keeping their jobs.

[61] *Makin v Grews Motors (Bridport) Ltd* (1986) The Times, 18 April, CA.

[62] *Caledonian Mining Co Ltd v Bassett* [1987] ICR 425, [1987] IRLR 165, applying *Martin v Glynwed Distribution Ltd* [1983] ICR 511, [1983] IRLR 198, CA; *Hellyer Bros Ltd v Atkinson* [1992] IRLR 540, EAT; *Lassman v De Vere University Arms Hotel* [2003] ICR 44.

[63] *East Sussex County Council v Walker* (1972) 7 ITR 280; *Martin*, n 63xyz. However, these cases must be carefully distinguished from (a) cases where the employer has merely indicated a general intention to dismiss at some time in the future (eg on a planned future factory closure): *Haseltine Lake & Co Ltd v Dowler* [1981] ICR 222, [1981] IRLR 25; *International Computers Ltd v Kennedy* [1981] IRLR 28; (b) cases where an employee under threat of dismissal reaches acceptable terms on which to leave. These will be ordinary resignations.

of who *really* terminated the employment. This question may also be of importance where there is an ambiguous or hot-headed 'resignation'; while an employer may rely on a clear statement by the employee, there may be an onus on it to investigate further if there are special factors or circumstances leading up to the employee's actions, and failure to do so may mean that what eventually occurred was actually a dismissal and, in all likelihood, an unfair dismissal.[64]

Where under category (1) an employee is given notice of dismissal, they may wish to leave the job before expiry of that notice (eg where, being about to be made redundant, they find another job which they wish to start immediately). In such circumstances the employee would normally be in a difficult position, as if they gave notice to leave, they might be construed as having resigned or terminated the employment by mutual consent with the employer;[65] in either case there would be no dismissal and so they would lose their unfair dismissal and redundancy rights. To avoid this pitfall, the legislation includes the concept of 'early notice',[66] so that if, during the currency of the employer's notice, the employee gives counter-notice to terminate the employment at an earlier date, they may leave and still be taken to have been dismissed by the employer. It must be noted here, however, that the provisions relating to early notice for redundancy purposes are narrower than those for unfair dismissal purposes, in two ways: (a) the employee must give their counter-notice in writing; and (b) the counter-notice must be given during the *obligatory* period of the employer's notice (ie the period which the employer must by law give, either under the individual contract, or by virtue of the minimum notice requirements,[67] whichever is the longer). These requirements used to exist for unfair dismissal purposes also, but were removed by the Employment Protection Act 1975.

The original version of category (2) existed to safeguard the position of employees under fixed-term contracts and used that terminology. In practice, most cases under this heading will still concern fixed-term (ie time limited) contracts, but in 2002 the wording was altered to cover all forms of limited-term contracts, to be consistent with the Fixed-term Worker Directive (in particular to cover 'task' or 'purpose' contracts). Expiry (whether by time or some other limiting event) without renewal is deemed to be a dismissal, so that in an unfair dismissal action, the employer will have to show that the reason for failure to renew was a fair one.[68] The meaning of 'limited-term contract' was considered earlier.[69]

7.2.1.2 **Constructive dismissal**

While categories (1) and (2) have not been without difficulties, it is category (3) which has been most contentious. This sets out the statutory definition of 'constructive dismissal', which was always in the redundancy payments legislation and was read into the unfair dismissal provisions[70] before being expressly included in 1974.

[64] *Willoughby v CF Capital Ltd* [2011] IRLR 985, CA; *Kwik Fit (GB) Ltd v Lineham* [1992] ICR 183, [1992] IRLR 156. One problem is, of course, that in such extreme circumstances the language used tends not to be that contained in s 95; more often a tribunal will have to decide instead whether telling the employer where to insert the job, in graphic anatomical detail, constitutes an unambiguous resignation.

[65] See 6.1.4.

[66] Employment Rights Act 1996, ss 95(2) and 136(3). The counter-notice given by the employee may be of any length; it does not have to be of the length required by their contract (or even the statutory minimum of one week under s 86): *Ready Case Ltd v Jackson* [1981] IRLR 312—*quaere* what if it was only a few hours, or even minutes? The employer must have given actual notice for these provisions to apply; it is not enough that it has made some general statement of a possible future dismissal.

[67] Employment Rights Act 1996, s 86.

[68] *Terry v East Sussex County Council* [1976] ICR 536, [1976] IRLR 332, approved by the Court of Appeal in *Fay v North Yorkshire County Council* [1986] ICR 133, [1985] IRLR 247.

[69] See 6.1.3.

[70] *Sutcliffe v Hawker Siddeley Aviation Ltd* [1973] ICR 560, [1973] IRLR 304, NIRC.

Constructive dismissal occurs where the employee appears to terminate the employment by walking out, but the real reason for termination was in some way the prior conduct of the employer. It is necessary in order to avoid the employer being able to force or goad the employee to leave their employment and then suggest that the employee resigned and cannot claim on grounds of dismissal.

When it is established, it means that for statutory purposes the contract is terminated by the employer. This is clearly the most contentious kind of dismissal, as there is no express act of dismissal by the employer. It must be remembered, however, that a constructive dismissal is *not* necessarily unfair and so a tribunal, even if it finds in the employee's favour on constructive dismissal, has only established the existence of a dismissal, and must still go on to consider fairness in the ordinary way; in many cases there will be little argument on this and the dismissal will, in the nature of things, be unfair, but this is not automatically so and there may be cases where, even though the employee had technically the right to walk out, the employer may be able to show that it was fair to act as it did.[71] It is an error of law for a tribunal to assume that a constructive dismissal is an unfair dismissal without findings on the reason for the dismissal (ie the reason for the act that constituted a repudiatory breach) and its 'fairness'.[72]

Definition of constructive dismissal

The key element of the definition of constructive dismissal is that the employee must have been *entitled* to leave without notice because of the employer's conduct. What does 'entitled' mean? At the outset of this legislation, there were two possible interpretations of this crucial word—first, that the employee could leave when the employer's behaviour towards them was so unreasonable that they could not be expected to stay, and second, that the employer's conduct had to be so grave that it constituted a repudiatory breach of the contract of employment, that is, that the employee was *contractually* entitled to leave. Clearly the second is a narrower approach, and it was argued that the first was more in line with the overall approach in unfair dismissal cases of looking at the reasonableness of the employer's conduct. Following an initial period of uncertainty, with conflicting decisions, the Court of Appeal held in *Western Excavating (ECC) Ltd v Sharp*[73] that the contractual approach is the correct one, Lord Denning MR defining it as follows:

> If the employer is guilty of conduct which is a significant breach going to the root of the contract of employment, or which shows that the employer no longer intends to be bound by one or more of the essential terms of the contract, then the employee is entitled to treat himself as discharged from any further performance. If he does so, then he terminates the contract by reason of the employer's conduct. He is constructively dismissed. The employee is entitled in those circumstances to leave at the instant without giving any notice at all or, alternatively, he may give notice and say that he is leaving at the end of the notice. But the conduct must in either case be sufficiently serious to entitle him to leave at once.

[71] *Savoia v Chiltern Herb Farms Ltd* [1982] IRLR 166, CA.

[72] *Stephenson & Co (Oxford) Ltd v Austin* [1990] ICR 609, EAT. See also *Wells v Countryside Estate Agents* UKEAT/0201/15 (11 February 2016, unreported) (the demotion was reasonable, and the demotion was the repudiatory breach, so the dismissal was reasonable).

[73] [1978] ICR 221, [1978] IRLR 27, CA; the passage cited is at 226 and 29xyz?229, respectively; *Courtaulds Northern Spinning Ltd v Sibson* [1988] ICR 451, [1988] IRLR 305, CA.

Thus, in a constructive dismissal case the tribunal is looking primarily for conduct by the employer[74] which is clearly a breach of one of the terms of the contract, and sufficiently important to be repudiatory on the part of the employer. This is a case-by-case determination and is a matter of mixed law and fact.[75] Certain examples may be fairly obvious, such as a refusal to pay wages,[76] an unjustified demotion or suspension,[77] failure to follow a contractually binding disciplinary procedure,[78] unilateral alteration of job content without contractual authority,[79] or insistence upon an unlawful or illegal order or the imposition of a penalty disproportionate to the offence.[80] A change to the location of work has been found to be a fundamental breach, but cannot be assumed to be so in every case.[81] Failure to provide the work an employee was contracted to provide is a repudiatory breach,[82] but failure of an agency employer to take any action to find work for an agency worker was not.[83] The breach in question may be of an implied term as well as an express one, and therefore it is important to be able to say exactly which term it is claimed that the

[74] Conduct by an immediate superior (eg a supervisor) may be enough to justify walking out, even if the employer later argues that that superior did not actually have the power to dismiss: *Hilton Industrial Hotels (UK) Ltd v Protopapa* [1990] IRLR 316.

[75] It has been held by the Court of Appeal that the question of whether a particular breach of contract is sufficient to be repudiatory (for the purpose of establishing constructive dismissal) is one of mixed fact and law, so that the EAT should rarely interfere with a tribunal's decision on this point, provided there was some evidence on which to base that decision: *Cetinsoy v London United Busways Ltd* UKEAT/0042/14 (23 May 2014, unreported); *Pedersen v Camden London Borough Council* [1981] ICR 674n, [1981] IRLR 173, CA. Although the test is contractual, seriously unreasonable conduct by the employer may be powerful evidence of breach of contract (in particular, the implied term of trust and respect): *Brown v Merchant Ferries Ltd* [1998] IRLR 682, NICA. Breach of statute by the employer should not be enough alone to find constructive dismissal: *Doherty v British Midland Airways Ltd* [2006] IRLR 90. However, in *Greenhof v Barnsley MBC* [2006] IRLR 98 such a result was achieved by arguing that the statutory breach (failure to make reasonable adjustments for a disabled employee) broke the implied contractual term of trust and respect.

[76] Even this major term is not sacrosanct, however, as every case must be considered on its facts; even a failure to pay wages might not be repudiatory in exceptional circumstances: *Adams v Charles Zub Associates Ltd* [1978] IRLR 551. Further, there is no implied term of an annual wage rise, so failure to give one will not necessarily amount to repudiatory conduct by the employer: *Murco Petroleum Ltd v Forge* [1987] ICR 282, [1987] IRLR 50; likewise, there is no implied term that there will never be a pay decrease: *White v Reflecting Roadstuds Ltd* [1991] ICR 733, [1991] IRLR 331. On the other hand, the Court of Appeal held in *Cantor Fitzgerald International v Callaghan* [1999] ICR 639, [1999] IRLR 234 (a common law action, but on the same point) that failure to pay any element of remuneration, however minor, will usually be repudiatory. For detailed consideration of matters held to be repudiatory in the past see *Harvey* DI [425].

[77] *McNeill v Charles Crimm (Electrical Construction) Ltd* [1984] IRLR 179, EAT.

[78] *Post Office v Strange* [1981] IRLR 515, EAT.

[79] *Millbrook Furnishing Industries Ltd v McIntosh* [1981] IRLR 309; where the alteration is only temporary and for pressing business need, it may be arguable that it is not enough to be repudiatory, but such an argument failed in the *Millbrook* case. One practical answer for the employer is to incorporate a flexibility clause in the contract in the first place, but even this may not be a panacea because in *Land Securities Trillium Ltd v Thornley* [2005] IRLR 765 such a clause was interpreted narrowly, not covering a wholesale change in job function.

[80] *BBC v Beckett* [1983] IRLR 43; *Cawley v South Wales Electricity Board* [1985] IRLR 89; this class of case is more interesting, for here the employer may technically have the contractual power to impose the penalty in question, but must still act in accordance with some sort of proportionality which is presumably implied into the contractual disciplinary rules.

[81] *Cetinsoy v London United Busways Ltd* UKEAT/0042/14 (23 May 2014, unreported), explaining *Musse v Abellio London Ltd* [2012] IRLR 360, EAT.

[82] *Lees v Imperial College of Science, Technology and Medicine* UKEAT/0288/15 (14 January 2016, unreported).

[83] *Sandle v Adecco* UKEAT/0028/16/JOJ (the outcome in this case might have been different had there been a contractual obligation to seek or provide work).

employer broke, and whether any such term ever actually existed in the contract.[84] The question of definition of contractual terms, considered in Chapter 3, has thus been given statutory significance.

Constructive dismissal in practice

The contractual test as laid down in *Western Excavating (ECC) Ltd v Sharp* appears to be much narrower and more precise than the 'reasonableness' test, and at first seemed to be a significant restriction on constructive dismissal. However, this has not been so, principally for two reasons. The first is that the Court of Appeal, while firmly basing the law upon ideas of contract, did not mean to impose a rigid test and envisaged some flexibility in its application. This can be seen particularly in the judgment of Lawton LJ:

> I do not find it either necessary or advisable to express any opinion as to what principles of law operate to bring a contract of employment to an end by reason of an employer's conduct. Sensible persons have no difficulty in recognising such conduct when they hear about it . . . Lay members of the [employment] tribunals . . . do not spend all their time in court and when out of court they may use, and certainly will hear, short words and terse phrases which describe clearly the kind of employer of whom an employee is entitled without notice to rid himself. This is what [constructive dismissal] is all about; and what is required for the application of this provision is a large measure of common sense.[85]

The second, and more far-reaching, reason is that in subsequent cases, the EAT has shown itself ready to read into contracts of employment a term obliging the employer to treat the employee with trust and respect.[86] This has also been called the '*Malik*' term, after the case that articulated it as an implied term of mutual trust and confidence.[87] According to this term, it can be a constructive dismissal for an employer to act in a way calculated or likely to destroy or seriously damage the relationship of confidence and trust between employer and employee.[88] To a large extent this development has outflanked the more purely contractual approach of the Court of Appeal in *Western Excavating (ECC) Ltd v Sharp*, so that harsh and unreasonable conduct by the employer might be construed by the tribunal as a breach of this implied term of mutual trust and confidence, giving rise to a constructive

[84] A good example is *Dryden v Greater Glasgow Health Board* [1992] IRLR 469 (no implied term allowing smoking); it was also held there that if a change of practice is lawful under the contract (there, the imposition of a no-smoking policy), the fact that it bears more heavily on one employee than on others is not a ground for constructive dismissal.

[85] [1978] ICR 221 at 229, [1978] IRLR 27 at 30, CA. Generally speaking, the test is objective, in that the employer's conduct does not have to be intentional or in bad faith before it may be repudiatory: *Post Office v Roberts* [1980] IRLR 347. In line with this, 'seriously unreasonable' conduct can be evidence of contractual breach: *Brown v Merchant Ferries Ltd* [1998] IRLR 682, NICA. However, one class of case has imported a potentially subjective test—in *Frank Wright & Co (Holdings) Ltd v Punch* [1980] IRLR 217 it was held that where there is a genuine dispute as to the meaning of a contractual term and the employer insists on implementing its genuine (but possibly mistaken) version of it, that is not a repudiatory breach (even if it is later proved to have been wrong). This principle has backing from the normal law of commercial contracts (see *Woodar Investment Development Ltd v Wimpey Construction (UK) Ltd* [1980] 1 All ER 571, [1980] 1 WLR 277, HL) but its application to the specialized area of constructive dismissal could have an unfortunately restrictive effect; it was treated with caution in *Financial Techniques (Planning Services) Ltd v Hughes* [1981] IRLR 32, CA, but mentioned with approval obiter by Sir John Donaldson MR in *Bridgen v Lancashire County Council* [1987] IRLR 58, CA, and so the point remains unresolved.

[86] See 3.3.4. [87] *Malik v Bank of Credit and Commerce International SA* [1997] ICR 606, 621.

[88] *Malik* (n xyz); *Leeds Dental Team Ltd v Rose* [2014] IRLR 8, EAT.

dismissal.[89] Thus, in the outcome, the contractual approach may differ only subtly from a simple 'reasonableness' approach,[90] and indeed a tribunal or court may now be impatient with an excessively contractual or technical argument by an employer which is aimed at frustrating the protective policy behind constructive dismissal.

This breadth of approach can be seen, for example, in the so-called last straw doctrine, namely that the employee's resignation can be in response to a long series of actions by the employer, with the result that the actual event over which they walk out need not in itself be a seriously repudiatory one; even a relatively minor event may need to be looked at in context.[91]

However, there remain two main qualifications. The *first* is that if the 'conduct' in question consists simply of the employer exercising one of its definite contractual rights (eg to make the employee move from site to site, where there is a mobility clause in the contract), the employee who refuses to comply *should* not, under the contractual approach, be able to claim constructive dismissal, as there has been no breach of contract;[92] however, it is argued elsewhere[93] that this may be changing, with the development by the courts of possible *overriding* implied terms, particularly that of mutual trust and confidence, which may impose limits on the *way* in which even express terms are applied, and in so doing increase the scope for constructive dismissal. The courts have already begun to put some limits on this approach, finding that where a constructive dismissal claim involves the exercise of a discretion afforded by the contract to the employer, the claimant must show *Wednesbury* unreasonableness—it must be demonstrated that no reasonable employer could have made the challenged exercise of the discretion.[94] The *second* qualification is that a particularly contractual approach has been taken by the Court of Appeal to the question of *anticipatory* breach by the employer; this is unlikely to occur often in practice, but if it does (eg by an employer announcing that it intends to implement unilateral changes of terms and conditions at some time in the future), it has been held that the employer may retract its intended repudiation as long as it does so before the employee has unequivocally accepted it and terminated the contract in anticipation.[95] It is also possible for an employer to prevent an act of unfair discipline from crossing the line of repudiation by investigating and retracting the disciplinary sanction before it can take effect.[96] However, it is also clear that once a repudiatory breach goes beyond being anticipatory to being a completed breach, the breach cannot be 'cured' by the employer (through, for

[89] Conduct which is serious enough to breach the term of trust and confidence will always be serious enough to constitute a repudiatory breach by the employer for the purpose of establishing constructive dismissal: *Amnesty International v Ahmed* [2009] IRLR 884, [2009] ICR 1450; *Morrow v Safeway Stores* [2002] IRLR 9.

[90] See *British Aircraft Corpn v Austin* [1978] IRLR 332 at 334, per Phillips J.

[91] *Omilaju v Waltham Forest LBC* [2005] IRLR 35, CA; although the last event need not be per se repudiatory, it must be serious enough to be a contributory factor to the decision to leave. Where the employee affirms the contract after events that were arguably repudiatory (eg by 'soldiering on', hoping it will all get better), that accumulation of breaches can be 'revived' by a less-than-repudiatory breach: *Kaur v Leeds Teaching Hospitals NHS Trust* [2018] IRLR 833.

[92] For example a threat by the employer to give lawful contractual notice of dismissal cannot establish constructive dismissal, so that an employee leaving because of it may be held to have jumped the gun: *Kerry Foods Ltd v Lynch* [2005] IRLR 680, not following *Greenaway Harrison v Wiles* [1994] IRLR 380.

[93] See 3.2.1.

[94] *IBM UK Holdings Ltd v Dalgleish* [2017] EWCA Civ 1212, [2018] IRLR 4; see also *Sharfugeen v T J Morris Ltd* UKEAT/0272/16 (3 March 2017, unreported).

[95] *Norwest Holst Group Administration Ltd v Harrison* [1985] ICR 668, [1985] IRLR 240, CA.

[96] *Assamoi v Spirit Pub Co* UKEAT/0050/11 (30 July 2012, unreported). Indeed, even a dismissal can be retracted by an internal appeal, and if it is the law treats the employment as never having been terminated: *Folkestone Nursing Home Ltd v Patel* UKEAT/0348/15 (1 June 2016, unreported).

example, retraction of an accusation or an apology and attempts at reconciliation) unless the employee chooses to affirm the contract.[97] This is true even if it means that where the employer finds in favour of the employee in a workplace grievance procedure and retracts the offending conduct, it is too late: the contract has been breached and the employee has been constructively dismissed. This principle goes both ways, of course: if an employee has engaged in repudiatory conduct but the employer has not yet accepted the repudiation by dismissing the employee, they remain in a position to leave and claim constructive dismissal on the basis of repudiatory conduct by the employer that happens after the employee's repudiatory conduct.[98]

Although the theory behind constructive dismissal is that it is the employer who terminates the contract for statutory purposes, in practice it will usually be the employee who takes the final step by resigning and walking out, thus showing that they have accepted the employer's repudiation as concluding the contract. If the employee does not take such action, or does so after a delay, there is the danger (particularly in cases where the employer's conduct consists of a unilateral proposal to change the terms of employment) of this being construed as an agreement by the employee to a variation in the contract; if this is so there is no constructive dismissal, even if the employee later resigns.[99] To avoid this danger, the employee should make up their mind quickly whether to leave,[100] or, if the economic circumstances are such that continued working for a short period is required, the employee should let it be known that any further work proceeds under protest. Those working under protest must comply with any changes imposed, even if they consider the changes repudiatory breaches of contract, because staying under protest but not complying can justify a dismissal for misconduct.[101]

The courts and tribunals have taken a realistic view of this,[102] but of course the employee cannot work under protest indefinitely and is expected to decide what their final response is to be within a reasonable period. This is because it remains the legal position that the employee must be able to show that they left *in response to* the employer's conduct (ie the causal link must be shown). However, this itself is to be viewed realistically (given the employee's difficult position), and so it has been held that (a) there can still be a constructive dismissal if the employee waits to leave until they have found another job to go to;[103]

[97] *Buckland v Bournemouth University* [2010] EWCA Civ 121.

[98] *Atkinson v Community Gateway Association* UKEAT/0457/12 (21 August 2014, unreported).

[99] A particularly harsh example of this can be found in *Colomar Mari v Reuters Ltd* UKEAT/0539/13 (30 January 2015, unreported), where an employee was deemed to have affirmed changes even though the employee's departure was only delayed by illness—it was seen as crucial that the employee had accepted sick pay during the delay. Fortunately, however, it has been affirmed that merely choosing to use the employer's grievance procedure to attempt a solution before leaving does *not* constitute affirmation: *Brooks v Leisure Employment Services Ltd* [2023] EAT 137.

[100] *Western Excavating (ECC) Ltd v Sharp* [1978] ICR 221 at 226, [1978] IRLR 27 at 29, respectively per Lord Denning MR; *Land and Wilson v West Yorkshire Metropolitan County Council* [1981] ICR 334, [1981] IRLR 87, CA. Note, however, that even if the employee must be taken to have consented to previous repudiations by the employer, it may be possible to rely on the fact of those repudiations having occurred as evidence of overall breach of the general implied term of trust and respect: *Lewis v Motorworld Garages Ltd* [1986] ICR 157, [1985] IRLR 465, CA.

[101] *Robinson v Tescom Corporation* [2008] IRLR 408, EAT.

[102] *Marriott v Oxford and District Co-operative Society Ltd* (No 2) [1970] 1 QB 186, [1969] 3 All ER 1126, CA; *Shields Furniture Ltd v Goff* [1973] 2 All ER 653, [1973] ICR 187; *Sheet Metal Components Ltd v Plumridge* [1974] ICR 373, [1974] IRLR 86; *W E Cox Toner (International) Ltd v Crook* [1981] ICR 823, [1981] IRLR 443. See too, in the context of *wrongful dismissal*, *Bliss v South East Thames Regional Health Authority* [1987] ICR 700, [1985] IRLR 308, CA.

[103] *Jones v F Sirl & Son (Furnishers) Ltd* [1997] IRLR 493; *Waltons and Morse v Dorrington* [1997] IRLR 488, EAT.

(b) the employee does not necessarily need to know that the employer conduct which forces them to leave is a repudiatory breach—it can suffice that they leave because of bad conduct, and that the conduct constitutes a repudiatory breach;[104] (c) an employee does not reaffirm the contract by staying to negotiate a termination package;[105] (d) similarly, an employee does not reaffirm the contract by using the employer's internal procedures to try to resolve matters before leaving;[106] and (e) as a matter of law there is no absolute requirement on the employee to tell the employer the real reason for leaving (given that the worse the employer's behaviour, the less likely the employee may be to want to dispute the position before getting out).[107] This last rule (highly inconvenient for HR professionals who may not have had reason to know what was going wrong until the employee left, thus giving them no chance to put it right) may in practice now be subject to qualification by the Employment Act 2008's provision for adjustments to compensation awards to penalize failure to exhaust internal grievance procedures. This of course does not prevent a tribunal from finding a dismissal (or ultimately an unfair dismissal) where the employee leaves without a word, as the acceptance of the employer's repudiation need not be express, but can take the form of conduct inconsistent with continued employment.[108]

7.2.1.3 **Resignation by the employee**

An employee may resign from their employment for any reason or none; if there is a reason and it is connected with the employer's conduct the employee may argue a constructive dismissal, but otherwise there can be no claim for unfair dismissal or a redundancy payment, as there is no dismissal.[109] An express resignation may be by unambiguous wording or, if the wording is ambiguous, by a combination of wording and circumstances from which a reasonable employer would understand the employee to be resigning.[110] However, the concept of resignation has caused problems when attempts have been made to apply it in circumstances other than those of express resignation by the employee.

[104] *Mruke v Khan* [2018] EWCA Civ 280, [2018] IRLR 526 (here the breach was paying well below minimum wage, which the Tanzanian worker did not know was illegal, but she knew it was intolerable).

[105] *Gibbs v Leeds United Football Club* [2016] EWHC 960 (QB), [2016] IRLR 493.

[106] *Gordon v J & D Pierce (Contracts) Ltd* UKEATS/0010/20; *Craig v Abellio Ltd* [2022] IRLR 596, EAT.

[107] *Weathersfield Ltd v Sargent* [1999] IRLR 94, CA, overruling on this point *Holland v Glendale Industries Ltd* [1998] ICR 493. Failure to make clear the reason for leaving when that might reasonably be expected could cast doubt on the genuineness of that reason, but only as a question of factual causation, not as a matter of law.

[108] *Atlantic Air v Hoff* (UKEAT/0602/07, 26 March 2008).

[109] Also a resignation under threat of dismissal may constitute a dismissal, unless the parties reach a mutually satisfactory agreement of terms (usually monetary) upon which the employee agrees to go; in that case it is a genuine resignation in spite of the previous threats—compare *Sheffield v Oxford Controls Co Ltd* [1979] ICR 396, [1979] IRLR 133 with *Thames Television Ltd v Wallis* [1979] IRLR 136. If the employer has already given the employee notice and the employee resigns during that period by giving counter-notice, they may still be 'dismissed' by virtue of ss 95(2) and 136(3) (see 7.2.1.1).

[110] *BG Gale Ltd v Gilbert* [1978] ICR 1149, [1978] IRLR 453; *Sothern v Franks Charlesly & Co* [1981] IRLR 278, CA. There may, however, be problems with a 'hotheaded' resignation which the employee seeks to retract almost immediately—theoretically a retraction would need the consent of the employer, but there have been cases where it has been said that a tribunal should take a broader, more common-sense approach to whether the employee must be taken to have unequivocally resigned (even if, for example, the wording at the time left little to the imagination!): *Willoughby v CF Capital Ltd* [2011] IRLR 985, CA; *Barclay v City of Glasgow District Council* [1983] IRLR 313; *Martin v Yeoman Aggregates Ltd* [1983] ICR 314, [1983] IRLR 49; *Sovereign House Security Services Ltd v Savage* [1989] IRLR 115, CA; *Kwik-Fit (GB) Ltd v Lineham* [1992] ICR 183, [1992] IRLR 156, EAT. The case law here is comprehensively reviewed in *Omar v Epping Forest District Citizens Advice* [2024] IRLR 92, [2024] ICR 301, EAT.

Such problems have arisen in two principal ways. The first occurs where the employee simply walks out or where, as in *British Leyland (UK) Ltd v Ashraf*,[111] the employee is allowed a definite period of leave from which they do not return on time. It is arguable that there needs to be a concept of 'resignation by conduct' to cover the first of these examples (ie where the employee never returns), but the problem with the second example was that it was tied in frequently with rather more spurious arguments on mutual termination or termination by agreement, as in such cases the employer may have allowed the leave on terms that 'if you do not return on time, your employment will terminate'; when the employee arrived back late, he was then told that his contract had ended automatically, without the need for a dismissal. This argument by the employer succeeded in *Ashraf*'s case, but its wider implications soon became obvious and a very different approach was taken. *Ashraf*'s case was first distinguished by the EAT,[112] and finally overruled by the Court of Appeal in *Igbo v Johnson Matthey Chemicals Ltd*,[113] on the ground that such an agreement for automatic termination (on failure to return from leave of absence) was void for contravening the Employment Rights Act 1996, s 203 which invalidates any agreement (whether in a contract of employment or not) which 'purports . . . to exclude or limit the operation of any provision of this Act'—this agreement limited the operation of ss 95 and 98, which give the right to claim unfair dismissal. The advantage from the employee's point of view of this reasoning is that even if they sign such an agreement in full knowledge of what they are signing (eg because the employer will only grant leave if they do so), the agreement will still be of no legal effect under the anti-contracting-out provisions of the section.

The second way in which problems arose had a far greater potential for driving the proverbial horse-drawn transport through the unfair dismissal legislation. This was the idea (known variously as 'constructive resignation' or 'self-dismissal') that in some cases the employee may commit such a grave breach of contract that they must be considered to have resigned by their own act.[114] Once again, this meant that there was no dismissal, and so no action for unfair dismissal. Moreover, such an agreement might arise not only from unusual or drastic facts but could also possibly be set up by an employer phrasing a final warning in terms such as 'if this happens again, you will be considered as having dismissed yourself'.[115] Fortunately, the position was clarified by the Court of Appeal in *London Transport Executive v Clarke*,[116] which concerned the taking of unauthorized leave by an employee in the knowledge that if he did so his name would be 'removed from the books'. When he returned the employers refused to take him back and he claimed unfair dismissal. The majority of the Court of Appeal (Templeman and Dunn LJJ) held that he had in fact been dismissed, applying the 'elective theory'[117] to repudiation of contracts of employment so that the employment was terminated by the employer's acceptance of the employee's repudiation; Lord Denning MR, dissenting, would have continued to apply the concept of self-dismissal, but the majority decision is clearly against it. Employers

[111] [1978] ICR 979, [1978] IRLR 330. For termination by mutual consent generally see 6.1.4.

[112] *Midland Electric Manufacturing Co Ltd v Kanji* [1980] IRLR 185; *Tracey v Zest Equipment Co Ltd* [1982] ICR 481, [1982] IRLR 268.

[113] [1986] ICR 505, [1986] IRLR 215, CA.

[114] The theoretical basis for this in contract law can be found in the previously current idea that contracts of employment formed an exception to the normal rule that a repudiation is only effective when accepted by the innocent party; thus, on this 'automatic termination' theory the contract was in fact ended by the employee's repudiation of it, which did not need any further action on the part of the employer and did not constitute a 'dismissal'.

[115] See eg *Smith v Avana Bakeries Ltd* [1979] IRLR 423 and *Kallinos v London Electric Wire* [1980] IRLR 11.

[116] [1981] ICR 355, [1981] IRLR 166, CA.

[117] See 6.4.2.

should not, however, throw up their hands in despair at this decision, as it was always arguable that the concept of self-dismissal was not particularly necessary anyway—if the employee's conduct was so drastic as to have been clearly repudiatory, then in most cases a tribunal is going to find the dismissal fair anyway (as was the ultimate conclusion of the Court of Appeal in *Clarke*'s case, unanimously).[118] The advantage of the majority's decision is that at least the fairness of the employer's conduct can be tested in such cases, rather than the employee's (possibly weak) claim being ruled out altogether on the jurisdictional point that technically there had been no dismissal.[119]

7.2.2 **The date of termination**

In the law relating to unfair dismissal and redundancy, it is necessary for several reasons[120] to know when the employment ended; for unfair dismissal purposes this is known as the 'effective date of termination' and for redundancy purposes the 'relevant date'. The principal rules relating to these dates are found in the Employment Rights Act 1996, ss 97 and 145, and are as follows:

1. Where the contract is terminated by notice (whether given by the employer or employee)—the date that the notice expires (whether or not the notice was of proper length).[121]
2. Where the contract is terminated without notice—the date on which the termination takes effect.[122]
3. Where a fixed-term or other limited-term contract expires without renewal—the date on which the termination takes effect.
4. Where the employee under notice gives counter-notice to terminate the employment sooner—the date of expiry of the counter-notice.

It is clear that (2) applies to summary dismissals, and in *Stapp v Shaftesbury Society*[123] the Court of Appeal affirmed that the simple rule that the date of termination is the date of the summary dismissal applies even if (a) that summary dismissal is effected while the employee is already under ordinary notice and (b) the effect of the summary dismissal bringing the date of termination forward is to deprive the employee of the qualifying period for unfair dismissal which they would otherwise have attained (except where the effective date of termination would thereby come before the expiration of the *statutory* notice period, in which case, only for the purpose of qualification, the date would be deemed to be the end of the statutory notice—see note 138). This rule will apply even if an internal appeal downgrades an original summary dismissal to an ordinary dismissal, and the claimant is paid for the notice period: the EDT will still be when the summary

[118] See also *Guernina v Thames Valley University* [2007] All ER (D) 156.

[119] Presumably there is now also the secondary ground that if the purported self-dismissal came from an agreement that 'if you do that again, you will be deemed to have dismissed yourself', that agreement itself will be void under s 203 (applying *Igbo v Johnson Matthey Chemicals Ltd*, above).

[120] For example for calculating the period of continuous employment (for calculation and possibly for qualification purposes) and for determining the date from which the three- and six-month limitation periods run.

[121] *Palfrey v Transco plc* [2004] IRLR 916.

[122] This may even mean a precise time on the date in question: *Octavius Atkinson & Sons Ltd v Morris* [1989] ICR 431, [1989] IRLR 158, CA.

[123] [1982] IRLR 326, CA. The fact that the summary dismissal was in breach of a contractually binding disciplinary procedure which would have taken some time to go through properly cannot be used to advance what is otherwise under the section the effective date of termination: *Batchelor v British Railways Board* [1987] IRLR 136, CA.

dismissal occurred (subject to the statutory notice).[124] The decision in *Geys*, to the effect that at common law the employee must accept a repudiation in order for it to terminate the contract,[125] does not change this interpretation of the statutorily determined date.[126]

7.2.2.1 Dismissal with wages in lieu of notice

However, summary dismissal is only one aspect of dismissal without notice. Far more common as a form of dismissal in practice is dismissal with wages in lieu of notice, whereby the employer is rid of the employee immediately (particularly vital where the employee under notice would otherwise have access at work to the firm's computers or confidential information), but with payment of what the employee would have earned had they worked out the notice period. What is to be the date of termination—the date when the notice would have expired (ie under (1)) or the date when the employee in fact leaves, albeit with a payment in lieu (ie under (2))? This could be particularly material on the question of whether a claim is brought in time, especially when the notice period is several weeks (eg from which date does the three-month limit for bringing an unfair dismissal action run?), and could also affect whether the employee has satisfied the qualifying period for the right in question. The interests of certainty would be best served by simply opting for the date when the employee actually leaves (ie treating it as under (2), as if a summary dismissal), and this was for several years thought to be the case, after the decision of the Court of Appeal in *Dedman v British Building and Engineering Appliances Ltd*.[127] However, confusion was caused by the decision of the EAT in *Adams v GKN Sankey Ltd*,[128] where it was suggested that the date of termination depends on the true construction to be placed on the dismissal—if it was expressed as a dismissal by notice (but with the employee not actually required to work out that notice), the date of termination should be the date of expiry of the notice; if, however, it was expressed as an instant dismissal (but with the payment of wages in lieu of notice as, in effect, compensation for wrongful dismissal), the date of termination should be the date the employee left. This distinction seems a thin one on which to base such an important concept as the date of termination and in practice may, one suspects, owe more to fortune than reality in its application. It certainly means that letters of dismissal should be drafted carefully, from the employer's point of view.

This 'construction' approach can also be seen in *Chapman v Letheby and Christopher Ltd*,[129] where it was stated that the mere fact that a dismissal was stated to be with payment in lieu did not mean that it constituted an instant dismissal, and that the effect of the dismissal depended on the construction which would be placed on it by an ordinary, reasonable employee. However, in *Robert Cort & Son Ltd v Charman*,[130] the EAT reverted to the straightforward *Dedman* view, stressing (a) the proper interpretation of the wording of

[124] *Rabess v London Fire and Emergency Planning Authority* [2016] EWCA Civ 1017, [2017] IRLR 147.

[125] *Société Générale London Branch v Geys* [2013] IRLR 122, [2013] ICR 177, SC; see 6.4.2.3.

[126] *Feltham Management Ltd v Feltham* UKEAT/0201/16 (21 December 2017, unreported); *Duniec v Travis Perkins Trading Co Ltd* UKEAT/0482/13 (11 March 2014, unreported).

[127] [1974] 1 All ER 520, [1974] ICR 53, CA, the leading case on the extension of time limits for commencing tribunal actions.

[128] [1980] IRLR 416.

[129] [1981] IRLR 440: the facts in the case were distinctly ambiguous, showing the difficulties that this 'construction' approach can cause, though the EAT did say that ultimately any ambiguity should be construed against the employer, who should have drafted the letter of dismissal more carefully. *Quaere*—how would this apply to an oral dismissal with wages in lieu where no one can remember exactly what was said?

[130] [1981] ICR 816, [1981] IRLR 437 (*Chapman v Letheby and Christopher Ltd* not referred to). The principal significance of the EAT's emphasis on the statutory interpretation of s 97 was that it enabled them to dispose of the employee's subtle arguments based on contractual ideas of repudiation and acceptance (see 7.2.1).

s 97 and (b) the need for absolute certainty on the effective date of termination, especially in the context of limitation periods (though the case itself concerned the question whether the employee had served the necessary qualifying period for an unfair dismissal action). This left the law in an uncertain state. The question was canvassed before the Court of Appeal in *Stapp v Shaftesbury Society*,[131] but that case concerned a different aspect of dismissal without notice (considered earlier in this chapter).[132] However, Stephenson LJ, giving the principal judgment, did allude to the present problem at two stages: at one point he expressly approved of the statement of Browne-Wilkinson J in *Chapman v Letheby and Christopher Ltd* that any ambiguity in a dismissal notice should be construed against the employer (though without commenting on the construction approach generally), but he later said:

> But the effect of summary dismissal in fixing the effective date of termination cannot be questioned. The case of *Cort* is a very recent application of what was laid down by this court some years ago in the case which it followed, *Dedman v British Building and Engineering Appliances Ltd.*

The judgment in *Stapp* is therefore at best ambiguous, and subsequently, in *Leech v Preston Borough Council*,[133] the EAT pointed out that the well-worn phrase 'wages in lieu of notice' has two distinct meanings;[134] it also applied the 'construction' approach in *Adams* and *Chapman*. That must now be considered to be the correct approach, since it is consistent with the explanation of dismissal with wages in lieu generally by Lord Browne-Wilkinson in the leading case on deductions from wages, *Delaney v Staples*;[135] he in fact isolated *four* possible forms of such a dismissal,[136] but they include the two principal forms alluded to in *Leech* and as, in his judgment, he explained that they operate on different grounds, it is reasonable to conclude that the EDT will be different, as the majority of the case law suggests. Therefore, if it is in the employer's interests to fix the EDT at the time the employee stops working, the notice of dismissal must be clear that the dismissal is without notice, and that the money is compensation for the lack of notice, as opposed to wages during a notice period the employee is not required to work.

7.2.2.2 **Additional points about the EDT**

Four further points should be noted. The *first* is that where the employee is dismissed by being given less notice than the employer is obliged to give them by statute,[137] the date of termination is deemed to be the date it would have been had that statutory minimum

[131] [1982] IRLR 326.

[132] The case was principally argued on the point whether an employer could avoid statutory rights by wrongfully dismissing the employee (and after having given him proper notice at that). It was, however, a case of dismissal with wages in lieu (in effect, though not in the usual way), for he had been given notice, then when summarily dismissed during the notice period was told that he would in fact be paid for the whole of the rest of what should have been his notice period.

[133] [1985] ICR 192, [1985] IRLR 337; *Cort*'s case is not cited in the judgment.

[134] The 'grammatically accurate sense of compensation for summary dismissal without notice' or the 'more colloquial sense of payment to someone who is excused or prohibited from attending the workplace during the notice period'.

[135] [1992] ICR 483, [1992] IRLR 191, HL.

[136] These are set out at 6.2, along with the suggested EDTs, in the light of this discussion.

[137] Employment Rights Act 1996, s 86. The employee can only claim an extension by the period of his or her statutory entitlement, not by the period of any more generous notice entitlement agreed in the contract: *Fox Maintenance Ltd v Jackson* [1978] ICR 110, [1977] IRLR 306. Note, however, that s 86(6) preserves the employer's right to dismiss summarily for gross misconduct, and so if an employer does so justifiably there can be no extension under the statute: *Lanton Leisure Ltd v White and Gibson* [1987] IRLR 119, EAT.

been given, for certain purposes. Those purposes are computation of any qualifying period required, calculation of the basic award for unfair dismissal, computation of the two-year qualifying period for a redundancy payment, and calculation of the period of continuous employment by which such a payment is determined.[138] The *second* point is that if the employee has been dismissed, the fact that they are actively pursuing an appeal under the firm's grievance procedure does *not* mean that the date of termination is extended to the completion of that appeal process.[139] Moreover, this is likely to be of most significance when deciding when the time limit for an unfair dismissal action begins to run, and the Court of Appeal affirmed strongly that the fact of pursuing an internal appeal will *not* be a good reason to extend the period in the tribunal's discretion.[140] The *third* point is that ss 97 and 145 do not state what the date of termination is to be in a case of constructive dismissal; it has been held that the EDT is the date of acceptance of the employer's repudiation of the contract, which will normally mean the date when the employee walks out, but it has also been held that an employee cannot use this argument to prolong the EDT past the date the employment *actually* ended.[141] The *fourth*, final, and perhaps most fundamental point on the EDT is that ultimately it is for the employer to get it right, so that any ambiguity is likely to be construed in the employee's favour.[142] In particular, there is in general no doctrine of *constructive* notice of dismissal, so that a dismissal by letter will only take effect when it is actually received by the employee,[143] even if that is later than expected by the employer (who will thus often be well advised to communicate the dismissal directly to the employee, or at the very least to use registered or recorded post so that the date of service can be ascertained).[144]

7.3 **Unfair dismissal—the right and the exclusions**

Just over 40 per cent of the cases heard by tribunals each year have claims of unfair dismissal as their primary concern. As is immediately obvious, such a claim is a much more realistic action to bring in most cases than the common law action for wrongful

[138] Employment Rights Act 1996, ss 97(2) and 145(5). The statutory extension is for these purposes only, it is not of general application: *Slater v John Swain & Son Ltd* [1981] ICR 554, [1981] IRLR 303; *Secretary of State for Employment v Cameron Iron Works* [1988] ICR 297 (revsd on other grounds [1989] ICR 664, [1989] IRLR 117, CA). In particular, note that it does not apply for the purposes of the three-/six-month limitation periods for bringing tribunal proceedings.

[139] *J Sainsbury Ltd v Savage* [1981] ICR 1, [1980] IRLR 109, CA. If, however, the appeal is successful there is no break in continuity, as the appeal decision applies as from the date of the original dismissal: *Howgate v Fane Acoustics Ltd* [1981] IRLR 161, EAT.

[140] *Palmer v Southend-on-Sea Borough Council* [1984] ICR 372, [1984] IRLR 119, CA.

[141] Contrast *G W Stephens & Son v Fish* [1989] ICR 324 with *BMK Ltd v Logue* [1993] ICR 601. Note, however, that there was introduced in 1982 an extension of time for certain purposes (akin to those in n 143) in the case of a constructive dismissal, the extension period being the amount of notice that should have been given under s 86 if it had been the employer who was terminating the employment: s 97(4).

[142] *Widdicombe v Longcombe Software Ltd* [1998] ICR 710 (ambiguous correspondence between employer and absent employee; EDT fixed as the date of the final, clearest letter, which came within the limitation period). As the EDT is a statutory concept, it cannot be altered by agreement between the parties: *Fitzgerald v University of Kent* [2004] ICR 737, [2004] IRLR 300, CA.

[143] *Newcastle upon Tyne NHS Foundation Trust v Haywood* [2018] UKSC 22, [2018] IRLR 644.

[144] *Gisda CYF v Barratt* [2010] IRLR 1073, [2010] ICR 1475, SC; *McMaster v Manchester Airport plc* [1998] IRLR 112 (sick employee not receiving dismissal letter on the expected day of delivery because on a day trip to France; limitation period only flowed from the day of his return).

dismissal, and since its inception in 1971[145] this branch of employment law has given rise to an enormous amount of case law. It is therefore particularly important in this context to bear in mind that the only way to cope successfully with the intimidating case law is to concentrate on those cases which establish principles, points of interpretation, or (at least when they are in fashion) general guidelines for the tribunals, and consider the rest as mere illustrations, interesting though they may be. One simple truth, so easy to overlook when surrounded by employment law reports, is that unfair dismissal is *not* primarily a case law subject—primacy must remain with the relevant wording of the statute. Further, the statute in most contexts puts matters into the discretion of the tribunals (and expressly gives a restricted right of appeal to the EAT, on points of law only) and so, although for the sake of exposition the following discussion will look at the law under certain headings and will concentrate on the evolving rules relating to certain categories of dismissal of practical importance, it must be remembered that in many instances the seeming rules of law under discussion may only be guidelines to the factors to be taken into consideration by the tribunal in deciding upon what is usually the central issue in an unfair dismissal case, namely whether the employer's conduct in the dismissal was reasonable.

7.3.1 **The right to claim**

Subject to certain exclusions, the Employment Rights Act 1996, s 94 gives to every employee the right not to be unfairly dismissed. There are two general qualifications to this, one continuing and one about to be significantly amended. The first is that the employee must have been 'dismissed' (considered above). The second is that from the very beginning there has always been a further requirement that the employee must have served a 'qualifying period' in the employment. This started off at six months, but was subject to variation and has latterly been the relatively long period of two years. However, one of the headline changes in the Employment Rights Bill as originally drafted was to make unfair dismissal a day one right, removing its qualifying period altogether (as had been specifically proposed in the Labour manifesto in 2024). However, this proved to be one of the most controversial elements of the Bill, leading to a difficult period of legislative ping pong between the Commons and Lords. Eventually, in order to secure the Bill's final stages late in 2025 the government compromised and substituted a reduction in the qualifying period from two years to six months. This is contained now in the Act and as part of the compromise is to come into force earlier than planned.

7.3.2 **The exclusions**

The right to bring an action has always been subject to exceptions. Part-timers were excluded for many years (indirectly, in that an employee working fewer than 16 hours per week could not count this towards the year qualification period) but this was

[145] The provisions relating to unfair dismissal were first enacted in the Industrial Relations Act 1971; they were re-enacted in the first Schedule to the Trade Union and Labour Relations Act 1974, amended by the Employment Protection Act 1975, and then consolidated, first in the Employment Protection (Consolidation) Act 1978 and then in the Employment Rights Act 1996. The scheme of the provisions follows ILO Recommendation 119 (1963); revised ILO standards on dismissal worked out subsequently have not been adopted; see (1984) 13 ILJ 130. For detailed consideration of this branch of law see *Harvey* Division DI, to which more detailed references are made later; also Dickens et al. *Dismissed* (1983); Collins 'The Meaning of Job Security' (1991) 20 ILJ 227; and, for a fundamental critique of the existing law, Collins *Justice in Dismissal* (1992) and Pitt 'Justice in Dismissal—A Reply to Hugh Collins' (1993) 22 ILJ 251.

repealed in 1995.[146] The exception that always caused the most difficulty and extensive litigation concerned employees over 65 or (if different) their 'normal retirement age'. This exception had to go with the advent of the Employment Equality (Age) Regulations 2006 (now superseded by the Equality Act 2010) and so there is now no upper age limit for a claim.[147] This change is somewhat illusory, however, as the Equality Act 2010 does not prohibit employers from adopting policies that require retirement at a specific age so long as the policy is a proportionate means to certain legitimate social aims.

The position on exclusions has thus been a fluid one, and indeed the Employment Relations Act 1999 had already made two important changes. First, it repealed the provisions in the Employment Rights Act 1996, s 197 which used to permit an employer to put into a fixed-term contract of one year or more a clause excluding unfair dismissal rights on termination. There had been long-standing criticisms of this power, on the basis of abuse by employers (especially by the device of putting employees onto successive such contracts, possibly over a long period of time), and the government decided to abolish it altogether. Second, the 1999 Act also repealed s 196 of the 1996 Act, which used to disapply most of the rights in the latter (including unfair dismissal) where 'under the employee's contract of employment he ordinarily works outside Great Britain'. What was to replace it? The government simply said that the matter would now be satisfactorily covered by the well-known rules of private international law(!), and a DTI (DBT predecessor) press release said that the normal provisions of the Brussels and Rome Conventions should be used. However, it is possible that this was a serious mistake, because while these rules and provisions are capable of governing the proper law of, and jurisdiction in relation to, a *contract* (such as a contract of employment), it is arguable that they cannot govern the position in relation to a purely statutory right such as unfair dismissal.[148] If this is correct, what the government actually did was to create a *hole* in the 1996 Act, so that we have a statute giving rights *without* the necessary statutory provisions on territorial jurisdiction.[149] The result was that it became a matter of statutory interpretation (not private international law) as to what was intended with regard to jurisdiction. After a period of uncertainty and conflicting decisions, the matter finally came before the House of Lords in *Lawson v Serco Ltd*,[150] a test case involving three appeals by British nationals working (a) for a British company but wholly on Ascension Island, (b) for the MoD on a base in Germany, and (c) as a pilot for a foreign airline but flying out of Heathrow. Accepting the gap in the legislation but declining to go down the route of judicial legislation or declaring it all to be a matter of discretion,

[146] See 2.5.1.

[147] The age exclusion used to be contained in the Employment Rights Act 1996, s 109, which was repealed as from October 2006.

[148] There is no implied contractual right not to be unfairly dismissed: *Focsa Services (UK) Ltd v Birkett* [1996] IRLR 325.

[149] Contrast this with the far more sensible amendments to the discrimination legislation in the Equal Opportunities (Employment Legislation) (International Limits) Regulations 1999, SI 1999/3163 (again seeking compliance with the Posted Workers Directive) which simply removed the wording 'or mainly' from the exclusion of employees working 'wholly or mainly outside Great Britain'. There may now be disputes over what is meant by 'wholly' outside GB (eg what level of involvement within GB could be ignored as de minimis), but at least we still have a statutory provision here to apply.

[150] [2006] ICR 250, [2006] IRLR 289, HL, noted Linden (2006) 35 ILJ 186.

the House of Lords laid down the applicable principles by dividing possible claimants into three categories:

1. *Standard cases*. Given that we cannot provide tribunals for the world, the necessary limitation is that the Employment Rights Act 1996 applies to an employee 'working in Great Britain'.[151] This appears to hark back to the pre-1999 law *except* that this current test is no longer based on what the contract says, but rather on what happened in practice (the contract only being a factor). In the context of unfair dismissal, Lord Hoffmann said that 'ordinarily the question should simply be whether he is working in Great Britain at the time when he is dismissed'.
2. *Peripatetic employees*. An example here would be airline staff, and in a peripatetic case the answer, according to the House of Lords, is in effect to go back to some earlier law in this area and apply what for many years was Lord Denning MR's 'base' test in *Todd v British Midland Airways Ltd*,[152] namely a wide factual test as to where the employee was effectively based (eg where they were living, paying tax, operating from, organized from; again, the contract could be evidence).
3. *Expatriate employees*. Cases of such employees (eg Mr Lawson on Ascension Island) have caused most problems. The fact of working for a GB company is *not* per se enough, and the 'base' test cannot help. Ostensibly this employee is *not* covered by the 1996 Act and must rely on the employment law (if any) of the country in which they are working. There are, however, two exceptions:
   (a) where the employee is *posted* abroad for the purposes of a business carried on in GB (an example being a foreign correspondent reporting for a GB television channel);
   (b) an expatriate 'operating in what amounts to an extra-territorial enclave in a foreign country' (the prime example being a British military base abroad).

On these principles, the MoD employee and the pilot clearly won their right to complain to an employment tribunal here and, on the facts,[153] the security guard on Ascension Island won, *just*, on the 'enclave' point. The availability of technology allowing people to work for a British company in a foreign location has opened the door even wider, to permit jurisdiction for non-British citizens who work remotely for British companies, provided that the only difference between working abroad or in Britain is the location (ie the work is essentially the same as if the employee was working from home in Britain).[154] In spite of these successes, however, there can remain serious dangers for an employee working abroad, including those 'on secondment' (a weasel word, having no inherent meaning in employment law), especially as the one thing that is clear is that being British, working for a British-owned concern, is *not* in itself enough to establish jurisdiction. Moreover, those who would not ordinarily attract tribunal jurisdiction under these principles cannot bootstrap jurisdiction through the use of a choice-of-law clause in their employment contracts.[155]

[151] Note that these principles apply to any claim under the 1996 Act, even though they are being considered here in the context of unfair dismissal.

[152] [1978] ICR 959; [1978] IRLR 370 (CA). Lord Hoffmann said that to hold otherwise would make airline pilots 'the flying Dutchmen of labour law' (presumably a double danger if employed by KLM).

[153] One factor being that Ascension Island, in addition to its odd constitutional position, has no indigenous population and so has never had much employment law.

[154] *Lodge v Dignity and Choice in Dying* UKEAT/0252/14 (2 December 2014, unreported).

[155] *Bleuse v MBT Transport and Tiefenbacher* [2008] IRLR 264.

To summarize, therefore, the law on excluded categories has always been difficult, even though the question posed ('who can claim?') appears simple. There are, however, three other exclusions which are long-standing and relatively certain:

1. two specific categories of share fishermen and the police;[156]
2. an employee governed by a dismissal procedures agreement between employers and trade unions in the industry, designated by the Secretary of State as operating in substitution for the statutory scheme;[157]
3. an employee whose dismissal was for the purpose of safeguarding national security.[158]

7.4 What is an unfair dismissal?

Once the employee has proved that they were dismissed (if that is a live issue in the case) the burden of proof then passes on to the employer, under s 98 of the 1996 Act, to show two things:

1. what was the reason for the dismissal (or the principal reason if more than one);
2. that it fell within one of the enumerated categories of prima facie fair dismissals, namely that the reason was:
   (a) related to the capability or qualifications of the employee for performing their work;
   (b) related to the conduct of the employee;
   (c) that the employee was redundant;
   (d) that the employee could not continue to work in that position without contravention of a legislative provision;[159]
   (e) 'some other substantial reason of a kind such as to justify the dismissal'.

It is then for the tribunal to decide whether in the circumstances (having regard to equity and the substantial merits of the case) the employer acted reasonably in treating that reason as a sufficient reason for dismissing the employee (s 98(4)).

This basic structure of an unfair dismissal action should be borne in mind (except in cases where the statute expressly provides that a certain type of dismissal shall be automatically fair or unfair), and the significance of the burden of proof being upon the employer is that if it fails to satisfy the tribunal at either of the first two stages ((1) reason and (2) prima facie fair) the dismissal will be held to be unfair.

[156] Employment Rights Act 1996, ss 199 and 200, respectively. On the meaning of 'share fisherman' see *Goodeve v Gilsons* [1985] ICR 401, CA.

[157] Section 110. Although this scheme was historically significant in showing a willingness to allow the parties to govern their own affairs, in fact only one industry (electrical contracting) ever used it, and that was discontinued in 2001.

[158] Employment Tribunal Act 1996, s 10.

[159] For example where an employee employed wholly or principally to drive a vehicle is disqualified and there is no alternative work for him or her: *Appleyard v F M Smith (Hull) Ltd* [1972] IRLR 19, IT; *Fearn v Tayford Motor Co* [1975] IRLR 336, IT. The tribunal must still go on to consider whether the dismissal was reasonable under s 98(4), as this is not an automatically fair reason for dismissal: *Sandhu v DES* [1978] IRLR 208. A mistaken belief by the employer that it cannot lawfully continue to employ the employee does not come under this heading, but may qualify as 'some other substantial reason': *Bouchaala v Trusthouse Forte Hotels Ltd* [1980] ICR 721, [1980] IRLR 382, EAT.

7.4.1 **Stage one: the reason**

The first stage is that the employer must show what the real reason was for the dismissal;[160] if it clearly relies upon one particular reason and the tribunal disbelieves it, the finding should be one of unfair dismissal and it should not normally be allowed to try to rely upon an entirely different reason either at the tribunal hearing (without applying for leave to amend its defence) or on appeal.[161] In *Robinson v Combat Stress*,[162] the employer had put forward three reasons at the tribunal, only one of which was free of serious procedural problems. The tribunal found it 'fair' to dismiss for that procedurally safe reason, but the EAT found that on the facts one of the procedurally flawed reasons was clearly the one on which the employer principally relied. The EAT held that the tribunal must deal with what was the employer's actual reason, not a reason that could have justified the dismissal. It has been said that the inquiry focuses on what motivated the actual decision-maker to act.[163]

7.4.1.1 **The implications of changing the reason**

However, tribunal proceedings are not meant to be as formal as High Court proceedings, and it must be accepted that, in the light of the complexity of certain of these areas of law, the employer may not always initially put the correct legal interpretation on the factors determining its decision to dismiss.[164] The general approach has therefore been that the tribunal's task is to discover the reason actually motivating the employer at the time of the dismissal. In *Abernethy v Mott, Hay and Anderson*,[165] in an oft-quoted passage, Cairns LJ said:

> A reason for the dismissal of an employee is a set of facts known to the employer, or it may be of beliefs held by him, which cause him to dismiss the employee. If at the time of his dismissal the employer gives a reason for it, that is no doubt evidence, at any rate as against him, as to the real reason, but it does not necessarily constitute the real reason. He may knowingly give a reason different from the real reason out of kindness or because he might have difficulty in proving the facts that actually led him to dismiss; or he may describe his reasons wrongly through some mistake of language or of law.

[160] The burden of proof is on the employer: if it leads evidence supporting its contention that it dismissed for reason A, that may cast an evidential burden on the employee to adduce some evidence to doubt reason A and/or suggest reason B; if they do so, the legal burden of proof remains with the employer at the end of the day: *Maund v Penwith District Council* [1984] ICR 143, [1984] IRLR 24, CA. If dismissal is with notice, it may be necessary to look at the reason(s) operating both at the giving and the expiry of the notice: *Parkinson v March Consulting Ltd* [1998] ICR 276, [1997] IRLR 308, CA; *West Kent College v Richardson* [1999] ICR 511.

[161] *Nelson v BBC* [1977] ICR 649, [1977] IRLR 148, CA; *ASLEF v Brady* [2006] IRLR 576. This is certainly so on appeal, as *Nelson* shows, if only because it is contrary to natural justice to decide an appeal on a ground that was not fully argued before the tribunal; a similar rule applies before the tribunal itself, but here a change of label may be permissible where the employee is in fact given a proper opportunity to refute the new ground: *Murphy v Epsom College* [1985] ICR 80, [1984] IRLR 271, CA; *Hotson v Wisbech Conservative Club* [1984] ICR 859, [1984] IRLR 422; *Burkett v Pendletons (Sweets) Ltd* [1992] ICR 407. Likewise, if the employer fails to establish the reason put forward, the tribunal should not cast around to try to find some other dismissible reason: *Adams v Derby City Council* [1986] IRLR 163.

[162] UKEAT/0310/14 (5 December 2014, unreported).

[163] *Beatt v Croydon Health Services NHS Trust* [2017] EWCA Civ 401, [2017] IRLR 748.

[164] 'Redundancy', for example, may cover a multitude of sins in layman's use, but in law it has a precise and restricted meaning.

[165] [1974] ICR 323, [1974] IRLR 213, CA; the passage cited was approved by the House of Lords in *W Devis & Sons Ltd v Atkins* [1977] ICR 662, [1977] IRLR 314, HL. For an example of wrong labelling see *Hannan v TNT-IPEC (UK) Ltd* [1986] IRLR 165.

Thus, a wrong label given by the employer is not fatal to its case and, further, it is clear from the cases that the approach here is basically subjective, particularly in cases where it is a *belief* on the part of the employer which led it to dismiss. The obvious example here is a belief that the employee is guilty of a crime (see 7.5.2), as in such cases, as with other 'belief' cases, it has been consistently held that what the employer is required to prove is its genuine belief, *not* that its belief was factually correct.[166] However, in the nature of things the approach cannot be totally subjective, as the employer has to *prove* that it held the belief in question and so in practice will have to go on to adduce some supporting evidence of the facts upon which it based its belief (even though it does not have to amount to clear proof of the correctness of that belief), otherwise there is the danger that the tribunal will not believe it.

At the heart of the matter of labelling lies a question of balance. It is clearly important in practice that a relatively lax approach should be taken to the label applied by the employer. On the other hand, too lax an approach could leave too much leeway for an employer to operate a 'shotgun' defence—to make multiple allegations, under different headings, against the employee and hope that one or two are accepted by the tribunal. A major step towards preventing improper use of such tactics was taken by the House of Lords in *Smith v City of Glasgow District Council*.[167] The employer put forward a mixture of reasons for dismissal, relating to incompetence and misconduct, crystallized into three substantive allegations; the tribunal found that one of them had not been made out but proceeded to find the dismissal generally fair. This reasoning was disapproved by the House of Lords, since what appeared to be an integral part of the reason for dismissal had not been proved (or, at least, proved to have been the subject of reasonable belief by the employer). This case does *not* mean that an employer cannot plead several reasons and win; it does mean, however, that if one of several reasons put forward collapses the employer must go further and show that the collapsed reason was not, or did not form a significant part of, the principal reason for the dismissal (ie that the remaining reasons were more important and justified the dismissal by themselves); according to the House of Lords, that had not been shown on the facts of this case. Clearly, the more reasons the employer loads into the shotgun (and the more it eventually fails to prove), the more difficult this will be to establish.

7.4.1.2 **Matters that may be considered in fixing the reason**

Two further points on this first stage of the action should also be noticed. The *first* is that the House of Lords held in *W Devis & Sons Ltd v Atkins*[168] that the employer can only rely on the facts as known to it at the date of dismissal; contrary to the position in a common law action for wrongful dismissal,[169] therefore, the employer cannot rely upon subsequently discovered misconduct (as in a case where there is a dubious dismissal for inefficiency, following which the employer checks the books and finds clear evidence of embezzlement by the ex-employee—there must still be a finding of unfair dismissal in

[166] *Trust House Forte Leisure Ltd v Aquilar* [1976] IRLR 251; *Ford v Libra Fair Trades* [2008] All ER (D) 106.

[167] [1987] ICR 796, [1987] IRLR 326, HL.

[168] [1977] ICR 662, [1977] IRLR 314, HL. Date of dismissal here means the effective date of termination, so that if the facts change between the giving and the expiry of notice (eg a redundancy situation is affected by the receipt of a new order during that period), the tribunal should look at the facts as known at the expiry date: *Stacey v Babcock Power Ltd* [1986] ICR 221, [1986] IRLR 3. Thus, further evidence coming to light during the notice period can be taken into account: *Alboni v Ind Coope Retail Ltd* [1998] IRLR 131, CA (employer's reasonable conduct looking for an alternative to dismissal during the notice period taken into account); *White v South London Transport Ltd* [1998] ICR 293 (further medical evidence during notice period backed up the original ill-health dismissal).

[169] *Boston Deep Sea Fishing and Ice Co v Ansell* (1888) 39 Ch D 339, CA.

such a case, though the subsequently discovered misconduct may be relevant on the question of compensation, discussed later in this chapter).

There is one major qualification to this fundamental rule. Where an initial decision to dismiss is subject to an internal appeal, further evidence may come to light during the course of the appeal and it has been held that the tribunal can look at this (it being unrealistic to do otherwise) *provided* that the new evidence relates to the original ground of dismissal.[170] However, this must not be taken too far and it has been held that (a) this exception does not allow an employer to use evidence from the appeal to set up an entirely new ground for dismissal[171] and (b) it does not render admissible evidence of matters occurring after the conclusion of the appeal.[172] The series of EAT decisions that established these principles were strongly affirmed by the House of Lords in *West Midland Co-operative Society Ltd v Tipton*,[173] where the approach was taken that internal appeal procedures are an integral part of the dismissal procedure and so should be taken into account; to do so does *not* offend the principle in *W Devis & Sons Ltd v Atkins*. Indeed, the *Tipton* case takes matters one stage further and holds that a *refusal* by an employer to allow an internal appeal may itself be evidence of unfairness.

The *second* point is that s 107 of the 1996 Act provides that in determining the reason for dismissal the tribunal may *not* take into account any industrial pressure (whether by strike or lesser action) which was exercised on the employer in order to procure the dismissal, or which was such that it was foreseeably likely to lead to dismissal.[174] This might apply where action was taken by a union or group of fellow employees against an employee who had refused to join in a strike, and if the employer sacks them solely because of the pressure, s 107 leads to the artificial position before the tribunal that the only reason for dismissal has to be ignored. The employer will then be found to have dismissed the employee unfairly, no reason having been shown, and, unless there was unreasonable conduct or undue obstinacy on the employee's part during the dispute, the employer may have to pay full compensation.[175] Where, however, the pressure was exercised on the employer because the applicant was not a member of the pressuring union, it is now provided that an action may be brought against the union (or other person exercising the pressure) either by the employer or by the applicant himself or herself and the union or other person may be ordered to pay some or all of the compensation awarded to the applicant.[176] These provisions supplement s 107 without replacing it.

7.4.1.3 **Establishing the reason in an organization**

The above discussion has concerned establishing the employer's reason, without considering who or what 'the employer' is for these purposes. Traditionally, it tended to be treated as if a natural person whose 'mind' contained that reason.[177] However, employment in reality is usually by some kind of organization, often corporate. In those circumstances, the question can arise as to *who within* that organization constitutes its 'mind' in relation to a decision to dismiss.

[170] *National Heart and Chest Hospitals v Nambiar* [1981] ICR 441, [1981] IRLR 196; *Sillifant v Powell-Duffryn Timber Ltd* [1983] IRLR 91.

[171] *Monie v Coral Racing Ltd* [1981] ICR 109, [1980] IRLR 464, CA.

[172] *Greenall Whitley plc v Carr* [1985] ICR 451, [1985] IRLR 289.

[173] [1986] ICR 192, [1986] IRLR 112, HL.

[174] *Ford Motor Co Ltd v Hudson* [1978] ICR 482, [1978] IRLR 66.

[175] *Hazell Offsets Ltd v Luckett* [1977] IRLR 430; *British United Trawlers (Grimsby) Ltd v Carr* [1977] ICR 622; Colwyn Borough Council v Dutton [1980] IRLR 420.

[176] Trade Union and Labour Relations (Consolidation) Act 1992, s 160.

[177] Linguistically, it was common to refer to the employer as 'he'.

In most cases, this does not arise and the tribunal will simply look at the reasoning and motivation of the dismissing manager. However, in some cases there can be a problem if some *other* manager has had some input/influence in the decision to dismiss, albeit not direct. Such situations have particularly arisen in the past few years in whistleblowing cases and have been tagged (with typical erudition) by Underhill LJ as 'Iago cases', for example where a line manager (Iago), embarrassed or annoyed by an episode of whistleblowing in their department, has concocted false charges to convince the dismissing manager (Othello) that the whistleblower (Desdemona) is guilty of them and has to go on *those* grounds, not the whistleblowing which would otherwise be protected. Can a tribunal look beyond the dismissing manager's (false but genuinely believed) reason and consider the motivation of the line manager (meaning here that 'the employer' may be liable under the whistleblower laws)?

At first, the reaction of the courts to this conundrum was that the logic of the unfair dismissal law meant that a tribunal could look only at the dismissing manager's motivation. As a dismissal can be fair if that manager had a reasonable *belief* in guilt (see below), this left a significant gap in employee protection in one of these cases. Fortunately, the whole question was reconsidered and the gap closed by the Supreme Court in *Royal Mail Group v Jhuti*.[178] Ms Jhuti made protected disclosures within the meaning of whistleblowing law to her line manager. The line manager's response to her disclosures was to seek to pretend over the course of several months that Ms Jhuti's performance of her duties under her contract of employment with the company was in various respects inadequate. In due course the company appointed another officer to decide whether Ms Jhuti should be dismissed and, having no reason to doubt the truthfulness of the material indicative of Ms Jhuti's inadequate performance, the other officer decided that she should be dismissed for that reason. What was 'the employer's' reason? The Court accepted that in most cases it will only be necessary to look at the dismissing manager, *but* held there can be cases where a wider enquiry will be appropriate. Lord Wilson summed this up as follows:

> In the present case, however, the reason for the dismissal given in good faith by [the decision-maker] turns out to have been bogus. If a person in the hierarchy of responsibility above the employee (here . . . Ms Jhuti's line manager) determines that, for reason A (here the making of protected disclosures), the employee should be dismissed but that reason A should be hidden behind an invented reason B which the decision-maker adopts (here inadequate performance), it is the court's duty to penetrate through the invention rather than to allow it also to infect its own determination. If limited to a person placed by the employer in the hierarchy of responsibility above the employee, there is no conceptual difficulty about attributing to the employer that person's state of mind rather than that of the deceived decision-maker.

This does leave one potential gap, namely where the poison is dripped into the dismissing manager's ear by a fellow employee of similar status, but otherwise it is a very welcome clarification in more normal (hierarchical) cases; however, it must be noted that subsequently the EAT has taken the view that, important though *Jhuti* is in these particular cases, it remains the exception to the rule that normally one should look at the reasons of the dismissing manager.[179]

[178] [2020] IRLR 129, [2020] ICR 731, SC, disapproving *Orr v Milton Keynes Council* [2011] IRLR 317, [2011] ICR 704, CA; see Hobby 'The Silencing of Public Interest Concerns and Hidden Motives' (2020) 49 ILJ 377.

[179] *University Hospital North Tees & Hartlepool NHS Foundation Trust v Fairhall* UKEAT/0150/20; *Kong v Gulf International Bank Ltd* EA-2020-000357 (upheld on other grounds: [2022] EWCA Civ 941).

7.4.2 **Stage two: prima facie fair grounds**

The second stage of the action is that the employer must prove that the reason for the dismissal fits into one of the enumerated categories. These are considered presently, but it should be noted here that the final residual category, 'some other substantial reason (SOSR) justifying dismissal', is deliberately wide and not to be restricted by being construed *ejusdem generis* with the previous categories.[180] Dismissal of a replacement for a woman temporarily absent on maternity leave (or for a person subject to compulsory medical suspension)[181] is expressly stated to be for a substantial reason (provided the replacement was told of the temporary nature of the job when engaged),[182] as is a dismissal because of a transfer of the employer's undertaking (see Chapter 8), but other than that all that can be said is that the question of what can be a substantial reason is an open one in respect of which the onus is clearly upon the employer to satisfy the tribunal on the facts of the particular case; the wider it is construed by the tribunals, the wider ostensibly is the area of management prerogative,[183] though of course any particular dismissal still has to be shown to be fair, even if for a substantial reason.[184] It has been held in the past to cover a range of miscellaneous reasons including the irretrievable breakdown of a working relationship,[185] an employer's mistaken belief that it had other fair grounds on which to dismiss,[186] dismissal at the behest of an important customer,[187] personality clashes,[188] awkward personality,[189] refusal to sign a restraint of trade clause,[190] refusal to work Sundays on religious grounds,[191] the dismissal of the spouse of a person already dismissed where they were engaged as a pair,[192] and a genuine but mistaken belief that the employee has resigned;[193] as will be seen in Chapter 8, it has been particularly important in cases of dismissals following necessary business reorganizations, but apart from this area, the extreme diversity of the examples given shows that there is *no* connecting theme as to what constitutes SOSR, in that each case depends on its facts.

[180] *RS Components Ltd v Irwin* [1973] ICR 535, [1973] IRLR 239.

[181] Under the Employment Rights Act 1996, s 64. [182] Section 106.

[183] Bowers and Clark 'Unfair Dismissal and Managerial Prerogative: A Study of "Other Substantial Reason"' (1981) 10 ILJ 34.

[184] *Gilham v Kent County Council (No 2)* [1985] ICR 233, [1985] IRLR 18, CA. A defence of some other substantial reason requires the tribunal 'to consider the reason established by the employer and decide whether it falls within the category of reason which could justify the dismissal of an employee—not that employee, but an employee—holding the position which that employee held': *Dobie v Burns International Security Services (UK) Ltd* [1984] IRLR 329 at 331, CA per Sir John Donaldson MR; the next stage is to consider whether the dismissal of that employee was fair on the facts, within s 98(4).

[185] *Ezsias v North Glamorgan NHS Trust* [2011] IRLR 550.

[186] *Klusova v London Borough of Hounslow* [2007] All ER (D) 105, CA (mistaken belief that employee was working contrary to immigration rules); *Taylor v Co-operative Retail Services Ltd* [1981] ICR 172, [1981] IRLR 1; affd [1982] ICR 600, [1982] IRLR 354, CA (mistaken belief that employer obliged to dismiss under a closed shop agreement); *Bouchaala v Trusthouse Forte Hotels Ltd* [1980] ICR 721, [1980] IRLR 382 (mistaken belief that continued employment would contravene a statutory enactment).

[187] *Scott Packing and Warehousing Ltd v Paterson* [1978] IRLR 166; *Grootcon* (UK) *Ltd v Keld* [1984] IRLR 302; *Dobie v Burns International Security Services (UK) Ltd* [1984] ICR 812, [1984] IRLR 329, CA.

[188] *Treganowan v Robert Knee & Co Ltd* [1975] ICR 405, [1975] IRLR 247.

[189] *Perkin v St George's Healthcare NHS Trust* [2006] ICR 606, [2005] IRLR 934, CA: the proper approach is to see first if dismissible misconduct had been caused, but if not the awkward personality can be SOSR in itself, if it has had sufficiently serious effects on the employer's business.

[190] *Willow Oak Developments Ltd v Silverwood* [2006] IRLR 607, CA.

[191] *Copsey v WWB Devon Clays Ltd* [2005] ICR 1789, [2005] IRLR 811, CA. This case arose before the Employment Equality (Religion or Belief) Regulations 2003 came into force, though it is by no means certain that they would produce a different decision on the facts.

[192] *Kelman v Oram* [1983] IRLR 432 (dismissal of publican's wife after (unfair) dismissal of publican).

[193] *Impact Recruitment Services Ltd v Korpysa* [2025] EAT 22.

7.4.3 **Stage three: fairness**

The third stage (not applicable in cases of 'automatically unfair dismissal', discussed in 7.5.4) is that the tribunal must consider under s 98(4) whether the employer acted reasonably in actually 'activating' the reason in question and dismissing the employee; this demonstrates clearly that it is not enough to show that the employer had a reason which would normally justify dismissal—it has to be shown that in all the circumstances of the case, it actually justified the particular dismissal in question. Unlike a wrongful dismissal action, this is not a technical exercise, looking at the parties' contractual entitlements and rights, but instead entails examination of the *substance* of the dismissal and consideration of the wider circumstances such as the employer's business needs (eg in a case of inefficiency or ineptitude by the employee) and any factors in mitigation of the employee's default, such as long service, lack of prior grounds for complaint, and the possibilities of improvement.

While the burden of proof on this overall question of fairness is technically neutral, the House of Lords in *Smith v City of Glasgow District Council*[194] approved the view of the Court of Session below that it remains logical to expect the employer to prove that the reason in question has been established—it cannot be reasonable to treat that reason as sufficient to justify dismissal unless the employer has shown either that it is true or that it believed it to be true. Although other factors (such as procedural considerations) may have to be considered, this emphasis on isolating the real reason(s) for dismissal may mean that in some cases the issue of overall fairness will tend to merge with the question of establishing the reason (on which the employer does still bear the burden of proof).

In applying the test of fairness, the tribunal must consider the reasonableness of the employer's conduct, *not* the injustice (or lack of it) done to the employee. This fundamental principle was reaffirmed by the House of Lords in *Polkey v A E Dayton Services Ltd*,[195] probably the most important decision on unfair dismissal since *W Devis & Sons Ltd v Atkins*[196] ten years earlier. An employee dismissed without warning for redundancy and sent home immediately had his claim for unfair dismissal turned down by the tribunal because they found that proper consultation would not have made any difference, that is, they looked at the eventual lack of injustice to the employee. The House of Lords held this to be clearly wrong and remitted the case to another tribunal, which was to apply the correct test of looking at the reasonableness of the employer's conduct in deciding not to consult or warn; the question of the amount of injustice done to the employee should only be relevant at the later stages of assessing compensation. This reasonableness test in s 98(4) has two overall effects. The first is that it is primarily responsible for giving the tribunals their wide discretion to reach just and equitable decisions in the light of 'good industrial practice' (the relevant wording in s 98(4) being 'in accordance with equity and the substantial merits of the case'); in the exercise of this discretion the tribunals have considerable freedom of action and in general the EAT will be reluctant to interfere with their decisions on such matters. The second effect is that it is the existence of s 98(4) which has led to the importance attached to the concept of 'procedural unfairness', that is, the possibility that a dismissal may be unfair if an unfair procedure is adopted by the employer (eg no warnings, lack of a hearing), even if there is prima facie a good substantive reason for the dismissal.

194 [1987] ICR 796, [1987] IRLR 326, HL; *Post Office (Counters) Ltd v Heavey* [1990] ICR 1, [1989] IRLR 513, EAT.

195 [1988] ICR 142, [1987] IRLR 503, HL.

196 [1977] IRLR 314, [1977] ICR 662, HL.

This concept, not to be found expressly stated in the legislation, was developed at an early stage in the history of the action[197] and remains a significant element in it. It has been subject to definable fluctuations in the amount of emphasis to be placed on it. Five particular phases can be seen. First, procedural fairness was a dominant factor in the early years of the new unfair dismissal law, during most of the 1970s while it was bedding in; the prospect of almost any lapse in procedure being held unfair concentrated employers' minds and meant that the new law had a rapid and significant normative effect on personnel practices. Second, however, procedural fairness suffered a definite wane in the later years of that decade and during the first half of the 1980s, for two reasons—(a) a generally less enthusiastic attitude by the Court of Appeal, seen most clearly in *Hollister v NFU*,[198] with a tendency to view procedural matters as merely one of the background factors; (b) the evolution and widespread application of the rule in *British Labour Pump Co Ltd v Byrne*,[199] to the effect that even if the employer failed to use the proper procedure on dismissal, it would still be fair if it could prove on a balance of probabilities that even if it had gone through the proper procedure the employee would still have been dismissed (and that dismissal would then have been fair)—that is, a lapse by the employer could be forgiven if with hindsight it made no difference.

Third, however, we saw a swing back of the pendulum in 1987 with the decision of the House of Lords in *Polkey v A E Dayton Services Ltd*,[200] in which *Byrne*'s case was overruled[201] for two reasons: (a) it is inconsistent with *W Devis & Sons Ltd v Atkins*,[202] since the tribunal should be considering what the employer actually did at the date of dismissal (and with its state of knowledge then), not what it might have done with hindsight; (b) more significantly, the *Byrne* approach was based on consideration of the (lack of) injustice to the employee, not the reasonableness of the employer's actions, and, as we have seen, that is a fundamentally flawed approach. In addition, the case of *Polkey* shows a generally more favourable approach to procedural unfairness;[203] Lord Mackay LC said that a lapse of procedure will not automatically make a dismissal unfair and accepted that (taking the facts of the case) a redundancy dismissal without consultation or warning might still be fair, *but* that would only be so if the employer could show that the decision not to consult or warn was a positive decision taken reasonably in the circumstances at the time, not justified merely as an *ex post facto* afterthought once the deed had been done. We saw, therefore, the reinstating of procedural fairness, not just as *a* factor but as one of *the* factors that are likely to dominate an unfair dismissal action, even if this stopped short of a return in full to its heyday in the early years of the unfair dismissal jurisdiction.

The fourth phase coincides with the relatively short lifespan of the statutory 'standard procedures'. In addressing the perceived problem of too many cases being taken to tribunals, the then government took the view that, of those so taken in the unfair

[197] *Earl v Slater and Wheeler (Airlyne) Ltd* [1973] 1 All ER 145, [1972] ICR 508; approved by the House of Lords in *W Devis & Sons Ltd v Atkins* [1977] ICR 662, [1977] IRLR 314, HL.

[198] [1979] ICR 542, [1979] IRLR 238, CA. See also *Retarded Children's Aid Society v Day* [1978] ICR 437, [1978] IRLR 128, CA and *Bailey v BP Oil (Kent Refinery) Ltd* [1980] ICR 642, [1980] IRLR 287, CA.

[199] [1979] ICR 347, [1979] IRLR 94.

[200] Note 195. In his speech, Lord Mackay LC, giving the judgment of the court, relied heavily on the strong criticisms of *Byrne*'s case by Browne-Wilkinson P in *Sillifant v Powell Duffryn Timber Ltd* [1983] IRLR 91.

[201] Also overruled is *W & J Wass Ltd v Binns* [1982] ICR 486, [1982] IRLR 283, in which the Court of Appeal had approved *Byrne*'s case, and 'all decisions supporting it'.

[202] Above.

[203] See also the post-*Polkey* decisions in *McLaren v National Coal Board* [1988] ICR 370, [1988] IRLR 215, CA; *Whitbread & Co plc v Mills* [1988] ICR 776, [1988] IRLR 501; *Spink v Express Foods Group Ltd* [1990] IRLR 320; *Stocker v Lancashire County Council* [1992] IRLR 75, CA; and Collins 'Procedural Fairness after Polkey' (1990) 19 ILJ 39.

dismissal jurisdiction, too many were based on procedural unfairness only (ie where the employer had good cause to dismiss but mishandled it). The Employment Act 2002 therefore attempted to limit procedural cases,[204] but in a relatively subtle way. It made the very minimal standard procedures mandatory, meaning that where an employer failed to comply with them the dismissal would automatically be unfair. However, it also provided that where employers had procedures in place that went beyond the statutory minimum (and many did, not least because the ACAS Code recommended that they do so) these could be ignored where the employer could demonstrate that observing them would have made no difference to the outcome. In short, the 2002 Act effected a statutory reintroduction of the rule in *British Labour Pump Co Ltd v Byrne* (cited earlier): if the employer could prove to the tribunal that it would have dismissed even if a wholly fair procedure had been adopted, the result was not just that little compensation was likely to be awarded (the *Polkey* solution) but that the dismissal would be *fair*.

This was a significant change, but as we have seen in Chapter 1, it was in practice a nightmare and was repealed by the Employment Act 2008; this ushered in the fifth phase, which amounts to a return to the *Polkey* position, only with more direct enforcement (through adjustments to compensation) of a reissued ACAS Code (see 7.1.3). In this phase it is clear that procedural unfairness can, by itself, make a dismissal unfair even if the dismissal would have occurred with a fair procedure. However, a tribunal commits error if it focuses on a single procedural flaw, to the exclusion of other aspects of the case, to find a dismissal unfair: the dismissal must be considered as a connected whole, and it must always be possible that a dismissal is fair despite the presence of an unfair procedure.[205] The ultimate question asked by the statute is whether the employer was 'reasonable' to dismiss in all the circumstances.

7.4.4 **The correct approach: the 'range of reasonable responses' test**

One aspect of s 98(4) has caused considerable disagreement in the earlier cases: whether the approach of the tribunal should be subjective or objective. To any lawyer versed in criminal law or tort, the concept of 'reasonableness' is clearly objective, and in earlier cases on s 98(4) the approach was indeed objective, viewing the tribunal as an 'industrial jury' with full powers to review the employer's conduct from their standpoint and decide, in the light of standard industrial practice (hence the lay membership), whether on the facts they would have dismissed.[206] Some later cases, however, adopted the view that the approach should be subjective (at least in part), particularly in cases where the employer's belief in a set of facts at the time of dismissal is important, so that the employer's own view that it acted reasonably should have some effect.[207] Thus, in *Alidair Ltd v Taylor*,[208] where an airline pilot's instant dismissal after damaging an aircraft in a faulty landing was held to be fair, Lord Denning MR said:

> [I]t must be remembered that [s 98] contemplated a subjective test. The tribunal have to consider the employer's reason and the employer's state of mind. If the company honestly

[204] The government's approach was that these cases, producing a basic finding of unfairness and little by way of compensation, had been a waste of tribunal time. Not all tribunal judges agreed.

[205] *NHS 24 v Pillar* UKEAT/0005/16 (4 July 2017, unreported); *Sharkey v Lloyds Bank plc* UKEATS/0005/15 (4 August 2015, unreported).

[206] *Bessenden Properties Ltd v Corness* [1977] ICR 821n, [1974] IRLR 338, CA.

[207] *Ferodo Ltd v Barnes* [1976] ICR 439, [1976] IRLR 302; *Post Office v Mughal* [1977] ICR 763, [1977] IRLR 178.

[208] [1978] ICR 445, [1978] IRLR 82, CA; the passages cited are at 450–51 and 84–85, respectively; *Vickers Ltd v Smith* [1977] IRLR 11. Cf *ILEA v Lloyd* [1981] IRLR 394, CA.

> believed on reasonable grounds that this pilot was lacking in proper capability to fly aircraft on behalf of the company, that was a good and sufficient reason for the company to determine the employment then and there . . . They clearly had no further confidence in him. He could not be trusted to fly their aircraft on their behalf. That being their honest belief on reasonable grounds, they were entitled to dismiss him. They acted reasonably in treating it as a sufficient reason for dismissing him.

Reinforcing this, his Lordship then said:

> If a man is dismissed for stealing, as long as the employer honestly believed it on reasonable grounds, that is enough to justify dismissal. It is not necessary for the employer to prove that he was in fact stealing. Whenever a man is dismissed for incapacity or incompetence it is sufficient that the employer honestly believes on reasonable grounds that the man is incapable or incompetent. It is not necessary for the employer to prove that he is in fact incapable or incompetent.

However, the approach cannot be totally subjective (otherwise the tribunal's discretion would be minimal when faced by an employer unshaken in its assertion that it thought it had acted reasonably), as can be seen from the above references to belief *on reasonable grounds*. Moreover, some later cases reaffirmed an objective element:

> [T]he [employment] tribunal, while using its own collective wisdom, is to apply the standard of the reasonable employer; that is to say, the fairness or unfairness of the dismissal is to be judged . . . by the objective standard of the way in which a reasonable employer in those circumstances, in that line of business, would have behaved.[209]

Thus, the correct position must lie in a clearer understanding of what counts as objective and subjective. The test is objective in the sense that it is about whether the decision in question was one open to a reasonable employer—it is not subjective in the sense that it considers what would be reasonable for *this* employer, with whatever individual characteristics it might have. What makes the test seem like it must have a subjective element is the fact that the question for the tribunal is: 'what would a reasonable employer *in these circumstances, with this information*, do?' It is therefore not helpful to think in terms of subjectivity: rather, the issue is that the tribunal is not asked to decide the dismissal decision anew, but to decide whether the employer was reasonable to make the challenged decision at the time it was made. That leads to two clear principles to guide the inquiry.

First, it is clear that in all but the most blatant and obvious case of misconduct or incapability, employers must have made a proper investigation of the grounds of the complaint against the employee and come to proper, tenable conclusions if they are to convince the tribunal that they had reasonable grounds for any belief which they put forward as a reason for the dismissal. Thus, in a suspected theft case employers must show reasonable investigations, reasonably allowing them to point the finger of accusation at the employee. Moreover, the requirement of reasonable investigation means that an employer cannot rely upon ignorance, at the time of dismissal, of a particular point in the employee's favour if a reasonable investigation would have revealed it; that is, the tribunal may look at the facts of which the employer knew or ought to have known.[210]

[209] *Watling & Co Ltd v Richardson* [1978] ICR 1049 at 1056, [1978] IRLR 255 and 257, per Phillips J, explaining *Vickers Ltd v Smith* above; see also *Mitchell v Old Hall Exchange Club Ltd* [1978] IRLR 160.

[210] *St Anne's Board Mill Co Ltd v Brien* [1973] ICR 444, [1973] IRLR 309, approved by the House of Lords in *W Devis & Sons Ltd v Atkins* [1977] ICR 662, [1977] IRLR 314, HL.

To this extent at least, the test is objective, as can be seen from the formula 'belief on reasonable grounds', and if the employer can show these reasonable grounds it may be in a strong position.[211]

Secondly, the tribunals must not look at the facts of every case *de novo* and simply apply their own view of those facts, deciding whether they would have done what the employer did in the circumstances.[212] Instead, they have to look at what the employer in fact did and decide whether that was a course of action which a reasonable employer could have taken in those circumstances (applying the standard of reasonableness as envisaged in the wording of s 98(4) itself). This becomes of particular significance in a case where in the circumstances the employer had several courses of action open to it, all of which were potentially what a reasonable employer might do, for example where the misconduct was such that it could dismiss, suspend without pay, or fine and it chose to dismiss, or where in a redundancy case it could dispense with A or B or C and it chose A. In such a case tribunals should not consider which course they would have taken and decide whether the dismissal was fair or not in accordance with that (eg holding dismissal unfair if they would on balance have decided upon suspension, or holding the dismissal of A unfair if on balance they would have dismissed C). Instead, they should decide whether the course of action in fact chosen was one which a reasonable employer *could* have decided upon, that is, whether the employer acted within the area of discretion covered by what would have been reasonable in the circumstances. Thus, in *Trust House Forte Leisure Ltd v Aquilar*,[213] Phillips J said:

> [W]hen the management is confronted with a decision to dismiss an employee in particular circumstances there may well be cases where reasonable managements might take either of two decisions: to dismiss or not to dismiss. It does not necessarily mean if they decide to dismiss that they have acted unfairly because there are plenty of situations in which more than one view is possible.

In *Watling & Co Ltd v Richardson*,[214] the same judge, using the redundancy example given previously as a warning to tribunals not simply to apply their own views, said:

> It has to be recognised that there are circumstances where more than one course of action may be reasonable . . . In such cases . . . if an industrial tribunal equates its view of what itself would have done with what a reasonable employer would have done, it may mean that an employer will be found to have dismissed an employee unfairly although in the circumstances many perfectly good and fair employers would have done as that employer did.[215]

[211] *Post Office v Mughal* [1977] ICR 763, [1977] IRLR 178.

[212] *Trust House Forte Hotels Ltd v Murphy* [1977] IRLR 186; *Meridian Ltd v Gomersall* [1977] ICR 597, [1977] IRLR 425; *Mansfield Hosiery Mills Ltd v Bromley* [1977] IRLR 301; *Watling & Co Ltd v Richardson* [1978] ICR 1049, [1978] IRLR 255.

[213] [1976] IRLR 251 at 254.

[214] [1978] ICR 1049 at 1056, [1978] IRLR 255 at 258; *Grundy (Teddington) Ltd v Willis* [1976] ICR 323, [1976] IRLR 118.

[215] It is worth noting that in all of these discussions of the many possible 'reasonable' options, dismissal is the harshest, and any time dismissal is reasonable, most would view something less harsh than dismissal as reasonable. However, nobody who thinks that dismissal is too harsh also thinks that dismissal is within the range of reasonable responses. If a judge believes that dismissal is unreasonable in a given case, no judgment has ever explained how that judge is supposed to comprehend someone finding dismissal reasonable in the same circumstances, other than by assuming that other people must be less reasonable than the judge.

7.4.4.1 The modern 'range' test

Indeed, the development of this 'range of reasonable responses' approach has been a major feature of unfair dismissal law and has had the effect of broadening the area of managerial discretion—it does not apply a test subjective to the respondent employer, but it does enjoin the tribunals to look at the matter from an employer standpoint generally (albeit that of a reasonable employer). This approach was approved by the Court of Appeal in *British Leyland (UK) Ltd v Swift*,[216] where Lord Denning MR said:

> The correct test is: was it reasonable for the employer to dismiss him? If no reasonable employer would have dismissed him, then the dismissal was unfair. But if a reasonable employer might reasonably have dismissed him, then the dismissal was fair. It must be remembered that in all these cases there is a band of reasonableness, within which one employer might reasonably take one view; another quite reasonably take a different view . . . if it was quite reasonable to dismiss him, then the dismissal must be upheld as fair: even though some other employers may not have dismissed him.

The 'range of reasonable responses' approach has been accepted by courts for years and was particularly well set out by Browne-Wilkinson P in *Iceland Frozen Foods Ltd v Jones*[217] as follows:

> [T]he correct approach for the Industrial Tribunal to adopt in answering the question posed by [s 98(4) of the 1996 Act] is as follows: (1) the starting point should always be the words of [s 98] themselves; (2) in applying the section an Industrial Tribunal must consider the reasonableness of the employer's conduct, not simply whether they [the members of the Industrial Tribunal] consider the dismissal to be fair; (3) in judging the reasonableness of the employer's conduct an Industrial Tribunal must not substitute its decision as to what was the right course to adopt for that of the employer; (4) in many (though not all) cases there is a band of reasonable responses to the employee's conduct within which one employer might reasonably take one view, another quite reasonably take another; (5) the function of the Industrial Tribunal, as an industrial jury, is to determine whether in the particular circumstances of each case the decision to dismiss the employee fell within the band of reasonable responses which a reasonable employer might have adopted. If the dismissal falls within the band the dismissal is fair; if the dismissal falls outside the band it is unfair.

A bombshell was dropped in late 1999 by the EAT under Morison P (in one of his final judgments in that court) in *Haddon v Van den Bergh Foods Ltd*,[218] where the panel stated that in their opinion the range of reasonable responses test is *wrong* (being said to be an unhelpful 'mantra', along with the general point that a tribunal should not substitute its

[216] [1981] IRLR 91, CA. The principle was well expounded by the EAT in *Rolls-Royce Ltd v Walpole* [1980] IRLR 343 and *British Gas plc v McCarrick* [1991] IRLR 305, CA is a strong decision reaffirming it.

[217] [1982] IRLR 439 at 442. The EAT was at pains to point out that this did not mean (as may have appeared from *Vickers Ltd v Smith* [1977] IRLR 11) that a dismissal could only be unfair if perverse (ie no reasonable employer could possibly have decided to dismiss). In a case depending on the credibility of a witness, the question is whether the employer could reasonably believe them, not whether the tribunal does: *Linfood Cash and Carry Ltd v Thomson* [1989] ICR 518, [1989] IRLR 235, EAT.

[218] [1999] ICR 1150, [1999] IRLR 672. The tribunal had held that the test forced it to find fair the dismissal of an employee who had been invited to a drinks party to celebrate 15 years of good service, who was then summarily dismissed for not returning for the last one and a half hours of his shift because he had been drinking! Arguably, the EAT could just have reversed this on ordinary grounds of perversity.

own view for that of the employer). This brief moment of reconsideration was based on the argument that the 'range' test made it too difficult for an employee to succeed in a misconduct case, and that it was too close to the administrative law concept of perversity.[219] The point at issue was so fundamental that the Court of Appeal expedited the hearing of the appeal in another case raising the same point and in *Foley v Post Office*[220] unambiguously disapproved *Haddon*, emphasizing the correctness of the range of reasonable responses test.

Subsequent case law has (mostly) followed this line, confirming that the test applies not just to the actual dismissal decision but also to the adequacy of the procedures adopted[221] and, in a misconduct case, to the reasonableness of the investigation carried out by the employer prior to the dismissal.[222] In more recent cases attention has been pointedly drawn to the statutory language calling for 'fairness' to be determined 'in accordance with equity and the substantial merits of the case' (s 98(4)(b)); tribunals may use their own understanding of equity and merits to some degree: 'an employment tribunal is entitled to find that dismissal was outside the band of reasonable responses without being accused of placing itself in the position of the employer'.[223] However, in the nature of things there will continue to be cases where tribunals appear to defer entirely to the employer because any attempt objectively to assess the decision will appear to 'substitute their judgment' for that of the employer, which is unacceptable at appeal level.

7.4.4.2 Criticisms of the 'range' or 'band'

There can be no doubt that the band of reasonable responses test has been frequently reaffirmed and is the established test for the 'fairness' of dismissal, though in one recent Supreme Court case there was more than a straw in the wind possibly inviting reconsideration at the highest level.[224] It has long been subjected to criticism, largely based on the logical problems considered above of marrying subjective and objective elements, arguably made more acute by the unfortunate legislative change to include unfair dismissal in the category of cases normally decided by employment judge alone, without the input of side members. These criticisms are set out extensively in an article by our late co-author Aaron Baker, published posthumously, which should be consulted on this continuing problem.[225]

[219] In keeping with the observations above, judges forced to assume that their own view that a particular dismissal was too harsh could not be relied upon, and that there must be a range, could only conclude that some reasonable people would not find it too harsh—how else to keep up the pretence that there is always a range? Thus only dismissals that were so harsh that one could not imagine anyone reasonable making the decision could be found outside the band.

[220] [2000] ICR 1283, [2000] IRLR 827, CA.

[221] *Whitbread plc v Hall* [2001] ICR 699, [2001] IRLR 275.

[222] *Sainsbury's Supermarkets Ltd v Hitt* [2002] EWCA Civ 1588, [2003] IRLR 23. In the context of misconduct, *Thomas v Hillingdon London Borough Council* (2002) The Times, 4 October is a particularly interesting (and strong) application of the test to the topical issue of internet abuse and downloading porn.

[223] *Newbound v Thames Water Utilities Ltd* [2015] EWCA Civ 677, [2015] IRLR 734, at para 61.

[224] In *Reilly v Sandwell Metropolitan Borough Council* [2018] UKSC 16, [2018] IRLR 558, [2018] ICR 705 Lady Hale, obiter but, significantly, on her own initiative and having no bearing on the disposition of the case, noted that the Supreme Court had never ruled on the validity of the Range test, observing that there seemed to be good arguments on both sides, and setting out some (probably intentionally) weak reasons for why it has not been properly challenged. The authors would not be the only ones to see this as an invitation to bring the Range test before the Supreme Court for a final reckoning.

[225] Baker, 'The "Range of Reasonable Responses" Test: a Poor Substitute for the Statutory Language' (2021) 50 ILJ 226.

7.5 Particular cases

Having considered the basis of an unfair dismissal action generally, we can now turn to four particular cases of practical importance. The first three (capability, conduct, and redundancy/reorganization) correspond to the major headings contained in s 98(2); the fourth (automatically unfair dismissals) concerns special protection added by subsequent legislation. Some heads of unfair dismissal (maternity dismissal, trade union reasons, and dismissal while taking part in industrial action) are treated separately in the context in which they arise elsewhere in the book (in Chapters 5, 9, and 10); they tend to be subject to more specialized rules, though some of the general principles discussed here lie behind them. The following discussion of these headings is, however, subject to the major caveat that the modern approach is to treat the accumulation of case law in these areas circumspectly and to deprecate overreliance on previous authorities (however venerable) if that either over-complicates the issue before the tribunal, or leads the tribunal to stray from the clear wording of the statute. Put shortly, precedents in this area are, to adapt Noel Coward's saying on wit, to be taken like caviar, not like marmalade.

7.5.1 Capability or qualifications

The first category of prima facie fair dismissals in s 98(2) is where the reason for dismissal is related to the capability or qualifications of the employee for performing his work.[226] 'Capability' is defined in s 98(3) as capability assessed by reference to skill, aptitude, health, or any other physical or mental quality, and 'qualifications' as any degree, diploma, or other academic, technical, or professional qualification relevant to the employee's position.[227] Lack of capability is of course the more important of these two categories, though the EAT has said that it should be viewed relatively narrowly as applying principally to cases where the employee is *incapable* of satisfactory work;[228] where the employee is capable of it, but refuses to exercise their ability, skills, and so on, that should preferably be viewed as a case of misconduct, with the result that the employer should apply any warnings procedure more strictly and with more emphasis on the disciplinary aspect.[229]

7.5.1.1 Incapability through incompetence

In the realm of dismissal for incapability, it is important that the employer's business should not have to suffer, to the detriment of all concerned, through the ineptitude or inefficiency of a particular employee. However, it is also important that the employee whose work is causing dissatisfaction should be treated fairly. The question for the tribunal is whether the employer has demonstrated that it genuinely believed on reasonable grounds that the employee was incapable.[230] The requirement of reasonable grounds means that the employer should make a proper and full investigation into the facts of the case, and give careful consideration to the decision to dismiss;[231] among other things, this consideration may include as a factor whether the employee was given proper training for the job, adequate supervision, and, where appropriate, proper support from the employer. Also, it

[226] Practical advice on handling cases of absence (medical and otherwise) and poor work performance is given in the current version of the ACAS Code of Practice on Disciplinary and Grievance Procedures and its accompanying Guide.

[227] *Blue Star Ship Management Ltd v Williams* [1978] ICR 770, [1979] IRLR 16.

[228] *Sutton and Gates (Luton) Ltd v Boxall* [1979] ICR 67, [1978] IRLR 486.

[229] *Littlewoods Organisation Ltd v Egenti* [1976] ICR 516, [1976] IRLR 334.

[230] *Alidair Ltd v Taylor* [1978] ICR 445, [1978] IRLR 82, CA.

[231] *Cook v Thomas Linnell & Sons Ltd* [1977] ICR 770, [1977] IRLR 132.

is well established that this area is amenable to the application of a warnings procedure,[232] though the emphasis may be different from that in misconduct cases, as here the constructive side of a warning may be more important, not only pointing out the employer's ground for complaint but also instructing the employee how to improve and giving them reasonable time in which to do so. Of course, warnings are not essential in every case, and may perhaps be irrelevant where it is clear that the employee is completely incapable of improvement or where they already clearly know what is expected of them.[233] That apart, however, the importance of a fair procedure in this area should not be underestimated, and lack of it (particularly if it leads to inadequate investigation by the employer) may make dismissal of an incompetent employee unfair (though it may still be open to the employer to argue that there should be little or no compensation where there was wilful default on the part of the employee, such as failure or refusal to improve).[234] One of the ways in which the ACAS Code of Practice on Disciplinary and Grievance Procedures was expanded in 2000 was by the inclusion of guidance on sub-standard work, which adopted and greatly simplified the results of this case law. Much of this guidance is now found in the non-statutory Guide to the current version of the Code.

7.5.1.2 **Incapability through illness**

One particular aspect of incapability which has given rise to much litigation is where the employee is incapable of performing their work due to prolonged and/or frequent illness. Four preliminary points may be made on this subject. The *first* is that an exceptionally severe and incapacitating illness could have the effect of frustrating the contract of employment, in which case there would be no dismissal and so no action could be brought; frustration is considered elsewhere,[235] and in general it should not be found readily by a tribunal because of its drastic effect on the employee's rights. The tests for a frustrating illness are therefore stringent, and are not the tests to be applied to the separate question whether a dismissal for illness was fair.[236] The *second* point is that many employees are covered by contractual sick pay schemes which will provide for payment during sickness up to a maximum period. A sick employee in most cases will expect to remain 'employed' during an illness at least until the sick pay period elapses. There is, however, no necessary link-up in law between the sick pay period and the question of dismissal for illness, for (a) a contractual sick pay term only covers payment while still employed and, although it would not normally be reasonable to dismiss before the end of the sick pay period, there may be cases where the employer's business needs are so urgent that dismissal (and replacement) *during* that period could be reasonable; (b) on the other hand, it is not necessarily fair to apply a policy of dismissing automatically once the sick pay period expires.[237] Thus, the two matters are conceptually separate. The *third* point is that if the medical cause of the absence is likely to be long-term and have a significant effect on the employee's life, the employer may now have to consider whether it could

[232] *Winterhalter Gastronom Ltd v Webb* [1973] ICR 245, [1973] IRLR 120, NIRC.

[233] *James v Waltham Holy Cross UDC* [1973] ICR 398, [1973] IRLR 202.

[234] *Sutton and Gates (Luton) Ltd v Boxall* [1979] ICR 67, [1978] IRLR 486, explaining *Kraft Foods Ltd v Fox* [1978] ICR 311, [1977] IRLR 431.

[235] See 6.1.2. The applicability of the doctrine of frustration in this context was reaffirmed by the Court of Appeal in *Notcutt v Universal Equipment Co (London) Ltd* [1986] ICR 414, [1986] IRLR 218, but would be on shaky ground in cases involving a disability under the Equality Act 2010.

[236] *Tan v Berry Bros and Rudd Ltd* [1974] ICR 586, [1974] IRLR 244, NIRC.

[237] *Hardwick v Leeds Area Health Authority* [1975] IRLR 319. For a later confirmation of this point, on rather unusual facts see *Smiths Industries Aerospace and Defence Systems Ltd v Brookes* [1986] IRLR 434.

constitute a 'disability' within the Equality Act 2010, in which case the following unfair dismissal law considerations may have to be supplemented by others under that Act, in particular any reasonable adjustments that might have to be made to help the employee to return.[238] *Fourth*, it is now clear that the ACAS disciplinary code does not apply to these cases, at least where only incapacity is involved, as opposed to malingering or other misconduct.[239]

Subject to these points, it is well established by leading cases such as *East Lindsey District Council v Daubney*[240] that the approach of the tribunal in assessing the reasonableness of the employer's decision to dismiss should be to consider whether it was reasonable to expect the employer to wait any longer before dismissing, in the light of such factors as the nature of the illness, the actual and potential length of the absence, the circumstances of the individual employee, the urgency of the need to fill the employee's job, and the size and nature of the employer's undertaking. The procedural steps to be taken by the employer will vary widely according to the facts of the case but, although a 'warning' as such is hardly appropriate, in most cases the employer will be expected to consult the employee and discuss the nature of their illness and their future prospects, bearing in mind the employer's need to have the work done.[241] The employer may also be expected to make such investigations as are necessary to establish the true facts of the case, which may mean taking further medical advice on the nature of the illness. It has been stressed by the EAT that the eventual decision whether to dismiss remains a managerial one, not a medical one,[242] but in the nature of things the employer may reasonably have to rely heavily upon a medical prognosis (even if it later turns out to have been wrong).

Where the employee is likely to be away for a considerable period and their position needs to be filled, the employer may still be expected to consider the possibility of alternative (perhaps lighter) work for the employee instead of dismissal; this may particularly be the case where the employer is a large concern, though even then it probably stops short of an obligation to create an entirely new job for that employee.[243] Some occupational pension schemes include provision for ill-health retirement; where this is true it can be unfair for an employer to dismiss a long-term sick employee without a reasonable investigation into whether such retirement is available to the employee.[244] There is, however, a very different possibility at the other end of the spectrum—if it becomes clear that the work is causing illness in that particular employee and there is no other work for them, might the employer argue that there is a common law obligation to dismiss,

[238] For disability discrimination law see 4.7.

[239] *Holmes v QinetiQ* [2016] ICR 1016, [2016] UKEAT 0206_15_2604.

[240] [1977] ICR 566, [1977] IRLR 181. This long-standing approach was reaffirmed (and said to be in line with the leading case on procedure generally, *Polkey v A E Dayton Services Ltd* [1988] ICR 142, [1987] IRLR 503, HL), in *A Links & Co Ltd v Rose* [1991] IRLR 353, Ct of Sess.

[241] *Spencer v Paragon Wallpapers Ltd* [1977] ICR 301, [1976] IRLR 373. There may, however, be special factors, perhaps in the nature of the job itself, rendering consultation unnecessary: *Leonard v Fergus and Haynes Civil Engineering Ltd* [1979] IRLR 235; *Taylorplan Catering (Scotland) Ltd v McInally* [1980] IRLR 53. Note also that persistent absenteeism through a series of unrelated medical complaints (often impossible to verify medically) may in fact be more amenable to treatment as misconduct (with warnings and a final decision) than under the illness principles in *Spencer and Lindsey: International Sports Co Ltd v Thomson* [1980] IRLR 340; *Lynock v Cereal Packaging Ltd* [1988] ICR 670, [1988] IRLR 510; this may be particularly so under the current system of self-certification for the first week of sickness.

[242] *East Lindsey District Council v Daubney* [1977] ICR 566, [1977] IRLR 181.

[243] *Merseyside and North Wales Electricity Board v Taylor* [1975] ICR 185, [1975] IRLR 60; *Bugden v Royal Mail Group Ltd* [2024] EAT 80.

[244] *First West Yorkshire v Haigh* [2008] IRLR 182.

on health and safety grounds, which should make the dismissal fair? Older case law was less paternalistic,[245] but in *Coxall v Goodyear GB Ltd*[246] (concerning occupational asthma) the only ground on which the employer was liable in tort for negligence was in not removing the employee from that work, the judge speculating that in an appropriate case the employer (faced with the desire of the employee to carry on and run the risks) might be 'under a duty in law to dismiss him for his own good so as to protect him against physical danger'.

It will be clear from the preceding that obtaining reliable medical evidence on the sick employee is of great importance. Medical confidentiality could be a problem since the employer may not simply demand a report from the employee's own doctor. It may of course invite the employee to allow such a report to be compiled and released to it; if the employee agrees, that covers the matter of confidentiality. However, there is the further complication that the Access to Medical Reports Act 1988 gives the employee a right to see such a report by their own doctor (provided they follow the prescribed procedure) in advance of its disclosure to the employer and, further, a right to object to part or all of it and, ultimately, to refuse to allow it to be disclosed (though of course in the latter, extreme, case there would be nothing to stop the employer drawing its own adverse inferences from the refusal and so in practice this may not be a realistic option). However, the Act is limited to reports compiled by the employee's *own* doctor, and so does not apply to a report compiled by an in-house company doctor, or an independent doctor nominated by the employer.[247] This factor now gives even more importance to the incorporation of a term into contracts of employment (as is now commonly done) that specifically gives the employer the right to require the employee to undertake a medical examination by a doctor nominated by the employer, with the results divulged to the employer. If there is no such term, the employer may only *request* such an examination.

The above discussion of illness has primarily envisaged physical illness as the incapacitating factor. Similar principles apply to mental illness, though in such a case it may be that the problem is more delicate and requires an even more understanding approach by the employer (particularly if it hired the employee knowing of their actual or potential condition). It is clear, for example, that a dismissal can be found unfair where the employer caused the illness through unreasonable stress, or even exacerbated an existing mental illness or vulnerability.[248] If, however, the employee actively concealed a mental condition when applying for the job, that may be a good reason for dismissal when the employer finds out (depending perhaps on the nature of the job), as that would not be primarily a dismissal for illness but rather for misconduct, as in other cases where an employee is taken on in some way under false pretences.[249]

[245] In *Withers v Perry Chain Co Ltd* [1961] 3 All ER 676, [1961] 1 WLR 1314, CA, Devlin LJ put it pithily that '[t]he relationship between employer and employee is not that of a schoolmaster and pupil'.

[246] [2002] EWCA Civ 1010, [2002] IRLR 742, CA. Simon Brown LJ did allude to the paradox that the law here is becoming more paternalistic (in the light of health and safety concerns) at the same time that a human rights approach elsewhere is stressing the autonomy of the individual, including the individual employee.

[247] This limitation is achieved indirectly by the drafting of the definition of 'medical report' in s 2(1) as 'a report . . . prepared by a medical practitioner who is or has been responsible for the clinical care of the individual'. Section 3 states that the employer must have the consent of the employee before requesting the report in the first place; s 7 contains exceptions where the doctor may withhold parts of the report if disclosure could cause the employee serious physical or medical harm. On the Act generally see Pitt (1988) 17 ILJ 239.

[248] *L v M UKEAT/0382/13* (16 May 2015, unreported).

[249] *O'Brien v Prudential Assurance Co Ltd* [1979] IRLR 140. Likewise, fraudulent use of a sick note might be good grounds for dismissal for misconduct: *Hutchinson v Enfield Rolling Mills Ltd* [1981] IRLR 318, EAT.

7.5.2 **Conduct**

As seen in Chapter 6, dismissal for misconduct[250] was an important concept at common law, primarily in the context of wrongful dismissal where the main factor was whether the misconduct was so bad that it repudiated the whole contract and so justified summary dismissal. In the modern context of unfair dismissal, dismissal for misconduct is obviously important (as one of the principal heads of prima facie fair dismissals) but it operates on a much broader base than at common law, so that the misconduct may or may not be dealt with by summary dismissal. The reason for this is that the tribunals can now look into the substantive fairness of any dismissal for misconduct, whereas at common law if an employer wished to be rid of an employee guilty of some lesser form of misconduct than that which would justify summary dismissal, it could just dismiss them with notice and, provided that notice was of the proper length, there could be no legal redress for the employee. Thus, the legal rules relating to the modern and the common law approaches to misconduct are different, so that many dismissals which at common law were unexceptionable can now be challenged as unfair; likewise, a dismissal could be wrongful at common law (because the conduct was not grave enough to warrant the summary dismissal which was inflicted upon the employee) but a tribunal might still hold that in the circumstances it was fair.[251] On the other hand, there will remain a practical relationship between the modern and the common law actions in that certain major heads of misconduct accepted as justifying summary dismissal at common law will remain major categories of fair dismissals, for example failure to obey proper and lawful orders,[252] breach of confidence by the employee by unfairly competing with the employer or prejudicing confidentiality necessary to the business,[253] and computer misuse by the employee.[254] One further influence of the common law could arise in the case of an employee who consistently plays practical jokes or is inclined to show physical aggression, as in such a case there is a common law duty upon the employer to take reasonable care for the safety of that employee's *fellow* employees,[255] which may ultimately require a dismissal.

These overlaps apart, misconduct in the modern statutory context fits into the overall pattern of unfair dismissal law in being essentially a matter of assessing the reasonableness of the employer's reaction to it in all the varied circumstances of the case, including the seriousness of the offence[256] and any extraneous matters such as length of service and previous good conduct which may act in mitigation of the offence; it is a particularly wide category of dismissal, ranging from gross misconduct (still justifying summary

[250] Practical advice on handling disciplinary matters is given in the non-statutory ACAS Code of Practice on Discipline and Grievances at Work (2015) with accompanying guidance notes.

[251] *Treganowen v Robert Knee & Co Ltd* [1975] ICR 405, [1975] IRLR 247. For more recent examples see *Hope v BMA* [2022] IRLR 206, EAT and *Brown v Castlerock Group* EA-2020-000174, EAT.

[252] As at common law, the employee may refuse to obey an unlawful order: *Morrish v Henlys (Folkestone) Ltd* [1973] ICR 482, [1973] IRLR 61, NIRC.

[253] *Mansard Precision Engineering Co Ltd v Taylor* [1978] ICR 44; *Golden Cross Hire Co Ltd v Lovell* [1979] IRLR 267; *Nova Plastic Ltd v Frogatt* [1982] IRLR 146.

[254] *Denco Ltd v Joinson* [1991] ICR 172, [1991] IRLR 63; *Thomas v Hillingdon London Borough Council* (2002) The Times, 4 October.

[255] *Hudson v Ridge Manufacturing Co Ltd* [1957] 2 QB 348, [1957] 2 All ER 229. Various statutory duties upon the employer to ensure compliance with safety regulations and the use of safety devices may be an important factor in the dismissal of an employee who consistently acts to the peril of himself or herself and other employees.

[256] This may also be important in determining how intrusively the employer is permitted to investigate the employee without breaching human rights or data protection laws. In *McGowan v Scottish Water* [2005] IRLR 167 a serious offence of timesheet falsification justified 'proportionate' covert surveillance by a private investigator.

dismissal) such as theft, violence, wilful refusal to obey an order, and gross negligence, down to lesser matters such as swearing and poor timekeeping which may only become serious if committed regularly. Faced with this wide diversity, there is sometimes an unfortunate tendency to attempt to over-classify, as if for example the many decided cases established a 'law on fighting at work'. While collecting together all the cases on one kind of misconduct may have some value, it must be stressed that that value is restricted to attempting to point out certain factors which may be important in certain of the more typical cases. Further than that, these matters remain clearly within the factual jurisdiction of the tribunals. Swearing is a good example of this, as there are ample cases on it but it remains purely a question of fact whether a particular incident merited dismissal, usually depending on factors such as the nature and place of the employment, the effect upon the recipient, whether it was gratuitous or provoked, and any previous incidents; thus, for example, words used to a fellow employee in the course of work on a building site could give rise to different considerations if used to a customer by an assistant at a perfume counter.

7.5.2.1 **Warnings and disciplinary procedure**

Except in cases of dismissal for a single act of gross misconduct, this area of dismissal is a prime one for the application of a warnings system (and in most cases for the granting of a hearing to allow employees to put forward either their view of the facts or mitigating circumstances having a bearing upon the question whether to dismiss).[257] A series of warnings may be particularly important in cases of persistent minor misconduct where it is primarily the fact of repetition which may eventually justify dismissal.[258] Moreover, the emphasis in the warnings in this context will normally be disciplinary and so the employer should ensure that they are given in accordance with any procedure laid down in the employee's contract or in the works rules; to this end, it is usually advisable for such terms or rules to lay down any types of misconduct which are particularly relevant to the job in question and the likely consequences of transgressions.[259]

Some employers may feel that by laying down such rules they are fettering their discretion, but this should not be the case. In general, disciplinary rules, if properly phrased, need not be viewed as exhaustive (and so employees cannot claim that they can only be disciplined for matters that fall neatly within a particular category in the rules);[260]

[257] The importance of following proper procedures in misconduct cases was given a welcome reaffirmation by the Court of Appeal in *McLaren v National Coal Board* [1988] ICR 370, [1988] IRLR 215 (dismissal without any form of hearing unfair, even though it was impossible to operate the normal procedures in the middle of the miners' strike); cf, however, the different decision on the facts in *Dillett v National Coal Board* [1988] ICR 218, CA (a pre-*Polkey* case).

[258] Warnings given in bad faith will undermine this effect; if dismissal is based on cumulative warnings, and one of the warnings was given in bad faith, the dismissal can be unfair: *Way v Spectrum Property Care Ltd* [2015] EWCA Civ 381, [2015] IRLR 657.

[259] An important and topical example of this is the desirability of clear policies on email and internet abuse by employees working with computers (given the potential legal difficulties for the employer, for example through the downloading and misuse of porn, especially if used for harassment of others). Such policies are strongly advised by the Data Protection Code of Practice, Pt III 'Monitoring of Employees'. If the correct procedures are carried out, dismissal for downloading porn at work is likely to be fair: *Thomas v Hillingdon London Borough Council* (2002) The Times, 4 October.

[260] *Distillers Co (Bottling Services) Ltd v Gardner* [1982] IRLR 47; *Macari v Celtic Football & Athletic Co Ltd* [1999] IRLR 787, Ct of Sess. An ambiguous approach by an employer (eg when setting out disciplinary rules) may, however, render a dismissal for a first breach of a particular rule unfair: *Trusthouse Forte (Catering) Ltd v Adonis* [1984] IRLR 382, EAT. For a prime example of the danger of an employer going straight to dismissal for a first offence where it was not clearly covered by a disciplinary rule see *Hewston v OFSTED* [2025] IRLR 457, CA.

moreover, the employer stands to gain, as if it wishes to treat as particularly heinous (in the circumstances) something which normally would not be viewed as serious (such as smoking at work or drinking at lunchtime), it is well advised to say so in the rules—if not it may have difficulty showing that a dismissal is fair when the subject matter of it would not normally be viewed as a dismissible offence in other contexts.[261] Being clear about this has the added advantage of making it easier to identify those dismissals that fall outside the category of conduct altogether: a dismissal resulting from the irretrievable breakdown of a working relationship was found not to be a conduct dismissal but a dismissal 'for some other substantial reason', which meant that it was not unfair for the employer not to have followed its disciplinary procedure for misconduct, including progressive warnings.[262]

The major conceptual problem here is in trying to achieve the right balance between certainty and flexibility. On the one hand, it is said to be an important principle that people committing like offences should be treated alike (equality is equity), which argues in favour of a consistent application of disciplinary rules, regardless of who the culprit is.[263] On the other hand, it is said that the key to unfair dismissal is flexibility by the employer, judging each case on its merits and not simply adopting a 'tariff' approach to misconduct based upon rigid disciplinary rules.[264] Inasmuch as the latter point means the matters of *mitigation* should be considered in each individual case (eg length of service, previous work record), it is consistent with a more certain approach to the offence itself (as in the former point), and so one possible approach (particularly in a larger organization) is that the employer should *start* by considering from the personnel records whether there have been any similar previous incidents and how they were dealt with, before going on to consider the specific facts and any mitigation in the instant case.[265] One thing that can be stated with some confidence, however, is that tribunals should be wary of simple 'disparity' arguments by applicants because, as any lawyer knows, few cases are so similar as to be directly comparable, particularly when the element of mitigation is taken into account.[266]

Suspension pending fuller investigation by the employer may be appropriate in serious cases (provided the employer has contractual authority to do so); the Code of Practice[267] states that normally this should be with pay and only for a brief period, and so in reality the employer may not be expected to do so for any great length of time and may reasonably have to take the decision to dismiss once it has had time to make reasonable investigations, even if other eventualities such as a criminal trial of the employee are still pending.[268] Indeed, any greater delay before the employer takes decisive action could conceivably make the eventual dismissal unfair.[269]

261 *Dairy Produce Packers Ltd v Beverstock* [1981] IRLR 265. One example might be particularly high standards of hygiene in food-processing establishments.

262 *Hawkes v Ausin Group (UK) Ltd* UKEAT/0070/18/BA (14 June 2018 unreported); *Ezsias v North Glamorgan NHS Trust* [2011] IRLR 550.

263 *Post Office v Fennell* [1981] IRLR 221, CA.

264 *MBNA Ltd v Jones* [2015] UKEAT 0120_15_0109; *Taylor v Parsons Peebles NEI Bruce Peebles Ltd* [1981] IRLR 119; *Hadjioannou v Coral Casinos Ltd* [1981] IRLR 352, EAT.

265 *Procter v British Gypsum Ltd* [1992] IRLR 7; *Harrow London Borough v Cunningham* [1996] IRLR 256.

266 *Paul v East Surrey District Health Authority* [1995] IRLR 305, CA.

267 Paragraph 8. Where the employee is suspended (and so not able to talk to fellow employees) it is particularly important that the employer's investigations should be even-handed and fair: *A v B* [2003] IRLR 405.

268 *Conway v Matthew Wright & Nephew Ltd* [1977] IRLR 89, EAT. The legal position here is well summarized in the judgment of Coulson LJ in North *West Anglia NHS Foundation Trust v Gregg* [2019] IRLR 570, CA at [107].

269 *Cf Refund Rentals Ltd v McDermott* [1977] IRLR 59.

As well as the application of warnings and hearings, dismissal for misconduct is also a prime area for the application of the principle that the function of the tribunal is to decide upon the reasonableness of the action taken by the employer, not simply to substitute their views for its; in a case as heavily dependent upon its facts as a misconduct case, there may well be a considerable area of discretion in which several solutions might have been reasonable, and as long as dismissal was within that area the employer is not to be penalized for choosing it in preference to any lesser measure.[270] One decision that will generally be outside that area will be a decision, after an internal appeal, to raise the sanction from the one that was initially applied (eg from a 'final warning' to dismissal).[271] Although there might be circumstances (such as ongoing abuse of children by the employee) where the discovery of evidence on appeal might make it reasonable to impose a higher sanction immediately, the proper course for the employer when more serious misconduct becomes known on appeal will be to confirm the earlier sanction and begin a new process with respect to the new evidence. On the other hand, it is acceptable, where a hearing has been conducted in bad faith (or suffers from other procedural shortcomings), to 'cure' the effect of that hearing with a proper appeal conducted without bad faith or procedural flaw.[272]

7.5.2.2 **Criminal offences**

The type of misconduct case which has caused most concern is the case where the employee has committed a criminal offence, particularly (though not necessarily) theft. Proved theft from the employer will usually be a clear ground for dismissal (regardless of the amount taken),[273] as will wilful concealment of previous convictions when applying for a job,[274] unless the conviction is 'spent' within the meaning of the Rehabilitation of Offenders Act 1974, in which case the employee is not obliged to disclose it and a dismissal because of it will be unfair.[275] The problems arise in cases where there is only a *suspicion* that the employee has committed an offence, as the employer may feel that it ought to dismiss the employee immediately even though it may be some time before a criminal case can be brought against the employee (which may of course result in their eventual acquittal). Where the criminal offence arose outside the employment (eg theft from another person or the commission of a sexual or drug offence outside working hours), the employer should not normally dismiss before the employee has been found guilty,[276] and even then should only do so if on the facts (looking at the nature of the offence, the type of job, and the potential effects on customers and fellow employees) the commission of that offence

[270] *Trust House Forte Leisure Ltd v Aquilar* [1976] IRLR 251; *Trust House Forte Hotels Ltd v Murphy* [1977] IRLR 186. See 7.4.4.

[271] *McMillan v Airedale NHS Foundation Trust* [2014] IRLR 803, [2015] ICR 400, CA.

[272] *Khan v Stripestar Ltd* UKEAT/0022/15 (10 May 2016, unreported).

[273] *Murphy v Epsom College* [1984] IRLR 271, [1985] ICR 80, CA.

[274] *Torr v British Railways Board* [1977] ICR 785, [1977] IRLR 184, EAT.

[275] *Property Guards Ltd v Taylor* [1982] IRLR 175. Certain categories of persons, primarily professional or connected with law enforcement, are excluded: Rehabilitation of Offenders Act 1974 (Exceptions) Order 1975, SI 1975/1023. These categories were significantly extended from 2001 onwards in relation to employments involving contact with children and vulnerable adults: see 2.4.3.

[276] *Securicor Guarding Ltd v R* [1994] IRLR 633. In the contrary case, where a criminal conviction comes before an internal disciplinary hearing, it will normally be reasonable for the employer to rely on the court's finding of guilt (including where the employee has pleaded), without going behind that finding, even where the employee still maintains his or her innocence: *P v Nottinghamshire County Council* [1992] ICR 706, [1992] IRLR 362, CA; *Secretary of State for Scotland v Campbell* [1992] IRLR 263, EAT.

renders the employee unsuitable for the job in question.[277] The Code of Practice, paragraph 30 puts it thus:

> 30. If an employee is charged with, or convicted of a criminal offence this is not normally in itself reason for disciplinary action. Consideration needs to be given to what effect the charge or conviction has on the employee's suitability to do the job and their relationship with their employer, work colleagues and customers.

Untypically, there are some enterprises or institutions where the accusation alone, especially if it is something like child sexual abuse, makes it necessary for the employer to dismiss, if only to disassociate itself with the scandal. In such cases of 'reputational risk' the reason for the dismissal is not conduct but SOSR, and the employer must identify with particularity why the making of the allegation made it impossible to continue employing the claimant.[278] If this is demonstrated, the employer must test the allegation's reliability by questioning the body making the allegations, but need not carry out its own investigation. Needless to say, these are sensitive and difficult cases, going against some basic ideas of fair dismissal.

Two possible complicating factors may be mentioned. The first is that if the employee's basic argument is that what they do outside work is their own business, this may now give rise to human rights issues (particularly Article 8 on respect for private life and Article 10 on freedom of expression, discussed in 7.5.2.4). However, the signs to date are that this extra element does *not* add much to the existing law on unfair dismissal and is unlikely to render unfair a dismissal that is fair under the general law. The second complicating factor, yet to be elaborated upon, is the suggestion that, in a case of misconduct away from work, it may be reasonable to expect a *large* employer at least to consider whether there was any other employment to which the employee could be transferred, rather than being dismissed.[279] The idea of alternative work is, of course, well known in capability and redundancy cases, but could be difficult to apply here.

7.5.2.3 **Reasonable investigation**

Where misconduct arises within the employment (an obvious example being theft of the employer's property) the employer's need to dismiss may appear to be more urgent, but at the same time the employee under suspicion must not be treated arbitrarily. The position as it has evolved (particularly since the seminal decision of the EAT in *British Home Stores*

[277] See *Nottinghamshire County Council v Bowly* [1978] IRLR 252; *Norfolk County Council v Bernard* [1979] IRLR 220; *Moore v C & A Modes* [1981] IRLR 71; *Mathewson v R B Wilson Dental Laboratory Ltd* [1988] IRLR 512. 'Conduct means actions of such a nature, whether done in the course of employment or outwith it, that reflects in some way on the employer–employee relationship': *Thomson v Alloa Motor Co* [1983] IRLR 403 at 404, per Lord McDonald.

[278] *Leach v Office of Communications (OFCOM)* [2012] EWCA Civ 959, [2012] IRLR 839. A slight twist on this idea emerged in *A v B (local authority)* [2016] EWCA Civ 766, [2016] IRLR 779, where a headmistress was dismissed for failing to reveal to her employer that a close male friend had been convicted of making indecent images of children. There was no evidence that she was involved in any way, or that the activities of the friend had anything to do with the school, but the failure to report it created enough uncertainty to make the dismissal fair. This was subsequently affirmed by the Supreme Court in *Reilly v Sandwell Metropolitan Borough Council* [2018] UKSC 16, [2018] IRLR 558, [2018] ICR 705.

[279] *P v Nottinghamshire County Council* [1992] IRLR 362, [1992] ICR 706, CA. If the employer does look for other work before dismissing, however, that is not to be used by the employee as an argument that the misconduct could not have been too serious: *Hamilton v Argyll and Clyde Health Board* [1993] IRLR 99, EAT.

Ltd v Burchell,[280] approved by the Court of Appeal in *W Weddel & Co Ltd v Tepper*[281] and *Whitbread plc v Hall*[282] and fully in line with the current, post-*Polkey* approach) is that the employer may dismiss if it has (a) a genuine belief in the employee's guilt, which is (b) based upon reasonable grounds provided (c) by a reasonable investigation; it does not have to be able to *prove* the employee's guilt and so, provided the employer has this genuine belief, it is irrelevant if the employee is later acquitted of the offence (or indeed if the police decline to bring charges).[283]

Thus, it is not the function of the tribunal to try a criminal action against the employee and the employer certainly does not have to prove guilt beyond reasonable doubt—the inquiry is a much more general one than that,[284] looking into the bona fides and reasonableness of the employer's claimed belief. The reasonableness of this belief will depend primarily upon whether the employer made a reasonable investigation to establish the facts and drew tenable conclusions from the results.

What constitutes a reasonable investigation will of course vary with the circumstances, so that in the case of red-handed theft with little attempt at explanation, the requirement may not be onerous. In less obvious cases, the employer should make a careful inquiry, allowing the employee to offer a defence. However, it must be remembered that the band of reasonable responses applies to the investigation as well, so the question of what investigatory steps must be taken falls to be judged against the standard of reasonable employers. Thus the Court of Appeal in *Sainsbury's Supermarkets Ltd v Hitt*[285] reversed the decisions of the tribunals below to the effect that the employer had failed to take reasonable investigative steps. The employee had been dismissed for stealing merchandise which was found in his locker at work; he alleged that it was planted, and that other employees had access to the locker. The ET and EAT found it unreasonable of the employer not to investigate those claims, but the Court of Appeal held that in doing so the tribunals below substituted their judgment for that of the employer: reasonable employers would not have taken these steps, so the investigation (and hence the dismissal) was reasonable.[286]

[280] [1980] ICR 303n, [1978] IRLR 379; see also *Ferodo Ltd v Barnes* [1976] ICR 439, [1976] IRLR 302; *Alidair Ltd v Taylor* [1978] ICR 445 at 451, [1978] IRLR 82 at 85, CA, per Lord Denning MR. The requirement is of actual belief, not just suspicion. However, a well-founded belief in the employee's intent to commit the offence may suffice, if they have been found out before committing it: *British Railways Board v Jackson* [1994] IRLR 235, CA. The principles in *British Home Stores Ltd v Burchell* apply to all forms of misconduct, not just to dishonesty cases: *Distillers Co (Bottling Services) Ltd v Gardner* [1982] IRLR 47; they were reaffirmed in *ILEA v Gravett* [1988] IRLR 497 and *Whitbread & Co plc v Mills* [1988] ICR 776, [1988] IRLR 501.

[281] [1980] ICR 286, [1980] IRLR 96, CA.

[282] [2001] ICR 699, [2001] IRLR 275.

[283] *Da Costa v Optolis* [1976] IRLR 178; *Harris (Ipswich) Ltd v Harrison* [1978] ICR 1256, [1978] IRLR 382. A difficult case might arise if an employee, having been (fairly) dismissed for theft, was later proved to have been innocent and brought defamation proceedings against the employer. Presumably the defence of justification would not be available and so the employer would have to rely on the protean defence of qualified privilege. For an example of findings of fair dismissal after acquittals by a criminal court see *Dhaliwal v British Airways Board* [1985] ICR 513, EAT.

[284] The strict rules of criminal evidence do not apply so that, for example, evidence of previous dishonesty is admissible, and indeed may be highly relevant: *Docherty v Reddy* [1977] ICR 365; *Coral Squash Clubs Ltd v Matthews* [1979] ICR 607, [1979] IRLR 390. In general, there is an onus on the claimant to specify the breach of procedure that they wish to rely on, not for the tribunal to go looking for it: *Elhalabi v Avis Budget UK Ltd* [2025] EAT 11.

[285] [2002] EWCA Civ 1588, [2003] IRLR 23.

[286] This is an excellent example of how the band of reasonable responses forces the threshold of reasonableness downward from the point of view of the reasonable tribunal: the Court of Appeal was able confidently to distinguish between the standard (of a reasonable investigation) that a tribunal would apply, and the standard that employers would apply, without any evidence of the latter standard other than the fact that this is what the employer in fact did do. This is also seen more recently in *Shrestha v Genesis Housing Association Ltd* [2015] EWCA Civ 94, [2015] IRLR 399, where the Court of Appeal held that where a dismissal was based on a claimed discrepancy in reporting mileage, and the employee offered several explanations of the discrepancy, the employer was reasonable in choosing not to investigate some of them.

Thus employers must perform a reasonable investigation, but no more than what other reasonable employers would do.

There is a major qualification on this, as the EAT has suggested that where the employee's actions are being actively investigated by the police with a view to criminal proceedings, it may be improper for the employer to hold a full investigation and to expect the employee to explain the conduct.[287] However, on at least one occasion,[288] the EAT has suggested that in such a case the employer might at least give the employee an opportunity to make representations particularly on the question whether the employer ought to go as far as to dismiss (which may involve matters in mitigation, such as long and satisfactory service); in many cases, the employer might in fact gain from doing so, and be seen to be acting in the spirit of a fair procedure. Also, any failure by the employee to put forward a defence might be held against them. When carrying out an investigation, the involvement of the police may be important, as if they give to the employer definite information about their findings, that may go far towards confirming the employer's suspicions;[289] on the other hand, the mere fact of police investigation may not be sufficient in itself to constitute reasonable grounds for a belief in guilt, and likewise an employer should not simply 'delegate' the matter to the police and the courts (eg deciding not to investigate but merely to await the outcome of the court case, dismissing automatically if the employee is found guilty).[290]

The employer must therefore have a genuine belief in the employee's guilt based upon such investigations as were reasonable in the circumstances; primarily, the belief must relate to the guilt of the particular individual, though it has been held by the Court of Appeal that if the employer can only narrow it down to one of two employees but holds a genuine belief that it must be one or the other of them, it may be reasonable to dismiss *both*, which seems distinctly hard on the innocent one.[291] This just highlights yet again how the emphasis of the unfair dismissal protection is not in fact on the unfairness to any given employee from the experience of dismissal, but on the reasonableness of the employer in deciding to dismiss.

Once the employer has the necessary belief, it will normally be considered reasonable to dismiss in the standard case of theft (in the absence of exceptionally strong mitigating factors of which the employer knew or ought to have known). It should be noted, however, that it has been suggested that minor participation in theft, or theft from someone other than the employer (eg from a fellow employee), *might* not warrant dismissal in some cases,[292] though it remains clear that theft from the employer will be a good ground for dismissal in almost all cases. One last thing that should be noted here is that *Burchell* has arguably been called into question by the recent Supreme Court decision in

[287] *Carr v Alexander Russell Ltd* [1979] ICR 469n, [1976] IRLR 220; *Conway v Matthew Wright & Nephew Ltd* [1977] IRLR 89; *Tesco (Holdings) Ltd v Hill* [1977] IRLR 63; *Parker v Clifford Dunn Ltd* [1979] ICR 463, [1979] IRLR 56. If the employee chooses to remain silent because of impending criminal charges, it may still be reasonable for the employer to dismiss on the basis of other evidence available: *Harris v Courage (Eastern) Ltd* [1981] ICR 496, [1981] IRLR 153.

[288] *Harris (Ipswich) Ltd v Harrison* [1978] ICR 1256, [1978] IRLR 382.

[289] As in *Carr*'s case and *Parker*'s case, above. However, actual police presence at an internal disciplinary hearing may well be held to render it invalid because of the pressure put on the employee: *Read v Phoenix Preservation Ltd* [1985] ICR 164, [1985] IRLR 93.

[290] *McLaren v National Coal Board* [1988] ICR 370, [1988] IRLR 215, CA. It will, however, normally be reasonable for the employer to rely on the fact of conviction when making its decision.

[291] *Monie v Coral Racing Ltd* [1981] ICR 109, [1980] IRLR 464, CA. This decision was applied to a case of suspected negligence by one of two fitters in *McPhie v Wimpey Waste Management Ltd* [1981] IRLR 316 and to a case of incapability in *Whitbread & Co plc v Thomas* [1988] ICR 135, [1988] IRLR 43. In *Parr v Whitbread & Co plc* [1990] ICR 427, [1990] IRLR 39 it was applied to one of four; the case contains useful guidance from Wood P.

[292] *Johnson Matthey Metals Ltd v Harding* [1978] IRLR 248, EAT.

Reilly v Sandwell Metropolitan Borough Council.[293] The Court questioned whether the test was properly applied to the 'fairness' inquiry in s 98(4), and instead more directed to ss 98(1)–98(3). It did not decide this question, so *Burchell* remains standing, but if the speculation of the Court is held to be correct, the *Burchell* test would no longer be subject to the 'range of reasonable responses' test. This is worth keeping an eye on.

7.5.2.4 **Human rights**

Although it seems that employment law ought to overlap extensively with human rights, that does not generally prove to be the case in the context of dismissals. The Human Rights Act 1998 applies the European Convention on Human Rights to employment tribunals as 'public authorities' (s 6(1)), so tribunals cannot, for example, confirm as 'fair' a dismissal that violates Convention rights. Although dismissals are unlikely to raise issues around the rights to, say, life or to be free from torture, dismissals can affect the qualified rights to privacy and family life, freedom of religion, freedom of expression, and freedom of association as protected under Articles 8–11 of the Convention. However, most dismissals are not themselves acts of the state, and they do not have the same significance as direct state interferences with the enjoyment of rights: no matter how 'unfair' they might be, dismissals are almost never able to engage a Convention right.[294] This means that even in the rare case where a dismissal engages a human right, the human rights question is ostensibly the same as the question asked in any ordinary dismissal case: was the dismissal justified? At least in theory, if it is 'reasonable' for an employer to dismiss under circumstances where the worker's privacy or religion are involved, then the burden on the enjoyment of the right will also be necessary in a democratic society in pursuit of a legitimate objective.[295] That is certainly how the courts and tribunals appear to see it.

In *X v Y*,[296] a dismissal for conviction of a sexual offence in a public toilet at a time outside work was upheld by the Court of Appeal in spite of human rights arguments. There the court helpfully explained that in cases where a Convention right was engaged, and where the right was of a kind (such as privacy, free expression, freedom of religion) where the state had a positive obligation to secure the enjoyment of the right, then the provisions of s 98 of the Employment Rights Act 1996 must be read and applied consistently with the Convention. However, the court opined that in most, if not all, cases the requirements of the unfair dismissal statute would produce an outcome consistent with human rights. In the case before it the court held that Article 8 of the Convention was not engaged, because the act that resulted in dismissal took place in public, and thus could not involve private life.[297] In *Pay v Lancashire Probation Service*,[298] the EAT reached a similar conclusion where a long-serving and well-regarded probation officer was dismissed when

[293] [2018] UKSC 16, [2018] IRLR 558, [2018] ICR 705.

[294] *Vining v London Borough of Wandsworth* [2017] EWCA Civ 1092, [2017] IRLR 1140.

[295] *Turner v East Midlands Trains Ltd* [2012] EWCA Civ 1470, [2013] IRLR 107.

[296] [2004] IRLR 625, CA. One point here was that there is no 'private life' interest in a public offence.

[297] Arguably the court failed to engage with the underlying argument of the claimant's case, which was that the dismissal punished the claimant, effectively, for *being* gay. The act was only unlawful because of its homosexual nature; the dismissal clearly resulted from the fact that it was a criminal offence involving a homosexual sex act. Dismissal on this ground therefore burdened the claimant's private decisions about sexual partners; Art 8 should have been found to be engaged on this ground, although perhaps the dismissal would have been 'justified' on the facts.

[298] [2004] ICR 187, [2004] IRLR 129, EAT. Once again the argument was adopted that he could have little 'privacy' interest when he had put himself on the internet. However, Art 8 was found to be engaged with regard to private performances, and Art 10 was also found to be engaged. The interference with human rights was held to be necessary in a democratic society because the dismissal was reasonable under ERA 1996, s 98.

his employers discovered his out-of-hours sideline of performing at various hedonist and fetish clubs and acting as a director of a company selling bondage, domination, and sado-masochistic products through the internet. In each case it was effectively the long-standing unfair dismissal rules that determined the case, not the human rights arguments, although the Court of Appeal in *X v Y* made it clear that tribunals must consider the effect the human rights element might have on how the 'reasonableness' enquiry is applied. Article 8 has been found to be engaged where surveillance was used to prove dishonesty, but the interference was found justified and the dismissal reasonable.[299] A dismissal that resulted from an employer's introduction of a requirement to work on Sundays was found to engage Article 9, but was reasonable under the circumstance and therefore not a human rights violation.[300] Article 10 can be engaged where a dismissal burdens free expression, but dismissals for offensive speech in the workplace are almost always upheld.[301] Disciplinary procedures in the workplace do not attract the protection of Article 6 of the Convention, although its protections do extend to procedure in the tribunals.[302]

In *Turner v East Midlands Trains Ltd*,[303] the Court of Appeal held that the damage to reputation, relationships, and future employment engendered by a dismissal for dishonest conduct can engage Article 8, thus requiring the justifying reason to be underpinned by a proper investigation. However, that decision was more interesting for what it had to say about the compatibility of the 'range of reasonable responses' test with human rights standards. The court ruled that the 'range of reasonable responses' test, as applied to questions of procedure in dismissals for dishonesty, satisfies the standard of fairness required by Strasbourg case law under Article 8. The decision emphasizes that the 'range' test is not subjective despite the insistence that tribunals must not substitute their judgment for that of the employer. Instead, it calls for procedures to be assessed 'by the objective standards of the hypothetical reasonable employer'.[304] The logic set out by Lord Justice Elias is attractive in that, when compared with how the standards for procedural fairness are expressed in the ECHR case law, the ostensibly objective standard represented by the 'range' must surely achieve the same outcome. The Strasbourg case law, in connection with the procedural requirements under Article 8, speaks of 'fairness', not proportionality, so his Lordship found it 'very difficult to see how a procedure which could be considered objectively fair if adopted by a reasonable employer could nonetheless be properly described as an unfair procedure within the meaning of Article 8'.

7.5.2.5 **E-misconduct**

As one might expect, there have been a number of dismissal cases in recent years involving the use of electronic media such as Facebook, X, email, and the Internet generally. The first observation that must be made about these cases is that they look much like other unfair dismissal cases, except that it is easier to engage in the relevant misconduct. The case of a school mentor who viewed and distributed pornography at work via the internet and email was treated much as a tribunal would treat the case of someone who did the same thing without the help of the Internet: the dismissal was fair because it showed poor

[299] *McGowan v Scottish Water* [2005] IRLR 167, EAT. See also *City and County of Swansea v Gayle* [2013] IRLR 768, EAT and *Garamukanwa v Solent NHS Trust* [2016] IRLR 476 (monitoring work emails did not engage Art 8; upheld by the ECtHR: [2019] IRLR 853). See further 3.3.7.2.

[300] *Copsey v WWB Devon Clays Ltd* [2005] EWCA Civ 932, [2005] IRLR 811. The tribunal had found that Art 9 was not engaged; the Court of Appeal held it was engaged, but that the interference was justified.

[301] For a full discussion see Pearson 'Offensive Expression and the Workplace' (2014) 43 ILJ 429.

[302] *Mattu v University Hospitals of Coventry and Warwickshire NHS Trust* [2012] EWCA Civ 641, [2012] 4 All ER 359.

[303] [2013] IRLR 107.

[304] [2012] EWCA Civ 1470 at para 16.

judgement and a reasonable employer would have dismissed in the circumstances.[305] Posting inappropriate comments about colleagues on Facebook can justify a dismissal much as bad-mouthing them in the lunchroom or a nightclub would do, if it undermines working relationships or damages the company's image, and a reasonable employer would dismiss.[306] Indeed, the EAT has made it clear that it has no intention of setting out guidelines of special principles to apply in internet or social media cases. In *Game Retail Ltd v Laws*,[307] the employee posted obscenity-laced rants on Twitter; although the rants were outside of work and purely personal, the employee had started his Twitter use for work purposes, and many of his followers were professional associates and employees of other stores in the employer's chain. It was found therefore to be reasonable to dismiss him for potentially damaging the company's image. Although the claimant's lawyers asked for clearer guidance from the EAT on Twitter use, Judge Eady (as she then was) flatly refused. She noted that the principles involved 'are either so obvious or so general as to be largely unhelpful'.[308] The principles for X, Facebook, and email are the same as the principles in other cases (eg 'the nature and seriousness of the alleged misuse; any previous warnings for similar misconduct in the past; actual or potential damage done to customer relationships and so on') except for one thing: the need for an IT or social media policy. This requirement appears in almost all cases on the subject,[309] suggesting that if there is one thing different about such cases it is that the new media call for clarity by employers as to what they expect.

7.5.3 **Redundancy and reorganization**

These two related causes of dismissal receive more thorough attention in Chapter 8, which focuses on issues including dismissal, surrounding redundancy, transfers of undertakings, and other large changes to the business that have effects on employees. However, they deserve a brief mention here in order to explain how and why they differ from other grounds of dismissal and hence call for separate treatment. The conceptual problem with a dismissal resulting from redundancy or reorganization is that it is a dismissal which is at the same time ostensibly fair (in that the employer has no option but to dismiss) and unfair (in that the employee has done no wrong). A redundancy occurs when some economic circumstance causes the employer to decide to reduce the workforce. This can happen in the context of closing a business, shutting down a part of a business (such as a branch, a department, or a distribution centre), or merely thinning out the ranks of workers. An employer typically makes the decision to take any of these kinds of action based on factors unrelated to the workers, such as insolvency, competitive pressure, or changes in demand. The same factors can, alternatively, lead to the decision to reorganize the business, rather than shutting part of it or reducing the workforce. Reorganization can nevertheless result in dismissals, because changes to the organization of work or to job

[305] *Henderson v London Borough of Hackney* UKEAT/0072/09/JOJ (unreported). This case also involved human rights claims and the dismissal was found to be proportionate for much the same reasoning as in *Pay*.

[306] *British Waterways Ltd v Smith* UKEATS/0004/15 (3 August 2015, unreported) (here the decision by the tribunal that the dismissal was unfair was criticized for treating misconduct on social media differently just because such conduct is increasingly common); *Crisp v Apple Retail UK Limited* [2011] ET/1500258/11 (unreported); *Teggart v TeleTech UK Ltd* [2012] NIIT 00704_11IT (unreported).

[307] [2014] UKEAT 0188_14_0311 (unreported).

[308] [2014] UKEAT 0188_14_0311 at para 52.

[309] It is also consistent with the holding of the European Court of Human Rights that the lawfulness of monitoring email and internet usage at work can turn on the presence or absence of a clear policy on its use: *Copland v UK* (2007) 45 EHRR 37, 25 BHRC 216; *Barbulescu v Romania* [2017] IRLR 1032.

responsibilities can lead to resistance from employees, who might rightly complain that the changes amount to breaches of their employment contracts. It can be reasonable, and hence 'fair', for an employer to dismiss employees who refuse to cooperate with changes called for by the economic needs of the business.

Both redundancy and reorganization are, in different ways, potentially fair reasons for dismissal. Redundancy is specifically identified in s 98(2) as a prima facie fair reason, and then subject to a detailed definition in s 139. If a dismissal falls within the statutory definition of redundancy, then it can still be fair or unfair; however, a redundancy dismissal is generally found unfair only on procedural grounds, such as lack of consultation or a flawed process for deciding which group of employees will be made redundant.[310] In these cases fairness will be assessed according to the 'range of reasonable responses test', meaning that the issue will be whether the procedure, the pool of employees subject to selection, or the selection from that pool were reasonable from the perspective of the employer and whether there was a reasonable consideration of possible alternative work[311] Even if the redundancy is 'fair', the employee is entitled to a redundancy payment, based on years of service, but this is almost always a significantly smaller amount than an employee could expect to receive in a successful unfair dismissal claim.

A reorganization dismissal—one that results not from a decision to reduce the workforce but from a decision to change the way the work is done—can be analysed as a special category of 'some other substantial reason',[312] or possibly of misconduct.[313] If the employee did not commit any disobedience or lack of cooperation that would support a conduct dismissal, the employer's reason will be that the economic circumstances required not just the reorganization but the dismissal of those who would not go along with the changes. This being a well-accepted form of 'some other substantial reason', the employee might get nothing at all if the dismissal falls within the range of reasonable responses; if it does not, the employer is liable to pay proper unfair dismissal compensation, not a mere redundancy payment.

Thus, if a dismissal happens in the context of an employer's response to economic pressures, and not because of something the employee did or did not do, in most cases it will fall within the definition of a redundancy, making it harder to prove unfair dismissal (procedural grounds only), but requiring at least some payment. If, however, the economic circumstances lead to changes that do not satisfy the definition of redundancy but nevertheless result in dismissals, the employee has a chance of winning the unfair dismissal claim on substantive grounds, but has an even better chance of losing altogether, and walking away with nothing.

7.5.4 **Automatically unfair dismissals**

We have seen over recent years the addition to the long-standing general rules on unfair dismissal of several specific categories of special protection to meet particular concerns. For example, the Trade Union Reform and Employment Rights Act 1993 gave such protection to health and safety representatives/complainants and to those asserting their statutory rights. In addition, there is now special coverage for (a) protected shop workers and betting workers, who may not be dismissed for refusing to work on Sundays,[314]

[310] See 8.1.1.

[311] *Wrexham Golf Club v Ingham* [2012] All ER (D) 209; *Hendy Group Ltd v Kennedy* [2025] EAT 106.

[312] *RS Components Ltd v Irwin* [1973] ICR 535, [1973] IRLR 239; *Robinson v Tescom Corporation* [2008] IRLR 408, EAT; *Hollister v National Farmers' Union* [1979] ICR 542, [1979] IRLR 238, CA; *Genower v Ealing, Hammersmith and Hounslow Area Health Authority* [1980] IRLR 297; *Farrant v Woodroffe School* [1998] ICR 184, [1998] IRLR 176.

[313] *Robinson v Tescom Corporation* [2008] IRLR 408.

[314] Employment Rights Act 1996, s 101.

(b) employees appointed as member-nominated trustees of their pension fund, under the Pensions Act 1995, who may not be dismissed for exercising their functions as such,[315] (c) employees elected (or seeking election) as employee representatives for the purposes of consultation over collective redundancies or transfers of undertakings, who may not be dismissed for performing, or proposing to perform, any such functions or activities,[316] and (d) employees exercising rights under the Working Time Regulations 1998, the Public Interest Disclosure Act 1998, the National Minimum Wage Act 1998, the Tax Credits Act 2002, or the Employment Act 2002, s 47 (flexible working), who may not be dismissed for any such reason.[317] In addition, the Part-time Worker Regulations 2000 and the Fixed-term Employee Regulations 2002 contain their own provisions rendering automatically unfair a dismissal due to exercising rights under the relevant Regulations.[318] In each case, there is also protection from victimization short of dismissal. The Enterprise and Regulatory Reform Act 2013 introduced a curious provision that removed the then-qualifying period for unfair dismissal if 'the dismissal is, or relates to, the employee's political opinions or affiliation', but did not make it an automatically unfair ground of dismissal.[319] A similarly odd version was introduced by the Employment Rights Act 2025 in relation to a 'fire and rehire' dismissal; this is declared to be automatically unfair *but* the employer is then given a statutory defence if the variation being forced through is necessary for its financial survival as a going concern, a form of qualified automatic dismissal.[320] Finally, where discrimination is the reason for a dismissal, the dismissal is effectively 'automatically unfair', because the claim will come under the Equality Act rather than s 94 of the Employment Rights Act 1996.

The form of the special protection has become familiar (in effect now being adopted 'off the peg' by the drafters of legislation)—a dismissal on these grounds is automatically unfair, as is any later selection for redundancy and any applicable qualifying period for unfair dismissal does not apply. In the case of whistleblowing, the statutory cap on compensation is removed (bringing it into line with the special protection for health and safety representatives and complainants with which it shares much ground). In the cases of pension trustees, employee representatives, and complaints by whistleblowers or under the Working Time Regulations there are further provisions making interim relief available. There is, however, one caveat to this regime of automatic unfairness. This is the 'separability principle', which applies across employment and discrimination law. It means that even if the employer has prima facie contravened the statutory protection, it is still open to the employer to seek to prove that that was not the real reason for the dismissal.

[315] Section 102.

[316] Collective Redundancies and Transfer of Undertakings (Protection of Employment) (Amendment) Regulations 1995, SI 1995/2587, reg 14.

[317] Employment Rights Act 1996, ss 101A, 103A, 104A, 104B, 104C, respectively. Dismissal for undertaking jury service is specifically covered by s 98B.

[318] SI 2000/1551, reg 7; SI 2002/2034, reg 6. There are similar protective provisions in the Transnational Information and Consultation of Employees ('European Works Council') Regulations 1999, SI 1999/3323, reg 28 and the Information and Consultation of Employees Regulations 2004, SI 2004/3426, reg 30 and all over the blossoming laws on family friendly rights.

[319] Section 13, amending s 108 of the Employment Rights Act 1996. This was introduced to implement the decision in *Redfearn v UK* [2012] ECHR 1878, 33 BHRC 713, [2013] 3 Costs LO 402, (2013) 57 EHRR 2, 57 EHRR 2, [2013] IRLR 51, that the UK failed adequately to protect the Art 11 ECHR rights of workers who did not satisfy the qualifying period.

[320] See 2.1.4.6.

In these cases[321] it is often argued that what the employer objected to was not the protected behaviour of the employee but the *way* they went about it. If this can be shown, the chain of causation is broken. That this can apply even in a case of automatic unfairness is shown by the leading Court of Appeal case[322] where it was accepted that the claimant had made a protected whistleblowing disclosure *but* the tribunal had been satisfied that the real reason for the subsequent dismissal was her conduct in abusing a colleague when dealing with her complaints. The EAT and Court of Appeal upheld that decision, holding that the tribunal had applied the idea of separability properly. Clearly, as case law has always accepted, a tribunal must treat such a defence cautiously, because otherwise it could give employers too easy a 'Get out of jail free' card, but it is beyond doubt that the principle itself does apply.

Despite the degree of commonality among these protections, some have provisions or raise issues that deserve particular attention: health and safety protection, assertion of statutory rights, and dismissals resulting from the transfer of an undertaking. The last of these is dealt with in 8.2.6, and the other two below.

7.5.4.1 **Health and safety protection**

In order to comply with the Framework Directive on the introduction of measures to encourage improvements in the safety and health of workers at work,[323] the Trade Union Reform and Employment Rights Act 1993 inserted what is now s 100 of the Employment Rights Act 1996. This makes a dismissal automatically unfair if the reason (or, if more than one, the principal reason) was that the employee:

(a) having been designated[324] by the employer to carry out health and safety functions, carries out or proposed to carry out such activities;

(b) being a safety representative or member of a safety committee, performed or proposed to perform such functions, or acted as an elected worker representative of employee safety (or took part in an election for such position);[325]

(c) where there was no representative or committee, or it was not reasonably practicable to raise the matter with them, brought to their employer's attention, by reasonable means, harmful or potentially harmful circumstances;[326]

321 The case normally cited here is *Martin v Devonshires Solicitors* [2011] ICR 352, EAT, a victimization case.

322 *Kong v Gulf International Bank (UK) Ltd* [2022] EWCA civ 941.

323 Directive 89/391/EEC; most of the requirements of this Directive were put into domestic law by the Management of Health and Safety at Work Regulations 1992 (reissued in 1999). However, the Directive also contains (in Arts 7.2, 8.4, 8.5, and 11.4) directions to member states requiring protection for workers and workers' representatives from detrimental treatment and rights to take direct action to counter imminent dangers.

324 This means formally designated by the employer, not just having general health and safety responsibilities when working: *Castano v London General Transport Services Ltd* [2020] IRLR 417, EAT.

325 To have this protection, the safety representative must have been acting within the scope of his or her responsibilities or jurisdiction: *Shillito v Van Leer (UK) Ltd* [1997] IRLR 495 (a case under the parallel provisions of s 44 on victimization short of dismissal on these grounds); once that is the case, the protection is wide, covering the exercise of the functions and the manner of doing so: *Goodwin v Cabletel UK Ltd* [1998] ICR 112, [1997] IRLR 665, EAT.

326 'Reasonable means' does not include concerted industrial action because the protection here is on an individual basis: *Balfour Kilpatrick Ltd v Acheson* [2003] IRLR 683.

(d) left the place of work, or refused to return to it, in circumstances of danger which they reasonably believed to be serious or imminent and which they could not reasonably have been expected to avert;[327] or

(e) in such circumstances, took or proposed to take appropriate steps to protect himself or herself or others from the danger.[328]

In addition to the automatic unfairness, extra protection is achieved in the following ways:

1. any applicable qualifying period does not apply;
2. any selection for redundancy because of the above factors is automatically unfair;[329]
3. the normal exclusions of tribunal jurisdiction in cases of dismissal while taking part in industrial action do not apply;[330]
4. interim relief is available;[331]
5. crucially, the statutory cap on the compensatory award for unfair dismissal does not apply.[332]
6. In addition to these unfair dismissal provisions, s 44 of the 1996 Act gives an employee a right not to have action *short of* dismissal taken against them on the above grounds, and a right to complain to a tribunal of any such detrimental treatment. In 2021 this protection was extended to 'workers' in relation to heads (d) and (e) above.[333]

While an employee dismissed for making health and safety complaints had some protection previously under the ordinary unfair dismissal law, it was patchy.[334] These provisions were therefore an important step forward. Finally note that a person making health and safety complaints in a more public arena may now also have protection under the Public Interest Disclosure Act 1998, as a protected 'whistleblower'.[335]

7.5.4.2 **Assertion of statutory rights**

The Trade Union Reform and Employment Rights Act 1993 inserted a provision (now s 104 of the Employment Rights Act 1996) making a dismissal automatically unfair if the reason (or principal reason) for it was that the employee had brought proceedings

[327] The danger in question can cover threats from another employee, not just for machinery or chemicals: *Harvest Press Ltd v McCaffrey* [1999] IRLR 778, EAT.

[328] Whether steps were appropriate must be judged by reference to all the circumstances, including the employee's state of knowledge, and the facilities and advice available to him or her: s 100(2). The special protection in (5) does not apply if the employer shows that it was so negligent for the employee to take those steps that a reasonable employer might have dismissed him or her for taking them: s 100(3). This derogation is specifically permitted by Art 8(3) of the Directive. The reference to danger to 'others' primarily means other employees but it has been held that it can apply more widely, eg to customers or members of the public: *Masiak v City Restaurants (UK) Ltd* [1999] IRLR 780, EAT.

[329] This protection is neutral; it does not put the representative/complainant into a better position in redundancy selection: *Smiths Industries Aerospace and Defence Systems v Rawlings* [1996] IRLR 656, EAT.

[330] For those exclusions see 10.2.2. [331] For interim relief see 9.2.1.

[332] Employment Rights Act 1996, s 124(1A); this also applies to dismissal of a whistleblower under s 103A.

[333] This was in response to the successful challenge in *Independent Workers Union of Great Britain v Secretary of State for Work and Pensions* [2021] IRLR 102 (Admin).

[334] An employee without the necessary continuous employment was unprotected, unless they could show that the dismissal was for trade union reasons; however, a health and safety complaint taken up on an individual basis was unlikely to qualify as 'union activities': *Chant v Aquaboats Ltd* [1978] 3 All ER 102, [1978] ICR 643, EAT.

[335] See 3.4.4.

against the employer to enforce a 'relevant statutory right' or had alleged infringement by the employer of such a right;[336] this does not apply if the dismissal was because of an allegation that was false and not made in good faith. The following rights are laid down as 'relevant statutory rights':

1. any right conferred by the 1996 Act, for which the remedy is by way of a complaint to an employment tribunal;
2. the right to notice laid down in s 86 of the 1996 Act;
3. the rights conferred by the Trade Union and Labour Relations (Consolidation) Act 1992 relating to deductions from pay, union activities, and time off;
4. the rights conferred by the Working Time Regulations 1998 and allied provisions;
5. rights conferred by the Transfer of Undertakings (Protection of Employment) Regulations 2006.

As with health and safety complaints (just discussed), any redundancy selection because of such assertion of statutory rights is made automatically unfair and the normal qualifying period does not apply. The latter point may be particularly significant where the alleged breach relates to the provisions on unlawful deductions (originally in the Wages Act 1986 and now in Part II of the 1996 Act), since that protection has no qualifying period, but in the past the exercise of the employee's rights under it was always dangerous if that employee lacked the qualifying period for ordinary unfair dismissal.

7.6 Remedies for unfair dismissal

The present statutory rules governing remedies for unfair dismissal were established as long ago as the Employment Protection Act 1975, which split compensation into a basic award and a compensatory award, and sought to strengthen the provisions relating to the direct remedies of reinstatement and re-engagement in an attempt to make them the primary remedies in practice as well as in theory; the figures have consistently shown that this aim has never been achieved,[337] and so compensation remains the prime remedy in most cases. The rules governing remedies are contained in ss 111–132 of the Employment Rights Act 1996. In addition, now that dismissal for trade union reasons is covered by the Trade Union and Labour Relations (Consolidation) Act 1992, there are special provisions in ss 161–166 of that Act relating to 'interim relief' which may serve to keep a contract of employment subsisting while a complaint in such cases is considered; such interim relief was extended by the Trade Union Reform and Employment Rights Act 1993 to the new head of dismissal for health and safety reasons and then to cases involving pension trustees, employee representatives, working time complaints, and whistleblowers, and so equivalent provisions now appear in the 1992 and 1996 Acts.

The normal remedies are now considered in turn, along with the important concepts of contributory fault and mitigation, either of which may decrease an award of compensation. As elsewhere in unfair dismissal law, it must be remembered that, although case law

[336] There are two gaps in the protection, due to this emphasis on the employee having complained of infringement: (a) if the employer has allowed the right in question (eg to time off for public duties), but then dismisses (before the qualifying period is served) because tired of having to allow it, that is not within the statutory protection; (b) it is not enough that on the facts the employee could have brought a complaint: *Mennell v Newell & Wright (Transport Contractors) Ltd* [1997] IRLR 519, CA. Note however that this was distinguished in *Simoes v DE Sede UK ltd* EA-2019-001209, EAT.

[337] See A C L Davies, Valuing Employment Rights: a Study of Remedies in Employment Law (Hart, 2024).

may be important in filling out the legislative bones (particularly in the area of the compensatory award), it is the wording of the statute which remains of paramount importance and the majority of cases are merely illustrations of the application of that wording.

7.6.1 **Reinstatement and re-engagement**

If a tribunal finds that a dismissal was unfair, it then proceeds to hear the parties on the question of remedies and by virtue of s 112 it must explain to the complainant the possible orders for reinstatement and re-engagement[338] and ask whether they wish the tribunal to make such an order.[339] An order for reinstatement means that the employer must take the employee back into their job; as this is in effect being treated as not having been dismissed, this means that the claimant is entitled to any benefits they might reasonably have expected to receive during the period of dismissal, principally back pay (including any *improvement* of terms and conditions which would have occurred during that period had there been no dismissal, but deducting any amounts actually received from the employer by way of wages in lieu or ex gratia payments, or from any employment during that period with another employer);[340] further, any other rights and privileges such as seniority and pension rights must be restored, and the tribunal must specify the date upon which reinstatement is to take effect. An order for re-engagement means that the employee must be taken back on by the employer (or by a successor or an associated employer)[341] in 'employment comparable to that from which he was dismissed or other suitable employment' on terms which are, so far as reasonably practicable, as favourable as if they had been reinstated; this too carries rights to back pay and preservation of accrued interests, and here the tribunal must specify not only the effective date of the order but also the identity of the re-engaging employer, the nature of the employment, and the rate of remuneration. In the case of either kind of order, the employee's continuity of employment is preserved and the time between dismissal and re-employment counts as a period of employment.[342]

7.6.1.1 **Practicability**

In a case where an employee expresses a desire for reinstatement or re-engagement, s 116 lays down a definite procedure to which the tribunal must adhere.[343] The tribunal must first decide whether to make an order for reinstatement and only if it decides not to do so should it go on to consider whether to order re-engagement and, if so, on what terms. In both exercises, it must take into account (a) the expressed wishes of the complainant,

[338] Dickens, Hart, Jones, and Weeks 'Re-Employment of Unfairly Dismissed Workers: The Lost Remedy' (1981) 10 ILJ 160; Williams and Lewis 'The Aftermath of Tribunal Reinstatement and Re-engagement' DE Research Paper No 23 (1981).

[339] The mandatory nature of this wording is not what it seems; a tribunal decision will not be rendered void by a failure to comply with this requirement: *Cowley v Manson Timber Ltd* [1995] ICR 367, [1995] IRLR 153, CA.

[340] Employment Rights Act 1996, s 114.

[341] Defined in the Employment Rights Act 1996, s 231; see 2.3.2. A tribunal should stick to the wording of the statute and make orders for either reinstatement or re-engagement, not just make an order that the employer should offer to re-employ: *Lilley Construction Ltd v Dunn* [1984] IRLR 483. An order may not be made to re-employ on significantly better terms: *Rank Xerox (UK) Ltd v Stryczek* [1995] IRLR 568.

[342] Employment Protection (Continuity of Employment) Regulations 1996, SI 1996/3147. These regulations apply where either there has been an application to a tribunal, or an agreed re-employment after the involvement of an ACAS conciliation officer or through a compromise agreement; thus an employee negotiating re-employment is advised to do so through ACAS or by a formal compromise agreement, otherwise there may be a break in continuity even if the employer had voluntarily taken the employee back: *Morris v Walsh Western UK Ltd* [1997] IRLR 562, EAT.

[343] *Pirelli General Cable Works Ltd v Murray* [1979] IRLR 190, EAT.

(b) whether it is *practicable* for the employer to comply with an order for reinstatement or re-engagement, and (c) whether the complainant caused or contributed to their dismissal and, if so, whether it would be just to make an order.[344] An employer who does not wish to take the dismissed employee back may therefore at this stage make representations on grounds (b) and (c) and, although (c) is important in ruling out important remedies for a 'rogue', it is (b) and the question of practicability which is likely to be the most pressing. It is for the employer to show impracticability, and as this is such an important matter it must discharge that onus properly—it is not enough for the tribunal to take a lax approach and decide that perhaps it would not be 'expedient' to put the employee back into employment.[345] Impracticability is a question of fact in each case, but may arise from inability to perform the work, unsuitability for it, definite opposition to their return among the workforce (either collectively or individually),[346] inability to take them back without having to dismiss another employee,[347] continued breakdown of trust and confidence between the parties,[348] or through an intervening factor arising since the dismissal such as redundancy or potential overmanning (though in such a case the tribunal should be satisfied that it is genuine).[349] In *Enessy Co SA v Minoprio*,[350] the Scottish EAT stated obiter that practicability may depend, inter alia, upon the size of the employer and that reinstatement into a small concern where a close personal relationship has to exist should only be ordered in exceptional cases; this may be a factor, particularly in domestic or quasi-domestic employment as in that case itself, but it is submitted that this approach should not be applied too widely, for as a principle it could come to bear an unfortunate resemblance to the old common law rules against enforcement of contracts of employment.[351]

7.6.1.2 **Employer non-compliance**

If an order for reinstatement or re-engagement is made and the employee is taken back but the employer does not comply fully with the terms of the order, the employee may complain under s 117 to the tribunal,[352] which is to order such compensation as it thinks fit having regard to the loss caused to the employee by the employer's actions. The more common form of complaint, however, will be that the employer has not complied with the order *at all* and has refused to take the employee back. In this case, s 117(3) provides that

[344] Lewis 'Interpretation of "Practicable" and "Just" in Relation to Re-Employment in Unfair Dismissal Cases' (1982) 45 MLR 384. Contributory conduct here is the same in content as contributory fault in a compensation case (see 7.6.2): *Boots Co plc v Lees-Collier* [1986] ICR 728, [1986] IRLR 485, EAT.

[345] *Qualcast (Wolverhampton) Ltd v Ross* [1979] ICR 386, [1979] IRLR 98, EAT. Similarly, the employer also may not rely on a belief that the employee will not accept contemplated conditions; if the claimant has requested reinstatement, and it is practicable with some alterations to employment permissible under the contract, it is error to find reinstatement impracticable because the employer believes the claimant might reject the changes: *McBride v Scottish Police Authority* [2016] UKSC 27, [2016] IRLR 633 (this decision features a useful up-to-date discussion of the principles of reinstatement).

[346] *Coleman v Magnet Joinery Ltd* [1975] ICR 46, [1974] IRLR 343, CA; *Langston v AUEW (No 2)* [1974] ICR 510, [1974] IRLR 182; *Meridian Ltd v Gomersall* [1977] ICR 597, [1977] IRLR 425.

[347] *Freemans plc v Flynn* [1984] ICR 874, [1984] IRLR 486, EAT.

[348] *Wood Group Heavy Industrial Turbines Ltd v Crossan* [1998] IRLR 680, EAT; *Kelly v PGA European Tour* [2021] IRLR 575, [2021] ICR 1124, CA. This may be more difficult for the employer to establish in a large organization where personal factors may be less important: *London Borough of Hammersmiuth & Fulham v Keable* EA-2019-000733, EAT.

[349] *Cold Drawn Tubes Ltd v Middleton* [1992] ICR 318, [1992] IRLR 160.

[350] [1978] IRLR 489. [351] See 6.4.2.

[352] One problem is whether s 117 can be relied upon where an employer uses more subtle tactics, eg taking the employee back but subtly victimizing them; also, where the employer takes the employee back on normally, but then later changes the terms of their employment (eg by downgrading them), that would have to be the subject of a separate unfair dismissal action.

the tribunal shall make an award of compensation in the normal way instead,[353] *and* an award of 'additional compensation' of between 26 and 52 weeks' pay. A 'week's pay' is subject to the same maximum as that in force at the time for the ordinary basic award[354] and, as the additional compensation is not expressly limited to compensation for loss actually suffered by the employee because of the employer's refusal to comply, it can include a punitive element.[355]

Once again, it is a defence to the granting of the additional compensation if the employer can satisfy the tribunal that it was not practicable to comply with the order; this may seem a strange provision, as it allows the employer a second opportunity to plead impracticability. In *Timex Corpn v Thomson*,[356] Browne-Wilkinson P held that the test effectively was the same (the latter stage *not* being confined to matters arising since the date of the order), so that it was possible for a tribunal merely to 'have regard' to practicability at the first stage and, if necessary, make the order on a fairly speculative basis and leave it to the employer to raise impracticability as a defence at this second stage if it did not work out in practice. This approach was generally approved by the Court of Appeal in *Port of London Authority v Payne*,[357] where it was said that, although a determination of sorts has to be made at the first stage, that will be 'of necessity provisional' and without prejudice to a fuller consideration of practicability at the second stage if necessary, with the burden of proof clearly on the employer (though only to show impracticability, not absolute impossibility). Finally, it should be noted that the statute provides that the fact that the employer has hired a replacement for the dismissed employee is not to be taken into account when deciding upon impracticability (at either stage at which it may arise) unless the employer can show that it was not practicable for it to arrange for the work to be done without engaging a permanent replacement, or (at the first stage, when deciding whether to make an order) that it only engaged the replacement after a reasonable period without hearing from the dismissed employee, and then had to do so in order that the work could be done.[358]

7.6.2 **Compensation**

The scheme of the present provisions on compensation is that the employee is eligible for a 'basic award' which is calculated mechanically in the same way as a redundancy payment and so rewards long service, and a 'compensatory award' which aims to put a realistic figure upon the employee's actual loss. The maximum for the basic award is determined by the maximum amount for a 'week's pay' for this purpose, and the compensatory award is subject to a maximum set figure in the statute.[359] This latter figure was allowed to fall behind inflation for much of the 1980s and 1990s, so that by 1999 it still stood at only

[353] If the tribunal finds that the employee himself or herself unreasonably prevented the order being complied with, that is to be considered as failure to mitigate their loss, with a view to decreasing the award of compensation: Employment Rights Act 1996, s 117(8).

[354] As from 6 April 2025 the figure is £719. For the calculation of a week's pay see 3.5.4.

[355] *George v Beecham Group* [1977] IRLR 43; IT; *Morganite Electrical Carbon Ltd v Donne* [1988] ICR 18, [1987] IRLR 363.

[356] [1981] IRLR 522, applied in *Freemans plc v Flynn* [1984] ICR 874, [1984] IRLR 486 and *Boots Co plc v Lees-Collier* [1986] ICR 728, [1986] IRLR 485.

[357] [1994] ICR 555, [1994] IRLR 9, CA, reversing the decision of the EAT which had been inconsistent with *Timex*. The case itself held the record for a tribunal hearing, having lasted 189 days.

[358] Section 116(5), (6).

[359] As at 6 April 2022 the maximum for a week's pay is £719 pw, giving a maximum basic award of £21,570.

£12,000, which had a depressing effect on unfair dismissal compensation[360] and caused problems when the equivalent maximum was removed from discrimination cases, so that it was in an applicant's interests to seek to bring a dismissal case as a discrimination claim whenever possible. The Labour government at first proposed in the White Paper 'Fairness at Work' to remove the limit altogether, but was prevailed upon only to raise it instead; this was done in the Employment Relations Act 1999, which increased the limit to £50,000 and at the same time instituted a system for raising all the award limits annually in line with the Retail Prices Index.[361] However, the Enterprise and Regulatory Reform Act 2013 introduced an additional cap of a year's pay, such that the cap which actually applies is the lesser of a year of the claimant's actual pay and the statutory cap as annually adjusted.[362] It will be interesting to see the effects when the Employment Rights Act 2025 removes the compensatory award cap altogether, as is the intention (as part of the retreat from making unfair dismissal a day-one right).

7.6.2.1 **The basic award**

The calculation method for this is similar to that for a redundancy payment; it is dependent upon the length of the employee's continuous employment as at the effective date of termination, and under s 119 the employee is to receive one and a half week's pay for each year of employment over the age of 41, one week's pay for each year between age 22 and age 41, and half a week's pay for each year under the age of 22; a maximum of 20 years may be counted and, as stated previously, the maximum weeks' pay for this purpose is limited to a fixed amount, subject to review.[363] The basic award is subject to reduction (a) by the amount of any redundancy payment received (either under the Act or by virtue of a private scheme),[364] (b) where the tribunal finds that there was contributory fault on the part of the employee[365] (discussed presently), (c) where the ex-employee has refused an offer of, in effect, reinstatement,[366] and (d) where the employer has made an ex gratia payment meant to offset or extinguish all legal rights (inasmuch as that amount may be set off against both basic and compensatory awards, if large enough).[367]

The basic award used to be subject to a minimum of two weeks' pay, but this was abolished by the Employment Act 1980, which also extended the idea of contributory fault to cover any conduct by the employee prior to the dismissal (not just conduct known to the employer and contributing positively to the decision to dismiss). A combination of these two reforms to the basic award ensured that an employee who is unfairly dismissed on ground A (eg unsatisfactory work) but who is later discovered to have been dismissible on ground B (eg concealed fraud, only coming to light after the employee left) cannot now claim the minimum basic award of two weeks' pay; the reforms were in response to fears expressed by the House of Lords in *W Devis & Sons Ltd v Atkins*[368] that the minimum basic award could be a 'rogue's charter' in such cases.

[360] Given that the figure stood at £6,250 in 1980, by the late 1990s inflation alone should have raised it to £30,000–£40,000. The latter figure was suggested by the CBI and IPD in their responses to 'Fairness at Work'.

[361] As at 6 April 2025 the maximum compensatory award stood at £118,223.

[362] Section 15, as implemented by the Unfair Dismissal (Variation of the Limit of Compensatory Award) Order 2013, art 2. When enacted, the Employment Rights Act 2025 will remove the statutory cap altogether.

[363] See *Harvey* DI [2503].

[364] Section 122(4); any excess over the amount of the basic award (which is thereby extinguished) is deducted from the compensatory award: s 123(7).

[365] Section 122(2). [366] Section 122(1).

[367] *Chelsea Football Club and Athletic Co Ltd v Heath* [1981] ICR 323, [1981] IRLR 73, EAT.

[368] [1977] ICR 662, [1977] IRLR 314, HL.

7.6.2.2 The compensatory award

Despite the fact that the cap on the compensatory award has been limited to one year's pay since 2013, the principles for arriving at an award up to that cap were not changed, so the jurisprudence developed under a more generous cap still applies.[369] Various aspects of the compensatory award can cause problems of quantification, and it is part of the tribunal's function to ensure that the relevant heads of compensation are considered.[370] However, since this award is meant to constitute realistic recompense and as such has to be approached from first principles in each case, the onus lies primarily upon the employee to adduce evidence of their losses;[371] the tribunal should not speculate unduly, but on the other hand the EAT has pointed out that only a realistic standard should be expected of the employee (who may have difficulty gaining certain evidence, even with the aid of discovery against the employer) and the tribunal should not hide behind the burden of proof where major problems of quantification arise.[372]

The basis of the compensatory award is contained in s 123(1), which provides that:

> the amount of the compensatory award shall be such amount as the tribunal considers just and equitable in all the circumstances having regard to the loss sustained by the complainant in consequence of the dismissal in so far as that loss is attributable to action taken by the employer.

In a potentially important and expansive decision, the Inner House of the Court of Session held in *Leonard v Strathclyde Buses Ltd*[373] that this statutory language is to be applied as it stands, and is not to have grafted on to it common law tests such as whether damage claimed was foreseeable or too remote; thus, when an unfairly dismissed employee had to sell back 6,000 company shares on leaving at the current price of £1.70, only to see them rise to £5.85 some months later (on a takeover), it was held that it was 'just and equitable' to award the difference on the facts, and that this was not to be defeated by technical arguments on remoteness of damage taken from other areas of the law. Such an expansive approach (leaving much in the discretion of the tribunal) became particularly important with the raising of the statutory limit to £50,000 in 1999 and the subsequent annual up-rating. On the other hand, it must also be remembered that ultimately the aim of an award is to reimburse the employee, not to punish the employer,[374] and this principle can have certain overall effects. In particular, it means that if the employee has in fact lost nothing, they are entitled to no compensatory award (only the basic award) and this may be held to be the case where it is clear that it would have made no difference even if they had not been unfairly dismissed; for example, in a redundancy dismissal where it is held to have been unfair through lack of consultation but it is clear that they would have been made redundant anyway, or in an incapacity or misconduct case where the dismissal was

[369] On the calculation of compensation generally see Upex *Termination of Employment* (7th edn, 2006); Collins 'The Just and Equitable Compensatory Award' (1991) 20 ILJ 201; Hough and Spowart-Taylor 'Liability, Compensation and Justice in Unfair Dismissal' (1996) 25 ILJ 308; and Crump, Pugsley, and Ashtiany *Butterworths Compensation Calculations* (1999).

[370] *Tidman v Aveling Marshall Ltd* [1977] ICR 506, [1977] IRLR 218.

[371] *Adda International Ltd v Curcio* [1976] ICR 407, [1976] IRLR 425; *Lifeguard Assurance Ltd v Zadrozny* [1977] IRLR 56; *Smith, Kline and French Laboratories Ltd v Coates* [1977] IRLR 220.

[372] *Barley v Amey Roadstone Corpn Ltd* (No 2) [1978] ICR 190, [1977] IRLR 299.

[373] [1998] IRLR 693, Ct of Sess; *Balmoral Group Ltd v Rae* (2000) The Times, 25 January, EAT.

[374] *Clarkson International Tools Ltd v Short* [1973] ICR 191, [1973] IRLR 90; *Lifeguard Assurance Ltd v Zadrozny* [1977] IRLR 56. It was said in *Townson v Northgate Group Ltd* [1981] IRLR 382 that the tribunal could look at how unfair the dismissal was when assessing compensation, but this was later disapproved in *Morris v Acco Ltd* [1985] ICR 306.

unfair because the proper procedure was not followed but it is clear that the employee would have been dismissed in any event.[375] In such a case it has long been clear that there may be a nil compensatory award, or a very limited one (eg where in a case of lack of redundancy consultation it appears that proper consultation would have lasted for four weeks but then the employee would have been dismissed; in such a case the compensatory award may only reflect four weeks' loss of wages).[376]

As we have already seen, the decision of the House of Lords in *Polkey v A E Dayton Services Ltd*[377] established as a general principle that it is *not* open to a tribunal to find a dismissal substantively fair merely because with hindsight a procedural lapse in fact made no difference, but on the other hand that decision did accept (and, indeed, emphasize) the important point for present purposes, namely that the injustice (or lack of it) to the employee at the end of the day *is* to be taken into account in fixing compensation, and that approach has been applied strongly in the post-*Polkey* case law,[378] to the extent that this is now widely known in employment lawyers' jargon as 'the *Polkey* reduction'. It means that the tribunals have to be proactive on this point in investigating the likelihood (or lack thereof) that the employee would be dismissed fairly in the foreseeable future, which can be done either on the basis of direct evidence as to when the employer would likely dismiss the employee fairly, or on the basis of a percentage estimate of that likelihood.[379] This adjustment should be distinguished from the adjustment introduced by the Employment Act 2008, allowing a 25 per cent reduction or increase in the compensatory award to reflect the failure of one party or the other to comply with applicable disciplinary or grievance procedures.[380]

Finally, and on an even more fundamental level, an employee may be said to have lost nothing if their *conduct* is such that it is not just and equitable to give any compensatory award, in spite of the finding of unfairness. This would be the case for example where the employer unfairly dismissed the employee on a weak ground (eg incapability) but then later found out about a cast-iron ground for dismissal (eg embezzlement) which the employee had kept hidden from it. In such a case, the House of Lords held in *W Devis &*

[375] *Clarkson International Tools Ltd v Short* [1973] ICR 191, [1973] IRLR 90; *British United Shoe Machinery Co Ltd v Clarke* [1978] ICR 70, [1977] IRLR 297; *Barley v Amey Roadstone Corpn Ltd (No 2)* [1978] ICR 190, [1977] IRLR 299; *Clyde Pipeworks Ltd v Foster* [1978] IRLR 313; *Brittains Arborfield Ltd v Van Uden* [1977] ICR 211.

[376] Note, however, that ultimately this remains a question of fact and what would be just and equitable, so that there is no 'tariff' of two or three weeks: *Elkouil v Coney Island Ltd* [2002] IRLR 174 (employers knew of redundancies ten weeks before telling employees; compensation given for ten weeks' loss of job searching opportunity).

[377] [1988] ICR 142, [1987] IRLR 503, HL.

[378] See particularly *Mining Supplies (Longwall) Ltd v Baker* [1988] ICR 676, [1988] IRLR 417; *Slaughter v C Brewer & Sons Ltd* [1990] ICR 730, [1990] IRLR 426; *Red Bank Manufacturing Co Ltd v Meadows* [1992] ICR 204, [1992] IRLR 209; *Campbell v Dunoon and Cowal Housing Association Ltd* [1993] IRLR 496, Ct of Sess; *Britool Ltd v Roberts* [1993] IRLR 481; *Rao v Civil Aviation Authority* [1994] ICR 495, [1994] IRLR 240, CA.

[379] *Contract Bottling Ltd v Cave* UKEAT/0100/14 (18 July 2014, unreported); *Dunlop Ltd v Farrell* [1993] ICR 885; *Wolesley Centers Ltd v Simmons* [1994] ICR 503; *Fisher v California Cake & Cookie Ltd* [1997] IRLR 212. The EAT have suggested two glosses to this rule, where the tribunal should not consider future likelihoods—(a) where the unfairness comes from a defect of substance (eg improper selection criteria) rather than of procedure: *Steel Stockholders (Birmingham) Ltd v Kirkwood* [1993] IRLR 515 (criticized by the Court of Appeal in *O'Dea v ISC Chemicals Ltd* [1996] ICR 222, [1995] IRLR 599, but reaffirmed by the Inner House of the Court of Session in *King v Eaton (No 2)* [1998] IRLR 686); (b) where the unfairness comes from positive steps taken by the employer (eg wrong application of criteria), rather than a sin of omission: *Boulton & Paul Ltd v Arnold* [1994] IRLR 532. Arguably, both of these are unfortunate complications in an already difficult area.

[380] Trade Union and Labour Relations (Consolidation) Act 1992, s 207A.

Sons Ltd v Atkins[381] that that subsequently discovered reason could not affect the fairness of the dismissal, or activate the provisions on contributory fault, for both of these matters have to be judged according to the employer's knowledge at the time of the dismissals; it could, however, justify the tribunal making a nil or nominal compensatory award on the ground of justice and equity, quite independently of any question of contributory fault.[382]

Given such general considerations, tribunals have to have a system of dividing up possible heads of loss, and this is well established, principally following the early NIRC case *Norton Tool Co Ltd v Tewson*,[383] which also established that the tribunal should set out in its judgment the relevant heads of compensation and the amounts awarded under each, not just one global sum.[384] The emphasis is very clearly upon pecuniary loss, and the following are the major heads.

Loss up to the date of hearing

This head requires a relatively simple mathematical calculation of the employee's actual loss of income during the period between the dismissal and the hearing; it is aimed at realistic compensation, so, as in the case of future loss (detailed later), the relevant figure is their previous weekly take-home pay (net of tax and National Insurance contributions), which may include matters such as overtime and tips which may *not* be counted under the stricter rules for calculating a 'week's pay' for the purpose of the basic award.[385] From this amount which the employee would have earned but for the dismissal the tribunal must deduct any sums earned in alternative employment during the period, or indeed in self-employment.[386] This is simply an example of the ordinary rules of mitigation of damage. However, there has always been an exception to this where the employee finds alternative employment during what should have been the notice period (in a case where no or short notice was given). Here, 'good industrial relations practice' dictates that mitigation should be suspended and the employee should receive any payments for the notice period without deduction.[387]

Problems arose when there were attempts to apply this exception for earnings during the (missing) notice period to the separate question of dismissal with wages in lieu of notice. Here, a non-deductibility rule would mean the employer paying twice and could have had a serious effect on the practicability of settlements. It was stopped at an early stage by the important decision of the Court of Appeal in *Addison v Babcock*

381 [1977] ICR 662, [1977] IRLR 314, HL.

382 [1977] ICR 662 at 680, [1977] IRLR 314 at 319, per Lord Dilhorne. This point was reaffirmed by the Court of *Appeal in Tele-Trading Ltd v Jenkins* [1990] IRLR 430.

383 [1973] 1 All ER 183, [1972] ICR 501. For a criticism of this whole approach see Collins (1991) 20 ILJ 201.

384 See also *Adda International Ltd v Curcio* [1976] ICR 407, [1976] IRLR 425, EAT.

385 *Brownson v Hire Service Shops Ltd* [1978] ICR 517, [1978] IRLR 73; *Palmanor Ltd v Cedron* [1978] ICR 1008, [1978] IRLR 303. Tax matters should not be considered in too great detail by the tribunal, which may, for example, ignore minor tax rebates: *MBS Ltd v Calo* [1983] ICR 459, [1983] IRLR 189. If there is a dispute as to what is the correct amount of wage payable at the date of dismissal, that must be resolved by the tribunal which is deciding upon compensation: *Kinzley v Minories Finance Ltd* [1988] ICR 113, [1987] IRLR 490, EAT.

386 *Ging v Ellward (Lancs) Ltd* (1978) [1991] ICR 222n; *Lee v IPC Business Press Ltd* [1984] ICR 306. This remains the case, even if the employee obtains new, permanent employment at higher pay, which eats into the compensation: *Dench v Flynn & Partners* [1998] IRLR 653, CA, applied in *Astha Ltd v Grewal* [2023] EAT 170.

387 *TBA Industrial Products Ltd v Locke* [1984] ICR 228, [1984] IRLR 48 (disapproving a contrary decision in *Tradewinds Airways Ltd v Fletcher* [1981] IRLR 272 and reverting to the original rule as laid down in *Norton Tool Co Ltd v Tewson*, above), approved in *Addison v Babcock FATA Ltd* [1987] IRLR 173, [1987] ICR 805, CA.

FATA Ltd[388]—even if it is accepted that non-deductibility applies to earnings during the notice period from elsewhere, it was made clear that it does *not* apply where the ex-employer has properly discharged the contract by paying wages in lieu of notice: there, the normal principle of mitigation applies and the employer is permitted to set that payment off against the compensation otherwise payable under this head; the employer will therefore *not* lose out by having to pay twice by reason of attempting to settle the case by, inter alia, the payment of wages in lieu. Moreover, it is clear that this principle applies to ex gratia payments generally[389]—again, the employer will normally[390] be given credit for such payments and be able to set them off against any compensation awarded later.[391]

As well as salary, wages, and other monetary receipts, the employee can claim compensation for past (and future) loss of other benefits such as a company car, a low-interest mortgage or loan, free or cheap accommodation, and other fringe benefits such as medical insurance and school fees; also, s 123(2) expressly includes any expenses reasonably incurred as a result of the dismissal (eg expenses incurred in seeking other employment), though this does not include the expense of bringing the unfair dismissal action itself.

Future loss

In contrast to the relative certainties of the first head, compensation for future loss may require the tribunal to perform a highly speculative exercise. The actual loss per week may be easy to quantify (where the ex-employee either has not obtained other employment, or has done so at a lower wage) and it may include the extra matters and perks mentioned above, but the tribunal has to fix a 'multiplier' (as in personal injury cases) of a number of weeks, months, or even years during which this loss might continue;[392] the state of the local labour market and conditions in the industry concerned will be factors, but there will be other discounting factors, such as the possibilities that the employee might have resigned in the future anyway, moved from the area, decided to focus on caring responsibilities, etc. Also, the principle mentioned previously that the employee will not be compensated if they have in fact suffered no loss must be borne in mind, so that if they would probably have lost their employment in the near future anyway (eg through impending redundancies), they may only be compensated in respect of that short extra period of likely employment.[393]

388 [1987] ICR 805, [1987] IRLR 173, CA, overruling *Finnie v Top Hat Frozen Foods* [1985] ICR 433, [1985] IRLR 365, EAT.

389 *Horizon Holidays Ltd v Grassi* [1987] ICR 851, [1987] IRLR 371, EAT.

390 The word 'normally' is used because there is an exception—if an ex gratia payment is made on dismissal which would have been made to the employee anyway even if no unfair dismissal had taken place (eg where a redundancy dismissal is unfair for lack of warning, but the facts show that the same ex gratia payment would have been made even if proper warning had been given), then it may be argued that that particular payment should not be taken into account as mitigation: *Roadchef Ltd v Hastings* [1988] IRLR 142; one complication in *Addison* was that there was (in addition to the payment in lieu) an ex gratia payment which was not taken into account, but it was for this reason.

391 Though even here the employer may lose out, for if the eventual amount of compensation is going to be over the statutory maximum, it has been held that the tribunal must deduct the ex gratia payment and then apply the maximum to what is left, which means that the employer may end up paying in total more than the statutory maximum: *McCarthy v BICC plc* [1985] IRLR 94; the order of making deductions is discussed presently. Thus the employer must be careful with ex gratia payments and, certainly in the case of higher earners, might be better advised to seek a binding settlement (either under the aegis of ACAS or under the rules on binding compromise agreements) rather than attempting a simple pay-off.

392 See eg *Cartiers Superfoods Ltd v Laws* [1978] IRLR 315. This must be viewed in the context of that individual claimant so that if their personal circumstances render new employment more difficult, the compensation may reflect that: *Fougère v Phoenix Motor Co Ltd* [1976] ICR 495, [1976] IRLR 259; *Gilham v Kent County Council (No 3)* [1986] ICR 52, [1986] IRLR 56, EAT.

393 *Young's of Gosport Ltd v Kendell* [1977] ICR 907, [1977] IRLR 433.

The number of factors in any particular case may thus be considerable and so, although as in other aspects of compensation the tribunal should explain in its decision how it arrived at the multiplier it used,[394] this is not an exercise in precision; the multiplier may be one general approximation of several different factors and, unless very clearly misguided, will not usually be altered by the EAT. In the past, even rough calculations could soon reach the low statutory maximum, rendering further precision unnecessary, but the raising of that maximum to £50,000 in 1999 (with annual increases) was expected to mean much more argument on exact calculation, in order to maximize compensation within (and up to) that limit, especially in cases of higher earners and/or likely long-term unemployment; in the large majority of cases, however, this will not be so and the multiplier will be relatively modest.

Loss of accrued rights

When an employee is dismissed and takes other employment, they lose any statutory (or other) rights against the dismissing employer which depend upon continuous service (eg redundancy and the employment protection rights) and must begin to accrue new rights against their new employer. This head of loss, established in *Norton Tool Co Ltd v Tewson*, was meant to reflect that disadvantage and initially caused some problems. Now, however, the major loss (of accrued redundancy rights) is in effect taken into account by the institution of the basic award and so any further compensation under this head will be less, though the EAT held in *Daley v A E Dorsett (Almar Dolls) Ltd*[395] that the right to the longer notice that accrues with service is itself valuable so that, independently of the power that a tribunal now has to award common law damages for loss of wages during the notice period, it is open to it to make an award including an amount reflecting the employee's loss of accrued statutory rights to longer notice.[396]

Loss due to the manner of dismissal

It was decided in 1972 (the year after the law on unfair dismissal was introduced) in *Norton Tool Co Ltd v Tewson* that the compensatory award was clearly tied to pecuniary loss and so, as at common law,[397] no amount could be awarded for loss of dignity, anguish, and so on simpliciter; an amount could only be granted under this head if the manner of dismissal could be said to affect the employee's future employment prospects, for example by blackening their name in the industry or in some way rendering them unfit for immediate re-employment.[398] This nostrum was followed consistently for three decades, until it was challenged entirely unexpectedly in a case concerning a very different point of law.

[394] *Qualcast (Wolverhampton) Ltd v Ross* [1979] ICR 386, [1979] IRLR 98. There is no 'conventional sum' of between six and 12 months—the period is to be determined by the tribunal in the light of all the evidence, subject only to the statutory maximum amount that can be awarded: *Morganite Electrical Carbon Ltd v Donne* [1988] ICR 18, [1987] IRLR 363 (impossible to say that an award covering 82 weeks was excessive).

[395] [1982] ICR 1, [1981] IRLR 385. Compensation may also reflect the loss of any extra redundancy rights that the ex-employee may have had under this contract over and above their ordinary statutory entitlement: *Lee v IPC Business Press Ltd* [1984] ICR 306.

[396] The EAT quantified this amount as half the wages for the statutory minimum of eight weeks' notice to which he was entitled. However, in the subsequent case of *S H Muffett Ltd v Head* [1987] ICR 1, [1986] IRLR 488 the EAT thought that in most cases it would be more appropriate merely to award a nominal sum of £100 under this head.

[397] *Addis v Gramophone Co Ltd* [1909] AC 488, HL; *Bliss v South East Thames Regional Health Authority* [1987] ICR 700, [1985] IRLR 308, CA; see 6.4.2.5.

[398] *Norton Tool Co Ltd v Tewson*, n 383; *Vaughan v Weighpack Ltd* [1974] ICR 261, [1974] IRLR 105; *BrittainsArborfield Ltd v Van Uden* [1977] ICR 211, EAT. This might be particularly relevant in a whistleblowing case.

Johnson v Unisys Ltd[399] was a common law claim for what had become known as 'stigma damages', that is, manner of dismissal damages, as part of a *wrongful* dismissal action.[400] In a strong decision putting an end to this development, one of the reasons given was that the common law should not be extended in such a way as to outflank or compromise statute law; in this context, that meant that 'manner of dismissal' damages should not be given at common law *because it was the function of unfair dismissal to do so*. This bombshell was contained in Lord Hoffmann's speech, in this short passage:

> I know that in the early days of the NIRC it was laid down that only financial loss could be compensated: see *Norton Tool Co Ltd v Tewson* . . . It was said that the word 'loss' can only mean financial loss. But I think that is too narrow a construction. The emphasis is upon the tribunal awarding such compensation as it thinks just and equitable. So I see no reason why in an appropriate case it should not include compensation for distress, humiliation, damage to reputation in the community or to family life.[401]

Not unsurprisingly, this was rapidly taken up by claimants' lawyers and representatives as a significant extension to unfair dismissal compensation. However, it split tribunals, with some granting such awards and others declining to. The issue was reconsidered by the House of Lords in *Dunnachie v Kingston-upon-Hull CC*,[402] which settled the matter. Giving the principal speech, Lord Steyn had little difficulty in finding that Lord Hoffmann's passage in *Johnson* was obiter, so that the House could consider the matter from first principles. Relying on the wording of s 123 and the long-standing authority of *Norton Tool Co v Tewson*, he held that 'loss' in s 123 is indeed restricted to financial loss, so that non-economic loss such as injury to feelings is *not* to be awarded in an unfair dismissal action. Stigma damages can be recovered to the extent that they are connected with pecuniary loss such as the loss of future employment, but not as a non-pecuniary injury to reputation.[403]

Loss of pension rights

Where the dismissed employee cannot find new employment, or can or may find new employment to which they cannot transfer their existing pension rights, this head of compensation may produce a considerable sum. It is, however, perhaps the most complicated head of all and the EAT has stressed that the tribunal should adopt a broad approach so that actuarial evidence, though of considerable help (bearing in mind that the claimant must adduce evidence of loss), is not conclusive. Once again the tribunal is aiming for a realistic, if approximate, estimate of actual loss so that if no loss is sustained overall, nothing is payable under this head; this might occur if the employee has to take, or opts for,[404] a deferred pension from their existing entitlement and can build up a suitable further entitlement from new employment, or if they move to employment with a better pension scheme (eg from a contributory to a non-contributory scheme), or if they can simply transfer the existing pension.

[399] [2001] ICR 480, [2001] IRLR 279.

[400] For this aspect of the case see 6.4.2.5.

[401] [2001] ICR 480 at 500, [2001] IRLR 279 at 288.

[402] [2004] ICR 1052, [2004] IRLR 727, HL. This appeal was heard alongside its companion case of *Eastwood v Magnox Electricity plc* [2004] ICR 1064, [2004] IRLR 733, HL which concerned the parallel position at common law see 6.4.2.5.

[403] *Chaggar v Abbey National* [2009] EWCA Civ 1202.

[404] Where there is an option the choice lies with the employee, who is not to be penalized by the tribunal if they opt not to take the deferred pension: *Sturdy Finance Ltd v Bardsley* [1979] ICR 249, [1979] IRLR 65.

In *Copson v Eversure Accessories Ltd*,[405] the NIRC said that there is no one correct way to quantify loss of pension rights, but isolated two types of loss: (a) loss of present pension position and (b) loss of future pension opportunity (ie the opportunity, had the employee not been dismissed, to improve their pension position during further service with that employer). Except in cases where the employee is close to retiring age (where the better approach may be to capitalize the cost of an annuity to produce a sum equal to the likely pension, discounting it for accelerated payment), the starting point for both (a) and (b) will be the contributions already paid to the scheme. The employee may have received back their own contributions, but can also claim (except in cases of transfer or deferment) credit for their legitimate interest in the contributions paid by the employer (plus interest thereon), which may be viewed as an adjunct to their salary.[406] As well as being the primary measure for the detriment to their present pension loss, lack of the employer's future contributions will be a guide to any future loss when compared with the position under any actual or likely pension scheme in new employment; the factors to be taken into account here may be numerous. Having arrived at a prima facie figure for loss, however, it is incorrect for the tribunal just to apply that for the number of years left to retirement age, because account must be taken of many contingencies, such as future resignation, future dismissal, early death, possible tax advantages, and the fact that any capital sum is being paid sooner than normal. The matter has been so testing for so long that a working party of employment judges have produced a guide 'Principles for compensating pension loss' which is essential for the tribunals in practice.[407]

Unemployment benefits?

One final point may be noted about the compensatory award. What is the position if the employee has received unemployment benefit (now Jobseeker's Allowance or Universal Credit) or some form of income support prior to the date of the hearing? Originally this was treated in the same way as receipt of income from another source during that period, and so was deductible. However, that meant that the employer was paying less compensation through a 'subsidy' from the state. Under the Employment Protection (Recoupment of Jobseeker's Allowance and Income Support) Regulations 1996,[408] the position now is that the tribunal is not to deduct the amount representing state benefits paid up to the date of the hearing, but instead must instruct the employer not to pay immediately that amount of the compensation it has awarded which represents loss of income during the period (called in the Regulations the 'prescribed element'). DBT will then serve upon the employer a recoupment notice (or a notice that no such notice will in fact be served), which requires it to pay back to them from the prescribed element the amount representing state benefits paid to the claimant prior to the hearing. After this has been done, the remainder of the prescribed element may be paid to the successful claimant. Thus, DBT obliges the employer to repay to them amounts made payable by them because of the unfair dismissal and the claimant still only receives what they have in fact lost. If no state benefits were in fact claimed during the period, the Regulations do not apply. Thus, the tribunal is relieved of the task of deducting benefits from the award (in return for the administrative chore

[405] [1974] ICR 636, [1974] IRLR 247, NIRC.

[406] *Copson*'s case; *Hill v Sabco Houseware (UK) Ltd* [1977] ICR 888; *Smith, Kline and French Laboratories Ltd v Coates* [1977] IRLR 220; *Sturdy Finance Ltd v Bardsley* [1979] ICR 249, [1979] IRLR 65.

[407] Regularly updated, the last at the time of writing being in 2021; see Harvey DI [2602] and S [3201].

[408] SI 1996/2349, replacing the original 1977 Regulations. *Mason v Wimpey Waste Management Ltd* [1982] IRLR 454. The Regulations do not apply to the settlement of an unfair dismissal action, so such a settlement may well take into account the state benefits in fact received, and those benefits will not be recoverable by the state. This may be an inducement to the employer to settle, since it may end up paying less.

of explaining the procedure to the parties) and, moreover, need not take the possibility of further receipt of benefit into account when deciding upon future loss either, as where compensation is awarded based on future loss for a set period of X weeks, months, or years, the claimant is disqualified from receiving benefit during that period.

7.6.2.3 **Contributory fault**

If a tribunal, having found in the claimant's favour on liability, considers that the dismissal was to any extent caused or contributed to by any action of the complainant, it must reduce both the basic award and the compensatory award by such proportion as it considers just and equitable.[409] The 'action' of the claimant must constitute blameworthy conduct in some way (so that it will not apply to proper and lawful activity on their part, such as refusing to obey an improper or unlawful order)[410] and this provision is aimed at giving the tribunal discretion to reach a just solution when both parties have been to blame,[411] as in the case of contributory negligence in a tort action. The employee's contribution must be to the *occurrence* of the dismissal, not to its *unfairness*: even if the employee's conduct had nothing to do with what made the dismissal unfair, it is contributory fault if it helped to cause the dismissal to happen.[412] Contributory fault constitutes a separate stage in the inquiry, once the tribunal has put a figure on the compensation, and should be explained by the tribunal as such.[413] In *Maris v Rotherham Corpn*,[414] the NIRC said that the tribunal should approach this question in a broad common-sense manner, looking at all the circumstances of the case and the employee's overall conduct (even if the actual ground of unfairness is a narrow, technical one); a slight change in the wording in 1975 strengthened this view.[415] The actual figure thus lies predominantly within the tribunal's discretion and may be difficult to challenge on appeal, provided that it has been properly considered at the hearing.[416]

Where the ground for dismissal was misconduct, but the dismissal is held to have been unfair (eg because of lack of warnings or a hearing) in spite of evidence of actual misconduct, that may be a clear case for reduction of compensation. Indeed, in *W Devis &*

[409] Employment Rights Act 1996, ss 122(2) and 123(6); by a combination of the Employment Acts 1980 and 1982, the contributory fault provision in the case of the basic award was widened to cover any conduct before the dismissal making it just and equitable to decrease that award; the reason for this is discussed presently. The procedure to be adopted (especially in a 'split' hearing) is considered by the EAT in *Iggesund Converters Ltd v Lewis* [1984] ICR 544 at 552, [1984] IRLR 431 at 435. There is no requirement that the basic and compensatory awards have to be reduced by the same percentage once contributory fault is found: *Charles Robertson (Developments) Ltd v White* [1995] ICR 349 (reviewing the previous, inconsistent case law); *Optikinetics Ltd v Whooley* [1999] ICR 984.

[410] *Morrish v Henlys (Folkestone) Ltd* [1973] ICR 482, [1973] IRLR 61, approved by the Court of Appeal in *Nelson v BBC (No 2)* [1980] ICR 110, [1979] IRLR 346, CA.

[411] The matter must be looked at between employer and employee, not involving the actions of third parties (eg other employees at fault): *Parker Foundry Ltd v Slack* [1992] ICR 302, [1992] IRLR 11, CA. Contributory fault can be applied even if the dismissal was constructive for, looking at the history of the matter, the employee may have been partly responsible for the employer taking the actual repudiatory action: *Garner v Grange Furnishing Ltd* [1977] IRLR 206; *Morrison v ATGWU* [1989] IRLR 361, NICA; *Polentarutti v Autokraft Ltd* [1991] ICR 757, [1991] IRLR 457 (not following *Holroyd v Gravure Cylinders Ltd* [1984] IRLR 259). 'Fault' on the part of the employee can include fault on the part of their agent, eg a solicitor: *Allen v Hammett* [1982] ICR 227, [1982] IRLR 89.

[412] *Parsons v Airplus International Limited* UKEAT/0023/16 (4 March 2016, unreported); *British Gas Trading Ltd v Price* UKEAT/0326/15 (22 March 2016, unreported).

[413] *Nudds v W and J B Eastwood Ltd* [1978] ICR 171.

[414] [1974] ICR 435, [1974] IRLR 147.

[415] *Brown v Rolls-Royce (1971) Ltd* (1977) 12 ITR 382 at 386, per Phillips J. There must still be a causal link between the conduct and the dismissal: *Hutchinson v Enfield Rolling Mills Ltd* [1981] IRLR 318, at least in the case of the compensatory award, though that link has been deliberately loosened in the case of the basic award.

[416] *Sutcliffe and Eaton Ltd v Pinney* [1977] IRLR 349; *Hollier v Plysu Ltd* [1983] IRLR 260, CA.

Sons Ltd v Atkins[417] Lord Dilhorne, disapproving earlier dicta that there may be a limit on the amount of reduction (eg 80 per cent maximum reduction), held that there is nothing inconsistent in finding unfairness but then using contributory fault in an extreme case to reduce compensation to nil or a merely nominal amount.

The position, however, is more difficult in the case of a dismissal for incapacity, for can an employee's unfortunate incapacity ever be considered to be 'fault' on their part? In *Kraft Foods Ltd v Fox*,[418] the EAT held that it could not, but in the subsequent case of *Moncur v International Paint Co Ltd*[419] it was explained that that was too sweeping a proposition and that the *Kraft* case envisaged the sort of incapability that was entirely outside the employee's control; even there, the EAT in *Moncur's* case doubted whether it was an absolute rule that such incapability could *never* amount to contributory fault, and a reduction in such circumstances was approved subsequently in *Finnie v Top Hat Frozen Foods.*[420] In *Slaughter v C Brewer & Sons Ltd*[421] a different tack was taken; the EAT said that a reduction of contributory fault would be rare in an incapability case *but* if it was clear that, even if the employee had been treated fairly, the employment would have had to end shortly, then compensation can be reduced accordingly under the general 'just and equitable' basis to the compensatory award, thus achieving much the same result. One matter that is well established is that where the incapability is in any way within the employee's control (eg where they are negligent, lazy, or unwilling to improve), that can clearly be contributory fault and indeed, according to the case of *Sutton and Gates (Luton) Ltd v Boxall*[422] (where a similar view was taken of the *Kraft* case), it may warrant a sizeable reduction.

A problem with contributory fault arose where the employer unfairly dismissed on one ground but then subsequently discovered other grounds which would certainly have justified dismissal. The House of Lords in *W Devis & Sons Ltd v Atkins*[423] held that in such a case the subsequently discovered misconduct cannot alter the finding of unfairness under s 57(3) *and* cannot be used as contributory fault as, being unknown at the time of dismissal, it could not have 'caused or contributed to' the dismissal. In such a case, however, justice could be done by giving a nil award under the general 'just and equitable' basis for compensation, *but* in that particular case the House of Lords were applying the old law on compensation which operated *before* the basic award was introduced in 1975. Once that award was introduced, the problem arose that a tribunal could not impose a nil basic award because the calculation is mathematical (not based on what is just and equitable) and it could only be reduced by contributory fault, which did not include subsequently discovered misconduct. Thus, in such a case, the employee whose dishonesty only came to light after being unfairly dismissed for laziness might still get a nil compensatory award but remain eligible for a basic award. Lord Diplock called this a 'rogue's charter' and in the Employment Act 1980 the government of the day took steps to prevent it, in two ways: first, the statutory minimum basic award of two weeks' pay was abolished; second, the tribunals were given a wider power to decrease (and possibly extinguish) a basic award where the conduct of the complainant before the dismissal was such that it would be just and equitable to reduce the award. This is wider than the previous rule on contributory

[417] [1977] ICR 662, [1977] IRLR 314, HL. See *Marley Homecare Ltd v Dutton* [1981] IRLR 380, *Chaplin v H J Rawlinson Ltd* [1991] ICR 553 and *Wilkinson v Driver and Vehicle Standard Agency* EA-2020-000048, EAT.

[418] [1978] ICR 311, [1977] IRLR 431.

[419] [1978] IRLR 223; *Brown's Cycles Ltd v Brindley* [1978] ICR 467.

[420] [1985] ICR 433, [1985] IRLR 365 (overruled later on other grounds in *Addison v Babcock FATA Ltd* [1987] ICR 805, [1987] IRLR 173, CA).

[421] [1990] ICR 730, [1990] IRLR 426.

[422] [1979] ICR 67, [1978] IRLR 486.

[423] [1977] IRLR 314, [1977] ICR 662, HL.

fault per se (which still applies to the compensatory award) in that it does not require a definite causal link between the conduct and the dismissal.[424] Thus, the undisclosed rogue may now be awarded no compensation at all.

7.6.2.4 **Mitigation**

Under s 123(4), the dismissed employee must take the same reasonable steps to mitigate their losses as they would have to at common law;[425] these might include answering job advertisements and going to the local job centre, though of course it might not be reasonable in the circumstances to expect them to take any job that occurs. Refusal of an offer of reinstatement by the same employer can constitute failure to mitigate,[426] but failure to use the company's appeal procedure once dismissed probably will not on general principles.[427] It may be reasonable in certain circumstances to leave one industry altogether and retrain for another, even if that necessarily means a longer period without work.

If the employee unreasonably refuses to mitigate, that can lead to a reduction in their compensatory award, though (on general principles) the onus lies upon the employer to prove failure to mitigate. The tribunal is not to account for failure to mitigate by means of a percentage reduction, but instead must determine a date by which the employee would have been expected to secure employment and cut off compensation at that date.

7.6.2.5 **The order of deductions**

In complex cases, where there may be several deductions to be made from an award of compensation (eg for mitigatory amounts, contributory fault, a *Polkey* reduction, and, of course, the statutory limit), a long-standing problem has been the order in which such deductions are to be made. This sounds very technical, but in practice can make a difference of thousands of pounds to the eventual award. It becomes particularly acute where the mitigatory amount in question is an ex gratia payment by the employer who, of course, wants to get full benefit of it when compensation is awarded. This, however, will only happen if that amount is deducted last (ie after the award has been subjected to all the other necessary adjustments).

After years of confusing and often inconsistent case law, the EAT reviewed the whole question in *Digital Equipment Co Ltd v Clements (No 2)* 427 and produced a definitive order of deductions, *starting* with mitigatory amounts including ex gratia payments (thus meaning that an employer may *not* get the full benefit of such a payment). When the case was appealed to the Court of Appeal, a complication was introduced—on the facts of the case the ex gratia payment was in fact a non-statutory (ie more generous) redundancy payment and the court held that Parliament's intent was that such payments were to be encouraged by being set off in full (subject only to the statutory limit), which could only be done by deducting them later. To that extent they allowed the employers' appeal;

[424] Employment Rights Act 1996, s 122(2).

[425] See 6.4.2.6. See particularly Potter LJ's summary of the approach to be taken by a tribunal in *Wilding v BT plc* [2002] EWCA Civ 349, [2002] IRLR 524. In that case Sedley LJ suggested that a test akin to the range of reasonable responses test should be applied (so that the employee would only fail to mitigate if no reasonable employee would have acted in that way) but the other two lords justices did not mention or support this idea.

[426] *Sweetlove v Redbridge and Waltham Forest Area Health Authority* [1979] ICR 477, [1979] IRLR 195; *Gallear v J F Watson & Son Ltd* [1979] IRLR 306; cf *Tiptools Ltd v Curtis* [1973] IRLR 276, where the offer of re-engagement included demotion. In *Wilding v BT plc*, above, Potter LJ said that a tribunal may have to take into account in such a case the attitude of the former employer, the way the employee was treated, and the employee's state of mind. The test may thus be both objective and subjective.

[427] *Seligman and Latz Ltd v McHugh* [1979] IRLR 130; cf *Hoover Ltd v Forde* [1980] ICR 239. The rule was approved (and *Hoover* not followed) in *William Muir (Bond 9) Ltd v Lamb* [1985] IRLR 95.

however, it is submitted that most of the reasoning of the EAT stands, subject only to this one qualification. On that basis, the order of deduction is:

1. any mitigatory amounts (from the ex-employer or new employment) *other than* a non-statutory redundancy payment exceeding the statutory amount;
2. any *Polkey* reduction (ie where a dismissal would have happened even if proper procedure had been observed);
3. any contributory fault;
4. any non-statutory redundancy payment;
5. the statutory limit, if applicable.

It is to be hoped that order has now been introduced into this complex area. There may, however, now be one further complication. If the employee wins but either party is found to have ignored the ACAS Code on discipline and grievance procedures there is to be a decrease or increase in compensation of up to 25 per cent. By virtue of the Employment Rights Act 1996, s 124A, this reduction is to be made to the compensatory award 'immediately before' any reduction for contributory fault (so that this punitive reduction applies in full); in the above scheme of things, in the case of a decrease because of the employee's default this means that it will occur between (2) and (3) in an appropriate case.

Review and Final Thoughts

- Although having clear rules and procedures governing discipline in the workplace has always been important, the cause of action for unfair dismissal gives them legal consequences, by taking procedure into account in deciding whether dismissals are fair. It is therefore important for employers to have such rules and procedures, patterned on the ACAS Code of Practice. See footnotes 4 and 48 for further reading.
- For the purposes of the unfair dismissal cause of action, a dismissal includes termination by the employer (with or without notice), constructive dismissal, and non-renewal of a fixed-term contract. Whether these have occurred is a matter of fact for a tribunal, and does not depend on formalities. Having the last two aspects of the definition means employers cannot avoid the consequences of a dismissal just by forcing workers to resign or by the use of fixed-term contracts. See footnote 59 for further reading.
- The unfair dismissal action consists of the following elements: (a) qualification to claim; (b) dismissal; (c) proof of the 'real' reason and that it is potentially fair; and (d) fairness (which really means the reasonableness of the employer's decision). The claimant must prove (a) and (b), the employer must prove (c), and although the burden in (d) is neutral, in practice the onus is on the employer in most cases, because the most potent defence for the employer is to demonstrate that it followed fair procedures and that dismissal under the circumstances was reasonable. See footnotes 150, 178, and 183 for further reading.
- Whether a dismissal is 'fair' depends entirely on the actions and reasoning of the employer, not on the impact on the employee. Tribunals must decide whether the dismissal decision fell within the 'band' or 'range' of reasonable employer responses, without substituting the tribunal's own judgment of what is reasonable. In practice that means that tribunals focus a lot on procedure (an area where they are less inclined to defer to the employer than with, say, the substantive fairness of the reason) and that generally tribunals and courts enforce a standard of minimal reasonableness which is artificially below the standard their own reason would apply. See footnotes 203 and 225 for further reading.
- Each of the 'potentially fair reasons' for dismissal under the statute (misconduct, capability or qualification, redundancy, compliance with statute, and SOSR) call for a slightly different

analysis of the fairness question: although the 'band' applies in the same way, the procedural expectations are different. Cases are not treated differently just because they involve computers or social media, and human rights are generally held to have little to add to the statutory fairness assessment. See footnotes 247 and 301 for further reading.

- A successful claimant can request reinstatement or re-engagement, but this is seldom practicable; most cases involve compensation in the form of a basic award (based on length of service) and a compensatory award (to replace any pecuniary loss to the claimant resulting from the dismissal). The size of the compensatory award is limited by a formal statutory cap which is the lesser of a year's pay or £118,223 (at the time of writing), and is limited even further by concepts of contributory fault, mitigation, and the exclusion of any damages for injury to feelings. See footnotes 338, 344, 369, and 383 for further reading.

8

Redundancy, reorganization, and transfers of undertakings

OVERVIEW

Redundancy, reorganization, and transfers of undertakings all involve significant employment consequences but happen for reasons unrelated to the individual worker. Economic circumstances or technical developments may cause the employer to shut down or reduce the size of the workforce, to change the structure or even the nature of the work, or to sell all or part of the business enterprise or contract out some part of the undertaking's activities. This chapter addresses the following matters:

- The legal consequences if jobs are lost through 'redundancy'—when an employer faces circumstances that require it to close or to reduce the size of its workforce. This includes the right to a statutory redundancy payment and what the law requires for a redundancy dismissal not to be unfair.

- What the law says about an employer's ability to change contracts of employment in order to meet economic or competitive challenges.
- The legal obligation to consult with workers collectively when an employer proposes to make people redundant or to change contracts of employment.
- What happens to employees when their employer sells the business they work for, or contracts out work they do to an external supplier (ie transfers the undertaking). In most cases the workers transfer with the work and the law protects many of their accrued rights.
- The obligation on an employer to consult with the workers collectively if it proposes to take action which will have the effect of transferring some of the employees to another employer.

Context

The unifying feature seen throughout this chapter is *change*, driven by economics, which has an impact on employees. However, the position of employees affected by such change is governed by four very different legal regimes:

1. Redundancy payments law—which is of entirely domestic UK origin and dates, virtually unchanged, from 1965.
2. The law of unfair dismissal, which constrains employers' freedom of action in:
   - selecting employees for redundancy;
   - imposing changes to contracts and working conditions in those reorganizations in which do not amount to redundancy.

   This law is again of entirely domestic UK origin.
3. Transfer of undertakings law, which preserves employees' jobs and terms and conditions when the activity in which they are employed is transferred to some other owner, operator, or contractor. This law dates from 1981 and is of EU origin (although UK law goes beyond the scope that was required by the EU). This law sits uncomfortably with both the common law of contract and UK unfair dismissal law. The typical EU vagueness of this legislation continues to cause difficulties.
4. The law requiring collective consultation with trade union or employee representatives in cases where a business transfer is forthcoming or a large-scale exercise is proposed which may involve terminating employees' contracts for economic reasons. This law is also of EU origin, but has been fairly comfortably incorporated into the UK legal system.

Most situations involving change for employees against a background of economic forces will involve considering two or three of these four fields. The different origins of these laws means that they do not always fit together well. However, the overall balance of these laws, with the exception of TUPE, used to be such that a determined and well-organized employer could usually achieve what it wanted to achieve, whether that be fewer employees or getting employees to accept less beneficial terms. The Employment Rights Act 2025 will change that state of affairs in relation to changes to terms and conditions of employment. Unions can help to resist jobs losses and pressure for change, but given their low level of presence now in the private sector, often they are not involved. It remains to be seen whether the pro-union measures in the 2025 Act will lead to an increase in union presence in private sector workplaces, but even where unions are recognized, their ability to resist the employer is often not great: calling a strike when the employer wants to reduce employee numbers or to cut pay is usually playing into the employer's hands.

8.1 Redundancy and reorganization

Questions of redundancy figure largely in the news in times of recession. However, research has shown[1] that even in recessionary times, compulsory redundancy is usually *not* the first option chosen and that other methods of reduction or reorganization of the workforce are usually considered more desirable, including natural wastage, redeployment, early retirement, and voluntary redundancy. Compulsory redundancy tends to be more common in the private sector, particularly where there is no recognized trade union.[2]

The difference between a redundancy dismissal on the one hand and a non-redundancy dismissal that happens as a result of a reorganization on the other hand is purely a function of the legal definition of redundancy. If company A responds to economic pressure by choosing to dismiss a specific number of employees, while company B reacts to similar circumstances by restructuring working processes and terms and conditions in such a way that several employees either leave or get dismissed for not cooperating with the changes, both situations could count, legally, as (a) redundancies, fair or unfair; or (b) dismissals 'for some other substantial reason', fair or unfair. The outcome turns on the question of whether the terminations satisfy the statutory redundancy definition by resulting from a diminished need for work of a particular kind. The answer to this question determines (a) whether the employees are entitled to redundancy payments and (b) what kind of legal analysis should apply in assessing whether the dismissals are unfair ones or not.

8.1.1 The definition of redundancy for redundancy payment and unfair dismissal purposes

The word 'redundancy' can mean different things to different people and in different contexts. For example, sometimes it is misused in the workplace to refer to dismissing a person whose 'face no longer fits'. Even in proper use by lawyers there are two definitions: a narrow one which applies to unfair dismissal and the redundancy payments scheme, and a wider one which applies to the obligations on an employer to consult collectively when collective dismissal are proposed.

For the purposes of unfair dismissal and the redundancy payments scheme, the definition is contained in the Employment Rights Act 1996, s 139, and this definition is exhaustive.[3] Whether redundancy is the principal reason for a dismissal is determined not by

[1] *Reasons for Leaving Last Job, 2011* (office of National Statistics 2011) available at <http://www.ons.gov.uk/ons/dcp171776_241679.pdf> (last accessed 10 March 2015); Millward et al. 'Workplace Industrial Relations in Transition' *The ED/ESRC/PSI/ACAS Survey*, (1992) ch 9.

[2] See n 1.

[3] *Hindle v Percival Boats Ltd* [1969] 1 All ER 836, [1969] 1 WLR 174, CA (Lord Denning MR dissenting). Per Widgery LJ at 847 and 187, respectively: 'It is not the policy of this Act to reward long service and good conduct as such, but only to compensate an employee who is dismissed for redundancy as defined in [s 139].' The function of the tribunal is to apply the statutory definition to the facts, *not* to seek to look behind the facts and assess the rights and wrongs of the employer's decision to make the redundancy: *Moon v Homeworthy Furniture (Northern) Ltd* [1977] ICR 117, [1976] IRLR 298; *AUT v Newcastle-upon-Tyne University* [1987] ICR 317, [1988] IRLR 10; *James W Cook & Co (Wivenhoe) Ltd v Tipper* [1990] ICR 716, [1990] IRLR 386, CA; this is subject to the point made previously, in the context of reorganization, that the tribunal may look into the reasons at least to the extent of being satisfied that they are genuine and not just a sham.

whether the employer claims it as the reason but by whether the definition applies to the factual circumstances. Under s 139 an employee is dismissed by reason of redundancy if the dismissal is attributable wholly or mainly to:

1. the fact that their employer has ceased, or intends to cease, (a) to carry on the business for the purposes of which the employee was employed by it, or (b) to carry on that business in the place where the employee was so employed; or
2. the fact that the requirements of that business (a) for employees to carry out work of a particular kind, or (b) for employees to carry out work of a particular kind in the place where the employee was employed by the employer, have ceased or diminished or are expected to cease or diminish.

This definition covers two principal cases—where the whole business closes down, and where the business carries on but its requirements for people to perform certain services cease or diminish. In either case, this can happen either generally or just in the place where the applicant was employed to work. These major elements will now be considered.

8.1.1.1 **Closure of the business**

This type of case is usually easy from the legal point of view (although, because of the large numbers of employees that are often affected, the compulsory collective consultation procedures will usually add a dimension of complexity—see 8.1.3).

The word 'business' is widely defined in the Employment Rights Act 1996, s 235 as including a trade or profession or any activity[4] carried on by a body of persons, whether corporate or unincorporated—so it includes public sector activities and charities. A legal person, such as a limited company or a public body, may have several businesses, so the focus is on whether the particular business in which the employee is employed is ceasing to trade, even if other businesses run by the organization are continuing—and quite possibly recruiting new employees.[5]

8.1.1.2 **Diminished requirements for employees to do work of a particular kind**

Section 139 is designed to cover the case where the business remains (or even expands), but the functions of particular employees disappear; this would occur for example when the function is automated or if work previously done by two employees is amalgamated and done by one, the other being dismissed.[6] It would also occur if the work is given instead to independent contractors,[7] however, in this situation the Employment Rights Act 2025 will, when s 28 is in force, add a complication since such a dismissal may be automatically unfair. This is discussed at 8.1.4.2, 'Employment Rights Act 2025—most reorganization dismissals to become automatically unfair'.

[4] *Dallow Industrial Properties Ltd v Else* [1967] 2 QB 449, [1967] 2 All ER 30.

[5] *Babar Indian Restaurant v Rawat* [1985] IRLR57, EAT.

[6] *Sutton v Revlon Overseas Corpn* [1973] IRLR 173; *Carry All Motors Ltd v Pennington* [1980] ICR 806, [1980] IRLR 455. The fact that the total amount of work to be done remains constant is irrelevant; there is a redundancy provided the number of employees required to do it has diminished: *McCrea v Cullen & Davison Ltd* [1988] IRLR 30, NICA.

[7] *Bromby & Hoare Ltd v Evans* [1972] ICR 113, 12 KIR 160; *Scarth v Economic Forestry Ltd* [1973] ICR 322, NIRC. Contracting out of services or activities has been a dominant theme in modern employment relations: 'The 1998 Workplace Employee Relations Survey—First Findings' (DTI/ACAS/ESRC/PSI; URN/98/934) p 7. Where the employee takes a job knowing that the work is subject to steady decline so that their employment can only be temporary, there may still be a redundancy when they are eventually dismissed: *Nottinghamshire County Council v Lee* [1980] ICR 635, [1980] IRLR 284, CA; this case must cast doubt on the correctness of the EAT's decision in *O'Hare v Rotaprint Ltd* [1980] ICR 94, [1980] IRLR 47.

Whose 'work of a particular kind'?

The question whether there has been a diminution in the requirements for employees to do work of a particular kind has caused problems for some time. For years courts and tribunals treated this as being a question of whether the work of the claimant employee had diminished. To decide whether an individual employee came within this wording, two rival tests evolved—the factual test (ie has the work they were actually doing gone?) and the contract test (has all the work that they *could* be required to do under the contract gone?). It was the latter that eventually gained ground,[8] based on two decidedly ambiguous Court of Appeal decisions.[9] This in some cases had the effect of making it more difficult to establish redundancy where the contractual obligations were drafted to include a level of flexibility.

However, there was then a major change of approach. This began with the judgment of Judge Clark in *Safeway Stores plc v Burrell*,[10] which went back to the pure wording of the section and held that both the factual and contractual tests are wrong, and are unnecessary glosses on that wording. It was pointed out that the wording considers the need for employees (plural), not that particular employee, and so what matters is whether a redundancy situation has arisen and whether any person has lost employment because of it. This approach was approved by House of Lords in *Murray v Foyle Meats Ltd*.[11] Giving the principal speech, Lord Irvine LC said:

> the language of [s 139(1)(b)] is in my view simplicity itself. It asks two questions of fact. The first is whether one or other of various states of economic affairs exists. In this case the relevant one is whether the requirements of the business for employees to carry out work of a particular kind have diminished. The second question is whether the dismissal is attributable, wholly or mainly to that state of affairs. This is a question of causation. In the present case, the Tribunal found as a fact that the requirements of the business for employees to work in the slaughter house had diminished. Secondly, they found that that state of affairs had led to the appellants being dismissed. That, in my opinion, is the end of the matter. This conclusion is in accordance with the analysis of the statutory provisions by Judge Peter Clark in *Safeway Stores plc v Burrell* and I need to say no more than that I entirely agree with his admirably clear reasoning and conclusions.

He went on to disapprove of the cases said to establish the contract test, and for good measure Lord Clyde, giving the other speech, castigated both previous tests as unnecessary.

This reinterpretation is very welcome. To summarize, it requires two questions to be considered:

1. Have the requirements of the business for employees to carry out work of a particular kind diminished—assessing the kind of work in a factual way rather than by looking at particular employees' contracts of employment?
2. If the answer to question 1 is 'Yes', then was this diminution the reason for the dismissal of the particular employee? If so, it is a dismissal for redundancy.

Murray v Foyle Meats also finally settled a long-standing uncertainty about whether an employee who was 'bumped' out of their job in a redundancy situation was dismissed for redundancy. This happens where, for example, within a department employee A's job disappears, but A (thought to be a good worker) is retained and given B's job, with B being

[8] *Cowen v Haden Ltd* [1983] ICR 1, [1982] IRLR 314, CA; *Pink v White* [1985] IRLR 489.

[9] *Nelson v BBC* [1977] ICR 649, [1977] IRLR 148, CA and *Nelson v BBC (No 2)* [1980] ICR 110, [1979] IRLR 346, CA.

[10] [1997] ICR 523, [1997] IRLR 200, EAT.

[11] [1999] ICR 827, [1999] IRLR 562, HL.

dismissed instead. Is B redundant—after all, his job still exists? *Murray v Foyle Meats* makes it clear that B has been dismissed for redundancy because the answer to both of questions 1 and 2 above is 'Yes'.

What is 'work of a particular kind'?

There remains, however, one further element of the definition of redundancy which is not affected by *Murray* (not being relevant on the facts of the case, and so not addressed). This is the question of what is meant by 'work of a particular kind', a particularly crucial concept where, for example, the numbers involved remain much the same (or indeed may even be increasing overall) but the *skills* required by the business change. There is much case law on this, and the law clearly looks at the *work function* of the employees within the organization, not necessarily at their particular job at the time, still less at any particular job title. Thus, the job may change over time in the way it is organized (and thereby, in some cases, in its suitability for, and attractiveness to, a particular employee) but, as long as the function remains, an employee who is dismissed for refusing to accept the changes (or who walks out because of them and then claims constructive dismissal under s 136(1)(c)) is *not* 'redundant'. They are not redundant because the requirement of the business for employees to do work of the particular kind has not diminished.

So, if an employer introduces new methods and technology to increase the efficiency of the function and the employee is either unwilling or unable to adapt to them, they may be dismissed without being redundant.[12] These reorganization dismissals could still be unfair, but they will be analysed either as misconduct dismissals (refusal to obey a lawful instruction) or as dismissals for 'some other substantial reason'.

The same approach often manifests itself in cases relating to changes in working hours. In *Johnson v Nottinghamshire Combined Police Authority*,[13] two clerks, whose work had been reorganized from a five-day week to a shift system operating over six days per week to increase overall efficiency, refused to accept this and claimed redundancy pay (in spite of the fact that they had been replaced by two new employees), but this was refused by the Court of Appeal on the ground that the particular kind of work remained the same and so the reorganization was not due to redundancy:

> It is settled . . . that an employer is entitled to reorganise his business so as to improve its efficiency and, in doing so, to propose to his staff a change in the terms and conditions of their employment; and to dispense with their services if they do not agree. Such a change does not automatically give the staff a right to redundancy payments. It only does so if the change in the terms and conditions is due to a redundancy situation.[14]

A similar result was achieved in *Lesney Products Ltd v Nolan*,[15] where the work of machine setters was altered from a day shift and a night shift to a double day shift system, with a consequent decrease in overtime payments; when six of the setters refused to work the

[12] *North Riding Garages Ltd v Butterwick* [1967] 2 QB 56, [1967] 1 All ER 644; *Hindle v Percival Boats Ltd* [1969] 1 All ER 836, [1969] 1 WLR 174, CA. It was argued earlier in this book that the courts might be willing to apply in such cases an implied term of reasonable adaptation to new methods and techniques: see 3.4.2 and *Cresswell v Board of Inland Revenue* [1984] 2 All ER 713, [1984] ICR 508.

[13] [1974] 1 All ER 1082, [1974] ICR 170, CA.

[14] Per Lord Denning MR [1974] 1 All ER 1082 at 1084, [1974] ICR 170 at 176; the phrase 'redundancy situation' is clarified in his Lordship's judgment in *Lesney Products Ltd v Nolan* (n 15). The last two sentences in the dictum are important because they make it clear that there *could* be a redundancy in certain circumstances; the EAT reaffirmed that there is no rule of law that a change of hours or shifts cannot produce a redundancy—it remains ultimately a question of fact for the tribunal: *MacFisheries Ltd v Findlay* [1985] ICR 160.

[15] [1977] ICR 235, [1977] IRLR 77, CA.

new system and claimed redundancy payments, the Court of Appeal held against them since the amount of work to be done remained constant, though reorganized onto a daytime basis (the undoubted overall 'redundancy situation' having been dealt with by the company by discontinuing the night shift worked by another class of employees who were not parties to the action).

An even more obvious instance of how the law approaches situations where work changes but the jobs remain is shown by *Chapman v Goonvean and Rostowrack China Clay Co Ltd*.[16] Ten employees were provided with free transport to work; when three were made redundant during a trade recession the transport became uneconomic and the employer discontinued it for the remaining seven, who responded by resigning and claiming redundancy payments. The Court of Appeal held that they were not redundant since the work that they performed had not ceased or diminished (the employer had shown that the seven were replaced by other employees taken on to do their work); the only change was in the organization and attractiveness of the jobs for the time being. There are limits, of course; a significant reduction in hours, effectively turning a full-time employee into a part-time one because there is a diminished need for their work, will be a redundancy if they refuse to accept the change and are dismissed.[17]

When does change go so far that there is a diminution in work of a particular kind?

It can be seen from the preceding discussion that under this head of redundancy, much will depend on the difficult question of fact—how radical does a change in the job, or the reorganization of it, have to be before it can be said that the function itself has changed? To put it in the language of s 139—what *is* work of that 'particular kind'? If the change is great enough to turn it into work of a different kind, then the employee who is unwilling or unable to perform the new function can claim that they are redundant since their old function has disappeared.[18]

In the earlier cases this was not easy, since the courts and tribunals in general took a fairly wide view of what constitutes one type of work (thus allowing the employer more scope for reorganization without having to make redundancy payments); thus, the function of 'barmaid' remained the same, even when an older style public house was transformed into a 'road house' requiring barmaids with certain attributes which no amount of retraining could possibly have produced in the original incumbent,[19] and the function of 'boatbuilder' remained the same even though the boatyard went over to fibreglass boats instead of the wooden ones which the dismissed employee was by long practice used to making.[20]

The approach in the later case of *Murphy v Epsom College*[21] shows a narrower approach to 'kind of work'. In that case the college's heating system was modernized, calling for new skills to maintain it. One of the existing two plumbers said that he was unwilling/unable to perform all the necessary new functions; he was dismissed and replaced with a

[16] [1973] 2 All ER 1063, [1973] ICR 310, CA, overruling *Dutton v C H Bailey Ltd* [1968] 2 Lloyd's Rep 122, 3 ITR 355; see also *Arnold v Thomas Harrington Ltd* [1969] 1 QB 312, [1967] 2 All ER 866.

[17] *Packman v Fauchon* UKEAT/0017/12 (16 May 2012, unreported) (changing course from *Aylward v Glamorgan Holiday Home Ltd* (EAT/0167/02), which had suggested that some reduction in head count was required for a redundancy).

[18] *Robinson v British Island Airways Ltd* [1978] ICR 304, [1977] IRLR 477, a case where the employee was arguing that he was *not* redundant, in order to claim the more generous remedies for unfair dismissal. A redundancy can arise from a change in specialisms within an overall job: *BBC v Farnworth* [1998] ICR 1116, EAT.

[19] *Vaux and Associated Breweries Ltd v Ward* (1968) 3 ITR 385.

[20] *Hindle v Percival Boats Ltd* [1969] 1 All ER 836, [1969] 1 WLR 174, CA.

[21] [1985] ICR 80, [1984] IRLR 271, CA.

heating technician. The Court of Appeal upheld the tribunal's decision that the dismissed employee was redundant since the employer's need for *plumbers* was reduced from two to one on the reorganization (with its corresponding requirement for a heating technician instead). However, more recently the EAT reminded employees that even extensive changes to the *terms and conditions* of work will not amount to a redundancy if the underlying *work* (in this case selling insurance) remains the same.[22]

This whole problem flows from the emphasis in s 139 on the overall work function and not the details of the job as organized at the material time; it has been argued that this should not be so, as it puts the financial risk of a particular way of doing a job becoming uneconomic upon the employee, rather than upon the employer.[23] The employee may lose their job because they are unable to meet the changed requirements but not receive any redundancy payment. However, the courts have stated that a *bogus* reorganization is not to be used by an employer as a cover for dismissals which are in fact due to redundancy.[24] It is also very important to note that although the employee may not be entitled to a redundancy payment, they can still challenge the fairness of the dismissal and, as will be seen in 8.1.4.2, the test imposed by an employment tribunal when considering the strength of the economic case for a non-redundancy reorganization appears to be more demanding than the test when reviewing the economic case for a redundancy. In other words, the employer may find it harder to show that the dismissal in a non-redundancy reorganization was fair because the tribunal may reject the employer's argument that the economic driver for the change was sufficient to justify dismissal. Therefore the topsy-turvy situation can easily arise of the employee (wanting more than the statutory redundancy payment) arguing that their dismissal was *not* for redundancy and that unfair dismissal compensation should be paid for an unjustified reorganization dismissal, and the employer (happy to keep the cost of the reorganization down to statutory redundancy payments) arguing that it was a redundancy and that the economic case for it cannot be reviewed by the tribunal.

8.1.1.3 'In the place where the employee was so employed'

Both of the above heads of redundancy envisage the relevant economic factors producing effects either generally or only in the place where the employee worked. It may therefore be vital to know what that 'place' is. It could cover the whole of the UK or be as small an area as one part of one city.[25] The problem often arises in cases where the employer orders the employee to move to a new workplace, for example if a company wishes to close down a factory in Ipswich and tells its employees there to work in its other factory in Norwich.

The (former) contractual approach

The approach generally adopted here in the past was to consider whether the employer has *contractual* authority to give the order to move, so that 'in the place where the employee was so employed' means in the place where they could be obliged to work under the terms of their contract of employment, not simply where they had in fact been working prior to the order to move.[26] If the contract envisages working in the new location (eg in the

[22] *Martland and Others v Cooperative Insurance Society Ltd* [2008] All ER (D) 166.

[23] See Freedland (1977) 6 ILJ 237.

[24] *Johnson v Nottinghamshire Combined Police Authority* [1974] 1 All ER 1082 at 1087, [1974] ICR 170 at 179, per Stephenson LJ.

[25] *Rowbotham v Arthur Lee & Sons Ltd* [1975] ICR 109, [1974] IRLR 377; *Air Canada v Lee* [1978] ICR 1202, [1978] IRLR 392, EAT.

[26] *Sutcliffe v Hawker Siddeley Aviation Ltd* [1973] ICR 560, [1973] IRLR 304, NIRC; *Rank Xerox Ltd v Churchill* [1988] IRLR 280, EAT.

example used, if the contract contained a term saying that the employee would work anywhere in East Anglia), then the employee who refuses is dismissed for failure to comply with the contract rather than for redundancy (even if they had in fact been working solely in Ipswich for years). If the contract does not envisage this (ie it refers only to working in Ipswich), then the employee has prima facie a redundancy claim based upon the closure of the Ipswich factory.

The practical approach

However, this contractual approach had long been criticized on the ground that a practical and geographical test (where was the employee *actually* working?) would fit better the purpose and intent of the legislation. The EAT in *Bass Leisure Ltd v Thomas*[27] agreed with that approach, held that the authority in favour of the contractual approach was only persuasive, and applied a geographical test. The case involved an employee whose work at a Coventry depot had ceased with its closure. The employer did have a contractual right to require her to work at another depot 20 miles away but it failed to exercise that right in the way the contract demanded, so the employee resigned, claiming that her constructive dismissal was because of redundancy. The EAT held that the reason for dismissal was redundancy because (1) her geographical place of work was the Coventry depot, (2) the requirement of the employer for employees at that depot had ceased, and (3) that was why she had been dismissed. The EAT said:

> the place where the employee was employed for the purposes of [ERA 1996 s 139(1)(*a*) and s 139(1)(*b*)] is to be established by a factual enquiry, taking account of the employee's fixed or changing place or places of work and any contractual terms which go to evidence or define the place of employment and its extent, but not those (if any) which make provision for the employee to be transferred to another.

This passage was cited with approval by the Court of Appeal in the case which confirmed that the correct approach to this question of determining the place of work is a practical one rather than a contractual one: *High Table Ltd v Horst*.[28] That case involved waitresses who were dismissed by a service company when the client no longer wanted their work. They were held to be redundant, in spite of a mobility clause in their contracts entitling the employer to move them to another location if it wished.

Usually, an employee will straightforwardly have a place where they work, but some jobs inherently involve a degree of movement, for example from site to site in the building trade, in which case the contractual definition of the place of work will be relevant to the factual enquiry as to what is that person's workplace. The contract may contain an express term,[29] which will usually dispose of the matter as the traditional view is that a clear express term should not normally be subject to extension or restriction by any claimed implied term.[30] If there is no such express term the tribunal must consider whether a term should be implied in the contract[31] by looking at all the relevant evidence. In *O'Brien*

[27] [1994] IRLR 104. [28] [1998] ICR 409, [1997] IRLR 513, CA.

[29] As eg in *Sutcliffe v Hawker Siddeley Aviation Ltd*, n 26 and *United Kingdom Atomic Energy Authority v Claydon* [1974] ICR 128, [1974] IRLR 6. If the employer wishes to rely on a mobility clause, it should do so clearly, and not as an afterthought: *Curling v Securicor Ltd* [1992] IRLR 549, EAT.

[30] *Nelson v BBC* [1977] ICR 649, [1977] IRLR 148, CA. However, modern cases have shown movement towards a concept of *overriding* implied terms (especially the term of trust and respect); it is possible that this development (if it continues) could spread into redundancy law.

[31] *GEC Telecommunications Ltd v McAllister* [1975] IRLR 346. For the implication of terms into contracts of employment see 3.2.

v Associated Fire Alarms Ltd,[32] two electricians worked for a company at its Liverpool office, working exclusively in that city (although the company operated throughout the United Kingdom and the Liverpool office controlled the whole of the north-west); when the company's business in Liverpool diminished and they were asked to work in Cumberland, they refused because it would have meant working away from home and they were dismissed. Their claims for redundancy payments were upheld by the Court of Appeal on the basis that, there being no relevant express term in their contracts, there was no implied term obliging them to work outside daily travelling distance from their homes, particularly as they had never been called upon to do so before and there was no clear evidence of any implied agreement to do so.[33] However, in *Stevenson v Teesside Bridge and Engineering Ltd*,[34] a steel erector who refused to move to another site when work on the existing site (which was close to his home) finished was not entitled to a redundancy payment since travelling from site to site was found by the Divisional Court to be an integral part of that trade (which there was evidence he had accepted when interviewed for the post) and the contract of employment, though not containing an express mobility clause, was held to envisage such mobility through terms relating to travelling and subsistence allowances and the transfer of contracts.

While it is now clear that the existence of a mobility clause entitling the employer to move the employee to a different place of work will not affect the assessment of the employee's place of work, the presence of such a clause in the contract of employment may still be very relevant to a redundancy situation. If such a clause exists but the employer, when faced with the reduced need for employees at the practical place of work, gives the employees notice of dismissal then the dismissals are for redundancy, following *Bass Leisure* and *Horst*. However if, instead, the employer requires the employees to move to another place in accordance with the mobility clause, then the employees must do that and if they fail to do so then they may be dismissed for refusal to obey the contract of employment—and that is a conduct dismissal, not a redundancy one.[35]

In both *Bass Leisure* and *Horst* the judges appeared to consider that the geographical approach is favourable to employees. However, the reality is that this is an area ripe for unanticipated boomerang effects: the overall result of the geographical approach is that it may make it easier for an employer to make an employee redundant (prima facie a fair reason for dismissal) at one location, even where there is a mobility clause in the contract. This could be significant where an employer wants to close down one whole location (where perhaps productivity and labour relations have not been good), dispense with the workforce there, and build up production elsewhere by taking on new staff.

Even where there is no mobility clause, a redundant employee may find themselves in effect compelled to move because, as will be seen in 8.1.2.4, a redundant employee will lose their entitlement to a redundancy payment if they unreasonably refuse to accept an offer of suitable alternative work. This means that although an employee may have a contractual right to refuse to transfer elsewhere, if the distance to the alternative place of work is not great then the offer of work in the new location may be an offer of suitable alternative employment—in which case, if the employee unreasonably rejects the offer, they will not be entitled to a redundancy payment.

[32] [1969] 1 All ER 93, [1968] 1 WLR 1916, CA; *Mumford v Boulton and Paul (Steel Construction) Ltd* (1970) 5 ITR 222; *Managers (Holborn) Ltd v Hohne* [1977] IRLR 230, EAT.

[33] While each case must depend on its facts, it is likely that a term that an employee may be required to work *within* reasonable daily travel will be easy to imply where the contract is silent on the matter: *Courtaulds Northern Spinning Ltd v Sibson* [1988] ICR 451, [1988] IRLR 305, CA.

[34] [1971] 1 All ER 296, 10 KIR 53.

[35] *Home Office v Evans* [2007] EWCA Civ 1089, [2008] IRLR 59, [2008] ICR, 302.

8.1.2 The redundancy payments scheme

The scheme requiring employers to make compulsory payments to redundant employees was introduced by the Redundancy Payments Act 1965 and is now contained in Part XI of the Employment Rights Act 1996. A first basic point to make about the scheme is that it is entirely separate from the dismissed employee's right to claim social security benefits; in one of the early cases on the 1965 Act, Lord Denning MR said:

> As I read the Act, a worker of long standing is now recognised as having an accrued right in his job, and his right gains in value with the years. So much so that, if the job is shut down, he is entitled to compensation for loss of the job . . . It is not unemployment pay. I repeat 'not'. Even if he gets another job straightaway, he nevertheless is entitled to full redundancy payment. It is, in a real sense, compensation for long service.[36]

There has been some controversy over the overall purpose of the legislation; ideas of increasing mobility of labour, giving greater job security, reducing the number of strikes over redundancies, and rewarding long service have been advanced, but none are complete answers and all are open to doubt.[37] What is clear that the payment is due irrespective of the 'rightness' or 'wrongness' of the dismissal: the redundancy payment is not intended to compensate the employee for unfair dismissal (they ought not to have been dismissed), nor for wrongful dismissal (dismissal without due contractual notice). A redundant employee is entitled to a redundancy payment and to notice of dismissal (or pay in lieu of notice) and may also claim that the dismissal was unfair. Fairness in redundancy is considered in 8.1.4.

Statutory redundancy payments are relatively modest. The maximum payment is for an employee with at least 20 years of continuous employment who is aged at least 62: they will receive 30 weeks' pay, although the value of a week's pay is capped and is £571 at the time of writing, making the maximum payment £17,130.[38] A worker aged 40 with ten years' service would get ten weeks' pay, with a maximum of £5,710. However, many employers now have private redundancy schemes[39] which are more generous than the legislative scheme, and it may be that it was the legislation which gave the spur to these improved schemes.

8.1.2.1 Reason for dismissal must be redundancy

In order to claim a redundancy payment, the ex-employee must have been 'dismissed', and that dismissal must have been 'by reason of redundancy'. Section 139 provides that a dismissal is to be taken to be by reason of redundancy if it is wholly or mainly attributable to a closure or diminution in requirements, as discussed in 8.1.1. The statutory definition of dismissal applies: dismissal by the employer, non-renewal of a limited-term contract, and constructive dismissal (see 7.2.1).[40] If a dispute about a former employee's entitlement

[36] *Lloyd v Brassey* [1969] 2 QB 98 at 102, [1969] 1 All ER 382 at 383, CA. Thus, receipt of a redundancy payment does not disentitle a person from Jobseeker's Allowance.

[37] See Fryer 'The Myths of the Redundancy Payments Act' (1973) 2 ILJ 1.

[38] See 8.1.2.3 for details of the calculation. The cap on a week's pay for this purpose is raised every 6 April.

[39] Also, certain specific redundancy schemes have in the past been established by statute in the public sector, eg the steelworkers' redundancy scheme, that relating to British shipbuilders, and the scheme applying to the NHS. The NHS scheme is much more generous than the statutory one: one month's pay for each year of service up to a maximum of 24 months, and with a much higher cap on weekly pay.

[40] Employment Rights Act 1996, s 136(1). Termination of contract by mutual consent will rarely be found in employment law, for it robs tribunals of jurisdiction; however, one application of it is particularly important here, namely a finding of mutual termination (not dismissal) on a voluntary early retirement/severance on satisfactory terms; in such a case, the volunteer *cannot* claim a redundancy payment as well: *Birch v University of Liverpool* [1985] ICR 470, [1985] IRLR 165, CA; *Scott v Coalite Fuels and Chemicals Ltd* [1988] ICR 355, [1988] IRLR 131, EAT.

to a redundancy payment comes before an employment tribunal, there is in s 163(2) a statutory presumption that the dismissal was for redundancy, so that the burden of proof is upon the *employer* to prove, on a balance of probabilities, that the dismissal was for some other reason.[41]

Three particular points may be noted. The first is that dismissal may not be necessary in certain cases if there has been instead a lay-off or short-time working (see 8.1.2.8). The second is that 'dismissal' cannot be stretched to include failure to employ in the first place. Thus, in *North East Coast Shiprepairers Ltd v Secretary of State for Employment*[42] it was argued that an apprentice was redundant for statutory purposes when he could not be taken on by the employer as a journeyman fitter at the end of his contract of apprenticeship, because there was no such work available. The EAT held, however, that there was no dismissal, only a refusal to employ him in a different capacity upon the proper termination of the previous contract.

The third point is that the legislation attempts to safeguard the position of an employee under notice of dismissal for redundancy who wishes to leave early (eg to take up other employment). The Employment Rights Act 1996, s 136(3) provides that they are still deemed to have been dismissed if they leave during the 'obligatory period' of the employer's notice and give written[43] notice of their intention to do so during that period. If, however, the employer has good reason to want that employee to stay for the full period and gives them a further written notice to that effect, but the employee still leaves early, they will only be eligible for a payment if the tribunal thinks it just and equitable that they should receive some or all of their entitlement, after considering the strength of the employer's reasons for wanting to prolong the employment and the employee's reasons for wanting to leave early.[44]

One major restriction on these provisions is that the employee's notice to leave early is only effective if given during the 'obligatory' period of the employer's notice. This means[45] the amount of time which, by statute[46] or under the individual contract of employment, the employer *has* to give to terminate the contract, and this is determined by working back from the expiry date of the notice. As a consequence, if the employer is generous and in fact gives longer notice than in law is required, the employee must wait until the start of the obligatory period before giving the counter-notice, otherwise that counter-notice is invalid and the employee may be deemed to have resigned, not to have been dismissed, and so will not be entitled to a redundancy payment.[47]

This is clearly a potential trap for the employee who, under longer notice than the contractual entitlement, finds a new job and needs to leave immediately to take it up, thus not being able to rely on s 136(3) if still outside the obligatory period. However, the EAT has suggested[48] a possible way round in one class of case: this is where the employee *requests*

[41] If unfair dismissal is also being claimed the employer may then have to prove that this other reason, if accepted by the tribunal, was fair. However, the presumption of redundancy will *not* apply to the latter claim: *Midland Foot Comfort Centre Ltd v Richmond* [1973] 2 All ER 294, [1973] ICR 219. For a relatively rare example of a case being decided by recourse to the statutory presumption see *Willcox v Hastings* [1987] IRLR 298, CA.

[42] [1978] ICR 755, [1978] IRLR 149.

[43] In s 95(2), the equivalent provision for unfair dismissal purposes, there is no longer the requirement of writing; before the requirement was dropped it caused problems in cases where the employee gave oral notice and the employer then contended that termination of the contract was in fact due to mutual agreement, not dismissal: *Lees v Arthur Greaves (Lees) Ltd* [1974] 2 All ER 393, [1974] ICR 501, CA; *McAlwane v Boughton Estates Ltd* [1973] 2 All ER 299, [1973] ICR 470. There appears to be no good reason why the requirement should remain in the redundancy provision.

[44] ERA 1996 s 142. [45] ERA 1996 s 136(4). [46] ERA 1996 s 86.

[47] *Armit v McLauchlin* (1965) 1 ITR 280; *Pritchard-Rhodes Ltd v Boon and Milton* [1979] IRLR 19; *Doble v Firestone Tyre and Rubber Co Ltd* [1981] IRLR 300, EAT.

[48] *CPS Recruitment Ltd v Bowen* [1982] IRLR 54, approving *Tunnel Holdings Ltd v Woolf* [1976] ICR 387.

to be allowed to leave early and the employer *agrees*. This is not a s 136(3) case (which is where the employee serves formal notice of their *intention* to leave early) and so can be construed on wider principles; in particular, it may be construed as a consensual variation of the employer's original notice of dismissal, meaning that the employee leaves at the earlier date, is still 'dismissed' by the employer, and can claim their redundancy payment. However, it must be remembered (a) that the employer must still have given *actual notice* in the first place (not just made vague statements about future job losses),[49] and (b) that this alternative approach only works if there is definite agreement between employer and employee—if the employee wants to (or has to) act unilaterally, they must still comply with s 136(3) and beware the 'obligatory period' trap.

What if there was on the facts prima facie a 'redundancy situation', but the employer claims to have acted on a genuine belief at the time that some other ground for dismissal existed (eg incompetence, suspected dishonesty): does that defeat the claim, or should the tribunal look at the facts objectively? It is now clear that to decide the reason for dismissal the employment tribunal must determine what were the facts that led to the employer's decision to dismiss. As it was put in *Abernethy v Mott Hay and Anderson*:[50] 'A reason for the dismissal of an employee is a set of facts known to the employer, or it may be beliefs held by him, which cause him to dismiss the employee.' Once that reason has been identified, the question is whether that reason amounts in law to being attributable to redundancy. The fact that the employer thinks that it is not redundancy makes no difference: the test is an objective one. This is of course consistent with *Murray v Foyle Meats Ltd*:[51] redundancy is defined, objectively, as the redundancy situation coupled with a factual finding that the dismissal was 'attributable to' that redundancy situation. On the other hand, if the tribunal finds as a matter of fact that a dismissal is mainly attributable to another genuinely believed ground, then there has not been, objectively, a redundancy. Widgery LJ said in *Hindle v Percival Boats Ltd*:[52]

> [T]he lesson of the *MacLaughlan* case in my opinion is that the tribunal must not accept the explanation put forward by the employer however honestly, without looking at the whole of the evidence to see if it positively established that the dismissal was not mainly due to a diminution in the requirement of the business for employees on work of a particular kind.[53]

8.1.2.2 **Exclusions**

The following classes of employee are excluded from the redundancy payments scheme:

1. employees with less than two years' continuous employment;[54]
2. employees who could have been dismissed for misconduct (see 8.1.2.5);
3. redundant employees refusing suitable alternative employment (see 8.1.2.4);

[49] Thus, certain previous cases such as *Pritchard-Rhodes Ltd v Boon and Milton* (n 47) remain good law and are reconcilable with *Bowen*'s case on the ground that the employer had not actually given notice, and so there was no notice there to be varied by agreement.

[50] [1974] ICR 323, CA.

[51] [1999] ICR 827, [1999] IRLR 562, HL. See 'What is 'work of a particular kind'?' above.

[52] [1969] 1 All ER 836, [1969] 1 WLR 174, CA.

[53] [1969] 1 All ER 836 at 848, [1969] 1 WLR 174 at 188, CA.

[54] ERA 1996 s 155. There used to be a further, frequently used, exclusion where, in a fixed-term contract of two years or more, the employee signed away their redundancy rights (or, in practice, were obliged to do so by the employer as a condition of getting the job) but this was abolished by the Fixed-term Employees (Prevention of Less Favourable Treatment) Regulations 2002, SI 2002/2034 because it constituted institutional discrimination against fixed-termers.

4. share fishermen,[55] employees of foreign governments,[56] civil servants, and certain public officials;[57]
5. classes of employees specifically excluded by order of the Secretary of State, where a collective agreement covers the question of redundancy.[58]

8.1.2.3 **Computation of a redundancy payment**

The method of calculating a payment is contained in s 162. It is done by reckoning back from the relevant date the number of whole years during which the employee was continuously employed.[59] The payment consists of (a) one and a half week's pay for each complete year of service in which the employee was over 41 years old; (b) one week's pay for each year not covered by (a) but in which the employee was over 22 years old; (c) half a week's pay for each other year. The maximum number of years which may be counted is 20, and a 'week's pay' is calculated in accordance with Part XIV, Chapter II of the 1996 Act, subject to a statutory maximum figure.[60]

When the laws on age discrimination were being framed, it was at first thought that the above scale would have to go, the age bands being direct age discrimination against younger employees and the years of service sliding scale being indirect discrimination against them. However, the government took the view that, although discriminatory, these provisions are still objectively justified. The Equality Act 2010 specifically licenses employers to have an age-discriminatory enhanced redundancy scheme provided it is, in summary, a multiplication of the statutory scheme.[61] If an employer operates an enhanced scheme which does not meet the terms of this provision, it may still be lawful if the employer can establish that it is objectively justified.[62]

8.1.2.4 **Offers of alternative employment**

If the employer makes an offer to an employee before the termination of their contract to renew the contract or re-engage them on suitable alternative work,[63] two consequences may flow. The first is that if the employee *accepts* that renewal or re-engagement (and there is either no gap, or a gap of less than four weeks between the contracts), there is in law (subject to the rules on trial periods, considered presently) no 'dismissal' at the end of

[55] Section 199(2). [56] Section 160. [57] Section 159. [58] Section 157.

[59] 'Relevant date' is defined in s 145 as (a) the date the employer's notice takes effect, (b) the date the dismissal takes effect, if no notice is given, (c) the date of termination of a limited-term contract, (d) the 'relevant date' (as already defined) of the last contract where there has been one or more trial periods, or (e) the date of expiry of the employee's notice where they have given valid early notice under s 136(3). Where, however, any notice given (including the case where no notice is given) is shorter than the legal minimum which is required by s 86, the relevant date may be deemed to be the later date of the notional expiry of that legal minimum period, for three purposes—the calculation of the two-year qualifying period, the computation of the length of service for calculation of the payment and the determination of the relevant statutory maximum on a 'week's pay' for calculation purposes (ie where that maximum has been raised by Regulations between the dismissal and the claim). The purpose of this complicated provision is to prevent an employer gaining an advantage in these three areas by wrongfully dismissing the employee with short or no notice.

[60] As at April 2022 the maximum for a week's pay is £571 pw, giving a maximum basic award of £17,130. For the purpose of calculation, actual pay as at the 'relevant date' is used, even if there is a later pay rise backdated to before that date: *Leyland Vehicles Ltd v Reston* [1981] ICR 403, [1981] IRLR 19.

[61] See generally 4.8.5. [62] See 4.8.3 at footnote 544.

[63] In *SI (Systems and Instrumentation) Ltd v Grist* [1983] ICR 788, [1983] IRLR 391 the EAT stated obiter that on the strict wording of the subsection, there is a distinction between 'renewal' (which automatically operates to deem there to have been no dismissal) and 're-engagement' (which only so operates if in pursuance of a formal offer, whether in writing or not, made before the end of the first contract).

the first contract and thus no entitlement to a redundancy payment.[64] The second is that if the employee *unreasonably refuses to accept* the offer and so still leaves employment when the notice of dismissal they have been given expires, they are disqualified from claiming a redundancy payment.[65]

Renewal and re-engagement

Cases of 'renewal' are not likely to cause many problems, for the word means renewal on the *same* terms (including possibly cases where any differences are negligible).[66] 'Re-engagement' may prove more difficult, for this envisages the new terms differing from the old ones, and raises two questions: first, was the alternative employment on offer suitable; second, was the employee's refusal of it reasonable? If the alternative employment is not 'suitable' then the employee is not disentitled from a redundancy payment if they turn it down. On the other hand, if the job is 'suitable' then the employee will lose the entitlement unless the refusal of the offer is reasonable.

In theory, the tribunal should start with the question of suitability, which entails consideration of the nature of the new employment in relation to the employee's skills and abilities. In many cases the offer will be of a similar type of employment, and it has been said that the mere offer of the same salary may not be enough if the job is totally different.[67] However, this is not an invariable rule, and an offer of a completely different job may on the facts be suitable, even for a skilled employee, particularly if it is part of a larger, generally beneficial scheme to protect jobs when the new role is temporary and the employee should be able to revert soon to their old job.[68] Naturally questions of pay may loom large, and difficulties may arise. Opportunities to earn overtime make a comparison of basic rates unreal, but on the other hand overtime may not be certain; the same problem applies to future prospects, which might soon recoup and perhaps surpass an initial drop in earnings. Thus, the tribunal must take a realistic view of the question of pay,[69] while at the same time accepting that the matter may be complicated by relevant changes in status and promotion prospects consequent upon acceptance of the new employment.[70]

Two further matters which might be material to suitability are the expected duration of the new employment and its location. If the new employment is likely to last only for a short time, it has nevertheless been held that it may be suitable provided that it is full-time and regular during that time.[71] Once again, however, this is not a definite rule as potential duration could be material in some cases, for example where the redundant employee, fearing a general recession in that particular industry, has found another job in another industry, particularly near retirement age, when employment for their last few working years is not easy to find anywhere.[72] The fact that the employment on offer is in a different location, necessitating a move of home or increased travelling, does not necessarily render it unsuitable; obviously this is very much a question of fact, but it is an important

[64] ERA 1996 s 138(1). [65] ERA 1996 s 141.

[66] *Devonald v J D Insulating Co Ltd* [1972] ICR 209, NIRC.

[67] The judgment of Lord Parker CJ in *Taylor v Kent County Council* [1969] 2 QB 560, [1969] 2 All ER 1080 is often cited on this point, as to whether the offer is of 'employment which is substantially equivalent to the employment which has ceased'. However, this is not part of the statutory wording, and ultimately the question is one of fact for the tribunal: *Standard Telephones and Cables Ltd v Yates* [1981] IRLR 21, EAT.

[68] *Dutton v Hawker Siddeley Aviation Ltd* [1978] ICR 1057, [1978] IRLR 390, EAT.

[69] *Kennedy v Werneth Ring Mills Ltd* [1977] ICR 206, EAT.

[70] *Harris v E Turner & Sons (Joinery) Ltd* [1973] ICR 31, NIRC; *Kane v Raine & Co Ltd* [1974] ICR 300, NIRC.

[71] *Morganite Crucible Ltd v Street* [1972] 2 All ER 411, [1972] ICR 110, NIRC.

[72] *Thomas Wragg & Sons v Wood* [1976] ICR 313, [1976] IRLR 145; *Paton Calvert & Co Ltd v Westerside* [1979] IRLR 108; cf *James and Jones v NCB* (1969) 4 ITR 70.

qualification on the employee's right, discussed earlier, not to be required to move to a new locality not covered by their contract of employment—they can insist upon that right and refuse an *order* to move, but if in fact the *offer* of work elsewhere is considered 'suitable' by a tribunal, they may still lose their redundancy payment.

Reasonableness of refusal

The second question, the reasonableness of a refusal, requires consideration of a wider range of different factors, looking at the matter more subjectively *from the point of view of the particular employee*. Even though the job offered is 'suitable', the employee may have reasons of a personal nature which make it reasonable to refuse it, such as health problems, family commitments, or a much longer journey to work. In addition, the employee may have personal objections to the job offered (eg perceived lack of status), even though under the first test the job is objectively 'suitable'.[73]

The two conditions in combination

This combination produces a test that is a mixture of subjective and objective factors. This is what is required by the legislation itself and it has been held that it is *not* necessary to go further and import an equivalent of the 'range of reasonable responses test', on analogy with unfair dismissal law.[74]

One effect of the test being partly subjective is that even where several employees of the same type are made redundant and are offered alternative work, a tribunal must look into the particular circumstances of each individual employee before disqualifying anyone for refusal.[75] To take an example, jobs in a different location may be suitable but it may be reasonable for one employee to turn the job down on the basis that their personal circumstances make the journey to work impracticable: perhaps because they have school transport obligations for children or because they live much further away from the new place of work than do the other employees.

Since the factors which may arise under the reasonableness of refusal question may be even more various than those under the suitability question, the one overall point about the law relating to suitable alternative employment is that each case is heavily dependent upon its own facts, with the results that the tribunal has a wide discretion to use its common sense, precedents from decided cases are of little use,[76] and the EAT will only reverse a decision if it is clear that the tribunal completely misdirected itself.[77]

In reality, although the questions of suitability and reasonableness of refusal are in theory separate, they may often be run together in practice in the process of reaching a fair and common-sense decision, particularly as it is well established that the employer bears the burden of proof on *both* questions.[78] Separate or not, the extent to which the alternative employment is suitable has bearing on the question of whether the employee acts reasonably in refusing it.[79] Another thing to keep clear is that if the tribunal finds that

[73] *Cambridge and District Co-operative Society Ltd v Ruse* [1993] IRLR 156, EAT.

[74] *Hudson v George Harrison Ltd* (2003) The Times, 15 January. For the range test in unfair dismissal law see 7.4.4.

[75] *John Fowler (Don Foundry) Ltd v Parkin* [1975] IRLR 89.

[76] In *Spencer and Griffin v Gloucestershire County Council* [1985] IRLR 393, CA, the EAT had stated as a principle that an employee could not reasonably object on the grounds that the quality of the work was not up to their standards, the setting of standards being a matter for the employer (the case concerned the dismissal of school cleaners and the offer to re-engage them on new, inferior contracts which would diminish the standard of cleaning). The Court of Appeal reversed this decision, holding that there is no room for any such principle and that reasonableness remains a question of fact for the tribunal.

[77] *Collier v Smith's Dock Co Ltd* (1969) 4 ITR 338.

[78] *Jones v Aston Cabinet Co Ltd* [1973] ICR 292.

[79] *Commission for Healthcare Audit and Inspection v Ward* [2008] All ER (D) 107 (Jun).

the refusal of alternative employment was 'unreasonable', this merely prevents a redundancy payment: it does not lead to a conclusion that the dismissal was fair—this can still be litigated.[80]

Trial periods

It may be the case that the employee is unsure about the new employment because it differs from the old employment in material ways, but wishes to give it a try. To improve the position of such a person, there is a statutory 'trial period' of four weeks from the end of the old employment.[81] If during that period the employee terminates the contract for any reason or the employer terminates it for a reason connected with the change of employment, the employee is treated as having been dismissed at the date of termination of the old contract, and for the reason or reasons prevalent at that date, and so has redundancy rights on that basis. Of course the tribunal *might* then decide that a redundancy payment was not due because the alternative employment was suitable and it was unreasonable for the employee to reject it.

In the ordinary case where the employee had been given notice of dismissal on the ground of redundancy, but an offer of other employment has been made, these provisions mean that the employee can try the new job and has the next four weeks in which to make up their mind, without prejudice to their rights.[82] However, one problem has arisen in the case of 'constructive dismissal' within s 136(1)(c): where a redundancy situation exists, but instead of giving the employee notice of dismissal combined with the offer of alternative employment, the employer simply states that it requires the employee to change to a different job. In this case, the employee could leave and claim to have been constructively dismissed on the basis that the employer committed a repudiatory breach of contract by requiring them to do a different job.[83] What happens, however, if the employee is unsure whether to resign and carries on with the employer, performing the new work on a trial basis, and only resigns at a later date, having decided that they do not like it?

In such circumstances it was held (in cases decided before the Employment Protection Act 1975 introduced the statutory trial period) that mere continuance at work did not show acceptance of the new terms and that the ordinary law about an innocent party having a reasonable period of time to decide whether to accept the other party's repudiatory breach meant that the employee had, in effect, a 'common law trial period' of an agreed or reasonable length during which the employee could still decide that they did not like the new work, leave, and still claim to have been constructively dismissed.[84] With the

[80] *Dunne v Colin & Avril Ltd* UKEAT/0293/16 (8 March 2017, unreported).

[81] ERA 1996 s 138(2): the trial period may be longer than four weeks if there is a written agreement to that effect so long as the purpose of the longer period is retraining. There may be more than one trial period, in which case the same rules apply with necessary modifications. The four weeks of the trial period are to be applied on a simple calendar basis; the period cannot be extended merely because there was no work available for part of the time (eg because of a Christmas closure): *Benton v Sanderson Kayser Ltd* [1989] ICR 136, [1989] IRLR 19, CA.

[82] If all that has happened is that the employee (already under notice) has agreed to work on temporarily, eg to finish a job, and is then dismissed, that remains an ordinary dismissal for redundancy, without the need to invoke those specialized provisions: *Mowlem Northern Ltd v Watson* [1990] ICR 751, [1990] IRLR 500, EAT.

[83] See eg *Lees v Imperial College of Science, Technology and Medicine* UKEAT/0288/15 (14 January 2016, unreported) (in this case the employee refused to do the new work and the employer responded by refusing to supply the old work—eventually the employee left and the non-provision of contracted-for work constituted a repudiatory breach and a constructive dismissal).

[84] *Marriott v Oxford and District Co-operative Society Ltd (No 2)* [1970] 1 QB 186, [1969] 3 All ER 1126, CA; *Shields Furniture Ltd v Goff* [1973] 2 All ER 653, [1973] ICR 187; *Sheet Metal Components Ltd v Plumridge* [1974] ICR 373, [1974] IRLR 86, NIRC.

introduction of the statutory trial period, the question arose whether it replaced the common law period or supplemented it (the practical point being that this period could be *longer* than the statutory four weeks—if a constructively dismissed employee left the new job more than four weeks after the change, could this still be within the common law's 'reasonable period' instead?). The EAT has clearly held that the common law period is *not* abrogated and that the statutory period is in addition.[85] In *Turvey v C W Cheyney & Son Ltd* the EAT said:

> This is an improvement in the position of the employee who is dismissed in [ordinary dismissal] circumstances. It is also an improvement in the protection of the employee in [constructive dismissal] circumstances. He has a period X in which to make up his mind. If his decision is not to take the new job, he is treated as dismissed at the moment he brings period X to an end by leaving the new job. If his decision is to take the new job and he brings period X to an end by making a new contract or renewing the old one with variations he then has the further trial period created by [s 138] in which to make up his mind, before losing his right to say, 'You dismissed me by repudiating the old contract' . . . So he has his common law period X protection plus his statutory trial period protection.[86]

There is a further possible special case, which is where there is a redundancy situation but, at the point when the employee agrees to a trial of alternative employment, notice of dismissal for redundancy has not been given. In such a case s 138 does not apply and if the trial is unsuccessful there is no redundancy dismissal to revive and it will be up to the employer to give notice of dismissal.[87]

8.1.2.5 **The effects of misconduct and industrial action**

Although an employee may be prima facie redundant, the employee may still commit misconduct (whether by going on strike or otherwise) so that the employer would in fact be justified in dismissing summarily because of that misconduct. In such a case, s 140 provides that the employee shall lose entitlement to a redundancy payment *provided* that the employer dismisses either (a) without notice, (b) with shorter notice than the employee is entitled to, or (c) with full notice, which must include a statement in writing that the employer would have been entitled to dismiss without notice (this last possibility being referred to in the cases as 'special notice').

This subsection has caused problems in its interpretation, particularly as it is clear that, if the employer dismisses for cause, that is *not* a dismissal for redundancy anyway, so in theory there is no need in such a case for s 140 in order to disentitle the employee. Two principal interpretations have been put forward:

- The first, following on from this basic point, is that s 140 is meant to apply where the employee is dismissed for redundancy, but in circumstances where the employer could have dismissed for cause (and makes this known to the employee, either impliedly by giving no or short notice, or expressly by giving special notice). This might happen where although the employer was *entitled* to dismiss because of gross misconduct, it would not actually have done so and instead decides that the employee must go as a response to the redundancy situation. The effect of this interpretation is that the employer might well give the employee more notice than a summary dismissal but does not have to pay the employee, who is guilty of gross misconduct, a redundancy payment.

85 *Air Canada v Lee* [1978] ICR 1202, [1978] IRLR 392; *Turvey v C W Cheyney & Son Ltd* [1979] ICR 341, [1979] IRLR 105.

86 *Turvey v C W Cheyney & Son Ltd* [1979] ICR 341 at 346, [1979] IRLR 105 at 108.

87 *East London NHS Foundation Trust v O'Connor* [2020] IRLR 16, EAT.

- The alternative interpretation is that the subsection applies to dismissals for cause (ie a dismissal *not* for redundancy) when there is a redundancy situation, in order to add the procedural rider that in order to prove this and so to rebut the presumption of redundancy, the employer must have given no, short, or special notice.

There is still no clear decision as to which view is right. The most important case so far, *Sanders v Ernest A Neale Ltd*,[88] clearly leans towards the first view, though at the same time stressing the importance of the procedural requirement of special notice:

> We agree . . . that neither section [now s 140(1) and (3), discussed below] has any application if the dismissal is neither wholly nor mainly attributable to redundancy . . . It seems therefore that, subject to [s 140(3)], a man who is dismissed solely on account of redundancy may lose his right to a redundancy payment if, by reason of the employee's conduct, his employer was actually entitled to dismiss him without notice.

> . . . We suggest that . . . Parliament thought that an employer should not be allowed to resist a claim for a redundancy payment upon the ground that the employee could have been dismissed without notice, unless the employee was warned of the facts upon which this defence is based at the time of the dismissal.

This approach can also be seen in the judgment of the EAT in *Simmons v Hoover Ltd*:[89]

> Certain matters can be stated with a fair amount of confidence:

(1) [s 140] operates only by way of exclusion and, accordingly, has no effect in the case of an applicant who is not prima facie entitled to a redundancy payment, eg where, although there is a redundancy situation, his dismissal is not attributable wholly or mainly to redundancy but to some other cause such as misconduct;

(2) the requirements of [s 140(1)(a), (b), or (c)] are presumably designed to ensure that the employee is put on notice that he is being dismissed otherwise than in the ordinary course of the contract; (3) a failure to serve such a notice under (a), (b) or (c) prevents the employer from relying on [s 140].

Whichever is the preferable interpretation in theory, the practical point is that an employer is advised to take the safe position by giving no, short, or special notice when dismissing an unsatisfactory employee for redundancy or, to be super-cautious, even when dismissing for misconduct in circumstances where the employee may claim to have been redundant.

The exclusory effect of s 140, however it is construed, is subject to two main qualifications, found in that section. The first is that under subsection (2), where an employee under notice of dismissal for redundancy is in fact dismissed during the obligatory period[90] of that notice because of misconduct, the complete exclusion does not apply and a tribunal has discretion to award all or only part of the payment to which they would otherwise have been entitled. This is a wide discretion, not likely to be altered on appeal unless the tribunal has clearly made an error in principle in exercising it.[91]

The second qualification applies where the misconduct in question is participation in a strike. This is classed as misconduct, entitling the employer to dismiss without notice, and

[88] [1974] 3 All ER 327 at 336, [1974] ICR 565 at 574.

[89] [1977] ICR 61 at 79, [1977] 1 All ER 775 at 787.

[90] Defined in s 136(4): see 8.1.2.1.

[91] *Lignacite Products Ltd v Krollman* [1979] IRLR 22.

so the exclusion in s 140(1) is applicable.[92] However, subsection (2) provides that where the strike and dismissal take place during the obligatory period of an existing notice of dismissal for redundancy the exclusion does not apply, and so the employee may still seek a redundancy payment, subject to the employer's statutory right to serve a written notice of extension on the employee requiring them to work extra days after the expiry of the notice, equivalent to the number of days lost due to the strike.[93] If the employee fails to comply with such a notice, they lose their right to claim.

So, the position of the redundant employee on strike during their notice period is safeguarded, but only if they are within the scheme of s 140(2). In *Simmons v Hoover Ltd*,[94] the unusual situation arose where the employee was already on strike when he was dismissed for redundancy (ie the opposite of the facts envisaged by s 140(2)). The EAT held that this fell outside the wording of the section, so that the employee remained disqualified under subsection (1) and could not claim a redundancy payment.

Finally on industrial action, it should be noted that there is no concept of 'self-induced redundancy' (operating to disqualify an employee); thus, even if the employee is a member of a group which has precipitated redundancies by continued industrial action, the employee will remain entitled to payment unless and until clearly disqualified in some way under the legislation:

> The court would like to take this opportunity of exorcising the ghost of self-induced redundancy. It can certainly occur, but as such it has no legal significance . . . the mere fact that the employee's action created the redundancy situation does not disentitle them to a redundancy payment. The entitlement depends upon the words of the statute and there is no room for any general consideration of whether it is equitable that the employee should receive a payment.[95]

8.1.2.6 Two years' continuous employment

In order to qualify for a redundancy payment, the dismissed employee must have been continuously employed for at least two years on the 'relevant date'.[96] Continuity of employment is considered in detail in 2.5.

8.1.2.7 Procedure for claiming a redundancy payment

A claim for a payment is subject to a prima facie time limitation of six months from the relevant date,[97] in that the employee will lose their entitlement unless during that period the payment has been agreed and paid or the employee has made a claim in writing to the employer, or has referred the question to an employment tribunal (either directly, or indirectly through making a complaint of unfair dismissal).[98] However, the employee is given a further six-month period in which to submit a claim, but in such a case the awarding of a payment is put into the discretion of the tribunal, which must have regard to whether an award would be 'just and equitable' in the light of the employee's reason for failure to claim during the first six months.[99]

[92] *Simmons v Hoover Ltd* [1977] 1 All ER 775, [1977] ICR 61. Notice that the exclusion also applies, indirectly, to the case where an employee walks out because of a lockout: s 143.

[93] Employment Rights Act 1996, s 143.

[94] See n 92.

[95] *Sanders v Ernest A Neale Ltd* [1974] 3 All ER 327 at 335, [1974] ICR 565 at 573.

[96] Section 155; for the 'relevant date' see n 59.

[97] Section 164. For the 'relevant date' see n 59.

[98] ERA 1996 s 164(1). Provided the employee has taken one of these steps (and so safeguarded their entitlement) they may still dispute the amount of the payment even after the expiry of the six months: *Bentley Engineering Co Ltd v Miller* [1976] ICR 225, [1976] IRLR 146.

[99] ERA 1996 s 164(2).

The claim in writing to the employer does not have to be in any particular form, the test being that it must be such that the employer could reasonably appreciate the employee's intention to claim;[100] however, it has been held that it must be submitted during the six-month period *beginning with* the relevant date, so that a claim submitted earlier than the date of termination of employment is invalid,[101] which seems to be an unnecessary complication capable of amounting to a trap for an unwary employee.

When an employer makes the redundancy payment it must give a written statement to the employee showing how the amount has been calculated.[102] The consequences of failure are, first, that the employer may be fined and, second, that they may in fact have to pay the sum again in a proper manner, particularly if, for example, the employer just gives the employee one unspecified lump sum upon termination with a vague indication that it is meant to include something for redundancy.[103]

There is a degree of state guarantee for redundancy payments. If the employer either refuses to pay after the employee has taken all reasonable steps (short of legal proceedings) to recover payment, or is insolvent, the employee may apply to the Secretary of State for payment of the amount directly out of the National Insurance Fund. For that reason the Secretary of State has a right to appear in any redundancy proceedings before a tribunal, for example to challenge the employee's assertion that they were dismissed by reason of redundancy.[104] When a payment is made from state funds the Secretary of State may exercise the employee's rights against the employer to attempt to recover the amount for the fund.[105]

8.1.2.8 **Lay-off and short time**

An ordinary claim for redundancy depends upon the existence of a 'dismissal'. In some cases of shortage of work, however, the employer may not dismiss, but instead may lay off the employee who has no work to do, or put the employee onto short time. If there is no contractual right to do so, this may constitute constructive dismissal so that the employee may walk out and still claim dismissal rights.[106] However, where the employer *has* such a contractual right this will not apply[107] and if the employee, short of money, walks out that will prima facie be a resignation, not a dismissal, to the prejudice of dismissal rights. To protect such a person, the legislation contains complicated provisions allowing the employee to claim a redundancy payment.

[100] *Price v Smithfield and Zwanenberg Group Ltd* [1978] ICR 93, [1978] IRLR 80, EAT.

[101] *Watts v Rubery Owen Conveyancer Ltd* [1977] ICR 429, [1977] IRLR 112; *Pritchard-Rhodes Ltd v Boon and Milton* [1979] IRLR 19, EAT.

[102] ERA 1996 s 165.

[103] It depends on the facts: *Barnsley Metropolitan Borough Council v Prest* [1996] ICR 85.

[104] Employment Tribunals (Constitution and Rules of Procedure) Regulations 2004, SI 2004/1861, reg 51.

[105] ERA 1996 s 166.

[106] *Powell Duffryn Wagon Co Ltd v House* [1974] ICR 123; *Jewell v Neptune Concrete Ltd* [1975] IRLR 147, IT; *Kenneth MacRae & Co Ltd v Dawson* [1984] IRLR 5. This may be an important argument if for some reason the employee cannot rely on the statutory procedure about to be described (eg owing to failure to comply with the detailed requirements); the employee can try to prove that there was *no* contractual right to lay off, resulting in a constructive dismissal on ordinary principles.

[107] This conclusion was avoided in *A Dakri & Co Ltd v Tiffen* [1981] ICR 256, [1981] IRLR 57 by arguing that even an express lay-off term is subject to an implied term that any lay-off would only last for a reasonable period (so that if it lasted longer an employee could still leave and claim constructive dismissal). This reasoning was disapproved in *Kenneth MacRae & Co Ltd v Dawson* (n 106) but surfaced again in *McClory v Post Office* [1992] ICR 758, [1993] IRLR 159 (in the context of a disciplinary suspension) and it can be seen to be consistent with other modern moves towards giving the implied term of trust and confidence overriding effect: see 3.2.1.3.

To take advantage of these provisions the employee must qualify strictly under their wording—it is not necessarily enough to say there was a 'lay-off', in common parlance. For statutory purposes, an employee is 'laid off' during any week when they receive no remuneration under this contract, and is on 'short time' if they receive during the week in question less than half their normal week's pay;[108] thus, if they receive more than half (eg under a guaranteed minimum pay clause in their contract), they are not within the statutory scheme.[109]

The employee may claim a redundancy payment where they have been laid off or on short time (as defined) for a period of four consecutive weeks, or for a total of six weeks in a 13-week period. The procedure is that they must give written notice to the employer of their intention to claim a redundancy payment by virtue of the lay-off or short time (within four weeks of the end of either of the specified periods) and must terminate their employment by giving the amount of notice required under the contract.[110] The employer may contest the claim by giving the employee a written counter-notice within seven days of receiving the employee's notice and by seeking to show that it could reasonably be expected (as the date of the employee's notice) that within four weeks the employee would enter a period of at least 13 weeks without any lay-offs or short time.[111] This question is then decided by the employment tribunal. Finally, the legislation provides that if the lay-off or short time in question is caused by a strike or lockout in *any* industry *anywhere*, these special provisions do not apply.[112]

8.1.3 **Collective consultation for collective dismissals**

The redundancy payments legislation creates individual rights to payments upon redundancy, but does not itself lay down any particular procedures for handling redundancies. However, pursuant to a European Directive on collective dismissals,[113] procedural requirements were established which are to be found in the Trade Union and Labour Relations (Consolidation) Act 1992, ss 188–198. There are two obligations laid upon the employer who is about to make 20 or more employees redundant: first, to consult employee or trade union representatives; second, to notify the Secretary of State.

8.1.3.1 **Both redundancy and reorganization dismissals**

It is crucial to note that these obligations arise in relation to a much wider range of proposed dismissals than just dismissals by reason of redundancy. This is because the definition of 'redundant' in TULR(C)A 1992, s 195 is derived from the EU Directive and is much wider, namely any dismissal 'for a reason not related to the individual concerned'.[114] For this reason, it is perhaps better to refer to this category of dismissal as 'collective dismissals' rather than to have to remind oneself that one is using the term 'redundant' in a special wider-than-usual sense.

[108] ERA 1996 s 147. An employee is not on short time if they refuse work that is offered (eg because they think it too poorly paid): *Spinpress Ltd v Turner* [1986] ICR 433.

[109] *Powell Duffryn Wagon Co Ltd v House*, n 106, at 126.

[110] ERA 1996 s 148. Note the time limit on giving notice: s 150.

[111] ERA 1996 s 152; if the tribunal finds with hindsight that the employee was in fact laid off or on short time during the whole four weeks following the date of the notice, that is conclusively deemed to decide the case against the employer on this point: s 152(2).

[112] ERA 1996 s 154.

[113] Earlier Directives are now consolidated in Directive 98/59/EC.

[114] The full definition in s 195(1) is 'dismissal for a reason not related to the individual concerned or for a number of reasons all of which are not so related'; under s 195(2) there is a rebuttable presumption that a dismissal or proposed dismissal is for redundancy.

It will be recalled that in the introduction to 8.1 and in the section 'When does change go so far that there is a diminution in work of a particular kind?' within 8.1.1.2 we noted that the redundancy payments scheme only extends to redundancy in the narrow sense used in the Employment Rights Act, and not to dismissals where there was a reorganization or change (such as to hours of work or place of work) but no reduction in the requirement of the employer for employees to do work of a particular kind. If an employer seeks to change employees' contracts to effect a change of this kind and the employees refuse to agree, the employer may give notice to end the employees' employment. Usually this is coupled with an offer of re-employment on the new contractual terms—a process which is often called 'fire and rehire'. While such employees will not be entitled to redundancy payments, such dismissals *will* fall within the definition of redundancy for collective consultation purposes, so that if at least 20 are proposed the consultation obligations will be triggered. Indeed, in such a case it is likely that the employer proposes this kind of wider 'redundancy' at the point in time when it decides to ask employees to agree to change their contractual terms, even though the employer hopes that all employees will agree so that no dismissals are necessary. This is discussed further at 8.1.3.3.

8.1.3.2 **Consultation with trade union representatives or other employee representatives**

Where an employer is proposing to dismiss as redundant (in the wider sense) within a period of 90 days or less more employees than the number specified by law as the threshold, it must consult about the dismissals all the persons who are appropriate representatives of any of the employees who may be affected by the dismissals or measures taken in relation to them. Appropriate representatives are defined as:

(a) if the employees are of a description in respect of which an independent trade union is recognized by their employer, representatives of that union; or

(b) in any other case, employee representatives already appointed or elected who have authority from the affected employees in relation to the proposed dismissals, or such representatives elected specifically for these purposes.[115] It is specifically provided that existing elected representatives can be used if 'it is appropriate (having regard to the purposes for which they were elected) for the employer to consult them about dismissals proposed'.[116]

Taken together with other consultation requirements (especially on TUPE) and the advantages to be gained from workforce agreements (eg in relation to the Working Time Regulations and the law on parental leave), this may argue strongly in favour of the employer having *standing* elected machinery for all of these purposes in employments where no union is recognized. If some of the employees proposed for dismissal are in a group for which a union is recognized and some are not in that group, the employer will have to consult with the union for one group and with elected or appointed employee representatives for the other group.

The consultation must begin in good time,[117] and in any event 45 days before the first dismissal takes effect (if the employer is proposing to dismiss 100 or more within the

[115] Trade Union and Labour Relations (Consolidation) Act 1992, s 188(1B). Where elections are held specifically for this purpose, they must comply with rules ensuring fair elections, laid down in s 188A.

[116] Section 196(1). They must be employed by the employer at the time when they are elected or appointed: s 196(2).

[117] Where an ad hoc election of employee representatives is being carried out, 'in good time' means as soon as reasonably practicable after the representatives are elected: s 188(7A). If the employees fail to elect representatives within a reasonable time, the employer can give each affected employee the information required by law, but is absolved from the requirement to consult collectively: s 188(7B).

90 days), or at least 30 days beforehand otherwise.[118] In reality, provided that the 30- and 45-day minima are observed, employee representatives, even trade unions, do not object that the consultation could have begun even earlier.

The 30- and 45-day periods are a matter of UK implementation (not the Directive itself) and the wording of s 188(1A) is that the consultation must begin 30/45 days 'before the first of the dismissals *takes effect*'. However, s 188 must be read in the light of the decision of the ECJ in *Junk v Kuhnel*,[119] where it was held that the (differently worded) Directive requires that notice should not be *given* until the necessary consultation is *completed.*

The interaction of this decision with the UK provision for the 30/45-day period remains uncertain. One school of thought is that it does *not* mean that the whole 30/45-day period must elapse before notice can be given, provided that consultation has been completed before notice is given. Thus, if consultation actually finishes early (or, indeed, if the parties have agreed that it shall last for a period less than the 30/45 days), the employer can proceed to give any necessary notice of dismissal. However, another school of thought is that the only safe way to comply with *Junk* is indeed to let the 30/45-day period elapse before giving any necessary notice.

According to s 188(2), the consultation must cover ways of avoiding the dismissals, reducing the numbers, and mitigating the consequences, and this must be undertaken by the employer with a view to reaching agreement with the appropriate representatives.[120] The case law also establishes that as a matter of general principle, 'consultation' requires (a) consultation while the proposals are still at a formative stage, (b) adequate information, (c) adequate time in which to respond, and (d) conscientious consideration of the responses to the consultation.[121]

With regard to information, s 188(4) specifies that an employer must disclose in writing to the appropriate representatives (a) the reason for the proposals, (b) the numbers and descriptions of employees proposed to be dismissed, (c) the total number of such employees at the establishment, (d) the proposed method of selection, (e) the proposed method of carrying out the dismissals, and (f) the proposed method of calculating any non-statutory redundancy payments to be made to those selected.

In a case where the proposed dismissals are to achieve changes to terms of employment (rather than because of redundancy in the narrow sense defined in s 139 ERA)—often referred to as 'fire and rehire'—there is a code of practice which was introduced in 2024: the Code of Practice on Dismissal and Re-engagement.[122] This Code contains guidance not only on individual consultation with employees but also on the collective information and consultation process under s 188.

Once the TUPE legislation came into force (see 8.2) a problem emerged when the intended transferee employer was proposing to make some of the transferring employees redundant. This fact would normally become apparent to the affected employees

[118] Until 6 April 2013 the period between the start of consultation and first dismissals was 90 days, but the Coalition government reduced the period in the interests of efficiency and generally making things easier for business.

[119] C-188/03 [2005] IRLR 310 ECJ; the Court also stressed the requirement in the Directive that the consultation should be undertaken 'with a view to reaching agreement'. On the question of timing, *Junk* means that *Middlesbrough BC v TGWU* [2002] IRLR 332 must now be considered wrong on this point.

[120] The consultation must be about all three topics: *Middlesbrough Borough Council v TGWU* [2002] IRLR 332.

[121] *R v British Coal Corpn and Secretary of State for Trade and Industry, ex p Price* [1994] IRLR 72, Div Ct (one of the 'pit closure' cases). Even if time limits are technically met, it may still be argued that in substance the whole exercise was a sham: *Transport and General Workers' Union v Ledbury Preserves (1928) Ltd* [1985] IRLR 412.

[122] Code of Practice on Dismissal and Re-engagement issued by the Secretary of State on 18 July 2024.

because the transferor employer is obliged under TUPE to give information to appropriate representatives of the workforce about any measures which the transferee employer envisages taking in relation to the employees (see 8.2.5). Once the worrying possibility of redundancy had been raised, the representatives would want to discuss it, probably with both the transferor employer and the transferee employer, and in practice this frequently happened. However, from the point of view of the transferee employer, any such consultations, during which issues such as selection methods and enhanced redundancy payments might well have been settled, could not count to discharge its obligation to consult collectively on the redundancies, because at the time when they were carried out the transferee was not 'the employer' within s 188. The transferee employer would have to engage in a further period of 30 or 45 days of consultation after the transfer had been effected, even though everything might already have been agreed.

In response to this issue, in 2014 ss 198A and 198B were inserted in the Trade Union and Labour Relations (Consolidation) Act 1992 to permit the transferee to begin consultations *before* the transfer takes place, so long as the transferor gives permission.[123]

8.1.3.3 **Meaning of 'proposing to dismiss'**

Three problems of definition have arisen under this section. The first is when it can be said that the employer is 'proposing' to make an employee redundant (as it is this that sets the wheels in motion). Under the existing law, it appears that the word 'proposing' requires a certain amount of planning and resolution on the part of the employer, not just speculation:

> [A] proposal to make redundant within the meaning of [s 188] connotes a state of mind directed to a planned or proposed course of events. The employer must have formed some view as to how many are to be dismissed, when this is to take place and how it is to be arranged. This goes beyond the mere contemplation of a possible event.[124]

However, this use of the word 'proposing' has led to the argument that the UK provisions do not properly enact the Directive. The latter states that an employer should begin consultation when 'contemplating' collective redundancies, a word which is capable of being construed as meaning *before* the employer has formed any definite views on the need for redundancies, whereas the domestic provision appears to apply only once that decision has been taken and therefore to apply principally to the question of *how* to deal with the proposed redundancies. When this was considered by the EAT in *MSF v Refuge Assurance plc*,[125] it was held that there is indeed a conflict between the Act and the Directive *but* that it was not possible to resolve it by reconstruing s 188.

However, the latest developments at the Court of Justice of the European Union suggest that in fact the difference between 'proposing' and 'contemplating' may not be as great as the UK courts had thought, because the CJEU appears to have construed the latter term in a way much closer to the meaning of 'proposing'. We say that the CJEU 'appears to

[123] Trade Union and Labour Relations (Consolidation) Act 1992, ss 198A and 198B.

[124] *Association of Pattern Makers and Allied Craftsmen v Kirvin Ltd* [1978] IRLR 318 at 320 per Lord McDonald. *Union of Shop, Distributive and Allied Workers v Leancut Bacon Ltd* [1981] IRLR 295; *Hough v Leyland-DAF Ltd* [1991] ICR 696, [1991] IRLR 194. It may be enough to trigger these provisions if the employer has decided *either* to go down the redundancy route *or* to adopt some other solution (eg sale of the business): *Scotch Premier Meat Ltd v Burns* [2000] IRLR 639.

[125] [2002] ICR 1365, [2002] IRLR 324, approving *R v British Coal Corpn and Secretary of State for Trade, ex p Vardy* [1993] IRLR 104.

have' done this because the Court's judgment in the key case, *Akavan Erityisdojen AEK v Fujitsu Siemens Computers*,[126] is somewhat contradictory. The Court in that case said:

> The consultation procedure must be started by the employer once a strategic or commercial decision compelling him to contemplate or to plan for collective redundancies has been taken.

However, the Court also said the following, which suggests a somewhat earlier start point for consultation:

> As is clear from the first subparagraph of that Article 2(2), the consultations must cover, inter alia, the possibility of avoiding or reducing the collective redundancies contemplated. A consultation which began when a decision making such collective redundancies necessary had already been taken could not usefully involve any examination of conceivable alternatives with the aim of avoiding them.

The UK Court of Appeal rightly commented on this in *United States of America v Nolan*[127] as follows:

> We have to say, again with respect, that we do not find the interpretation of the ECJ's decision on [this question] straightforward. Putting in stark form the question arising in the present case, does the ECJ explain whether the consultation obligation arises (i) when the employer is proposing, but has not yet made, a strategic business or operational decision that will foreseeably or inevitably lead to collective redundancies; or (ii) only when that decision has actually been made and he is then proposing consequential redundancies?

The Court of Appeal therefore referred the *Nolan* case to the CJEU for further guidance on this issue but unfortunately the European Court ruled that it did not have jurisdiction,[128] so the question remains unresolved. On an allied point about determining whether the number of redundancies intended triggers the consultation requirement, the ECJ held in the post -Brexit case of *JLOG v Resorts Mallorca Hotels International SL*[129] that the obligation to consult arises when the employer 'contemplates or plans' a reduction in employment positions the number of which may exceed the limit which triggers consultation. Since Brexit, the question of what amounts to a proposal is a matter for the UK courts to determine, but they may well still take account of the EU jurisprudence on the matter. However, it does seem clear that in at least one category of case early consultation may be required, and that is where a complete closure of a workplace is contemplated. In such a case the EAT said in *UK Coal Mining Limited v National Union of Mineworkers (Northumberland Area)*[130] that if it is reasonably clear that closure of an operation will 'almost inevitably' result in dismissals, the employer is deemed to have 'proposed dismissals' at the time of proposing closure and so must consult before the final closure decision is made rather than after it has been made. The Appeal Tribunal's reasoning was that since one of the consultation obligations is to consult over ways of avoiding the proposed redundancies that 'inevitably involves engaging with the reasons for the dismissals, and that in turn requires consultation over the reasons for the closure'. To give

[126] C-44/08, [2009] IRLR 944. [127] [2010] EWCA Civ 1223, [2011] IRLR 40.

[128] C-583/10, [2012] IRLR 1020, [2013] ICR 193. Although the UK legislation on collective consultation on redundancies covers all employers, the Directive does not extend to public bodies such as the US government and so the CJEU held that it had no jurisdiction.

[129] C-589/22, [2024] IRLR 524. [130] [2008] IRLR 4.

another illustration, if an employer is considering closing one of two factories, the way to avoid redundancies at factory A is to close factory B, and vice versa, so the employer needs to consult with representatives before it has decided which factory to close.

An employer may want employees to agree to a change in their contractual terms, for example to change the place of work or the timing of shifts or to reduce pay or benefits. The normal route for an employer is to seek to agree such changes with employees, but to indicate that if agreement cannot be reached it will give notice of dismissal, usually coupled with an offer of immediate re-engagement on the new terms. Such an employer will hope not to have to give anyone notice of termination, but if it does do so such dismissals will be within the wide scope of the definition of redundancy for collective consultation purposes. So the question arises: does the employer propose redundancies only when it gets to the point that some employees have refused to agree to change their contracts (in which case the employer will need to consult collectively only if there are at least 20 such refuseniks) or does the employer propose redundancy from the moment that it proposes to change contractual terms? In *Hardy v Tourism South East*,[131] the EAT held that the latter approach is correct, saying: 'If the employer only proposes to keep the employee in his employment on what is in reality a different contract of employment, he will be proposing to terminate the existing one.'

8.1.3.4 **The threshold number of proposed dismissals**

The trigger for collective consultation is a proposal by an employer to dismiss as redundant (in the wider sense) 20 or more employees at one establishment within a period of 90 days or less. This threshold presents a definitional problem about what is meant by an 'establishment', for the purpose of counting the number of employees proposed for redundancy and thus determining whether the obligation to consult is triggered and also for the purpose of determining whether the 30-day or 45-day period applies. For example, in a case where the employer operates at several locations, if each location is a separate 'establishment' and there are fewer than 20 redundancies at each, the requirements of the section will not apply, even if the overall number of redundancies is high.

The word 'establishment' appears in the Collective Redundancies Directive, but is not defined. This issue came before the ECJ in the Danish case of *Rockfon A/S v Nielsen*.[132] The vital background to this case is that the Directive gives member states two options for determining how large a redundancy programme must be to trigger the consultation obligation, and the option selected by the Danish government was the one that was based on more than 10 per cent of the workforce at an establishment being proposed for redundancy. This had the consequence that if 'establishment' was interpreted in an atomistic way, so that branches of a company were each separate establishments, then consultation would be more often triggered. For example, if a company had 300 employees spread among 10 branches with 30 employees in each, then a proposal to make four employees in each of three of the branches would trigger consultation because four is more than 10 per cent of 30 (whereas if all the branches were a single 'establishment' then the 12 proposed redundancies would be less than 10 per cent of 300). The ECJ ruled that the protective intent of the Directive must be kept in mind and not frustrated by the technicalities of corporate structure, and in consequence the court held that each branch is a separate

131 [2005] IRLR 242.

132 Case C-449/93 [1996] ICR 673, [1996] IRLR 168, ECJ. In particular, they held that a company in a group can still be an 'establishment' even if the power to make redundancies as a matter of policy lies elsewhere in the group. On the other hand (applying *Rockfon*), central management is not enough in itself to constitute one establishment where the organization emphasis remains at the branch level: *MSF Refuge Assurance plc*, [2002] ICR 1365, [2002] IRLR 324.

establishment. This same approach was taken by the ECJ in a later case to mean that three distinct production units for three kinds of paper, each with its own chief production officer, equipment, and specialized workforce, were separate establishments despite the fact that the head office made financial decisions for all three.[133]

However, the UK had taken the other option in the Directive for setting the trigger, namely that the employer was proposing at least 20 redundancies in the establishment. This means that if each separate branch is an establishment then consultation may well not be triggered when a small number of redundancies at each branch is proposed, even when more than 20 employees—hundreds even—are affected nationwide by the proposal. After a period of nervousness amongst UK lawyers, in 2015 the CJEU confirmed that this was indeed the position. The case involve the closure of dozens of Woolworths and Ethel Austin stores throughout the UK.[134] Many of those stores had fewer than 20 employees and the employers declined to consult in relation to those small stores. The CJEU decided that the employers were not required by the Directive to consult at any store where there were fewer than 20 redundancies proposed. The unfortunate result, of course, is that employees of the same chain might or might not receive consultation protection depending on the number of workers made redundant at each shop—on the other hand, it also means that workers in chain shops are in roughly the same position as those in similarly sized non-chain shops. It has since been held that a place of work can be an establishment even if the employer does not in fact control or own the location—for example where the employer has a service contract to supply workers to work at a number of locations owned and operated by the customer each of those locations may well, depending on the facts, amount to a separate establishment.[135]

The Employment Rights Act 2025 takes steps to address this position. When section 29 is in force it will make amendments to TULR(C)A 1992 to introduce powers for the Secretary of State to specify an alternative threshold which will count all employees of an employer who are proposed for dismissal whether or not they are at the same establishment. Collective consultation will be required if either the existing 20 threshold or the new one is reached. As for the minimum duration of the consultation, the longer period of 90 days will apply if, using either threshold, the number of dismals proposed is 100 or more.

8.1.3.5 Associated employers and future employers

Even where the 'establishment' has been discerned, it may still be necessary to decide who is the 'employer', and here there may be a problem because the concept of 'associated employers', so important elsewhere in employment law,[136] is surprisingly *not* adopted by s 188 and the EAT has held that it will not unilaterally lift the veil of incorporation in this context. Thus, in *E Green & Son (Castings) Ltd v Association of Scientific, Technical and Managerial Staffs*[137] three companies were making redundancies of 97, 36, and 24 employees, respectively, but the relevant consultation period was 30 days (not 90, as the period for 100 employees then was) since they were each separate employers, even though (a) they were all subsidiaries of one holding company (and so would be associated employers in other contexts) and (b) they all operated from the same physical 'establishment'.

133 *Athinaiki Chartoposia AE v Panagiotidis* (C-270/05) [2007] IRLR 284.

134 *USDAW v WW Realisation 1 Ltd* (C-80/14) [2015] IRLR 577.

135 *Seahorse Maritme Ltd v Nautilus International* [2018] EWCA Civ 2789, [2019] IRLR 286.

136 See 2.1.6. 137 [1984] ICR 352, [1984] IRLR 135.

8.1.3.6 **The remedy for non-compliance**

The sanction for failure to consult is the 'protective award'. This may be sought by employee representatives, by the trade union, or (if there are no representatives or the failure relates to the election of representatives) by any of the employees affected or dismissed.[138] Where employees are represented by a trade union or elected representatives, only those representatives can bring the claim,[139] and trade unions in multi-union workforces cannot bring a claim regarding parts of the workforce they do not represent.[140]

The matter is referred to a tribunal which, if it finds the complaint established, must make a declaration to that effect and may make a protective award, which is an order that the employer shall continue to pay wages to the employees concerned for a 'protected period'.[141] This period is within the tribunal's discretion, subject to a maximum of 90 days. When s 30 of the Employment Rights Act 2025 is in force the maximum will become 180 days. The employee is entitled to a 'week's pay'[142] for each week of the protected period; if the employer fails to make any or all of the payments due for this period, the individual employee may complain within three months to a tribunal, which may order payment. The employee may be disqualified from claiming under the protective award if they are fairly dismissed for a reason other than redundancy, unreasonably resign during the period, or unreasonably refuse suitable alternative employment.[143]

The only guidance given to the tribunals by the statute on the way to apply a protective award is that it should be 'just and equitable in all the circumstances having regard to the seriousness of the employer's default'; this, however, could mean either a compensatory approach (looking at the employee's actual loss) or a punitive one (looking at the seriousness of the employer's default and its effect on industrial relations). In *Susie Radin Ltd v GMB*,[144] the Court of Appeal held that the purpose of the award is punitive and to act as a deterrent to employers. On that basis, advice was given to tribunals to start in each case at the 90-day maximum, thus putting the burden on the employer to bid it down by proving mitigation. However, it has since been held that *Susie Radin* requires starting with the maximum only where there has been no attempt at compliance by the employer; otherwise the tribunal decides the starting point at its own discretion.[145] This means that protective awards are likely to be lower, and on occasion employers decide that the likely level of the award is such that it makes economic sense to press ahead with the redundancies with inadequate consultation or even no consultation. However, with a large redundancy programme the risk of paying up to a quarter of a year's pay to each employee is a substantial one.

In a case where the proposed dismissals were to achieve changes to terms of employment (rather than because of redundancy in the narrow sense defined in s 139 ERA) then if the tribunal determines that there has been an unreasonable failure in connection

[138] Trade Union and Labour Relations (Consolidation) Act 1992, s 189.

[139] *Northgate HR Ltd v Mercy* [2008] IRLR 222.

[140] *Transport & General Workers' Union v Brauer Coley Ltd* [2007] IRLR 207.

[141] Trade Union and Labour Relations (Consolidation) Act 1992, ss 189, 190. The period starts with the *proposed* date of the first dismissal, whether or not the *actual* date is different: *E Green & Son (Castings) Ltd v Association of Scientific, Technical and Managerial Staffs* [1984] ICR 352, [1984] IRLR 135, applied in *Transport and General Workers' Union v Ledbury Preserves (1928) Ltd* [1986] ICR 855, [1986] IRLR 492.

[142] As defined in the Employment Rights Act 1996, Pt XIV, Ch II.

[143] Trade Union and Labour Relations (Consolidation) Act 1992, s 191; where there is an offer of alternative employment, the 'trial period' provisions are specially applied.

[144] [2004] ICR 893, [2004] IRLR 400, CA.

[145] *Todd v Strain* [2011] IRLR 11, EAT affirmed the context of redundancy consultation; *London Borough of Barnet v UNISON* UKEAT/0191/13 (14 January 2014, unreported).

with collective consultation to comply with the Code of Practice on Dismissal and Re-engagement[146] then the protective award may be increased by up to 25 per cent.[147]

It can occur that an employer has been unable to consult fully because of external events which do not reach the threshold to amount to special circumstances which relieve the employer of liability for failure to consult (see 8.1.3.8). Alternatively, the external events may amount to special circumstances but the employer did not carry out as much consultation as was reasonably practicable. In such cases the tribunal must consider whether the length of the protective award should be reduced.[148]

8.1.3.7 **Notification to the Secretary of State**

Where an employer proposes to dismiss as redundant 20 or more employees at one establishment within 30 days, it must give the Secretary of State written notice of the proposal at least 30 days before the first dismissal takes effect; where it proposes to dismiss 100 or more within 90 days, it must give 45 days' notice.[149] A copy of the notice must be sent to the appropriate representatives. If the employer fails to give this notice, the Secretary of State may prosecute the employer, and any director or manager of the employer if the offence was committed with their consent or connivance of by reason of their neglect (the maximum fine being level 5 on the standard scale).[150]

8.1.3.8 **The 'special circumstances' defence**

It is expressly provided, in the case of both consultation and notification, that if there are special circumstances rendering it not reasonably practicable for an employer to comply with the statutory requirements, it need only take such steps towards compliance as are reasonably practicable.[151] The burden of proof is upon the employer to establish special circumstances, but if it can do so, and can show that it did what was reasonably practicable (which may in some cases be nothing), it has a good case that there should be *no* protective award, not just a reduction in it. The meaning of 'special circumstances' has been left to the tribunals and courts, and will be a question of fact in each case. It has been made clear that events which occur after the obligation to consult arises cannot form the basis of a special circumstances defence.[152] Additionally, the Court of Appeal in *Clarks of Hove Ltd v Bakers' Union*[153] held that the employer's insolvency and collapse were not in themselves special circumstances:

> [I]nsolvency is, on its own, neither here nor there. It may be a special circumstance, it may not be a special circumstance. It will depend entirely on the cause of the insolvency whether the circumstance can be described as special or not. If, for example, a sudden disaster strikes a company, making it necessary to close the concern, then plainly that would be a matter which was capable of being a special circumstance; and that is so whether the disaster is

[146] Code of Practice on Dismissal and Re-engagement issued by the Secretary of State on 18 July 2024.

[147] Trade Union and Labour Relations (Consolidation) Act 1992, s 2907A.

[148] *Keeping Kids Company v Smith* [2018] IRLR 484, *Shanahan Engineering Ltd v UNITE* UKEAT/411/09 (22 February 2010, unreported).

[149] Trade Union and Labour Relations (Consolidation) Act 1992, s 193; the requirement of notice does not apply where less than 20 are dismissed. The wording of s 193 was amended in 2006 to require that the notice is also given before giving any notices of dismissal; this was to bring it into line with *Junk v Kuhnel*, n 119.

[150] Section 194. The offence, in relation to the employer at least, is one of strict liability and no mens rea is required: *R (Palmer) v Northern Derbyshire Magistrates Court* [2022] ICR 531.

[151] Sections 188(7) and 193(7).

[152] *Keeping Kids Company v Smith* [2018] IRLR 484.

[153] [1978] ICR 1076, [1978] IRLR 366, CA, confirmed as still good law in *Carillion Services Ltd v Benson* [2022] IRLR 39, EAT.

> physical or financial. If the insolvency however were merely due to a gradual run-down of the company, as it was in this case, then those are facts on which the industrial tribunal can come to the conclusion that the circumstances were not special. In other words, to be special the event must be something out of the ordinary, something uncommon.[154]

Thus, although insolvency itself may not be special, the employer has been held to have a good defence where the company carried on trading in the face of insolvency in the genuine hope that it would be able to sell the company as a going concern and so prevent redundancies, but had to appoint a receiver (without any consultation) when the last prospective purchaser disappeared.[155] In such a case, extensive consultation could be fatal to delicate negotiations, but on the other hand it may still be reasonable to expect *some* consultation, and if that is the case the employer will not have shown that it did all that was reasonably practicable and so will remain liable.[156] The requirement of doing all that is reasonable puts a considerable onus on the employer to know and understand these legal requirements, so that in general a mistaken view of the law and its application will not be a 'special circumstance' unless it was a reasonable mistake,[157] even if the employer was acting upon wrong advice, though in such a case the facts may support an argument for reduction of the protective award if the 'employer's default' is considered less.[158]

To protect employees of transnational concerns who may be made redundant by decisions taken at higher levels than their immediate employer the Act provides that where the decision leading to the proposed dismissals is that of a person controlling the employer, a failure on the part of that person to provide information to the employer does *not* constitute special circumstances.[159]

8.1.3.9 **Protection of representatives**

Where the 'appropriate representatives' are officials of a recognized trade union they will have the ordinary protection for such offices when taking part in union activities, and the ordinary right to time off work for these duties.[160] However, these provisions would not apply to the category of elected employee representatives, and so the Act contains parallel provisions for them. Thus, an elected representative (or candidate for that office) has a statutory right not to be victimized (short of dismissal), dismissed, or later selected for redundancy on the grounds of having performed or proposed to perform such duties, and similar protection is extended to employees participating in the election of representatives.[161] A representative or candidate also has the right to paid time off work in order to perform such duties or to undergo training.[162]

8.1.4 **Unfair dismissal in redundancy and reorganization**

Redundancy is a potentially fair reason for dismissal. As for a dismissal resulting from an employee's refusal to acquiesce to changes made by an employer in response to economic pressures, this may be fair for 'some other substantial reason' (SOSR), although

[154] [1978] ICR 1076 at 1085, [1978] IRLR 366 at 369, per Geoffrey Lane LJ. Sudden financial deterioration following collapse of negotiations to sell the firm's shares to a third party was held to constitute a special circumstance in *USDAW v Leancut Bacon Ltd* [1981] IRLR 295; the shedding of labour normal on an insolvency was held not to in *GMB v Rankin and Harrison* [1992] IRLR 514.

[155] *APAC v Kirvin Ltd* [1978] IRLR 318.

[156] *Hamish Armour v ASTMS* [1979] IRLR 24; cf *USDAW v Leancut Bacon Ltd*, n 154.

[157] *Joshua Wilson & Bros Ltd v USDAW* [1978] ICR 614, [1978] IRLR 120.

[158] *UCATT v Rooke & Son Ltd* [1978] ICR 818, [1978] IRLR 204, applied in *Secretary of State for Employment v Helitron Ltd* [1980] ICR 523.

[159] Sections 188(7) and 193(7).

[160] See Chapter 9.

[161] Employment Rights Act 1996, ss 47, 103, 105(6).

[162] Section 61.

once amendments contained in the Employment Rights Act 2025 have been brought into force, such a change may, instead, be automatically unfair.[163]

Only redundancy is in play if the employer reacts to difficult times by going out of business or shutting down part of the operation, or reducing the number of employees. However, when the employer makes other changes to the operation and this leads to terminations then, as explained at 8.1.1.2, the dismissals might not satisfy the 'diminished need for work of a particular kind' definition, and would, at the time of writing, need to be defended on an SOSR basis. This can occur if an employee refuses to agree to changes in their contract of employment and the employer responds by terminating the contract (a dismissal) and offering re-engagement on the new contracts ('fire and rehire'). Alternatively, the employer may simply press ahead and introduce the new terms unilaterally; this is likely to be a repudiatory breach of contract and if the employee resigns in response that will be a constructive dismissal and again the potentially fair reason will be SOSR, although the dismissal is likely to be unfair because a reasonable employer would not proceed in this high-handed unilateral way.

What determines whether a dismissal is a redundancy dismissal, as opposed to an SOSR one, is not how the employer conceives of its decision, but whether the dismissals can be factually 'attributed to' a diminished need for work of a particular kind (WOPK). Thus, even if the employer thinks it is making workers redundant, and supplies all of the appropriate consultation and notice, the dismissals will need to be defended under SOSR logic if the evidence does not support a causal link with diminished WOPK. Similarly (and more likely), if the employer reorganizes, and employees are dismissed for refusing to agree to contract changes effected by the reorganization (or the employees resigned in the face of such changes being introduced unilaterally by the employer), the dismissals will be unintended redundancies if they are factually attributable to a diminished need for WOPK.

In an unfair dismissal case, as discussed in Chapter 7, the employer must establish the principal reason for dismissal. This means proving the factual reason for which the employer carried out the dismissal. It is then the role of the employment tribunal to decide if those facts satisfy the redundancy definition: if so, the dismissal is a redundancy and cannot be something else. Equally, if those facts do not show that the dismissal was attributable to redundancy as defined then the tribunal will have to assess whether they amount to some other substantial reason. The statutory presumption of redundancy that exists in the redundancy payments scheme[164] is not applicable in an unfair dismissal claim.[165]

Another implication of the redundancy definition is that once the facts are shown to satisfy the definition, a tribunal may not look behind that reason and consider whether the employer really was obliged to make employees redundant and, if so, whose fault it was—even if *another* employer might have decided to try to solve the economic problem another way, the fact that *this* employer has decided to reduce the number of employees is sufficient to make redundancy the reason for dismissal, because *this* employer's requirement for employees to carry out work of a particular kind has diminished. As we will see, that economic decision cannot even be reviewed by the tribunal when considering the next question, which is whether the decision to dismiss for redundancy was reasonable in all the circumstances.[166] The position is very different when the dismissal falls within

[163] See 8.1.4.2, 'Employment Rights Act 2025—most reorganization dismissals to become automatically unfair'.

[164] ERA 1996 s 170(2).

[165] *Midland Foot Comfort Centre Ltd v Richmond* [1973] 2 All ER 294, [1973] IRLR 141.

[166] See 'No review of economic case for redundancy' in 8.1.4.1.

the SOSR category (see 8.1.4.2). In addition, once s 28 of the Employment Rights Act 2025 is in force, the economic pressure on the employer will be very relevant to fairness if the redundancy occurs because the employer is replacing employees with workers who are not employees. This is discussed at 8.1.4.2, 'Employment Rights Act 2025—most reorganization dismissals to become automatically unfair'.

8.1.4.1 **Unfair redundancy**

Automatically unfair redundancies

A redundancy dismissal is deemed to be unfair if the person made redundant was on maternity leave, adoption leave, or shared parental leave and was not offered any alternative employment that was available. This provision, which gives such employees priority for alternative employment over other employees, is discussed under 'Return to old job' at 5.2.2.2.[167]

A redundancy dismissal is also deemed to be unfair by a combination of s 153 of the Trade Union and Labour Relations (Consolidation) Act 1992 and s 105 of the Employment Rights Act 1996 if the employee can show that the circumstances producing the redundancy applied equally to other comparable employees[168] in the same undertaking who were not dismissed, and the applicant employee was chosen for dismissal because of union membership or activities, or non-membership,[169] or for an 'inadmissible reason' (covering the categories where dismissal is made automatically unfair, for example where the reason for dismissal is contrary to the special protection afforded to pregnancy or childbirth, making health and safety complaints, asserting statutory rights, being a protected shop-worker, acting as an employee representative or pension fund trustee, or exercising rights to the national minimum wage or under the Working Time Regulations, Part-time Worker Regulations, or Fixed-term Employee Regulations or the protection given to whistleblowers). The aim of these provisions is to prevent an employer from avoiding the automatic unfairness of dismissals for this reason by using the more subtle technique of getting rid of perceived troublemakers or difficult cases by a later redundancy selection.

Finally, once s 28 of the Employment Rights Act 2025 is in force, a redundancy may be automatically unfair if the employer is replacing employees with workers who are not employees. This is discussed at 8.1.4.2, 'Employment Rights Act 2025—most reorganization dismissals to become automatically unfair'.

Unreasonable redundancy

Setting apart redundancies which are automatically unfair by reason of being for trade union membership or some other inadmissible reason, complaints by employees that their dismissals for redundancy are unfair are considered under the ordinary unfair dismissal regime. The question is whether, under the Employment Rights Act 1992, s 98(4), the employer's conduct was unreasonable having regard to equity and the substantial merits of the case.

No review of economic case for redundancy

An important first point is that in considering the reasonableness of the decision to dismiss, it has been held that the tribunal is not permitted to review the employer's decision to employ fewer workers. For example, a tribunal will not entertain an argument that a

[167] MPL etc Regulations 1999, reg 20(1)(b), PAL Regulations, regs 26 and 29(5) and SPL Regulations, regs 39, 40(2).

[168] *Powers v A Clarke & Co (Smethwick) Ltd* [1981] IRLR 483.

[169] This head of unfair dismissal generally is considered at 9.4.3.

reasonable employer would have decided to seek to restore the profitability of a business in some other way than closing a factory,[170] or an argument that the employer should have waited longer to see if business picked up.[171] This is in illogical contrast with the position when a tribunal is assessing the fairness of a dismissal in a reorganization case which does not involve redundancy, where the balance between the economic case for action against the impact on employees has always been a matter to be reviewed by the tribunal—moreover the Employment Rights Act 2025 will impose even stricter control on what an employer can do in such cases (see 'Was the reorganization necessary?' in 8.1.4.2).

Williams v Compair Maxam Ltd

The case law has developed three general requirements upon an employer who is about to make an employee redundant if the dismissals are to be fair:[172]

- The employee must not be *selected* unfairly. Blatant unfairness may be challenged in this way but in many cases it will be difficult to establish, as many different factors may be involved, such as efficiency and suitability of the employee.
- The employer should make reasonable efforts where practicable to look for alternative employment within the organization,[173] although tribunals should not expect unrealistic efforts to be made in what may be difficult circumstances.[174]
- The employer should usually consult affected employees and give them reasonable warning of impending redundancy.[175] The significance of consultation was strengthened by the emphasis on procedure in *Polkey* (considered presently), in the light of which it has been subsequently said by the EAT that 'the importance of such consultation cannot be over-emphasised'.[176]

These guidelines were reaffirmed and recast by the EAT in *Williams v Compair Maxam Ltd*,[177] giving particular emphasis to two issues: consultation and the method of selection.

170 *Moon v Homeworthy Furniture (Northern) Ltd* [1977] ICR 117, [1976] IRLR 298, EAT.

171 *James W Cook & Co (Wivenhoe) Ltd v Tipper* [1990] ICR 716, [1990] IRLR 386, CA.

172 These three requirements are now so well established that they should automatically be considered by a tribunal in an unfair redundancy case, even if not specifically raised by an applicant (eg where they are a litigant in person): *Langston v Cranfield University* [1998] IRLR 172, EAT.

173 *Vokes Ltd v Bear* [1974] ICR 1, [1973] IRLR 363; *Modern Injection Moulds Ltd v Price* [1976] ICR 370, [1976] IRLR 172. However, a requirement to look within the group, not just within the firm itself, was looked on with disfavour by the Scottish EAT in *Barratt Construction Ltd v Dalrymple* [1984] IRLR 385, and by the English EAT in *MDH Ltd v Sussex* [1986] IRLR 123, EAT.

174 *British United Shoe Machinery Co Ltd v Clarke* [1978] ICR 70, [1977] IRLR 297. In *Thomas and Betts Manufacturing Ltd v Harding* [1980] IRLR 255, CA, it was said that s 98 is so wide that this may mean looking for other jobs for A to do, even if that means dismissing B instead (if B has less seniority than A), ie a 'bumping' redundancy (though for the problems with this concept see 8.1.1.2); once again, however, the Scottish EAT was unwilling to apply this wider approach: *Green v A&I Fraser (Wholesale Fish Merchants) Ltd* [1985] IRLR 55. Note that statutory preference (in finding other work) is given to (1) women on maternity leave when made redundant, (2) employees on adoption leave when made redundant, and (3) disabled employees, where the employer is making reasonable adjustments: *Kent County Council v Mingo* [2000] IRLR 90.

175 *Clarkson International Tools Ltd v Short* [1973] ICR 191, [1973] IRLR 90; *Kelly v Upholstery and Cabinet Works (Amesbury) Ltd* [1977] IRLR 91; *British United Shoe Machinery Co Ltd v Clarke* [1978] ICR 70, [1977] IRLR 297; cf *Atkinson v George Lindsay & Co* [1980] IRLR 196, Ct of Sess. The importance of this factor was reaffirmed by the EAT in *Freud v Bentalls Ltd* [1983] ICR 77, [1982] IRLR 443 and *Holden v Bradville Ltd* [1985] IRLR 483. The requirement is for both warning and consultation: *Rowell v Hubbard Group Services* [1995] IRLR 195, EAT.

176 *Dyke v Hereford and Worcester County Council* [1989] ICR 800 at 807, per Wood J. A particularly useful summary of the consultation requirements is to be found in the judgment of Judge Clark in *Mugford v Midland Bank plc* [1997] ICR 399, [1997] IRLR 208.

177 [1982] ICR 156, [1982] IRLR 83.

Consultation

For redundancy dismissals to be fair there may have to be both collective consultation, with employee representatives, and individual consultation with those employees who are at risk of redundancy. So far as collective consultation is concerned, the EAT said in *Williams v Compair Maxam* that where the employer recognizes a union the necessary consultations will normally of course be with that union, and where this is the case the employer should give as much warning as possible of the impending redundancies, seek to agree criteria for selection with the union, review the eventual selection with the union to consider whether it is in accordance with those criteria, and consider union representations on selection. This point is now understood to apply to cases where there is no recognized union but, because of the added rules requiring consultation with employee representatives in all cases where 20 or more redundancies are proposed,[178] consultation is required by law; lack of it may affect the fairness of any eventual individual redundancies. Moreover, even if the number of redundancies is not sufficient to trigger the statutory consultation requirements, if there is a recognised union, a failure to consult with it is likely to render the dismissals that follow unfair.[179]

One area of difficulty had been the dividing line or overlap between collective consultation with a union or with employee representatives on the one hand and individual consultation with affected employees on the other hand. Typically collective consultation will be about ways of avoiding redundancy and selection criteria. If there has been such collective discussion then the individual consultations with employees will usually take place subsequently, once they have been provisionally selected for redundancy, and will be for the purpose of discussing their own personal situations, to let them comment on the application of the selection criteria to them and to discuss the possibility of alternative employment. The EAT noted in *Mugford v Midland Bank plc*[180] that unions will generally want to consult over selection criteria, but rarely want to be involved in the invidious process of selecting individuals by the application of those criteria.

The case law in this area was reviewed by the Court of Appeal in *Haycocks v ADP RPO UK Ltd* and a helpful overall statement of the law on this matter was given by Underhill LJ as follows:

> I agree with the EAT that there are dangers in the unthinking application of labels 'individual' and 'collective' consultation. Collective consultation in ordinary usage refers to consultation between the employer and representatives of the affected workforce (that is, those who are at risk of dismissal) as a whole. Typically it is the appropriate forum to discuss issues that are common to the group. The most obvious such issue is whether there are ways in which redundancies can be avoided, or at least the numbers reduced, but there will also be procedural issues relevant to the group as a whole, such as the choice of selection criteria. Where collective consultation occurs, it may be sufficient for individuals to be consulted about issues peculiar to them. The most obvious such issue is alternative employment, to which the EAT specifically refers; but it may not be the only issue on which fairness requires that there be individual consultation (not least because the distinction between 'common' and 'individual' issues may not always be clear-cut). But where there is no collective consultation the situation is different. In such a case it is good practice for employees to be given, in the course of individual consultation, the opportunity to express

[178] See 8.1.3.2.

[179] See *Haycocks v ADP RPO UK Ltd* [2024] EWCA Civ 1291, [2025] IRLR 123 at [55] where it was noted that for unfair dismissal purposes union consultation would be required either because the statutory process is triggered or, where it is not, whether there is a recognised trade union.

[180] [1997] IRLR 208, EAT.

> their views on any issue that may affect the risk of their dismissal or its consequences, whether it is peculiar to them as an individual or common to the affected workforce as a whole. It should certainly not be assumed that they will have nothing useful to contribute on common issues: it depends on the particular case. For the avoidance of doubt, I am not to be taken as saying that a failure to afford that opportunity will necessarily render any subsequent dismissal unfair: again, that will depend on the circumstances (see points (f) and (g) [in a summary of the law that had been given by the EAT]). But if there is a widespread view among employers that individual consultation need only ever address individual matters the sooner they are disabused of it the better.

The fact that some aspect of an employer's consultation was deficient does not necessarily mean that a dismissal is unfair. In the passage just cited, the points (f) and (g) were, first, that it is a question of fact and degree as to whether consultation is adequate and it is not automatically unfair that there is a lack of consultation in a particular respect (*Mugford v Midland Bank plc*)[181] and, second, that any particular aspect of consultation, such as the provision of scoring, is not essential to a fair process (*Camelot Group plc v Hogg*).[182] One final point is that consultation is particularly important when the employer has 'selected' from a 'pool of one'. Such consultation should be before the employer has decided to use such a restricted pool.[183]

Selection—the pool and the selection criteria

Clearly if not all employees doing work of a particular kind are to be made redundant, there will be a need to establish a pool from which to make the selection. There is no hard rule of law about the composition of the pool: what unfair dismissal law requires is that the pool should be within the range of reasonable responses of the employer to the situation it faces.[184] The pool might be all employees doing similar jobs, or could be wider if the workers might be interchangeable.

As to the selection criteria, the EAT in *Williams v Compair Maxam* said that when working out criteria for selection (whether or not with union agreement) the emphasis must be on criteria which leave as little as possible to subjective assessments by the people making the selection, but rather are capable of being objectively applied on the basis of matters such as length of service, experience, and efficiency.[185] However, this has now been substantially qualified in later cases: the mere fact that individual judgement, as opposed to purely quantifiable metrics, plays some role in the decision does not make it unfair, and so long as the decision is not completely subjective, there is no need for selection decisions to be reduced to 'box-ticking exercises'.[186] The consequence is that employers frequently create a 'selection matrix' where each employee is scored against several criteria, some of which may be objective, such as disciplinary record or attendance record,

[181] [1997] IRLR 208, EAT.

[182] UKEATS/0019/10, (23 September 2011, unreported)

[183] *Mogane v Bradford Teaching Hospitals NHS Foundation Trust* [2002] EAT 139, [2023] IRLR 44; *Valimulia v Bradford Teaching Hospitals NHS Trust* [2023] EAT 1331, [20124] IRLR 713.

[184] There is a helpful summary at para 31 of *Capita Hartshead Ltd v Byard* [2012] IRLR 814; see also *Wrexham Golf Club v Ingham* UKEAT/0190/12 (10 July 2012, unreported).

[185] Thus, in *Williams v Compair Maxam Ltd* the redundancy was held to be unfair, partly on the ground that the criteria established by the employer (that those retained would be those 'who, in the opinion of the managers concerned, would be able to keep the company viable') lacked the necessary objectivity. See also *E-Zec Medical Transport Service Ltd v Ms S A Gregory* UKEAT/0192/08/MAA.

[186] *Mitchells of Lancaster (Brewers) v Tattersall* UKEAT/0605/11/SM (29 May 2012, unreported). See also *Nicholls v Rockwell Automation Ltd* UKEAT/0540/11 (25 June 2012, unreported) and *Canning v National Institute for Health and Care Excellence* UKEAT/0241/13 (6 March 2019, unreported).

and some more subjective, such as range of skills and potential for development. Some criteria may be weighted more heavily than others. Wise employers try to reduce the risk of the scores being influenced by personal prejudice on the part of managers by having the scoring carried out by several managers.

This has led to an important question: should a tribunal just look at the general fairness of the system set up by the employer, or should it (as the applicant will probably want) investigate in detail the scoring of *all* the employees involved, in order to decide whether the applicant had been wrongly scored or harshly treated, and so unfairly selected? One point of procedure which may act as the focus for this whole question is the power of the tribunal to order disclosure; if the employee made redundant has been given their score, but the employer has refused to divulge the scores of the other employees under consideration, should a tribunal accede to that employee's request for an order for disclosure of that further information (without which a detailed analysis of the application of the employer's selection scheme probably cannot be made in practice)?

In *British Aerospace plc v Green*,[187] the Court of Appeal refused an order for disclosure of the scores of other employees who were not selected for redundancy. Waite LJ summed up the view of the whole court as follows:

> Employment law recognises, pragmatically, that an over-minute investigation of the selection process by the tribunal members may run the risk of defeating the purpose which the tribunals were called into being to discharge, namely, a swift, informal disposal of disputes arising from redundancy in the workplace. So in general the employer who sets up a system of selection which can reasonably be described as fair and applies it without any overt sign of conduct which mars its fairness will have done all that the law requires of him.[188]

It must be said at the outset that there was indeed a 'pragmatic' reason for refusing disclosure in this case because of its very scale—it involved the making redundant (following the cancellation of a fighter contract) of 530 employees out of a workforce of approximately 7,000. However, only one judge (Stuart-Smith LJ) made any reference to the court's approach being restricted to mass redundancy cases, and the two other judgments are in broad terms, which are capable of causing severe problems because their premise is a denial that redundancy selection operates on a comparative and competitive basis at all:

> Documents relating to retained employees are not likely to be relevant in any but the most exceptional circumstances. The question for the industrial tribunal, which must be determined separately for each applicant, is whether the applicant was unfairly dismissed, *not whether some other employee could have been fairly dismissed.*[189]

This cannot, with respect, be correct; given that X redundancies have to be made (which cannot be challenged) and that an inherently competitive points-scoring system has been put into place to select who is to be made redundant, any consideration of the fairness of selecting employee A *must* involve their comparison with those not chosen, and whether the criteria have been properly applied, however distasteful it may be, a challenge to the fairness of selecting A must include within it at least an implied assertion that B or C should have been chosen instead. *British Aerospace* denies this completely.

[187] [1995] ICR 1006, [1995] IRLR 433, CA. There may be a novel complication, given recent developments, concerning the lawfulness of disclosing information on other employees and whether to do so might contravene the data protection legislation; see particularly the Data Protection Employment Code of Practice, Part II: Employee Records.

[188] [1995] ICR 1006 at 1010, [1995] IRLR 433 at 434.

[189] [1995] ICR 1006 at 1019, [1995] IRLR 433 at 438, per Millett LJ (emphasis added).

Moreover, only two months later the EAT in *FDR Ltd v Holloway*[190] effectively ignored *British Aerospace* and upheld an order for disclosure of information on employees not selected,[191] stating that this was essential in order to dispose of the issue of whether the selection criteria had been applied fairly, and that a tribunal was *not* to take at face value an employer's assertion that it had all been done properly. These decisions are, quite simply, conflicting and, in spite of the pure argument of precedent that the decision of the Court of Appeal should always apply, it would be dangerous for an employer to assume that simple reliance could be placed on that decision in order to refuse disclosure of other scores as a matter of course.

The Scottish EAT in *John Brown Engineering Ltd v Brown*[192] upheld a tribunal decision of unfair dismissal where the employers had refused to divulge to employees their own scores, stating that such a refusal may make individual consultation worthless, and the Court of Session in *King v Eaton Ltd (No 2)*[193] (the remedies stage of the original decision) simply stated in passing that 'the general reasons for trying to avoid that kind of inquiry [ie into individual scores] do not seem to us to be absolute'.

There are not many cases where employers do not divulge to employees their own scores. In relation to the scores of other employees the general approach in the tribunals, as far as one can gather, has been to continue to order disclosure where appropriate, though it must be accepted that there is a problem of law here because of the uncompromising language in *British Aerospace*, which may eventually have to be referred to the Supreme Court. For now the state of affairs appears best represented by the decision in *Nichols v Rockwell Automation Ltd*: there the EAT read *British Aerospace* as standing for the proposition that disclosure can be had for the purposes of cross-examination to challenge the motives and genuineness of management, but that once the selection procedure has been shown to be reasonable on its face, evidence of the scores of other employees cannot be relied upon by a tribunal to critique the fairness of a specific dismissal.[194]

Must the employer offer an appeal?

This was considered in *Gwynedd Council v Barratt*.[195] If the employer's procedures provide for an appeal in redundancy cases then it is likely to be unfair not to allow appeals. However, very often the employer's procedures only provide for appeals in conduct and capability dismissals, in which case a redundancy dismissal will not be unfair *solely* because the

[190] [1995] IRLR 400. Quantitatively the case is at the opposite end of the scale, involving the making redundant of one employee out of eight.

[191] On the question of disclosure, the case is distinguishable—in *British Aerospace* the employees wanted the information to see if there were any faults in the selection, and this was disallowed on the ordinary principle of disclosure that the court will not allow it for a 'fishing expedition'; in *FDR* the EAT held that 'an issue' had already arisen (to which disclosure could be attached) because the employee's suspicions were aroused by the retention of an employee with less service and a poorer record. In spite of this, it must be said that the EAT's treatment of *British Aerospace* is on the cavalier side of brusque—the judgment is short, citing hardly anything of the Court of Appeal judgments, and dismissing their ratio decidendi as 'certain observations' which had been 'misread' by counsel for the employers. Lord Denning himself could hardly have done better. Where a recognized trade union is involved, it may be able instead to seek the information required on a collective level, under TULR(C)A, s 181, since the CAC have held that redundancy selection methods may remain in the sphere of collective bargaining, for the purpose of disclosure of bargaining information: see 9.8.

[192] [1997] IRLR 90; analytically the case is less than helpful, because all it does is to rehearse the arguments for both sides and then decide it as a question of fact; arguably it is the actual decision that is significant.

[193] [1998] IRLR 686; see particularly para 21.

[194] [2012] UKEAT 0540_11_2506 (25 June 2012) at para 28: ('Once granted that there is a fair system of selection applied without overt signs of unfairness it was not for the Tribunal to embark on a detailed critique of individual items of scoring').

[195] [2021] EWCA Civ 1322, [2021] IRLR 1028.

employer has not offered or allowed an appeal, but the absence of an appeal process can if there are other deficiencies contribute to a decision that the dismissal was unfair.

Making employees apply for future employment

Where a number of jobs are to disappear to be replaced by a smaller number of different jobs, employers often ask the affected employees to apply for the new roles and then put them through a process more akin to a recruitment selection process of tests and/or interviews. If the new roles are significantly different from the old ones, a tribunal may find this to be fair, on the basis that a *Williams v Compare Maxam* approach of selection by reference to ability to perform the old job is not a good guide to who will be best at the new roles.[196] However, this only applies if the roles are different: if the roles are identical or substantially similar then the *Williams v Compair Maxam* approach (as developed in the subsequent cases) applies.[197] This is a helpful caution: if the purpose of the selection process is to retain the best employees in a reduced number of unchanged roles, the reasonable way to identify them must be to assess their past performance rather than to give the jobs to those employees who happen to be best at being interviewed.

The approach to 'reasonableness' in redundancy unfair dismissal cases

The EAT has stressed that when deciding whether a redundancy dismissal is fair it is particularly important that the tribunal should apply the 'range of reasonable responses' test[198] and not simply impose its own view as to how its members might have handled the redundancy.[199]

As seen in Chapter 7, *Polkey v A E Dayton Services Ltd*,[200] with its emphasis on the continuing importance of procedures, was a landmark case generally, and in this context it is useful to remember that it was in fact an unfair redundancy case. *Williams v Compair Maxam Ltd* was not specifically approved in *Polkey* but, although the House of Lords in *Polkey* did not hold that a breach of normal procedure would invariably make a dismissal unfair, the overall effect of *Polkey* in reinstating procedural fairness as a central factor must be taken as backing for *Williams*. This was certainly the tenor of subsequent reported cases.[201]

However, *Polkey* does not require slavish adherence to procedures in cases where they could have no effect and there has been a tendency to look to Lord Bridge's speech for the exceptional case,[202] which he described as being where the employer (subjectively) thought reasonably *at the time* that to go through the usual procedures would be meaningless; in such a case, the dismissal could still be fair. However, in *Duffy v Yeomans & Partners Ltd*[203] the Court of Appeal held that the proper description of this exception is that given by Lord Mackay LC, that is, an objective test of whether the employer *could reasonably have concluded* at the time that to go through the usual procedures would be meaningless. This is more than semantics because the latter, objective, test could (if applied too loosely) come

196 *Morgan v Welsh Rugby Union* [2011] IRLR 376, EAT.

197 *Green v London Borough of Barking and Dagenham* UKEAT/0157/16 (10 March 2001, unreported); Gwynedd *Council v Barratt* [2020] IRLR 847, EAT (appealed on other grounds to CA).

198 See 7.4.4.

199 *Grundy (Teddington) Ltd v Willis* [1976] ICR 323, [1976] IRLR 118; *Watling & Co Ltd v Richardson* [1978] ICR 1049, [1978] IRLR 255.

200 [1988] ICR 142, [1987] IRLR 503, HL.

201 *Walls Meat Co Ltd v Selby* [1989] ICR 601, CA; *Dyke v Hereford and Worcester County Council* [1989] ICR 800; *Ferguson v Prestwick Circuits Ltd* [1992] IRLR 266; *De Grasse v Stockwell Tools Ltd* [1992] IRLR 269; *Rolls-Royce Motor Cars Ltd v Price* [1993] IRLR 203, EAT.

202 See *Robertson v Magnet Ltd* [1993] IRLR 512, EAT.

203 [1995] ICR 1, [1994] IRLR 642, CA.

to bear an unfortunate resemblance to the old 'but it made no difference' test in *British Labour Pump Co Ltd v Byrne*,[204] which was disapproved in *Polkey*. There is a difference in principle (under *Duffy* the tribunal must still look at the date of dismissal, whereas *Byrne* allowed the unrestrained use of hindsight), but it is a point that needs careful handling by the tribunals.

Selection procedures and indirect discrimination

An employer needs to be careful if there is a risk that a criterion for selection is indirectly discriminatory against employees with a particular protected characteristic. If a selection criterion puts employees in a protected group at a particular disadvantage it will be unlawful discrimination unless it can be justified as a proportionate means of achieving a legitimate aim (see 4.2.5). Thus, redundancy selection will need to meet the standards required by the Equality Act 2010 as well as the unfair dismissal provisions; if the selection criteria are unlawful direct or indirect discrimination, the dismissal will probably also be unfair on the basis that adopting discriminatory selection criteria would be outside the range of reasonable responses to a redundancy situation.

In *Clarke v Eley (IMI) Kynoch Ltd*,[205] it was held that selecting part-timers for redundancy before full-timers was indirect sex discrimination because women were more likely to be part-time workers and applying this PCP was not justified. One selection criterion that was once common—indeed it often used to be the sole criterion—is length of service, where the procedure adopted was often 'last in, first out' (LIFO). In many cases the use of LIFO was the product of negotiation with a trade union, and in general trade unions have been in favour of such an approach. In the *Clarke* case, the EAT expressed the opinion, obiter, that although length of service might be discriminatory against women, it was likely to be justified for the legitimate aim of reaching agreement with the trade union about a reasonable and common-sense method of selection with a limited discriminatory impact. In *Brook v London Borough of Haringey*,[206] where length of service was one of four criteria used, the EAT accepted this as justified with very little examination.

The matter was more fully examined in the context of the clearly *age*-discriminatory effect of length of service in *Rolls Royce plc v Unite the Union*.[207] Shortly after age discrimination became unlawful, Rolls Royce sought to get out of a selection agreement with its trade union which applied LIFO as one criterion among others. The company applied to the High Court for declaration that this provision meant that the agreed selection method amounted to unjustified indirect age discrimination. The Court of Appeal ruled that the inclusion of the length of service criterion was a proportionate means of achieving a legitimate aim, namely the reward of loyalty, and the overall desirability of achieving a stable workforce in the context of a fair process of redundancy selection. At the High Court the judge had been influenced in addition by the desirability of having a method of selection which was agreed with the recognized trade union representing the workforce. The Court of Appeal held that the length of service criterion was a proportionate means of achieving the aim since it was only one of a substantial number of criteria for selection for redundancy, and was by no means determinative, and that younger employees appeared to accept it as fair. This suggests that the position might be different were length of service the sole criterion. The ECJ more recently confirmed that age discrimination legislation need not forbid long service as a factor in employment decisions (in this case pay scales) so long as the link to service, as opposed to age, was justified.[208]

[204] [1979] ICR 347, [1979] IRLR 94; see 7.4.3. [205] [1983] ICR 165, [1982] IRLR 482.
[206] [1992] IRLR 478, EAT. [207] [2009] EWCA Civ 387, [2002] IRLR 576.
[208] *Tyrolean Airways Tiroler Luftfahrt Gesellschaft v Betriebsrat Tiroler Luftfahrt Gesellschaft* C-132/11, [2012] All ER (D) 38.

Returning to part-timers, selecting them first would now come within the Part-time Workers (Prevention of Less Favourable Treatment) Regulations 2000 and so there would be an obligation on the employer to justify it, presumably on grounds similar to those required by sex discrimination law. A similar development has taken place in relation to any 'fixed-termers first' policy because of the Fixed-term Employees (Prevention of Less Favourable Treatment) Regulations 2002.[209]

8.1.4.2 Reorganization—redundancy and SOSR dismissals

As the law stands at the time of writing, cases where employees are dismissed consequent to a reorganization that involves a diminution in the requirement for employees to carry out the particular kind of work are potentially fair under the head of redundancy, and cases where employees are dismissed so as to enable the employer to employ people to do that same work but on different contractual terms are potentially fair under the head of 'some other substantial reason'. This subset of SOSR has evolved through the cases and demonstrates how difficult it is to draw the line between fairness and unfairness where there is a clear conflict between the employer's legitimate business interests and the employee's contractual rights. The problem arises where the employer wishes to reorganize the operation in such a way that there will have to be changes in the employee's job, or in the way it is carried out (eg changes relating to hours, shifts, wages, job content, or location). The employee's contract, however, is static and so prima facie they can insist upon continued performance of it as it stands. The employer will want to make changes necessary for the efficiency (and in an extreme case the survival) of the enterprise,[210] but in ordinary contract law they may not make unilateral alterations to existing contracts of employment. If they attempt to do so, the employee has a common law action for breach of contract[211] and, more significantly, may under the legislation walk out because of it and claim to have been constructively dismissed through the employer's breach.[212] Because of this, normally an employer who cannot persuade employees to agree to change their contracts will dismiss them by giving proper notice, which is lawful at common law but is of course a dismissal for statutory purposes. Either way, the employer is open to an unfair dismissal claim. From the decided cases, it appears that there are three possibilities in these reorganization cases:

209 This has, of course, been a common policy in the past (especially where fixed-term contracts were due to expire anyway), but it had not been challenged under discrimination law in the way that 'part-timers first' had been. Ironically, shortly before the 2002 Regulations came in, there arose the first major, successful challenge to a 'fixed-termers first' policy on the basis of sex discrimination: *Whiffen v Milham Ford Girls' School* [2001] EWCA Civ 385, [2001] ICR 1023, [2001] IRLR 468.

210 This has been recognized in the context of redundancy law: *Chapman v Goonvean and Rostowrack China Clay Co Ltd* [1973] 1 All ER 218, [1973] ICR 50; *Johnson v Nottinghamshire Combined Policy Authority* [1974] ICR 170, [1974] IRLR 20, CA; *Lesney Products & Co Ltd v Nolan* [1977] ICR 235, [1977] IRLR 77, CA.

211 This can take the form of an action for wages due under the old contract, on the old terms, and can be an effective tactic: *Burdett-Coutts v Hertfordshire County Council* [1984] IRLR 91 (concerning unilateral changes to dinner ladies' terms and conditions, a fruitful source of important case law in the mid-1980s); *Rigby v Ferodo Ltd* [1988] ICR 29, [1987] IRLR 516, HL. Unless the employer can show a variation of contract, assented to by the employee, it will lose the common law action, and will then have to force the issue by dismissing those who refuse to accept the changes and taking its chances in an unfair dismissal action (discussed later in the chapter).

212 *Greenaway Harrison Ltd v Wiles* [1994] IRLR 380, EAT. To be clear, redundancies can be constructive as well: it depends on whether the action that constitutes a repudiatory breach is causally attributable to a redundancy situation. See eg *Lees v Imperial College of Science, Technology and Medicine* UKEAT/0288/15 (14 January 2016, unreported).

Possibility 1: change is within the contract

It may be that the proposed changes fall within the permissible range of managerial discretion to organize the work,[213] or indeed within the proper ambit of the contractual job description for that employee anyway. This will be particularly so if the changes are minor or of an administrative nature, if they can be construed merely as an updating of essentially the same job (seen in the light possibly of an implied term of the contract that the employee will adapt to new methods and techniques reasonably required).[214] Alternatively it may be that the job description in fact covers jobs A and B but the employee, used to doing only A in practice, refuses to do B instead. In consequence, a skilfully drafted contractual job description (and/or a flexibility clause) could perhaps anticipate and cover subsequent reorganizations.

In this situation the changes do not constitute a breach of contract and so if the employee still refuses to accept them and is dismissed, that will be a dismissal for refusal to obey a lawful order and so will probably be fair on conduct grounds.[215] Likewise, if the employee walks out because of such changes, it will not constitute constructive dismissal since there will have been no repudiatory breach of contract by the employer (unless there was something seriously objectionable about the way it was handled, capable of independently producing a breach of contract). They will therefore not receive a redundancy payment or compensation for unfair dismissal.[216]

Possibility 2: the reorganization results in a redundancy situation

If the changes are more major and either cause or result from a diminished need for work of a particular kind, that may constitute redundancy within the definition in the Employment Rights Act 1996, s 139.[217] If so, the dismissed employee may be eligible for a redundancy payment and the fairness of the dismissal will be assessed against the principles set out in 8.1.4.1.

The dismissal of employees followed by replacing them with non-employed workers also amounts to a redundancy dismissal since there has been a diminution in the requirement of the employer for *employees* to carry out the work.[218] Again the dismissed employee may be eligible for a redundancy payment and, as the law stands at the time of writing, the fairness of the dismissal will be assessed against the principles set out in 8.1.4.1. However, increasing concern about this practice has led to the insertion by the Employment Rights Act 2025 of new section 104K into ERA 1996. Once this is in force if the new, non-employed, workers are contracted to do work with is the same or substantially the same activities as the dismissed employees, then the dismissals are prima facie unfair. The employer can only get out of the automatic unfairness if it can prove both:

- that the reason for the replacement with non-employees was to 'eliminate, prevent or significantly reduce, or significantly mitigate the effect of, any financial difficulties

[213] See 2.6.2.

[214] *Cresswell v Board of Inland Revenue* [1984] ICR 508, [1984] IRLR 190 (computerization of PAYE system still within the ambit of the existing contracts of those operating the system, who were expected to adapt).

[215] *Rochford v WNS Global Services UK Ltd* [2017] EWCA Civ 2205.

[216] *George Wimpey & Co Ltd v Cooper* [1977] IRLR 205; *Glitz v Watford Electric Co Ltd* [1979] IRLR 89. In the latter case the EAT pointed out that in a small firm or unit the job descriptions may necessarily be more vague, allowing the employer to expect greater flexibility and adaptability from its employees. Note also, more generally, the successful attack on an unconscionable reliance on an apparently wide flexibility clause in *Land Securities Trillium Ltd v Thornley* [2005] IRLR 765: see 3.1.3 and White, 'Working under Protest and Variation of Employment Terms' (2008) 37 ILJ 365.

[217] See 8.1.1. See also Bennett 'Interpreting Unfair Dismissal and Redundancy Payments Law: The Judicial Reluctance to Disapprove Employer Decisions to Dismiss' (2002) 23 Statute Law Review 135.

[218] *Bromby & Hoare Ltd v Evans* [1972] ICR 113, 12 KIR 160; *Scarth v Economic Forestry Ltd* [1973] ICR 322, NIRC.

which at the time of the dismissal were affecting, or were likely in the immediate future to affect the employer's ability to carry on the business as a going concern' (or in the public sector to affect the financial sustainability of carrying out the employer's statutory functions); and

- that in all the circumstances the employer could not reasonably have avoided the need to make the replacement.

This is clearly a very substantial double hurdle for an employer to jump: it will be difficult to prove such an economic case to a tribunal, and thus in reality this provision will amount to a ban on dismissing employees so as to replace them with non-employee workers. In the unlikely event that an employer can jump this hurdle, that only means that the dismissal is not *automatically* unfair, and the employer will still need to show that the dismissal was fair in the ordinary way. Presumably the ordinary redundancy fairness principles discussed at 8.1.4.1 will apply, so that issues such as consultation and selection will be considered. Rather superfluously, new section 104K(7) in ERA 1996, will require a tribunal when deciding whether the dismissal is fair or unfair to include in the matters it considers any consultation with the employees and employee representatives. However regulations may add to the matters which must be considered.

Possibility 3: no redundancy so dismissal may be for SOSR

If the changes are major but do not produce in law a redundancy (eg where the work is undiminished but the hours or the remuneration have to change), it is well established that the reorganization *can* constitute 'some other substantial reason' within s 98(1), and so the employee may not be able to succeed in a claim for unfair dismissal.[219] (They will certainly not be entitled to a redundancy payment because the s 139 definition of redundancy has not been met.) This is the type of case which causes most problems, because to decide on fairness the tribunal in effect has to make a decision as to the precedence between the employer's business needs and the employee's normal contractual and statutory rights. If the tribunal decides that the dismissal is fair then it is in reality allowing the employer to insist upon a unilateral variation of the contract.[220]

In recent years this ability of employers to 'fire and rehire' has become very controversial. The Conservative government introduced a new Code of Practice to seek to address apparent misuse and unreasonable behaviour on the part of employers.[221] This Code is considered below. It mainly affects what an employer should do in procedural terms in connection with consulting employees and their representatives about the proposals (and therefore whether a dismissal is unfair for procedural reasons) rather than affecting what might or might not amount to fairness in relation to the substance of the decision to dismiss. However the new Labour government elected in July 2024 considered that fire and

[219] *RS Components Ltd v Irwin* [1973] ICR 535, [1973] IRLR 239; and *Robinson v British Island Airways Ltd* [1978] ICR 304, [1977] IRLR 477; *Hollister v National Farmers' Union* [1979] ICR 542, [1979] IRLR 238, CA; *Genower v Ealing, Hammersmith and Hounslow Area Health Authority* [1980] IRLR 297; *Farrant v Woodroffe School* [1998] ICR 184, [1998] IRLR 176. Cf, however, *Labour Party v Oakley* [1988] ICR 403, [1988] IRLR 34, CA, where the reorganization was shown on the facts to be a pretext for dismissing someone they had already decided to dispense with.

[220] See Bowers and Clark 'Unfair Dismissal and Managerial Prerogative: A Study of "Other Substantial Reason"' (1981) 10 ILJ 34. The existence of a 'dismissal' will normally be clear, through either (a) an express dismissal by the employer of the refusenik, (b) a constructive dismissal if the employee leaves, or (c) an application of the rule that a unilateral change can be so fundamental as to constitute termination of the old contract by the employer, even where the employee in fact carries on working (under, in effect, a new contract), as in *Hogg v Dover College* [1990] ICR 39, affirmed in *Alcan Extrusions Ltd v Yates* [1996] IRLR 327, EAT.

[221] Code of Practice on Dismissal and Re-engagement issued by the Secretary of State on 18 July 2024.

rehire should be subject to much more extensive restrictions, and in consequence dramatic changes to the law on unfair dismissal in such cases will be made by amendments under s 28 of the Employment Rights Act 2025. These are also discussed below.

Consultation in SOSR case

Consultation with the employee and with employee representatives has long been seen as one of the major requirements of a fair dismissal in these cases and it is clear that if the employer does negotiate a reorganization with the relevant union or with the majority of the employees and one employee still holds out, that agreement will considerably strengthen the case for dismissal of that employee. Thus, it has been said by the EAT that there must be proper consultation, not just the presentation of a fait accompli or ultimatum,[222] and that the employer should consider any counter-proposals put forward by the employee and should bear in mind the position of the individual employee, which may not be done if all cases are treated as one, for example by just consulting a weak union or staff association.[223]

However, in *Hollister v National Farmers' Union*[224] the Court of Appeal held that too much emphasis had been placed upon consultation in past cases, to the point that the EAT was in danger of putting a gloss upon the simple reasonableness test in s 98(4)—consultation is only one of the factors to be considered when looking at the circumstances of the case, and so lack of it (as in that case, where the changes were just announced to the employee) is not necessarily fatal to the employer's case.

With effect from July 2024, there is guidance in a new Code of Practice which a tribunal must take into account in assessing the reasonableness of an employer's approach to consultation in a reorganization case.[225] The Code aims to encourage employers and employees to agree the contractual changes so that dismissals (whether outright or for fire and rehire purposes) can be avoided. The key steps which the Code says an employer should take are as follows:

1. As early as reasonably possible the employer should provide information in writing about the proposals, including what the proposed changes to terms are, who will be affected, the business reasons for the proposed changes, the anticipated timings, and the other options that have been considered (Code paras 21–25).
2. The employer should engage in meaningful consultation in good faith and with a view to reaching an agreed outcome (Code paras 28–30).
3. Consultation should last as long as is reasonably possible (Code para 30)
4. The Code is rather unclear, and potentially contradictory, about when the employer should indicate that if agreement cannot be reached dismissal and re-engagement will take place. It says: 'If, at any point, the employer intends, if an agreed outcome cannot be reached, to opt for dismissal and re-engagement, it is important that the employer be clear about that. However, raising the prospect of dismissal can be detrimental to attempts to reach an agreed outcome, so the employer should not do so unreasonably early' (Code para 31).
5. Once it has become clear that contractual change by agreement cannot be achieved, the employer must re-examine its proposals and consider whether it still needs to implement the changes (Code para 33).

[222] *Ellis v Brighton Co-operative Society Ltd* [1976] IRLR 419.

[223] *Martin v Automobile Proprietary Ltd* [1979] IRLR 64. Presumably this would require some form of individual consultation in the case of a non-unionist.

[224] [1979] ICR 542, [1979] IRLR 238.

[225] Code of Practice on Dismissal and Re-engagement issued by the Secretary of State on 18 July 2024.

6. The employer should consider whether there is any practical support it might offer to employees such as relocation assistance, or career coaching or counselling for emotional support (Code para 50).
7. The employer might commit to reviewing the changes at a fixed point in the future to see if they are still necessary (Code para 51). Additionally, if more than 20 dismissals are proposed then s 188 TULR(C)A 1992 will require collective consultation as they will constitute collective dismissals under EU law. This is considered, in relation to both contract change dismissals and redundancy dismissals, in 8.1.3.1 and 8.1.3.3.

Clearly these steps are not an inviolable set of rules—rather they are matters which must be taken account in deciding whether the employer's actions fall within the reasonable range of responses. We may never get any appellate case law on the application of the Code of Practice, since it is likely to become much less important when changes to be made under the Employment Rights Act 2025 make most fire and rehire dismissals automatically unfair.

Note that if more than the threshold number of dismissals are proposed then s 188 TULR(C)A 1992 will require collective consultation. This is considered at 8.1.3.1.

Substantive fairness in an SOSR case

Assuming that an employer has proceeded in a reasonable way, the issue becomes whether the dismissal is *substantively* fair. As the law stands at the time of writing it is the s 98(4) concept of reasonableness which is central to this question: given that the reorganization is a substantial reason which *can* justify dismissal, was the dismissal of the employee *in fact* justified on the facts of the particular case? The tribunal looks at the reasonableness of the employer's actions leading to dismissal, and in essence decides whether the time had come when the employer had no further option but to dismiss the employee in order to put into effect the necessary changes. In doing so, the tribunal may have to consider three matters:

Was the reorganization necessary? Although it is not for the tribunal to decide how the employer ought to run the business and the employer's genuine belief in the necessity for changes is likely to be paramount, a tribunal may expect the employer to lead evidence showing why it thought change necessary and how it reached the particular decisions in question.[226] In one of the original cases, *Ellis v Brighton Co-operative Society Ltd*,[227] the EAT seemed to assume that in order to justify eventual dismissals for non-compliance, the changes had to be so vital that if they were not put into effect the whole business would be brought to a standstill, but this was held by the Court of Appeal to be too restrictive in *Hollister v National Farmers' Union*,[228] where it was said that it is sufficient if there is a good, sound business reason for the reorganization.

That approach leaves a great deal to the employer's discretion and, indeed, the area of business reorganizations has produced many findings of fair dismissal. In *Evans v Elemeta Holdings Ltd*,[229] the EAT appeared to move in the direction of redressing this

[226] *Banerjee v City and East London Area Health Authority* [1979] IRLR 147; *Ladbroke Courage Holidays Ltd v Asten* [1981] IRLR 59; in *Orr v Vaughan* [1981] IRLR 63 it was said that, while business reorganizations are basically for the employer to decide upon, the tribunal must be satisfied that, at the least, the employer came to his decision on reasonable information reasonably acquired.

[227] [1976] IRLR 419.

[228] [1979] ICR 542, [1979] IRLR 238; *Bowater Containers Ltd v McCormack* [1980] IRLR 50. Outside pressure for change, eg from customers or insurers, may be a relevant factor, but the employer must still establish that it handled the pressure reasonably: *Scott Packing and Warehousing Ltd v Paterson* [1978] IRLR 166; *Dobie v Burns International Security Services (UK) Ltd* [1984] ICR 812, [1984] IRLR 329, CA.

[229] [1982] ICR 323, [1982] IRLR 143.

imbalance by concentrating more upon examining the changes imposed by the employer and considering whether it was *reasonable for the employee to reject them* (the case itself concerning major changes to overtime obligations, disadvantageous to the employee). However, in the event this case did not lead to a significant development in this area, for it did not decide what was to happen in the most difficult class of case, that is, where it was reasonable for the employee to reject the changes because of their effect on their livelihood, but equally it was reasonable for the employer to insist upon them because of the needs of its business; the fact that one party was acting reasonably does *not* mean that the other was therefore acting unreasonably.

On those grounds, a differently constituted EAT soon afterwards refused to follow *Evans* in *Chubb Fire Security Ltd v Harper*.[230] In that case, a middle way of sorts was suggested, namely that a tribunal might consider whether the employer had acted reasonably in deciding that the advantages of the reorganization to it outweighed the disadvantages to the employee. This is an interesting approach but it was stressed subsequently that this is only a *factor* (not a test) for a tribunal to consider when deciding whether the dismissal was fair within s 98(4) (as being within the range of reasonable responses that an employer faced with the employee's refusal to change might have adopted);[231] this is ultimately the test and its application, here as elsewhere, is a question of fact for the tribunal, as the Court of Appeal has emphasized.[232] In considering this question of fact, the EAT recently observed that acquiescence of most employees to a pay cut could be indicative of the reasonableness of dismissing those who refuse to accept it, but that the tribunal should consider 'the extent to which the workforce were or were not persuaded by reasons which were not good and proper reasons for adopting a common approach in favour of cuts'.[233]

So, there is some ability for an employee to challenge the economic case for the reorganization. This is in stark, and illogical, contrast with the position when the tribunal is considering a claim of unfair dismissal in relation to redundancy, where this is not open for review (see 8.1.4.1, 'No review of economic case for redundancy').

Was it necessary to insist on the change? An allied question is: given the reorganization plan, was it necessary to insist upon changing the employee's job in order to put that plan into effect? In many cases, the answer may simply be 'Yes', particularly where the employee is in a key position. It may be, however, that if only one or two employees are holding out, and their concurrence is not absolutely vital, the employer may be expected to consider any minor alterations to its plan which might accommodate those employees without frustrating the reorganization—especially if they have good reason to hold out, for example family care commitments which mean they cannot accept the whole of a proposed change in the hours of work.[234] Also, when the alteration is a pay cut owing to

[230] [1983] IRLR 311; applied in *Catamaran Cruisers Ltd v Williams* [1994] IRLR 386.

[231] *Richmond Precision Engineering Ltd v Pearce* [1985] IRLR 179. One point in this case had to be rectified subsequently, for it was suggested that the test is the reasonableness of the employer's offer; in fact, the correct test (under s 98) is the reasonableness of the decision to dismiss because of the employee's refusal of the offer: *St John of God (Care Services) Ltd v Brooks* [1992] ICR 715, [1992] IRLR 546. Further factors to consider may include how many other employees had accepted the changes and the attitude of any trade union involved: *Catamaran Cruisers Ltd v Williams* [1994] IRLR 386. The existence of a financial inducement to 'buy out' the old terms may also be relevant.

[232] *Gilham v Kent County Council (No 2)* [1985] ICR 233, [1985] IRLR 18, CA.

[233] *Garside & Laycock Ltd v Booth* [2011] IRLR 735, at para 23.

[234] *Martin v Automobile Proprietary Ltd* [1979] IRLR 64.

straitened economic circumstances, a tribunal might look into whether one employee or a group of them bears an unfair proportion of the burden:

> [T]here may be situations in which management proposes a cut to the pay of those who are not in management, but retains the pay of those who are in management as it has always been. A Tribunal would have to consider whether equity, with its implied sense of fair dealing in order to meet a combined challenge of reduced trading profits, would be served by dismissals of those refuseniks not in management in such a case.[235]

Factors which the Code of Practice says the employer should consider. Although the new Code of Practice[236] deals mainly with procedural matters, it does indicate in paragraphs 33 to 34 that before making a final decision to press ahead with dismissals an employer should re-examine the position and consider a number of questions which are more matters of substance rather than procedure. Paragraph 34 reads:

> Factors which an employer should consider include, but are not necessarily limited to:
>
> - the objectives which it is seeking to achieve
> - the negative consequences of imposing the proposed changes—these could include:
>   - risks to the employer's reputation
>   - damage to relationships with its workforce or representative trade unions
>   - the potential for strikes or other industrial action
>   - the risk of losing valued employees
>   - the risk of facing legal claims, and the associated costs and management time
> - whether its proposals could have a greater impact on some employees than others—this might be on the basis that they share a protected characteristic under the Equality Act 2010
> - whether there are any reasonable alternative ways of achieving the employer's objectives

Employment Rights Act 2025—most reorganization dismissals to become automatically unfair

In response to concern some quarters about 'fire and rehire', the Labour government elected in 2024 took steps impose much stricter controls by enacting the Employment Rights Act 2025. When section 28 of this is in force a new section 104I of the Employment Rights Act 1996 will make many such dismissals automatically unfair and will also introduce some changes for fire and rehire dismissals that fall outside the automatic unfairness.

First of all, it will prima facie be automatically unfair to dismiss an employee if either the reason is that they refused to agree to a 'restricted variation' to their contract or the reason for the dismissal is to enable the employer to re-engage the employee, or engage someone else, to carry out substantially the same duties but with a 'restricted variation' made to the terms of the contact of employment. The list of restricted variations covers reduction of pay, variation of a contractual term relating to pension, a change to working hours, a reduction in the amount of time off to which them employee is entitled, or any

[235] See n 233.

[236] Code of Practice on Dismissal and Re-engagement issued by the Secretary of State on 18 July 2024.

other category of variation prescribed in regulations. This prima facie automatic unfairness will apply unless the employer can prove both:

- that the reason for the restricted variation was to 'eliminate, prevent or significantly reduce, or significantly mitigate the effect of, any financial difficulties which at the time of the dismissal were affecting, or were likely in the immediate future to affect the employer's ability to carry on the business as a going concern' (or in the public sector to affect the financial sustainability of carrying out the employer's statutory functions); and
- that in all the circumstances the employer could not reasonably have avoided the need to make the restricted variation.

This is clearly a very substantial double hurdle for an employer to jump: it will be difficult to prove such an economic case to a tribunal, and thus in reality this provision will amount to a ban on restriction variations. In the unlikely event that an employer can jump this hurdle, that only means that the dismissal is not *automatically* unfair, and the employer will still need to show that the dismissal was reasonable in the same way as for fire and rehire dismissals carried out to achieve variations which are not on the restricted list, such as changes in the employees' duties.

Such dismissals—ones carried out so as to achieve contractual change which are not automatically unfair—will in principle remain potentially justifiable as SOSR dismissals, but with a twist. The twist is that a new section 104I(11) and 104J(5) in ERA 1996 will require a tribunal when deciding whether the dismissal is fair or unfair to include in the matters it considers any consultation with the employees and employee representatives, anything offered to the employees by the employer in return for agreeing to the variation and any other matter specified in regulations. In the case of a dismissal to achieve a non-restricted variation the tribunal must also consider the reason for the variation. The reality is that this adds little if anything to what is already relevant in considering fairness in an SOSR case. Moreover it seems clear that the assessment of fairness, bearing in mind factors such as these, will remain a matter of deciding whether the employer's decision fell within the 'range of reasonable responses'.

The Employment Rights Act 2025 will also introduce provisions to address the situation where an employer dismisses employees in order to engage *non-employees* to carry out substantially the same work. As discussed in 8.1.1.2, such dismissals are for redundancy since they result from the employer requiring fewer employees to carry out work of a particular kind. Under new s 104K, such dismissals will be automatically unfair unless the employer can establish that the facts meet the same exceptions as for dismissal to achieve a 'restricted variation'. If the employer can meet those requirements then in deciding whether the dismissal is fair or unfair, the tribunal will be required to consider similar factors, such as the consultation carried out, to those which apply in the case of dismissal to achieve a restricted variation.

8.2 Transfers of undertakings

8.2.1 Introduction

8.2.1.1 Background

This part of the chapter considers the rules relating to transfers of undertakings. Domestic law has had rules since 1963 preserving continuity of employment through a business transfer but these only operated if the new owner *chose* to take on the existing staff and even if the new owner did so choose the law did not prevent it employing the workers on different terms—which could be less favourable terms. European law has, since the early

1980s, required member states to have laws which go much further in that they enact a system of compulsory transfer under which most of the existing terms of employment are preserved, with accompanying consultation and information obligations. The resulting UK provisions were the TUPE Regulations, which were often suggested as a likely target for post-Brexit deregulation, but so far little has happened in relation to this.

8.2.1.2 What the regulations do

In short, where all or part of an undertaking is transferred to a new operator, whether by sale or otherwise, then the law automatically transfers the employees assigned to that undertaking, or part of the undertaking, to the new operator. The new operator inherits them on their existing contractual terms (save in relation to pension) and also inherits any employment-related rights and liabilities (eg liability for any discriminatory act or any personal injury done before the transfer and any liability for arrears of pay). The law also constrains the new employer's ability to dismiss such employees or to change their terms of employment. In addition, any union recognition in relation to the workers may transfer. Further, prior to the transfer, the old employer must inform and consult with any recognized trade union (or, if there is none, with employee representatives).

8.2.1.3 The legislation and its deficiencies

The compulsory transfer rules were contained for a quarter of a century in the Transfer of Undertakings (Protection of Employment) Regulations 1981, which implemented the Business Transfers Directive 77/187/EC, also known as the Acquired Rights Directive. That Directive was replaced in 2001 by an amended Directive 2001/23/EC. The UK TUPE regulations were amended and reissued in 2006. The Directive and the Regulations have been the cause of a great deal of uncertainty and many appeal cases have been brought in order to settle uncertain areas. The difficulties stem from two main issues.

First, the Directive is framed in typically vague EU legislative language so the meaning of parts of it was unclear. This was compounded by the fact that these new laws were not wanted by the Conservative government in power in 1981 and this affected their eventual form—they took the form of regulations simply placed on top of existing UK law with little or no attempt to integrate them. Moreover, in an exercise of minimum compliance, the government adopted the 'copy-out' technique of drafting, lifting large parts directly from the Directive with no attempt to 'translate' them into concepts more akin to existing law.[237]

Second, the Directive is so framed as to work better in states where large proportions of the workforce have terms governed by collectively agreed terms and conditions—terms which often have legislative support. Some aspects of the Directive did not therefore fit well with either the UK legal framework or the industrial relations realities of the UK. This again led to uncertainty as to the meaning of TUPE in the UK and as to how to deliver the Directive's aims in the UK.

Some of the uncertainties of interpretation were resolved by ECJ decisions in the 1980s and 1990s and so when the UK regulations were updated in 2006 the opportunity was taken to supplement the previous wording of the 1981 regulations to spell out those matters now settled by case law. Some minor amendments to the 2006 TUPE regulations were made in 2014.

TUPE has had a major effect on commercial practice because the possible liabilities to be inherited by an acquiring organization are often a significant consideration in commercial dealings. TUPE applies not only to the paradigm case where a business or part

[237] The best example is the transposition of the 'economic, technical or organizational reasons' defence to unfair dismissal, which had and still has no counterpart in domestic law.

of a business is sold to a new owner, but also—in the UK at least—to the contracting-out and contracting-in of services such as cleaning, catering, IT support, and human resources operations. As will be discussed below at 8.2.4, the unpredictability of the tribunals' application of TUPE to such contracting was so great that in 2006 the UK took the unusual step of legislating beyond the scope set out in the Directive so as to make the transfer laws apply more widely than European law required.

Two further points may be noted by way of introduction. The first is that the genesis of the Regulations in an EU Directive may well be important in any case requiring their interpretation, because it means that a purposive interpretation of the TUPE Regulations is required, resolving any ambiguity in the light of the intent of the Directive. This remains the case notwithstanding Brexit, although the UK courts now have some freedom to move away from European Court of Justice case law where they are satisfied that such authority misunderstands the Directive. The second point is that there may be further considerations than the TUPE Regulations in the public sector; transfers within and from the Civil Service (widely defined) have for many years been governed by the Cabinet Office Statement of Practice: Staff Transfers in the Public Sector,[238] which seeks to ensure that TUPE principles are always the norm and which does require protection of pension position.

8.2.2 **The two kinds of TUPE transfer**

The 2006 Regulations apply to two situations:

1. Transfers within the core definition: the transfer of an undertaking, business, or part of an undertaking to another person where there is a transfer of an economic entity which retains its identity.[239]
2. Contracting-out and -in transfers: this is called in the TUPE Regulations a 'service provision change' and is where an organized grouping of employees which has as its principal purpose the carrying out of the activities of the employer is contracted out or, if already contracted out, is either moved to a new contractor or taken back in-house.[240]

Situation 1 is the core European concept of a TUPE transfer and the definition is taken directly from the Directive. Situation 2 is a UK-only extension which was adopted in order to try to resolve uncertainty in contracting-out and contracting-in cases, by expressly providing that all such cases are governed by TUPE. In the UK the law of TUPE has the same effect on both categories of transfer, but before examining those rules we need to consider in detail the scope of the two categories of transfer.

8.2.3 **Transfers within the core definition**

This is defined as the transfer of an undertaking, business, or part of an undertaking to another person where there is a transfer of an economic entity which retains its identity.[241] The reference to a transfer 'to another person' imposes the major limitation that TUPE does not apply to the takeover of a company by the purchase of its shares because in such a case the employer remains the same—the limited company concerned. This is the case even if such an arrangement is adopted deliberately to avoid the Regulations.[242] However, there are occasions when the shares in a company are sold (which is not a TUPE transfer)

[238] May 2014: <https://www.gov.uk/government/publications/staff-transfers-in-the-public-sector>.
[239] Regulation 3(1)(a). [240] Regulation 3(1)(b). [241] Regulation 3(1)(a).
[242] *Brooks v Borough Care Services* [1998] ICR 1198, [1998] IRLR 636.

but subsequently the new corporate parent begins to merge its management with that of the new subsidiary to the extent that the right characterization of the situation is that the business of the subsidiary has been moved into the business of the parent and therefore, at that later point in time, there has been a TUPE transfer.[243]

'Economic entity' is defined in reg 3(2) as 'an organised grouping of resources which has the objective of pursuing an economic activity, whether or not that activity is central or ancillary'. This formulation is taken primarily from the leading and often cited ECJ decision in *Spijkers v Gebroeders Benedik Abbattoir BV*[244] and has two principal effects. The first is that it places emphasis on the continued viability of that which is transferred; the DTI guidance refers to the transfer of a business 'as a going concern' (a useful phrase, though it does not appear in the Regulations) and this may be particularly important where (as in *Spijkers* itself) it is a *part* that is being transferred, raising possibly the question whether it was the transfer of part of a business or merely the sale of an asset. The second effect is that the test concentrates on the reality of the situation (potentially from the employees' standpoint) rather than requiring any particular form of legal transfer.[245] Thus, early ECJ case law upheld the application of the Directive to the transfer merely of some form of business lease or franchise, with the employees going into the employment of the new lessee or franchisee.[246] The fact that the business was closed at the time of the transfer does not prevent the conclusion that an undertaking has been transferred.[247]

The economic entity must 'retain its identity' and the *Spijkers* case says the following factors much be considered when determining this:

- The type of undertaking or business concerned
- Whether tangible assets, such as buildings and movable property, are transferred
- Whether or not the majority of the employees assigned to the undertaking are taken over by the new employer
- Whether or not the customers of the business are transferred
- The degree of similarity between the activities carried on before and after the transfer
- The period, if any, for which the activities are suspended in connection with the transfer.

[243] *Guvera Ltd v Butler* UKEAT/0265/16 (21 November 2017, unreported); *Jackson Lloyd Ltd and Mears Group plc v Smith* UKEAT/0127/13 (4 April 2014, unreported); cf *ICAP Management Services Ltd v Berry* [2017] EWHC 1321 (QB), [2017] IRLR 811.

[244] 24/85 [1986] ECR 1119, [1986] 2 CMLR 296, ECJ. See also, at ECJ level, *Franciso Hernandez SA v Gomez Perez* C-127/96 [1999] IRLR 132; *Sanchez Hidalgo v ASEN* C-173/96 [1999] IRLR 136; and *Allen v Amalgamated Construction Ltd* C-234/98 [2000] IRLR 119.

[245] That is, reg 3(6)(b) states that a transfer may take place whether or not any property is transferred.

[246] *Foreningen af Arbejdsledere i Danmark v Daddy's Dance Hall A/S*: 324/86 [1988] IRLR 315, ECJ; *Landsoganisationen i Danmark v Ny Molle Kro* C-287/86 [1989] ICR 330, [1989] IRLR 37, ECJ; *Berg v Besselsenn*: C-144/87 [1990] ICR 396, [1989] IRLR 447, ECJ. A much-reported case showing such an approach in a more mainstream context is the *Christel Schmidt* case: C-392/92 [1994] ECR I-1311, [1995] 2 CMLR 331, ECJ. There can be a relevant transfer between two companies in the same group: *Allen v Amalgamated Construction Ltd* C-234/98 [2000] ICR 436, [2000] IRLR 119, ECJ. However, the definition is not infinitely elastic, and domestic courts have held that there was no transfer on the redeployment of a bank's staff from a subsidiary to a new department (*BIFU v Barclays Bank plc* [1987] ICR 495) or where employees were changed from direct staff to agency workers (*Wynnwith Engineering Co Ltd v Bennett* [2002] IRLR 170).

[247] *Bork International A/S (in liquidation) v Foreningen of Arbejdsledere i Danmark* 101/87 [1989] IRLR 41, ECJ and *Sigüenza v Ayuntamiento de Valladolid In-Pulso Musical Sociedad Cooperativa*: C-472/16, [2018] IRLR 1056, CJEU. See also *Wood v Caledon Social Club Limited* UKEAT/0528/09, [2010] AllER (d) 79 (Sep), where the business was closed for four months.

This is not a checklist: every factor need not point in the direction of a transfer; rather, it is a list of factors which needs to be considered in reaching a conclusion on the legal question of whether or not the identity of the economic entity has been retained.

The ECJ has held that the Acquired Rights Directive applies to transfer employees from transferor to transferee 'where the part of the undertaking or business transferred does not retain its organisational autonomy, provided that the functional link between the various elements of production transferred is preserved, and that that link enables the transferee to use those elements to pursue an identical or analogous economic activity'.[248] In other words, a transferee cannot avoid the application of the Directive (and hence TUPE) by breaking up the transferred undertaking and integrating it into the transferee's existing management structure.

In addition to the general definition, there are subsidiary rules stating that immediately before the transfer the undertaking, business, or part must have been situated in the UK,[249] that the Regulations apply to public and private undertakings engaged in economic activities whether or not they are operated for gain,[250] but that an administrative reorganization of public administrative authorities or the transfer of administrative functions between public authorities does not constitute a transfer for these purposes.[251] It is further specifically provided that a relevant transfer may be effected by a series of two or more transactions,[252] but some care may be needed here because the ECJ has held that ultimately a transfer must take place at one moment, that is, it is not possible to have it take place over an extended period.[253] Further, that moment is when responsibility for conducting the business changes hands, and this might, for example, be either before or after the date of sale of a business and also might, in a case involving transfer in stages, be part way through the serios of transactions.[254] Inevitable this is vague, but it is hard to see how a more precise definition of when the transfer takes place could be laid down without opening up the possibility of unfairness and indeed without creating the opportunity for well-advised employers to evade the intended effect of TUPE in protecting employees.

TUPE regulation 8(7) excludes from the transfer of employment contracts and liabilities and form the control of dismissals of employees because of relevant transfer cases where the transferor is the subject of bankruptcy proceedings or any analogous insolvency proceedings which have been instituted with a view to the liquidation of the assets of the transferor and are under the supervision of an insolvency practitioner. Note that this does not mean that all cases involving insolvency proceedings are excluded from the scope of TUPE;

[248] *Klarenberg v Ferrotron Technologies* [2009] All ER (D) 133 (Feb). See, further, McMullen 'Leaving a Legacy: Recent Jurisprudence of the European Court on Transfers of Undertakings' (2021) 50 ILJ 130 at p 144.

[249] Regulation 3(1)(a). Note, however, that if this is the case the Regulations apply even if the transfer or the employment of the employees is governed by foreign law (reg 3(4)(b)) and/or persons employed by the undertaking transferred ordinarily work outside the UK (reg 3(4)(c)).

[250] Regulation 3(4)(a). The original 1981 Regulations excluded undertakings of a non-commercial nature but ECJ case law showed that this was contrary to the Directive (particularly in *Dr Sophie Redmond Stichting v Bartol* C-29/91 [1992] IRLR 366) and it was removed in 1993.

[251] Regulation 3(5); this codifies the decision in *Henke v Gemeinde Schievke* C-298/94 [1996] IRLR 701, ECJ.

[252] Regulation 3(6)(a); *Longden v Ferrari Ltd* [1994] ICR 443, [1994] IRLR 157. This may be particularly relevant on a re-tendering of a contracted-out service: *Dines v Initial Health Care Services Ltd* [1994] IRLR 336, CA.

[253] *Celtec Ltd v Astley* C-478/03 [2005] IRLR 647, ECJ. On a partial privatization in 1990, civil servants went on secondment to the new body for three years before formally taking employment with it. The ECJ ruled against any 'continuing' transfer over three years. Applying this, a divided House of Lords held that they had actually transferred in 1990, even though no one had realized(!): see [2006] ICR 992, [2006] IRLR 635, HL.

[254] *Rajput v Commerzbank AG* [2023] EAT 116, [2023] IRLR 957.

in particular in *some* 'pre-pack' cases (where a business is put into liquidation and then immediately sold to a buyer which has been lined up in in advance) TUPE may still apply.[255]

8.2.4 **Contracting-out and contracting-in transfers**

8.2.4.1 **Developments before the 2006 regulations**

Organizations often contract out certain services (such as catering or cleaning), on the basis that such services can be more efficiently and cheaply provided by specialists. When this happens, staff who previously performed these services in-house will often be taken on by the successful contractors, but before TUPE when this happened there would be a clean break with the old employer, so that (a) the contractor did not assume any responsibility for any accrued rights (in particular, accrued redundancy rights) and (b) it was free to take on only some of the old workforce and/or then to 'adjust' (ie diminish) their old terms and conditions, to reduce labour costs. Clearly, if the TUPE Regulations applied, neither of those assumptions would survive and some of the attraction of contracting-out would be called into question—although there would still be some scope for saving labour costs because a contractor might be able to do the work with fewer staff and because TUPE does not transfer full pension rights to the new employer.

In *Rask v ISS Kantineservice A/S*,[256] the ECJ held that the Directive applied where a large private company had contracted out the running of a staff canteen to a service company and an existing employee entered the latter's employment; the result was that when the service company changed one of the employee's terms of employment she could claim the protection of the Danish legislation enacting the Directive.[257] This was followed by the British courts when interpreting TUPE.[258]

This broad approach seemed to be taken to its logical conclusion by the decision of the ECJ in the *Christel Schmidt* case.[259] The ECJ held that where an employee who was the sole cleaner of a particular branch of a bank was dismissed when that service function was contracted out to the firm that already provided it with other cleaning services, this dismissal was contrary to the Acquired Rights Directive. This was so in spite of the facts that (a) all that was 'transferred' was a purely ancillary function (not part of the bank's principal business), (b) only one employee was involved, and (c) there was no transfer whatsoever of any tangible assets.

However, *Schmidt* was followed by another ECJ judgment which appeared to pull back from this very generous interpretation of a 'transfer of an undertaking'. This was the case of *Ayse Süzen*,[260] and it caused heartache even to TUPE-hardened employment lawyers. The ECJ stated that a contracting-out of an activity where no significant tangible or

[255] Contrast *Federatie Nederlandes Vakvereniging v Smallsteps BV* C-1126, [2017] IRLR 852 and *Federatie Nederlandse Vakbeweging v Heiploeg Seafood International BV* C-237/20, [2023] IRLR 405.

[256] C-209/91 [1993] IRLR 133, ECJ.

[257] At least in *Rask* it concerned an employee who wanted to be there and whom the transferee wanted to employ; automatic transfer means that a firm contracting for a service would notionally have to take on *all* the employees currently doing the job (even those it had not planned on keeping), with all their accrued rights.

[258] *Kenny v South Manchester College* [1993] ICR 934, [1993] IRLR 265, and TUPE was also held to apply when a contract-out service was contract moved from one supplier to another (*Dines v Initial Health Care Services* [1995] ICR 11, [1994] IRLR 336, CA) and when a contracted-out service was brought back in-house (*Isles of Scilly Council v Brintel Helicopters Ltd* [1995] ICR 249, [1995] IRLR 6, EAT).

[259] *Schmidt v Spar und Leihkasse der früheren Ämter Bordesholm, Kiel und Cronshagen* C-392/92 [1994] ECR I-1311, [1995] 2 CMLR 331, ECJ.

[260] *Süzen v Zehnacker Gebäudereinigung GmbH Krankenhausservice*: C-13/95 [1997] ICR 662, [1997] IRLR 255, ECJ. A similar approach was taken subsequently by the ECJ in *Francisco Hernández Vidal SA v Gomez Perez*: C-127/96 [1999] IRLR 132, ECJ and *Sánchez Hidalgo v Asociación de Servicios Aser and Sociedad Cooperativa Minerva* C-173/96 [2002] ICR 73, [1999] IRLR 136, ECJ, though (it has been argued) with more emphasis on the importance of the workforce itself as the 'economic entity' in a labour-intensive industry.

intangible assets are used, referred to as a labour-intensive undertaking, will be covered by the Directive *so long as* the new contractor takes over a major part, in terms of their numbers and skills, of the employees assigned by his predecessor to that task. This raises the possibility that the question 'Is the new contractor obliged by the law of TUPE to employer these workers?' is answered by considering whether the new employer did in fact *choose* to employ them. This highly circular argument is of course unsatisfactory and its adoption by the ECJ also appeared to open the way for 'evasion' of TUPE by the simple expedient of the new contractor not taking on many of the old contractor's employees. The concern about evasion was quickly addressed by the Court of Appeal in *ECM (Vehicle Delivery Service) Ltd v Cox*,[261] which held that *all* the circumstances of the transfer must be considered, *including* any intent to evade the Regulations.

However, the main problem with *Ayse Süzen* remained: the circularity and therefore the illogicality of making whether the law had the effect of transferring employees depend on whether the major part, in terms of their numbers and skills, of the employees were in fact taken on by the alleged transferee employer. In practice the UK tribunals tended to decide that TUPE did apply to contracting-out cases, but nevertheless there was a period of huge uncertainty where lawyers could only advise the parties that TUPE probably applied to particular service provision changes (or, occasionally, that it probably did not). The practical difficulties were demonstrated by the fact that the courts in most other EU states took a narrower view than the UK tribunals as to when a contracting-out was covered by their TUPE laws, so that where an international business sought to contract out, say, its IT support function, the company would be advised that the UK staff would probably transfer to the new contractor and the staff in other countries probably would not.

One other aspect of *Ayse Süzen* should be noted. The Court indicated that in a case where significant tangible assets are used, then the transfer of those assets, or not, to the new contractor will be important in determining whether there has been a TUPE transfer. On that basis, in *Oy Liikenne AB v Liskojarvi and Juntunen*[262] the ECJ held that there was no TUPE transfer when a bus company lost a contract to run seven bus routes and the new contractor did not take over any of the buses used. However, no single factor is likely ever to be decisive: all the relevant *Spijkers* circumstances mast be assessed. This is illustrated by a decision of the CJEU in a subsequent bus contract case, *Grafe and Pohle v Südbrandenburger Nahverkehrs GmbH.*[263] In that case the new contractor did not take over any buses, nor any depots. It was argued that there were good reasons for the new contractor not to take on the bus assets since more stringent requirements applied for the future: there were tougher emission requirements and disabled access had to be provided. The court held that the taking over of the buses, or not, was not the sole determining factor and in a case like the one under consideration where there were legal, environmental, or technical constraints on doing so a court might still decide that other factual circumstances, such as the taking over of the majority of the employees, whose skills were rare in the rural area where the service operated, and the pursuit, without interruption, of the service, meant that this was a transfer governed by the Directive.

8.2.4.2 **The reforms in the 2006 regulations**

The government acted fairly quickly to resolve the uncertainty stemming from *Ayse Süzen* when it made the new 2006 TUPE Regulations, by introducing a new category of situation, the service provision change, which would be governed by TUPE. This means

[261] [1999] ICR 1162, [1999] IRLR 559, CA.
[262] C-172/99, [2001] IRLR 171.
[263] C 298/18, [2020] IRLR 399. These two bus contract cases are discussed, and the *Grafe* decision welcomed, in McMullen 'Leaving a Legacy: Recent Jurisprudence of the European Court on Transfers of Undertakings' (2021) 50 ILJ 130 at p 138.

that in practice all, or perhaps nearly all, contracting-out cases in the UK are governed by TUPE even if the Directive would not require them to be covered.

One purpose of enacting a regime where TUPE should be the norm is to create the proverbial level playing field so that all parties know the rules and can tender and contract on that basis (including as to price, which may be sensitive to the employment liabilities to be taken on by a successful tenderer). This endeavour has been successful and the service provision industries have proceeded since 2006 on that basis. When the Conservative–Liberal Democrat government consulted in 2013, as part of its deregulation initiative, on abolishing the service provision change part of TUPE on the basis that it constituted unnecessary 'gold-plating' of EU legal requirements, there was almost unanimous support from employers and unions to retain this component of TUPE. The government abandoned the proposal,[264] which ironically confirms that in one of the few cases where it could be clearly shown that UK implementation of European employment law *was* 'gold-plated', this was actually something which was as welcome to the representatives of capital as to the representatives of labour.

Regulation 3(1)(b) applies the statutory scheme to a first-generation contracting-out, a second-generation contracting-out, and a contracting-back-in-again, provided that:

(a) immediately before the service provision change—

  (i) there is an organized grouping of employees[265] situated in Great Britain which has as its principal purpose the carrying out of the activities concerned on behalf of the client;[266]

  (ii) the client intends that the activities will, following the service provision change, be carried out by the transferee other than in connection with a single specific event or task of short-term duration;[267] and

(b) the activities concerned do not consist wholly or mainly of the supply of goods for the client's use.[268]

There is a further condition in reg 3(2A) that the activities must remain 'fundamentally the same' before and after the transfer.[269] In assessing this question a tribunal must approach the matter in a common-sense and pragmatic way. Activities should not be defined at such a level of generality that they do not really describe the specific activities at all but nevertheless the definition of the activities should be holistic and avoid too narrow a focus since a pedantic and excessively detailed

[264] Transfer of Undertakings (Protection of Employment) Regulations 2006 Government Response to Consultation, September 2013.

[265] This includes a single employee (reg 2(1)), thus covering the position in *Cristel Schmidt*, n 259; see also *Rynda (UK) Ltd v Rhijnsburger* [2015] EWCA Civ 75, [2015] IRLR 394.

[266] 'Client' can be read as 'clients' where they act with a common intention—for example a number of residents' management companies who engaged a property maintenance service provider and who changed to a new provider: *Duncan v Ottimo Property Services Ltd* [2015] IRLR 806.

[267] This single/short-term exception requires that the client intends the work only to be a single task or short-term; if the client intends the activities to go on for some time, but only intends a specific transferee to do them short-term, this does not satisfy the exception and a TUPE transfer will have occurred: *Mustafa v Trek Highways Services Ltd and other companies* [2016] IRLR 326, EAT; see also *Heathman Ltd t/a County Contractors v Quadron Property Services Ltd* UKEAT/0451/15 (22 January 2016, unreported).

[268] Regulation 3(3). Head (b) is there to prevent an 'accidental' TUPE transfer when the client swaps supplier of, for example, a photocopier (ie the engineer who had always serviced it is not inadvertently transferred by law from that supplier to the new one).

[269] As to what happens where an activity is split between several different contractors see 8.2.7.2.

definition of 'activities' would risk defeating the purpose of the service provision change provisions.[270]

The overall aim of this new formulation is to avoid the uncertainties of the previous case law[271] to ensure that TUPE protection will be the norm (protecting all those who need it to retain their employment), but at the same time to ensure that TUPE does not apply where it would be unnecessary and indeed positively harmful. Some examples may illustrate this:

- A small cleaning company with three employees loses its one big contract on which the three employees have spent all of their time; there is no replacement work. In this case the employees need TUPE protection and the reference in reg 3(3)(a)(i) to an organized grouping of employees with the principal purpose of serving that client ensures that there is a TUPE transfer, so that they are transferred to the company obtaining the contract.[272]
- A major security company has many contracts in a particular town. Its long-standing employee AB is moved around from one contract to another from time to time but happens to be working at one contracted client at the time that contract is lost to a competitor. Employee AB simply expects that the following day they will be sent to work at another client's premises and has no desire whatsoever to change employment to the competitor company winning the contract.[273] The wording of reg 3(3)(a) (i) should ensure that there is no undesired application of automatic transfer because AB is not part of an organized grouping of employees which has as its principal purpose the carrying out of the activities concerned on behalf of the client.[274]
- The affairs of a major client of a law firm are handled by one 'dedicated' team of lawyers and the firm loses that client to another law firm. The lawyers and support staff in the team would probably expect, and wish, to remain with their old firm, but TUPE may have a different result: clearly the original firm remains in existence, but the question is whether the team that handled the work of the client is an organized grouping of employees which has as its principal purpose the carrying out of the activities concerned on behalf of the client. It is entirely possible that an employment

[270] *Salvation Army Trustee Company v Coventry Cyrenians Ltd* [2017] IRLR 410, EAT. For appeal cases holding particular activities to be or not to be fundamentally the same see *Enterprise Management Services Ltd v Connect-up Ltd* [2012] IRLR 190, EAT, *Johnson Controls v UK Atomic Energy Authority* UKEAT/0041/12 (14 February 2012, unreported), *OCS Group Uk Ltd v Jones* UKEAT/0038/09 (4 August 2009, unreported) and *Tuitt v LB of Richmond on Thames* [2022]EAT 124, [2022] IRLR 1035.

[271] Particularly the regrettable decision in *Ayse Süzen*, n 260. For a definitive discussion of the recent case law in this area see McMullen 'The Developing Case Law on TUPE and Service Provision Change' (2016) 45 ILJ 220.

[272] This logic was applied, for example, in *Salvation Army v Bahi* UKEAT/0120/16/RN (unreported), where the employees of one of 20 small charities supplying homelessness support to the council were TUPE transferred to the Salvation Army when it won the contract to consolidate the work of the 20 charities. Compare this to *Amaryllis Ltd v McLeod* UKEAT/0273/15 (9 June 2016, unreported), where no TUPE transfer occurred because there was no organized grouping providing work to the client at the time of the new tender, even though there had historically been one.

[273] *C T Plus (Yorkshire) CIC v Stagecoach*, [2016] UKEAT 0035_16_0308 (this case is not on all fours with the example, but involves a client (Hull City Council) who decided to cancel a contractor's services when a third party set up a competing business in roughly the same place, making the services unnecessary—there was no TUPE transfer here, and the third party was not required to take on the employees of the original contractor).

[274] However, the exact facts of each case are important: if one or more workers are assigned to one particular client for a period of time the point will come where they constitute an organized grouping which has as its principal purpose providing a service to that client.

tribunal would decide that TUPE transferred this team to the new law firm.[275] As will be seen, however, the employees could if they wish opt out of the transfer—and may do so if the old firm indicates it is happy to continue to employ them.

8.2.5 **Consultation on transfers of undertaking**

If a projected transfer does qualify as a 'TUPE transfer', reg 13 imposes duties to inform and consult and reg 15 contains enforcement provisions similar in part to those applying to redundancy consultation, but with one significant difference: there is no minimum number of affected employees—even if only one employee will be affected by the transfer, the collective information and consultation rules apply.

8.2.5.1 **Appropriate representatives**

The law on whether the appropriate representatives for consultation are trade union officials or elected or nominated employee representatives, and on elections for employee representatives, is contained in regs 13 and 14. For an account of the identical collective redundancy provisions see 8.1.3.2.

The 2014 TUPE amendments introduced a provision allowing small businesses to consult directly with individual employees if there are no 'appropriate representatives' in place, rather than having to call an election for the purpose of consultation. This was expanded in 2024, and now applies in any case where the employer has fewer than 50 employees or, even if there are more than 50 employees where the transfer is in respect of fewer than ten employees.[276]

As in the case of consultation on impending collective redundancies, employee representatives are given special legal protection against victimization, dismissal, and subsequent selection for redundancy, on the grounds of having fulfilled those functions; there is also a statutory right to time off work with pay for fulfilling them or for training.[277]

8.2.5.2 **The duty to inform**

Long enough before a relevant transfer to enable the employer of any affected employees[278] to consult all their appropriate representatives, the employer must give those representatives information regarding (a) the fact that the relevant transfer is to take place, when, and the reasons[279] for it; (b) the legal, economic, and social implications[280] for the

[275] *Royden v Barnetts Solicitors* ET Case No 21043451/07 is an example. But see the rather surprising conclusion in *Ward Hadaway Solicitors v Love* UKEAT/0471/09/SM (25 March 2010, unreported) where a client moved its regular flow of work from one law firm to another, that the activities carried out by the first firm were just the cases that had been allocated to it already, and which were to be completed by that firm, and not the new cases which went to the second law firm and so there was no transfer of activities.

[276] Regulation 13A.

[277] Employment Rights Act 1996, ss 47,103, 105, and 61, respectively.

[278] An affected employee is defined as an employee of either the transferor or transferee who may be affected by the transfer or may be affected by measures taken in connection with it: reg 13(1). This is a very wide definition, particularly as it also says that the employee does not have to be employed in the undertaking or part thereof to be transferred. As such, it seems open-ended, given that a transfer 'may' affect practically anyone in the two businesses in some way, which could cause problems of line drawing in businesses which recognize several unions (particularly if they know their Donne: no man is an island; any man's transfer diminishes me).

[279] These must be the real reasons, and a breach will occur if the employer misrepresents its reasons: *LLDY Alexandria Ltd v Unite the Union and Peopleforwork Ltd* UKEATS/0002/14/SM (30 April 2014, unreported).

[280] It suffices for the employer to tell employees what it genuinely believes will be the legal, economic, and social implications of the transfer, even if it is wrong: *Royal Mail Group v Communication Workers Union* [2009] All ER (D) 07.

affected employees; (c) the measures the employer envisages will be taken in relation to those employees in connection with the transfer; and (d) if the employer is the transferor, the measures which the transferee envisages will be taken.[281] In order to enable the transferor to discharge this last obligation under (d) the transferee must give him the necessary information.[282]

One possible problem relates to the timing. The Regulations say that the information must be given 'long enough before a relevant transfer to enable consultations to take place', which is not further defined or qualified (contrast this with the provisions on collective redundancies); moreover, as has been pointed out,[283] head (a) of the information to be given concerns the *fact* that the transfer is to take place, that is, there need be no information or consultation at the stage of *proposals* for a transfer.[284]

8.2.5.3 **Consultation**

Where an employer of affected employees envisages that it will be 'taking measures' in relation to them in connection with the transfer, it must enter into consultations with the appropriate representatives with a view to seeking their agreement to measures to be taken, and in doing so must (a) consider any representations and (b) reply to them, giving reasons for any rejections.[285] If there are special circumstances making it not reasonably practicable for an employer to inform or consult as required, it must take all steps as are reasonably practicable in the circumstances to comply; this means that an employer cannot say that, merely because full compliance was impossible, it did not need to do anything at all.[286]

In practice the transferor rarely envisages that it will be taking any measures in relation to the transferring workforce: it will just be saying 'goodbye' to them. That means that although the transferor must provide the employee representatives with the information outlined above, it is not obliged to enter into any consultation. The *transferee* may well envisage taking measures, such as changing the place of work or the working hours, or making some redundancies or perhaps devising a new incentive scheme. However, the transferee is only obliged to consult about measures which will affect its employees and, before the transfer, the employees who will be affected by the measures which the transferee intends to take are not employed by the transferee.[287] Moreover, it has been held that the consultation obligation is a pre-transfer obligation so the transferee employer does not come under any obligation to consult *under TUPE* after the workers have become its employees.[288]

[281] Regulation 13(2). [282] Regulation 13(4).

[283] Hepple (1982) 11 ILJ at 38.

[284] Again this may be contrasted with the provisions on collective redundancies, where the Trade Union and Labour Relations (Consolidation) Act 1992, s 188 requires an employer 'proposing' to make redundancies to consult recognized unions: see 8.1.3.3. Regulation 10(10) provides that where the employer is going through the process of electing representatives, the employer complies with the time requirement if it acts as soon as reasonably practicable after the representatives are elected. If the employees fail to elect representatives within a reasonable time, the employer may give individual affected employees the information required by law, and is then absolved from collective consultation: reg 10(11).

[285] Regulation 13(6), (7). In *Institution of Professional Civil Servants v Secretary of State for Defence* [1987] IRLR 373 (decided under the Dockyard Services Act 1986, which adopted and applied the provisions of this regulation), Millett J emphasized that although the obligation to give information applied to all four heads above, the obligation to consult only applies to head (3), the measures which are envisaged; his judgment gives guidance on the meaning of 'measures', which is not defined in the Regulations.

[286] Regulation 13(9). This establishes a 'special circumstances' defence in similar terms to that applying to collective redundancies (see 8.1.3.8). Presumably the case law which has arisen in that context will be applied here.

[287] Of course post-transfer measures envisaged by the employer may also affect people who *are* already the transferee's employees (its current workforce), in which case TUPE obliges the transferee to consult, before the transfer, with the representatives of its current employees about those measures.

[288] *AMICUS and others v City Building (Glasgow) LLP and others* [2009] IRLR 253.

The nonsensical situation therefore is that although affected employees must be informed in advance by the transferor employer, through their representatives, about any measures that the new employer envisages taking, they have no right to be consulted through their representatives about these changes in advance of the transfer. In practice, because of the risk that a workforce which is told that significant measures will be taken by the transferee may become very unsettled, the transferor employer usually permits the transferee employee to consult with the representatives in advance of the transfer date. Indeed, as seen in 8.1.3.5, the law now provides that if this happens when redundancies are envisaged by the transferee employer, that employer may discharge its collective redundancy consultation obligation before the transfer.

8.2.5.4 **Enforcement provision**

As in the case of a failure to consult on impending redundancies, a complaint of failure to comply with reg 13 may be presented to a tribunal by the employee representatives, or the recognized trade union, or, in any other case, by any affected employee.[289] Where employees are represented by a trade union or elected representatives, only those representatives can bring the claim.[290] The employer may raise the 'special circumstances' defence (ie that there were such circumstances making performance of the obligations not reasonably practicable *and* that it did all that was reasonably practicable in the circumstances), in which case the burden of proof is upon it.[291]

Prior to the 2006 Regulations liability for a failure by the transferor to consult on an impending transfer was one of the liabilities which transferred to the transferee under what is now reg 4 of TUPE,[292] but there is now joint liability on transferor and transferee.[293] The policy behind this is to stop the transferor deliberately flouting the requirement in the knowledge that the transferee would pick up the bill if challenged.

If the tribunal finds the complaint well founded it must make a declaration to that effect and award compensation to affected employees up to a maximum of 13 weeks' pay.[294] This became of particular significance when it was subsequently held in *Sweetin v Coral Racing*[295] that (in line with the protective award in collective redundancy law) this award is punitive (not merely compensatory) and meant to act as a deterrent; the result is that a tribunal should start in each case at the maximum and only reduce it if the employer proves mitigation.

[289] Regulation 15(1). The complaint must be brought within three months of the date on which the transfer was completed (undefined): reg 15(12); it may be brought *before* the transfer is effected: *Banking Insurance and Finance Union v Barclays Bank plc* [1987] ICR 495; *South Durham Health Authority v UNISON* [1995] ICR 495, [1995] IRLR 407.

[290] *Northgate HR Ltd v Mercy* [2008] IRLR 222.

[291] Regulation 15(2). If the complaint is against the transferor, who maintains that the reason for default was that the transferee had not provided the necessary information, the transferor cannot raise the special circumstances defence unless the transferee is joined as a party to the proceedings: reg 15(5).

[292] *Alamo Group (Europe) Ltd v Tuckes* [2003] ICR 829, [2003] IRLR 266.

[293] Regulation 15(9).

[294] Regulation 15(8). If it is not paid, the employee may complain to the tribunal within three months of the date of the order: reg 15(10)–(12). One innovation in the 2006 Regulations was to make the transferor and transferee employers jointly and severally liable (reg 15(9)); it will be interesting to see how this works. 'Week's pay' is calculated in accordance with the Employment Rights Act 1996, Pt XIV, Ch II.

[295] [2006] IRLR 252, applying *Susie Radin v GMB*.

8.2.6 **What transfers?**

8.2.6.1 **Transfer of contract and other rights and liabilities related to the employee**

Regulation 4(1) lies at the heart of the statutory regime and provides that a relevant transfer does not terminate the contract of employment of an employee of the transferor, but instead that contract is to 'have effect after the transfer as if originally made between the person so employed and the transferee'. This has been described as a form of statutory novation of the contract, which overrides the basic common law tenet that an employee may not be transferred to a new employer without that employee's consent.[296] The CJEU has strongly affirmed the automatic nature of the transfer, irrespective of the views or even the wishes of the parties,[297] and the EAT have held that a transfer can occur even if the employee has no knowledge of the facts or the identity of the new employer.[298]

Regulation 4(2) expands on this by stating that on completion of the transfer 'all the transferor's rights, powers, duties and liabilities' are to be transferred to the transferee and (following the logic of reg 4(1)) any act or omission (before the transfer is completed) of the transferor is to be deemed to be an act or omission of the transferee. By virtue of reg 10, rights under occupational pension schemes do not transfer. Instead employees who have been transferred are given a much more basic level of pension protection under the Pensions Act 2004, which could leave the employee with a much lesser pension entitlement after the transfer. The exclusion of pensions is a derogation and so, according to the ECJ, is to be construed narrowly: it only applies to old age, invalidity, or survivors' benefits, so that any other aspects of a pension scheme (eg early retirement benefits) *do* transfer.[299] Criminal liabilities of the transferor which relate to employees are not transferred.[300]

The automatic transfer provisions are of wide, general application. They obviously cover the transferred employee's existing terms and conditions of employment, along with accrued rights such as those in relation to redundancy payments and continuity of employment generally. A transferee can find itself the respondent before a tribunal in a case involving a pre-transfer dispute such as a discrimination claim,[301] or even the defendant in a personal injury action brought by an employee where the accident happened before the transfer.[302] On the 'rights' side, it has been held that the transferee employer can exercise rights under a restraint of trade clause imposed by the transferor.[303]

[296] *Nokes v Doncaster Amalgamated Collieries* [1940] AC 1014, HL.

[297] *Berg and Busschers v Besselsen* C-144/87 [1989] IRLR 447, ECJ; *Celtec Ltd v Astley*, n 253.

[298] *Secretary of State for Trade & Industry v Cook* [1997] IRLR 150.

[299] Regulation 10(2), codifying *Beckman v Dynamco Whicheloe Macfarlane Ltd* C-164/00 [2002] IRLR 578, ECJ. See Pollard 'Pensions and TUPE' (2005) 34 ILJ 127.

[300] Regulation 4(6).

[301] *DJM International Ltd v Nicholas* [1996] ICR 214, [1996] IRLR 76 (transferee inheriting a sex discrimination claim). Liability transfers even if the fellow employee who was the perpetrator of the discrimination or harassment did not transfer: *Vernon v Azure Support Services Ltd* UKEAT/0192/13 (7 November 2014, unreported). However the opposite has been held not to be the case: where a victim of harassment did not transfer under TUPE but the perpetrator did transfer, the new employer did not inherit under TUPE the transferor's vicarious liability for harassment (*Sean Pong Tyres Ltd v Moore* [2024] EAT 1, [2024] IRLR 363.

[302] *Bernadone v Pall Mall Services Group* [2001] ICR 197, [2000] IRLR 487, CA. Where the transferor was in the private sector and obliged to insure under the Employers' Liability (Compulsory Insurance) Act 1969, the transferee also inherits the benefit of that insurance. Certain public employers are not obliged to insure under the Act; in such a case, reg 17 now provides that there is to be joint liability for the transferor and transferee.

[303] *Morris Angel & Son Ltd v Hollande* [1993] ICR 71, [1993] IRLR 169, CA; *P14 Medical Ltd v Mahon* [2021] IRLR 39, HC.

Problems have arisen where part of a business was transferred under TUPE and the employee was entitled under the contract to a bonus based on the success of the business overall. So far as the entitlement relates to back-pay before the transfer, the transferee owes the amount based on the transferor's performance,[304] but in the problematic matter of the employee's future entitlement the EAT has attempted to square the circle by suggesting that the transferee would be required to establish an *equivalent* payment system, based on its own performance.[305] A similar approach applies where a transferring employee is entitled to a reward in the form of shares in the employing company: the new employer must provide some substantially equivalent share incentive.[306]

Clearly there is a risk for the transferee employer that it will inherit obligations and liabilities it was not aware of: it could find itself breaching the contract of employment without being aware that it is doing so and it could find itself inheriting a complaint by an employee about their treatment and not being aware that remedial action is required. To provide some protection to the transferee, TUPE requires transferors to provide transferees, 28 days before the transfer, with 'employee liability information', which is the following information about each employee who will transfer:

- identity and age;
- particulars of employment required by the Employment Rights Act 1996, s 1;
- information about any disciplinary or grievance procedures relating to the transferring employees in the last two years—defined as procedures to which the ACAS Code of Practice is applicable;
- information about any court or tribunal case brought by an employee against the transferor in the previous two years or that the transferor has reasonable grounds to believe that an employee may bring against the transferee arising out of the employer's employment with the transferor;
- information on any applicable collective agreement.[307]

It has also been held (logically but oddly) that where an employee dismissed for misconduct before the transfer brought an appeal which was heard after the transfer, the transferor could still take the decision to reinstate them, even though they were reinstating them into the *transferee's* employment.[308]

One particular issue relating to the continuance post-transfer of a term relating to the previous employment caused problems which have now been resolved. In *Whent v T Cartledge Ltd*,[309] local authority employees whose contracts stated that their pay was as determined from time to time by a nationally negotiated collective agreement in the public sector were TUPE transferred to a private company. When the pay rates in that agreement were increased post-transfer, the employees argued that they were entitled to the increase since their contracts of employment had been preserved by TUPE and those contracts stated that they were to be paid in accordance with the collective agreement. The EAT agreed even though the employees' new employer was not a party to the collective agreement and, indeed, had derecognized the union. The same issue came up in *Alemo-Herron v Parkwood Leisure*[310] and was referred to the CJEU. The European Court held that obliging

[304] *Unicorn Consultancy Services Ltd v Westbrook* [2000] IRLR 80.
[305] *MITIE Managed Services Ltd v French* [2002] IRLR 512.
[306] *Ponticelli UK Ltd v Gallagher* [2023] CSIH 32, [2023] IRLR 934.
[307] Regulation 11.
[308] *G4S Justice Services (UK) Ltd v Austey* [2006] IRLR 588. The case was given an extra frisson because the transferee was the transferor's *competitor*, to which it had just lost the contract!
[309] [1997] IRLR 153.
[310] C-426/11, [2013] IRLR 744.

the transferee to pay the increase would mean that the Acquired Rights Directive was interfering with the new employer's freedom to conduct its business because it had no ability to participate in the process which determined its employees' pay. Accordingly it was contrary to European law as a matter of principle for the transferee to be bound by such a provision in the transferred contract of employment. This led ultimately to TUPE being amended in 2014 as so specifically to exclude, from the bundle of rights that transfer, any provisions of a transferor's collective bargaining agreement that are agreed after the transfer, and with regard to which the transferee did not participate in the bargaining process.[311]

Case law on what transfers has been expansive, and as the case law stands at the time of writing, the only matters which have been held not to transfer (because they do not arise under the employee's contract) are liability under an order for interim relief,[312] an employee's normal (as opposed to contractual) retirement age,[313] and a lease on working premises held by the transferor, even where termination of the lease upon transfer could result in the dismissal of the employees.[314] A transferee was recently held to be permitted to remove an 'outdated and unjustified' expense allowance after the transfer: although all of the terms of the contract, including the allowance in question, were deemed to transfer, the transferee could drop the allowance because it no longer applied to the new circumstances.[315]

8.2.6.2 **Transfer of collective agreements and union recognition**

Regulation 6 provides that where prior to the transfer an independent union was recognized in respect of any category of employees which include employees transferred under TUPE then the recognition transfers to the new employer, *provided* that the organized grouping of resources (in a standard TUPE case) or the organized grouping of employees (in a service provision case) retains an identity distinct from the remainder of the transferee's undertaking. Of course, sometimes a distinct identity will not be maintained, in which case the recognition will evaporate on transfer. This provision makes more sense in a continental context where, if the transferred unit does not retain its identity, the expectation is that the transferee will already have a recognition agreement with a union in place in respect of its existing workforce, which will automatically be extended to the transferred employees. In the UK situation it is statistically more likely that there will be no other recognition in place to replace the one which disappears.

However, even when the recognition disappears, reg 5 ensures that any provision in a pre-transfer collective agreement which has an impact on a transferred employee will be deemed to remain in effect as part of a collective agreement between the union and the transferee employer. This would cover, for example, a clause in a collective agreement which required the employer to consult with the union before making shift changes permitted by the contracts of employment.

Traditionally, these regulations did not in fact give much protection to the relevant union or its members because in the UK neither a collective agreement nor a recognition agreement is legally enforceable, so a transferee with the necessary industrial power would be able to withdraw from the agreement and/or derecognize the union after the transfer. However, the position might now be different in the case of recognition if that recognition had been obtained by the union by invoking the statutory recognition procedure[316] against the transferor; in that case, any limitations on derecognition by the transferor would presumably continue to apply to the transferee.

[311] Regulation 4A. [312] *Dowling v ME Ilic Haulage* [2004] ICR 1176.

[313] *Cross v British Airways plc* [2006] ICR 1239, [2006] IRLR 804, CA.

[314] *Kirtruna SL, Elisa Vigano v Red Elite de Electrodomesticos SA and others* Case C-313/07, ECJ.

[315] *Tabberer v Mears Ltd* [2018] UKEAT 0064_17_0502 (5 February 2018).

[316] See 9.7.3.

8.2.7 **Who transfers?**

TUPE applies to 'employees' but the definition is not the usual one in employment law statutes. Regulation 2(1) defines an employee as 'any individual who works for another person whether under a contract of service or apprenticeship *or otherwise*, but does not include anyone who provides services under contract for services'. The Directive says in Article 2.1(d) that 'employee' means 'any person who, in the member state concerned, is protected as an employee under national law'. As the gig economy grows, cases may well start to come before employment tribunals where individuals who are not 'employees' within the definition in the Employment Rights Act 1996 but are 'workers' as defined by that Act[317] claim that they are entitled to benefit from TUPE. In one such case[318] the employment tribunal decided that such workers are covered by TUPE, because the fact that these individuals have some employment law rights (eg to paid holiday and the national minimum wage) and have protection as 'employees' under the extended definition in the Equality Act 2010 means that they should benefit from the Directive. There will no doubt be appellate decisions on this question in due course.[319] In May 2024 the Conservative government issued a consultation paper seeking views on whether the TUPE Regulations should be amended so as to clarify that they apply only to employees in the normal employment law sense. Since that government left office, no further step has yet been takin in relation to this.

Apart from that issue, in many cases, the question of who transfers is simple; it is the whole workforce of the acquired undertaking, with the transferee having no power to pick or choose. However, there are some tricky questions, some of which have been addressed specifically by the 2006 Regulations: namely whether the law can be evaded by dismissals before the transfer, who transfers if only a part of the undertaking is acquired or if the undertaking is split up, and what happens if an employee objects.

8.2.7.1 **Who transfers: pre-transfer dismissals**

The original version of reg 4 applied wherever an employee was employed by the transferor employer 'immediately before' the transfer. So a pre-transfer dismissal was perceived as a possible way for the transferee to exercise selection by getting the transferor to dismiss those employees the transferee did not want in *advance* of the transfer. At first, this seemed to succeed, because of the decision in *Secretary of State for Employment v Spence*[320] that automatic transfer only applied to those in the employment of the transferor at the time of the transfer.

However, this position changed radically in the light of two decisions—that of the ECJ in *P Bork International A/S (in liquidation) v Foreningen of Arbejdsledere i Danmark*[321] on the meaning of Directive 77/187/EEC on which the regulations were based, and that of the House of Lords in *Litster v Forth Dry Dock and Engineering Co Ltd*,[322] which followed and applied the decision of the ECJ. The end result was that if the transferor dismissed the employee because of the transfer (eg at the transferee's request) and that dismissal was unfair under reg 7 (which it would be unless it came within the 'economic, technical or organizational reasons' defence in reg 7(2)), then for the purposes of the Transfer

[317] See 2.1.3. [318] *Dewhurst v Revisecatch Ltd* (ET Case No 2201909/2018).

[319] This topic is considered in McMullen 'Leaving a Legacy: Recent Jurisprudence of the European Court on Transfers of Undertakings' (2021) 50 ILJ 130 at p 132.

[320] [1986] ICR 651, [1986] IRLR 248, CA. Ironically, *Spence* was a case where it was the employees who wanted it *not* to be a transfer (in order to cash in their accrued redundancy rights against the transferor and start afresh with the transferee), but in winning they appeared to worsen the position of employees in more normal cases.

[321] 101/87 [1989] IRLR 41, ECJ. [322] [1989] ICR 341, [1989] IRLR 161, HL.

Regulations the employee would be deemed to have been still employed by the transferor immediately before the transfer, so that automatic transfer of their contract to the transferee would apply. The decision in *Litster* was specifically adopted in the 2006 Regulations, which provide that automatic transfer applies to those employed by the transferor immediately before the transfer 'or who would have been so employed if . . . not dismissed in the circumstances described in regulation 7(1)'.[323] Thus, it is clear that prior dismissal will not be effective to prevent the transfer—however, it has been held that the dismissal is still a dismissal, so what the transferee inherits under TUPE is not a current employee but the former employee's claims under and in connection with the contact of employment, such as a claim for unfair dismissal.[324]

8.2.7.2 **Who transfers: only part of undertaking is transferred—or undertaking is split**

Regulation 4(1) adopts wording from the leading ECJ case authority of *Botzen v Rotterdamsche Droogdok Maatschappij BV*,[325] stating that the transfer affects any employee 'assigned to the organized grouping of resources or employees that is subject to the relevant transfer'; reg 2(1) states that 'assigned' means 'assigned other than on a temporary basis'.

The *Botzen* 'assignment' test is thus codified, but it can still lead to considerable problems in applying it to the facts, especially where what is being transferred is a part of a complex organization or group of companies. For example, if the old employer is facing financial disaster, can an employee who worked for several parts of the organization or group claim to be attached to the part transferred, and so 'jump ship' to the employment of the financially viable transferee/purchaser? Another example would be where a company has several service contracts with customers and some of those contracts are lost: what happens to a manager who was responsible for several contracts, including the lost contracts as well as others?

In *Sunley Turriff Holdings Ltd v Thomson*,[326] two companies (LC Ltd and LC Scotland Ltd) went into receivership and the latter was sold to Co X. The employee had been company secretary and chief accountant for both companies. Although his contract had been with LC Ltd, he had done substantial work for LC Scotland Ltd and so, when he was made redundant by the receivers, the EAT held that he was able to claim that he was covered by the Regulations and so technically taken on by Co X, against whom he could claim unfair dismissal. On the other hand, in *Michael Peters Ltd v Farnfield*,[327] when receivers were called in to a group of a holding company and 25 subsidiaries, the EAT held that the chief executive of the group could not invoke the Regulations and claim to go with the transfer when (only) four viable subsidiaries were sold to Co Y. In both cases the court applied the *Botzen* test, that is, to look as a question of fact at 'to which part of the undertaking or business the employee was assigned' or allocated.

It is clear from the first of these two cases that the issue is not resolved simply by looking at the technicalities of where the contract of employment lies. Other than that (which presumably must at least be a factor) this is a wide question of fact and degree and the courts have not laid down rules of thumb, such as at least X per cent of work being done for the part transferred. This can make advising on this point in advance of a transfer very difficult, especially as the EAT subsequently added that tribunals should be astute to ensure that protection of the individual (and the intent of the Directive and Regulations)

[323] Regulation 4(3). [324] of *Wilson v St Helens BC* [1998] ICR 1141, [1998] IRLR 706, HL.
[325] 186/83 [1985] ECR 519, [1986] 2 CMLR 50, CJEU. [326] [1995] IRLR 184.
[327] [1995] IRLR 190. See also *CPL Distribution Ltd v Todd* [2003] IRLR 28, where a manager's PA was held not to transfer, on similar grounds.

should not be prejudiced by too formalistic an emphasis being placed on the intricacies of the corporate structure of the transferor organization.[328]

Difficulties also arise where the service is transferred from one transferor to more than one transferee. The UK approach has been to consider whether it can properly be said that the employees were 'assigned' to the part of the activity that has been transferred to a particular transferee. The leading case is *Kimberley Group Housing v Hambley and others*,[329] where the only information available to the EAT was that 71 per cent of the work of providing services to asylum seekers in Stockton was transferred to Kimberley and 29 per cent to Angel. The EAT held that the employees were to be regarded as having been assigned to the activities that were taken over by Kimberley and accordingly the employees were all transferred by TUPE to Kimberley.[330] In contrast, there are cases where the former service becomes so fragmented after the new contracts are awarded that there is no longer any organized grouping of employees or no new contractor can be identified as having taken over the pre-transfer activities. In such cases there is no TUPE transfer.[331]

However, the UK courts will need to reconsider their past approach to fragmentation in the light of the CJEU's recent judgment in *ISS Facility Services v Govaerts*. This decision may be difficult to implement in UK law. The judgment says:

> Where there is a transfer of undertaking involving a number of transferees, Article 3(1) of [the Directive] must be interpreted as meaning that the rights and obligations arising from a contract of employment are transferred to each of the transferees, in proportion to the tasks performed by the worker concerned, provided that the division of the contract of employment as a result of the transfer is possible and neither causes a worsening of working conditions nor adversely affects the safeguarding of the rights of workers guaranteed by that directive, which it is for the referring court to determine. If such a division were to be impossible to carry out or would adversely affect the rights of that worker, the transferee(s) would be regarded as being responsible for any consequent termination of the employment relationship, under Article 4 of that directive, even if that termination were to be initiated by the worker.[332]

This appears to mean that each contract of employment should be split and the fragments shared out among the new contractors, which would be a novel and difficult thing to do. Where this is not possible without worsening working conditions or adversely affecting rights protected by the Directive, the European Court is suggesting that the new contractors would be responsible for any 'consequent' termination—implying that some formula would need to be devised to share between them the cost of notice pay and any unfair dismissal liability. Since the dismissals would be because of the transfer it would appear that they would be automatically unfair (see 8.2.8), which seems tough on the employers. So far, we have limited domestic guidance on *ISS Facility Services*. In *McTear Contracts Ltd v Bennett*,[333] the employment tribunal had held, before the *ISS Facility Services* decision, that where work had been split between two new contractors

[328] *Duncan Web Offset (Maidstone) Ltd v Cooper* [1995] IRLR 633.

[329] [2008] IRLR 682, [2008] ICR 1030.

[330] In *Kimberly* the split was quantitative, in the sense of different subsets of employees going to different transferees; in *Arch Initiatives v Greater Manchester West Mental Health NHS Foundation Trust* [2016] IRLR 406, EAT the activities were split functionally, and this was held to be no bar to TUPE coverage as a service provision transfer.

[331] See eg *Ankers v Clearsprings Management Ltd* UKEAT 0054/08 (24 February 2009, unreported).

[332] *ISS Facility Services v Govaerts* C-244/18, [2020] IRLR 639, ECJ at para 39.

[333] [2021] IRLR 444.

there was no transfer. This case came before the EAT after *ISS Facility Services* had been decided and the EAT sent the case back to the tribunal to reconsider its decision in the light of that CJEU decision. The EAT took the view that the principles laid down in *ISS Facility* Services should apply not only to traditional transfers of undertakings under the Acquired Rights Directive, but also to the UK extension of TUPE to service provision changes. At the time of writing we await further developments. It would not be surprising if the UK courts were to conclude that it is not possible to read TUPE in such a way as to deliver the split between the new contractors required by *ISS Facility Services*—and leave the matter to the government to address in legislation. It is also possible that this might be a situation where the Court of Appeal or the Supreme Court could use their exceptional post-Brexit power under s 6(4) of the European Union (Withdrawal) Act 2018 to depart from a pre-Brexit CJEU decision which they consider to be wrong.[334] In May 2024, shortly before leaving office, the Conservative government issued a consultation paper about whether TUPE should be amended to seek to tackle the problems raised by *ISS Facility Services*. No action has been proposed yet by the new Labour government.

8.2.7.3 **Who transfers: employees are working in a service company**

In corporate groups it is not unusual for various subsidiaries to conduct a number of separate undertakings, but for the employees to be employed by a special subsidiary which then contracts to provide those employees to the operating subsidiaries. If one of those subsidiaries sells its business to another company, there are no employees in the undertaking to transfer. This would defeat the purpose of the Directive and so in *Albron Catering BV v FNV Bondgenoten*[335] the ECJ held that the Directive must be read purposively to transfer those employees to the new owner of the undertaking. It is likely that TUPE would be read so as to deliver the same result.[336]

8.2.7.4 **Who transfers: employee does not want to transfer**

The Regulations give the employee various powers to object. First of all, reg 4(9) states that where a transfer involves or would involve a 'substantial change in working conditions to the material detriment' of a person threatened with transfer, they may treat the contract as having been terminated, resulting in a dismissal by the employer. In effect this enacts an additional form of constructive dismissal[337]—one which does not require a repudiatory breach of contract by the employer. This dismissal can then lead to a claim for unfair dismissal.[338] However, reg 4(10) states that where reg 4(9) applies no damages are to be

[334] The difficulties thrown up by the *ISS Facilities Services* case are discussed in McMullen 'Leaving a Legacy: Recent Jurisprudence of the European Court on Transfers of Undertakings' (2021) 50 ILJ 130 at p 150.

[335] C-242/09, [2011] IRLR 76, [2011] ICR 373.

[336] Graham J did so in the High Court in *ICAP Management Services Ltd v Berry* [2017] EWHC 1321 (QB), [2017] IRLR 811, but distinguished *Albron* on the basis that only applies when the assignment to the transferred business was a permanent one. See also *Hyde Housing Association Ltd v Hyde* [2016] IRLR 107, [2016] ICR 261, which cited *Albron* as representing the law in the UK.

[337] Under the (differently worded) version in the 1981 Regulations it had been held that, like ordinary constructive dismissal, this required the employee to prove a repudiatory breach of contract by the employer. The current, more generalized wording aims to remove that requirement. Where, however, there *is* a repudiatory breach, reg 4(11) preserves the employee's ordinary right to claim constructive dismissal.

[338] If the employee's resignation is before the transfer, it appears that he is not employed immediately before the transfer and so the claim is against the transferor, even though it will usually be the case that the imposition of the change to working conditions was something that the *transferee* planned to do. This was the conclusion of the Court of Appeal in *University of Oxford v Humphreys* [2000] IRLR 305 (a case where the transferee was in face proposing a contractual change).

awarded in respect of any unpaid notice pay, that is, there is to be no *wrongful* dismissal action, which seems odd.[339]

The second possibility is that the employer commits a repudiatory breach of contract—most likely the transferee makes a substantial contractual change. In such a case the employee can resign and claim constructive dismissal on ordinary principles. It appears that if the transferee's breach is an anticipatory one where it indicates before the transfer that it will make the change after the transfer, that this is still effective as a breach of contract by the employer (even though the transferee is not at that point the employer) and so the employee can resign and claim constructive dismissal against the transferor (who is the employer at the moment of resignation). This was the conclusion of the Court of Appeal in *University of Oxford v Humphreys*[340] more than 20 years ago and it has gone unchallenged since, even though it appears to be contrary to contractual principle and to operate unfairly on the transferor which has done nothing to breach the contractual terms.

The third possibility is that any employee can exercise a *general* right to object to being transferred. Regulation 4(7) states that an employee will not be transferred if they inform the transferor or the transferee that they 'object to becoming employed by the transferee'.[341] However, reg 4(8) then goes on to state that 'subject to paragraphs (9) and (11)' where such objection is made, 'the relevant transfer shall operate so as to terminate his contract of employment with the transferor *but he shall not be treated, for any purpose, as having been dismissed by the transferor*'.

We will come back to the proviso 'subject to paragraphs (9) and (11)' in a moment, but in the ordinary case where reg 4(9) is not applicable to the circumstances and there is no repudiatory breach of contract, the result of reg 4(8) is that the employee has a theoretical right of objection but exercising this right causes the contract of employment to evaporate with no right to bring any kind of dismissal claim against the transferee or the transferor. The danger created by this provision is that if an employee is unhappy about the proposed transfer any objection could result in them losing their job with no entitlement to compensation. However this risk is mitigated by the words 'subject to paragraphs (9) and (11)'. The EAT held in *London United Busways Ltd v De Marchi*[342] that if the employee objects because either there is a substantial change to working conditions (ie reg 4(9) applies) or there is a repudiatory breach of contract (ie reg 4(11) applies) then although the objection to transfer does stop the employee transferring, they have a claim under reg 4(9) or reg 4(11) against the transferor.

Note that reg 4(7) comes in useful where both the transferor and the employee want the employee to stay with the transferor after the transfer: the employee can object to the transfer in return for a promise from the transferor of post-transfer employment.

[339] The validity of these provisions has been called into question by the Delphic ECJ decision in *Juuri v Fazer Amica Oy* [2008] All ER (D) 302 (Nov), which appears to say that (a) member states need not provide any compensation remedy for employees who elect not to transfer owing to substantial changes in conditions but (b) they must at least award whatever compensation is awarded under national law for termination of the employment contract. So it seems that reg 4(10) must be disapplied for excluding compensation for the notice period (unless of course it is treated as representing the national law on compensation in such situations). It is nice to get that cleared up.

[340] [2000] IRLR 305.

[341] No particular form is laid down for objection, which may therefore be inferred from words or conduct: *Hay v George Hanson (Building Contractors) Ltd* [1996] IRLR 427, though notice the more cautious approach in *Senior Heat Treatment Ltd v Bell* [1997] IRLR 614.

[342] [2024] EAT 191, [2025] IRLR 352.

8.2.8 **Unfair TUPE dismissal**

Regulation 7 creates a regime of possible *automatic* unfairness, subject to a defence whose wording was taken straight from the Acquired Rights Directive and which has caused repeated problems in its interpretation. The original form of reg 7 raised problems and so when the regulations were updated in 2006 the opportunity was taken to rephrase it, arguably with little change in substance but some clarification. There was then a further change in the 2014 amendments, so reg 7(1)–(2) now means that where there is a TUPE transfer there are three unfair dismissal possibilities:

1. The transfer is not the sole or principal reason for the dismissal. Such a dismissal is not affected by reg 7, and falls to be considered as an ordinary unfair dismissal case.
2. The sole or principal reason for the dismissal is an economic, technical, or organizational reason entailing changes in the workforce (commonly known as an 'ETO reason').[343] Such a dismissal is deemed for unfair dismissal purposes to have been for 'some other substantial reason' (or redundancy if the definition of redundancy is satisfied by the facts of the case) and so the employer must go on to show that the dismissal was fair in the ordinary way under the Employment Rights Act 1996, s 98(4).[344] Note that in *Hynd v Armstrong*[345] it was held by the Court of Session that if the transferor needs all the employees up until the moment of transfer, and it is the transferee who will not need all the employees, then the redundancy reason is only available to the transferee and so a dismissal by the transferor in anticipation of the redundancy will not be for an ETO reason and will therefore be automatically unfair.[346]
3. The sole or principal reason for the dismissal is the transfer itself (and is not an ETO reason).[347] Such a dismissal is automatically unfair.[348]

Before the 2014 amendments, category 3 was wider in that a non-ETO dismissal was automatically unfair if the reason or principal reason for it was the TUPE transfer *or a reason connected* with the TUPE transfer. This wording was certainly wider than the wording of the Directive, and arguably was wider in effect than ECJ case law under the Directive required. In consequence, as part of its attempts to deregulate employment law, the Conservative–Liberal Democrat government consulted on removing this piece of 'gold-plating' of European law.[349] In due course this was done in the 2014 amendments to TUPE. Since 2014, such non-ETO dismissals which are only connected with the transfer fall within category 1.

[343] Regulation 7(2).

[344] *McGrath v Rank Leisure Ltd* [1985] ICR 527, [1985] IRLR 323. Where the defence works in a redundancy context, reg 7(3)(b) specifically preserves the redundancy option and the tribunal should go on to decide on fairness on the ordinary principles of unfair redundancy selection: *Warner v Adnet Ltd* [1998] IRLR 394, CA.

[345] [2007] CSIH 16, [2007] IRLR 338.

[346] It is submitted that this decision may not be correct, and it can be awkward in practice since employees who know they are going to lose their jobs may prefer to be made redundant by their long-standing employer who they know and trust (and who may provide non-contractual enhanced redundancy payments) than by the transferee. Although the dismissals must be left until after the transfer, ss 198A and 198B of the Trade Union and Labour Relations (Consolidation) Act 1992 were introduced to enable collective consultation about the impending redundancies to be conducted by the transferee prior to the transfer date (see 8.1.3.2).

[347] Regulation 7(1).

[348] This could arise where employees are dismissed to 'slim down' the business to facilitate an actual or impending sale: *Morris v John Grose Group Ltd* [1998] ICR 655, [1998] IRLR 499, following on this point *Harrison Bowden Ltd v Bowden* [1994] ICR 186 and disapproving the narrower view in *Ibex Trading Co Ltd v Walton* [1994] ICR 907, [1994] IRLR 564, EAT.

[349] Transfer of Undertakings (Protection of Employment) Regulations 2006 Government Response to Consultation, September 2013.

An example of such a case might arise where the transferee wished to harmonize the terms and conditions of the newly acquired workforce with those of its existing employees. If the employees inherited under TUPE refused to agree to such a change the employer might give them all notice of dismissal and offers of re-engagement on new terms. Such a dismissal would clearly be *connected* with the TUPE transfer and so automatically unfair prior to the 2014 amendments.[350] In contrast, it is not clear that under the post-2014 law such a dismissal is automatically unfair—can it be said that 'the reason for this dismissal is the transfer'? It is true that but for the transfer there would have been no harmonization, but on the other hand a decision to harmonize by the transferee is not an inevitable consequence of a TUPE transfer. Moreover, the ECJ has held that the Directive does not preclude a variation of the employment relationship with the new employer insofar as national law allows the employment relationship to be altered in a manner unfavourable to employees provided that the transfer of the undertaking itself is not the reason for the alteration.[351]

To date there is little case law to guide us on this post-2014 issue. The only reported decision on the new wording is *Hare Wines Ltd v Kaur*,[352] where there had been longstanding difficulties between Mrs Kaur and a fellow employee, Mr Chatha. The transferee employer was to be a new company of which Mr Chatha was a director, and at the transferee's request the transferor employer dismissed Mrs Kaur, who claimed that the dismissal was because of the transfer and thus automatically unfair. The employer claimed that the reason was not the transfer but the wish to solve a problem of a poor working relationship. The Court of Appeal held that the employment tribunal had been entitled to decide that since the difficulties between the two employees existed before the transfer was mooted and yet Mrs Kaur had not been dismissed until the transfer came along, the transfer was the reason for the dismissal, with the consequence that the dismissal was automatically unfair.

The 'ETO' formulation in category 3 was transposed directly from the Directive in 1981 and had no prior equivalent in UK law. It is important to note that there must not only be a reason for dismissal which is 'economic', 'technical', or 'organizational', but also it must be a reason which 'entails changes in the workforce'. The potential effect of this, greatly to the transferee employer's disadvantage, was disclosed at an early stage by the decision of the Court of Appeal in *Berriman v Delabole Slate Ltd*[353] that 'changes in the workforce' in the defence means changes in the *composition* of the workforce, such as the number of employees or their duties; mere changes in the terms and conditions of the workforce are not enough. New reg 4(5A), introduced in 2014, deems a change in the location of an employee's work to be 'a change in the workforce' for the purposes of the ETO exception—some lawyers had understood the judgment in *Delabole Slate* to suggest the contrary.

If there are actual changes to the jobs of those transferred (eg as part of a reorganization, but with a knock-on effect on terms and conditions), it was confirmed in *Crawford v Swinton Insurance Brokers Ltd*[354] that that *can* constitute a 'change in the workforce' and so give rise to the reg 7 (ETO) defence.

[350] See eg *Manchester College v Hazel* [2014] EWCA Civ 72, [2014] IRLR 392: choosing as part of a reorganization to dismiss and rehire some workers on new terms for the purpose of harmonizing terms and conditions between existing and transferred employees was not ETO and was, under TUPE as it was then worded, automatically unfair.

[351] *Rask v ISS Kantineservice A/S* C-209/91 [1993] IRLR 133, ECJ. See also the discussion of *Manchester College v Hazel* in McMullen 'TUPE, Variation of Employment Terms, and the ETO Reason' (2014) 43 ILJ 364.

[352] [2019] EWCA Civ 216, [2019] IRLR 555.

[353] [1985] ICR 546, [1985] IRLR 305, CA, noted McMullen (1986) 49 MLR 524.

[354] [1990] ICR 85, [1990] IRLR 42, EAT.

The tribunals have shown a willingness, after the 2014 amendments, to interpret the ETO exception strictly, such that an 'organizational' reason will only be found if changes are made with the purpose of effecting a change to organization—changes for other purpose which simply result in organizational change will not be ETO reasons.[355]

8.2.9 **What can be changed after the transfer?**

The rules in TUPE on this question have been subject to a number of fairly recent amendments. As with the changes to the rules on dismissal, it is unclear how far-reaching the effects will be.

8.2.9.1 **Non-insolvency cases**

Given that the transferee employer has to take on all the transferred employees on their existing terms and conditions of employment, what can that employer then do if that cohort of new employees are on different terms and conditions from those of its existing employees doing similar work? The obvious desire may be to rationalize the newcomers' terms and conditions into those applying generally (if only to avoid a future equal pay issue), but employers suffered an early shock in *Berriman v Delabole Slate Ltd*,[356] where the Court of Appeal held that the employer's 'economic, technical or organisational reason' (ETO) defence had to involve a change in the *composition* of the workforce on transfer, not just a change to their terms and conditions, so that it could *not* apply to a straightforward rationalization. At that time the ETO defence only arose in the unfair dismissal provisions (see 8.2.8), but this decision did give the transferred employees' existing terms and conditions considerable protection because it meant that any threat to dismiss an employee who would not agree to change their contracts voluntarily was legally dangerous under TUPE.

For some time after *Berriman* it was assumed that the answer therefore lay in negotiation, in other words, that contractual terms could be changed after a transfer so long as the employees agreed to the changes. However, it was then held by the House of lords in *Wilson v St Helens Borough Council*[357] that the protection of the Directive (and hence the Regulations) is intended to be stronger than that, with the result that a transferee may *not* lawfully change the existing terms and conditions *if* the change is 'transfer-related', and that any attempt to do so will be void, even if for good consideration and with the ostensible agreement of the employees.

The House of Lords held that there are two circumstances where a post-transfer contractual change is lawful: (a) where either transferor or transferee dismisses the employees and re-engages them on the new terms (this being effective because domestic law does not acknowledge the possibility of a dismissal being void, even under the Directive); (b) where the transferee can break the chain of causation by showing that the changes were *not* 'transfer-related', that is, that they were made for some other, independent reason such as a reorganization of the whole workplace involving all employees (both long-standing and transferred), in which case the ordinary rules of contract law apply. Category (a) is not as attractive as it seems, because it lays the employer open to claims from the employees of automatically unfair dismissal (see 8.2.8). Category (b) could be fraught with problems of proof and timing (there being no rule of thumb that a change will not be transfer-related after a certain period from the transfer), and assumptions made by employers about their ability to impose or even negotiate changes after the

[355] *Davies v Droylsden Academy* UKEAT/0044/16 (11 October 2016, unreported).

[356] [1985] ICR 546, [1985] IRLR 305, CA.

[357] [1998] ICR 1141, [1998] IRLR 706, HL; see McMullen (1998) 28 ILJ 76.

transfer could sometimes be proved to have been entirely wrong.[358] In two recent cases, however, the need to correct a pay anomaly that could and should have been corrected before the transfer[359] and a harmonization of terms triggered by the demands of a contract with a customer (even where that new contract came with the transfer)[360] were found by the EAT not to be by reason of the transfer and were therefore permissible.

When it came to drafting the 2006 Regulations, the government decided to codify *Wilson* into clearer language and in doing so to increase the scope of the ETO defence to cover agreed contract changes as well as unfair dismissal provisions. The result was that the Regulations made it clear that a contract change connected with a transfer was void unless if it was for an ETO reason. Subsequently, as with the unfair dismissal provisions, further amendments in 2014 narrowed the scope of the ban on contract changes. Regulation 4(4) now makes void only changes whose sole or principal reason is the transfer (whereas previously changes that were *connected with* the transfer would also be void).[361] The removal of reasons 'connected' with a transfer seems to clearly open the door for more variations. It has been suggested that under the new rules employers 'are more likely to be able to call on new circumstances, such as a cut in funding, loss of an order, increased competition and so forth, to construct a non-transfer related reason for the change, even if it may be said there is some "connection" with the transfer'.[362] As with the unfair dismissal provisions, new reg 4(5A) confirms that a change in the location of work falls under 'changes of the workforce' for the ETO exception regarding contract variations.

Regulation 4(5) says that changes in terms where the terms of the contract expressly permit the variation are not void under TUPE, but this really goes without saying as a matter of law since they are changes *within* the contract.

New reg 4(5B) also attempts to permit some changes once more than a year has passed since the transfer, although it has to be said that the wording is unclear. The provision attempts to make use of a flexibility given by the Directive under which a member state can limit the period of time for which a transferee employer is bound by a transferred collective agreement so long as the period is not less than one year. What the new regulation says is that after one year contract terms can be changed if both:

- the terms being changed are ones incorporated into the employment contracts by a collective bargaining agreement; and
- the new contract terms as a whole are no less favourable to the employee after the variation than before.

[358] In two cases, restraint of trade clauses negotiated into contracts by the transferee shortly after the transfer were held to be unenforceable because they were transfer-related and therefore void changes: *Crédit Suisse First Boston (Europe) Ltd v Padiachy* [1999] ICR 569, [1998] IRLR 504; *Crédit Suisse First Boston (Europe) Ltd v Lister* [1999] ICR 794, [1998] IRLR 700, CA. In the latter case, this was despite the employee having been paid £625,000 for the change in terms.

[359] *Smith v Trustees of Brooklands College* (UKEAT/0128/11) and *Tabberer v Mears Ltd* [2018] UKEAT 0064_17_0502 (5 February 2018).

[360] *Enterprise Managed Services Ltd v Dance* (UKEAT/0200/11).

[361] A striking recent example is *Ferguson v Astrea Asset Management Ltd* [2020] IRLR 577, EAT, where the directors of a company which was going to lose a service contract awarded themselves substantial rights to bonuses and termination payments so as to benefit from these provisions after the new contractor inherited them as employees under TUPE. The EAT held that the reason for the changes was the TUPE transfer and thus the changes were void since reg 4(4) applies to all changes and not just to changes which are adverse to the employee. For a criticism of this conclusion see Wynn-Evans 'The Use and Abuse of TUPE' (2020) 49 ILJ 459.

[362] McMullen 'TUPE: Ringing the (Wrong) Changes. The Collective Redundancies and Transfer of Undertakings (Protection of Employment) (Amendment) Regulations 2014' (2014) 43 ILJ 149. This article also argues that the new rules are in conflict with the EU law principles laid down in *Foreningen of Arbejdsledere i Danmark v Daddy's Dance Hall A/S* 324/86 [1988] IRLR 315, ECJ.

It is not clear from the wording whether the new terms must be agreed by collective bargaining or whether the new terms could be agreed by employees individually. It is also far from clear how a tribunal would assess whether or not the terms were overall not less favourable, for example if a reduction in the duration of sick pay were balanced by an increase in basic wages. It is also not clear whether 'overall less favourable' applies separately to each employee or to the workforce as a whole: the logic suggests the latter but the wording is more consistent with the former. It is likely in practice that this power to make changes will be used only in cases where the new terms are agreed by collective bargaining with a union representing the workers concerned—and in such cases the employer will probably want the union to record its view that the terms are overall no less favourable.

8.2.9.2 **Insolvency cases**

The renegotiated Directive introduced a further new flexibility to make changes which applies if (but only if) at the time of the transfer the transferor is subject to certain insolvency proceedings. This was adopted in the UK so that a workforce can lawfully agree different (and, of course, possibly worse) terms and conditions as the 'price' of keeping the undertaking going under new management and so keeping their jobs. The protection given by reg 9 is that this may not be done on an individual basis; instead, any such agreement must be reached with 'appropriate representatives' of the transferred employees. Where a trade union is recognized, that means representatives of the union. Where there is no recognition, it means directly elected or appointed employee representatives.

In such a case reg 9 says that the transferor, the transferee, or an insolvency practitioner may agree with the representatives of transferred employees to make 'permitted variations' to the latter's terms and conditions. These are defined as variations where:

(1) the sole or principal reason for the variation is the transfer and is not an economic, technical, or organizational reason entailing changes in the workforce; and

(2) it is designed to safeguard employment opportunities by ensuring the survival of the undertaking, business, or part of the undertaking or business that is the subject of the relevant transfer.

8.2.10 **Conclusions**

The 2006 Regulations with their 2014 amendments might be viewed as a welcome attempt at clarification and simplification of the law relating to transfers. The parts that codify the existing case law have increased clarity and lessened the need to refer back to those cases. The continued exclusion of pensions may be seen, especially by employees and unions, as a disappointment.

However, serious uncertainties persist. One is the lack of clarity about when post-transfer changes in terms and conditions are permitted. Another is the huge doubt about what happens when a business or service contract is split between several new operators. These difficulties are not surprising given the obscureness of EU law on these matters. This might be one of the rare situations where Brexit might assist employment law: the government could now introduce more precise and comprehensive regulations.

Such new regulations could also address some matters which hitherto have not been addressed by the Regulations at all. Two examples are (a) 'dumping' (ie putting the least desirable employees on to a contract about to be lost to have them transferred to another employer), and (b) late changes to employees' terms and conditions before a TUPE transfer (leaving the transferee to pick up the tab).

In many cases the various employers involved in a business change cope with the uncertainties and omissions of TUPE by 'legislating' for themselves, that is to say, dealing in their contracts for business sales or outsourcing with matters such as which employees transfer to which new employer and preventing dumping. Intending transferee employers also spend a considerable amount of time in 'due diligence' to identify all the liabilities that they might inherit. There is a breed of practising employment lawyers who spend much of their time on such transfer-related work.

Review and Final Thoughts

- While closure of a business uncontroversially results in redundancy dismissals accompanied by redundancy payments and no other compensation (unless consultation obligations were violated), reducing the size of or reorganizing a business might produce redundancies or it might, depending on the circumstances, end in dismissals for 'some other substantial reason' (SOSR).
- If the reorganization leads to job losses which can be attributed to 'a diminished need for . . . work of a particular kind', employees can expect a redundancy payment and, rarely, obtain unfair dismissal compensation if their employer failed to follow a fairly comprehensive list of procedural expectations.
- On the other hand, if job losses cannot be attributed to a diminished need for work of a particular kind, there will be no redundancy payment and the SOSR dismissal may be more easily challenged as unfair because the tribunal will consider not only procedural questions such as consultation but also whether the business need for the change was sufficiently compelling for the dismissals to be within the range of reasonable responses. SOSR dismissals will in most cases be automatically unfair once the Employment Rights Act 29025 is in force.
- Alternatively, even if there are reductions in the need for work of a particular kind, the employer may respond by instructing employees to do other work which is within the scope of their contracts. If employees refuse to do so then any consequent dismissals will be for misconduct and again there will be no entitlement to redundancy payment but there will be a possibility of a successful claim for unfair dismissal.
- So, in the most complicated cases, where a business responds to economic circumstances by reorganizing with some loss of jobs, whether or not those losses are redundancies depends on whether they can be attributed to 'a diminished need for . . . work of a particular kind'. Regardless of what the employer intends, if the need for work is the same, but the employer reorganizes for efficiency and the employee refuses to cooperate, a dismissal that follows will be either for misconduct or SOSR. For further reading see footnotes 23, 37, 216–17, and 220.
- Straightforward, intentional redundancies require that employers consult with workers as soon as redundancies are contemplated, seriously consider alternatives to redundancies, accept advice from the union (if there is one) on selection criteria and employ a fair set of selection criteria, and offer redundant employees suitable alternative employment where available.
- When a business is sold this is a transfer of an undertaking governed by the TUPE regulations. The employees go with the business and their employment contracts remain in force and bind the transferee whose ability to change those contracts is restricted. This applies

even if only part of a business is sold, so long as there is an organized grouping of employees dedicated to the functions sold. For further reading see footnotes 319, 353, and 357.

- When an employer decides to 'contract out' (ie pay an outside organization to do work that used to be done inside the company) the TUPE regulations apply, so that an organized grouping of employees assembled primarily to serve the client—who will now be served by the new contractor—must be transferred to the contractor if the client intends the relevant work to continue. For further reading see footnotes 271 and 361.
- The TUPE Regulations are often suggested as a likely target for post-Brexit deregulation. However, since many outsourcing contracts are drafted on the assumption that TUPE does apply, it is far from clear that this would be welcomed by those businesses which are active in this field.

9

Collective labour law

OVERVIEW

This chapter considers the laws that affect trade unions and employment relations at a collective level. Historically, collective relations between employers and employees have been conducted through trade unions, but more recently EU law had intervened in connection with another collective approach, which is to set up 'information and consultation' arrangements with elected or appointed worker representatives. This chapter deals first with union-related law and then with other worker representation as follows:

- Historical background and statistics
- The legal status of a trade union and the concept of trade union independence
- Freedom of association, a fundamental concept in trade unionism, and how it is protected and promoted by the law by giving protection to union members against discrimination and by the provision of a right to time off work, sometimes paid, for union activities and duties
- The important concept of 'recognition' of a union by an employer
- Statutory recognition: historically recognition was obtained by a union persuading an employer to negotiate with the union. Since 2000 there has been a mechanism in place by which a union with a sufficient level of membership at a workplace can force an employer to recognize it
- The right of a recognized trade union to compel an employer to disclose information for the purposes of collective bargaining
- The EU-derived laws which provide for consultation with elected or appointed employee representatives:
  - in 'domestic' works councils under the Information and Consultation of Employees Regulations 2004;
  - in 'European Works Councils' for European multinational companies.

Context

Collective labour law deals with relations between workers acting together and their employer (or sometimes several employers in the same industry). Usually this collective action is organized by a trade union. The need for workers to have a collective voice stems from the weak bargaining position of a single worker relative to an employer: the employer controls access to a job which is suitable for the worker and the number of alternative employers available to the worker may be very limited. Therefore a right for workers to form unions and to bargain collectively with employers is recognized in the Universal Declaration of Human Rights, in the European Convention on Human Rights, and in various instruments of the International Labour Organization and the European Union. Within the UK, the policy for over a century has been that the law should facilitate collective bargaining by giving trade unions and their members legal rights and protections in order to enable unions to represent their members effectively in negotiations with employers and to arrange strikes and other industrial action so as. Over the past 45 years or so that has been supplemented by giving individual workers protection against discrimination because they are union members or activists.

Union membership levels have fallen steadily over the past 40 years, and far fewer workers in the private sector are represented by unions in collective negotiations than in the past. In consequence, unions have no impact on the working lives of many workers. This is even more the case for the millions of people who work as 'self-employed' contractors—it is only very recently that unions have even sought to represent such individuals and, so far, the unions have made limited headway with this.[1] In contrast, unions remain strong in the public sector, where they are of great significance in relation to the terms of employment and the day-to-day treatment of all those working in the public sector—whether union members or not.

Ultimately the bargaining strength of unions stems from the ability to organize workers to take industrial action. Rights for unions to exist and to represent workers—a 'freedom of association'—are of limited value if unions are not able lawfully to organize industrial action. In recent decades UK governments have often shown themselves to be much less keen on freedom to strike than on freedom of association. However the Labour government elected in 2024 has legislated both to strengthen unions generally and also to make it easier for them to organize industrial action. The new statutory provisions are enacted in the Employment Rights Act 2025, and will be discussed in the main text of this chapter. The law on industrial action is covered in Chapter 10.

9.1 Background and some statistics relating to the level of union influence in the workplace

9.1.1 The importance of union density

Union membership levels have declined in most years since the 1980s. In 2024 the proportion of employees who were union members, which is known as 'union density', was 24.0 per cent, but this hides a very mixed picture. Union density in the public sector was 49.2 per cent, but it was only 11.2 per cent in the private sector.[2] This is linked to a

[1] See Bertolini and Dukes 'Trade Unions and Platform Workers in the UK: Worker Representation in the Shadow of the Law' 50 ILJ 662.

[2] Trade Union Membership, UK 1995–2024 (Department for Business, Energy & Industrial Strategy Statistical Bulletin May 2025).

reduction in the absolute numbers of union members in the UK from a peak of more than 12.5 million in 1980 to 6.4 million in 2024.[3]

9.1.2 **The reduced significance of union bargaining**

There has also been a declining trend in the number of workplaces in which terms and conditions are, for some categories of worker at least, determined by collective bargaining. In 2024 only 20.1 per cent of workers in the private sector had their terms set by union bargaining, while in the public sector the proportion was 89.2 per cent.[4] These figures have remained fairly stable since about 2010, prior to which they had dropped significantly, especially in the private sector.

9.1.3 **The future?**

For some time it was thought that perhaps where union influence disappeared it would be replaced by worker representation in elected works councils. Such representation is encouraged by a number of legal provisions derived from EU law, but in fact they seem to have gained little traction: while works councils, joint staff consultative committees, and similar bodies are quite widespread, they are proving to have little influence over the workplace (see 9.10.1 and 9.10.2.7). The Employment Rights Act 2025 seeks to enhance the ability of unions to gain membership, and therefore traction, in workplaces and to make it easier for them to win recognition for bargaining from employers and easier to organise industrial action. The Act will also introduce nationwide collective bargaining in relation to adult social care and school support staff—the details of which are outside the scope of this book.

9.2 The legal position of a trade union

9.2.1 **Definition of 'trade union'**

A trade union is defined in the Trade Union and Labour Relations (Consolidation) Act 1992, s 1 as an organization which consists wholly or mainly of workers of one or more description and whose principal purposes include the regulation of relations between workers of that description or those descriptions and employers or employers' associations.[5] The definition also extends to organizations which consist of constituent or affiliated trade unions, or the representatives of such organizations. This definition contains three elements: first, there must be an 'organization', whether temporary or permanent, which indicates that there must be some degree of formal structure as opposed to a casual grouping of workers.[6] Second, the organization must be composed wholly or mainly of workers[7] or trade

[3] Trade Union Membership, UK 1995–2024 n 2.

[4] Annual Survey of Hours and Earnings, cited in Trade Union Membership, UK 1995–2024 n 1.

[5] An employers' association is similarly defined in s 122.

[6] *Frost v Clarke & Smith Manufacturing Co Ltd* [1973] IRLR 216; *Weeks v National Amalgamated Stevedores and Dockers' Union* (1940) 67 Ll L Rep 282; *Midland Cold Storage v Turner* [1972] ICR 230.

[7] 'Worker' is defined for these purposes as including those working or seeking to work under contracts of employment and those who contract personally to perform work or services for another, but excluding contracts with professional clients (see eg *Carter v Law Society* [1973] ICR 113): Trade Union and Labour Relations (Consolidation) Act 1992, s 296(1). However, in some circumstances union rights under article 11 of the European Convention on Human Rights requires the definition in s 296(1) to be read more widely. See further 9.3.4. There are specific exclusions for members of the armed forces (s 296(1)) and the police service (s 280).

unions.[8] In the 'gig' economy there is an increasing number of individuals who are highly dependent on a single 'customer' but who may well not be covered because they fall outside the definition of 'worker'. This exclusion may be in breach of Article 11 of the European Convention on Human Rights: see 9.3.4. Third, the principal purposes of the organization must include industrial relations with employers or their associations.[9]

In *Midland Cold Storage v Turner*,[10] a joint shop stewards' committee was held not to meet this definition because it had not itself entered into negotiations with employers, but had merely acted as a pressure group, seeking to influence the decisions of the dock workers' unions on the taking of industrial action. In contrast, in *British Association of Advisers and Lecturers in Physical Education v National Union of Teachers*,[11] a professional association whose objects clause stated that it 'shall be concerned with the professional interests of its members' was held to be a trade union, although to describe industrial relations as one of its principal purposes might seem on the facts to be stretching the point.

9.2.2 **Listing as a trade union**

If an organization satisfies the definition in s 1 then it is a trade union and has the rights and duties of a union without the need for formal approval. However, in practice, nearly all unions apply to be included in the list of trade unions maintained by the Certification Officer[12] under s 2. If listing is refused, the organization may appeal to the EAT.[13]

Entry on the list is declared to be evidence that the organization is a trade union, but it is not conclusive evidence.[14] There are three principal advantages for a trade union in being listed. The first is that the fact of listing constitutes evidence that the organization falls within the legal definition of a trade union. Second, the union gains tax exemptions for its provident benefits funds, and third, listing is a precondition for the far more important step of gaining a certificate of independence,[15] which is the key that unlocks the door to most of the statutory union rights.

9.2.3 **The legal status of a trade union**

Trade unions are not bodies corporate:[16] a trade union is an unincorporated association, a collection of individuals bound together by the contract of membership with no separate legal personality. However, trade unions are invested by statute with some of the most important attributes of legal personality, including the power to make contracts, to sue

[8] Trade Union and Labour Relations (Consolidation) Act 1992, s 1(b). This covers union federations such as the International Transport Workers' Federation: see eg *Camellia Tanker Ltd SA v ITWF* [1976] ICR 274, [1976] IRLR 190, CA.

[9] There is an exception in the case of union federations, where the definition is satisfied if the organization's principal purposes include the regulation of relations between its constituent or affiliated organizations: Trade Union and Labour Relations (Consolidation) Act 1992, s 1(b).

[10] [1972] ICR 230.

[11] [1986] IRLR 497, CA.

[12] See 1.3.3. The Certification Officer also maintains a list of employers' associations, to which similar rules apply: see s 123. On 31 March 2020 there were 139 trade unions and 85 employers' associations of which the Certification Officer was aware (in 1983, there had been 502 trade unions and 375 employers' associations) and there were 6,695,098 union members reported to her by those unions. See Annual Report of the Certification Officer 2019/20.

[13] Trade Union and Labour Relations (Consolidation) Act 1992, ss 9 and 126.

[14] Trade Union and Labour Relations (Consolidation) Act 1992, ss 2(4) and 123(4).

[15] Trade Union and Labour Relations (Consolidation) Act 1992, s 6: see 9.2.4.2.

[16] Trade Union and Labour Relations (Consolidation) Act 1992, s 10; a professional organization which is a 'special register body' as defined in s 117 (eg the British Medical Association) is permitted to have corporate status. An employers' association may be incorporated or unincorporated: s 127.

and be sued, and to be prosecuted for criminal offences.[17] All property belonging to the union must be vested in trustees in trust for the union and that property may be attached for the satisfaction of any judgment, order, or award in the same way as if the union were a body corporate.[18]

Part 1 of the 1992 Act contains extensive provisions which regulate many aspects of the administration and governance of trade unions, including annual returns and accounts, officers, elections, rights of union members as against their union, political funds, and amalgamations. These provisions are beyond the scope of this work, but it is worth mentioning that further requirements were added by the Trade Union Act 2016.

Section 11 of the 1992 Act contains a provision which historically was of great significance, because it removed from unions the threat of being found to be illegal on the basis of constituting a restraint of trade.[19] This provision states that the purposes of a trade union are not, by reason only that they are in restraint of trade, to be regarded as unlawful so as (a) to make any union member liable to criminal proceedings for conspiracy[20] or otherwise, or (b) to make any agreement or trust void or voidable. This protection also extends to the union's rules, which are not to be regarded as unlawful or unenforceable by reason only that they are in restraint of trade.[21]

9.2.4 **Independent trade unions**

9.2.4.1 **The importance of independence**

Many rights of unions and union members and officials are only available if the union is *independent*. For example, only an independent trade union can compel the employer to provide bargaining information,[22] or apply to the CAC to force an employer to recognize the union for bargaining purposes.[23] Only an independent union can demand to be consulted on pending redundancies or a planned transfer of the employer's undertaking.[24] Likewise, only a member of an independent trade union has a right to time off work for union activities,[25] and a right not to have detrimental action taken against them or to be dismissed because of their union activities.[26]

[17] On a literal interpretation of s 10 it has been held that a union cannot sue for libel in its own name, as it lacks sufficient legal personality: *EETPU v Times Newspapers Ltd* [1980] QB 585, [1980] 1 All ER 1097. This formulation also gives rise to the argument that the doctrine of ultra vires should not now apply to trade unions: Wedderburn (1985) 14 ILJ 127, commenting on the case of *Taylor v NUM (Derbyshire Area)* [1985] IRLR 99, in which the doctrine was applied; Clayton and Tomlinson 'Vicarious Liability and Trade Unions' [1985] NLJ 361.

[18] Trade Union and Labour Relations (Consolidation) Act 1992, s 12. Section 129 applies similar provisions to an unincorporated employers' association.

[19] Section 128 of the 1992 Act gives similar protection to the purposes and rules of an unincorporated employers' association. For an example of the application of this section see *Goring v British Actors Equity Association* [1987] IRLR 122, Ch D.

[20] Possible liability for conspiracy on more general grounds (where the object of the conspiracy is not itself unlawful) is excluded in the criminal context by the Criminal Law Act 1977, s 1(1) and in the tortious context by s 219 of the 1992 Act.

[21] The protection was extended to union rules as a direct result of certain views expressed in *Edwards v SOGAT* [1971] Ch 354, [1970] 3 All ER 689, CA, where the Court of Appeal asserted a jurisdiction to supervise the content of union rules, not just to secure their proper enforcement.

[22] See 9.8. [23] See 9.7.3.

[24] See 9.7.1. This refers to the position where a trade union of some sort is involved; however, the consultation requirements for redundancies and business transfers apply to elected worker representatives, in cases where no trade union is involved.

[25] See 9.5.1. [26] See 9.4.3.

Staff associations (or 'house' unions) have been particularly at risk of failing to be certified as independent, since they may have evolved from little more than social clubs or may have been set up by an employer in the hope of deterring employees from joining an external union. Also at risk are non-TUC-affiliated bodies and breakaway groups from larger unions, where they may face opposition from established affiliated unions.[27]

9.2.4.2 **Certification of independence**

A listed[28] trade union may apply to the Certification Officer (CO)[29] for a certificate of independence, under the Trade Union and Labour Relations (Consolidation) Act 1992, s 6. If a union meets the definition of independence in s 5 then it is an independent trade union whether or not it has a certificate. However, a certificate is conclusive evidence that the union is independent and a refusal of a certificate is conclusive evidence that the union is not independent.[30] If in any legal proceedings a dispute arises as to whether a union which does not have a certificate is in fact an independent union then the court or tribunal must refer that issue to the CO for them to determine.[31]

If the CO decides that a union is 'independent' they must grant the certificate, and if their conclusion is against independence the CO must give reasons for refusal. The CO is at liberty to make such inquiries as they think fit and 'shall take into account any relevant information submitted to him [or her] by any person', which will of course include any other union which has an interest in the area in question and may wish to oppose the application for a certificate. If an applicant union is refused a certificate, it may appeal against that decision to the EAT on a point of law.[32] An application can be made more than once, so that if a union is at first refused a certificate it may decide to make changes and then apply again.[33]

9.2.4.3 **The tests of 'independence'**

An independent trade union is defined in s 5 as one which (a) is not under the domination or control of an employer or a group of employers or of one or more employers' associations, and (b) is not liable to interference by an employer or any such group or association (arising out of the provision of financial or material support or by any other means whatsoever) tending towards such control. The CO has evolved certain criteria, which are

[27] The *Annual Report of the Certification Office 1987* showed a cumulative total of 52 refusals of applications in the important first ten years of operation—a large proportion of these were staff associations; 231 certificates had been issued and were still in force at the end of 1987; 140 had been issued and subsequently cancelled (largely due to union amalgamation). Far fewer applications for certificates of independence are now made because only a handful of new unions are formed every year.

[28] That is, listed under the Trade Union and Labour Relations (Consolidation) Act 1992, s 2—see 9.2.2.

[29] See 1.3.3.

[30] Trade Union and Labour Relations (Consolidation) Act 1992, s 8(1). Such a certificate may, if necessary, be retrospective, ie also declaring that the body has been independent at an earlier stage: *Bone v North Essex Partnership NHS Foundation Trust* [2014] ICR 1053, [2014] IRLR 635, CA.

[31] Trade Union and Labour Relations (Consolidation) Act 1992, s 8(4) and 8(5).

[32] Trade Union and Labour Relations (Consolidation) Act 1992, s 9, as amended by the Employment Relations Act 2004.

[33] *Blue Circle Staff Association v Certification Officer* [1977] ICR 224, [1977] IRLR 20; *HSD (Hatfield) Employees Association v Certification Officer* [1978] ICR 21, [1977] IRLR 261.

currently set out in 'Independence: a guide for trade unions wishing to apply for a certificate of independence' (revised, April 2020).[34] These criteria are:

- *History.* If the union began with employer support and encouragement, or even as a creature of management, and this was recent, it is a powerful argument against independence, but the CO recognizes that some unions evolve from a dependent to an independent state.
- *Membership base.* A union, especially a small one with few resources, whose membership is confined to the employees of one employer is more vulnerable to employer interference than a broadly based union. The CO says experience has confirmed that a narrow membership base may make the union's task of proving its independence more difficult but that it does not make it impossible.
- *Organization and structure.* These are considered both as they are set out in the union's rule book and as they work in practice. The main requirement is that the union should be organized in a way which enables the members to play a full part in the decision-making process and excludes any form of employer involvement or influence in the union's internal affairs. If senior managers can belong to the union then it will be relevant whether there are restrictions on the part which they can play in the union's affairs.
- *Finance.* A union with weak finances and inadequate reserves is obviously more likely to be vulnerable to employer interference than one whose financial position is strong.
- *Employer-provided facilities.* These may take the form of premises, time off, and office or other services provided by the employer. The free provision of such facilities is in fact common practice so the important issue is how easy the union would find it to cope if they were withdrawn.
- *Negotiating record.* The CO states that this is almost always an important consideration. While a weak record does not of itself indicate dependence, a strong record in negotiation may outweigh other factors unfavourable to the union's case. In assessing the record, account is taken of such factors as the particular environment in which the union operates—for example, the kind of employer with whom it negotiates and the traditions and attitudes of the employees whom it represents. An effective union is more likely to be independent than an ineffective one.

In order to qualify as independent, the union must not only be free from domination or control by an employer; it must also not be *liable* to interference, perhaps indirectly.[35] This second stage of the test requires a certain amount of speculation and foresight, and raises a question of interpretation—what is meant by 'liable' to interference? The more trusting view is that 'liable' means 'likely to suffer in practice', so that even if there are some provisions in the union's rules which might in theory permit interference by the management, they should be ignored if in practice this is unlikely to happen. The more cautious view is that 'liable' means 'vulnerable to' or 'exposed to the risk of' interference, so that any factors raising a possibility of interference should disentitle the union to a certificate of independence even if, as things stand at the time of the application, there is little likelihood in practice of it happening. In *Squibb UK Staff Association v Certification*

[34] These are similar to criteria used by the CO in 1977 which were implicitly approved by the EAT in the first case to come before it on certification, *Blue Circle Staff Association v Certification Officer* [1977] ICR 224, [1977] IRLR 20.

[35] *HSD (Hatfield) Employees Association v Certification Officer* [1978] ICR 21, [1977] IRLR 261.

Officer, the applicant association was recognized by the employer for bargaining purposes and a large proportion of employees were members; however, it was dependent upon the employer for material support such as accommodation and communications and was in a weak financial position, though there was found to be little likelihood of withdrawal of the employer's support. The Court of Appeal held that the correct interpretation was the more cautious one so that on the facts the CO's decision to refuse the certificate was correct.[36] The Court said:

> One has to envisage the possibility that there may be a difference of opinion in the future between the employers and the staff association. It does not matter whether it is likely or not . . . It may be a mere possibility. But when it arises the questions have to be asked. What is the strength of the employers? What pressures could they bring to bear against the staff association? What facilities could they withdraw?[37]

9.3 Freedom of association—general issues

9.3.1 History: British common law

Trade unions can only exist where individuals are free to combine together in associations. This freedom to associate[38] was granted in Britain as long ago as 1824 with the repeal of the Combination Acts,[39] which had made it unlawful for workers to combine together in trade unions. At common law, therefore, individuals were free to form and join trade unions.[40] However, the common law did not grant positive *rights* of association, enforceable against others, so that at common law there was no protection against discriminatory action by an employer on grounds of union membership, whether in the form of a refusal to hire, dismissal, or some other action aimed at discouraging union membership or participation in union activities. Furthermore, the common law did not give a worker any right *not* to belong to a union: an employer could refuse to employ such a person in a 'closed shop'. Finally, with one possible exception,[41] there was no common law right to insist on being admitted to a trade union of one's choice: admission to a union presupposed the willingness of that union to admit the applicant into membership. As Lord Diplock put it in *Cheall v APEX*:[42] 'My Lords, freedom of association can only be mutual; there can be no right of an individual to associate with other individuals who are not willing to associate with him.'

Some rights to associate, and not to associate, in a trade union have been granted by statute. This was not done by enacting a general right to associate, but instead through the

[36] [1979] ICR 235, [1979] IRLR 75, CA. For an application of these principles, see *A Monk & Co Staff Association v Certification Officer* [1980] IRLR 431, EAT. The staff association formed at GCHQ, Cheltenham (after the government's decision in 1984 to ban unions there on the grounds of national security) was refused a certificate of independence on this second limb of the test and that refusal was upheld by the EAT: *Government Communications Staff Federation v Certification Officer* [1993] ICR 163, [1993] IRLR 260.

[37] [1979] ICR 235 at 245, [1979] IRLR 75 at 78, per Lord Denning MR. The staff association was eventually granted a certificate by the Certification Officer (Employment News No 62 (May/June 1979)).

[38] See, generally, Von Prondzynski *Freedom of Association and Industrial Relations* (1987); Wedderburn 'Freedom of Association and Philosophies of Labour Law' (1989) 18 ILJ 1.

[39] Combination Laws Repeal Act 1824. Repeal of the legal restrictions on union activities did not come until much later—see 10.1.1.

[40] With the exception of the police and those working in the intelligence services.

[41] Lord Denning's 'right to work' principle in *Nagle v Feilden* [1966] 2 QB 633, CA.

[42] [1983] ICR 398, [1983] IRLR 215, HL.

adoption of a complex set of measures (now contained in Part III of the Trade Union and Labour Relations (Consolidation) Act 1992). These give specific protection to those who are refused employment, discriminated against, or dismissed for union reasons, and they control admission to and expulsion from trade unions. When in force, new provisions enacted in the Employment Rights Act 2025 will for the first time require employers to notify workers, in their statement of employment particulars issued when they start work of their right to join a union, and trade unions will be given a right to demand access to workplaces and to communicate with workers in order to support, recruit, and organize workers. The approach in English law has therefore been to build a collective right to associate 'out of the bricks of certain individual employment rights'.[43]

9.3.2 **International law—does British law comply?**

British union rights exist against the backdrop of an array of international treaties and conventions guaranteeing the principle of freedom of association, including Article 11 of the European Convention on Human Rights and Fundamental Freedoms and ILO Conventions No 87 (on Freedom of Association and Protection of the Right to Organize) and No 98 (on the Right to Organize and Bargain Collectively).[44]

For many years there has been a lively debate over the extent to which the UK law on freedom of association complies with these international standards.[45] The debate took on an entirely new dimension in the UK as a result of the incorporation in English law of the European Convention on Human Rights by the Human Rights Act 1998.[46] Article 11 of the Convention states:

(1) Everyone has the right to freedom of peaceful assembly and to freedom of association with others, including the right to form and to join trade unions for the protection of his interests.

(2) No restrictions shall be placed on the exercise of these rights other than such as are prescribed by law and are necessary in a democratic society in the interests of national security or public safety, for the prevention of disorder or crime, for the protection of health or morals or for the protection of the rights and freedoms of others.

Initially, the judgments of the European Court of Human Rights under Article 11 gave little reason to think that the incorporation of the Convention would lead to a strengthening of the right to associate in the UK.[47] Indeed, individuals seeking to assert a right *not* to associate had had greater success under Article 11 than had trade unions and their

[43] Wedderburn (1976) 39 MLR 168. For a more recent discussion of this issue see Bogg '"Individualism" and "Collectivism" in Collective Labour Law' (2017) 46 ILJ 72.

[44] See generally Ewing *Britain and the ILO* (2nd edn, 1994); Morris 'Freedom of Association and the Interests of the State' in Ewing, Gearty, and Hepple (eds) *Human Rights and Labour Law: Essays for Paul O'Higgins* (1994).

[45] See eg Morris [1985] PL 177 on the 1984 ban on union membership at the Government Communications Headquarters (GCHQ): *Council of Civil Service Unions v Minister for the Civil Service* [1985] ICR 14, [1985] IRLR 28, HL.

[46] See Ewing (ed) *Human Rights at Work* (2000); O'Dempsey et al. *Employment Law and the Human Rights Act 1998* (2001); Hepple 'The Impact on Labour Law' in Markesinis (ed) *The Impact of the Human Rights Bill on English Law* (1998); Ewing 'The Human Rights Act and Labour Law' (1998) 27 ILJ 275; Palmer 'Human Rights: Implications for Labour Law' (2000) 59 CLJ 168; Ewing and Hendy 'The Trade Union Act 2016 and the Failure of Human Rights' (2016) 45 ILJ 391.

[47] See eg Council of Civil Service Unions v United Kingdom (1987) 10 EHRR 269, EComHR.

members,[48] hence Ewing's comment in 1998 that 'the contribution of Article 11 to date has been disappointing, failing to deliver any meaningful protection for trade union activities, while being used as an instrument for undermining trade union security'.[49]

The impact of the Convention started to grow with later decisions of the European Court of Human Rights, beginning with *Wilson and National Union of Journalists; Palmer, Wyeth and National Union of Rail, Maritime and Transport Workers v United Kingdom*.[50] Although the actual point at issue is now covered by legislation (discussed later in this chapter), the general tenor and approach in *Wilson and Palmer* is still important in debates about other aspects of the right to union representation.

In both cases the employers had offered a substantial pay increase to those employees who agreed to give up their right to have their terms and conditions negotiated through collective bargaining and to sign individual contracts instead. The applicants complained that this constituted a breach of their statutory right not to have 'action short of dismissal' taken against them for trade union reasons.[51] The House of Lords[52] ruled against the applicants, on the grounds, first, that the statutory protection only applied to 'actions' and not 'omissions'[53] and secondly, that the statutory protection only applied to action taken for the purpose of preventing or deterring union membership, and that on the facts there was no evidence that the employer's ultimate purpose was to deter union membership.

The European Court of Human Rights ruled in *Wilson and Palmer*[54] that UK law was in violation of Article 11 of the European Convention on Human Rights. The Court set out some important general principles:

- members of a trade union 'have a right, in order to protect their interests, that the trade union should be heard';[55]
- furthermore, 'it is of the essence of the right to join a trade union . . . that employees should be free to instruct or permit the union to make representations to their employer or to take action in support of their interests on their behalf';
- and 'it is the role of the State to ensure that trade union members are not prevented or restrained from using their union to represent them in attempts to regulate their relations with their employers'.[56]

The Court considered that the UK had failed to do what was required of it as a state, because UK law had 'permitted employers to treat less favourably employees who were not prepared to renounce a freedom that was an essential feature of union membership'.[57] Furthermore, under UK law 'it was . . . possible for an employer effectively to undermine or frustrate a trade union's ability to strive for the protection of its members' interests'.[58] The Court concluded that 'by permitting employers to use financial incentives to induce employees to surrender important union rights, the respondent State failed in its positive obligation to secure the enjoyment of the rights under Article 11 of the Convention'.[59]

[48] *Young, James and Webster v United Kingdom* [1981] IRLR 408, ECtHR.

[49] Ewing *Britain and the ILO* (2nd edn, 1994) 279.

[50] [2002] IRLR 568, ECtHR (hereinafter referred to as *Wilson and Palmer*).

[51] Then contained in the Employment Protection (Consolidation) Act 1978, s 23; see now the Trade Union and Labour Relations (Consolidation) Act 1992, s 146. As to this right see 9.4.3.

[52] [1995] ICR 406, [1995] IRLR 258, HL.

[53] The statute has since been amended to include omissions.

[54] See n 50.

[55] *Wilson and Palmer*, n 50, at para 42.

[56] *Wilson and Palmer*, n 50, at para 46.

[57] *Wilson and Palmer*, n 50, at para 47.

[58] *Wilson and Palmer*, n 50, at para 48.

[59] *Wilson and Palmer*, n 50, at para 48.

Since the decision in *Wilson and Palmer* a number of aspects of the trade union freedom under Article 11 have been explored by the European Court:

A right to be a union activist? The European Court has held that the Article 11 right includes being active in the union including acting as a union representative.[60]

A human right for the union and not just its members? The collective right to associate is protected under UK law by a means of a series of rights for individuals. In *Wilson and Palmer*, the European Court held that the UK was in violation of Article 11 'as regards both the applicant unions and the individual applicants',[61] the clear implication being that 'trade unions have freedom of association rights in addition to and separate from the rights of their members'.[62] Initially the Court held that contracting states 'enjoy a wide margin of appreciation as to how trade union freedom may be secured'[63] and reasserted its consistently held view that the freedom of a union to make its voice heard does not extend to an obligation on an employer to recognize a union.[64]

A human right to union recognition? The Court's view on this changed in the case of *Demir v Turkey*,[65] in which the Court declared that the right to bargain collectively was one of the essential elements in the human right to associate. It is clear from *Demir* that a state must not interfere with collective bargaining between an employer and union unless there is a 'pressing social need' to justify such interference. There is some doubt about whether this means that a state must provide a legal means by which a union can compel an employer to bargain with the union. The UK Supreme Court has held that the ECHR case law does not require this. This is considered in 9.7.3.2.

A human right to strike? With regard to industrial action, the European Court has held that Article 11 safeguards the freedom of trade unions to protect the occupational interests of their members,[66] and that '[t]he grant of a right to strike represents without any doubt one of the most important of [the] means' by which a state could seek to secure the protection of the Article 11 rights.[67] So far the Court has not decided that the right to strike is an essential component of the right to associate, but restrictions on industrial action will be taken into account in assessing whether a state is in breach of Article 11. This is considered in 10.1.6.

[60] For example *Sánchez Navajas v Spain* [2001] ECHR VI–507, ECtHR; *Straume v Latvia* (App no 59402/14) [2022] IRLR 802, ECtHR). This does not, however, protect those who abuse such rights or who exceed the limits of acceptable criticism (eg *Palomo Sánchez v Spain* [2011] IRLR 934, 54 EHRR 872, ECtHR; Szima v Hungary [2013] IRLR 59, ECtHR).

[61] *Wilson and Palmer*, n 50, at para 48. According to the court, a trade union 'must . . . be free to strive for the protection of its members interests': para 42.

[62] Ewing 'The Implications of *Wilson and Palmer*' (2003) 32 ILJ 1.

[63] *Wilson and Palmer*, n 50, at para 44. 'Article 11 does not . . . secure any particular treatment of trade unions or their members and leaves each state a free choice of the means to be used to secure the right to be heard': para 42.

[64] 'Although collective bargaining may be one of the ways by which trade unions may be enabled to protect their members' interests, it is not indispensable for the effective enjoyment of trade union freedom': *Wilson and Palmer*, n 50, at para 44. However, there have since been further cases relating to the question of recognition.

[65] [2009] IRLR 766, 48 EHRR 1272, ECtHR.

[66] *UNISON v United Kingdom* [2002] IRLR 497, ECtHR; see also *Swedish Engine Drivers' Union v Sweden* (1976) 1 EHRR 617, ECtHR; *National Union of Belgian Police v Belgium* (1975) 1 EHRR 578. It was accepted in *Gate Gourmet London Ltd v TGWU* [2005] IRLR 881, QBD that Convention rights are relevant in an industrial dispute case when deciding on the 'balance of convenience' test for an injunction.

[67] *Schmidt and Dahlström v Sweden* (1976) 1 EHRR 632, ECtHR.

9.3.3 **Restrictions on freedom of association stemming from EU law**

Collective agreements about the contractual terms of workers were in principle in breach of EU competition law, but the European Court of Justice established an exception based on social policy objectives in relation to agreements intended to improve conditions of work and employment.[68] However, following Brexit EU competition law is no longer part of UK law, so this issue has disappeared. Similarly, prior to Brexit, industrial action to protect collectively agreed terms of employment could in some circumstances be unlawful because it interfered with the EU freedoms relating to establishment and supplying services across member state boundaries, as discussed in 10.2.6.1.

9.3.4 **Atypical workers and union representation**

UK law gives some trade union rights to 'workers' and other rights to 'trade unions' and their members, with trade unions being defined as organizations consisting of 'workers'.[69] The term 'worker' is defined in s 296 of the Trade Union and Labour Relations (Consolidation) Act 1992 as someone working or seeking to work under a contract of employment and/or who contracts personally to perform work or services for another, but excluding those cases where the other party to the contract is a professional client. Increasing numbers of people work in what has been termed the 'gig economy', where they have no guaranteed hours and are often offered work in discrete pieces through the internet. Frequently the provider of the work seeks to secure that those doing the work are regarded in law as being neither 'employees' nor 'workers', for example by issuing contracts which permit the other party to perform the service either personally or by supplying someone else.

Gig economy workers are among the most vulnerable in the workforce, both because of the precarious nature of their flow of work and because they often do not qualify for the protections and rights given to employees and workers. Arguably, they need union protection and representation more than most.[70] Article 11 of the European Convention on Human Rights gives the right to join a union and to benefit from its protection to 'everyone'. The UK appellate courts have held in two recent rulings that in deciding whether in accordance with Article 11 union rights should be accorded to an individual it must be decided whether they are in an 'employment relationship' with the alleged employer and in determining this European Court of Human Rights case law required that account must be taken of the guidance in Employment Relationship Recommendation No 198 of the International Labour Organization. This says that the determination of the existence of such a relationship should be guided primarily by the facts relating to the performance

[68] C-67/96 *Albany International BV v Stichting Bedrijfspensioenfond Textielindustrie* [1999] ECR I-5751, [2000] 4 CMLR 446. Although a judgment of the European Free Trade Association Court, applying these principles to the identical EFTA law on competition, indicated that the interest in self-preservation held by a non-profit-making body set up to implement a collective agreement might go beyond improving the conditions of workers, with the result that the agreement infringed competition law: *Holship Norge AS v Norsk Transport Arbeiderforbund* [2016] 4 CMLR 29. The EFTA Court is required to pay due account to the principles laid down by the Court of Justice of the European Union (Art 3(2) of the EFTA Surveillance and Court Agreement). See Hendy and Novitz 'The Holship Case' (2018) 47 ILJ 315.

[69] See 9.2.1.

[70] On the extent to which unions have sought to protect such workers, and how they have gone about it, see Bertolini and Dukes 'Trade Unions and Platform Workers in the UK: Worker Representation in the Shadow of the Law' 50 ILJ 662. On how platform workers have sought to organize themselves see Katsabian 'Collective Action in the Digital Reality: the Case of Platform-Based Workers', 920210 84(5) MLR 1005.

of the work and the remuneration of the worker and should not turn on how the relationship is characterised by the parties. The Guidance say that relevant factors, which point towards such are relationship, include:

(a) the fact that the work: is carried out according to the instructions and under the control of another party; involves the integration of the worker in the organization of the enterprise; is performed solely or mainly for the benefit of another person; must be carried out personally by the worker; is carried out within specific working hours or at a workplace specified or agreed by the party requesting the work; is of a particular duration and has a certain continuity; requires the worker's availability; or involves the provision of tools, materials and machinery by the party requesting the work;

(b) periodic payment of remuneration to the worker; the fact that such remuneration constitutes the worker's sole or principal source of income; provision of payment in kind, such as food, lodging or transport; recognition of entitlements such as weekly rest and annual holidays; payment by the party requesting the work for travel undertaken by the worker in order to carry out the work; or absence of financial risk for the worker.

Accordingly, in the first case, *National Union of Professional Foster Carers v Certification Officer*,[71] the Court of Appeal held that foster carers were in an employment relationship sufficient to engage the Article 11 right to union representation, notwithstanding that they have no contractual relationship with the local authorities who recruit and pay them. In consequence they should be entitled in law to form a union. In order to achieve that, the Court said, the definition of 'worker' must be read so as to include foster carers.

The decision went the other way in the second recent case, which concerned a more typical 'gig' or platform working situation. This case was *Independent Workers' Union of Great Britain v Central Arbitration Committee*,[72] where Deliveroo riders again sought to rely on Article 11 so that their 'union' could apply to the CAC for a declaration that it was recognized for bargaining with Deliveroo. The problem was that the case law on definition of 'worker' in the Trade Union and Labour Relations (Consolidation) Act 1992 excludes people who usually do work personally but have the contractual right to send a substitute.[73] Was there an unjustified interference with the Article 11 rights of the Deliveroo delivery operatives? The Supreme Court said that 'employment relationship' for Article 11 purposes is an autonomous concept that does not depend on the definitions of workers or employees used in domestic law. The correct approach requires the application of a multifactorial test, focusing on the practicalities of the relationship and how it operates in reality. The genuine and unrestricted right to use a substitute was decisive in determining that they were not in an 'employment relationship' as interpreted by the European Court of Human Rights. The Court pointed out that in fact other aspects of the relationship also in accordance with Recommendation No 198 supported this conclusion, namely that riders were free to reject offers of work, to make themselves unavailable and to undertake work for competitors.

[71] [2021] EWCA Civ 548, [2021] IRLR 588, CA.

[72] [2023] UKSC 43, [2024] IRLR 148, [2024] ICR 189.

[73] See 2.1.3.

9.4 Right of association through laws against union discrimination

The Trade Union and Labour Relations (Consolidation) Act 1992 gives workers protection against an employer declining to recruit them, subjecting them to a detriment at work, or dismissing them on the grounds of workers' union membership or activities.

9.4.1 Refusal of employment on grounds of union membership

9.4.1.1 The basic protection for union membership

Section 137 of the Act makes it unlawful to refuse a person employment on grounds related to union membership or non-membership.[74] While the government's primary aim may have been to abolish the pre-entry closed shop (where employers only offered jobs to people who already belonged to a union),[75] in the event the protection was extended to union members and non-members alike.

Unusually in relation to trade union rights, it is only prospective employees in the narrow sense of those who will receive a contract of *service* who benefit from this protection,[76] something which may well be in breach of Article 11 of the European Convention on Human Rights.[77] 'Refusal' includes a positive refusal or a 'deliberate omission' to entertain and process an application or to offer employment to the applicant, or causing the applicant to withdraw or cease to pursue their application, or making an offer on terms designed to cause the employee to refuse it (terms 'which are such as no reasonable employer who wished to fill the post would offer').[78]

It will normally be for the applicant to prove that the refusal of employment was on grounds related to union membership and not for some other reason, but in certain specific circumstances a refusal of employment will be deemed to be unlawful without such proof. In particular, where a job advertisement is published which indicates (or might reasonably be understood as indicating) that a particular job is only open to union members or to non-union members, a person who does not satisfy that requirement and who applies unsuccessfully for that job will be conclusively presumed to have been refused employment unlawfully, whatever the employer's reason for not appointing.[79]

9.4.1.2 Protection for union activities?

Section 137 refers to refusal of employment on grounds of union *membership*; it does not expressly cover an applicant who is refused employment because of their past union *activities*. In contrast, the protection against discrimination *within* employment specifically

[74] This includes a situation where a person is refused employment because they are unwilling to accept a requirement not to join or to cease to be a union member: s 137(1)(b). There is an important causative requirement that the employer's actions must have been 'because' of the relevant union factor; if the employer can show some other reason there is no contravention of s 137: *Miller v Interserve Industrial Services Ltd* UKEAT/0244/12.

[75] The provision was originally introduced by Employment Act 1990, s 1. See in particular the Green Paper which led to this enactment, 'Removing Barriers to Employment' (Cm 655, 1989).

[76] Trade Union and Labour Relations (Consolidation) Act 1992, s 143(1).

[77] See, on the personal scope of trade union rights, 9.3.4.

[78] Trade Union and Labour Relations (Consolidation) Act 1992, s 137(5).

[79] Trade Union and Labour Relations (Consolidation) Act 1992, s 137(3). A refusal of employment will also be deemed unlawful where it is in pursuance of a union labour-supply arrangement and the applicant is not a member of the relevant union (s 137(4)), and where the applicant rejects a job offer because they are unable or unwilling to accept or comply with conditions attached to it concerning union membership (s 137(6)).

extends to dismissal or detriment because of union activities.[80] However, in the context of s 137 the EAT, in *Harrison v Kent County Council*,[81] refused to draw a rigid distinction between membership of a trade union and taking part in union activities, holding that if a person was refused employment because they were a trade union activist or because of their union activities, it is open to a tribunal to conclude that they were refused employment because they were a member of a union.

Some doubt was cast on this broad, purposive interpretation of s 137 by the later case of *Wilson and Palmer*.[82] However, the question was re-examined in *Jet2.com Ltd v Denby*,[83] where the EAT concluded that the wide interpretation in *Harrison* not only reflected the intention of Parliament but was consistent with the tribunal's duty under s 3 of the Human Rights Act 1998 to interpret UK legislation so as to be compatible with the right to participate in a trade union under Article 11 of the European Convention on Human Rights. However, it remains unresolved whether a point comes at which an individual's union activities go beyond the incidents of membership and so take the person concerned outside the protection of s 137. Is a union 'troublemaker' protected, or someone who has organized and taken part in industrial action? As to the latter point, the Supreme Court's judgment in *Secretary of State for Business and Trade v Mercer*[84] may be relevant. That case concerned whether the protection of workers against detriment (s 146) or dismissal (s 152) for taking part in trade union activities extends to taking part in industrial action. The Court held that Parliament had always made separate provision for protection from dismissal and detriment for taking part in industrial action, on the one hand, (contained in Part V of the 1992 Act) and for detriment and dismissal for other trade union activities, on the other hand, (under ss 146 and 152 which are in Part III of the Act). Section 137 also falls in Part III. However, the Court was not expressly considering s 137 and that provision does have a different legislative history from ss 146 and 152, so we cannot be sure how much reliance should be placed on *Mercer* in identifying the true scope of s 137.

9.4.1.3 **Remedies**

Complaints of a breach of this right lie to an employment tribunal,[85] which may make a declaration, order the employer to pay compensation (up to the limit of the compensatory award for unfair dismissal),[86] and/or recommend that the respondent take remedial action 'for the purpose of obviating or reducing the adverse effect on the complainant of any conduct to which the complaint relates'.[87]

[80] See 9.4.3. [81] [1995] ICR 434, EAT.

[82] [1995] ICR 408, [1995] IRLR 258, a case involving an allegation of detriment in employment contrary to s 146. The House of Lords denied the existence of any general principle that a reference to union membership includes union activities, which seemed to place the correctness of the decision in *Harrison* in some doubt. However, subsequently the European Court of Human Rights made it plain in *Wilson and Palmer v UK* [2002] IRLR 568, 35 EHRR 523 that accessing the essential services of a union is intrinsic to exercising the right to belong to a union.

[83] [2018] ICR 597, [2018] IRLR 417. [84] [2024] UKSC 12, [2024] IRLR 599, [2024] ICR 814.

[85] Trade Union and Labour Relations (Consolidation) Act 1992, s 137(2). Complaints must be brought within three months of the conduct complained of, subject to the usual extension where not reasonably practicable: s 139(1).

[86] Compensation is assessed on the same basis as an award of damages in tort for breach of statutory duty, and may include an amount for injury to feelings: s 140(2).

[87] Failure to comply with such an order without reasonable justification may lead to an increased award of compensation, but still subject to the statutory maximum: s 140(3).

9.4.2 **Blacklisting**

While the introduction in 1990 of the right not to be refused employment on grounds of union membership went some way towards plugging the gaps in the protection of the right to associate, in practice it is very difficult for a worker to discover that they were refused a job for this reason—and even harder to prove this. The controversial practice continued of compiling 'blacklists' of union officials or members so that users of the blacklists could deny them employment. The practice of blacklisting was well documented in the UK during the 1980s, and the failure of the UK government to prohibit the practice was criticized by the International Labour Organization.[88]

In 1999 the government enacted s 3 of the Employment Relations Act 1999, which conferred a power on the Secretary of State to make Regulations prohibiting blacklists.[89] However, it was not until evidence emerged in 2009 of widespread blacklisting in the construction industry that steps were taken to make the Regulations.[90]

The Employment Relations Act 1999 (Blacklists) Regulations 2010[91] make it unlawful to compile, use, sell, or supply[92] a blacklist (referred to as a 'prohibited list') of trade union members or persons who have taken part in trade union activities, and which is compiled 'with a view to being used by employers or employment agencies for the purposes of discrimination in relation to recruitment or in relation to the treatment of workers'.[93] There are limited exceptions in the case of those who use a blacklist in order to expose its existence (eg investigative journalists) and situations where significant trade union knowledge or experience is a necessary requirement of the job.[94] Under amendments made by the Employment Relations Act 2025, it is likely that in 2027 regulations will be made so that even if a list was not created for the purpose of discrimination against union members or activists, the use of a list for that purpose will be prohibited.

A worker may bring a claim in the employment tribunal if an employer refuses a person employment as a worker, or subjects a worker to any detriment, including termination of their contract, because that person's name is, or is not, on a prohibited list.[95] Compensation can be awarded for both financial losses and for injury to feelings and is usually a minimum of £5,000.[96] A dismissal for this reason is automatically unfair.[97] A person who suffers loss due to blacklisting is in addition entitled under reg 13 to seek damages from the county court, which (unlike an employment tribunal) could grant an injunction to prevent further damage from occurring.

In *Ryanair DAC v Morais*,[98] the employer complied a spreadsheet of those pilots who had taken part in a strike, and used the spreadsheet to withdraw concessionary travel benefits from them. The pilots claimed that this was a detriment related to a prohibited

[88] See eg ILO 287th Report of the Freedom of Association Committee (1992) para 267.

[89] 'List' is defined widely to mean 'any index or other set of items whether recorded electronically or by any other means': Employment Relations Act 1999, s 3(5).

[90] In the meantime the Construction Industry cases led to prosecution of the list compiler by the Information Commissioner under the Data Protection Act.

[91] SI 2010/493.

[92] The requirement in reg 3(4) for a person to sell or supply a prohibited list 'knowingly or recklessly' would clearly provide a defence for organizations such as the Royal Mail that distribute such lists unknowingly or accidentally.

[93] Employment Relations Act 1999, s 3(1), (2).

[94] Regulation 4(3), (4).

[95] Regulations 5 and 9.

[96] Regulations 8 and 11.

[97] Section 104F Employment Rights Act 1996, inserted by reg 12.

[98] [2025] EWCA Civ 19, [2025] IRLR 297, [2025] ICR 863.

list. The Court of Appeal agreed, holding that the protection extended to a case where someone was blacklisted for taking part in industrial action so long as it was organized by a trade union, even if the action had not been properly balloted so as to make it 'protected' action under s 238A (see 10.7.3). This is an important decision, since until s 76 of the Employment Rights Act 2025 is brought into force there is no other protection for workers against detriment for taking part in industrial action.

9.4.3 **Dismissal, and detriment short of dismissal, on trade union grounds and anti-union inducements**

This section starts with a summary of the various legal protections and then examines the elements which are common to them all. This is followed by a consideration of the aspects which are special to each provision.

9.4.3.1 **The protections in brief**

Detriment

Under s 146 of the Trade Union and Labour Relations (Consolidation) Act 1992,[99] a worker has a right not to be subjected to any detriment as an individual by their employer, whether by an act or a deliberate failure to act, for the purpose of:

(1) preventing or deterring them from being or seeking to become a member of an independent trade union, or penalizing them for doing so;
(2) preventing or deterring them from taking part in the activities of an independent trade union at an appropriate time, or penalizing them for doing so;
(3) preventing or deterring them from making use of trade union services[100] at an appropriate time, or penalizing them for doing so; or
(4) compelling them to be or become a member of a trade union.

Dismissal

Under s 152 of the Trade Union and Labour Relations (Consolidation) Act 1992, a dismissal of an employee will be *automatically unfair* if the reason for it (or, if more than one, the principal reason) was that the employee:

(1) was, or proposed to become, a member of an independent trade union;
(2) had taken part, or proposed to take part, in the activities of an independent trade union at an appropriate time;
(3) had made use, or proposed to make use, of trade union services at an appropriate time; or
(4) was not a member of any trade union, or of a particular trade union, or of one of a number of particular trade unions, or had refused, or proposed to refuse, to become or remain a member.

[99] As amended by the Employment Relations Act 1999 and the Employment Relations Act 2004 (which extended the protection from 'employees' to 'workers'). Note the analogous protection in Pt V of the Employment Rights Act 1996, for example, for health and safety representatives and pension scheme trustees.

[100] This means services made available by virtue of their membership; this includes consenting to a matter being raised on their behalf by the union: s 146(2A)–(2C).

A dismissal for redundancy will be deemed to be unfair under s 153 of the 1992 Act if it is shown that the circumstances producing the redundancy applied equally to other comparable employees in the same undertaking who were not dismissed,[101] and the employee was selected for dismissal for any of the above reasons.

Anti-union inducements

Under s 145A of the Trade Union and Labour Relations (Consolidation) Act 1992, a worker has a right not to have an offer made to them by the employer for the sole or main purpose of inducing them:

(1) not to be or seek to become a member of an independent trade union;
(2) not to take part at an appropriate time in the activities of an independent trade union;
(3) not to make use (at an appropriate time) of trade union services; or
(4) to be or become a member of any trade union or of a particular trade union or of one of a number of particular trade unions.

Heads (1) to (3) are there to protect union members in their membership and activities, whereas head (4) serves the totally different purpose of protecting *non*-union members, and is therefore considered in 9.6 in the context of the closed shop.

9.4.3.2 **Elements common to trade union dismissal, detriment, and inducement**

Common issue 1: scope of application

These protections apply to 'workers' as defined in s 296 of the Trade Union and Labour Relations (Consolidation) Act 1992—with the exception of dismissal, because unfair dismissal can only extend to 'employees'. However, a non-employee worker whose contract is terminated for a trade union reason can seek a remedy for this as a detriment.[102] The confining of protection to 'workers' may be narrower than required by the European Convention on Human Rights, as discussed in 9.3.4.

Common issue 2: membership of a union—which union?

This question arises in cases of inter-union rivalry. In *National Coal Board v Ridgway*,[103] a pay rise was given by the employer to members of a new miners' union, the UDM, but not to members of the traditional union, the NUM, because the NUM had rejected a pay deal negotiated between the employer and the UDM. Two of the NUM members complained that this constituted a breach of s 146 because they were in effect being penalized for being members of the NUM rather than the UDM. The Court of Appeal held that the protection in the section applies to penalizing membership of a particular union as well as membership of unions generally.[104] The Court therefore accepted the potential application of s 146 to inter-union disputes which lead to differential treatment by the employer.

[101] In making the comparison with the position of other employees, anything that the employee did or had a right to do as a trade union official must be left out of account, lest the purpose of the section be defeated: *O'Dea v ISC Chemicals Ltd* [1995] IRLR 599, CA.

[102] Trade Union and Labour Relations (Consolidation) Act 1992, s 146(5A).

[103] [1987] ICR 641, [1987] IRLR 80, CA; rvsg [1986] IRLR 379, EAT; see Simpson (1987) 50 MLR 639.

Common issue 3: does 'membership' also cover union activities?

The protection for union activities and for making use of union services only applies in relation to such actions while in the employment of the current employer.[105] An employee who is dismissed when their employer discovers that in a *previous* job they were a union activist is only protected if the protection against detriment or dismissal for 'membership' can be read as covering activities. This issue also arises in relation to non-recruitment contrary to s 137,[106] but the answer the law gives to the question may well not be the same.

At first, in *Discount Tobacco and Confectionery Ltd v Armitage*,[107] the EAT declined to draw a sharp distinction between union membership and making use of the essential services of a union. However, in *Associated Newspapers Ltd v Wilson; Associated British Ports v Palmer*,[108] the House of Lords said, obiter, that while the decision in *Discount Tobacco* might have been correct on its facts, it did not establish any general principle that membership of a union was to be equated with making use of the union's services. In their Lordships' opinion there was no justification for reading into the statute extra words such as 'or making use of the essential services of the union'.[109]

This narrow interpretation of 'membership' reduces the protection of union membership under limb (a) almost to vanishing point,[110] as in practice employers are far more likely to be concerned about the consequences of union membership than they are about the mere fact of membership. In *Speciality Care plc v Pachela*,[111] the EAT made a bold attempt to salvage something from the wreckage of the House of Lords' decision in *Wilson and Palmer*, noting that the relevant passage was obiter and holding that it was still open to a tribunal to find that an employee dismissed for engaging the assistance of a union in a dispute with the employer over working hours was dismissed on grounds of union membership. Subsequently it became clear in the light of the European Court of Human Rights' decision in *Wilson and Palmer* that the broader interpretation of 'membership' was to be preferred, and the issue was resolved by the Employment Relations Act 2004, which inserted limb (3) to cover detriment and dismissal for the purpose of preventing or deterring the worker from 'making use of trade union services at an appropriate time'. Notwithstanding the *Pachela* decision, in the light of this implicit acceptance by Parliament that 'membership' could not extend to cover making use of union services, it would appear that in ss 145A, 146, and 152 the meaning of 'membership' is confined to the narrow fact of being a member.

Nevertheless, a worker dismissed for being a union activist while working for a previous employer might still succeed for either of two reasons. First, it seems likely that Article 11 of the European Convention on Human Rights as interpreted by the European Court means that UK tribunals should interpret the legislation to give such a worker protection—for example, by reading these sections as applying to union activities and to use of union service at an appropriate time *at a previous employer*—although this would be contrary to two UK authorities which pre-dated the Human Rights Act 1998.[112] Second, the protection under these sections does clearly apply where action is taken to *prevent or*

[104] Although *Ridgway* was subsequently overruled on other grounds in *Associated Newspapers Ltd v Wilson; Associated British Ports v Palmer* (see n 108), the reasoning of the Court of Appeal on this point would appear still to be valid.

[105] In *City of Birmingham District Council v Beyer* [1978] 1 All ER 910, [1977] IRLR 211, EAT, a well-known union activist gained employment with the council by using a false name, and was subsequently dismissed because of the deceit; the EAT held that the employee could not benefit from the statutory protection, because it did not extend to pre-employment activities. This was considered to be correct by the Court of Appeal in *Fitzpatrick v British Railways Board* [1991] IRLR 376.

[106] See 9.4.1.2.

[107] [1995] ICR 431n, [1990] IRLR 15, EAT.

[108] [1995] ICR 406, [1995] IRLR 258, HL.

[109] See Lord Bridge at 264; Lord Lloyd at 266. Cf Lord Slynn at 265, taking a somewhat broader view.

deter an employee from engaging in union activity within the current employment, and as the Court of Appeal indicated in *Fitzpatrick v British Railways Board*,[113] it may be difficult for an employer to persuade the tribunal that it was entirely motivated by the employee's previous conduct and not by fears that it might be repeated in the present employment.

Common issue 4: 'at an appropriate time'

To be protected, the union activities, or use of union services, must take place at an 'appropriate time'. This is defined as either outside the worker's working hours or during their working hours but with the agreement or consent of the employer.[114] 'Working hours' are defined as the time when the worker is contractually obliged to be at work, which has been construed as meaning when they are actually performing work, so that when an employee takes part in activities during a meal break that will be an 'appropriate time', even if they are still on the premises and being paid by the employer during the break.[115]

One potentially contentious area is whether the employer has in fact consented to an activity where it takes place during working hours. The case of *Robb v Leon Motor Services Ltd*[116] showed a fairly rigorous approach to the issue. The employee, a shop steward, was transferred to a department where he was no longer in contact with other employees because of his over-enthusiastic pursuit of union activities in working hours. The union was not recognized and there was no express agreement allowing union activities during working hours, but the employee's written statement of terms of employment stated that he would be permitted to take part in union activities 'at the appropriate time', though without defining it. The EAT dismissed the employee's claim under what is now s 146, holding that there was not the necessary agreement or consent to his union activities (the written term being too vague to be construed as such).

In contrast, in *Bass Taverns Ltd v Burgess*,[117] the employee, a pub manager who was also a shop steward of the National Association of Licensed House Managers, was regularly permitted by the company to make presentations on behalf of the union at induction courses for new employees. On one occasion he made some remarks which were highly critical of the company, and which led to his demotion. He resigned and claimed constructive dismissal, arguing that his dismissal was for taking part in union activities at an appropriate time, and was therefore automatically unfair under s 152. The Court of Appeal held that the employer's consent to his participation should not be considered as subject to an implied limitation that nothing critical of the company would be said, so that, despite his remarks, he was still taking part in trade union activities at an appropriate time, and his claim therefore succeeded.

It is clear from the cases that consent does not have to be express. This was accepted by the Court of Appeal in *Marley Tile Co Ltd v Shaw*,[118] but the case also shows that consent

[110] Per Knox J in *Discount Tobacco and Confectionery Ltd v Armitage* [1995] ICR 431n, [1990] IRLR 15 at 16.

[111] [1996] ICR 633, [1996] IRLR 248.

[112] See n 105.

[113] *Fitzpatrick v British Railways Board* [1991] IRLR 376.

[114] Sections 145A(2), 146(2), and 152(2).

[115] *Post Office v UPOW* [1974] 1 All ER 229, [1974] ICR 378, HL; *Zucker v Astrid Jewels Ltd* [1978] ICR 1088, [1978] IRLR 385, EAT.

[116] [1978] ICR 506, [1978] IRLR 26, EAT.

[117] [1995] IRLR 596, CA. Cf the suggestion in the case that the activities might fall outside the protection of s 152 if the employee indulged in malicious, untruthful, or irrelevant invective; see also *Shillito v Van Leer (UK) Ltd* [1997] IRLR 495, EAT (on the analogous provisions on victimization for health and safety reasons).

[118] [1980] ICR 72, [1980] IRLR 25, CA; *Zucker v Astrid Jewels Ltd* [1978] ICR 1088, [1978] IRLR 385, EAT. In *Marley*'s case the Court of Appeal upheld the EAT on the possibility of implied consent, but reversed its decision on the facts, holding that no consent could be inferred in the circumstances.

will not be readily implied merely from the employer's silence (particularly on an ad hoc basis, where it is being argued that on one particular occasion the employee proposed to do something during working hours and the employer did not strenuously object), and that implied consent is not easy to establish where the union member is not accredited by the employer, or the union is not recognized. On the other hand, where the union presence is accepted by the employer it is possible that, even in the absence of express agreement, consent might be implied over a period of time on the basis of established workplace practice or good industrial relations practice.

If the employer permits employees to talk about anything they wish while working (eg while working on a production line), then an employment tribunal can conclude that there was implied consent to chat while working about union matters.[119]

It is possible that by confining protection to union activities undertaken outside working hours (or at such other times as are permitted by the employer) the UK legislation fails to give full effect to Article 11 of the European Convention of Human Rights. In *Sadrettin Guler v Turkey*,[120] a civil servant had been issued with a warning for being absent from work without leave to attend a demonstration on Labour Day that had been organized by his union. The European Court of Human Rights held that this was an unjustified interference with his right to participate in union activity. The judgment is a short one and it is possible that the determining factor was that the employer had simply issued the warning for absence without considering whether, given that the absence was for a union activity, it was justifiable to issue the warning. Nevertheless, since dismissal or detriment for taking part in a strike can be an interference with the Article 11 right,[121] it does seem possible that dismissal or detriment for union activities other than 'at an appropriate time' might be a breach of Article 11.

Common issue 5: activities of a trade union

To be protected, the activities in question must be those of a trade union, in the sense of having a genuine trade union connection rather than just being the type of activity which one might expect a union to engage in. Thus, protected activities would include taking part in union meetings,[122] consulting a shop steward or union official,[123] and attempting to recruit new members or form a workplace union group.[124] However, they would not include actions on an individual basis without any union involvement, as in *Chant v Aquaboats Ltd*[125] where the EAT held that the applicant's actions, in personally complaining about woodworking machinery which did not comply with safety standards and organizing a petition of other employees to support the claim, did not qualify as trade union activities and so were not protected.[126]

A point comes at which activities done allegedly for trade union reasons are so extreme that they are not regarded as trade union activities, for example if they are 'wholly

[119] *Zucker v Astrid Jewels Ltd* [1978] IRLR 385, [1978] ICR 1088, EAT.

[120] App No 56237/08, [2018] IRLR 880.

[121] See 10.1.6.

[122] *Miller v Rafique* [1975] IRLR 70, IT; this may apply to attendance at a meeting which is critical of the union: *British Airways Engine Overhaul Ltd v Francis* [1981] ICR 278, [1981] IRLR 9, EAT.

[123] *Marley Tile Co Ltd v Shaw* [1978] ICR 828, [1978] IRLR 238, EAT (rvsd on other grounds: [1980] ICR 72, [1980] IRLR 25, CA).

[124] *Brennan v Ellward (Lancs) Ltd* [1976] IRLR 378, EAT; *Lyon and Scherk v St James Press Ltd* [1976] ICR 413, [1976] IRLR 215, EAT; *Dixon and Shaw v West Ella Developments Ltd* [1978] ICR 856, [1978] IRLR 151, EAT.

[125] [1978] 3 All ER 102, [1978] ICR 643, EAT (an unfair dismissal case); *Gardner v Peeks Retail Ltd* [1975] IRLR 244, IT; *Drew v St Edmundsbury Borough Council* [1980] ICR 513, [1980] IRLR 459, EAT.

[126] An employee raising health and safety concerns today may well be protected under the specific provisions concerning dismissal or other detriment for health and safety reasons in the Employment Rights Act 1996, ss 44 and 100: see 7.5.4.1.

unreasonable, extraneous or malicious acts', but 'the right to take part in the affairs of a trade union must not be obstructed too easily' by finding that acts were not trade union activities.[127] So, for example, a shop steward making remarks to new recruits about management's attitude to health and safety which he later accepted were 'over the top' nevertheless fell within the scope of trade union activities,[128] as did a trade union official keeping a copy of, and referring in a grievance to, a surreptitious photograph of a manager's diary entry which had been supplied to him because it might be relevant to a redundancy exercise.[129] On the other hand, the dismissal of a union representative for disclosing to her members some confidential information with which she had been supplied by the employers in the course of negotiations on a expressly confidential basis was not a dismissal for taking part in trade union activities.[130]

A key question is whether ss 146 and 152 give protection against detriment and dismissal for taking part in industrial action. One might think that participation in industrial action is a classic example of taking part in trade union activities, and therefore protected. However, there are two problems. First, it can be argued that protection—at least against dismissal, if not detriment—for taking part in industrial action is dealt with elsewhere in the 1992 Act. Secondly, even if participation in industrial action could in principle constitute an activity of a trade union it will rarely be undertaken at an 'appropriate time', as it is unlikely to be an activity undertaken outside working hours or within working hours but with the employer's consent (see 'Common issue 4' above).[131]

The Supreme Court held in *Secretary of State for Business and Trade v Mercer*[132] that s 146 and s 152 do not extend to detriment or dismissal imposed for participating in industrial action, because dismissal is indeed dealt with elsewhere in the Act (ss 238–238A),[133] and the provision on detriment is parallel and must be construed in the same way. This creates a lacuna, where there is nothing to prevent an employer imposing a penalty short of dismissal on an employee who has taken part in industrial action, such as the issuing of a warning, the denial of overtime or refusing to increase pay when the pay of other workers is increased. The Supreme Court recognized in *Mercer* that this meant that UK law did not meet the standard required by Article 11 of the European Convention on Human Rights. This is considered further in 10.7.4. Note that some protection is available through Blacklisting Regulations (see 9.4.2) and that once s 76 of the Employment Rights Act is in force there will be specific statutory protection for industrial action detriment (see 10.7.4).

The next question is whether ss 146 and 152 apply if the trade union activity is not *participating* in industrial action but *organizing* it. Is detriment or dismissal for organizing covered by s 146 and s 152? EAT has held in the past that participating in the preliminary planning and organization of industrial action can amount to taking part in trade union activities within the meaning of s 152.[134] Unlike with participating, if s 146 and s 152 cover organizing there is there is no conflict with s 238A since that concerns only dismissal for *participation* in industrial action. Although the Court of Appeal in *Mercer*[135] said that

[127] *Morris v Metrolink RATP Dev Ltd* [2018] EWCA Civ 1358, CA, unreported, approving statements in *Lyon and Scherk v St James Press Ltd* [1976] ICR 413, [1976] IRLR 215, EAT.

[128] *Bass Taverns Ltd v Burgess* [1995] IRLR 596, CA.

[129] *Morris v Metrolink RATP Dev Ltd* [2018] EWCA Civ 1358, [2018] IRLR 853.

[130] *Azam v Ofqual* [2015] UKEAT 0407/17/1903, unreported.

[131] *Britool Ltd v Roberts* [1993] IRLR 481, EAT. One example of industrial action which could conceivably be held to be at an 'appropriate time' is a ban on voluntary (ie non-contractual) overtime, as noted by the Supreme Court in *Secretary of State for Business and Trade v Mercer* [2024] UKSC 12, [2024] IRLR 599, [2024] ICR 814 at para 45.

[132] [2024] UKSC 12, [2024] IRLR 599, [2024] ICR 814.

[133] See 10.7.3.

[134] *Britool Ltd v Roberts* [1993] IRLR 481, EAT.

[135] [2022] EWCA Civ 379, [2022] IRLR 517, at paras 51 and 54.

s 146 and s 152 does not apply to organizing industrial action, the Supreme Court did not address this point. It is submitted that what the Court of Appeal said was obiter and incorrect.

9.4.3.3 **Detriment for trade union reasons**

The elements of this which are common with dismissal for trade union reasons are dealt with in 9.4.3.2.

Detriment by 'action' or 'omission'

The section applies where a worker is 'subjected to any detriment' by the employer, whether by an act or a deliberate failure to act (ie an omission). Note that the beneficiary of this section is any 'worker', and not merely any 'employee'.[136] If the work contract of someone who is not an employee is terminated for trade union reasons, they cannot bring a claim for unfair dismissal under s 152, but the termination is a detriment and they can claim under s 146 instead.

Detriment 'as an individual'

The worker must be subjected to a detriment 'as an individual'. This requirement is designed to ensure that the protection cannot be used to claim what are essentially collective rights belonging to the union. Action taken by the employer against a trade union (eg derecognition of the union, or the withdrawal of union facilities) may well have an indirect adverse effect on union members, but it is unlikely to constitute a detriment to them as individuals within the scope of the statutory protection unless it affects them personally, for example through their pay packets, rather than affecting them only as union members or officials. A good example of action taken against a union which affected the members personally can be seen in *National Coal Board v Ridgway*,[137] where a pay rise was negotiated by a breakaway union, the UDM, but was rejected by the long-standing union, the NUM, and the increase was paid to UDM members but not to NUM members. The Court of Appeal held that this constituted action taken against the applicants (who were NUM members) as individuals, because the action against the union also affected them as individuals through their pay packets.

It seems that derecognition of an individual shop steward (as opposed to derecognition of the union) can constitute action taken against that person as an individual, even though it may not directly affect them as an employee.[138] In the context of dismissal for union membership or activities, it has been held that the protection does not apply where action is taken by the employer in retaliation for activities by the union generally, unless those affected were singled out for attention because of their own trade union membership or activities.[139]

[136] See 9.3.4 for the width of this term.

[137] *National Coal Board v Ridgway* [1987] ICR 641, [1987] IRLR 80, CA. See also *Cheall v Vauxhall Motors Ltd* [1979] IRLR 253, where the employer's refusal to allow union representation in disciplinary proceedings was held to be action taken against individual employees. Although *Ridgway* was overruled by the House of Lords in *Associated Newspapers Ltd v Wilson; Associated British Ports v Palmer* (n 114) on other grounds, the reasoning of the Court of Appeal on this point still appears to be valid.

[138] *F W Farnsworth Ltd v McCoid* [1999] ICR 1047, CA, upholding the EAT decision on this point: [1998] IRLR 362.

[139] *Carrington v Therm-A-Stor Ltd* [1983] ICR 208, [1983] IRLR 78, CA; the decision has been heavily criticized, and rightly so.

Was the employer's sole or main purpose on the list of prohibited purposes?

Once a worker has established that they were subjected to some detriment short of dismissal, it then falls to the employer to show the 'sole or main purpose' for which it acted or failed to act.[140] The courts have tended to take a narrow approach to this issue, and have refused to equate the employer's *purpose* with the *effect* of the action complained of. In *Gallacher v Department of Transport*,[141] the employee, a civil servant who for several years had spent most of his time on trade union duties, was advised by his career development officer that in order to gain promotion he would need to acquire greater line management experience, which would necessitate a sharp reduction in his union activities. The tribunal held that this recommendation was intended to deter him from continuing with his union activities, and that the employers had therefore taken action short of dismissal against him for the purpose of deterring him from taking part in trade union activities. However, the Court of Appeal held that the tribunal had misconstrued the meaning of the word 'purpose', by failing to distinguish between purpose and effect. According to Neill LJ, in this context the phrase 'for the purpose of' 'connotes an object which the employer desires or seeks to achieve'; on the facts, the employers' purpose was to ensure that only those with sufficient management experience were promoted, not to deter the employee from continuing with his union activities.

A useful way of thinking about this distinction is the example given by counsel to the EAT in *North Essex NHS Foundation Trust v Bone*.[142] Counsel pointed out that if she ate a large chocolate cake because she liked cake, she was aware that she was likely to get fat, but her *purpose* in eating the cake was not to get fat. The case, which went on to the Court of Appeal, concerned a member of a small union acting in opposition to a large, recognized union, where the employer subjected him to detriments in order to dissuade him from union activities, with the intention of marginalizing the small union and also placating the recognized union and so achieving a quiet life. The Court held that the employer's *purpose* in acting the way it did was clearly to deter the claimant from undertaking activities for the small union, and so the employer's actions were contrary to s 146.[143]

Provided that the employer's *purpose* is not on the proscribed list, then the fact that the employer is pleased that the *effect* of its actions would be to deter union activities does not mean there has been a breach of s 146. This was the conclusion in *Serco Ltd v Dahou*,[144] where disciplinary action was taken against a member of a union (ultimately leading to dismissal) against the background of possible disruption of the Olympic Games. The EAT ruled that if the disciplinary action was held to have been properly taken in its own terms (ie for the actual misconduct) and not to have been for the purpose outlawed in the section then there was no breach of ss 146 or 152, and that would remain the case if the management welcomed, because of the claimant's union activism, the opportunity to suspend him and were pleased to be able to dismiss him.

Remedies

An worker subjected to a detriment in contravention of s 146 may complain to an employment tribunal.[145] If the tribunal finds the complaint justified, it must make a declaration to that effect and may order such compensation as it thinks just and equitable.[146] The tribunal must have regard to the infringement of the worker's rights under s 146 and

[140] Trade Union and Labour Relations (Consolidation) Act 1992, s 148(1).

[141] [1994] IRLR 231, CA. [142] UKEAT/0352/12, 10 July 2014.

[143] *Bone v North Essex Partnership NHS Foundation Trust (No 2)* [2016] EWCA Civ 45, [2016] IRLR 295.

[144] [2015] IRLR 30, EAT. This issue was not discussed by the Court of Appeal when the case was appealed: [2016] EWCA Civ 832, [2017] IRLR 81.

[145] Trade Union and Labour Relations (Consolidation) Act 1992, s 147.

[146] Trade Union and Labour Relations (Consolidation) Act 1992, s 149(2).

to any loss sustained by the worker, in particular any expenses incurred by them and any loss of benefits which they might reasonably have expected but for the employer's act or failure to act. The tribunal is not restricted to the worker's pecuniary loss, and may also award compensation for any non-pecuniary injury such as stress and anxiety caused to the worker, for deprivation of benefits which might have come from trade union membership,[147] and for injury to feelings.[148]

9.4.3.4 **Dismissal for union reasons**

The elements of this which are common with detriment short of dismissal for trade union reasons are dealt with in 9.4.3.2.

A dismissal contrary to s 152 is automatically unfair. What is more, there is no minimum qualifying period of continuous employment to bring such a claim.[149] The remedies available are also better than in an ordinary case of unfair dismissal. Note that a claim of unfair dismissal for union reasons cannot be brought by a person who is not an employee but is, because they have contracted to do work personally, a 'worker' within the meaning of s 296 of the Act. Such a person can, however, claim that the termination of their contract is a detriment contrary to s 146.

'Sole or principal reason' for dismissal

Establishing that the sole or principal reason for a dismissal or a redundancy selection was one of the specified trade union grounds can give rise to considerable evidential problems, particularly where the employer claims that there was some other reason (eg misconduct) for the dismissal. It is not enough that the employer's actions are 'connected with' or 'tainted with' considerations of the employee's union activities.[150] The EAT has emphasized that the scope of the factual enquiry into the reason for the dismissal should not be restricted.[151] It is also clear that malice or anti-union feeling on the part of the employer is not enough: in *Therm A Stor v Atkins*,[152] an employer responded to a request to recognize a union by dismissing 20 recent recruits who were selected without reference to whether they were union members. Since it could not be shown that any particular employee was dismissed for their union membership or activities, the protection of ss 152 and 153 did not apply. See 7.4.1.3 on *Royal Mail Group v Jhuti*.

Interim relief from dismissal for union reasons

In cases where an employee complains of unfair dismissal for trade union reasons, ss 161–166 of the 1992 Act make special provision for 'interim relief' pending the full hearing. The aim is to safeguard the position of the employee by seeking to ensure that they remain in employment until the tribunal is able to hear the case. One rationale for this special provision is that dismissals for union reasons are particularly likely to trigger industrial disputes and therefore it is wise to seek to keep the alleged victim in employment until the fairness or otherwise of the dismissal has been determined by the tribunal.

[147] *Brassington v Cauldon Wholesale Ltd* [1978] ICR 405, [1977] IRLR 479, EAT.

[148] *Cleveland Ambulance NHS Trust v Blane* [1997] IRLR 332, EAT.

[149] Trade Union and Labour Relations (Consolidation) Act 1992, s 154. Cf. the normal two-year qualifying period for unfair dismissal claims. This section was substituted by the Employment Relations Act 2004, to make it clear that the burden of proof remains on the employer in all complaints of unfair dismissal on trade union-related grounds.

[150] *North West Ambulance Services v Rice* UKEAT/0152/18, 30 January 2019, unreported.

[151] See *Driver v Cleveland Structural Engineering Co Ltd* [1994] ICR 372, [1994] IRLR 636, EAT, where the employer's failure to select the applicant, a former shop steward, for alternative employment in a redundancy situation was held to be legally relevant in determining whether he was unfairly dismissed on account of his trade union activities under s 152.

[152] [1983] IRLR 78, [1983] ICR 208, [1983] 1 All ER 796, CA.

An application for interim relief must be presented to a tribunal within seven days of the effective date of termination,[153] and must be backed by a certificate from an official of the union concerned,[154] stating (a) that the applicant is a member of the union (or proposed to become one) and (b) that in the official's opinion there are reasonable grounds for supposing that the dismissal was for union reasons. The tribunal must hear the application as soon as is practicable.[155] If the tribunal thinks it likely[156] that the employee's complaint will be upheld at the full hearing, it must ask the employer if it is willing to reinstate or re-engage the employee pending the hearing. If so, the tribunal will make an order to that effect; if not, the tribunal will make an order for the continuation of the employee's contract pending the full hearing.[157] If the employer fails to comply with either kind of order, the applicant may complain to the tribunal, which can order the employer to pay compensation (or, if the employer has broken a reinstatement or re-engagement order, can make a continuation order).[158] In practice, in addition to granting interim relief, the tribunal will direct that the substantive unfair dismissal claim should be listed for an early hearing.

Interim relief is available only when notice of dismissal has been given, but it is possible that if steps are being taken that may lead to dismissal a worker may be able to get an injunction to halt those steps by relying on the implied trust and confidence term—arguing that that the action being taken is unlawful detriment under s 146 and that to act contrary to that section is to act in a way which seriously damages trust and confidence.[159]

Remedies for union reason unfair dismissal

For a dismissal which is unfair under ss 152 or 153 there is a minimum basic award (£8,763 at the time of writing).[160] As in other unfair dismissal cases, compensation may be reduced where there is contributory fault, but a failure on the part of the employee to comply with a requirement (whether or not contractual) to join or not to join a union, or not to take part in union activities, is not to be regarded as 'fault' for these purposes.[161]

[153] On which see 7.2.2.

[154] The official must be authorized by the union to act for this purpose: s 161(4). If the authority of the official is challenged, it will be for the union to prove that the official was authorized to sign the certificate: *Sulemany v Habib Bank* [1983] ICR 60, EAT. For obvious reasons there is no requirement for a certificate where an application for interim relief is made in a case of dismissal for non-membership.

[155] Trade Union and Labour Relations (Consolidation) Act 1992, s 162.

[156] That is, the applicant must have a 'pretty good' chance of success, which means more than a 51 per cent chance: *Taplin v C Shippam Ltd* [1978] ICR 1068, [1978] IRLR 450, EAT; *Mihaj v Sodexho Ltd* [2014] ICR D25, EAT. In *Wollenberg v Global Gaming Ventures (Leeds) Ltd* UKEAT/0053/18/DA, 4 April 2018, unreported (a claim for interim relief in a whistleblowing case), this was described as 'a significantly higher degree of likelihood' than 'more likely than not'.

[157] Trade Union and Labour Relations (Consolidation) Act 1992, ss 163–164.

[158] Trade Union and Labour Relations (Consolidation Act 1992), s 166.

[159] *Avsar v Wilson James Ltd* [2020] EWHC 3412 (QB), [2021] IRLR 300. An injunction was not granted because on the facts of the case the judge decided that damages would be an adequate remedy.

[160] Trade Union and Labour Relations (Consolidation) Act 1992, s 156. In common with most other statutory compensation limits, the minimum basic award is subject to indexation under the Employment Relations Act 1999, s 34.

[161] Trade Union and Labour Relations (Consolidation) Act 1992, s 155. In determining whether there has been contributory fault the tribunal is entitled to take into account the employee's conduct *leading up* to the dismissal, although clearly it must disregard the conduct which in fact led to the dismissal: *TGWU v Howard* [1992] ICR 106, [1992] IRLR 170, EAT.

9.4.3.5 **Anti-union inducements**

In the two cases of *Associated Newspapers Ltd v Wilson* and *Associated British Ports v Palmer*,[162] the employers offered a pay rise only to those employees who agreed to sign personal contracts differing from the terms collectively negotiated by the unions. The House of Lords held that neither employer had the purpose of deterring union membership contrary to s 146: in *Wilson* the purpose was to smooth the transition from collective bargaining to individual contracting, and in *Palmer* to achieve greater flexibility.[163] This reasoning was undermined by the decision of the European Court of Human Rights in *Wilson and Palmer*[164] that it was contrary to the right created by Article 11 to belong to and be represented by a union for the law to allow employers to offer financial inducements to workers on condition that they surrender their rights to union representation, or to make it a condition of entering individualized contracts that workers must relinquish those rights.

The result was legislative amendment by the Employment Relations Act 2004, which added s 145A–145F to the 1992 Act so as to deal specifically with sweeteners.

Inducements not to belong to a union or not to take part in union activities

Section 145A bans the offering of payments or other benefits to workers for any of the familiar union-related reasons listed in 9.4.3.1.

Inducements to depart from collective bargaining

Section 145B states that a worker who is a member of a recognized trade union (or one seeking recognition) has a right not to have an offer made to them if (a) acceptance of the offer (together with other workers' acceptance) would lead to one or more of their terms of employment not being (or no longer being) determined by collective agreement negotiated by or on behalf of the union, and (b) the employer's sole or main purpose is to achieve this result. The reference to the offer being made to the worker together with other workers (in the plural) appears to mean that the offer must be made to at least three workers.

In determining the employer's purpose, s 145D(3) requires a tribunal to include in the matters taken into account whether the employer had changed or sought to change collective bargaining arrangements or did not wish to enter into such arrangements, and also whether the offers were made only to some employees for the purpose of rewarding them for good performance or retaining them because of their special value.

The question arises as to whether it is enough to put an employer in breach of s 145B for it to wish to adopt a non-negotiated term, or whether the section only applies if the employer wishes to depart, to some extent at least, from future collective bargaining. A classic situation where this issue arises is when an employer has been unable in annual collective negotiations to agree a new term, such as the amount of a pay rise, with its recognized union. If the employer does not wish to get out of collective bargaining in subsequent years but seeks to break the deadlock in the current year, and so offers that pay rise directly to the union members, the employer clearly has the intention that they should accept that non-negotiated increase. Does that mean the employer has the prohibited purpose?

[162] [1995] ICR 406, [1995] IRLR 258, HL.

[163] See also Lord Lloyd, at 266, on the importance of distinguishing between the *purposes* and the *consequences* of derecognition.

[164] [2002] IRLR 568, ECtHR.

In *Kostal UK Ltd v Dunkley*,[165] the Supreme Court held that the mischief which s 145B was intended to prevent was the bypassing of collective bargaining and that this was how the meaning of 'prohibited result' should be understood. So, in cases where the union is already recognized, s 145B is breached if at the time the offers were made there was a real possibility that but for those offers the workers' terms would have been determined by collective agreement; and, said the majority, where there is an agreed bargaining procedure in place it must ordinarily be assumed that there was such a possibility if the agreed procedure had not been exhausted. In the subsequent case of *Ineos Infrastructure Grangemouth Ltd v Jones*,[166] the EAT stressed that the question of whether negotiations were at an end when the offer was made must be objectively assessed as a matter of fact. In that case, after the rejection by the union of what the employer had called a 'best and final offer', the employer had made an offer direct to its employees. Unlike in the *Kostal* case, the collective agreement between the employer and the union did not contain a formalized series of steps in the negotiation process and the employment tribunal had heard evidence that the parties had contemplated further rounds of negotiation, so the EAT said the tribunal had been right to conclude the parties had been near to reaching agreement at the time the offer had been made. The EAT upheld the decision that the offer had the purpose of bypassing collective bargaining and was contrary to s 145B.

Turning to cases where a union is not yet recognized, but it is seeking recognition, the Supreme Court in *Kostal* was clear that making offers to workers asking them to agree that collective bargaining would not determine their terms of employment would amount to making offers which had the effect and purpose of achieving the prohibited result contrary to s 145B. However, the majority said that merely offering new terms directly to workers at time when a union is seeking recognition would not be a breach of s 145B. This is because, in such cases, at the time when the offers are made there is no possibility of agreeing the terms through collective bargaining since the union is not yet recognized for collective bargaining.

Remedies

A worker or former worker can complain to a tribunal if an inducement contrary to s 145A or 145B is made.[167] If the complaint is upheld, the tribunal is to make a declaration to that effect and award compensation of £5,735 (at the time of writing).

Even without any tribunal decision on the applicability of s 145A or 145B, any acceptance by the worker of an offending offer is unenforceable by the employer, and also the employer cannot recover any inducement already paid over.[168] In apparent contradiction, it is also provided that if, as a result of an offending offer, the terms of employment have been varied, then nothing in s 145A or 145B makes the variation unenforceable.[169] The resolution of the contradiction is presumably that an employee cannot be compelled to continue with a new term which has not yet been implemented, but that once the change has been made to their contract then it is enforceable.

[165] [2022] ICR 434, [2022] IRLR 66. Some of the difficulties thrown up by this case are examined in Bogg and Ewing 'Collective Bargaining in the Supreme Court' (2022) 138 LQR 337 and in Brodie 'Collectivism in Labour Law: Only by Exception' (2022) 51 ILJ 464.

[166] [2022] EAT 22. [2022] IRLR 768.

[167] Trade Union and Labour Relations (Consolidation) Act 1992, ss 145A(5) and 145B(5). The burden of proof on what was the sole or main purpose of the offer is on the employer: s 145D. Note that a worker is also protected against 'detriment' due to their failure to accept the offer: s 146(2C).

[168] Trade Union and Labour Relations (Consolidation) Act 1992, s 145E(4)(a).

[169] Trade Union and Labour Relations (Consolidation) Act 1992, s 145E(4)(b).

9.5 Right of association through laws providing time off work

At a workplace where an independent trade union is recognized, officials of that union have a right to reasonable *paid* time off work to carry out trade union duties and to undertake trade union training, and both union officials and members of that union have a statutory right to reasonable *unpaid* time off work to take part in trade union activities. In addition, union learning representatives have a right to take paid time off during working hours to undertake their duties and to undertake relevant training.

The relevant provisions are contained in ss 168–173 of the Trade Union and Labour Relations (Consolidation) Act 1992, and are supplemented by the ACAS Code of Practice No 3 on *Time Off for Trade Union Duties and Activities*,[170] which recommends the negotiation of specific agreements on time off between employers and unions, to take into account the particular features of each workplace and to provide clear guidelines against which applications for time off can be determined, thereby avoiding misunderstanding, facilitating better planning, and ensuring fair and reasonable treatment.[171] Such agreements are important because the Code itself gives no guidance about what is one of the most disputed issues between unions and employers, namely *how much* time off is reasonable.

9.5.1 Time off for trade union duties

An employer is obliged by s 168 of the 1992 Act to allow an employee who is an official of an independent trade union recognized[172] by that employer to have a reasonable amount of paid time off during working hours[173] for the purposes of carrying on official duties concerned with:

1. negotiations with the employer over matters falling within s 178(2) (which defines the subject matter of collective bargaining) in relation to which the union is recognized by the employer;
2. the performance of functions related to matters falling within s 178(2) which the employer has agreed to the union performing on behalf of its employees;
3. consultation in relation to collective redundancies under s 188 of the Trade Union and Labour Relations (Consolidation) Act 1992 or in relation to a transfer governed by the Transfer of Undertakings (Protection of Employment) Regulations 2006;
4. the negotiation or execution of an agreement under reg 9 of the Transfer of Undertakings (Protection of Employment) Regulations 2006.Time off is also permitted for:
5. training in aspects of industrial relations relevant to the matters in heads (1)–(4).

'Official' is defined as covering union officers and also employee representatives, typically shop stewards, elected or appointed under the union rules.[174] Head (3) is dealt with

[170] The Code is admissible in evidence and is to be taken into account when deciding what time off would be reasonable: s 168(3).

[171] COP No 3, s 4. The Code is set out in *Harvey* S [101].

[172] As to the meaning of 'recognized' see 9.7.2.

[173] See *Davies v Neath Port Talbot County Borough Council* discussed at 9.5.1.6 for a possible challenge to this restriction.

[174] Trade Union and Labour Relations (Consolidation) Act 1992, s 119.

elsewhere[175] and head (4) is of very minor relevance. The other heads deserve a little more attention here.

9.5.1.1 **Time off in relation to negotiation**

The time off must be in order to deal with negotiation about one of the matters in relation to which the union is recognized. The ACAS Code of Practice gives examples such as negotiations about terms and conditions of employment, recruitment and selection policies, redundancy and dismissal arrangements, job grading and job evaluation, flexible working practices, disciplinary and grievance procedures, facilities for union officials, and collective bargaining machinery. The Code suggests that reasonable time off may be sought to prepare for negotiations, inform members of progress, explain outcomes to members, and prepare for meetings with the employer about matters for which the union has only representational rights.

9.5.1.2 **Time off for other functions on behalf of employees**

This covers union officials' duties in relation to matters where the union is recognized but the time off is to perform an activity that falls short of collective negotiation with the employer. It could cover meeting employees to discuss concerns they have about one of the matters in the s 178(2) list, such as a matter of discipline or connected to the allocation of work, or writing to a manager about such an issue on behalf of one or more employees. This right only applies to the extent that the employer has agreed that the union can perform such duties. In reality such agreement is rarely express. Often the agreement is by custom and practice and in other cases the recognition agreement between an employer and a union will, in specifying the time off which the official will be granted, implicitly indicate functions falling under this heading.

9.5.1.3 **Time off for training**

The Code suggests that employers should consider releasing employees for initial basic training in employment relations duties as soon as possible after their election or appointment, and subsequently for further training covering special responsibilities and changing circumstances.

9.5.1.4 **Reasonable time off**

There are two stages in a claim to this right: (a) is the activity one envisaged by the Act (bearing in mind the Code of Practice); (b) if so, is it reasonable to give time off in all the circumstances? The time off must be reasonable in relation to all of the following: the amount of time off, the purpose for which the time off is wanted, the occasions on which it is taken, and any conditions imposed by the employer.[176] The Code of Practice does not give any useful help on *how much* time is reasonable other than to urge unions and employers to enter into an agreement about the issue. Ultimately this is a matter to be decided by an employment tribunal through the means of an employee who is a union official commencing proceedings complaining that the employer has been in breach of their right to time off. In relation to time off for union *activities* it has been held that what constitutes 'reasonable' time off may include a consideration of how much time off has already been given to the employee on previous occasions.[177] In *Ministry of Defence*

[175] See 8.1.3 and 8.2.3.1.

[176] Trade Union and Labour Relations (Consolidation) Act 1992, s 168(3).

[177] *Wignall v British Gas Corpn* [1984] ICR 716, [1984] IRLR 493, EAT.

v Crook and Irving,[178] the EAT suggested that the question of reasonableness is to be approached by applying the 'range of reasonable responses' test evolved in the context of unfair dismissal, but this view is not universally accepted.

9.5.1.5 Time off to attend disciplinary and grievance meetings

While the right to time off for trade union duties only applies with regard to recognized unions, a worker attending a disciplinary or grievance hearing has a right to be accompanied by any fellow employee of their choice even if they are not a union official.[179] Such a companion has a right to a reasonable amount of paid time off to accompany the worker.

9.5.1.6 The right is for *paid* time off

Under s 169 of the 1992 Act, the employee is entitled to be paid the amount which they would normally have received during the time off in question, as if they had worked their normal hours (or, where their remuneration varies with the amount of work done, on the basis of an average of their hourly earnings for that work).[180] This causes problems where the employee is a shift worker or part-time worker, and the duties are carried out at a time when the employee would not otherwise have been at work. The EAT has ruled that as the right is to paid time off 'during his working hours', a shift worker who undertakes trade union duties outside their working hours has no right to paid time off in lieu or to payment in lieu.[181]

However, the ECJ has held[182] that it may be unlawful indirect sex discrimination not to pay a part-time female worker for the total number of hours spent on trade union duties (including those outside her normal working hours) in circumstances where a full-time male worker would have been paid for all the hours spent undertaking those duties because he would have been at work if he had not been carrying out such duties. Such an outcome hinges upon whether the time off in question is for 'work' within the meaning of EU law. It is clear from the ECJ decisions that time off to attend the employer's staff council, or to undergo training necessary for performing staff council functions, does constitute 'work' for that purpose,[183] and the EAT confirmed in *Davies v Neath Port Talbot County Borough Council*[184] that attendance at a union-organized health and safety training course also constitutes 'work', because it is 'by reason of the existence of an employment relationship': 'attending a training course organised by a recognized trade union is still related to the employment relationship and is safeguarding staff interests which

[178] [1982] IRLR 488.

[179] Employment Relations Act 1999, s 10. Alternatively, the worker can choose to be accompanied by an official who is employed by the union. Section 10(7) gives both categories of companion the right to paid time off in accordance with ss 168 and 169 of the 1992 Act.

[180] Trade Union and Labour Relations (Consolidation) Act 1992, s 169.

[181] *Hairsine v Kingston upon Hull City Council* [1992] ICR 212, [1992] IRLR 211, EAT.

[182] *Arbeiterwohlfahrt der Stadt Berlin v Botel* [1992] IRLR 423, ECJ.

[183] *Arbeiterwohlfahrt der Stadt Berlin v Botel* [1992] IRLR 423, ECJ. See also *Kuratorium für Dialyse und Nierentransplantation v Lewark* [1996] IRLR 637, where the ECJ considered the scope of the justification defence.

[184] [1999] ICR 1132, [1999] IRLR 769. The EAT also declared that its previous decision in *Manor Bakeries v Nazir* [1996] IRLR 604, to the effect that attendance at a union's annual conference is not 'work', 'should not be followed'. Arguably, it would have been open to the EAT in *Davies* to distinguish *Manor Bakeries* on the basis that while attendance at a union health and safety training course is 'work' because it is 'by reason of the existence of an employment relationship', attendance at a union's annual conference is not 'work' because it lacks sufficient nexus with the employment relationship. (*Manor Bakeries* was an unusual case, because normally a union official would not be entitled to *paid* time off to attend a union annual conference since such attendance is not within the range of duties set out in s 168; however, the collective agreement in place at Manor Bakeries provided for paid time off for this purpose. The case relied entirely on Art 119 and not on ss 168–169.)

is ultimately beneficial to the employer'.[185] Significantly, the EAT rejected the employer's argument that paying part-time workers only for their contractual working hours was not indirectly discriminatory because it was objectively justified: 'The issue is whether part-time workers (predominantly female) engaged on a full-time course should receive full-time pay. There cannot, it seems to us, be a justifiable policy or aim which maintains the inequality.' The EAT held that s 169(2) on paid time off was to be read subject to the right to equal pay under Article 119.

The position of part-timers in relation to time off is now reinforced by the Part-time Workers (Prevention of Less Favourable Treatment) Regulations 2000,[186] which give part-time workers the right not to be treated less favourably in relation to terms and conditions of employment than comparable full-time workers, unless the employer can show some objective justification for the less favourable treatment. The Regulations do not deal expressly with time off, but the BIS guidance on the Regulations recommends that training should be scheduled so that part-time workers can attend so far as possible. The ACAS Code of Practice on Time Off takes the position that staff who work part time will be entitled to be paid if staff who work full time would be entitled to be paid.

9.5.1.7 **Provision of facilities for trade union duties**

At the time of writing there is no legal obligation on any employer to provide facilities such as accommodation for meetings; telephones; use of noticeboards, intranets, and email; and possibly even dedicated office space. The Code suggests that management should consider making such facilities so that representatives can perform their duties efficiently and effectively and this clearly opens up the possibility that if an employer denies such facilities to a union, then the amount of time off that is reasonable may be greater—because, for example, officials have to travel off site for meetings or to make use of computers at home or in the union branch office. However the Employment Rights Act 2025 introduces new s 168(3A) into TULR(C)A 1992 which, once it is in force will require an employer that permits an employee to take time off for trade union duties to provide, where requested, such accommodation and other facilities as are reasonable for carrying out the duties or undergoing training. The Code of Practice will be amended to give guidance on what would be reasonable.

9.5.2 **Unpaid time off for trade union members to take part in trade union activities**

An employee is entitled, under the Trade Union and Labour Relations (Consolidation) Act 1992, s 170, to reasonable *unpaid* time off during working hours to take part in any activities of an independent trade union to which the employee belongs and which is recognized by the employer in respect of employees in the category in which they fall.

The section specifically excludes activities which themselves consist of industrial action. The ACAS Code of Practice suggests that the right should extend to activities such as attending workplace meetings to discuss and vote on the outcome of negotiations with the employer, meeting full-time officials to discuss issues relevant to the workplace, and voting in industrial action ballots and union elections. Where the member is acting as a representative of the union, the activities may also include taking part in branch, area, or regional meetings of the union; attending meetings of official policy-making bodies such as the executive committee or annual conference; and attending meetings with full-time officials to discuss issues relevant to the workplace.

[185] *Davies v Neath Port Talbot Country Borough Council*, per Morison J.

[186] SI 2000/1551: see 2.1.5.1.

In *Luce v Bexley London Borough Council*,[187] it was held that time off may only be claimed for union activities that are in some way connected with the employment relationship between the employer, the employee, and the union. In that case the employee, a member of the National Union of Teachers, was refused unpaid time off to attend a TUC lobby of Parliament in protest against the Education Reform Bill. The EAT held that the tribunal was entitled to take the view on the facts that as the lobby was intended to convey only political or ideological objections to the proposed legislation, attendance at it could not be regarded as a trade union activity within the meaning of the section.

As with time off for union duties, the amount of time off which may be taken for union activities, and the occasions on which it may be taken, is whatever is 'reasonable'.[188] The Code of Practice does not give any useful help on this other than to urge unions and employers to enter into an agreement about the issue. Ultimately this is a matter to be decided by an employment tribunal through the means of an employee commencing proceedings complaining that the employer has been in breach of their right to time off. It has been held that what constitutes 'reasonable' time off may include a consideration of how much time off has already been given to the employee on previous occasions.[189]

9.5.3 **Paid time off for union learning and equality representatives**

To qualify for time off as a learning representative, the employee must be a member of a recognized independent trade union and have been appointed or elected as a union learning representative, in accordance with the union's rules.[190] A union learning representative is entitled to reasonable paid time off to analyse learning or training needs, provide information and advice about learning or training matters, arrange learning or training, or promote the value of learning and training, and also for the purpose of consulting the employer about carrying on any of those activities.[191] The union must have notified the employer in writing that the employee is a union learning representative, and the employee must have undergone sufficient training to be capable of fulfilling the role (or be going to receive such training within six months).[192] In addition, union members are entitled to reasonable unpaid time off during working hours to access the services of a union learning representative.[193] Similar arrangements will be introduced for trade union equality representatives once s 168B of TULR(C)A 1992 is in force.

9.5.4 **Remedies for breach by the employer**

Where an employer has failed to permit an employee to take time off in accordance with these statutory provisions, the employee may make a complaint to an employment tribunal. Union officials and union learning representatives may also complain if the employer has failed to pay them for the time necessary to perform their duties, in which case the tribunal may order payment of the amount due.

The EAT has held that in order for a trade union official to show that the employer has failed to permit them to take time off in order to carry out union duties, the request for

[187] [1990] ICR 591, [1990] IRLR 422, EAT.

[188] Trade Union and Labour Relations (Consolidation) Act 1992, s 170(3).

[189] *Wignall v British Gas Corpn* [1984] ICR 716, [1984] IRLR 493, EAT.

[190] Trade Union and Labour Relations (Consolidation) Act 1992, s 168A(11).

[191] Trade Union and Labour Relations (Consolidation) Act 1992, s 168A(1) (2).

[192] Trade Union and Labour Relations (Consolidation) Act 1992, s 168A(3), (4). The employee may be entitled to paid time off to undergo training relevant to the functions of a union learning representative: s 168A(7).

[193] Trade Union and Labour Relations (Consolidation) Act 1992, s 170(2B).

time off must have come to the notice of the employer's appropriate representative, and it must be established that they have either refused it, ignored it, or in some other way, knowing of it, simply failed to deal with it; the same principle will surely apply to time off for union activities.[194]

In the case of failure to permit time off, the tribunal must grant a declaration to that effect and may in addition award such compensation as it thinks just and equitable, having regard to the employer's default and any loss sustained by the employee attributable to the failure to permit time off.[195] This is analogous to the similar provision on compensation for detriment short of dismissal on trade union grounds,[196] which means that it is not viewed as a penal fine on the employer, but at the same time the tribunal is not limited to awarding compensation only for pecuniary loss and can include an amount for non-pecuniary matters such as interference with the employee's rights and desires to participate in the activities in question.[197] Unlike in a case of detriment for union activities or membership, compensation for injury to feelings appears not to be available in a refusal of time off case.[198] In *Ryford Ltd v Drinkwater*,[199] the EAT confirmed that an employee does not lose the right to receive compensation for refusal of time off if they still take the time off without permission.

It has been decided by the EAT that the tribunal's powers are only those of awarding a declaration and compensation; the tribunal cannot go further and lay down conditions upon which time off shall be allowed in future.[200]

9.6 The right to dissociate and the closed shop

9.6.1 Protection of individual non-members

While the right to associate[201] has been protected since 1974 through the statutory controls on dismissal and detriment short of dismissal for trade union reasons, the protection afforded in English law to those not wishing to associate with others is of more recent origin.

This reflected the long-standing tradition in British industrial relations of the closed shop, where a job was only available if the worker became, or was already, a member of a specified trade union. In the 1980s the political climate became increasingly hostile towards the closed shop, which led to a succession of legal measures which made it increasingly difficult for employers and trade unions to enforce a closed shop arrangement. This culminated in the Employment Act 1988, which provided that a dismissal is automatically unfair if the reason (or principal reason) was that the employee 'was not a member of any trade union, or of a particular trade union, or of one of a number of particular

194 *Ryford Ltd v Drinkwater* [1996] IRLR 16, EAT.

195 Trade Union and Labour Relations (Consolidation) Act 1992, s 172(2).

196 Trade Union and Labour Relations (Consolidation) Act 1992, s 149(2), as explained by the EAT in *Brassington v Cauldon Wholesale Ltd* [1978] ICR 405, [1977] IRLR 479; see 9.4.3.3, *Remedies*.

197 *Skiggs v South West Trains Ltd* [2005] IRLR 459, EAT.

198 See *Rowe v London Underground Ltd* UKEAT/0125/16, 17 October 2016, where this conclusion was expressed obiter, but after full argument in a case relating to a refusal of time off for a union safety representative under the Safety Representatives and Safety Committees Regulations 1977, SI 1977/500.

199 [1996] IRLR 16, EAT.

200 *Corner v Buckinghamshire County Council* [1978] ICR 836, [1978] IRLR 320, EAT.

201 See Davies and Freedland *Kahn-Freund's Labour and the Law* (3rd edn, 1983) 236–70; Millward, Bryson, and Forth *All Change at Work? British Employee Relations, 1980–1998* (2000).

trade unions, or had refused or proposed to refuse to become or remain a member'.[202] Similarly, all discriminatory action short of dismissal against non-members was made unlawful.[203] In short, the position is that the protection against dismissal or detriment short of dismissal enjoyed by non-members is the same as that enjoyed by union members. Amendments made by the Employment Act 1990 covered non-recruitment for not being a union member by introducing the right not to be refused employment on grounds of union membership or non-membership.[204]

For the remedies available see the 'Remedies' headings in 9.4.1.3 (non-recruitment), 9.4.3.3 (detriment short of dismissal), and 9.4.3.4 (dismissal). Note, however, that in a situation of inter-union rivalry, or in the nowadays very rare case where a union is seeking to enforce a closed shop, it may be claimed that the employer was induced to dismiss the complainant, or to subject him to detriment, by industrial pressure exercised by a union or other third party (whether by strike or otherwise). In such a case the employer or the dismissed employee can ask the tribunal to join the third person as a party to the proceedings.[205] Any award of compensation may then be made wholly or partly against the union or other person, as the tribunal considers just and equitable, instead of against the employer. As a consequence of these measures the closed shop is now rare, if not indeed extinct.

9.6.2 **Other measures restricting the closed shop**

There is a series of further measures restricting enforcement of closed shops through contract compliance or by industrial pressure. The Employment Act 1982 introduced measures designed to render illegal the practice of encouraging closed shops by making it a condition of contracts or tenders that the contractor must use employees who are union members. Any such term in a contract is void and any person who refuses to contract or to accept tenders on such grounds may be liable in tort for breach of statutory duty to anyone adversely affected by their actions.[206] The Act provided that if any other person (in practice a union) exerts industrial pressure in order to secure a union labour-only clause in a contract or to induce an unlawful refusal to contract or tender on the ground of the employment of non-union labour, the usual immunities from suit in tort are expressly withdrawn from that industrial pressure,[207] so that the union may be sued for an injunction or damages.

This process was taken an important stage further by the Employment Act 1988, which removed the immunity from suit in tort from any industrial action taken because a particular employer is employing, has employed, or might employ a non-union member, or

[202] See now the Trade Union and Labour Relations (Consolidation) Act 1992, s 152(1)(c). It will also be an automatically unfair dismissal to select an employee for redundancy because of their non-membership if other employees holding similar positions were equally affected and have not been dismissed: s 153.

[203] See now the Trade Union and Labour Relations (Consolidation) Act 1992, s 146(1)(c).

[204] See 9.4.1.

[205] Trade Union and Labour Relations (Consolidation) Act 1992, ss 150 and 160. Such a request must be granted if made before the hearing but thereafter the tribunal has a discretion to refuse it, save that no such request may be made after the tribunal has made a declaration that the complaint is well founded: s 150(2) and s 160(2).

[206] See now the Trade Union and Labour Relations (Consolidation) Act 1992, ss 144, 145; s 145 also applies to refusals to contract or tender on the ground that the contractor or tenderer uses union labour. Sections 186 and 187 impose similar restrictions on such refusals where the aim is to oblige the contractor or tenderer to recognize or consult with a particular trade union.

[207] See now the Trade Union and Labour Relations (Consolidation) Act 1992, s 222(3). For the statutory immunities see Ch 10.

is failing, has failed, or might fail to discriminate against such a non-union member.[208] Any person affected by such industrial action (directly or indirectly) may, if they have been injured tortiously by it, sue the union for an injunction and for damages without the union having its normal trade dispute immunity.

9.7 Collective bargaining (1): recognition of trade unions

9.7.1 What is 'recognition'?

In everyday 'industrial' terms, a union is recognized by an employer if the employer accepts that the union has a practical right to be dealt with by the employer in connection with a particular category of employees. This may be a right for the union to make representations, or to be consulted about certain issues, or it may be a right to negotiate with the employer about, for example, terms and conditions of employment. Such a right is 'practical' in the sense that in most cases it is not legally enforceable.

However, if a union is recognized to any extent as having a right not just to represent workers but to *negotiate collectively* with an employer then this does bring with it legal consequences. In particular:

1. A recognized independent trade union has rights:
    - to receive bargaining information;[209]
    - to be consulted on impending redundancies;[210]
    - to receive information and be consulted about an impending transfer of the employer's undertaking;[211]
    - to appoint safety representatives;[212]
    - to be notified about certain matters relating to company pension schemes and to be consulted about certain changes to pension schemes.[213]
2. Members and officials of unions recognized by an employer have rights to time off for union duties and activities.[214]

For the purpose of these rights, 'recognition' is defined by the law. This important definition is considered in 9.7.2.

There is one further area of statutory intervention in relation to recognition, and this relates to the circumstances in which an employer can be compelled by law to recognize a union for collective bargaining. A system providing for this was added to the 1992 Act in 2000 and it is considered in 9.7.3. Machinery for consultation and negotiation, including recognition for collective bargaining, is expressly covered as a proper subject for a 'trade dispute' so a union does not have to adopt this statutory route to win recognition from an

[208] See now the Trade Union and Labour Relations (Consolidation) Act 1992, s 222(1), (2), discussed at 10.2.8.3.

[209] See 9.8.

[210] See 8.1.3. Equivalent rights have been extended to directly elected worker representatives.

[211] Transfer of Undertakings (Protection of Employment) Regulations 2006, SI 2006/246, reg 13; see 8.2.3.1.

[212] Health and Safety at Work etc Act 1974, s 2, as amended by the Employment Protection Act 1975, s 116. Again, there has been an extension to directly elected worker representatives.

[213] Pension Schemes Act 1993, s 113; Occupational and Personal Pension Schemes (Disclosure of Information) Regulations 2013 SI 2013/2734; Occupational and Personal Pension Schemes (Consultation by Employers and Miscellaneous Amendment) Regulations, SI 2006/349, as amended.

[214] See 9.5.

unwilling employer—it can instead organize its members to take industrial action against the employer unless the employer will agree 'voluntarily' to recognize the union.[215]

9.7.2 **The definition of recognition**

Section 178(3) of the Trade Union and Labour Relations (Consolidation) Act 1992, states that a recognized trade union is one which is recognized by an employer, or two or more associated employers,[216] to any extent for the purposes of collective bargaining. 'Collective bargaining' is in turn defined by s 178(1) and (2) as negotiation relating to or connected with one of the following matters:

- terms and conditions of employment;
- physical conditions of work;
- engagement or non-engagement or termination or suspension of employment;
- allocation of work between workers;
- matters of discipline;
- workers' membership or non-membership of a union;
- facilities for union officials;
- the machinery for negotiation or consultation about any of these matters, including the recognition by the employer of the right of a union to represent workers in such negotiation or consultation.

The phrase 'recognition . . . to any extent' means that although there must be full agreement to recognize the union for *bargaining*, this need only be on one topic in this list.[217] As long as the necessary level of agreement can be shown, this form of partial recognition will be sufficient in law.[218] In contrast, a form of 'recognition' involving only the right of a union *to represent* its members in individual matters, for example under a grievance or discipline procedure,[219] falls short of an agreement to negotiate and bargain and so does *not* qualify as recognition in law.[220]

The clearest cases are where there is an express recognition agreement between employer and union. However, recognition may also be implied if it exists in practice, no matter what the employer might call it.[221] In *National Union of Gold, Silver and Allied Trades v Albury Bros Ltd*,[222] the Court of Appeal held that the concept of recognition is so important and so fundamental to the statutory union rights that, in the absence of an express agreement, it should not be held to be established unless there is clear and

[215] Trade Union and Labour Relations (Consolidation) Act 1992, ss 218(1)(g), 244(1)(g).

[216] For associated employers see 2.1.6.

[217] *Transport and General Workers' Union v Dyer* [1977] IRLR 93; *National Union of Gold, Silver and Allied Trades v Albury Bros Ltd* [1978] ICR 62, [1977] IRLR 173 (upheld on appeal by the Court of Appeal—n 222).

[218] For example, in *Pharmacists' Defence Association Union v Boots Management Services Ltd* [2017] EWCA Civ 66, [2017] IRLR 355 recognition of the Boots Pharmacists Association for the purposes of bargaining only about facilities for the Association's officials and the machinery for consultation was sufficient to amount to recognition.

[219] This is now backed by the employee's statutory right to be accompanied by a trade union official (or fellow worker) before a disciplinary or grievance procedure: Employment Relations Act 1999, ss 10–15.

[220] *Distributive and Allied Workers v Sketchley Ltd* [1981] ICR 644, [1981] IRLR 291.

[221] *Joshua Wilson & Bros Ltd v Union of Shop, Distributive and Allied Workers* [1978] ICR 614, [1978] IRLR 120.

[222] [1979] ICR 84, [1978] IRLR 504, CA. See also *National Union of Tailors and Garment Workers v Charles Ingram & Co Ltd* [1977] ICR 530, [1977] IRLR 147.

unequivocal evidence of conduct (probably over a period of time) from which recognition can be inferred. On the facts of the case, evidence of recruitment by the union of a few employees followed shortly after by a letter to the employer raising the question of rates of pay, leading to one inconclusive meeting, was held to be too insubstantial to establish the recognition that would have obliged the employer to consult the union over subsequent redundancies.

This case also established that even if an employer observes terms and conditions negotiated elsewhere—the employer in the case was a member of an employers' association which *did* conduct collective bargaining with the union in question—this cannot of itself be construed as recognition by that employer.[223]

9.7.3 **The statutory recognition procedure**

9.7.3.1 **History**

In most cases unions are recognized by employers 'voluntarily': the employer has chosen (albeit possibly in the light of a threat that otherwise the union will organize industrial action) to negotiate with the union in respect of a group of workers. In the 1970s two attempts were made to provide legal machinery for resolving disputes about union recognition. These were unsuccessful and the machinery was abolished by the Employment Act 1980.[224] The Labour government that came to power in 1997 introduced a new statutory scheme for obtaining recognition which was designed so as to try to avoid the delays and other shortcomings of the pre-1980 procedures. The procedure is contained in Schedule A1 to the Trade Union and Labour Relations (Consolidation) Act 1992. Once the relevant provisions in the Employment Rights Act 2025 are in force, this procedure will be amended so as to make it easier for unions to succeed with recognition applications.

9.7.3.2 **The European Convention on Human Rights**

There is some important human rights law background here. The European Convention on Human Rights says in Article 11 that a person's freedom of association includes the freedom to form and join a union for the protection of their interests. The European Court of Human Rights has held that this means that the citizen has a right to join a union which is *effective* for that purpose.[225] However, until 2009 the Court's view was that collective bargaining was not always an indispensable part of that right.[226] The Court's view, however, developed in the case of *Demir v Turkey*,[227] where a local authority had entered into a collective agreement with a trade union. The Turkish courts annulled the agreement on the ground that the Constitution did not authorize public sector unions to negotiate collective agreements. The European Court of Human Rights held that a right to bargaining collectively was an essential element of the right to join an effective union

[223] The *NUGSAT* case was applied in *Cleveland County Council v Springett* [1985] IRLR 131, EAT (concerning health and safety representatives), where it was held that the addition of the union to the Burnham Committee by the Secretary of State did *not* per se mean that the union became recognized by one of the employers represented on that committee.

[224] For details of the repealed procedure see the early editions of this book; particularly interesting historically is ch 8 of the *ACAS Annual Report 1980*, giving their own assessment of the operation of the procedure from 1976 until its demise in 1980.

[225] *National Union of Belgian Police v Belgium* (1979) 1 EHRR 578, [1975] ECHR 4464/70, ECtHR; *Wilson, Palmer and Doolan v United Kingdom* [2002] IRLR 568, 35 EHRR 523, ECtHR.

[226] *Swedish Engine Drivers' Union v Sweden* (1976) 1 EHRR 617, [1976] ECHR 5614/72, ECtHR; *Schettini; UNISON v United Kingdom* [2002] IRLR 497, ECtHR; *Wilson, Palmer and Doolan v United Kingdom* [2002] IRLR 568, 35 EHRR 523, ECtHR.

[227] [2009] IRLR 766, 48 EHRR 1272, ECtHR.

under Article 11, and that in preventing the union and the employer from negotiating and reaching a collective agreement, the Turkish government had infringed this Article.

What the *Demir* case decided for the first time was that it was contrary for a state to *prohibit* an employer and a union from bargaining collectively: it did not rule that a member state must provide a system to *compel* employers to bargain with unions. This was underlined by the Court in 2016 in the case of *Unite the Union v United Kingdom*,[228] which concerned the abolition of the Agricultural Wages Board. This Board had for many decades fixed legal minimum terms and conditions for workers in agriculture by means of collective bargaining between a trade union and representatives of the employers. Unite's complaint was that the abolition of this system was an unjustified interference with the right to join an effective union under Article 11. The Court pointed out in this case that *Demir* related to a state prohibiting collective bargaining and not to the question of whether a state must provide a means by which a union could force an employer to bargain with it.

The Court recognized, however, that in contrast the *Unite the Union* case *did* require a decision on whether a state is required to provide a means by which employers can be compelled to agree terms and conditions by collective bargaining, but unfortunately the Court applied a narrow focus to this question by confining itself to a ruling in relation to UK agriculture. It held that 'the positive obligations of the state to secure the effective enjoyment of the right to bargain collectively' did not go so far as to oblige the UK to provide a mandatory mechanism for collective bargaining *in the agricultural sector*. It is far from clear from the judgment whether a state is however required to provide some general legal mechanism through which a union can obtain recognition—there are passages in the judgment which can be used to support either of the available answers to the question. These passages were considered by the Supreme Court in *Independent Workers' Union of Great Britain v Central Arbitration Committee*[229] which held that the ECtHR had not decided that a member state was obliged to provide a mechanism under which a union could couple an employer to bargain with it. Moreover, if a state had, as in the UK, provided such a mechanism, the adequacy of that mechanism was not subject to legal assessment by reference to Article 11 of the ECHR. For the time being the position is settled in the UK by the Supreme Court decision, but of course the position might change were this issue to come before the ECtHR again.

9.7.3.3 **The statutory recognition procedure—overview**

The procedure is contained in Schedule A1 to the Trade Union and Labour Relations (Consolidation) Act 1992.[230] The procedure is set out in great detail and is combined with very tight time limits. Amendments will be made when s 60 of the Employment Rights Act 2025 comes in to force. Those amendments are intended to make it easier for a union to win recognition.

Applications for recognition are dealt with by the Central Arbitration Committee, whose role is mainly to act as referee to the process: in particular, it is not the responsibility of the CAC to decide whether the employer *ought* to recognize the union—that issue is determined by the level of support for the union among the workforce of the employer.

[228] (Application 65397/13) (2016) 63 EHRR SE7, [2017] IRLR 438. This case is considered in detail in Arabadjieva 'Another Disappointment in Strasbourg: Unite the Union v United Kingdom' (2017) 46 ILJ 289.

[229] [2023] UKSC 43, [2024] IRLR 148, [2024] ICR 189.

[230] For a critical and comparative analysis of these provisions see Wood and Goddard 'The Statutory Union Recognition Procedure in the Employment Relations Bill: A Comparative Analysis' (1999) 37 BJIR 203; Simpson (1998) 27 ILJ 253 and Wedderburn 'Collective Bargaining or Legal Enactment' (2000) 29 ILJ 1 at 33 ff; Dukes, 'The Statutory Recognition Procedure 1999: No Bias in Favour of Recognition' (2008) 37 ILJ 236. For detailed consideration of the CAC case law see *Harvey* Div NI7.

The system applies to 'workers' as defined in the Trade Union and Labour Relations (Consolidation) Act 1992, s 296(1), so if the individuals concerned have a right to send a substitute to carry out the work then this may be fatal.[231] A union can only seek recognition by the organization which is the employer of those workers and not, for example, recognition by another body which in truth determines the terms and conditions of the workers.[232] The Schedule only applies if the employer has at least 21 workers.[233]

There are two other key aspects to the new system. First, statutory recognition will only extend to collective bargaining about pay, hours, and holidays, unless widened by voluntary agreement between the parties.[234] (Where the CAC has declared a union to be recognized and has specified a method of bargaining then the employer must also regularly *consult* the union about worker training.)[235] Secondly, in order to prevent an employer from facing repeated attempts by a union to win recognition, if a union gets an application past the threshold stage (see 'The threshold for admissibility' in 9.7.3.4) but then fails to win recognition, it cannot submit a fresh application for substantially the same bargaining unit for a period of three years.[236]

9.7.3.4 **The detailed provisions**

Part 1 of the Schedule contains the principal provisions on statutory recognition, which may be requested by one union or jointly by more than one. For the rest of this account we shall assume that a single union is seeking recognition. The paragraphs of Part 1 do not follow a very logical order and much turning back and forth of pages in the Schedule is needed to understand the process.

Making the application for recognition

In contrast to other rights under the Act, for this purpose it is not enough for the union to be in law independent; it must actually possess a certificate of independence issued by the Certification Officer.[237] In order to promote a voluntarist approach, before applying to the CAC the union must make a request for recognition to the employer.[238] The employer has ten working days to agree to recognize or to indicate that it is willing to negotiate about the possibility.[239] If this leads to agreement (possibly after assistance from ACAS), that is the end of the procedure.[240] If, however, the employer rejects the request or agrees to negotiate but negotiations fail, the union may apply to the CAC to decide (a) what is to be the appropriate bargaining unit for these purposes and (b) whether the union has the support of the majority of workers in that bargaining unit so that it is entitled to be declared recognized.[241]

[231] See eg *Independent Workers' Union of Great Britain v Central Arbitration Committee and Roofoods Ltd* [2021] EWCA Civ 952, [2022] ICR 84, [2021] IRLR 796. See also 9.3.4.

[232] *R (on the application of Independent Workers' Union of Great Britain) v Central Arbitration Committee* [2019] EWHC 728 (Admin), [2019] IRLR 530.

[233] Schedule A1, para 7, which contains a calculation method. Workers of any associated employer are included.

[234] Schedule A1, para 3(4). The CAC held that 'pay' could include employer contributions to company pension schemes (*UNIFI v Union Bank of Nigeria plc* [2001] IRLR 712, CAC) but this was specifically reversed by the 2004 Act, inserting a new para 171A into the Schedule. The right to bargain applies to both contractual and non-contractual matters; eg it covers shift rosters: *British Airline Pilots Association v Jet2.com Ltd* [2017] EWCA Civ 20, [2017] ICR 457, [2017] IRLR 233.

[235] Trade Union and Labour Relations (Consolidation) Act 1992, s 70A.

[236] Paragraph 39.

[237] Schedule A1, para 6. As to the issuing of certificates of independence see 9.2.4.2.

[238] Paragraph 4.

[239] Paragraph 10.

[240] Paragraph 10. The CAC may, however, be subsequently involved in any dispute over operating the agreement; also, such an agreement may not be unilaterally terminated by the employer for three years: paras 52–63.

[241] Paragraphs 11, 12.

The threshold for admissibility

Once the application has been made to the CAC, a threshold test is applied before the case is allowed to proceed any further:

- the CAC must be satisfied that at least 10 per cent of the workers in the bargaining unit proposed by the union are union members (under the Employment Rights Act 2025 regulations may be made to reduce this percentage, with a minimum of 2 per cent); and
- the CAC must conclude that a majority of workers in the bargaining unit 'would be likely to favour recognition of the union as entitled to conduct collective bargaining on behalf of the bargaining unit'.[242] Once s 60 of under the Employment Rights Act 2025 is in force this second requirement will cease to exist.

A union will ensure that it has well over 10 per cent membership before making an application, so the important part of the threshold test is, until the Employment Rights Act 2025 is in force, the second limb. The CAC will expect the union to produce evidence of support in the form of membership levels and/or petitions. The CAC will invite the union to submit to a CAC official the names of its members and copies of any petitions and will ask the employer to submit a list of the names of workers in the bargaining unit proposed by the union. The official then compares the lists and calculates the percentage support levels, and reports to the CAC panel and to the parties without disclosing the workers' names.[243] A long line of cases decided by the CAC shows that if the combined support from membership levels and petitions is 40 per cent or above, the CAC will almost always conclude that it is likely that in due course a majority of the members of the proposed bargaining unit will support recognition. If the level of support falls between 30 per cent and 40 per cent, much will depend on other factors, such as whether membership levels are rising or falling. Below about 30 per cent an application is likely to fail the threshold test.

Paragraph 35 provides that an application may not proceed if 'there is already in force a collective agreement under which a union is . . . recognised as entitled to conduct collective bargaining on behalf of any workers falling within the relevant bargaining unit'.[244] This important exception (obviously meant to avoid the process becoming involved in inter-union rivalry) is drafted very widely and applies even if the existing union is not independent. This rule can stop recognition by the applicant union even if the range of bargaining under the existing arrangement is substantially lower than that sought by the applicant union,[245] or the applicant union has substantially more members in the bargaining unit than the existing union, and thus is more representative.[246] This 'first-in-the-field' rule is open to manipulation by an employer working with a second union, however unrepresentative.[247]

[242] Paragraph 37(1).

[243] Examples of this threshold test in action are *RMT and J W Filshill* (TUR1/897/2014, 30 December 2014), *CAC and Unite the Union and Aeroprofessional Ltd* (TUR1/899/2014, 16 January 2015).

[244] Paragraph 35. The Schedule adopts the *wide* definition of collective bargaining for this particular purpose (para 3(6); s 178), and note the reference to *any* workers, not a majority.

[245] *TGWU v ASDA* [2004] IRLR 836, CAC ('partnership' agreement with union A covering only facilities for shop stewards was held to rule out an application by union B wanting to represent on pay etc).

[246] *R (NUJ) v CAC* [2005] ICR 493, [2005] IRLR 28, Admin (existing arrangement with (breakaway) journalist union A kept out an application by the NUJ, even though (a) union A only had one member in the bargaining unit and (b) union A had only been recognized by the employer after negotiations with the NUJ had started).

[247] This is illustrated by the fact of *Pharmacists' Defence Association Union v Boots Management Services Ltd* [2017] EWCA Civ 66, [2017] IRLR 355. Note however that the discussion this case of the impact of the ECHR is no longer helpful in the light of the decision of the Supreme Court in *Independent Workers' Union of Great Britain v Central Arbitration Committee* n 229.

Clearly an employer has ready access to all its workers in order to seek to persuade them against recognition. Since 2014 the law has provided that once the CAC has accepted a recognition application, the union may apply to the CAC for a 'suitable independent person' (SIP) to be appointed. The CAC must then make such an appointment and obtain from the employer the names and addresses of all workers in the proposed bargaining unit. These are passed on to the 'SIP' and the union can pay for the SIP to send communications to those workers' home addresses.[248] The access rights of unions will be significantly enhanced by amendments to be made under s 60 of the Employment Rights Act 2025. Under those provisions, as soon as the CAC has accepted an application, the union give notice requesting access to the workers in the bargaining unit. The CAC is then required to try to help the union and the employer reach agreement on the terms on which the union is to have access to the workers, and failing agreement the CAC will prescribe the terms of access. The legislation does not define what is meant by access, but it is clear from the wording that this will include meetings between union officials and workers.

Determination of the bargaining unit

Once an application has been accepted by the CAC the next issue, unless the union and the employer are in agreement on this point, is to determine the unit of workers for whom the union will be entitled to bargain if recognition is granted, which is called the bargaining unit.[249] Clearly there are considerations of workability for both the union and the employer. For example, if the union does not have a high level of support across the represented workforce, it may not be able to 'deliver' on any changes to terms and conditions agreed by it with the employer. Again, an employer may be keen to limit a union's influence to a small part of the workforce. However, in fact tactical issues in relation to the Schedule A1 process for determining recognition claims often influence the parties' contentions on what should be the appropriate bargaining unit: a small unit consisting of categories in the workforce where union support is high will increase the chance of the union winning recognition and a wider unit may dilute the level of support and thus increase the employer's chances of defeating the application.

The emphasis in the Schedule is on encouraging the parties to agree the bargaining unit, but in default of that the CAC must determine the appropriate unit.[250] In doing so, paragraph 19B requires it to take into account the need for the unit to be compatible with effective management and, so far as they do not conflict with that need, also some additional factors:

- the views of the employer and the union;
- existing national and local bargaining arrangements;
- the desirability of avoiding small fragmented bargaining units;
- the characteristics of the workers falling inside and outside the unit;
- the location of workers.

Any alternative unit proposed by the employer must be taken into account by the CAC,[251] but it is not the role of the CAC to decide which is *the most appropriate* bargaining unit; rather, it must decide whether or not the unit proposed by the union is *an appropriate* bargaining unit. A good example is the case which confirmed this interpretation, *R v CAC, ex p Kwik-Fit (GB) Ltd*,[252] where the union proposed a bargaining unit

[248] Paragraphs 19C–19F. [249] Paragraph 18. [250] Paragraph 18. [251] Paragraph 19B(4).

[252] *R v CAC, ex p Kwik-Fit (GB) Ltd* [2002] IRLR 395, CA. In general, a court may be reluctant to interfere with a CAC decision on a point such as this, given the deliberately wide discretion allowed to it by Parliament: *R (Cable & Wireless Services Ltd) v CAC* [2008] IRLR 425, Admin.

comprising workers at the 110 workshops within the employer's two London divisions, while the employer contended that since there was no difference in terms and conditions between those workers and those at the 536 other workshops across the country (other than a London weighting to pay rates), the bargaining unit should be nationwide. The CAC decided that the union's proposed unit was compatible with effective management and it was irrelevant therefore whether a nationwide unit would be more compatible with effective management. The Court of Appeal upheld that approach. In addition to geographical issues, the job categories within a unit are often a matter of contention; for example, employers often argue, usually unsuccessfully, that all workers are treated the same and regarded as part of one team, so the bargaining unit should be all workers save senior management.[253]

Retesting admissibility

If the CAC decides on a unit other than the one proposed by the union, then the admissibility tests are reapplied.[254]

Has the union sufficient support to be declared recognized?

Once the application has been accepted by the CAC and the bargaining unit has been determined, the CAC proceeds to the main question, namely whether the level of support for collective bargaining among the workers is sufficient for it to make an order for recognition. There are two routes:

- If the CAC is satisfied that a majority of workers in the unit are union members, it must declare the union recognized unless one of the exceptions applies.[255] No ballot is held: the union gains recognition by the sheer weight of numbers in the bargaining unit. The exceptions are that the CAC must arrange a secret ballot if it considers that (a) it would be in the interests of good industrial relations to do so, or (b) a significant number of members in the unit inform the CAC that they do not want collective bargaining, or (c) there are doubts about the membership evidence.[256]
- If the majority of workers in the unit are not union members there must be a secret ballot.[257]

The procedure for a ballot is set out in paragraphs 24–28. Those provisions, supplemented by a Code of Practice, set out a system for deciding whether the ballot is to be at the workplace or by post, or a combination of both. They also give the union rights to access to the workers at the workplace—in mass meetings, in small groups, and by noticeboard and leaflets.[258] The union can also pay for the 'qualified independent person' which

[253] For an interesting exception where this argument was successful see *Unite the Union and Kettle Foods Ltd* TUR1/557(2007), 29 June 2007.

[254] Paragraphs 20 and 43–5. As to the admissibility provisions see 9.7.3.4, '*The threshold for admissibility*'.

[255] Once Employment Rights Act 2025 s 60 is in force, any workers who joined the bargaining unit after the day on which the union applied to the CAC for recognition will be ignored. This is intended to prevent an employer flooding the bargaining unit with new workers who it believes are not union members or will vote against union recognition.

[256] Paragraph 22. The CAC's discretion here, as elsewhere in the Schedule, is wide and difficult to challenge; as there is no obligation to give reasons there can be no challenge on the basis of inadequacy of reasons, only on the basis that any reasons that are given are erroneous in law or perverse: *Fullarton Computer Industries Ltd v Central Arbitration Committee* [2001] IRLR 752. In fact, the incidence of judicial review applications has been very low.

[257] Paragraph 23. The ballot must be conducted by an appointed independent person.

[258] Paragraphs 24–28 and Code of Practice: Access and unfair practices during recognition and derecognition ballots (2005).

the CAC has appointed to conduct the ballot to send communications written by the union to the workers' homes. The parties are encouraged by the Schedule to agree access arrangements themselves but the CAC will settle them if necessary and it will also rule on alleged unfair practices. If a party does not put any misconduct right when ordered to do so, the CAC's ultimate sanction is to rule against that party on the recognition issue.[259] Pre-ballot election campaigns are often highly charged but there are very few successful complaints to the CAC.

To win recognition by ballot the union must jump two hurdles: a majority of those voting must support recognition *and* those voting in favour must constitute at least 40 per cent of the workers in the bargaining unit.[260] Once s 60 of the Employment Rights Act 2025 is in force, the second hurdle will disappear, making it significantly easier for a union to win recognition. Following such a result, the CAC must issue a declaration that the union is entitled to recognition; otherwise, the application is dismissed.

Unfair practices

At the time of writing there is a regime aimed at preventing either the employer or the union using unfair practices during the pre-ballot period., such as making an offer of a benefit to workers if they vote in a particular way. Unions have been very concerned that this arrangement is too limited, since it does not prevent improper behaviour at any other point in the process and because it is very hard to succeed with a complaint—the CAC can only decide that a complaint is well-founded and impose a remedy if it is satisfied that not only had an employer engaged in an unfair practice but also that the unfair practice had changed, or was likely to, change the way a worker voted.

In response to this concern, the Employment Rights Act 2025 will, when s 60 is in force, make substantial changes to the rules on unfair practices. First, it will remove the rule that there is only a well-founded complaint if it can be shown that a worker did change, or was likely to change, the way they voted,[261] and second, the period of protection will be extended to cover the whole application process. Under the new regime, once an application for recognition has been accepted by the CAC then neither the union nor the employer must use any unfair practice if it is undertaken 'with a view to influencing the outcome of the application' (which it might do by, for example, removing someone for the bargaining unit, or persuading someone to abandon union membership, or to vote against recognition in a ballot). The forbidden practices are:

- Dismissing or threating to dismiss a worker
- Taking or threatening disciplinary action
- Subjecting a worker to any other detriment
- Offering money or money's worth in return for voting a particular way or abstaining from voting
- Making an outcome-specific offer to a worker (i.e. of money or money's worth to be given if there is a particular result from the recognition application)
- Coercing or attempt to coerce a worker to disclose how they will vote or have voted
- Using undue influence on a worker (a phrase which is not defined)[262]

[259] Paragraph 27D.

[260] Paragraph 29. Once Employment Rights Act 2025 s 60 is in force, any workers who joined the bargaining unit after the day on which the union applied to the CAC for recognition will not be entitled to vote. This is intended to prevent an employer flooding the bargaining unit with new workers who it believes will vote against union recognition.

[261] Paragraph 19N(4).

[262] Paragraph 19M.

If a complaint of unfair practice is well-founded then the CAC can order the guilty party to take such steps are a reasonable to mitigate the effect of the unfair practice,[263] and if the party fails to comply the CAC can, if the party in breach was the employer, order recognition straight away, and if the party in breach is the union can declare straight away that the application for recognition has failed.[264]

Settling and enforcing the method of collective bargaining

Once a union has been declared recognized, the parties are given a period of 30 working days (or longer by agreement) to negotiate a method by which they will conduct collective bargaining on pay, hours, and holidays. If no agreement is reached, either side may apply to the CAC for assistance.[265] A further period is allowed for CAC-assisted negotiations, but after that the CAC must specify a method and in doing so is required to take account of the method specified by the Secretary of State under paragraph 168.[266] This method provides for a minimalist annual negotiation process. In practice the CAC makes only small departures from this method (in order to take account of the particular circumstances of the employer and the union). It is rare for the CAC to need to specify a method of bargaining,[267] but the existence of the specified method as the default option inevitably influences what the union and the employer agree.

If the method is specified by the CAC then it has effect as contract between the parties enforceable by an order for specific performance. If the method is settled by agreement then in a case of non-compliance the other party must first complain about that to the CAC and get the CAC to formally specify the bargaining method, after which any further breach can be enforced by an order for specific performance.[268]

Subsequent changes to bargaining arrangements

The Schedule contains provisions which address what happens if there are changes in the bargaining unit. In summary, Part III (paragraphs 64–95) enables the employer or the union to apply for an amendment. The CAC, after consultation with the union and the employer, will if appropriate amend the bargaining unit or, if the bargaining unit has ceased to exist, will declare that the union is no longer recognized.

9.7.3.5 **Derecognition**

The Schedule also provides various routes to derecognition. The procedures are straightforward where the relevant workers fall below the threshold of 21[269] and where the union loses its independence.[270] In other cases, the procedure is more complex: once three years have passed from the declaration of recognition, the employer or one or more workers may apply for derecognition. The employer must satisfy a threshold test suggesting that the majority of workers no longer support recognition and then a derecognition ballot will be held.[271]

[263] Paragraph 19O.

[264] Paragraph 19P. These remedies of immediate declarations of recognition or no recognition also apply, without any need for an attempt to mitigate their impact, if the unfair practice involved the use of violence or the dismissal of a union official.

[265] Paragraph 30. [266] Paragraph 31.

[267] On average in only 10 per cent of cases: *CAC Annual Report 2017/18*.

[268] Paragraphs 31 and 32. [269] Paragraphs 99–103. [270] Part VII (paras 149–55).

[271] The procedure is set out in paras 104–11 (in Part V (paras 122–33) if the recognition was achieved without a ballot).

9.7.3.6 Semi-voluntary agreement

Sometimes after the compulsory recognition procedure has been started an employer will recognize the union voluntarily. There is clearly a danger that having done so it will back out of the agreement, so paragraph 56 provides that an employer may not terminate such an agreement for three years. This gives the union the same minimum period of recognition as it would have obtained if it had won a declaration of recognition from the CAC. Another possibility is that having agreed the principle of recognition the parties cannot agree a method of bargaining, so if this happens paragraphs 58–61 enable a party to apply to the CAC for a method to be specified.

9.7.3.7 Overall effect

When the statutory recognition system was introduced in 2000, views varied as to its significance. Some thought that it was more important politically than industrially, both as something delivered by the Labour government in return for union electoral support and as a measure aimed principally at a small number of employers with high levels of union membership which did not recognize unions (and in some cases had positively derecognized them in the preceding decade). Others thought it might lead to an increase in collective bargaining, in some cases because the mere existence of the statutory procedure might lead to voluntary recognition. Such a shift might have reversed or stemmed the ongoing decline in union membership levels.

By March 2025 there had been 1,459 applications in just under 25 years of operation. These led to 434 declarations of union recognition, an average of 17 a year.[272] Many of the applications involved quite small groups of employees.[273] It is probably fair to say that CAC declarations of recognition have had little effect on the prevalence of collective bargaining and have affected the negotiation of the terms and conditions of very few workers. Studies have shown that the total number of workers to whom recognition had been extended by the statutory scheme over the first 20 years was only about 79,000, of which 56,000 were in the first 10 years. However, these studies went on to consider the far larger numbers of *voluntary* recognition agreements signed over the period—covering at least 1 million workers, and possibly 2.5 million. There was a substantial surge in these for a few years after the new system was announced in 1997, which suggests the introduction of a compulsory system caused many employers to agree recognition voluntarily rather than face an application to the CAC. However, after a few years the number of new voluntary agreements every year fell back to a level consistent with what was typical before the compulsory system existed.[274] It is important to remember, as discussed in 9.1.2, that the overall prevalence of collective bargaining has fallen rather than increased since the year 2000.

[272] Progress Chart in Central Arbitration Committee Annual Report 2024–25.

[273] For instance, in the years to March 2024 and 2025, the average size of the bargaining units in relation to which recognition was sought were 98 and 93, and the proportion of employers subject to applications who had fewer than 200 workers were 40 per cent, and 43 per cent, respectively: Central Arbitration Committee Annual Report 2024–25.

[274] Gall 'The First Ten Years of the Third Statutory Union Recognition Procedure in Britain' (2010) 39 ILJ 444 and Gall 'Twenty Years of the Third Statutory Union Recognition Procedure in Britain' (2020) 49 ILJ 657. For an assessment of CAC adjudication on the procedure in its first five years see Bogg 'Politics, Community, Democracy; Appraising CAC Decision Making in the First Five Years' (2006) 35 ILJ 245.

9.7.4 TUPE and recognition

By virtue of the Transfer of Undertakings (Protection of Employment) Regulations 2006, where there has been a 'relevant transfer' of an undertaking or of an organized grouping of employees to a new employer, then the recognition of a union may also transfer. This occurs if, after the transfer, the grouping of resources or employees keeps an identity distinct from the rest of the transferee employer's business.[275] This applies whether the recognition of the union was voluntary or statutory.

9.7.5 Forcing recognition on third parties

By virtue of the Trade Union and Labour Relations (Consolidation) Act 1992, ss 186 and 187, it is unlawful to insert into a contract for the supply of goods or services a condition that a party to that contract must recognize a particular union or unions, and any such clause is declared to be void. Likewise, it is unlawful to refuse to contract with or accept tenders from an employer on the ground that it does not recognize a particular trade union. The imposition of such a condition or the refusal to contract or accept tenders on the ground of non-recognition is made tortious as a breach of statutory duty. These provisions go along with the wider provisions in ss 144 and 145 aimed at outlawing union labour-only contracts and tenders. Finally, although a union and its members benefit from immunity from suit if they organize industrial action in order to persuade the employer of those members to recognize the union, s 225 provides that the immunity does not cover industrial action aimed at securing that a contracting party puts a requirement in a contract that the other party should recognize a union.

9.8 Collective bargaining (2): disclosure of bargaining information

Whether a union has been recognized voluntarily or through the statutory procedure, rational collective bargaining is supported by the imposition upon an employer of a duty to disclose certain information to an independent trade union which is recognized by it. This duty is contained in the Trade Union and Labour Relations (Consolidation) Act 1992, ss 181–185 and the Code of Practice No 2 'Disclosure of Information to Trade Unions for Collective Bargaining Purposes'.[276]

9.8.1 The duty to disclose

Section 181 lays upon an employer a duty to disclose information which is in its possession and relates to its undertaking or that of an associated employer, if:

1. it is information without which the union would be impeded to a material extent in carrying out collective bargaining with it, *and*
2. it is information which the employer ought to disclose in the interests of good industrial relations.

[275] SI 2006/246, reg 6. Of course, there is nothing to stop the transferee employer later rescinding the deemed recognition agreement.

[276] See Kahn-Freund *Labour and the Law* (3rd edn, 1983) 106–18; Gospel 'Disclosure of Information to Trade Unions' (1976) 5 ILJ 223; Gospel and Williams 'Disclosure of Information: The CAC Approach' (1981) 10 ILJ 10; Gospel and Lockwood 'Disclosure of Information for Collective Bargaining: The CAC Approach Revisited' (1999) 28 ILJ 233.

The Code of Practice states that the detail, form, and depth of information in any given case will vary with the level of bargaining involved, and goes on in paragraph 11 to give examples of information which an employer may be required to disclose:

- 'pay and benefits': pay systems, job evaluation and grading schemes, total pay bill, fringe benefits, and the way that the overall pay bill is analysed;
- 'conditions of service': recruitment, training, promotion, and redundancy policies; appraisal systems; health and safety matters;
- 'man-power': analysis of workforce, manpower, and investment plans; any planned changes;
- 'performance': productivity, efficiency, and their savings; return on capital; state of order book;
- 'financial': cost structures, gross and net profits, sources of earnings, assets, liabilities; allocation of profits; government aid; transfer prices; loans within the group and interest charged.

The Code emphasizes that these examples are not an exhaustive checklist[277] and it stresses the desirability of reaching joint agreement on what should be disclosed.

As seen above, the union must be 'recognized' in order to make a claim, but that recognition might only be partial (eg restricted to negotiating rights only in respect of certain matters). Disclosure is confined by s 181(1) to information relevant to negotiation about matters 'in respect of which the trade union is recognized'. Thus, in *R v CAC, ex p BTP Tioxide Ltd*[278] the union had bargaining rights in respect of certain terms and conditions of employment, but in respect of a particular job evaluation scheme it only had the right to make representations on behalf of members seeking re-evaluation of their job.[279] Because of this, the Divisional Court held that the CAC had exceeded its jurisdiction in ordering disclosure by the employer of information relating to the scheme.

9.8.2 **Exceptions to the duty to disclose**

The duty to disclose is subject to exceptions which are contained in s 182. Three obvious exceptions are where disclosure would be against the interests of national security or in contravention of other legislation, and where the information was obtained by the employer for the purpose of bringing or defending legal proceedings. The other exceptions are:

1. Information which has been communicated to the employer in confidence, or in some way in consequence of a confidence; this is not further defined, either in the Act or in the Code.[280]

[277] One marginal area of interest is redundancy selection; in *Rolls Royce plc and AEEU* (CAC Award 94/1) the CAC upheld a union request for further information on how a points-based selection system had been applied, accepting that this process fell within the sphere of collective bargaining. In the individual context, this question has caused severe difficulties to the tribunals and courts (see the discussion of *Eaton Ltd v King* and other cases in 8.1.2; see the *CAC Annual Report 1994* for a contrasting of the CAC and the tribunal approach).

[278] [1981] ICR 843, [1982] IRLR 60. For a good example see *Babtie Shaw & Morton and UKAPE* (CAC Award 82/4).

[279] This form of recognition for representation is not sufficient to qualify as 'recognition' for the purpose of claiming statutory union rights: see 9.7.2.

[280] This exception was held to apply to information included in a commercial tender submitted to the employer in confidence: *Civil Service Union v CAC* [1980] IRLR 274.

2. Information relating specifically to an individual (unless they have consented to its disclosure). So, while the union may be able to require disclosure of the wages bill for a whole department, the employer may resist a request for details of each individual's salary. This exception has caused some difficulties in areas where the trend has been towards individual contracting and performance-related pay.[281]
3. Information the disclosure of which could cause 'substantial injury' to the employer's undertaking for reasons other than its effect on collective bargaining.

The proviso to this last exception is of course a very necessary one—otherwise an employer could refuse to disclose information on the basis that it would enable the union to drive a harder bargain. When will harm to the employer amount to substantial injury? There is a difficulty inherent in the word 'substantial': does it mean 'large' or just 'more than trivial'?

The Code gives some guidance in paragraphs 14 and 15 on the kinds of information that might fall within this exception and the circumstances in which substantial injury might occur, for example, cost information on individual products; detailed analysis of proposed investment, marketing, or pricing policies; and price quotas or tender prices. It also states:

> Substantial injury may occur if, for example, certain customers would be lost to competitors, or suppliers would refuse to supply necessary materials, or the ability to raise funds to finance the company would be seriously impaired as a result of disclosing certain information. The burden of establishing that disclosure of certain information would cause substantial injury lies with the employer.

This exception may have the result that the union is hindered in effective negotiation. For example, in *Unite the Union and Vanderlande Industries UK Ltd*[282] the employer's position was that any pay increases had to be funded out of the revenue on the service contract on which the employees worked, but resisted disclosure of turnover and profit margin information on the basis that if this information were disclosed that would cause substantial injury because it would be useful to competitors. The CAC concluded that the absence of information about the profit margins would make it 'extremely difficult for the union to formulate a pay claim' but nevertheless disclosure was not ordered because it could potentially affect the employer's competitive position and thereby cause substantial injury.

An unresolved question is whether the giving of an undertaking by union officials to keep the sensitive information secret would mean that disclosure could be ordered because it would not then be 'likely' that competitors would get to know the information.[283]

Section 182(2) gives some practical protection to an employer by providing that it need not produce original documentation (so that a specially prepared report can be supplied)

[281] *CAC Annual Report 1991* p 3.

[282] DI/10/2021, 15 February 2022, CAC.

[283] In a case where no such undertaking has been given by the union officials it is an open question whether, since the statute only obliges disclosure to the officials concerned, and then only for the purposes of conducting collective bargaining with that employer, an employer could restrain further use of that information by the union by an action for breach of confidence. Even if such an action would be available, the CAC might not consider that this justified disclosure: in a European Works Council case where a worker representative sought disclosure of confidential information, the CAC held that the information could be withheld by the employer because the statutory remedy for breach of confidence in an EWC case would not put right the harm the employer would suffer if the representative broke the confidence: *Verizon European Works Council and Verizon Group* (EWC/26/20, 3 April 2020).

and that it need not compile or assemble information where to do so would involve work or expenditure 'out of reasonable proportion to the value of the information in the conduct of collective bargaining'.

9.8.3 **Enforcement provisions**

If a union considers that an employer is wrongly refusing to disclose information, it may complain to the CAC under s 183. If the CAC thinks that a solution may be reached by conciliation, it must, and most often does, refer the matter to ACAS for that purpose. If the matter is not referred to conciliation (or if it is but no settlement is reached), the CAC must hear and determine the complaint. There are only a handful of applications to the CAC each year and in most years they are resolved by agreement between the parties.[284] If the CAC upholds the complaint, its declaration to that effect must specify the material which ought to be divulged and a period during which the employer should do so.

If at the expiry of this period the employer has still failed to disclose the specified information, the union may make a further complaint to the CAC under s 184, and this time may attach a claim on behalf of some or all of the employees in question (for higher pay, better benefits, etc). It is this procedure which gives teeth to this provision, for if the CAC finds the union's further complaint well founded it may make a declaration to that effect *and* award all or part of the claim for new terms and conditions, which are then automatically incorporated into the contracts of employment of the employees concerned. Given the severity of this sanction it would be a foolish employer who failed to obey a disclosure order made by the CAC.

One unfortunate limitation of these disclosure provisions is that the CAC is limited to deciding upon information which has in fact already been refused by the employer; this means that it cannot go on to give guidance on information which should be divulged in the future, even if to do so might avoid future litigation on linked matters where it is foreseeable that disputes may well arise.[285]

9.8.4 **Other obligatory disclosure**

The employer must also disclose information to a recognized trade union concerning pending redundancies and in relation to proposed transfers of business or service contracts falling within TUPE.[286] Further, an employer must disclose certain information (relating to safety) to safety representatives appointed by a recognized union or elected by employees.[287]

There are also disclosure obligations in relation to pension schemes. First, there are regulations providing for the disclosure of information generally about the running of

[284] See 'Outcomes' on the CAC website.

[285] *R v CAC, ex p BTP Tioxide Ltd* [1981] ICR 843, [1982] IRLR 60.

[286] Trade Union and Labour Relations (Consolidation) Act 1992, ss 188–92 (see 8.1.3) and Transfer of Undertakings (Protection of Employment) Regulations 2006, reg 13 (see 8.2.3.1). Both of these obligations have been extended to elected worker representatives.

[287] For union representatives see Safety Representatives and Safety Committees Regulations 1977, SI 1977/500, reg 7; this contains grounds upon which an employer may refuse to disclose similar to those in the Trade Union and Labour Relations (Consolidation) Act 1992, s 182. See also the Health and Safety Commission's Code of Practice on Safety Representatives (1978) para 6. For the extension to elected worker representatives see Health and Safety (Consultation with Employees) Regulations 1996, SI 1996/1513. The latter Regulations provide that where there are no representatives at all, the employer must consult directly with employees and must disclose information to them.

occupational pension schemes.[288] Second, where there is a proposal to make a 'listed change' (essentially an adverse change) to a pension scheme, then there must be prior disclosure of certain information to, and consultation with, employee representatives. Where there is a recognized union in place or there are representatives under the Information and Consultation of Employees Regulations 2004 or under a 'pre-existing agreement' as defined in those Regulations,[289] then the disclosure and consultation must be with that union or those representatives. Where there are no such representatives and no union then ad hoc elections must be organized.[290]

9.9 A right of union access to the workforce

9.9.1 Overview

One of the difficulties facing trade unions in workplaces where they are not recognized is getting to speak to workers in order to encourage them to become members with a view to the union bargaining with the employer. Without a significant level of membership in a workplace, a union will be unable to win recognition, whether voluntary or under the statutory regime, from the employer. The Employment Rights Act 2025 seeks to address this by introducing a new right of trade union access—both physical and digital—to workers. Under new s 70ZA of the Trade Union and Labour Relations Act 1992, once it is in force, a union will be able to seek access from an employer and, if this is not granted will be entitled to apply to the Central Arbitration Committee for an order that access be granted. The CAC will in those such cases specify the details of such access, bearing in mind certain principles set out in s 70ZF and also any instructions issued by the Secretary of State as part of the implementation of the Act.

9.10 Informing and consulting the workforce generally—the new approach?

9.10.1 Overview

British employment relations have been subject to major changes in the past four decades, and that has been reflected in some of the legal changes explored in this chapter. One of those changes, the statutory recognition law, has had little impact on the decline of collective negotiation, but for a time it seemed possible that we might see the emergence of an alternative legal form of, at least, employee *involvement* in decision-taking which, while falling significantly short of the old model of co-determination with recognized unions, might fill some of the voids left in many areas by the demise of that old model. This new model is a system of consultation with representatives drawn from the workforce who meet managers to discuss matters in what is often called a joint consultative committee or works council.

[288] Occupational and Personal Pension Schemes (Disclosure of Information) Regulations 2013 SI 2013/2734.

[289] See 9.10.

[290] Occupational and Personal Pension Scheme (Consultation by Employers and Miscellaneous Amendment) Regulations 2006, SI 2006/349, as amended.

In reality, this model is not 'new' at all; indeed, the number of workplaces with a JCC has fallen steadily since the 1980s.[291] A significant number of large and medium-sized employers organize such systems voluntarily, but in recent years there has been some statutory underpinning as a result of EU legislation.[292] First of all, some EU directives provided an incentive to set up such systems because they permit employers to use them to agree with employee representatives to depart from EU legal default rules; for example, the Working Time Regulations 1998 lay down rules on working hours and breaks, but then allow 'derogations' from them if this is agreed by means of a collective agreement with a recognized union or, in the case of a non-unionized workplace, by means of a 'workforce agreement', that is, a written agreement with elected employee representatives.[293]

The final component in the EU drive towards worker consultation consisted of two Directives requiring an element of information and consultation more generally. The first deals with large organizations operating across member states and is of reduced significance in the UK following Brexit; the second applies to medium-sized and large employers *within* the member state and is still in full force in the UK—and so will be considered first below.

9.10.2 'Domestic' works councils: the Information and Consultation of Employees Regulations 2004

9.10.2.1 A minimum worker consultation obligation in EU states

Many EU member states have long had legal obligations on employers to set up works councils. The Information and Consultation Directive[294] introduced a minimum 'floor' level of provision for works councils across the whole of the EU even where the employer operates only within one member state. Two key points are, first, that the Directive only applies to employers of at least 50 employees, and secondly, that there is no obligation on an employer to set up a works council unless a prescribed minimum number of employees make a request for one.[295] Rules are set out for calculating numbers and an employee or employees' representative has a right to information from the employer to establish the relevant number.[296]

The Directive was transposed into UK law in the Information and Consultation of Employees Regulations 2004, commonly known as 'ICER', which regulations remain

[291] See Hall 'A Cool Response to the ICE Regulations? Employer and Trade Union Approaches to the New Legal Framework for Information and Consultation' (2006) 37–35 IRJ 456 and the underlying data included with '2011 Workplace Employment Relations Study First Findings' Brigid van Wanrooy et al. There is, however, some evidence of an increase in JCCs (reported in Hall 'EU Regulation and the UK Employee Consultation Framework' (2010) Economic and Industrial Democracy 31(4S) 55).

[292] See generally Hyman 'The Future of Employee Representation' (1997) 35 BJIR 309 and Pollert 'The Unorganized Worker: The Decline in Collectivism and New Hurdles to Individual Employment Rights' (2005) 34 ILJ 217.

[293] See 5.3.2.

[294] Directive 2002/14/EC; Bercusson 'The European Social Model Comes to Britain' (2002) 31 ILJ 209; Young 'Common Sense or Nonsense' [2002] NLJ 794.

[295] The employer can be public or private but at least a part of its activities (and more than a de minimis part) must be the carrying out of an economic activity: Regulation 2 as interpreted in *Advisory Conciliation and Arbitration Service v Public and Commercial Services Union* UKEAT/0160/17, 5 February 2018, unreported.

[296] The Regulations apply to 'employees', not 'workers'. An average of numbers employed is taken over the previous 12 months. An employer may count a part-timer working for 75 hours or less per month as a half: reg 4.

in force following Brexit.[297] The Regulations are supplemented by detailed DTI guidance.[298]

9.10.2.2 **The 'trigger'**

These Regulations only apply if either the employer or the employees choose to make them apply. An employer can start the process,[299] but more usually this happens when the 'trigger' mechanism is operated by the required proportion of the employees in the undertaking, recently reduced to 2 per cent, submitting a written 'employee request' for an information and consultation system.[300] This request will normally be to the employer but can also be directly to the CAC if more confidentiality is wanted.[301] Any dispute as to whether a valid request has been made may be referred to the CAC.[302]

This trigger works on an 'undertaking' basis, even though the ICE system eventually agreed could be wider. 'Undertaking' means a public or private undertaking carrying out an economic activity, whether or not operating for gain.[303] In determining that ACAS was an undertaking for this purpose the Employment Appeal Tribunal applied case law interpreting the same definition in TUPE and the Acquired Rights Directive.[304]

If a valid employee request has been made, this leads to three possibilities under the Regulations:

1. the employer proceeds to negotiate an information and consultation (ICE) system;
2. the employer resists having to do so on the basis of a pre-existing agreement(s) (PEA); or
3. there is no PEA and negotiations either do not start or they fail, in which case the employer becomes bound by the 'standard information and consultation provisions' set out in the Regulations (which operate as the default option).

[297] SI 2004/3426; *Harvey* N III [101]; since the Regulations were made under the Employment Relations Act 2004 rather than the European Communities Act 1972, they would not be revoked as 'EU-derived subordinate legislation' under the Retained EU Law (Revocation and Reform) Bill as drafted on first publication of the Bill. See Hall 'Assessing the ICE Regulations' (2005) 34 ILJ 103 and Hall et al. 'Implementing Information and Consultation—Early Experience under the ICE Regulations: Interim Update Report' (BERR Employment Relations Occasional Paper, October 2008).

[298] The ICE Regulations 2004: DTI Guidance (January 2006). This guidance is hard to find, but it is available by clicking the link at <https://webarchive.nationalarchives.gov.uk/ukgwa/20121212135622/http://www.bis.gov.uk/files/file25934.pdf>. ACAS has also issued its own practical guidance on its website (<http://www.acas.org.uk>). The Regulations complete with annotations from the guidance are set out at *Harvey* R [2195].

[299] Regulation 11.

[300] Regulation 7(1), (2) as amended by the Employment Rights (Miscellaneous Amendments) Regulations 2019 SI 731 reg 16. For the reason for this change see 9.10.2.7. The 2 per cent can be in a single request, or as an aggregate of requests over a six-month period.

[301] Regulation 7(4)–(6).

[302] Regulation 13. Note that where an existing ICE system has been set up (or the employees have voted against one: see 9.10.2.4) there is a three-year moratorium before another request can be made, unless there have been material changes in the undertaking: reg 12.

[303] Regulation 2. The BIS advice makes clear that, in the commercial sector, this operates on a *company* basis (even if that company is itself part of a larger group); the concept of associated employers does not apply.

[304] *Advisory Conciliation and Arbitration Service v Public and Commercial Services Union* [2018] IRLR 1110, [2018] ICR 1793. It was enough that some of the activities of ACAS were in the nature of an economic activity even though some other activities were the exercise of public powers.

9.10.2.3 **Negotiated agreements**

As soon as is reasonably practicable after the trigger has been pulled, the employer must make arrangements for the election and appointment by the employees of negotiating representatives, inform the employees in writing of the identity of those representatives, and invite them to enter into negotiations to reach a negotiated agreement.[305] The employer is in effect given nine months to get the representatives in place and to complete the negotiations.[306] If agreement is not reached before the expiry of the time limit then the default arrangements will apply from a date six months after that expiry date.[307]

Any agreement reached in such negotiations must satisfy certain statutory requirements, namely that it (a) sets out the circumstances in which the employer must inform and consult the employees, (b) is in writing and dated, (c) is signed by the employer, and (d) provides for the appointment or election of 'information and consultation representatives' or, in a surprising alternative, provides that the employer must inform and consult the employees directly.[308] In addition, the negotiated agreement must be approved by the workforce. This means that it must be *either*:

- signed by all the negotiating representatives *or*
- signed by a majority of the negotiating representatives and either approved in writing by at least 50 per cent of the undertaking's employees or approved in a ballot of those employees (in which at least 50 per cent of those voting voted in favour of approval).[309]

Although the Regulations contain these definite procedural requirements, what is striking is the lack of regulation of the *substance* of any negotiated agreement. In theory the consultation arrangements agreed with the negotiating representatives could fall well short of the default rules (the 'standard information and consultation provisions'), but of course in practice the existence of those default arrangements sets a benchmark since the negotiating parties will know that if agreement cannot be reached within the time limit then those default arrangements will come in to force.

9.10.2.4 **Pre-existing agreements**

One key concern when drafting the Regulations was that the new system should not be allowed to wreck existing systems too easily. However, as already seen, these new provisions operate very differently from traditional collective bargaining and do *not* entrench trade unions as the proper conduit for employee representation. The Regulations address this through the 'pre-existing agreement' (PEA) exception, stating that the employer

[305] Regulation 14(1)–(2). It is not clear by whom the choice is to be made as to whether the section of negotiating representatives is by election or appointment but it is clear from reg 14(2)(a) that all employees must eventually be represented by those representatives. The CAC has held that by virtue of reg 14(2)(b) all employees must be allowed to stand to be elected or appointed as such representatives (so that an exclusion of employees with short service or a disciplinary record is not permitted) and all employees may participate in the choice: *Mcguire and DHL eCommerce UK* (IC/0066 (2024) 11 July 2025).

[306] Regulation 14(3) provides that the negotiations are (subject to certain exceptions) to last for a maximum of six months, beginning three months from the date of the request: *Darnton v Bournemouth University* [2009] IRLR 4, CAC. The parties may agree to extend this period: reg 14(5). A complaint about the election on appointment of representatives may be made to the CAC: reg 15.

[307] Regulation 18(1)(b).

[308] Regulation 16(1). There is no presumption that the negotiating representatives will eventually become the ICE representatives.

[309] Regulation 16(3). If a ballot is used it must be secret and fair: reg 16(5). The DTI guidance para 40 suggests the use of an independent scrutineer but this is not a legal requirement. A complaint about a ballot may be made to the CAC: reg 17.

need not proceed with an employee request if there exists one or more such agreements—unless a large proportion of the workforce vote to override the existing arrangements.

The PEA rules are complex. First, the employer can only seek to use the exception if the initial request under ICER was made by fewer than 40 per cent of the undertaking's employees. Secondly, all the employees in the undertaking must be covered by one or more PEAs, and the PEA(s) must have been approved by the employees and set out how the employer is to give information to the employees or their representatives and seek their views.[310] If these conditions are met, the employer (on receipt of the ICER request) may arrange a ballot to see if the request is endorsed by the employees.[311] If at least 40 per cent of the undertaking's employees *and* the majority of the employees voting cast their votes in favour of endorsing the request then the employer must proceed to negotiate under ICER. However, if this double threshold is not attained by those seeking a new system, the employer can refuse to proceed to negotiate a new ICE system.[312]

Some of the difficulties that might arise under these requirements were seen in the first case to be heard by the EAT under the Regulations, *Stewart v Moray Council*.[313] Faced with an employee request for a new ICE system, the council relied on three existing union agreements for a PEA defence. The EAT held against the council because one of the three agreements did not actually specify how information and consultation was to work (possibly a general problem where the employer is relying on long-standing collective bargains which are largely about terms and conditions). The Appeal Tribunal went on to give guidance on two of the other requirements, particularly in cases of existing trade union involvement. With regard to the requirement of full coverage of all employees, it said that this could be shown by the existence of trade union recognition agreements covering the whole workforce (even if there are large numbers, possibly a majority, of non-members). However, there was then a shot across the bows in relation to the prior approval requirement: while trade union 'approval' might be effective to jump this hurdle, this would only be so if (a) trade union members are a majority of the workforce and (b) there is no evidence of any split within the union itself on the issue. Thus 'coverage' can be purely collective, but 'approval' is based on an individualistic model.

So, while the Regulations as a whole might be an opportunity for a trade union trying to establish itself in a non-union organization, the stringent requirements of the PEA defence might be a *threat* to an established trade union which retains long-standing recognition with the employer but on a reduced membership base, since even a shared desire by employer and union to continue the existing system might be trumped by a request for something new by non-members or dissidents.

9.10.2.5 **The statutory default: the standard ICE provisions**

If the employer fails to initiate negotiations when the ICER trigger is pulled, or those negotiations fail to produce an agreement within the time limit, then at most six months later the standard information and consultation provisions apply.[314] The employer must

[310] Regulation 8(1). The Regulations do not specify how employee approval is to be gauged, but the BIS guidance para 20 suggests support by a simple majority in a workforce ballot, a majority of the workforce expressed through signatures or the agreement of employee representatives who represent a majority of the workforce; different agreements covering the undertaking could be approved in different ways. The agreement or agreements in question must pre-date the employee request under reg 7: *AMICUS v Macmillan Publishers Ltd* [2007] IRLR 378, CAC.

[311] Regulation 8(2). The usual rules apply as to the fairness of the ballot: reg 8(3)–(5). Complaint about irregularities lies to the CAC: reg 8(7)–(9).

[312] Regulation 8(5)(b). [313] [2006] IRLR 592. [314] Regulation 18.

arrange within that six-month period a ballot to elect a set number of ICE representatives[315] and the substantive provisions will apply from their election.[316] Those substantive provisions set out the requirements on the employer, which are:

1. to inform the representatives on 'the recent and probable development of the undertaking's activities and economic situation';[317]
2. to inform and consult the representatives on 'the situation, structure and probable development of employment within the undertaking, and on any anticipatory measures envisaged, in particular where there is a threat to employment within the undertaking';[318]
3. to inform and consult the representatives with a view to reaching agreement on 'decisions likely to lead to substantial changes in work organisation or in contractual relations'.[319]

This is fleshed out in paragraphs 55–61 of the BIS Guidance. One limitation is that, as pointed out there, none of this applies to issues of pay or benefits with a monetary value.[320] Apart from that, however, these default requirements are in broad terms and it is suggested that they could, subject to the points made in 9.10.2.7 about the limited impact of ICER in practice, have at least three effects on established tenets of employment law.

First, the reference in (2) to 'anticipatory measures envisaged, in particular where there is a threat to employment' could be important in redundancy situations—as discussed in 8.1.3.1, it is arguable that the law on collective redundancies only requires consultation on how they are to be handled (ie the primary economic decision making has always been managerial), but this could be altered if the standard provisions apply because they appear to push the consultation obligation backwards into the area of the economic need for the redundancies.[321]

Second, the requirement in (3) to consult (with a view to agreement) on 'decisions likely to lead to substantial changes in work organisation' might well cover changes to non-contractual matters (traditionally called 'works rules' and now often found in company handbooks)[322] which employers have often kept in their prerogative, precisely in order *not* to have to involve the workforce in any changes.

[315] Regulation 19(1). The ballot must be conducted under rules set out in Sch 2. The set number of representatives is one per 50 employees (with a minimum of two and a maximum of 25): reg 19(3). Complaint of breach of these requirements lies to the CAC: reg 19(4).

[316] Regulation 18.

[317] Regulation 20(1)(a). Information under reg 20 must be given in such a manner as to allow the representatives to conduct an adequate study and prepare for consultation: reg 20(2).

[318] Regulation 20(1)(b). Consultation under reg 20 must be appropriate in its timing, method, and content; it must be on the basis of the information supplied and any opinion expressed by the representatives; it must permit the representatives to meet an appropriate level of management and to obtain a reasoned response from the employer: reg 20(4)(a)–(c); DTI guidance, para 61.

[319] Regulation 20(1)(c), (4)(d). In addition, reg 21 puts a duty on the parties (when negotiating or implementing either a negotiated agreement or the standard provisions) to 'work in a spirit of co-operation and with due regard for their reciprocal rights and obligations, taking into account the interests of both the undertaking and the employees'.

[320] BIS Guidance para 55. This is because the Directive's treaty base is Art 137, which itself excludes matters of pay as an area of EU competence.

[321] This was expressly envisaged in the government's original consultation document on the Directive. One point of interpretation is that head (3) specifically includes issues coming within the existing laws on collective redundancies and TUPE consultation, with reg 20(5) allowing the employer to disapply the ICE requirement if it notifies the representatives in writing that it intends to go down one of those routes instead. However, the 'threat to employment' limb is contained in head (2), which is *not* covered by reg 20(5) and so cannot be disapplied in this way.

[322] See 2.6.1 and 2.6.2.

Third, the reference in (3) to consultation (with a view to agreement) on changes in 'contractual relations' could be used to counter an employer seeking to force through changes in terms and conditions by suddenly 'proposing' changes on a 'take-it-or-leave-it' basis, putting the onus on the employees to object or face the prospect of having consented by acquiescence.[323] It may be that the language of head (3) will cover this and so diminish significantly the scope for change by employer ambush.

9.10.2.6 **Enforcement**

Finally, what is to happen if the Regulations are breached? Two preliminary points are (a) that there are duties on employees not to misuse information received from the employer in confidence, breach of which are declared to be actionable in a civil suit for breach of statutory duty[324] and (b) that the normal panoply of rights (to time off and not to be dismissed or subjected to a detriment) are applied to employees acting as negotiating or ICE representatives.[325]

In addition, reg 22 provides that an ICE representative (or an employee or employee representative if there are no ICE representatives) can present a complaint to the CAC that the employer has failed to comply with the terms of a negotiated agreement or the standard ICE provisions (whichever is applicable). If the CAC finds for the complainant, it must make a declaration to that effect and may make an order requiring the employer to take specified steps to comply.[326]

The complainant may in addition (within three months of the CAC making the declaration) apply to the EAT for a penalty notice. This is to be issued unless the EAT is satisfied, on hearing representations for the employer, that the failure resulted from a reason beyond the employer's control or that it has some other reasonable excuse for the failure. Regulation 23 sets out the factors to be taken into account when fixing the penalty (which is to be paid to the Secretary of State), and sets the maximum penalty at £75,000.[327]

9.10.2.7 **Have the ICE regulations had much impact?**

In quantitative terms, the evidence as to the use of ICER is limited. The First Findings of the 2011 Workplace Employment Relations Study[328] suggested a continued reduction after 2004 in the proportion of employers with joint consultative committees, but other evidence suggests some increase.[329] The majority of JCCs pre-date the ICER regulations, but there is some evidence that many employers reviewed their arrangements around the time that ICER came into force. They appear in the main not to have sought to adjust

[323] See 2.6.3 and 2.6.4.

[324] Regulation 25. Advice on this vital issue for employers is given in the ACAS advice and the DTI guidance, with the latter going out of its way to state that (contrary to early employer concerns) the giving of information under these Regulations should *not* involve the employer in breaches of the UK Listing Rules or the City Code on Takeovers and Mergers (see para 77). Regulation 26 permits the employer to withhold information where its disclosure 'would seriously harm the functioning of, or would be prejudicial to, the undertaking'. Where the parties disagree over this exemption, the matter may be referred to the CAC for adjudication.

[325] Regulations 27–33.

[326] The level of this form of enforcement remains low. In the five years to July 2018 the CAC received only 14 complaints, on which the CAC made only three final decisions: CAC website, 'Outcomes'.

[327] In *AMICUS v Macmillan Publishers Ltd* [2007] IRLR 885, EAT a fine of £55,000 was imposed in a case of consistent failure by the employer to abide by the procedure, showing a 'cavalier attitude'; on the other hand, in *Darnton v Bournemouth University* UKEAT/0039/09 the university's default was largely due to a misunderstanding and the fine was only £10,000.

[328] Brigid van Wanrooy et al. '2011 Workplace Employment Relations Study First Findings'.

[329] See Hall 'EU Regulation and the UK Employee Consultation Framework' (2010) Economic and Industrial Democracy 31(4S) 55; Hall et al. 'Promoting Effective Consultation? Assessing the Impact of the ICE Regulations' (2013) 51(2) BJIR 355.

their JCCs in order for them to qualify as 'pre-existing agreements', but simply to ensure that no group of employees and no union chooses to 'pull the trigger'.[330] JCCs are much more common in public sector workplaces (65 per cent) than in private sector workplaces (20 per cent).[331] The Taylor 'Good Work' review of 2017 reported that only 14 per cent of workplaces in organizations employing 50 or more employees had an on-site JCC in 2011[332] (but made no mention of some 38 per cent of workplaces where the JCC was at a higher level, such as a national JCC) and suggested that one reason for this was the difficulty in assembling enough employee signatures to meet the then 10 per cent threshold to pull the trigger under ICER. The report recommended a reduction to 2 per cent, which was implemented in April 2020. It remains to be seen whether this makes any difference.

The Trade Union Congress welcomed ICER, which clearly does present an opportunity for unions for organize and to ensure that the employee voice is heard even in employers where the union is not recognized, but the evidence suggests that in practice unions have not used ICER to any great degree. It appears that ICER has not had the effect of marginalizing the representational or bargaining influence of unions and it also appears that in some cases, even though it was the employer which instigated or relaunched an information and consultation system, the standing of the union within the organization was in fact reinforced.[333]

9.10.3 **European Works Councils**

9.10.3.1 **Organizations covered—and the impact of Brexit**

The original European Works Council Directive of 1994[334] was implemented in the UK by the Transnational Information and Consultation of Employees Regulations 1999.[335] Amendments were made to those Regulations in 2011 to reflect the replacement EU Directive of 2009.[336] The law applied to a 'community-scale undertaking', meaning one with at least 1,000 employees within the EU and at least 150 employees in each of at least two member states. Under the Directive, each EU state was required to adopt laws implementing the Directive and it is the law of the member state where the group has its 'central management' that applies to the European Works Council (EWC).

Clearly Brexit has had an impact. Under EU law, the UK no longer counts as a member state for EWC purposes from 31 December 2020, which was 'IP Completion Day' (short for Implementation Period Completion Day). A series of amendments to the UK EWC regulations took effect on that date,[337] and since then it has not been possible to start the process under the UK regulations to set up a new EWC. As for EWCs that were already in existence and which were governed by the UK regulations, the amendments made to

[330] See n 329.

[331] Adams et al. 'Joint Consultative Committees under the Information and Consultation of Employees Regulations: A WERS Analysis' ACAS Research Paper 01/14.

[332] 'Good Work: The Taylor Review of Modern Working Practices', July 2017. It is not clear where the 14 per cent figure came from, but it may well be linked to the 13 per cent given in the WERS analysis by Duncan Adams et al. (see n 331).

[333] Hall et al. 'Trade Union Approaches towards the ICE Regulation: Defensive Realism or Missed Opportunity?' (2015) 53(2) BJIR 350.

[334] Directive 94/45; *Harvey* PII [1150]. See Wedderburn 'Consultation and Collective Bargaining in Europe: Success or Ideology' (1997) 26 ILJ 1 at 21.

[335] SI 1999/3323.

[336] The current Directive is 2009/38 and the 1999 Regulations were amended by SI 2010/1088.

[337] The amendments to the UK EWC regulations are made by the Employment Rights (Amendment) (EU Exit) Regulations 2019 SI 2019/535 Schedule 2, and are expressed as coming into force on exit day, 31 January 2020. However, by virtue of the European Union (Withdrawal Agreement) Act 2020 s 41 and Sch 5 para 1 this is to be read as 'IP Completion Day'.

accommodate Brexit appeared to remove from scope the biggest category of EWC governed by them—those where the central management was situated in the UK—with the result that the UK regulations remained applicable only to EWCs where the headquarters were outside the EU but a UK representative agent had been designated. This was probably unintended and in *easyJet v easyJet European Works Council*,[338] the Court of Appeal ruled that the UK regulations do still apply to EWCs where the central management is in the UK.

Although this is what the UK regulations say, the EU Commission has taken a different stance in a Notice to Stakeholders:[339] this says that UK employees will no longer count for the thresholds used in determining whether an organization is a community-scale one, and takes the view that this not only applied to workers' requests to set up new EWCs but also resulted in existing EWCs ceasing to be governed by the Directive if they depended on a UK component for the enterprise to qualify as a community-scale one. Moreover, even if the number of employees in other states are sufficient to mean that the undertaking is still a community-scale one after IP Completion Day, the Commission takes the view that for undertakings where the central management (either the headquarters or the representative agent) was in the UK, the central management had to be moved to another member state and that if central management did not take steps to do this prior to 1 January 2021 then default rules in the Directive moved the location to another member state automatically.

The consequence of this divergence between the UK and the EU is that a transnational undertaking may, post-Brexit, have to continue to operate an EWC covering UK employees under the UK legislation and also be required to set up, under the laws of an EU state, a new EWC to cover EU employees. The Court of Appeal recognized that this might be the case in the *easyJet* decision.[340] The reality is that most if not all undertakings with a UK central management had before IP Completion Day date taken steps to designate a representative agent in another member state.

The following text concentrates on the UK law governing the ongoing operation of EWCs and only summarises the law that dealt with setting them up.

9.10.3.2 The 'trigger' and negotiating to establish a European Works Council

The Regulations provided for an undertaking covered by them to set up a special negotiating body, either of its own motion or in response to a written request from at least 100 employees or their representatives in at least two member states—sometimes referred to as the 'trigger'. The purpose of this special negotiating body was to negotiate on the establishment of a EWC or, as a lesser form, an 'information and consultation procedure'. If the central management refused to commence negotiations within six months of a request, or if negotiations were still fruitless after three years, the 'default' provisions of Schedule 1 to the Regulations applied, that is, a 'statutory EWC' was imposed.

The default provisions in Schedule 1 laid down the basic rules for composition of the EWC, for the appointment or election of UK members, conduct of ballots, yearly

338 [2023] EWCA Civ 756, [2023] IRLR 782, [2023] ICR 1394.

339 Notice to Stakeholders, *Withdrawal of the United Kingdom and EU Rules on European Works Councils*, 21 April 2020. This view may well not be correct since Arts 4(1) and 4(2) seem to concentrate on the numbers of employees and the locations of the group's establishments at the time the 'trigger' was pulled to set up the EWC.

340 *easyJet v easyJet European Works Council* [2023] EWCA Civ 756, [2023] IRLR 782, [2023] ICR 1394. However in the subsequent case of *HSBC EWC v HSBC Continental Europe* [2024] EAT 104, [2024] IRLR 916, [2024] ICR 1284, the EAT held that wording of the negotiated agreement that had set up the EWC in that case was such that it did not apply to any employees in a location that was no longer part of the EU.

information and consultation meetings on the progress of the business, and exceptional information and consultation meetings.[341]

9.10.3.3 The information and consultation requirements

The subject matter of the yearly meetings should be 'the structure, economic and financial situation, the probable development of the business and of production and sales, the situation and probable trend of employment, investments, and substantial changes concerning organization, introduction of new working methods or production processes, transfers of production, mergers, cut-backs or closures of undertakings, establishments or important parts thereof, and collective redundancies'.[342] Exceptional meetings should be held where exceptional circumstances affect the employers' interests to a considerable extent,[343] particularly in the event of relocations, closure of establishments or undertakings, or collective redundancies.

The employer must supply information to the employee representatives and consult them in relation to 'transnational matters', that is to say, matters which concern the undertaking or group of undertakings as a whole or at least two of its establishments in different member states.[344] The employer must provide information early enough to permit representatives to make a detailed assessment of the possible impact of the information provided and to prepare for consultation.[345] The EWC is entitled to sufficient information to enable it to understand the rationale behind a proposal so that it can represent the interests of the employees affected. However, the EWC is not entitled to information relating to the impact on customers as opposed to employees, nor is it entitled to information solely for the purpose of seeking to reverse a management proposal.[346] The Regulations say that the content and timing of the consultation itself must be such as to enable the representatives to express an opinion on the matter,[347] but the EAT has held that so long as consultation has taken place the employer need not wait for the delivery of the opinion before commencing implementation of its proposals.[348] As to the degree of detail needed in the information provided, the CAC has ruled that in order to fulfil its role the EWC must understand a decision and the rationale for it but that it did not have to be given access to the full range of information that it would need if it were in the shoes of the employer as the decision-maker.[349]

[341] This may be done through a 'select committee' of the EWC, comprising no more than three members acting on its behalf: para 2(4).

[342] Para 7(2). In relation to EWCs set up under the arrangements introduced by the original 1994 Directive, the scope of these 'default' consultation topics is narrower.

[343] If the matter is transnational (see 9.10.3.3) then consultation is required even if the impact on workers is only 'considerable' in one member state: *Princes Group EWC and Clegg and The Central Management of Princes Group* (EWC/21/2019, 17 January 2020) CAC.

[344] Regulation 2(4A) and 18A(7). In order for collective redundancy proposals affecting undertakings in two countries to be transnational, there must be a common link or nexus of some kind or there must be some way in which each proposal affects or has potential effects on undertakings in each of two different countries: *Olsten (UK) Holdings Ltd v Adecco Group European Works Council* [2023] EWCA Civ 883, [2023] IRLR 859, [2024] ICR 1.

[345] Regulation 18A(3). [346] Regulation 18A(3). [347] Regulation 18A(3) and (5).

[348] *Hinrichs v Oracle Corporation UK Ltd* [2019] IRLR 1051. The CAC had said in its decision in this case that although management need not wait for an opinion to be delivered, it 'must do all it can' to supply information to the EWC early enough for it to give an 'opinion which will be useful to the decision-making process' (*Hans-Peter Hinrichs and Oracle Corporation UK Ltd* EWC/17/2017, 12 February 2018, CAC, relying on Recital 23 of Directive 2009/38). The EAT did not address this issue but it did indicate that there would be cases where it might be argued that the consultation obligation had not been discharged if it had not been conducted in good faith (para 48).

[349] *Verizon EWC and the Central Management of the Verizon Group* (EWC/23/2019, 20 December 2019) CAC.

The employer must provide the EWC representatives with 'the means required to fulfil their duty'.[350] This is taken to mean paying for travel and accommodation, for interpreters and translators, and for communications with the employees they represent; and in relation to cases to which the default arrangements apply, it is expressly provided that this includes paying for an expert to advise the EWC.[351] This could include the fees of a lawyer retained to bring a complaint to the CAC that management had failed to comply with EWC law.[352]

Provision is made for certain information not to be divulged by the central management where it would cause serious harm to the undertaking,[353] and any disclosure by an individual representative of information given to them by the central management on the basis that it is to be held in confidence is declared to be a breach of statutory duty.[354]

The usual series of employment protection laws (paid time off and protection from detriment or dismissal) are extended to members of the body in question.[355]

9.10.3.4 **Disputes relating to an EWC**

The CAC hears complaints of failure to operate the information and consultation system adopted in a company under the regulations.[356] Employment protection disputes go to an employment tribunal in the ordinary way.

9.10.3.5 **Have the EWC regulations had much impact?**

The impact of these Regulations has been a matter of some speculation. Their use is limited by two factors. The first is that many UK multinationals were, because of their activities elsewhere in the EU, already covered by the Directive when it was extended to the UK, and although they could have set up an EWC only in relation to employees in other member states, in practice they had in most cases already included UK employees as a matter of good practice and so had pre-empted the UK Regulations. The second is that in any event the Directive extending the EWC Directive to the UK allowed undertakings here until December 1999 to reach voluntary agreements on transnational information and consultation, in which case the Regulations did not apply. A significant number of these 'Article 13' agreements were entered.

[350] Regulation 19A.

[351] Schedule para 9(5) and (6).

[352] *Verizon EWC and the Central Management of the Verizon Group* (EWC/22/2109, 9 October 2019) CAC and *Princes Group EWC and Clegg and the Central Management of Princes Group* (EWC/21/2019, 17 January 2020) CAC.

[353] Regulation 24; the operation of this exception may be challenged before the CAC: see eg *Verizon EWC and the Central Management of the Verizon Group* (EWC/22/2019, 3 April 2020) CAC (employer justified in withholding all information until a sale contract had been entered into because of 'genuine fears' that any rumours would make the business hard to sell).

[354] Regulation 23. Even though disclosure of confidential information by a member of the EWC would be a breach of that duty, management may still be justified in not disclosing the information to the EWC if the harm would already have been done once the breach had occurred: *Verizon EWC and the Central Management of the Verizon Group* (EWC/22/2019, 3 April 2020) CAC.

[355] Regulations 25–32.

[356] Regulations 20, 21, 21A. The CAC may declare what steps are to be taken to remedy the default. If the CAC makes a finding against a party then the other party may apply to the EAT for order for a penalty of up to £75,000 to be paid to the Secretary of State: reg 22.

Review and Final Thoughts

- UK collective labour law largely reflects the historical 'voluntarist' approach to law and policy in connection with collective bargaining between trade unions and employers. The three broad themes of the law are:
  - Protection of union members and union officials from adverse treatment meted out by current and prospective employers. This is coupled with protection for those who do not wish to join a union (see 9.4).
  - A degree of support for union organizing in workplaces where the union is recognized for collective bargaining purposes. In particular, the granting of certain rights to time off work for union members and officials so as to enable them to play a part in running the union (see 9.5).
  - Support for union bargaining, in particular through rights given to a recognized union to demand disclosure by an employer of information to assist the union in negotiating effectively (see 9.8), and also through the granting of rights to be consulted in situations of large-scale change affecting security of employment (see 8.1.3).
- On to these relatively long-standing arrangements there was grafted in 2000 a new right for a union to compel an employer to bargain collectively in cases where the union can show that the majority of workers in the bargaining unit are in favour. This right only confers rights to bargain on pay, hours, and holiday. This topic was considered in 9.7.3.
- These legal arrangements have been arrived at through piecemeal legislation over many decades. Although they can be presented as components of a right to associate, there is no such overarching right or principle expressed in UK law. However, UK law must now be interpreted so far as possible so as to comply with the European Convention on Human Rights, and that does declare an overall principle in the form of a right to be a member of an effective trade union. The Convention's principles-based approach has already affected UK law in relation to collective bargaining and may continue to do so. However, the influence of the Convention in this field has always been limited by the determination of the European Court of Human Rights to reserve for member state governments a wide margin of appreciation in delivering, and making exceptions to, the right to be a member of an effective trade union. The impact of the Convention is discussed in many parts of this chapter, in particular 9.3.2.1, 9.3.2.2, 9.3.4, 9.4.1.2, and 'Common issue 5: Activities of a trade union' in 9.4.3.2.
- The relevance of all these union-related aspects of collective labour law to the situation of the worker in their job has steadily diminished in recent decades because of the ever-falling level of union membership and union influence in the workplace. That reduction in influence is no doubt to some degree a consequence of the growing 'individualist' nature of British society, but it is probably also strongly related to the substantial curbs on industrial action introduced by legislation in the 1980s, in 1990, and, most recently, in 2016 (see Chapter 10). The fall in union membership has appears to have levelled off in the past four years, so this trend may now have halted.
- Some commentators have seen a prospect of continued collective worker influence in the workplace through a growth in the number of bodies with names such as works council, staff committee, and joint consultative committee. EU legislation adopted more than 15

years ago enables workers to compel an employer to set up a structure for information and consultation—but not negotiation—with worker representatives. It is not clear that existence of the legislation led to any increase in consultative arrangements. The law was considered in 9.10. The question of the effectiveness of these consultative bodies is beyond the scope of this work, but it may well be that in many cases they are rightly seen by employees as merely being 'talking shops'.

10

Industrial action

OVERVIEW

The law relating to industrial action has always been one of the most difficult areas of employment law. There has never been any positive right to strike or take other action, and any such action has always been potentially illegal at common law, under one or other of the 'economic torts' such as conspiracy or inducement of breach of contract. A key issue has always been, therefore, the extent to which such action is then legalized by statutory immunities. On occasion, new common law torts have been 'discovered' which have evaded statutory immunities, followed by new Acts being passed in response. One result of this is that in order to understand the current position it is necessary to look at the history of the law.

There are two broad areas of law considered in this chapter:

- Law operating mainly at a collective level relating to the impact of industrial action on the employer and on others, including:
  - civil claims in tort for injunctions against trade unions and their members to stop industrial action and to recover compensation for any losses suffered;
  - how unions can avoid civil liability by confining action to protests about 'industrial' matters and by meeting balloting and notice requirements
  - criminal offences that may be committed by those participating in industrial action and, especially, by pickets.
- Law relating to the rights of the individual worker who participates in industrial action. This covers the question of whether they are in breach of contract, whether any remuneration is due during such action, and whether there is any statutory protection against dismissal or detriment for taking part in industrial action.

This chapter will deal with these matters in the following order:

1. Some important history which is vital in order to understand the current law, followed by some considerations stemming from the European Convention on Human Rights (10.1).

2. The laws primarily operating at a collective level:

   (a) liability in tort for industrial action, immunity from such liability granted by statute, and the conditions on that immunity (10.2);

   (b) the preconditions for immunity relating to secret ballots and notices of industrial action (10.3);

   (c) criminal liability for industrial action (10.4);

   (d) picketing, tortious and criminal liability for picketing, and the statutory immunity for some picketing (10.5);

   (e) the rules relating to trade union liability in tort (10.6.1–10.6.3);

   (f) the use injunctions to stop industrial action (10.6.4).

3. The law relating to the position and the protection, or otherwise, of the individual participant in industrial action (10.7).

Context

Industrial action is a key component of collective bargaining since a union's negotiating strength derives from its ability to organize its members to withdraw their labour from the employer's operations. However, strikes tend to have serious adverse effects not only on the employer but also on the general public. It is not surprising therefore that the extent to which workers and their unions should be free to organize industrial action, and the conditions or restrictions which should apply to such action, have long been controversial. The law in this field has in consequence changed many times over the past two centuries, and indeed the most recent changes are effected by the Employment Rights Act 2025.

A further consequence of this controversiality is that much of the academic writing in this field has a tendency towards the polemical, with writers much more often arguing in favour of union freedom to organize strikes and criticizing the content of legislation and the judgments of the courts than arguing to the contrary. It is important when thinking about the law in this field to keep separate three things: first, what the current law actually provides for; second, how the law might develop (eg through case law interpretation in the United Kingdom or at the European Court of Human Rights); and third, the political question of what the law *ought* to say.

In day-to-day industrial disputes, the law is most relevant in relation to the rules on balloting union members for industrial action and the notices which unions have to give to employers about both intended ballots and the actual calling of industrial action. Employers sometimes seek to nullify the impact of industrial action by applying to the courts for injunctions to stop the action on the basis of some alleged non-compliance with the law on balloting and notices. The *Serco* decision of the Court of Appeal in 2011[1] reduced the chance of success with such applications, and the Employment Rights Act 2025, by reducing the procedural requirements that must be complied with by unions, will further reduce the ability of employers to interfere with industrial action on legal grounds.

[1] See 10.3.1 and 10.3.4.

10.1 History—still relevant in understanding the current law—and the European Convention on Human Rights

As Maurice Kay LJ put it in 2009: 'In this country, the right to strike has never been much more than a slogan or a legal metaphor. What has happened is that . . . legislation has provided limited immunities from a liability in tort.'[2] This section explains how this situation is a consequence of a long and convoluted history.[3]

10.1.1 Historical background

Until the last quarter of the nineteenth century, important aspects of trade union aims and methods were in danger of being construed as criminal, either under certain statutes which outlawed certain forms of combination[4] or under the general law relating to conspiracy. The Trade Union Act 1871 provided that the *purposes* of a union should not be deemed unlawful merely because they were in restraint of trade so as to render members liable to criminal prosecution for conspiracy or otherwise.[5] Moreover, the Conspiracy and Protection of Property Act 1875 provided that an agreement by two or more persons to do or procure any act in contemplation or furtherance of a trade dispute was not to be indictable as a conspiracy if such an act, when committed by one person alone, would not be punishable as a crime.[6] Thus, the mere fact of combination is not criminal.[7]

While this Act had removed the fear of prosecution for *criminal* conspiracy, it had no application to civil actions and so did not protect unions or their members from liability for damages in a *civil* suit. Unsurprisingly, it was to the civil remedy that aggrieved persons now turned. In *Allen v Flood*,[8] the House of Lords prevented the evolution of one general tort of intentionally causing harm to a person without justification, by holding that an act lawful in itself is not converted by a malicious or bad motive into an unlawful act leading to civil liability. However, in this same period the courts did create or approve the specific torts of conspiracy[9] and of inducement of breach of contract.[10] In consequence, if there was an element of combination or of contractual breach, there could be civil liability.

Moreover, in the famous *Taff Vale* case[11] the House of Lords held that a trade union could be sued in tort in spite of not being a body corporate and its assets could be taken in satisfaction of judgment. As a result all the funds of the union became attachable, including those to which members had subscribed for the receipt of benefits such as union sick pay. However, in 1906 the Trade Disputes Act (a) gave complete immunity to unions

[2] *Metrobus v Unite the Union* [2009] EWCA Civ 829.

[3] For more of this historical background see Ewing *The Right to Strike* (1991); Auerbach *Legislating for Conflict* (1992); Davies and Freedland *Labour Legislation and Public Policy* (1993); Millward, Bryson, and Forth *All Change at Work? British Employee Relations, 1980–1998* (2000); Morris and Archer *Collective Labour Law* (2000) ch 6.

[4] Combination Act 1800; Molestation of Workmen Act 1825. For the history of the intervention of criminal law see Wedderburn *The Worker and the Law* (3rd edn, 1986) 513–21.

[5] See now the Trade Union and Labour Relations (Consolidation) Act 1992, s 11.

[6] This is still the criminal law position under s 3 of the Criminal Law Act 1977, which extends the principle to all conspiracies by restricting criminal conspiracies to agreements to commit crimes (with two exceptions, neither of which is relevant in industrial cases).

[7] Agreements to commit acts which are themselves criminal are not protected, although summary offences may be disregarded in certain circumstances. See 10.4.

[8] [1898] AC 1, HL.

[9] *Mogul Steamship Co v McGregor, Gow & Co* [1892] AC 25, HL; *Quinn v Leathem* [1901] AC 495, HL.

[10] *South Wales Miners' Federation v Glamorgan Coal Co* [1905] AC 239, HL.

[11] *Taff Vale Rly Co v ASRS* [1901] AC 426, HL.

in respect of actions in tort, (b) gave immunity to officers and members of unions from liability for conspiracy and inducement of breach of contract provided they acted in 'contemplation or furtherance of a trade dispute'(a phrase dubbed the 'golden formula' by Wedderburn in recognition of the crucial role which it plays in determining the existence of the statutory immunities), and (c) gave statutory backing to *Allen v Flood* by declaring, for the avoidance of doubt, that an act done in contemplation or furtherance of a trade dispute is not actionable in tort simply because it interferes with the legitimate interests of another person. This statutory protection was extended in the Trade Disputes Act 1965 to give immunity from liability (within the golden formula) for the tort of intimidation, which had in 1964 been exhumed and applied by the House of Lords in *Rookes v Barnard*.[12]

The whole scheme was then altered by the Industrial Relations Act 1971, which removed complete immunity from unions and introduced certain 'unfair industrial practices' based on the old heads of civil liability.[13] The Act was considered by many to have been a failure—leading the parties to industrial disputes to concentrate on litigation rather than seeking to negotiate a settlement of the underlying industrial issues. In 1974 the pre-Industrial Relations Act law was reinstated by the Trade Union and Labour Relations Act 1974 and the immunities were further extended by the Trade Union and Labour Relations (Amendment) Act 1976, which widened the immunity from the tort of inducement of breach of contract to cover commercial contracts as well as contracts of employment (thereby removing possible liability for secondary boycotts and 'blackings'), and extended the immunity to cover a possible new tort which appeared to be emerging in the courts of interference with contract (ie short of an actual breach).

By 1976, therefore, the immunities appeared almost watertight. However, for a time in the late 1970s it seemed that the Court of Appeal had succeeded in restricting the scope of the immunities, not by finding loopholes in the individual immunities themselves but instead by taking a more stringent approach to what fell within the golden formula, upon which the immunities depend; however, this approach was subsequently disapproved by the House of Lords in three landmark cases.[14]

10.1.2 **Major change under the Conservative governments**

The Conservative government elected in 1979 embarked on a step-by-step reform of the law on industrial action over 14 years which produced a remarkable transformation. There were no fewer than six Acts of Parliament and they:

- removed the immunities from most forms of secondary industrial action (ie action against employers not directly concerned in the dispute);[15]
- narrowed the definition of 'trade dispute' and withdrew the immunities where unions take action designed to achieve the insertion into commercial contracts of requirements for union labour only or union recognition;[16]
- exposed union funds to liability in tort subject to special rules limiting the amount recoverable and the funds that can be attacked;[17]

[12] [1964] AC 1129, [1964] 1 All ER 367, HL.

[13] For a discussion of the law under the 1971 Act see Cooper's *Outlines of Industrial Law* (6th edn, 1972) ch XI.

[14] *NWL Ltd v Nelson* [1979] ICR 867, [1979] IRLR 478, HL; *Express Newspapers Ltd v McShane* [1980] 1 All ER 65, [1980] IRLR 35, HL; *Duport Steels Ltd v Sirs* [1980] 1 All ER 529, [1980] IRLR 116, HL.

[15] Employment Act 1980 s 17.

[16] Employment Act 1982 s 18; s 14.

[17] Employment Act 1982 s 15.

- made the unions' golden formula immunity from tort conditional on there being a ballot of the workers who are to be called upon to take action;[18]
- imposed extensive controls on internal union affairs;[19]
- removed the statutory immunities from industrial action taken to support or enforce union membership, thereby restricting a union's ability to defend a closed shop by means of industrial pressure;[20]
- amended the strike ballot provisions to require separate ballots to be held at each workplace unless certain stringent conditions were satisfied;[21]
- introduced a series of measures designed to discourage secondary industrial action and unofficial industrial action.[22]

This series of changes was no doubt a major factor in the significant reduction in the number of instances of industrial action in the 1990s and later decades as compared with the 1970s and 1980s.[23]

This series of Acts was consolidated into one massive statute: the Trade Union and Labour Relations (Consolidation) Act 1992. Although there have been many subsequent changes, these have been effected by making amendments to the 1992 Act. These later changes included several very significant and highly controversial reforms of the law on industrial action. There were major changes to the law on industrial action ballots, including compulsory postal ballots, independent scrutiny of the ballot process, and a requirement to give notice of a ballot, and of any subsequent industrial action, to the employers of those involved. Furthermore, individuals were given a right to seek an injunction restraining unlawful industrial action where that action affects the supply of goods or services to that person—although very little use has been made of this citizen's right in practice.

10.1.3 **Continuity under the following governments**

After 18 years of Conservative rule, a Labour government was elected in 1997. The party's general election manifesto had made it clear that a Labour government would not repeal the key elements of the Conservative trade union laws,[24] although the new government signalled its intention to simplify the law on industrial action ballots and to extend unfair dismissal protection to those dismissed for taking part in lawfully organized official industrial action. The Employment Relations Act 1999 duly enacted measures implementing those proposals. The measures protecting employees from dismissal for taking part in lawful, official industrial action were significant, as while they cannot be said to guarantee a 'right to strike' as such (on account of the qualified nature of the protection against dismissal, and the absence of any protection against victimization short of dismissal), they are undoubtedly the closest that UK law has ever come to such a right.

On the change of government in 2010, the incoming Coalition government launched a wide-ranging review of employment law, but this did not include further measures in relation to industrial action.

[18] Trade Union Act 1984 ss 10–11.

[19] Trade Union Act 1984 and Employment Act 1988. Further elaborate controls since have been added by the Transparency of Lobbying, Non-party Campaigning and Trade Union Administration Act 2014 and the Trade Union Act 2016.

[20] Employment Act 1988 s 10.

[21] Employment Act 1988 s 17.

[22] Employment Act 1990 ss 4–9.

[23] For the numbers of stoppages from 1891 to 2017 see figure 3 in *Labour Disputes in the UK: 2017* (Office for National Statistics).

[24] *New Labour: Because Britain Deserves Better* (1997) 17.

10.1.4 The Conservative government of 2015

After the 2015 general election the Conservative Party was able to form a government without a coalition, and it fairly quickly proceeded to enact the Trade Union Act 2016. This Act introduced more demanding requirements in terms of the votes cast in ballots for industrial action so that a vote in favour was only effective if at least 50 per cent of those entitled to vote to actually returned a ballot paper. Moreover, if the majority of those being balloted were normally engaged in the provision of important public services (as defined by regulations) then the number of votes in favour had to constitute at least 40 per cent of the electorate. These provisions reflect concern on the part of some that industrial action was often called on the basis of a ballot in favour of which only a small number of union members had bothered to vote. There was also the view that before important public services are disrupted there should be a really substantial level of support among union members. However, others discerned an intention on the part of the government to reduce the number of strikes and to weaken the collective bargaining power of unions, especially in public transport and the health service.

In the final year of the Conservative government the Strikes (Minimum Service Levels) Act 2024 enabled regulations to be made requiring certain minimum levels of service to be provided in so-called essential industries during industrial action. Such provisions are found in other countries and there is some scope for this within Article 11 of the European Convention on Human Rights. This Act was repealed by the Labour Government in 2025 without ever having been used.[25]

10.1.5 Labour government makes significant changes

The Labour government formed in 2025 has taken steps, by means of the Employment Rights Act 2025, to relax the restrictions placed on unions organizing industrial action, undoing not only most of the Conservative changes made since 2010 but also cancelling some of the requirements imposed in the 1980s, which the previous period of Labour government had left undisturbed.

10.1.6 Relevance of human rights law

One important dimension is the impact of the Human Rights Act 1998.[26] As seen in Chapter 9, Article 11 of the European Convention on Human Rights confers a right to freedom of association with others, including the right to form and join trade unions. Unlike the European Social Charter, Article 11 does not expressly include a right to strike, but the European Court of Human Rights has held that Article 11 safeguards the freedom of trade unions to protect the occupational interests of their members[27] and that '[t]he grant of a right to strike represents without any doubt one of the most important of [the] means' by which a state could seek to secure the protection of the Article 11 rights.[28] In the UK this understanding of Article 11 has been recognized by the Supreme Court, which said 'the core right to advocate for the interests for trade union members is devoid

25 Employment Rights Act 2025, s 78.

26 See Hendy 'Article 11 and the Right to Strike' in Ewing (ed) *Human Rights at Work* (2000); O'Dempsey et al. *Employment Law and the Human Rights Act 1998* (2001) ch 4.

27 *UNISON v United Kingdom* [2002] IRLR 497, ECtHR; see also *Swedish Engine Drivers' Union v Sweden* (1976) 1 EHRR 617, ECtHR; *National Union of Belgian Police v Belgium* (1975) 1 EHRR 578. It was accepted in *Gate Gourmet London Ltd v TGWU* [2005] IRLR 881, QBD that Convention rights are relevant in an industrial dispute case when deciding on the 'balance of convenience' test for an injunction.

28 *Schmidt and Dahlström v Sweden* (1976) 1 EHRR 632, ECtHR.

of substance if it is not backed by a right to take strike action'.[29] Crucially, however, Article 11 leaves each state a free choice of the means to be used for safeguarding the freedom of unions to protect their members,[30] and the Court has readily acknowledged that a right to strike may be subject to restrictions under national laws.[31] The Supreme Court has drawn from the ECtHR case law understanding that on the question of legislative interference with the right to strike there is a narrower margin of appreciation in assessing such restrictions where the state is the employer facing industrial action dispute than when the European Court is assessing the law of a nation in relation to non-state employers.[32]

In recent years the arguments have tended to concentrate on the Court's decision in *Demir v Turkey*,[33] in which it was held that the Article 11 protection included as an essential element the right to conduct collective bargaining. It is argued that this must mean that the right to strike is also an essential element of Article 11 since industrial action is the indispensable corollary of collective bargaining if a union is to have any negotiating power in the bargaining.[34] However, the European Court of Human Rights has expressly held back from deciding whether a right to strike is an essential element of collective bargaining; although it has confirmed that industrial action is part of collective bargaining so that if industrial action was, in a particular situation, not permitted that might mean that Article 11 was infringed. Once again, however, the weak link in this argument in practice has been that, even if Article 11(1) is engaged in an industrial dispute case, the margin of appreciation given to member states by Article 11(2) in deciding what restrictions on such action are necessary tends to trump this and lead to a conclusion that the existing laws are not contrary to the Article. In the most recent decision on this topic, *Humpert v Germany*,[35] the Court confirmed that in assessing the acceptability of restrictions the Court must carry out a proportionality assessment which takes into account all the circumstances of the case and the totality of the measures taken by the state to secure trade union freedom.

In *UNISON v United Kingdom*,[36] the European Court of Human Rights held that the prohibition of the strike in that case was a restriction on the union's power to protect the interests of its members, and therefore it engaged the freedom of association guaranteed by Article 11(1). The Court's ruling was not as significant as it might at first appear, however, because on the facts the Court dismissed the union's application as inadmissible, holding that this restriction under national law was justified under Article 11(2) as being 'necessary in a democratic society for the prevention of disorder or crime, for

[29] *Secretary of State for Business and Trade v Mercer* [2024] UKSC 12, [2024] IRLR 599, [2024] ICR 814 at para 70.

[30] In *Gustafsson v Sweden* (1996) 22 EHRR 409, the ECtHR emphasized that states enjoy 'a wide margin of appreciation' in the choice of means to be employed.

[31] *Schmidt and Dahlström v Sweden* (1976) 1 EHRR 632. See eg *NATFHE v United Kingdom* (1998) 25 EHRR 122, where the Commission held that the then requirement under ss 226A and 234A of the 1992 Act to disclose to an employer the names of those to be balloted or to take part in industrial action was not 'a significant limitation on the right to take collective action'. Likewise, reliance on Art 11 failed at a domestic level in *Ministry of Justice v Prison Officers Association* [2008] IRLR 380, QBD.

[32] *Secretary of State for Business and Trade v Mercer* [2024] UKSC 12, [2024] IRLR 599, [2024] ICR 814 at paras 75–80.

[33] [2009] IRLR 766.

[34] See eg Bogg and Ewing 'The Implications of the RMT Case' (2014) 43 ILJ 221.

[35] [2024] IRLR 222.

[36] [2002] IRLR 497, ECtHR. The union had threatened industrial action against the employer, University College London Hospitals NHS Trust, because it refused to give an undertaking that the terms and conditions of staff to be transferred to a consortium which was to build and run a new private finance initiative hospital would be maintained for a period of 30 years at an equivalent level to employees who were not transferred. The application to the ECtHR followed the issue of an injunction by the Court of Appeal ([1999] IRLR 31) restraining the industrial action on the grounds that the dispute was not a trade dispute.

the protection of the health or morals or for the protection of the rights and freedoms of others' (in this case, the economic interests of the employer). In *Metrobus Ltd v Unite the Union*,[37] the Court of Appeal held that the detailed rules on strike ballots (the usual target of union litigation in the UK) fell within that margin of appreciation.

When the UK rules went again to the European Court of Human Rights in *NURMTW v United Kingdom*,[38] the result was a disappointment for both the challenging union and indeed anyone hoping for clarification. A challenge to the law restricting secondary action was dismissed, again on the basis that it fell within governmental discretion. A second challenge to the law on strike ballots was not even considered, being ruled inadmissible because it only concerned a procedural requirement relating to the union's notice of ballot to the employer, and, after an injunction had been granted against the union because of that procedural point, the union had in fact been able to gather the information needed to serve a new and compliant ballot notice.[39]

Thus, challenges along these lines do not seem, on the basis of results to date, to be a promising avenue for the unions. Moreover, the significant relaxation of the procedural rules applying to unions wishing to organize industrial action which have been introduced under the Employment Rights Act 2025 make it even less likely that any aspect of UK law on this topic will now be held to be in breach of the European Convention. The single possible exception is in relation to gig economy workers, which is discussed next.

10.1.6.1 Industrial action and the gig economy

Article 11 may also be relevant in relation to the application of UK law to industrial action in the growing 'gig economy', where workers have no guaranteed hours and are often offered work in discrete pieces through the internet. Frequently the provider of the work seeks to secure that those doing the work are regarded in law as being neither 'employees' nor 'workers', for example by issuing contracts which permit the other party to perform the service either personally or by supplying someone else. The immunities from injunctions and claims for damages which are provided by the 'golden formula' apply only in relation to a 'trade dispute', which is defined to mean a dispute between workers and their employer.[40] Article 11 of the European Convention on Human Rights gives the right to join a union and to benefit from its protection to 'everyone' and so it is arguable that UK law is deficient as a result of the exclusions contained in the definition of 'worker', which in effect deny the right to strike to those who usually do work personally but have the contractual right to send a substitute, and also to those who are professionals working for clients.[41] In relation to the right to obtain union recognition for collective bargaining the Court of Appeal has held that the Convention case law applies Article 11 to those who are in 'employment relationship'. In consequence foster carers had to be treated as 'workers' even though they fall outside the express wording of the definition of 'worker' because they have no contract.[42] On the other hand, the Supreme Court held that people

[37] [2010] ICR 173, [2009] IRLR 851, CA. [38] C-31045/10 [2014] IRLR 467.

[39] The *RMT* case is considered in detail in Bogg and Ewing 'The Implications of the RMT Case' (2014) 43 ILJ 221. This seeks to put a more positive spin on some of the Court's dicta about *Demir* but could equally be seen as a valiant effort to retrieve something from the wreckage.

[40] See 10.2.7.2 on the definition of 'trade dispute'. The definition of 'worker' in s 296 of the Trade Union and Labour Relations (Consolidation) Act 1992 is considered in 9.3.4.

[41] For a fuller discussion of this issue see Freedland and Kountouris 'Some Reflections on the "Personal Scope" of Collective Labour Law' (2017) 46 ILJ 52 and De Stefano 'Non-Standard Work and Limits on Freedom of Association: A Human Rights-Based Approach' (2017) 46 ILJ 185.

[42] *National Union of Professional Foster Carers v Certification Officer* [2021] EWCA Civ 548, [2021] IRLR 588, CA. For more on this case see 9.3.4.

delivering meals for Roofoods were not in an employment relationship because they genuinely could send substitutes to do their work.[43]

Even when the gig workers are 'workers' in law, complying with UK law's requirements for ballots and notices to employers may be particularly hard to achieve with a casual, 'gig' workforce[44] and this too may be a source of incompatibility with Article 11, unless UK law can be mitigated by the courts taking a less stringent approach to compliance.[45]

10.2 **Liability in tort and the statutory immunities**

10.2.1 **The law in a nutshell**

It is the law of tort, and the statutory immunity from liability in tort which is granted in certain circumstances, which matter most in relation to the legal regulation of strikes and industrial action. If the immunity does not on the facts apply, the employer will be able to obtain an injunction to halt any proposed industrial action.[46] The law is complex so it is best to start with a simplified summary:

1. Industrial action and picketing have some legal issues in common but are best considered separately.
2. Organizing or participating in industrial action is tortious and so an employer can obtain an injunction to stop such action (and compensation too, although this is rarely sought). The courts created many different torts during the nineteenth and twentieth centuries. There was some simplification of those torts in a House of Lords decision of 2007.
3. In order to enable unions to organize industrial action, and employees to participate in such action, the 'golden formula' grants immunity in tort for action in contemplation or furtherance of a trade dispute. This wide immunity was first granted by the Trade Disputes Act 1906 but since 1980 many restrictions on the application of the golden formula have been imposed by statute.
4. In relation to a trade union organizing industrial action, the golden formula immunity is only available if it observes a set of detailed rules about getting the support of a ballot and about giving notices to the employer of the action. While individual workers and union organizers do not have to comply with these ballot and notice rules, the golden formula is only available to a union in respect of its actions (and its vicarious liability for the actions of its officials) if the balloting and notice rules have been complied with.

[43] *Independent Workers' Union of Great Britain v Central Arbitration Committee* [2023] UKSC 43, [2024] IRLR 148, [2024] ICR 189. For more on this topic see 9.3.4.

[44] See De Stefano 'Non-Standard Work and Limits on Freedom of Association: A Human Rights-Based Approach' (2017) 46 ILJ 185 at p 200.

[45] See 10.3.4 and especially the possibility that the courts may in due course hold that only 'substantial compliance' is required.

[46] See generally *Harvey* N II [701]ff; Elias and Ewing 'Economic Torts and Labour Law: Old Principles and New Liabilities' (1982) 41 CLJ 321; Carty 'Intentional Violation of Economic Interests: The Limits of Common Law Liability' (1988) 104 LQR 250; Sales and Stilitz 'Intentional Infliction of Harm by Unlawful Means' (1999) 115 LQR 411; Carty *An Analysis of the Economic Torts* (2001).

5. Even if the action has been properly balloted and notified, the golden formula immunity will not be available if the action is in one of the prohibited categories. The various amendments made since 1980 mean that immunity is never available for:
    - secondary action;
    - unlawful picketing;
    - industrial action to enforce a 'closed shop' (where only union members are employed);
    - industrial action taken because of the dismissal of unofficial strikers;
    - industrial action designed to impose a union recognition requirement on a third-party employer (industrial action intended to persuade the strikers' own employer to recognize the union does fall within the immunity).
6. These questions normally come before the courts because an employer is seeking an injunction to prevent industrial action. The most frequent legal issues in such cases are:
    - whether the golden formula applies at all—usually because of an allegation that the union's dispute is with someone other than the employer or is of a political nature not falling within the definition of a 'trade dispute'; and
    - whether the balloting and notice rules have been complied with.

10.2.1.1 **The detail**

In practice it is likely to be fairly clear that a tort has been committed by organizing the industrial action, so the key legal issue is therefore whether the action is covered by the *immunity* granted by statute. For purposes of analysis, however, it is still necessary to set out the requirements of the applicable torts as they now stand, before going on to consider immunity.

10.2.2 **Liability in tort—judge-led developments followed by simplification in the *OBG* case**

As seen in 10.1.1, the decision in *Allan v Flood*[47] prevented the evolution of one 'super-tort' of injuring someone without justification. Instead, the emphasis was on the development of specific torts. Conspiracy was evolving as a tort as well as a crime, and the case of *Lumley v Gye*[48] established the tort of inducement of breach of contract. It was against the background of these fundamental torts that the widespread immunities in the Trade Disputes Act 1906 were granted, as a result of which there were relatively few developments in this area for a further half a century because the law was largely removed as a means of resolving industrial disputes.

That began to change in the late 1950s and 1960s with renewed interest in use of the law. This led in particular to extensions and elaborations of the *Lumley v Gye* tort of inducement of breach of contract,[49] and the exhumation of the tort of intimidation.[50]

[47] [1898] AC 1, HL. [48] (1853) 2 E & B 216.

[49] *Thomson & Co Ltd v Deakin* [1952] CL 646, [1952] 2 All ER 361, CA; *J T Stratford & Sons Ltd v Lindley* [1965] AC 269, [1964] 3 All ER 102, HL; *Associated Newspapers Group v Wade* [1979] ICR 664, [1979] IRLR 201, CA; *Torquay Hotel Co Ltd v Cousins* [1969] 2 Ch 106, [1969] 1 All ER 522, CA; *Merkur Island Shipping Corpn v Laughton* [1983] ICR 490, [1983] IRLR 218, HL.

[50] *Rookes v Barnard* [1964] AC 1129, [1964] 1 All ER 367, HL. The tort had last been heard in *Tarleton v M'Gawley* (1793) Peake 270. The Trades Disputes Act 1965 was passed by a sympathetic Labour government to extend the statutory immunities to cover it. This is now contained in the Trade Union and Labour Relations (Consolidation) Act 1992, s 219(1)(b), which may now be otiose because of the *OBG* case.

The definition of the relevant torts was reviewed in 2007 in what is now the leading case, *OBG Ltd v Allan*.[51] This was not an industrial dispute case, but was in fact three consolidated commercial cases[52] in which the House of Lords took the opportunity to review the economic torts generally. The decision is long and complex, but on the economic torts the principal speeches are by Lord Hoffmann and Lord Nicholls and are largely in agreement (although with some differences in terminology). In the case of any conflict, it is Lord Hoffmann's speech with which the remaining judges agreed. The principal points established are as follows:

1. The two torts accepted in the case are inducing breach of contract ('the *Lumley v Gye* tort') and causing economic loss by unlawful means.[53] Although they are separate, they can both arise on one set of facts.
2. The idea that these two torts are merely subdivisions of one larger tort (the 'unifying theory') is wrong: inducing breach of contract is a form of secondary liability (requiring a breach of contract by the primary wrongdoer), whereas causing economic loss by unlawful means is a form of primary liability.
3. The extension of the economic torts into areas such as mere interference with contract (direct or indirect) was improper; interference with contract or business will now only be unlawful if it comes within the ambit of the modern tort of causing economic loss by unlawful means.
4. The tort of intimidation (threatening to act unlawfully against another party unless that party acts as demanded) should no longer be considered a separate form of liability, but is instead only a factual example of the tort of causing economic loss by unlawful means, with the threat of unlawful action constituting the unlawful means.[54]

There are two final points on *OBG*. The first is that nothing in *OBG* addresses the tort of conspiracy, which must be considered (unless we are ever told to the contrary) to have been left unaffected. The second is that Lord Hoffmann cautioned that this radical reappraisal of the tort base must not be read as meaning that on their facts the multitude of previous cases had necessarily been wrongly *decided*; indeed, many of them would have had the same result under the new rules.

10.2.3 **Inducing breach of contract**

10.2.3.1 **The cause of action**

Reliance in industrial action cases has tended to be placed largely on the tort of inducing breach of contract, a cause of action established in *Lumley v Gye*,[55] where a theatre owner induced an opera singer to break her existing contract so that she could sing for

[51] [2007] IRLR 608, [2007] 4 All ER 545, HL. See Simpson 'Economic Tort Liability in Labour Disputes: The Potential Impact of the House of Lords' Decision in *OBG Ltd v Allan*' (2007) 36 ILJ 468, which sets the decision into the context of the existing statutory immunities.

[52] There had been a renewal of interest in the economic torts in this commercial sphere. *OBG* concerned alleged unlawful action by receivers causing loss to the claimant company.

[53] Confusingly, Lord Nicholls refers to this tort as 'interference with the claimant's business by unlawful means'. Lord Hoffmann's terminology is used here.

[54] Lord Hoffmann uses the old 'intimidation' case of *Tarleton v M'Gawley* (n 50) as an early authority for the modern tort, stating that the confusion had arisen from an early edition of *Salmond on Tort*. Unfortunately, however, he does not directly discuss *Rookes v Barnard*, the key modern case on intimidation, hence Simpson's remark ((2007) 36 ILJ at 476) that '[t]he potential which the House of Lords' decision in *Rookes v Barnard* has always had for undermining the whole structure on which the legal basis for the right to strike rests in English law has certainly not been diminished by the decision in *OBG Ltd v Allan*'.

[55] (1853) 2 E & B 216.

him instead. In the context of an industrial dispute such an inducement may arise where a union calls upon members to strike in breach of their contracts of employment or (in a secondary action case) where it puts pressure on one of the suppliers or customers of the employer in dispute to break a commercial contract (of supply or purchase) with that employer.

According to *OBG Ltd v Allan*,[56] the constituent elements of the tort are that:

1. the defendant knows that they are inducing a breach of contract;
2. there must be an actual breach of contract, mere 'interference' no longer being sufficient.[57]

On the first issue of knowledge, what is required is actual knowledge, not what a reasonable person would realize. However, it is clear from *OBG* that the defendant turning a blind eye where they had the means of knowledge, which they deliberately disregarded, would be enough.[58] The majority in the earlier case of *Emerald Construction Co Ltd v Lowthian*[59] appeared to suggest that in addition to such 'Nelsonian' knowledge it would be enough if the defendant was reckless as to whether what he was seeking to persuade someone to do would cause a breach of contract—that is to say if the defendant did not care if it would cause a breach. Although this case was cited with approval in *OBG*, the judgments in *OBG* did not reassert this point. More recently, in *Adam v Pollock* Lewison LJ said: 'You must actually *realize* that the act you are procuring *will have* the effect of breaching the contract in question. "Will have" is not the same as "might have".'[60]

One tactic historically has been for the employer's lawyers to ensure that the defendant has the requisite knowledge by serving on the union details of commercial contracts that could be breached. Lawyers may come into the matter in another way too: what if the defendant took legal advice on whether what they intended to procure would be a breach of contract and the lawyers' advice was to the effect of 'the position is arguable'? At the moment that question remains unresolved.[61]

The conventional wisdom has always been that there is a defence of justification available, but its scope is uncertain, and it is not as wide as that for conspiracy by lawful means. Thus, in *South Wales Miners' Federation v Glamorgan Coal Co Ltd*[62] it was held that there was no defence of justification available on the facts, in spite of the fact that the workers involved were merely acting in genuine furtherance of their own interests and bore no ill will towards the employers. While self-interest cannot, it seems, amount to justification, the observance of some kind of 'duty' may be enough.[63] For example, in *Brimelow v Casson*[64] the justification defence was that the union had a duty, as a representative

[56] [2007] IRLR 608, [2007] 4 All ER 545, HL.

[57] *Torquay Hotel Co Ltd v Cousins* [1969] 2 Ch 106, [1969], All ER 522, CA and *Merkur Island Shipping Corpn v Laughton* [1983] 2 AC 570, [1983] 2 All ER 189, HL disapproved. Previous cases decided on interference grounds (such as *Dimbleby & Sons v NUJ* [1984] IRLR 67, [1984] 1 All ER 117, HL) would now have to come (if at all) under the tort of causing loss by unlawful means (see 10.2.4).

[58] *OBG Ltd v Allan* [2007] IRLR 608, [2007] 4 All ER 545, HL.

[59] [1966] 1 WLR 691, CA.

[60] [2020] 2 WLR 1010, [2020] IRLR 387 (sub nom. *Allen v Dodd*), CA (italics in the original judgment).

[61] See *Adam v Pollock* and *Meretz Investments NV v ACP Ltd* [2008] Ch 244.

[62] [1905] AC 239, HL; and see *British Motor Trade Association v Salvadori* [1949] Ch 556, [1949] 1 All ER 208.

[63] See the *South Wales Miners* case, in the Court of Appeal [1903] 2 KB 545, at 573 per Romer LJ and in the House of Lords [1905] AC 239 at 249 per Lord James; *Greig v Insole* [1978] 3 All ER 449, [1978] 1 WLR 302 at 491 and 340, respectively, per Slade J. See also *TimePlan Education Group Ltd v National Union of Teachers* [1997] IRLR 457, CA, at para 21 per Peter Gibson LJ.

[64] [1924] 1 Ch 302; *Camden Nominees Ltd v Forcey* [1940] Ch 352, [1940] 2 All ER 1. The suggestion in *British Industrial Plastics Ltd v Ferguson* [1938] 4 All ER 504, CA at 510 per Slesser LJ that a desire not to break the law might amount to justification must be doubtful.

association, to secure the payment of reasonable wages by a theatrical manager in order that chorus girls in his employ could live without having to resort to immoral earnings. The idea of a 'duty' to act providing justification for the tort of inducement is a nebulous one; it is theoretically capable of being extended to cover many union activities on the basis that a union officer may have certain legal and moral 'duties' towards the membership, but in practice the defence rarely succeeds.[65] This question of justification was not addressed in *OBG Ltd v Allan*; it did not arise on the facts and so did not have to be addressed, and so presumably the old case law on it still stands until directly reconsidered.

10.2.3.2 **The immunity**

Section 219(1)(a) of the Trade Union and Labour Relations (Consolidation) Act 1992 provides that an act done in contemplation or furtherance of a trade dispute is not actionable in tort on the ground only that it induces another person to break a contract.

10.2.4 **Causing loss by unlawful means**

10.2.4.1 **The cause of action**

According to *OBG Ltd v Allan* there are two elements to this tort. The first is that the defendant must commit acts in relation to a third party with the intention of causing loss to the claimant. As with the tort of inducement, this means actual intention (the loss being the defendant's end or being a means to that end), and mere foresight of possible loss is not sufficient.[66] The second element is that the defendant must use 'unlawful means' against the third party. As this phrase is capable of covering a multitude of sins, Lord Hoffmann was keen to give a definition capable of keeping the tort within reasonable bounds.[67] He did so by limiting it in two ways. First, the means are only unlawful if they constitute an actionable wrong which the third party could sue the perpetrator for—it is not enough to show that the perpetrator has done an act which they were not in law at liberty to commit. Secondly, the unlawful acts against a third party must impinge directly on the relationship between the third party and the claimant:

> Unlawful means therefore consists of acts intended to cause loss to the claimant by interfering with the freedom of a third party in a way which is unlawful as against that third party and which is intended to cause loss to the claimant. It does not in my opinion include acts which may be unlawful against a third party, but which do not affect his freedom to deal with the claimant.[68]

This should prevent the tort from being committed through some random illegality, unconnected with the dispute.

An example of this tort would be where a union is in dispute with Employer A and in support of that dispute a union official asks the union's members at Employer B not to handle goods or services going to or coming from Employer A. Employer B can of course sue the official for the tort of inducing a breach by its workers of their contacts of

[65] *Posluns v Toronto Stock Exchange* (1964) 46 DLR (2d) 210 at 270, per Gale J. Cf *Pete's Towing Services Ltd v NIUW* [1970] NZLR 32 at 51 per Speight J.

[66] Deliberate disregard when the defendant had the means to know—turning a blind eye—would be sufficient, however. See the fuller discussion in 10.2.3.1.

[67] As he put it, not to permit it to extend beyond the original ambit envisaged for it in the foundation cases of *Allen v Flood* [1898] AC 1, HL and *Quinn v Leathem* [1901] AC 495, HL.

[68] At para [51]. Confirmed in *Secretary of State for Health v Servier Laboratories Ltd* [2021] UKSC 24, [2021] 3 WLR 370, [2022] 1 All ER 1.

employment. Employer A can sue the official for causing loss by unlawful means—those means being the official's tort against Employer B. Another example is where a union threatens to induce its members to strike unless the employer takes certain action, such as to dismiss on full notice a non-unionist. This threat of breach of contract amounts to unlawful means against the employer, and the non-unionist can sue the union for his loss caused by the unlawful means.[69]

One question which arises is whether the unlawful means must be a tort: could a breach of contract be unlawful means? This is highly controversial. This issue was considered in *Barretts & Baird (Wholesale) Ltd v IPCS*,[70] where fatstock officers staffing private abattoirs took industrial action in a dispute with their employers, the Meat and Livestock Commission. The abattoir owners brought proceedings for injunctions against the union and against an individual fatstock officer. As against the former, the case relied on inducement to breach of statutory duty (see 10.2.6.2), but against the latter the argument was that the officers had interfered with the claimant's business, the unlawful means being quite simply their own breaches of employment contracts with their employer. If such an action were accepted it would have the astonishing result that the union officials organizing a strike would be immune,[71] but the individual employees could be sued by anyone affected by their action. The problem here is that it has never been authoritatively decided whether or not simple breach of contract could be unlawful means for the economic torts.[72] Henry J was therefore driven to conclude that it was arguable that simple breach could constitute unlawful means.[73] In the event he avoided finding the fatstock officers individually liable, on the basis, first, that they lacked the necessary intention to injure the claimant,[74] and second, that the remedy sought could not be granted against the individual employee defendant because of the statutory restrictions on the enforcement of contracts of employment against employees.[75] Subsequently, in *OBG* their Lordships assumed that a breach of contact can amount to unlawful means but did not consider the arguments for and against. The possibility of such an argument succeeding in the future has been referred to as 'a time-bomb in our labour law'.[76]

Another form of unlawful means which is of potentially great practical significance is the tort of inducement of breach of statutory duty. As discussed in 10.2.6.2, this tort may provide a cause of action in its own right, but there its impact is restricted by the requirement that the breach of statutory duty be independently actionable at the suit of the claimant. However, in *Associated British Ports v TGWU*,[77] a majority of the Court of

[69] These were the facts of *Rookes v Barnard* [1964] AC 1129, [1964] 1 All ER 367, HL.

[70] [1987] IRLR 3, noted Simpson (1987) 50 MLR 506, Napier (1987) 46 CLJ 222, Benedictus (1987) 16 ILJ 191.

[71] Assuming there had been a ballot and that it remained primary action, the officials would have the protection of s 219(1) covering their inducement of the breaches of contract by the employees; that inducement would therefore not be actionable per se, nor would it constitute unlawful means, eg for the tort of causing loss on their part.

[72] Although *Rookes v Barnard* [1964] AC 1129, [1964] 1 All ER 367, HL appeared to be against it. Section 13(3)(b) of the Trade Union and Labour Relations Act 1974 used to state 'for the avoidance of doubt' that a breach on contract in contemplation or furtherance of a trade dispute was not to be treated as unlawful means, but that subsection was repealed by the Employment Act 1980.

[73] In so deciding (at p 9) the judge cites Wedderburn *The Worker and the Law* (3rd edn, 1986) at 637, where the author pointed out this danger of the repeal of s 13(3)(b).

[74] This aspect was approved by Lord Hoffmann in *OBG Ltd v Allan*: see 10.2.2.

[75] Now contained in the Trade Union and Labour Relations (Consolidation) Act 1992, s 236.

[76] Davies and Freedland *Labour Law Texts and Materials* (2nd edn, 1984) 755. The restriction on the enforcement of contracts of employment would not, of course, apply to an action for damages (actual or threatened) against employees taking industrial action.

[77] [1989] 3 All ER 796, [1989] IRLR 305, CA (reversed on other grounds, [1989] 3 All ER 822, [1989] IRLR 399, HL).

Appeal considered that it was 'strongly arguable' that a breach of statutory duty could be relied upon as unlawful means even if not actionable at the suit of the claimant.

10.2.4.2 **The immunity**

One of the problems in this area has been in trying to keep the statutory immunities up to date with the twists and turns in the case law on liabilities. As this particular tort was only put into its present form in *OBG Ltd v Allan* in 2007 it is hardly surprising that the immunities do not cover it specifically by name. However, the statutory immunities were worded to deal with possible liabilities of a fairly wide nature and it is likely that they will in fact cover the situations likely to arise under this new tort, which in most cases subsumes those earlier possible torts.[78] The first instance of this is that the immunity extends to any act which 'interferes or induces another person to interfere with [a contract's] performance' and although interference with contract does not now (following *OBG Ltd v Allan*) qualify as an independent tort, these words may well cover many actions which constitute the new tort of causing loss by unlawful means. The second instance is that although there may now be no separate tort of 'intimidation', intimidatory conduct could also come within the new tort, in which case it would be covered by s 219(1)(b), which was originally enacted in 1965 to deal with the invention of intimidation in *Rookes v Barnard*[79] and which provides immunity for an act that 'consists in his threatening that a contract . . . will be broken or its performance interfered with, or that [the defendant] will induce another person to break a contract or interfere with its performance'.

A further likely protection against liability for causing loss by unlawful means is that the immunity in s 219 may result in the means adopted to cause the loss, which would otherwise be unlawful, *not being unlawful*; and if the means is not unlawful then the tort is not committed. For example, if in an industrial dispute with Employer A a trade union induces its members employed by A to take strike action, and this inflicts loss on Employer B who is a customer of Employer A, it is likely that that strike call will itself be immune under s 219(1)(a) and so Employer B will not be able to sue because the union's inducement of its members to break their contracts will not constitute 'unlawful means'.

For these reasons it is hoped that the effect of the realignment of this tort in *OBG* should *not* be the accidental creation of yet another judicial bypassing of the statutory immunities, though in this tortious area nothing is ever completely certain.[80]

10.2.5 **Conspiracy**

10.2.5.1 **The cause of action**

That conspiracy is a head of civil, as well as criminal, liability was clearly established by the House of Lords at the end of the nineteenth century in the famous 'trilogy' of conspiracy cases.[81] The tort of conspiracy may take either of two forms.

[78] One of the problems of *OBG* concerning commercial disputes rather than industrial ones is that the House of Lords did not have to consider this question of immunity.

[79] See n 12. [80] See Simpson (2007) 36 ILJ at 476–9.

[81] *Mogul Steamship Co v McGregor, Gow & Co* [1892] AC 25, HL; *Allen v Flood* [1898] AC 1, HL: *Quinn v Leathem* [1901] AC 495, HL. See the recent discussion of this history in *Revenue and Customs Commissioner v Total Network SL* [2008] 2 All ER 413, HL.

Conspiracy by lawful means

'Conspiracy by lawful means'[82] is committed where two or more persons combine together with intent to injure the claimant by the use of means which are lawful in themselves, but with a predominant purpose to harm the claimant rather than to advance the legitimate interests of the combiners.

The emergence of this form of conspiracy could have constituted a serious impediment to the lawfulness of industrial action, for almost any strike will require concerted action and will lead to loss to the employer. This consideration led to the immunity which was first granted in the Trade Disputes Act 1906, but in fact, as the tort was developed in subsequent cases (in particular by the House of Lords in *Sorrell v Smith*[83] and *Crofter Hand Woven Harris Tweed Co Ltd v Veitch*),[84] it is arguable that the immunity is in fact unnecessary, for the courts have taken a liberal approach to what constitutes the legitimate interests of organized labour. If the union can show a genuine trade union reason for the industrial action[85] then the conspiracy will not be actionable, in spite of the loss caused to the employer, because the employer will be unable to show that the union's *predominant* purpose was to harm it: rather, it was to advance the workers' interests in the industrial dispute.[86] It is this element of the tort of conspiracy by lawful means which has become dominant, whether it be called lack of an improper purpose or, more commonly, a defence of 'justification'. In the light of this, this particular head of liability has played little part in the modern cases.

Conspiracy to use unlawful means

The second type of tortious conspiracy is 'conspiracy to use unlawful means'. This is committed where two or more persons combine together with intent to injure the claimant by the employment of means which are unlawful *in themselves*. The scope of this kind of conspiracy is as wide as the scope of unlawful means, and so it covers a conspiracy to injure by means that are criminal[87] or tortious. At one point it was thought[88] that for this form of the tort it was also necessary to show that the predominant purpose of the combiners must be to injure the claimant. However, the House of Lords in *Lonrho plc v Fayed*[89] made it clear that under the second form there is no such requirement, and that it is sufficient to show that the defendants acted with intent to injure the claimant.

[82] This version of the tort, sometimes referred to as 'conspiracy to injure' or 'simple' conspiracy or 'conspiracy to effect an unlawful purpose', was described as an 'anomalous tort' in *Lonrho Ltd v Shell Petroleum Co Ltd (No 2)* [1982] AC 173, [1981] 2 All ER 456, HL.

[83] [1925] AC 700, HL.

[84] [1942] AC 435, [1942] 1 All ER 142, HL.

[85] See eg *Reynolds v Shipping Federation* [1924] 1 Ch 28 (action to enforce a closed shop); the *Crofters'* case [1942] AC 435, [1942] 1 All ER 142, HL (action to force up wages); *Scala Ballroom (Wolverhampton) Ltd v Ratcliffe* [1958] 3 All ER 220, [1958] 1 WLR 1057, CA (action to stamp out a colour bar operated by the employer).

[86] *Quinn v Leathem* [1901] AC 495 is perhaps best explained as a rare case where the jury decided that the defendants' predominant purpose was vindictive; see also *Huntley v Thornton* [1957] 1 All ER 234, [1957] 1 WLR 321.

[87] *Revenue and Customs Commissioner v Total Network SL* [2008] 2 All ER 413, HL (see Mitchell [2008] NLJ 773 where the point is made that the ruling that a crime is enough per se, as long as it was the necessary 'means', is significant given the large expansion in the number of regulatory offences in recent years). The House of Lords accepted that the concept of unlawful means is wider in the tort of conspiracy than in the tort of causing economic loss by unlawful means.

[88] Based on a dictum of Lord Diplock in *Lonrho Ltd v Shell Petroleum Co Ltd (No 2)* [1982] AC 173, [1981] 2 All ER 456, HL.

[89] [1992] 1 AC 448, [1991] 3 All ER 303, HL, overruling *Metall und Rohstoff AG v Donaldson Lufkin & Jenrette Inc* [1990] 1 QB 391, [1989] 3 All ER 14, CA. Cf also *Lonrho plc v Fayed (No 5)* [1994] 1 All ER 188, CA (the claimant must prove actual pecuniary or financial loss for both forms of the tort, as opposed, for example, to loss of reputation).

10.2.5.2 **The immunity**

Section 219(2) of the Trade Union and Labour Relations (Consolidation) Act 1992 provides that an agreement or combination to do any act in contemplation or furtherance of a trade dispute is not actionable in tort if the act is one which, if done by one person alone, would not be actionable. This therefore gives protection from liability for conspiracy by lawful means (ie means which would not be actionable if done by only one person), but does *not* give immunity from suit for conspiracy by unlawful means (ie means which *would* be actionable if done by only one person). However, in the latter case there will be an indirect immunity if the means are covered by one of the other immunities and are therefore removed from being 'unlawful' by the immunity.

The result is that in most cases conspiracy will be a dead letter as a cause of action in industrial action cases, but it is important to remember that it is not abolished, only held in abeyance while within the golden formula. If the act complained of is outside that formula, for example a personal vendetta or clear misuse of union power for improper purpose, conspiracy could still be used as a cause of action.[90]

10.2.6 **Outflanking the immunities—two further possibilities**

It is clear from the preceding that much of the stimulus for the development of the economic torts during the twentieth century came from attempts to outflank the statutory immunities. There are two further possibilities. The fact that these major areas of uncertainty exist (along with the other unresolved questions relating to the nature and extent of the established economic torts, referred to earlier) shows how deeply unsatisfactory and unpredictable our current law on industrial action is.

10.2.6.1 **Possibility (1): a tort of inducing a breach of statutory duty**

The first possible development is the extension of the tort of inducement of breach of contract to other situations which involve the violation of legal rights, and in particular to inducement of breach of statutory duty.[91] The basis for this new tort was laid by the Court of Appeal in *Meade v London Borough of Haringey*,[92] a case concerning the legality (under the Education Act 1944) of a decision by a local authority to close its schools because of strike action by caretakers and ancillary staff. In the course of their judgments, both Lord Denning MR and Eveleigh LJ stated obiter that it was tortious for the union to induce the local authority to be in breach of its statutory duty, and moreover that such tortious action would not be covered by the statutory immunities. The existence of the tort was subsequently confirmed by the Court of Appeal in *Associated British Ports v TGWU*,[93] but with the important caveat that the statutory duty in question must be independently actionable.[94] The tort of inducement of breach of statutory duty could be of particular significance in the public sector, where employers are more likely to be under a statutory duty to provide and maintain goods or services, not least because there is no statutory immunity covering it.

[90] As in *Huntley v Thornton* [1957] 1 All ER 234, [1957] 1 WLR 321.

[91] See also *Prudential Assurance Co Ltd v Lorenz* (1971) 11 KIR 78 (inducement of breach of equitable obligation).

[92] [1979] 2 All ER 1016, [1979] ICR 494, CA. See also *Associated Newspapers Group Ltd v Wade* [1979] ICR 664, [1979] IRLR 201, CA and *Barretts & Baird (Wholesale) Ltd v IPCS* [1987] IRLR 3.

[93] *Associated British Ports v TGWU* [1989] 3 All ER 796, [1989] IRLR 305, CA; revsd on other grounds [1989] 3 All ER 822, [1989] IRLR 399, HL.

[94] This is a matter of construction of the statute; to be independently actionable the claimant will usually need to show that the statute was passed for the benefit of a class which includes them, or that they have suffered some special damage: see *Cutler v Wandsworth Stadium Ltd* [1949] AC 398, HL; *Lonrho Ltd v Shell Petroleum Co Ltd (No 2)* [1982] AC 173, [1981] 2 All ER 465, HL.

10.2.6.2 **Possibility (2): the importation of the contractual doctrine of economic duress**

The second possibility concerns the importation into industrial disputes of the contractual doctrine of 'economic duress', that is, that if a party to a contract is obliged to enter into it, or to agree to certain terms, because of illegitimate coercion by the other party, they may claim that the contract is voidable for duress and so claim repayment of anything paid under it.[95] In *Universe Tankships Inc of Monrovia v International Transport Workers' Federation*,[96] the International Transport Workers' Federation (ITWF), as part of its campaign against ships under flags of convenience, caused the blacking of the claimant's ship until certain demands were met, including making a payment to a seamen's welfare fund. Once the ship was released, the claimants sought the return of this payment on the basis that it had been paid under duress. The House of Lords allowed recovery by a majority of three to two. The first point to note about this application of the doctrine of duress is that it does *not* constitute a new head of tort; rather, it gives rise to an action for restitution of moneys paid over, and given that such arrangements between unions and employers are not common, it is likely that in practice the occasions when such a claim will be brought will be few.[97] However, if a claim is brought, it raises an exceptionally difficult point—when does pressure by a union on an employer overstep the line between hard bargaining on the one hand and illegitimate coercion (giving rise to economic duress) on the other? The answer given by the House of Lords was as follows: although the doctrine of duress does not give rise to an action in tort, so that the immunities in the Trade Union and Labour Relations (Consolidation) Act 1992, s 219 are not directly applicable, those immunities can be used *indirectly* to draw the line, the reasoning being that it would be contrary to Parliament's intention to hold voidable for duress actions which, had a suit been pleaded in tort, would have been covered by the statutory immunities. Thus, if an action would have been immune from a suit in tort, it will probably not be held to amount to economic duress. The majority went on to hold that the actions of the ITWF in fact would not have come within the statutory immunity, and so the claimants could recover the money paid over by them.

10.2.7 **Immunity—the golden formula**

10.2.7.1 **Introduction**

For the statutory immunities to apply, the industrial action in question must be within the 'golden formula', that is, it must be 'in contemplation or furtherance of a trade dispute'; if it falls outside that, the immunities will not apply, and in most cases it will be easy for the claimant employer to show all the elements of one or more of the above torts and on that basis claim an interim injunction to stop the industrial action. For many years, if the formula applied then that was the end of the matter: there was immunity from liability in tort for organizing or participating in industrial action. The immunity would cover not just the classic case of the effect of a strike on the employer's business but also,

[95] Originally duress in contract law only covered threats of violence, but it was widened to economic duress: see *North Ocean Shipping Co Ltd v Hyundai Construction Co Ltd* [1979] QB 705, [1978] 3 All ER 1170; *Pao On v Lau Yiu Long* [1980] AC 614, [1979] 3 All ER 65, PC; *Syros Shipping Co SA v Elaghill Trading Co* [1981] 3 All ER 189; *B & S Contracts and Design Ltd v Victor Green Publications Ltd* [1984] ICR 419, CA; *CTN Cash and Carry Ltd v Gallagher Ltd* [1994] 4 All ER 714, CA.

[96] [1982] 2 All ER 67, [1982] ICR 262, HL, noted (1982) 45 MLR 556; see Sterling 'Actions for Duress, Seafarers and Industrial Disputes' (1982) 11 ILJ 156.

[97] Although cf *Dimskal Shipping Co SA v International Transport Workers' Federation, The Evia Luck (No 2)* [1992] ICR 37, [1992] IRLR 78, HL.

for example, an instruction given by a union to members working for a customer of the employer in dispute with the union not to handle goods supplied by that employer.

However, since the 1980s, determining whether the golden formula applies is only the first stage in identifying whether the immunity applies. As a result of a series of amendments:

- In relation to those cases where the potential defendant is a trade union, before the defendant can benefit from the immunity it must comply with an elaborate scheme of balloting union members about the proposed industrial action and must also give advance notice of the industrial action to the employer. These rules are contained in ss 226 and 234A of the Act and, because the immunity of trade unions from liability for organizing industrial action is conditional upon compliance with them, the effect of the law is that unions are compelled to observe these procedures. These conditions are therefore of great significance and they are dealt with in 10.3.
- In all cases, organizing certain kinds of industrial action is now excluded from the immunity. These exclusions are contained in ss 222–225 of the Trade Union and Labour Relations (Consolidation) Act 1992 and are considered in 10.2.8.

We must turn first to examine the scope of the golden formula: two matters must be shown—there must be a 'trade dispute', and the acts in question must be 'in contemplation or furtherance' of it.

10.2.7.2 **Is there a trade dispute?**

The statutory definition

Section 244 of the Trade Union and Labour Relations (Consolidation) Act 1992 defines a trade dispute as a dispute between 'workers[98] and their employer' which relates 'wholly or mainly to' one or more of the following:[99]

1. terms and conditions of employment,[100] or the physical conditions in which any workers are required to work;
2. engagement or non-engagement, or termination or suspension of employment, or the duties of employment,[101] of one or more workers;

[98] 'Worker' is defined in s 296 and includes an independent contractor, provided they undertake to perform work or services personally (other than in a professional capacity): *Broadbent v Crisp* [1974] ICR 248; cf *Writers' Guild of Great Britain v BBC* [1974] ICR 234. For a discussion of whether this is compatible with the European Convention on Human Rights see 10.1.6.1.

[99] A dispute which relates to matters occurring outside the UK qualifies as a trade dispute only if those taking action within the UK are likely to be affected by the outcome of the dispute in relation to one or more of the matters specified in s 244(1)(a)–(g): s 244(3).

[100] The use of the composite expression 'terms and conditions of employment' shows that the phrase was intended to be given a broad meaning, as covering both the rules of employment and the application of those rules: *P v National Association of Schoolmasters/Union of Women Teachers* [2003] IRLR 307, [2003] 1 All ER 993, per Lord Hoffmann; there must, however, be some limitation of it to terms which regulate the relationship between employer and employee, excluding any matters extraneous to that relationship: *Universe Tankships Inc of Monrovia v International Transport Workers' Federation* [1982] 2 All ER 67, [1982] ICR 262, HL.

[101] A trade dispute arising out of fears for jobs in a period of high unemployment (involving, for example, a demand that what work there is should be done by existing employees, not by outside contractors) was said by Lord Diplock in *Hadmor Productions Ltd v Hamilton* [1982] 1 All ER 1042, [1982] ICR 114, HL to be a classic instance of a dispute covered by head (2); the Court of Appeal had held that there was no trade dispute in such a case.

3. allocation of work or the duties of employment between workers or groups of workers;[102]
4. matters of discipline;
5. the membership or non-membership of a trade union on the part of a worker;[103]
6. facilities for officials of trade unions;
7. machinery for negotiation or consultation, and other procedures, relating to any of the above matters, including recognition of a union by an employer or employer's association.[104]

It is further provided in s 244(4) that there can still be a 'dispute' even if the employer in fact submits to the union's demands, so that the initial making of the demands can still be considered as within the golden formula.[105]

Subject matter

'Trade dispute' is thus given a wide definition, capable of covering most disputes between employees and their employer about the job the employees are employed to do or the terms and conditions on which they are employed to do it, and therefore the actual definition will not normally be a significant legal restriction on a union's activities, provided it acts generally within an employment relations context. If, however, it goes outside that and engages in what, for want of a better word, might be called 'political' action, then arguably it might be outside a trade dispute. Thus, industrial action taken *purely* as a protest against government action might be of dubious legality.[106] However, the mere fact that there is a 'political' aspect will not remove a dispute from the statutory definition, so that anti-government action might still be included if there is a genuine employment aspect, as, for example, where the government is a significant employer of the union's members,[107] or where those members may be directly affected by government policies in question (eg on questions of nationalization or privatization of the industry concerned or where a teachers' union was seeking to persuade the government to provide more funding for sixth form colleges so that those colleges could pay teachers better).[108]

[102] This covers demarcation disputes, but note that the employer must be a party to such a dispute for it to qualify under head (3) because of the general requirement that the dispute be between 'workers and their employer'; moreover, that requirement means that head (3) only applies to the allocation of work between the employer's own workers—it does not apply to a dispute over reallocation of work from the employer's own workers to an outside company: *Dimbleby & Sons Ltd v NUJ* [1984] ICR 386, [1984] IRLR 161, HL.

[103] While the definition of trade dispute still includes disputes over non-membership, s 222 provides that the immunities will be withdrawn where industrial action is taken to enforce union membership: see 10.2.8.3.

[104] However, the action must clearly be connected with the recognition issue, not just an aftermath: *J T Stratford & Son Ltd v Lindley* [1965] AC 269, [1964] 3 All ER 102, HL.

[105] Nullifying statements to the contrary in *Cory Lighterage Ltd v TGWU* [1973] ICR 339, [1973] IRLR 152, CA.

[106] *Associated Newspapers Group Ltd v Flynn* (1970) 10 KIR 17; in *National Sailors' and Firemen's Union v Reed* [1926] Ch 536, Astbury J held that the 1926 General Strike was illegal, sed quaere (see Goodhart (1927) 36 Yale LJ 464). In *Sherard v AUEW* [1973] ICR 421, [1973] IRLR 188, CA, at 433 and 189, respectively, Lord Denning MR stated as his opinion that a dispute between the TUC and the government (simpliciter) would not be a trade dispute. See also *Express Newspapers v Keys* [1980] IRLR 247, and *University College London Hospitals NHS Trust v UNISON* [1999] IRLR 31.

[107] *Sherard v AUEW* [1973] ICR 421, [1973] IRLR 188, CA.

[108] *General Aviation Services (UK) Ltd v TGWU* [1974] ICR 35, [1973] IRLR 355 and *Secretary of State for Education v NUT* [2016] EWHC 812 (QB), [2016] IRLR 512. Section 244(2) provides that a dispute between workers and a government minister who is not their employer will be treated as a trade dispute with their employer where the dispute cannot be settled without the minister's involvement or approval: see eg *Wandsworth London Borough Council v NASUWT* [1993] IRLR 344, CA.

The Employment Act 1982 narrowed the trade dispute definition considerably by requiring that the dispute relate 'wholly or mainly to' one or more of the listed matters, rather than simply be 'connected with' them. The importance of this can clearly be seen in *Mercury Communications Ltd v Scott-Garner*.[109] The case concerned action taken by the union representing British Telecom (BT) workers to try to prevent the licensing of a private company by BT (a process referred to as 'liberalization'). The company brought proceedings for an injunction to restrain this action. The union pleaded the immunity, on the basis that this was a trade dispute concerning possible job losses. However, the Court of Appeal granted the injunction on the basis that the facts did not show that fear of job losses was the major factor behind the action (particularly as there was in existence a job security agreement with BT), and that on the facts the dispute related wholly or mainly to the union's political objection to liberalization, which was seen as a precursor to the entire privatization of BT (that in the event followed).

In contrast, in *Wandsworth London Borough Council v NASUWT*,[110] the Court of Appeal had to decide whether industrial action by teachers which included a boycott of testing under the national curriculum was a 'trade dispute' and therefore covered by the statutory immunities. The local authority argued that the main impetus for the dispute was the objection of the union and its members to the principle of testing, so that it was not wholly or mainly related to terms and conditions, etc, but on the facts the Court of Appeal accepted the union's argument that the dispute related mainly to the increased workload on teachers in conducting the tests (a point stressed by union leaders at every turn and also emphasized in the wording of the strike ballot), and held that there was in fact a trade dispute. The court attached 'considerable importance' to the fact that the wording of the question posed in the ballot paper referred to 'protest against the excessive workload and unreasonable imposition made upon teachers' as a result of the new national curriculum assessment and testing requirements.

Parties to dispute

The dispute must be between 'workers and *their* employer', which raises the question of the legality of industrial action aimed at securing for the future the terms and conditions of employees following a business transfer. In *University College London Hospitals NHS Trust v UNISON*,[111] the union threatened industrial action after the Trust refused to give an undertaking that the terms and conditions of staff to be transferred to a new consortium which was to build and run a private finance initiative hospital would be maintained for a period of 30 years at an equivalent level to those of Trust employees who were not transferred. The Court of Appeal issued an injunction restraining the action, on the grounds that the trade dispute definition does not cover a dispute about the terms and conditions offered by an as yet unidentified employer. Insofar as the decision relates to the as yet unidentified *future* employees of an as yet unidentified employer, it is perhaps unexceptionable, but the Court of Appeal's suggestion that the trade dispute definition does

[109] [1984] ICR 74, [1983] IRLR 494, CA.

[110] [1994] ICR 81, [1993] IRLR 344, CA. See also *University College London Hospitals NHS Trust v UNISON* [1999] IRLR 31, CA, and *Westminster City Council v UNISON* [2001] EWCA Civ 443, [2001] ICR 1046.

[111] [1999] IRLR 31, CA. See also *UNISON v United Kingdom* [2002] IRLR 497, ECtHR, discussed in 10.1.6, where the ECtHR rejected the union's claim that the Court of Appeal's interpretation was an unjustified restriction on the right to freedom of assembly and association in Art 11 of the European Convention on Human Rights.

not include industrial action to protect the terms and conditions of *existing* employees after they are transferred to a new employer is arguably an undesirably narrow interpretation of the trade dispute definition.[112]

10.2.7.3 Is the action 'in contemplation or furtherance'?

It is not enough for there to be a trade dispute in existence: to be within the golden formula, the industrial action must be taken 'in contemplation or furtherance' of it. This raises requirements as to timing and the nature of the connection with the dispute. On timing, the trade dispute must either be about to or likely to happen ('contemplation'), or it must already be in existence ('furtherance'). An action could be too far in advance of any possible dispute to be in contemplation of it,[113] and action taken after the conclusion of the dispute (eg to 'punish' certain participants in it or to regain prestige for the union) might be too late to be considered in furtherance of it.[114] Even if the employer believes that a dispute has been settled, action can still be in furtherance of a trade dispute if the union genuinely and honestly believe there is still a dispute.[115] In *Conway v Wade*,[116] Lord Shaw said:

> The contemplation of such a dispute must be the contemplation of something impending or likely to occur and . . . [it does] not cover the case of coercive interference in which the intervener may have in his own mind that if he does not get his own way he will thereupon take ways and means to bring a trade dispute into existence . . . With regard to the term 'furtherance' of a trade dispute, I think that must apply to a trade dispute in existence and that the act done must be in the course of it and for the purpose of promoting the interests of either party or both parties to it.

The House of Lords has ruled that the question whether a person acts in contemplation or furtherance of a trade dispute is a subjective one which must be decided in the light of the intentions and beliefs of the actors; if a person has a genuine and honest belief that his actions will further the interests of one party to the dispute, the fact that those actions, considered objectively, are not reasonably capable of furthering the dispute will be relevant only insofar as it casts doubt on the genuineness of that person's subjective belief.[117] In the words of Lord Scarman in *Express Newspapers Ltd v McShane*:

> It follows therefore that, once it is shown that a trade dispute exists, the person who acts, but not the court, is the judge of whether his acts will further the dispute. If he is acting honestly, Parliament leaves to him the choice of what to do. I confess that I am relieved to find that this is the law. It would be a strange and embarrassing task for a judge to be called upon to review the tactics of a party to a trade dispute and to determine whether in the view of the court the tactic employed was likely to further or advance that party's side of the dispute . . . It would need very clear statutory language to persuade me that Parliament intended to allow the courts to act as some sort of backseat driver in trade disputes.[118]

[112] A dispute over whether a proposed transfer should go ahead would clearly fall within the definition, as the identity of the employer is a term of the contract: see eg *Westminster City Council v UNISON* [2001] EWCA Civ 443, [2001] ICR 1046.

[113] *Bents Brewery Co Ltd v Hogan* [1945] 2 All ER 570.

[114] *J T Stratford & Son Ltd v Lindley* [1965] AC 269, [1964] 3 All ER 102, HL; *Stewart v AUEW* [1973] ICR 128, [1973] IRLR 57, NIRC.

[115] *Newham London Borough v National and Local Government Officers' Association* [1993] IRLR 83, CA; *Warrington Borough Council v Unite the Union* [2023] EWHC 3093 (KB), [2024] IRLR 190, [2024] ICR 599.

[116] [1909] AC 506, HL at 522. The case remains good law on this point.

[117] *NWL Ltd v Nelson* [1979] ICR 867, [1979] IRLR 478, HL; *Express Newspapers Ltd v McShane* [1980] ICR 42, [1980] IRLR 35, HL; *Duport Steels Ltd v Sirs* [1980] ICR 161, [1980] IRLR 116, HL.

[118] [1980] ICR 42 at 64, [1980] IRLR 35 at 78.

10.2.8 **Restrictions on the statutory immunities—kinds of industrial action which are never protected**

Even if industrial action is in contemplation or furtherance of a trade dispute and so falls within the golden formula, it may still be rendered illegal if it falls within one of the categories of industrial action from which the immunities have been removed by the legislation introduced since 1980.[119]

10.2.8.1 **Secondary action**

The statutory immunities are severely curtailed in the case of 'secondary action', that is, action which is taken against an employer other than the employer in dispute. Such action might be against a supplier or customer of the employer in dispute, with the union instructing its members employed by that supplier or customer not to handle goods to or from the employer in dispute. The golden formula immunity does not apply to any kind of secondary action unless it occurs in the course of 'lawful picketing' (see 10.5). An attempt to challenge this ban on secondary action on the basis that it was incompatible with Article 11 of the European Convention on Human Rights failed in *NURMTW v United Kingdom*. The European Court of Human Rights held that, although Article 11(1) was engaged, the decision to impose these restrictions was within the margin of appreciation given to governments by Article 11(2).[120]

The law is contained in s 224(2) of the Trade Union and Labour Relations (Consolidation) Act 1992, which provides that there is 'secondary action' in relation to a trade dispute when two conditions apply: *first*, a person either:

1. induces another to break a contract of employment[121] or interferes or induces another to interfere with its performance; or
2. threatens that a contract of employment under which they or another are employed will be broken or its performance interfered with, or that they will induce another to break a contract of employment or to interfere with its performance;

and *second*, the employer under the contract of employment is not the employer party to the dispute.

The gist of the definition is that to be secondary action the action must be directed against an employer *who is not a party to the trade dispute* and, moreover, must involve *interference with the contracts of employment* of that employer. Action which is in fact aimed at the employer in dispute, but which causes loss to that employer's customers or suppliers (ie 'primary action'[122] which has what might be termed secondary *effects*), is not 'secondary action' within the meaning of the section.

The result of the tightening of the restrictions on secondary action since 1980 is that the scope of lawful industrial action may be determined by the corporate structure of the employer in dispute,[123] and the refusal of the courts to lift the corporate veil means that action taken against another employer, even one in the same group as (or otherwise closely related to) the employer in dispute, will not be covered by the statutory immunities, unless it is possible to identify a separate trade dispute with that employer.

[119] See Auerbach *Legislating for Conflict* (1992).

[120] [2014] IRLR 467, (2015) 60 EHRR 10; see Bogg and Ewing 'The Implications of the RMT Case' (2014) 43 ILJ 221.

[121] Section 224(6) adopts a wide definition of 'contract of employment' which includes self-employed and freelance workers, and others who personally do work or perform services for another.

[122] As defined in s 224(5).

[123] This was an important part of the union's argument in the *NURMTW v UK* case.

10.2.8.2 **Unlawful picketing**

The second removal of the immunities relates to any acts done in the course of picketing which fall outside the scope of the picketing immunity conferred by s 220.[124] The details and effect of this exclusion are considered in 10.5.

10.2.8.3 **Action to enforce union membership**

Sections 137, 146, and 152 of the Trade Union and Labour Relations (Consolidation) Act 1992 outlaw the closed shop by making it unlawful for an employer to refuse employment because someone is not a member of a trade union or refuses to join one, and also making it unlawful for an employer to dismiss an employee for such a reason or to subject an employee to a detriment for such a reason.[125] Nevertheless it is possible that an employer might be put under pressure by a union either to operate a closed shop itself or to demand that a supplier should operate a closed shop. Accordingly, s 222(1) of the Act withdraws the golden formula immunity where the reason for the industrial action is the fact or belief that a particular employer (a) 'is employing, has employed or might employ a person' who is not a member of a trade union,[126] or (b) 'is failing, has failed or might fail to discriminate against such a person'. While the main target of this provision when it was introduced by the Employment Act 1988 was to outlaw industrial action taken in defence of a closed shop, in fact it goes further by removing the immunities from *all* industrial action taken for reasons of non-union membership, irrespective of whether there is a closed shop in operation. For example, it would apply to a situation where a union is, through industrial action, seeking to persuade an employer to treat fellow workers who are members of a rival union less favourably than its own members.[127]

10.2.8.4 **Pressure to impose union recognition requirements**

Sections 186 and 187 of the Trade Union and Labour Relations (Consolidation) Act 1992 make it unlawful to refuse to deal with a supplier of goods or services on the grounds that the supplier does not or is not likely to recognize, negotiate, or consult with a trade union.[128] Section 225 of the Act removes the statutory immunities from industrial action taken to persuade an employer to impose a union recognition requirement on a customer or supplier. It does this in two ways:

1. by removing the immunity from any industrial action aimed at inducing an employer to breach any of the above restrictions (eg by inserting a term requiring union recognition in a commercial contract); and
2. by removing the immunity from industrial action taken against Employer A which interferes (or can reasonably be expected to interfere) with the supply of goods or services between that employer and the supplier, Employer B, where the reason or one of the reasons for the action is the fact or belief that Employer B does not or might not recognize, negotiate with, or consult with one or more trade unions.

[124] Section 219(3). [125] See 9.4.1 and 9.4.3.

[126] Whether the person in question is not a member of any trade union or of a particular trade union or of one of a number of particular trade unions: s 222(5).

[127] This was the allegation in *Birmingham City Council v Unite the Union* [2019] IRLR 423, HC, where the industrial action organized by Union A was held not to be intended to persuade the employer to treat members of Union B less favourably; rather, it was intended to win for members of Union A a benefit that had already been awarded by the employer to members of Union B. In consequence s 222 did not remove Union A's immunity.

[128] See 9.7.5.

Note, however, that the golden formula immunity is available if a union organizes industrial action in order to persuade the workers' own employer to recognize the union.

10.2.8.5 **Action taken because of the dismissal of unofficial strikers**

Those taking part in unofficial industrial action cannot bring a complaint of unfair dismissal.[129] In a related provision, s 223 of the Trade Union and Labour Relations (Consolidation) Act 1992 aims to discourage a collective response to such dismissals by removing the statutory immunities where the reason (or *one* of the reasons) for the industrial action is the fact or belief that an employer has dismissed an employee taking part in unofficial industrial action.

10.3 **Balloting and notice requirements**

10.3.1 **Introduction—and trends in interpretation**

The most important potential restrictions on the availability of the golden formula immunity are those contained in:

- s 226 of the Trade Union and Labour Relations (Consolidation) Act 1992, which makes a union's immunity conditional on the industrial action having the support of a ballot in relation to which the detailed rules set out in ss 226–234 have been observed; and
- s 234A, which makes a union's immunity conditional on notice being given to the employer of the taking of industrial action.

These rules remove the immunity in relation to any act done by, or deemed to have been done by, a trade union.[130] The rules have been controversial. An unsuccessful attempt was made in *Metrobus v Unite the Union*[131] to challenge these rules in the Court of Appeal on the basis that they made lawful strike action so difficult to organize that they contravened the right to associate in Article 11 of the European Convention on Human Rights.

However, although *Metrobus Ltd v Unite the Union* appeared to show that these procedural requirements are in effect absolute, so that any lapse in them puts the union in breach—subject only to the 'small accidental failures' exception in s 232B, which applies only to a minority of the ballot requirements—within a year the Court of Appeal adopted a significantly different approach in two decisions. Those cases demonstrated at the very least the courts running out of patience with the highly technical arguments commonly put forward by employers. In *British Airways plc v Unite the Union*,[132] the employer applied for an injunction to prevent strike action on a technical point about informing the membership of the results of a ballot. The majority in the Court of Appeal said that the relevant section in the 1992 Act was poorly drafted and that in the light of that it was inappropriate to apply an overly literal approach in order to comply with the overall aims of the legislation.

[129] See 10.7.3.1.

[130] This is the combined effect of Trade Union and Labour Relations (Consolidation) Act 1992 ss 219(4), 226, and 234A. As to when a union is responsible for the acts of its officials see 10.6.2.

[131] [2010] ICR 173, [2009] IRLR 851, CA. The facts of the case well illustrate the complexity here—the union did not give the employer notice of the ballot result (required by the Trade Union and Labour Relations (Consolidation) Act 1992, s 213A) until two days later, when giving actual strike notice (required by s 234A). It was held that these are two separate requirements and that the union had not given the s 231A notice 'as soon as reasonably practicable', and an injunction was granted to stop the strike.

[132] [2010] ICR 1316, [2012] IRLR 809, CA.

More important was the second case, *NURMT v Serco Ltd*,[133] in which the Court of Appeal clearly set out to rebalance the practical operation of the law by preventing the use by employers of highly technical breaches on the part of a union to obtain interim injunctions banning industrial action. Elias LJ's judgment will be considered in more detail later in this chapter after the balloting and notice requirements have been explained in full, but at this point it is important to say that breaches of many of the detailed requirements may now be interpreted generously by the courts if their impact on the democratic validity of the ballot is in reality minor. Judgments pre-dating the *Serco* judgment should be read subject to the more liberal approach set out by the Court of Appeal in *Serco*. Indeed, it is possible that there may be even further liberality to come: Elias LJ suggested that there might be an even more generous principle that only 'substantial compliance' with the balloting provisions is required, but he left this for argument on another day.

One further key point about the *Serco* case is worth making now. The court's judgment starts with a general point that this legislation is to be construed and applied in a normal way, without any presumption that it will be applied strictly against a union wishing to claim its statutory protection (or indeed that the employer's interest must prevail), and in a way that will give it a 'likely and workable construction', giving due weight to freedom of association as enshrined in Article 11 of the European Convention on Human Rights.

A recent important development is the Employment Rights Act 2025, which significantly reduces the procedural requirements placed on unions and makes the balloting system as a whole easier for unions to comply with—or, to put it another way, makes it harder for an employer to stop industrial action by persuading a court that the balloting has not been correctly carried out by the union.

10.3.2 **The balloting requirements**

10.3.2.1 **Overview**

Section 226 of the Trade Union and Labour Relations (Consolidation) Act 1992 provides that the immunities in s 219 do not apply where an act is 'done by a trade union'[134] to induce a person to take part (or continue to take part) in industrial action,[135] unless the industrial action 'has the support of a ballot'. The ballot only supports the action if it relates to the action to be taken rather than some other industrial action and the ballot must relate to the same dispute as the action relates.[136] Section 226(2) spells out that to provide support the ballot must comply with a long list of requirements set out in the succeeding sections of the Act. Where the immunities are removed the full weight of the common law liabilities will be restored, and so anyone suffering loss or damage through a tort committed by the union could sue, even ordinary customers or suppliers of the employer in dispute.[137]

The balloting provisions were originally introduced in the Trade Union Act 1984, and were further tightened up by three more Acts which followed soon after. That basic structure has remained in place ever since but with successive loosening of the requirements,

[133] [2011] ICR 848, [2011] IRLR 399, CA. [134] See 10.6.2.

[135] This is not defined for present purposes. For its interpretation in the context of dismissal of those taking part in industrial action see 'The definitions of "strike", "other industrial action", and "lockout"' in 10.7.3.3.

[136] *Westminster Kingsway College v University and College Union* [2014] EWHC 4409 (QB) (13 October 2014, unreported); *Warrington Borough Council v Unite the Union* [2023] EWHC 3093 (KB), [2024] IRLR 190, [2024] ICR 599.

[137] See eg *Falconer v ASLEF and NUR* [1986] IRLR 331. Since the withdrawal of immunity is so immediate and so total, the only defence a union will have might be that no tort was committed in the first place—an uphill battle at the best of times.

followed by tightening and then loosening again by successive governments of different political colours.

One important source is the Code of Practice on Industrial Action Ballots and Notice to Employers,[138] which gives guidance as to 'desirable practices' in relation to industrial action ballots. The Code is not law but any provision which appears relevant can be taken into account by a court in determining any issue before it.[139] The Code covers preparations for a ballot (including providing notice to the employer, establishing the balloting constituency, balloting at more than one workplace, and producing the voting forms), holding the ballot (including independent scrutiny and secrecy), and action to be taken after the ballot (including guidance on continuous and discontinuous industrial action).

10.3.2.2 **Entitlement to vote**

Section 227(1) states:

> Entitlement to vote in the ballot must be accorded equally to all the members of the trade union who it is reasonable at the time of the ballot for the union to believe will be induced by the union to take part . . . in the industrial action in question, and to no others.[140]

The union must take great care when defining the balloting constituency, for if a member is not accorded entitlement to vote in the ballot and is subsequently induced to take part in the industrial action, the entire ballot may be invalidated and the immunity lost (subject to the statutory dispensation permitting small accidental failures to be disregarded and subject to the court being generous because of *Serco*).[141]

What is the position in relation to workers who become part of the workforce after the ballot has been held, for example new workers who did not start working for the employer, or working within the balloting constituency, until after the ballot? And what of new members who did not join the union until after the ballot? Can they be induced to take part in the industrial action? In *London Underground v RMT*,[142] the issue was whether the statutory immunities were lost because some 692 workers who had joined the union since the date of the ballot were called upon to take part in the industrial action. The Court of Appeal held that the industrial action still had the support of a ballot:

> The union is required to ballot those, *and only those*, of *its members* who *at the time of the ballot* it is reasonable to believe will be called upon to take part in the industrial action. It cannot identify future members, but even if it could it must not ballot them, since the ballot is confined to persons who were members at the time of the ballot.[143]

But what of existing union members who were not working for the employer in dispute at the time of the ballot? Could they also be called upon to take part in the action? The logic

[138] Revised in 2017 to reflect the changes made by the Trade Union Act 2016.

[139] See Trade Union and Labour Relations (Consolidation) Act 1992, s 207.

[140] Trade Union and Labour Relations (Consolidation) Act 1992, s 227(1). A failure to comply will not be condoned simply because a union's complex structure makes full compliance difficult: *RJB Mining (UK) Ltd v National Union of Mineworkers* [1997] IRLR 621, QBD. On the other hand, an attempt by an employer to restrict entitlement to vote only to those due to *work* on the days or shifts affected was rejected: *United Closures and Plastics Ltd* [2012] IRLR 29, Ct of Sess (OH).

[141] Trade Union and Labour Relations (Consolidation) Act 1992, s 232B.

[142] [1995] IRLR 636, CA. Millett LJ also stated, obiter, that nothing in the statutory balloting provisions curtails a union's right to induce *non-members* to support industrial action called by the union, as those provisions are concerned exclusively with the relationship between the union and its members, and are intended for the protection of members, not the protection of the employer or the public.

[143] [1995] IRLR 636 at 639. Millett LJ's emphasis.

of the decision in *London Underground v RMT* applies equally to such members, since it would not have been reasonable *at the time of the ballot* for the union to believe that those members would be called upon to take part in the action, in view of the fact that they were not employed by the employer in dispute at that time. However, the position is put beyond doubt by s 232A, which deals with this in a back-to-front way by stating that industrial action will not be regarded as having the support of the ballot if (a) a person was a member of the union at the time when the ballot was held; (b) it was reasonable at that time for the union to believe that the person would be induced to take part in the industrial action; (c) the person was not accorded entitlement to vote in the ballot; and (d) the person was induced by the union to take part in the industrial action. Unless the union knew that the member was going to change job and join the group who were going to be called on to take industrial action, condition (b) is not fulfilled and so the immunity is not lost.

A union may fully intend to send ballot papers to some workers, because it intends to call on them to take part in the industrial action, but may fail by accident to do so. In relation to this issue it is necessary to distinguish *according the entitlement* to vote from actually giving a person *the opportunity to cast the vote* to which they are entitled:

- s 227(1), which we have just considered, is concerned with ensuring that the union gives the right categories of workers the *entitlement* to vote even if, by some accident, some of those workers do not get sent a ballot paper;
- s 230(2) adds that so far as is reasonably practicable, everyone with the entitlement to vote should *actually be given the opportunity to vote.*

This is important because, as has been judicially recognized, in the real world it will normally be impossible for a union to compile an accurate list of all its members within a particular balloting constituency:

> It is a fact of life that no trade union of any size can keep completely full and accurate records of the names and addresses of its ever-changing body of members, still less their current places of work, trade categories and pay grades.[144]

A union is required by law to maintain a register of members' names and addresses, and so far as is reasonably practicable to keep it accurate and up to date,[145] but the union's record-keeping duty does not extend to the occupations, grades, or workplaces of its members, nor is there any duty on members to inform the union when they change jobs or move house. In practice, therefore, it is very likely that if, for example, a union intends to call out on strike all members who are fitters in grades 1 to 4, some members who are within that balloting constituency may not be given an opportunity to vote—for example because the union's records are inaccurate, or because mistakes occur during the ballot process (such as ballot papers getting lost in the post), or because members change jobs or indeed join the union during the balloting process. Such failures do not necessarily mean that those members were not accorded entitlement to vote within the meaning of s 227(1)—the union did not intend to deny them a vote. As the House of Lords has confirmed, whether or not failures of that kind invalidate the ballot must be determined by applying the other provisions of the Act which deal with the administration of the ballot, including s 230(2) (which states that 'so far

[144] *P v National Union of Schoolmasters/Union of Women Teachers* [2003] IRLR 307, [2003] 1 All ER 993, HL per Lord Walker at [65].

[145] Trade Union and Labour Relations (Consolidation) Act 1992, s 24.

as is reasonably practicable, every person who is entitled to vote in the ballot must . . . be given a convenient opportunity to vote by post')[146] and s 232B (which makes both s 227(1) and s 230(2) subject to a dispensation for small accidental errors): 'If failure to send a ballot paper to a person within the constituency falls within either of these exceptions, he is not by reason of that failure to be treated as having not been accorded entitlement to vote.'[147]

Even before the introduction of the dispensation for small accidental failures in 1999, it had been recognized that it would be unrealistic to expect a union to achieve total compliance by supplying a ballot paper to every single member of the balloting constituency. In one of the earliest cases on the strike ballot provisions, the Court of Appeal held that an inadvertent failure to give someone the opportunity of voting did not necessarily constitute an infringement of the balloting requirements,[148] and the House of Lords confirmed in *P v National Union of Schoolmasters/Union of Women Teachers*[149] that, despite the changes in the wording of the balloting provisions in 1999,[150] the position remains the same.

10.3.2.3 **Aggregate ballots across several workplaces**

There must be separate workplace ballots where a union wishes to organize industrial action at more than one place of work.[151] The aim is to prevent a union from manipulating the outcome of a ballot by creating 'artificial' balloting constituencies, combining different groups of workers together so as to ensure an overall vote in favour of industrial action. However, as an insistence on separate workplace ballots in every case would have been a recipe for industrial relations chaos, a union may hold one aggregated ballot across several workplaces where those to be balloted have some particular factor in common.

A union may hold an aggregated ballot across more than one workplace[152] if one of the following is satisfied:

- Each workplace concerned is the workplace of at least one member of the union who is 'affected by the dispute'.[153] A union is permitted to ask members not affected by a dispute to take industrial action in support of fellow employees of the same employer, but this provision limits the circumstances in which such employees can be included in an *aggregate* ballot: if none of the union members at a workplace is directly affected by the dispute then they must be balloted separately.
- The union reasonably believes that it is balloting all its members of a particular occupational description (or descriptions) who are employed by an employer (or

[146] This provision is considered in 10.3.2.6.

[147] *P v National Union of Schoolmasters/Union of Women Teachers* [2003] UKHL 8, [2003] 1 All ER 993, per Lord Hoffmann at [44].

[148] *British Railways Board v National Union of Railwaymen* [1989] ICR 678, [1989] IRLR 349, CA.

[149] [2003] IRLR 307, [2003] 1 All ER 993, HL.

[150] Before 1999, s 227(2) stated that the balloting requirements were not satisfied if a member who was induced to take part in the action was 'denied' entitlement to vote. That provision was replaced by s 232A, which used the expression 'not accorded' in place of 'denied'.

[151] Trade Union and Labour Relations (Consolidation) Act 1992, ss 228 and 228A.

[152] For these purposes, 'workplace' means, if the person works at or from a single set of premises, those premises, and in any other case, the premises with which the person's employment has the closest connection: s 228(4). Under the pre-1999 provisions, it was held that the freedom to hold an aggregate ballot was not confined to situations where the different workplaces all belonged to the same employer (see *University of Central England v NALGO* [1993] IRLR 81), and this is believed still to be the case.

[153] Section 228A(5) sets out four categories of union member who are to be regarded as 'affected by a dispute', for example if the dispute relates wholly or partly to a proposed or actual decision of the employer and the member is directly affected by that decision.

employers) with whom the union is in dispute. This would cover, for example, a ballot of all helpdesk staff or all grade 1 drivers at all UK depots employed by John Smith Ltd and Mary Jones Ltd

- The union reasonably believes that it is balloting all its members who are employed by an employer (or employers) with whom the union is in dispute.

10.3.2.4 **Notice of ballot to the employer**

A union must give the employers of those entitled to vote in the ballot at least seven days' notice in writing of the ballot,[154] the apparent aim being to give employers the opportunity to makes plans to respond to the disruptive effects of the industrial action.[155] In reality, until the reduction by the Employment Rights Act 2025 of the amount of information that must be given in the ballot notice, employers have often been able to use deficiencies in the notice of ballot as the basis of a legal challenge to the efficacy of the ballot.

Section 226A of the Trade Union and Labour Relations (Consolidation) Act 1992 provides that the notice must state the intention to hold a ballot and give its opening date, together with information about the members to be balloted in the form of lists of the categories of employees and the workplaces affected and the total number of workers being balloted.[156] Slightly different rules apply where the employer deducts union subscriptions from employees' pay—a system which is known as 'checkoff' or DOCAS (deduction of contributions at source). In such a case, instead of giving numbers, the union merely needs to give the employer such information as will enable it readily to deduce the numbers, categories, and workplaces of those being balloted.[157] Where some union members pay by checkoff and some do not, the union can use a mixture of methods to give the requisite information.[158]

One area of contention has been what is meant by 'categories' of employee. It appears that the union is only obliged to provided category information based on the membership information which it possesses.[159] However, using such information as the union has, how specific must the categories be? The starting point is that what is meant is the general type of the worker.[160] Moreover, there is no obligation to adopt the categories used by the employer for pay purposes.[161] In *British Airways plc v British Airline Pilots Association*,[162] the Court of Appeal said that the sufficiency of the information is to be judged by reference to the two policy objectives of the legislation: first, to allow the employer to make plans to mitigate the effects of industrial action; second, to achieve notification requirements that were capable of being clearly and certainly applied by unions without creating too great a burden on them and that did not create a series of legislative traps. The Court

[154] Trade Union and Labour Relations (Consolidation) Act 1992, s 226A, as amended by the Employment Relations Act 1999, Sch 3.

[155] As noted by the Court of Appeal in *British Airways Plc v British Airline Pilots Association* [2020] IRLR 43.

[156] Section 226A(2)–(2B) as amended by Employment Rights Act 2025 s 70. The notice must be given not later than the seventh day before the opening of the ballot, and a copy of the voting paper must be given not later than the third day before: s 226A(1). Previously, the union also had to give details of the numbers involved in each and workplace and a brief explanation of how the figures had been arrived at, but in *Metrobus Ltd v Unite the Union* [2010] ICR 173, [2009] IRLR 851, CA, it was held that, in spite of their complexity, these provisions do not infringe the right to free association in Art 11 of the European Convention on Human Rights; they are within the margin of appreciation given to states.

[157] Sections 226A(2) and 226A(2C) as amended by Employment Rights Act 2025 s 70.

[158] *Metrobus Ltd v Unite the Union* [2010] ICR 173, [2009] IRLR 851, CA.

[159] *NURMT v Serco Ltd* [2011] ICR 848, [2011] IRLR 399, CA, paras 70–75.

[160] *Westminster City Council v Unison* [2001] IRLR 524, CA.

[161] *NURMT v Serco Ltd* [2011] ICR 848, [2011] IRLR 399, CA.

[162] [2020] IRLR 43, CA.

also said that provided the information is sufficient against these criteria, the fact that the union could have given more precise job categories does not mean that it must do so. In that case the ballot notice had indicated how many of those being balloted were captains and how many were co-pilots, but did not separate them into long-haul and short-haul categories. The Court of Appeal held that sufficient information had been given.[163]

It is specifically stated that '[n]othing in this section requires a union to supply an employer with the names of the employees concerned'.[164] The lists and figures supplied must be 'as accurate as is reasonably practicable in the light of the information in the possession of the union at the time when it complies' with these requirements. Reasonable practicability is to be judged in the light of the information in the union's possession at the time when it sends its notice to the employer.[165] For a time the courts appeared to require extensive steps to be taken to audit membership records for the purpose of the notice of ballot, but in *NURMT v Serco Ltd*[166] the Court of Appeal held that this was not required, although the union should obtain any relevant documents from its officers and employees and collate and analyse that information in order to supply the lists and figures as accurately as the union reasonably can, and it would be a breach of this duty for a union to provide information drawn solely from documentary records when it knew that the information was actually wrong. One recent potential problem for unions came with the introduction in April 2015 of an obligation on each union to appoint an 'assurer' to conduct an annual audit and to issue a certificate—which must be lodged with the Certification Officer and is a public document—as to whether the union's system for compiling and maintaining its register of members' names and addresses is satisfactory.[167] Clearly, if the certificate says that the system is not satisfactory, there must be scope for the argument that the union has not taken all reasonably practicable steps.

10.3.2.5 **The voting paper**

The content of the voting paper is specified in great detail. There are now six requirements.

1. The voting paper must contain at least one of the two 'statutory questions', asking the voter to say, by answering 'yes' or 'no', whether they are prepared to take part in a 'strike', or in 'industrial action short of a strike'.[168] If the union contemplates taking both types of action these two questions must be put separately, and separate approval must be obtained for each type of action.[169] In *West Midlands Travel Ltd v TGWU*,[170] the employers argued that where separate questions are put, the union must obtain majority approval of all those who had participated in the voting process, including those who had abstained on one of the questions, and not just a simple majority in respect of each individual question on the ballot paper;[171]

[163] In the earlier case of *Virgin Atlantic Airways Ltd v PPU* [2018] EWHC 3645 (QB) the High Court had held that the union should have separated those being balloted into the categories of captain and co-pilot because this was needed by the airline to be able to plan to minimize disruption, since captains could be used as co-pilots but co-pilots could not step up to the captain's seat.

[164] Section 226A(2D), (2G). [165] Section 226A(2D).

[166] *NURMT v Serco Ltd* [2011] ICR 848, [2011] IRLR 399, CA.

[167] Trade Union and Labour Relations (Consolidation) Act 1992, ss 24ZA–24ZD inserted by the Transparency of Lobbying, Non-party Campaigning and Trade Union Administration Act 2014.

[168] Trade Union and Labour Relations (Consolidation) Act 1992, s 229(2). Overtime bans and call-out bans are to be treated as industrial action short of a strike for these purposes: Trade Union and Labour Relations (Consolidation) Act 1992, s 229(2A).

[169] *Post Office v Union of Communication Workers* [1990] ICR 258, [1990] IRLR 143, CA.

[170] [1994] ICR 978, [1994] IRLR 578, CA.

[171] The wording of the statute is certainly ambiguous, in that s 226(2) provides that 'the majority voting in [the] ballot' must have answered the relevant question affirmatively.

however, the Court of Appeal sensibly held that where separate questions are posed, one relating to strike action and the other to industrial action short of a strike, each question must be regarded as a separate matter to be voted on individually, and the result of the ballot in respect of each question must be considered separately.

2. The voting paper must contain a statement informing members that industrial action may be unlawful but reminding them about the strong unfair dismissal protection applying to strikers,[172] as follows:

> If you take part in a strike or other industrial action, you may be in breach of your contract of employment. However, if you are dismissed for taking part in strike or other industrial action which is called officially and is otherwise lawful, the dismissal will be unfair.

This statement may not be qualified or commented on by anything else on the ballot paper,[173] even if it is clear that the action in question does not involve a breach of contract (as, for example, in the case of withdrawal from voluntary overtime).[174]

3. The voting paper must identify the person or persons authorized by the union to call upon members to take part in industrial action in the event of a vote in favour.[175]
4. The voting paper must give the name of the independent scrutineer.[176]
5. The voting paper must specify the address to which it must be retuned and the date by which this must be done.[177]
6. Each paper must be marked with a unique number.[178]

If any of the ballot paper requirements is omitted the industrial action will not be regarded as having the support of a ballot, and the statutory immunities will be withdrawn. To facilitate a challenge on the ground of a defective ballot, a union is required to provide the employers of those entitled to vote in the ballot with a sample voting paper at least three days before the start of the ballot.[179]

10.3.2.6 **Conduct of the ballot**

Members must be allowed to vote in a postal ballot without interference from the union (although interference from other quarters will not invalidate the ballot), and, so far as is reasonably practicable, the voting must be secret and at no direct cost to those voting.[180] The government has announced an intention to permit electronic balloting, and possibly also workplace voting.[181] The ballot paper must so far as is reasonably practicable be sent to every member entitled to vote at their home address (or any other address they have notified).[182] In *Royal Mail Group Ltd v Communication Workers Union*,[183]

[172] Trade Union and Labour Relations (Consolidation) Act 1992, s 229(4).

[173] There does not appear to be anything to prevent a union from commenting on the statement in material enclosed with the voting paper, provided nothing appears on the voting paper itself.

[174] *Power Packing Casemakers Ltd v Faust* [1983] ICR 292, [1983] IRLR 117, CA.

[175] Trade Union and Labour Relations (Consolidation) Act 1992, s 229(3).

[176] Trade Union and Labour Relations (Consolidation) Act 1992, s 1A(a)

[177] Trade Union and Labour Relations (Consolidation) Act 1992, s 1A(b).

[178] Trade Union and Labour Relations (Consolidation) Act 1992, s 1A(c)(d).

[179] Trade Union and Labour Relations (Consolidation) Act 1992, s 226A(1).

[180] Trade Union and Labour Relations (Consolidation) Act 1992, s 230(1). This means that the union must pay the postage (eg by providing pre-paid envelopes).

[181] This may be permitted by regulations under the Employment Relations Act 2004, s 54.

[182] Trade Union and Labour Relations (Consolidation) Act 1992, s 230(2).

[183] [219] EWCA Civ 2150, [2020] IRLR 213.

the voters were postal workers and although the ballot papers were put in the post addressed to their home addresses, the union encouraged members to take the envelopes out of the sorting frame as soon as they arrived at those members' sorting offices and then to mark their ballot forms and to participate in mass events to post the form back. This was held to be an interference and also a breach of the duty to take reasonable steps to send the ballot to members home addresses. The Act does not specify how long must be allowed for voting, but the Code of Practice recommends a minimum of seven days if first class post is used in both directions, and 14 days if second class post is used.[184]

It was argued on behalf of the union in *National Union of Rail, Maritime and Transport Workers v Midland Mainline* that the test of whether it was reasonably practicable for the union to supply ballot papers to members within the balloting constituency must be assessed in the light of the facts as they were on the day that the ballot papers were sent out, that is, in the light of the information available to the union at that time. The Court of Appeal rejected that reading:

> It cannot have been intended that a ballot will be regarded as having been properly conducted if the union does not properly record changes of address notified to it. Where, on the other hand, the union has a system for reminding members of the need to keep the union notified of any changes of addresses but a member fails to notify the union of such a change and the union is in fact ignorant of that change of address and sends a ballot paper to the old address then a court would probably find that the union will have done all that is reasonably practicable.[185]

New provisions introduced in 2015 require each union to appoint an 'assurer' to audit annually its system for maintaining up-to-date registers of members' names and addresses. If the assurer concludes that the system is not 'satisfactory' that may lead to arguments that a union has not done all that is reasonably practicable.[186]

It is frequently the case that some of the union members entitled to vote do not in fact receive ballot papers. This situation is addressed in the Act by s 232B, which provides that accidental failures in sending ballot papers which, taken together, are on a scale which is unlikely to affect the result of the ballot are to be disregarded.

10.3.2.7 **The ballot result**

Votes must be fairly and accurately counted (although accidental errors may be disregarded if incapable of affecting the result),[187] and the detailed results must be made known both to those voting and to their employers as soon as is reasonably practicable after the holding of the ballot.[188]

When compulsory balloting for industrial action was introduced, the rule was that action had the support of a ballot if the majority of those voting answered 'Yes' to the

[184] Code of Practice on Industrial Action Ballots and Notice to Employers, para 27.

[185] [2001] EWCA Civ 1206, [2001] IRLR 813, at para 32.

[186] For the membership assurer see Trade Union and Labour Relations (Consolidation) Act 1992, ss 24ZA–24ZD inserted by the Transparency of Lobbying, Non-party Campaigning and Trade Union Administration Act 2014.

[187] Trade Union and Labour Relations (Consolidation) Act 1992, s 230(4).

[188] Trade Union and Labour Relations (Consolidation) Act 1992, ss 231 and 231A. This applies whether or not the union proceeds with industrial action: *Metrobus Ltd v Unite the Union* [2010] ICR 173, [2009] IRLR 851, CA.

question applicable to the type of industrial action being taken, with spoilt votes being disregarded. However, two very significant changes were made by the Trade Union Act 2016, which are now on their way to becoming history:

- For all ballots, at least 50 per cent of those who were entitled to vote must in fact cast a vote.[189] This means that if more than half of the electorate cannot be bothered to vote, the union will not be able to organize industrial action without losing immunity from suit in tort. This requirement will be repealed once s 68 of the Employment Rights Act 2025 is brought into force, but the government's intention is that this will not happen until electronic balloting is permitted.[190]
- For ballots where the majority of those entitled to vote are at the relevant time 'normally engaged in the provision of important public services', it used to be necessary for 40 per cent of the electorate to vote 'Yes'.[191] Although this sometimes presented a significant hurdle for unions in fact in many cases it was avoided by ensuring that a significant number of workers who fell outside the definition of important public services were included (eg by balloting all hospital doctors and not just those working A&E). This requirement has been removed by s 69 of the Employment Rights Act 2025.

For the time being those counted as voting in the ballot includes those submitting spoilt papers, so spoilt papers count as 'No' votes in determining whether there is a majority in favour of industrial action and they also count in assessing whether the turnout threshold has been met.[192] However, this will be repealed at the same time as the 50 per cent turnout threshold is abolished.[193]

The notice of the result given to the voters and to the employer must set out the votes cast in favour and against and the number of spoiled papers. For the time being the notice must also state the number of members who were entitled to vote and whether the turnout threshold has been met, but both these requirements will be removed when the turnout threshold is abolished.[194]

10.3.2.8 **Period of effectiveness of ballot**

A ballot in favour of industrial action is valid to support the action for twelve months from the date of the ballot (the last voting day).[195] If a union wishes to continue with action after this time period it must ballot its members afresh.

[189] Trade Union and Labour Relations (Consolidation) Act 1992, s 226(2)(a)(iia).

[190] Electronic balloting may be permitted by regulations under the Employment Relations Act 2004, s 54.

[191] Trade Union and Labour Relations (Consolidation) Act 1992, s 226(2A)–(2F).

[192] Trade Union and Labour Relations (Consolidation) Act 1992, s 297A.

[193] Employment Rights Act 2025, s 68(4).

[194] Trade Union and Labour Relations (Consolidation) Act 1992, s 231 as amended by Employment Rights Act 2025 s 68(3).

[195] Trade Union and Labour Relations (Consolidation) Act 1992, s 234(1) as amended by Employment Rights Act 2025, s 72. The 'date of the ballot' is defined in s 246. There is a discretion in the court to extend the period of validity where the union has been prohibited from calling or organizing industrial action by a court order or an undertaking given to the court, and that order or undertaking has subsequently lapsed: s 234(2)–(6). Prior to the 2016 Act there was no defined end to the validity period of the ballot, but industrial action had to be *commenced* within four weeks of the date of the ballot. This was thought to have the disadvantage of encouraging unions to press ahead with industrial action rather than use a favourable ballot result to persuade the employer to make concessions. Hence the change to the new six-month validity period.

10.3.2.9 **The calling of industrial action**

Any strike call by the union in advance of the ballot will normally be fatal in that the action will be deemed not to have the support of a ballot.[196] In determining whether there has been a 'call' by the union, the statutory test of vicarious liability applies,[197] which means that an unauthorized and unballoted call by, for example, a shop steward will be regarded as a call *by the union*, and the resulting action will consequently be denied the protection of the statutory immunities. The only way in which the union can avoid liability in such a case is to repudiate the unauthorized call,[198] but by doing so it exposes those who continue to take part in the action to the risk of selective dismissal.[199]

To add to the complications, for the immunity to apply the industrial action must be called by a 'specified person'[200] (ie a person specified by the union on the voting paper), to prevent local officials 'jumping the gun' without authorization by calling on members to take industrial action without waiting for the union leadership to decide whether or not to implement the ballot decision. If action is called by someone *other* than a specified person, that action will not be regarded as having the support of a ballot, even where there was a clear vote in favour of the action and all the other statutory requirements were satisfied. There are, however, signs that this requirement will be interpreted flexibly, and that some limited degree of delegation may be acceptable; in *Tanks and Drums Ltd v TGWU*,[201] the Court of Appeal held that the section was satisfied where the specified person, the union's general secretary, authorized a district official to implement the industrial action if further negotiations with the employer the following day were not successful. Neill LJ stated that

> in the field of industrial relations it would be impracticable to leave matters in such a way that there was no possibility for the exercise of judgment on the ground. Some matters must be left for the judgment of those on the ground who have to decide how and when as a matter of common sense the call for action is to be put into operation.

However, Neill LJ also considered that a blanket delegation of authority to a local official would not be acceptable, and stressed the need for 'a close link in time between the call for the strike and the event, for example, an unsuccessful meeting which precipitates the final action'.

10.3.3 **Notice of industrial action to employers**

To benefit from the golden formula immunity a union must not only comply with all the balloting rules considered in 10.3.2, but also give the employer a detailed notice of industrial action. The earliest date that notice may be given is the day on which the employer

[196] Trade Union and Labour Relations (Consolidation) Act 1992, s 233(1)(b). The prohibition on calling for industrial action before the date of the ballot is not infringed by a union recommendation to its members to vote in favour of industrial action: *Newham London Borough Council v NALGO* [1993] ICR 189, [1993] IRLR 83, CA. However, it appears that a premature call for one kind of industrial action, eg a refusal to carry out some duties, will destroy the authority of the ballot for all kinds of action in that trade dispute: *Govia Thameslink Railway Ltd v ASLEF* [2016] EWHC 1320 (QB), [2016] IRLR 686, HC.

[197] Trade Union and Labour Relations (Consolidation) Act 1992, s 20. See 10.6.2.

[198] Trade Union and Labour Relations (Consolidation) Act 1992, s 21. See 10.6.2.

[199] Trade Union and Labour Relations (Consolidation) Act 1992, s 237. See 10.7.3.1.

[200] Trade Union and Labour Relations (Consolidation) Act 1992, s 233(1). The union can decide whom to specify, but the person (or description of persons) specified must come within the list of those for whom the union is deemed responsible under s 20.

[201] [1992] ICR 1, [1991] IRLR 372, CA.

is informed of the result of the ballot[202] and the notice must give at least 10 days before the action starts.[203] The information which must be given in the notice parallels what is required in the notice of the ballot under s 226A but goes slightly further. Details must be given of the categories and workplaces of the members who the union reasonably believes will be induced to take part in the action. The notice must also indicate the total number of members and the number of them at each workplace.[204] The notice must state whether the industrial action is intended to be continuous or discontinuous. If the action is to be continuous, the notice must state when it is to start; if intended to be discontinuous (ie if the union does not intend to take action on all the days on which it could do so), the notice must specify the particular dates on which it is to take place.

The result is that unions cannot use the threat of random discontinuous action to bring pressure to bear on employers, although there is still some potential for disruption in that, having given notice of the dates on which it intends the discontinuous action to take place, the union does not then have to call for that action to take place on all (or indeed any) of those dates. Furthermore, there is no obligation on the union to specify what kind of industrial action is intended.

There is nothing to prevent a union giving several notices under s 234A. For example, it might give notice of four one-day strikes over several weeks. If the dispute is still continuing it can later give notice of further days of strike action, so long as at least 14 days' notice is given and the necessary information about those who will be induced to take part in the action is given in the notice. Furthermore, where the industrial action has been suspended by joint agreement between the employer and the union, the action can be resumed after an agreed date ('the resumption date') without the need for the union to issue a fresh notice.[205]

10.3.4 **A rebalancing of the system?**

As mentioned in 10.3.1, in 2011 the Court of Appeal appears to have set out to rebalance the operation of the law in relation to the complex balloting requirements. (It is reasonable to take this rebalancing as applying also to the strike notice requirements, although they were not the subject of the court's judgment.) The decision of the Court of Appeal in *NURMT v Serco Ltd*[206] shows a *general* move against granting injunctive relief on the basis of highly technical breaches by a union. Elias LJ's judgment on behalf of the whole court starts with a general point that this legislation is to be construed and applied in a normal way, without any presumption that it will be applied strictly against a union wishing to claim its statutory protection (or indeed that the employer's interest must prevail), and in a way that will give it a 'likely and workable construction', giving due weight to freedom of association as enshrined in Article 11 of the European Convention on Human Rights.

The principal alleged defaults by the union in *NURMT v Serco Ltd* were that it had informed the employer that there were 21 affected members at one depot instead of 20, and 33 at another depot instead of 32 (at that date the statute required that the ballot

[202] Trade Union and Labour Relations (Consolidation) Act 1992, s 234A(4)(a).

[203] Trade Union and Labour Relations (Consolidation) Act 1992, s 234A(4)(b). Before the Employment Rights Act 2025 the period was 14 days.

[204] Trade Union and Labour Relations (Consolidation) Act 1992, s 234A(3B), (3C) as amended by the Employment Rights Act 2025

[205] Trade Union and Labour Relations (Consolidation) Act 1992, s 234A(7B). The period of suspension may be extended by joint agreement.

[206] [2011] ICR 848, [2011] IRLR 399, CA.

notice should include the numbers to be balloted at each workplace). Moreover, objection was taken to the form in which the union provided the employer with 'an explanation of how those figures were arrived at' (s 226A(2)(c)), which consisted of the statement:

> The lists and figures accompanying this notice were arrived at by retrieving information from the union's database and workplaces of members and the numbers in and at each, the database having been audited and updated for the purpose of the statutory notification and balloting requirements to ensure accuracy.

It was argued that not only was this too anodyne, but it was also inaccurate because there had not actually been an 'audit'. The judge found for the employer on all of these points and disallowed the union's attempt to use the 'small accidental failures' (s 232B), ruling that these mistakes were not accidental because they could have been avoided if steps had been taken to be more accurate. He also held against a more general defence that there was a common law de minimis principle permitting minor errors of all kinds to be forgiven.

The Court of Appeal disagreed fundamentally. It held as follows:

1. In relation to the small accidental failures defence in s 232B, the court accepted the union's argument that in insisting that the failure be both unintentional and unavoidable the judge had erected a test of perfection which could frustrate the whole purpose of the section. This was not a case where the union had known of the mistakes and continued; it had believed it was balloting the relevant members and no one else, and the mistakes were caused by human error. As Elias LJ put it, 'section 232B was designed to cater for precisely this kind of case'.
2. In relation to the requirement (s 226A(2D)) that the information given to the employer must be accurate, the whole of the relevant phrase must be considered, and that shows that the requirement is to provide information which is 'as accurate as is reasonably practicable *in the light of the information in the possession of the union*'. This materially diminishes the scope for arguing for a positive duty on the union to have gone out and found more such information; essentially, the union can draw on such information as it already has.
3. In relation to the de minimis point, the employer had argued that the enactment of s 232B had left no scope for a general defence of this nature but the court disagreed: there is a de minimis principle which means that injunctions should not be granted to prevent industrial action because of 'trifling errors which should not be allowed to form a basis for invalidating the ballot'.[207] This is very significant since it overcomes the problem that the statutory de minimis provision in s 232B only applies to a very limited range of errors. In a tantalizing comment, Elias LJ went on to indicate that he found 'very persuasive' the view of Smith LJ in *British Airways plc v Unite the Union*[208] that only 'substantial compliance' with the balloting rules was required of a union. However, he left this for argument on another day.
4. In relation to the adequacy of the union's explanation of the figures given in notice, the court took into consideration paragraph 16 of the Industrial Action Ballots Code of Practice to hold that 'the duty on the union is not a very onerous one' and so the statement could be relatively formulaic or anodyne. The fact that more

[207] The Court based this particularly on *British Railways Board v National Union of Railwaymen* [1989] ICR 678, [1989] IRLR 349, CA.

[208] [2010] ICR 1316, [2012] IRLR 809, CA.

information could have been given did not mean that the union had failed in the statutory obligation.

5. The court held that it was not misleading to use in the explanation of the information the words 'audit' and 'updating', which could be construed as covering the sort of basic checking that the union had done.

Thus, the claim for the injunction was comprehensively rejected. This decision diminishes the scope for arguments based on technical defaults by a union and it is possible that, to précis one commentator, by trial and error we have now reached a workable system.[209] Some specific questions remain. The first is just *how* incorrect a union's actions must be for them to fall foul of what are still complex and difficult procedural requirements. The second is to what extent the *Serco* approach will apply to the new voting threshold requirements, as discussed previously.[210] These question are less likely to arise in practice now that the detail that must be given in notices of ballot and of action have been significantly reduced by the Employment Rights Act 2025.

10.4 Potential criminal liability

As seen in the introduction to this chapter, criminal law does not play any significant role in the regulation of industrial action, outside the specialized law relating to picketing, and the application of the ordinary laws relating to violence and public order if a dispute gives rise to violence and disruption. Those matters are considered in 10.5.6 on picketing. However, there are two other contexts in which, in exceptional cases, there might be criminal liability.

10.4.1 Sit-ins—criminal trespass

The first arises where employees occupy their employer's premises, for example by way of a sit-in or work-in. In civil law they become trespassers when they refuse to leave, and the employer may take civil action to regain possession of its premises. However, English law has always been wary of imposing criminal sanctions for trespass, a position strengthened by the Criminal Law Act 1977, which provided that it could not be a criminal conspiracy for people to agree to commit an act which was merely tortious, such as trespass.[211] At the same time, Part II of that Act created several new trespass offences which could conceivably be committed by workers engaged in occupying the employer's premises, and in respect of which the police have powers of arrest and entry on to the property in question. Thus, it is an offence to use violence to secure entry when there is someone already on the premises,[212] or to enter as a trespasser with a 'weapon of offence'.[213] In most sit-ins or work-ins, the former will not arise, as possession of the premises is usually gained by failing to leave (or, at least, by entry by stealth);[214] the occupiers may, however, be at risk

[209] Walker 'Striking a Balance' [2012] NLJ 1171. [210] See 10.3.2.7.

[211] Criminal Law Act 1977, s 1(1), overruling the decision of the House of Lords in *Kamara v DPP* [1974] AC 104, [1973] 2 All ER 1242, HL.

[212] Criminal Law Act 1977, s 6, as amended by the Criminal Justice and Public Order Act 1994, s 72.

[213] Criminal Law Act 1977, s 8.

[214] Indeed, once inside the occupiers could themselves be protected by s 6, which will render criminal any attempt by the factory owner to use violence to enter to evict them! Note, however, the decision of the Scottish High Court of Justiciary that a work-in can constitute 'watching or besetting' (under the Trade Union and Labour Relations (Consolidation) Act 1992, see 10.5.6.1) even though the people concerned are inside the premises: *Galt (Procurator Fiscal) v Philp* [1984] IRLR 156; this decision is potentially more damaging to occupations than the Criminal Law Act 1977.

under the latter, as many articles (even working tools) can constitute 'weapons of offence' if the person carrying them has the intention of using them to inflict injury on others. It is also an offence to resist bailiffs who are seeking to regain possession of the premises under a court order.[215]

10.4.2 **Situations where industrial action might itself be a crime**

The second area of possible criminal liability is under certain remaining (and in some cases anomalous) statutory provisions creating offences which limit the freedom to take industrial action.

First, there is a general offence, dating from the Conspiracy and Protection of Property Act 1875 and now contained in the Trade Union and Labour Relations (Consolidation) Act 1992, s 240, which makes it an offence for a person

> wilfully and maliciously [to break] a contract of service or hiring, knowing or having reasonable cause to believe that the probable consequences of his so doing, either alone or in combination with others, will be to endanger human life or cause serious bodily injury, or to expose valuable property, whether real or personal, to destruction or serious injury.

This provision is potentially of significance in industrial disputes, particularly in the context of industrial action by workers in the essential services such as nurses, doctors, fire-fighters, and ambulance workers. The penalty is small, and there appears to be no record of any prosecution under it, but it is conceivable that the main significance of such a provision could lie in its use as the basis of an application for an injunction to restrain a threatened breach of it, rather than in the possibility of prosecution directly under it. In *Gouriet v UPOW*,[216] the claimant sought an injunction to prevent a threatened boycott of mail to South Africa, on the basis that the action would contravene the Post Office Act 1953. This was ultimately refused by the House of Lords, which reaffirmed the traditional limitation on this use of a civil law remedy to prevent anticipated breaches of criminal law—that an action may only be brought by the Attorney General or by an individual whose private rights were about to be infringed or who would suffer 'special damage'. As the claimant in *Gouriet* had failed to persuade the Attorney General to bring the action, and had brought it himself merely as a member of the general public, he did not have the necessary locus standi. An action for an injunction to restrain a threatened breach of the criminal law would, however, be open to someone who did have the necessary legal interest, and this could conceivably arise in the circumstances envisaged by s 240, for example where someone stands to risk personal injury or property damage as a result of a strike.

There are also certain more specific offences in certain jobs:

- Industrial action by postal workers may involve the commission of the offence of intentionally delaying a postal packet under the Postal Services Act 2000,[217] and telecommunications workers may commit an offence if they intentionally intercept a communication in the course of its transmission.[218]

[215] Criminal Law Act 1977, s 10. [216] [1978] AC 435, [1977] 3 All ER 70, HL.

[217] Postal Services Act 2000, s 83. The offence is not committed where a postal packet is delayed as a result of industrial action in contemplation or furtherance of a trade dispute (a dispensation which did not apply under the previous provisions in the Post Office Act 1953, ss 58, 68; see *Gouriet v Union of Post Office Workers* [1978] AC 435, [1977] 3 All ER 70, HL).

[218] Regulation of Investigatory Powers Act 2000, s 1.

- There are criminal provisions in the merchant shipping legislation which may affect the legality of a strike by merchant seamen.[219]
- There are statutory restrictions on union membership[220] and the organization of strike action in the police force,[221] and on inducing prison officers to withhold their services or to commit breaches of discipline.[222]

10.4.3 One kind of crime not criminal if done for a trade dispute

There is also one anomalous case of *decriminalization* of one kind of crime in an industrial action context. Normally agreements to commit acts which are themselves criminal constitute the crime of conspiracy, and so if persons involved in industrial action agree among themselves to commit offences, for example to assault or intimidate people or destroy property, they may be prosecuted for those offences and also for criminal conspiracy.[223] However, there is an exception to this where the offence in question is a summary offence not punishable by imprisonment, as s 242 of the Trade Union and Labour Relations (Consolidation) Act 1992 provides[224] that any such offence which is committed in contemplation or furtherance of a trade dispute shall be disregarded for the purposes of the law of criminal conspiracy.

10.5 Picketing

10.5.1 What is picketing?

What is meant by 'picketing' as a matter of ordinary usage of language? Essentially it is the attendance of protesters at or near the entrance to premises for the purpose of communicating with those entering or leaving the premises. In an industrial context the premises are usually those of an employer in dispute with workers and the communication is normally aimed at persuading other workers and customers and suppliers not to enter the premises or preventing them physically from doing so. It is therefore a species of public demonstration.

10.5.2 Introduction

The act of picketing the premises of another person may not be unlawful in itself,[225] but in reality it can very easily become so, either as a tort, such as public or private nuisance or trespass to the highway, or under one of several specific or general criminal offences. For

[219] Merchant Shipping Act 1995, s 59(1).

[220] Police Act 1996, s 64. A person who belonged to a union before becoming a member of a police force may continue to be a union member: s 64(2).

[221] Police Act 1996, s 91.

[222] Criminal Justice and Public Order Act 1994, s 127; the section operates by imposing a statutory duty owed to the Home Secretary, not by imposing criminal liability. This duty is breached even if the prison officers' action is to decline to carry out voluntary non-contractual tasks: *Ministry of Justice v The Prison Officers' Association* [2017] EWHC 1839 (QB), [2018] ICR 181, [2017] IRLR 1121.

[223] As in *R v Jones* [1974] ICR 310, 59 Cr App Rep 120, CA (the Shrewsbury pickets' case).

[224] Re-enacting Criminal Law Act 1977, s 1(3).

[225] *Hubbard v Pitt* [1975] 3 All ER 1, [1975] ICR 308, CA, per Lord Denning MR (dissenting); the majority decided the case on procedural points relating to interlocutory injunctions, not primarily upon the substantive law on picketing. See Wallington 'Injunctions and the Right to Demonstrate' (1976) 35 CLJ 86.

that reason there is a statutory immunity for peaceful picketing during a trade dispute, now contained in the Trade Union and Labour Relations (Consolidation) Act 1992, s 220.

Picketing will be considered in the following order:

- first, an overview of the law in a 'nutshell';
- second, the relevance of the European Convention on Human Rights;
- third, the ways in which a picket may prima facie fall foul of the law;
- fourth, the extent to which a picket in connection with industrial action is protected.

10.5.3 **The law in a nutshell**

In relation to picketing, criminal law is as important as tort law, and the statutory immunity is relevant to both. The law is complex and heavily influenced by history, so it is best to start with a simplified summary:

1. Industrial action and picketing have some legal issues in common but are best considered separately.
2. Nearly all picketing activities are tortious and some of them are criminal.
3. This means these picketing activities would be unlawful were it not for the immunity granted by s 220 of the Trade Union and Labour Relations (Consolidation) Act 1992. The immunity only applies if the picketing is in contemplation of furtherance of a trade dispute.
4. That immunity only covers a very narrow range of activities: the immunity renders it lawful to attend for the purposes only of peacefully obtaining or communicating information or peacefully persuading any person to abstain from working.
5. Workers can only picket their own workplaces: the immunity only applies to attendance by persons at or near their workplace and by union officials representing such workers.
6. Activities falling outside point (4) or point (5) are not immune and so may lead to injunctions or to arrest and prosecution.
7. Picketing is a sub-species of public protest and the European Convention on Human Rights is relevant. Aspects of the statutory provisions picketing in industrial disputes and the associated Code of Practice may not comply with the rights to freedom of speech and of assembly set out in the Convention. This may influence the interpretation of the statute and will also affect the willingness of courts to grant injunctions and the nature of the restrictions which courts are willing to impose in such injunctions.

10.5.4 **The relevance of the European Convention on Human Rights**

Since picketing is a form of public demonstration, the imposition of restrictions on picketing has important civil liberties implications, particularly for freedom of assembly and freedom of speech. The right to freedom of expression in Article 10 of the European Convention on Human Rights and the right to freedom of peaceful assembly in Article 11 could conceivably be used to challenge some of the existing legal restrictions on picketing.[226]

[226] See O'Dempsey et al. *Employment Law and the Human Rights Act 1998* (2001) 217–23.

An example is *Middlebrook Mushrooms Ltd v TGWU*,[227] where the claimants, a firm of mushroom growers, sought an injunction restraining the union from distributing leaflets outside supermarkets asking customers not to buy their mushrooms, in support of members dismissed by the claimants for taking industrial action. The Court of Appeal emphasized the importance of keeping the civil law constraints on picketing within proper limits, Neill LJ stating that Article 10 should be taken into consideration 'in all cases which involve a proposed restriction on the right of free speech'.[228] Similarly, in *DPP v Jones*,[229] Lord Irvine LC expressed the view, obiter, that if English law did not give a right of peaceful assembly on the highway, Article 11 of the European Convention might in future require the common law to develop such a right.

As in other areas of employment law potentially affected by human rights law, the key issue here will be the extent to which the guarantee of freedom of peaceful assembly in Article 11(1) is found to be qualified by Article 11(2), which permits restrictions on that freedom 'where necessary in a democratic society . . . for the prevention of disorder or crime . . . or for the protection of rights and freedoms of others'.[230]

In the first reported case to consider the lawfulness of an industrial picket in the light of the Convention, *Gate Gourmet London Ltd v TGWU*,[231] the High Court took account of the Convention, saying that its incorporation into UK law arguably had created a 'right to picket' to the extent that the right to peaceful assembly is guaranteed by Article 11 of the Convention and Article 10 contains the right to freedom of expression. Accordingly, when considering granting an injunction which would infringe such rights, the court had an obligation to give due weight to the importance of those rights. The judge did that by imposing the minimum restrictions on freedom of expression and assembly that were necessary for the prevention of crime.

Increasingly unions are seeking to involve people other than the workers affected in industrial disputes, and to organize protests at locations other than the workplace, as part of wider campaigns which are often orchestrated or conducted through social media. Neither kind of protest can qualify as a potentially lawful picket under Trade Union and Labour Relations (Consolidation) Act 1992 s 220 because, as will be seen in 10.5.7.1, the s 220 immunity applies only to workers at or near their own workplace. This means that all the potential crimes and torts covered in the next section may apply and may lead to injunctions being granted. However, this is subject to a balance being struck with the rights of assembly and freedom of expression.

For example, in *Thames Cleaning and Support Services Ltd v United Voice of the World*[232] a union threatened to organize protests outside the workplaces of its members in support of industrial action which the members were taking. It was anticipated that many protesters would not be workers involved in the industrial action. Video evidence of similar actions elsewhere had shown very noisy and disorderly protests involving upwards of 40 people, substantial obstructions to the public, and a police officer being jostled. One clip showed someone explaining to a crowd that a woman had come to 'face her oppressors

[227] [1993] ICR 612, CA.

[228] [1993] ICR 612 at 620.

[229] [1999] 2 All ER 257, HL. The case demonstrates the difficulties in store for the courts in interpreting Art 11, for Lord Slynn and Lord Hope saw no necessary conflict between the common law and the Convention on this point.

[230] There are similar restrictions in Art 10(2). In *Steel v United Kingdom* (1998) 28 EHRR 603, the ECtHR ruled that the detention for breach of the peace of protestors who were merely holding banners and distributing leaflets infringed Art 10, observing that while states have a margin of appreciation in deciding what restrictions are necessary, the overriding consideration was that the measures used should be proportionate to the end to be achieved. See Fenwick (1999) 62 MLR 491.

[231] *Gate Gourmet London Ltd v TGWU* [2005] IRLR 881.

[232] [2016] IRLR 695, HC.

and tell them to fuck off'. The judge noted that speech of that kind was not unlawful and that freedom of speech includes the right to embarrass or offend. However, he said, such activities can tip into public disorder, harassment, intimidation, and other interferences with the rights of others which it is necessary and proportionate to prevent, as one of the legitimate aims identified in Articles 10(2) and 11(2). He expressed the view that the more protests involve physical confrontation at close quarters between the protesters and those seeking to go about their lawful daily activities, the more likely they are to go beyond the lawful limits of protest. The judge granted an injunction to prevent protests taking place within 10 metres of any entrance, with a specific exception permitting picketing being conducted by union members in accordance with s 220.

In relation to criminal liability for picketing, the UK courts have held that if an offence is subject to a 'lawful excuse' or 'reasonable excuse' defence, then the court trying the case must consider the balance between the rights of the defendant under Articles 10 and 11 and the wrongs they have done in order to determine if the excuse is made out.[233] On the other hand if the provision contains no such defence, then the courts must proceed on the basis that this balancing has already been done by Parliament in defining the offence.[234]

10.5.5 **Potential civil liability**

Pickets may commit one or more of the economic torts, so picketing may therefore, subject to s 220, be restrainable at the suit of the employer or some other person involved. For example, a picket who persuades a delivery driver to turn around and not cross a picket line probably induces that driver to break his contract of employment, and may also indirectly induce a breach of (or at least interfere with) the commercial supply contracts of the driver's employer.[235] The presence of pickets may also give rise to the tort of trespass to the highway[236] or nuisance,[237] and in *Thomas v NUM (South Wales Area)*,[238] Scott J granted an injunction against mass picketing on the grounds of a new common law tort of 'harassment' (a variant of private nuisance) at the suit of working miners who were being

[233] *DPP v Ziegler* [2021] UKSC 23, [2021] 4 All ER 985, [2021] 3 WLR 179, where the Supreme Court set out a long list of factual matters to be taken into account such as the duration of the protest, the location of the protesters, the importance of the issues raised etc.

[234] *DPP v Cuciurean* [2022] EWHC 736 (Admin) [2022] QB 888, [2022] 4 All ER 1043.

[235] In *Union Traffic Ltd v TGWU* [1989] ICR 98, [1989] IRLR 127, the Court of Appeal held that the mere presence of pickets may constitute the tort of inducing breach of contract if it is clear that the presence of the pickets is intended to induce a breach of contract and it achieves its objective.

[236] See *DPP v Jones* [1999] 2 All ER 257, a landmark case on the law on trespassory assemblies arising from a protest at Stonehenge, where the House of Lords held that there is a public right of peaceful assembly on the highway for any reasonable purpose, provided the activity does not obstruct the highway by unreasonably impeding the rights of others to pass and repass, and does not amount to a public or private nuisance.

[237] *Hubbard v Pitt* [1975] 3 All ER 1, [1975] ICR 308, CA. In *Sheffield Environmental Services and others v Personson Unknown* [2025] EWHC 2141 (KB) (13 August 2025, unreported) where between 9 and 20 protesters supported industrial action by walking slowly in a circle on the highway so as to block vehicular access to the claimant's site, this was held to amount to a private nuisance and an injunction was granted to prohibit it.

[238] [1985] 2 All ER 1, [1985] IRLR 136. See Benedictus 'The Use of the Law of Tort in the Miners' Dispute' (1985) 14 ILJ 176. In *News Group Newspapers Ltd v SOGAT '82 (No 2)* [1987] ICR 181, [1986] IRLR 337 Stuart-Smith J expressed obiter reservations about the decision in *Thomas*. In *Khorasandjian v Bush* [1993] QB 727, [1993] 3 All ER 669 (a non-industrial case), the Court of Appeal accepted the existence of a common law tort of harassment as a form of private nuisance available to a person without an interest in land, but that case was overruled on that point in *Hunter v Canary Wharf Ltd* [1997] AC 655, HL.

prevented from going to work, even though they were not the owners of the land being picketed. That case also illustrates that a legal claim may be brought by people other than the employer in dispute. Picketing could also conceivably involve the commission of the statutory tort of harassment under the Protection from Harassment Act 1997, although to date the civil remedy under that Act has not been used in the context of picketing.[239] The Protection from Harassment Act 1997 makes it both a tort and a criminal offence for a person to pursue a 'course of conduct'[240] which amounts to harassment of another and which they know or ought to know amounts to harassment of another.[241] Although primarily aimed at 'stalkers', harassment as defined by the Act is clearly wide enough to apply to pickets; its significance in practice is likely to turn on the extent to which pickets are able to rely on the statutory defence in the Act 'that in the particular circumstances the pursuit of the course of conduct was reasonable'.[242]

An injunction to prevent unlawful picketing may have the effect of stopping the picketing altogether, or may instead impose conditions on picketing activity (eg on the numbers of pickets and their location).

10.5.6 **Potential criminal liability**

10.5.6.1 **Miscellaneous crimes**

If picketing is violent, there will of course be criminal liability for (eg) assault, criminal damage, and public order offences (see 10.5.8) in the ordinary way, as seen most dramatically in the miners' strike of 1984–85.[243] Even if it is peaceful, however, picketing may constitute the crime of obstruction of the highway[244] or public nuisance[245] and any refusal to obey lawful police orders may constitute the offence of wilfully obstructing a police officer in the execution of their duty, contrary to the Police Act 1996, s 89. Picketing may also constitute the crime of harassment under the Protection from Harassment Act 1997.[246]

[239] In *Majrowski v Guy's & St Thomas' NHS Trust* [2006] UKHL 34, [2006] IRLR 695 it was held that the Act may apply across employment law (see 3.3.3.2).

[240] This must involve conduct on at least two occasions: Protection from Harassment Act 1997, s 7(3); 'conduct' in this context includes speech: s 7(4).

[241] Protection from Harassment Act 1997, ss 1(1), 2(1). 'Harassment' is not defined, save that references to harassing a person include alarming the person or causing the person distress: s 7(2). A person convicted of an offence under these provisions may be subjected to a restraining order for the purpose of protecting the victim (or any other person named in the order) from further harassment: s 5.

[242] Protection from Harassment Act 1997, s 1(3)(c).

[243] During the course of the strike, 10,372 criminal charges were brought, including 468 for assaults of sorts, 360 for assaulting a police officer, 137 for riot, 509 for unlawful assembly, 21 for affray, 4,107 for conduct conducive to breach of the peace (Public Order Act 1936, s 5), 1,019 for criminal damage, 352 for theft, 1,682 for obstructing a police officer, 640 for obstruction of the highway, and 275 for intimidation. Subsequently, however, many of the major charges (especially those including riot) were not proceeded with.

[244] Highways Act 1980, s 137; see eg *Broome v DPP* [1974] 1 All ER 314, [1974] ICR 84, HL. It seems that picketing will only be an offence under the Highways Act where it involves an unreasonable use of the highway: see *Hubbard v Pitt* [1975] 3 All ER 1, [1975] ICR 308.

[245] When this was a common law offence it was held that the offence was not committed by a public protest assembly on a highway unless it causes unreasonable obstruction of the highway: *Hubbard v Pitt* [1975] 3 All ER 1, [1975] ICR 308, CA. This offence has been replaced by a statutory codification in the Police, Crime, Sentencing and Courts Act 2022, s 78 which requires serious harm (as defined), or a risk of it, to the public and contains a defence of reasonable excuse.

[246] See Mullender (1998) 61 MLR 236. For more on what constitutes harassment under the Act see 10.5.5.

In addition to the above, s 241 of the Trade Union and Labour Relations (Consolidation) Act 1992[247] makes it an offence for a person 'with a view to compelling[248] another person to abstain from doing or to do any act which that person has a legal right to do or abstain from doing, wrongfully and without legal authority' to:

1. use violence to or intimidate[249] that person or his wife or children, or injure his property;
2. persistently follow that person about from place to place;[250]
3. hide any tools, clothes, or other property owned or used by that person, or deprive him of or hinder him in the use thereof;[251]
4. watch or beset[252] the house or other place where that person resides, works, carries on business, or happens to be, or the approach to such house or place;
5. follow that person with two or more other persons in a disorderly manner in or through any street or road.

The prosecution must establish that the person whom the accused sought to influence had a legal right to do, or not to do, the act. For example, where a protester was seeking to persuade a workman not to cut down a tree, and claimed that cutting it down would be a criminal offence, the protester was acquitted because the prosecutor failed to prove the cutting down the tree would not be an offence.[253] The inclusion of the words 'wrongful and without legal authority' means that the acts complained of under heads (1)–(5) must already be unlawful (ie either tortious[254] or criminal)—the aim of the section is to make them amenable to summary trial in addition to any other unlawfulness:

> [Section 242] legalises nothing, and it renders nothing wrongful that was not so before. Its object is solely to visit certain selected classes of acts which were previously wrongful, ie were at least civil torts, with penal consequences capable of being summarily inflicted.[255]

[247] Re-enacting the Conspiracy and Protection of Property Act 1875, s 7. The offence is not necessarily restricted to industrial cases: see eg *DPP v Todd* [1996] Crim LR 344 (anti-road protesters).

[248] The defendant must have acted with a view to *compelling* someone to do something they had a right not to do, or vice versa; an intention to persuade is not enough: *DPP v Fidler* [1992] 1 WLR 91 (another non-industrial case involving a picket outside an abortion clinic).

[249] Actual violence or threats of immediate personal injury are not necessary, but there must be some definite element of causing someone to feel afraid: *Judge v Bennett* (1887) 36 WR 103; *Gibson v Lawson* [1891] 2 QB 545; *Curran v Treleaven* [1891] 2 QB 545; *R v Jones* [1974] ICR 310, 59 Cr App Rep 120, CA.

[250] *Smith v Thomasson* (1891) 16 Cox CC 740; *R v Wall* (1907) 21 Cox CC 401. For a rare example of a prosecution under this limb in Scotland see *Elsey v Smith (Procurator Fiscal)* [1983] IRLR 292.

[251] *Fowler v Kibble* [1922] 1 Ch 487, CA.

[252] This limb is particularly relevant to picketing (see *R v Bonsall* [1985] Crim LR 150), and it is significant that the statutory immunity now contained in s 220 of the 1992 Act was originally a proviso to s 7 of the 1875 Act, which deemed attendance for the purpose of obtaining or communicating information not to be watching or besetting. According to the Scottish High Court of Justiciary in *Galt (Procurator Fiscal) v Philp* [1984] IRLR 156, a person can be guilty of watching and besetting from inside the property, ie by occupying it, but this has been doubted.

[253] *Roblyn v DPP* [2021] EWHC 3055 (Admin), [2022] EnvLR 16.

[254] The converse of this is that the fact that the conduct in question constitutes an offence under this section does not automatically mean that it is an actionable tort: *Thomas v NUM (South Wales Area)* [1985] 2 All ER 1, [1985] IRLR 136. cf *Galt (Procurator Fiscal) v Philp* [1984] IRLR 156, where it was held that tortious acts protected by the statutory immunities remain 'wrongful' for the purposes of these provisions. If correct, the decision could have profound implications for the legality of picketing.

[255] *Ward Lock & Co Ltd v Operative Printers' Assistants' Society* (1906) 22 TLR 327, CA, at 329 per Fletcher Moulton LJ; *Fowler v Kibble* [1922] 1 Ch 487, CA; cf *J Lyons & Sons v Wilkins* [1899] 1 Ch 255, where the Court of Appeal had previously held that the section created new offences complete in themselves. The approach in Ward Lock was preferred by Scott J in *Thomas v NUM (South Wales Area)* [1985] 2 All ER 1, [1985] IRLR 136.

10.5.6.2 **The importance of an anticipated breach of the peace**

The discussion so far has centred on substantive offences which might be committed by pickets. However, one concept which, in practice, has tended to be dominant in the physical control of picketing by the police is that of breach of the peace[256] (either actual or reasonably apprehended). It is a police officer's duty to prevent such a breach, if necessary by positive action to limit the numbers and placings of pickets. If a picket disregards an instruction from a police officer, and that officer can show grounds for reasonably anticipating[257] a breach of the peace at the time, then that picket is guilty of wilfully obstructing the police officer in the execution of their duty, contrary to s 89 of the Police Act 1996. Thus, breach of the peace acts as an umbrella head of liability which may justify the police in limiting numbers, as in *Piddington v Bates*,[258] or holding back from the factory gates some, or even all, of the pickets[259] even if that means that there is little practical likelihood of the pickets being able to communicate with a person seeking to enter the premises (the very purpose of picketing), provided that the drastic nature of any police action is justified by the magnitude of the risk of a breach of the peace.

These powers have long been used to control the activities of pickets at the premises being picketed. However, the miners' strike of 1984–85 saw a significant development when the police, faced with major disorders outside pits, began to close off areas altogether to would-be pickets, preventing them from reaching the premises in question at all, if necessary by the use of roadblocks. Any pickets proceeding past such a barrier risked being arrested for obstruction of the police.[260] The legality of such drastic preventive tactics was questioned in *Moss v McLachlan*[261] in the case of four such would-be pickets charged with obstruction for trying to pass a police cordon. They were convicted by magistrates and their appeal was dismissed by the Divisional Court, which held that, on the facts, the police had reasonably anticipated a breach of the peace and so their preventive action was justified. One important holding was that in forming their reasonable anticipation the police were entitled to take into account their common knowledge of the course of the dispute and the likelihood of further major violence. The problem with the case as a precedent is that in fact the police cordon was between one and a half and four miles from four working pits within one area served by that particular road. Thus, the physical nexus between the cordon and the premises was relatively close. It is perhaps unfortunate that the legality of certain more controversial actions taken by the police (such as the stopping of Kent miners on their way to the northern coalfields at the Dartford tunnel) was not properly tested in the courts. Were similar facts to arise today, the courts would have to give due weight to the exercise by the pickets of their Convention rights to freedom of

[256] See *R v Howell (Errol)* [1982] QB 416, [1981] 3 All ER 383, CA, per Watkins LJ: 'There is a breach of the peace whenever harm is actually done or is likely to be done to a person or in his presence to his property or a person is in fear of being so harmed through an assault, an affray, a riot, an unlawful assembly or other disturbance.' See also *Percy v DPP* [1995] 1 WLR 1382; *Nicol and Selvanayagam v DPP* (1995) 160 JP 155. The common law offence of breach of the peace was specifically retained by the Public Order Act 1986, s 40(4).

[257] See *Foulkes v Chief Constable of the Merseyside Police* [1998] 3 All ER 705, CA, per Beldam LJ: 'There must . . . be a sufficiently real and present threat to the peace to justify the extreme step of depriving of his liberty a citizen who is not at the time acting unlawfully.'

[258] [1960] 3 All ER 660, [1961] 1 WLR 162.

[259] *Kavanagh v Hiscock* [1974] 2 All ER 177, [1974] ICR 282.

[260] Arrested pickets were routinely subjected to stringent bail conditions aimed at preventing them from returning; see eg *R v Mansfield Justices, ex p Sharkey* [1985] 1 All ER 193, [1984] IRLR 496, where the Divisional Court upheld the validity of what was then a common bail condition 'not to visit any premises or place for the purpose of picketing or demonstrating in connection with the current trade dispute between the NUM and the NCB other than peacefully to picket or demonstrate at his usual place of employment'.

[261] [1985] IRLR 76. Police powers to use roadblocks are now codified: Police and Criminal Evidence Act 1984, s 4.

expression and of peaceful assembly in deciding whether a police officer had reasonable grounds for apprehending a breach of the peace.[262]

10.5.6.3 **Public order offences**

Picketing which is not 'peaceful' may bring liability not only under specific criminal offences applying to industrial disputes, but also under the general laws relating to public order.[263] The measures relevant to picketing lie principally in the following areas: (a) offences against public order; (b) controls over public processions and assemblies.

The Public Order Act replaces older offences with six graduated offences, all carrying powers of arrest. The offences are as follows:[264]

Disorderly behaviour

Using threatening, abusive, or insulting words or behaviour, or disorderly behaviour (or displaying anything to like effect) within the hearing or sight of a person likely to be caused harassment, alarm, or distress thereby, with the intention or the awareness that the words or behaviour may be threatening, abusive, insulting, or disorderly.[265] This offence (perhaps best summed up colloquially as 'generally loutish behaviour') was particularly strongly criticized upon its introduction; it covers a multitude of sins, but is not of great importance in picketing cases since any such behaviour in that context is likely to lead to a breach of the peace (actual or reasonably apprehended), to which the present section probably adds little.[266] The offence is triable summarily only, with a maximum penalty of a level 3 fine.

The words 'threatening', 'abusive' and 'disorderly' must be read in the context of Article 10 of the European Convention on Human Rights, and in the light of Parliament's decision to omit the word 'insulting'. The Article 10 context includes the principle that behaviour which is an affront to other people, or is disrespectful or contemptuous of them, is not prohibited, nor is behaviour which is merely 'distressing', 'offensive', 'distasteful', 'insulting', or 'intemperate'.[267] As Sedley LJ said in *Redmond-Bate v DPP*:[268] 'Free speech includes not only the inoffensive but the irritating, the contentious, the eccentric, the heretical, the unwelcome and the provocative provided it does not tend to provoke violence. Freedom only to speak inoffensively is not worth having.'

Intentional harassment

This offence is based on the offence of disorderly behaviour (discussed above), but with the additional requirements that the person must intend to cause, and the victim must actually be caused, harassment, alarm, or distress.[269] It carries a much stiffer

[262] See Fenwick 'The Right to Protest, the Human Rights Act and the Margin of Appreciation' (1999) 62 MLR 491.

[263] See Smith *Offences against Public Order* (1987); Wallington [1987] Crim LR 180; Carty 'The Public Order Act 1986: Police Powers and the Picket Line' (1987) 16 ILJ 146.

[264] The following are condensed versions of the offences; for the full wording see the text of the Act.

[265] Public Order Act 1986, s 5. The test of intention or awareness here is subjective: see *DPP v Clarke* (1991) 94 Cr App Rep 359.

[266] Section 5 is principally aimed at conduct which is a social nuisance but which falls short of an actual breach of the peace because there is no actual or threatened harm to a person or their property; in that light, note the inclusion of mere 'disorderly behaviour'.

[267] *Hicks v DPP* [2023] EWHC 1089 (Admin), [2023] 2 CrAppR 12, Div Ct.

[268] [2000] HRLR 249.

[269] Public Order Act 1986, s 4A. Compare the offence of harassment under the Protection from Harassment Act 1997, where it is enough to show that the accused ought to have known that their course of conduct amounted to harassment: see 10.5.6.1.

penalty than the non-intentional version, being punishable on summary conviction by up to six months' imprisonment and/or a level 5 fine. Although apparently aimed at serious, persistent racial harassment, it is clearly of potential significance to picketing.

Violent behaviour

Using threatening, abusive, or insulting words or behaviour (or distributing or displaying anything to like effect) to another person with intent to cause that person to fear immediate unlawful violence (to himself, herself, or another) or to provoke that person or another to use immediate unlawful violence.[270] This offence is triable summarily only and carries a maximum penalty of six months' imprisonment and/or a level 5 fine.

Affray

Using or threatening unlawful violence towards another, such as would cause a person of reasonable firmness present at the scene to fear for their personal safety.[271] The maximum penalty here is three years' imprisonment and/or a fine on indictment, or six months' imprisonment and/or the maximum scale fine on summary conviction.

Violent disorder

Three or more persons present together using or threatening unlawful violence, their conduct being such as would cause a person of reasonable firmness present at the scene to fear for their personal safety.[272] Anyone using or threatening unlawful violence is liable on indictment to five years' imprisonment and/or a fine, or on summary conviction to six months' imprisonment and/or the maximum scale fine. This offence replaced the old common law offence of unlawful assembly, and is envisaged as being the major offence in practice in the case of serious disorder.

Riot

Twelve or more persons present together using or threatening unlawful violence for a common purpose, their conduct being such as would cause a person of reasonable firmness present at the scene to fear for their personal safety.[273] Anyone using unlawful violence for the common purpose is liable on indictment to a maximum of ten years' imprisonment, a fine, or both.

Controls on public processions and assemblies

Sections 11–13 of the Public Order Act 1986 require the giving of advance notice to the police of public processions, and empower the police to impose conditions on them or to prohibit them altogether in order to prevent disorderly or intimidatory conduct. These powers are considered in full elsewhere[274] and are not of immediate application to picketing (except in the case of, for example, marches in support of pickets). Of more obvious relevance to picketing is the power to regulate public assemblies in s 14.[275] This permits a

[270] Public Order Act 1986, s 4. Violence includes violence to property; s 8.

[271] Public Order Act 1986, s 3.

[272] Public Order Act 1986, s 2.

[273] Public Order Act 1986, s 1.

[274] See n 263.

[275] There is also a power to ban trespassory assemblies, introduced by the 1994 Act, which could conceivably be used where picketing (eg persistent mass picketing) results in 'serious disruption to the life of the community': Public Order Act 1986, s 14A; see *DPP v Jones* [1999] 2 All ER 257, HL.

senior police officer to impose conditions on a 'public assembly',[276] either in advance or at the scene, where the officer reasonably believes that:

> (a) [the assembly] may result in serious public disorder, serious damage to property or serious disruption to the life of the community, or
>
> (b) the purpose of the persons organising it is the intimidation of others with a view to compelling them not to do an act they have a right to do, or to do an act they have a right not to do.

The potential application of this provision to picketing is obvious. If the senior police officer has such a reasonable belief, they may:

> give directions imposing on the persons organising or taking part in the assembly such conditions as to the place at which the assembly may be (or continue to be) held, its maximum duration, or the maximum number of persons who may constitute it, as appear to him necessary to avoid disorder, damage, disruption or intimidation.

As we have seen, the concept of breach of the peace (which remains unaffected by the 1986 Act) already gives a police officer on the spot some of these directional powers, but s 14 puts them into a wider, clearer, and more comprehensive statutory form[277] (backed by criminal sanctions on those organizing or taking part in an assembly in breach of conditions), and of course allows conditions to be attached in advance. Particularly significant are possible conditions as to place, time (perhaps times of shift changes for working employees?), and, of course, numbers, where a provision in the Code of Practice on picketing suggesting a limit of six pickets per entrance (considered presently) assumes great significance.

10.5.7 **The picketing immunity**

10.5.7.1 **Introduction**

In view of the many and varied ways in which picketing can potentially fall foul of the law, the scope of the statutory immunity for picketing becomes of crucial significance, as it in effect defines the extent of the right to picket. Section 220 of the Trade Union and Labour Relations (Consolidation) Act 1992 provides that:

> It is lawful for a person in contemplation or furtherance of a trade dispute to attend—
>
> (a) at or near his own place of work, or
>
> (b) if he is an official of a trade union, at or near the place of work of a member of the union whom he is accompanying and whom he represents,[278]

[276] This is defined as 'an assembly of 20 or more persons in a public place which is wholly or partly open to the air' (s 16), which clearly covers a picket line with that number of people (except in the unlikely event of it being entirely on private property). The requirement of advance notice and the power to ban (which apply to processions) do not apply to assemblies, although note the power to ban *trespassory* assemblies: see n 275.

[277] 'The crucial difference is that reasons other than the need to preserve the peace may be relied upon, in particular the reasonable belief of the senior officer present that the picket organizers' purpose is to intimidate others' (Wallington [1987] Crim LR 180, at 190).

[278] An official who is elected or appointed to represent some members of the union is to be regarded as representing only those members: s 220(4). This is to prevent the drafting in of large numbers of union officials, shop stewards, etc, from different parts of the country to do the picketing. A national officer, however, will be regarded as representing all members.

for the purpose only of peacefully obtaining or communicating information, or peacefully persuading any person to work or abstain from working.[279]

If an employee normally works at more than one place, or at a location which is such that attendance there for picketing is impracticable, then their place of work is deemed for these purposes to be any premises of the employer from which that employee's work is administered.[280]

10.5.7.2 **It is only attendance for communication and persuasion that is rendered lawful**

It is important to appreciate that s 220 does not confer a general 'right' to picket as such; it gives a limited right to *attend* for the stated purposes of peacefully obtaining or communicating information or peacefully persuading a person to work or abstain from working (ie 'peaceful picketing'), but it does not legitimize the *activities* of pickets. The s 220 immunity has therefore been described as 'narrow but real'[281] in that by protecting attendance for the purposes of peaceful picketing, it ensures that pickets will not incur either tortious liability (eg for nuisance) or criminal liability[282] (eg for obstruction of the highway or watching and besetting) from the mere fact of their *attendance*. Any liability which arises from the *activities* of pickets is protected, if at all, under the general trade dispute immunities contained in s 219 of the 1992 Act.

However, even mere attendance is affected by s 219 because if that attendance falls outside the s 220 immunity then it loses any protection which it might otherwise have enjoyed under s 219. On the other hand, picketing which is within s 220 retains the s 219 immunities, even if it constitutes secondary action which would normally not be immune because of the exclusion of secondary action from immunity under s 224. The interrelationship of the immunities is discussed further in 10.5.7.5.

As seen, the s 220 immunity applies to attendance for the purposes of peaceful picketing. It follows that if some other purpose can be inferred from the actions of the pickets (eg intimidation of those seeking to enter the workplace, or blockading the entrance), the immunity does not apply. Thus, in *Tynan v Balmer*,[283] where pickets walked in a circle around the factory gates in such a way as to seal off the entrance from traffic, the court was able to infer a purpose other than one of those in the section. Similarly, in *Broome v DPP*[284] the House of Lords held that the defendant's purpose in standing in front of a lorry to prevent its passage (having failed to persuade the driver not to enter the picketed premises) was to obstruct rather than to persuade or communicate; the justices had acquitted the defendant on a charge of obstruction because they thought that he had only spent a reasonable time in trying to exercise his 'statutory right' of peaceful persuasion, a right which they considered would be meaningless if he was not allowed actually to stop the vehicle. The House of Lords held that this was entirely misconceived—the section gives

[279] The 'persuasion' limb was introduced by the Trade Disputes Act 1906, s 2; it had not been included in the immunity given by the Conspiracy and Protection of Property Act 1875: *J Lyons & Sons v Wilkins* [1899] 1 Ch 255, CA.

[280] Trade Union and Labour Relations (Consolidation) Act 1992, s 220(2).

[281] *Broome v DPP* [1974] 1 All ER 314, [1974] ICR 84, HL at 325 and 96. respectively, per Lord Salmon.

[282] The Code of Practice of Picketing, para 46, states that there is no immunity from the criminal law, but there are dicta in *Broome v DPP* to the contrary.

[283] [1967] 1 QB 91, [1966] 2 All ER 133. The case is a good example of the offence of obstruction of the highway: see 10.5.6.1.

[284] See n 281.

no 'right' to picket, and certainly does not allow a picket to compel someone to stop and listen if that person does not wish to do so (a point reaffirmed shortly afterwards by the Divisional Court in *Kavanagh v Hiscock*).[285] Lord Salmon put it thus:

> [The] words make it plain that it is nothing but the attendance of the pickets at the places specified which is protected; and then only if their attendance is for one of the specified purposes. The section gives no protection in relation to anything the pickets may say or do whilst they are attending if what they say or do is itself unlawful. But for the section, the mere attendance of pickets might constitute an offence under [s 241(1)(b) and (d) of the 1992 Act or under the Highways Act 1980] or constitute a tort, for example, nuisance. The section, therefore, gives a narrow but nevertheless real immunity to pickets. It clearly does no more.

10.5.7.3 **Location of picket**

Since 1980, the statutory immunity has been restricted to a person picketing at or near[286] their *own* place of work[287] (and to a union representative accompanying such a person). Since the golden formula immunity in s 219 is expressly removed from acts done in the course of any picketing which falls outside the scope of s 220[288] (eg because it is not at that person's place of work, or is not peaceful), the effect of this is to allow an employer not a party to a dispute to obtain an injunction to stop employees of some other employer in dispute picketing its premises in the course of their dispute.[289]

10.5.7.4 **Picket supervisor**

For a period from 2016 the availability of the statutory immunity for any picketing organized by a trade union was subject to the union complying with a series of requirements in relation to the 'picket supervisor'. This has now been repealed by the Employment Rights Act 2025, s 75. However, the Code of Practice on picketing[290] has long recommended that there should be such a supervisor. At the time of writing the Code has not been revised to reflect this repeal, but the amended code is likely to continue to recommend that a supervisor should be appointed.

10.5.7.5 **Picketing as secondary action**

In one important respect the immunity for picketing is wider than the immunity for other forms of industrial action, because in certain circumstances pickets enjoy immunity for *secondary* action occurring during picketing.[291] This exception exists for the

[285] [1974] 2 All ER 177, [1974] ICR 282.

[286] A realistic approach must be taken to the meaning of 'at or near': *Rayware Ltd v TGWU* [1989] ICR 457, [1989] IRLR 134, CA (pickets at the entrance to a private industrial estate which contained the employer's factory were held to be attending 'at or near' their place of work, even though 1,200 yards from their employer's premises).

[287] Those with no fixed place of work, or whose workplace makes picketing impracticable (eg the proverbial lighthouse keeper), may picket 'any premises' from which they work or from which their work is administered: s 220(2); see *Union Traffic Ltd v Transport and General Workers' Union* [1989] IRLR 127, CA. Workers who have been dismissed because of the dispute (and so who technically have no place of work) may picket their former place of work: s 220(3), although note that if the employer moves production to a new plant, the dismissed workers may not lawfully picket that plant because it was never their place of work: *News Group Newspapers Ltd v SOGAT 1982 (No 2)* [1987] ICR 181, [1986] IRLR 337.

[288] Trade Union and Labour Relations (Consolidation) Act 1992, s 219(3); see 10.2.8.2.

[289] As in *Mersey Docks and Harbour Co v Verrinder* [1982] IRLR 152. One problem for an employer may be to identify the pickets in order to bring civil proceedings against them; it is no part of the police function to do so (see the Code of Practice on Picketing, para 51).

[290] The Code of Practice is discussed in 10.5.8.

[291] Trade Union and Labour Relations (Consolidation) Act 1992, s 244(3). The protection is, of course, subject to the other restrictions on the statutory immunities, such as the need to hold a valid ballot.

simple reason that without it the immunity for attendance conferred by s 220 would in practice be worthless. Workers peacefully picketing at their own place of work can very easily become involved in secondary action—for example, the actions of a picket who persuades a delivery driver who works for a third party not to cross a picket line (thereby probably inducing that driver to break his contract of employment and also interfering with the commercial supply contracts of the driver's employer) are likely to constitute secondary action if the driver is not employed by the employer in dispute. If there were no immunity for secondary action occurring during picketing, it would be virtually impossible for any lawful picketing to take place. Secondary action committed during peaceful picketing is therefore protected, but *only* if done by pickets employed (or last employed) by the employer in dispute, and union officials lawfully accompanying them. Those not employed by the employer in dispute (eg sympathy pickets who picket their own place of work in support of other workers) enjoy no protection against secondary action which occurs during picketing.

10.5.7.6 **Number of pickets**

One issue which has been the cause of much controversy is mass picketing. This is not in itself unlawful, and s 220 places no limits on the numbers of pickets who may lawfully attend. However, the section does require that the picketing be 'peaceful', that is, for the stated purposes of obtaining or communicating information or peacefully persuading any person to work or abstain from working. Thus, while mass picketing is not unlawful in itself, it is in the nature of things easier, as the numbers grow larger, to infer a purpose other than that of peaceful communication or persuasion. In *Broome v DPP*,[292] Lord Salmon said that each case would depend on its facts, with the number of pickets being just one of the factors in deciding whether the attendance was for statutory purposes, but Lord Reid said, perhaps more realistically, that in a case of mass picketing 'it would not be difficult to infer as a matter of fact that pickets who assemble in unreasonably large numbers do have the purpose of preventing free passage', that is, a purpose outside those permitted in s 220. Lord Reid's approach was echoed in the judgment of Scott J in *Thomas v NUM (South Wales Area)*.[293] When the 1980 Employment Bill was going through Parliament, there was some pressure to supplement this general position with a statutory provision limiting numbers of pickets. This was not done in the Act, but an attempt was made to achieve the same result indirectly in the Code of Practice on picketing, issued later in the year.[294] Paragraph 52 of the current Code states that

> the law does not impose a specific limit on the number of people who may picket at any one place; nor does this Code affect in any way the discretion of the police to limit the number of people on a particular picket line.

However, paragraph 56, after discussing the problems caused by large numbers, goes on to state that 'pickets and their organisers should ensure that in general the number of pickets does not exceed six at any entrance to, or exit from, a workplace; frequently a smaller number will be appropriate'. Although the Code itself is not legally binding it is expressly made admissible in tribunal or court proceedings,[295] and this suggested maximum of six pickets per entrance has in the past been seized upon by the courts as a guide 'to a sensible number for a picket line in order that the weight of numbers should

[292] [1974] 1 All ER 314, [1974] ICR 84, HL.
[293] [1985] 2 All ER 1, [1985] IRLR 136.
[294] The Code of Practice is discussed in 10.5.8.
[295] Trade Union and Labour Relations (Consolidation) Act 1992, s 207.

not intimidate those who wish to go to work',[296] the implication being that the presence of pickets in numbers greater than six may be taken to indicate a purpose outside those permitted by the section.

In the light of the rights of freedom of expression and freedom of assembly contained in Articles 10 and 11 of the European Convention on Human Rights, it would seem that the lawfulness of a picket should be assessed as a matter of substance and not on the basis of numbers as numbers. In the first reported case to consider the lawfulness of an industrial picket in the light of the Convention, *Gate Gourmet London Ltd v TGWU*,[297] the High Court refused to limit the 200 or so people protesting at a site some 500 metres from the entrance to the workplace but did limit to six the number at a site opposite the works entrance where there had been intimidation. At the former site there had been only some 'unlawful threats and abuse', and the judge concluded that he should initially seek to deal with that by prohibiting the pickets from approaching employees who were on their way to or from work, and hold in reserve the possibility of limiting numbers.

10.5.8 **The Code of Practice on picketing**

The current Code was published in 1980 by the Secretary of State for Employment,[298] and at the time of writing the current revision was issued in 2017. It is likely to be revised in order to take account of the repeal of the requirement to have a picket supervisor—although it is likely that the Code will still recommend that unions should appoint picket supervisor. The Code is not legally binding but it is admissible in evidence and can be taken into account by a court in determining any question to which it is relevant.[299] Much of it is concerned with explaining the relevant law. However, as seen in 10.5.7.5, one aspect of the Code—the suggested maximum number of six pickets per entrance—has in the past been given indirect legal effect through being taken into account by the courts when deciding whether the picketing was 'peaceful' and so within the immunity. Other than that, the Code's general exhortations as to prior consultations with the police and proper organization of picketing by officials[300] are of little legal significance. The Code includes the following recommendations: (a) where an entrance or exit is used jointly by the workers of more than one employer, pickets should not interfere with those workers or call upon them to join in the dispute; (b) picketing should be confined to a location or locations as near as is practicable to the place of work; (c) a picket should not be designated as official unless it is actually organized by a trade union and the union is prepared to accept responsibility for it.

[296] *Thomas v NUM (South Wales Area)* [1985] ICR 886, [1985] IRLR 136, per Scott J; see also *News Group Newspapers Ltd v SOGAT 1982 (No 2)* [1987] ICR 181, [1986] IRLR 337, per Stuart-Smith J. In *Thomas v NUM*, the terms of the injunction were clearly drafted with the Code of Practice in mind, for they restrained the organizing of picketing at the colliery in question in numbers greater than six for any purpose other than peaceful persuasion or communication. Similarly, in *Gate Gourmet London Ltd v TGWU* [2005] IRLR 881 the judge limited the pickets near the employer's entrance (where there had been intimidation) to six in number even though the employer had, it appears, argued only for a limit of ten pickets.

[297] Gate *Gourmet London Ltd v TGWU* [2005] IRLR 881.

[298] Under powers now contained in the Trade Union and Labour Relations (Consolidation) Act 1992, s 203, which allows him to promulgate codes of practice (with parliamentary approval) after consultation with ACAS. The Code of Practice is set out in *Harvey* S [2101].

[299] Trade Union and Labour Relations (Consolidation) Act 1992, s 207.

[300] One irony here is that, while the Code stresses the importance of good organization and marshalling by officials, the law has never accepted that 'official pickets' should have any rights (other than the right of attendance) over and above ordinary pickets, eg a right to go through police cordons to talk to lorry drivers (see *Kavanagh v Hiscock* [1974] 2 All ER 177, [1974] ICR 282).

One part of the Code is open to serious objection as a misuse of the idea of codes of practice. This is Section G (Essential Supplies and Services), which states that pickets should ensure that such supplies and services are not impeded or prevented.[301] The problem is that it is difficult to see what legal effect this could have—it would be stretching several points to argue that picketing which did interfere with such services or supplies was thereby not 'peaceful', and it is the peaceful or other nature of it which is normally in issue in deciding whether or not the s 220 immunity can be relied upon. If it is correct that Section G has no legal effect, its inclusion can be seen either as merely pious hope or, more objectionably, an attempt to legislate by code of practice. If there are to be measures on something as important as the protection of essential supplies and services, it is surely not expecting too much that they should be properly enacted in a statute.[302]

10.6 Injunctions and damages

10.6.1 Introduction

So far in this chapter we have been concerned with the legal niceties concerning the existence of a cause of action on which a party injured by industrial action can rely for an injunction or damages. However, the next major question concerns enforcement. This is a matter of civil law: it is up to injured parties to bring proceedings against either the trade union or its officials for an injunction to stop the action or for damages for the losses incurred. The claimant is usually the employer but it can be a member of the public who is affected.[303] In addition, a union member who is called upon to take part in industrial action which does not have the support of a ballot can apply to court for an injunction to stop the action.[304]

Since the employer's legal action is now normally brought against the union, as opposed to the union's members or officials, the key issues are:

- When is a union to be liable in tort for the acts of its officers and members?
- What remedies can be sought against it?
- Out of which union funds can an award of damages be satisfied?

10.6.2 When can a union be liable in tort for acts of its officers and members?

A union is responsible for acts which had been 'authorised or endorsed by a responsible person', viz:

1. the union's principal executive committee;
2. any other person empowered by the union rules to authorize or endorse such acts;

[301] Paragraph 66. Paragraph 67 lists such supplies and services as including pharmaceutical and medical products; hospitals; fuel for institutions; supplies needed in a crisis for public health and safety; goods and services necessary to the maintenance of plant and machinery; livestock; food and animal feeding stuffs; the operation of essential public services and mortuaries, burial and cremation services.

[302] On industrial action in the essential services generally see Morris *Strikes in Essential Services* (1986), and 'Industrial Action in Essential Services: The New Law' (1991) 29 ILJ 89.

[303] The Trade Union and Labour Relations (Consolidation) Act 1992, s 235A gives an individual the right to apply for an injunction restraining unlawful industrial action where an effect (or a likely effect) of that action will be to (a) prevent or delay the supply of goods or services to that individual or (b) reduce the quality of goods or services supplied to them: see 10.6.4.4.

[304] Trade Union and Labour Relations (Consolidation) Act 1992, s 62.

3. the president or general secretary;
4. any other official, employed by the union or not; or
5. any other committee of the union.

A 'committee' includes any group constituted under the rules of the union.[305]

This means that the ability of a union to repudiate unauthorized actions by its officials and committees becomes of crucial importance. Such repudiation is only available in relation to the acts of people in categories (4) and (5) and the requirements are very specific:[306]

- the repudiation must take place as soon as is reasonably practicable after the relevant act has come to the knowledge of the repudiator;
- written notice of the repudiation must be given to the committee or official in question without delay;
- the union must 'do its best' to give individual written notice of the fact and date of the repudiation, without delay, to every member of the union who the union has reason to believe is taking part (or might otherwise take part) in industrial action as a result of the act which is being repudiated, and to the employer of every such member;
- the notice to union members must contain the following statement:

> Your union has repudiated the call (or calls) for industrial action to which this notice relates and will give no support to unofficial industrial action taken in response to it (or them). If you are dismissed while taking unofficial industrial action, you will have no right to complain of unfair dismissal.

- the repudiation will be deemed to be ineffective if the executive, president, or general secretary subsequently behaves in a manner which is inconsistent with the purported repudiation,[307] or fails to confirm forthwith and in writing on request by a party to a commercial contract whose performance has been interfered with as a result of the act in question that it has been repudiated.

10.6.3 **What remedies can be sought against a union?**

While the primary aim in most cases will be an injunction, the possibility of unions having to pay damages raises one of the principal objections to laying unions open to actions in tort, namely that a strike or other industrial action could well cause vast losses by impeding production—losses which, if fully reflected in damages, could bankrupt the union. Section 22 of the 1992 Act attempts to meet that argument by laying down maximum amounts of damages to be awarded against unions in tort actions (other than actions for personal injury or arising out of the ownership, occupation, possession, control, or use of property, or product liability, where the statutory maxima do not apply). The limits were increased for the first time in 40 years in 2022 and are now: (a) £40,000 if

[305] Trade Union and Labour Relations (Consolidation) Act 1992, s 20(3)(a).

[306] Trade Union and Labour Relations (Consolidation) Act 1992, s 21.

[307] For a case where a purported repudiation was held on the facts to have been a sham see *Express and Star Ltd v NGA (1982)* [1985] IRLR 455 ('nods, winks, turning of blind eyes and similar clandestine methods of approval', per Skinner J); see also *Gate Gourmet London Ltd v TGWU* [2005] IRLR 881.

the union has fewer than 5,000 members; (b) £200,000 if more than 5,000 but fewer than 25,000 members; (c) £500,000 if more than 25,000 but fewer than 100,000 members; (d) £1,000,000 if more than 100,000 members.[308]

In addition, s 23 of the 1992 Act creates a class of 'protected property' which may not be taken to satisfy any award of damages, costs, or expenses. This covers any property (a) belonging to trustees of the union in any other capacity (including personally); (b) belonging to any union member (otherwise than jointly or in common with the other members); (c) belonging to any union official who is neither a member nor a trustee; (d) comprised in a political fund;[309] or (e) comprised in a provident benefits fund.[310]

10.6.4 **The use of injunctions in industrial cases**

10.6.4.1 **The most important remedy**

Although the establishment of a viable cause of action in an industrial dispute case could, in theory, lead to an award of damages against the defendant union or its leaders or members, the practical importance of such a cause of action has always been that it permits the claimant to seek an injunction to *stop* the industrial action. Moreover, as industrial disputes and stoppages may arise very quickly, the pattern has been for the claimant to apply for an interim injunction as quickly as possible. An interim injunction may stop the industrial action and although in theory it only does so in order to preserve the status quo pending the full trial of the substantive action, in practice the claimant has achieved their aim and so the vast majority of these cases never proceed to trial. This means that the granting of the interim injunction in effect decides the issue.[311] This raises two problems for a potential defendant.

10.6.4.2 **Speed**

First, an interim injunction may be sought and granted at great speed.[312] Such an injunction can be sought without notice to the defendant, but in practice this is rare because s 221(1) of the Trade Union and Labour Relations (Consolidation) Act 1992 provides that

[308] Trade Union and Labour Relations (Consolidation) Act 1992 s 22 as amended by the Liability of Trade Unions in Proceedings in Tort (Increase of Limits on Damages) Order 2022 SI 2022/699. These limits presumably the maximum amounts at the suit of one particular claimant, so that if there are several claimants, damages up to the maximum can be awarded in the case of each successful claimant, even if the actions arise from the same event. The section is not specific on this point. Note that the restrictions on amount in s 22 only apply to damages; they do not apply to any interest awarded on damages (*Boxfoldia Ltd v National Graphical Association (1982)* [1988] IRLR 383) or to fines for contempt of court, and neither this section nor s 23 on protected property prevents the sequestration of the whole of a union's property if a fine is not paid.

[309] The political fund must be subject to rules of the union which prevent its contents from being used for financing strikes or other industrial action: s 23(2)(d).

[310] 'Provident benefits' are defined in s 23(3) as including payments expressly authorized by the union rules, in respect of sickness, injury, or unemployment; superannuation; accidents; loss of tools through fire or theft; funeral expenses; and provision for the children of deceased members.

[311] See Anderman and Davies 'Injunction Procedure in Labour Disputes' (1973) 2 ILJ 213 and (1974) 3 ILJ 30; Evans 'The Use of Injunctions in Industrial Disputes' (1987) 25 BJIR 419; Gall and McKay 'Injunctions as a Legal Weapon in Industrial Disputes' (1996) 34 BJIR 567.

[312] See eg *Barretts & Baird* (see n 70), where the injunction that Henry J discharged had originally been granted by another judge over the telephone on a Sunday afternoon. In *Gate Gourmet London Ltd v TGWU* [2005] IRLR 881 the injunction was granted not just against a named individual, but also against unnamed persons who could be defined by their unlawful activities.

a court shall not grant the injunction in a case where the defendant is likely to claim that they acted in contemplation or furtherance of a trade dispute unless it is

> satisfied that all steps which in the circumstances were reasonable have been taken with a view to securing that notice of the application and an opportunity of being heard with respect to the application have been given to [the defendant].

Nevertheless, although the union is usually given notice and is usually present in court to argue against the injunction, it often has very little time to prepare the relevant evidence and to formulate its legal arguments.

10.6.4.3 How strong must the claim be?

The second problem relates to how strong the claimant's case must be in order to obtain an interim injunction. In theory, an application for an interim injunction does not involve a trial of the issue, merely a decision whether to give a temporary remedy pending the full trial of the claim. If, however, the matter never goes any further (as in most industrial injunction cases), the interim stage is the only one at which the defendant can put forward their case. It used to be thought that, to be granted an interim injunction, the claimant had to show a 'prima facie' or 'strong prima facie' case that they would succeed at trial.[313] In a case which was not about industrial action, *American Cyanamid Co v Ethicon Ltd*,[314] the House of Lords held that all that has to be shown by the claimant is that there is a 'serious question to be tried', in other words, an arguable case fit to go on trial. Once that has been shown, the question whether to grant the injunction was to be decided on the 'balance of convenience', that is, whether the claimant would suffer more damage in the meantime if it were not granted than the defendant would suffer if it were. In ordinary commercial cases, this may make perfect sense and may be backed up by other devices such as an undertaking by a claimant seeking the injunction that if it ultimately loses the case after a full trial, it will pay damages to the defendant for the losses suffered by being prevented from proceeding with its intended course of action.

In employment cases, however, application of these ordinary principles on interim injunctions would be likely to favour the claimant employer,[315] as the balance of convenience will usually fall in the employer's favour, for it can usually point to definite pecuniary loss if the strike is allowed to continue, whereas the defendant union can only point to the intangible 'damage' of loss of a tactical advantage in the dispute if the strike is postponed until its lawfulness has been determined by the court. In an attempt to meet the potential problem, the Employment Protection Act 1975 added a new requirement, now contained in s 221(2) of the Trade Union and Labour Relations (Consolidation) Act 1992, which provides that where an application is made to a court for an interim injunction pending the trial of an action, and the party against whom the injunction is sought claims that they acted in contemplation or furtherance of a trade dispute:

[313] *J T Stratford & Son Ltd v Lindley* [1965] AC 269, [1964] 3 All ER 102, HL.

[314] [1975] AC 396, [1975] 1 All ER 504, HL. See *Hubbard v Pitt* [1975] 3 All ER 1, [1975] ICR 308, CA, the judgment of Henry J in *Barretts & Baird (Wholesale) Ltd v IPCS* [1987] IRLR 3 and Gray 'Interlocutory Injunctions since *Cyanamid*' (1981) 40 CLJ 307.

[315] As was acknowledged by Lord Diplock in *NWL Ltd v Nelson* [1979] ICR 867, [1979] IRLR 478, HL. Moreover, in *British Airways plc v Unite the Union* [2010] IRLR 423 Cox J, in granting an injunction to restrain strike action at airports over Christmas, took the interests of the travelling public into account too, in deciding on the balance of convenience.

> [T]he court shall, in exercising its discretion whether or not to grant the injunction, have regard to the likelihood of that party's succeeding at the trial of the action in establishing any matter which would afford a defence to the action.

Section 221(2) was first considered by the House of Lords in *NWL Ltd v Nelson*,[316] where Lord Diplock said that the section was enacted to enable judges to take into account the practical reality of employment disputes when applying the 'balance of convenience' principle:

> [Section 221(2)] . . . appears to me to be intended as a reminder addressed to English judges that where industrial action is threatened that is prima facie tortious because it induces a breach of contract they should in exercising their discretion whether or not to grant an interim injunction, put into the balance of convenience in favour of the defendant those countervailing practical realities and, in particular, that the grant of an injunction is tantamount to giving final judgment against the defendant . . . My Lords, when properly understood, there is in my view nothing in the decision of this House in *American Cyanamid Co v Ethicon Ltd* to suggest that in considering whether or not to grant an interim injunction the judge ought not to give full weight to all the practical realities of the situation to which the injunction will apply . . . Cases of this kind are exceptional, but when they do occur they bring into the balance of convenience an important additional element . . . it was clearly prudent of the draftsman of the section to state expressly that in considering whether or not to grant an interim injunction the court should have regard to the likelihood of the defendant's succeeding in establishing that what he did or threatened was done and threatened in contemplation or furtherance of a trade dispute.[317]

In practice, s 221(2) has placed little restraint upon the granting of interim injunctions in industrial disputes: it is the case that if there is little chance of the claimant employer succeeding, an injunction will not be granted, but otherwise the odds seem to be stacked in the employer's favour, particularly as it appears that the 'public interest' may in appropriate cases be taken into account at this stage[318] (a factor that could be particularly influential where the dispute may give rise to significant disruption to the public). The odds often favour the claimant employer because a judge hearing an application for an interim injunction, who may well not have much previous knowledge of collective employment law, will usually give some (albeit often hurried) consideration to the points of law involved, particularly on the applicability or otherwise of the immunities, but the relevant law is so complex that it has often not been difficult for the employer's counsel to put together an arguable case that there may have been some (perhaps technical) infringement by the union that renders the immunities inapplicable,[319] and that therefore there is sufficient likelihood of the claims succeeding at the full trial. However, since the *Serco*[320] judgment of the Court of Appeal (considered in 10.3.1 and 10.3.4), the balance has

[316] [1979] ICR 867, [1979] IRLR 478, HL. [317] [1979] ICR 867 at 879, [1979] IRLR 478 at 484.

[318] *Beaverbrook Newspapers Ltd v Keys* [1978] ICR 582, [1978] IRLR 34, CA; *United Biscuits (UK) Ltd v Fall* [1979] IRLR 110; *Express Newspapers Ltd v McShane* [1980] 1 All ER 65, [1980] IRLR 35, HL; *Associated British Ports v TGWU* [1989] 3 All ER 822, [1989] ICR 557, HL.

[319] This is much more likely as a result of the narrowing of the immunities since 1980, particularly with the introduction of the highly complex balloting and notice requirements: see 10.3. The development of torts *not* covered by an immunity (eg inducing breach of statutory duty) is also highly significant here. See eg *Associated British Ports v TGWU* [1989] 3 All ER 796, [1989] IRLR 305, CA (reversed on other grounds, [1989] 3 All ER 822, [1989] IRLR 399, HL).

[320] *NURMT v Serco Ltd* [2011] ICR 848, [2011] IRLR 399, CA.

been to some extent restored because the union's counsel may well be able to undermine the damage done by various small infringements of the balloting or notice provisions by arguing that they are 'trifling errors which should not be allowed to form a basis for invalidating the ballot'.

10.6.4.4 **Other points**

Finally, four points should be noted. The first is that an appeal against the granting or refusal of an interim injunction will not be allowed merely on the basis that the judge's exercise of discretion as to the issuing of an injunction was wrong. An appeal will succeed only where the decision of the trial judge was wrong in law or was unjust because of a serious procedural or other irregularity in the proceedings,[321] or where there has been a change of circumstances since the order was made. The issue was considered in *Hadmor Productions Ltd v Hamilton*,[322] where Lord Diplock emphasized that the appellate court's function is one of review only; an interim injunction is a discretionary remedy, lying essentially within the discretion of the trial judge, so that the appellate court should not on appeal treat the matter *de novo* and substitute its own view on the facts.[323]

The second point is that events during the miners' strike of 1984–85 showed how potent a weapon an injunction[324] can be when it is granted against a union itself, not a named individual, as breach of or failure to comply with it is a contempt of court[325] for which the union may be fined (the fine not being subject to the statutory maxima on damages); if the fine is not paid, the claimant may apply for sequestration of the union's assets, and the fact of sequestration could give rise to a claim by disaffected union members for the union to be placed in receivership. Indeed, it has been argued that sequestration and, to a lesser extent, receivership can be viewed as remedies in their own right (especially as sequestration is not merely an administrative means of gathering the fine, since even after the fine is recovered by the sequestrators the sequestration continues until the union purges its contempt). This is why trade unions do obey injunctions in industrial action cases.[326]

The third point is that it must be remembered that an employment dispute is an employment relations problem, and at some stage the two sides will have to try to resume normal relations; this is unlikely to be helped by taking legal action, and a delicate balance may have to be preserved between the enforcement of legal rights in the short term, and the resolution of issues in the employment relations context in the long term. ACAS has certainly found its collective conciliation efforts materially complicated in cases where

[321] CPR 52.11(3). There is no right of appeal against a grant or refusal of an interim injunction without the permission of a judge: CPR 52.3.

[322] [1982] 1 All ER 1042, [1982] ICR 114, HL, applied in *Dimbleby & Sons Ltd v NUJ* [1984] ICR 386, [1984] IRLR 161.

[323] Under the Civil Procedure Rules, the court can hold a rehearing if it considers that it would be in the interests of justice to do so in the circumstances: CPR 52.11(1).

[324] The principal injunctions during the strike were in fact granted to working miners, not employers, but the principles are the same. See Ewing (1985) 14 ILJ at 170; Lightman (1987) 40 CLP 25.

[325] On contempt of court and its remedies see *Harvey* N II [4162] and Kidner 'Sanctions for Contempt by a Trade Union' (1986) 6 LS 18. For an example of a contempt fine for half-hearted and delayed compliance with a court order see *Kent Free Press v NGA* [1987] IRLR 267. When dealing with a contempt the court must consider the offending party's rights under the European Convention on Human Rights in deciding whether the imposing of a sanction is justified: *Cuadrilla Bowland Ltd v Persons Unknown* [2020] EWCA Civ 9, [2020] 4 WLR 29, [2020] EnvLR 20.

[326] However, see McCluskey 'Can the Unions Stay Within the Law Any Longer' (2015) 44 ILJ 439, where the General Secretary of the Unite union argued that recent developments such as the Trade Union Act 2016 might lead to unions having to decide to cease to obey the law.

there is the threat or actuality of legal proceedings, and at one point suggested that there should be some procedure whereby legal proceedings in industrial dispute cases could be temporarily stayed by the courts to allow at least an attempt at conciliation before final steps are taken,[327] but the idea has not been taken up.

Finally, the fourth point is that in practice many employers faced with industrial action which is unlawful choose not to pursue legal remedies for fear of inflaming an already difficult situation and reducing the chances of an early negotiated settlement. In theory such a strategy on the part of an employer could be frustrated by s 235A of the 1992 Act,[328] which gives an individual who is deprived of goods or services[329] as a result of unlawful industrial action a right (dubbed the 'Citizen's Right', or, to trade unionists at the time, a 'nutters' charter') to apply for an injunction restraining that action.[330] It seems that the claimant need not have suffered any quantifiable financial loss or damage as a result of it. The potential impact of this procedure was graphically illustrated in *P v National Association of Schoolmasters/Union of Women Teachers*,[331] which arose out of the refusal of NASUWT members to accept the 'unreasonable direction' of the head teacher to teach a disruptive pupil who had been permanently excluded from school only to be reinstated following a successful appeal to the school governors. The pupil sought an injunction restraining the industrial action on the grounds that it was unlawful, and that the separate tuition arrangements which had been made for him interfered with the provision of educational services to him and placed him at a disadvantage. In fact, the application was rejected on the facts,[332] and that decision was upheld on appeal by both the Court of Appeal and the House of Lords, but the fact that the application was made at all is significant.

The Citizen's Right is significant on three levels: first, when introduced in 1993 (to considerable political controversy) it represented in theory a breathtaking extension of liability, and could be said to render much of the earlier discussion on the scope of the economic torts irrelevant, for as long as the industrial action is in theory actionable by at least one person, anyone else adversely affected by that action may seek an injunction to restrain it. Second, it could have a damaging effect on attempts to reach negotiated settlements to industrial disputes. In explaining the rationale of the Citizen's Right, the then minister of state posed the question 'Why should citizens be inconvenienced because a gutless and spineless employer fails to see a remedy for unlawful action which results in loss?'[333]—a view which arguably failed to recognize the employment relations realities of the situation. Third, however, this apparently wide extension of liability has in fact hardly ever been raised since the *NASUWT* case and is now largely forgotten, though of course it is still on the statute book and so potentially an unexploded land mine.

[327] ACAS Annual Report, 1983 paras 1.16–1.18.

[328] Introduced by the Trade Union Reform and Employment Rights Act 1993, s 22.

[329] The original proposals in the Green Paper 'Industrial Relations in the 1990s' (Cm 1602, 1991) would have confined the right to customers of the public services within the scope of the Citizen's Charter, but as enacted the right goes considerably further.

[330] The section does not give a right to damages.

[331] [2003] IRLR 307, [2003] 1 All ER 993, HL.

[332] The claimant had alleged (a) that the dispute was not a trade dispute because it did not relate wholly or mainly to terms and condition of employment; and (b) that the statutory balloting requirements had not been complied with because two members of staff to whom ballot papers should have been sent did not receive them. Morison J at first instance found for the union on both points.

[333] Minister of State, Mr Michael Forsyth, Hansard, HC (Standing Committee F).

10.7 The effect of industrial action on the participating employee

As was seen in 10.1, the approach traditionally taken in the law on industrial action has been to preserve the freedom to strike by providing immunities at the collective level (albeit within increasingly narrow boundaries) rather than by conferring any positive right to strike on the individual participants. We now turn to consider how the law deals with the position of a striker as an individual.

10.7.1 The effect of industrial action on individual contracts of employment

Since the most fundamental contractual obligation of an employee is to be ready and willing to serve the employer, the action of going on strike is likely to be a repudiatory breach of contract, giving the employer the right to dismiss summarily. In theory it may also entitle the employer to sue the employee for damages,[334] although in practice the employer's common law power to withhold wages in respect of non-performance (or indeed partial performance) of contractual obligations is likely to be of far greater significance. It is not surprising to anyone that workers would not be paid during a strike; however, when the industrial action takes the form of action short of a strike, such as not undertaking certain duties, the question of how much, if anything, the employer must pay in wages or salary is not only controversial between unions and employers as a matter of industrial fairness but is also controversial—and at present unclear—as a matter of law. It is a common tactic for an employer faced with industrial action short of a strike to notify employees that it will not accept partial performance and that any work done will be done voluntarily, and then to pay nothing or to pay only a very reduced level of remuneration. The law on this is considered in 3.5.1.3.

The orthodox view is that industrial action will be a breach of contract however it is organized, and if advance notice is given it will be construed merely as notice of an impending breach rather than as a notice of resignation—even if the length of the notice equals or exceeds the period prescribed in the contract of employment.[335] However, this orthodox view was challenged by Lord Denning MR in *Morgan v Fry*,[336] where he suggested that where strike notice was given which was at least equal to the length required to terminate the contracts of employment, the strike was not unlawful, since the notice had the effect of suspending the contracts, not breaking them:

> The truth is that neither employer nor workmen wish to take the drastic action of termination [of the contracts of employment] if it can be avoided. The men do not wish to leave their work for ever. The employers do not wish to scatter their labour force to the four winds. Each side is, therefore, content to accept a 'strike notice' of proper length as lawful.

[334] *National Coal Board v Galley* [1958] 1 All ER 91, [1958] 1 WLR 16, CA; *Neil v Strathclyde Regional Council* [1984] IRLR 14 (not an industrial dispute case).

[335] See principally *Rookes v Barnard* [1964] AC 1129, [1964] 1 All ER 367, HL, at 1204 and 396, respectively, per Lord Devlin; *Stratford & Son Ltd v Lindley* [1965] AC 269 at 285, [1964] 2 All ER 209 at 217, CA, per Lord Denning MR.

[336] [1968] 2 QB 710, [1968] 3 All ER 452, CA; Davies LJ supported Lord Denning's view, but Russell LJ did not and decided the case on other grounds.

> It is an implication read into the modern law as to trade disputes. If a strike takes place, the contract of employment is not terminated. It is suspended during the strike and revives again when the strike is over.[337]

The whole question arose (obliquely) for consideration by the EAT in *Simmons v Hoover Ltd*,[338] where, in reaffirming that an employer has a right to dismiss a striking employee (who is thereby disentitled to a redundancy payment), Phillips J held that there is no common law doctrine of suspension by strike notice, and refused to apply Lord Denning's views in *Morgan v Fry*. He considered that those views were out of line with the modern statutory provisions relating to strikes (in contexts such as unfair dismissal, redundancy claims, and continuity of employment), which operate on the assumption that participation in a strike is repudiatory conduct entitling the employer to dismiss, and then graft on special rules (depending on the context).[339]

While it is clear that strike action will be a breach of contract, the position as regards industrial action short of a strike is less certain. Where the industrial action is inconsistent with express or implied contractual obligations, there is little doubt that it will be in breach of contract.[340] But what if the industrial action in question is a work to rule, or a ban on voluntary overtime? In relation to overtime, in *Burgess v Stevedoring Services Ltd*,[341] the Privy Council held that a ban on voluntary overtime was not in breach of the contracts of the participants, Lord Hoffmann stating that employees are not in breach of their contracts 'for refusing to do things altogether outside their contractual obligations (like going to work on Sunday) merely because they do not have a bona fide reason for refusal. They do not have to have any reason at all'.[342] As for a work to rule, employees will be in breach of contract if their interpretation of the rules is an unreasonable one designed to frustrate the purpose of the employment.[343]

10.7.2 **The effect of industrial action on miscellaneous statutory employment rights**

Participation in a strike or other industrial action is likely to have a highly detrimental impact on an employee's statutory employment rights. The most serious consequence is likely to be the potential loss of the right to bring proceedings for unfair dismissal,

[337] [1968] 2 QB 710 at 728, [1968] 3 All ER 452 at 458.

[338] [1977] ICR 61, [1976] IRLR 266, EAT; applied in *Wilkins v Cantrell and Cochrane (GB) Ltd* [1978] IRLR 483, EAT and *Haddow v ILEA* [1979] ICR 202, EAT.

[339] This view could be said to be implicit in the Trade Union and Labour Relations (Consolidation) Act 1992, s 229(4), which requires a ballot paper to point out that a person who takes part in a strike or other industrial action may be in breach of his contract of employment. Note, however, the judgment of Saville J in *Boxfoldia Ltd v NGA (1982)* [1988] ICR 752, [1988] IRLR 383 to the effect that the question of whether a purported strike notice avoids a breach of contract is a matter of interpretation of the notice (which, in order to be effective, would have to be an unambiguous notice of termination of contracts by the strikers).

[340] *Burgess v Stevedoring Services Ltd* [2002] UKPC 39, [2002] IRLR 810 and *British Telecommunications plc v Ticehurst* [1992] ICR 383, [1992] IRLR 219, CA, which considered employees exercising a discretion within their contract of employment in a way intended to disrupt the employer's business. This case is discussed at 3.4.4.6.

[341] [2002] UKPC 39, [2002] IRLR 810.

[342] [2002] UKPC 39, [2002] IRLR 810 at 813.

[343] *Secretary of State for Employment v ASLEF (No 2)* [1972] 2 QB 455, CA. This case has been argued by some to support the proposition that if the motive of workers is to harm the employer then actions which are within the contract of employment are nevertheless in breach of contract when done as part of collective action with the intention of harming the employer's interests. This wider interpretation has not found favour in the later cases of *Burgess* (see n 340) and *Ministry of Justice v The Prison Officers' Association* [2017] EWHC 1839 (QB), [2017] ICR 181, [2017] IRLR 1121.

discussed in this chapter; but other statutory rights of a striking employee will also be affected, in particular:

1. the restrictions on deductions from pay do not apply to deductions in respect of a strike or other industrial action in which the employee took part;[344]
2. a striking employee's rights to a redundancy payment may be jeopardized;[345]
3. a week during which an employee takes part in a strike will not count for the purposes of calculating that employee's continuity of employment, although it will not break continuity;[346]
4. an employee is not entitled to a statutory guarantee payment where the failure to provide work is in consequence of a strike, lockout, or other industrial action involving their employer or an associated employer;[347]
5. an employee may be disqualified from receiving statutory sick pay where there is a stoppage of work due to a trade dispute at their place of work;[348]
6. rights to state benefits (in particular those relating to unemployment) will be materially affected.

10.7.3 **Industrial action and unfair dismissal**

As discussed above, when employees take part in industrial action, their employer usually has the contractual right to dismiss them.[349] However, while a dismissal in such circumstances is lawful at common law, it may still be unfair. In determining whether a dismissed striker can bring a claim for unfair dismissal there are four different possible legal regimes which may apply, which will each be examined in detail in what follows. It should be noted that none of these regimes afford any protection to workers who provide personal service but are not 'employees'.[350]

In summary, the four unfair dismissal regimes are as follows:

1. If the dismissal took place while the employee was taking part in unofficial industrial action. In such a case the employee has no right to complain of unfair dismissal.[351]
2. If dismissal was because the employee took part in 'protected industrial action', that is to say, official action which was properly balloted and notified. Such dismissals are automatically unfair.
3. If the dismissal took place during a lockout by the employer or during official industrial action which is not covered by (2). As to the latter possibility, this could happen if there was a failure by the union to comply with the balloting and notice requirements or, in a case where the action was properly balloted and notified, when the dismissal occurred after the 12-week period. In this third regime the employment tribunal may not consider an unfair dismissal claim unless there has been selective

[344] Employment Rights Act 1996, s 14(5): see 3.5.5.2, *Exceptions*. For the common law power to withhold wages in such circumstances see 3.5.1.3.

[345] Employment Rights Act 1996, s 140: see 8.1.4.6.

[346] Employment Rights Act 1996, s 216: see 2.5.3.

[347] Employment Rights Act 1996, s 29(3): see 3.5.3.2.

[348] Social Security Contributions and Benefits Act 1992, Sch 11, paras 2(g) and 7.

[349] *Simmons v Hoover Ltd* [1977] ICR 61, [1976] IRLR 266, EAT; *Wilkins v Cantrell and Cochrane (GB) Ltd* [1978] IRLR 483, EAT; *Haddow v ILEA* [1979] ICR 202, EAT.

[350] See further 10.1.6.1.

[351] Trade Union and Labour Relations (Consolidation) Act 1992, s 237: see 10.7.3.1.

dismissal of some only of the workers involved, or they have all been dismissed but only some have been offered re-engagement. If such selectivity has occurred the employment tribunal must consider whether the dismissal was unfair.[352]

4. If the dismissal took place *after* a lockout by the employer or *after* industrial action (other than a case covered by (2)). In such a case the employment tribunal must consider whether the dismissal was fair.[353]

To gain a clear picture of the current position, it is necessary to explore how this intricate state of affairs has come about. For this purpose reference will be made to 'Regimes (1)–(4)', but it should be noted that these names have been created for this book and are not in wider currency. The approach of those responsible for drafting the original unfair dismissal legislation was to seek to protect the neutrality of employment tribunals by relieving them of the necessity of investigating the rights and wrongs of an industrial dispute, while at the same time preserving the employer's ultimate freedom to dismiss the participants. This was achieved by providing that where, at the date of dismissal, the employee was taking part in a strike or other industrial action, or the employer was conducting a lockout, the tribunal would have no jurisdiction to hear an unfair dismissal complaint by that employee unless the employer had discriminated between the participants, either by selectively dismissing only some of them, or by selectively offering re-engagement.[354] The Employment Act 1990 took matters further, by completely removing the right to complain of unfair dismissal from those dismissed while taking part in *unofficial* industrial action.[355]

In 1999 the Labour government introduced protection from dismissal for employees taking part in lawfully organized official industrial action by enacting the Employment Relations Act 1999, which created the concept of protected industrial action and made it automatically unfair to dismiss someone taking in part in such action for the first eight weeks (now 12) of the action. The Employment Rights Act 2025 removed the time limit altogether. The current position is therefore as follows.

10.7.3.1 Regime (1): unofficial action

By virtue of s 237 of the Trade Union and Labour Relations (Consolidation) Act 1992, an employee has no right to bring an unfair dismissal complaint where at the time of the dismissal the employee was taking part in an unofficial strike or other unofficial industrial action.[356] Action is 'unofficial' if at least one person taking part is a union member but the action has not been authorized or endorsed by the union.[357]

The effect of this provision is that an employer may selectively dismiss the ringleaders of unofficial action without fear of having to defend an unfair dismissal complaint. The

[352] Trade Union and Labour Relations (Consolidation) Act 1992, s 238: see 10.7.3.3.

[353] See 10.7.3.4.

[354] See *Gallagher v Wragg* [1977] ICR 174, EAT, per Phillips J; the neutrality explanation is arguably undermined by the fact that, where a dismissal or re-engagement is selective, the tribunal will have to decide whether the dismissal was fair or unfair.

[355] See now the Trade Union and Labour Relations (Consolidation) Act 1992, s 237.

[356] The meanings of 'taking part', 'strike', and 'industrial action' are considered in 10.7.3.3 in respect of s 238 (ie Regime (3)).

[357] This is the effect of the complex wording in s 237(2). Section 237(3) applies the statutory test of vicarious liability in s 20 to determine whether there has been union authorization or endorsement (see 10.6.2). Where industrial action is repudiated by the union under s 21 of the 1992 Act, s 237(4) provides that it does not become unofficial before the end of the next working day after the day on which the repudiation takes place, in effect giving those involved a day's grace to decide whether to continue with the action.

only exception is where it is shown that even though at the time of dismissal the employee was taking part in industrial action, the reason for the dismissal was jury service or specified family reasons; or because the employee had taken certain specified action in relation to certain specified matters, in particular health and safety or flexible working, or had acted as an employee representative, or had made a protected disclosure under the 'whistleblowing' provisions.[358] In such cases, the dismissal will be automatically unfair; in all other cases, the reason for the dismissal is wholly irrelevant.

10.7.3.2 Regime (2): properly balloted and notified official industrial action

Section 238A of the Trade Union and Labour Relations (Consolidation) Act 1992 provides that industrial action is deemed for the purposes of this unfair dismissal regime to be 'protected industrial action' if the employee is induced to take part in the industrial action 'by an act which by virtue of section 219 is not actionable in tort'.[359] In other words, the protection for the individual participants is contingent upon them having been induced to take part by a union and that union having complied with the legal preconditions for immunity: the balloting requirements and the restrictions on certain forms of industrial action which are considered in 10.3 and 10.2.8, respectively.[360] A dismissal of such an employee will be automatically unfair[361] if the reason (or, if more than one, the principal reason) for the dismissal is that the employee took 'protected industrial action'.[362] (As for what counts as taking parting in industrial action see 'Taking part industrial action' in 10.7.3.3.)

10.7.3.3 Regime (3): dismissal during a lockout or official action where regime (2) does not apply

Summary of Regime (3)

Until the introduction of 'protected industrial action', which made dismissal for industrial action unfair, Regime (3) was the most common situation in practice, and it applied to all employees taking part in official industrial action and also to employees locked out by their employer as part of an industrial dispute. Nowadays Regime (3), which is set out in s 238 of the Act, is in reality a peculiar residual category containing a 'ragbag' of factual situations which do not frequently occur:

- The employee was taking part in industrial action which was official but was *not* 'protected' within the meaning of s 238A, most likely because there was a failure by the union to comply with some aspect of the balloting or notice provisions.

[358] Trade Union and Labour Relations (Consolidation) Act 1992, s 237(1A). The health and safety exception was introduced to alleviate fears that employees dismissed for refusing to work in circumstances of danger might be held to be taking part in industrial action, and therefore excluded from the protection against unfair dismissal.

[359] On a strict interpretation, this could be taken to mean that if the industrial action is not tortious, or it involves the commission of a tort which is not covered by the s 219 immunities, the unfair dismissal protection does not apply! See Ewing (1999) 28 ILJ 283, at 292.

[360] The legislation also protects a person taking part in industrial action in which no participant is a union member. By virtue of s 237(2) such action is not regarded as unofficial and, since no union is involved, the rules on balloting and notice which a union must observe in order to benefit from the s 219 immunity do not apply. If such industrial action is in contemplation or furtherance of a trade dispute then the s 219 immunity applies to its organizers and it is therefore 'protected industrial action'.

[361] The usual qualifying period and age restriction for unfair dismissal claims do not apply in complaints under s 238A: s 239(1). No reinstatement or re-engagement order may be made until after the end of the industrial action: s 239(4).

[362] Trade Union and Labour Relations (Consolidation) Act 1992, s 238A.

- The employee was dismissed while taking part in 'protected industrial action' but the reason or, if more than one, the principal reason for his dismissal was something other than taking part in industrial action.
- The employee was at the time locked out by the employer (or directly interested in the dispute which was the reason for the lockout).

In any of these situations a tribunal will not have jurisdiction to consider an unfair dismissal complaint unless either there has been selectivity in dismissal or re-engagement or the dismissal is because the employee has taken certain specified action in relation to employment rights or health and safety, or has acted as an employee representative.[363]

Tribunals have jurisdiction only if there is selective dismissal or re-engagement

In a Regime (3) case, where at the date of dismissal[364] the employer was conducting or instituting a lockout or the complainant was taking part in a strike or other industrial action, then the tribunal cannot determine an unfair dismissal complaint unless the employee shows that either:

1. one or more relevant employees have not been dismissed; or
2. a relevant employee has, before the expiry of the period of three months beginning with that employee's date of dismissal, been offered re-engagement and the complainant has not been offered re-engagement.[365]

As defined in s 238(3), 'relevant employees' means:

1. in relation to a lockout, employees who were directly interested in the dispute in contemplation or furtherance of which the lockout occurred;
2. in relation to a strike or other industrial action, those employees at the establishment of the employer at or from which the complainant works who at the date of his dismissal were taking part in the action.

This enables an employer to issue an ultimatum to those taking industrial action to return to work or face dismissal and then to dismiss all those who fail to comply, while still retaining the protection of the section against unfair dismissal proceedings brought by the dismissed employees.[366]

A significant limit on the 'no selectivity' principle is that in relation to re-engagement it only applies where a relevant employee is offered re-engagement within three months of their dismissal. Thereafter the employer is free to re-engage strikers selectively without

[363] Section 238(2A). In the latter category, the dismissal will be automatically unfair.

[364] This is defined in s 238(5). See *Heath v J F Longman (Meat Salesmen) Ltd* [1973] ICR 407, [1973] IRLR 214, where it was taken to mean that the employee must be taking part in industrial action at the time of dismissal, and not merely on the same date. A dismissal before the industrial action has started (*Midland Plastics v Till* [1983] ICR 118, [1983] IRLR 9, EAT) or after it has ended (*Seed v Crowther (Dyers)* [1973] IRLR 199) will not fall within the section.

[365] Re-engagement means taking the employee back into the same job or in a different job which would be reasonably suitable in his case: s 238(4). The definition of 'job' (Employment Rights Act 1996, s 235(1)) allows the employer a certain leeway on the precise terms on which it takes the employee back: see *Williams v National Theatre Board Ltd* [1982] ICR 715, [1982] IRLR 377, CA. An advertising campaign offering job vacancies is unlikely to be interpreted as an offer of re-engagement to a particular employee within the meaning of the section: *Crosville (Wales) Ltd v Tracey* [1993] IRLR 60, EAT.

[366] In contrast, an employee who was locked out but has returned to work by the time of the dismissal will still be a relevant employee: *Fisher v York Trailer Co Ltd* [1979] ICR 834, [1979] IRLR 385, EAT; *H Campey & Sons Ltd v Bellwood* [1987] ICR 311, EAT.

conferring jurisdiction on the tribunal.[367] The time limit also enables the employer to make an earlier limited offer of re-engagement—perhaps to those employees regarded as not being troublemakers—so long as the remainder of the workforce are offered re-engagement within three months of their dismissal.[368]

A second limitation is that 'relevant employees' are only those employed 'at the establishment of the employer at or from which the complainant works',[369] so that the employer can dismiss all employees at one establishment and not those at another establishment. One potential difficulty for a large employer operating from several sites is that an employee dismissed for taking part in industrial action might be mistakenly re-engaged at another site within the three-month period, so opening up the employer to unfair dismissal complaints by those not re-engaged. However, the EAT has held that for there to be an effective offer of re-engagement, the employer must have actual or constructive knowledge (in the sense that it has the means of finding out) of the job from which the employee was dismissed and the reason why they were dismissed.[370]

It has been argued that Regime (3), by excluding industrial action dismissals from unfair dismissal, can be exploited by an employer who is in fact willing to dispense with one whole group of employees, who may be deprived of their unfair dismissal rights in two ways—either by the employer instituting a lockout affecting them all or by goading the employees in question into taking industrial action and then dismissing them all. In *Thompson v Eaton Ltd*,[371] Phillips J suggested that this second possibility might be countered by the concept of an 'engineered' strike (ie one produced by 'gross provocation' by the employer), which would not fall within the exclusion. However, in *Marsden v Fairey Stainless Ltd*,[372] the EAT disapproved of the idea of an engineered strike, pointing out that the wording of the section simply requires the employee to have been dismissed *while* on strike,[373] so that the exclusion will apply even if the industrial action was provoked by the employer.[374] Of course, since the introduction of protected industrial action under Regime (2) the viability of goading employees into strike action as a means of being able to dismiss them all without consequences is less attractive since, as long as the union

[367] This could cause limitation problems where the complainant and the relevant employee's dismissals took place at the same time, for the normal limitation period for the claimant to bring their action is also three months. Because of this, the limitation period is extended to six months in a case where the complainant is relying on the re-engagement of a relevant employee as a ground for arguing that the s 238 or s 238A exclusion should not apply: Trade Union and Labour Relations (Consolidation) Act 1992, s 239(2). The six-month limit also applies to complaints under s 238A (protected industrial action).

[368] *Highland Fabricators Ltd v McLaughlin* [1985] ICR 183, [1984] IRLR 482, EAT.

[369] There is no definition here of 'establishment'. This word is used elsewhere (again without definition) in the very different context of redundancy consultation; for the case law there, which could by analogy apply here, see 8.1.3.1, 'Definitional problems'. However, in the case of redundancy consultation this word was adopted in TULR(C)A 1992 because it is the word used in the EU Directive on this topic (98/59/EC), whereas in relation to industrial action dismissal the statutory provisions have an entirely British origin.

[370] *Bigham and Keogh v GKN Kwikform* [1992] ICR 113, [1992] IRLR 4, EAT; the EAT also confirmed that a re-engagement resulting from fraud on the part of the employee will not deprive the employer of the protection of the section.

[371] [1976] ICR 336 at 342, [1976] IRLR 308 at 311, EAT.

[372] [1979] IRLR 103, EAT. See also *Wilkins v Cantrell and Cochrane (GB) Ltd* [1978] IRLR 483, EAT.

[373] Phillips J had been able to argue for the concept of an engineered strike because, as originally drafted, the section provided that the real reason for dismissal must be that the employee was on strike; however, the requirement of such a causal link was removed by the Employment Protection Act 1975, Sch 16, Part III, para 13.

[374] A particularly controversial application of the exclusion was in the dispute between the printing unions and News International; see Ewing and Napier 'The Wapping Dispute and Labour Law' (1986) 45 CLJ 285, at 291. For an ingenious attempt to devise an argument avoiding this unfortunate state of affairs see Elias 'The Strike and Breach of Contract: A Reassessment' in Ewing, Gearty, and Hepple (eds) *Human Rights and Labour Law: Essays for Paul O'Higgins* (1994).

organized the strike correctly, the employer would need to wait at least 12 weeks before dismissing the employees.

If there has been selectivity

If there has been selectivity in dismissal or if all relevant employees are dismissed but only some are selected for re-engagement, the tribunal will then have jurisdiction to consider the case in the ordinary way, which means that it must consider the reason for the dismissal.[375] If the reason is one of the potentially fair reasons under s 98 of the Employment Rights Act 1996 the tribunal must determine in the ordinary way where it was reasonable to dismiss that particular employee in those circumstances and thus decide whether the dismissal was fair or unfair. If the reason is an automatically unfair one, such as union membership or activities at an appropriate time, then the dismissal will be automatically unfair.[376] So, a selective dismissal is not automatically unfair as such (unlike a dismissal for taking protected industrial action), and the employer may be able to show that it was reasonable in all the circumstances to dismiss or not to re-engage some of the strikers. The question of whether dismissal for taking part in industrial action is fair or not is considered in 10.7.3.5.

The definitions of 'strike,' 'other industrial action,' and 'lockout'

The interpretation of the provisions just set out has proved to be especially problematic, not least because a number of key phrases are not defined. There is no definition of 'lockout' or 'other industrial action', and until 1992 there was no definition of 'strike' either. The term 'strike' is now defined in this context as 'any concerted stoppage of work'.[377] There are definitions of 'strike' and 'lockout' in s 235 of the Employment Rights Act 1996, but it has previously been held that those definitions are only for the purposes of continuity of employment and so are not to be applied under s 238,[378] although they may provide some guidance to the tribunal in interpreting the section. However, at the end of the day the words should be given their ordinary and natural meaning, and their interpretation remains strictly a question of fact for the tribunal. This is entirely in line with the modern anti-legalism approach and the unpredictability and inconsistency that it can produce was commented on adversely by Browne-Wilkinson P in *Naylor v Orton and Smith Ltd*;[379] however, that approach was reaffirmed by the Court of Appeal in *Express and Star Ltd v Bunday*,[380] where May LJ said:

> What are the necessary elements of a lockout, or for that matter of a bicycle or an elephant, is not in my opinion a question of law. Nor I think is it necessarily a question of law whether a court or tribunal was correct in thinking that the presence of a particular element or ingredient in a given state of affairs is necessary before that can be, for instance, a 'lockout'. This may be a mixed question of law and fact. Alternatively it may be solely a question of fact, which it is for the expert tribunal to determine.[381]

[375] See *Baxter v Limb Group of Companies* [1994] IRLR 572, CA.

[376] See 9.4.3. Note, however, that taking part in industrial action is unlikely to be 'activities at an appropriate time'.

[377] Trade Union and Labour Relations (Consolidation) Act 1992, s 246.

[378] *McCormick v Horsepower Ltd* [1980] ICR 278, [1980] IRLR 182, EAT (upheld on other grounds on appeal) [1981] ICR 535, [1981] IRLR 217, CA and *Rasool v Hepworth Pipe Co Ltd* [1980] ICR 494, [1980] IRLR 88, EAT in relation to 'strike'; *Express and Star Ltd v Bunday* [1988] ICR 379, [1987] IRLR 422, CA in relation to 'lockout'.

[379] [1983] ICR 665, [1983] IRLR 233, EAT.

[380] See n 378.

[381] At 388 and 425, respectively. However, there is one apparent rule of law here, which is that, as what is being covered here is some form of collective action, acts purely by an individual employee cannot constitute industrial action: *Norris v London Fire and Emergency Planning Authority* [2013] IRLR 428, EAT (disapproving *Lewis & Britton v E Mason & Sons* [1994] IRLR 4, EAT).

In some cases, the dominant consideration for the tribunals in determining whether the circumstances amount to a strike or other industrial action within the meaning of the Act has been the purpose for which the action in question was taken, and in particular whether it involved the application of pressure on the employer.[382] So, for example, in *Rasool v Hepworth Pipe Co (No 2)*,[383] the EAT held that attendance at an unauthorized union meeting during working hours did not amount to industrial action because the purpose was to discuss wages and not to apply pressure on the employer, even though the meeting did in fact result in some disruption of production. However, while it is undoubtedly true that industrial action will usually be taken for the purpose of putting pressure on the employer, there may be circumstances where action is taken for a social or political rather than an industrial motive (eg in protest at government policy), and it is highly likely that such action would in practice be held to be industrial action. Greater emphasis is therefore likely to be placed on the nature and effect of the action, rather than on the reasons for it.[384]

It is clear that the technical question of whether the action is in breach of contract is not conclusive, although once again it may be taken into account as a factor. Usually a strike will involve a breach of contract, but not always; for example, an overtime ban, if done collectively and with a coercive purpose, may constitute industrial action even though individually each employee was perfectly entitled to refuse the overtime.[385]

'Taking part' in industrial action

In Regimes (1) and (3) the right to complain of unfair dismissal is only removed from employees who were 'taking part' in a strike or other industrial action at the date of the dismissal. This enables an employer in cases other than protected industrial action under Regime (2) to issue an ultimatum to those taking industrial action to return to work or face dismissal and then to dismiss all those who fail to comply, while still retaining the protection of the section against unfair dismissal proceedings brought by the dismissed employees.

The Court of Appeal has emphasized that the question of whether or not an individual is 'taking part' is ultimately a question of fact for the tribunal,[386] but the cases nevertheless provide some guidance as to the correct approach. In *Coates v Modern Methods and Materials Ltd*,[387] the employee had stayed away from work during the strike because she was frightened of crossing a picket line. The majority of the Court of Appeal held that the test to be applied is an objective one, focusing on what the employee in fact did, and not on

[382] cf Stephenson LJ in *Power Packing Casemakers Ltd v Faust* [1983] ICR 292, [1983] IRLR 117, CA: 'the continued application of pressure is industrial action in the commonsense of the words'. See also *Fire Brigades Union v Knowles* [1996] IRLR 337, EAT (under s 65(2)(a)).

[383] [1980] IRLR 137, EAT. The case is a good illustration of the potentially fine dividing line between union activity and industrial action. The EAT has held that the two situations are mutually exclusive: *Drew v St Edmundsbury Borough Council* [1980] ICR 513, [1980] IRLR 459.

[384] See *Rasool v Hepworth Pipe Co (No 2)*, n 389, where the EAT acknowledged that it was 'probably incorrect to attempt to interpret [industrial action] narrowly in terms of specific intention and that the nature and effect of the concerted action are probably of greater importance'.

[385] *Power Packing Casemakers Ltd v Faust* [1983] ICR 292, [1983] IRLR 117, CA. The decision has been heavily criticized.

[386] *Coates v Modern Methods and Materials Ltd* [1982] ICR 763, [1982] IRLR 318, CA; *Naylor v Orton and Smith Ltd* [1983] ICR 665, [1983] IRLR 233, EAT.

[387] See n 386. See also *Bolton Roadways Ltd v Edwards* [1987] IRLR 392, EAT; *Manifold Industries Ltd v Sims* [1991] ICR 504, [1991] IRLR 242, EAT.

her motivation: as Stephenson LJ put it, 'participation in a strike must be judged by what the employee does and not by what he thinks or why he does it'.[388]

It follows that employees who are absent from work due to sickness or who are on holiday leave during the industrial action may still be held to be taking part in it, particularly if they associate themselves with the strike (eg by attending at the picket line).[389] However, it seems that clear evidence of participation will be required before an employee who is off sick when the action begins will be found to be participating in it.[390] Just as the employee's subjective motivation is irrelevant, so also is subjective knowledge on the part of the employer, so that an employer's reasonable but mistaken belief that the employee is taking part in the industrial action will not be sufficient if the employee's actions and omissions do not justify the conclusion that they were in fact taking part in that action.[391] A threat to take industrial action does not of itself amount to taking part in industrial action within the meaning of the Act,[392] but where an employee has stated their intention of joining in existing industrial action, they may be held to be taking part in that action before the time when they are contractually due to work in fact arrives.[393] In *Lewis and Britton v E Mason & Sons*,[394] an employee was dismissed for refusing to drive a heavy goods vehicle which did not have an overnight heater unless he was given an allowance to cover the cost of overnight accommodation. On learning of the dismissal, one of his colleagues threatened the employer that there would be a strike the following day unless the dismissed employee was reinstated. The EAT controversially held that it was open to the tribunal to find that by making a definite threat not to come to work the following day, at a time when further negotiation could not have been expected to take place and where the work for the following day had been allocated by the employer, the employees were taking part in industrial action.[395]

10.7.3.4 **Regime (4): dismissal *after* the industrial action or lockout**

Some employees dismissed *after* industrial action benefit from the automatic protection conferred by s 238A in the form of Regime (2). For example, if a six-week strike which constitutes 'protected industrial action' leads to a settlement of the trade dispute and then a return to work, a subsequent dismissal for taking part in the strike will be automatically unfair whenever that dismissal takes place. However, for dismissals falling outside Regime (2), the special rules excluding tribunals from determining complaints of unfair

[388] Kerr LJ expressed a similar view.

[389] *Bolton Roadways Ltd v Edwards* [1987] IRLR 392, EAT, per Scott J. In *Hindle Gears Ltd v McGinty* [1985] ICR 111, [1984] IRLR 477, the EAT overturned as perverse the tribunal's decision that a sick employee who spent time talking to pickets while handing in his medical certificate was participating in the industrial action.

[390] *Rogers v Chloride Systems Ltd* [1992] ICR 198, EAT.

[391] *Bolton Roadways Ltd v Edwards*, see n 389; in *McKenzie v Crosville Motor Services Ltd* 1990] ICR 172, [1989] IRLR 516, the EAT held that the reasonable belief of the employer that the employee was participating would be sufficient, but this was rejected in favour of the approach in *Bolton* by the EAT in *Manifold Industries Ltd v Sims*, n 387 (followed in *Jenkins v P&O European Ferries (Dover) Ltd* [1991] ICR 652).

[392] *Midland Plastics v Till* [1983] ICR 118, [1983] IRLR 9, EAT.

[393] See *Winnett v Seamarks Bros Ltd* [1978] ICR 1240, [1978] IRLR 387, EAT, where an employee who had made clear his intention to join a strike when his next shift began was held to be taking part in industrial action from the time when he made that intention clear.

[394] [1994] IRLR 4, EAT.

[395] The decision goes considerably further than *Winnett v Seamarks Bros Ltd* [1978] ICR 1240, [1978] IRLR 387, because that case involved a threat to join an existing strike, rather than a threat to commence strike action. cf Browne-Wilkinson J in *Midland Plastics v Till* [1983] ICR 118, [1983] IRLR 9: 'The actual taking of industrial action is ... quite distinct from the stage at which the threat of it is being used as a negotiating weapon.'

dismissal (under both Regime (1) and Regime (3)) are not relevant because they only apply to dismissals that take place *while* the employee is taking part in the industrial action, or during a lockout.

That means that in relation to a dismissal after a return to work, if Regime (2) does not on the facts apply to the dismissal, then the ordinary law of unfair dismissal applies. In such a case a claim can be made whether or not there has been selectivity in the dismissal of strikers. The question of whether such a dismissal would be fair is considered in the next section.

10.7.3.5 **Are industrial action dismissals fair?**

Clearly, dismissals falling within Regime (2) relating to protected industrial action are automatically unfair. But what of other dismissals, for example selective dismissal under Regime (3) for taking part in official industrial action which lasted longer than 12 weeks, or in relation to which the union had failed to observe one of the complex balloting requirements? The fact that Regime (2) protection is contingent on the industrial action in question being lawful may make reliance by a striker on the protection something of a gamble, as an individual union member has no way of knowing whether the union has in fact complied with the Byzantine laws governing industrial action.[396]

There is hardly any reported authority on the fairness of dismissal for taking part in industrial action. In *Sehmi v Gate Gourmet London Ltd*[397] it was argued that the enactment of s 238A and/or the incorporation into UK law of the right to strike under Article 11 of the European Convention on Human Rights meant that taking part in a strike was no longer conduct always entitling an employer in *contract* to summarily dismiss the employee. The EAT rejected that contention but pointed out that this was not the same thing as deciding that summary dismissal for going on strike is for *unfair dismissal* purposes within the band of reasonable responses of an employer. The *Gate Gourmet* case concerned a large-scale unofficial strike and the claimant had been dismissed when he presented himself to restart work. Since he was no longer taking part in an unofficial strike at the time when he was dismissed, TULR(C)A 1992 s 237 did not prevent him bringing a claim for unfair dismissal. The EAT said:

> Properly stated, the question is whether the tribunal was entitled to find that it was within the range of reasonable responses for the company to dismiss Mr Mathew for taking part in industrial action by absenting himself without leave over two (or three) consecutive shifts. In our view the answer to that question is straightforward. We do not say that the withdrawal by an employee of his labour, even if it is in breach of contract, will necessarily and in every conceivable circumstance justify the sanction of dismissal. But in a case, such as the present, where large numbers of employees deliberately absent themselves from work, in a manner which is plainly liable to do serious damage to the employer's business, it seems to us plain beyond argument that dismissal of those taking part in the action will be within the range of reasonable responses, even where the absence is (as in Mr Mathew's case) not very prolonged . . . [T]he fact that Parliament excluded certain types of dismissal related to industrial action from the jurisdiction of the tribunal does not imply any view on the necessary outcome of claims where jurisdiction remained.

It appears therefore that dismissal even after a fairly short period of absence on strike may be within the range of reasonable responses. However, as the EAT also indicated, not

[396] A satisfactory report on the ballot by the independent scrutineer may provide some reassurance that the union has safely navigated the legal minefield, but it will probably come too late to be of any help, and in any event it does not guarantee that the industrial action is lawful.

[397] [2009] IRLR 807, EAT.

every short withdrawal of labour will justify a dismissal. It seems likely that *a fortiori* dismissal for action less damaging than a strike may not be fair. If the industrial action takes the form of a ban on voluntary overtime, and is thus not action in breach of contract, it seems particularly likely that this would not justify a fair dismissal.

It is also significant that the *Gate Gourmet* case related to unofficial action called without a ballot. The position might well be different in a Regime (3) case where the dismissed employee had been participating in official industrial action and had then been treated differently from some other participants (who had not been dismissed). Such a selective dismissal for taking part in official action might well be held by an employment tribunal to be outside the range of reasonable responses of an employer and so to be unfair, especially if the industrial action had been properly balloted and called but was no longer protected because the protected period had expired. Even if the industrial action had never qualified as 'protected' under Regime (2), perhaps because of a balloting error, the employee would not be aware of that error and it seems likely that selectively dismissing them might well be regarded as unfair.

It appears that when considering the fairness of an industrial action dismissal under Regime (3), a tribunal must not consider the merits of the industrial dispute, but it can consider the conduct of the parties not only in relation to the selective dismissal or re-engagement of the employees participating in the industrial action but also to the parties' conduct more generally:

> [I]t may well be essential to compare the treatment accorded to [the] employee with the treatment accorded to others, and to have regard to the employer's conduct and to the general merits of the case. But even here I would stop short of accepting that the consideration of the matter by the tribunal must necessarily extend to the collective merits or demerits of the industrial action.[398]

If the dismissal is held to be unfair, the tribunal is not entitled to take into account the mere act of participating in industrial action in deciding whether to reduce the award of compensation on the grounds of contributory fault, but the award may be reduced where there is individual blameworthy conduct by the applicant, additional to or separate from the mere act of participation in the industrial action, which contributed to the dismissal and which was sufficiently blameworthy to make it just and equitable for the tribunal to reduce the compensation (eg if the claimant is a strike leader who has contributed to their own dismissal by their over-zealous or inflammatory actions).[399]

10.7.4 **Detriment short of dismissal for taking part in industrial action**

For many years there was no special protection from the employer imposing a detriment *short* of dismissal, which meant that an employee who is victimized by the employer (eg by being denied promotion) for taking part in lawfully organized official industrial action was unprotected under English law. In *Secretary of State for Business and Trade v Mercer*,[400] the Supreme Court confirmed that the complete absence of protection from detriment was contrary to Article 11 of the European Convention

[398] *Crosville Wales Ltd v Tracey (No 2)* [1998] AC 167, [1997] IRLR 691, [1997] ICR 862, HL, obiter per Lord Nolan, giving the unanimous judgment of the House of Lords.

[399] *Tracey v Crosville Wales Ltd* [1997] ICR 862, [1997] IRLR 691, HL, overruling *TNT Express (UK) Ltd v Downes* [1994] ICR 1, [1993] IRLR 432, EAT. Contributory fault in unfair dismissal complaints is considered at 7.6.2.3.

[400] [2024] UKSC 12, [2024] IRLR 599, [2024] ICR 814.

on Human Rights. However, the Supreme Court decided that it could not remedy the deficiency by reading words into the legislation. This was because of the policy choices that would have to be made in deciding what should be the extent of the protection against detriment bearing in mind the wide margin of appreciation accorded to member states in determining the balance to be adopted between the various social and economic factors involved in the regulation of industrial action. The Supreme Court said that those policy choices should be made by Parliament rather than the judiciary. The court issued a declaration that the absence of any protection from detriment for participation in lawful industrial action was a breach of Article 11.

The Employment Rights Act 2025 addressed this by enacting new s 236A of TULR(C)A 1992. This provides a remedy for detriment for taking part in industrial action. However this is confined to detriments of a kind which, at the time of writing, are still to be prescribed in regulations. In the meantime, it should be noted that public sector employers do not have a licence to impose detriments on workers who take part in industrial action since, as part of the state, such employers have an obligation under the Human Rights Act 1998 s 6 not to act in a way which is incompatible with the Convention

Even before the new statutory protection against detriment for taking part in industrial action was brought in to force, the courts had found one route for providing some remedy to workers who are subjected to such action. This is through the medium of the Employment Relations Act 1999 (Blacklists) Regulations 2010 which make it unlawful to compile, use, sell, or supply a list of trade union members or persons who have taken part in trade union activities, and which is compiled 'with a view to being used by employers or employment agencies for the purposes of discrimination in relation to recruitment or in relation to the treatment of workers'.[401] Very often, in order to impose a detriment on workers who have taken part in industrial action the employer will need to compile or use a list of those who were involved. In *Ryanair DAC v Morais*,[402] the employer complied a spreadsheet of those pilots who had taken part in a strike, and used the spreadsheet to withdraw concessionary travel benefits from them. The pilots claimed that they had been subjected to a detriment by use of a blacklist contrary to these regulations. The Court of Appeal agreed, holding that the protection extended to a case where someone was blacklisted for taking part in industrial action so long as it was organized by a trade union. Moreover that was the case *even if* the action had not been properly balloted so as to make it 'protected' action under s 238A (see 10.7.3).

10.8 **Use by employers of replacement labour**

An employer faced with industrial action may attempt to mitigate the effect by finding other workers. In general there is no legal brake on this, but there is one exception. Under the Conduct of Employment Agencies and Employment Businesses Regulations, SI 2003/3319, reg 7 it is a criminal offence for what is called an 'employee business' (in normal parlance what we would refer to as an 'employment agency') to provide replacement labour for workers taking part in industrial action. The repeal of this provision in 2022 was struck down by the High Court because of a failure to consult with interested parties.[403] Clearly the Labour government will not seek to revive this attempted repeal.

[401] See 9.4.2.

[402] [2025] EWCA Civ 19, [2025] IRLR 297, [2025] ICR 863.

[403] *R (on the application of ASLEF and others) v Secretary of State for Business and Trade* [2023] EWHC 1781 (Admin), [2023] IRLR 823, [2023] ICR 1405.

Review and Final Thoughts

- Organizing industrial action is nearly always tortious. In consequence, both union members and unions need immunity from suit if they are to be able to take such action. See 10.2.2 to 10.2.6 for details of the various torts.
- Such immunity has been provided by statute since 1906 in the 'golden formula' and is currently contained in s 219 of the Trade Union and Labour Relations (Consolidation) Act 1992 (see 10.2.7). In its current form the immunity applies to action taken in contemplation or further of a trade dispute between employees and their own employer, but it is subject to two major restrictions. First, some kinds of action, such as 'secondary action' and action to secure the reinstatement of dismissed unofficial strikers, are never protected by the immunity (see 10.2.8). Second, the immunity only benefits a union if the elaborate rules on arranging and notifying a secret postal ballot are complied with and if formal notice of industrial action is given to affected employers (see 10.3).
- The latest in a series of amendments to the rules on ballots was introduced by the Trade Union Act 2016 (discussed in appropriate places in 10.3). The impact of these latest restrictions on industrial action remains to be seen.
- As for the individual striker, as a matter of contract law they can be dismissed instantly without compensation, but this is very rare in practice. However, dismissal during at least the first 12 weeks of properly balloted industrial action has since 2000 been automatically unfair. Outside that very important special protection which covers most strikers, the law is complicated, but a fair general summary is that those participating are unlikely to be able to bring a complaint of unfair dismissal. Industrial action and unfair dismissal were discussed in 10.7.3.
- British law relating to strikes and other industrial action is about as complicated as one could make it. This affects not only the question of whether organizing and participating in such action is lawful in any particular case, but also the extent to which participants are protected from dismissal or other punishment for taking part. This complexity stems from a number of factors, each of which is touched on next.
- The first source of complexity is the flexibility of the common law, including the willingness of judges over the past two centuries to use that flexibility. The many instances of creation or revival of judge-made torts and crimes have resulted in many kinds of unlawfulness that can 'trip up' a striker or a picket. This in turn led to many legislative attempts, and some judicial ones, to clear a path through for workers to take industrial action in furtherance of genuine trade disputes. See in particular section 10.1.
- Governments vary in their views about the proper scope of industrial action, about how easy it should be to initiate such action, and about how much protection should be given to third parties. This has resulted in frequent amendments to the legislation, which makes it complex and has filled the law with exceptions and special rules for particular situations. The latest iteration of this is the Trade Union Act 2016, which has made a number of changes to the law governing industrial action, including the introduction of a whole set of new complications relating to industrial action in 'important public services'—which promises to be a fertile area for new legal disputes.
- Confusion has often been bred by the high stakes involved in industrial disputes and the prospect that legal proceedings to obtain an injunction may provide a relatively cheap and speedy winning tactic for an employer.[404] As a consequence, employers and their lawyers

[404] A dramatic recent illustration is *Govia Thameslink Railway Ltd v ASLEF* [2016] EWHC 1320 (QB), [2016] IRLR 686, HC, where a message from the general secretary to members about what certain train drivers were obliged to do was interpreted as a premature call for industrial action before a ballot had been completed. Whether or not that interpretation is accepted, the significant point is that the consequence was that the union was banned from ever organizing industrial action on this issue because that premature call made it impossible for any such action to have 'the support of a ballot' (see 10.3.2.9).

have expended much effort and ingenuity in identifying ways to argue that a particular proposed strike is unlawful. Such arguments have often succeeded on an urgent application for an interim injunction and it is rare for this to be followed by a careful and detailed examination at a full hearing. From time to time, for example in Allen v Flood, *OBG Ltd v Allan*, and *NURMT v Serco Ltd*, the appellate courts have brought some simplification and even-handedness to the law, but the pressure from employers never ends.

- A final source of confusion is the absence of any positive right to strike in UK law. While that may have been understandable in a recently industrialized economy in the nineteenth century, it seems a remarkable state of affairs in the modern world. Many would argue that this is the root of the problem and that from this stem all the other complexities and uncertainties. It can be argued that the freedom to join an effective union and to engage in collective bargaining which must, in conformity with Article 11 of the European Convention on Human Rights, be granted by the state to citizens would be best served by legislating for such a positive right to strike. However, the reality is that starting with a positive statement of lawfulness would not avoid much of the complexity since clearly there would still be limits imposed on what could be done by strikers; moreover, secret ballots to authorize industrial action are surely here to stay. It is also noteworthy that neither the Convention nor the European Court of Human Rights has declared that a right to strike is unequivocally an essential part of the Article 11 freedom. The relevance of the Convention is examined in 10.1.6, 10.3.1, and (in relation to picketing) 10.5.4.
- While one might expect the law to intervene so as to restrain industrial action which involved very high levels of injury to what might be termed innocent third parties, one only has to read the facts of a handful of the many cases cited in this chapter where an injunction was granted to see that the typical case in fact relates to a 'normal' strike or other instance of industrial action by employees in dispute with their employer about what should be their terms and conditions of employment. Ultimately such disputes should surely be resolved by the employer and the union reaching a compromise containing terms acceptable to both sides—and usually they are in the end resolved in that way. It is arguably unsatisfactory that the law from time to time delivers a knock-out blow in favour of the employer.

Index

References to notes contain the letter 'n' following the page number